T0135323

Lecture Notes in Computer Science 13679

More information about this series at https://link.springer.com/bookseries/558

Editors
Shai Avidan
Tel Aviv University
Tel Aviv, Israel

Gabriel Brostow (iD)
University College London
London, UK

Moustapha Cissé
Google AI
Accra, Ghana

Giovanni Maria Farinella (iD)
University of Catania
Catania, Italy

Tal Hassner (iD)
Facebook (United States)
Menlo Park, CA, USA

ISSN 0302-9743   ISSN 1611-3349 (electronic)
Lecture Notes in Computer Science
ISBN 978-3-031-19799-4   ISBN 978-3-031-19800-7 (eBook)
https://doi.org/10.1007/978-3-031-19800-7

This Springer imprint is published by the registered company Springer Nature Switzerland AG
The registered company address is: Gewerbestrasse 11, 6330 Cham, Switzerland

Shai Avidan · Gabriel Brostow ·
Moustapha Cissé · Giovanni Maria Farinella ·
Tal Hassner (Eds.)

Computer Vision – ECCV 2022

17th European Conference
Tel Aviv, Israel, October 23–27, 2022
Proceedings, Part XIX

 Springer

Foreword

Organizing the European Conference on Computer Vision (ECCV 2022) in Tel-Aviv during a global pandemic was no easy feat. The uncertainty level was extremely high, and decisions had to be postponed to the last minute. Still, we managed to plan things just in time for ECCV 2022 to be held in person. Participation in physical events is crucial to stimulating collaborations and nurturing the culture of the Computer Vision community.

There were many people who worked hard to ensure attendees enjoyed the best science at the 16th edition of ECCV. We are grateful to the Program Chairs Gabriel Brostow and Tal Hassner, who went above and beyond to ensure the ECCV reviewing process ran smoothly. The scientific program includes dozens of workshops and tutorials in addition to the main conference and we would like to thank Leonid Karlinsky and Tomer Michaeli for their hard work. Finally, special thanks to the web chairs Lorenzo Baraldi and Kosta Derpanis, who put in extra hours to transfer information fast and efficiently to the ECCV community.

We would like to express gratitude to our generous sponsors and the Industry Chairs, Dimosthenis Karatzas and Chen Sagiv, who oversaw industry relations and proposed new ways for academia-industry collaboration and technology transfer. It's great to see so much industrial interest in what we're doing!

Authors' draft versions of the papers appeared online with open access on both the Computer Vision Foundation (CVF) and the European Computer Vision Association (ECVA) websites as with previous ECCVs. Springer, the publisher of the proceedings, has arranged for archival publication. The final version of the papers is hosted by SpringerLink, with active references and supplementary materials. It benefits all potential readers that we offer both a free and citeable version for all researchers, as well as an authoritative, citeable version for SpringerLink readers. Our thanks go to Ronan Nugent from Springer, who helped us negotiate this agreement. Last but not least, we wish to thank Eric Mortensen, our publication chair, whose expertise made the process smooth.

October 2022

Rita Cucchiara
Jiří Matas
Amnon Shashua
Lihi Zelnik-Manor

Preface

Welcome to the proceedings of the European Conference on Computer Vision (ECCV 2022). This was a hybrid edition of ECCV as we made our way out of the COVID-19 pandemic. The conference received 5804 valid paper submissions, compared to 5150 submissions to ECCV 2020 (a 12.7% increase) and 2439 in ECCV 2018. 1645 submissions were accepted for publication (28%) and, of those, 157 (2.7% overall) as orals.

846 of the submissions were desk-rejected for various reasons. Many of them because they revealed author identity, thus violating the double-blind policy. This violation came in many forms: some had author names with the title, others added acknowledgments to specific grants, yet others had links to their github account where their name was visible. Tampering with the LaTeX template was another reason for automatic desk rejection.

ECCV 2022 used the traditional CMT system to manage the entire double-blind reviewing process. Authors did not know the names of the reviewers and vice versa. Each paper received at least 3 reviews (except 6 papers that received only 2 reviews), totalling more than 15,000 reviews.

Handling the review process at this scale was a significant challenge. To ensure that each submission received as fair and high-quality reviews as possible, we recruited more than 4719 reviewers (in the end, 4719 reviewers did at least one review). Similarly we recruited more than 276 area chairs (eventually, only 276 area chairs handled a batch of papers). The area chairs were selected based on their technical expertise and reputation, largely among people who served as area chairs in previous top computer vision and machine learning conferences (ECCV, ICCV, CVPR, NeurIPS, etc.).

Reviewers were similarly invited from previous conferences, and also from the pool of authors. We also encouraged experienced area chairs to suggest additional chairs and reviewers in the initial phase of recruiting. The median reviewer load was five papers per reviewer, while the average load was about four papers, because of the emergency reviewers. The area chair load was 35 papers, on average.

Conflicts of interest between authors, area chairs, and reviewers were handled largely automatically by the CMT platform, with some manual help from the Program Chairs. Reviewers were allowed to describe themselves as senior reviewer (load of 8 papers to review) or junior reviewers (load of 4 papers). Papers were matched to area chairs based on a subject-area affinity score computed in CMT and an affinity score computed by the Toronto Paper Matching System (TPMS). TPMS is based on the paper's full text. An area chair handling each submission would bid for preferred expert reviewers, and we balanced load and prevented conflicts.

The assignment of submissions to area chairs was relatively smooth, as was the assignment of submissions to reviewers. A small percentage of reviewers were not happy with their assignments in terms of subjects and self-reported expertise. This is an area for improvement, although it's interesting that many of these cases were reviewers hand-picked by AC's. We made a later round of reviewer recruiting, targeted at the list of authors of papers submitted to the conference, and had an excellent response which helped provide enough emergency reviewers. In the end, all but six papers received at least 3 reviews.

The challenges of the reviewing process are in line with past experiences at ECCV 2020. As the community grows, and the number of submissions increases, it becomes ever more challenging to recruit enough reviewers and ensure a high enough quality of reviews. Enlisting authors by default as reviewers might be one step to address this challenge.

Authors were given a week to rebut the initial reviews, and address reviewers' concerns. Each rebuttal was limited to a single pdf page with a fixed template.

The Area Chairs then led discussions with the reviewers on the merits of each submission. The goal was to reach consensus, but, ultimately, it was up to the Area Chair to make a decision. The decision was then discussed with a buddy Area Chair to make sure decisions were fair and informative. The entire process was conducted virtually with no in-person meetings taking place.

The Program Chairs were informed in cases where the Area Chairs overturned a decisive consensus reached by the reviewers, and pushed for the meta-reviews to contain details that explained the reasoning for such decisions. Obviously these were the most contentious cases, where reviewer inexperience was the most common reported factor.

Once the list of accepted papers was finalized and released, we went through the laborious process of plagiarism (including self-plagiarism) detection. A total of 4 accepted papers were rejected because of that.

Finally, we would like to thank our Technical Program Chair, Pavel Lifshits, who did tremendous work behind the scenes, and we thank the tireless CMT team.

October 2022

Gabriel Brostow
Giovanni Maria Farinella
Moustapha Cissé
Shai Avidan
Tal Hassner

Organization

General Chairs

Rita Cucchiara	University of Modena and Reggio Emilia, Italy
Jiří Matas	Czech Technical University in Prague, Czech Republic
Amnon Shashua	Hebrew University of Jerusalem, Israel
Lihi Zelnik-Manor	Technion – Israel Institute of Technology, Israel

Program Chairs

Shai Avidan	Tel-Aviv University, Israel
Gabriel Brostow	University College London, UK
Moustapha Cissé	Google AI, Ghana
Giovanni Maria Farinella	University of Catania, Italy
Tal Hassner	Facebook AI, USA

Program Technical Chair

Pavel Lifshits	Technion – Israel Institute of Technology, Israel

Workshops Chairs

Leonid Karlinsky	IBM Research, Israel
Tomer Michaeli	Technion – Israel Institute of Technology, Israel
Ko Nishino	Kyoto University, Japan

Tutorial Chairs

Thomas Pock	Graz University of Technology, Austria
Natalia Neverova	Facebook AI Research, UK

Demo Chair

Bohyung Han	Seoul National University, Korea

Social and Student Activities Chairs

Tatiana Tommasi   Italian Institute of Technology, Italy
Sagie Benaim   University of Copenhagen, Denmark

Diversity and Inclusion Chairs

Xi Yin   Facebook AI Research, USA
Bryan Russell   Adobe, USA

Communications Chairs

Lorenzo Baraldi   University of Modena and Reggio Emilia, Italy
Kosta Derpanis   York University & Samsung AI Centre Toronto,
                                   Canada

Industrial Liaison Chairs

Dimosthenis Karatzas   Universitat Autònoma de Barcelona, Spain
Chen Sagiv   SagivTech, Israel

Finance Chair

Gerard Medioni   University of Southern California & Amazon,
                                   USA

Publication Chair

Eric Mortensen   MiCROTEC, USA

Area Chairs

Lourdes Agapito   University College London, UK
Zeynep Akata   University of Tübingen, Germany
Naveed Akhtar   University of Western Australia, Australia
Karteek Alahari   Inria Grenoble Rhône-Alpes, France
Alexandre Alahi   École polytechnique fédérale de Lausanne,
                                   Switzerland
Pablo Arbelaez   Universidad de Los Andes, Columbia
Antonis A. Argyros   University of Crete & Foundation for Research
                                   and Technology-Hellas, Crete
Yuki M. Asano   University of Amsterdam, The Netherlands
Kalle Åström   Lund University, Sweden
Hadar Averbuch-Elor   Cornell University, USA

Matthijs Douze	Facebook AI Research, USA
Mohamed Elhoseiny	King Abdullah University of Science and Technology, Saudi Arabia
Sergio Escalera	University of Barcelona, Spain
Yi Fang	New York University, USA
Ryan Farrell	Brigham Young University, USA
Alireza Fathi	Google, USA
Christoph Feichtenhofer	Facebook AI Research, USA
Basura Fernando	Agency for Science, Technology and Research (A*STAR), Singapore
Vittorio Ferrari	Google Research, Switzerland
Andrew W. Fitzgibbon	Graphcore, UK
David J. Fleet	University of Toronto, Canada
David Forsyth	University of Illinois at Urbana-Champaign, USA
David Fouhey	University of Michigan, USA
Katerina Fragkiadaki	Carnegie Mellon University, USA
Friedrich Fraundorfer	Graz University of Technology, Austria
Oren Freifeld	Ben-Gurion University, Israel
Thomas Funkhouser	Google Research & Princeton University, USA
Yasutaka Furukawa	Simon Fraser University, Canada
Fabio Galasso	Sapienza University of Rome, Italy
Jürgen Gall	University of Bonn, Germany
Chuang Gan	Massachusetts Institute of Technology, USA
Zhe Gan	Microsoft, USA
Animesh Garg	University of Toronto, Vector Institute, Nvidia, Canada
Efstratios Gavves	University of Amsterdam, The Netherlands
Peter Gehler	Amazon, Germany
Theo Gevers	University of Amsterdam, The Netherlands
Bernard Ghanem	King Abdullah University of Science and Technology, Saudi Arabia
Ross B. Girshick	Facebook AI Research, USA
Georgia Gkioxari	Facebook AI Research, USA
Albert Gordo	Facebook, USA
Stephen Gould	Australian National University, Australia
Venu Madhav Govindu	Indian Institute of Science, India
Kristen Grauman	Facebook AI Research & UT Austin, USA
Abhinav Gupta	Carnegie Mellon University & Facebook AI Research, USA
Mohit Gupta	University of Wisconsin-Madison, USA
Hu Han	Institute of Computing Technology, Chinese Academy of Sciences, China

Bohyung Han	Seoul National University, Korea
Tian Han	Stevens Institute of Technology, USA
Emily Hand	University of Nevada, Reno, USA
Bharath Hariharan	Cornell University, USA
Ran He	Institute of Automation, Chinese Academy of Sciences, China
Otmar Hilliges	ETH Zurich, Switzerland
Adrian Hilton	University of Surrey, UK
Minh Hoai	Stony Brook University, USA
Yedid Hoshen	Hebrew University of Jerusalem, Israel
Timothy Hospedales	University of Edinburgh, UK
Gang Hua	Wormpex AI Research, USA
Di Huang	Beihang University, China
Jing Huang	Facebook, USA
Jia-Bin Huang	Facebook, USA
Nathan Jacobs	Washington University in St. Louis, USA
C. V. Jawahar	International Institute of Information Technology, Hyderabad, India
Herve Jegou	Facebook AI Research, France
Neel Joshi	Microsoft Research, USA
Armand Joulin	Facebook AI Research, France
Frederic Jurie	University of Caen Normandie, France
Fredrik Kahl	Chalmers University of Technology, Sweden
Yannis Kalantidis	NAVER LABS Europe, France
Evangelos Kalogerakis	University of Massachusetts, Amherst, USA
Sing Bing Kang	Zillow Group, USA
Yosi Keller	Bar Ilan University, Israel
Margret Keuper	University of Mannheim, Germany
Tae-Kyun Kim	Imperial College London, UK
Benjamin Kimia	Brown University, USA
Alexander Kirillov	Facebook AI Research, USA
Kris Kitani	Carnegie Mellon University, USA
Iasonas Kokkinos	Snap Inc. & University College London, UK
Vladlen Koltun	Apple, USA
Nikos Komodakis	University of Crete, Crete
Piotr Koniusz	Australian National University, Australia
Philipp Kraehenbuehl	University of Texas at Austin, USA
Dilip Krishnan	Google, USA
Ajay Kumar	Hong Kong Polytechnic University, Hong Kong, China
Junseok Kwon	Chung-Ang University, Korea
Jean-Francois Lalonde	Université Laval, Canada

Ivan Laptev	Inria Paris, France
Laura Leal-Taixé	Technical University of Munich, Germany
Erik Learned-Miller	University of Massachusetts, Amherst, USA
Gim Hee Lee	National University of Singapore, Singapore
Seungyong Lee	Pohang University of Science and Technology, Korea
Zhen Lei	Institute of Automation, Chinese Academy of Sciences, China
Bastian Leibe	RWTH Aachen University, Germany
Hongdong Li	Australian National University, Australia
Fuxin Li	Oregon State University, USA
Bo Li	University of Illinois at Urbana-Champaign, USA
Yin Li	University of Wisconsin-Madison, USA
Ser-Nam Lim	Meta AI Research, USA
Joseph Lim	University of Southern California, USA
Stephen Lin	Microsoft Research Asia, China
Dahua Lin	The Chinese University of Hong Kong, Hong Kong, China
Si Liu	Beihang University, China
Xiaoming Liu	Michigan State University, USA
Ce Liu	Microsoft, USA
Zicheng Liu	Microsoft, USA
Yanxi Liu	Pennsylvania State University, USA
Feng Liu	Portland State University, USA
Yebin Liu	Tsinghua University, China
Chen Change Loy	Nanyang Technological University, Singapore
Huchuan Lu	Dalian University of Technology, China
Cewu Lu	Shanghai Jiao Tong University, China
Oisin Mac Aodha	University of Edinburgh, UK
Dhruv Mahajan	Facebook, USA
Subhransu Maji	University of Massachusetts, Amherst, USA
Atsuto Maki	KTH Royal Institute of Technology, Sweden
Arun Mallya	NVIDIA, USA
R. Manmatha	Amazon, USA
Iacopo Masi	Sapienza University of Rome, Italy
Dimitris N. Metaxas	Rutgers University, USA
Ajmal Mian	University of Western Australia, Australia
Christian Micheloni	University of Udine, Italy
Krystian Mikolajczyk	Imperial College London, UK
Anurag Mittal	Indian Institute of Technology, Madras, India
Philippos Mordohai	Stevens Institute of Technology, USA
Greg Mori	Simon Fraser University & Borealis AI, Canada

Vittorio Murino   Istituto Italiano di Tecnologia, Italy
P. J. Narayanan   International Institute of Information Technology,
                                  Hyderabad, India

Ram Nevatia   University of Southern California, USA
Natalia Neverova   Facebook AI Research, UK
Richard Newcombe   Facebook, USA
Cuong V. Nguyen   Florida International University, USA
Bingbing Ni   Shanghai Jiao Tong University, China
Juan Carlos Niebles   Salesforce & Stanford University, USA
Ko Nishino   Kyoto University, Japan
Jean-Marc Odobez   Idiap Research Institute, École polytechnique
                                  fédérale de Lausanne, Switzerland
Francesca Odone   University of Genova, Italy
Takayuki Okatani   Tohoku University & RIKEN Center for
                                  Advanced Intelligence Project, Japan

Manohar Paluri   Facebook, USA
Guan Pang   Facebook, USA
Maja Pantic   Imperial College London, UK
Sylvain Paris   Adobe Research, USA
Jaesik Park   Pohang University of Science and Technology,
                                  Korea
Hyun Soo Park   The University of Minnesota, USA
Omkar M. Parkhi   Facebook, USA
Deepak Pathak   Carnegie Mellon University, USA
Georgios Pavlakos   University of California, Berkeley, USA
Marcello Pelillo   University of Venice, Italy
Marc Pollefeys   ETH Zurich & Microsoft, Switzerland
Jean Ponce   Inria, France
Gerard Pons-Moll   University of Tübingen, Germany
Fatih Porikli   Qualcomm, USA
Victor Adrian Prisacariu   University of Oxford, UK
Petia Radeva   University of Barcelona, Spain
Ravi Ramamoorthi   University of California, San Diego, USA
Deva Ramanan   Carnegie Mellon University, USA
Vignesh Ramanathan   Facebook, USA
Nalini Ratha   State University of New York at Buffalo, USA
Tammy Riklin Raviv   Ben-Gurion University, Israel
Tobias Ritschel   University College London, UK
Emanuele Rodola   Sapienza University of Rome, Italy
Amit K. Roy-Chowdhury   University of California, Riverside, USA
Michael Rubinstein   Google, USA
Olga Russakovsky   Princeton University, USA

Mathieu Salzmann	École polytechnique fédérale de Lausanne, Switzerland
Dimitris Samaras	Stony Brook University, USA
Aswin Sankaranarayanan	Carnegie Mellon University, USA
Imari Sato	National Institute of Informatics, Japan
Yoichi Sato	University of Tokyo, Japan
Shin'ichi Satoh	National Institute of Informatics, Japan
Walter Scheirer	University of Notre Dame, USA
Bernt Schiele	Max Planck Institute for Informatics, Germany
Konrad Schindler	ETH Zurich, Switzerland
Cordelia Schmid	Inria & Google, France
Alexander Schwing	University of Illinois at Urbana-Champaign, USA
Nicu Sebe	University of Trento, Italy
Greg Shakhnarovich	Toyota Technological Institute at Chicago, USA
Eli Shechtman	Adobe Research, USA
Humphrey Shi	University of Oregon & University of Illinois at Urbana-Champaign & Picsart AI Research, USA
Jianbo Shi	University of Pennsylvania, USA
Roy Shilkrot	Massachusetts Institute of Technology, USA
Mike Zheng Shou	National University of Singapore, Singapore
Kaleem Siddiqi	McGill University, Canada
Richa Singh	Indian Institute of Technology Jodhpur, India
Greg Slabaugh	Queen Mary University of London, UK
Cees Snoek	University of Amsterdam, The Netherlands
Yale Song	Facebook AI Research, USA
Yi-Zhe Song	University of Surrey, UK
Bjorn Stenger	Rakuten Institute of Technology
Abby Stylianou	Saint Louis University, USA
Akihiro Sugimoto	National Institute of Informatics, Japan
Chen Sun	Brown University, USA
Deqing Sun	Google, USA
Kalyan Sunkavalli	Adobe Research, USA
Ying Tai	Tencent YouTu Lab, China
Ayellet Tal	Technion – Israel Institute of Technology, Israel
Ping Tan	Simon Fraser University, Canada
Siyu Tang	ETH Zurich, Switzerland
Chi-Keung Tang	Hong Kong University of Science and Technology, Hong Kong, China
Radu Timofte	University of Würzburg, Germany & ETH Zurich, Switzerland
Federico Tombari	Google, Switzerland & Technical University of Munich, Germany

James Tompkin	Brown University, USA
Lorenzo Torresani	Dartmouth College, USA
Alexander Toshev	Apple, USA
Du Tran	Facebook AI Research, USA
Anh T. Tran	VinAI, Vietnam
Zhuowen Tu	University of California, San Diego, USA
Georgios Tzimiropoulos	Queen Mary University of London, UK
Jasper Uijlings	Google Research, Switzerland
Jan C. van Gemert	Delft University of Technology, The Netherlands
Gul Varol	Ecole des Ponts ParisTech, France
Nuno Vasconcelos	University of California, San Diego, USA
Mayank Vatsa	Indian Institute of Technology Jodhpur, India
Ashok Veeraraghavan	Rice University, USA
Jakob Verbeek	Facebook AI Research, France
Carl Vondrick	Columbia University, USA
Ruiping Wang	Institute of Computing Technology, Chinese Academy of Sciences, China
Xinchao Wang	National University of Singapore, Singapore
Liwei Wang	The Chinese University of Hong Kong, Hong Kong, China
Chaohui Wang	Université Paris-Est, France
Xiaolong Wang	University of California, San Diego, USA
Christian Wolf	NAVER LABS Europe, France
Tao Xiang	University of Surrey, UK
Saining Xie	Facebook AI Research, USA
Cihang Xie	University of California, Santa Cruz, USA
Zeki Yalniz	Facebook, USA
Ming-Hsuan Yang	University of California, Merced, USA
Angela Yao	National University of Singapore, Singapore
Shaodi You	University of Amsterdam, The Netherlands
Stella X. Yu	University of California, Berkeley, USA
Junsong Yuan	State University of New York at Buffalo, USA
Stefanos Zafeiriou	Imperial College London, UK
Amir Zamir	École polytechnique fédérale de Lausanne, Switzerland
Lei Zhang	Alibaba & Hong Kong Polytechnic University, Hong Kong, China
Lei Zhang	International Digital Economy Academy (IDEA), China
Pengchuan Zhang	Meta AI, USA
Bolei Zhou	University of California, Los Angeles, USA
Yuke Zhu	University of Texas at Austin, USA

Todd Zickler   Harvard University, USA
Wangmeng Zuo   Harbin Institute of Technology, China

Technical Program Committee

Davide Abati
Soroush Abbasi
    Koohpayegani
Amos L. Abbott
Rameen Abdal
Rabab Abdelfattah
Sahar Abdelnabi
Hassan Abu Alhaija
Abulikemu Abuduweili
Ron Abutbul
Hanno Ackermann
Aikaterini Adam
Kamil Adamczewski
Ehsan Adeli
Vida Adeli
Donald Adjeroh
Arman Afrasiyabi
Akshay Agarwal
Sameer Agarwal
Abhinav Agarwalla
Vaibhav Aggarwal
Sara Aghajanzadeh
Susmit Agrawal
Antonio Agudo
Touqeer Ahmad
Sk Miraj Ahmed
Chaitanya Ahuja
Nilesh A. Ahuja
Abhishek Aich
Shubhra Aich
Noam Aigerman
Arash Akbarinia
Peri Akiva
Derya Akkaynak
Emre Aksan
Arjun R. Akula
Yuval Alaluf
Stephan Alaniz
Paul Albert
Cenek Albl

Filippo Aleotti
Konstantinos P.
    Alexandridis
Motasem Alfarra
Mohsen Ali
Thiemo Alldieck
Hadi Alzayer
Liang An
Shan An
Yi An
Zhulin An
Dongsheng An
Jie An
Xiang An
Saket Anand
Cosmin Ancuti
Juan Andrade-Cetto
Alexander Andreopoulos
Bjoern Andres
Jerone T. A. Andrews
Shivangi Aneja
Anelia Angelova
Dragomir Anguelov
Rushil Anirudh
Oron Anschel
Rao Muhammad Anwer
Djamila Aouada
Evlampios Apostolidis
Srikar Appalaraju
Nikita Araslanov
Andre Araujo
Eric Arazo
Dawit Mureja Argaw
Anurag Arnab
Aditya Arora
Chetan Arora
Sunpreet S. Arora
Alexey Artemov
Muhammad Asad
Kumar Ashutosh

Sinem Aslan
Vishal Asnani
Mahmoud Assran
Amir Atapour-Abarghouei
Nikos Athanasiou
Ali Athar
ShahRukh Athar
Sara Atito
Souhaib Attaiki
Matan Atzmon
Mathieu Aubry
Nicolas Audebert
Tristan T.
    Aumentado-Armstrong
Melinos Averkiou
Yannis Avrithis
Stephane Ayache
Mehmet Aygün
Seyed Mehdi
    Ayyoubzadeh
Hossein Azizpour
George Azzopardi
Mallikarjun B. R.
Yunhao Ba
Abhishek Badki
Seung-Hwan Bae
Seung-Hwan Baek
Seungryul Baek
Piyush Nitin Bagad
Shai Bagon
Gaetan Bahl
Shikhar Bahl
Sherwin Bahmani
Haoran Bai
Lei Bai
Jiawang Bai
Haoyue Bai
Jinbin Bai
Xiang Bai
Xuyang Bai

Yang Bai
Yuanchao Bai
Ziqian Bai
Sungyong Baik
Kevin Bailly
Max Bain
Federico Baldassarre
Wele Gedara Chaminda
   Bandara
Biplab Banerjee
Pratyay Banerjee
Sandipan Banerjee
Jihwan Bang
Antyanta Bangunharcana
Aayush Bansal
Ankan Bansal
Siddhant Bansal
Wentao Bao
Zhipeng Bao
Amir Bar
Manel Baradad Jurjo
Lorenzo Baraldi
Danny Barash
Daniel Barath
Connelly Barnes
Ioan Andrei Bârsan
Steven Basart
Dina Bashkirova
Chaim Baskin
Peyman Bateni
Anil Batra
Sebastiano Battiato
Ardhendu Behera
Harkirat Behl
Jens Behley
Vasileios Belagiannis
Boulbaba Ben Amor
Emanuel Ben Baruch
Abdessamad Ben Hamza
Gil Ben-Artzi
Assia Benbihi
Fabian Benitez-Quiroz
Guy Ben-Yosef
Philipp Benz
Alexander W. Bergman

Urs Bergmann
Jesus Bermudez-Cameo
Stefano Berretti
Gedas Bertasius
Zachary Bessinger
Petra Bevandić
Matthew Beveridge
Lucas Beyer
Yash Bhalgat
Suvaansh Bhambri
Samarth Bharadwaj
Gaurav Bharaj
Aparna Bharati
Bharat Lal Bhatnagar
Uttaran Bhattacharya
Apratim Bhattacharyya
Brojeshwar Bhowmick
Ankan Kumar Bhunia
Ayan Kumar Bhunia
Qi Bi
Sai Bi
Michael Bi Mi
Gui-Bin Bian
Jia-Wang Bian
Shaojun Bian
Pia Bideau
Mario Bijelic
Hakan Bilen
Guillaume-Alexandre
   Bilodeau
Alexander Binder
Tolga Birdal
Vighnesh N. Birodkar
Sandika Biswas
Andreas Blattmann
Janusz Bobulski
Giuseppe Boccignone
Vishnu Boddeti
Navaneeth Bodla
Moritz Böhle
Aleksei Bokhovkin
Sam Bond-Taylor
Vivek Boominathan
Shubhankar Borse
Mark Boss

Andrea Bottino
Adnane Boukhayma
Fadi Boutros
Nicolas C. Boutry
Richard S. Bowen
Ivaylo Boyadzhiev
Aidan Boyd
Yuri Boykov
Aljaz Bozic
Behzad Bozorgtabar
Eric Brachmann
Samarth Brahmbhatt
Gustav Bredell
Francois Bremond
Joel Brogan
Andrew Brown
Thomas Brox
Marcus A. Brubaker
Robert-Jan Bruintjes
Yuqi Bu
Anders G. Buch
Himanshu Buckchash
Mateusz Buda
Ignas Budvytis
José M. Buenaposada
Marcel C. Bühler
Tu Bui
Adrian Bulat
Hannah Bull
Evgeny Burnaev
Andrei Bursuc
Benjamin Busam
Sergey N. Buzykanov
Wonmin Byeon
Fabian Caba
Martin Cadik
Guanyu Cai
Minjie Cai
Qing Cai
Zhongang Cai
Qi Cai
Yancheng Cai
Shen Cai
Han Cai
Jiarui Cai

Bowen Cai
Mu Cai
Qin Cai
Ruojin Cai
Weidong Cai
Weiwei Cai
Yi Cai
Yujun Cai
Zhiping Cai
Akin Caliskan
Lilian Calvet
Baris Can Cam
Necati Cihan Camgoz
Tommaso Campari
Dylan Campbell
Ziang Cao
Ang Cao
Xu Cao
Zhiwen Cao
Shengcao Cao
Song Cao
Weipeng Cao
Xiangyong Cao
Xiaochun Cao
Yue Cao
Yunhao Cao
Zhangjie Cao
Jiale Cao
Yang Cao
Jiajiong Cao
Jie Cao
Jinkun Cao
Lele Cao
Yulong Cao
Zhiguo Cao
Chen Cao
Razvan Caramalau
Marlène Careil
Gustavo Carneiro
Joao Carreira
Dan Casas
Paola Cascante-Bonilla
Angela Castillo
Francisco M. Castro
Pedro Castro

Luca Cavalli
George J. Cazenavette
Oya Celiktutan
Hakan Cevikalp
Sri Harsha C. H.
Sungmin Cha
Geonho Cha
Menglei Chai
Lucy Chai
Yuning Chai
Zenghao Chai
Anirban Chakraborty
Deep Chakraborty
Rudrasis Chakraborty
Souradeep Chakraborty
Kelvin C. K. Chan
Chee Seng Chan
Paramanand Chandramouli
Arjun Chandrasekaran
Kenneth Chaney
Dongliang Chang
Huiwen Chang
Peng Chang
Xiaojun Chang
Jia-Ren Chang
Hyung Jin Chang
Hyun Sung Chang
Ju Yong Chang
Li-Jen Chang
Qi Chang
Wei-Yi Chang
Yi Chang
Nadine Chang
Hanqing Chao
Pradyumna Chari
Dibyadip Chatterjee
Chiranjoy Chattopadhyay
Siddhartha Chaudhuri
Zhengping Che
Gal Chechik
Lianggangxu Chen
Qi Alfred Chen
Brian Chen
Bor-Chun Chen
Bo-Hao Chen

Bohong Chen
Bin Chen
Ziliang Chen
Cheng Chen
Chen Chen
Chaofeng Chen
Xi Chen
Haoyu Chen
Xuanhong Chen
Wei Chen
Qiang Chen
Shi Chen
Xianyu Chen
Chang Chen
Changhuai Chen
Hao Chen
Jie Chen
Jianbo Chen
Jingjing Chen
Jun Chen
Kejiang Chen
Mingcai Chen
Nenglun Chen
Qifeng Chen
Ruoyu Chen
Shu-Yu Chen
Weidong Chen
Weijie Chen
Weikai Chen
Xiang Chen
Xiuyi Chen
Xingyu Chen
Yaofo Chen
Yueting Chen
Yu Chen
Yunjin Chen
Yuntao Chen
Yun Chen
Zhenfang Chen
Zhuangzhuang Chen
Chu-Song Chen
Xiangyu Chen
Zhuo Chen
Chaoqi Chen
Shizhe Chen

Xiaotong Chen
Xiaozhi Chen
Dian Chen
Defang Chen
Dingfan Chen
Ding-Jie Chen
Ee Heng Chen
Tao Chen
Yixin Chen
Wei-Ting Chen
Lin Chen
Guang Chen
Guangyi Chen
Guanying Chen
Guangyao Chen
Hwann-Tzong Chen
Junwen Chen
Jiacheng Chen
Jianxu Chen
Hui Chen
Kai Chen
Kan Chen
Kevin Chen
Kuan-Wen Chen
Weihua Chen
Zhang Chen
Liang-Chieh Chen
Lele Chen
Liang Chen
Fanglin Chen
Zehui Chen
Minghui Chen
Minghao Chen
Xiaokang Chen
Qian Chen
Jun-Cheng Chen
Qi Chen
Qingcai Chen
Richard J. Chen
Runnan Chen
Rui Chen
Shuo Chen
Sentao Chen
Shaoyu Chen
Shixing Chen

Shuai Chen
Shuya Chen
Sizhe Chen
Simin Chen
Shaoxiang Chen
Zitian Chen
Tianlong Chen
Tianshui Chen
Min-Hung Chen
Xiangning Chen
Xin Chen
Xinghao Chen
Xuejin Chen
Xu Chen
Xuxi Chen
Yunlu Chen
Yanbei Chen
Yuxiao Chen
Yun-Chun Chen
Yi-Ting Chen
Yi-Wen Chen
Yinbo Chen
Yiran Chen
Yuanhong Chen
Yubei Chen
Yuefeng Chen
Yuhua Chen
Yukang Chen
Zerui Chen
Zhaoyu Chen
Zhen Chen
Zhenyu Chen
Zhi Chen
Zhiwei Chen
Zhixiang Chen
Long Chen
Bowen Cheng
Jun Cheng
Yi Cheng
Jingchun Cheng
Lechao Cheng
Xi Cheng
Yuan Cheng
Ho Kei Cheng
Kevin Ho Man Cheng

Jiacheng Cheng
Kelvin B. Cheng
Li Cheng
Mengjun Cheng
Zhen Cheng
Qingrong Cheng
Tianheng Cheng
Harry Cheng
Yihua Cheng
Yu Cheng
Ziheng Cheng
Soon Yau Cheong
Anoop Cherian
Manuela Chessa
Zhixiang Chi
Naoki Chiba
Julian Chibane
Kashyap Chitta
Tai-Yin Chiu
Hsu-kuang Chiu
Wei-Chen Chiu
Sungmin Cho
Donghyeon Cho
Hyeon Cho
Yooshin Cho
Gyusang Cho
Jang Hyun Cho
Seungju Cho
Nam Ik Cho
Sunghyun Cho
Hanbyel Cho
Jaesung Choe
Jooyoung Choi
Chiho Choi
Changwoon Choi
Jongwon Choi
Myungsub Choi
Dooseop Choi
Jonghyun Choi
Jinwoo Choi
Jun Won Choi
Min-Kook Choi
Hongsuk Choi
Janghoon Choi
Yoon-Ho Choi

Yukyung Choi
Jaegul Choo
Ayush Chopra
Siddharth Choudhary
Subhabrata Choudhury
Vasileios Choutas
Ka-Ho Chow
Pinaki Nath Chowdhury
Sammy Christen
Anders Christensen
Grigorios Chrysos
Hang Chu
Wen-Hsuan Chu
Peng Chu
Qi Chu
Ruihang Chu
Wei-Ta Chu
Yung-Yu Chuang
Sanghyuk Chun
Se Young Chun
Antonio Cinà
Ramazan Gokberk Cinbis
Javier Civera
Albert Clapés
Ronald Clark
Brian S. Clipp
Felipe Codevilla
Daniel Coelho de Castro
Niv Cohen
Forrester Cole
Maxwell D. Collins
Robert T. Collins
Marc Comino Trinidad
Runmin Cong
Wenyan Cong
Maxime Cordy
Marcella Cornia
Enric Corona
Huseyin Coskun
Luca Cosmo
Dragos Costea
Davide Cozzolino
Arun C. S. Kumar
Aiyu Cui
Qiongjie Cui

Quan Cui
Shuhao Cui
Yiming Cui
Ying Cui
Zijun Cui
Jiali Cui
Jiequan Cui
Yawen Cui
Zhen Cui
Zhaopeng Cui
Jack Culpepper
Xiaodong Cun
Ross Cutler
Adam Czajka
Ali Dabouei
Konstantinos M. Dafnis
Manuel Dahnert
Tao Dai
Yuchao Dai
Bo Dai
Mengyu Dai
Hang Dai
Haixing Dai
Peng Dai
Pingyang Dai
Qi Dai
Qiyu Dai
Yutong Dai
Naser Damer
Zhiyuan Dang
Mohamed Daoudi
Ayan Das
Abir Das
Debasmit Das
Deepayan Das
Partha Das
Sagnik Das
Soumi Das
Srijan Das
Swagatam Das
Avijit Dasgupta
Jim Davis
Adrian K. Davison
Homa Davoudi
Laura Daza

Matthias De Lange
Shalini De Mello
Marco De Nadai
Christophe De
    Vleeschouwer
Alp Dener
Boyang Deng
Congyue Deng
Bailin Deng
Yong Deng
Ye Deng
Zhuo Deng
Zhijie Deng
Xiaoming Deng
Jiankang Deng
Jinhong Deng
Jingjing Deng
Liang-Jian Deng
Siqi Deng
Xiang Deng
Xueqing Deng
Zhongying Deng
Karan Desai
Jean-Emmanuel Deschaud
Aniket Anand Deshmukh
Neel Dey
Helisa Dhamo
Prithviraj Dhar
Amaya Dharmasiri
Yan Di
Xing Di
Ousmane A. Dia
Haiwen Diao
Xiaolei Diao
Gonçalo José Dias Pais
Abdallah Dib
Anastasios Dimou
Changxing Ding
Henghui Ding
Guodong Ding
Yaqing Ding
Shuangrui Ding
Yuhang Ding
Yikang Ding
Shouhong Ding

Haisong Ding
Hui Ding
Jiahao Ding
Jian Ding
Jian-Jiun Ding
Shuxiao Ding
Tianyu Ding
Wenhao Ding
Yuqi Ding
Yi Ding
Yuzhen Ding
Zhengming Ding
Tan Minh Dinh
Vu Dinh
Christos Diou
Mandar Dixit
Bao Gia Doan
Khoa D. Doan
Dzung Anh Doan
Debi Prosad Dogra
Nehal Doiphode
Chengdong Dong
Bowen Dong
Zhenxing Dong
Hang Dong
Xiaoyi Dong
Haoye Dong
Jiangxin Dong
Shichao Dong
Xuan Dong
Zhen Dong
Shuting Dong
Jing Dong
Li Dong
Ming Dong
Nanqing Dong
Qiulei Dong
Runpei Dong
Siyan Dong
Tian Dong
Wei Dong
Xiaomeng Dong
Xin Dong
Xingbo Dong
Yuan Dong

Samuel Dooley
Gianfranco Doretto
Michael Dorkenwald
Keval Doshi
Zhaopeng Dou
Xiaotian Dou
Hazel Doughty
Ahmad Droby
Iddo Drori
Jie Du
Yong Du
Dawei Du
Dong Du
Ruoyi Du
Yuntao Du
Xuefeng Du
Yilun Du
Yuming Du
Radhika Dua
Haodong Duan
Jiafei Duan
Kaiwen Duan
Peiqi Duan
Ye Duan
Haoran Duan
Jiali Duan
Amanda Duarte
Abhimanyu Dubey
Shiv Ram Dubey
Florian Dubost
Lukasz Dudziak
Shivam Duggal
Justin M. Dulay
Matteo Dunnhofer
Chi Nhan Duong
Thibaut Durand
Mihai Dusmanu
Ujjal Kr Dutta
Debidatta Dwibedi
Isht Dwivedi
Sai Kumar Dwivedi
Takeharu Eda
Mark Edmonds
Alexei A. Efros
Thibaud Ehret

Max Ehrlich
Mahsa Ehsanpour
Iván Eichhardt
Farshad Einabadi
Marvin Eisenberger
Hazim Kemal Ekenel
Mohamed El Banani
Ismail Elezi
Moshe Eliasof
Alaa El-Nouby
Ian Endres
Francis Engelmann
Deniz Engin
Chanho Eom
Dave Epstein
Maria C. Escobar
Victor A. Escorcia
Carlos Esteves
Sungmin Eum
Bernard J. E. Evans
Ivan Evtimov
Fevziye Irem Eyiokur
   Yaman
Matteo Fabbri
Sébastien Fabbro
Gabriele Facciolo
Masud Fahim
Bin Fan
Hehe Fan
Deng-Ping Fan
Aoxiang Fan
Chen-Chen Fan
Qi Fan
Zhaoxin Fan
Haoqi Fan
Heng Fan
Hongyi Fan
Linxi Fan
Baojie Fan
Jiayuan Fan
Lei Fan
Quanfu Fan
Yonghui Fan
Yingruo Fan
Zhiwen Fan

Zicong Fan
Sean Fanello
Jiansheng Fang
Chaowei Fang
Yuming Fang
Jianwu Fang
Jin Fang
Qi Fang
Shancheng Fang
Tian Fang
Xianyong Fang
Gongfan Fang
Zhen Fang
Hui Fang
Jiemin Fang
Le Fang
Pengfei Fang
Xiaolin Fang
Yuxin Fang
Zhaoyuan Fang
Ammarah Farooq
Azade Farshad
Zhengcong Fei
Michael Felsberg
Wei Feng
Chen Feng
Fan Feng
Andrew Feng
Xin Feng
Zheyun Feng
Ruicheng Feng
Mingtao Feng
Qianyu Feng
Shangbin Feng
Chun-Mei Feng
Zunlei Feng
Zhiyong Feng
Martin Fergie
Mustansar Fiaz
Marco Fiorucci
Michael Firman
Hamed Firooz
Volker Fischer
Corneliu O. Florea
Georgios Floros

Wolfgang Foerstner
Gianni Franchi
Jean-Sebastien Franco
Simone Frintrop
Anna Fruehstueck
Changhong Fu
Chaoyou Fu
Cheng-Yang Fu
Chi-Wing Fu
Deqing Fu
Huan Fu
Jun Fu
Kexue Fu
Ying Fu
Jianlong Fu
Jingjing Fu
Qichen Fu
Tsu-Jui Fu
Xueyang Fu
Yang Fu
Yanwei Fu
Yonggan Fu
Wolfgang Fuhl
Yasuhisa Fujii
Kent Fujiwara
Marco Fumero
Takuya Funatomi
Isabel Funke
Dario Fuoli
Antonino Furnari
Matheus A. Gadelha
Akshay Gadi Patil
Adrian Galdran
Guillermo Gallego
Silvano Galliani
Orazio Gallo
Leonardo Galteri
Matteo Gamba
Yiming Gan
Sujoy Ganguly
Harald Ganster
Boyan Gao
Changxin Gao
Daiheng Gao
Difei Gao

Chen Gao
Fei Gao
Lin Gao
Wei Gao
Yiming Gao
Junyu Gao
Guangyu Ryan Gao
Haichang Gao
Hongchang Gao
Jialin Gao
Jin Gao
Jun Gao
Katelyn Gao
Mingchen Gao
Mingfei Gao
Pan Gao
Shangqian Gao
Shanghua Gao
Xitong Gao
Yunhe Gao
Zhanning Gao
Elena Garces
Nuno Cruz Garcia
Noa Garcia
Guillermo
    Garcia-Hernando
Isha Garg
Rahul Garg
Sourav Garg
Quentin Garrido
Stefano Gasperini
Kent Gauen
Chandan Gautam
Shivam Gautam
Paul Gay
Chunjiang Ge
Shiming Ge
Wenhang Ge
Yanhao Ge
Zheng Ge
Songwei Ge
Weifeng Ge
Yixiao Ge
Yuying Ge
Shijie Geng

Zhengyang Geng
Kyle A. Genova
Georgios Georgakis
Markos Georgopoulos
Marcel Geppert
Shabnam Ghadar
Mina Ghadimi Atigh
Deepti Ghadiyaram
Maani Ghaffari Jadidi
Sedigh Ghamari
Zahra Gharaee
Michaël Gharbi
Golnaz Ghiasi
Reza Ghoddoosian
Soumya Suvra Ghosal
Adhiraj Ghosh
Arthita Ghosh
Pallabi Ghosh
Soumyadeep Ghosh
Andrew Gilbert
Igor Gilitschenski
Jhony H. Giraldo
Andreu Girbau Xalabarder
Rohit Girdhar
Sharath Girish
Xavier Giro-i-Nieto
Raja Giryes
Thomas Gittings
Nikolaos Gkanatsios
Ioannis Gkioulekas
Abhiram
    Gnanasambandam
Aurele T. Gnanha
Clement L. J. C. Godard
Arushi Goel
Vidit Goel
Shubham Goel
Zan Gojcic
Aaron K. Gokaslan
Tejas Gokhale
S. Alireza Golestaneh
Thiago L. Gomes
Nuno Goncalves
Boqing Gong
Chen Gong

Yuanhao Gong
Guoqiang Gong
Jingyu Gong
Rui Gong
Yu Gong
Mingming Gong
Neil Zhenqiang Gong
Xun Gong
Yunye Gong
Yihong Gong
Cristina I. González
Nithin Gopalakrishnan
    Nair
Gaurav Goswami
Jianping Gou
Shreyank N. Gowda
Ankit Goyal
Helmut Grabner
Patrick L. Grady
Ben Graham
Eric Granger
Douglas R. Gray
Matej Grcić
David Griffiths
Jinjin Gu
Yun Gu
Shuyang Gu
Jianyang Gu
Fuqiang Gu
Jiatao Gu
Jindong Gu
Jiaqi Gu
Jinwei Gu
Jiaxin Gu
Geonmo Gu
Xiao Gu
Xinqian Gu
Xiuye Gu
Yuming Gu
Zhangxuan Gu
Dayan Guan
Junfeng Guan
Qingji Guan
Tianrui Guan
Shanyan Guan

Denis A. Gudovskiy
Ricardo Guerrero
Pierre-Louis Guhur
Jie Gui
Liangyan Gui
Liangke Gui
Benoit Guillard
Erhan Gundogdu
Manuel Günther
Jingcai Guo
Yuanfang Guo
Junfeng Guo
Chenqi Guo
Dan Guo
Hongji Guo
Jia Guo
Jie Guo
Minghao Guo
Shi Guo
Yanhui Guo
Yangyang Guo
Yuan-Chen Guo
Yilu Guo
Yiluan Guo
Yong Guo
Guangyu Guo
Haiyun Guo
Jinyang Guo
Jianyuan Guo
Pengsheng Guo
Pengfei Guo
Shuxuan Guo
Song Guo
Tianyu Guo
Qing Guo
Qiushan Guo
Wen Guo
Xiefan Guo
Xiaohu Guo
Xiaoqing Guo
Yufei Guo
Yuhui Guo
Yuliang Guo
Yunhui Guo
Yanwen Guo

Akshita Gupta
Ankush Gupta
Kamal Gupta
Kartik Gupta
Ritwik Gupta
Rohit Gupta
Siddharth Gururani
Fredrik K. Gustafsson
Abner Guzman Rivera
Vladimir Guzov
Matthew A. Gwilliam
Jung-Woo Ha
Marc Habermann
Isma Hadji
Christian Haene
Martin Hahner
Levente Hajder
Alexandros Haliassos
Emanuela Haller
Bumsub Ham
Abdullah J. Hamdi
Shreyas Hampali
Dongyoon Han
Chunrui Han
Dong-Jun Han
Dong-Sig Han
Guangxing Han
Zhizhong Han
Ruize Han
Jiaming Han
Jin Han
Ligong Han
Xian-Hua Han
Xiaoguang Han
Yizeng Han
Zhi Han
Zhenjun Han
Zhongyi Han
Jungong Han
Junlin Han
Kai Han
Kun Han
Sungwon Han
Songfang Han
Wei Han

Xiao Han
Xintong Han
Xinzhe Han
Yahong Han
Yan Han
Zongbo Han
Nicolai Hani
Rana Hanocka
Niklas Hanselmann
Nicklas A. Hansen
Hong Hanyu
Fusheng Hao
Yanbin Hao
Shijie Hao
Udith Haputhanthri
Mehrtash Harandi
Josh Harguess
Adam Harley
David M. Hart
Atsushi Hashimoto
Ali Hassani
Mohammed Hassanin
Yana Hasson
Joakim Bruslund Haurum
Bo He
Kun He
Chen He
Xin He
Fazhi He
Gaoqi He
Hao He
Haoyu He
Jiangpeng He
Hongliang He
Qian He
Xiangteng He
Xuming He
Yannan He
Yuhang He
Yang He
Xiangyu He
Nanjun He
Pan He
Sen He
Shengfeng He

Songtao He
Tao He
Tong He
Wei He
Xuehai He
Xiaoxiao He
Ying He
Yisheng He
Ziwen He
Peter Hedman
Felix Heide
Yacov Hel-Or
Paul Henderson
Philipp Henzler
Byeongho Heo
Jae-Pil Heo
Miran Heo
Sachini A. Herath
Stephane Herbin
Pedro Hermosilla Casajus
Monica Hernandez
Charles Herrmann
Roei Herzig
Mauricio Hess-Flores
Carlos Hinojosa
Tobias Hinz
Tsubasa Hirakawa
Chih-Hui Ho
Lam Si Tung Ho
Jennifer Hobbs
Derek Hoiem
Yannick Hold-Geoffroy
Aleksander Holynski
Cheeun Hong
Fa-Ting Hong
Hanbin Hong
Guan Zhe Hong
Danfeng Hong
Lanqing Hong
Xiaopeng Hong
Xin Hong
Jie Hong
Seungbum Hong
Cheng-Yao Hong
Seunghoon Hong

Yi Hong
Yuan Hong
Yuchen Hong
Anthony Hoogs
Maxwell C. Horton
Kazuhiro Hotta
Qibin Hou
Tingbo Hou
Junhui Hou
Ji Hou
Qiqi Hou
Rui Hou
Ruibing Hou
Zhi Hou
Henry Howard-Jenkins
Lukas Hoyer
Wei-Lin Hsiao
Chiou-Ting Hsu
Anthony Hu
Brian Hu
Yusong Hu
Hexiang Hu
Haoji Hu
Di Hu
Hengtong Hu
Haigen Hu
Lianyu Hu
Hanzhe Hu
Jie Hu
Junlin Hu
Shizhe Hu
Jian Hu
Zhiming Hu
Juhua Hu
Peng Hu
Ping Hu
Ronghang Hu
MengShun Hu
Tao Hu
Vincent Tao Hu
Xiaoling Hu
Xinting Hu
Xiaolin Hu
Xuefeng Hu
Xiaowei Hu

Yang Hu
Yueyu Hu
Zeyu Hu
Zhongyun Hu
Binh-Son Hua
Guoliang Hua
Yi Hua
Linzhi Huang
Qiusheng Huang
Bo Huang
Chen Huang
Hsin-Ping Huang
Ye Huang
Shuangping Huang
Zeng Huang
Buzhen Huang
Cong Huang
Heng Huang
Hao Huang
Qidong Huang
Huaibo Huang
Chaoqin Huang
Feihu Huang
Jiahui Huang
Jingjia Huang
Kun Huang
Lei Huang
Sheng Huang
Shuaiyi Huang
Siyu Huang
Xiaoshui Huang
Xiaoyang Huang
Yan Huang
Yihao Huang
Ying Huang
Ziling Huang
Xiaoke Huang
Yifei Huang
Haiyang Huang
Zhewei Huang
Jin Huang
Haibin Huang
Jiaxing Huang
Junjie Huang
Keli Huang

Lang Huang
Lin Huang
Luojie Huang
Mingzhen Huang
Shijia Huang
Shengyu Huang
Siyuan Huang
He Huang
Xiuyu Huang
Lianghua Huang
Yue Huang
Yaping Huang
Yuge Huang
Zehao Huang
Zeyi Huang
Zhiqi Huang
Zhongzhan Huang
Zilong Huang
Ziyuan Huang
Tianrui Hui
Zhuo Hui
Le Hui
Jing Huo
Junhwa Hur
Shehzeen S. Hussain
Chuong Minh Huynh
Seunghyun Hwang
Jaehui Hwang
Jyh-Jing Hwang
Sukjun Hwang
Soonmin Hwang
Wonjun Hwang
Rakib Hyder
Sangeek Hyun
Sarah Ibrahimi
Tomoki Ichikawa
Yerlan Idelbayev
A. S. M. Iftekhar
Masaaki Iiyama
Satoshi Ikehata
Sunghoon Im
Atul N. Ingle
Eldar Insafutdinov
Yani A. Ioannou
Radu Tudor Ionescu

Umar Iqbal
Go Irie
Muhammad Zubair Irshad
Ahmet Iscen
Berivan Isik
Ashraful Islam
Md Amirul Islam
Syed Islam
Mariko Isogawa
Vamsi Krishna K. Ithapu
Boris Ivanovic
Darshan Iyer
Sarah Jabbour
Ayush Jain
Nishant Jain
Samyak Jain
Vidit Jain
Vineet Jain
Priyank Jaini
Tomas Jakab
Mohammad A. A. K.
    Jalwana
Muhammad Abdullah
    Jamal
Hadi Jamali-Rad
Stuart James
Varun Jampani
Young Kyun Jang
YeongJun Jang
Yunseok Jang
Ronnachai Jaroensri
Bhavan Jasani
Krishna Murthy
    Jatavallabhula
Mojan Javaheripi
Syed A. Javed
Guillaume Jeanneret
Pranav Jeevan
Herve Jegou
Rohit Jena
Tomas Jenicek
Porter Jenkins
Simon Jenni
Hae-Gon Jeon
Sangryul Jeon

Boseung Jeong
Yoonwoo Jeong
Seong-Gyun Jeong
Jisoo Jeong
Allan D. Jepson
Ankit Jha
Sumit K. Jha
I-Hong Jhuo
Ge-Peng Ji
Chaonan Ji
Deyi Ji
Jingwei Ji
Wei Ji
Zhong Ji
Jiayi Ji
Pengliang Ji
Hui Ji
Mingi Ji
Xiaopeng Ji
Yuzhu Ji
Baoxiong Jia
Songhao Jia
Dan Jia
Shan Jia
Xiaojun Jia
Xiuyi Jia
Xu Jia
Menglin Jia
Wenqi Jia
Boyuan Jiang
Wenhao Jiang
Huaizu Jiang
Hanwen Jiang
Haiyong Jiang
Hao Jiang
Huajie Jiang
Huiqin Jiang
Haojun Jiang
Haobo Jiang
Junjun Jiang
Xingyu Jiang
Yangbangyan Jiang
Yu Jiang
Jianmin Jiang
Jiaxi Jiang

Jing Jiang
Kui Jiang
Li Jiang
Liming Jiang
Chiyu Jiang
Meirui Jiang
Chen Jiang
Peng Jiang
Tai-Xiang Jiang
Wen Jiang
Xinyang Jiang
Yifan Jiang
Yuming Jiang
Yingying Jiang
Zeren Jiang
ZhengKai Jiang
Zhenyu Jiang
Shuming Jiao
Jianbo Jiao
Licheng Jiao
Dongkwon Jin
Yeying Jin
Cheng Jin
Linyi Jin
Qing Jin
Taisong Jin
Xiao Jin
Xin Jin
Sheng Jin
Kyong Hwan Jin
Ruibing Jin
SouYoung Jin
Yueming Jin
Chenchen Jing
Longlong Jing
Taotao Jing
Yongcheng Jing
Younghyun Jo
Joakim Johnander
Jeff Johnson
Michael J. Jones
R. Kenny Jones
Rico Jonschkowski
Ameya Joshi
Sunghun Joung

Felix Juefei-Xu
Claudio R. Jung
Steffen Jung
Hari Chandana K.
Rahul Vigneswaran K.
Prajwal K. R.
Abhishek Kadian
Jhony Kaesemodel Pontes
Kumara Kahatapitiya
Anmol Kalia
Sinan Kalkan
Tarun Kalluri
Jaewon Kam
Sandesh Kamath
Meina Kan
Menelaos Kanakis
Takuhiro Kaneko
Di Kang
Guoliang Kang
Hao Kang
Jaeyeon Kang
Kyoungkook Kang
Li-Wei Kang
MinGuk Kang
Suk-Ju Kang
Zhao Kang
Yash Mukund Kant
Yueying Kao
Aupendu Kar
Konstantinos Karantzalos
Sezer Karaoglu
Navid Kardan
Sanjay Kariyappa
Leonid Karlinsky
Animesh Karnewar
Shyamgopal Karthik
Hirak J. Kashyap
Marc A. Kastner
Hirokatsu Kataoka
Angelos Katharopoulos
Hiroharu Kato
Kai Katsumata
Manuel Kaufmann
Chaitanya Kaul
Prakhar Kaushik

Yuki Kawana
Lei Ke
Lipeng Ke
Tsung-Wei Ke
Wei Ke
Petr Kellnhofer
Aniruddha Kembhavi
John Kender
Corentin Kervadec
Leonid Keselman
Daniel Keysers
Nima Khademi Kalantari
Taras Khakhulin
Samir Khaki
Muhammad Haris Khan
Qadeer Khan
Salman Khan
Subash Khanal
Vaishnavi M. Khindkar
Rawal Khirodkar
Saeed Khorram
Pirazh Khorramshahi
Kourosh Khoshelham
Ansh Khurana
Benjamin Kiefer
Jae Myung Kim
Junho Kim
Boah Kim
Hyeonseong Kim
Dong-Jin Kim
Dongwan Kim
Donghyun Kim
Doyeon Kim
Yonghyun Kim
Hyung-Il Kim
Hyunwoo Kim
Hyeongwoo Kim
Hyo Jin Kim
Hyunwoo J. Kim
Taehoon Kim
Jaeha Kim
Jiwon Kim
Jung Uk Kim
Kangyeol Kim
Eunji Kim

Daeha Kim
Dongwon Kim
Kunhee Kim
Kyungmin Kim
Junsik Kim
Min H. Kim
Namil Kim
Kookhoi Kim
Sanghyun Kim
Seongyeop Kim
Seungryong Kim
Saehoon Kim
Euyoung Kim
Guisik Kim
Sungyeon Kim
Sunnie S. Y. Kim
Taehun Kim
Tae Oh Kim
Won Hwa Kim
Seungwook Kim
YoungBin Kim
Youngeun Kim
Akisato Kimura
Furkan Osman Kınlı
Zsolt Kira
Hedvig Kjellström
Florian Kleber
Jan P. Klopp
Florian Kluger
Laurent Kneip
Byungsoo Ko
Muhammed Kocabas
A. Sophia Koepke
Kevin Koeser
Nick Kolkin
Nikos Kolotouros
Wai-Kin Adams Kong
Deying Kong
Caihua Kong
Youyong Kong
Shuyu Kong
Shu Kong
Tao Kong
Yajing Kong
Yu Kong

Zishang Kong
Theodora Kontogianni
Anton S. Konushin
Julian F. P. Kooij
Bruno Korbar
Giorgos Kordopatis-Zilos
Jari Korhonen
Adam Kortylewski
Denis Korzhenkov
Divya Kothandaraman
Suraj Kothawade
Iuliia Kotseruba
Satwik Kottur
Shashank Kotyan
Alexandros Kouris
Petros Koutras
Anna Kreshuk
Ranjay Krishna
Dilip Krishnan
Andrey Kuehlkamp
Hilde Kuehne
Jason Kuen
David Kügler
Arjan Kuijper
Anna Kukleva
Sumith Kulal
Viveka Kulharia
Akshay R. Kulkarni
Nilesh Kulkarni
Dominik Kulon
Abhinav Kumar
Akash Kumar
Suryansh Kumar
B. V. K. Vijaya Kumar
Pulkit Kumar
Ratnesh Kumar
Sateesh Kumar
Satish Kumar
Vijay Kumar B. G.
Nupur Kumari
Sudhakar Kumawat
Jogendra Nath Kundu
Hsien-Kai Kuo
Meng-Yu Jennifer Kuo
Vinod Kumar Kurmi

Yusuke Kurose
Keerthy Kusumam
Alina Kuznetsova
Henry Kvinge
Ho Man Kwan
Hyeokjun Kweon
Heeseung Kwon
Gihyun Kwon
Myung-Joon Kwon
Taesung Kwon
YoungJoong Kwon
Christos Kyrkou
Jorma Laaksonen
Yann Labbe
Zorah Laehner
Florent Lafarge
Hamid Laga
Manuel Lagunas
Shenqi Lai
Jian-Huang Lai
Zihang Lai
Mohamed I. Lakhal
Mohit Lamba
Meng Lan
Loic Landrieu
Zhiqiang Lang
Natalie Lang
Dong Lao
Yizhen Lao
Yingjie Lao
Issam Hadj Laradji
Gustav Larsson
Viktor Larsson
Zakaria Laskar
Stéphane Lathuilière
Chun Pong Lau
Rynson W. H. Lau
Hei Law
Justin Lazarow
Verica Lazova
Eric-Tuan Le
Hieu Le
Trung-Nghia Le
Mathias Lechner
Byeong-Uk Lee

Chen-Yu Lee
Che-Rung Lee
Chul Lee
Hong Joo Lee
Dongsoo Lee
Jiyoung Lee
Eugene Eu Tzuan Lee
Daeun Lee
Saehyung Lee
Jewook Lee
Hyungtae Lee
Hyunmin Lee
Jungbeom Lee
Joon-Young Lee
Jong-Seok Lee
Joonseok Lee
Junha Lee
Kibok Lee
Byung-Kwan Lee
Jangwon Lee
Jinho Lee
Jongmin Lee
Seunghyun Lee
Sohyun Lee
Minsik Lee
Dogyoon Lee
Seungmin Lee
Min Jun Lee
Sangho Lee
Sangmin Lee
Seungeun Lee
Seon-Ho Lee
Sungmin Lee
Sungho Lee
Sangyoun Lee
Vincent C. S. S. Lee
Jaeseong Lee
Yong Jae Lee
Chenyang Lei
Chenyi Lei
Jiahui Lei
Xinyu Lei
Yinjie Lei
Jiaxu Leng
Luziwei Leng

Jan E. Lenssen
Vincent Lepetit
Thomas Leung
María Leyva-Vallina
Xin Li
Yikang Li
Baoxin Li
Bin Li
Bing Li
Bowen Li
Changlin Li
Chao Li
Chongyi Li
Guanyue Li
Shuai Li
Jin Li
Dingquan Li
Dongxu Li
Yiting Li
Gang Li
Dian Li
Guohao Li
Haoang Li
Haoliang Li
Haoran Li
Hengduo Li
Huafeng Li
Xiaoming Li
Hanao Li
Hongwei Li
Ziqiang Li
Jisheng Li
Jiacheng Li
Jia Li
Jiachen Li
Jiahao Li
Jianwei Li
Jiazhi Li
Jie Li
Jing Li
Jingjing Li
Jingtao Li
Jun Li
Junxuan Li
Kai Li

Kailin Li
Kenneth Li
Kun Li
Kunpeng Li
Aoxue Li
Chenglong Li
Chenglin Li
Changsheng Li
Zhichao Li
Qiang Li
Yanyu Li
Zuoyue Li
Xiang Li
Xuelong Li
Fangda Li
Ailin Li
Liang Li
Chun-Guang Li
Daiqing Li
Dong Li
Guanbin Li
Guorong Li
Haifeng Li
Jianan Li
Jianing Li
Jiaxin Li
Ke Li
Lei Li
Lincheng Li
Liulei Li
Lujun Li
Linjie Li
Lin Li
Pengyu Li
Ping Li
Qiufu Li
Qingyong Li
Rui Li
Siyuan Li
Wei Li
Wenbin Li
Xiangyang Li
Xinyu Li
Xiujun Li
Xiu Li

Xu Li
Ya-Li Li
Yao Li
Yongjie Li
Yijun Li
Yiming Li
Yuezun Li
Yu Li
Yunheng Li
Yuqi Li
Zhe Li
Zeming Li
Zhen Li
Zhengqin Li
Zhimin Li
Jiefeng Li
Jinpeng Li
Chengze Li
Jianwu Li
Lerenhan Li
Shan Li
Suichan Li
Xiangtai Li
Yanjie Li
Yandong Li
Zhuoling Li
Zhenqiang Li
Manyi Li
Maosen Li
Ji Li
Minjun Li
Mingrui Li
Mengtian Li
Junyi Li
Nianyi Li
Bo Li
Xiao Li
Peihua Li
Peike Li
Peizhao Li
Peiliang Li
Qi Li
Ren Li
Runze Li
Shile Li

Sheng Li
Shigang Li
Shiyu Li
Shuang Li
Shasha Li
Shichao Li
Tianye Li
Yuexiang Li
Wei-Hong Li
Wanhua Li
Weihao Li
Weiming Li
Weixin Li
Wenbo Li
Wenshuo Li
Weijian Li
Yunan Li
Xirong Li
Xianhang Li
Xiaoyu Li
Xueqian Li
Xuanlin Li
Xianzhi Li
Yunqiang Li
Yanjing Li
Yansheng Li
Yawei Li
Yi Li
Yong Li
Yong-Lu Li
Yuhang Li
Yu-Jhe Li
Yuxi Li
Yunsheng Li
Yanwei Li
Zechao Li
Zejian Li
Zeju Li
Zekun Li
Zhaowen Li
Zheng Li
Zhenyu Li
Zhiheng Li
Zhi Li
Zhong Li

Zhuowei Li
Zhuowan Li
Zhuohang Li
Zizhang Li
Chen Li
Yuan-Fang Li
Dongze Lian
Xiaochen Lian
Zhouhui Lian
Long Lian
Qing Lian
Jin Lianbao
Jinxiu S. Liang
Dingkang Liang
Jiahao Liang
Jianming Liang
Jingyun Liang
Kevin J. Liang
Kaizhao Liang
Chen Liang
Jie Liang
Senwei Liang
Ding Liang
Jiajun Liang
Jian Liang
Kongming Liang
Siyuan Liang
Yuanzhi Liang
Zhengfa Liang
Mingfu Liang
Xiaodan Liang
Xuefeng Liang
Yuxuan Liang
Kang Liao
Liang Liao
Hong-Yuan Mark Liao
Wentong Liao
Haofu Liao
Yue Liao
Minghui Liao
Shengcai Liao
Ting-Hsuan Liao
Xin Liao
Yinghong Liao
Teck Yian Lim

Che-Tsung Lin
Chung-Ching Lin
Chen-Hsuan Lin
Cheng Lin
Chuming Lin
Chunyu Lin
Dahua Lin
Wei Lin
Zheng Lin
Huaijia Lin
Jason Lin
Jierui Lin
Jiaying Lin
Jie Lin
Kai-En Lin
Kevin Lin
Guangfeng Lin
Jiehong Lin
Feng Lin
Hang Lin
Kwan-Yee Lin
Ke Lin
Luojun Lin
Qinghong Lin
Xiangbo Lin
Yi Lin
Zudi Lin
Shijie Lin
Yiqun Lin
Tzu-Heng Lin
Ming Lin
Shaohui Lin
SongNan Lin
Ji Lin
Tsung-Yu Lin
Xudong Lin
Yancong Lin
Yen-Chen Lin
Yiming Lin
Yuewei Lin
Zhiqiu Lin
Zinan Lin
Zhe Lin
David B. Lindell
Zhixin Ling

Zhan Ling
Alexander Liniger
Venice Erin B. Liong
Joey Litalien
Or Litany
Roee Litman
Ron Litman
Jim Little
Dor Litvak
Shaoteng Liu
Shuaicheng Liu
Andrew Liu
Xian Liu
Shaohui Liu
Bei Liu
Bo Liu
Yong Liu
Ming Liu
Yanbin Liu
Chenxi Liu
Daqi Liu
Di Liu
Difan Liu
Dong Liu
Dongfang Liu
Daizong Liu
Xiao Liu
Fangyi Liu
Fengbei Liu
Fenglin Liu
Bin Liu
Yuang Liu
Ao Liu
Hong Liu
Hongfu Liu
Huidong Liu
Ziyi Liu
Feng Liu
Hao Liu
Jie Liu
Jialun Liu
Jiang Liu
Jing Liu
Jingya Liu
Jiaming Liu

Jun Liu
Juncheng Liu
Jiawei Liu
Hongyu Liu
Chuanbin Liu
Haotian Liu
Lingqiao Liu
Chang Liu
Han Liu
Liu Liu
Min Liu
Yingqi Liu
Aishan Liu
Bingyu Liu
Benlin Liu
Boxiao Liu
Chenchen Liu
Chuanjian Liu
Daqing Liu
Huan Liu
Haozhe Liu
Jiaheng Liu
Wei Liu
Jingzhou Liu
Jiyuan Liu
Lingbo Liu
Nian Liu
Peiye Liu
Qiankun Liu
Shenglan Liu
Shilong Liu
Wen Liu
Wenyu Liu
Weifeng Liu
Wu Liu
Xiaolong Liu
Yang Liu
Yanwei Liu
Yingcheng Liu
Yongfei Liu
Yihao Liu
Yu Liu
Yunze Liu
Ze Liu
Zhenhua Liu

Zhenguang Liu
Lin Liu
Lihao Liu
Pengju Liu
Xinhai Liu
Yunfei Liu
Meng Liu
Minghua Liu
Mingyuan Liu
Miao Liu
Peirong Liu
Ping Liu
Qingjie Liu
Ruoshi Liu
Risheng Liu
Songtao Liu
Xing Liu
Shikun Liu
Shuming Liu
Sheng Liu
Songhua Liu
Tongliang Liu
Weibo Liu
Weide Liu
Weizhe Liu
Wenxi Liu
Weiyang Liu
Xin Liu
Xiaobin Liu
Xudong Liu
Xiaoyi Liu
Xihui Liu
Xinchen Liu
Xingtong Liu
Xinpeng Liu
Xinyu Liu
Xianpeng Liu
Xu Liu
Xingyu Liu
Yongtuo Liu
Yahui Liu
Yangxin Liu
Yaoyao Liu
Yaojie Liu
Yuliang Liu

Yongcheng Liu
Yuan Liu
Yufan Liu
Yu-Lun Liu
Yun Liu
Yunfan Liu
Yuanzhong Liu
Zhuoran Liu
Zhen Liu
Zheng Liu
Zhijian Liu
Zhisong Liu
Ziquan Liu
Ziyu Liu
Zhihua Liu
Zechun Liu
Zhaoyang Liu
Zhengzhe Liu
Stephan Liwicki
Shao-Yuan Lo
Sylvain Lobry
Suhas Lohit
Vishnu Suresh Lokhande
Vincenzo Lomonaco
Chengjiang Long
Guodong Long
Fuchen Long
Shangbang Long
Yang Long
Zijun Long
Vasco Lopes
Antonio M. Lopez
Roberto Javier
    Lopez-Sastre
Tobias Lorenz
Javier Lorenzo-Navarro
Yujing Lou
Qian Lou
Xiankai Lu
Changsheng Lu
Huimin Lu
Yongxi Lu
Hao Lu
Hong Lu
Jiasen Lu

Juwei Lu
Fan Lu
Guangming Lu
Jiwen Lu
Shun Lu
Tao Lu
Xiaonan Lu
Yang Lu
Yao Lu
Yongchun Lu
Zhiwu Lu
Cheng Lu
Liying Lu
Guo Lu
Xuequan Lu
Yanye Lu
Yantao Lu
Yuhang Lu
Fujun Luan
Jonathon Luiten
Jovita Lukasik
Alan Lukezic
Jonathan Samuel Lumentut
Mayank Lunayach
Ao Luo
Canjie Luo
Chong Luo
Xu Luo
Grace Luo
Jun Luo
Katie Z. Luo
Tao Luo
Cheng Luo
Fangzhou Luo
Gen Luo
Lei Luo
Sihui Luo
Weixin Luo
Yan Luo
Xiaoyan Luo
Yong Luo
Yadan Luo
Hao Luo
Ruotian Luo
Mi Luo

Tiange Luo
Wenjie Luo
Wenhan Luo
Xiao Luo
Zhiming Luo
Zhipeng Luo
Zhengyi Luo
Diogo C. Luvizon
Zhaoyang Lv
Gengyu Lyu
Lingjuan Lyu
Jun Lyu
Yuanyuan Lyu
Youwei Lyu
Yueming Lyu
Bingpeng Ma
Chao Ma
Chongyang Ma
Congbo Ma
Chih-Yao Ma
Fan Ma
Lin Ma
Haoyu Ma
Hengbo Ma
Jianqi Ma
Jiawei Ma
Jiayi Ma
Kede Ma
Kai Ma
Lingni Ma
Lei Ma
Xu Ma
Ning Ma
Benteng Ma
Cheng Ma
Andy J. Ma
Long Ma
Zhanyu Ma
Zhiheng Ma
Qianli Ma
Shiqiang Ma
Sizhuo Ma
Shiqing Ma
Xiaolong Ma
Xinzhu Ma

Gautam B. Machiraju
Spandan Madan
Mathew Magimai-Doss
Luca Magri
Behrooz Mahasseni
Upal Mahbub
Siddharth Mahendran
Paridhi Maheshwari
Rishabh Maheshwary
Mohammed Mahmoud
Shishira R. R. Maiya
Sylwia Majchrowska
Arjun Majumdar
Puspita Majumdar
Orchid Majumder
Sagnik Majumder
Ilya Makarov
Farkhod F.
    Makhmudkhujaev
Yasushi Makihara
Ankur Mali
Mateusz Malinowski
Utkarsh Mall
Srikanth Malla
Clement Mallet
Dimitrios Mallis
Yunze Man
Dipu Manandhar
Massimiliano Mancini
Murari Mandal
Raunak Manekar
Karttikeya Mangalam
Puneet Mangla
Fabian Manhardt
Sivabalan Manivasagam
Fahim Mannan
Chengzhi Mao
Hanzi Mao
Jiayuan Mao
Junhua Mao
Zhiyuan Mao
Jiageng Mao
Yunyao Mao
Zhendong Mao
Alberto Marchisio

Diego Marcos
Riccardo Marin
Aram Markosyan
Renaud Marlet
Ricardo Marques
Miquel Martí i Rabadán
Diego Martin Arroyo
Niki Martinel
Brais Martinez
Julieta Martinez
Marc Masana
Tomohiro Mashita
Timothée Masquelier
Minesh Mathew
Tetsu Matsukawa
Marwan Mattar
Bruce A. Maxwell
Christoph Mayer
Mantas Mazeika
Pratik Mazumder
Scott McCloskey
Steven McDonagh
Ishit Mehta
Jie Mei
Kangfu Mei
Jieru Mei
Xiaoguang Mei
Givi Meishvili
Luke Melas-Kyriazi
Iaroslav Melekhov
Andres Mendez-Vazquez
Heydi Mendez-Vazquez
Matias Mendieta
Ricardo A. Mendoza-León
Chenlin Meng
Depu Meng
Rang Meng
Zibo Meng
Qingjie Meng
Qier Meng
Yanda Meng
Zihang Meng
Thomas Mensink
Fabian Mentzer
Christopher Metzler

Gregory P. Meyer
Vasileios Mezaris
Liang Mi
Lu Mi
Bo Miao
Changtao Miao
Zichen Miao
Qiguang Miao
Xin Miao
Zhongqi Miao
Frank Michel
Simone Milani
Ben Mildenhall
Roy V. Miles
Juhong Min
Kyle Min
Hyun-Seok Min
Weiqing Min
Yuecong Min
Zhixiang Min
Qi Ming
David Minnen
Aymen Mir
Deepak Mishra
Anand Mishra
Shlok K. Mishra
Niluthpol Mithun
Gaurav Mittal
Trisha Mittal
Daisuke Miyazaki
Kaichun Mo
Hong Mo
Zhipeng Mo
Davide Modolo
Abduallah A. Mohamed
Mohamed Afham
    Mohamed Aflal
Ron Mokady
Pavlo Molchanov
Davide Moltisanti
Liliane Momeni
Gianluca Monaci
Pascal Monasse
Ajoy Mondal
Tom Monnier

Aron Monszpart
Gyeongsik Moon
Suhong Moon
Taesup Moon
Sean Moran
Daniel Moreira
Pietro Morerio
Alexandre Morgand
Lia Morra
Ali Mosleh
Inbar Mosseri
Sayed Mohammad
    Mostafavi Isfahani
Saman Motamed
Ramy A. Mounir
Fangzhou Mu
Jiteng Mu
Norman Mu
Yasuhiro Mukaigawa
Ryan Mukherjee
Tanmoy Mukherjee
Yusuke Mukuta
Ravi Teja Mullapudi
Lea Müller
Matthias Müller
Martin Mundt
Nils Murrugarra-Llerena
Damien Muselet
Armin Mustafa
Muhammad Ferjad Naeem
Sauradip Nag
Hajime Nagahara
Pravin Nagar
Rajendra Nagar
Naveen Shankar Nagaraja
Varun Nagaraja
Tushar Nagarajan
Seungjun Nah
Gaku Nakano
Yuta Nakashima
Giljoo Nam
Seonghyeon Nam
Liangliang Nan
Yuesong Nan
Yeshwanth Napolean

Dinesh Reddy
    Narapureddy
Medhini Narasimhan
Supreeth
    Narasimhaswamy
Sriram Narayanan
Erickson R. Nascimento
Varun Nasery
K. L. Navaneet
Pablo Navarrete Michelini
Shant Navasardyan
Shah Nawaz
Nihal Nayak
Farhood Negin
Lukáš Neumann
Alejandro Newell
Evonne Ng
Kam Woh Ng
Tony Ng
Anh Nguyen
Tuan Anh Nguyen
Cuong Cao Nguyen
Ngoc Cuong Nguyen
Thanh Nguyen
Khoi Nguyen
Phi Le Nguyen
Phong Ha Nguyen
Tam Nguyen
Truong Nguyen
Anh Tuan Nguyen
Rang Nguyen
Thao Thi Phuong Nguyen
Van Nguyen Nguyen
Zhen-Liang Ni
Yao Ni
Shijie Nie
Xuecheng Nie
Yongwei Nie
Weizhi Nie
Ying Nie
Yinyu Nie
Kshitij N. Nikhal
Simon Niklaus
Xuefei Ning
Jifeng Ning

Yotam Nitzan
Di Niu
Shuaicheng Niu
Li Niu
Wei Niu
Yulei Niu
Zhenxing Niu
Albert No
Shohei Nobuhara
Nicoletta Noceti
Junhyug Noh
Sotiris Nousias
Slawomir Nowaczyk
Ewa M. Nowara
Valsamis Ntouskos
Gilberto Ochoa-Ruiz
Ferda Ofli
Jihyong Oh
Sangyun Oh
Youngtaek Oh
Hiroki Ohashi
Takahiro Okabe
Kemal Oksuz
Fumio Okura
Daniel Olmeda Reino
Matthew Olson
Carl Olsson
Roy Or-El
Alessandro Ortis
Guillermo Ortiz-Jimenez
Magnus Oskarsson
Ahmed A. A. Osman
Martin R. Oswald
Mayu Otani
Naima Otberdout
Cheng Ouyang
Jiahong Ouyang
Wanli Ouyang
Andrew Owens
Poojan B. Oza
Mete Ozay
A. Cengiz Oztireli
Gautam Pai
Tomas Pajdla
Umapada Pal

Simone Palazzo
Luca Palmieri
Bowen Pan
Hao Pan
Lili Pan
Tai-Yu Pan
Liang Pan
Chengwei Pan
Yingwei Pan
Xuran Pan
Jinshan Pan
Xinyu Pan
Liyuan Pan
Xingang Pan
Xingjia Pan
Zhihong Pan
Zizheng Pan
Priyadarshini Panda
Rameswar Panda
Rohit Pandey
Kaiyue Pang
Bo Pang
Guansong Pang
Jiangmiao Pang
Meng Pang
Tianyu Pang
Ziqi Pang
Omiros Pantazis
Andreas Panteli
Maja Pantic
Marina Paolanti
Joao P. Papa
Samuele Papa
Mike Papadakis
Dim P. Papadopoulos
George Papandreou
Constantin Pape
Toufiq Parag
Chethan Parameshwara
Shaifali Parashar
Alejandro Pardo
Rishubh Parihar
Sarah Parisot
JaeYoo Park
Gyeong-Moon Park

Hyojin Park
Hyoungseob Park
Jongchan Park
Jae Sung Park
Kiru Park
Chunghyun Park
Kwanyong Park
Sunghyun Park
Sungrae Park
Seongsik Park
Sanghyun Park
Sungjune Park
Taesung Park
Gaurav Parmar
Paritosh Parmar
Alvaro Parra
Despoina Paschalidou
Or Patashnik
Shivansh Patel
Pushpak Pati
Prashant W. Patil
Vaishakh Patil
Suvam Patra
Jay Patravali
Badri Narayana Patro
Angshuman Paul
Sudipta Paul
Rémi Pautrat
Nick E. Pears
Adithya Pediredla
Wenjie Pei
Shmuel Peleg
Latha Pemula
Bo Peng
Houwen Peng
Yue Peng
Liangzu Peng
Baoyun Peng
Jun Peng
Pai Peng
Sida Peng
Xi Peng
Yuxin Peng
Songyou Peng
Wei Peng

Weiqi Peng
Wen-Hsiao Peng
Pramuditha Perera
Juan C. Perez
Eduardo Pérez Pellitero
Juan-Manuel Perez-Rua
Federico Pernici
Marco Pesavento
Stavros Petridis
Ilya A. Petrov
Vladan Petrovic
Mathis Petrovich
Suzanne Petryk
Hieu Pham
Quang Pham
Khoi Pham
Tung Pham
Huy Phan
Stephen Phillips
Cheng Perng Phoo
David Picard
Marco Piccirilli
Georg Pichler
A. J. Piergiovanni
Vipin Pillai
Silvia L. Pintea
Giovanni Pintore
Robinson Piramuthu
Fiora Pirri
Theodoros Pissas
Fabio Pizzati
Benjamin Planche
Bryan Plummer
Matteo Poggi
Ashwini Pokle
Georgy E. Ponimatkin
Adrian Popescu
Stefan Popov
Nikola Popović
Ronald Poppe
Angelo Porrello
Michael Potter
Charalambos Poullis
Hadi Pouransari
Omid Poursaeed

Shraman Pramanick
Mantini Pranav
Dilip K. Prasad
Meghshyam Prasad
B. H. Pawan Prasad
Shitala Prasad
Prateek Prasanna
Ekta Prashnani
Derek S. Prijatelj
Luke Y. Prince
Véronique Prinet
Victor Adrian Prisacariu
James Pritts
Thomas Probst
Sergey Prokudin
Rita Pucci
Chi-Man Pun
Matthew Purri
Haozhi Qi
Lu Qi
Lei Qi
Xianbiao Qi
Yonggang Qi
Yuankai Qi
Siyuan Qi
Guocheng Qian
Hangwei Qian
Qi Qian
Deheng Qian
Shengsheng Qian
Wen Qian
Rui Qian
Yiming Qian
Shengju Qian
Shengyi Qian
Xuelin Qian
Zhenxing Qian
Nan Qiao
Xiaotian Qiao
Jing Qin
Can Qin
Siyang Qin
Hongwei Qin
Jie Qin
Minghai Qin

Yipeng Qin
Yongqiang Qin
Wenda Qin
Xuebin Qin
Yuzhe Qin
Yao Qin
Zhenyue Qin
Zhiwu Qing
Heqian Qiu
Jiayan Qiu
Jielin Qiu
Yue Qiu
Jiaxiong Qiu
Zhongxi Qiu
Shi Qiu
Zhaofan Qiu
Zhongnan Qu
Yanyun Qu
Kha Gia Quach
Yuhui Quan
Ruijie Quan
Mike Rabbat
Rahul Shekhar Rade
Filip Radenovic
Gorjan Radevski
Bogdan Raducanu
Francesco Ragusa
Shafin Rahman
Md Mahfuzur Rahman
   Siddiquee
Hossein Rahmani
Kiran Raja
Sivaramakrishnan
   Rajaraman
Jathushan Rajasegaran
Adnan Siraj Rakin
Michaël Ramamonjisoa
Chirag A. Raman
Shanmuganathan Raman
Vignesh Ramanathan
Vasili Ramanishka
Vikram V. Ramaswamy
Merey Ramazanova
Jason Rambach
Sai Saketh Rambhatla

Clément Rambour
Ashwin Ramesh Babu
Adín Ramírez Rivera
Arianna Rampini
Haoxi Ran
Aakanksha Rana
Aayush Jung Bahadur
   Rana
Kanchana N. Ranasinghe
Aneesh Rangnekar
Samrudhdhi B. Rangrej
Harsh Rangwani
Viresh Ranjan
Anyi Rao
Yongming Rao
Carolina Raposo
Michalis Raptis
Amir Rasouli
Vivek Rathod
Adepu Ravi Sankar
Avinash Ravichandran
Bharadwaj Ravichandran
Dripta S. Raychaudhuri
Adria Recasens
Simon Reiß
Davis Rempe
Daxuan Ren
Jiawei Ren
Jimmy Ren
Sucheng Ren
Dayong Ren
Zhile Ren
Dongwei Ren
Qibing Ren
Pengfei Ren
Zhenwen Ren
Xuqian Ren
Yixuan Ren
Zhongzheng Ren
Ambareesh Revanur
Hamed Rezazadegan
   Tavakoli
Rafael S. Rezende
Wonjong Rhee
Alexander Richard

Christian Richardt
Stephan R. Richter
Benjamin Riggan
Dominik Rivoir
Mamshad Nayeem Rizve
Joshua D. Robinson
Joseph Robinson
Chris Rockwell
Ranga Rodrigo
Andres C. Rodriguez
Carlos Rodriguez-Pardo
Marcus Rohrbach
Gemma Roig
Yu Rong
David A. Ross
Mohammad Rostami
Edward Rosten
Karsten Roth
Anirban Roy
Debaditya Roy
Shuvendu Roy
Ahana Roy Choudhury
Aruni Roy Chowdhury
Denys Rozumnyi
Shulan Ruan
Wenjie Ruan
Patrick Ruhkamp
Danila Rukhovich
Anian Ruoss
Chris Russell
Dan Ruta
Dawid Damian Rymarczyk
DongHun Ryu
Hyeonggon Ryu
Kwonyoung Ryu
Balasubramanian S.
Alexandre Sablayrolles
Mohammad Sabokrou
Arka Sadhu
Aniruddha Saha
Oindrila Saha
Pritish Sahu
Aneeshan Sain
Nirat Saini
Saurabh Saini

Takeshi Saitoh
Christos Sakaridis
Fumihiko Sakaue
Dimitrios Sakkos
Ken Sakurada
Parikshit V. Sakurikar
Rohit Saluja
Nermin Samet
Leo Sampaio Ferraz
    Ribeiro
Jorge Sanchez
Enrique Sanchez
Shengtian Sang
Anush Sankaran
Soubhik Sanyal
Nikolaos Sarafianos
Vishwanath Saragadam
István Sárándi
Saquib Sarfraz
Mert Bulent Sariyildiz
Anindya Sarkar
Pritam Sarkar
Paul-Edouard Sarlin
Hiroshi Sasaki
Takami Sato
Torsten Sattler
Ravi Kumar Satzoda
Axel Sauer
Stefano Savian
Artem Savkin
Manolis Savva
Gerald Schaefer
Simone Schaub-Meyer
Yoni Schirris
Samuel Schulter
Katja Schwarz
Jesse Scott
Sinisa Segvic
Constantin Marc Seibold
Lorenzo Seidenari
Matan Sela
Fadime Sener
Paul Hongsuck Seo
Kwanggyoon Seo
Hongje Seong

Dario Serez
Francesco Setti
Bryan Seybold
Mohamad Shahbazi
Shima Shahfar
Xinxin Shan
Caifeng Shan
Dandan Shan
Shawn Shan
Wei Shang
Jinghuan Shang
Jiaxiang Shang
Lei Shang
Sukrit Shankar
Ken Shao
Rui Shao
Jie Shao
Mingwen Shao
Aashish Sharma
Gaurav Sharma
Vivek Sharma
Abhishek Sharma
Yoli Shavit
Shashank Shekhar
Sumit Shekhar
Zhijie Shen
Fengyi Shen
Furao Shen
Jialie Shen
Jingjing Shen
Ziyi Shen
Linlin Shen
Guangyu Shen
Biluo Shen
Falong Shen
Jiajun Shen
Qiu Shen
Qiuhong Shen
Shuai Shen
Wang Shen
Yiqing Shen
Yunhang Shen
Siqi Shen
Bin Shen
Tianwei Shen

Xi Shen
Yilin Shen
Yuming Shen
Yucong Shen
Zhiqiang Shen
Lu Sheng
Yichen Sheng
Shivanand Venkanna
    Sheshappanavar
Shelly Sheynin
Baifeng Shi
Ruoxi Shi
Botian Shi
Hailin Shi
Jia Shi
Jing Shi
Shaoshuai Shi
Baoguang Shi
Boxin Shi
Hengcan Shi
Tianyang Shi
Xiaodan Shi
Yongjie Shi
Zhensheng Shi
Yinghuan Shi
Weiqi Shi
Wu Shi
Xuepeng Shi
Xiaoshuang Shi
Yujiao Shi
Zenglin Shi
Zhenmei Shi
Takashi Shibata
Meng-Li Shih
Yichang Shih
Hyunjung Shim
Dongseok Shim
Soshi Shimada
Inkyu Shin
Jinwoo Shin
Seungjoo Shin
Seungjae Shin
Koichi Shinoda
Suprosanna Shit

Palaiahnakote
    Shivakumara
Eli Shlizerman
Gaurav Shrivastava
Xiao Shu
Xiangbo Shu
Xiujun Shu
Yang Shu
Tianmin Shu
Jun Shu
Zhixin Shu
Bing Shuai
Maria Shugrina
Ivan Shugurov
Satya Narayan Shukla
Pranjay Shyam
Jianlou Si
Yawar Siddiqui
Alberto Signoroni
Pedro Silva
Jae-Young Sim
Oriane Siméoni
Martin Simon
Andrea Simonelli
Abhishek Singh
Ashish Singh
Dinesh Singh
Gurkirt Singh
Krishna Kumar Singh
Mannat Singh
Pravendra Singh
Rajat Vikram Singh
Utkarsh Singhal
Dipika Singhania
Vasu Singla
Harsh Sinha
Sudipta Sinha
Josef Sivic
Elena Sizikova
Geri Skenderi
Ivan Skorokhodov
Dmitriy Smirnov
Cameron Y. Smith
James S. Smith
Patrick Snape

Mattia Soldan
Hyeongseok Son
Sanghyun Son
Chuanbiao Song
Chen Song
Chunfeng Song
Dan Song
Dongjin Song
Hwanjun Song
Guoxian Song
Jiaming Song
Jie Song
Liangchen Song
Ran Song
Luchuan Song
Xibin Song
Li Song
Fenglong Song
Guoli Song
Guanglu Song
Zhenbo Song
Lin Song
Xinhang Song
Yang Song
Yibing Song
Rajiv Soundararajan
Hossein Souri
Cristovao Sousa
Riccardo Spezialetti
Leonidas Spinoulas
Michael W. Spratling
Deepak Sridhar
Srinath Sridhar
Gaurang Sriramanan
Vinkle Kumar Srivastav
Themos Stafylakis
Serban Stan
Anastasis Stathopoulos
Markus Steinberger
Jan Steinbrener
Sinisa Stekovic
Alexandros Stergiou
Gleb Sterkin
Rainer Stiefelhagen
Pierre Stock

Ombretta Strafforello
Julian Straub
Yannick Strümpler
Joerg Stueckler
Hang Su
Weijie Su
Jong-Chyi Su
Bing Su
Haisheng Su
Jinming Su
Yiyang Su
Yukun Su
Yuxin Su
Zhuo Su
Zhaoqi Su
Xiu Su
Yu-Chuan Su
Zhixun Su
Arulkumar Subramaniam
Akshayvarun Subramanya
A. Subramanyam
Swathikiran Sudhakaran
Yusuke Sugano
Masanori Suganuma
Yumin Suh
Yang Sui
Baochen Sun
Cheng Sun
Long Sun
Guolei Sun
Haoliang Sun
Haomiao Sun
He Sun
Hanqing Sun
Hao Sun
Lichao Sun
Jiachen Sun
Jiaming Sun
Jian Sun
Jin Sun
Jennifer J. Sun
Tiancheng Sun
Libo Sun
Peize Sun
Qianru Sun

Shanlin Sun
Yu Sun
Zhun Sun
Che Sun
Lin Sun
Tao Sun
Yiyou Sun
Chunyi Sun
Chong Sun
Weiwei Sun
Weixuan Sun
Xiuyu Sun
Yanan Sun
Zeren Sun
Zhaodong Sun
Zhiqing Sun
Minhyuk Sung
Jinli Suo
Simon Suo
Abhijit Suprem
Anshuman Suri
Saksham Suri
Joshua M. Susskind
Roman Suvorov
Gurumurthy Swaminathan
Robin Swanson
Paul Swoboda
Tabish A. Syed
Richard Szeliski
Fariborz Taherkhani
Yu-Wing Tai
Keita Takahashi
Walter Talbott
Gary Tam
Masato Tamura
Feitong Tan
Fuwen Tan
Shuhan Tan
Andong Tan
Bin Tan
Cheng Tan
Jianchao Tan
Lei Tan
Mingxing Tan
Xin Tan

Zichang Tan
Zhentao Tan
Kenichiro Tanaka
Masayuki Tanaka
Yushun Tang
Hao Tang
Jingqun Tang
Jinhui Tang
Kaihua Tang
Luming Tang
Lv Tang
Sheyang Tang
Shitao Tang
Siliang Tang
Shixiang Tang
Yansong Tang
Keke Tang
Chang Tang
Chenwei Tang
Jie Tang
Junshu Tang
Ming Tang
Peng Tang
Xu Tang
Yao Tang
Chen Tang
Fan Tang
Haoran Tang
Shengeng Tang
Yehui Tang
Zhipeng Tang
Ugo Tanielian
Chaofan Tao
Jiale Tao
Junli Tao
Renshuai Tao
An Tao
Guanhong Tao
Zhiqiang Tao
Makarand Tapaswi
Jean-Philippe G. Tarel
Juan J. Tarrio
Enzo Tartaglione
Keisuke Tateno
Zachary Teed

Ajinkya B. Tejankar
Bugra Tekin
Purva Tendulkar
Damien Teney
Minggui Teng
Chris Tensmeyer
Andrew Beng Jin Teoh
Philipp Terhörst
Kartik Thakral
Nupur Thakur
Kevin Thandiackal
Spyridon Thermos
Diego Thomas
William Thong
Yuesong Tian
Guanzhong Tian
Lin Tian
Shiqi Tian
Kai Tian
Meng Tian
Tai-Peng Tian
Zhuotao Tian
Shangxuan Tian
Tian Tian
Yapeng Tian
Yu Tian
Yuxin Tian
Leslie Ching Ow Tiong
Praveen Tirupattur
Garvita Tiwari
George Toderici
Antoine Toisoul
Aysim Toker
Tatiana Tommasi
Zhan Tong
Alessio Tonioni
Alessandro Torcinovich
Fabio Tosi
Matteo Toso
Hugo Touvron
Quan Hung Tran
Son Tran
Hung Tran
Ngoc-Trung Tran
Vinh Tran

Phong Tran
Giovanni Trappolini
Edith Tretschk
Subarna Tripathi
Shubhendu Trivedi
Eduard Trulls
Prune Truong
Thanh-Dat Truong
Tomasz Trzcinski
Sam Tsai
Yi-Hsuan Tsai
Ethan Tseng
Yu-Chee Tseng
Shahar Tsiper
Stavros Tsogkas
Shikui Tu
Zhigang Tu
Zhengzhong Tu
Richard Tucker
Sergey Tulyakov
Cigdem Turan
Daniyar Turmukhambetov
Victor G. Turrisi da Costa
Bartlomiej Twardowski
Christopher D. Twigg
Radim Tylecek
Mostofa Rafid Uddin
Md. Zasim Uddin
Kohei Uehara
Nicolas Ugrinovic
Youngjung Uh
Norimichi Ukita
Anwaar Ulhaq
Devesh Upadhyay
Paul Upchurch
Yoshitaka Ushiku
Yuzuko Utsumi
Mikaela Angelina Uy
Mohit Vaishnav
Pratik Vaishnavi
Jeya Maria Jose Valanarasu
Matias A. Valdenegro Toro
Diego Valsesia
Wouter Van Gansbeke
Nanne van Noord

Simon Vandenhende
Farshid Varno
Cristina Vasconcelos
Francisco Vasconcelos
Alex Vasilescu
Subeesh Vasu
Arun Balajee Vasudevan
Kanav Vats
Vaibhav S. Vavilala
Sagar Vaze
Javier Vazquez-Corral
Andrea Vedaldi
Olga Veksler
Andreas Velten
Sai H. Vemprala
Raviteja Vemulapalli
Shashanka
    Venkataramanan
Dor Verbin
Luisa Verdoliva
Manisha Verma
Yashaswi Verma
Constantin Vertan
Eli Verwimp
Deepak Vijaykeerthy
Pablo Villanueva
Ruben Villegas
Markus Vincze
Vibhav Vineet
Minh P. Vo
Huy V. Vo
Duc Minh Vo
Tomas Vojir
Igor Vozniak
Nicholas Vretos
Vibashan VS
Tuan-Anh Vu
Thang Vu
Mårten Wadenbäck
Neal Wadhwa
Aaron T. Walsman
Steven Walton
Jin Wan
Alvin Wan
Jia Wan

Jun Wan
Xiaoyue Wan
Fang Wan
Guowei Wan
Renjie Wan
Zhiqiang Wan
Ziyu Wan
Bastian Wandt
Dongdong Wang
Limin Wang
Haiyang Wang
Xiaobing Wang
Angtian Wang
Angelina Wang
Bing Wang
Bo Wang
Boyu Wang
Binghui Wang
Chen Wang
Chien-Yi Wang
Congli Wang
Qi Wang
Chengrui Wang
Rui Wang
Yiqun Wang
Cong Wang
Wenjing Wang
Dongkai Wang
Di Wang
Xiaogang Wang
Kai Wang
Zhizhong Wang
Fangjinhua Wang
Feng Wang
Hang Wang
Gaoang Wang
Guoqing Wang
Guangcong Wang
Guangzhi Wang
Hanqing Wang
Hao Wang
Haohan Wang
Haoran Wang
Hong Wang
Haotao Wang

Hu Wang
Huan Wang
Hua Wang
Hui-Po Wang
Hengli Wang
Hanyu Wang
Hongxing Wang
Jingwen Wang
Jialiang Wang
Jian Wang
Jianyi Wang
Jiashun Wang
Jiahao Wang
Tsun-Hsuan Wang
Xiaoqian Wang
Jinqiao Wang
Jun Wang
Jianzong Wang
Kaihong Wang
Ke Wang
Lei Wang
Lingjing Wang
Linnan Wang
Lin Wang
Liansheng Wang
Mengjiao Wang
Manning Wang
Nannan Wang
Peihao Wang
Jiayun Wang
Pu Wang
Qiang Wang
Qiufeng Wang
Qilong Wang
Qiangchang Wang
Qin Wang
Qing Wang
Ruocheng Wang
Ruibin Wang
Ruisheng Wang
Ruizhe Wang
Runqi Wang
Runzhong Wang
Wenxuan Wang
Sen Wang

Shangfei Wang
Shaofei Wang
Shijie Wang
Shiqi Wang
Zhibo Wang
Song Wang
Xinjiang Wang
Tai Wang
Tao Wang
Teng Wang
Xiang Wang
Tianren Wang
Tiantian Wang
Tianyi Wang
Fengjiao Wang
Wei Wang
Miaohui Wang
Suchen Wang
Siyue Wang
Yaoming Wang
Xiao Wang
Ze Wang
Biao Wang
Chaofei Wang
Dong Wang
Gu Wang
Guangrun Wang
Guangming Wang
Guo-Hua Wang
Haoqing Wang
Hesheng Wang
Huafeng Wang
Jinghua Wang
Jingdong Wang
Jingjing Wang
Jingya Wang
Jingkang Wang
Jiakai Wang
Junke Wang
Kuo Wang
Lichen Wang
Lizhi Wang
Longguang Wang
Mang Wang
Mei Wang

Min Wang
Peng-Shuai Wang
Run Wang
Shaoru Wang
Shuhui Wang
Tan Wang
Tiancai Wang
Tianqi Wang
Wenhai Wang
Wenzhe Wang
Xiaobo Wang
Xiudong Wang
Xu Wang
Yajie Wang
Yan Wang
Yuan-Gen Wang
Yingqian Wang
Yizhi Wang
Yulin Wang
Yu Wang
Yujie Wang
Yunhe Wang
Yuxi Wang
Yaowei Wang
Yiwei Wang
Zezheng Wang
Hongzhi Wang
Zhiqiang Wang
Ziteng Wang
Ziwei Wang
Zheng Wang
Zhenyu Wang
Binglu Wang
Zhongdao Wang
Ce Wang
Weining Wang
Weiyao Wang
Wenbin Wang
Wenguan Wang
Guangting Wang
Haolin Wang
Haiyan Wang
Huiyu Wang
Naiyan Wang
Jingbo Wang

Jinpeng Wang
Jiaqi Wang
Liyuan Wang
Lizhen Wang
Ning Wang
Wenqian Wang
Sheng-Yu Wang
Weimin Wang
Xiaohan Wang
Yifan Wang
Yi Wang
Yongtao Wang
Yizhou Wang
Zhuo Wang
Zhe Wang
Xudong Wang
Xiaofang Wang
Xinggang Wang
Xiaosen Wang
Xiaosong Wang
Xiaoyang Wang
Lijun Wang
Xinlong Wang
Xuan Wang
Xue Wang
Yangang Wang
Yaohui Wang
Yu-Chiang Frank Wang
Yida Wang
Yilin Wang
Yi Ru Wang
Yali Wang
Yinglong Wang
Yufu Wang
Yujiang Wang
Yuwang Wang
Yuting Wang
Yang Wang
Yu-Xiong Wang
Yixu Wang
Ziqi Wang
Zhicheng Wang
Zeyu Wang
Zhaowen Wang
Zhenyi Wang

Zhenzhi Wang
Zhijie Wang
Zhiyong Wang
Zhongling Wang
Zhuowei Wang
Zian Wang
Zifu Wang
Zihao Wang
Zirui Wang
Ziyan Wang
Wenxiao Wang
Zhen Wang
Zhepeng Wang
Zi Wang
Zihao W. Wang
Steven L. Waslander
Olivia Watkins
Daniel Watson
Silvan Weder
Dongyoon Wee
Dongming Wei
Tianyi Wei
Jia Wei
Dong Wei
Fangyun Wei
Longhui Wei
Mingqiang Wei
Xinyue Wei
Chen Wei
Donglai Wei
Pengxu Wei
Xing Wei
Xiu-Shen Wei
Wenqi Wei
Guoqiang Wei
Wei Wei
XingKui Wei
Xian Wei
Xingxing Wei
Yake Wei
Yuxiang Wei
Yi Wei
Luca Weihs
Michael Weinmann
Martin Weinmann

Congcong Wen
Chuan Wen
Jie Wen
Sijia Wen
Song Wen
Chao Wen
Xiang Wen
Zeyi Wen
Xin Wen
Yilin Wen
Yijia Weng
Shuchen Weng
Junwu Weng
Wenming Weng
Renliang Weng
Zhenyu Weng
Xinshuo Weng
Nicholas J. Westlake
Gordon Wetzstein
Lena M. Widin Klasén
Rick Wildes
Bryan M. Williams
Williem Williem
Ole Winther
Scott Wisdom
Alex Wong
Chau-Wai Wong
Kwan-Yee K. Wong
Yongkang Wong
Scott Workman
Marcel Worring
Michael Wray
Safwan Wshah
Xiang Wu
Aming Wu
Chongruo Wu
Cho-Ying Wu
Chunpeng Wu
Chenyan Wu
Ziyi Wu
Fuxiang Wu
Gang Wu
Haiping Wu
Huisi Wu
Jane Wu

Jialian Wu
Jing Wu
Jinjian Wu
Jianlong Wu
Xian Wu
Lifang Wu
Lifan Wu
Minye Wu
Qianyi Wu
Rongliang Wu
Rui Wu
Shiqian Wu
Shuzhe Wu
Shangzhe Wu
Tsung-Han Wu
Tz-Ying Wu
Ting-Wei Wu
Jiannan Wu
Zhiliang Wu
Yu Wu
Chenyun Wu
Dayan Wu
Dongxian Wu
Fei Wu
Hefeng Wu
Jianxin Wu
Weibin Wu
Wenxuan Wu
Wenhao Wu
Xiao Wu
Yicheng Wu
Yuanwei Wu
Yu-Huan Wu
Zhenxin Wu
Zhenyu Wu
Wei Wu
Peng Wu
Xiaohe Wu
Xindi Wu
Xinxing Wu
Xinyi Wu
Xingjiao Wu
Xiongwei Wu
Yangzheng Wu
Yanzhao Wu

Yawen Wu
Yong Wu
Yi Wu
Ying Nian Wu
Zhenyao Wu
Zhonghua Wu
Zongze Wu
Zuxuan Wu
Stefanie Wuhrer
Teng Xi
Jianing Xi
Fei Xia
Haifeng Xia
Menghan Xia
Yuanqing Xia
Zhihua Xia
Xiaobo Xia
Weihao Xia
Shihong Xia
Yan Xia
Yong Xia
Zhaoyang Xia
Zhihao Xia
Chuhua Xian
Yongqin Xian
Wangmeng Xiang
Fanbo Xiang
Tiange Xiang
Tao Xiang
Liuyu Xiang
Xiaoyu Xiang
Zhiyu Xiang
Aoran Xiao
Chunxia Xiao
Fanyi Xiao
Jimin Xiao
Jun Xiao
Taihong Xiao
Anqi Xiao
Junfei Xiao
Jing Xiao
Liang Xiao
Yang Xiao
Yuting Xiao
Yijun Xiao

Yao Xiao
Zeyu Xiao
Zhisheng Xiao
Zihao Xiao
Binhui Xie
Christopher Xie
Haozhe Xie
Jin Xie
Guo-Sen Xie
Hongtao Xie
Ming-Kun Xie
Tingting Xie
Chaohao Xie
Weicheng Xie
Xudong Xie
Jiyang Xie
Xiaohua Xie
Yuan Xie
Zhenyu Xie
Ning Xie
Xianghui Xie
Xiufeng Xie
You Xie
Yutong Xie
Fuyong Xing
Yifan Xing
Zhen Xing
Yuanjun Xiong
Jinhui Xiong
Weihua Xiong
Hongkai Xiong
Zhitong Xiong
Yuanhao Xiong
Yunyang Xiong
Yuwen Xiong
Zhiwei Xiong
Yuliang Xiu
An Xu
Chang Xu
Chenliang Xu
Chengming Xu
Chenshu Xu
Xiang Xu
Huijuan Xu
Zhe Xu

Jie Xu
Jingyi Xu
Jiarui Xu
Yinghao Xu
Kele Xu
Ke Xu
Li Xu
Linchuan Xu
Linning Xu
Mengde Xu
Mengmeng Frost Xu
Min Xu
Mingye Xu
Jun Xu
Ning Xu
Peng Xu
Runsheng Xu
Sheng Xu
Wenqiang Xu
Xiaogang Xu
Renzhe Xu
Kaidi Xu
Yi Xu
Chi Xu
Qiuling Xu
Baobei Xu
Feng Xu
Haohang Xu
Haofei Xu
Lan Xu
Mingze Xu
Songcen Xu
Weipeng Xu
Wenjia Xu
Wenju Xu
Xiangyu Xu
Xin Xu
Yinshuang Xu
Yixing Xu
Yuting Xu
Yanyu Xu
Zhenbo Xu
Zhiliang Xu
Zhiyuan Xu
Xiaohao Xu

Yanwu Xu
Yan Xu
Yiran Xu
Yifan Xu
Yufei Xu
Yong Xu
Zichuan Xu
Zenglin Xu
Zexiang Xu
Zhan Xu
Zheng Xu
Zhiwei Xu
Ziyue Xu
Shiyu Xuan
Hanyu Xuan
Fei Xue
Jianru Xue
Mingfu Xue
Qinghan Xue
Tianfan Xue
Chao Xue
Chuhui Xue
Nan Xue
Zhou Xue
Xiangyang Xue
Yuan Xue
Abhay Yadav
Ravindra Yadav
Kota Yamaguchi
Toshihiko Yamasaki
Kohei Yamashita
Chaochao Yan
Feng Yan
Kun Yan
Qingsen Yan
Qixin Yan
Rui Yan
Siming Yan
Xinchen Yan
Yaping Yan
Bin Yan
Qingan Yan
Shen Yan
Shipeng Yan
Xu Yan

Yan Yan
Yichao Yan
Zhaoyi Yan
Zike Yan
Zhiqiang Yan
Hongliang Yan
Zizheng Yan
Jiewen Yang
Anqi Joyce Yang
Shan Yang
Anqi Yang
Antoine Yang
Bo Yang
Baoyao Yang
Chenhongyi Yang
Dingkang Yang
De-Nian Yang
Dong Yang
David Yang
Fan Yang
Fengyu Yang
Fengting Yang
Fei Yang
Gengshan Yang
Heng Yang
Han Yang
Huan Yang
Yibo Yang
Jiancheng Yang
Jihan Yang
Jiawei Yang
Jiayu Yang
Jie Yang
Jinfa Yang
Jingkang Yang
Jinyu Yang
Cheng-Fu Yang
Ji Yang
Jianyu Yang
Kailun Yang
Tian Yang
Luyu Yang
Liang Yang
Li Yang
Michael Ying Yang

Yang Yang
Muli Yang
Le Yang
Qiushi Yang
Ren Yang
Ruihan Yang
Shuang Yang
Siyuan Yang
Su Yang
Shiqi Yang
Taojiannan Yang
Tianyu Yang
Lei Yang
Wanzhao Yang
Shuai Yang
William Yang
Wei Yang
Xiaofeng Yang
Xiaoshan Yang
Xin Yang
Xuan Yang
Xu Yang
Xingyi Yang
Xitong Yang
Jing Yang
Yanchao Yang
Wenming Yang
Yujiu Yang
Herb Yang
Jianfei Yang
Jinhui Yang
Chuanguang Yang
Guanglei Yang
Haitao Yang
Kewei Yang
Linlin Yang
Lijin Yang
Longrong Yang
Meng Yang
MingKun Yang
Sibei Yang
Shicai Yang
Tong Yang
Wen Yang
Xi Yang

Xiaolong Yang
Xue Yang
Yubin Yang
Ze Yang
Ziyi Yang
Yi Yang
Linjie Yang
Yuzhe Yang
Yiding Yang
Zhenpei Yang
Zhaohui Yang
Zhengyuan Yang
Zhibo Yang
Zongxin Yang
Hantao Yao
Mingde Yao
Rui Yao
Taiping Yao
Ting Yao
Cong Yao
Qingsong Yao
Quanming Yao
Xu Yao
Yuan Yao
Yao Yao
Yazhou Yao
Jiawen Yao
Shunyu Yao
Pew-Thian Yap
Sudhir Yarram
Rajeev Yasarla
Peng Ye
Botao Ye
Mao Ye
Fei Ye
Hanrong Ye
Jingwen Ye
Jinwei Ye
Jiarong Ye
Mang Ye
Meng Ye
Qi Ye
Qian Ye
Qixiang Ye
Junjie Ye

Sheng Ye
Nanyang Ye
Yufei Ye
Xiaoqing Ye
Ruolin Ye
Yousef Yeganeh
Chun-Hsiao Yeh
Raymond A. Yeh
Yu-Ying Yeh
Kai Yi
Chang Yi
Renjiao Yi
Xinping Yi
Peng Yi
Alper Yilmaz
Junho Yim
Hui Yin
Bangjie Yin
Jia-Li Yin
Miao Yin
Wenzhe Yin
Xuwang Yin
Ming Yin
Yu Yin
Aoxiong Yin
Kangxue Yin
Tianwei Yin
Wei Yin
Xianghua Ying
Rio Yokota
Tatsuya Yokota
Naoto Yokoya
Ryo Yonetani
Ki Yoon Yoo
Jinsu Yoo
Sunjae Yoon
Jae Shin Yoon
Jihun Yoon
Sung-Hoon Yoon
Ryota Yoshihashi
Yusuke Yoshiyasu
Chenyu You
Haoran You
Haoxuan You
Yang You

Quanzeng You
Tackgeun You
Kaichao You
Shan You
Xinge You
Yurong You
Baosheng Yu
Bei Yu
Haichao Yu
Hao Yu
Chaohui Yu
Fisher Yu
Jin-Gang Yu
Jiyang Yu
Jason J. Yu
Jiashuo Yu
Hong-Xing Yu
Lei Yu
Mulin Yu
Ning Yu
Peilin Yu
Qi Yu
Qian Yu
Rui Yu
Shuzhi Yu
Gang Yu
Tan Yu
Weijiang Yu
Xin Yu
Bingyao Yu
Ye Yu
Hanchao Yu
Yingchen Yu
Tao Yu
Xiaotian Yu
Qing Yu
Houjian Yu
Changqian Yu
Jing Yu
Jun Yu
Shujian Yu
Xiang Yu
Zhaofei Yu
Zhenbo Yu
Yinfeng Yu

Zhuoran Yu
Zitong Yu
Bo Yuan
Jiangbo Yuan
Liangzhe Yuan
Weihao Yuan
Jianbo Yuan
Xiaoyun Yuan
Ye Yuan
Li Yuan
Geng Yuan
Jialin Yuan
Maoxun Yuan
Peng Yuan
Xin Yuan
Yuan Yuan
Yuhui Yuan
Yixuan Yuan
Zheng Yuan
Mehmet Kerim Yücel
Kaiyu Yue
Haixiao Yue
Heeseung Yun
Sangdoo Yun
Tian Yun
Mahmut Yurt
Ekim Yurtsever
Ahmet Yüzügüler
Edouard Yvinec
Eloi Zablocki
Christopher Zach
Muhammad Zaigham
    Zaheer
Pierluigi Zama Ramirez
Yuhang Zang
Pietro Zanuttigh
Alexey Zaytsev
Bernhard Zeisl
Haitian Zeng
Pengpeng Zeng
Jiabei Zeng
Runhao Zeng
Wei Zeng
Yawen Zeng
Yi Zeng

Yiming Zeng
Tieyong Zeng
Huanqiang Zeng
Dan Zeng
Yu Zeng
Wei Zhai
Yuanhao Zhai
Fangneng Zhan
Kun Zhan
Xiong Zhang
Jingdong Zhang
Jiangning Zhang
Zhilu Zhang
Gengwei Zhang
Dongsu Zhang
Hui Zhang
Binjie Zhang
Bo Zhang
Tianhao Zhang
Cecilia Zhang
Jing Zhang
Chaoning Zhang
Chenxu Zhang
Chi Zhang
Chris Zhang
Yabin Zhang
Zhao Zhang
Rufeng Zhang
Chaoyi Zhang
Zheng Zhang
Da Zhang
Yi Zhang
Edward Zhang
Xin Zhang
Feifei Zhang
Feilong Zhang
Yuqi Zhang
GuiXuan Zhang
Hanlin Zhang
Hanwang Zhang
Hanzhen Zhang
Haotian Zhang
He Zhang
Haokui Zhang
Hongyuan Zhang

Hengrui Zhang
Hongming Zhang
Mingfang Zhang
Jianpeng Zhang
Jiaming Zhang
Jichao Zhang
Jie Zhang
Jingfeng Zhang
Jingyi Zhang
Jinnian Zhang
David Junhao Zhang
Junjie Zhang
Junzhe Zhang
Jiawan Zhang
Jingyang Zhang
Kai Zhang
Lei Zhang
Lihua Zhang
Lu Zhang
Miao Zhang
Minjia Zhang
Mingjin Zhang
Qi Zhang
Qian Zhang
Qilong Zhang
Qiming Zhang
Qiang Zhang
Richard Zhang
Ruimao Zhang
Ruisi Zhang
Ruixin Zhang
Runze Zhang
Qilin Zhang
Shan Zhang
Shanshan Zhang
Xi Sheryl Zhang
Song-Hai Zhang
Chongyang Zhang
Kaihao Zhang
Songyang Zhang
Shu Zhang
Siwei Zhang
Shujian Zhang
Tianyun Zhang
Tong Zhang

Tao Zhang
Wenwei Zhang
Wenqiang Zhang
Wen Zhang
Xiaolin Zhang
Xingchen Zhang
Xingxuan Zhang
Xiuming Zhang
Xiaoshuai Zhang
Xuanmeng Zhang
Xuanyang Zhang
Xucong Zhang
Xingxing Zhang
Xikun Zhang
Xiaohan Zhang
Yahui Zhang
Yunhua Zhang
Yan Zhang
Yanghao Zhang
Yifei Zhang
Yifan Zhang
Yi-Fan Zhang
Yihao Zhang
Yingliang Zhang
Youshan Zhang
Yulun Zhang
Yushu Zhang
Yixiao Zhang
Yide Zhang
Zhongwen Zhang
Bowen Zhang
Chen-Lin Zhang
Zehua Zhang
Zekun Zhang
Zeyu Zhang
Xiaowei Zhang
Yifeng Zhang
Cheng Zhang
Hongguang Zhang
Yuexi Zhang
Fa Zhang
Guofeng Zhang
Hao Zhang
Haofeng Zhang
Hongwen Zhang

Hua Zhang
Jiaxin Zhang
Zhenyu Zhang
Jian Zhang
Jianfeng Zhang
Jiao Zhang
Jiakai Zhang
Lefei Zhang
Le Zhang
Mi Zhang
Min Zhang
Ning Zhang
Pan Zhang
Pu Zhang
Qing Zhang
Renrui Zhang
Shifeng Zhang
Shuo Zhang
Shaoxiong Zhang
Weizhong Zhang
Xi Zhang
Xiaomei Zhang
Xinyu Zhang
Yin Zhang
Zicheng Zhang
Zihao Zhang
Ziqi Zhang
Zhaoxiang Zhang
Zhen Zhang
Zhipeng Zhang
Zhixing Zhang
Zhizheng Zhang
Jiawei Zhang
Zhong Zhang
Pingping Zhang
Yixin Zhang
Kui Zhang
Lingzhi Zhang
Huaiwen Zhang
Quanshi Zhang
Zhoutong Zhang
Yuhang Zhang
Yuting Zhang
Zhang Zhang
Ziming Zhang

Zhizhong Zhang
Qilong Zhangli
Bingyin Zhao
Bin Zhao
Chenglong Zhao
Lei Zhao
Feng Zhao
Gangming Zhao
Haiyan Zhao
Hao Zhao
Handong Zhao
Hengshuang Zhao
Yinan Zhao
Jiaojiao Zhao
Jiaqi Zhao
Jing Zhao
Kaili Zhao
Haojie Zhao
Yucheng Zhao
Longjiao Zhao
Long Zhao
Qingsong Zhao
Qingyu Zhao
Rui Zhao
Rui-Wei Zhao
Sicheng Zhao
Shuang Zhao
Siyan Zhao
Zelin Zhao
Shiyu Zhao
Wang Zhao
Tiesong Zhao
Qian Zhao
Wangbo Zhao
Xi-Le Zhao
Xu Zhao
Yajie Zhao
Yang Zhao
Ying Zhao
Yin Zhao
Yizhou Zhao
Yunhan Zhao
Yuyang Zhao
Yue Zhao
Yuzhi Zhao

Bowen Zhao
Pu Zhao
Bingchen Zhao
Borui Zhao
Fuqiang Zhao
Hanbin Zhao
Jian Zhao
Mingyang Zhao
Na Zhao
Rongchang Zhao
Ruiqi Zhao
Shuai Zhao
Wenda Zhao
Wenliang Zhao
Xiangyun Zhao
Yifan Zhao
Yaping Zhao
Zhou Zhao
He Zhao
Jie Zhao
Xibin Zhao
Xiaoqi Zhao
Zhengyu Zhao
Jin Zhe
Chuanxia Zheng
Huan Zheng
Hao Zheng
Jia Zheng
Jian-Qing Zheng
Shuai Zheng
Meng Zheng
Mingkai Zheng
Qian Zheng
Qi Zheng
Wu Zheng
Yinqiang Zheng
Yufeng Zheng
Yutong Zheng
Yalin Zheng
Yu Zheng
Feng Zheng
Zhaoheng Zheng
Haitian Zheng
Kang Zheng
Bolun Zheng

Haiyong Zheng
Mingwu Zheng
Sipeng Zheng
Tu Zheng
Wenzhao Zheng
Xiawu Zheng
Yinglin Zheng
Zhuo Zheng
Zilong Zheng
Kecheng Zheng
Zerong Zheng
Shuaifeng Zhi
Tiancheng Zhi
Jia-Xing Zhong
Yiwu Zhong
Fangwei Zhong
Zhihang Zhong
Yaoyao Zhong
Yiran Zhong
Zhun Zhong
Zichun Zhong
Bo Zhou
Boyao Zhou
Brady Zhou
Mo Zhou
Chunluan Zhou
Dingfu Zhou
Fan Zhou
Jingkai Zhou
Honglu Zhou
Jiaming Zhou
Jiahuan Zhou
Jun Zhou
Kaiyang Zhou
Keyang Zhou
Kuangqi Zhou
Lei Zhou
Lihua Zhou
Man Zhou
Mingyi Zhou
Mingyuan Zhou
Ning Zhou
Peng Zhou
Penghao Zhou
Qianyi Zhou

Shuigeng Zhou
Shangchen Zhou
Huayi Zhou
Zhize Zhou
Sanping Zhou
Qin Zhou
Tao Zhou
Wenbo Zhou
Xiangdong Zhou
Xiao-Yun Zhou
Xiao Zhou
Yang Zhou
Yipin Zhou
Zhenyu Zhou
Hao Zhou
Chu Zhou
Daquan Zhou
Da-Wei Zhou
Hang Zhou
Kang Zhou
Qianyu Zhou
Sheng Zhou
Wenhui Zhou
Xingyi Zhou
Yan-Jie Zhou
Yiyi Zhou
Yu Zhou
Yuan Zhou
Yuqian Zhou
Yuxuan Zhou
Zixiang Zhou
Wengang Zhou
Shuchang Zhou
Tianfei Zhou
Yichao Zhou
Alex Zhu
Chenchen Zhu
Deyao Zhu
Xiatian Zhu
Guibo Zhu
Haidong Zhu
Hao Zhu
Hongzi Zhu
Rui Zhu
Jing Zhu

Jianke Zhu
Junchen Zhu
Lei Zhu
Lingyu Zhu
Luyang Zhu
Menglong Zhu
Peihao Zhu
Hui Zhu
Xiaofeng Zhu
Tyler (Lixuan) Zhu
Wentao Zhu
Xiangyu Zhu
Xinqi Zhu
Xinxin Zhu
Xinliang Zhu
Yangguang Zhu
Yichen Zhu
Yixin Zhu
Yanjun Zhu
Yousong Zhu
Yuhao Zhu
Ye Zhu
Feng Zhu
Zhen Zhu
Fangrui Zhu
Jinjing Zhu
Linchao Zhu
Pengfei Zhu
Sijie Zhu
Xiaobin Zhu
Xiaoguang Zhu
Zezhou Zhu
Zhenyao Zhu
Kai Zhu
Pengkai Zhu
Bingbing Zhuang
Chengyuan Zhuang
Liansheng Zhuang
Peiye Zhuang
Yixin Zhuang
Yihong Zhuang
Junbao Zhuo
Andrea Ziani
Bartosz Zieliński
Primo Zingaretti

Contents – Part XIX

Learning Mutual Modulation for Self-supervised Cross-Modal Super-Resolution

Xiaoyu Dong[1,2], Naoto Yokoya[1,2(✉)], Longguang Wang[3], and Tatsumi Uezato[4]

[1] The University of Tokyo, Tokyo, Japan
dong@ms.k.u-tokyo.ac.jp, yokoya@k.u-tokyo.ac.jp
[2] RIKEN AIP, Tokyo, Japan
[3] National University of Defense Technology, Changsha, China
[4] Hitachi, Ltd., Tokyo, Japan
https://github.com/palmdong/MMSR

Abstract. Self-supervised cross-modal super-resolution (SR) can overcome the difficulty of acquiring paired training data, but is challenging because only low-resolution (LR) source and high-resolution (HR) guide images from different modalities are available. Existing methods utilize pseudo or weak supervision in LR space and thus deliver results that are blurry or not faithful to the source modality. To address this issue, we present a mutual modulation SR (MMSR) model, which tackles the task by a mutual modulation strategy, including a source-to-guide modulation and a guide-to-source modulation. In these modulations, we develop cross-domain adaptive filters to fully exploit cross-modal spatial dependency and help induce the source to emulate the resolution of the guide and induce the guide to mimic the modality characteristics of the source. Moreover, we adopt a cycle consistency constraint to train MMSR in a fully self-supervised manner. Experiments on various tasks demonstrate the state-of-the-art performance of our MMSR.

Keywords: Mutual modulation · Self-supervised super-resolution · Cross-modal · Multi-modal · Remote sensing

1 Introduction

Multi-modal data, e.g., visible RGB, depth, and thermal, can reflect diverse physical properties of scenes and objects and are widely applied in practice [1, 3,21,61]. While high-resolution (HR) visible data is easy to acquire, non-visible modalities are usually low-resolution (LR) due to sensor limitations [2,11]. This hinders practical applications and introduces the necessity of cross-modal super-resolution (SR).

Supplementary Information The online version contains supplementary material available at https://doi.org/10.1007/978-3-031-19800-7_1.

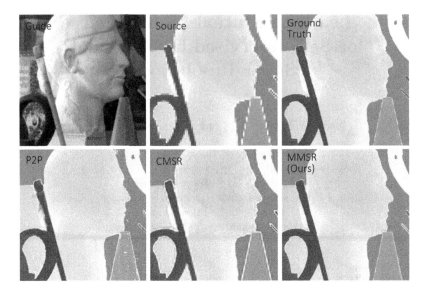

Fig. 1. ×4 depth SR results from CMSR [47], P2P [36], and our MMSR. Our MMSR achieves results that are HR and faithful to the source modality

Cross-modal SR aims at increasing the resolution of an LR modality (source) by using as guidance the structural cues from an HR modality (guide). This is difficult due to the spatial discrepancy between different modalities [8,11,55].

In recent years, deep CNNs have been widely studied to explore source-guide spatial dependency for cross-modal SR, and numerous networks have been developed [2,8,11,17,19,28,50]. However, these methods rely on HR source images (i.e., ground truth) for supervised learning and suffer limited generalization performance, since large-scale training data with paired ground truth is hard to collect [16,36,47].

To address this issue, several efforts [36,47] have been made to learn cross-modal SR in a self-supervised[1] manner. Such methods do not require external training data and perform online learning on each combination of LR source and HR guide, thus providing a strong generalization capability. However, they face two technical challenges: **First**, training SR models using two images that have modality difference and cannot form a direct LR-to-HR mapping. **Second**, achieving high spatial resolution as well as faithful image modality without accessing the supervision from HR source. To find a solution, CMSR [47] further downsampled the LR source to generate pseudo paired data in LR space. P2P [36] formulated the task as a modality transformation problem of the HR guide, and employed the LR source as weak supervision. While succeeding in training the models, these methods cannot overcome the second challenge and

---

[1] In this paper, self-supervised learning [13] refers to learning from data without paired ground truth in source modality, i.e., only an LR source and an HR guide.

deliver results that are blurry or not faithful to the source modality (Fig. 1). Overall, robust self-supervised cross-modal SR remains an open problem.

In this paper, we tackle self-supervised cross-modal SR by modulating the source and the guide with a cycle consistency constraint (Fig. 2). Specifically, we introduce a mutual modulation strategy, which includes a source-to-guide modulation (Fig. 3) to induce the source to emulate the resolution of the guide, and a guide-to-source modulation (Fig. 4) to bring the guide closer to the source with respect to the characteristics of the imaging modality. During the modulations, we develop cross-domain adaptive filters to fully exploit the spatial dependency between the source and the guide and drive our mutual modulation. Moreover, we adopt a cycle consistency loss between the downsampled SR result and the original LR source input to train our mutual modulation SR (MMSR) model in a fully self-supervised manner. It is demonstrated that our MMSR achieves state-of-the-art performance and produces results with both fine spatial detail and faithful image modality (Fig. 1).

Contributions: (**1**) We address an open problem in cross-modal SR, and develop a robust self-supervised MMSR model. (**2**) We propose a mutual modulation strategy, and show correlation-based filtering provides an effective inductive bias for deep self-supervised cross-modal SR models. (**3**) We validate our MMSR on depth, digital elevation model (DEM), and thermal SR, which involve benchmark data, noisy data, and real-world remote sensing data, demonstrating its robustness, generalizability, and applicability. (**4**) We compare our MMSR with state-of-the-art supervised and self-supervised methods, comprehensively demonstrating both its quantitative and qualitative superiority.

2   Related Work

In this section, we first review several mainstream works in cross-modal SR. Then we discuss techniques that are related to our work, including modulation networks, image filtering, and cycle-consistent learning.

2.1   Cross-Modal SR

Cross-modal SR has evolved from filtering-based [15,33,34,65], optimization-based [7,10,41], and dictionary-based methods [23,26] to learning-based methods [2,11,36] over the past decades. We focus on learning-based methods and review several supervised and self-supervised methods.

Supervised methods, as in other SR tasks [54,56,59,62,66,68], have made great progress. Early pioneers [2,17,27,28] have cast the task in a learning-based manner. Recent works [8,11,12,19,40,53] have studied the spatial dependency between the source and guide images. Representative work includes the weighted analysis sparse representation model [11,12] and the spatially variant linear representation model [8,40]. While obtaining promising performance, these methods suffer limited generalization performance in real-world scenes since large-scale paired training data is hard to acquire [16,36,47].

To address this issue, self-supervised methods without external training have been studied [36,47]. Such methods perform online learning on each combination of LR source and HR guide, and so can be adapted to any given scenario. Existing methods conduct the task by forming pseudo supervision in LR space [47] or interpret the task as cross-modal transformation in a weakly supervised manner [36]. While successfully training the models, their delivered results, caused by the non-ideal supervisions, are blurry or not faithful to the source modality.

2.2   Modulation Networks

Modulation networks are emerging in different research fields [25,32,64]. In image restoration, researchers have developed modulation networks to control restoration capability and flexibility [14,58,60]. Wang et al. [57] presents a degradation-aware modulation block to handle different degradations in blind SR. Xu et al. [63] designs a temporal modulation network to achieve arbitrary frame interpolation in space-time video SR. In speech separation, Lee et al. [24] introduces a cross-modal affinity transformation to overcome the frame discontinuity between audio and visual modalities. In image retrieval, Lee et al. [25] introduces content-style modulation to handle the task by exploiting text feedback.

We propose a mutual modulation strategy to tackle self-supervised cross-modal SR. Our strategy enables our model to achieve results with both high spatial resolution and faithful image modality, and outperform even state-of-the-art supervised methods.

2.3   Image Filtering

Many vision applications involve image filtering to suppress and/or extract content of interests in images [15]. Simple linear filters have been extensively used in image tasks such as sharpening, stitching [42], and matting [51]. In the area of image restoration, local [43] and non-local [5,6] filtering have been studied. Liu et al. [31] first incorporated non-local operations in a neural network for denoising and SR. Later researchers used non-local layers to exploit the self-similarity prior for restoration quality improvement [38,39,49,69].

Differently, we aim at handling multi-modal images that have local spatial dependency [8,40], discrepancy, and resolution gap. Therefore, we learn filters confined to pixel neighborhoods across features from the source and guide modality domains to exploit the local spatial dependency of different modalities and drive our mutual modulation. Experiments in Sect. 4.3 show that our filters can eliminate the spatial discrepancy and resolution gap of multi-modal images, providing an effective inductive bias for cross-modal SR models.

2.4   Cycle-Consistent Learning

Given a data pair A and B, cycle-consistent learning aims to train deep models by establishing a closed cycle with a forward A-to-B mapping and a backward

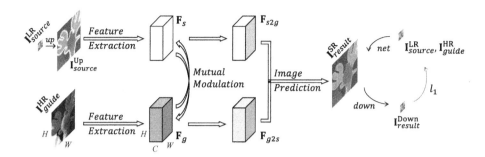

Fig. 2. An illustration of our MMSR model. During mutual modulation, the source is induced to emulate the resolution of the guide, while the guide is induced to mimic the characteristics of the source. A cycle consistency constraint is adopted to conduct training in a fully self-supervised manner. '*up*', '*net*', '*down*', and 'l_1' represent upsampling, our network, downsampling, and loss term, respectively

B-to-*A* mapping. This idea has been investigated in vision tasks such as visual tracking [18,52], dense semantic alignment [70,71], and image translation [67,72]. In image restoration, researchers imposed cycle consistency constraint to image dehazing [48] and unpaired SR [37].

We introduce cycle-consistent learning to cross-modal SR, and adopt a cycle consistency loss to encourage the downsampled SR source and the original LR source input to be consistent with each other. This allows our model to be trained in a fully self-supervised manner.

3   Method

As illustrated in Fig. 2, our MMSR starts from an LR source $\mathbf{I}_{source}^{LR}$ and the HR guide $\mathbf{I}_{guide}^{HR}$. It then modulates the source feature $\mathbf{F}_s$ extracted from the bilinearly upsampled source $\mathbf{I}_{source}^{Up}$, which still presents low resolution and lacks of spatial detail, and the guide feature $\mathbf{F}_g$ extracted from $\mathbf{I}_{guide}^{HR}$, which contains HR structural cues important to the source and also discrepancy patterns. Finally, it predicts the SR source $\mathbf{I}_{result}^{SR}$ from the fusion of the modulated $\mathbf{F}_{s2g}$ and $\mathbf{F}_{g2s}$, and constrains itself by casting $\mathbf{I}_{result}^{SR}$ back to $\mathbf{I}_{source}^{LR}$.

3.1   Mutual Modulation

In our mutual modulation, $\mathbf{F}_s$ and $\mathbf{F}_g$ are optimized by taking each other as reference. Cross-domain adaptive filters are developed as basic operators to drive the modulation.

In the ***Source-to-Guide Modulation*** (Fig. 3), $\mathbf{F}_s$ is modulated to emulate the high resolution of $\mathbf{F}_g$. Specifically, to each pixel in $\mathbf{F}_s$ (denoted as $\mathbf{s}_{(i,j)}$), we learn a filter $f_{(i,j)}^{s2g}(\cdot)$ confined to its neighbor pixels in an $n \times n$ neighborhood

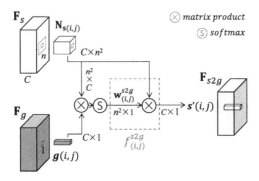

Fig. 3. An illustration of the source-to-guide modulation. Filters update the pixels in $\mathbf{F}_s$ by targeting the counterparts in $\mathbf{F}_g$ to induce $\mathbf{F}_s$ to become HR

(denoted as $\mathbf{N}_{\mathbf{s}_{(i,j)}}$)) and target its counterpart pixel in $\mathbf{F}_g$ (denoted as $\mathbf{g}_{(i,j)}$)[2]. The filter weight is calculated as[3]:

$$\mathbf{w}_{(i,j)}^{s2g} = \mathrm{softmax}\Big(\big(\mathbf{N}_{\mathbf{s}_{(i,j)}}\big)^{\mathrm{T}}\mathbf{g}_{(i,j)}\Big), \tag{1}$$

and evaluates the correlation value between $\mathbf{g}_{(i,j)}$ and each pixel in $\mathbf{N}_{\mathbf{s}_{(i,j)}}$ [4, 31]. Thus our filters allow fully exploitation of the local dependency between the source and guide modalities. In Sect. 4.3, we experimentally show that such adaptive filters with learning cross-domain correlations can deliver product that is spatially approaching a given target from a different domain, and are effective modulators to $\mathbf{F}_s$ and $\mathbf{F}_g$ in a case in which neither an HR source feature nor a guide feature without spatial discrepancy is available. Here, a filtering operation is expressed as[4]:

$$\mathbf{s}'_{(i,j)} = f_{(i,j)}^{s2g}\big(\mathbf{N}_{\mathbf{s}_{(i,j)}}\big) = \mathbf{N}_{\mathbf{s}_{(i,j)}}\mathbf{w}_{(i,j)}^{s2g}, \tag{2}$$

where the resulting $\mathbf{s}'_{(i,j)}$ is the update of $\mathbf{s}_{(i,j)}$ and is induced to spatially emulate $\mathbf{g}_{(i,j)}$, which is in HR domain. The whole source-to-guide modulation is conducted by updating all the pixels in $\mathbf{F}_s$ by targeting the counterpart guide pixels, resulting in $\mathbf{F}_{s2g}$, which inherits the HR property of the guide.

The **_Guide-to-Source Modulation_** (Fig. 4) suppresses the discrepancy in $\mathbf{F}_g$ to make its characteristics more like those of $\mathbf{F}_s$. To guide pixel $\mathbf{g}_{(p,q)}$, we learn a filter $f_{(p,q)}^{g2s}(\cdot)$ specific to the neighbor pixels in an $m \times m$ neighborhood

---

[2] $\mathbf{s}_{(i,j)}$ or $\mathbf{g}_{(i,j)}$ denotes the pixel at the i-th row and j-th column in $\mathbf{F}_s$ or $\mathbf{F}_g$ and is a vector of size $C \times 1$. $\mathbf{N}_{\mathbf{s}_{(i,j)}}$ contains $n \times n$ pixels and is a tensor of shape $C \times n \times n$.

[3] $\mathbf{N}_{\mathbf{s}_{(i,j)}}$ is first reshaped to a $C \times n^2$ matrix. Matrix multiplication is then taken between the transpose of the matrix and $\mathbf{g}_{(i,j)}$, which results in a $n^2 \times 1$ vector. Filter weight $\mathbf{w}_{(i,j)}^{s2g}$ is obtained by taking a softmax normalization to the resulting vector and is also of size $n^2 \times 1$.

[4] $\mathbf{w}_{(i,j)}^{s2g}$ weights the reshaped $\mathbf{N}_{\mathbf{s}_{(i,j)}}$ by taking matrix multiplication to result in a $C \times 1$ vector, i.e., $\mathbf{s}'_{(i,j)}$.

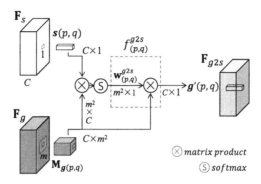

Fig. 4. An illustration of the guide-to-source modulation. Filters update the pixels in $\mathbf{F}_g$ by targeting $\mathbf{F}_s$ to bring $\mathbf{F}_g$ closer to the source on modality characteristics

$\mathbf{M}_{\mathbf{g}_{(p,q)}}$ and target the source pixel $\mathbf{s}_{(p,q)}$. The filter weight measuring the cross-domain correlation between $\mathbf{M}_{\mathbf{g}_{(p,q)}}$ and $\mathbf{s}_{(p,q)}$ is calculated as:

$$\mathbf{w}_{(p,q)}^{g2s} = \mathrm{softmax}\Big(\big(\mathbf{M}_{\mathbf{g}_{(p,q)}}\big)^{\mathrm{T}}\mathbf{s}_{(p,q)}\Big). \tag{3}$$

$\mathbf{g}_{(p,q)}$ is updated as:

$$\mathbf{g}'_{(p,q)} = f_{(p,q)}^{g2s}\big(\mathbf{M}_{\mathbf{g}_{(p,q)}}\big) = \mathbf{M}_{\mathbf{g}_{(p,q)}}\mathbf{w}_{(p,q)}^{g2s}. \tag{4}$$

Updating the guide pixels by considering the correlation to the pixels from the source modality domain allows our model to recognize which patterns in the guide are highly relevant to the source. Thus the guide-to-source modulation can adaptively suppress the discrepancy patterns in $\mathbf{F}_g$, resulting in $\mathbf{F}_{g2s}$, which has modality characteristics that are close to the source and the structural cues necessary to super-resolve the source.

Ablation studies in Sect. 4.3 demonstrate that both the mutual modulation and the cross-domain adaptive filtering play critical roles in developing a model that can yield results with high spatial resolution and faithful image modality.

3.2   Cycle-Consistent Self-supervised Learning

One technical challenge in self-supervised cross-modal SR is using source and guide images that cannot form direct LR-to-HR mapping to train SR models.

We argue the SR result should stay fully in the source modality domain, and therefore train our model with a cycle consistency constraint in which the start is the LR source along with the HR guide, while the end is still the LR source, as illustrated in Fig. 2. In the forward mapping, our network works as a regularizer that optimizes both the source and the guide to make a prediction induced to reach the guide in terms of spatial resolution and be faithful to the source in terms of image modality. In the backward mapping, we incentivize the consistency between the downsampled prediction and the original LR source input by minimizing l_1 norm:

$$\mathbb{C} = \left\| f_{down}\big(f_{net}(\mathbf{I}_{source}^{LR}, \mathbf{I}_{guide}^{HR})\big) - \mathbf{I}_{source}^{LR} \right\|_1, \tag{5}$$

where f_{net} denotes our network and f_{down} denotes average pooling downsampling. Our mutual modulation strategy enables our MMSR to successfully avoid a trivial solution of Eq. 5, i.e., an identity function for f_{net}. Experimental support is provided in Sect. 4.3.

Unlike other self-supervised methods that utilize pseudo or weak supervision in LR space, our model starts from the source modality, seeks an optimal prediction in HR space, and then constrains itself by getting back the start. In this way, both high resolution and faithful modality can be achieved and the whole process is fully self-supervised.

4   Experiments

4.1   Experimental Settings

Network Architecture. We adopt conventional convolution layers and the residual block from [30] to construct our network. The feature extraction branch of the source image (source branch) and the feature extraction branch of the guide image (guide branch) each consists of two convolution layers and two residual blocks. The image prediction part contains three residual blocks and one convolution layer. In the source branch and the prediction part, the convolution kernel size is set as 1×1. In the guide branch, the kernel size is 3×3. Before the prediction part, a 1×1 convolution is adopt to fuse $\mathbf{F}_{s2g}$ and $\mathbf{F}_{g2s}$. The number of channels is 1 for the first convolution in source branch and the last convolution in prediction part; is 3 for the first convolution in guide branch; is 64 for the other convolutions.

Implementation Details. We implement our MMSR model with PyTorch on an NVIDIA RTX 3090 GPU, and train it through the cycle consistency loss in Eq. 5 for 1000 epochs on each combination of LR source and HR guide. Adam optimizer [20] is employed. The learning rate starts from 0.002 and decays by 0.9998 every 5 epochs. We do not use data augmentation techniques [47].

Comparison Methods. We compare MMSR with five state-of-the-art cross-modal SR methods, including three supervised methods (FDSR [16], DKN [19], and FDKN [19]) and two self-supervised methods (CMSR [47] and P2P [36]). We implement these methods fully following the settings suggested in their papers.

Datasets and Evaluation Metric. We conduct experiments on depth, DEM, and thermal modalities. For depth SR, we sample three test sets from the widely used Middlebury 2003 [46], 2005 [45], and 2014 [44] benchmarks. These three test sets include 14, 37, and 43 visible-depth pairs of size 320×320, respectively. The

Table 1. Depth SR on the Middlebury 2003, 2005, and 2014 datasets. We report the average RMSE. The best and the second best results are in red and blue, respectively

Dataset	Scale	Supervised			Self-supervised		
		DKN [19]	FDKN [19]	FDSR [16]	P2P [36]	CMSR [47]	Ours
2003	×4	2.11	1.84	1.83	2.94	2.52	1.78
	×8	2.71	2.74	2.55	3.03	–	2.63
2005	×4	3.14	2.79	2.74	3.78	3.51	2.47
	×8	4.45	4.52	4.27	3.99	–	3.92
2014	×4	2.88	2.51	2.41	3.90	2.87	2.30
	×8	4.21	4.06	4.00	4.13	–	3.60

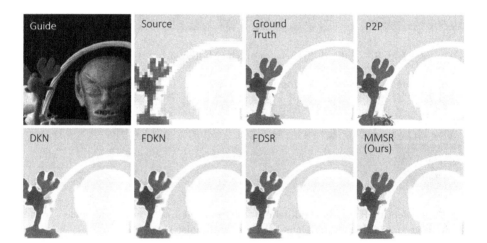

Fig. 5. ×8 depth SR results on the Middlebury 2005 dataset. All the compared methods [16,19,47], except for P2P [36], take both LR source and HR guide as input

three supervised comparison methods are trained on 1000 data pairs from the NYU v2 benchmark [21]. For DEM SR, we choose the remote sensing data used in the 2019 IEEE GRSS Data Fusion Contest (DFC) [22] and create a test set that includes 54 visible-DEM pairs. We train the supervised methods on 1000 data pairs. We follow the protocols in [35,36] and adopt pooling to generate LR depth and DEM. For thermal SR, we use the visible and thermal hyperspectral remote sensing data from the 2014 IEEE GRSS DFC [29], and select one band from the original thermal hyperspectral imagery as LR source. As the evaluation metric, we use the Root Mean Squared Error (RMSE).

4.2   Evaluation on Benchmark Depth Data

In this section, we compare MMSR with five state-of-the-art methods [16,19, 36,47] on the Middlebury benchmarks. In the source-to-guide modulation of

Fig. 6. ×8 depth SR results on the Middlebury 2014 dataset

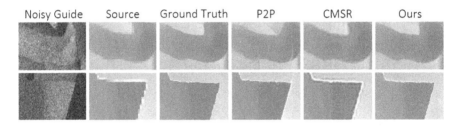

Fig. 7. ×4 depth SR on the Middlebury 2003 dataset under noisy guidance. 'Noisy Guide' is generated by adding Gaussian noise with noise level 50

MMSR, the neighborhood size for filtering is set as 11×11. In the guide-to-source modulation, it is 5×5. The effect of the neighborhood size is analyzed in Sect. 4.3.

Table 1 quantitatively reports ×4 and ×8 SR results. We do not provide the ×8 SR results of CMSR [47] because its training settings for high scale factors is not reported in its paper. As we can see, our MMSR consistently outperforms previous self-supervised methods [36,47], as well as fully supervised methods [16,19] that are trained under the supervision from HR source.

Figure 5 and Fig. 6 visualize ×8 SR results on the Middlebury 2005 and 2014 datasets. We can observe that performing cross-modal SR as weakly-supervised cross-modal transformation allows P2P [36] to maintain the resolution of the guide yet incurs serious discrepancy artifacts. FDSR [16], DKN [19], and FDKN [19] produce results that are faithful to the source modality but spatially blurry, because supervised methods cannot easily generalize well the test data. In contrast, our MMSR does not require external training and optimizes both the source and the guide with a cycle-consistent constraint, thus achieving

Table 2. Effectiveness study of mutual modulation strategy

	$Model_0$	$Model_1$	$Model_2$	$Model_3$
Source-to-Guide	✗	✗	✓	✓
Guide-to-Source	✗	✓	✗	✓
RMSE	4.30	4.08	3.72	3.67

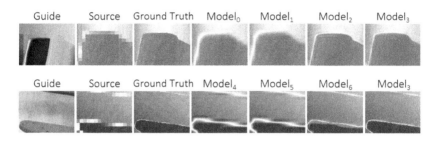

Fig. 8. SR results from models with different modulation settings (upper row) or variant filters (lower row)

strong generalization performance and resulting in both high spatial resolution and faithful modality characteristics.

In Fig. 7, we further compare our MMSR with the two self-supervised methods (CMSR [47] and P2P [36]) to study their robustness to noisy guidance. Thanks to our mutual modulation strategy which filters and updates multimodal inputs by considering their correlation at a pixel level, our MMSR shows stronger robustness to guide images with heavy noise.

4.3 Ablation Study

We analyze MMSR by observing ×8 SR results on the Middlebury 2014 dataset.

Mutual Modulation Strategy. We first clarify the effectiveness and necessity of the proposed source-to-guide and guide-to-source modulations with setting the both neighborhood sizes for filtering as 11×11. Table 2 reports models that adopt different modulation settings. Visual examples are shown in Fig. 8 (upper row). We can see $Model_0$ without mutual modulation tends toward the unimproved solution of Eq. 5. $Model_1$ with only the guide-to-source modulation also produces blurred results since the input source stays unimproved. $Model_2$ yields better performance as the source-to-guide modulation increases the resolution of the source. By performing mutual modulation between source and guide, $Model_3$ successfully overcomes the challenge that limits existing self-supervised methods, and yields results that are HR and faithful to the source modality, though no any supervision from ground truth is given.

Cross-Domain Adaptive Filtering. Based on $Model_3$, we highlight our developed filters with regard to two factors: **(1)** cross-domain learning (our filters

Table 3. Effectiveness study of cross-domain adaptive filters

	Model$_4$	Model$_5$	Model$_6$	Model$_3$
Cross-Domain	✗	✓	✗	✓
Adaptive	✗	✗	✓	✓
RMSE	4.87	4.88	3.84	3.67

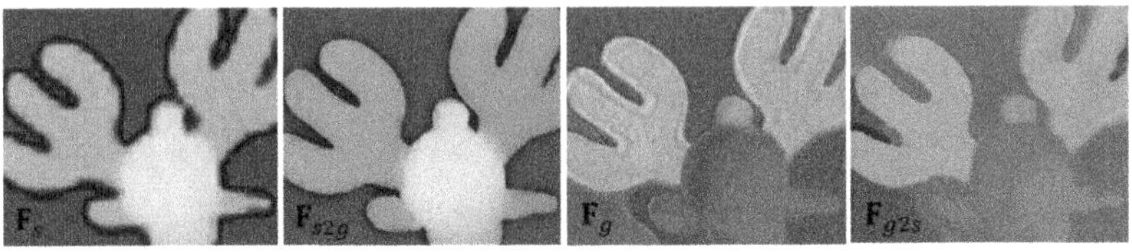

Fig. 9. Visualization of features before and after cross-domain adaptive filtering

measure the correlation across the source and guide modality domains) and (**2**) adaptiveness (our filter weights are variant for different pixel neighborhoods). Table 3 compares Model$_3$ and three models with variant filters. Visual examples are in Fig. 8 (lower row). Note that, in Model$_3$, our filters $f_{(i,j)}^{s2g}$ and $f_{(p,q)}^{g2s}$ are of size 11×11. In Model$_4$, we replace $f_{(i,j)}^{s2g}$ with an 11×11 convolution to filter $\mathbf{F}_s$, replace $f_{(p,q)}^{g2s}$ with another 11×11 convolution to filter $\mathbf{F}_g$, and fuse the filtering products using a 1×1 convolution. In Model$_5$, we first concatenate $\mathbf{F}_s$ and $\mathbf{F}_g$, then fuse them using an 11×11 convolution. Due to insufficient consideration of the dependency between source and guide domains and the weight invariance of conventional convolutions [9], Model$_4$ and Model$_5$ show inferior performance. In Model$_6$, we change the target pixel of $f_{(i,j)}^{s2g}(\cdot)$ (i.e., $\mathbf{g}_{(i,j)}$) to $\mathbf{s}_{(i,j)}$, and change the target pixel of $f_{(p,q)}^{g2s}(\cdot)$ (i.e., $\mathbf{s}_{(p,q)}$) to $\mathbf{g}_{(p,q)}$, resulting in adaptive filters $f_{(i,j)}^{s2s}(\cdot)$ and $f_{(p,q)}^{g2g}(\cdot)$ similar to non-local filtering [31]. As we can observe, Model$_6$ gets improvement by suppressing artifacts caused by bilinear interpolation, but is still inferior as its filters cannot update $\mathbf{F}_s$ and $\mathbf{F}_g$ properly due to the no measurement of cross-domain correlations. In Model$_3$, our cross-domain adaptive filters $f_{(i,j)}^{s2g}(\cdot)$ and $f_{(p,q)}^{g2s}(\cdot)$ fully exploit cross-modal spatial dependency, update $\mathbf{F}_s$ by considering pixel correlation to $\mathbf{F}_g$ from the HR guide domain, and update $\mathbf{F}_g$ by considering pixel correlation to $\mathbf{F}_s$ from the source modality domain. Figure 9 visualizes features before and after filtering. Our filters optimize the resolution of the source feature and suppress the discrepancy of the guide feature, enabling an effective inductive bias and the superior performance of Model$_3$.

Effect of Asymmetric Neighborhood Sizes. As introduced in Sect. 3.1, our mutual modulation is driven by filtering confined neighborhoods in the source and guide features. In general image restoration, properly increasing filtering size benefits model performance [31]. In our experiments, to Model$_3$ in Table 2, if the

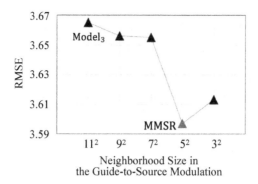

Fig. 10. Effect of asymmetric neighborhood sizes. The neighborhood in the source-to-guide modulation is fixed as 11×11

Table 4. DEM SR evaluation by observing average RMSE. The best and the second best results are in red and blue, respectively

Scale	Supervised			Self-supervised		
	DKN [19]	FDKN [19]	FDSR [16]	P2P [36]	CMSR [47]	MMSR (ours)
×4	0.80	0.80	0.81	1.57	0.78	0.73
×8	1.39	1.25	1.55	1.70	-	1.02

neighborhood sizes in the source-to-guide and guide-to-source modulations are both set as 3×3 or 7×7, the obtained RMSE values are correspondingly 4.23 and 3.91. When both are increased to 11×11, as in Table 2, the RMSE is 3.67. Considering GPU memory limitations, we did not increase the sizes further. Since our modulation strategy is bidirectional, we further investigate the effect of asymmetric neighborhood sizes. Based on Model$_3$, we fix the neighborhood size in the source-to-guide modulation as 11×11, while reducing that in the guide-to-source modulation, as shown in Fig. 10. The performance peaks at 5×5, which shows that there is an optimal setting on specific types of image data. On the Middlebury data, when the neighborhood sizes in the source-to-guide and guide-to-source modulations are respectively 11×11 and 5×5, our model can modulate the source and the guide optimally. Therefore, we adopt this setting to our model in Sect. 4.2. When we fixed the neighborhood in the guide-to-source modulation and reduced that in the source-to-guide modulation, the results were overly decided by the source. Visual results and more analyses of these two cases are in the supplementary material.

4.4 Validation on Real-World DEM and Thermal

Given the importance of SR techniques in Earth observation, we apply our MMSR to real-world remote sensing data that covers DEM and thermal modal-

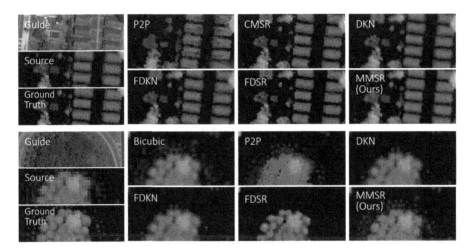

Fig. 11. DEM SR. The upper and lower rows show ×4 and ×8 SR results, respectively

ities. The neighborhood sizes in the source-to-guide and guide-to-source modulations are set as 5×5 and 3×3, respectively.

We compare MMSR with the five state-of-the-art methods [16,19,36,47] in terms of ×4 and ×8 DEM SR. As reported in Table 4, our MMSR yields the best quantitative performance under both scale factors, and outperforms the three supervised methods by a large margin. It can be seen qualitatively from Fig. 11 that our MMSR shows superiority by preserving finer spatial details for the buildings and plants and the modality characteristics of DEM.

We further compare MMSR with CMSR [47] on the visible-thermal data from [29]. We do not provide numerical evaluation since only LR thermal data is available. As presented in Fig. 12, our MMSR shows robust performance and superior generalizability. More visual results are in the supplementary material.

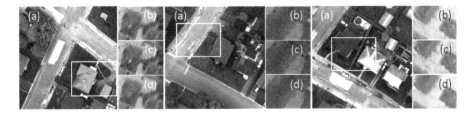

Fig. 12. ×5 thermal SR. (a) Guide. (b) Source. Results from (c) CMSR and (d) Ours

5 Conclusions

We study cross-modal SR and present a robust self-supervised MMSR model. Within MMSR, we introduce a mutual modulation strategy to overcome the LR problem of the source and the discrepancy problem of the guide, and adopt a cycle consistency constraint to conduct training in a fully self-supervised manner, without accessing ground truth or external training data. We demonstrate the superior generalizability of our MMSR on depth, DEM, and thermal modalities, and its applicability to noisy data and real-world remote sensing data. Extensive experiments demonstrate the state-of-the-art performance of our MMSR.

We believe our concept of modulating different modalities to achieve self-supervised cross-modal SR can inspire further progress in this field, and believe our MMSR can contribute to Earth observation applications where images in various modalities are available but HR ones are rare and expensive.

Acknowledgements. XD was supported by the RIKEN Junior Research Associate (JRA) Program. NY was supported by JST, FOREST Grant Number JPMJFR206S, Japan.

References

1. Adriano, B., et al.: Learning from multimodal and multitemporal earth observation data for building damage mapping. ISPRS J. Photogramm. Remote. Sens. **175**(1), 132–143 (2021)
2. Almasri, F., Debeir, O.: Multimodal sensor fusion in single thermal image super-resolution. In: Carneiro, G., You, S. (eds.) ACCV 2018. LNCS, vol. 11367, pp. 418–433. Springer, Cham (2019). https://doi.org/10.1007/978-3-030-21074-8_34
3. Arar, M., Ginger, Y., Danon, D., Bermano, A.H., Cohen-Or, D.: Unsupervised multi-modal image registration via geometry preserving image-to-image translation. In: CVPR, pp. 13407–13416 (2020)
4. Buades, A., Coll, B., Morel, J.M.: A non-local algorithm for image denoising. In: CVPR (2005)
5. Burger, H., Schuler, C., Harmeling., S.: Image denoising: can plain neural networks compete with BM3D? In: CVPR (2012)
6. Dabov, K., Foi, A., Katkovnik, V., Egiazarian, K.: Image denoising by sparse 3-D transform-domain collaborative filtering. IEEE Trans. Image Process. **16**(8), 2080–2095 (2007)
7. Diebel, J., Thrun, S.: An application of Markov random fields to range sensing. In: NeurIPS (2005)
8. Dong, J., Pan, J., Ren, J., Lin, L., Tang, J., Yang, M.H.: Learning spatially variant linear representation models for joint filtering. IEEE Trans. Pattern Anal. Mach. Intell. (2021)
9. Esser, P., Rombach, R., Ommer, B.: Taming transformers for high-resolution image synthesis. In: CVPR (2021)
10. Ferstl, D., Reinbacher, C., Ranftl, R., Ruether, M., Bischof, H.: Image guided depth upsampling using anisotropic total generalized variation. In: ICCV (2013)
11. Gu, S., et al.: Learned dynamic guidance for depth image reconstruction. IEEE Trans. Pattern Anal. Mach. Intell. **42**(10), 2437–2452 (2020)

12. Gu, S., Zuo, W., Guo, S., Chen, Y., Chen, C., Zhang, L.: Learning dynamic guidance for depth image enhancement. In: CVPR, pp. 712–721 (2017)

13. Hajjar, A.J.: In-depth guide to self-supervised learning: benefits & uses. (2020) https://research.aimultiple.com/self-supervised-learning/

14. He, J., Dong, C., Qiao, Y.: Modulating image restoration with continual levels via adaptive feature modification layers. In: CVPR, pp. 11056–11064 (2019)

15. He, K., Sun, J., Tang, X.: Guided image filtering. IEEE Trans. Pattern Anal. Mach. Intell. **35**(6), 1397–1409 (2013)

16. He, L., et al.: Towards fast and accurate real-world depth super-resolution: benchmark dataset and baseline. In: CVPR (2021)

17. Hui, T.-W., Loy, C.C., Tang, X.: Depth map super-resolution by deep multi-scale guidance. In: Leibe, B., Matas, J., Sebe, N., Welling, M. (eds.) ECCV 2016. LNCS, vol. 9907, pp. 353–369. Springer, Cham (2016). https://doi.org/10.1007/978-3-319-46487-9_22

18. Kalal, Z., Mikolajczyk, K., Matas, J.: Forward-backward error: automatic detection of tracking failures. In: ICPR, pp. 2756–2759 (2010)

19. Kim, B., Ponce, J., Ham, B.: Deformable kernel networks for joint image filtering. Int. J. Comput. Vision **129**(4), 579–600 (2021)

20. Kingma, D., Ba, J.: Adam: a method for stochastic optimization. In: ICLR (2015)

21. Silberman, N., Hoiem, D., Kohli, P., Fergus, R.: Indoor segmentation and support inference from RGBD images. In: Fitzgibbon, A., Lazebnik, S., Perona, P., Sato, Y., Schmid, C. (eds.) ECCV 2012. LNCS, vol. 7576, pp. 746–760. Springer, Heidelberg (2012). https://doi.org/10.1007/978-3-642-33715-4_54

22. Kunwar, S., et al.: Large-scale semantic 3-D reconstruction: outcome of the 2019 IEEE GRSS data fusion contest - part A. IEEE J. Sel. Topics Appl. Earth Observ. Remote Sens. **14**, 922–935 (2020)

23. Kwon, H., Tai, Y.W., Lin, S.: Data-driven depth map refinement via multi-scale sparse representation. In: CVPR, pp. 159–167 (2015)

24. Lee, J., Chung, S.W., Kim, S., Kang, H.G., Sohn, K.: Looking into your speech: learning cross-modal affinity for audio-visual speech separation. In: CVPR, pp. 1336–1345 (2021)

25. Lee, S., Kim, D., Han, B.: CoSMo: content-style modulation for image retrieval with text feedback. In: CVPR, pp. 802–812 (2021)

26. Li, Y., Xue, T., Sun, L., Liu, J.: Joint example-based depth map super-resolution. In: ICME, pp. 152–157 (2012)

27. Li, Y., Huang, J.-B., Ahuja, N., Yang, M.-H.: Deep joint image filtering. In: Leibe, B., Matas, J., Sebe, N., Welling, M. (eds.) ECCV 2016. LNCS, vol. 9908, pp. 154–169. Springer, Cham (2016). https://doi.org/10.1007/978-3-319-46493-0_10

28. Li, Y., Huang, J.B., Ahuja, N., Yang, M.H.: Joint image filtering with deep convolutional networks. IEEE Trans. Pattern Anal. Mach. Intell. **41**(8), 1909–1923 (2019)

29. Liao, W., et al.: Processing of multiresolution thermal hyperspectral and digital color data: outcome of the 2014 IEEE GRSS data fusion contest. IEEE J. Sel. Topics Appl. Earth Observ. Remote Sens. **8**(6), 2984–2996 (2015)

30. Lim, B., Son, S., Kim, H., Nah, S., Lee, K.M.: Enhanced deep residual networks for single image super-resolution. In: CVPRW (2017)

31. Liu, D., Wen, B., Fan, Y., Loy, C.C., Huang, T.S.: Non-local recurrent network for image restoration. In: NeurIPS, pp. 1680–1689 (2018)

32. Liu, J., et al.: Overfitting the data: compact neural video delivery via content-aware feature modulation. In: ICCV (2021)

33. Liu, M.Y., Tuzel, O., Taguchi, Y.: Joint geodesic upsampling of depth images. In: CVPR, pp. 169–176 (2013)
34. Lu, J., Forsyth, D.: Sparse depth super resolution. In: CVPR, pp. 2245–2253 (2015)
35. de Lutio, R., Becker, A., D'Aronco, S., Russo, S., Wegner, J.D., Schindler, K.: Learning graph regularisation for guided super-resolution. In: CVPR (2022)
36. de Lutio, R., D'Aronco, S., Wegner, J.D., Schindler, K.: Guided super-resolution as pixel-to-pixel transformation. In: ICCV, pp. 8828–8836 (2019)
37. Maeda, S.: Unpaired image super-resolution using pseudo-supervision. In: CVPR (2020)
38. Mei, Y., Fan, Y., Zhou, Y.: Image super-resolution with non-local sparse attention. In: CVPR, pp. 3517–3526 (2021)
39. Mei, Y., Fan, Y., Zhou, Y., Huang, L., Huang, T.S., Shi, H.: Image super-resolution with cross-scale non-local attention and exhaustive self-exemplars mining. In: CVPR (2020)
40. Pan, J., Dong, J., Ren, J., Lin, L., Tang, J., Yang, M.H.: Spatially variant linear representation models for joint filtering. In: CVPR, pp. 1702–1711 (2019)
41. Park, J., Kim, H., Tai, Y.W., Brown, M.S., Kweon, I.: High quality depth map upsampling for 3D-TOF cameras. In: ICCV, p. 1623–1630 (2011)
42. Perez, P., Gangnet, M., Blake, A.: Guided image filtering. ACM Trans. Graph. **22**(3), 313–318 (2003)
43. Rudin, L., Osher, S.: Total variation based image restoration with free local constraints. In: ICIP (1994)
44. Scharstein, D., et al.: High-resolution stereo datasets with subpixel-accurate ground truth. In: GCPR (2014)
45. Scharstein, D., Pal, C.: Learning conditional random fields for stereo. In: CVPR (2007)
46. Scharstein, D., Szeliski, R.: High-accuracy stereo depth maps using structured light. In: CVPR, pp. 195–202 (2003)
47. Shacht, G., Danon, D., Fogel, S., Cohen-Or, D.: Single pair cross-modality super resolution. In: CVPR (2021)
48. Shao, Y., Li, L., Ren, W., Gao, C., Sang, N.: Domain adaptation for image dehazing. In: CVPR (2020)
49. Shim, G., Park, J., Kweon, I.S.: Robust reference-based super-resolution with similarity-aware deformable convolution. In: CVPR (2020)
50. Su, H., Jampani, V., Sun, D., Gallo, O., Learned-Miller, E., Kautz, J.: Pixel-adaptive convolutional neural networks. In: CVPR, pp. 11166–11175 (2019)
51. Sun, J., Jia, J., Tang, C.K., Shum, H.Y.: Poisson matting. In: ACM SIGGRAPH (2004)
52. Sundaram, N., Brox, T., Keutzer, K.: Dense point trajectories by GPU-accelerated large displacement optical flow. In: Daniilidis, K., Maragos, P., Paragios, N. (eds.) ECCV 2010. LNCS, vol. 6311, pp. 438–451. Springer, Heidelberg (2010). https://doi.org/10.1007/978-3-642-15549-9_32
53. Tang, J., Chen, X., Zeng, G.: Joint implicit image function for guided depth super-resolution. In: ACMMM (2021)
54. Tian, Y., Zhang, Y., Fu, Y., Xu, C.: TDAN: temporally-deformable alignment network for video super-resolution. In: CVPR (2020)
55. Uezato, T., Hong, D., Yokoya, N., He, W.: Guided deep decoder: unsupervised image pair fusion. In: Vedaldi, A., Bischof, H., Brox, T., Frahm, J.-M. (eds.) ECCV 2020. LNCS, vol. 12351, pp. 87–102. Springer, Cham (2020). https://doi.org/10.1007/978-3-030-58539-6_6

56. Wang, L., et al.: Exploring fine-grained sparsity in convolutional neural networks for efficient inference. IEEE Trans. Pattern Anal. Mach. Intell. (2022)

57. Wang, L., et al.: Unsupervised degradation representation learning for blind super-resolution. In: CVPR (2021)

58. Wang, W., Guo, R., Tian, Y., Yang, W.: CFSNet: toward a controllable feature space for image restoration. In: ICCV, p. 4140–4149 (2019)

59. Wang, X., Li, Y., Zhang, H., Shan, Y.: Towards real-world blind face restoration with generative facial prior. In: CVPR (2021)

60. Wang, X., Yu, K., Dong, C., Tang, X., Loy, C.C.: Deep network interpolation for continuous imagery effect transition. In: CVPR, pp. 1692–1701 (2019)

61. Wang, Y., Wang, L., Liang, Z., Yang, J., An, W., Guo, Y.: Occlusion-aware cost constructor for light field depth estimation. In: CVPR (2022)

62. Wang, Y., et al.: Disentangling light fields for super-resolution and disparity estimation. IEEE Trans. Pattern Anal. Mach. Intell. (2022)

63. Xu, G., Xu, J., Li, Z., Wang, L., Sun, X., Cheng, M.M.: Temporal modulation network for controllable space-time video super-resolution. In: CVPR, pp. 6388–6397 (2021)

64. Yang, L., Wang, Y., Xiong, X., Yang, J., Katsaggelos, A.K.: Efficient video object segmentation via network modulation. In: CVPR (2018)

65. Yang, Q., Yang, R., Davis, J., Nister, D.: Spatial-depth super resolution for range images. In: CVPR (2007)

66. Zhang, K., Li, Y., Zuo, W., Zhang, L., Van Gool, L., Timofte, R.: Plug-and-play image restoration with deep denoiser prior. IEEE Trans. Pattern Anal. Mach. Intell. (2021)

67. Zhang, P., Zhang, B., Chen, D., Yuan, L., Wen, F.: Cross-domain correspondence learning for exemplar-based image translation. In: CVPR (2020)

68. Zhang, Y., Li, K., Li, K., Fu, Y.: MR image super-resolution with squeeze and excitation reasoning attention network. In: CVPR, pp. 13425–13434 (2021)

69. Zhang, Y., Li, K., Li, K., Zhong, B., Fu, Y.: Residual non-local attention networks for image restoration. In: ICLR (2019)

70. Zhou, T., Jae Lee, Y., Yu, S.X., Efros, A.A.: FlowWeb: joint image set alignment by weaving consistent, pixel-wise correspondences. In: CVPR (2015)

71. Zhou, T., Krahenbuhl, P., Aubry, M., Huang, Q., Efros, A.A.: Learning dense correspondence via 3D-guided cycle consistency. In: CVPR (2016)

72. Zhu, J.Y., Park, T., Isola, P., Efros, A.A.: Unpaired image-to-image translation using cycle-consistent adversarial networks. In: ICCV (2017)

Spectrum-Aware and Transferable Architecture Search for Hyperspectral Image Restoration

Wei He[1], Quanming Yao[2], Naoto Yokoya[3,4], Tatsumi Uezato[5],
Hongyan Zhang[1(✉)], and Liangpei Zhang[1]

[1] LIESMARS, Wuhan University, Wuhan, China
{weihe1990,zhanghongyan,zlp62}@whu.edu.cn
[2] Department of Electronic Engineering, Tsinghua University, Beijing, China
qyaoaa@tsinghua.edu.cn
[3] The University of Tokyo, Tokyo, Japan
yokoya@k.u-tokyo.ac.jp
[4] RIKEN AIP, Tokyo, Japan
[5] Hitachi, Ltd., Tokyo, Japan
tatsumi.uezato.ay@hitachi.com

Abstract. Convolutional neural networks have been widely developed for hyperspectral image (HSI) restoration. However, making full use of the spatial-spectral information of HSIs still remains a challenge. In this work, we disentangle the 3D convolution into lightweight 2D spatial and spectral convolutions, and build a spectrum-aware search space for HSI restoration. Subsequently, we utilize neural architecture search strategy to automatically learn the most efficient architecture with proper convolutions and connections in order to fully exploit the spatial-spectral information. We also determine that the super-net with global and local skip connections can further boost HSI restoration performance. The proposed STAS is optimized in a noise independent mode to increase transferability. The searched architecture on the CAVE dataset has been adopted for various reconstruction tasks, and achieves remarkable performance. On the basis of fruitful experiments, we conclude that the transferability of searched architecture is dependent on the spectral information and independent of the noise levels.

Keywords: Hyperspectral restoration · Spatial-spectral · Convolutional neural networks · Denoising

---

W. He and Y. Yao—Equal contribution.

Supplementary Information The online version contains supplementary material available at https://doi.org/10.1007/978-3-031-19800-7_2.

1   Introduction

As three-dimensional (3D) cubes, hyperspectral images (HSIs) have the ability to distinguish precise details between similar materials [21], and therefore have been widely utilized in various applications [15,19,32,36,45]. However, due to the sensitive imaging process and complex external imaging environment, HSIs tend to suffer from various degradations, *i.e.*, noise [4,5,13,16], missing [20,44], and undersampling [28,39]. Thus, HSI restoration is an important preprocessing step, essential to improving image quality and the subsequent applications.

Unlike RGB, *the main challenge of HSI processing is the exploration of high spectral information.* To that end, low-rank regularization has been successfully utilized to explore the spectral correlation and achieves remarkable restoration results [7,33,50,53]. The further spatial-spectral regularizations [5,11,20,28,41] boost restoration performance to the state-of-the-art (SOTA). However, the complexity of these methods is unacceptable for real-time processing [28,43].

Recently, convolutional neural networks (CNNs) have been introduced for HSI restoration [48]. The CNN-based methods utilize numerous simulated degradation datasets to train the model, and then apply the trained model to denoise the HSIs. Generally, the training stage is time consuming, but the test stage is fast. Initially, separable 3DUnet [14] and recurrent architecture [42] were proposed to denoise the HSI. Following, attention module [30,31,35] and multi-scale architecture [48] were also embedded into the CNN architecture.

In contrast to traditional RGB restoration tasks where CNN models tend to be promising, training CNN models for HSI restoration is difficult due to the large number of spectral bands. First, it has been pointed out that simultaneously processing the whole spectrum can improve restoration accuracy [20]. However, because of the huge computation burden, previous networks [3,14] fail to fully exploit the spatial-spectral information of HSIs. Second, the hand-crafted CNN models, such as 3DUnet [14] and TSA [30] are efficient for specific dataset, but may be suboptimal for different HSI dataset with spectra/noise diversity. In summary, the main challenge of CNN model for HSI restoration is the exploration of spatial-spectral information, including full-spectrum processing and the proper choice of convolution operations with proper connections.

The past few years have witnessed the development of automatic architecture design. Compared to hand-crafted architectures, the learned architectures have achieved excellent performance in various applications, *e.g.,* classification [56], objection detection [37], and super-resolution [22,25]. Inspired by these works, we propose the Spectrum-aware and Transferable Architecture Search (STAS) to build a lightweight and efficient network for HSI restoration tasks. The proposed super-net STAS is composed of repeated super-cell modules with global and local skip connections. Inspired by the previous works [14,24], we design a spectrum-aware search space that takes into consideration spatial convolution, spectral convolution, and spatial-spectral separable convolution. Specifically, *we utilize STAS to automatically choose the efficient convolutions with proper connections for the adaptive spatial-spectral information exploration of HSI.*

For different HSI restoration tasks, the noise type is different, *i.e.*, the Gaussian/stripe noise in denoising [14], and model errors in HSI imaging [31]. Without unified noise analysis framework, existing CNN-based methods [14,30] are mostly designed for specific dataset and tasks. Therein, we introduce the noise-independent analysis for the proposed STAS, to increase the transferability of the searched architectures across different datasets and different tasks. The contributions are summarized as follows:

- We disentangle the 3D convolution into lightweight 2D spatial and spectral convolutions, and introduce a spectrum-aware search space. The proposed STAS, which includes local and global skip connections, is utilized to automatically learn an adaptive spatial-spectral network for efficient HSI restoration. The searched architectures can be successfully applied to various dataset restoration tasks.
- We conclude that the transferability of searched architecture is dependent on the spectral information and independent of the noise levels. Specifically, for CAVE with fewer spectral bands, spatial convolution is effective. For Pavia with larger spectral bands, separable convolution is effective.

2   Related Work

CNN-Based HSI Restoration. For HSI restoration, *The main principles of deep network are the spatial-spectral exploration and transferability across tasks.* Unfortunately, the pioneering methods HSI-DeNet [3] and HSID-CNN [48] ignored the global spectral information. Following, Dong *et al.* proposed the separable 3D convolution with Unet architecture [14] to efficiently capture the spatial-spectral features of 3D HSI. Fu *et al.* introduced an efficient spectrum based recurrent architecture [42]. For HSI imaging reconstruction, the spatial-spectral attention [30,31] and plug-and-play framework [49,54] are also introduced to enhance the spectral information, and improve the restoration performance.

In summary, 3D convolution [9,24] is appearing to explore spatial-spectral information, but the balance analysis between spatial and spectral modes is missing. Furthermore, most of existed works simply focus on one specific task and lose the transferability. The proposed STAS learns an adaptive spatial-spectral 3D convolution, and analyzes the transferability across different tasks.

One-Shot Neural Architecture Search (NAS). Since proposed in [56], NAS techniques have achieved great progress, and have been utilized in various applications, such as classification [26,29,56], object detection [37], and restoration [17,22,25,51], among others.

At the outset, reinforcement learning [56], evolution [34], and sequential model-based optimization [26] were utilized to optimize the NAS. However, these algorithms are time-consuming and cost more than hundreds of GPU days for training on a small dataset. Subsequently, one-shot NAS was proposed to share weights during the training progress and significantly save search time [10,27,40,46]. Specifically, one-shot NAS builds a super-net [27] to subsume all candidate architectures for the whole search space. Each candidate architecture is regarded as a discrete structure from the super-net and inherits the weight of the super-net, which is trained only once. In this case, the training time is significantly reduced.

We also utilize the one-shot NAS to design efficient architecture for HSI restoration. To make NAS workable for this problem, we design a spectrum-aware super-net that includes spatial, spectral and spatial-spectral convolutions. The gradient-based algorithm [27] is utilized to optimize the proposed super-net.

3   Method

In this section, we introduce the proposed spectrum-aware and transferable architecture search. We first discuss the limitation of existing methods for HSI restoration. Subsequently, we introduce the spectrum-aware search space design for STAS, including global architecture (Fig. 1(a)), micro architecture (Fig. 1(b)), and mixed residual block (Fig. 1(c)). Finally, we present the Noise level independent one-shot search algorithm for the STAS.

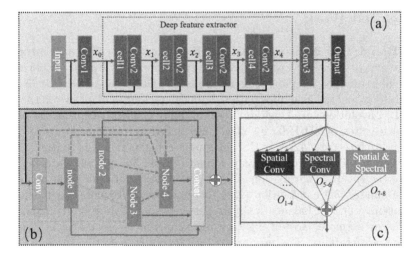

Fig. 1. Overview of the proposed STAS. (a) Global architecture used in STAS. (b) The architecture of super-cell. (c) MRB to connect the nodes in the super-cell

Until now, many works have been proposed for HSI restoration [2,3,24,31, 52]. Inspired by these works, we summarize a baseline global architecture for the HSI restoration task, as presented in Fig. 1(a). The baseline global architecture consists of a shallow feature extractor, a deep feature extractor, a feature reconstruction module, and a global skip connection [3,52]. The channel number of the input x is c. The shallow feature extractor Conv1 outputs x_0 with $8 \times c$ channels. The extracted x_0 will be distilled by the deep feature extractor of n-layer repeated modules, with each module composed of the `cell` block and `Conv2`. We fix the layer of repeated modules as 4. The procedure is formulated as the following:

$$x_i = \text{Conv2}\big\{\text{Concat}(\text{cell}(x_{i-1}), x_{i-1})\big\}, \tag{1}$$

where $i = 1, \cdots, 4$. `cell` is the main block with $8 \times c$ channels for the input/output features. The input and output of the current `cell` block are stacked together, followed by `Conv2` to generate the input of the next `cell`. Subsequently, the distilled features from the deep feature extractor are processed by feature reconstruction `Conv3` to output the residual image. Finally, the output residual and the input images are combined by the global skip connection to formulate the final reconstructed HSI y.

By replacing `cell` with different operations, the baseline can approach different hard-crafted networks, such as HSI-DeNet [3] with spatial convolution and SIP [24] with separable 3D convolution. Regarding the operation choice for `cell`, 3D convolution has been proved efficient for the spatial-spectral exploration of 3D HSI data [14]. However, it is always associated with a huge computation burden and prevents the large-scale processing of HSIs. SIP combines a 2D depthwise convolution and a 2D pointwise convolution to formulate the separable 3D convolution, but the simple combination of the two cannot learn the spatial-spectral features well. To confirm this finding, we formulate 4 different nets, *i.e.*, `spe` net, `spa` net (in HSI-DeNet [3]), `SS1` of separable convolution (in SIP [24]), and finally `SS2` net with another composition of depthwise and pointwise convolutions. The 4 nets are illustrated in Fig. 7 of Supplementary Materials. The experiments presented in Fig. 8 of Supplementary materials shows that well composed spatial and spectral architecture of `SS2` can achieve better learning ability. That is to say, *the composition strategy between* `spa` *and* `spe` *is also important to efficiently learning the HSI features. Therefore, we are inspired to decouple the* `spe` *and* `spa`, *and learn an adaptive 3D convolution through the use of NAS.*

HSIs are always corrupted by different noise due to sensors and imaging condition; meanwhile different tasks always introduce different type of model errors. Due the uncertain noise in different dataset/tasks, the essence features exploration for HSIs are blocked by the limited hard-crafted architectures. On the other hand, from [20], different HSI restoration tasks can be integrated in an unified paradigm with different types of noise. This motivates us to explore the intrinsic architectures across HSI datasets/tasks by injecting the noise-independent analysis, with the intention of extending the applicability of proposed STAS.

3.1   Spectrum-Aware Search Space

In this subsection, we present the search space design of the proposed STAS. The search space can be represented by a super-net, which consists of global architecture (Fig. 1(a)), micro architecture (Fig. 1(b)) and mixed residual block (MRB) (Fig. 1(c)). Similar to [27], we consider a fixed global architecture as the same of baseline but search for a better micro architecture and MRB, because cheap of the search in computational resource requirements. To implement the global architecture, we define the details of convolution in Fig. 1(a), *i.e.*, Conv1 composed of 1×1 convolution, ReLU (rectified linear units), and BN (batch normalization); Conv2 composed of spatial depthwise 3×3 convolution, spectral pointwise 1×1 convolution, ReLU, and BN; and Conv3 composed of 1×1 convolution and 3×3 convolution.

Micro Level. The cell topology structure is based on [27] with appropriate adjustment for HSI restoration. As presented in Fig. 1(b), we build a super-cell to integrate all possible convolutions. The super-cell is composed of one Conv and 4 nodes. The Conv is a series of operations that include the 1×1 convolution, ReLU, and BN. Specifically, the channel of input features is $8 \times c$, and Conv reduces it to $2 \times c$. We denote the features after Conv as x^0. The super-cell adopts x^0 as input, utilizes a directed acyclic graph to collect the sequence of 4 nodes, and outputs a tensor x_i by concatenating the outputs of 4 nodes with a local skip connection.

Mixed Residual Block (MRB). As presented in Fig. 1(c), we introduce the MRB to connect the possible two nodes, and fully exploit the spatial-spectral information. Our designed operation search space consists of 4 spatial convolutions, 2 spectral convolutions, and 2 spatial-spectral convolutions, as presented in Table 1.

Table 1. Operations utilized in the MRB.

Conv type	Label	Operation
Spatial	o1	3×3 convolution
	o2	5×5 convolution
	o3	3×3 dilated convolution
	o4	3×3 dilated group convolution
Spectral	o5	1×1 convolution
	o6	1×1 group convolution
Spatial-spectral	o7	3×3 separable dilated convolution
	o8	3×3 separable dilated group convolution

3.2 Noise Level Independent Search Algorithm

Based on the above introduction, the overall search complexity of our proposed STAS is estimated as 9^{10}, which is challengeable for optimization. Inspired by [12, 27,40], we are motivated to use one-shot NAS, which greatly reduce search time by training a super-net that contains all candidate architectures.

Search Objective. The connection between the paired nodes (j, k) $(0 \leq j \leq 3, 1 \leq k \leq 4, j < k)$ using MRB can be formulated as

$$\text{MRB}(x^j) = x^j + \sum_{l=1}^{8} o_l(x^j), \tag{2}$$

where x^j is the output of node j, and l indicates the operation from Table 1. To discriminate the importance of different operations in Table 1 and make the search space continuous, a weight vector α^{jk} with softmax is utilized to improve MRB as the following:

$$\text{MRB}^{jk}(x^j) = x^j + \sum_{l=1}^{8} \frac{\exp(\alpha_l^{jk})}{\sum_{p=1}^{8} \exp(\alpha_p^{jk})} o_l(x^j). \tag{3}$$

Taking into consideration all the node pairs presented in Fig. 1(c), the task of STAS is to learn a set of continuous variables $\alpha = \{\alpha^{jk}\}$. After the training of the super-net STAS, for each MRB, the operator with the largest weight α_l^{jk} $(1 \leq l \leq 8)$, denoted as o^{jk}, is selected to replace the MRB, and finally a discrete operation of MRB is obtained.

Given a set of images $\mathcal{D} = \{x_i(\sigma), y_i\}$ where y_i is the clean image and $x_i(\sigma)$ is the noisy version of y_i with noise level σ. Let net_α be the STAS net with architecture represented by α. The goal of STAS net is to recover the clean image from $x(\sigma)$. We use the square loss to measure the recovered image to the clean one. Subsequently, the recovery performance of net_α on $\mathcal{D}$ is

$$\mathcal{L}(\theta, \alpha, \mathcal{D}) = 1/2 \sum_{y \in \mathcal{D}} \left\| \text{net}_\alpha(x(\sigma); \theta) - y \right\|_2^2. \tag{4}$$

Thus, we have the following bi-level objective function for searching α:

$$\min_{\alpha} \quad \mathbb{E}_\sigma[\mathcal{L}(\theta^\star(\alpha, \sigma), \alpha, \mathcal{D}_{\text{val}})], \tag{5}$$

$$\text{s.t.} \quad \theta^\star(\alpha, \sigma) = \arg\min_{\theta} \mathcal{L}(\theta, \alpha, \mathcal{D}_{\text{tra}}) \tag{6}$$

where $\mathcal{D}_{\text{tra}}$ and $\mathcal{D}_{\text{val}}$ denote training set and validation set respectively.

Search Algorithm. Unlike classical NAS, the network parameter θ in (6) depends on noise level, but α in (5) does not. In this way, we hope architectures can focus more on the statistics of the images not the noise. Thus, we do not need to search architectures for different noise levels. However, this requires us to propose new search algorithm to deal with $\mathbb{E}_\sigma$. Thus, we generate the inputs via adding random noise during the training and combine this process with DARTS, which leads to Algorithm 1.

Algorithm 1. Spectrum-aware and Transferable Architecture Search (STAS).

Input: Training data, validation data, MRB via (3)

1: Initialize network parameter θ and architecture parameter α
2: **while** not converged **do**
3:    Generate inputs via adding random noise on the training/validation data
4:    Update α by descending $\mathcal{L}(\theta(\alpha, \sigma), \alpha, \mathcal{D}_{val})$
5:    Update θ by descending $\nabla_\theta \mathcal{L}_{train}(\theta(\alpha), \alpha)$
6: **return** architecture α

Output: Discrete architecture from α.

Following our idea, more recent NAS works can also be adopted. Examples are DrNAS [6], SPOS [18], NASP [46], and DARTS- [10], which seek to improve the classical one-shot NAS method, *i.e.*, DARTS, from different directions. In experiments, we will further replace DARTS update rules in Algorithm 1 with SPOS as an usage of example.

3.3   Difference with Existing Works

Compared to representative hand-crafted architectures HSI-DeNet [3], SIP [24] and QRNN3D [42], we also expect that the learned architecture STAS can be utilized with different dataset and different noise cases. First, the proposed spectrum-aware search space of STAS explores the domain-specific information of the HSI. Second, the learned architectures via STAS can be adapted to different noise levels. However, we can simply train STAS once, and apply the searched architecture to the restoration task on HSIs with similar spectral information, regardless of the noise level.

Table 2. Dataset introduction and implementation.

Task	Training set		Test set	
	Patch size	Number	Size	Number
STAS on CAVE (STAS$_C$)	$40 \times 40 \times 31$	22K	—	—
STAS on Pavia (STAS$_P$)	$40 \times 40 \times 60$	15K	—	—
CAVE denoising	$40 \times 40 \times 31$	120K	$300 \times 300 \times 31$	7
ICVL denoising	$40 \times 40 \times 31$	162K	$300 \times 300 \times 31$	7
Pavia denoising	$40 \times 40 \times 60$	15K	$200 \times 200 \times 60$	4
KAIST Imaging	$256 \times 256 \times 28$	5K	$256 \times 256 \times 28$	10

4 Experiments

In this section, we first introduce the datasets, including CAVE[1], ICVL [1], Pavia center, Pavia University[2], and KAIST [8]. Subsequently, we utilize the searched architecture for the different restoration tasks. Third, we analyze the learned discrete architectures via STAS, including the efficient understanding and transferability of the searched architecture.

4.1 Datasets and Implementation Details

The CAVE dataset contains 32 images of size $512 \times 512 \times 31$. We split it into training and test sets of 25 and 7 images, respectively. The images from ICVL are of size $1392 \times 1300 \times 31$. We select 120 images for the training, and 7 images of size $300 \times 300 \times 31$ for the test. Paiva datasets are from the remote sensing database, and we select the Pavia center of $1096 \times 715 \times 60$ for the training, and crop 4 patches of size $200 \times 200 \times 60$ from Pavia University for the test. In accordance with [30], we also choose 10 images of size $256 \times 256 \times 28$ from the KAIST dataset for the test of the imaging reconstruction task.

For the architecture search of STAS, we execute on the training sets of CAVE and Pavia Center. 2% of the training samples are chosen as the valid dataset, which is used to update the STAS architecture parameters. We train the STAS 100 epochs with a batch size of 8. The parameters of the network and the architecture are optimized separately by Adam. For the update of network parameters, we set the weight decay as $4e^{-4}$, and utilize the cosine annealing strategy to decay the learning rate from $1e^{-3}$ to $1e^{-6}$. For the update of architecture parameters, we set the weight decay as $1e^{-3}$, and the learning rate as $3e^{-4}$. In the training of STAS, we generate inputs by randomly adding noise of variations from $30, 50$, and 70 on the training/valid images.

For the denoising task, we retrain the discrete model learned from STAS on the training dataset, and apply the trained model to the related test dataset. We keep the optimizer, weight decay, and learning rate the same as that of STAS. For the imaging reconstruction task, we train on the whole CAVE dataset, and test on the KAIST dataset. The imaging mask and the coded image are utilized to generate an initialization that is the same size as the output HSI. The input settings of this network are the same as that of [30].

We generate small patches from the training dataset, and utilize crop and rotation to augment the trained images. The patch size and related numbers for different tasks are presented in Table 2. We refer to the network obtained by STAS on CAVE as $STAS_C$, and on Pavia as $STAS_P$. The experiments are performed on a single NVIDIA Tesla V100 GPU.

In the following, we apply the searched architecture from CAVE dataset for denoising (Subsect. 4.2) and imaging reconstruction (Subsect. 4.3). Subsection 4.4 presents the understanding of the searched architecture, and Subsect. 4.5

---

[1] http://www1.cs.columbia.edu/CAVE/databases/.

[2] http://www.ehu.eus/ccwintco/index.php/.

explains why the searched architecture STAS$_C$ can be applied to different datasets and different HSI restoration tasks.

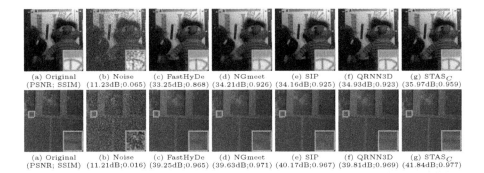

(a) Original	(b) Noise	(c) FastHyDe	(d) NGmeet	(e) SIP	(f) QRNN3D	(g) STAS$_C$
(PSNR; SSIM)	(11.23dB;0.065)	(33.25dB;0.868)	(34.21dB;0.926)	(34.16dB;0.925)	(34.93dB;0.923)	(35.97dB;0.959)
(a) Original	(b) Noise	(c) FastHyDe	(d) NGmeet	(e) SIP	(f) QRNN3D	(g) STAS$_C$
(PSNR; SSIM)	(11.21dB;0.016)	(39.25dB;0.965)	(39.63dB;0.971)	(40.17dB;0.967)	(39.81dB;0.969)	(41.84dB;0.977)

Fig. 2. Denoised results of different methods with noise variance 70. Top: CAVE toy image (R:28, G:11, B:6), bottom: ICVL image (R:30, G:11, B:6)

4.2   Denoising Results

As elaborated in Sect. 4.4 and 4.5, STAS is spectrum-aware and independent of noise level. We only train the STAS on the CAVE images once, and apply the learned STAS$_C$ to the denoising of different datasets (CAVE and ICVL from Table 2) with different noise levels (30, 50, and 70).

We compare the proposed STAS$_C$ to classical SOTA methods FastHyDe [55], NGmeet [20], and learning-based methods, including SIP [24], and QRNN3D [42]. The peak signal-to-noise ratio (PSNR) and the structural similarity (SSIM) are adopted to evaluate the performance. Higher PSNR and SSIM mean better performance in spatial information.

Denoising on CAVE. Table 3 presents the average quantitative evaluation results of different methods on the 7 CAVE test images. The noise variance changes from 30, 50, to 70. In the low noise case, the NGmeet achieves the best performance. As the noise level increases, the learning-based methods, *i.e.*, QRNN3D and STAS$_C$, can beat NGmeet. In particular, in the noise case of 70, the proposed STAS$_C$ can improve 1.5dB on average compared to that of NGmeet. On the other hand, compared to other learning-based methods SIP and QRNN3D, our proposed STAS$_C$ can always achieve the best performance on average. Figure 2 shows the visual results of different methods on the CAVE toy image with noise variance 70. It can be observed that the proposed STAS$_C$ achieves the best visual result in the balance of noise removal and details restoration.

Table 3. Denoising experiments on CAVE and ICVL datasets. The best result is in bold, while the second best is underlined.

	Method	FastHyDe		NGmeet		SIP		QRNN3D		STAS$_C$	
	Noise	PSNR	SSIM	PSNR	SSIM	PSNR	SSIM	PSNR	SSIM	PSNR	SSIM
CAVE	30	38.00	0.949	**39.05**	**0.963**	36.97	0.948	37.65	0.957	<u>38.39</u>	<u>0.961</u>
	50	35.53	0.911	<u>36.38</u>	<u>0.941</u>	35.81	0.937	35.84	0.935	**36.80**	**0.949**
	70	33.70	0.871	34.34	0.916	34.64	<u>0.929</u>	<u>34.96</u>	0.927	**35.83**	**0.940**
ICVL	30	42.96	0.971	<u>43.42</u>	<u>0.973</u>	41.58	0.960	42.08	0.967	**43.92**	**0.978**
	50	40.58	0.958	<u>40.85</u>	<u>0.962</u>	40.03	0.950	40.62	0.959	**42.01**	**0.969**
	70	38.86	0.941	<u>39.21</u>	<u>0.950</u>	38.88	0.930	39.21	0.943	**41.13**	**0.961**

Denoising on ICVL. Table 3 shows the average evaluation results of different methods on the 7 ICVL test images. Compared to NGmeet, QRNN3D can achieve similar PSNR values, but lower MSA values (in Supplementary Materials). That is to say, QRNN3D can achieve similar spatial restoration performance, but lower spectral performance. This is mainly because the advantage of NGmeet in spectral regularization. However, the proposed STAS$_C$ beats the classical methods and learning-based methods in the three evaluation indices of various noise levels. This indicates that our learned STAS$_C$ on CAVE can be successfully transferred to the ICVL denoising problem. Figure 2 shows the visual results of different methods on ICVL images with noise variance 70. From the enlarged rectangle, we can see that our proposed method can clearly recover window edge, while other compared methods produce blurry details. Detailed evaluation results are presented in Supplementary Materials.

Table 4. Imaging reconstruction on the KAIST dataset. The best result is in bold, while the second best is underlined.

Method	DeSCI		HSSP		λ-net		TSA		GSM-based		STAS$_C$	
Index	PSNR	SSIM	PSNR	SSIM	PSNR	SSIM	PSNR	SSIM	PSNR	SSIM	PSNR	SSIM
1	27.15	0.787	31.07	0.851	30.82	0.874	<u>31.26</u>	0.882	32.17	<u>0.915</u>	**32.52**	**0.918**
2	22.26	0.687	26.31	0.799	26.30	0.845	26.88	0.856	<u>27.20</u>	<u>0.897</u>	**28.55**	**0.898**
3	26.56	0.873	29.00	0.879	29.42	0.915	**30.03**	<u>0.921</u>	30.02	**0.925**	29.57	0.915
4	39.00	**0.964**	38.24	0.926	37.37	0.961	**39.90**	<u>0.963</u>	39.20	<u>0.963</u>	38.83	0.955
5	24.66	0.774	27.98	0.831	27.84	0.865	<u>28.89</u>	0.878	28.19	<u>0.882</u>	**29.62**	**0.921**
6	24.80	0.742	29.16	0.819	30.69	0.892	31.30	0.891	<u>32.84</u>	**0.937**	**33.47**	<u>0.933</u>
7	20.03	0.763	24.11	0.854	24.20	0.874	25.16	<u>0.886</u>	<u>25.29</u>	<u>0.886</u>	**25.81**	**0.890**
8	23.98	0.725	27.94	0.804	28.86	0.873	29.69	0.880	<u>31.38</u>	<u>0.923</u>	**31.65**	**0.936**
9	25.94	0.809	29.14	0.829	29.33	0.898	<u>30.03</u>	0.898	29.67	<u>0.911</u>	**31.23**	**0.917**
10	24.28	0.647	26.44	0.731	27.66	0.836	28.32	0.841	**30.52**	**0.925**	<u>30.13</u>	<u>0.911</u>
Average	25.86	0.777	28.94	0.832	29.25	0.883	30.15	0.890	<u>30.65</u>	<u>0.916</u>	**31.14**	**0.919**

4.3   Imaging Reconstruction Results

In accordance with [30], we directly utilize the proposed $STAS_C$ instead of TSA net for the HSI imaging reconstruction task, with the CAVE dataset for training and the KAIST dataset for testing. We slightly adjust the input and output channels of $STAS_C$ to fit the KAIST images. We compare our proposed method to DeSCI [28], HSSP [38], λ-net [31], TSA [30], and GSM-based [23]. Table 4 presents the evaluation results on 10 images from the KAIST dataset. From the table, it can be observed that in most cases, our proposed $STAS_C$ can achieve the best accuracy compared to the previous methods. Specifically, our proposed $STAS_C$ can improve nearly 1dB in PSNR compared to TSA and 0.5dB compared to GSM-based. The proposed $STAS_C$ has $1.43M$ parameters, much less than the $44.3M$ of TSA and the $3.76M$ of GSM-based, further indicating the efficiency of our STAS architecture. The visual results of different methods are presented in Supplementary Materials.

4.4   Understanding of STAS for HSIs

Effectiveness of the Search Space. Table 5 presents the ablation study of proposed STAS with different attributes. Firstly, compared to *baseline* HSI-DeNet [3] and search space DARTS [27], our proposed search space of STAS can achieve better accuracy. Secondly, from *architecture design*, the local skip connections used in Figs. 1(b–c), and the global skip connection are proved to be efficient.

Table 6 shows the results of STAS replaced with different operations and improved algorithms. Regarding *operation*, we replace the learned operations of STAS with other operations, including spe, spa, SS1 (in Subsect. 3) and random selection (in [27]). It is obvious that the learned adaptive spatial-spectral convolution via STAS is more suitable for the restoration of HSIs. Regarding *algorithm*, although we replace different improved algorithms [10,18] to optimize STAS, the improvement is limited. It indicates that the designed search space of STAS is good enough for HSI processing. Since the skip connections has been adjusted in STAS, The DARTS- [10] decreases the result on our designed search space.

Table 5. Ablation study of the proposed STAS on the CAVE with noise 50. In *baseline*, "DARTS" means search space used in [27].

Attribute	Baseline		Architecture design				
	HSI-DeNet	DARTS	STAS	STAS	STAS	STAS	STAS
skip in Fig. 1(b)					$\checkmark$		$\checkmark$
skip in Fig. 1(c)				$\checkmark$	$\checkmark$	$\checkmark$	$\checkmark$
Global *skip*	$\checkmark$					$\checkmark$	$\checkmark$
PSNR (dB)	33.85	32.18	33.87	34.52	35.73	35.22	36.80

Table 6. Ablation study of the proposed STAS with different operations and algorithms on the CAVE with noise 50.

Attribute	Operation				Algorithm		
	Random	spe	spa	SS1	DARTS-	SPOS	STAS
PSNR (dB)	35.25	32.81	34.72	35.67	36.42	36.89	36.80

Figure 3 presents the PSNR values with the GPU hours of the proposed search space STAS and the well-known search space DARTS on the CAVE dataset. STAS(SPOS) means the proposed search space optimized by SPOS [18]. We slightly adjust the last layer of DARTS for the HSI restoration task. In fact, STAS(SPOS) achieves the best accuracy faster, but the final accuracy is similar to STAS. Overall, the performance of proposed search space is much better than that of DARTS. Therein, it motivates us to pay more attention to the search space design for HSIs, but not the optimization algorithms.

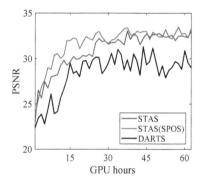

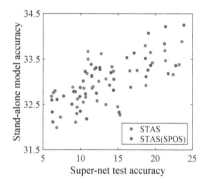

Fig. 3. PSNR values with the GPU hours on different search spaces STAS/DARTS.

Fig. 4. Comparison of super-nets and stand-alone model accuracies from a statistical sample of architectures

Quality of the Trained Super-Net. We attempt to access the quality of the trained super-net STAS. Based on [47], we randomly select the operations and connections from the super-cell (Fig. 1(b)) to formulate the discrete architecture (such as Fig. 5), and remove the rest from the super-cell. With this randomly selected architecture, we can obtain a super-net test accuracy by using the weight of the super-net STAS trained on CAVE. From another perspective, we retrain this random architecture on a small training set, and obtain the test accuracy, which we call the stand-alone model accuracy. We randomly select 40 architectures; the obtained accuracy pairs of the super-net STAS and the stand-alone model are presented in Fig. 4. It can be seen that higher super-net test accuracy means higher stand-alone model accuracy, indicating that the searched architectures from super-net STAS can predict the importance of the weight and operations in the final discrete architecture. We also utilize SPOS to optimize the proposed designed architecture, and achieve similar results compared to that STAS.

Table 7. Quantitative evaluation with noise variance 50 on CAVE/Pavia denoising.

Method	Index	FastHyDe	NGmeet	$STAS_C$	$STAS_P$
CAVE	PSNR	33.53	36.38	**36.80**	35.92
	SSIM	0.911	0.941	**0.949**	0.936
	MSA	9.33	6.12	**5.34**	6.04
Pavia	PSNR	33.93	34.80	33.10	**34.96**
	SSIM	0.913	0.926	0.917	**0.933**
	MSA	4.86	3.98	4.20	**3.64**

Table 8. Training (hour) and testing (second) cost of different methods on CAVE denoising and KAIST imaging tasks.

Time (s)	FastHyDe	NGmeet	SIP	QRNN3D	STAS
			Train (h)/test	Train (h)/test	Train (h)/test
CAVE denoising	21	68	35 h/1.5 s	23 h/1.2 s	12 h/0.8 s
Time (s)	GAP-TV	DeSCI	Lambda net	TSA	STAS
			Train (h)/test	Train (h)/test	Train (h)/test
KAIST imaging	120	7,928	31 h/1.2 s	25 h/1.6 s	11 h/0.6 s

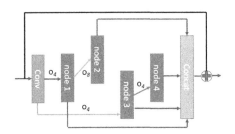 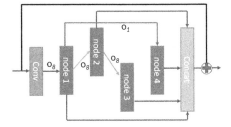

Fig. 5. The cell learned on CAVE dataset.

Fig. 6. The cell learned on Pavia dataset

Computational Efficiency. Table 8 presents the time cost of learned $STAS_C$ and the compared methods on CAVE denoising and KAIST imaging reconstruction tasks. From the table, it can be observed that the deep-learning-based methods can be very fast in the test stage compared to the classical methods. Compared to other deep-learning-based methods, the proposed $STAS_C$ can achieve better performance with many fewer parameters and less training time, demonstrating the efficiency of the searched architecture.

Visualization of Searched Architectures. The searched cell structure of STAS on CAVE denoising is presented in Fig. 5, while on Paiva denoising is illustrated in Fig. 6. From the comparison of these two cell structures on two HSI datasets, we make the following observations.

- For the CAVE dataset with fewer spectral bands, the discrete operators are dominated by the spatial group dilated convolution. This indicates that the spatial convolution is enough to explore the prior knowledge of CAVE images.
- For the Paiva with larger spectral bands, the separable convolution dominates the cell block, indicating the necessity of joint spatial/spectral exploration.
- The proposed STAS is dependent on the spectral information, and independent of the noise level. We will further illustrate this in Subsect. 4.5.

4.5   Transferability

Dependency of Spectral Information. The experimental results of $STAS_C$ on CAVE denoising, ICVL denoising, and KAIST imaging reconstruction demonstrate the transferability of the spectrum-aware searched architecture. We also extend our learned $STAS_C$ and $STAS_P$ to cross-validate the performance on CAVE and Pavia image denoising tasks. We adjust the input/output channels of $STAS_C$ to denoise Pavia images with different spectral information. From Table 7, it can be observed that the $STAS_C$ performs worse to the baseline NGmeet on the Pavia denoising task, whereas $STAS_P$ can achieve much better performance. For the CAVE image denoising task, the $STAS_C$ can obtain much better performance compared to $STAS_P$. We can see that the transferability of $STAS_C$ from CAVE to Pavia datasets gets stuck. This is mainly because the spectral information of the two datasets is different. By comparing the architectures of $STAS_C$ (Fig. 5) and $STAS_P$ (Fig. 6), we can conclude that the transferability is dependent on spectral information. For HSIs with fewer spectral bands, the spatial convolution is important, while, the spatial-spectral convolution is efficient for HSIs with higher spectral bands.

Table 9. Denoising results on CAVE test images with different noise levels. $STAS_{adap}$ means the network learned by STAS on the corresponding noise level.

Noise	30	50	70
$STAS_C$	38.39	**36.80**	35.83
$STAS_{adap}$	**38.52**	36.67	**35.99**

Independency of the Noise Level. We train STAS only once with the mixed noise, and apply the learned $STAS_C$ to different noise level denoising of the CAVE and ICVL datasets. The experiments presented in Subsect. 4.2 prove the efficiency of $STAS_C$ on different noise levels. Furthermore, we retrain STAS on the CAVE dataset with the fixed noise level, *e.g.* train the STAS on CAVE with noise variance 30 and apply the searched architecture (marked as $STAS_{adap}$) for the CAVE denoising with 30 of noise variance. Table 9 presents the comparison of $STAS_C$ and $STAS_{adap}$. We can see that the differences between the two searched architectures are not that significant, further demonstrating the independency of the noise level.

5   Conclusions

In this work, we propose a spectrum-aware and transferable architecture search for HSI restoration across different datasets. To make the proposed STAS workable for HSI restoration, we design a spectrum-aware search space that includes spatial, spectral, and spatial-spectral convolutions. Furthermore, the proposed super-net STAS is equipped with local and global skip connections to boost performance. The fruitful experiments also demonstrate that the proposed $STAS_C$ can be successfully transferred to different dataset (ICVL) denoising and different tasks (KAIST imaging reconstruction), and achieve SOTA performance. The transferability of searched architecture is dependent on the spectral information, and independent of the noise levels. Specifically, the spatial convolution is efficient for fewer spectral band HSI processing, whereas the spatial-spectral convolution is meaningful for higher spectral band HSI.

Acknowledgments. This work is partially supported by the National Natural Science Foundation of China under grants 61871298 and 42071322, and partially supported by the JST, FOREST Grant Number JPMJFR206S, Japan.

References

1. Arad, B., Ben-Shahar, O.: Sparse recovery of hyperspectral signal from natural RGB images. In: Leibe, B., Matas, J., Sebe, N., Welling, M. (eds.) ECCV 2016. LNCS, vol. 9911, pp. 19–34. Springer, Cham (2016). https://doi.org/10.1007/978-3-319-46478-7_2
2. Bodrito, T., Zouaoui, A., Chanussot, J., Mairal, J.: A trainable spectral-spatial sparse coding model for hyperspectral image restoration. In: Advances in Neural Information Processing Systems, vol. 34 (2021)
3. Chang, Y., Yan, L., Fang, H., Zhong, S., Liao, W.: HSI-DeNet: hyperspectral image restoration via convolutional neural network. IEEE Trans. Geosci. Remote Sens. **57**(2), 667–682 (2019). https://doi.org/10.1109/TGRS.2018.2859203
4. Chang, Y., Yan, L., Zhao, X.L., Fang, H., Zhang, Z., Zhong, S.: Weighted low-rank tensor recovery for hyperspectral image restoration. IEEE Trans. Cybern. **50**(11), 4558–4572 (2020)
5. Chang, Y., Yan, L., Zhong, S.: Hyper-Laplacian regularized unidirectional low-rank tensor recovery for multispectral image denoising. In: CVPR, pp. 4260–4268 (2017)
6. Chen, X., Wang, R., Cheng, M., Tang, X., Hsieh, C.J.: DRNAS: Dirichlet neural architecture search. In: ICLR (2021)
7. Chen, Y., Huang, T.Z., He, W., Zhao, X.L., Zhang, H., Zeng, J.: Hyperspectral image denoising using factor group sparsity-regularized nonconvex low-rank approximation. IEEE Trans. Geosci. Remote Sens. **60**, 1–16 (2021)

8. Choi, I., Jeon, D.S., Nam, G., Gutierrez, D., Kim, M.H.: High-quality hyperspectral reconstruction using a spectral prior. ACM Trans. Graph. (TOG) **36**(6), 1–13 (2017)
9. Chollet, F.: Xception: deep learning with depthwise separable convolutions. In: Proceedings of the IEEE Conference on Computer Vision and Pattern Recognition (CVPR), July 2017
10. Chu, X., Wang, X., Zhang, B., Lu, S., Wei, X., Yan, J.: Darts-: robustly stepping out of performance collapse without indicators. In: International Conference on Learning Representations (2020)
11. Dian, R., Fang, L., Li, S.: Hyperspectral image super-resolution via non-local sparse tensor factorization. In: Proceedings of CVPR, pp. 3862–3871, July 2017. https://doi.org/10.1109/CVPR.2017.411
12. Ding, Y., Yao, Q., Zhao, H., Zhang, T.: DiffMG: differentiable meta graph search for heterogeneous graph neural networks. In: Proceedings of the 27th ACM SIGKDD Conference on Knowledge Discovery and Data Mining. KDD 2021, New York, NY, USA, pp. 279–288 (2021). https://doi.org/10.1145/3447548.3467447
13. Dong, W., Li, G., Shi, G., Li, X., Ma, Y.: Low-rank tensor approximation with Laplacian scale mixture modeling for multiframe image denoising. In: ICCV, pp. 442–449 (2015)
14. Dong, W., Wang, H., Wu, F., Shi, G., Li, X.: Deep spatial spectral representation learning for hyperspectral image denoising. IEEE Trans. Comput. Imaging **5**(4), 635–648 (2019). https://doi.org/10.1109/TCI.2019.2911881
15. Dong, Y., Liang, T., Zhang, Y., Du, B.: Spectral spatial weighted kernel manifold embedded distribution alignment for remote sensing image classification. IEEE Trans. Cybern. **51**(6), 3185–3197 (2021). https://doi.org/10.1109/TCYB.2020.3004263
16. Fu, Y., Zheng, Y., Sato, I., Sato, Y.: Exploiting spectral-spatial correlation for coded hyperspectral image restoration. In: Proceedings of CVPR, pp. 3727–3736, Jun 2016. https://doi.org/10.1109/CVPR.2016.405
17. Gou, Y., Li, B., Liu, Z., Yang, S., Peng, X.: Clearer: multi-scale neural architecture search for image restoration. In: Advances in Neural Information Processing Systems, vol. 33 (2020)
18. Guo, Z., et al.: Single path one-shot neural architecture search with uniform sampling. In: Vedaldi, A., Bischof, H., Brox, T., Frahm, J.-M. (eds.) ECCV 2020. LNCS, vol. 12361, pp. 544–560. Springer, Cham (2020). https://doi.org/10.1007/978-3-030-58517-4_32
19. He, W., Chen, Y., Yokoya, N., Li, C., Zhao, Q.: Hyperspectral super-resolution via coupled tensor ring factorization. Pattern Recogn. **122**, 108280 (2022)
20. He, W., et al.: Non-local meets global: an integrated paradigm for hyperspectral image restoration. IEEE Trans. Pattern Anal. Mach. Intell. **44**(4), 2089–2107 (2022). https://doi.org/10.1109/TPAMI.2020.3027563
21. Hong, D., et al.: Interpretable hyperspectral artificial intelligence: when nonconvex modeling meets hyperspectral remote sensing. IEEE Geosci. Remote Sens. Mag. **9**(2), 52–87 (2021). https://doi.org/10.1109/MGRS.2021.3064051
22. Huang, H., Shen, L., He, C., Dong, W., Huang, H., Shi, G.: Lightweight image super-resolution with hierarchical and differentiable neural architecture search. In: Proceedings of the IEEE/CVF Conference on Computer Vision and Pattern Recognition (2021)
23. Huang, T., Dong, W., Yuan, X., Wu, J., Shi, G.: Deep Gaussian scale mixture prior for spectral compressive imaging. In: Proceedings of the IEEE/CVF Conference on Computer Vision and Pattern Recognition (CVPR), pp. 16216–16225, June 2021

24. Imamura, R., Itasaka, T., Okuda, M.: Zero-shot hyperspectral image denoising with separable image prior. In: Proceedings of the IEEE/CVF International Conference on Computer Vision (ICCV) Workshops, October 2019

25. Lee, R., et al.: Journey towards tiny perceptual super-resolution. In: Vedaldi, A., Bischof, H., Brox, T., Frahm, J.-M. (eds.) ECCV 2020. LNCS, vol. 12371, pp. 85–102. Springer, Cham (2020). https://doi.org/10.1007/978-3-030-58574-7_6

26. Liu, C., et al.: Progressive neural architecture search. In: Ferrari, V., Hebert, M., Sminchisescu, C., Weiss, Y. (eds.) ECCV 2018. LNCS, vol. 11205, pp. 19–35. Springer, Cham (2018). https://doi.org/10.1007/978-3-030-01246-5_2

27. Liu, H., Simonyan, K., Yang, Y.: Darts: differentiable architecture search. In: International Conference on Learning Representations (2019)

28. Liu, Y., Yuan, X., Suo, J., Brady, D.J., Dai, Q.: Rank minimization for snapshot compressive imaging. IEEE Trans. Pattern Anal. Mach. Intell. **41**(12), 2990–3006 (2019). https://doi.org/10.1109/TPAMI.2018.2873587

29. Ma, A., Wan, Y., Zhong, Y., Wang, J., Zhang, L.: SceneNet: remote sensing scene classification deep learning network using multi-objective neural evolution architecture search. ISPRS J. Photogramm. Remote. Sens. **172**, 171–188 (2021)

30. Meng, Z., Ma, J., Yuan, X.: End-to-end low cost compressive spectral imaging with spatial-spectral self-attention. In: Vedaldi, A., Bischof, H., Brox, T., Frahm, J.-M. (eds.) ECCV 2020. LNCS, vol. 12368, pp. 187–204. Springer, Cham (2020). https://doi.org/10.1007/978-3-030-58592-1_12

31. Miao, X., Yuan, X., Pu, Y., Athitsos, V.: λ-net: Reconstruct hyperspectral images from a snapshot measurement. In: Proceedings of ICCV, October 2019

32. Pan, Z., Healey, G., Prasad, M., Tromberg, B.: Face recognition in hyperspectral images. IEEE Trans. Pattern Anal. Mach. Intell. **25**(12), 1552–1560 (2003). https://doi.org/10.1109/TPAMI.2003.1251148

33. Peng, Y., Meng, D., Xu, Z., Gao, C., Yang, Y., Zhang, B.: Decomposable nonlocal tensor dictionary learning for multispectral image denoising. In: CVPR, pp. 2949–2956 (2014)

34. Real, E., Aggarwal, A., Huang, Y., Le, Q.V.: Regularized evolution for image classifier architecture search. In: Proceedings of the AAAI Conference on Artificial Intelligence, vol. 33, pp. 4780–4789 (2019)

35. Shi, Q., Tang, X., Yang, T., Liu, R., Zhang, L.: Hyperspectral image denoising using a 3-D attention denoising network. IEEE Trans. Geosci. Remote Sens. 1–16 (2021). https://doi.org/10.1109/TGRS.2020.3045273

36. Stein, D.W., Beaven, S.G., Hoff, L.E., Winter, E.M., Schaum, A.P., Stocker, A.D.: Anomaly detection from hyperspectral imagery. IEEE Sig. Process. Mag. **19**(1), 58–69 (2002)

37. Sun, P., Zhang, W., Wang, H., Li, S., Li, X.: Deep RGB-D saliency detection with depth-sensitive attention and automatic multi-modal fusion. In: Proceedings of the IEEE/CVF Conference on Computer Vision and Pattern Recognition, pp. 1407–1417 (2021)

38. Wang, L., Sun, C., Fu, Y., Kim, M.H., Huang, H.: Hyperspectral image reconstruction using a deep spatial-spectral prior. In: Proceedings of CVPR, pp. 8032–8041 (2019)

39. Wang, L., Xiong, Z., Shi, G., Wu, F., Zeng, W.: Adaptive nonlocal sparse representation for dual-camera compressive hyperspectral imaging. IEEE Trans. Pattern Anal. Mach. Intell. **39**(10), 2104–2111 (2016)

40. Wang, R., Cheng, M., Chen, X., Tang, X., Hsieh, C.J.: Rethinking architecture selection in differentiable NAS. In: International Conference on Learning Representations (2021)

41. Wang, Y., Peng, J., Zhao, Q., Leung, Y., Zhao, X.L., Meng, D.: Hyperspectral image restoration via total variation regularized low-rank tensor decomposition. IEEE J. Sel. Topics Appl. Earth Observ. Remote Sens. **11**(4), 1227–1243 (2018)
42. Wei, K., Fu, Y., Huang, H.: 3D quasi recurrent neural network for hyperspectral image denoising. IEEE Trans. Neural Netw. Learn. Syst. **32**(1), 363–375 (2021). https://doi.org/10.1109/TNNLS.2020.2978756
43. Xie, Q., Zhao, Q., Meng, D., Xu, Z.: Kronecker-basis-representation based tensor sparsity and its applications to tensor recovery. IEEE Trans. Pattern Anal. Mach. Intell. **40**(8), 1888–1902 (2018)
44. Xie, T., Li, S., Fang, L., Liu, L.: Tensor completion via nonlocal low-rank regularization. IEEE Trans. Cybern. **49**(6), 2344–2354 (2019). https://doi.org/10.1109/TCYB.2018.2825598
45. Xiong, F., Zhou, J., Qian, Y.: Material based object tracking in hyperspectral videos. IEEE Trans. Image Process. **29**, 3719–3733 (2020). https://doi.org/10.1109/TIP.2020.2965302
46. Yao, Q., Xu, J., Tu, W.W., Zhu, Z.: Efficient neural architecture search via proximal iterations. In: Proceedings of the AAAI Conference on Artificial Intelligence, vol. 34, pp. 6664–6671 (2020)
47. Yu, K., Ranftl, R., Salzmann, M.: An analysis of super-net heuristics in weight-sharing NAS. IEEE Trans. Pattern Anal. Mach. Intell. (2021)
48. Yuan, Q., Zhang, Q., Li, J., Shen, H., Zhang, L.: Hyperspectral image denoising employing a spatial spectral deep residual convolutional neural network. IEEE Trans. Geosci. Remote Sens. **57**(2), 1205–1218 (2019). https://doi.org/10.1109/TGRS.2018.2865197
49. Yuan, X., Liu, Y., Suo, J., Durand, F., Dai, Q.: Plug-and-play algorithms for video snapshot compressive imaging. arXiv preprint arXiv:2101.04822 (2021)
50. Zhang, H., He, W., Zhang, L., Shen, H., Yuan, Q.: Hyperspectral image restoration using low-rank matrix recovery. IEEE Trans. Geosci. Remote Sens. **52**(8), 4729–4743 (2014)
51. Zhang, H., Li, Y., Chen, H., Shen, C.: Memory-efficient hierarchical neural architecture search for image denoising. In: Proceedings of the IEEE/CVF Conference on Computer Vision and Pattern Recognition, pp. 3657–3666 (2020)
52. Zhang, K., Zuo, W., Chen, Y., Meng, D., Zhang, L.: Beyond a gaussian denoiser: residual learning of deep CNN for image denoising. IEEE Trans. Image Process. **26**(7), 3142–3155 (2017)
53. Zhang, S., Wang, L., Fu, Y., Zhong, X., Huang, H.: Computational hyperspectral imaging based on dimension-discriminative low-rank tensor recovery. In: Proceedings of ICCV, October 2019
54. Zheng, S., et al.: Deep plug-and-play priors for spectral snapshot compressive imaging. Photon. Res. **9**(2), B18–B29 (2021)
55. Zhuang, L., Bioucas-Dias, J.M.: Fast hyperspectral image denoising and inpainting based on low-rank and sparse representations. IEEE J. Sel. Topics Appl. Earth Observ. Remote Sens. **11**(3), 730–742 (2018)
56. Zoph, B., Le, Q.V.: Neural architecture search with reinforcement learning. In: International Conference on Learning Representations (2017)

Neural Color Operators for Sequential Image Retouching

Yili Wang[1], Xin Li[2], Kun Xu[1(✉)], Dongliang He[2], Qi Zhang[2], Fu Li[2], and Errui Ding[2]

[1] BNRist, Department of CS&T, Tsinghua University, Beijing, China
xukun@tsinghua.edu.cn
[2] Department of Computer Vision Technology (VIS), Baidu Inc., Beijing, China
{lixin41,hedongliang01,zhangqi44,lifu,dingerrui}@baidu.com

Abstract. We propose a novel image retouching method by modeling the retouching process as performing a sequence of newly introduced trainable *neural color operators*. The neural color operator mimics the behavior of traditional color operators and learns pixelwise color transformation while its strength is controlled by a scalar. To reflect the homomorphism property of color operators, we employ equivariant mapping and adopt an encoder-decoder structure which maps the non-linear color transformation to a much simpler transformation (i.e., translation) in a high dimensional space. The scalar strength of each neural color operator is predicted using CNN based strength predictors by analyzing global image statistics. Overall, our method is rather lightweight and offers flexible controls. Experiments and user studies on public datasets show that our method consistently achieves the best results compared with SOTA methods in both quantitative measures and visual qualities. Code is available at https://github.com/amberwangyili/neurop.

Keywords: Image retouching · Image enhancement · Color operator · Neural color operator

1 Introduction

In the digital eras, images are indispensable components for information sharing and daily communication, which makes improving the perceptual quality of images quite demanding in many scenarios. While professional retouching software such as Adobe Photoshop and Lightroom provide various retouching operations, the effectiveness and proficiency of using them still require expertise

---

Work done during Yili Wang's internship at VIS, Baidu.

Supplementary Information The online version contains supplementary material available at https://doi.org/10.1007/978-3-031-19800-7_3.

S. Avidan et al. (Eds.): ECCV 2022, LNCS 13679, pp. 38–55, 2022.
https://doi.org/10.1007/978-3-031-19800-7_3

on the part of the users. Automation of such tedious editing works is highly desirable and has been extensively studied for decades.

Recently, deep learning has exhibited stunning success in many computer vision and image processing tasks [20,34], which generally uses networks to learn sophisticated mappings from paired data. In the pioneering work by Bychkovsky *et al.* [6], a large scale of input and expert-retouched image pairs have been collected: the constructed MIT-Adobe FiveK dataset has enabled high-quality supervised learning and drives the mainstream towards data-driven methods.

Among these methods, *sequential image retouching* [16,38,39,45] is rather attractive. Following human's step-by-step workflow, they model the image retouching process as a sequence of standard color operators (*i.e.*, brightness or contrast adjustments), each of which is controlled by a scalar parameter. Besides generating a retouched image, they also produce a semantically meaningful history of retouching operators. With the retouching history on hand, the process is more interpretable, offers convenient controls for re-editing, and could be used in applications like photo manipulation tutorial generation [12] and image revision control [8]. However, due to the limited expressiveness of standard color operators, these methods require a relatively large number of operators to reproduce the complex retouching effects, which makes it less robust to accurately predict the operator parameters and hard to achieve high-fidelity retouched results (*i.e.*, high PSNR scores) compared to other state-of-the-art retouching methods [14,33,49,50].

To address this issue, we introduce a novel trainable color operator, named *neural color operator*. It is designed to mimic the behavior of traditional color operators, which maps a 3D RGB color to a modified color according to a scalar indicating the operator's strength. Instead of using a fixed function as in standard color operators, we allow the parameters of a neural color operator to be learned in order to model more general and complex color transformations. To reflect the *homomorphism property* of color operators (*i.e.*, adjusting exposure by +2, followed a second +3 adjustment, is approximately equivalent to a single operator that adjusts exposure by +5), we employ *equivariant mapping* and adopt an encoder-decoder structure, which maps the color transformation in 3D RGB space to a much simpler transformation (*i.e.*, translation) in a high dimensional feature space where the scalar strength controls the amount of translation.

We further propose an automatic, lightweight yet effective sequential image retouching method. We model the retouching process as applying a sequence of pixel-wise neural color operators to the input image. The strength of each neural color operator is automatically determined by the output of a CNN based *strength predictor* using global statistics of deep image features computed from downsampled intermediate adjusted images. The neural color operators and strength predictors are jointly trained in an end-to-end manner, with a carefully designed initialization scheme.

Contributions. Our contributions are summarized as follows: First, we introduce neural color operator—a novel, trainable yet interpretable color operator. It mimics the behavior of color operators whose strength is controlled by a scalar, and could effectively model sophisticated global color transformations. Second, based on neural color operators, we propose a lightweight and efficient method with only 28k parameters for sequential image retouching. Without any bells and whistles, experiments and user studies show that our method consistently achieves the best performance on two public datasets, including MIT-Adobe FiveK [6] and PPR10K [30], compared with state-of-the-art methods from both qualitative measures and visual qualities. Furthermore, our method inherits the nice properties of sequential image retouching, which allows flexible controls and convenient re-editing on results by intuitively adjusting the predicted scalar strengths using three sliders in real-time.

2 Related Works

Computational methods for automatic image retouching have kept evolving over the years—from traditional heuristics such as spatial filters [4], to histogram-based methods [3,26,28,40,44], and recent learning-based approaches. Here we give a general review on this most recent branch of researches.

Image-to-Image Translation Based Methods. These methods generally consider image retouching as a special case of image-to-image translation and use neural networks to directly generate the enhanced images from input images [9,18,19,21,24,37,48,50]. While these methods can produce visually pleasing results, they have some common limitations: they usually employ large networks and consume too much computational resources when applied to high-resolution images; besides, the use of downsampled convolutional layers may easily lead to artifacts in high frequency textures. Some methods have been proposed to alleviate these issues by decomposition of reflectance and illumination [42,47], representative color transform [25], or Laplacian pyramid decomposition [1,31].

Sequential Image Retouching. This category of methods [16,38,39,45] follow the step-by-step retouching workflow of human experts, which models the process as a sequence of several color operators where the strength of each operator is controlled by a scalar. This modeling paradigm is quite challenging because it requires more supervision of editing sequences. Some researchers [16,38] resort to deep reinforcement learning algorithms which are known to be highly sensitive to their numerous hyper-parameters [15]. Shi *et al.* [39] propose an operation-planning algorithm to generate pseudo ground-truth sequences, hence making the network easier to train. However, it needs extra input text as guidance. Overall, these methods provide an understandable editing process, and allow convenient further controls on results through intuitive adjustments of the color operators. However, due to the limited expressiveness of standard color operators, they require a sequence with a relatively large number of operators to reproduce complex retouching effects, which is harder to learn and leads to less satisfactory performance (*i.e.*, lower PSNR scores).

Color Transformation Based Methods. These methods usually use a low-resolution image to extract features and predict the parameters of some prede-fined global or local color transformation, and later apply the predicted color transformation to the original high-resolution image. Different color transformations have been used in existing works, including quadratic transforms [7,32, 41,46], local affine transforms [11], curve based transforms [6,13,23,29,36], filters [10,35], lookup tables [43,49], and customized transforms [5]. Compared with image-to-image translation based methods, these methods usually use smaller models and are more efficient. However, their capabilities are constrained by the predefined color transformation and might be inadequate to approximate highly non-linear color mappings between low and high quality images.

Recently, He *et al.* [14,33] proposed Conditional Sequential Retouching Network (CSRNet), which models the global color transformation using a 3-layer multi-layer perceptron (MLP). The MLP is influenced through global feature modulation via a 32D conditional vector extracted from the input image through a conditional network. Their method is lightweight and achieves nice performance. However, the 32D condition vector is hard to interpret and control. While CSRNet is named with 'sequential', we prefer to regard it as a color transformation based method instead of a sequential image retouching method. This is because it does not explicitly model retouching operators or generate a meaningful retouching sequence, nor does it produce intermediate adjusted images, all of which are important features of sequential image retouching.

Our Motivation. We are motivated by the seemingly intractable dilemma in the context of previous retouching methods: while "black-boxing" the standard operators [14,33] can improve model expressiveness such non-interpretable parameterization leads to the lack of controllability; though good interpretability can be achieved by using sequential methods with standard post-processing operators [16,38,39,45], these methods require a relatively large number of operators to reproduce the complex retouching effects but also make it less robust to accurately predict the parameters and fail to achieve satisfactory results.

Specifically, we seek to resolve this dilemma by disentangling the complex nonlinear retouching process into a series of easier transformations modeled by our trainable neural color operators with interpretable controls, while still maintaining high efficacy and lightweight structures.

3 Neural Color Operator

Definition. A neural color operator (short as neural operator or neurOp) mimics the behavior of traditional global color operators. It is defined to learn a pixel-wise global color mapping $\mathcal{R}$ from an input 3D RGB color $\mathbf{p}$, with a 1D scalar v indicating the operator's strength, to an output 3D RGB color $\mathbf{p}'$:

$$\mathbf{p}' = \mathcal{R}(\mathbf{p}, v). \tag{1}$$

For simplicity, we restrict the scalar strength v to be normalized in $[-1, 1]$.

Color Operator Properties. By carefully studying standard global color operators, such as exposure, black clipping, vibrance in *Lightroom*, and contrast, `brightness` in *Snapseed*, and general hue, saturation and gamma adjustments, we find those operators usually satisfy the following properties:

- – 1. The effect of a color operator is controlled in a continuous way by adjusting the scalar strength.
- – 2. The color value should keep unchanged if strength is zero, *i.e.*, $\mathbf{p} = \mathcal{R}(\mathbf{p}, 0)$.
- – 3. The larger the strength is, the larger the color changes. For example, adjusting brightness by $+2$ should incur more changes than $+1$ adjustment.
- – 4. From a mathematical aspect, the operator should approximately satisfy the *homomorphism property*, *i.e.*, $\mathcal{R}(\mathbf{p}, v_1 + v_2) \approx \mathcal{R}(\mathcal{R}(\mathbf{p}, v_1), v_2)$. For example, adjusting exposure by $+3$, followed by a second operator that adjusts exposure by $+2$, is approximately equivalent to a single operator that adjusts exposure by $+5$.

Recall that our goal is to mimic the behavior of traditional color operators. Hence, The above color operator properties should be considered in the design of our neural color operators. Our main observation is: since the translation function naturally satisfies those properties, *i.e.*, for $f(x, v) = x + v$ we easily have $f(x, v_1 + v_2) = f(f(x, v_1), v_2))$, if we could map the non-linear color transformation in the 3D RGB space to a simple translation function in a high-dimensional feature space, the neural color operators would also satisfy those properties.

Network Structure. Based on the observation, we employ *equivariant mapping*, which has been widely used in other applications like geometric deep learning [22,27], for the purpose. Specifically, we adopt an encoder-decoder structure, as shown in Fig. 1 (top right). The encoder E transforms the input 3D RGB color $\mathbf{p}$ to a high-dimensional (*i.e.*, 64D) feature vector $\mathbf{z}$, then we perform a simple translation in the feature space $\mathbf{z}' = \mathbf{z} + v \cdot \mathbf{i}$, where the translation direction $\mathbf{i}$ is simply set as an all-one vector in the feature space and v controls the distance of translation. Finally, the decoder D transforms the feature vector $\mathbf{z}'$ back to the 3D RGB space to obtain the output color $\mathbf{p}'$. In general, we define the mapping of a neural color operator $\mathcal{R}$ as:

$$\mathbf{p}' = \mathcal{R}(\mathbf{p}, v) = D(E(\mathbf{p}) + v \cdot \mathbf{i}). \tag{2}$$

To maintain a lightweight structure, the encoder contains only one fully connected (FC) layer (without any hidden layers), and the decoder contains two FC layers where the first layer uses ReLU activations. Different from traditional encoders which usually map data to a lower dimensional latent space, our encoder maps colors to a higher dimensional feature space. We provide visualization of the 64D feature vectors in the supplemental document.

Note that our neural color operator can only approximately (but not strictly) satisfy the above color operator properties, since the decoder is not theoretically guaranteed to be the exact inverse of the encoder, i.e., $D(E(\mathbf{p})) \approx \mathbf{p}$.

4   Automatic Sequential Image Retouching

In this section, we present how to develop an automatic, lightweight yet effective sequential image retouching method based on our proposed neurOps.

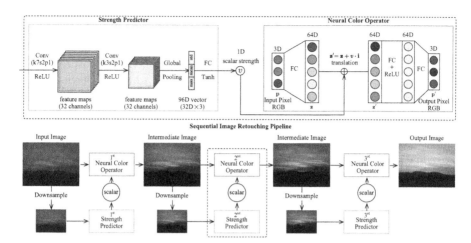

Fig. 1. Pipeline of our approach and network structures. Top left: structure of a strength predictor. Parameters of two convolutional layers are shared among all strength predictors (k7s2p1 denotes a kernel size 7×7, a stride of 2 and a padding of 1). Top right: network structure of a neural color operator. Parameters are not shared among different neural color operators. Bottom: the overall pipeline of our method. (Color figure online)

4.1   Problem Setup

Given an input image $I \in \mathbb{R}^{H \times W \times C}$ with an arbitrary resolution, our goal is to generate a retouched image $I^R \in \mathbb{R}^{H \times W \times C}$ by sequentially applying K pixel-wise color transformations modeled by neurOps:

$$I_k = \mathcal{R}_k(I_{k-1}, v_k), \quad 1 \leq k \leq K, \tag{3}$$

where $I_0 = I$ is the input image, I_k $(1 \leq k \leq K - 1)$ are intermediate images, and $I^R = I_K$ is the output image. $\mathcal{R}_k$ is the k-th neurOp, and v_k is a scalar that controls its strength. A neurOp maps each pixel's input color to an output color in a pixel-wise manner. In our experiments, we use $K = 3$ neurOps for the best trade-off between model size and efficacy. H, W and C denote the height, width, and channel size of the image, respectively.

To make the retouching process automatic, we predict the strength of each neurOp by strength predictors:

$$v_k = \mathcal{P}_k(I_{k-1}^{\downarrow}), \quad 1 \leq k \leq K, \tag{4}$$

where $\mathcal{P}_k$ is the k-th strength predictor, and $I_{k-1}^{\downarrow}$ is the bilinearly downsampled image from intermediate image I_{k-1} by shortening the longer image edge to 256. We use intermediate images instead of always using the original input image I to infer the strength parameter. This is motivated by human's editing workflow: an artist also needs intermediate visual feedbacks to decide the next editing step [16]. Figure 1 (bottom) illustrates the overall pipeline of our approach. Note that we do not share parameters between the 3 neurOps.

4.2   Strength Predictor

A strength predictor is used to predict the scalar strength used in a neurOp. Global image information is required for such prediction, i.e., an exposure adjustment needs the average intensity of the image. Hence, we use a downsampled intermediate edited image from the previous editing step as the input to the strength predictor.

The strength predictor contains 4 layers: two convolutional layers, a global pooling layer, and a FC layer. First, we use the first two convolutional layers to extract 32-channel feature maps. Then, we apply global pooling to obtain a 96D vector. Specifically, we employ three different pooling functions to compute channel-wise maximum, average, and standard deviation, respectively, and concatenate the three 32D vectors together. Finally, the FC layer, which acts as a predicting head, maps the 96D vector to a scalar strength in $[-1, 1]$. The top left of Fig. 1 shows the network structure of a strength predictor.

To reduce the overall size of our network, we force the parameters of the two convolutional layers to be shared among all 3 strength predictors. The parameters of the predicting head (*i.e.*, the last FC layer) are not shared.

Our strength predictor is inspired by the conditional network in CSR-Net [14,33] in order to maintain a lightweight structure. It is improved in several ways. First, we take intermediate images instead of the original image as input to better reflect human's editing workflow. Second, their conditional network outputs a 32D vector while our strength predictor generates a scalar. Third, we use three pooling functions instead of only one average pooling function which are demonstrated to be more helpful.

4.3   Loss Function and Training

We jointly train our neurOps and strength predictors by optimizing a predefined loss function in an end-to-end fashion. In practice, we find that a carefully designed initialization for the neurOps is also rather helpful.

Loss Function. For a single training image I, denoting its ground truth retouched image as I^{GT} and the predicted retouched image as I^R, respectively, the loss $\mathcal{L}$ is defined as the weighted sum of a reconstruction loss $\mathcal{L}_r$, a total variation (TV) loss $\mathcal{L}_{tv}$, and a color loss $\mathcal{L}_c$:

$$\mathcal{L} = \mathcal{L}_r + \lambda_1 \mathcal{L}_{tv} + \lambda_2 \mathcal{L}_c, \tag{5}$$

where λ_1 and λ_2 are two balancing weights empirically set as $\lambda_1 = \lambda_2 = 0.1$. The reconstruction loss measures L1 difference between the predicted image and the ground truth:

$$\mathcal{L}_r = \frac{1}{CHW} \|I^R - I^{GT}\|_1. \tag{6}$$

A TV loss [2] is included to encourage spatially coherent predicted images:

$$\mathcal{L}_{tv} = \frac{1}{CHW} \|\nabla I^R\|_2, \tag{7}$$

where $\nabla(\cdot)$ denotes the gradient operator. Besides, we include a color loss [32,42], which regards RGB colors as 3D vectors and measures their angular differences. Specifically, the color loss is defined as:

$$\mathcal{L}_c = 1 - \frac{1}{HW}\angle(I^R, I^{GT}), \tag{8}$$

where $\angle(\cdot)$ is an operator that computes the pixel-wise average of the cosine of the angular differences. The overall loss is computed as the sum of losses (Eq. 5) over all training images.

Initialization Scheme for Neural Color Operators. Instead of initializing the neurOps from scratch, we find that initializing them with standard color operators is a better choice. By analyzing the retouching histories in the MIT-Adobe FiveK dataset [6], we picked up the 3 most commonly used standard operators in the dataset, which are `black clipping`, `exposure`, and `vibrance` in *Lightroom*. For initialization, we intend to let our 3 neurOps reproduce the above 3 standard operators, respectively.

Since the formulas of those Lightroom operators are not publicly available, we have selected a small number of images (*i.e.*, 500 images) from the training set of MIT-Adobe FiveK, and manually retouched those images using those standard operators. Specifically, for each standard operator, for each input image I, we manually generate M (*i.e.*, $M = 40$) retouched images (*i.e.*, $\{I_m\}$, $1 \leq m \leq M$) with uniformly distributed levels of strengths. The strength used for each retouched image I_m is denoted as v_m.

Then, we enforce each neurOp $\mathcal{R}$ to reproduce the manually retouched images from each standard operator as much as possible. To do so, we optimize each neurOp by minimizing the sum of a unary loss and a pairwise loss over all selected images. The unary loss $\mathcal{L}_1$ enforces that the color keeps unchanged when the strength is zero:

$$\mathcal{L}_1 = \frac{1}{M}\sum_m \|\mathcal{R}(I_m, 0) - I_m\|_1. \tag{9}$$

The pairwise loss $\mathcal{L}_2$ enforces that the neurOp behaves the same as the given standard operator for specific strength values:

$$\mathcal{L}_2 = \frac{1}{M(M-1)}\sum_{m \neq n} \|\mathcal{R}(I_m, v_n - v_m) - I_n\|_1. \tag{10}$$

For optimization, we use the Adam optimizer with an initial learning rate of $5e^{-5}$, $\beta_1 = 0.9$, $\beta_2 = 0.99$, and a mini-batch size of 1, and run 100,000 iterations.

Joint Training. After initializing neurOps using the scheme described above, and initializing the strength predictors with random parameters, we jointly train our neurOps and strength predictors in an end-to-end fashion towards minimizing the overall loss function (Eq. 5). We also use the Adam optimizer with the same configurations as in the initialization scheme, and run 600,000 iterations. For data augmentation, we randomly crop images and then rotate them by multiples of $90°$.

5   Experiments

Datasets. The MIT-Adobe FiveK dataset [6] has been widely used for global image retouching and enhancement tasks. It consists of 5000 images in RAW format and an Adobe Lightroom Catalog that contains the adjusted rendition setting by five experts. We follow the common practice and use rendition version created by expert C as the ground truth. There are two public variations in terms of input rendition setting. The first variation is provided by Hu *et al.* [16], which choose the input `with Daylight WhiteBalance minus 1.5` and export them to 16 bits ProPhotoRGB TIFF images. We refer to it as *MIT-Adobe-5K-Dark*. The second variation is provided by Hwang *et al.* [17] which adopt the input `As Shot Zeroed` and export them to 8 bits sRGB JPEG images. We refer to it as *MIT-Adobe-5K-Lite*.

PPR10K [30] is a recently released image retouching dataset. It contains more than 11,000 high-quality portrait images. For each image, a human region mask is given and three retouched images by three experts are provided as ground truth. We refer to the three retouched variations as *PPR10K-a*, *PPR10K-b*, and *PPR10K-c*, respectively.

We train and evaluate our method on all 5 variations of both datasets. We follow the same split of training and testing sets as in previous works. For the MIT-Adobe FiveK dataset, all images are resized by shortening the longer edge to 500. For the PPR10K dataset, we use image resolution of 360p. All the experiments are performed on a PC with an NVIDIA RTX2080 Ti GPU. It takes about 2 h for initialization, and takes about 9 and 15 h for training on MIT-Adobe FiveK and PPR10K, respectively.

5.1   Comparison and Results

Comparison. We compare our method with a series of state-of-the-art methods, including White-Box [16], Distort-and-Recover [38], HDRNet [11], DUPE [42], MIRNet [48], Pix2Pix [20], 3D-LUT [49], CSRNet [14,33] on *MIT-Adobe-5K-Dark*, and DeepLPF [35], IRN [50] on *MIT-Adobe-5K-Lite*, and CSRNet, 3D-LUT, 3D-LUT+HRP [30] on *PPR10K*.

For the PPR10K dataset, since each image is associated with a human region mask, we also provide a variant of our method that additionally considers human region priority (HRP) [30] in training, which we refer to as NeurOp+HRP. This is done by slightly modifying the L1 loss in Eq. 6 to be a weighted one, *i.e.*, pixels inside human region have larger weights (e.g., 5) while other pixels have smaller weights (e.g., 1).

As shown in Table 1, our method consistently achieves the best performance on all dataset variations, demonstrating the robustness of our method. In contrast, while CSRNet performs relatively well on MIT-Adobe-5K-Dark, it performs less satisfactory on PPR10K, *i.e.*, their PSNR is lower than ours by 2 db on PPR10K-a, which is consistent with the benchmark carried out in [30]. Furthermore, our method is the most lightweight one (*i.e.*, only 28k parameters).

Table 1. Quantitative comparison with state-of-the-art methods. The best results are boldface and the second best ones are underlined.

Dataset	Method	PSNR↑	SSIM↑	ΔE_{ab}^*↓	#params
MIT-Adobe-5K-Dark	White-Box [16]	18.59	0.797	17.42	8,561,762
	Dis.& Rec. [38]	19.54	0.800	15.44	259,263,320
	HDRNet [11]	22.65	0.880	11.83	482,080
	DUPE [42]	20.22	0.829	16.63	998,816
	MIRNet [48]	19.37	0.806	16.51	31,787,419
	Pix2Pix [20]	21.41	0.749	13.26	11,383,427
	3D-LUT [49]	23.12	0.874	11.26	593,516
	CSRNet [14,33]	<u>23.86</u>	<u>0.897</u>	<u>10.57</u>	<u>36,489</u>
	NeurOp (ours)	**24.32**	**0.907**	**10.10**	**28,108**
MIT-Adobe-5K-Lite	DeepLPF [35]	23.63	0.875	10.55	<u>1,769,347</u>
	IRN [50]	<u>24.27</u>	<u>0.900</u>	<u>10.16</u>	11,650,752
	NeurOp (ours)	**25.09**	**0.911**	**9.93**	**28,108**

Dataset	Method	PSNR↑	SSIM↑	ΔE_{ab}^*↓
PPR 10K-a	CSRNet [14,33]	24.24	0.937	9.75
	3D-LUT [49]	25.64	–	–
	3D-LUT+HRP [30]	25.99	0.952	8.95
	NeurOp (ours)	<u>26.32</u>	<u>0.953</u>	<u>8.81</u>
	NeurOp+HRP (ours)	**26.46**	**0.955**	**8.80**
PPR 10K-b	CSRNet [14,33]	23.93	0.938	9.83
	3D-LUT [49]	24.70	–	–
	3D-LUT+HRP [30]	25.06	0.945	9.36
	NeurOp (ours)	<u>25.45</u>	<u>0.946</u>	<u>9.21</u>
	NeurOp+HRP (ours)	**25.82**	**0.951**	**8.97**
PPR 10K-c	CSRNet [14,33]	24.35	0.929	9.92
	3D-LUT [49]	25.18	–	–
	3D-LUT+HRP [30]	25.46	0.939	9.43
	NeurOp (ours)	<u>26.02</u>	<u>0.946</u>	<u>8.94</u>
	NeurOp+HRP (ours)	**26.23**	**0.947**	**8.86**

Figure 2 shows visual comparisons. 3D-LUT sometimes generates color banding artifacts due to the use of color space interpolation. Other methods easily lead to color shifting problems especially when the input image has a very low exposure or has a very different temperature. Generally, the results of our method have fewer artifacts and are closer to the ground truth. More visual comparisons are given in the supplemental document.

User Study. We have conducted a user study to evaluate the subjective visual quality of our method on both dataset variations of MIT-Adobe-5K. For MIT-Adobe-5K-Dark, we compare with CSRNet [14,33], while for MIT-Adobe-5K-Lite, we choose IRN [50] for comparison, since the two methods achieve the second best performance on the two variations, respectively. For each dataset variation, we randomly select 50 images from the testing set and invite 10 participants (totally 20 participants are invited). For each selected image, for each participant, three retouched images are displayed: the ground truth image, and the two images generated by our method and the competing method (the latter two are displayed in random order). The participant is asked to vote which one of the latter two is visually more pleasing and more similar to the ground truth. Figure 3 (a) shows the results of user study, which suggest that our retouched images are visually more appreciated than those of competing approaches.

Controllability. While our method could generate the retouched images in a fully automatically way, we still allow users to intuitively adjust the results by changing the predicted scalar strengths using three sliders in real-time. Figure 3 (b) shows some examples. We find that adjusting the strengths could result in meaningful edits. For example, increasing the strength of the first neurOp amplifies the shadow and adds more contrast. Increasing the second tends to give more brightness to the middle tone while preserving the highlight proportion unchanged. Adjusting the third makes the image look cooler or warmer. More

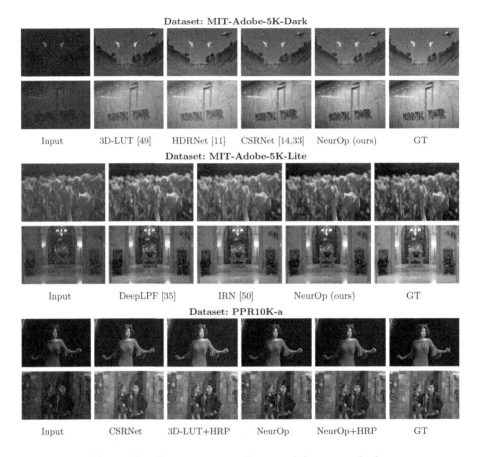

Fig. 2. Visual comparison with state-of-the-art methods.

examples of controllability as well as the intermediate images are provided in the supplemental document.

Existing methods such as CSRNet [14,33] achieve controlling through a linear interpolation between the retouched image and the original image by adjusting the interpolation weight. However, such controllability is rather limited. First, linear interpolation cannot faithfully reproduce sophisticated and highly non-linear color transformations. Second, only one degree of freedom is usually not enough for detailed color adjustments.

Timing and Memory Consumption. Our method runs in real-time. It takes 4 ms for a 500×333 image or 19 ms for an image with 1M pixels, which is slightly slower than CSRNet and 3D-LUT. However, it is worthy since our method has smaller model size (*i.e.*, only 28k parameters), achieves better performance (*i.e.*, higher PSNR scores), and inherits advantages of sequential image retouching which they do not possess.

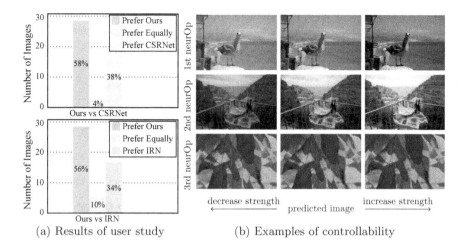

(a) Results of user study   (b) Examples of controllability

Fig. 3. User study and controllability. (a) Results of user study. (b) Examples of controllability. The middle column shows our automatically retouched images. The left and right columns show the results by further adjusting strengths of specific neurOps.

Table 2. Ablation study for neural color operators. (a) Different initialization schemes. (b) Initialization with different ordering of standard operators. $\overrightarrow{\text{vbe}}$ denotes using the order of `vibrance`, `black clipping`, and `exposure` for initialization. (c) Different number of neurOps. (d) Our method (final model).

Configs	(a) Initialization		(b) Order					(c) Number			(d) Ours
	Random	Standard fix	$\overrightarrow{\text{vbe}}$	$\overrightarrow{\text{veb}}$	$\overrightarrow{\text{evb}}$	$\overrightarrow{\text{ebv}}$	$\overrightarrow{\text{bve}}$	$K=1$	$K=2$	$K=4$	Finetune, $\overrightarrow{\text{bev}}$, $K=3$
PSNR↑	22.61	23.78	23.93	24.17	24.11	24.12	24.23	21.97	23.5	24.17	24.32

For memory consumption, our strength predictor takes less than 5M, our neroOp takes less than 1K per pixel. Overall, by processing pixels in batches (*i.e.*, 4096 pixels a batch), our method takes less than 10M memory for input images with arbitrary resolutions (storage for input/output images not included).

Benefits of Our Method. Due to the nice properties of neural color operators, the advantages of our method are multi-fold. First, it is rather lightweight and runs in real-time, hence, it could be easily deployed in mobile devices. Second, it inherits the advantages of sequential image retouching methods: providing an understandable editing history and offering convenient and flexible controls. Last but not least, besides the above advantages, our method still consistently achieves the best performance compared to state-of-the-art methods on two public datasets in both quantitative measures and visual qualities, as demonstrated by experiments and user studies.

Table 3. Ablation study for strength predictors and loss function. (a) Different pooling configurations in strength predictors. (b) Other design components in strength predictors. (c) Different configurations for the loss function. (d) Our method (final model).

Configs	(a) Pooling layer			(b) Strength predictor		(c) Loss function			(d) Ours
	aver	aver+max	aver+std	ori-img-input	non-share-layer	$\mathcal{L}_r$	$\mathcal{L}_r + \mathcal{L}_c$	$\mathcal{L}_r + \mathcal{L}_{tv}$	
PSNR↑	23.96	24.27	24.11	23.91	24.35	24.22	24.30	24.26	24.32
#Params	27,916	28,012	28,012	28,108	56,076	28,108	28,108	28,108	28,108

5.2   Ablation Study

We conduct a series of ablation studies to justify our training strategy as well as the design choices of our neurOps and strength predictors. Except for the ablated parts, we retrain the ablated models adopting the same setting as our final models. We make quantitative comparisons using average PSNR achieved on the testing images of MIT-Adobe-5K-Dark as it is generally more challenging.

Neural Color Operators. We first verify the effectiveness of the initialization strategy for neurOps. Recall that we first initialize all neurOps with standard operators and then finetune their parameters in a later joint training step. We compare our choice with two alternatives: random initialization from scratch, initialization with standard operators without allowing further finetuning (*i.e.*, in later steps, only strength predictors are trained while neurOps keep fixed). The performance is given in Table 2 (a) and (d). The results verify that initialization using standard operators is clearly superior to random initialization (PSNR: 24.32 db vs 22.61 db). Besides, using trainable neurOps is also shown to be a better choice than using fixed functional standard operators (PSNR: 23.78 db), due to better model expressiveness.

Recall that we choose the three most commonly used standard operators to initialize our neurOps. We then test whether the order of standard operators matters. As shown in Table 2 (b) and (d), we test all 6 permutations of different ordering, and find that initializing the first, second and third neural operators with `black clipping`, `exposure` and `vibrance`, respectively, is the best choice.

We further conduct experiments to find out how many neurOps are suitable. We test four choices: $K = 1, 2, 3$ and 4. For $K = 1$, we use `black clipping` for initialization. For $K = 2$, we use `black clipping` and `exposure` for initialization. For $K = 4$, we use another standard operator `highlight recovery` to initialize the 4th neurOp. We could find that $K = 3$ achieves the best performance, as shown in Table 2 (c–d). This is possibly due to that fewer neural operators (*i.e.*, $K = 1$ or 2) lead to insufficient expressiveness while a larger number of neural operators (*i.e.*, $K = 4$) result in harder training of strength predictors due to longer sequence. Overall, $K = 3$ is the best choice.

Strength Predictors. In the global pooling layer of a strength predictor, recall that we have combined three pooling functions that compute average, maximum, and standard deviation, respectively. We test cases when a part of or all pooling functions are used, as shown in Table 3 (a) and (d). Notice that each pooling function is useful, and combining all of them achieves the best performance.

We also verify other design choices of strength predictors in Table 3 (b). Recall that we feed intermediate images from previous editing steps as the input to strength predictors. An alternative choice would be always feeding the original input image, however, that would result in a drop in performance, *i.e.*, PSNR: 24.32 db → 23.91 db. It verifies that following human's editing workflow to use intermediate visual feedbacks is a better choice. Besides, recall that we force all strength predictors to share parameters for convolutional layers. We also test the case when parameters are not forced sharing. Unsurprisingly, the performance slightly gains, *i.e.*, increasing PSNR by 0.03 db. However, it doubles the network size (28k → 56k). Sharing parameters for all strength predictors leads to a good trade-off between maintaining high performance and lightweight structures.

Loss Function. Our loss function (Eq. 5) includes a reconstruction loss term, a TV loss term, and a color loss term. In Table 3 (c), we evaluate the choice of terms in the loss function. The results verify that combining all terms produces the best performance.

6   Conclusion and Limitations

In this paper, we have proposed a lightweight sequential image retouching method. The core of our method is the newly introduced neural color operator. It mimics the behavior of traditional color operators and learns complex pixel-wise color transformation whose strength is controlled by a scalar. We have also designed CNN based strength predictors to automatically infer the scalar strengths. The neural color operators and strength predictors are trained in an end-to-end manner together with a carefully designed initialization scheme.

Extensive experiments show that our model achieve the state-of-the-art performance on public datasets with only 28k parameters and provide more convenient parametric controls compared with previous competitive works.

Limitations. Our method has several limitations and could be further improved in the future. First, our method is limited to global color retouching. A possible way to handle local effects is extending strength predictors to infer strength maps instead of scalar strengths. Second, we only support pixel-wise color editing. It would be an interesting topic to extend neural color operators to handle spatial filtering. Third, from a theoretical aspect, our encoder-decoder structure for neural color operators cannot guarantee accurate homomorphism properties. It is worthwhile to investigate other network structures with better theoretical properties, such as invertible networks. As for future works, we are also interested in applying the idea of neural color operators to other related applications such as image editing.

Acknowledgements. This work is supported by the National Natural Science Foundation of China (Project Number: 61932003).

References

1. Afifi, M., Derpanis, K.G., Ommer, B., Brown, M.S.: Learning multi-scale photo exposure correction. In: Proceedings of the IEEE Conference on Computer Vision and Pattern Recognition (2021)
2. Aly, H.A., Dubois, E.: Image up-sampling using total-variation regularization with a new observation model. IEEE Trans. Image Process. **14**(10), 1647–1659 (2005)
3. Arici, T., Dikbas, S., Altunbasak, Y.: A histogram modification framework and its application for image contrast enhancement. IEEE Trans. Image Process. **18**(9), 1921–1935 (2009)
4. Aubry, M., Paris, S., Hasinoff, S.W., Kautz, J., Durand, F.: Fast local Laplacian filters: theory and applications. ACM Trans. Graph. (TOG) **33**(5), 1–14 (2014)
5. Bianco, S., Cusano, C., Piccoli, F., Schettini, R.: Content-preserving tone adjustment for image enhancement. In: Proceedings of the IEEE/CVF Conference on Computer Vision and Pattern Recognition Workshops (CVPRW) (2019)
6. Bychkovsky, V., Paris, S., Chan, E., Durand, F.: Learning photographic global tonal adjustment with a database of input / output image pairs. In: Proceedings of the IEEE Conference on Computer Vision and Pattern Recognition (CVPR), pp. 97–104. IEEE (2011)
7. Chai, Y., Giryes, R., Wolf, L.: Supervised and unsupervised learning of parameterized color enhancement. In: The IEEE Winter Conference on Applications of Computer Vision (WACV), pp. 992–1000 (2020)
8. Chen, H.T., Wei, L.Y., Chang, C.F.: Nonlinear revision control for images. ACM Trans. Graph. **30**(4) (2011). https://doi.org/10.1145/2010324.1965000
9. Chen, Y.S., Wang, Y.C., Kao, M.H., Chuang, Y.Y.: Deep photo enhancer: unpaired learning for image enhancement from photographs with GANs. In: Proceedings of the IEEE Conference on Computer Vision and Pattern Recognition (CVPR), pp. 6306–6314 (2018)
10. Deng, Y., Loy, C.C., Tang, X.: Aesthetic-driven image enhancement by adversarial learning. In: 2018 ACM Multimedia Conference on Multimedia Conference (MM), pp. 870–878. ACM (2018)
11. Gharbi, M., Chen, J., Barron, J.T., Hasinoff, S.W., Durand, F.: Deep bilateral learning for real-time image enhancement. ACM Trans. Graph. (TOG) **36**(4), 118 (2017)
12. Grabler, F., Agrawala, M., Li, W., Dontcheva, M., Igarashi, T.: Generating photo manipulation tutorials by demonstration. ACM Trans. Graph. **28**(3) (2009). https://doi.org/10.1145/1531326.1531372
13. Guo, C., et al.: Zero-reference deep curve estimation for low-light image enhancement. In: Proceedings of the IEEE/CVF Conference on Computer Vision and Pattern Recognition (CVPR), pp. 1780–1789 (2020)

14. He, J., Liu, Y., Qiao, Yu., Dong, C.: Conditional sequential modulation for efficient global image retouching. In: Vedaldi, A., Bischof, H., Brox, T., Frahm, J.-M. (eds.) ECCV 2020. LNCS, vol. 12358, pp. 679–695. Springer, Cham (2020). https://doi.org/10.1007/978-3-030-58601-0_40

15. Henderson, P., Islam, R., Bachman, P., Pineau, J., Precup, D., Meger, D.: Deep reinforcement learning that matters. In: Proceedings of the AAAI Conference on Artificial Intelligence (2018)

16. Hu, Y., He, H., Xu, C., Wang, B., Lin, S.: Exposure: a white-box photo post-processing framework. ACM Trans. Graph. (TOG) 37(2), 1–17 (2018)

17. Hwang, S.J., Kapoor, A., Kang, S.B.: Context-based automatic local image enhancement. In: Fitzgibbon, A., Lazebnik, S., Perona, P., Sato, Y., Schmid, C. (eds.) ECCV 2012. LNCS, vol. 7572, pp. 569–582. Springer, Heidelberg (2012). https://doi.org/10.1007/978-3-642-33718-5_41

18. Ignatov, A., Kobyshev, N., Timofte, R., Vanhoey, K., Van Gool, L.: DSLR-quality photos on mobile devices with deep convolutional networks. In: Proceedings of the IEEE International Conference on Computer Vision (ICCV), pp. 3277–3285 (2017)

19. Ignatov, A., Kobyshev, N., Timofte, R., Vanhoey, K., Van Gool, L.: WESPE: weakly supervised photo enhancer for digital cameras. In: Proceedings of the IEEE Conference on Computer Vision and Pattern Recognition Workshops (CVPRW), pp. 691–700 (2018)

20. Isola, P., Zhu, J.Y., Zhou, T., Efros, A.A.: Image-to-image translation with conditional adversarial networks. In: Proceedings of the IEEE Conference on Computer Vision and Pattern Recognition (CVPR), pp. 1125–1134 (2017)

21. Jiang, Y., et al.: EnlightenGAN: deep light enhancement without paired supervision. IEEE Trans. Image Process. (TIP) 30, 2340–2349 (2021)

22. Jimenez Rezende, D., Eslami, S., Mohamed, S., Battaglia, P., Jaderberg, M., Heess, N.: Unsupervised learning of 3D structure from images. Adv. Neural. Inf. Process. Syst. 29, 4996–5004 (2016)

23. Kim, H.-U., Koh, Y.J., Kim, C.-S.: Global and local enhancement networks for paired and unpaired image enhancement. In: Vedaldi, A., Bischof, H., Brox, T., Frahm, J.-M. (eds.) ECCV 2020. LNCS, vol. 12370, pp. 339–354. Springer, Cham (2020). https://doi.org/10.1007/978-3-030-58595-2_21

24. Kim, H.-U., Koh, Y.J., Kim, C.-S.: PieNet: personalized image enhancement network. In: Vedaldi, A., Bischof, H., Brox, T., Frahm, J.-M. (eds.) ECCV 2020. LNCS, vol. 12375, pp. 374–390. Springer, Cham (2020). https://doi.org/10.1007/978-3-030-58577-8_23

25. Kim, H., Choi, S.M., Kim, C.S., Koh, Y.J.: Representative color transform for image enhancement. In: Proceedings of the IEEE/CVF International Conference on Computer Vision (ICCV), pp. 4459–4468, October 2021

26. Kim, Y.T.: Contrast enhancement using brightness preserving bi-histogram equalization. IEEE Trans. Consum. Electron. 43(1), 1–8 (1997)

27. Kulkarni, T.D., Whitney, W., Kohli, P., Tenenbaum, J.B.: Deep convolutional inverse graphics network. arXiv preprint arXiv:1503.03167 (2015)

28. Lee, C., Lee, C., Kim, C.S.: Contrast enhancement based on layered difference representation of 2D histograms. IEEE Trans. Image Process. 22(12), 5372–5384 (2013)

29. Li, C., Guo, C., Ai, Q., Zhou, S., Loy, C.C.: Flexible piecewise curves estimation for photo enhancement (2020)

30. Liang, J., Zeng, H., Cui, M., Xie, X., Zhang, L.: Ppr10k: a large-scale portrait photo retouching dataset with human-region mask and group-level consistency.

In: Proceedings of the IEEE/CVF Conference on Computer Vision and Pattern Recognition (CVPR), pp. 653–661, June 2021

31. Liang, J., Zeng, H., Zhang, L.: High-resolution photorealistic image translation in real-time: A laplacian pyramid translation network. In: Proceedings of the IEEE Conference on Computer Vision and Pattern Recognition (2021)
32. Liu, E., Li, S., Liu, S.: Color enhancement using global parameters and local features learning. In: Ishikawa, H., Liu, C.-L., Pajdla, T., Shi, J. (eds.) ACCV 2020. LNCS, vol. 12623, pp. 202–216. Springer, Cham (2021). https://doi.org/10.1007/978-3-030-69532-3_13
33. Liu, Y., et al.: Very lightweight photo retouching network with conditional sequential modulation. CoRR abs/2104.06279 (2021). http://arxiv.org/abs/2104.06279
34. Long, J., Shelhamer, E., Darrell, T.: Fully convolutional networks for semantic segmentation. In: IEEE Conference on Computer Vision and Pattern Recognition (CVPR), pp. 3431–3440 (2015)
35. Moran, S., Marza, P., McDonagh, S., Parisot, S., Slabaugh, G.: DeepLPF: deep local parametric filters for image enhancement. In: IEEE Conference on Computer Vision and Pattern Recognition (CVPR), pp. 12826–12835 (2020)
36. Moran, S., McDonagh, S., Slabaugh, G.: CURL: neural curve layers for global image enhancement. In: 2020 25th International Conference on Pattern Recognition (ICPR), pp. 9796–9803. IEEE (2021)
37. Ni, Z., Yang, W., Wang, S., Ma, L., Kwong, S.: Towards unsupervised deep image enhancement with generative adversarial network. IEEE Trans. Image Process. (TIP) **29**, 9140–9151 (2020)
38. Park, J., Lee, J.Y., Yoo, D., So Kweon, I.: Distort-and-recover: color enhancement using deep reinforcement learning. In: Proceedings of the IEEE Conference on Computer Vision and Pattern Recognition (CVPR), pp. 5928–5936 (2018)
39. Shi, J., Xu, N., Xu, Y., Bui, T., Dernoncourt, F., Xu, C.: Learning by planning: language-guided global image editing. In: Proceedings of the IEEE/CVF Conference on Computer Vision and Pattern Recognition, pp. 13590–13599 (2021)
40. Stark, J.A.: Adaptive image contrast enhancement using generalizations of histogram equalization. IEEE Trans. Image Process. **9**(5), 889–896 (2000)
41. Wang, B., Yu, Y., Xu, Y.Q.: Example-based image color and tone style enhancement. ACM Trans. Graph. (TOG) **30**(4), 1–12 (2011)
42. Wang, R., Zhang, Q., Fu, C.W., Shen, X., Zheng, W.S., Jia, J.: Underexposed photo enhancement using deep illumination estimation. In: Proceedings of the IEEE Conference on Computer Vision and Pattern Recognition (CVPR), pp. 6849–6857 (2019)
43. Wang, T., et al.: Real-time image enhancer via learnable spatial-aware 3D lookup tables. In: Proceedings of the IEEE/CVF International Conference on Computer Vision (ICCV), pp. 2471–2480, October 2021
44. Wang, Y., Chen, Q., Zhang, B.: Image enhancement based on equal area dualistic sub-image histogram equalization method. IEEE Trans. Consum. Electron. **45**(1), 68–75 (1999)
45. Yan, J., Lin, S., Bing Kang, S., Tang, X.: A learning-to-rank approach for image color enhancement. In: Proceedings of the IEEE Conference on Computer Vision and Pattern Recognition (CVPR), pp. 2987–2994 (2014)
46. Yan, Z., Zhang, H., Wang, B., Paris, S., Yu, Y.: Automatic photo adjustment using deep neural networks. ACM Trans. Graph. (TOG) **35**(2), 11 (2016)
47. Ying, Z., Li, G., Ren, Y., Wang, R., Wang, W.: A new low-light image enhancement algorithm using camera response model. In: Proceedings of the IEEE International Conference on Computer Vision Workshops (CVPRW), pp. 3015–3022 (2017)

48. Zamir, S.W., et al.: Learning enriched features for real image restoration and enhancement. In: Vedaldi, A., Bischof, H., Brox, T., Frahm, J.-M. (eds.) ECCV 2020. LNCS, vol. 12370, pp. 492–511. Springer, Cham (2020). https://doi.org/10.1007/978-3-030-58595-2_30
49. Zeng, H., Cai, J., Li, L., Cao, Z., Zhang, L.: Learning image-adaptive 3D lookup tables for high performance photo enhancement in real-time. IEEE Trans. Pattern Anal. Mach. Intell. (TPAMI) (2020)
50. Zhao, L., Lu, S.P., Chen, T., Yang, Z., Shamir, A.: Deep symmetric network for underexposed image enhancement with recurrent attentional learning. In: Proceedings of the IEEE/CVF International Conference on Computer Vision (ICCV), pp. 12075–12084, October 2021

Optimizing Image Compression via Joint Learning with Denoising

Ka Leong Cheng, Yueqi Xie, and Qifeng Chen$^{(\boxtimes)}$

The Hong Kong Univeristy of Science and Technology, Hong Kong, China
{klchengad,yxieay}@connect.ust.hk, cqf@ust.hk

Abstract. High levels of noise usually exist in today's captured images due to the relatively small sensors equipped in the smartphone cameras, where the noise brings extra challenges to lossy image compression algorithms. Without the capacity to tell the difference between image details and noise, general image compression methods allocate additional bits to explicitly store the undesired image noise during compression and restore the unpleasant noisy image during decompression. Based on the observations, we optimize the image compression algorithm to be noise-aware as joint denoising and compression to resolve the bits misallocation problem. The key is to transform the original noisy images to noise-free bits by eliminating the undesired noise during compression, where the bits are later decompressed as clean images. Specifically, we propose a novel two-branch, weight-sharing architecture with plug-in feature denoisers to allow a simple and effective realization of the goal with little computational cost. Experimental results show that our method gains a significant improvement over the existing baseline methods on both the synthetic and real-world datasets. Our source code is available at: https://github.com/felixcheng97/DenoiseCompression.

Keywords: Joint method · Image compression · Image denoising

1 Introduction

Lossy image compression has been studied for decades with essential applications in media storage and transmission. Many traditional algorithms [50,60] and learned methods [3,5,13,44,65] are proposed and widely used. Thanks to the fast development of mobile devices, smartphones are becoming the most prevalent and convenient choice of photography for sharing. However, the captured images usually contain high levels of noise due to the limited sensor and aperture size in smartphone cameras [1]. Since existing compression approaches are designed for general images, the compressors treat the noise as "crucial" information and explicitly allocate bits to store it, even though noise is usually undesired for common users. The image noise can further degrade the compression quality, especially at medium and high bit rates [2,48]. Concerning these aspects, we see

---

K. L. Cheng and Y. Xie—Joint first authors

S. Avidan et al. (Eds.): ECCV 2022, LNCS 13679, pp. 56–73, 2022.
https://doi.org/10.1007/978-3-031-19800-7_4

the crucial need for an image compression method with the capacity of noise removal during the compression process.

A natural and straightforward solution is to go through a sequential pipeline of individual denoising and compression methods. However, a simple combination of separate models can be sub-optimal for this joint task. On the one hand, sequential methods introduce additional time overhead due to the intermediate results, leading to a lower efficiency than a united solution. The inferior efficiency can limit their practical applications, especially on mobile devices. On the other hand, a sequential solution suffers from the accumulation of errors and information loss in the individual models. Most image denoising algorithms have strong capabilities of noise removal for the flat regions but somehow over-smooth the image details [66]. However, the details are the critical parts of information that need to be kept for compression. Lossy image compression algorithms save bits through compressing local patterns with a certain level of information loss, particularly for the high-frequency patterns. However, both image details and noise are considered high-frequency information, so a general image compressor is likely to eliminate some useful high-frequency details while misallocating bits to store the unwanted noise instead. In the area of image processing, many researchers explore to develop joint solutions instead of using sequential approaches, such as combined problems of joint image demosaicing, denoising, or super-resolution [21,40,66].

In this paper, we contribute a joint method to optimize the image compression algorithm via joint learning with denoising. The key challenge of this joint task is to resolve the bit misallocation issue on the undesired noise when compressing the noisy images. In other words, the joint denoising and compression method needs to eliminate only the image noise while preserving the desired high-frequency content so that no extra bits are wastefully allocated for encoding the noise information in the images. Some existing works attempt to integrate the denoising problem into image compression algorithms. Prior works [22,49] focus on the decompression procedure and propose joint image denoise-decompression algorithms, which take the noisy wavelets coefficients as input to restore the clean images, but leave the compressing part untouched. A recent work [54] attempts to tackle this task by adding several convolutional layers into the decompressor to denoise the encoded latent features on the decoding side. However, their networks can inevitably use additional bits to store the noise in the latent features since there are no particular designs of modules or supervision for denoising in the compressor, leading to their inferior performance compared to the sequentially combined denoising and compression solutions.

We design an end-to-end trainable network with a simple yet effective novel two-branch design (a denoising branch and a guidance branch) to resolve the bit misallocation problem in joint image denoising and compression. Specifically, we hope to pose explicit supervision on the encoded latent features to ensure it is noise-free so that we can eliminate high-frequency noise while, to a great extent, preserving useful information. During training, the denoising and guidance branches have shared encoding modules to obtain noisy features from the noisy input image and the guiding features from the clean input image, respectively; efficient denoising modules are plugged into the denoising branch to denoise the noisy features as noise-free latent codes. The explicit supervision is posed in high-dimensional space from the guiding features to the encoded latent codes. In this way, we can train the denoiser to help learn a noise-free representation. Note that the guidance branch is disabled during inference.

We conduct extensive experiments for joint image denoising and compression on both the synthetic data under various noise levels and the real-world SIDD [1]. Our main contributions are as follows:

- We optimize image compression on noisy images through joint learning with denoising, aiming to avoid bit misallocation for the undesired noise. Our method outperforms baseline methods on both the synthetic and real-world datasets by a large margin.
- We propose an end-to-end joint denoising and compression network with a novel two-branch design to explicitly supervise the network to eliminate noise while preserving high-frequency details in the compression process.
- Efficient plug-in feature denoisers are designed and incorporated into the denoising branch to enable the denoising capacity of the compressor with only little addition of complexity during inference time.

2   Related Work

2.1   Image Denoising

Image denoising is an age-long studied task with many traditional methods proposed over the past decades. They typically rely on certain pre-defined assumptions of noise distribution, including sparsity of image gradients [9,53] and similarity of image patches [16,24]. With the rapid development of deep learning, some methods [11,25,62] utilize CNNs to improve the image denoising performance based on the synthetic [20,61,64] and real-world datasets, including DND [47], SIDD [1], and SID [11]. Some works [26,33,69] focus on adapting solutions from synthetic datasets to real-world scenarios. Some current state-of-the-art methods are proposed to enhance performance further, including DANet [68] utilizing an adversarial framework and InvDN [41] leveraging the invertible neural networks. However, many learning-based solutions rely on heavy denoising models, which are practically inefficient for the joint algorithms, especially in real-world applications.

2.2   Lossy Image Compression

Many traditional lossy image compression solutions [7,23,31,50,60] are widely proposed for practical usage. They map an image to quantized latent codes through hand-crafted transformations and compress them using entropy coding. With vast amounts of data available these days, many learning-based solutions are developed to learn a better transformation between image space and feature space. RNN-based methods [30,56,58] are utilized to iteratively encode residual information in the images, while most of the recent solutions are based on variational autoencoders (VAEs) [4,55] to optimize the whole image compression process directly. Some methods [5,13,27,29,37,44,45] focus on improving the entropy models to parameterize the latent code distribution more accurately. Some others [38,65] design stronger architectures to learn better transformations for image compression. For example, Lin et al. [38] introduce spatial RNNs to reduce spatial redundancy, Mentzer et al. [42] integrate generative adversarial networks for high-fidelity generative image compression, and Xie et al. [65] utilize invertible neural networks to form a better reversible process. However, these existing compression methods generally do not consider the image noise in their designs.

2.3 Joint Solutions

A series of operations are usually included in a whole image or video processing pipeline, while a pipeline with separate solutions can suffer from the accumulation of errors from individual methods. Thus, many joint solutions have been proposed for various combinations of tasks. Several widely-studied ones for image processing include joint denoising and demosaicing [15,18,21,32,35], joint denoising and super-resolution [70], and joint demosaicing and super-resolution [19,59,67]. Recently, Xing et al. [66] further propose to solve a joint triplet problem of image denoising, demosaicing, and super-resolution. As for video processing, Norkin et al. [46] integrate the idea of separating film grain from video content into the AV1 video codec, which can be viewed as a joint solution of video denoising and compression. However, the task for joint image denoising and compression has not received much attention yet important. Some works like [22,49] only target at building decompression methods that restore clean images from the noisy bits by integrating the denoising procedure in the decompression process. A recent work [54] also incorporates the denoising idea into image decompression by performing denoising on the encoded latent codes during decompression. These approaches cannot achieve our goal of solving the bits misallocation problem and cannot achieve pleasant rate-distortion performance since denoising during decompression cannot produce noise-free bits.

3   Problem Specification

We wish to build an image compression method that takes noise removal into consideration during compression since noise is usually unwanted for general users while requiring additional bits for storage. Hence, the benefit of such a compressor lies in saving storage for the unwanted noise during the compression process. Formally, given a noisy image $\tilde{x}$ with its corresponding clean ground truth image x, the compressor takes $\tilde{x}$ as input to denoise and compress it into denoised bitstreams. We can later decompress the bitstreams to get the denoised image $\hat{x}$. Meanwhile, instead of sequentially doing denoising and successive compression or vice versa, we require the whole process to be end-to-end optimized as a united system to improve efficiency and avoid accumulation of errors.

3.1 Selection of Datasets

It is desirable to have a large number of diverse samples to train a well-performing learned image compression network. Many real-world datasets such as DND [47], SIDD [1], and SID [11] have been proposed for image denoising with noisy-clean image pairs. However, they generally have limited training samples, scene diversities, or noise levels because collecting a rich (large scale, various gains, illuminance, etc.) real-world dataset typically includes much time-consuming labor work. In contrast, synthetic data is cheap and unlimited, and it is flexible to synthesize images with different levels of noise. Therefore, the main experiments in this paper are carried out using synthetic data; additional experiments on the SIDD [1] are also conducted to further verify the effectiveness of our method. We use the SIDD only for real-world datasets because RNI15 [36] has no clean ground truths; SID [11] is for image denoising in the dark; DND [47] only allows 5 monthly submissions, which is not suitable for the image compression task that requires evaluations at various bit rates.

3.2 Noise Synthesis

We use a similar strategy as in [43] to do noise synthesis in raw, where the following sRGB gamma correction function Γ is used to transform between the image sRGB domain $\mathbf{X}$ and the raw linear domain $\mathbf{Y}$:

$$\mathbf{X} = \Gamma(\mathbf{Y}) = \begin{cases} m\mathbf{Y}, & \mathbf{Y} \le b, \\ (1+a)\mathbf{Y}^{1/\gamma} - a, & \mathbf{Y} > b, \end{cases} \tag{1}$$

where $a = 0.055$, $b = 0.0031308$, $m = 12.92$, $\gamma = 2.4$. Specifically, the inverse function Γ^{-1} is first applied on sRGB image $\mathbf{x}$ to get the raw image $\mathbf{y} = \Gamma^{-1}(\mathbf{x})$. The noise in raw images is defined as the standard deviation of the linear signal, ranging from 0 to 1. Given a true signal intensity y_p at position p, the corresponding noisy measurement $\tilde{y}_p$ in the noisy raw image $\tilde{\mathbf{y}}$ is estimated by a two-parameter signal-dependent Gaussian distribution [28]:

$$\tilde{y}_p \sim \mathcal{N}(y_p, \sigma_s y_p + \sigma_r^2), \tag{2}$$

where σ_s and σ_r denote the shot and readout noise parameters, respectively, indicating different sensor gains (ISO). After the noise synthesis in raw space, we obtain our noisy sRGB image $\tilde{\mathbf{x}} = \Gamma(\tilde{\mathbf{y}})$.

4 Method

Our joint denoising and compression method is inherently an image compression algorithm with the additional capacity to remove undesirable noise. Hence, the proposed method for image denoise-compression is built upon the learned image compression methods. Figure 1 shows an overview of the proposed method. Our network contains a novel two-branch design for the training process, where the guiding features in the guidance branch pose explicit supervision on the denoised features in the denoising branch during the compression process.

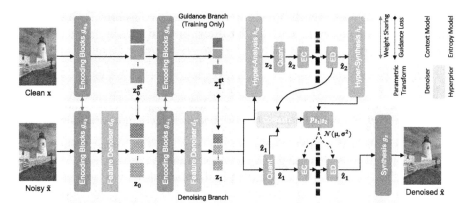

Fig. 1. Overview of the two-branch design of our proposed network, which is first pre-trained on clean images and successively fine-tuned on noisy-clean image pairs. In the top left of the figure, the clean image goes through the guidance branch for the two-level guiding features; in the bottom left, the noisy image is fed into the denoising branch to obtain the two-level denoised features. Note that the guidance branch is for training only, and that the denoising branch (orange part) and the denoisers (orange blocks) are only activated during fine-tuning and used for inference. The right half of the figure contains the common hyperprior, entropy models, context model, and synthesis transform used in the recent learned compression methods [13,44]. (Color figure online)

4.1 Network Design

Overall Workflow. The network contains a parametric analysis transform g_a (containing g_{a_0} and g_{a_1}) with plug-in feature denoisers d (containing d_0 and d_1) to encode and denoise the input noisy image $\tilde{\mathbf{x}}$ into some denoised latent features $\mathbf{z}_1$. Discrete quantization is then applied to obtain the quantized latent features $\hat{\mathbf{z}}_1$. Instead of using the non-differentiable discrete rounding function during training, we add a uniform noise $\mathcal{U}(-0.5, 0.5)$ on top of $\mathbf{z}_1$ to get $\tilde{\mathbf{z}}_1$, which can be view as an approximation of the discrete quantization process [4]. For notation simplicity, we use $\hat{\mathbf{z}}_1$ to represent both $\hat{\mathbf{z}}_1$ and $\tilde{\mathbf{z}}_1$ in this paper. Then accordingly, we have a parametric synthesis transform g_s that decodes $\hat{\mathbf{z}}_1$ to obtain the denoised image $\hat{\mathbf{x}}$. The parametric transforms g_a, g_s and the denoiser d formulate a basic variational model for the joint image denoising and compression task.

As discussed in Ballé et al. [5], there still remain significant spatial dependencies within the latent features $\hat{\mathbf{z}}_1$ using a basic variational model. Hence, a similar scale hyperprior is appended on top of the basic variational model. In particular, the hyperprior contains parametric transform h_a to model the spatial dependencies and obtain the additional latent features $\mathbf{z}_2$, so that we can assume that the target variables $\mathbf{z}_1$ conditioned on the introduced latent $\mathbf{z}_1$ are independent [8]. We adopt the same uniform noise strategy on $\mathbf{z}_2$ to obtain $\tilde{\mathbf{z}}_2$ during training and perform discrete quantization for $\hat{\mathbf{z}}_2$ during testing. Similarly, we use $\hat{\mathbf{z}}_2$ to represent $\hat{\mathbf{z}}_2$ and $\tilde{\mathbf{z}}_2$ for notation simplicity. Together with the causal context model c, another parametric synthesis transform h_s transforms $\hat{\mathbf{z}}_2$ to estimate the means $\hat{\boldsymbol{\mu}}$ and standard deviations $\hat{\boldsymbol{\sigma}}$ for the latent features $\hat{\mathbf{z}}_1$ so that each element of the latent features is modeled as mean and scale Gaussian [44]:

$$p_{\hat{\mathbf{z}}_1|\hat{\mathbf{z}}_2} \sim \mathcal{N}(\hat{\boldsymbol{\mu}}, \hat{\boldsymbol{\sigma}}^2). \tag{3}$$

Similar to [4], the distribution of $\hat{\mathbf{z}}_2$ is modeled as $p_{\hat{\mathbf{z}}_2|\theta}$ by a non-parametric, factorized entropy model θ because the prior knowledge is not available for $\hat{\mathbf{z}}_2$.

Two-Branch Architecture. The noisy image $\tilde{\mathbf{x}}$ and the corresponding clean image $\mathbf{x}$ are fed into the denoising and guidance branches, respectively. Similar to many denoising methods [10,12], the plug-in denoisers d_0 and d_1 are designed in a multiscale manner. The two-level guiding features $\mathbf{z}_0^{\mathbf{gt}}$ and $\mathbf{z}_1^{\mathbf{gt}}$ are obtained by the parametric analysis g_{a_0} and g_{a_1}, respectively; the two-level denoised features $\mathbf{z_0}$ and $\mathbf{z_1}$ are obtained by the parametric analysis g_{a_0} and g_{a_1} plus the denoisers d_0 and d_1, respectively:

$$\begin{aligned}
\mathbf{z}_0^{\mathbf{gt}} &= g_{a_0}(\mathbf{x}), & \mathbf{z_0} &= g_{a_0}(\tilde{\mathbf{x}}) + d_0(g_{a_0}(\tilde{\mathbf{x}})), \\
\mathbf{z}_1^{\mathbf{gt}} &= g_{a_1}(\mathbf{z}_0^{\mathbf{gt}}), & \mathbf{z_1} &= g_{a_1}(\mathbf{z_0}) + d_1(g_{a_1}(\mathbf{z_0})).
\end{aligned} \tag{4}$$

Note that the weights are shared for the parametric analysis g_{a_0} and g_{a_1} in two branches, and the denoisers are implemented in a residual manner. To enable direct supervision for feature denoising, a multiscale guidance loss is posed on the latent space to guide the learning of the denoisers. Specifically, the two-level guidance loss $\mathcal{G}$ is to minimize the $\mathcal{L}_1$ distance between the denoised and guiding features:

$$\mathcal{G} = ||\mathbf{z_0} - \mathbf{z}_0^{\mathbf{gt}}||_1 + ||\mathbf{z_1} - \mathbf{z}_1^{\mathbf{gt}}||_1. \tag{5}$$

4.2 Rate-Distortion Optimization

Some entropy coding methods like arithmetic coding [52] or asymmetric numeral systems (ANS) [17] are utilized to losslessly compress the discrete latent features $\hat{\mathbf{z}}_1$ and $\hat{\mathbf{z}}_2$ into bitstreams, which are the two parts of information needed to be stored during compression. As an inherent compression task, we hope the storing bitstreams are as short as possible; as a joint task with denoising, we hope to minimize the difference between the decoded image $\hat{\mathbf{x}}$ and the clean image $\mathbf{x}$. Hence, it is natural to apply the rate-distortion (RD) objective function $\mathcal{L}_{rd}$ in this joint task:

$$\mathcal{L}_{rd} = \mathcal{R}(\hat{\mathbf{z}}_1) + \mathcal{R}(\hat{\mathbf{z}}_2) + \lambda_d \mathcal{D}(\mathbf{x}, \hat{\mathbf{x}}). \tag{6}$$

In the context of rate-distortion theory, the to-be-coded sources are the noisy images $\tilde{\mathbf{x}}$, and the distortion is measured with respect to the corresponding clean counterparties $\mathbf{x}$. Similar to [13,44], the rate $\mathcal{R}$ denotes the rate levels for the bitstreams, which is defined as the entropy of the latent variables:

$$\begin{aligned}
\mathcal{R}(\hat{\mathbf{z}}_1) &= \mathbb{E}_{\tilde{\mathbf{x}} \sim p_{\tilde{\mathbf{x}}}}[-\log_2 p_{\hat{\mathbf{z}}_1|\hat{\mathbf{z}}_2}(\hat{\mathbf{z}}_1|\hat{\mathbf{z}}_2)], \\
\mathcal{R}(\hat{\mathbf{z}}_2) &= \mathbb{E}_{\tilde{\mathbf{x}} \sim p_{\tilde{\mathbf{x}}}}[-\log_2 p_{\hat{\mathbf{z}}_2|\theta}(\hat{\mathbf{z}}_2|\theta)].
\end{aligned} \tag{7}$$

The formulation of the distortion $\mathcal{D}$ is different for MSE and MS-SSIM [63] optimizations, which is either $\mathcal{D} = \text{MSE}(\mathbf{x}, \hat{\mathbf{x}})$ or $\mathcal{D} = 1 - \text{MS-SSIM}(\mathbf{x}, \hat{\mathbf{x}})$. The factor λ_d governs the trade-off between the bit rates $\mathcal{R}$ and the distortion $\mathcal{D}$.

4.3 Training Strategy

Pre-training as Image Compression. Given that our joint image denoising and compression method is an inherent image compression algorithm, we first pre-train our network with only the guidance branch, where to-be-coded sources are the clean images $\mathbf{x}$ and the distortion is also measured with respect to $\mathbf{x}$. In this way, the compression capacity is enabled for our model with properly trained parameter weights, except for the denoiser d. In the supplements, we further present some ablation studies showing that the pre-training process on image compression can benefit and significantly boost the performance of the joint network.

Fine-Tuning Under Multiscale Supervision. The next step is to properly train the plug-in denoisers d_1, d_2 to enable the denoising capacity in the denoising branch. Specifically, noisy-clean image pairs are fed into the denoising and guidance branches accordingly for model fine-tuning, with both the rate-distortion loss $\mathcal{L}_{rd}$ and the guidance loss $\mathcal{G}$. In this way, the full objective function $\mathcal{L}$ during fine-tuning becomes

$$\mathcal{L} = \mathcal{R}(\hat{\mathbf{z}}_1) + \mathcal{R}(\hat{\mathbf{z}}_2) + \lambda_d \mathcal{D}(\mathbf{x}, \hat{\mathbf{x}}) + \lambda_g \mathcal{G}(\mathbf{z}_0, \mathbf{z}_0^{\mathbf{gt}}, \mathbf{z}_1, \mathbf{z}_1^{\mathbf{gt}}), \qquad (8)$$

where $\lambda_g = 3.0$ is empirically set as the weight factor for the guidance loss.

5 Experiments

5.1 Experimental Setup

Synthetic Datasets. The Flicker 2W dataset [39] is used for training and validation, which consists of $20,745$ general clean images. Similar to [65], images smaller than 256 pixels are dropped for convenience, and around 200 images are selected for validation. The Kodak PhotoCD image dataset (Kodak) [14] and the CLIC Professional Validation dataset (CLIC) [57] are used for testing, which are two common datasets for the image compression task. There are 24 high-quality 768×512 images in the Kodak dataset and 41 higher-resolution images in the CLIC dataset.

We use the same noise sampling strategy as in [43] during training, where the readout noise parameter σ_r and the shot noise parameter σ_s are uniformly sampled from $[10^{-3}, 10^{-1.5}]$ and $[10^{-4}, 10^{-2}]$, respectively. As for the validation and testing, the 4 pre-determined parameter pairs $(\sigma_r, \sigma_s)^1$ in [43]'s official test set are used. Please note that Gain $\propto$ 4 (slightly noisier) and Gain $\propto$ 8 (significantly noisier) levels are unknown to the network during training. We test at

---

1 Gain $\propto$ 1 $= (10^{-2.1}, 10^{-2.6})$, Gain $\propto$ 2 $= (10^{-1.8}, 10^{-2.3})$, Gain $\propto$ 4 $= (10^{-1.4}, 10^{-1.9})$, Gain $\propto$ 8 $= (10^{-1.1}, 10^{-1.5})$.

full resolution on the Kodak and CLIC datasets with pre-determined levels of noise added.

Real-World Datasets. The public SIDD-Medium [1] dataset, containing 320 noisy-clean sRGB image pairs for training, is adopted to further validate our method on real-world noisy images. The SIDD-Medium dataset contains 10 different scenes with 160 scene instances (different cameras, ISOs, shutter speeds, and illuminance), where 2 image pairs are selected from each scene instance. Following the same settings in image denoising tasks, the models are validated on the 1280 patches in the SIDD validation set and tested on the SIDD benchmark patches by submitting the results to the SIDD website.

Training Details. For implementation, we use the anchor model [13] as our network architecture (without d_1 and d_2) and choose the bottlenect of a single residual attention block [13] for the plug-in denoisers d_1 and d_2. During training, the network is optimized using randomly cropped patches at a resolution of 256 pixels. All the models are fine-tuned on the pre-trained anchor models [13] provided by the popular CompressAI PyTorch library [6] using a single RTX 2080 Ti GPU. Some ablation studies on the utilized modules and the training strategy can be found in our supplements.

The networks are optimized using the Adam [34] optimizer with a mini-batch size of 16 for 600 epochs. The initial learning rate is set as 10^{-4} and decayed by a factor of 0.1 at epoch 450 and 550. Some typical techniques are utilized to avoid model collapse due to the random-initialized denoisers at the start of the fine-tuning process: 1) We warm up the fine-tuning process for the first 20 epochs. 2) We have a loss cap for each model so that the network will skip the optimization of a mini step if the training loss is beyond the set threshold value.

We select the same hyperparameters as in [13] to train compression models target a high compression ratio (relatively low bit rate) for practical reasons. Lower-rate models (q_1, q_2, q_3) have channel number $N = 128$, usually accompanied with smaller λ_d values. The channel number N is set as 192 for higher-rate models (q_4, q_5, q_6) and optimized using larger λ_d values. We train our MSE models under all the 6 qualities, with λ_d selected from the set {0.0018, 0.0035, 0.0067, 0.0130, 0.0250, 0.0483}; the corresponding λ_d values for MS-SSIM (q_2, q_3, q_5, q_6) are chosen from {4.58, 8.73, 31.73, 60.50}.

Evaluation Metrics. For the evaluation of rate-distortion (RD) performance, we use the peak signal-to-noise ratio (PSNR) and the multiscale structural similarity index (MS-SSIM) [63] with the corresponding bits per pixel (bpp). The RD curves are utilized to show the denoising and coding capacity of various models, where the MS-SSIM metric is converted to $-10\log_{10}(1 - \text{MS-SSIM})$ as prior work [13] for better visualization.

5.2   Rate-Distortion Performance

The sequential methods contains individual models of the state-of-the-art denoising DeamNet [51] and the anchor compression model Cheng2020 [13]. We compare our method with the following baseline methods: 1) "Cheng2020+DeamNet":

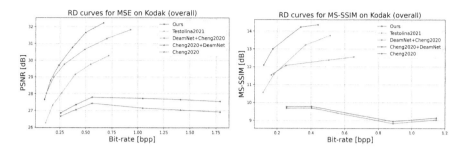

Fig. 2. Overall RD curves on the Kodak dataset at all noise levels. Our method has better RD performance over the pure compression, the sequential, and the joint baseline methods. (Color figure online)

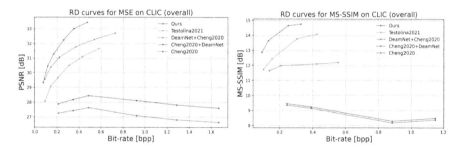

Fig. 3. Overall RD curves on the CLIC dataset at all noise levels. Our method has better RD performance over the pure compression, the sequential, and the joint baseline methods. (Color figure online)

sequential method of Cheng2020 and DeamNet; 2) "DeamNet+Cheng2020": sequential method of DeamNet and Cheng2020; 3) "Testolina2021": the joint baseline method [54]. We also report the performance of the pure image compression model "Cheng2020" on noisy-clean image pairs. Note that since a pure image compression model is trained to faithfully reconstruct the input image and is not expected to do any extra noisy-to-clean mapping, "Cheng2020" is only for qualitatively demonstrating the limitation of the current pure compression models as a reference.

For compression models, we use the pre-trained model provided by CompressAI [6]. For the denoising models on SIDD, we use the officially pre-trained DeamNet; for models on synthetic data, we retrain DeamNet from stretch on the same synthetic training data as ours. We re-implement "Testolina2021" as the joint baseline method according to their original paper [54]. The RD results are obtained from the CompressAI evaluation platform and the official SIDD website. More quantitative results are available in our supplements.

Synthetic Noise (Overall). We show the overall (containing all the 4 noise levels) RD curves for both the MSE and MS-SSIM methods evaluated on the Kodak dataset in Fig. 2 and on the CLIC dataset in Fig. 3. We can observe that our method (the blue RD curves) yields much better overall performance than

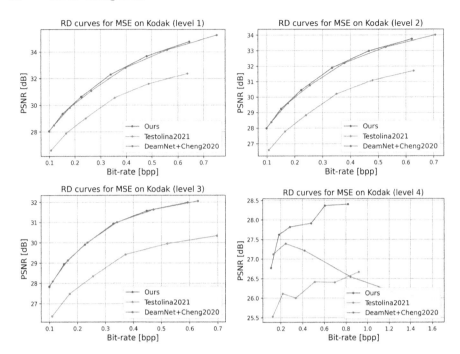

Fig. 4. RD curves on the Kodak dataset at individual noise level. Our method outperforms the baseline solutions, especially at the highest noise level. (Color figure online)

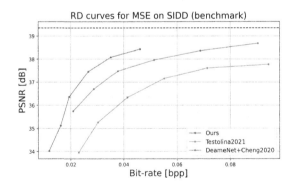

Fig. 5. RD curves optimized for MSE on the SIDD. Our method outperforms all the baseline solutions. The black dotted line is the DeamNet ideal case without compression for reference. (Color figure online)

the pure compression method, the sequential methods, and the joint baseline method.

For sequential methods, the green and red RD curves show that both sequential solutions have inferior performance compared to our joint solution. The execution order of the individual methods also matters. Intuitively, the sequential method that performs compression and successively denoising can suffer from the information loss and waste of bits allocating to image noise caused by the bottleneck of the existing general image compression method (see the purple RD curves for reference). The compressed noisy image with information loss makes the successive denoiser harder to reconstruct a pleasing image. Hence, in our remaining discussions, the sequential method specifically refers to the one that does denoising and successive compression.

The orange RD curves show that the joint baseline method [54] cannot outperform the sequential one and have a more significant performance gap between our method due to the better design of our compressor to learn a noise-free representation compared to previous works.

Synthetic Noise (Individual). To further discuss the effects of different noise levels, Fig. 4 shows the RD curves at individual noise levels for the MSE models on the Kodak dataset. We can see that our joint method is slightly better than the sequential method at the first three noise levels and significantly outperforms the sequential one at the highest noise level. Not to mention that our method has a much lower inference time as detailed in Sect. 5.3.

It is interesting to know that the pure denoiser DeamNet (black dotted line) drops significantly down to around 24 PSNR at noise level 4, which is the direct cause of the degraded performance for the sequential method (green curve) in the fourth chart in Fig. 4. Recall that all the models are not trained on synthetic images at noise level 3 (Gain $\propto$ 4) and 4 (Gain $\propto$ 8), where the Gain $\propto$ 4 noise is slightly higher while Gain $\propto$ 8 noise is considerably higher than the noisiest level during training. This indicates that the performance of the sequential solutions is somehow limited by the capacity of individual modules and suffers from the accumulation of errors. Our joint method has a beneficial generalization property to the unseen noise level to a certain extent.

Real-World Noise. We also provide the RD curves optimized for MSE on the SIDD with real-world noise in Fig. 5. We plot DeamNet (black dotted line) as a pure denoising model to show an ideal case of denoising performance without compression (at 24 bpp) for reference. The results show that our proposed method works well not only on the synthetic dataset but also on the images with real-world noise.

It is worth mentioning that given the same compressor, the compressed bit lengths of different images vary, depending on the amount of information (entropy) inside the images. Here, we can see that all the evaluated RD points are positioned in the very low bpp range (< 0.1 bpp). The very low bit-rate SIDD results are consistent among all methods, indicating inherently low entropy in the test samples, where the official SIDD test patches of size 256×256 contain relatively simple patterns.

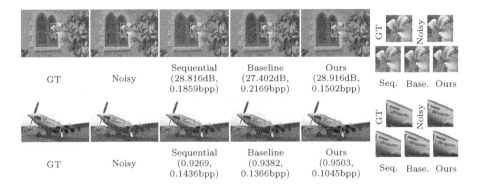

Fig. 6. Comparison results at noise level 4 (Gain ∝ 8) on Kodak image *kodim07* for MSE models and on Kodak image *kodim20* for MS-SSIM models. Apart from the better PSNR values and lower bpp rates, we can see that our solution has a better capacity to restore structural texture and edges.

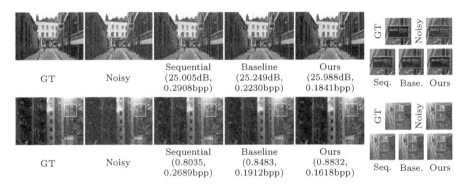

Fig. 7. Comparison results at noise level 4 (Gain ∝ 8) on sample CLIC images for both MSE and MS-SSIM models. Apart from the better PSNR values and lower bpp rates, we can observe that the text and edges are better restored for our method.

5.3   Efficiency Performance

We also compare the efficiency between our method and the sequential solution on the Kodak dataset, where the main difference comes from the compression process. The average elapsed encoding time under all qualities and noise levels for the sequential method is 75.323 s, while our joint solution is only 7.948 s. The elapsed running time is evaluated on Ubuntu using a single thread on Intel(R) Xeon(R) Gold 5118 CPU with 2.30 GHz frequency. The sequential method has considerably longer running time than our joint method, where the additional overhead mainly comes from the heavy individual denoising modules in the encoding process of the sequential method. On the contrary, our joint formulation with efficient plug-in feature denoising modules, which pose little burden upon running time, is more attractive in real-world applications.

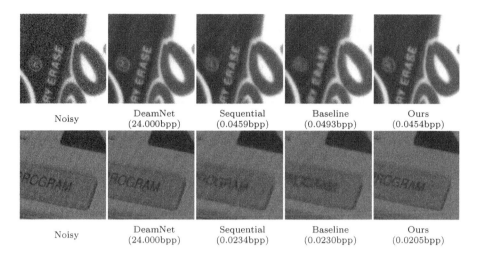

| Noisy | DeamNet (24.000bpp) | Sequential (0.0459bpp) | Baseline (0.0493bpp) | Ours (0.0454bpp) |

| Noisy | DeamNet (24.000bpp) | Sequential (0.0234bpp) | Baseline (0.0230bpp) | Ours (0.0205bpp) |

Fig. 8. Sample results on the SIDD. Since no ground-truth image is available for SIDD benchmark dataset, the visual results of DeamNet is shown as a reference for ground truth. We can see that the texts in our results is clearer at even slightly lower bpp rate.

5.4 Qualitative Results

Some qualitative comparisons are presented to further demonstrate the effectiveness of our method. We show the visual results at noise level 4 (Gain $\propto$ 8) of the sample Kodak images in Fig. 6 and CLIC images in Fig. 7 for both MSE and MS-SSIM models. Figure 8 shows the results of two sample patches from the SIDD. These results show that our method can obtain better quality images with even lower bit rates. Please check our supplements for more visual results.

6 Conclusion

We propose to optimize image compression via joint learning with denoising, motivated by the observations that existing image compression methods suffer from allocating additional bits to store the undesired noise and thus have limited capacity to compress noisy images. We present a simple and efficient two-branch design with plug-in denoisers to explicitly eliminate noise during the compression process in feature space and learn a noise-free bit representation. Extensive experiments on both the synthetic and real-world data show that our approach outperforms all the baselines significantly in terms of visual and metrical results. We hope our work can inspire more interest from the community in optimizing the image compression algorithm via joint learning with denoising and other aspects.

References

1. Abdelhamed, A., Lin, S., Brown, M.S.: A high-quality denoising dataset for smartphone cameras. In: Proceedings of CVPR (2018)
2. Al-Shaykh, O.K., Mersereau, R.M.: Lossy compression of noisy images. IEEE Trans. Image Prpcess.**7**(12), 1641–1652 (1998)
3. Ballé, J., Laparra, V., Simoncelli, E.P.: End-to-end optimization of nonlinear transform codes for perceptual quality. In: Proceedings of PSC (2016)
4. Ballé, J., Laparra, V., Simoncelli, E.P.: End-to-end optimized image compression. In: Proceedings of ICLR (2017)
5. Ballé, J., Minnen, D., Singh, S., Hwang, S.J., Johnston, N.: Variational image compression with a scale hyperprior. In: Proceedings of ICLR (2018)
6. Bégaint, J., Racapé, F., Feltman, S., Pushparaja, A.: CompressAI,: a pytorch : a PyTorch library and evaluation platform for end-to-end compression research. arXiv:2011.03029 (2020)
7. Bellard, F.: Bpg imagae format (2015). https://bellard.org/bpg/
8. Bishop, C.M.: Latent variable models. In: Jordan, M.I. (eds.) Learning in Graphical Models. NATO ASI Series, vol. 89, pp. 371–403. Springer, Netherlands (1998). https://doi.org/10.1007/978-94-011-5014-9_13
9. Chambolle, A.: An algorithm for total variation minimization and applications. J. Math. Imaging Vis. **20**(1), 89–97 (2004)
10. Chang, M., Li, Q., Feng, H., Xu, Z.: Spatial-Adaptive network for single image denoising. In: Vedaldi, A., Bischof, H., Brox, T., Frahm, J.-M. (eds.) ECCV 2020. LNCS, vol. 12375, pp. 171–187. Springer, Cham (2020). https://doi.org/10.1007/978-3-030-58577-8_11
11. Chen, C., Chen, Q., Xu, J., Koltun, V.: Learning to see in the dark. In: Proceedings of CVPR (2018)
12. Cheng, S., Wang, Y., Huang, H., Liu, D., Fan, H., Liu, S.: Nbnet: Noise basis learning for image denoising with subspace projection. In: Proceedings of CVPR (2021)
13. Cheng, Z., Sun, H., Takeuchi, M., Katto, J.: Learned image compression with discretized Gaussian mixture likelihoods and attention modules. In: Proceedings of CVPR, pp. 7939–7948 (2020)
14. Company, E.K.: Kodak lossless true color image suite (1999). https://www.r0k.us/graphics/Kodak
15. Condat, L., Mosaddegh, S.: Joint demosaicking and denoising by total variation minimization. In: Proceedings of ICIP (2012)
16. Dabov, K., Foi, A., Katkovnik, V., Egiazarian, K.: Color image denoising via sparse 3D collaborative filtering with grouping constraint in luminance-chrominance space. In: Proceedings of ICIP (2007)
17. Duda, J.: Asymmetric numeral systems. arXiv:0902.0271 (2009)
18. Ehret, T., Davy, A., Arias, P., Facciolo, G.: Joint demosaicking and denoising by fine-tuning of bursts of raw images. In: Proceedings of ICCV, pp. 8868–8877 (2019)
19. Farsiu, S., Elad, M., Milanfar, P.: Multiframe demosaicing and super-resolution from undersampled color images. In: Computational Imaging II (2004)
20. Foi, A., Trimeche, M., Katkovnik, V., Egiazarian, K.O.: Practical poissonian-gaussian noise modeling and fitting for single-image raw-data. IEEE Trans. Image Process. **17**(10), 1737–1754 (2008)
21. Gharbi, M., Chaurasia, G., Paris, S., Durand, F.: Deep joint demosaicking and denoising. ACM TOG **35**(6), 191:1–191:12 (2016)

22. González, M., Preciozzi, J., Musé, P., Almansa, A.: Joint denoising and decompression using cnn regularization. In: Proceedings of CVPR Workshops (2018)
23. Google: Web picture format (2010). http://chromium.googlesource.com/webm/libwebp
24. Gu, S., Zhang, L., Zuo, W., Feng, X.: Weighted nuclear norm minimization with application to image denoising. In: Proceedings of CVPR (2014)
25. Guan, H., Liu, L., Moran, S., Song, F., Slabaugh, G.G.: NODE: extreme low light raw image denoising using a noise decomposition network. arXiv:1909.05249 (2019)
26. Guo, S., Yan, Z., Zhang, K., Zuo, W., Zhang, L.: Toward convolutional blind denoising of real photographs. In: Proceedings of CVPR. pp. 1712–1722 (2019)
27. Guo, Z., Wu, Y., Feng, R., Zhang, Z., Chen, Z.: 3-D context entropy model for improved practical image compression. In: Proceedings of CVPR Workshops, pp. 116–117 (2020)
28. Healey, G., Kondepudy, R.: Radiometric CCD camera calibration and noise estimation. IEEE Trans. Pattern Anal. Mach. Intell. **16**(3), 267–276 (1994)
29. Hu, Y., ,ang, W., Liu, J.: Coarse-to-fine hyper-prior modeling for learned image compression. In: Proceedings of AAAI. pp. 11013–11020 (2020)
30. Johnston, N., et al.: Improved lossy image compression with priming and spatially adaptive bit rates for recurrent networks. In: Proceedings of CVPR (2018)
31. (JVET), J.V.E.T.: VVC official test model VTM (2021). http://vcgit.hhi.fraunhofer.de/jvet/VVCSoftware/_VTM/-/tree/master
32. Khashabi, D., Nowozin, S., Jancsary, J., Fitzgibbon, A.W.: Joint demosaicing and denoising via learned nonparametric random fields. IEEE Trans. Image Process. **23**(12), 4968–4981 (2014)
33. Kim, Y., Soh, J.W., Park, G.Y., Cho, N.I.: Transfer learning from synthetic to real-noise denoising with adaptive instance normalization. In: Proceedings of CVPR, pp. 3482–3492 (2020)
34. Kingma, D.P., Ba, J.: Adam: a method for stochastic optimization. In: Proceedings of ICLR (2015)
35. Klatzer, T., Hammernik, K., Knobelreiter, P., Pock, T.: Learning joint demosaicing and denoising based on sequential energy minimization. In: Proceedings of ICCP (2016)
36. Lebrun, M., Colom, M., Morel, J.: The noise clinic: a blind image denoising algorithm. Image Process. Online **5**, 1–54 (2015)
37. Lee, J., Cho, S., Beack, S.: Context-adaptive entropy model for end-to-end optimized image compression. In: Proceedings of ICLR (2019)
38. Lin, C., Yao, J., Chen, F., Wang, L.: A spatial RNN codec for end-to-end image compression. In: Proceedings of CVPR (2020)
39. Liu, J., Lu, G., Hu, Z., Xu, D.: A unified end-to-end framework for efficient deep image compression. arXiv:2002.03370 (2020)
40. Liu, L., Jia, X., Liu, J., Tian, Q.: Joint demosaicing and denoising with self guidance. In: Proceedings of CVPR, pp. 2237–2246 (2020)
41. Liu, Y., et al.: Invertible denoising network: a light solution for real noise removal. In: Proceedings of CVPR, pp. 13365–13374 (2021)
42. Mentzer, F., Toderici, G., Tschannen, M., Agustsson, E.: High-fidelity generative image compression. In: Advances in NeurIPS (2020)
43. Mildenhall, B., Barron, J.T., Chen, J., Sharlet, D., Ng, R., Carroll, R.: Burst denoising with kernel prediction networks. In: Proceedings of CVPR (2018)
44. Minnen, D., Ballé, J., Toderici, G.: Joint autoregressive and hierarchical priors for learned image compression. In: Advances in NeurIPS, pp. 10794–10803 (2018)

45. Minnen, D., Singh, S.: Channel-wise autoregressive entropy models for learned image compression. In: Proceedings of ICIP (2020)
46. Norkin, A., Birkbeck, N.: Film grain synthesis for AV1 video codec. In: Proceedings of DCC, pp. 3–12 (2018)
47. Plotz, T., Roth, S.: Benchmarking denoising algorithms with real photographs. In: Proceedings of CVPR (2017)
48. Ponomarenko, N.N., Krivenko, S.S., Lukin, V.V., Egiazarian, K.O., Astola, J.: Lossy compression of noisy images based on visual quality: A comprehensive study. EURASIP 2010 (2010)
49. Preciozzi, J., González, M., Almansa, A., Musé, P.: Joint denoising and decompression: a patch-based bayesian approach. In: Proceedings of ICIP (2017)
50. Rabbani, M.: Jpeg 2000: Image compression fundamentals, standards and practice. J. Electron. Imag. **11**(2), 286 (2002)
51. Ren, C., He, X., Wang, C., Zhao, Z.: Adaptive consistency prior based deep network for image denoising. In: Proceedings of CVPR, pp. 8596–8606 (2021)
52. Rissanen, J., Langdon, G.G.: Universal modeling and coding. IEEE Trans. Inf. Theory **27**(1), 12–23 (1981)
53. Rudin, L.I., Osher, S., Fatemi, E.: Nonlinear total variation based noise removal algorithms. Physica D **60**(1–4), 259–268 (1992)
54. Testolina, M., Upenik, E., Ebrahimi, T.: Towards image denoising in the latent space of learning-based compression. In: Applications of Digital Image Processing XLIV. vol. 11842, pp. 412–422 (2021)
55. Theis, L., Shi, W., Cunningham, A., Huszár, F.: Lossy image compression with compressive autoencoders. In: Proceedings of ICLR (2017)
56. Toderici, G., et al.: Variable rate image compression with recurrent neural networks. In: Proceedings of ICLR (2016)
57. Toderici, G., et al.: Workshop and challenge on learned image compression (2021). http://compression.cc/
58. Toderici, G., et al.: Full resolution image compression with recurrent neural networks. In: Proceedings of CVPR (2017)
59. Vandewalle, P., Krichane, K., Alleysson, D., Süsstrunk, S.: Joint demosaicing and super-resolution imaging from a set of unregistered aliased images. In: Digital Photography III (2007)
60. Wallace, G.K.: The jpeg still picture compression standard. IEEE TCE :38(1), xviii–xxxiv (1992)
61. Wang, W., Chen, X., Yang, C., Li, X., Hu, X., Yue, T.: Enhancing low light videos by exploring high sensitivity camera noise. In: Proceedings of ICCV (2019)
62. Wang, Y., Huang, H., Xu, Q., Liu, J., Liu, Y., Wang, J.: Practical deep raw image denoising on mobile devices. In: Vedaldi, A., Bischof, H., Brox, T., Frahm, J.-M. (eds.) ECCV 2020. LNCS, vol. 12351, pp. 1–16. Springer, Cham (2020). https://doi.org/10.1007/978-3-030-58539-6_1
63. Wang, Z., Simoncelli1, E.P., Bovik, A.C.: Multiscale structural similarity for image quality assessment. In: Proceedings of ACSSC (2003)
64. Wei, K., Fu, Y., Yang, J., Huang, H.: A physics-based noise formation model for extreme low-light raw denoising. In: Proceedings of CVPR (2020)
65. Xie, Y., Cheng, K.L., Chen, Q.: Enhanced invertible encoding for learned image compression. In: Proceedings of ACM MM, pp. 162–170 (2021)
66. Xing, W., Egiazarian, K.O.: End-to-end learning for joint image demosaicing, denoising and super-resolution. In: Proceedings of CVPR, pp. 3507–3516 (2021)
67. Xu, X., Ye, Y., Li, X.: Joint demosaicing and super-resolution (JDSR): Network design and perceptual optimization. IEEE Trans. Image Prpcess. **6**, 968–980 (2020)

68. Yue, Z., Zhao, Q., Zhang, L., Meng, D.: Dual adversarial network: toward real-world noise removal and noise generation. In: Vedaldi, A., Bischof, H., Brox, T., Frahm, J.-M. (eds.) ECCV 2020. LNCS, vol. 12355, pp. 41–58. Springer, Cham (2020). https://doi.org/10.1007/978-3-030-58607-2_3
69. Zhang, K., Zuo, W., Zhang, L.: FfdNet: toward a fast and flexible solution for CNN-based image denoising. IEEE Trans. Image Prpcess. **27**(9), 4608–4622 (2018)
70. Zhang, K., Zuo, W., Zhang, L.: Learning a single convolutional super-resolution network for multiple degradations. In: Proceedings of CVPR (2018)

Restore Globally, Refine Locally: A Mask-Guided Scheme to Accelerate Super-Resolution Networks

Xiaotao Hu[1,2], Jun Xu[2(✉)], Shuhang Gu[3], Ming-Ming Cheng[1], and Li Liu[4]

[1] College of Computer Science, Nankai University, Tianjin, China
[2] School of Statistics and Data Science, Nankai University, Tianjin, China
nankaimathxujun@gmail.com
[3] The University of Sydney, Camperdown, Australia
[4] Inception Institute of Artificial Intelligence, Abu Dhabi, United Arab Emirates

Abstract. Single image super-resolution (SR) has been boosted by deep convolutional neural networks with growing model complexity and computational costs. To deploy existing SR networks onto edge devices, it is necessary to accelerate them for large image (4K) processing. The different areas in an image often require different SR intensities by networks with different complexity. Motivated by this, in this paper, we propose a Mask Guided Acceleration (MGA) scheme to reduce the computational costs of existing SR networks while maintaining their SR capability. In our MGA scheme, we first decompose a given SR network into a Base-Net and a Refine-Net. The Base-Net is to extract a coarse feature and obtain a coarse SR image. To locate the under-SR areas in the coarse SR image, we then propose a Mask Prediction (MP) module to generate an error mask from the coarse feature. According to the error mask, we select K feature patches from the coarse feature and refine them (instead of the whole feature) by Refine-Net to output the final SR image. Experiments on seven benchmarks demonstrate that our MGA scheme reduces the FLOPs of five popular SR networks by 10%–48% with comparable or even better SR performance. The code is available at https://github.com/huxiaotaostasy/MGA-scheme.

Keywords: Single image super-resolution · Network acceleration

1 Introduction

Single image super-resolution (SR) aims to recover high-resolution (HR) images from the corresponding low-resolution (LR) ones. During the last decades, this problem is widely studied in academia and industry of the computer vision field [8,19,25,26,30,47]. Ever since the pioneer work of SRCNN [7], numerous

Supplementary Information The online version contains supplementary material available at https://doi.org/10.1007/978-3-031-19800-7_5.

methods [5,19,33,47,48] have been developed to improve the SR performance along with the advances in network backbones [13,15,16,39,41]. However, this advancement is achieved at the expense of designing larger SR networks with more computational costs [6,7,14,23,33,34,47,50], hindering the corresponding SR networks from being deployed on edge devices such as cameras and mobiles.

For real-world applications, researchers shift to developing efficient SR networks for high-resolution image processing. The efficiency is mainly judged by three aspects: running time, number of parameters, or floating-point operations (FLOPs). Early works mainly report the running time [7,9,19], which is largely determined by the hardware and implementations of basic operations (e.g., 3×3 conv.) in deep learning frameworks [1,35]. Later works mainly resort to reducing the number of parameters [27,37,38] or FLOPs [29,40] for network efficiency. However, pursuing reduction on parameters (or FLOPs) may increase the running time [37] and FLOPs (or parameters) amount. In all, expertise knowledge on deep neural networks is essential for developing efficient SR networks.

Instead of developing new SR networks, a recent trend is to reduce the parameter amount and/or FLOPs of existing ones while maintaining their SR capability [21]. As far as we know, ClassSR [21] is a pioneer work in this direction. It classifies the patches of an LR image into the "easy" (restoration difficulty), "medium", and "hard" categories, and restores these patches by three SR networks in different widths. However, the extra classification network in ClassSR largely limits its practical efficiency due to the additional computational costs. Besides, since the three SR networks in [21] share the same network architecture but with different widths, ClassSR suffers from a huge growth on parameters.

In this paper, we develop a new scheme to reduce the FLOPs and running time on edge devices of popular SR networks. Our scheme divides an existing SR network along the depth, e.g., RCAN [47], into a base network (Base-Net) and a refine network (Refine-Net). The Base-Net restores globally the LR image to extract a coarse feature and output a coarse SR image. Then we propose a Mask Prediction (MP) module to estimate an error mask from the coarse feature by Base-Net, indicating the gap between the coarse and desired SR images. This mask is used to select the feature patches of under super-resolved (under-SR) areas in the coarse SR image. The selected feature patches will be fed into the Refine-Net for further refinement. Since Refine-Net only needs to refine the selected areas, instead of the whole coarse SR image, the computational costs (e.g., FLOPs) of the original SR network, i.e., RCAN [47], can be largely reduced. The refined image is output as the final SR image.

Our Mask-Guided Acceleration (MGA) scheme is different from ClassSR [21] on at least two aspects. Firstly, ClassSR has an extra classification network and three parallel SR networks, resulting in a huge growth on the number of parameters. But our MGA scheme only brings a marginal increment on parameters by our lightweight MP module. Secondly, ClassSR has to perform classification and SR sequentially during the inference, making the SR process time-consuming. However, in our MGA scheme, after the coarse SR by the Base-Net, the Refine-Net of an existing SR network only needs to handle a few selected complex

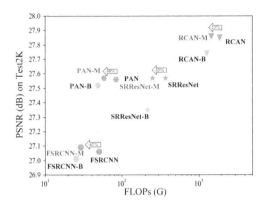

Fig. 1. Average PSNR (dB) and FLOPs (G) of different SR networks $w/$ **or**
w/o **our Mask-Guided Acceleration scheme** on Test2K [12] at scale factor 4. "B"
and "M" denote the baseline and mask-guided models, respectively.

areas. As shown in Fig. 1, our MAG scheme reduces the computational FLOPs
of FSRCNN [9], SRResNet [49], and RCAN [47] by 42%, 33%, and 23%, respectively, while arriving at comparable PSNR results on Test2K [12]. Experiments
on seven benchmark datasets validate the effectiveness of our MGA Scheme on
accelerating five popular SR networks [9,29,47,49].

Our main contributions are summarized as follows:

- **We propose a Mask-Guided Acceleration (MGA) scheme to reduce
  the FLOPs amount and running time of existing SR networks while
  preserving their SR capability**. Given an existing SR network, our MGA
  scheme divides it into a Base-Net to restore the LR image globally and a
  Refine-Net to further refine the selected under-SR areas locally.
- **We propose a lightweight Mask Prediction module** to adaptively select
  the feature patches of under-SR areas, which are from the coarse SR image
  by the Base-Net and further refined by the Refine-Net.
- Experiments on seven benchmark datasets demonstrate that **our Mask-
  Guided Acceleration scheme can accelerate five popular SR networks in different scales** while achieving comparable SR performance.

2   Related Work

2.1   Single Image Super-Resolution

Single image SR has been advanced by convolutional neural networks (CNNs)
ever since SRCNN [7]. The work of VDSR [19] introduces a residual learning
scheme to avoid direct SR prediction. The integration of residual and dense
connections is later exploited in RDN [48]. Despite the discriminative learning
framework, generative learning [10] is also employed in SRGAN [23] to produce

visually pleasing SR results. Attention mechanisms have also been utilized in many SR networks. For example, RCAN [47] incorporates channel attention [15] into residual learning [13]. Self-attention is adopted in [33] to provide global correlation information for SR. The success of the transformer framework in natural language processing inspires the work of IPT [5]. These SR networks achieve performance gain at the expense of increasing parameters and FLOPs, hindering their applications on edge devices [3,24,29]. In this work, we aim to accelerate general SR networks while preserving their SR capability.

2.2 Lightweight Super-Resolution

Lightweight super-resolution aims to achieve efficient SR by reducing the running time, the number of parameters and/or floating point operations (FLOPs). To reduce the running time, FSRCNN [9] performs upsampling at the final stage and uses small convolution kernels, while LapSRN [22] gradually upsamples the feature maps. But running time is greatly influenced by the hardware, the actual implementations, and the deep learning frameworks [1,35,46]. The parameter amount is also a useful criterion to evaluate model efficiency [37,49]. To this end, DRRN [37] learns shared residual blocks in a recursive manner, while PAN [49] incorporates the self-calibrated convolution [28] and introduces a pixel attention module. However, the reduction on parameter amount does not necessarily bring clear improvements on the model efficiency [46]. Recent works [29,40] often tend to reduce the number of FLOPs. RFDN [29] replaces standard residual blocks with shallow variants, arriving at similar SR results with fewer FLOPs. Overall, it is challenging to design better lightweight SR networks. In this paper, we propose a general scheme to accelerate general SR networks.

2.3 Accelerating Super-Resolution Networks

Accelerating super-resolution networks is an alternative way for lightweight SR. Along this direction, SMSR [40] adaptively tackles different areas by efficient convolutions, which are not plug-and-play to general SR networks. AdderSR [36] replaces amounts of multiplications by additions in convolutions to reduce the energy consumption. But it suffers from clear degradation in SR performance. ClassSR [21] is a pioneer framework to accelerate SR networks. It assigns suitable SR networks to process local areas with different restoration difficulties, which are determined by a classification network. Though with less computational costs, ClassSR also brings a huge amount of extra parameters. FADN [44] replaces the original residual block with an efficient one to accelerate SR networks. However, each replacement increases the parameter amounts of the SR networks. In this paper, we introduce a mask-guided scheme to accelerate popular SR networks by performing coarse SR on the LR image and further refinement on under-SR areas only. This provides a flexible trade-off between SR capability and network efficiency with a little parameter growth.

3   Our Mask-Guided Acceleration Scheme

3.1   Motivation and Overview

In image super-resolution (SR), the quality of SR images is mainly degraded by the information loss that occurs in complex areas such as edges and textures [40]. To well recover these areas, most SR methods resort to developing networks larger than those required for the plain areas [11].

Increasing the network width (*i.e.*, number of channels) is a feasible choice to improve its capability of restoring complex areas [21]. But for different areas of an image, an SR network with a single branch can only extract the features with equal channel dimension. Thus, the work of [21] restores the areas with different complexities by multiple SR networks with respective widths. However, this brings a great increase in the amount of network parameters [21].

Increasing the network depth (*i.e.*, number of layers) is an alternative way to well recover complex areas. However, handling different areas simply by multiple SR networks with adaptive depths still suffers from significant parameter growth. To alleviate this problem, we propose to process different areas by the sub-networks with adaptive depths of a single-branch SR network. This is feasible by decomposing an SR network into different parts along the depth dimension: the shallow part restores the whole image while the deep part only recovers the complex areas. Since complex areas are sparse in the image, the computational costs of the decomposed SR network can be largely reduced.

Take the PAN network [49] for example. The original PAN has 16 SCPA blocks. We denote as PAN-B the PAN with 12 SCPA blocks. Given an LR image in Fig. 2 (1), we employ PAN-B and PAN to obtain a coarse SR image and a final SR image in Fig. 2 (2) and Fig. 2 (3), respectively. The absolute difference (error map) between these two SR images is calculated on the luminance channel and shown in Fig. 2 (4). We plot its histogram in Fig. 2 (5), and observe that most areas are smooth with small errors (<0.1) while large errors (*e.g.*, >0.1) are sparsely dispersed in textures and edges. This demonstrates that most areas in the LR image can be well recovered by the shallower PAN-B, while only a few areas need "stronger" restoration by the deeper PAN. This motivates us to accelerate an SR network by decomposing it into a base network for coarse restoration and a refine network to further enhance the (sparsely) complex areas.

Overview. In this work, we propose a Mask-Guided Acceleration (MGA) scheme to accelerate general SR networks. Specifically, we design a Mask Prediction (MP) module (will be introduced in Sect. 3.3) to indicate the areas with large errors between coarse and final SR images. We then incorporate the MP module into a decomposed SR network (D-Net) to contain three parts: the base network (Base-Net), the MP module, and the refine network (Refine-Net). Our MGA scheme is illustrated in Fig. 3. The LR image is first fed into the Base-Net to obtain a feature map F_c, which is upsampled to produce a coarse SR image I_c. Then we use the proposed MP module to generate an error mask M from F_c. Guided by the mask M, we select a few areas with the largest errors and crop the respective feature patches from F_c. The feature patches are fed into

(1) Input LR Image   (2) Coarse SR Image   (3) Final SR Image   (4) Error Map   (5) Histogram of (4)

Fig. 2. Difference between the coarse and final SR images. The LR image (1) is restored by PAN-B and PAN to produce the coarse SR image (2) and the final SR image (3), respectively. (4): the error map between (2) and (3).

Refine-Net for further refinement. Finally, we replace the respective patches in the coarse SR image I_c by the refined patches to output the final SR image I_{SR}.

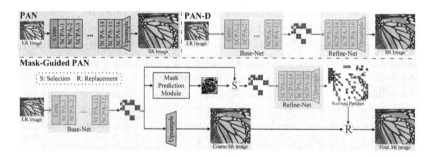

Fig. 3. Illustration of our Mask-Guided Acceleration (MGA) scheme to accelerate super-resolution (SR) networks, *e.g.*, **PAN** [49]. **PAN** (top-left) mainly contains 16 SCPA blocks. **PAN-D** (top-right) is the decomposed PAN consisting of a Base-Net with 12 SCPA blocks and a Refine-Net with 4 SCPA blocks. **Mask-Guided PAN** (bottom) is built upon the PAN-D, but accelerated by our MGA scheme. Here, the LR image is fed into the Base-Net to output a coarse feature. This coarse feature is upsampled to produce a coarse SR image, and used to estimate an error mask by the proposed Mask Prediction module. K patches from coarse feature with largest errors are selected for further refinement by the Refine-Net. The refined image patches are used to replace the respective patches in the coarse SR image to output the final SR image.

3.2 Base Network for Global Super-Resolution

Given an input LR image I_{LR}, the goal of Base-Net is to extract its coarse feature map F_c, which is upsampled to output a coarse SR image I_c. The smooth areas dominating the LR image I_{LR} can be well restored with no need of further processing. Since the Base-Net is shallower than the decomposed SR network, the complex areas like edges and textures are still relatively under-SR when compared to the smooth areas. By varying the depth of Base-Net, it is feasible to trade-off its SR capability and model efficiency.

3.3 Mask Prediction and Feature Patch Selection

To locate the under-SR areas in I_c for further refinement, we feed the coarse feature F_c into our Mask-Prediction module to obtain an error mask M, and accordingly select K feature patches $\{F_k\}_{k=1}^K$ from F_c with the largest errors.

Mask prediction. Given the coarse feature $F_c \in \mathbb{R}^{H \times W \times C}$, our Mask Prediction (MP) module is to estimate an adaptive error mask M indicating the under-SR areas in the coarse SR image I_c. Specifically, as shown in Fig. 4, the coarse feature F_c is input into two 3×3 convolutional layers with a Global Average Pooling (GAP) to produce a spatial feature map $F_s \in \mathbb{R}^{\frac{1}{p}H \times \frac{1}{p}W \times 2}$, where $p \geq 1$ is the spatial size of the feature patch F_k. Note that each spatial element of F_s corresponds to a feature patch $F_k \in \mathbb{R}^{p \times p \times C}$. Then, a softmax operation is performed on F_s along the channel dimension to output a spatial mask $M_s \in \mathbb{R}^{\frac{1}{p}H \times \frac{1}{p}W \times 2}$. The two channels in M_s, denoted as M_s^1 and M_s^2, indicate the possibilities of being well-SR and under-SR patches, respectively.

The under-SR mask $M_s^2 \in \mathbb{R}^{\frac{1}{p}H \times \frac{1}{p}W}$, obtained by the spatial-wise softmax operation, only reflects the position-wise possibilities of being under-SR patches. To integrate the surrounding information for more comprehensive mask prediction, we utilize a convolution operation over the M_s^2 for larger spatial perception. To achieve position-adaptive interaction, here we implement the dynamic convolution (D-Conv) [18] over the M_s^2 to generate position-wise filters by integrating the corresponding surrounding features in F_c. The mask M_s^2 processed by the D-Conv is employed as the final error mask, denoted as $M \in \mathbb{R}^{\frac{1}{p}H \times \frac{1}{p}W}$.

Feature Patch Selection. Here, each element in the error mask M corresponds to a feature patch in the coarse feature F_c. We select K feature patches from F_c by the K largest elements in M. These selected feature patches $\{F_k \in \mathbb{R}^{p \times p \times C}\}_{k=1}^K$, instead of F_c, will be fed into the Refine-Net for further refinement. This greatly reduces the amounts of computational costs for the original SR network.

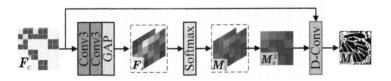

Fig. 4. Our Mask Prediction module. The feature F_c is fed into two 3×3 convolutional layers and a Global Average Pooling (GAP) to produce a spatial feature F_s. A softmax operation is performed on F_s along the channel dimension to output a spatial mask $M_s = [M_s^1, M_s^2]$. The feature F_c and mask M_s^2 are fed into a dynamic convolution (D-Conv) to output final error mask M.

3.4 Refine Network for Local Enhancement

The K feature patches $\{F_k\}_{k=1}^K$ selected by our MP module, mainly from the complex areas under-SR by the Base-Net, are fed into the Refine-Net for further enhancement. The outputs are the reconstructed high-resolution image patches $\{P_k \in \mathbb{R}^{sp \times sp \times 3}\}_{k=1}^K$, where s is the SR scale factor ($e.g.$, 4). In this way, the Refine-Net avoids processing the whole coarse feature $F_c \in \mathbb{R}^{H \times W \times C}$. Since one can set $Kp^2 \ll HW$, the computational costs of the original SR network can be largely reduced on the Refine-Net. This is the key reason that our MGA scheme is able to accelerate the original SR network. Finally, the refined patches $\{P_k\}_{k=1}^K$ are used to replace the respective patches in the coarse SR image I_c, to output the final SR image I_{SR}.

3.5 Training Strategy

When directly trained end-to-end from scratch, the mask-guided SR network suffers from clear performance drops, as will be shown in Sect. 4.4 (Table 4). The main reason is that, in the early training, the initial features extracted by the Base-Net are of low quality and change greatly, making our MP-module unstably updated and failing to reach a good local optimum. To avoid this problem, we propose to train the Mask-Guided SR network in a three-step strategy.

Step 1. We train the decomposed SR network (D-Net) on all the training data (will be introduced in Sect. 4.2) with an ℓ_1 loss function.

Step 2. This step aims to endow the Refine-Net with the capability to process small feature patches. To this end, once the Base-Net extracts the coarse feature F_c, we first crop small feature patches from it and then feed these cropped feature patches into the Refine-Net. The D-Net trained with all cropped feature patches is denoted as All-Net, which is trained with the same setting as that in **Step 1**.

Step 3. This step aims to train the mask-guided SR network, in which the Base-Net and Refine-Net are initialized by the All-Net in **Step 2**. Now we fix the learned weights of the Base-Net and Refine-Net, and only train our MP-module. To supervise the mask prediction process for better SR performance, we deploy the absolute difference between the coarse and final SR images obtained by the Base-Net and All-Net in **Step 2**, respectively, as the "ground-truth" for the corresponding mask M predicted by our MP module. Here, we also penalty the mask prediction by an ℓ_1 loss function.

4 Experiments

4.1 Implementation Details

Firstly, we train the decomposed SR network (D-Net). The mini-batch size per GPU is set as 32. We use the Adam optimizer [20] with the default setting. We set $p = 4$. The total number of iterations is 600K and divided into three identical periods. For each period, we use a cosine annealing strategy with warm-up to adjust the learning rate. Each period contains 200K iterations and is subdivided into two stages. In the first 2K iterations, called warmup, the learning rate is increased from 4×10^{-5} to 4×10^{-4}. In the remaining 198K, the learning rate is decayed from 4×10^{-4} to 1×10^{-7}. Secondly, we use the trained D-Net as the initialization model of the All-Net. Then we train the All-Net for another 600K iterations in the same way as that for D-Net. Finally, we employ the pre-trained All-Net to initialize the Mask-Guided SR network, and only train the MP module while fixing the Base-Net and Refine-Net. We train the MP module for 100K iterations using the cosine annealing learning rate strategy, with 2K iterations for warm-up. The other settings are the same as the training of D-Net. We perform data argumentation with randomly horizontal/vertical flipping and rotation with 90°. For a fair comparison with the Base-Net of the original SR network, we also retrain it from scratch with the same settings as training the D-Net. All models are trained on two GeForce RTX 2080Ti GPUs.

4.2 Datasets and Metrics

Training Set. We use the DIV2K [2] and Flickr2K [42] datasets for network training. We crop the HR images in DIV2K and Flickr2K into 480×480 sub-images, and use these sub-images as the HR images. We downsample the HR images by scale factors of 2, 3, or 4 to obtain the corresponding LR images. We randomly crop a 64×64 patch from each LR image and a 128×128 (or 192×192, 256×256) patch from the corresponding HR image as the paired training samples for the ×2 (or ×3, ×4) SR task.

Test Set. We evaluate different methods on seven standard datasets: Set5 [4], Set14 [45], B100 [31], Manga109 [32], Urban100 [17], Test2K and Test4K. For Test2K (or Test4K), as suggested in ClassSR [21], we downsample the 200 images (index: 1201–1400) from DIV8K [12] to 2K (or 4K) resolution as HR images. Here, we only provide the results for ×3 and ×4 SR tasks on Urban100, Test2K, and Test4K. Please refer to the *Supplementary File* for more comparison results.

Metric. We calculate PSNR and SSIM [43] on the Y channel of the YCbCr color space to evaluate different comparison methods.

4.3 Comparison Results

Comparison of SR Network Variants. We implement our MGA scheme into five popular SR networks with diverse parameter amounts, *i.e.*, FSRCNN [9] (~42K), PAN [49] (~300K), RFDN [29] (~700K), SRResNet [23] (~2M) and RCAN [47] (~16M). The details of decomposing different SR networks are provided in the *Supplementary File*. For each network, we evaluate its Base network (-B), the Decomposed network (-D) before acceleration, the All-Net trained with all cropped feature patches (-A), and the mask-guided network accelerated by our scheme (-M). The results on ×3 and ×4 SR tasks are listed in Table 1. One can see that the mask-guided networks (appended by "-M") achieve comparable PSNR/SSIM results with the decomposed ones (appended by "-D", achieving close SR performance to their original networks, respectively), but

Table 1. Comparison results of different SR networks on the Urban100, Test2K and Test4K datasets. "-B": Base-Net. "-D": D-Net. "-A": ALL-Net. "-M": network accelerated by our MGA scheme. See Sect. 3.5 and Sect. 4.3.

Scale	Method	# Params	Urban100			Test2K			Test4K		
			PSNR	SSIM	FLOPs(G)	PSNR	SSIM	FLOPs(G)	PSNR	SSIM	FLOPs(G)
×3	FSRCNN-B	23K	25.87	0.7919	11.25	28.47	0.8187	26.27	29.87	0.8573	100.77
	FSRCNN-D	42K	26.07	0.7986	22.08	28.56	0.8211	51.55	29.99	0.8594	197.76
	FSRCNN-A	42K	26.24	0.8036	22.36	28.60	0.8220	52.20	30.05	0.8603	200.26
	FSRCNN-M	43K	26.22	0.8025	13.45	28.59	0.8216	28.61	30.03	0.8598	103.85
	PAN-B	204K	27.80	0.8453	27.69	29.10	0.8387	64.66	30.71	0.8749	248.07
	PAN-D	296K	27.97	0.8481	49.42	29.17	0.8395	115.38	30.80	0.8757	442.68
	PAN-A	296K	28.04	0.8499	67.18	29.20	0.8407	156.84	30.84	0.8768	601.75
	PAN-M	311K	27.96	0.8475	36.34	29.17	0.8396	74.94	30.78	0.8757	266.49
	RFDN-B	424K	27.89	0.8473	34.42	29.15	0.8393	80.37	30.79	0.8759	308.37
	RFDN-D	698K	28.08	0.8507	57.04	29.21	0.8405	133.18	30.85	0.8765	510.98
	RFDN-A	698K	28.32	0.8556	81.35	29.26	0.8420	189.94	30.91	0.8780	728.73
	RFDN-M	721K	28.28	0.8545	45.16	29.23	0.8403	93.67	30.84	0.8761	334.38
	SRResNet-B	1.10M	27.62	0.8420	120.13	28.93	0.8361	280.49	30.36	0.8712	1076.11
	SRResNet-D	1.67M	28.06	0.8501	194.93	28.93	0.8393	455.14	30.76	0.8751	1746.16
	SRResNet-A	1.67M	28.08	0.8503	234.22	29.20	0.8397	546.86	30.78	0.8753	2098.07
	SRResNet-M	1.71M	28.01	0.8485	144.70	29.18	0.8391	309.26	30.76	0.8747	1125.70
	RCAN-B	11.05M	28.57	0.8613	934.84	29.37	0.8456	2182.72	31.03	0.8808	8374.18
	RCAN-D	16.07M	29.10	0.8705	1360.41	29.55	0.8497	3176.36	31.25	0.8845	12186.37
	RCAN-A	16.07M	29.16	0.8717	1851.63	29.56	0.8499	4323.29	31.25	0.8847	16586.64
	RCAN-M	16.11M	29.10	0.8706	1110.19	29.55	0.8493	2362.27	31.23	0.8841	8574.54
×4	FSRCNN-B	23K	24.32	0.7192	10.93	27.01	0.7499	25.43	28.22	0.7984	97.57
	FSRCNN-D	42K	24.43	0.7230	21.63	27.06	0.7512	50.31	28.29	0.7997	193.01
	FSRCNN-A	42K	24.52	0.7271	21.78	27.09	0.7525	50.67	28.33	0.8009	194.41
	FSRCNN-M	43K	24.50	0.7261	14.60	27.09	0.7523	29.19	28.31	0.8004	101.74
	PAN-B	215K	25.87	0.7780	20.84	27.52	0.7716	48.47	28.91	0.8187	185.96
	PAN-D	313K	26.01	0.7828	36.05	27.56	0.7725	83.86	28.96	0.8195	321.74
	PAN-A	313K	26.05	0.7840	45.53	27.57	0.7730	105.91	28.97	0.8200	406.34
	PAN-M	328K	26.02	0.7825	29.74	27.57	0.7728	58.30	28.96	0.8195	200.37
	RFDN-B	433K	26.01	0.7839	19.89	27.53	0.7730	46.27	28.95	0.8202	177.51
	RFDN-D	717K	26.09	0.7862	33.11	27.60	0.7743	77.03	29.02	0.8213	295.53
	RFDN-A	717K	26.18	0.7886	46.83	27.63	0.7751	108.95	29.05	0.8221	418.02
	RFDN-M	740K	26.17	0.7878	29.94	27.61	0.7741	57.75	29.03	0.8210	196.15
	SRResNet-B	1.25M	25.74	0.7773	92.59	27.35	0.7696	215.40	28.49	0.8144	826.38
	SRResNet-D	1.97M	26.08	0.7857	159.59	27.57	0.7731	371.26	28.94	0.8195	1424.36
	SRResNet-A	1.97M	26.08	0.7859	181.77	27.57	0.7736	422.85	28.93	0.8199	1622.31
	SRResNet-M	2.01M	26.07	0.7850	124.04	27.57	0.7735	249.20	28.92	0.8197	871.89
	RCAN-B	11.02M	26.56	0.8002	547.86	27.74	0.7791	1274.50	29.16	0.8251	4889.71
	RCAN-D	16.00M	26.95	0.8115	808.21	27.85	0.7838	1880.14	29.31	0.8296	7213.30
	RCAN-A	16.00M	27.00	0.8128	1085.53	27.86	0.7842	2525.29	29.32	0.8300	9688.46
	RCAN-M	16.04M	26.96	0.8119	728.52	27.86	0.7837	1457.51	29.31	0.8295	5084.44

Table 2. Results of different SR networks accelerated by ClassSR and our MGA scheme on the Urban100, Test2K and Test4K datasets. "-M": network accelerated by our MGA scheme. "-C": network accelerated by ClassSR.

Scale	Method	# Params	Urban100		Test2K		Test4K	
			PSNR(RGB)	FLOPs(G)	PSNR(RGB)	FLOPs(G)	PSNR(RGB)	FLOPs(G)
×4	FSRCNN-C	113K	22.89	20.07	25.61	36.77	26.91	139.72
	FSRCNN-M	43K	23.01	14.60	25.66	29.19	26.94	101.74
	SRResNet-C	3.06M	24.53	149.92	26.20	298.18	27.66	1135.60
	SRResNet-M	2.01M	24.55	124.04	26.20	249.20	27.66	871.89
	RCAN-C	30.11M	25.14	741.76	26.39	1380.80	27.88	5255.70
	RCAN-M	16.04M	25.43	728.52	26.46	1457.51	27.96	5084.44

Fig. 5. SR images by different methods on the ×4 SR task. "-B": Base-Net. "-C": network accelerated by ClassSR. "-M": network accelerated by our MGA scheme. "-D": D-Net. Please refer to Sect. 3.5 and Sect. 4.3 for more details.

reducing the FLOPs amounts of these five SR networks by 10%–48% with a little parameter growth. We also compare the visual results by different variants of RCAN/SRResNet in Fig. 5. We observe that the mask-guided variants (-M) obtain comparable or better quality than the decomposed ones (-D), validating the effectiveness of our MGA scheme on preserving their SR capability.

Comparison with ClassSR [21]. We compare our MGA scheme with ClassSR on the Urban100, Test2K, and Test4K datasets. For a fair comparison, we retrain each SR network accelerated by ClassSR [21] on DIV2K and Flickr2K, while the other settings are kept unchanged. In Table 2, we compare the PSNR results on RGB color space, and the average FLOPs of ClassSR processing a whole image as our MGA does. Note that the ClassSR here obtains higher FLOPs than those reported in [21]. The reason is that the original ClassSR only calculates the average FLOPs on the cropped 32×32 image patches, while needing to consider the FLOPs of the overlapping areas between 32×32 image patches when processing a whole image. From Fig. 5, we observe that the SR networks of RCAN and SRResNet accelerated by our MGA scheme recover the structure and textures more clearly than those accelerated by ClassSR.

Speed on Mobile Devices. To test the speed of SR networks accelerated by our MGA scheme and ClassSR on mobile devices, we deploy the accelerated RCAN on Kirin 980 using the Pytorch Mobile framework[1]. The average speed is calculated for the ×4 SR task with $256 \times 256 \times 3$ images. The average speeds of RCAN-D, RCAN-C and RCAN-M are 45.61 s, 38.91 s and 35.51 s, respectively.

---

[1] https://pytorch.org/mobile/home/.

Fig. 6. Visualization of the LR image, the HR image, the "ground-truth" error mask (MASK_GT), and the error mask predicted by our MP module.

4.4   Ablation Study

Now we conduct a more detailed examination of our MGA scheme on SR to assess: 1) the design of our Mask Prediction (MP) module; 2) effectiveness of our MP module on mask prediction; 3) how to train mask-guided SR networks with our MP module; 4) the impact of decomposing manner to SR networks in our MGA scheme; 5) how the size of feature patches affects our MGA scheme; 6) how the order of selecting elements from the error mask influences the SR performance. More ablation studies are provided in the *Supplementary File*.

1) How to design our MP module? A trivial design of our MP module is to generate the spatial feature map F_s with only one channel, which needs to remove the softmax function. Taking PAN as an example, we denote this variant as "PAN-M (1C)". The comparison results bewteen PAN-M and "PAN-M (1C)", on Urban100, Test2K, and Tesk4K at ×4 SR task, are listed in Table 3: PAN-M outperforms clearly "PAN-M (1C)" on PSNR and SSIM, but with close FLOPs. This shows the necessity to design a two-channel spatial feature map F_s.

Table 3. Results of PAN-M with the spatial feature map F_s of one channel or two channels in our MP module on Urban100, Test2K, and Test4K. "1C": the spatial feature F_s is of one channel. The scale factor is 4.

Method	Urban100			Test2K			Test4K		
	PSNR	SSIM	FLOPs(G)	PSNR	SSIM	FLOPs(G)	PSNR	SSIM	FLOPs(G)
PAN-B	25.87	0.7780	20.84	27.52	0.7716	48.47	28.91	0.8187	185.96
PAN-M(1C)	25.96	0.7812	29.74	27.55	0.7725	58.30	28.94	0.8193	200.37
PAN-M	26.02	0.7825	29.74	27.57	0.7728	58.30	28.96	0.8195	200.37
PAN-D	26.01	0.7828	36.05	27.56	0.7725	83.86	28.96	0.8195	321.74

2) Effectiveness of our MP module. To study this problem, we visualize the mask predicted by our MP module in Fig. 6. We observe that most of the under-SR pixels are successfully predicted by our MP module. The ℓ_1 error between the predicted MASK and the "ground-truth" mask "MASK_GT" (as described in Sect. 3.5) is very small (*i.e.*, 0.0346). This demonstrates that our MP module can indeed accurately predict the error masks indicating under-SR areas.

3) How to train the mask-guided SR networks with our MP module? To answer this question, we propose to train the mask-guided network with two other strategies. The first is to train the mask-guided network with our MP

Table 4. Results of FSRCNN-M with different training strategies for our Mask Prediction (MP) module on the Urban100, Test2K, and Test4K datasets. "E2E": end-to-end train the mask-guided network with our MP module from scratch. "w/o S": train our MP module separately in **Step 3** (see Sect. 3.5) without supervision. The scale factor is 2.

Method	Urban100			Test2K			Test4K		
	PSNR	SSIM	FLOPs(G)	PSNR	SSIM	FLOPs(G)	PSNR	SSIM	FLOPs(G)
FSRCNN-B	29.15	0.8913	12.38	31.52	0.9107	28.65	33.32	0.9326	109.92
FSRCNN-M(E2E)	29.10	0.8910	13.63	31.50	0.9110	30.23	33.27	0.9326	113.15
FSRCNN-M(w/o S)	29.50	0.8970	13.63	31.64	0.9124	30.23	33.47	0.9341	113.15
FSRCNN-M	29.56	0.8973	13.63	31.67	0.9128	30.23	33.49	0.9343	113.15
FSRCNN-D	29.38	0.8951	23.80	31.62	0.9122	55.08	33.43	0.9337	211.33

module end-to-end from scratch, denoted as "E2E". The second is to train the mask-guided network by the strategy introduced in Sect. 3.5, but without supervision on our MP module in **Step 3**, denoted as "w/o S". By taking FSRCNN for example, the results listed in Table 4 show that FSRCNN-M achieves higher PSNR and SSIM results than those of FSRCNN-M (E2E) and FSRCNN (w/o S). This validates the advantages of our training strategy in Sect. 3.5 over the two variant strategies of "E2E" and "w/o S", for our MGA scheme.

4) How the depths of the Base-Net and Refine-Net influence the SR performance of the decomposed network? To study this problem, by taking PAN for example, we compare the three mask-guided SR networks obtained by decomposing the PAN-D into three variants: "PAN-M(10+6)" with 10 SCPAs in Base-Net and 6 SCPAs in Refine-Net; "PAN-M(12+4)" with 12 SCPAs in Base-Net and 4 SCPAs in Refine-Net; "PAN-M(14+2)" with 14 SCPAs in Base-Net and 2 SCPAs in Refine-Net. The results listed in Table 5 show that, by varying the depth of Refine-Net, our MGA scheme provides a flexible trade-off between the capability (on PSNR/SSIM) and efficiency (FLOPs) of an SR network.

Table 5. Results of PAN-M with different decomposing manners on the Urban100, Test2K, and Test4K datasets. "$a + b$" means that the Base-Net has a SCPA blocks and the Refine-Net has b SCPA blocks. The scale factor is 2.

Method	Urban100			Test2K			Test4K		
	PSNR	SSIM	FLOPs(G)	PSNR	SSIM	FLOPs(G)	PSNR	SSIM	FLOPs(G)
PAN-M(10 + 6)	31.67	0.9236	50.58	32.41	0.9234	110.33	34.39	0.9428	408.74
PAN-M(12 + 4)	31.81	0.9252	55.14	32.45	0.9240	122.25	34.45	0.9433	457.42
PAN-M(14 + 2)	31.90	0.9263	59.69	32.50	0.9247	134.17	34.50	0.9439	506.09
PAN-D	31.86	0.9259	73.91	32.46	0.9242	171.09	34.48	0.9436	656.39

5) How does the size p of feature patches influence the performance of the mask-guided SR networks? To this end, we compare the mask-guided SR networks with different sizes of feature patches in our MGA scheme. By taking FSRCNN for example, we implement the FSRCNN-M with $p = 2, 4, 8$ and denote

Table 6. Results of FSRCNN-M with different sizes of feature patches (selected between MP module and Refine-Net) on the Urban100, Test2K, and Test4K datasets. "2": 2 × 2. "4": 4 × 4. "8": 8 × 8. The scale factor is 4.

Method	Urban100			Test2K			Test4K		
	PSNR	SSIM	FLOPs(G)	PSNR	SSIM	FLOPs(G)	PSNR	SSIM	FLOPs(G)
FSRCNN-B	24.32	0.7192	10.93	27.01	0.7499	25.43	28.22	0.7984	97.57
FSRCNN-M(2)	24.50	0.7264	14.73	27.08	0.7527	29.26	28.30	0.8003	101.82
FSRCNN-M(4)	24.50	0.7261	14.60	27.09	0.7523	29.19	28.31	0.8004	101.74
FSRCNN-M(8)	24.48	0.7226	14.52	27.07	0.7517	28.64	28.29	0.7999	101.71
FSRCNN-D	24.43	0.7230	21.63	27.06	0.7512	20.31	28.29	0.7997	193.01

Table 7. Results of RFDN-M with different orders of selecting K elements from error mask, on the Urban100, Test2K, and Test4K datasets. "S", "R" or "L" means selecting K smaller, random or larger errors, respectively. "All": selecting all errors for each image. The scale factor is 2.

Method		K = 0	K = 1000, S	K = 1000, R	K = 1000, L	K = All/2, S	K = All/2, R	K = All/2, L	K = All
Urban100	PSNR	31.99	31.99	32.01	32.26	32.03	32.14	32.36	32.36
	SSIM	0.9265	0.9265	0.9270	0.9296	0.9273	0.9283	0.9304	0.9306
Test2K	PSNR	32.48	32.48	32.49	32.57	32.49	32.55	32.62	32.62
	SSIM	0.9246	0.9246	0.9248	0.9254	0.9249	0.9253	0.9261	0.9262
Test4K	PSNR	34.51	34.51	34.53	34.59	34.53	34.59	34.66	34.66
	SSIM	0.9440	0.9440	0.9441	0.9445	0.9441	0.9445	0.9451	0.9451

the resulting variants as FSRCNN-M(2), FSRCNN-M(4), and FSRCNN-M(8). The results are listed in Table 6. One can see that, on Urban100 and Test2K, FSRCNN-M(2) (or FSRCNN-M(4)) slightly outperforms FSRCNN-M(4) (or FSRCNN-M(8)) with a little growth on FLOPs. In summary, larger p reduces the FLOPs amount but usually degrades the SR performance.

6) How does the order of selecting elements from error mask M influence our MGA on SR? In our MGA scheme, we select K largest elements from the error mask M. To validate this point, we change the order of selecting the K elements from "Larger" (L) to "Smaller" (S) or "Random" (R). By taking RFDN for example, we list the results of different variants in Table 7. We observe that RFDN-M with "L" outperforms the other variants obviously. This validates the effectiveness of selecting K largest elements in our MGA scheme.

5 Conclusion

In this paper, we proposed a Mask Guided Acceleration (MGA) scheme to accelerate popular single image super-resolution (SR) networks. Our MGA scheme decomposes an SR network into a Base-Net to extract a coarse feature and a Refine-Net to refine the mostly under-SR areas. To locate these areas, we designed a Mask Prediction module for error mask generation. Some feature patches were selected accordingly from the coarse feature to trade-off model capability and efficiency. Experiments on seven benchmark datasets demonstrated that, our MGA scheme largely reduces the computational costs of five SR networks with different complexities, while preserving well their SR capability.

Acknowledgements. This work was supported by The National Natural Science Foundation of China (No. 62002176 and 62176068).

References

1. Abadi, M., et al.: TensorFlow: a system for large-scale machine learning. In: Proceedings of the 12th USENIX Conference on Operating Systems Design and Implementation, pp. 265–283. USENIX Association, USA (2016)
2. Agustsson, E., Timofte, R.: NTIRE 2017 challenge on single image super-resolution: dataset and study. In: IEEE Conference on Computer Vision and Pattern Recognition Workshop, pp. 126–135 (2017)
3. Ahn, N., Kang, B., Sohn, K.A.: Fast, accurate, and lightweight super-resolution with cascading residual network. In: European Conference on Computer Vision, pp. 252–268 (2018)
4. Bevilacqua, M., Roumy, A., Guillemot, C., Alberi-Morel, M.L.: Low-complexity single-image super-resolution based on nonnegative neighbor embedding (2012)
5. Chen, H., et al.: Pre-trained image processing transformer. In: IEEE Conference on Computer Vision and Pattern Recognition, pp. 12299–12310 (2021)
6. Dai, T., Cai, J., Zhang, Y., Xia, S.T., Zhang, L.: Second-order attention network for single image super-resolution. In: IEEE Conference on Computer Vision and Pattern Recognition, pp. 11065–11074 (2019)
7. Dong, C., Loy, C.C., He, K., Tang, X.: Learning a deep convolutional network for image super-resolution. In: Fleet, D., Pajdla, T., Schiele, B., Tuytelaars, T. (eds.) ECCV 2014. LNCS, vol. 8692, pp. 184–199. Springer, Cham (2014). https://doi.org/10.1007/978-3-319-10593-2_13
8. Dong, C., Loy, C.C., He, K., Tang, X.: Image super-resolution using deep convolutional networks. IEEE Trans. Pattern Anal. Mach. Intell. **38**(2), 295–307 (2015)
9. Dong, C., Loy, C.C., Tang, X.: Accelerating the super-resolution convolutional neural network. In: Leibe, B., Matas, J., Sebe, N., Welling, M. (eds.) ECCV 2016. LNCS, vol. 9906, pp. 391–407. Springer, Cham (2016). https://doi.org/10.1007/978-3-319-46475-6_25
10. Goodfellow, I., et al.: Generative adversarial nets. Adv. Neural Inform. Process. Syst. **27** (2014)
11. Gu, J., Dong, C.: Interpreting super-resolution networks with local attribution maps. In: IEEE Conference on Computer Vision and Pattern Recognition, pp. 9199–9208 (2021)
12. Gu, S., Lugmayr, A., Danelljan, M., Fritsche, M., Lamour, J., Timofte, R.: DIV8K: DIVerse 8k resolution image dataset. In: International Conference on Computer Vision Workshop, pp. 3512–3516. IEEE (2019)
13. He, K., Zhang, X., Ren, S., Sun, J.: Deep residual learning for image recognition. In: IEEE Conference on Computer Vision Pattern Recognition, pp. 770–778 (2016)

14. He, X., Mo, Z., Wang, P., Liu, Y., Yang, M., Cheng, J.: Ode-inspired network design for single image super-resolution. In: IEEE Conference on Computer Vision on Pattern Recognition, pp. 1732–1741 (2019)
15. Hu, J., Shen, L., Sun, G.: Squeeze-and-excitation networks. In: IEEE Conference on Computer Vision on Pattern Recognition, pp. 7132–7141 (2018)
16. Huang, G., Liu, Z., Van Der Maaten, L., Weinberger, K.Q.: Densely connected convolutional networks. In: IEEE Conference on Computer Vision and Pattern Recognition, pp. 4700–4708 (2017)
17. Huang, J.B., Singh, A., Ahuja, N.: Single image super-resolution from transformed self-exemplars. In: IEEE Conference on Computer Vision and Pattern Recognition, pp. 5197–5206 (2015)
18. Jia, X., De Brabandere, B., Tuytelaars, T., Gool, L.V.: Dynamic filter networks. Adv. Neural Inform. Process. Syst. **29**, 667–675 (2016)
19. Kim, J., Lee, J.K., Lee, K.M.: Accurate image super-resolution using very deep convolutional networks. In: IEEE Conference on Computer Vision and Pattern Recognition, pp. 1646–1654. IEEE Computer Society (2016)
20. Kingma, D.P., Ba, J.: Adam: a method for stochastic optimization. In: International Conference on Learning Representation (2015)
21. Kong, X., Zhao, H., Qiao, Y., Dong, C.: ClassSR: a general framework to accelerate super-resolution networks by data characteristic. In: IEEE Conference on Computer Vision and Pattern Recognition, pp. 12016–12025 (2021)
22. Lai, W.S., Huang, J.B., Ahuja, N., Yang, M.H.: Deep Laplacian pyramid networks for fast and accurate super-resolution. In: IEEE Conference on Computer Vision and Pattern Recognition, pp. 624–632 (2017)
23. Ledig, C., et al.: Photo-realistic single image super-resolution using a generative adversarial network. In: IEEE Conference on Computer Vision and Pattern Recognition, pp. 4681–4690 (2017)
24. Li, W., Zhou, K., Qi, L., Jiang, N., Lu, J., Jia, J.: LAPAR: linearly-assembled pixel-adaptive regression network for single image super-resolution and beyond. In: Advances in Neural Information Processing Systems (2020)
25. Li, Y., Gu, S., Mayer, C., Gool, L.V., Timofte, R.: Group sparsity: the hinge between filter pruning and decomposition for network compression. In: IEEE Conference on Computer Vision and Pattern Recognition, pp. 8018–8027 (2020)
26. Lim, B., Son, S., Kim, H., Nah, S., Lee, K.M.: Enhanced deep residual networks for single image super-resolution. In: IEEE Conference on Computer Vision and Pattern Recognition Workshop, pp. 136–144 (2017)
27. Lin, S., Ryabtsev, A., Sengupta, S., Curless, B.L., Seitz, S.M., Kemelmacher-Shlizerman, I.: Real-time high-resolution background matting. In: IEEE Conference on Computer Vision and Pattern Recognition, pp. 8762–8771 (2021)
28. Liu, J.J., Hou, Q., Cheng, M.M., Wang, C., Feng, J.: Improving convolutional networks with self-calibrated convolutions. In: IEEE Conference on Computer Vision and Pattern Recognition, pp. 10096–10105 (2020)
29. Liu, J., Tang, J., Wu, G.: Residual feature distillation network for lightweight image super-resolution. In: Bartoli, A., Fusiello, A. (eds.) ECCV 2020. LNCS, vol. 12537, pp. 41–55. Springer, Cham (2020). https://doi.org/10.1007/978-3-030-67070-2_2
30. Liu, J., Zhang, W., Tang, Y., Tang, J., Wu, G.: Residual feature aggregation network for image super-resolution. In: IEEE Conference on Computer Vision and Pattern Recognition, pp. 2359–2368 (2020)

31. Martin, D., Fowlkes, C., Tal, D., Malik, J.: A database of human segmented natural images and its application to evaluating segmentation algorithms and measuring ecological statistics. In: International Conference on Computer Vision, vol. 2, pp. 416–423. IEEE (2001)

32. Matsui, Y., et al.: Sketch-based manga retrieval using manga109 dataset. Multimedia Tools Appl. **76**(20), 21811–21838 (2017)

33. Mei, Y., Fan, Y., Zhou, Y.: Image super-resolution with non-local sparse attention. In: IEEE Conference on Computer Vision and Pattern Recognition, pp. 3517–3526 (2021)

34. Niu, B., et al.: Single image super-resolution via a holistic attention network. In: Vedaldi, A., Bischof, H., Brox, T., Frahm, J.-M. (eds.) ECCV 2020. LNCS, vol. 12357, pp. 191–207. Springer, Cham (2020). https://doi.org/10.1007/978-3-030-58610-2_12

35. Paszke, A., et al.: Pytorch: an imperative style, high-performance deep learning library. In: Advances in Neural Information Processing Systems (2019)

36. Song, D., Wang, Y., Chen, H., Xu, C., Xu, C., Tao, D.: AdderSR: towards energy efficient image super-resolution. In: IEEE Conference on Computer Vision and Pattern Recognition, pp. 15648–15657 (2021)

37. Tai, Y., Yang, J., Liu, X.: Image super-resolution via deep recursive residual network. In: IEEE Conference on Computer Vision and Pattern Recognition, pp. 2790–2798. IEEE Computer Society (2017)

38. Tai, Y., Yang, J., Liu, X., Xu, C.: MemNet: a persistent memory network for image restoration. In: International Conference on Computer Vision, pp. 4549–4557. IEEE Computer Society (2017)

39. Vaswani, A., et al.: Attention is all you need. In: Advances in Neural Information Processing Systems, pp. 5998–6008 (2017)

40. Wang, L., et al.: Exploring sparsity in image super-resolution for efficient inference. In: IEEE Conference on Computer Vision and Pattern Recognition, pp. 4917–4926 (2021)

41. Wang, X., Girshick, R., Gupta, A., He, K.: Non-local neural networks. In: IEEE Conference on Computer Vision and Pattern Recognition, pp. 7794–7803 (2018)

42. Wang, X., et al.: ESRGAN: enhanced super-resolution generative adversarial networks. In: European Conference on Computer Vision (2018)

43. Wang, Z., Bovik, A.C., Sheikh, H.R., Simoncelli, E.P.: Image quality assessment: from error visibility to structural similarity. IEEE Trans. Image Process. **13**(4), 600–612 (2004)

44. Xie, W., Song, D., Xu, C., Xu, C., Zhang, H., Wang, Y.: Learning frequency-aware dynamic network for efficient super-resolution. In: Proceedings of the IEEE/CVF International Conference on Computer Vision, pp. 4308–4317 (2021)

45. Zeyde, R., Elad, M., Protter, M.: On single image scale-up using sparse-representations. In: Boissonnat, J.-D., et al. (eds.) Curves and Surfaces 2010. LNCS, vol. 6920, pp. 711–730. Springer, Heidelberg (2012). https://doi.org/10.1007/978-3-642-27413-8_47

46. Zhang, K., et al.: AIM 2020 challenge on efficient super-resolution: methods and results. In: Bartoli, A., Fusiello, A. (eds.) ECCV 2020. LNCS, vol. 12537, pp. 5–40. Springer, Cham (2020). https://doi.org/10.1007/978-3-030-67070-2_1

47. Zhang, Y., Li, K., Li, K., Wang, L., Zhong, B., Fu, Y.: Image super-resolution using very deep residual channel attention networks. In: European Conference on Computer Vision, pp. 286–301 (2018)

48. Zhang, Y., Tian, Y., Kong, Y., Zhong, B., Fu, Y.: Residual dense network for image super-resolution. In: IEEE Conference on Computer Vision and Pattern Recognition, pp. 2472–2481 (2018)
49. Zhao, H., Kong, X., He, J., Qiao, Yu., Dong, C.: Efficient image super-resolution using pixel attention. In: Bartoli, A., Fusiello, A. (eds.) ECCV 2020. LNCS, vol. 12537, pp. 56–72. Springer, Cham (2020). https://doi.org/10.1007/978-3-030-67070-2_3
50. Zhou, S., Zhang, J., Zuo, W., Loy, C.C.: Cross-scale internal graph neural network for image super-resolution. Adv. Neural Inform. Process. Syst. **33**, 3499–3509 (2020)

Compiler-Aware Neural Architecture Search for On-Mobile Real-time Super-Resolution

Yushu Wu[1], Yifan Gong[1], Pu Zhao[1], Yanyu Li[1], Zheng Zhan[1], Wei Niu[2], Hao Tang[3], Minghai Qin[1], Bin Ren[2], and Yanzhi Wang[1(✉)]

[1] Northeastern University, Boston, MA 02115, USA
{wu.yushu,gong.yifa,yanz.wang}@northeastern.edu
[2] College of William and Mary, Williamsburg, VA 23185, USA
[3] CVL, ETH Zürich, 8092 Zürich, Switzerland

Abstract. Deep learning-based super-resolution (SR) has gained tremendous popularity in recent years because of its high image quality performance and wide application scenarios. However, prior methods typically suffer from large amounts of computations and huge power consumption, causing difficulties for real-time inference, especially on resource-limited platforms such as mobile devices. To mitigate this, we propose a compiler-aware SR neural architecture search (NAS) framework that conducts depth search and per-layer width search with adaptive SR blocks. The inference speed is directly taken into the optimization along with the SR loss to derive SR models with high image quality while satisfying the real-time inference requirement. Instead of measuring the speed on mobile devices at each iteration during the search process, a speed model incorporated with compiler optimizations is leveraged to predict the inference latency of the SR block with various width configurations for faster convergence. With the proposed framework, we achieve real-time SR inference for implementing 720p resolution with competitive SR performance (in terms of PSNR and SSIM) on GPU/DSP of mobile platforms (Samsung Galaxy S21). Codes are available at link.

Keywords: Super resolution · Real-time · On-mobile · NAS

1 Introduction

As a classic vision task, single-image-super-resolution (SISR) restores the original high-resolution (HR) image based on a down-sampled low-resolution (LR) one. It can be applied in various applications, such as low-resolution media data

---

Y. Wu and Y. Gong–Contributed equally.

Supplementary Information The online version contains supplementary material available at https://doi.org/10.1007/978-3-031-19800-7_6.

S. Avidan et al. (Eds.): ECCV 2022, LNCS 13679, pp. 92–111, 2022.
https://doi.org/10.1007/978-3-031-19800-7_6

enhancement or video/image upscaling for high resolution display panels. Various classic [24,38,66,67] and deep learning (DL)-based [20,21,52,62,81] SR methods have been proposed in the past. Compared with classic interpolation algorithms to improve image/video resolution, DL-based methods take advantage of learning mappings from LR to HR images from external datasets. Thus most recent SR works emerge in the DL area. However, one major limitation of existing DL-based SR methods is their high computation and storage overhead to achieve superior image quality, leading to difficulties to implement real-time SR inference even on powerful GPUs, not to mention resource limited edge devices. Due to the ever-increasing popularity of mobile devices and interactive on-mobile applications (such as live streaming), it is essential to derive lightweight SR models with both high image quality and low on-mobile inference latency.

There exist several works targeting at efficient SR models, including using upsampling operator at the end of a network [21,62], adopting channel splitting [34], using wider activation [81], and combining lightweight residual blocks with variants of group convolution [52]. Neural architecture search (NAS) is applied to derive the optimal architecture in many vision tasks. Latest works [15,16,44,63] try to derive fast, lightweight, and accurate SR networks via NAS. However, their models are still too large to be implemented on mobile devices. Furthermore, these methods usually take the parameter numbers and computation counts (such as multiply-accumulate (MAC) operations) into the optimization for model efficiency, without considering the actual on-mobile implementation performance such as the inference latency. The actual mobile deployment of SR mobiles has rarely been investigated. The most relevant works are the winner of the PIRM challenge [68], MobiSR [45], and work [85]. But they either require nearly one second per frame for inference, far beyond real-time, or take a long search time.

Targeting at achieving real-time inference of accurate SR model for 720p resolution on various resource-limited hardware such as mobile GPU and DSP, this paper proposes a compiler-aware NAS framework. An adaptive SR block is introduced to conduct the depth search and per-layer width search. Each convolution (CONV) layer is paired with a mask layer in the adaptive SR block for the width search, while the depth search is reached by choosing a path between the skip connection and the masked SR block. The mask can be trained along with the network parameters via gradient descent optimizers, significantly saving training overhead. Instead of using MACs as the optimization target, the latency performance is directly incorporated into the objective function with the usage of a speed model. Our implementation can support real-time SR inference with competitive SR performance on various resource-limited platforms, including mobile GPU and DSP. The contributions are summarized below:

- We propose a framework to search for the appropriate depth and per-layer width with adaptive SR blocks.
- We introduce a general compiler-aware speed model to predict the inference speed on the target device with corresponding compiler optimizations.
- The proposed framework can directly optimize the inference latency, providing the foundations for achieving real-time SR inference on mobile.

– Our proposed framework can achieve real-time SR inference (with only tens of milliseconds per frame) for the implementation of 720p resolution with competitive SR performance (in terms of PSNR and SSIM) on mobile (Samsung Galaxy S21). Our achievements can facilitate various practical SR applications with real-time requirements such as live streaming or video communication.

2   Related Work

SR Works. In recent years, most SR works have shifted their approaches from classic methods to DL-based methods with significant SR performance improvements. From the pioneering SRCNN [20] to later works with shortcut operator, dense connection, and attention mechanism [17,41,48,87,88], the up-scaling characteristic have dramatically boosted at the cost of high storage and computation overhead. Most of the works mentioned above even take seconds to process only one image on a powerful GPU, let alone mobile devices or video applications.

Efficient SR. Prior SR works are hard to be implemented on resource-limited platforms due to high computation and storage cost. To obtain more compact SR models, FSRCNN [21] postpones the position of the upsampling operator. IDN [35] and IMDN [34] utilize the channel splitting strategy. CARN-M [7] explores a lightweight SR model by combining efficient residual blocks with group convolutions. SMSR [70] learns sparse masks to prune redundant computation for efficient inference. ASSLN [89] and SRPN [90] leverage structure-regularized pruning and impose regularization on the pruned structure to guarantee the alignment of the locations of pruned filters across different layers. SR-LUT [40] uses look-up tables to retrieve the precomputed HR output values for LR input pixels, with a more significant SR performance degradation. However, these SR models do not consider the actual mobile deployment, and the sizes of the models are still too large. The actual SR deployment is rarely investigated. The winner of the PIRM challenge [68], MobiSR [45], and work [85] explore the on-device SR, but the models take seconds for a single image, far from real time, or require long search time. Work [37] considers real-time SR deployed on the powerful mobile TPU, which is not widely adopted such as mobile CPU/GPU.

NAS for SR. NAS has been shown to outperform heuristic networks in various applications. Recent SR works start to leverage NAS to find efficient, lightweight, and accurate SR models. Works [15,16,85] leverage reinforced evolution algorithms to achieve SR as a multi-objective problem. Work [6] uses a hierarchical search strategy to find the connection with local and global features. LatticeNet [56] learns the combination of residual blocks with the attention mechanism. Work [19,32,74] search lightweight architectures at different levels with differentiable architecture search (DARTS) [51]. DARTS based methods introduce architecture hyper-parameters which are usually continuous rather than binary, incurring additional bias during selection and optimization. Furthermore, the above-mentioned methods typically take the number of parameters or MACs into the objective function, rather than on-mobile latency as discussed in Sect. 3. Thus they can hardly satisfy the real-time requirement.

Hardware Acceleration. A significant emphasis on optimizing the DNN execution has emerged in recent years [22,25,29,36,39,43,60,75,79]. There are several representative DNN acceleration frameworks including Tensorflow-Lite [1], Alibaba MNN [2], Pytorch-Mobile [3], and TVM [13]. These frameworks include several graph optimization techniques such as layer fusion, and constant folding.

3   Motivation and Challenges

With the rapid development of mobile devices and real-time applications such as live streaming, it is essential and desirable to implement real-time SR on resources-limited mobile devices. However, it is challenging. To maintain or upscale the spatial dimensions of feature maps based on large input/output size, SR models typically consume tens of or hundreds of GMACs (larger than several GMACs in image classification [54,69]), incurring difficulties for real-time inference. For example, prior works on mobile SR deployment [45] and [68] achieve 2792ms and 912ms on-mobile inference latency, respectively, far from real-time.

We can adopt NAS or pruning methods to find a lightweight SR model with fast speed on mobile devices. But there are several challenges: (C1) tremendous searching overhead with NAS, (C2) misleading magnitude during pruning, (C3) speed incorporation issues, and (C4) heuristic depth determination.

Tremendous Searching Overhead with NAS. In NAS, the exponentially growing search space leads to tremendous search overhead. Specifically, the RL-based [91,93,94] or evolution-based NAS methods [61,64,78] typically need to sample large amounts of candidate models from the search space and train each candidate architecture with multiple epochs, incurring long search time and high computation cost. Besides, differentiable NAS methods [8,11,51] build super-nets to train multiple architectures simultaneously, causing significant memory cost and limited discrete search space up-bounded by the available memory. To mitigate these, there are certain compromised strategies, such as proxy tasks (to search on CIFAR and target on ImageNet) [61,78,92] and performance estimation (to predict/estimate the architecture performance with some metrics) [4,49,65].

Misleading Magnitude During Pruning. Pruning can also be adopted to reduce the model size, which determines the per-layer pruning ratio and pruning positions. With the assumption that weights with smaller magnitudes are less important for final accuracy, magnitude-based pruning [26,30,31,47,57,58,72, 84,86] is widely employed to prune weights smaller than a threshold. However, the assumption is not necessarily true, and weight magnitudes can be misleading. Magnitude-based pruning is not able to achieve importance shifting during pruning. As detailed in Appendix ??, in iterative magnitude pruning, small weights pruned first are not able to become large enough to contribute to the accuracy. Thus layers pruned more at initial will be pruned more and more, causing a non-recoverable pruning policy. It becomes pure exploitation without exploration.

Speed Incorporation Issues. To achieve real-time inference on mobile, it is essential to obtain the on-mobile speed performance when searching architectures.

However, it is non-trivial to achieve this since testing speed requires an additional process to interact with the mobile device for a few minutes, which can hardly be incorporated into a typical model training. To mitigate this, certain methods [53,54,69] adopt weight number or computation counts as an estimation of the speed performance. Other methods [18,73,77] first collect on-mobile speed data and then build lookup tables with the speed data to estimate the speed.

Heuristic Depth Determination. Reducing model depth can avoid all computations in the removed layers, thus significantly accelerating the inference. Since previous NAS works do not incorporate a practical speed constraint or measurement during optimization, their search on model depth is usually heuristic. Designers determine the model depth according to a simple rule that the model should satisfy an inference budget, without a specific optimization method [8,49–51,78,92]. More efforts are devoted to searching other optimization dimensions such as kernel size or width rather than model depth.

4 Our Method

We first introduce the framework, then discuss the components of the framework in detail. We also specify how it can deal with the challenges in Sect. 3.

4.1 Framework with Adaptive SR Block

In the framework, we perform a compiler-aware architecture depth and per-layer width search to achieve real-time SR on mobile devices. The search space contains the width for each CONV layer and the number of stacked SR blocks in the model, which is too large to be explored with a heuristic method. Therefore, we propose an adaptive SR block to implement the depth and per-layer width search, and the model is composed of multiple adaptive SR blocks. Figure 1 shows the architecture of the adaptive SR block. It consists of a masked SR block, a speed model, and an aggregation layer. The adaptive SR block has two inputs (and outputs) corresponding to the SR features and the accumulated speed, respectively. It achieves per-layer width search with mask layers in the masked SR blocks and depth search with aggregation layer to choose a path between the skip connection and the masked SR block. Besides, to obtain the on-mobile speed performance, we adopt a speed model to predict the speed of the masked SR block. The speed model is trained on our own dataset with speed performance of various block width configurations measured through compiler optimizations for significant inference acceleration to achieve accurate speed prediction.

4.2 Per-Layer Width Search with Mask Layer for C1 and C2

Width search is performed for each CONV layer in a typical WDSR block [81]. WDSR is chosen as our basic building blocks since it has demonstrated high efficiency in SR tasks [14,82,83]. Note that our framework is not limited to the WDSR block and can be easily extended to various residual SR blocks [7,35,48]

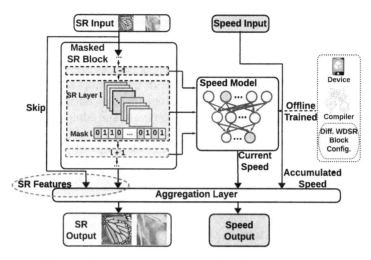

Fig. 1. Architecture of the adaptive SR block search.

in the literature. To satisfy the real-time requirement, we perform a per-layer width search to automatically select an appropriate number of channels for each CONV layer in the WDSR block. Specifically, we insert a differentiable mask layer (a depth-wise 1×1 CONV layer) after each CONV layer to serve as the layer-wise trainable mask, as shown below,

$$a_l^n = m_l^n \odot (w_l^n \odot a_{l-1}^n), \tag{1}$$

where $\odot$ denotes the convolution operation. $w_l^n \in R^{o \times i \times k \times k}$ is the weight parameters in the lth CONV layer of the nth block, with o output channels, i input channels, and kernels of size $k \times k$. $a_l^n \in R^{B \times o \times s \times s'}$ represents the output features of lth layer (with the trainable mask), with o channels and $s \times s'$ feature size. B denotes the batch size. $m_l^n \in R^{o \times 1 \times 1 \times 1}$ is the corresponding weights of the depth-wise CONV layer (i.e., the mask layer).

We use each element of m_l^n as the pruning indicator for the corresponding output channel of $w_l^n \odot a_{l-1}^n$. Larger elements of m_l^n mean that the corresponding channels should be preserved while smaller elements indicate pruning the channels. Formally, we use a threshold to convert m_l^n into a binary mask,

$$b_l^n = \begin{cases} 1, m_l^n > thres. \\ 0, m_l^n \leq thres. \end{cases} \text{(element-wise)}, \tag{2}$$

where $b_l^n \in \{0,1\}^{o \times 1 \times 1 \times 1}$ is the binarized m_l^n. We initialize m_l^n with random values between 0 and 1, and the adjustable $thres$ is set to 0.5 in our case. The WDSR block with the proposed mask layers is named as masked SR block.

Thus we are able to obtain a binary mask for each CONV layer. The next problem is how to make the mask trainable, as the binarization operation is non-differentiable, leading to difficulties for back-propagation. To solve this, we integrate Straight Through Estimator (STE) [9] as shown below,

$$\frac{\partial \mathcal{L}}{\partial m_l^n} = \frac{\partial \mathcal{L}}{\partial b_l^n}, \tag{3}$$

where we directly pass the gradients through the binarization. The STE method is originally proposed to avoid the non-differentiable problems in quantization tasks [55,80]. Without STE, some methods adopt complicated strategies to deal with the non-differentiable binary masks such as [27,28].

With the binarization and the STE method, we are able to build a trainable mask to indicate whether the corresponding channel is pruned or not. Our mask generation and training are more straightforward and simpler. For example, proxyless-NAS [12] transforms the real-valued weights to binary gates with a probability distribution, and adopts complex mask updating procedure (such as task factorizing). SMSR [70] adopts Gumbel softmax to perform complex sparse mask CONV. Unlike proxylessNAS or SMSR, we generate binary masks simply via a threshold and train the masks directly via STE.

4.3   Speed Prediction with Speed Model for C3

To achieve real-time SR inference on mobile devices, we take the inference speed into the optimization to satisfy a given real-time threshold. It is hard to measure the practical speed or latency of various structures on mobile devices during optimization. Traditionally, the inference speed may be estimated roughly with the number of computations [53,54,69] or a latency lookup table [18,73,77], which can hardly provide an accurate speed. To solve this problem, we adopt a DNN-based speed model to predict the inference speed of the block. The input of the speed model is the width of each CONV layer in the block, and it outputs the block speed. As shown in Fig. 1, the width of each CONV layer can be obtained through the mask layer. Thus the speed model can work perfectly with the width search, dealing with C3 to provide speed performance of various architectures.

To train such a speed model, we first need to build a speed dataset with block latency of various layer width configurations in the block. Next, we can train a speed model based on the dataset to predict the speed. We find that the trained speed model is accurate in predicting the speed of different layer widths in the block (with 5% error at most). We show the details about the dataset, speed model, and the prediction accuracy in Sect. 5 and Appendix B.

We highlight that our speed model not only takes the masks as inputs to predict the speed, but also back-propagates the gradients from the speed loss (Eq. (10)) to update the masks as detailed in Sect. 4.5, rather than just predicting performance forwardly such as [71]. That is why we build the speed model based on DNNs instead of loop-up tables. The trainable masks and the speed model are combined comprehensively to solve the problem more efficiently.

4.4   Depth Search with Aggregation Layer for C4

Although reducing the per-layer width can accelerate the inference, removing the whole block can avoid the computations of the whole block, thus providing higher speedup. Hence, besides width search, we further incorporate depth search to automatically determine the number of adaptive SR blocks in the model. Note that although per-layer width search may also converge to zero width, which eliminates the entire block, we find that in most cases, there are usually a few channels left in each block to promote the SR performance, leading to difficulties in removing the whole block. Thus it is necessary to incorporate depth search.

To perform depth search, we have two paths in each adaptive SR block. As shown in Fig. 1, one path is the skip connection, and the other path is the masked SR block. In the aggregation layer, there is a parameter like a switch to control which path the SR input goes through. If the SR input chooses the skip path, the masked SR block is skipped, and the latency of this block is just 0, leading to significant inference acceleration. The aggregation layer plays a key role in the path selection. It contains two trainable parameters α_s and α_b. In the forward pass, it selects the skip path or the masked WDSR block path based on the relative relationship of α_s and α_b, as shown below,

$$\beta_s = 0 \text{ and } \beta_b = 1, \text{if } \alpha_s \leq \alpha_b, \tag{4}$$
$$\beta_s = 1 \text{ and } \beta_b = 0, \text{if } \alpha_s > \alpha_b, \tag{5}$$

where the binarized variables β_s and β_b denote the path selection ($\beta_s{=}1$ means choosing the skip path and $\beta_b{=}1$ means choosing the masked SR block path). Since the comparison operation is non-differentiable, leading to difficulties for back-propagation, similarly we adopt STE [9] to make it differentiable as below,

$$\frac{\partial \mathcal{L}}{\partial \alpha_s} = \frac{\partial \mathcal{L}}{\partial \beta_s}, \quad \frac{\partial \mathcal{L}}{\partial \alpha_b} = \frac{\partial \mathcal{L}}{\partial \beta_b}. \tag{6}$$

In the aggregation layer, the forward computation can be represented below,

$$\boldsymbol{a}^n = \beta_s \cdot \boldsymbol{a}^{n-1} + \beta_b \cdot \boldsymbol{a}^n_L, \tag{7}$$
$$v_n = v_{n-1} + \beta_b \cdot v_c, \tag{8}$$

where $\boldsymbol{a}^n$ is the SR output features of the nth adaptive SR block. $\boldsymbol{a}^n_L$ is the SR output features of masked SR block in the nth adaptive SR block, and L is the maximum number of CONV layers in each block and we have $l{\leq}L$. v_n is the accumulated speed or latency until the nth adaptive SR block and v_c is the speed of the current block which is predicted by the speed model. By training α_s and α_b, the model can learn to switch between the skip path and the SR path to determine the model depth, thus dealing with C4.

4.5   Training Loss

Multiple adaptive SR blocks can form the SR model, which provides two outputs including the typical SR outputs and the speed outputs. The training loss is a combination of a typical SR loss and a speed loss as below,

$$\mathcal{L}_{SPD} = \max\{0, v_N - v_T\}, \tag{9}$$
$$\mathcal{L} = \mathcal{L}_{SR} + \gamma \mathcal{L}_{SPD}, \tag{10}$$

where v_T is the real-time threshold, v_N is the accumulated speed of N blocks, and γ is a parameter to control their relative importance. The objective is to

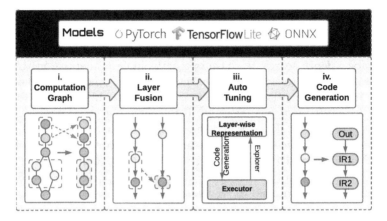

Fig. 2. The overview of compiler optimizations.

achieve high SR performance while the speed can satisfy a real-time threshold. To summarize, with the trainable masks, the speed model, and the aggregation layer in the adaptive SR block, our search algorithm achieves the following advantages:

- The mask can be trained along with the network parameters via gradient descent optimizers, thus dealing with C1 to save search overhead compared with previous one-shot pruning [23,31] or NAS methods [91,93] to train multiple epochs for each candidate architecture with huge searching efforts.
- Compared with magnitude-based threshold pruning, we decouple the trainable masks from original model parameters, thus enabling exploitation and overcoming the drawbacks of magnitude-based pruning, dealing with C2.
- We use the speed model for predicting the speed to solve C3, which is differentiable regarding the trainable mask. Thus the mask is trained to find a model with both high SR performance and fast inference speed.
- We also incorporate depth search though aggregation layers to deal with C4.

5   Compiler Awareness with Speed Model

To satisfy the speed requirement with a given latency threshold on a specific mobile device, it is required to obtain the actual inference latency on the device. It is non-trivial to achieve this as the model speed varies with different model width and depth. It is unrealistic to measure the actual on-mobile speed during the search, as the search space is quite large, and testing the mobile speed of each candidate can take a few minutes, which is not compatible with DNN training.

To solve this problem, we adopt a speed model to predict the inference latency of the masked SR block with various width configurations. With the speed model, we can obtain the speed prediction as outputs by providing the width of each CONV layer in the SR block as inputs. It is fully compatible with the trainable mask, enabling differentiable model speed with respect to the layer width.

To obtain the speed model, we first build a latency dataset with latency data measured on the hardware platforms incorporated with compiler optimizations. Then the DNN speed model is trained based on the latency dataset.

Compiler Optimization. To build a latency dataset, we need to measure the speed of various block configurations on mobile devices. Compiler optimizations are adopted to accelerate the inference speed during speed testing. It is essential to incorporate compiler optimizations as they can significantly accelerate the inference speed. The overview of the compiler optimizations is shown in Fig. 2.

To fully exploit the parallelism for a higher speedup, the key features of SR have to be considered. As the objective of SR is to obtain a HR image from its LR counterpart, each layer has to maintain or upscale the spatial dimensions of the feature, leading to larger feature map size and more channels compared with classification tasks. Therefore, the data movements between the memory and cache are extremely intensive. To reduce the data movements for faster inference, we adopt two important optimization techniques: 1) operator fusion and 2) decreasing the amount of data to be copied between CPU and GPU.

Operator fusion is a key optimization technique adopted in many state-of-the-art DNN execution framework [1–3]. However, these frameworks usually adopt fusion approaches based on certain patterns that are too restrictive to cover the diversity of operators and layer connections. To address this problem, we classify the existing operations in the SR model into several groups based on the mapping between the input and output, and develop rules for different combinations of the groups in a more aggressive fusion manner. For instance, CONV operation and depth-to-space operation can be fused together. With layer fusion, both the memory consumption of the intermediate results and the number of operators can be reduced. An auto-tuning process is followed to determine the best-suited configurations of parameters for different mobile CPUs/GPUs and Domain Specific Language (DSL) based code generation. After that, a high-level DSL is leveraged to specify the operator in the computational graph of a DNN model. We show more details about compiler optimization in Appendix C.

Latency Dataset. To train the speed model, we first measure and collect the inference speed of the WDSR block under various CONV layer width configurations. After that, a dataset of the WDSR block on-mobile speed with different configurations can be built. We vary the number of filters in each CONV layer as the different width configurations. The inference time is measured on the target device (Samsung Galaxy S21) by stacking 20 WDSR blocks with the same configuration, and the average latency is used as the inference time to mitigate the overhead of loading data on mobile GPU. As the maximum number of CONV layers in each masked WDSR block is L, each data point in the dataset can be represented as a tuple with $L+2$ elements: $\{\mathcal{F}_{CONV^1}, \cdots, \mathcal{F}_{CONV^{L+1}}, \mathcal{T}_{inference}\}$, where $\mathcal{F}_{CONV^i}$, for $i \in \{1, \cdots, L\}$, indicates the number of input channels for the ith CONV layer, $\mathcal{F}_{CONV^{L+1}}$ is the number of output channels for the last CONV layer, and $\mathcal{T}_{inference}$ is the inference speed for this configuration measured in milliseconds. The entire dataset is composed of 2048 data points.

Table 1. Comparison with SOTA efficient SR models for implementing 720p.

Scale	Method	Params (K)	MACs (G)	Latency (ms)	PSNR				SSIM			
					Set5	Set14	B100	Urban100	Set5	Set14	B100	Urban100
×2	FSRCNN [21]	12	6.0	128.47	37.00	32.63	31.53	29.88	0.9558	0.9088	0.8920	0.9020
	MOREMNAS-C [16]	25	5.5	–	37.06	32.75	31.50	29.92	0.9561	0.9094	0.8904	0.9023
	TPSR-NOGAN [44]	60	14.0	–	37.38	33.00	31.75	30.61	0.9583	0.9123	0.8942	0.9119
	LapSRN [42]	813	29.9	–	37.52	33.08	31.80	30.41	0.9590	0.9130	0.8950	0.9100
	CARN-M [7]	412	91.2	1049.92	37.53	33.26	31.92	31.23	0.9583	0.9141	0.8960	0.9193
	FALSR-C [15]	408	93.7	–	37.66	33.26	31.96	31.24	0.9586	0.9140	0.8965	0.9187
	ESRN-V [63]	324	73.4	–	37.85	33.42	32.10	31.79	0.9600	0.9161	0.8987	0.9248
	EDSR [48]	1518	458.0	2031.65	37.99	33.57	32.16	31.98	0.9604	0.9175	0.8994	0.9272
	WDSR [81]	1203	274.1	1973.31	38.10	33.72	32.25	32.37	0.9608	0.9182	0.9004	0.9302
	SMSR [70]	985	131.6	–	38.00	33.64	32.17	32.19	0.9601	0.9179	0.8990	0.9284
	SRPN-L [90]	609	139.9	–	38.10	33.70	32.25	32.26	0.9608	0.9189	0.9005	0.9294
	Ours ($v_T = 100$ ms)	47	11.0	**98.90**	37.64	33.16	31.91	31.08	0.9591	0.9136	0.8961	0.9170
	Ours ($v_T = 70$ ms)	28	6.6	**66.09**	37.49	33.05	31.81	30.76	0.9584	0.9123	0.8946	0.9135
	Ours ($v_T = 40$ ms, real-time)	11	2.5	**34.92**	37.19	32.80	31.60	30.15	0.9572	0.9099	0.8919	0.9054
×4	FSRCNN [21]	12	4.6	98.13	30.71	27.59	26.98	24.62	0.8657	0.7535	0.7150	0.7280
	TPSR-NOGAN [44]	61	3.6	55.82	31.10	27.95	27.15	24.97	0.8779	0.7663	0.7214	0.7456
	FEQE-P [68]	96	5.6	82.81	31.53	28.21	27.32	25.32	0.8824	0.7714	0.7273	0.7583
	CARN-M [7]	412	32.5	374.15	31.92	28.42	27.44	25.62	0.8903	0.7762	0.7304	0.7694
	ESRN-V [63]	324	20.7	–	31.99	28.49	27.50	25.87	0.8919	0.7779	0.7331	0.7782
	IDN [35]	600	32.3	–	31.99	28.52	27.52	25.92	0.8928	0.7794	0.7339	0.7801
	EDSR [48]	1518	114.5	495.90	32.09	28.58	27.57	26.04	0.8938	0.7813	0.7357	0.7849
	DHP-20 [46]	790	34.1	–	31.94	28.42	27.47	25.69	–	–	–	–
	IMDN [34]	715	40.9	–	32.21	28.58	27.56	26.04	0.8948	0.7811	0.7353	0.7838
	WDSR [81]	1203	69.3	533.02	32.27	28.67	27.64	26.26	0.8963	0.7838	0.7383	0.7911
	SR-LUT-S [40]	77	–	–	29.77	26.99	26.57	23.94	0.8429	0.7372	0.6990	0.6971
	SMSR [70]	1006	41.6	–	32.12	28.55	27.55	26.11	0.8932	0.7808	0.7351	0.7868
	SRPN-L [90]	623	35.8	–	32.24	28.69	27.63	26.16	0.8958	0.7836	0.7373	0.7875
	Ours ($v_T = 100$ ms)	188	10.8	**93.50**	32.02	28.50	27.51	25.83	0.8922	0.7778	0.7328	0.7769
	Ours ($v_T = 70$ ms)	116	6.7	**64.95**	31.88	28.43	27.46	25.69	0.8905	0.7760	0.7312	0.7715
	Ours ($v_T = 40$ ms, real-time)	66	3.7	**36.46**	31.73	28.28	27.34	25.44	0.8878	0.7725	0.7281	0.7620

∗ Some latency results are not reported as the models are not open-source or contain operators that cannot run on mobile GPU.

† The latency results are measured on the GPU of Samsung Galaxy S21.

Speed Model. With the latency dataset, the speed model can be trained on the collected data points. The inference speed estimation is a regression problem, thus, a network with 6 fully-connected layers combined with ReLU activation is used as the speed model. During the speed model training, 90% of the data is used for training and the rest is for validation. After training, the speed model can predict the inference time of various block configurations with high accuracy. From our results, the speed model only incurs 5% of deviation for the speed prediction. The speed model has two advantages: (1) It is compatible with the width search framework as the trainable mask can be directly fed into the speed model. (2) It makes the model speed differentiable with respect to the masks, and back-propagates gradients to update the masks, thus the model can update the model speed by adjusting the layer width though back-propagation.

6   Experiments

6.1   Experimental Settings

SR Datasets. All SR models are trained on the training set of DIV2K [5] with 800 training images. For evaluation, four benchmark datasets Set5 [10], Set14 [76], B100 [59], and Urban100 [33] are used for test. The PSNR and SSIM are calculated on the luminance channel (a.k.a. Y channel) in the YCbCr color space.

Evaluation Platforms and Running Configurations. The training codes are implemented with PyTorch. 8 GPUs are used to conduct the search, which usually finishes in 10 h. The latency is measured on the GPU of an off-the-shelf Samsung Galaxy S21 smartphone, which has the Qualcomm Snapdragon 888 mobile platform with a Qualcomm Kryo 680 Octa-core CPU and a Qualcomm Adreno 660 GPU. Each test takes 50 runs on different inputs with 8 threads on CPU, and all pipelines on GPU. The average time is reported.

Training Details. 48×48 RGB image patches are randomly sampled from LR images for each input minibatch. We use the architecture of WDSR with 16 blocks as the backbone of our NAS process. Considering the huge input size of SR (normally nHD–640×360 inputs or higher resolution for ×2 task), a compact version of the WDSR block is chosen to fit the mobile GPU, where the largest filer number for each CONV layer is 32, 146, and 28, respectively. The backbone is initialized with the parameters of the pretrained WDSR model. Traditional MAE loss is used to measure the differences between the SR image and the ground-truth as the SR loss. The parameter γ in the training loss denoted as Eq. (10) is set to 0.01. The first 20 epochs are used for the NAS process, and the following 30 epochs for fine-tuning the searched model. ADAM optimizers with

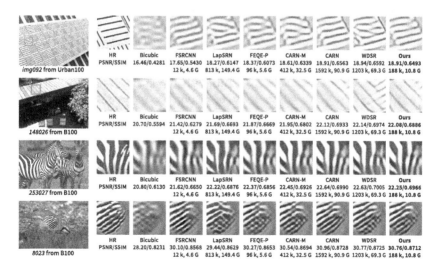

Fig. 3. Visual Comparisons with other methods on Urban100/B100 for ×4 SR.

$\beta_1 = 0.9$, $\beta_2 = 0.999$, and $\epsilon = 1 \times 10^{-8}$ are used for both model optimization and fine-tuning process. The learning rate is initialized as 1×10^{-4} and reduced by half at 10, 16 epochs and at 20, 25 epochs in the NAS and fine-tuning process, respectively. The details of the searched architecture are in Appendix D.

Baseline Methods. We compare with some traditional human-designed SR models such as FSRCNN and EDSR. Besides, some baselines optimizing the speed or hardware with NAS approaches are also covered. For example, TPSR-NOGAN, FALSR-C, ESRN-V optimize the SR efficiency to facilitate the deployment on end devices. Moreover, we compare with some methods exploring the sparsity in SR models such as DHP, SMSR, and SRPN-L for efficient inference.

6.2   Experimental Results

Comparison with Baselines on SR Performance. The comparisons of the models obtained by the proposed framework with state-of-the-art efficient SR works are shown in Table 1. Two commonly used metrics (PSNR and SSIM) are adopted to evaluate image quality. The evaluations are conducted on $\times 2$ and $\times 4$ scales. For a fair comparison, we start from different low-resolution inputs but the high-resolution outputs are 720p (1280$\times$720). To make a comprehensive study, the latency threshold v_T is set to different values. Specifically, as real-time execution typically requires at least 25 frames/sec (FPS), the latency threshold v_T is set as 40 ms to obtain SR models for real-time inference.

For $\times 2$ scale, the model obtained with latency threshold $v_T = 100$ ms outperforms TPSR-NOGAN, LAPSRN, and CARN-M in terms of PSNR and SSIM with fewer parameters and MACs. Compared with FALSR-C, ESRN-V, EDSR, WDSR, SMSR, and SRON-L, our model greatly reduces the model size and computations with a competitive image quality performance. By setting v_T as 70 ms, our model has similar parameters and MACs as MOREMNAS-C, but achieves higher PSNR and SSIM performance. Similar results can be obtained on the $\times 4$ scale. Furthermore, for both scales, by setting v_T as 40 ms, we obtain extremely

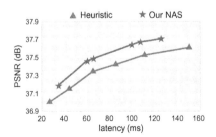

Fig. 4. Comparison of $\times 2$ SR results between searched models and heuristic models on Set5 with latency measured on the GPU of Samsung Galaxy S21.

Table 2. Comparison of different search schema for $\times 2$ scales. The performance is evaluated on Set5 and Urban100 datasets

Search method		Latency (ms)	Set 5		Urban100	
Width search	Depth search		PSNR	SSIM	PSNR	SSIM
✗	✗	150.92	37.62	0.9589	31.03	0.9164
✗	✓	111.58	37.65	0.9591	31.10	0.9172
✓	✗	108.38	37.65	0.9591	31.02	0.9161
✓	✓	**98.90**	37.64	0.9591	31.08	0.9170

lightweight models and the models still maintain satisfying PSNR and SSIM performance on all four datasets. Although SR-LUT uses look-up tables for efficient SR inference, it suffers from more significant SR performance degradation.

The visual comparisons with other SR methods for ×4 up-scaling task are shown in Fig. 3. Our model can recover the details comparable or even better than other methods by using fewer parameters and computations.

Comparison with Baselines on Speed Performance. In general, our method can achieve real-time SR inference (higher than 25 FPS) for implementing 720p resolution up-scaling with competitive image quality in terms of PSNR and SSIM on mobile platforms (Samsung Galaxy S21). Compared with [70] which also explore the sparsity of SR models, our method can achieve more significant model size and computation reduction (our 11GMACs v.s. 131.6GFLOPs [70] for ×2 scale), leading to faster speed (our 11.3 ms v.s. 52 ms [70] on Nvidia A100 GPU).

Comparison with Heuristic Models. We compare our searched models with heuristic models, which are obtained by evenly reducing the depth and width from the WDSR model. Since we do not search per-layer width in heuristic models, the width is the same among all blocks in one heuristic model. For a fair comparison, the same compiler optimization framework is adopted for both searched models and heuristic models. As shown in Fig. 4, we can see that the NAS approach can achieve faster inference than the heuristic models under the same PSNR, demonstrating the effectiveness of the search approach.

Compiler Optimization Performance. To demonstrate the effectiveness of our compiler optimizations, we implement CARN-M [7], FSRCNN [21], and our searched model with the open-source MNN framework. By comparing their PSNR and FPS performance, we find that our model can achieve higher FPS and PSNR than the baseline models, with detailed results in Appendix E. We also compare with the compilation of [36] detailed in Appendix F.

Performance on Various Devices. Our main results are trained and tested on the mobile GPU. We highlight that our method can be easily applied to all kinds of devices with their corresponding speed models. To demonstrate this, we perform compiler optimizations for the DSP on the mobile device and train the corresponding speed model. With the new speed model, we use our method to search an SR model for the DSP, which can achieve 37.34 PSNR on Set5 with 32.51 ms inference speed for ×2 up-scaling task, detailed in Appendix G.

6.3 Ablation Study

For the ablation study, we investigate the influence of depth search and per-layer width search separately for ×2 scale task. Multiple runs are taken for each search method with different latency threshold v_T so that the searched models have similar PSNR and SSIM on Set5 to provide a clear comparison. From the results in Table 2, we can see that both depth search only and width search only can greatly reduce the latency with better image quality than non-search case.

Specifically, as a missing piece in many prior SR NAS works, depth search provides better PSNR and SSIM performance than width search on Urban100 with a slightly higher latency, which shows the importance of this search dimension. By combining depth search and width search, we could reach faster inference with similar PSNR and SSIM than conducting either search alone.

7   Conclusion

We propose a compiler-aware NAS framework to achieve real-time SR on mobile devices. An adaptive WDSR block is introduced to conduct depth search and per-layer width search. The latency is directly taken into the optimization objective with the leverage of a speed model incorporated with compiler optimizations. With the framework, we achieve real-time SR inference for the implementation of 720p with competitive SR performance on mobile.

Acknowledgements. The research reported here was funded in whole or in part by the Army Research Office/Army Research Laboratory via grant W911-NF-20-1-0167 to Northeastern University. Any errors and opinions are not those of the Army Research Office or Department of Defense and are attributable solely to the author(s). This research is also partially supported by National Science Foundation CCF-1937500 and CNS-1909172.

References

1. https://www.tensorflow.org/mobile/tflite/
2. https://github.com/alibaba/MNN
3. https://pytorch.org/mobile/home
4. Abdelfattah, M.S., Mehrotra, A., Dudziak, Ł., Lane, N.D.: Zero-cost proxies for lightweight NAS. In: International Conference on Learning Representations (2021). https://openreview.net/forum?id=0cmMMy8J5q
5. Agustsson, E., Timofte, R.: NTIRE 2017 challenge on single image super-resolution: dataset and study. In: The IEEE Conference on Computer Vision and Pattern Recognition (CVPR) Workshops, July 2017
6. Ahn, J.Y., Cho, N.I.: Neural architecture search for image super-resolution using densely constructed search space: DeCoNAS. In: 2020 25th International Conference on Pattern Recognition (ICPR), pp. 4829–4836. IEEE (2021)
7. Ahn, N., Kang, B., Sohn, K.A.: Fast, accurate, and lightweight super-resolution with cascading residual network. In: Proceedings of the European Conference on Computer Vision (ECCV), pp. 252–268 (2018)
8. Bender, G., Kindermans, P.J., Zoph, B., Vasudevan, V., Le, Q.: Understanding and simplifying one-shot architecture search. In: International Conference on Machine Learning, pp. 550–559 (2018)
9. Bengio, Y., Léonard, N., Courville, A.C.: Estimating or propagating gradients through stochastic neurons for conditional computation. CoRR abs/1308.3432 (2013), arxiv:1308.3432
10. Bevilacqua, M., Roumy, A., Guillemot, C., Alberi-Morel, M.L.: Low-complexity single-image super-resolution based on nonnegative neighbor embedding (2012)

11. Brock, A., Lim, T., Ritchie, J.M., Weston, N.: Smash: one-shot model architecture search through hypernetworks. arXiv preprint arXiv:1708.05344 (2017)
12. Cai, H., Zhu, L., Han, S.: ProxylessNAS: direct neural architecture search on target task and hardware. ICLR (2019)
13. Chen, T., Moreau, T., et al.: TVM: an automated end-to-end optimizing compiler for deep learning. In: USENIX, pp. 578–594 (2018)
14. Cheng, G., Matsune, A., Li, Q., Zhu, L., Zang, H., Zhan, S.: Encoder-decoder residual network for real super-resolution. In: Proceedings of the IEEE/CVF Conference on Computer Vision and Pattern Recognition (CVPR) Workshops, June 2019
15. Chu, X., Zhang, B., Ma, H., Xu, R., Li, Q.: Fast, accurate and lightweight super-resolution with neural architecture search. arXiv preprint arXiv:1901.07261 (2019)
16. Chu, X., Zhang, B., Xu, R.: Multi-objective reinforced evolution in mobile neural architecture search. In: Bartoli, A., Fusiello, A. (eds.) ECCV 2020. LNCS, vol. 12538, pp. 99–113. Springer, Cham (2020). https://doi.org/10.1007/978-3-030-66823-5_6
17. Dai, T., Cai, J., Zhang, Y., Xia, S.T., Zhang, L.: Second-order attention network for single image super-resolution. In: Proceedings of the IEEE/CVF Conference on Computer Vision and Pattern Recognition, pp. 11065–11074 (2019)
18. Dai, X., et al.: ChamNet: towards efficient network design through platform-aware model adaptation. In: Proceedings of the IEEE/CVF Conference on Computer Vision and Pattern Recognition, pp. 11398–11407 (2019)
19. Ding, M., et al.: HR-NAS: searching efficient high-resolution neural architectures with lightweight transformers. In: Proceedings of the IEEE/CVF Conference on Computer Vision and Pattern Recognition (CVPR) (2021)
20. Dong, C., Loy, C.C., He, K., Tang, X.: Learning a deep convolutional network for image super-resolution. In: Fleet, D., Pajdla, T., Schiele, B., Tuytelaars, T. (eds.) ECCV 2014. LNCS, vol. 8692, pp. 184–199. Springer, Cham (2014). https://doi.org/10.1007/978-3-319-10593-2_13
21. Dong, C., Loy, C.C., Tang, X.: Accelerating the super-resolution convolutional neural network. In: Leibe, B., Matas, J., Sebe, N., Welling, M. (eds.) ECCV 2016. LNCS, vol. 9906, pp. 391–407. Springer, Cham (2016). https://doi.org/10.1007/978-3-319-46475-6_25
22. Dong, P., Wang, S., et al.: RTMobile: beyond real-time mobile acceleration of RNNs for speech recognition. arXiv:2002.11474 (2020)
23. Frankle, J., Carbin, M.: The lottery ticket hypothesis: finding sparse, trainable neural networks. ICLR (2018)
24. Freeman, W.T., Jones, T.R., Pasztor, E.C.: Example-based super-resolution. IEEE Comput. Graph. Appl. **22**(2), 56–65 (2002)
25. Gong, Y., et al.: Automatic mapping of the best-suited DNN pruning schemes for real-time mobile acceleration. ACM Trans. Des. Autom. Electron. Syst. (TODAES) **27**(5), 1–26 (2022)
26. Gong, Y., et al.: A privacy-preserving-oriented DNN pruning and mobile acceleration framework. In: Proceedings of the 2020 on Great Lakes Symposium on VLSI, pp. 119–124 (2020)
27. Guan, Y., Liu, N., Zhao, P., Che, Z., Bian, K., Wang, Y., Tang, J.: DAIS: automatic channel pruning via differentiable annealing indicator search (2020)
28. Guo, S., Wang, Y., Li, Q., Yan, J.: DMCP: differentiable Markov channel pruning for neural networks. In: Proceedings of the IEEE/CVF Conference on Computer Vision and Pattern Recognition, pp. 1539–1547 (2020)

29. Han, S., Shen, H., Philipose, M., Agarwal, S., Wolman, A., Krishnamurthy, A.: MCDNN: an approximation-based execution framework for deep stream processing under resource constraints. In: Proceedings of the 14th Annual International Conference on Mobile Systems, Applications, and Services (MobiSys), pp. 123–136, ACM (2016)

30. Han, S., Mao, H., Dally, W.J.: Deep compression: compressing deep neural networks with pruning, trained quantization and Huffman coding. In: International Conference on Learning Representations (ICLR) (2016)

31. He, Y., Zhang, X., Sun, J.: Channel pruning for accelerating very deep neural networks. In: Proceedings of the IEEE International Conference on Computer Vision (ICCV), pp. 1389–1397 (2017)

32. Huang, H., Shen, L., He, C., Dong, W., Huang, H., Shi, G.: Lightweight image super-resolution with hierarchical and differentiable neural architecture search. arXiv preprint arXiv:2105.03939 (2021)

33. Huang, J.B., Singh, A., Ahuja, N.: Single image super-resolution from transformed self-exemplars. In: Proceedings of the IEEE Conference on Computer Vision and Pattern Recognition, pp. 5197–5206 (2015)

34. Hui, Z., Gao, X., Yang, Y., Wang, X.: Lightweight image super-resolution with information multi-distillation network. In: Proceedings of the 27th ACM International Conference on Multimedia, pp. 2024–2032 (2019)

35. Hui, Z., Wang, X., Gao, X.: Fast and accurate single image super-resolution via information distillation network. In: Proceedings of the IEEE Conference on Computer Vision and Pattern Recognition, pp. 723–731 (2018)

36. Huynh, L.N., Lee, Y., Balan, R.K.: DeepMon: Mobile GPU-based deep learning framework for continuous vision applications. In: Proceedings of the 15th Annual International Conference on Mobile Systems, Applications, and Services (MobiSys), pp. 82–95. ACM (2017)

37. Ignatov, A., Timofte, R., Denna, M., Younes, A.: Real-time quantized image super-resolution on mobile NPUs, mobile AI 2021 challenge: report. In: Proceedings of the IEEE/CVF Conference on Computer Vision and Pattern Recognition, pp. 2525–2534 (2021)

38. Irani, M., Peleg, S.: Improving resolution by image registration. CVGIP: Graph. Models Image Process. **53**(3), 231–239 (1991)

39. Jian, T., et al.: Radio frequency fingerprinting on the edge. IEEE Trans. Mob. Comput. **21**, 4078–4093 (2021)

40. Jo, Y., Kim, S.J.: Practical single-image super-resolution using look-up table. In: CVPR (2021)

41. Kim, J., Lee, J.K., Lee, K.M.: Accurate image super-resolution using very deep convolutional networks. In: Proceedings of the IEEE Conference on Computer Vision and Pattern Recognition, pp. 1646–1654 (2016)

42. Lai, W.S., Huang, J.B., Ahuja, N., Yang, M.H.: Deep Laplacian pyramid networks for fast and accurate super-resolution. In: Proceedings of the IEEE Conference on Computer Vision and Pattern Recognition, pp. 624–632 (2017)

43. Lane, N.D., et al.: DeepX: a software accelerator for low-power deep learning inference on mobile devices. In: Proceedings of the 15th International Conference on Information Processing in Sensor Networks, p. 23. IEEE Press (2016)

44. Lee, R., et al.: Journey towards tiny perceptual super-resolution. In: Vedaldi, A., Bischof, H., Brox, T., Frahm, J.-M. (eds.) ECCV 2020. LNCS, vol. 12371, pp. 85–102. Springer, Cham (2020). https://doi.org/10.1007/978-3-030-58574-7_6

45. Lee, R., Venieris, S.I., Dudziak, L., Bhattacharya, S., Lane, N.D.: MobiSR: efficient on-device super-resolution through heterogeneous mobile processors. In: The 25th Annual International Conference on Mobile Computing and Networking, pp. 1–16 (2019)

46. Li, Y., Gu, S., Zhang, K., Van Gool, L., Timofte, R.: DHP: differentiable meta pruning via HyperNetworks. In: Vedaldi, A., Bischof, H., Brox, T., Frahm, J.-M. (eds.) ECCV 2020. LNCS, vol. 12353, pp. 608–624. Springer, Cham (2020). https://doi.org/10.1007/978-3-030-58598-3_36

47. Li, Z., et al.: SS-auto: a single-shot, automatic structured weight pruning framework of DNNs with ultra-high efficiency. arXiv preprint arXiv:2001.08839 (2020)

48. Lim, B., Son, S., Kim, H., Nah, S., Lee, K.M.: Enhanced deep residual networks for single image super-resolution. In: Proceedings of the IEEE Conference on Computer Vision and Pattern Recognition Workshops, pp. 136–144 (2017)

49. Lin, M., et al.: Zen-NAS: a zero-shot NAS for high-performance deep image recognition. In: 2021 IEEE/CVF International Conference on Computer Vision, ICCV 2021 (2021)

50. Liu, C., et al.: Progressive neural architecture search. In: Proceedings of the European Conference on Computer Vision (ECCV), pp. 19–34 (2018)

51. Liu, H., Simonyan, K., Yang, Y.: DARTS: differentiable architecture search. arXiv preprint arXiv:1806.09055 (2018)

52. Liu, H., Lu, Z., Shi, W., Tu, J.: A fast and accurate super-resolution network using progressive residual learning. In: IEEE International Conference on Acoustics, Speech and Signal Processing (ICASSP), pp. 1818–1822. IEEE (2020)

53. Liu, S., et al.: EVSRNet: efficient video super-resolution with neural architecture search. In: 2021 IEEE/CVF Conference on Computer Vision and Pattern Recognition Workshops (CVPRW), pp. 2480–2485 (2021). https://doi.org/10.1109/CVPRW53098.2021.00281

54. Liu, Z., et al.: MetaPruning: meta learning for automatic neural network channel pruning. In: Proceedings of the IEEE/CVF International Conference on Computer Vision, pp. 3296–3305 (2019)

55. Liu, Z.G., Mattina, M.: Learning low-precision neural networks without straight-through estimator (STE). arXiv preprint arXiv:1903.01061 (2019)

56. Luo, X., Xie, Y., Zhang, Y., Qu, Y., Li, C., Fu, Y.: LatticeNet: towards lightweight image super-resolution with lattice block. In: Vedaldi, A., Bischof, H., Brox, T., Frahm, J.-M. (eds.) ECCV 2020. LNCS, vol. 12367, pp. 272–289. Springer, Cham (2020). https://doi.org/10.1007/978-3-030-58542-6_17

57. Ma, X., et al.: BLK-REW: a unified block-based DNN pruning framework using reweighted regularization method. arXiv preprint arXiv:2001.08357 (2020)

58. Mao, H., Han, S., et al.: Exploring the regularity of sparse structure in convolutional neural networks. arXiv:1705.08922 (2017)

59. Martin, D., Fowlkes, C., Tal, D., Malik, J.: A database of human segmented natural images and its application to evaluating segmentation algorithms and measuring ecological statistics. In: Proceedings Eighth IEEE International Conference on Computer Vision. ICCV 2001, vol. 2, pp. 416–423. IEEE (2001)

60. Niu, W., et al.: PatDNN: achieving real-time DNN execution on mobile devices with pattern-based weight pruning. arXiv preprint arXiv:2001.00138 (2020)

61. Real, E., Aggarwal, A., Huang, Y., Le, Q.V.: Regularized evolution for image classifier architecture search. In: Proceedings of the AAAI Conference on Artificial Intelligence, vol. 33, pp. 4780–4789 (2019)

62. Shi, W., Caballero, J., Huszar, F., et al.: Real-time single image and video super-resolution using an efficient sub-pixel convolutional neural network. In: Proceedings of the IEEE Conference on Computer Vision and Pattern Recognition, pp. 1874–1883 (2016)
63. Song, D., Xu, C., Jia, X., Chen, Y., Xu, C., Wang, Y.: Efficient residual dense block search for image super-resolution. In: Proceedings of the AAAI Conference on Artificial Intelligence, vol. 34, pp. 12007–12014 (2020)
64. Tan, M., Le, Q.V.: EfficientNet: rethinking model scaling for convolutional neural networks. arXiv preprint arXiv:1905.11946 (2019)
65. Tanaka, H., Kunin, D., Yamins, D.L., Ganguli, S.: Pruning neural networks without any data by iteratively conserving synaptic flow. arXiv preprint arXiv:2006.05467 (2020)
66. Timofte, R., De Smet, V., Van Gool, L.: Anchored neighborhood regression for fast example-based super-resolution. In: Proceedings of the IEEE International Conference on Computer Vision, pp. 1920–1927 (2013)
67. Timofte, R., De Smet, V., Van Gool, L.: A+: adjusted anchored neighborhood regression for fast super-resolution. In: Cremers, D., Reid, I., Saito, H., Yang, M.-H. (eds.) ACCV 2014. LNCS, vol. 9006, pp. 111–126. Springer, Cham (2015). https://doi.org/10.1007/978-3-319-16817-3_8
68. Vu, T., Van Nguyen, C., Pham, T.X., Luu, T.M., Yoo, C.D.: Fast and efficient image quality enhancement via Desubpixel convolutional neural networks. In: Proceedings of the European Conference on Computer Vision (ECCV) Workshops (2018)
69. Wan, A., et al.: FBNetV2: differentiable neural architecture search for spatial and channel dimensions. In: Proceedings of the IEEE/CVF Conference on Computer Vision and Pattern Recognition, pp. 12965–12974 (2020)
70. Wang, L., et al.: Exploring sparsity in image super-resolution for efficient inference. In: CVPR (2021)
71. Wen, W., Liu, H., Chen, Y., Li, H., Bender, G., Kindermans, P.-J.: Neural predictor for neural architecture search. In: Vedaldi, A., Bischof, H., Brox, T., Frahm, J.-M. (eds.) ECCV 2020. LNCS, vol. 12374, pp. 660–676. Springer, Cham (2020). https://doi.org/10.1007/978-3-030-58526-6_39
72. Wen, W., Wu, C., et al.: Learning structured sparsity in deep neural networks. In: NeurIPS, pp. 2074–2082 (2016)
73. Wu, B., et al.: FBNet: hardware-aware efficient convnet design via differentiable neural architecture search. In: Proceedings of the IEEE Conference on Computer Vision and Pattern Recognition (CVPR), pp. 10734–10742 (2019)
74. Wu, Y., Huang, Z., Kumar, S., Sukthanker, R.S., Timofte, R., Van Gool, L.: Trilevel neural architecture search for efficient single image super-resolution. arXiv preprint arXiv:2101.06658 (2021)
75. Xu, M., Zhu, M., Liu, Y., Lin, F.X., Liu, X.: DeepCache: principled cache for mobile deep vision. In: Proceedings of the 24th Annual International Conference on Mobile Computing and Networking, pp. 129–144. ACM (2018)
76. Yang, J., Wright, J., Huang, T.S., Ma, Y.: Image super-resolution via sparse representation. IEEE Trans. Image Process. **19**(11), 2861–2873 (2010)
77. Yang, T.J., et al.: NetAdapt: platform-aware neural network adaptation for mobile applications. In: Proceedings of the European Conference on Computer Vision (ECCV), pp. 285–300 (2018)
78. Yang, Z., et al.: CARs: continuous evolution for efficient neural architecture search. In: Proceedings of the IEEE/CVF Conference on Computer Vision and Pattern Recognition, pp. 1829–1838 (2020)

79. Yao, S., Hu, S., Zhao, Y., Zhang, A., Abdelzaher, T.: DeepSense: a unified deep learning framework for time-series mobile sensing data processing. In: Proceedings of the 26th International Conference on World Wide Web, pp. 351–360 (2017)
80. Yin, P., Lyu, J., Zhang, S., Osher, S., Qi, Y., Xin, J.: Understanding straight-through estimator in training activation quantized neural nets. arXiv preprint arXiv:1903.05662 (2019)
81. Yu, J., et al.: Wide activation for efficient and accurate image super-resolution. arXiv preprint arXiv:1808.08718 (2018)
82. Yu, J., Huang, T.: Autoslim: towards one-shot architecture search for channel numbers. arXiv preprint arXiv:1903.11728 (2019)
83. Yu, J., Lin, Z., Yang, J., Shen, X., Lu, X., Huang, T.S.: Free-form image inpainting with gated convolution. In: Proceedings of the IEEE/CVF International Conference on Computer Vision (ICCV), October 2019
84. Yuan, G., et al.: MEST: accurate and fast memory-economic sparse training framework on the edge. Adv. Neural Inf. Process. Syst. **34**, 20838–20850 (2021)
85. Zhan, Z., et al.: Achieving on-mobile real-time super-resolution with neural architecture and pruning search. In: ICCV (2021)
86. Zhang, T., et al.: A unified DNN weight pruning framework using reweighted optimization methods. In: 2021 58th ACM/IEEE Design Automation Conference (DAC), pp. 493–498. IEEE (2021)
87. Zhang, Y., Li, K., Li, K., Wang, L., Zhong, B., Fu, Y.: Image super-resolution using very deep residual channel attention networks. In: Proceedings of the European Conference on Computer Vision (ECCV), pp. 286–301 (2018)
88. Zhang, Y., Tian, Y., Kong, Y., Zhong, B., Fu, Y.: Residual dense network for image super-resolution. In: Proceedings of the IEEE Conference on Computer Vision and Pattern Recognition, pp. 2472–2481 (2018)
89. Zhang, Y., Wang, H., Qin, C., Fu, Y.: Aligned structured sparsity learning for efficient image super-resolution. Adv. Neural Inf. Process. Syst. **34**, 2695–2706 (2021)
90. Zhang, Y., Wang, H., Qin, C., Fu, Y.: Learning efficient image super-resolution networks via structure-regularized pruning. In: International Conference on Learning Representations (2021)
91. Zhong, Z., Yan, J., Wu, W., Shao, J., Liu, C.L.: Practical block-wise neural network architecture generation. In: Proceedings of the IEEE Conference on Computer Vision and Pattern Recognition, pp. 2423–2432 (2018)
92. Zhou, D., et al.: EcoNAS: finding proxies for economical neural architecture search. In: Proceedings of the IEEE/CVF Conference on Computer Vision and Pattern Recognition, pp. 11396–11404 (2020)
93. Zoph, B., Le, Q.V.: Neural architecture search with reinforcement learning. In: ICLR (2017)
94. Zoph, B., Vasudevan, V., Shlens, J., Le, Q.V.: Learning transferable architectures for scalable image recognition. In: Proceedings of the IEEE Conference on Computer Vision and Pattern Recognition (CVPR), pp. 8697–8710 (2018)

Modeling Mask Uncertainty in Hyperspectral Image Reconstruction

Jiamian Wang[1(⊠)], Yulun Zhang[2], Xin Yuan[3], Ziyi Meng[4], and Zhiqiang Tao[1]

[1] Department of Computer Science and Engineering, Santa Clara University,
Santa Clara, USA
{jwang16,ztao}@scu.edu
[2] ETH Zürich, Zürich, Switzerland
[3] Westlake University, Hangzhou, China
xyuan@westlake.edu.cn
[4] Kuaishou Technology, Beijing, China

Abstract. Recently, hyperspectral imaging (HSI) has attracted increasing research attention, especially for the ones based on a coded aperture snapshot spectral imaging (CASSI) system. Existing deep HSI reconstruction models are generally trained on paired data to retrieve original signals upon 2D compressed measurements given by a particular optical hardware mask in CASSI, during which the mask largely impacts the reconstruction performance and could work as a "model hyperparameter" governing on data augmentations. This mask-specific training style will lead to a hardware miscalibration issue, which sets up barriers to deploying deep HSI models among different hardware and noisy environments. To address this challenge, we introduce mask uncertainty for HSI with a complete variational Bayesian learning treatment and explicitly model it through a mask decomposition inspired by real hardware. Specifically, we propose a novel Graph-based Self-Tuning (GST) network to reason uncertainties adapting to varying spatial structures of masks among different hardware. Moreover, we develop a bilevel optimization framework to balance HSI reconstruction and uncertainty estimation, accounting for the hyperparameter property of masks. Extensive experimental results validate the effectiveness (over 33/30 dB) of the proposed method under two miscalibration scenarios and demonstrate a highly competitive performance compared with the state-of-the-art well-calibrated methods. Our source code and pre-trained models are available at https://github.com/Jiamian-Wang/mask_uncertainty_spectral_SCI

1 Introduction

Hyperspectral imaging (HSI) provides richer signals than the traditional RGB vision and has broad applications across agriculture [28,30], remote sensing [54,59], medical imaging [17,29], etc. Various HSI systems have been built

---

Supplementary Information The online version contains supplementary material available at https://doi.org/10.1007/978-3-031-19800-7_7.

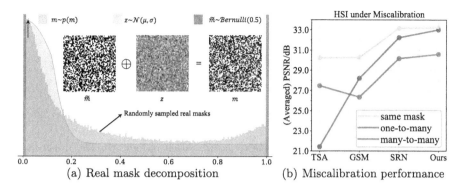

(a) Real mask decomposition   (b) Miscalibration performance

Fig. 1. (a) A real mask $m \sim p(m)$ can be decomposed into an unknown clean mask $\tilde{m}$ plus random noise z. The mask distribution is plotted by realistic hardware mask values. Note that the distributions are demonstrated in a `symlog` scale. (b) Performance comparison under three different settings, including 1) the same mask for training/testing, 2) training on one mask and testing on multiple masks (one-to-many), and 3) training with random masks and testing on a held-out mask set (many-to-many).

and studied in recent years, among which, the coded aperture snapshot spectral imaging (CASSI) system [11,52] stands out due to its passive modulation property and has attracted increasing research attentions [16,27,34,36,47,50,55] in the computer vision community. The CASSI system adopts a hardware encoding & software decoding schema. It first utilizes an optical hardware mask to compress hyperspectral signals into a 2D measurement and then develops software algorithms to retrieve original signals upon the coded measurement conditioning on one particular mask used in the system. Therefore, the hardware mask generally plays a key role in reconstructing hyperspectral images and may exhibit a strongly-coupled (*one-to-one*) relationship with its reconstruction model.

While deep HSI networks [16,34,44,46,56] have shown a promising performance on high-fidelity reconstruction and real-time inference, they mainly treat the hardware mask as a fixed "model hyperparameter" (governing data augmentations on the compressed measurements) and train the reconstruction network on the paired hyperspectral images and measurements given the same mask. Empirically, this will cause a **hardware miscalibration** issue – the mask used in the pre-trained model is mismatched with the real captured measurement, when 1) deploying a single deep network among arbitrary uncalibrated hardware systems of different masks, or 2) having distinct responses of the same mask due to the fabrication errors. As shown in Fig. 1, the performance of deep reconstruction networks pre-trained with one specific mask will badly degrade when applied to multiple unseen masks (*one-to-many*). Rather than re-training models on each new mask, which is inflexible for practical usage, we are more interested in training a single model that could adapt to different hardware by exploring and exploiting uncertainties among masks.

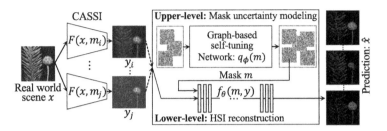

Fig. 2. Illustration of the proposed bilevel optimization framework. The upper-level models the mask uncertainty by approximating a mask posterior distribution, and the lower-level adopts a reconstruction network $f_\theta(m, y)$ which takes masks as hyperparameters. Our model could be applied in multiple CASSIs using different masks.

One possible solution is to train a deep network over multiple CASSI systems, *i.e.*, using multiple masks and their corresponding encoded measurements following the deep ensemble [23] strategy. However, due to the distinct spatial patterns of each mask and its hyperparameter property, directly training the network with randomly sampled masks still cannot achieve a well-calibrated performance and sometimes performs even worse, *e.g.*, *many-to-many* of TSA-Net [34] in Fig. 1. Hence, we delve into one possible mask decomposition observed from the real hardware, which treats a mask as the unknown clean one plus random noise like Gaussian (see Fig. 1). We consider the noise stemming from two practical sources: 1) the hardware fabrication in real CASSI systems and 2) the functional mask values caused by different lighting environments. Notably, rather than modeling the entire mask distribution, which is challenging due to the high-dimensionality of a 2D map, we explicitly model the mask uncertainty as Gaussian noise centering around a given mask through its decomposition and resort to learn *self-tuning variances* adapting to different mask spatial patterns.

In this study, we propose a novel Graph-based Self-Tuning (GST) network to model mask uncertainty upon variational Bayesian learning and hyperparameter optimization techniques. On the one hand, we approximate the mask posterior distribution with variational inference under the given prior from real mask values, leading to a smoother mask distribution with smaller variance supported by empirical evidence. On the other hand, we leverage graph convolution neural networks to instantiate a stochastic encoder to reason uncertainties varying to different spatial structures of masks. Moreover, we develop a bilevel optimization framework (Fig. 2) to balance the HSI reconstruction performance and the mask uncertainty estimation, accounting for the high sensitive network responses to the mask changes. We summarize the contributions of this work as follows.

– We introduce *mask uncertainty* for CASSI to calibrate a single deep reconstruction network applying in multiple hardware, which brings a promising research direction to improve the robustness and flexibility of deploying CASSI systems to retrieve hyperspectral signals in real-world applications.

To our best knowledge, this is the first work to explicitly explore and model mask uncertainty in the HSI reconstruction problem.

– A complete variational Bayesian learning framework has been provided to approximate the mask posterior distribution based on a mask decomposition inspired by real hardware mask observations. Moreover, we design and develop a bilevel optimization framework (see Fig. 2) to jointly achieve high-fidelity HSI reconstruction and mask uncertainty estimation.

– We propose a novel Graph-based Self-Tuning (GST) network to automatically capture uncertainties varying to different spatial structures of 2D masks, leading to a smoother mask distribution over real samples and working as an effective data augmentation method.

– Extensive experimental results on both simulation and real data demonstrate the effectiveness (over 33/30 dB) of our approach under two miscalibration cases. Our method also shows a highly competitive performance compared with state-of-the-art methods under the traditional well-calibrated setting.

2   Related Work

Recently, many advanced algorithms have been designed from diverse perspectives to reconstruct the HSI data from measurements encoded by CASSI system. Among them, the optimization-based methods solve the problem by introducing different priors, *e.g.*, GPSR [7], TwIST [2] GAP-TV [51], and DeSCI [27]. Another mainstream direction is to empower optimization-based method by deep learning. For example, deep unfolding methods [13,31,45] and Plug-and-Play (PnP) structures [36,38,39,53] have been raised. Despite their interpretability and robustness to masks to a certain degree, they may suffer from low efficiency and unstable convergence. Besides, a number of deep reconstruction networks [4,15,16,25,34,35,37,44] have been proposed for HSI, yielding the state-of-the-art performance with high inference efficiency. For instances, TSA-Net [34] retrieves hyperspectral images through modeling spatial and spectral attentions. SRN [44] provides a lightweight reconstruction backbone based on nested residual learning. More recently, a Gaussian Scale Mixture (GSM) based method [16] shows robustness on masks by enabling an approximation on multiple sensing matrices. However, all the above pre-trained networks perform unsatisfactorily on distinct unseen masks, raising the question of how to deploy a single reconstruction network among different hardware systems.

Previous works mainly consider mask calibration from a hardware perspective. For example, a high-order model [1] is proposed to calibrate masks with a single fixed wavelength for various wavelengths adaptation, enabling a band-limited signal approximation. One recent work [41] proposes to calibrate the point-spread-function upon existing CASSI setups for better quality. Yet, the impact of software (reconstruction model) has been barely considered in the mask calibration process. In this work, we calibrate a single deep reconstruction network to adapt to different real masks (hardware systems) by estimating mask uncertainties with a Bayesian variational approach. Popular uncertainty estimation methods include 1) Bayesian neural networks (BNN) [3,10,32] and 2) deep

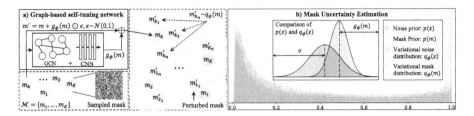

Fig. 3. Illustration of modeling mask uncertainty with the proposed Graph-based Self-Tuning (GST) network. a) GST takes as input a real mask m_k randomly sampled from different hardware masks $\mathcal{M}$ and obtains perturbed masks m'_{k_n} by learning self-tuning variance centering on m_k. b) GST estimates mask uncertainty by approximating the mask posterior with a variational distribution $q_\phi(m)$, leading to a smoother mask distribution over the mask prior $p(m)$. More discussions are given in Sect. 4.2.

ensemble [8, 23, 26]. The former usually approximates the weight posterior distribution by using variational inference [3] or MC-dropout [10], while the latter generally trains a group of networks from random weight initializations. However, it is challenging to directly quantify mask uncertainty via BNNs or deep ensemble, since treating masks as model weights contraries to their hyperparameter properties. The proposed method solves this challenge by marrying uncertainty estimation to hyperparameter optimization in a bilevel framework [33, 42, 58].

3   Methodology

3.1   Preliminaries

HSI Reconstruction. The reconstruction based on the CASSI system [34, 52] generally includes a hardware-encoding forward process and a software-decoding inverse process. Let x be a 3D hyperspectral image with the size of $H \times W \times \Lambda$, where H, W, and Λ represent the height, width, and the number of spectral channels. The optical hardware encoder will compress the datacube x into a 2D measurement y upon a fixed physical mask m. The forward model of CASSI is

$$y = F(x; m) = \sum_\lambda^\Lambda \mathtt{shift}(x)_\lambda \odot \mathtt{shift}(m)_\lambda + \zeta, \tag{1}$$

where λ refers to a spectral channel, $\odot$ represents the element-wise product, and ζ denotes the measurement noise. The shift operation is implemented by a single disperser as $\mathtt{shift}(x)(u, v, i) = x(h, w + d(i - \lambda), i)$. In essence, the measurement y is captured by spectral modulation[1] conditioning on the hardware mask m.

In the inverse process, we adopt a deep reconstruction network as the decoder: $\widehat{x} = f_\theta(m, y)$ where $\widehat{x}$ is the retrieved hyperspectral image, and θ represents all the learnable parameters. Let $\mathcal{D} = \{(x_i, y_i)\}_{i=1}^N$ be the dataset. The reconstruction network f_θ is generally trained to minimize an ℓ_1 or ℓ_2 loss as the following:

---

[1] We used a two-pixel shift for neighbored spectral channels following [34, 44]. More details about spectral modulation could be found in [52].

$$\min_{\theta} \sum_{x,y \in \mathcal{D}} \ell(f_\theta(m,y) - x) \quad \text{where} \quad y = F(x;m). \tag{2}$$

We instantiate f_θ as a recent HSI backbone model provided in [44], which benefits from nested residual learning and spatial/spectral-invariant learning. We employ this backbone for its lightweight structure to simplify the training.

Hardware Miscalibration. As shown in Eq. (2), there is a *paired relationship* between the parameter θ and mask m in deep HSI models. Thus, for different CASSI systems (i.e., distinct masks), multiple pairs $\{m_1; \theta_1\}, ..., \{m_K; \theta_K\}$ are expected for previous works. Empirically, the miscalibration between m and θ will lead to obvious performance degradation. This miscalibration issue inevitably impairs the flexibility and robustness of deploying deep HSI models across real systems, considering the expensive training time and various noises existing in hardware. To alleviate such a problem, one straight-forward solution is to train the model f_θ with multiple masks, i.e., $\mathcal{M} = \{m_1, ..., m_K\}$, falling in a similar strategy to deep ensemble [23]. However, directly training a single network with random masks cannot provide satisfactory performance to unseen masks (see Sect. 4), since the lack of explicitly exploring the relationship between uncertainties and different mask structures.

3.2   Mask Uncertainty

Modeling mask uncertainty is challenging due to the high dimensionality of a 2D mask, limited mask set size (*i.e.*, K for $\mathcal{M}$), and the varying spatial structures among masks. In this section, we first estimate uncertainties around each mask through one possible mask decomposition, and then we adapt the mask uncertainty to the change of mask structures with a self-tuning network in Sect. 3.3.

Inspired by the distribution of real mask values (Fig. 1 and Fig. 3), which renders two peaks at 0 and 1 and appears a Gaussian shape spreading over the middle, we decompose a mask as two components:

$$m = \tilde{m} + z, \tag{3}$$

where we assume each pixel in z follows a Gaussian distribution. For simplicity, we slightly abuse the notations by denoting the noise prior as $p(z) = \mathcal{N}(\mu, \sigma)$. The $\tilde{m}$ denotes the underlying clean binary mask with a specific spatial structure.

We estimate the mask uncertainty by approximating the mask posterior $p(m|X, Y)$ following [3,9,49], where $X = \{x_1, ..., x_N\}$ and $Y = \{y_1, ..., y_N\}$ indicate hyperspectral images and their corresponding measurements. To this end, we aim to learn a variational distribution $q_\phi(m)$ parameterized by ϕ to minimize the KL-divergence between $q_\phi(m)$ and $p(m|X, Y)$, $\min_\phi KL[q_\phi(m)||p(m|X, Y)]$, equivalent to maximizing the evidence lower bound (ELBO) [14,21] as

$$\max_{\phi} \underbrace{\mathbb{E}_{q_\phi(m)}[\log p(X|Y, m)]}_{\text{reconstruction}} - \underbrace{KL[q_\phi(m)||p(m)]}_{\text{regularization}}, \tag{4}$$

where the first term measures the reconstruction (i.e., reconstructing the observations X based on the measurements Y and mask m via $f_\theta(m, y)$), and the second term regularizes $q_\phi(m)$ given the mask prior $p(m)$. Following the mask decomposition in (3), we treat the clean mask $\tilde{m}$ as a 2D constant and focus on mask uncertainties arising from the noise z. Thus, the variational distribution $q_\phi(m)$ is defined as a Gaussian distribution centering on a given $m \in \mathcal{M}$ by

$$q_\phi(m) = \mathcal{N}(m, g_\phi(m)), \tag{5}$$

where $g_\phi(m)$ learns *self-tuning variance* to model the uncertainty adapting to real masks sampled from $\mathcal{M}$. Correspondingly, the underlying variational noise distribution $q_\phi(z)$ follows Gaussian distribution with variance $g_\phi(m)$. We adopt the reparameterization trick [21] for computing stochastic gradients for the expectation w.r.t $q_\phi(m)$. Specifically, let $m' \sim q_\phi(m)$ be a random variable sampled from the variational distribution, we have

$$m' = t(\phi, \epsilon) = m + g_\phi(m) \odot \epsilon, \quad \epsilon \sim \mathcal{N}(0, 1). \tag{6}$$

Notably, we clamp all the pixel values of m' in range $[0, 1]$.

The first term in Eq. (4) reconstructs x with $p(x|y, m) \propto p(x|\hat{x} = f_\theta(m, y))$, yielding a squared error when $x|\hat{x}$ follows a Gaussian distribution [43]. Similar to AutoEncoders, we implement the negative log-likelihood $\mathbb{E}_{q_\phi(m)}[-\log p(X|Y, m)]$ as a ℓ_2 loss and compute its Monte Carlo estimates with Eq. (6) as

$$\ell(\phi, \theta; \mathcal{D}) = \frac{N}{B} \sum_{i=1}^{B} \| f_\theta(y_i, t(\phi, \epsilon_i)) - x_i \|^2, \tag{7}$$

where $(x_i, y_i) \in \mathcal{D}$, B denotes the mini-batch size, and $t(\phi, \epsilon_i)$ represents the i-th sample from $q_\phi(m)$. We leverage $t(\phi, \epsilon_i)$ to sample B perturbed masks from $q_\phi(m)$ centering on one randomly sampled mask $m \in \mathcal{M}$ per batch.

Since $p(m)$ is unknown due to various spatial structures of masks, we resort to approximating the KL term in Eq. (4) with the entropy of $q_\phi(m)$. Eventually, we implement the $\mathrm{ELBO}(q(m))$ with the following loss:

$$\mathcal{L}(\phi, \theta; \mathcal{D}) = \ell(\phi, \theta; \mathcal{D}) + \beta \mathbb{H}[\log q_\phi(m)], \tag{8}$$

where $\mathbb{H}[\log q_\phi(m)]$ is computed by $\ln(g_\phi(m)\sqrt{2\pi e})$ and $\beta > 0$ interprets the objective function between variational inference and variational optimization [19,33].

3.3 Graph-Based Self-tuning Network

We propose a graph-based self-tuning (GST) network to instantiate the variance model $g_\phi(m)$ in Eq. (5), which captures uncertainties around each mask and leads to a smoother mask distribution over real masks (see Fig. 3). The key of handling unseen masks (new hardware) is to learn how the distribution will change along with the varying spatial structures of masks. To this end, we implement the GST as a visual reasoning attention network [5,24,57]. It firstly computes pixel-wise correlations (visual reasoning) based on neural embeddings and then generates

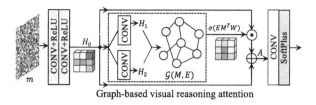

Graph-based visual reasoning attention

Fig. 4. Structure of Graph-based Self-Tuning (GST) network. The model takes mask m as input and outputs a 2D variance map, globally handling mask in a graph domain.

attention scores based on graph convolutional networks (GCN) [22,40]. Unlike previous works [5,24,57], the proposed GST model is tailored for building a stochastic probabilistic encoder to capture the mask distribution.

We show the network structure of GST in Fig. 4. Given a real mask m, GST produces neural embedding H_0 by using two concatenated CONV-ReLU blocks. Then, we employ two CONV layers to convert H_0 into two different embeddings H_1 and H_2, and generate a graph representation by matrix multiplication $H_1^T H_2$, resulting in $\mathcal{G}(M, E)$, where the node matrix M represents mask pixels and the edge matrix E denotes the pixel-wise correlations. Let W be the weight matrix of GCN. We obtain an enhanced attention cube by pixel-wise multiplication

$$A = H_0 \odot (\sigma(EM^TW) + \mathbf{1}), \tag{9}$$

where σ is the sigmoid function. Finally, the self-tuning variance is obtained by

$$g_\phi(m) = \delta(\text{CONV}(A)), \tag{10}$$

where δ denotes the softplus function and ϕ denotes all the learnable parameters. Consequently, GST enables adaptive variance modeling to multiple real masks.

3.4 Bilevel Optimization

While it is possible to jointly train the HSI reconstruction network f_θ and the self-tuning network g_ϕ using the Eq. (8), it is more proper to formulate the training of these two networks as a bilevel optimization problem accounting for the hyperparameter properties of masks. Deep HSI methods [34,44] usually employ a single mask and

---
Algorithm 1: GST Training Algorithm

Input: $\mathcal{D}^{trn}, \mathcal{D}^{val}, \mathcal{M}$; initialized θ, ϕ;
Output: θ^*, ϕ^*
1   Pre-train $f_\theta(\cdot)$ on $\mathcal{D}^{trn}$ with α_0 for T^{init} epochs;
2   **while** *not converge* **do**
3   **for** $t = 1, ..., T^{trn}$ **do**
4       $\{(x_i, y_i)\}_{i=1}^{B} \sim \mathcal{D}^{trn}$;
5       $\theta \leftarrow \theta - \alpha_1 \frac{\partial}{\partial\theta}\ell(\phi, \theta; \mathcal{D}^{trn})$;
6   **end**
7   **for** $t = 1, ..., T^{val}$ **do**
8       $\{(x_i, y_i)\}_{i=1}^{B} \sim \mathcal{D}^{val}, m \sim \mathcal{M}, \epsilon \sim \mathcal{N}(0,1)$;
9       $\phi \leftarrow \phi - \alpha_2 \frac{\partial}{\partial\phi}\mathcal{L}(\phi, \theta; \mathcal{D}^{val})$;
10   **end**
11 **end**

---

shifting operations to lift the 2D measurements as multi-channel inputs, where the mask works as a hyperparameter similar to the data augmentation purpose. Thus, the reconstruction network is highly-sensitive to the change/perturbation of masks (model weight θ is largely subject to a mask m).

To be specific, we define the lower-level problem as HSI reconstruction and the upper-level problem as mask uncertainty estimation, and propose the final objective function of our GST model as the following:

$$\min_{\phi} \mathcal{L}(\phi, \theta^*; \mathcal{D}^{val}) \quad \text{s.t.} \quad \theta^* = \arg\min_{\theta} \ell(\phi, \theta; \mathcal{D}^{trn}), \tag{11}$$

where $\ell(\phi, \theta; \mathcal{D}^{trn})$ is provided in Eq. (7) with a training set and $\mathcal{L}(\phi, \theta^*; \mathcal{D}^{val})$ is given by Eq. (8) in a validation set. Upon Eq. (11), f_θ and g_ϕ are alternatively updated by computing gradients $\frac{\partial l}{\partial \theta}$ and $\frac{\partial \mathcal{L}}{\partial \phi}$. To better initialize the parameter θ, we pre-train the reconstruction network $f_\theta(m, y)$ for several epochs. The entire training procedure of the proposed method is summarized in Algorithm 1. Notably, introducing Eq. (11) brings two benefits. 1) It could balance the solutions of HSI reconstruction and mask uncertainty estimation. 2) It enables the proposed GST as a hyperparameter optimization method, which could provide high-fidelity reconstruction even working on a single mask (see Table 3).

4   Experiments

Simulation Data. We adopt the training set provided in [34]. Simulated measurements are obtained by mimicking the compressing process of SD-CASSI system [34]. For metric and perceptual comparisons, we employ a benchmark test set that contains ten $256 \times 256 \times 28$ hyperspectral images following [16,36,44]. We build a validation set by splitting 40 hyperspectral images from the training set.

Real Data. We adopt five real 660×714 measurements provided in [34] for the qualitative evaluation. We train the model on the expanded simulation training set by augmenting 37 HSIs originating from the KAIST dataset [6]. Also, the Gaussian noise ($\mathcal{N}(0, \varphi), \varphi \sim U[0, 0.05]$) is added on the simulated measurements during training, for the sake of mimicking practical measurement noise ζ. All the other settings are kept the same as the compared deep reconstruction methods.

Mask Set. We adopt two 660×660 hardware masks in our experiment. Both are produced by the same fabrication process. For the training, the mask set $\mathcal{M}$ is created by randomly cropping (256×256) from the mask provided in [34]. For the testing, both masks are applied. In simulation, testing masks are differentiated from the training ones. For real HSI reconstruction, the second mask [35] is applied, indicating a hardware miscalibration scenario.

Implementation Details. The training procedures (Algorithm 1) for simulation and real case follow the same schedule: We apply the `xavier uniform` [12] initializer with `gain=1`. Before alternating, the reconstruction network is trained for T^{init}=20 epochs (learning rate α_0=4× 10^{-4}). Then, the reconstruction network $f_\theta(\cdot)$ is updated on training phase for T^{trn}=5 epochs (α_1=4× 10^{-4}) and the GST network is updated on validation phase for T^{val}=3 epochs (α_2=1× 10^{-5}). The learning rates are halved per 50 epochs and we adopt Adam optimizer [20] with the default setting. In this work, we adopt SRN (`v1`) [44] as the reconstructive backbone, i.e., the full network without rescaling pairs. All the experiments were conducted on four NVIDIA GeForce GTX 3090 GPUs.

Compared Methods. For hardware miscalibration, masks for data pair setup (i.e., CASSI compressing procedure) and network training should be different from those for testing. We specifically consider two scenarios: 1) many-to-many, i.e., training the model on mask set $\mathcal{M}$ and testing it by unseen masks; 2) One-to-many, i.e., training the model on single mask and testing it by diverse unseen masks, which brings more challenges. For quantitative performance comparison, in this work all the testing results are computed upon 100 testing trials (100 random unseen masks). We compare with four state-of-the-art methods: TSA-Net [34], GSM-based method [16], SRN [44], and PnP-DIP [36], among which the first three are deep networks and the last one is an iterative optimization-based method. Note that 1) PnP-DIP is a self-supervised method. We test it by feeding the data encoded by different masks in the testing mask set and compute the performance over all obtained results. 2) For real-world HSI reconstruction, all models are trained on the same mask while tested on the other. Specifically, the network inputs are initialized by testing mask for TSA-Net and SRN. For

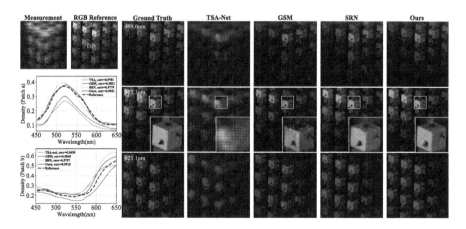

Fig. 5. Reconstruction results on one simulation scene under hardware miscalibration (many-to-many). All methods are trained on the mask set $\mathcal{M}$ and tested by one unseen mask. Density curves computed on chosen patches are compared to analysis the spectra.

GSM, as demonstrated by the authors, we directly compute the sensing matrix of testing mask and replace the corresponding approximation in the network. We use PSNR and SSIM [48] as metrics for quantitative comparison.

4.1 HSI Reconstruction Performance

We evaluate our method under different settings on both simulation and real data. More visualizations and analyses are provided in the supplementary.

Miscalibration (Many-to-Many). Training the deep reconstruction networks with a mask ensemble strategy could improve the generalization ability, such as training TSA-Net, GSM, and SRN on a mask set. However, as shown in Table 1 and Table 3, these methods generally suffer from a clear performance degradation under miscalibration compared with their well-calibrated performance. Benefiting from modeling mask uncertainty, our approach achieves high-fidelity results (over 33 dB) on both cases, with only a 0.2 dB drop. As shown in Fig. 5, our method retrieves more details at different spectral channels.

Miscalibration (One-To-Many). In Table 2, all the methods are trained on a single mask and tested on multiple unseen masks. We pose this setting to further demonstrate the hardware miscalibration challenge. Except for the mask-free method PnP-DIP, the others usually experience large performance descent compared with those in Table 1. This observation supports the motivation of modeling mask uncertainty – 1) simply using mask ensemble may aggravate the miscalibration (TSA-Net using ensemble performs even worse) and 2) the model trained with a single mask cannot be effectively deployed in different hardware.

Table 1. PSNR(dB)/SSIM by different methods on 10 simulation scenes under the **many-to-many** hardware miscalibration. All the methods are trained with a mask set $\mathcal{M}$ and tested by random unseen masks. TSA-Net [34], GSM [16], and SRN [44] are obtained with a mask ensemble strategy. We report $\mathbf{mean_{\pm std}}$ among 100 testing trials.

Scene	TSA-Net [34]		GSM [16]		PnP-DIP[†] [36]		SRN [44]		GST (Ours)	
	PSNR	SSIM	PSNR	SSIM	PSNR	SSIM	PSNR	SSIM	PSNR	SSIM
1	$23.45_{\pm0.29}$	$0.6569_{\pm0.0051}$	$31.38_{\pm0.20}$	$0.8826_{\pm0.0032}$	$29.24_{\pm0.98}$	$0.7964_{\pm0.0532}$	$33.26_{\pm0.16}$	$0.9104_{\pm0.0018}$	$\mathbf{33.99}_{\pm0.14}$	$\mathbf{0.9258}_{\pm0.0013}$
2	$18.52_{\pm0.12}$	$0.5511_{\pm0.0049}$	$25.94_{\pm0.22}$	$0.8570_{\pm0.0041}$	$25.73_{\pm0.54}$	$0.7558_{\pm0.0117}$	$29.86_{\pm0.23}$	$0.8809_{\pm0.0029}$	$\mathbf{30.49}_{\pm0.17}$	$\mathbf{0.9002}_{\pm0.0022}$
3	$18.42_{\pm0.30}$	$0.5929_{\pm0.0127}$	$26.11_{\pm0.20}$	$0.8874_{\pm0.0034}$	$29.61_{\pm0.45}$	$0.8541_{\pm0.0125}$	$31.69_{\pm0.20}$	$0.9093_{\pm0.0020}$	$\mathbf{32.63}_{\pm0.16}$	$\mathbf{0.9212}_{\pm0.0013}$
4	$30.44_{\pm0.15}$	$0.8940_{\pm0.0043}$	$34.72_{\pm0.35}$	$0.9473_{\pm0.0023}$	$38.21_{\pm0.66}$	$0.9280_{\pm0.0078}$	$39.90_{\pm0.22}$	$0.9469_{\pm0.0012}$	$\mathbf{41.04}_{\pm0.23}$	$\mathbf{0.9667}_{\pm0.0014}$
5	$20.89_{\pm0.23}$	$0.5648_{\pm0.0077}$	$26.15_{\pm0.24}$	$0.8256_{\pm0.0061}$	$28.59_{\pm0.79}$	$0.8481_{\pm0.0183}$	$30.86_{\pm0.16}$	$0.9232_{\pm0.0019}$	$\mathbf{31.49}_{\pm0.17}$	$\mathbf{0.9379}_{\pm0.0017}$
6	$23.04_{\pm0.19}$	$0.6099_{\pm0.0060}$	$30.97_{\pm0.29}$	$0.9224_{\pm0.0025}$	$29.70_{\pm0.51}$	$0.8484_{\pm0.0186}$	$34.20_{\pm0.23}$	$0.9405_{\pm0.0014}$	$\mathbf{34.89}_{\pm0.29}$	$\mathbf{0.9545}_{\pm0.0009}$
7	$15.97_{\pm0.14}$	$0.6260_{\pm0.0042}$	$22.58_{\pm0.24}$	$0.8459_{\pm0.0054}$	$27.13_{\pm0.31}$	$0.8666_{\pm0.0079}$	$27.27_{\pm0.16}$	$0.8515_{\pm0.0026}$	$\mathbf{27.63}_{\pm0.16}$	$\mathbf{0.8658}_{\pm0.0024}$
8	$22.64_{\pm0.18}$	$0.6366_{\pm0.0066}$	$29.76_{\pm0.22}$	$0.9059_{\pm0.0021}$	$28.38_{\pm0.35}$	$0.8325_{\pm0.0203}$	$32.35_{\pm0.22}$	$0.9320_{\pm0.0015}$	$\mathbf{33.02}_{\pm0.26}$	$\mathbf{0.9471}_{\pm0.0013}$
9	$18.91_{\pm0.11}$	$0.5946_{\pm0.0083}$	$27.23_{\pm0.11}$	$0.8899_{\pm0.0021}$	$33.63_{\pm0.26}$	$0.8779_{\pm0.0073}$	$32.83_{\pm0.13}$	$0.9205_{\pm0.0016}$	$\mathbf{33.45}_{\pm0.13}$	$\mathbf{0.9317}_{\pm0.0013}$
10	$21.90_{\pm0.18}$	$0.5249_{\pm0.0110}$	$28.05_{\pm0.21}$	$0.8877_{\pm0.0055}$	$27.24_{\pm0.43}$	$0.7957_{\pm0.0226}$	$30.25_{\pm0.14}$	$0.9053_{\pm0.0019}$	$\mathbf{31.49}_{\pm0.15}$	$\mathbf{0.9345}_{\pm0.0015}$
Avg.	$21.42_{\pm0.07}$	$0.6162_{\pm0.0030}$	$28.20_{\pm0.01}$	$0.8852_{\pm0.0001}$	$29.66_{\pm0.38}$	$0.8375_{\pm0.0093}$	$32.24_{\pm0.10}$	$0.9121_{\pm0.0010}$	$\mathbf{33.02}_{\pm0.01}$	$\mathbf{0.9285}_{\pm0.0001}$

[†]PnP-DIP is a mask-free method which reconstructs from measurements encoded by random masks.

Table 2. PSNR(dB)/SSIM by different methods on 10 simulation scenes under the **one-to-many** hardware miscalibration. All the methods are trained by a single mask and tested by random unseen masks. We report $\text{mean}_{\pm\text{std}}$ among 100 testing trials.

Scene	TSA-Net [34]		GSM [16]		PnP-DIP† [36]		SRN [44]		GST (Ours)	
	PSNR	SSIM	PSNR	SSIM	PSNR	SSIM	PSNR	SSIM	PSNR	SSIM
1	$28.49_{\pm0.58}$	$0.8520_{\pm0.0081}$	$28.20_{\pm0.95}$	$0.8553_{\pm0.0185}$	$29.24_{\pm0.98}$	$0.7964_{\pm0.0532}$	$31.24_{\pm0.77}$	$0.8878_{\pm0.0117}$	$\mathbf{31.72}_{\pm0.76}$	$\mathbf{0.8939}_{\pm0.0119}$
2	$24.96_{\pm0.51}$	$0.8332_{\pm0.0064}$	$24.46_{\pm0.96}$	$0.8330_{\pm0.0189}$	$25.73_{\pm0.54}$	$0.7558_{\pm0.0117}$	$27.87_{\pm0.82}$	$0.8535_{\pm0.0131}$	$\mathbf{28.22}_{\pm0.85}$	$\mathbf{0.8552}_{\pm0.0144}$
3	$26.14_{\pm0.76}$	$0.8829_{\pm0.0108}$	$23.71_{\pm1.18}$	$0.8077_{\pm0.0221}$	$29.61_{\pm0.45}$	$0.8541_{\pm0.0125}$	$28.31_{\pm0.88}$	$0.8415_{\pm0.0213}$	$28.77_{\pm1.13}$	$0.8405_{\pm0.0257}$
4	$35.67_{\pm0.47}$	$0.9427_{\pm0.0028}$	$31.55_{\pm0.75}$	$0.9385_{\pm0.0074}$	$38.21_{\pm0.66}$	$0.9280_{\pm0.0078}$	$\mathbf{37.93}_{\pm0.72}$	$\mathbf{0.9476}_{\pm0.0057}$	$37.60_{\pm0.81}$	$0.9447_{\pm0.0071}$
5	$25.40_{\pm0.59}$	$0.8280_{\pm0.0108}$	$24.44_{\pm0.96}$	$0.7744_{\pm0.0291}$	$28.59_{\pm0.79}$	$0.8481_{\pm0.0183}$	$27.99_{\pm0.79}$	$0.8680_{\pm0.0194}$	$28.58_{\pm0.79}$	$\mathbf{0.8746}_{\pm0.0208}$
6	$29.32_{\pm0.60}$	$0.8796_{\pm0.0047}$	$28.28_{\pm0.92}$	$0.9026_{\pm0.0094}$	$29.70_{\pm0.51}$	$0.8484_{\pm0.0186}$	$32.13_{\pm0.87}$	$\mathbf{0.9344}_{\pm0.0061}$	$\mathbf{32.72}_{\pm0.79}$	$0.9339_{\pm0.0061}$
7	$22.80_{\pm0.65}$	$0.8461_{\pm0.0101}$	$21.45_{\pm0.79}$	$0.8147_{\pm0.0162}$	$27.13_{\pm0.31}$	$0.8666_{\pm0.0079}$	$24.84_{\pm0.73}$	$0.7973_{\pm0.0150}$	$\mathbf{25.15}_{\pm0.76}$	$0.7935_{\pm0.0173}$
8	$28.09_{\pm0.43}$	$0.8738_{\pm0.0043}$	$28.08_{\pm0.76}$	$0.9024_{\pm0.0089}$	$28.38_{\pm0.35}$	$0.8325_{\pm0.0203}$	$31.32_{\pm0.59}$	$0.9324_{\pm0.0043}$	$\mathbf{31.84}_{\pm0.56}$	$\mathbf{0.9323}_{\pm0.0042}$
9	$27.75_{\pm0.55}$	$0.8865_{\pm0.0054}$	$26.80_{\pm0.78}$	$0.8773_{\pm0.0144}$	$33.63_{\pm0.26}$	$0.8779_{\pm0.0073}$	$31.06_{\pm0.66}$	$0.8997_{\pm0.0091}$	$31.11_{\pm0.72}$	$\mathbf{0.8988}_{\pm0.0104}$
10	$26.05_{\pm0.48}$	$0.8114_{\pm0.0072}$	$26.40_{\pm0.77}$	$0.8771_{\pm0.0124}$	$27.24_{\pm0.43}$	$0.7957_{\pm0.0226}$	$29.01_{\pm0.61}$	$0.9028_{\pm0.0092}$	$\mathbf{29.50}_{\pm0.68}$	$\mathbf{0.9030}_{\pm0.0098}$
Avg.	$27.47_{\pm0.46}$	$0.8636_{\pm0.0060}$	$26.34_{\pm0.06}$	$0.8582_{\pm0.0012}$	$29.66_{\pm0.38}$	$0.8375_{\pm0.0093}$	$30.17_{\pm0.63}$	$0.8865_{\pm0.0108}$	$\mathbf{30.60}_{\pm0.08}$	$\mathbf{0.8881}_{\pm0.0013}$

†PnP-DIP is a mask-free method which reconstructs from measurements encoded by random masks.

Same Mask (One-to-One). Table 3 reports the well-calibrated performance for all the methods, *i.e.*, training/testing models on the same real mask. While our approach is specially designed for training with multiple masks, it still consistently outperforms all the competitors by leveraging a bilevel optimization.

Results on Real Data. Figure 6 visualizes reconstruction results on the real dataset, where the *left* corresponds to the same mask and the *right* is under the one-to-many setting. For the same mask, the proposed method is supposed to perform comparably. For the one-to-many, we train all the models on a single real mask provided in [34] and test them on the other one [35]. The proposed method produces plausible results and improves over other methods visually.

Table 3. PSNR (dB) and SSIM values by different algorithms on the simulation dataset under the well-calibrated setting (training/test on the *same mask*). We adopt the same 256×256 real mask provided in previous works [16,34] for a fair comparison.

Scene	λ-net [37]		HSSP [45]		TSA-Net [34]		GSM [16]		PnP-DIP [36]		SRN [44]		GST (Ours)	
	PSNR	SSIM	PSNR	SSIM	PSNR	SSIM	PSNR	SSIM	PSNR	SSIM	PSNR	SSIM	PSNR	SSIM
1	30.82	0.8492	31.07	0.8577	31.26	0.8920	32.38	0.9152	31.99	0.8633	34.13	0.9260	**34.19**	**0.9292**
2	26.30	0.8054	26.30	0.8422	26.88	0.8583	27.56	0.8977	26.56	0.7603	30.60	0.8985	**31.04**	**0.9014**
3	29.42	0.8696	29.00	0.8231	30.03	0.9145	29.02	0.9251	30.06	0.8596	32.87	0.9221	**32.93**	**0.9224**
4	37.37	0.9338	38.24	0.9018	39.90	0.9528	36.37	0.9636	38.99	0.9303	**41.27**	**0.9687**	40.71	0.9672
5	27.84	0.8166	27.98	0.8084	28.89	0.8835	28.56	0.8820	29.09	0.8490	31.66	0.9376	**31.83**	**0.9415**
6	30.69	0.8527	29.16	0.8766	31.30	0.9076	32.49	0.9372	29.68	0.8481	35.14	**0.9561**	**35.14**	0.9543
7	24.20	0.8062	24.11	0.8236	25.16	0.8782	25.19	0.8860	27.68	0.8639	27.93	**0.8638**	**28.08**	0.8628
8	28.86	0.8307	27.94	0.8811	29.69	0.8884	31.06	0.9234	29.01	0.8412	33.14	**0.9488**	**33.18**	0.9486
9	29.32	0.8258	29.14	0.8676	30.03	0.8901	29.40	0.9110	33.35	0.8802	33.49	0.9326	**33.50**	**0.9332**
10	27.66	0.8163	26.44	0.8416	28.32	0.8740	30.74	0.9247	27.98	0.8327	31.43	**0.9338**	**31.59**	0.9311
Avg.	29.25	0.8406	28.93	0.8524	30.24	0.8939	30.28	0.9166	30.44	0.8529	33.17	0.9288	**33.22**	**0.9292**

Table 4. Ablation study and complexity analysis. All the methods are tested on simulation test set under the many-to-many setting with one NVIDIA RTX 3090 GPU. We report the PSNR (dB)/SSIM among 100 testing trials, the total training time, and the test time per sample. PnP-DIP is self-supervised, thus no training is required.

Settings	PSNR	SSIM	#params (M)	FLOPs (G)	Training (day)	Test (sec.)
TSA-Net [34]	$21.42_{\pm 0.07}$	$0.6162_{\pm 0.0030}$	44.25	110.06	1.23	0.068
GSM [16]	$28.20_{\pm 0.01}$	$0.8852_{\pm 0.0001}$	3.76	646.35	6.05	0.084
PnP-DIP [36]	$29.66_{\pm 0.38}$	$0.8375_{\pm 0.0093}$	33.85	64.26	–	482.78
w/o GST	$32.24_{\pm 0.10}$	$0.9121_{\pm 0.0010}$	1.25	81.84	1.14	0.061
w/o Bi-Opt	$32.43_{\pm 0.02}$	$0.9206_{\pm 0.0001}$	1.27	82.87	1.83	0.061
w/o GCN	$32.82_{\pm 0.01}$	$0.9262_{\pm 0.0001}$	1.27	82.78	1.63	0.062
Ours (full model)	$33.02_{\pm 0.01}$	$0.9285_{\pm 0.0001}$	1.27	82.87	2.56	0.062

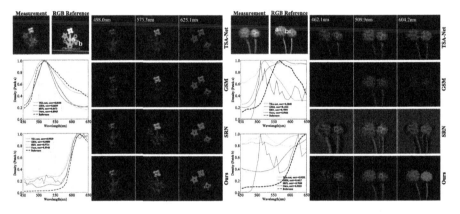

Fig. 6. Real HSI reconstruction. *Left*: same mask (one-to-one) reconstruction, i.e., all methods are trained and tested on the same 660×660 real mask. *Right*: miscalibration (one-to-many) setting, i.e., all methods are trained on a single mask and tested by unseen masks (Here we adopt another 660×660 real mask).

4.2   Model Discussion

Ablation Study. Table 4 compares the performance and complexity of the proposed `full model` with three ablated models as follows. 1) The model `w/o GST` is equivalent to training the reconstruction backbone SRN [44] with a mask ensemble strategy. 2) The model `w/o Bi-Opt` is implemented by training the proposed method without using the Bilevel optimization framework. 3) In the model `w/o GCN`, we replace the GCN module in GST with convolutional layers carrying a similar size of parameters. The bilevel optimization achieves 0.59dB improvement without overburdening the complexity. The GCN contributes 0.2dB with 0.09G FLOPs increase. Overall, the proposed GST yields 0.8 dB improvement with negligible costs (i.e., +0.02M #params, +1.03G FLOPs, and +1.14 d training), and could be used in multiple unseen masks without re-training.

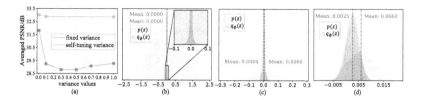

Fig. 7. Discussion on self-tuning variance. (a) Performance comparison between self-tuning variance and fixed ones. (b) The standard normal prior $\mathcal{N}(0,1)$. (c) Set the prior as $\mathcal{N}(0.006, 0.1)$ by observing real masks. (d) Set the prior as $\mathcal{N}(0.006, 0.005)$ by observing real masks and the performance curve in (a).

Complexity Comparison. In Table 4, we further compare the complexity of the proposed method with several recent HSI methods. The proposed method possess one of the smallest model size. Besides, our method shows a comparable FLOPs and training time as others. Notably, given M distinct masks, TSA-Net, GSM, and SRN require $M\times$ training time as reported to achieve well-calibrated performance. Instead, the proposed method only needs to be trained one time to provide calibrated reconstructions over multiple unseen masks.

Self-tuning Variance Under Different Priors. We first validate the effectiveness of the self-tuning variance by comparing it with the fix-valued variance, i.e., scalars from 0 to 1. As shown by the green curve in Fig. 7 (a), fixed variance only achieves less than 32 dB performance. The best performance by 0.005 indicates a strong approximation nature to the mask noise. The self-tuning variance upon different noise priors achieves no less than 32.5 dB performance (red curve in Fig. 7 (a)). Specifically, we implement the noise prior $p(z)$ by exchanging the standard normal distribution of auxiliary variable ϵ in Eq. (6). We start from $\mathcal{N}(0,1)$, which is so broad that the GST network tries to centralize variational noise and restrict the randomness as Fig. 7 (b) shown. Then, we constraint the variance and approximate the mean value by the minimum of the real mask histogram to emphasize the near-zero noise, proposing $\mathcal{N}(0.006, 0.1)$. Figure 7

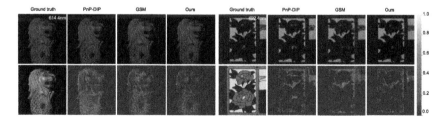

Fig. 8. Illustration of epistemic uncertainty induced by multiple masks. For each block, the first row shows the averaged reconstruction results of selected channels given by different methods and the second demonstrates the corresponding epistemic uncertainty.

(c) indicates the underlying impact of GST network. We further combine the previous fixed-variance observation and propose $\mathcal{N}(0.006, 0.005)$. The best performance is obtained by observing the red curve in Fig. 7 (a). In summary, the proposed method restricts the posited noise prior, leading to the variational noise distribution with a reduced range.

From Mask Uncertainty to Epistemic Uncertainty. The hardware mask plays a similar role to model hyperparameter and largely impacts the weights of reconstruction networks. Thus, marginalizing over the mask posterior distribution will induce the epistemic uncertainty (also known as model uncertainty [9,18]) and reflect as pixel-wise variances (the second row in Fig. 8) of the reconstruction results over multiple unseen masks. As can be seen, the mask-free method PnP-DIP [36] still produces high uncertainties given measurements of the same scene coded by different hardware masks. While employing a deep ensemble strategy could alleviate this issue, such as training GSM [16] with mask ensemble, it lacks an explicit way to quantify mask uncertainty and may lead to unsatisfactory performance (see Table 1). Differently, the proposed GST method models mask uncertainty by approximating the mask posterior through a variational Bayesian treatment, exhibiting high-fidelity reconstruction result with low epistemic uncertainties across different masks as shown in Fig. 8.

5   Conclusions

In this work, we have explored a practical hardware miscalibration issue when deploying deep HSI models in real CASSI systems. Our solution is to calibrate a single reconstruction network via modeling mask uncertainty. We proposed a complete variational Bayesian learning treatment upon one possible mask decomposition inspired by observations on real masks. Bearing the objectives of variational mask distribution modeling and HSI retrieval, we introduced and implemented a novel Graph-based Self-Tuning (GST) network that proceeds HSI reconstruction and uncertainty reasoning under a bilevel optimization framework. The proposed method enabled a smoothed distribution and achieved promising performance under two different miscalibration scenarios. We hope the proposed insight will benefit future work in this novel research direction.

References

1. Arguello, H., Rueda, H., Wu, Y., Prather, D.W., Arce, G.R.: Higher-order computational model for coded aperture spectral imaging. Appl. Opt. **52**(10), D12–D21 (2013)
2. Bioucas-Dias, J.M., Figueiredo, M.A.: A new twist: two-step iterative shrinkage/thresholding algorithms for image restoration. IEEE Trans. Image Process. **16**(12), 2992–3004 (2007)
3. Blundell, C., Cornebise, J., Kavukcuoglu, K., Wierstra, D.: Weight uncertainty in neural network. In: ICML (2015)

4. Cai, Y., et al.: Mask-guided spectral-wise transformer for efficient hyperspectral image reconstruction. In: CVPR (2022)
5. Chen, X., Li, L.J., Fei-Fei, L., Gupta, A.: Iterative visual reasoning beyond convolutions. In: CVPR (2018)
6. Choi, I., Kim, M., Gutierrez, D., Jeon, D., Nam, G.: High-quality hyperspectral reconstruction using a spectral prior. Tech. rep. (2017)
7. Figueiredo, M.A., Nowak, R.D., Wright, S.J.: Gradient projection for sparse reconstruction: application to compressed sensing and other inverse problems. IEEE J. sel. top. sig. process. $\mathbf{1}(4)$, 586–597 (2007)
8. Fort, S., Hu, H., Lakshminarayanan, B.: Deep ensembles: a loss landscape perspective. arXiv preprint arXiv:1912.02757 (2019)
9. Gal, Y.: Uncertainty in deep learning. Ph.D. thesis, University of Cambridge (2016)
10. Gal, Y., Ghahramani, Z.: Dropout as a bayesian approximation: representing model uncertainty in deep learning. In: ICML (2016)
11. Gehm, M.E., John, R., Brady, D.J., Willett, R.M., Schulz, T.J.: Single-shot compressive spectral imaging with a dual-disperser architecture. Opt. Express $\mathbf{15}(21)$, 14013–14027 (2007)
12. Glorot, X., Bengio, Y.: Understanding the difficulty of training deep feedforward neural networks. In: Proceedings of the Thirteenth International Conference on Artificial Intelligence and Statistics, pp. 249–256. JMLR Workshop and Conference Proceedings (2010)
13. Hershey, J.R., Roux, J.L., Weninger, F.: Deep unfolding: model-based inspiration of novel deep architectures. arXiv preprint arXiv:1409.2574 (2014)
14. Hoffman, M.D., Johnson, M.J.: Elbo surgery: yet another way to carve up the variational evidence lower bound. In: NeurIPS Workshop (2016)
15. Hu, X., et al.: Hdnet: high-resolution dual-domain learning for spectral compressive imaging. In: CVPR (2022)
16. Huang, T., Dong, W., Yuan, X., Wu, J., Shi, G.: Deep gaussian scale mixture prior for spectral compressive imaging. In: CVPR (2021)
17. Johnson, W.R., Wilson, D.W., Fink, W., Humayun, M.S., Bearman, G.H.: Snapshot hyperspectral imaging in ophthalmology. J. Biomed. Opt. $\mathbf{12}(1)$, 014036 (2007)
18. Kendall, A., Gal, Y.: What uncertainties do we need in bayesian deep learning for computer vision. In: NeurIPS (2017)
19. Khan, M., Nielsen, D., Tangkaratt, V., Lin, W., Gal, Y., Srivastava, A.: Fast and scalable bayesian deep learning by weight-perturbation in adam. In: ICML (2018)
20. Kingma, D.P., Ba, J.: Adam: a method for stochastic optimization. arXiv preprint arXiv:1412.6980 (2014)
21. Kingma, D.P., Welling, M.: Auto-encoding variational bayes. arXiv preprint arXiv:1312.6114 (2013)
22. Kipf, T.N., Welling, M.: Semi-supervised classification with graph convolutional networks. In: ICLR (2017)
23. Lakshminarayanan, B., Pritzel, A., Blundell, C.: Simple and scalable predictive uncertainty estimation using deep ensembles. In: NeurIPS (2017)
24. Li, K., Zhang, Y., Li, K., Li, Y., Fu, Y.: Visual semantic reasoning for image-text matching. In: ICCV (2019)
25. Lin, J., et al.: Coarse-to-fine sparse transformer for hyperspectral image reconstruction. arXiv preprint arXiv:2203.04845 (2022)
26. Liu, J.Z., Paisley, J., Kioumourtzoglou, M.A., Coull, B.: Accurate uncertainty estimation and decomposition in ensemble learning. arXiv preprint arXiv:1911.04061 (2019)

27. Liu, Y., Yuan, X., Suo, J., Brady, D.J., Dai, Q.: Rank minimization for snapshot compressive imaging. IEEE Trans. Pattern Anal. Mach. Intell. **41**(12), 2990–3006 (2018)
28. Lorente, D., Aleixos, N., Gómez-Sanchis, J., Cubero, S., García-Navarrete, O.L., Blasco, J.: Recent advances and applications of hyperspectral imaging for fruit and vegetable quality assessment. Food Bioprocess Technol. **5**(4), 1121–1142 (2012)
29. Lu, G., Fei, B.: Medical hyperspectral imaging: a review. J. Biomed. Opt. **19**(1), 010901 (2014)
30. Lu, R., Chen, Y.R.: Hyperspectral imaging for safety inspection of food and agricultural products. In: Pathogen Detection and Remediation for Safe Eating, vol. 3544, pp. 121–133. International Society for Optics and Photonics (1999)
31. Ma, J., Liu, X.Y., Shou, Z., Yuan, X.: Deep tensor admm-net for snapshot compressive imaging. In: ICCV (2019)
32. MacKay, D.J.C.: Bayesian methods for adaptive models. Ph.D. thesis, California Institute of Technology (1992)
33. MacKay, M., Vicol, P., Lorraine, J., Duvenaud, D., Grosse, R.: Self-tuning networks: bilevel optimization of hyperparameters using structured best-response functions. arXiv preprint arXiv:1903.03088 (2019)
34. Meng, Z., Ma, J., Yuan, X.: End-to-end low cost compressive spectral imaging with spatial-spectral self-attention. In: ECCV (2020)
35. Meng, Z., Qiao, M., Ma, J., Yu, Z., Xu, K., Yuan, X.: Snapshot multispectral endomicroscopy. Opt. Lett. **45**(14), 3897–3900 (2020)
36. Meng, Z., Yu, Z., Xu, K., Yuan, X.: Self-supervised neural networks for spectral snapshot compressive imaging. In: ICCV (2021)
37. Miao, X., Yuan, X., Pu, Y., Athitsos, V.: l-net: reconstruct hyperspectral images from a snapshot measurement. In: ICCV (2019)
38. Qiao, M., Liu, X., Yuan, X.: Snapshot spatial-temporal compressive imaging. Opt. Lett. **45**(7), 1659–1662 (2020)
39. Qiao, M., Meng, Z., Ma, J., Yuan, X.: Deep learning for video compressive sensing. Apl Photonics **5**(3), 030801 (2020)
40. Scarselli, F., Gori, M., Tsoi, A.C., Hagenbuchner, M., Monfardini, G.: The graph neural network model. IEEE Trans. Neural Networks **20**(1), 61–80 (2008)
41. Song, L., Wang, L., Kim, M.H., Huang, H.: High-accuracy image formation model for coded aperture snapshot spectral imaging. IEEE Trans. Comput. Imaging **8**, 188–200 (2022)
42. Tao, Z., Li, Y., Ding, B., Zhang, C., Zhou, J., Fu, Y.: Learning to mutate with hypergradient guided population. In: NeurIPS (2020)
43. Vincent, P., Larochelle, H., Lajoie, I., Bengio, Y., Manzagol, P.A., Bottou, L.: Stacked denoising autoencoders: learning useful representations in a deep network with a local denoising criterion. J. Mach. Learn. Res. **11**(12), 3371–3408 (2010)
44. Wang, J., Zhang, Y., Yuan, X., Fu, Y., Tao, Z.: A new backbone for hyperspectral image reconstruction. arXiv preprint arXiv:2108.07739 (2021)
45. Wang, L., Sun, C., Fu, Y., Kim, M.H., Huang, H.: Hyperspectral image reconstruction using a deep spatial-spectral prior. In: CVPR (2019)
46. Wang, L., Sun, C., Zhang, M., Fu, Y., Huang, H.: Dnu: deep non-local unrolling for computational spectral imaging. In: CVPR (2020)
47. Wang, L., Xiong, Z., Shi, G., Wu, F., Zeng, W.: Adaptive nonlocal sparse representation for dual-camera compressive hyperspectral imaging. IEEE Trans. Pattern Anal. Mach. Intell. **39**(10), 2104–2111 (2016)

48. Wang, Z., Bovik, A.C., Sheikh, H.R., Simoncelli, E.P.: Image quality assessment: from error visibility to structural similarity. IEEE Trans. Image Process. **13**(4), 600–612 (2004)
49. Wilson, A.G., Izmailov, P.: Bayesian deep learning and a probabilistic perspective of generalization. arXiv preprint arXiv:2002.08791 (2020)
50. Yuan, X., Liu, Y., Suo, J., Durand, F., Dai, Q.: Plug-and-play algorithms for video snapshot compressive imaging. IEEE Trans. Pattern Anal. Mach. Intell. **01**, 1–1 (2021)
51. Yuan, X.: Generalized alternating projection based total variation minimization for compressive sensing. In: ICIP (2016)
52. Yuan, X., Brady, D.J., Katsaggelos, A.K.: Snapshot compressive imaging: theory, algorithms, and applications. IEEE Signal Process. Mag. **38**(2), 65–88 (2021)
53. Yuan, X., Liu, Y., Suo, J., Dai, Q.: Plug-and-play algorithms for large-scale snapshot compressive imaging. In: CVPR (2020)
54. Yuan, Y., Zheng, X., Lu, X.: Hyperspectral image superresolution by transfer learning. IEEE J. Sel. Top. Appl. Earth Observations Remote Sens. **10**(5), 1963–1974 (2017)
55. Zhang, S., Wang, L., Fu, Y., Zhong, X., Huang, H.: Computational hyperspectral imaging based on dimension-discriminative low-rank tensor recovery. In: ICCV (2019)
56. Zhang, T., Fu, Y., Wang, L., Huang, H.: Hyperspectral image reconstruction using deep external and internal learning. In: ICCV (2019)
57. Zhang, Y., Li, K., Li, K., Fu, Y.: Mr image super-resolution with squeeze and excitation reasoning attention network. In: CVPR (2021)
58. Zhu, R., Tao, Z., Li, Y., Li, S.: Automated graph learning via population based self-tuning GCN. In: The 44th International ACM SIGIR Conference on Research and Development in Information Retrieval, pp. 2096–2100. ACM (2021)
59. Zou, Y., Fu, Y., Zheng, Y., Li, W.: Csr-net: camera spectral response network for dimensionality reduction and classification in hyperspectral imagery. Remote Sens. **12**(20), 3294–3314 (2020)

Perceiving and Modeling Density
for Image Dehazing

Tian Ye[1], Yunchen Zhang[2], Mingchao Jiang[3], Liang Chen[4], Yun Liu[5],
Sixiang Chen[1], and Erkang Chen[1(✉)]

[1] School of Ocean Information Engineering, Jimei University, Xiamen, China
{201921114031,201921114013,ekchen}@jmu.edu.cn
[2] China Design Group Co.,Ltd., Nanjing, China
cydiachen@cydiachen.tech
[3] Joyy Ai Group, Guangzhou, China
[4] Fujian Provincial Key Laboratory of Photonics Technology,
Fujian Normal University, Fuzhou, China
[5] College of Artificial Intelligence, Southwest University, Chongqing, China
yunliu@swu.edu.cn

Abstract. In the real world, the degradation of images taken under haze
can be quite complex, where the spatial distribution of haze varies from
image to image. Recent methods adopt deep neural networks to recover
clean scenes from hazy images directly. However, due to the generic
design of network architectures and the failure in estimating an accurate
haze degradation model, the generalization ability of recent dehazing
methods on real-world hazy images is not ideal. To address the problem
of modeling real-world haze degradation, we propose a novel Separable
Hybrid Attention (SHA) module to perceive haze density by capturing positional-sensitive features in the orthogonal directions to achieve
this goal. Moreover, a density encoding matrix is proposed to model the
uneven distribution of the haze explicitly. The density encoding matrix
generates positional encoding in a semi-supervised way – such a haze density perceiving and modeling strategy captures the unevenly distributed
degeneration at the feature-level effectively. Through a suitable combination of SHA and density encoding matrix, we design a novel dehazing network architecture, which achieves a good complexity-performance trade-
off. Comprehensive evaluation on both synthetic datasets and real-world
datasets demonstrates that the proposed method surpasses all the state-
of-the-art approaches with a large margin both quantitatively and qualitatively. The code is released in https://github.com/Owen718/ECCV22-
Perceiving-and-Modeling-Density-for-Image-Dehazing.

Keywords: Image dehazing · Image restoration · Deep learning

T. Ye, Y. Zhang and M. Jiang—Equal contribution.

Supplementary Information The online version contains supplementary material
available at https://doi.org/10.1007/978-3-031-19800-7_8.

1   Introduction

Single image dehazing aims to generate a haze-free image from a hazy image. It is a classical image processing problem, which has been an important research topic in the vision communities within the last decade [3,4,21,23]. Numerous real-world vision tasks (e.g., object detection and auto drive) require high-quality clean images, while the fog and haze usually lead to degraded images. Therefore, it is of great interest to develop an effective algorithm to recover haze-free images.

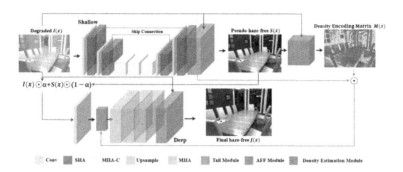

Fig. 1. Overview of network architecture. The Tail Module is formulated by a convolution layer and an activation layer. The shallow layers, consisting of a stack of Multi-branch Hybrid Attention modules with Contextual Transformer (MHAC) blocks and a Tail Module, are used to generate a pseudo-haze-free image. Then, the density encoding matrix is generated by a density estimation module. The deep layers emphasize on detailed reconstruction by using the Adaptive Features Fusion (AFF) module and Multi-branch Hybrid Attention Block (MHA). α is a learnable factor.

Haze is a common atmospheric phenomenon in our daily life. Images with haze and fog lose details and color fidelity. Mathematically, the image degradation caused by haze can be formulated by the following model:

$$\mathbf{I}(\mathbf{x}) = \mathbf{J}(\mathbf{x})t(\mathbf{x}) + \mathbf{A}(\mathbf{x})(1 - t(\mathbf{x})), \tag{1}$$

where $\mathbf{I}(\mathbf{x})$ is the hazy image, $\mathbf{J}(\mathbf{x})$ is the clear image, $t(\mathbf{x})$ is the transmission map and $\mathbf{A}(\mathbf{x})$ stands for the global atmospheric light.

Methods [5,9,11,14] based on priors first estimate the above two unknown parameters $t(\mathbf{x})$ and $\mathbf{A}(\mathbf{x})$, then infer $\mathbf{J}(\mathbf{x})$ according the Eq. 1 inversely. Unfortunately, these hand-crafted priors do not always hold in diverse real-world hazy scenes, resulting in inaccurate estimation of $t(\mathbf{x})$. Therefore, in recent years, more and more researchers have begun to pay attention to data-driven learning algorithms [8,12,16,21,23]. Different from traditional methods, deep learning methods achieve superior performance via training on large-scale datasets. However, methods introduce generic network architectures by simply stacking more layers or using wider layers, ignoring the uneven distribution that causes the unknown depth information which varies at different positions. Some approaches aim at introducing complex loss functions and designing fancy training strategies, leads to high training-costs and poor convergence. Due to the airlight-albedo ambiguity and the limited number of datasets with ground-truth data of transmission maps, these methods result in poor performance degradation in real-world scenes. Moreover, inaccurate estimation of transmission map can significantly deteriorate the clean image restoration.

To address the above problems, we learn the implicit representation and estimate the explicit supervision information for modeling the uneven haze distribution. From Eq. 1, we can notice that the haze degradation model is highly associated with the absolute position of image pixels. The key to solve the dehazing problem lies in accurately encoding the haze intensity with its absolute position. As is demonstrated in Fig. 1, we propose a network to perceive the density of haze distribution with tailor designed modules that captures the positional-sensitive features. Moreover, we introduce a haze density encoding matrix to encode the image-level co-relationship between haze intensity and its absolute position.

We propose the method from three different levels: primary block of the network, architecture of the network and map of haze density information to refine features:

• *Primary Block:* We propose an efficient attention mechanism to perceive the uneven distribution of degradation of features among channel and spatial dimensions: Separable Hybrid Attention (SHA), which effectively samples the input features through a combination of different pooling operations, and strengthens the interaction of different kinds of dimensional information by scaling and shuffling channels. Our SHA based on horizontal and vertical encoding can obtain sufficient spatial clues from input features.

• *Density Encoding Matrix:* We design a coefficient matrix called as density encoding matrix, which encodes the co-relationship between haze intensity and absolute position. The density encoding matrix explicitly models the intensity of the haze degradation model at corresponding spatial locations. The density encoding matrix is obtained in an end-to-end manner, and semantic information of the scene is also introduced implicitly, which makes the density encoding matrix more consistent with the actual distribution.

• *Network Architecture:* We design a novel network architecture that restores hazy images with the coarse-to-fine strategy. The architecture of our network mainly consists of three parts: shallow layer, deep layer and density encoding matrix. We build the shallow layer and deep layer of our method based on SHA. The shallow layer will generate the coarse haze-free image, which we call as the pseudo-haze-free image. For modeling the uneven degradation of a hazy image to refine features explicitly, we utilize the pseudo-haze-free image and the input hazy sample to generate the density encoding matrix.

Our main contributions are summarized as follows:

– We propose the SHA as a task-specified attention mechanism, which perceives haze density effectively from its design of operation on orthogonal separated direction operations and enlarged perception fields.
– We propose the density encoding matrix as an explicit model of haze density, which enhances the coupling of our model. In addition, the proposed method

demonstrates the potential of dealing with the non-homogeneous haze distribution.

– We formulate a novel dehazing method that incorporates the implicit perception of haze features and explicit model of haze density in a unified framework. Our method confirms the necessity of perceiving and modeling of haze density and achieves the best performance compared with the state-of-the art approaches.

2 Related Works

2.1 Single Image Dehazing

Single image dehazing is mainly divided into two categories: a prior-based defogging method [11,15] and a data-driven method based on deep learning. With the introduction of large hazy datasets [17,20], image dehazing based on the deep neural network has developed rapidly. MSBDN [8] uses the classic Encoder-Decoder architecture, but repeated up-sampling and down-sampling operations result in texture information loss. The number of parameters of MSBDN [8] is large, and the model is complex. FFA-Net [21] proposes an Feature Attention (FA) block based on channel attention and pixel attention, obtains the final haze-free image by fusing features of different levels. With the help of two different-scale attention mechanisms, FFA-Net has obtained impressive PSNR and SSIM, but the entire model performs convolutional operations at the resolution of the original image, resulting in a large amount of calculation and slow speed. AECR-Net [23] reuses the FA block and proposes to use a novel loss function based on the contrast learning to make full use of hazy samples, and use a deformable convolution block to improve the expression ability of the model, pushing the index on SOTS [17] to a new height, but memory consumption of the loss function is so high. Compared with AECR-Net [23], our model only needs to utilize a simple Charbonnier [7] loss function to achieve higher PSNR and SSIM.

2.2 Attention Mechanism

Attention mechanisms have been proven essential in various computer vision tasks, such as image classification [13], segmentation [10], dehazing [12,21,23] and deblurring [24]. One of the classical attention mechanisms is SENet [13], which is widely used as a comparative baseline of the plugin of the backbone network. CBAM [22] introduces spatial information encoding via convolutions with large-size kernels, which sequentially infers attention maps along the channel and spatial dimension. The modern attention mechanism extends the idea of CBAM [22] by adopting different dimension attention mechanisms to design the advanced attention module. This shows that the key of the performance of the attention mechanism is to sample the original feature map completely. There is no effective information exchange of attention encoding across different dimensions in existing networks, thus limiting the promotion of networks. In response to the above problems, we utilize two types of pooling operations to sample the original feature map and smartly insert the channel shuffle block in our attention module. Experiments demonstrate that the performance of our attention mechanism has been dramatically improved due to sufficient feature sampling and efficient feature exchange among different dimensions.

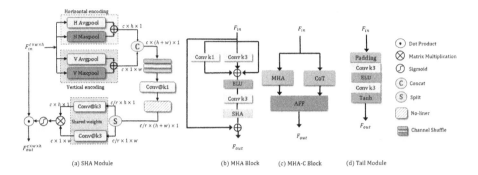

Fig. 2. Illustrations of the Separable Hybrid Attention (SHA) Module and our basic blocks. (a) The Separable Hybrid Attention Module. (b) The Multi-branch Hybrid Attention (MHA) Block. (c) The MHAC block of shallow layers. (d) The tail module of the shallow and deep layers. Our SHA focuses on directional embedding, which consists of unilateral directional pooling and convolution. **@k** denotes the kernel size of the convolution layer.

3   Proposed Methods

We formulate the image dehazing task from two aspects: designing basic blocks to capture positional-sensitive features from orthogonal directions, and modeling haze density from the image-level to the feature-level explicitly.

3.1   Implicit Perception of Haze Density - Separable Hybrid Attention Mechanism and Its Variants

Previous image dehazing methods [12,21,23] follow the paradigm of subsequently calculating attention weights on spatial dimensions and channel dimensions, which lacks useful information exchange among dimensions and leads to the sub-optimal perceptual ability in capturing uneven distributions.

In order to introduce the effective cross-dimension information exchange, we propose a novel attention mechanism called Separable Hybrid Attention (SHA). Different from previous methods that treat attention across the dimension individually, the SHA mechanism acts in a unified way: It harvests contextual information by compressing features from the horizontal and vertical axes, which guarantees that a pixel at any position perceives contextual information from all pixels. Specifically, it first compresses spatial information in separated directions, exchanges information across channel dimensions, reduces the channel dimension and then recovers channel information and spatial information sequentially.

Specifically, a hybrid design of the pooling layer is proposed to preserve abundant spatial information. It combines the maximum pooling layer and the average pooling layer to minimize the loss on capturing high-frequency information and maximize noise resistances among spatial dimensions.

The details and formulas are as follows:

$$v_{avg}^h = \mathbf{AvgPool_h}(F_{in}), v_{avg}^v = \mathbf{AvgPool_v}(F_{in}), \tag{2}$$

$$v_{max}^h = \mathbf{MaxPool_h}(F_{in}), v_{max}^v = \mathbf{MaxPool_v}(F_{in}), \tag{3}$$

We get the direction encode features v^h and v^v from Eq. 2 and Eq. 3 respectively, so we can make distribution of features like a normal distribution, which can better preserve the important information of input features:

$$v^h = v_{avg}^h + v_{max}^h, v^v = v_{avg}^v + v_{max}^v, \tag{4}$$

We concatenate the encoded features and utilize the channel shuffle to interaction channel information, aiming to exchange the encoding information between different channels. Then, we utilize the 1x1 convolution to reduce the dimension of features, which pass through the nonlinear activation function, so that the features of different channels are fully interactive. The formulas are as follows:

$$[y_{c/r}^h, y_{c/r}^v] = \delta(\mathbf{Conv}(\mathbf{cat}([v_c^h, v_c^v]))), \tag{5}$$

wherein Eq. 5, δ is $ReLU6$ activation function, c is the number of dimensions and r is the channel scaling factor, r is usually 4. We use the shared 3x3 convolution to restore the number of channel dimensions for encoded features of different directions, making the isotropic features get similar attention weight values. The final weights can be determined by the larger receptive field of the input features.

$$y_c^h = \mathbf{Conv}(y_{c/r}^h), y_c^v = \mathbf{Conv}(y_{c/r}^v), \tag{6}$$

After restoring the channel of the feature, multiply y_c^h and y_c^w to obtain the attention weight matrix with the same size as the input feature. Finally, a *Sigmoid* function works to get the attention map $W_{c \times h \times w}$:

$$W_{c \times h \times w} = \mathbf{Sigmoid}(y_c^h \times y_c^v), \tag{7}$$

We multiply the attention weight matrix $W_{c \times h \times w}$ with the input feature F_{in} to get the output feature F_{out}:

$$F_{out} = W_{c \times h \times w} \otimes F_{in}. \tag{8}$$

Multi-branch Hybrid Attention. We design the Multi-branch Hybrid Attention (MHA) Block, mainly consisting of the SHA module with parallel convolution. The multi-branch design will improve the expressive ability of the network by introducing multi-scale receptive-filed. The multi-branch block comprises parallel 3x3 convolution, 1x1 convolution, and a residual connection, as shown in Fig. 2

(a). The degradation is often uneven in space in degraded images, such as hazy images and rainy images, and the spatial structure and color of some areas in the picture are not affected by the degradation of the scene, so we set the local residual learning to let the feature pass the current block directly without any process, which also avoids the disappearance of the gradient.

Adaptive Features Fusion Module. We hope that the network can adjust the proportion of feature fusion adaptively according to the importance of different kinds of information. Different from the MixUP [23] operation that fuses the information from different layers for feature preserving in AECR-Net, we utilize the Adaptive Features Fusion Module to combine two different blocks. The formula is as follows:

$$\begin{aligned} F_{out} &= \mathbf{AFF}(\mathbf{block1}, \mathbf{block2}), \\ &= \sigma(\theta) * \mathbf{block1} + (1 - \sigma(\theta)) * \mathbf{block2}, \end{aligned} \tag{9}$$

wherein, *block* denotes the block module, which has the same output size, σ is the *Sigmoid* activation function, and θ is a learnable factor.

Multi-branch Hybrid Attention with Contextual Transformer. Long-range dependence is essential for feature representation, so we introduce an improved Contextual Transformer (CoT) [18] block combined with the MHA block in the shallow layers to mine the long-distance dependence of sample features that further expand the receptive field. Specifically, we design a parallel block that uses the MHA block and the improved CoT block to capture local features and global dependencies simultaneously. To fuse the attention result, an Adaptive Features Fusion module is followed back as shown in Fig. 2 (b), we call this as MHAC block. The formulas are as follows:

$$\begin{aligned} F_{out} &= \mathbf{AFF}(\mathbf{MHAB}(F_{in}), \mathbf{CoT}(F_{in})), \\ &= \sigma(\theta) * (\mathbf{MHAB}(F_{in}) + (1 - \sigma(\theta)) * \mathbf{CoT}(F_{in}), \end{aligned} \tag{10}$$

F_{in} denotes the input features, F_{out} is the adaptive mixing results from MHA and CoT block. Considering that the BN layer will destroy the internal features of the sample, we use the IN layer to replace the BN layer in the improved CoT Block and use ELU as the activation function.

3.2   Shallow Layers

The shallow layers are stacked by several Multi-branch Hybrid Attention modules with CoT [18] blocks. We use the shallow layers to generate the pseudo-haze-free image, which has high-level semantic information.

Tail Module. As shown in Fig. 2 (c), we design the Tail module, which fuses the extracted features and restores the hazy image. The *tanh* activation function is often used on degradation reconstructions. Therefore, we use that as the activation of the output after a stack of 3x3 convolution.

Architecture of Shallow Layers. As shown in Fig. 1, we use the shallow layers to reconstruct the degraded image context content. In order to effectively reduce the amount of calculation and expand the receptive field of the convolution of MHAC, we utilize 2 convolutions with a stride of 2 to reduce the resolution of the feature map to 1/4 of the original input firstly; each convolution follows a SHA module. Then, we use a stack of 8 MHAC blocks with 256 channels, which has 2 skip connections to introduce shallow features before up-sampling, and utilize the Tail module for obtaining the residual of the restored image of the shallow layers:

$$S(x) = \textbf{Shallowlayers}(x) + x, \tag{11}$$

wherein $S(x)$ denotes the pseudo-haze-free image, x denotes the hazy input image.

3.3 Explicit Model of Haze Density - Haze Density Encoding Matrix

Previous methods mainly focus on modeling haze density in an implicit manner. Methods based on physical model focus on obtaining an approximate estimation of haze distribution with direct supervision (e,g. transmission maps, K estimation) , which is limited with their inherent incompleteness in haze density modeling and their vulnerability in error that is introduced by degraded sub-tasks. Methods based on implicit constraints mainly rely on a complicated regularization term of loss functions, which only boosts the perception ability of the feature-level, ignoring the hidden spatial clue in the image-level. Some approaches based on explicit modeling haze density from haze images, lacks careful consideration of the mismatching between explicit image-level information and implicit feature-level distribution, resulting in sub-optimal dehazing results.

The proposed haze density encoding matrix addresses these problems from these aspects: Firstly, the haze density encoding matrix is an attention map that shares the shape prior of haze degradation. Secondly, the haze density encoding matrix, which is derived from haze image, encodes spatial clue from image-level to feature-level, bridging the gap between the channel mismatching between image space and feature space . Thirdly, the haze density encoding matrix is fully optimized with the network, which does not require any direct supervision, avoiding the incompleteness of hand-crafted priors.

As is mentioned in Fig. 2, the SHA mechanism perceives haze density effectively with its spatial-channel operation. It is obvious that shallow layers have the ability to generate sub-optimal results. The proposed density estimation module encodes spatial clues in the image-level information by a concatenation of input haze image I(x) and sub-optimal haze-free image $\bar{J}(x)$. The formulas are as follows:

$$F(x) = G(I(x); \bar{J}(x)) \tag{12}$$

The simple convolution network encodes the spatial clues in image-level to a 64-channel feature map with a 3x3 convolution after utilizing the Reflected Padding

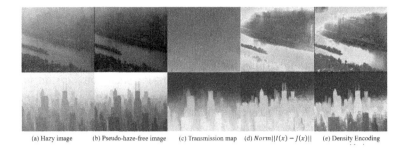

(a) Hazy image   (b) Pseudo-haze-free image   (c) Transmission map   (d) $Norm\|I(x) - J(x)\|$ (e) Density Encoding

Fig. 3. Visualization of different representations of haze density. The transmission map in (c) are predicted by DehazeNet [6]. The $Norm\|I(x) - J(x)\|$ [12] in (d) is the normalized result of the difference map. Our Density Encoding Matrix is shown in (e).

Fig. 4. (i) An illustration of the pipeline that generates the density encoding matrix. (ii) An illustration of the histogram of the difference map and density encoding matrix. The difference map is the numerical difference between the pseudo-haze-free images and haze images. The value of the density encoding matrix is mapped from [0, 1] to [0, 255]. The difference map and density encoding matrix are visualized by ColorJet for observation and comparison. Note that the histograms of the difference map and density encoding matrix have similar intensity distributions.

to avoid the detail loss of the feature edge. Afterwards, we utilize the SHA module to explore perceiving the uneven degeneration of input features fully, and finally use a convolution operation to compress the shape of the feature. The sigmoid function is used to get the density encoding matrix $M \in \mathbb{R}^{1 \times H \times W}$. After getting the density encoding matrix M, we multiply M by the input feature $F_{in} \in \mathbb{R}^{C \times H \times W}$ to get the final output $F_{out} \in \mathbb{R}^{C \times H \times W}$:

$$F_{out} = F_{in} \otimes M, \tag{13}$$

3.4   Deep Layers

To preserve abundant pixel-level texture details, we utilize the deep layers with the supervised signal from density encoding matrix. As shown in Fig. 1, we utilize 10 MHA blocks with 16 channels to extract features at the resolution of the original input. In order to avoid unnecessary calculations caused by repeated extraction of features, we use the AFF module to introduce and mix features refined by our density encoding matrix from the shallow layers adaptively.

4   Experiments

4.1   Datasets and Metrics

We choose the PSNR and SSIM as experimental metrics to measure the performance of our network. We perform comprehensive evaluation on both synthetic datasets and real datasets.

To evaluate performance on synthetic datasets, we train on two large synthetic datasets, RESIDE [17] and Haze4K [20], and testing on SOTS [17] and Haze4K [20] testing sets, respectively. The indoor training set of RESIDE [17] contains 1,399 clean images and 13,990 hazy images generated by corresponding clean images. The indoor testing set of SOTS contains 500 indoor images. The outdoor testing set of SOTS contains 500 outdoor images. The training set of Haze4K [20] contains 3,000 hazy images with ground truth images and the testing set of Haze4K [20] contains 1,000 hazy images with ground truth images.

To evaluate performance on real-world datasets, i.e., Dense-Haze [1], NH-HAZE [3] and O-HAZE [2], we train the network following the official train-val split for fair comparison with other methods.

4.2   Loss Function

We only use Charbonnier loss [7] as our optimization objective:

$$\mathcal{L}(\Theta) = \mathcal{L}_{\text{char}}\left(S(x), J_{gt}(x)\right) + \mathcal{L}_{\text{char}}\left(D(x), J_{gt}(x)\right)), \tag{14}$$

where Θ denotes the parameters of our network, the $S(x)$ denotes pseudo-haze-free image, $D(x)$ denotes output of deep layers, which is the final output image, J_{gt} stands for ground truth, and $\mathcal{L}_{\text{char}}$ is the Charbonnier loss [7]:

$$\mathcal{L}_{\text{char}} = \frac{1}{N} \sum_{i=1}^{N} \sqrt{\|X^i - Y^i\|^2 + \epsilon^2}, \tag{15}$$

with constant ϵ emiprically set to $1e^{-3}$ for all experiments.

4.3   Ablation Study

To demonstrate the effectiveness of separated hybrid attention mechanism, we design a baseline network with the minimized design. The network consists of one convolution with kernel size of 3 and stride of 2, followed by four residual blocks, one upsample layer and one tail module. The baseline network is trained and evaluated on the Haze4K [20] dataset. We employ the Charbonnier loss [7] as the training loss function for ablation study, and utilize Haze4K [20] dataset for both training and testing. Detailed implementation of the baseline model is demonstrated in the supplementary material.

Effectiveness of Separated Hybrid Attention Module. In order to make a fair comparison between attention modules on implicit perceiving haze density, we replace the residual blocks in our baseline model with different kinds of attention blocks. The performance of above models are summarized in Table 1. We provide visualization results of high-level feature maps in the supplementary material.

Table 1. Comparisons on Haze4K [20] testset for different configurations of Shallow Layers. The number of parameters and flops is calculated only on the attention modules.

Settings	Model	# of Params	# of Flops	PSNR
1	Baseline	–	–	24.40
2	SE	512	520	24.71
3	ECA	3	114	24.78
4	CBA	4.9 K	78.69 M	25.36
5	FA	8.25 K	4.6 M	25.30
6	SWRCA	10.3 K	302 M	25.87
7	SHA (Ours)	2.6 K	368 K	26.39
8	MHAB (Ours)	22.2 K	321 M	27.02
9	MHA-C (Ours)	38.3 K	587.3 M	27.58

As is depicted in Table 1, we can see that attention modules boost the performance of image dehazing network. Comparing with the models of Setting 1, Setting 2, Setting 3, haze specific attention mechanisms gain a noticeable performance boost. Unfortunately, the performance of Setting 5 is worse than the performance of Setting 4, indicate the brute design of Setting 5 is not optimal. Compared with Setting 5 and Setting 6, the proposed modules obtain higher PSNR scores while maintaining the appropriate efficiency. The key to the performance lies in the mutual interaction between spatial and channel dimensions, and the extracted positional-sensitive features is effective in perceiving haze density. Furthermore, We find that MHAC and MHAB can achieve better performance, but the number of parameters also increases. Therefore, the careful design of shallow layers and deep layers is essential.

Effectiveness of Density Encoding Matrix. Compared with previous methods that explores haze density from a variety of forms, we perform an experiment on validating the effectiveness of the proposed Density Encoding Matrix. Since the haze density representation can be obtained by attaching direct supervisions on the density estimation module, we compare different forms of haze density. First, we replace the haze density encoding matrix (as is denoted with doted orange line in Fig. 1) with the identity matrix as the baseline. Second, We replace the haze density encoding matrix with a ground-truth transmission map provided with Haze4K [20] as the validation of the effectiveness of classical model derives from the physical model. Third, we modify the Density Estimation Module with an extra transmission map supervision, enabling the output of online estimation of transmission map. As is depicted in KDDN, a normed difference map is introduced as another unsupervised haze density representations. Finally, the proposed Density Encoding Matrix is optimized without any direction supervision.

As is depicted in Table 2, we can observe that different kinds of density representations boost the performance of the dehazing network than the identity matrix, which indicates that the ability of the implicit perception of haze distribution is limited and it is necessary to introduce external image-level guidance to the dehazing network. The comparison between Setting 2 and Setting 3 indicates that methods with direct supervisions are vulnerable to error introduced by the auxiliary task, which suffer from more severe performance degradation in real-world scenes. Compared with Settings 2, 3 and Setting 4, the online estimation of the normalized difference map achieves a higher score than online estimation of the transmission map, which indicates no direct constraint or joint optimization allows better performance in feature-level. Unfortunately, it suffers from serious performance degradation than ground-truth transmission map, which indicates that image-level spatial distribution is mismatched with feature-level distribution. The proposed density encoding matrix achieves the highest score than its competitors, which adopts a fully end-to-end manner in training, shares a shape prior with haze degradation model and aligns the uneven image-level distribution with feature-level distribution. In addition, we provide visualization results of different representations of haze density.

Table 2. Comparison with different forms of haze representations.

Settings	Density representations	Online inference/Supervision Type	PSNR
1	Identity matrix	Offline/-.	30.33
2	GT Transmission Map	Offline/Sup.	31.42
3	Est. Transmission Map	Online/Sup.	31.17
4	Norm $\|I(x) - J(x)\|$ [12]	Online / UnSup	32.21
5	Density Encoding Matrix	Online / UnSup	<u>33.49</u>

Fig. 5. Visual comparison of dehazing results of one image from Haze4k [20] dataset.

5   Compare with SOTA Methods

5.1   Implementation Details

We augment the training dataset with randomly rotated by 90, 180, 270 degrees and horizontal flip. The training image patches with the size 256×256 are extracted as input I_{in} of our network. The network is trained for 7.5×10^5, 1.5×10^6 steps on Haze4K [20] and RESIDE [17] respectively. We use the Adam optimizer with initial learning rate of 2×10^{-4}, and adopt the CyclicLR to adjust the learning rate, where on the triangular mode, the value of gamma is 1.0, base momentum is 0.8, max momentum is 0.9, base learning rate is initial learning rate and max learning rate is 3×10^{-4}. PyTorch is used to implement our model with 4 RTX 3080 GPUs with total batchsize of 40.

Fig. 6. Visual comparison of dehazing results on Haze4k [20] dataset.

Fig. 7. Visual comparision of dehazing results on real-world images.

5.2   Qualitative and Quantitative Results on Benchmarks

Visual Comparisons. To validate the superiority of our method, as shown in Fig. 5, 6, 7, firstly we compare the visual results of our method with previous SOTA methods on synthetic hazy images from Haze4K [20] and real-world hazy images. It can be seen that other methods are not able to remove the haze in all the cases, while the proposed method produced results close to the real clean scenes visually. Additionally, the visualization results of the density encoding matrix demonstrates the ability of capturing uneven haze distribution. Our method is superior in the recovery performance of image details and color fidelity. Please refer to the supplementary materials for more visual comparisons on the synthetic hazy images and real-world hazy images.

Quantitative Comparisons. We quantitatively compare the dehazing results of our method with SOTA single image dehazing methods on Haze4 K [20], SOTS [17] datasets, Dense-Haze [1], NH-Haze [3] and O-HAZE [2]. As shown in Table 3, our method outperforms all SOTA methods, achieving 33.49 dB PSNR and 0.98 SSIM on Haze4 K [20]. It increases the PSNR by 4.93 dB compared to the second-best method. On the SOTS [17] indoor test set, our method also outperforms all SOTA methods, achieving 38.41 dB PSNR and 0.99 SSIM. It increases the PSNR by 1.24 dB, compared to the second-best method. Our method also outperforms all SOTA methods on the SOTS [17] outdoor test set, achieving 34.74 dB PSNR and 0.97 SSIM. In conclusion, our method achieves the best performance on the 6 synthetic and real-world benchmarks compared to previous methods.

Table 3. Quantitative comparisons of our method with the state-of-the-art dehazing methods on Haze4K [20] and SOTS [17] datasets (PSNR(dB)/SSIM). Best results are underlined.

Method	Haze4K [20]		SOTS Indoor [17]		SOTS Outdoor [17]		Dense-Haze [1]		NH-HAZE [3]		O-HAZE [2]	
	PSNR↑	SSIM↑	PSNR↑	SSIM↑	PSNR↑	SSIM↑	PSNR↑	SSIM↑	PSNR↑	SSIM↑	PSNR↑	SSIM↑
DCP [11]	14.01	0.76	15.09	0.76	19.13	0.8148	10.06	0.39	10.57	0.52	16.78	0.653
DehazeNet [6]	19.12	0.84	20.64	0.80	20.29	0.88	13.84	0.43	16.62	0.52	17.57	0.77
AOD-Net [16]	17.15	0.83	19.82	0.82	24.14	0.92	13.14	0.41	15.40	0.57	15.03	0.54
GDN [19]	23.29	0.93	32.16	0.98	30.86	0.98	–	–	–	–	23.51	0.83
MSBDN [8]	22.99	0.85	33.79	0.98	23.36	0.88	15.37	0.49	19.23	0.71	24.36	0.75
FFA-Net [21]	26.96	0.95	36.39	0.98	33.57	0.98	14.39	0.45	19.87	0.69	22.12	0.77
AECR-Net [23]	–	–	37.17	0.99	–	–	15.80	0.47	19.88	0.72	–	–
DMT-Net [20]	28.53	0.96	–	–	–	–	–	–	–	–	–	–
Ours	33.49	0.98	38.41	0.99	34.74	0.99	16.79	0.51	20.42	0.73	24.64	0.83

6   Conclusion

In this paper, we propose a powerful image dehazing method to recover haze-free images directly. Specifically, the Separable Hybrid Attention is designed to better perceive the haze density, and a density encoding matrix is to further refine extracted features. Although our method is simple, it is superior to all the previous state-of-the-art methods with a very large margin on two large-scale hazy datasets. Our method has a powerful advantage in the restoration of image detail and color fidelity. We hope to further promote our method to other low-level vision tasks such as deraining, super-resolution, denoising and desnowing.

Limitations: The proposed method recovers high-fidelity haze-free images in common scenarios. However, as is shown in Fig. 7 (top), the dense hazy area with high-light scenes still has residues of haze. Following the main idea of this work, future research can be made in various aspects to generate high-quality images with pleasant visual perceptions.

Acknowledgement. This work is supported partially by the Natural Science Foundation of Fujian Province of China under Grant (2021J01867), Education Department of Fujian Province under Grant (JAT190301), Foundation of Jimei University under Grant (ZP2020034), the National Nature Science Foundation of China under Grant (61901117), Natural Science Foundation of Chongqing, China under Grant (No. cstc2020jcyj-msxmX0324).

References

1. Ancuti, C.O., Ancuti, C., Sbert, M., Timofte, R.: Dense haze: a benchmark for image dehazing with dense-haze and haze-free images. In: IEEE International Conference on Image Processing (ICIP). IEEE ICIP 2019 (2019)
2. Ancuti, C.O., Ancuti, C., Timofte, R., Vleeschouwer, C.D.: O-haze: a dehazing benchmark with real hazy and haze-free outdoor images. In: IEEE Conference on Computer Vision and Pattern Recognition, NTIRE Workshop. NTIRE CVPR'18 (2018)
3. Ancuti, C.O., Ancuti, C., Vasluianu, F.A., Timofte, R.: Ntire 2020 challenge on nonhomogeneous dehazing. In: Proceedings of the IEEE/CVF Conference on Computer Vision and Pattern Recognition Workshops, pp. 490–491 (2020)
4. Ancuti, C.O., Ancuti, C., Vasluianu, F.A., Timofte, R.: Ntire 2021 nonhomogeneous dehazing challenge report. In: Proceedings of the IEEE/CVF Conference on Computer Vision and Pattern Recognition, pp. 627–646 (2021)
5. Berman, D., Avidan, S., et al.: Non-local image dehazing. In: Proceedings of the IEEE Conference on Computer Vision and Pattern Recognition, pp. 1674–1682 (2016)
6. Cai, B., Xu, X., Jia, K., Qing, C., Tao, D.: Dehazenet: an end-to-end system for single image haze removal. IEEE Trans. Image Process. **25**(11), 5187–5198 (2016)
7. Charbonnier, P., Blanc-Feraud, L., Aubert, G., Barlaud, M.: Two deterministic half-quadratic regularization algorithms for computed imaging. In: Proceedings of 1st International Conference on Image Processing, vol. 2, pp. 168–172. IEEE (1994)
8. Dong, H., et al.: Multi-scale boosted dehazing network with dense feature fusion. In: Proceedings of the IEEE/CVF Conference on Computer Vision and Pattern Recognition, pp. 2157–2167 (2020)
9. Fattal, R.: Dehazing using color-lines. ACM Trans. Graph. **34**(1), 13:1–13:14 (2014)
10. Fu, J., et al.: Dual attention network for scene segmentation. In: Proceedings of the IEEE/CVF Conference on Computer Vision and Pattern Recognition, pp. 3146–3154 (2019)
11. He, K., Sun, J., Tang, X.: Single image haze removal using dark channel prior. IEEE Trans. Pattern Anal. Mach. Intell. **33**(12), 2341–2353 (2010)
12. Hong, M., Xie, Y., Li, C., Qu, Y.: Distilling image dehazing with heterogeneous task imitation. In: Proceedings of the IEEE/CVF Conference on Computer Vision and Pattern Recognition, pp. 3462–3471 (2020)
13. Hu, J., Shen, L., Sun, G.: Squeeze-and-excitation networks. In: Proceedings of the IEEE Conference on Computer Vision and Pattern Recognition, pp. 7132–7141 (2018)
14. Jiang, Y., Sun, C., Zhao, Y., Yang, L.: Image dehazing using adaptive bi-channel priors on superpixels. Comput. Vis. Image Underst. **165**, 17–32 (2017)
15. Katiyar, K., Verma, N.: Single image haze removal algorithm using color attenuation prior and multi-scale fusion. Int. J. Comput. Appl. **141**(10), 037–042 (2016). https://doi.org/10.5120/ijca2016909827

16. Li, B., Peng, X., Wang, Z., Xu, J., Feng, D.: Aod-net: all-in-one dehazing network. In: Proceedings of the IEEE International Conference on Computer Vision, pp. 4770–4778 (2017)
17. Li, B.: Benchmarking single-image dehazing and beyond. IEEE Trans. Image Process. **28**(1), 492–505 (2018)
18. Li, Y., Yao, T., Pan, Y., Mei, T.: Contextual transformer networks for visual recognition. arXiv preprint arXiv:2107.12292 (2021)
19. Liu, X., Ma, Y., Shi, Z., Chen, J.: Griddehazenet: attention-based multi-scale network for image dehazing. In: Proceedings of the IEEE/CVF International Conference on Computer Vision, pp. 7314–7323 (2019)
20. Liu, Y., et al.: From synthetic to real: image dehazing collaborating with unlabeled real data. arXiv preprint arXiv:2108.02934 (2021)
21. Qin, X., Wang, Z., Bai, Y., Xie, X., Jia, H.: Ffa-net: feature fusion attention network for single image dehazing. In: Proceedings of the AAAI Conference on Artificial Intelligence, vol. 34, pp. 11908–11915 (2020)
22. Woo, S., Park, J., Lee, J.Y., Kweon, I.S.: Cbam: convolutional block attention module. In: Proceedings of the European Conference on Computer Vision (ECCV), pp. 3–19 (2018)
23. Wu, H., et al.: Contrastive learning for compact single image dehazing. In: Proceedings of the IEEE/CVF Conference on Computer Vision and Pattern Recognition, pp. 10551–10560 (2021)
24. Zamir, S.W., et al.: Multi-stage progressive image restoration. In: Proceedings of the IEEE/CVF Conference on Computer Vision and Pattern Recognition, pp. 14821–14831 (2021)

Stripformer: Strip Transformer for Fast Image Deblurring

Fu-Jen Tsai[1], Yan-Tsung Peng[2], Yen-Yu Lin[3], Chung-Chi Tsai[4], and Chia-Wen Lin[1]($\boxtimes$)

[1] National Tsing Hua University, Hsinchu, Taiwan
fjtsai@gapp.nthu.edu.tw, cwlin@ee.nthu.edu.tw
[2] National Chengchi University, Taipei City, Taiwan
ytpeng@cs.nccu.edu.tw
[3] National Yang Ming Chiao Tung University, Taipei City, Taiwan
lin@cs.nycu.edu.tw
[4] Qualcomm Technologies, Inc., San Diego, USA
chuntsai@qti.qualcomm.com

Abstract. Images taken in dynamic scenes may contain unwanted motion blur, which significantly degrades visual quality. Such blur causes short- and long-range region-specific smoothing artifacts that are often directional and non-uniform, which is difficult to be removed. Inspired by the current success of transformers on computer vision and image processing tasks, we develop, Stripformer, a transformer-based architecture that constructs intra- and inter-strip tokens to reweight image features in the horizontal and vertical directions to catch blurred patterns with different orientations. It stacks interlaced intra-strip and inter-strip attention layers to reveal blur magnitudes. In addition to detecting region-specific blurred patterns of various orientations and magnitudes, Stripformer is also a token-efficient and parameter-efficient transformer model, demanding much less memory usage and computation cost than the vanilla transformer but works better without relying on tremendous training data. Experimental results show that Stripformer performs favorably against state-of-the-art models in dynamic scene deblurring.

1 Introduction

Blur coming from object movement or camera shaking causes a smudge in taken images, often unwanted for photographers and affecting the performance of subsequent computer vision applications. Dynamic scene image deblurring aims to recover sharpness from a single blurred image, which is difficult since such blur is usually globally and locally non-uniform, and only limited information can be utilized from the single image.

Supplementary Information The online version contains supplementary material available at https://doi.org/10.1007/978-3-031-19800-7_9.

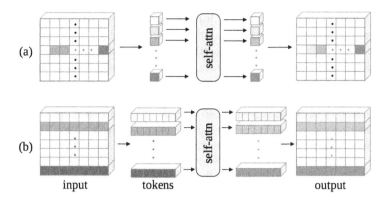

Fig. 1. (a) Horizontal intra-strip attention (Intra-SA-H) encodes pixel dependence within the same horizontal strip. Vertical intra-strip attention (Intra-SA-V) is symmetrically constructed. (b) Horizontal inter-strip attention (Inter-SA-H) captures strip-wise correlations. Inter-SA-V is similarly established for vertical strips. Horizontal and vertical intra-strip and inter-strip attention works jointly to explore blur orientations. Stacking interlaced intra-strip and inter-strip attention layers reveals blur magnitudes.

Conventional approaches usually exploit prior knowledge for single image deblurring due to its ill-posedness. Some methods simplify this task by assuming that only uniform blur exists [6,10]; However, it is often not the case for real-world dynamic scenes. Some works utilize prior assumptions to remove non-uniform blur [16,21,22]. However, non-uniform blur is usually region-specific, which is hard to be modeled by the specific priors, often making these works fail. In addition, these methods typically involve solving a non-convex optimization problem, leading to high computation time.

Deblurring has made significant progress using deep learning. Based on convolutional neural networks (CNNs), several studies have improved the deblurring performance based on recurrent architectures, such as multi-scale (MS) [11,20], multi-patch (MP) [31,42], and multi-temporal (MT) [23] recurrent architectures. However, blur from dynamic scenes, in general, is non-uniform and regionally directional, requiring a better model design to explore global and local correlations from blur in one image.

Recently, motivated by the success of transformers [34] which exploit attention mechanisms for natural language processing, researchers have explored transformer-based architectures to address computer vision tasks and obtained promising results, such as image classification [9], object detection [1] and low-level vision [2]. We explore the self-attention mechanisms used in transformers to deal with blurred patterns with different magnitudes and orientations.

Transformer architectures can be generally classified into two categories: a pure encoder-decoder architecture [34] and a hybrid architecture [1]. The former treats image patches of a fixed size $n \times n$ as tokens and takes these tokens as input. To preserve fine-grained information, the number of parameters grows proportional to n^2, like IPT [2], which requires numerous parameters and relies on a large amount of training data (over $1M$ images) to achieve competitive results. The hybrid architecture extracts embedding features of an input image using additional models such as CNNs before the transformer is applied. The architecture demands high memory and computation consumption due to its pixel-wise attention, up to $\mathcal{O}(H^2W^2)$ for an input image or feature maps of resolution $H \times W$. A trade-off between compactness and efficiency is present.

In transformers, similar tokens mutually attend to each other. The attention mechanism can capture all-range information, which is essential to superior performance in image deblurring but tends to have a large memory requirement. In addition, since blur patterns are often region-specific and hard to catch by a deblurring model, we instead try to specify each region-specific pattern using its orientation and magnitude. Thus, it suffices to attain orientation and magnitude information at each position for deblurring.

We leverage these observations to address the trade-off between a pure transformer and a hybrid transformer. In turn, we propose a token-efficient and parameter-efficient hybrid transformer architecture, called Stripformer, exploiting both intra-strip and inter-strip attention, shown in Fig. 1, to reassemble the attended blur features. The intra-strip tokens, forming the intra-strip attention, carry local pixel-wise blur features. In contrast, the inter-strip tokens, forming the inter-strip attention, bear global region-wise blur information.

The designs of intra-strip and inter-strip attention are inspired by [32], which projects blur motions into horizontal and vertical directions in the Cartesian coordinate system for estimating the motion blur field of a blurred image. The intra- and inter-strip attention contains horizontal and vertical branches to capture blur patterns. The captured horizontal and vertical features stored at each pixel offer sufficient information for the subsequent layer to infer the blur pattern orientation at that pixel. Moreover, sequential local-feature extraction by successive intra-strip blocks obtains multi-scale features, which reveal blur pattern magnitudes. It turns out that we stack multi-head intra-strip and inter-strip attention blocks to decompose dynamic blur into different orientations and magnitudes, and can remove short- and long-range blurred artifacts from the input image.

The intra- and inter-strip attention in our Stripformer is developed based on the inductive bias of image deblurring. It also results in an efficient transformer model. Since the intra-strip and inter-strip tokens are fewer than those used in the vanilla attention, Stripformer requires much less memory and computation costs than the vanilla transformer. Therefore, Stripformer works better without relying on tremendous training data. Extensive experimental results show that Stripformer performs favorably against state-of-the-art (SOTA) deblurring models in recovered image quality, memory usage, and computational efficiency. The source code is available at https://github.com/pp00704831/Stripformer.

2   Related Work

Deblurring via CNN-Based Architectures. Single image deblurring using CNN-based architectures has achieved promising performance. Most of these successful architectures are recurrent and can be roughly classified into three types: Multi-scale (MS), multi-patch (MP), and multi-temporal (MT) models. Nah *et al.* [20] propose an MS network by a *coarse-to-fine* strategy to restore a sharp image on different resolutions gradually. Zhang *et al.*[42] utilize an MP method by building a hierarchical deblurring model. Motivated by MS and MP, Park *et al.*[23] propose an MT deblurring model via incremental temporal training in the original spatial scale to preserve more high-frequency information for reliable deblurring. In addition, Kupyn *et al.*[17] suggest using conditional generative adversarial CNN networks to restore high-quality visual results.

Attention Mechanism. Attention mechanisms [34] have been commonly used in the fields of image processing [24,41] and computer vision [13,35] to encode long-range dependency in the extracted features. Specifically to deblurring, attention mechanisms can help learn cross-pixel correlations to better address non-uniform blur [25,31]. Hence, transformers with multi-head self-attention to explore local and global correlations would be a good choice for deblurring.

Hou *et al.*[12] exploit horizontal and vertical one-pixel long kernels to pool images and extract context information for scene parsing, called strip pooling, initially designed for contextual information extraction instead of deblurring. We extend strip tokens to intra- and inter-strip attentions for better capturing blurred patterns. CCNet [15] utilizes the criss-cross attention to capture the global image dependencies for semantic segmentation, working a bit similar to the proposed intra-strip attention. The criss-cross attention computes pixel correlations horizontally and vertically in a joint manner. In contrast, we construct horizontal and vertical intra-strips separately and calculate their intra-strip attentions parallelly. Moreover, intra-strip attention works together with the region-wise inter-strip attention to capture blurred patterns locally and globally.

Vision Transformer. Unlike conventional CNN architectures, the transformers are originally proposed for natural language processing (NLP), utilizing multi-head self-attention to model global token-to-token relationships. Recently, transformers have achieved comparable or even better performance than CNN models in several vision applications such as image classification [9], object detection [1], semantic segmentation [27], inpainting [40], and super-resolution [37]. Take Vision Transformers (ViT) [9] for image classification as an example. ViT generates tokens for the Multi-head Self-Attention (MSA) from the pixels or patches of an image. The former flattens the three-dimensional feature maps $X \in \mathbb{R}^{H \times W \times C}$ produced by a CNN model to a two-dimensional tensor of size $\mathbb{R}^{HW \times C}$. Its global self-attention mechanism requires up to $\mathcal{O}(H^2W^2)$ space complexity for each head of MSA, which is memory-demanding. The latter uses

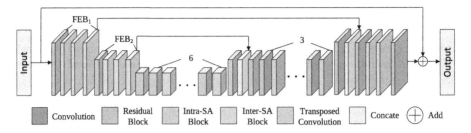

Fig. 2. Architecture of Stripformer. We utilize shallow convolution embedding with intra- and inter-strip attention blocks for image deblurring.

patches instead of pixels as tokens, like [2], where each token is a patch of size 8×8. However, it needs lots of parameters ($114M$ used in [2]) to preserve all the channel dimensions and keep the spatial information. Moreover, transformers with more parameters rely on more training data for stable optimization. In [2], the model requires to be pre-trained on ImageNet with more than one million annotated images for deraining, denoising, and super-resolution to obtain competitive results.

To address the issue of high memory consumption of transformers, Liu *et al.*propose Swin [19], a transformer architecture that uses a sliding window to make it token-efficient and realize local attention. However, Swin [19] does not consider high-resolution global attention, which is crucial to some dense prediction tasks. For example, images with dynamic scene blur commonly have local and global blur artifacts, requiring deblurring models to consider short-range and long-range pixel correlations. Chu *et al.* [7] proposed Twins, which utilizes locally-grouped self-attention (LSA) by local window attention and global sub-sampled attention (GSA) by pooling key and value features to the size 7×7 for classification. However, it is not suitable for high-resolution dense prediction tasks such as image deblurring by only using 7×7 features. In our design, we simultaneously leverage the prior observation of blurred patterns to reduce the number of tokens and parameters.

The proposed Stripformer is a token-efficient transformer with its space complexity of only $\mathcal{O}(HW(H+W))$ and $\mathcal{O}(H^2+W^2)$ for intra- and inter-strip attention, respectively, where H and W are the height and width of the input image. It is much less than the vanilla transformer's $\mathcal{O}(H^2W^2)$. In addition, our model uses much fewer parameters ($20M$) than IPT [2] ($114M$), thus not needing a large amount of training data to achieve even better performance.

3   Proposed Method

Images captured in dynamic scenes often suffer from blurring, where the blur artifacts could have various orientations and magnitudes. The proposed Stripformer is a transformer-based architecture that leverages intra- and inter-strip tokens to extract blurred patterns with different orientations and magnitudes.

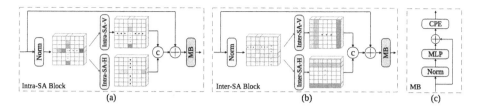

Fig. 3. Illustration of (a) Intra-Strip Attention (Intra-SA) Block, (b) Inter-Strip Attention (Inter-SA) Block, where ⓒ denotes concatenation, and (c) MLP Block (MB), where CPE denotes the conditional position encoding [8].

The intra- and inter-strip tokens contain horizontal and vertical strip-wise features to form multi-head intra-strip attention and inter-strip attention blocks to break down region-specific blur patterns into different orientations. Through their attention mechanisms, intra-strip and inter-strip features can be reweighted to fit short- and long-range blur magnitudes.

Figure 2 demonstrates the model design of Stripformer, which is a residual encoder-decoder architecture starting with two Feature Embedding Blocks (FEBs) to generate embedding features. Since a FEB downsamples the input, the output resolution is one-fourth of the input after two FEBs. Next, it stacks a convolution layer with interlaced Intra-SA and Inter-SA blocks on the smallest and second-smallest scales. As shown in Fig. 3, in Intra-SA and Inter-SA blocks, we perform horizontal and vertical intra-strip or inter-strip attention to produce multi-range strip-shaped features to catch blur with different magnitudes and orientations. We adopt transposed convolution for upsampling. Its output features are concatenated with those generated from the encoder on the same scale. Lastly, Stripformer ends with two residual blocks and a convolution layer with a residual connection to the input blurred image. In the following, we detail the main functional modules: FEBs, Intra-SA blocks, and Inter-SA blocks.

3.1 Feature Embedding Block (FEB)

For a vanilla transformer, the input image is usually divided into patches before feeding them to a transformer [2,9], meaning that features in each patch are flattened to yield a token. However, this could cause spatial pixel correlations to be lost due to flattened pixels and require numerous parameters because of its self-attention mechanism. Instead, we use two FEBs, each of which consists of one convolutional layer and three residual blocks to generate feature embedding without losing spatial information.

3.2 Intra-SA and Inter-SA Blocks

The core of Stripformer is Intra-SA and Inter-SA blocks. We detail their designs as follows.

Intra-SA Block. As shown in Fig. 3 (a), an Intra-SA block consists of two paralleled branches: horizontal intra-strip attention (Intra-SA-H) and vertical intra-strip attention (Intra-SA-V). Let the input features of an intra-strip block be $X \in \mathbb{R}^{H \times W \times C}$, where H, W, and C represent the height, the width, and the number of channels, respectively. We first process them with a LayerNorm layer (**Norm**) followed by a 1×1 convolution layer (**Conv**) with C filters to obtain the input features, described as

$$(X^h, X^v) = \mathbf{Conv}(\mathbf{Norm}(X)), \tag{1}$$

where X^h and $X^v \in \mathbb{R}^{H \times W \times D}$ stand for the input features for Intra-SA-H and Intra-SA-V, respectively, where $D = \frac{C}{2}$.

For the horizontal intra-strip attention, we split the input features X^h into H non-overlapping horizontal strip $X_i^h \in \mathbb{R}^{W \times D}$, $i = \{1, 2, ..., H\}$. Each strip X_i^h has W tokens with D dimensions. Next, we generate queries, keys, and values associated with X_i^h as Q_{ij}^h, K_{ij}^h, and $V_{ij}^h \in \mathbb{R}^{W \times \frac{D}{m}}$ for the multi-head attention mechanism as

$$(Q_{ij}^h, K_{ij}^h, V_{ij}^h) = (X_i^h P_j^Q, X_i^h P_j^K, X_i^h P_j^V), \tag{2}$$

where P_j^Q, P_j^K, and $P_j^V \in \mathbb{R}^{D \times \frac{D}{m}}$, $j \in \{1, ..., m\}$, representing linear projection matrices for the query, key, and value with the multi-head attention. Here, we set the number of heads to five, $m = 5$. The multi-head attended feature $O_{ij}^h \in \mathbb{R}^{W \times \frac{D}{m}}$ for one horizontal strip is calculated as

$$O_{ij}^h = \mathbf{Softmax}(\frac{Q_{ij}^h(K_{ij}^h)^T}{\sqrt{D/m}})V_{ij}^h, \tag{3}$$

whose space complexity is $\mathcal{O}(W^2)$. We concatenate the multi-head horizontal features $O_{ij}^h \in \mathbb{R}^{W \times \frac{D}{m}}$ along the channel dimension to generate $O_i^h \in \mathbb{R}^{W \times D}$ and fold all of them into three-dimensional tensors $O^h \in \mathbb{R}^{H \times W \times D}$ as the Intra-SA-H output. Symmetrically, the vertical intra-strip attention produces the multi-head attended feature for one vertical strip, denoted as $O_{ij}^v \in \mathbb{R}^{H \times \frac{D}{m}}$, whose space complexity is $\mathcal{O}(H^2)$. After folding all the vertical features, the Intra-SA-V output denotes as $O^v \in \mathbb{R}^{H \times W \times D}$.

We then concatenate them to feed into a 1×1 convolution layer with a residual connection to the original input features X to obtain the attended features $O_{attn} \in \mathbb{R}^{H \times W \times C}$ as

$$O_{attn} = \mathbf{Conv}(\mathbf{Concate}(O^h, O^v)) + X. \tag{4}$$

An MLP block, as illustrated in Fig. 3 (c), is then applied to O_{attn}. Specifically, we use LayerNorm, feed-forward MultiLayer Perceptron (**MLP**) with a residual connection, and the Conditional Positional Encodings [8] (**CPE**), a 3×3 depth-wise convolution layer with a residual connection, to generate the final output $O_{intra} \in R^{H \times W \times C}$ as

$$O_{intra} = \mathbf{CPE}(\mathbf{MLP}(\mathbf{Norm}(O_{attn})) + O_{attn}. \tag{5}$$

The total space complexity of Intra-SA is $\mathcal{O}(HW^2 + WH^2)$ for H horizontal and W vertical strips.

Inter-SA Block. As shown in Fig. 3 (b), an Inter-SA block also consists of two paralleled branches: horizontal inter-strip attention (Inter-SA-H) and vertical inter-strip attention (Inter-SA-V). Inter-SA is a strip-wise attention that regards each strip feature as a token. We process the input like Intra-SA using Eq. (1) to generate input features X^h and $X^v \in \mathbb{R}^{H \times W \times D}$ for Inter-SA-H and Inter-SA-V, respectively.

For the horizontal inter-strip attention, we generate the multi-head queries, keys, and values by linear projection matrices as Eq. (2), where we abused the notation for simplicity as Q_j^h, K_j^h, and $V_j^h \in \mathbb{R}^{H \times W \times \frac{D}{m}}$. Next, we reshape Q_j^h, K_j^h, and V_j^h to two-dimensional tensors with the size of $H \times \frac{D^h}{m}$, where $D^h = W \times D$, representing H horizontal strip tokens with the size of $\frac{D^h}{m}$. Then, the output features $O_j^h \in \mathbb{R}^{H \times \frac{D^h}{m}}$ is calculated as

$$O_j^h = \mathbf{Softmax}(\frac{Q_j^h (K_j^h)^T}{\sqrt{D^h/m}})V_j^h, \tag{6}$$

whose space complexity is $\mathcal{O}(H^2)$. Symmetrically, the vertical inter-strip attention generates the multi-head attended features $O_j^v \in \mathbb{R}^{W \times \frac{D^v}{m}}$, where $D^v = H \times D$. Its space complexity is $\mathcal{O}(W^2)$ in the attention mechanism.

Lastly, we concatenate the multi-head horizontal and vertical features along the channel dimension to be $O^h \in \mathbb{R}^{H \times D^h}$ and $O^v \in \mathbb{R}^{W \times D^v}$ and reshape them back to three-dimensional tensors with the size of $H \times W \times D$. Similar to Intra-SA in Eq. (4) and Eq. (5), we can generate the final output $O_{inter} \in R^{H \times W \times C}$ for an Inter-SA block. The total space complexity of Inter-SA is $\mathcal{O}(W^2 + H^2)$.

Compared to the vanilla transformer, whose space complexity takes up to $\mathcal{O}(H^2 W^2)$, our Stripformer is more token-efficient, which only takes $\mathcal{O}(HW(H + W) + H^2 + W^2) = \mathcal{O}(HW(H + W))$. Furthermore, the proposed horizontal and vertical multi-head Intra-SA and Inter-SA can help explore blur orientations. Stacking interlaced Intra-SA and Inter-SA blocks can reveal blur magnitudes. Therefore, even though Stripformer is a transformer-based architecture, our meticulous design for deblurring not only demands less memory but also achieves superior deblurring performance.

3.3   Loss Function

Contrastive Learning. Contrastive learning [3] is known to be an effective self-supervised technique. It allows a model to generate universal features from data similarity and dissimilarity even without labels. Recently, it has been adopted in vision tasks [2,36] by pulling close "positive" (similar) pairs and pushing apart "negative" (dissimilar) pairs in the feature space. Motivated by [36], we utilize contrastive learning to make a deblurred output image similar to its ground truth but dissimilar to its blurred input. Let the blurred input be X, its deblurred result be R, and the associated sharp ground truth be S, where X, R, and $S \in R^{H \times W \times 3}$. We regard X, R, and S as the negative, anchor, and positive samples. The contrastive loss is formulated as

$$L_{con} = \frac{L_1\big(\psi(S) - \psi(R)\big)}{L_1\big(\psi(X) - \psi(R)\big)}, \tag{7}$$

where ψ extracts the hidden features from conv3-2 of the fixed pre-trained VGG-19 [30], and L_1 represents the L_1 norm. Minimizing L_{con} helps pull the deblurred result R close to the sharp ground truth S (the numerator) while pushing R away from its blurred input X (the denominator) in the same latent feature space.

Optimization. The loss function of Stripformer for deblurring is

$$L = L_{char} + \lambda_1 L_{edge} + \lambda_2 L_{con}, \tag{8}$$

where L_{char} and L_{edge} are the Charbonnier loss and the edge loss the same as those used in MPRNet [39], and L_{con} is the contrastive loss. Here, we set to $\lambda_1 = 0.05$ as set in [39] and $\lambda_2 = 0.0005$.

4   Experiments

In this section, the proposed Stripformer is evaluated. We first describe the datasets and implementation details. Then we compare our method with the state-of-the-arts quantitatively and qualitatively. At last, the ablation studies are provided to demonstrate the effectiveness of the Stripformer design.

4.1   Datasets and Implementation Details

For comparison, we adopt the widely used GoPro dataset [20] which includes $2,103$ blurred and sharp pairs for training and $1,111$ pairs for testing. The HIDE dataset [29] with $2,025$ images is included only for testing. To address real-world blurs, we evaluate our method on the RealBlur dataset [28], which has $3,758$ blurred and sharp pairs for training and 980 pairs for testing.

We train our network with a batch size of 8 on the GoPro dataset. Adam optimizer is used with the initial learning rate of 10^{-4} that is steadily decayed to 10^{-7} by the cosine annealing strategy. We adopt random cropping, flipping, and rotation for data augmentation, like [23,38]. We train Stripformer on the GoPro training set and evaluate it on the GoPro testing set and HIDE dataset. For the RealBlur dataset, we use the RealBlur training set to train the model and evaluate it on the RealBlur testing set. We test our method on the full-size images using an NVIDIA 3090 GPU.

The authors from the universities in Taiwan completed the experiments.

4.2   Experimental Results

Quantitative Analysis. We compare our model on the GoPro testing set with several existing SOTA methods [2,4,5,11,14,17,18,23,25,26,31,33,38,39,42,43]. In Table 1, all of the compared methods utilize CNN-based architectures to build the deblurring networks except for IPT [2] and our network, where transformers serve as the backbone for deblurring. As shown in Table 1, Stripformer performs favorably against all competing methods in both PSNR and SSIM on the GoPro test set. It is worth mentioning that Stripformer can achieve state-of-the-art performance by only using the GoPro training set. It has exceeded the expectation that transformer-based architectures tend to have suboptimal performance compared to most of the CNN-based methods without using a large amount of training data [2,9]. That is, a transformer-based model typically requires a large dataset, *e.g.*more than one million annotated data, for pre-training to compete with a CNN-based model in vision tasks. For example, IPT fine-tunes the models with pre-training on ImageNet for deraining, denoising, and super-resolution tasks to achieve competitive performance. We attribute Stripformer's success

Table 1. Evaluation results on the benchmark GoPro testing set. The best two scores in each column are highlighted in bold and underlined, respectively. † represents the work did not release the code or pre-trained weight. Params and Time are calculated in (M) and (ms), respectively.

Method	PSNR ↑	SSIM ↑	Params ↓	Time ↓
CNN-based				
DeblurGAN-v2 [17]	29.55	0.934	68	60
EDSD† [38]	29.81	0.937	**3**	**10**
SRN [33]	30.25	0.934	<u>7</u>	650
PyNAS† [14]	30.62	0.941	9	<u>17</u>
DSD [11]	30.96	0.942	**3**	1300
DBGAN† [43]	31.10	0.942	–	–
MTRNN [23]	31.13	0.944	**3**	30
DMPHN [42]	31.20	0.945	22	303
SimpleNet† [18]	31.52	0.950	25	376
RADN† [25]	31.85	0.953	–	38
SAPHN† [31]	32.02	0.953	–	770
SPAIR† [26]	32.06	0.953	–	–
MIMO [5]	32.45	0.957	16	31
TTFA† [4]	32.50	0.958	–	–
MPRNet [39]	32.66	0.959	20	148
Transformer-based				
IPT† [2]	32.58	–	114	–
Stripformer	**33.08**	**0.962**	20	52

on deblurring to being able to better leverage the local and global information with our intra-strip and inter-strip attention design. In addition, Stripformer can run efficiently without using recurrent architectures compared to the [31,39,42]. Table 2 and Table 3 report more results on the HIDE and RealBlur datasets, respectively. As can be seen, Stripformer again achieves the best deblurring performance among the SOTA methods for both synthetic and real-world blur datasets.

Qualitative Analysis. Fig. 4 and Fig. 5 show the qualitative comparisons on the GoPro test set and the HIDE dataset among our method and those in [5,11,23,39,42]. They indicate that our method can better restore images, especially on highly textured regions such as texts and vehicles. It can also restore fine-grained information like facial expressions on the HIDE dataset. In Fig. 6, we show the qualitative comparisons on the RealBlur test set among our method and those in [5,17,33,39]. This dataset contains images in low-light environments where motion blurs usually occur. As can be observed, our model can better restore these regions than the competing works. In Fig. 7, we show the qualitative comparisons on the RWBI [43] dataset, which contains real images without ground truth. As shown, our model produces sharper deblurring results than the other methods [5,17,33,39]. Overall, the qualitative results demonstrate that Stripformer works well on blurred images in both synthetic and real-world scenes.

Table 2. Evaluation results on the benchmark HIDE dataset. Note that all the models are trained on the GoPro training set. The best two scores in each column are highlighted in bold and underlined, respectively. Params and Time are calculated in (M) and (ms), respectively.

Method	PSNR ↑	SSIM ↑	Params ↓	Time ↓
DeblurGAN-v2 [17]	27.40	0.882	68	57
SRN [33]	28.36	0.904	<u>7</u>	424
HAdeblur [29]	28.87	0.930	–	–
DSD [11]	29.01	0.913	**3**	1200
DMPHN [42]	29.10	0.918	22	310
MTRNN [23]	29.15	0.918	22	<u>40</u>
SAPHN[†] [31]	29.98	0.930	–	–
MIMO [5]	30.00	0.930	16	**30**
TTFA[†] [4]	30.55	0.935	–	–
MPRNet [39]	<u>30.96</u>	<u>0.939</u>	20	140
Stripformer	**31.03**	**0.940**	20	43

Table 3. Evaluation results on the RealBlur testing set. The best and the second scores in each column are highlighted in bold and underlined, respectively. Params and Time are calculated in (M) and (ms), respectively.

Model	RealBlur-J		RealBlur-R		RealBlur	
	PSNR ↑	SSIM ↑	PSNR ↑	SSIM ↑	Params ↓	Time ↓
DeblurGANv2 [17]	29.69	0.870	36.44	0.935	68	60
SRN [33]	31.38	0.909	38.65	0.965	**7**	412
MPRNet [39]	31.76	<u>0.922</u>	<u>39.31</u>	<u>0.972</u>	20	113
SPAIR† [26]	31.82	–	–	–	–	–
MIMO [5]	<u>31.92</u>	0.919	–	–	<u>16</u>	**39**
Stripformer	**32.48**	**0.929**	**39.84**	**0.974**	20	<u>42</u>

4.3 Ablation Studies

Here, We conduct ablation studies to analyze the proposed design, including component and computational analyses and comparisons against various modern attention mechanisms.

Component Analysis. Stripformer utilizes intra-strip and inter-strip attention blocks in horizontal and vertical directions to address various blur patterns with diverse magnitudes and orientations. Table 4 reports the contributions of individual components of Stripformer. The first two rows of Table 4 show the

Fig. 4. Qualitative comparisons on the GoPro testing set. The deblurred results from left to right are produced by DSD [11], DMPHN [42], MTRNN [23], MIMO [5], MPRNet [39], and our method, respectively.

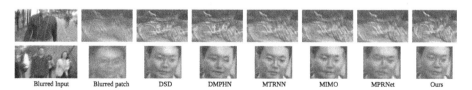

Fig. 5. Qualitative comparisons on the HIDE dataset. The deblurred results from left to right are produced by DSD [11], DMPHN [42], MTRNN [23], MIMO [5], MPRNet [39] and our method, respectively.

Table 4. Component analysis of Stripformer trained and tested on the GoPro training and test sets.

Intra-SA	Inter-SA	CPE	L_{con}	PSNR
√				32.84
	√			32.88
√	√			33.00
√	√	√		33.03
√	√	√	√	33.08

performance of using either the intra-strip or inter-strip attention blocks only, respectively. The two types of attention blocks are synergistic since combining them results in better performance, as given in the third row. It reveals that Stripformer encoders feature both pixel-wise and region-wise dependency, more suitable to solve the regional-specific blurred artifacts. In the fourth row, the conditional positional encoding (CPE) [8] is included for positional encoding and boosts the performance, which shows it works better for arbitrary input sizes compared to the fixed, learnable positional encoding. The last row shows that the contrastive loss can further improve deblurring performance.

Analysis on Transformer-Based Architectures and Attention Mechanisms. We compare Stripformer against efficient transformer-based architectures, including Swin [19] and Twins [7], and the attention mechanism CCNet [15]. Note that these three compared methods are designed for efficient attention computation rather than deblurring. For fair comparisons, we replace

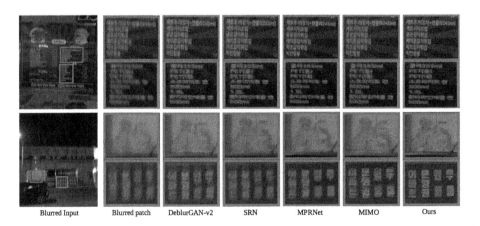

Blurred Input   Blurred patch   DeblurGAN-v2   SRN   MPRNet   MIMO   Ours

Fig. 6. Qualitative comparisons on the RealBlur dataset. The deblurred results from left to right are produced by DeblurGAN-v2 [17], SRN [33], MPRNet [39], MIMO [5] and our method.

Table 5. Comparison among various attention mechanisms. FLOPs are calculated the same way as IPT. The inference time (Time) is measured based on the GoPro and HIDE datasets on average for full-resolution (1280×720) images.

Method	IPT [2]	Swin [19]	CCNet [15]	Twins [7]	Ours
Params (M)	114	20	20	20	20
FLOPs (G)	32	6.7	7.4	6.5	6.9
Time (ms)	–	48	47	43	48
GoPro (PSNR)	32.58	32.39	32.73	32.89	**33.08**
HIDE (PSNR)	–	30.19	30.61	30.82	**31.03**

our attention mechanism in Stripformer with theirs using a similar parameter size and apply the resultant models to deblurring. As reported in Table 5, the proposed intra-strip and inter-strip attention mechanism in Stripformer works better in PSNR than all the other competing attention mechanisms. The reason is that Stripformer takes the inductive bias of image deblurring into account to design the intra-strip and inter-strip tokens and attention mechanism. It strikes a good balance among the image restorability, model size, and computational efficiency for image deblurring. Besides, SWin works with a shifted windowing scheme, restricting its self-attention computed locally. Thus, it is not enough to obtain sufficient global information for deblurring like our intra- and inter-strip attention design. CCNet extracts pixel correlations horizontally and vertically in a criss-cross manner. Twins uses local window attention and global sub-sampled attention (down to the size of 7×7). Both of them consider more global information, working better than SWin. Our strip-wise attention design can better harvest local and global blur information to remove short-range and long-range blur artifacts, performing favorably against all these compared attention mechanisms.

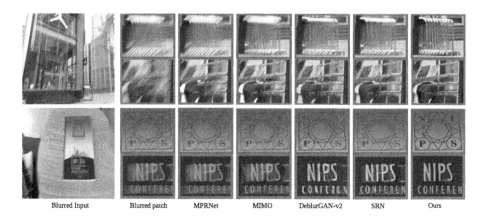

Blurred Input   Blurred patch   MPRNet   MIMO   DeblurGAN-v2   SRN   Ours

Fig. 7. Qualitative comparisons on the RWBI [43]. The deblurred results from left to right are produced by MPRNet [39], MIMO [5], DeblurGAN-v2 [17], SRN [33], and our method.

5   Conclusions

In this paper, we propose a novel model, called Stripformer, for dynamic scene image deblurring. Stripformer is a token- and parameter-efficient transformer-based model designed for region-specific blur artifacts in images taken in dynamic scenes. To better address such blur having diverse orientations and magnitudes, Stripformer utilizes both intra- and inter-strip attentions to demand not only less memory and computation costs than a vanilla transformer but to achieve excellent deblurring performance. Experimental results show that our method achieves SOTA performance on three benchmarks, including the GoPro, HIDE, and Realblur datasets, without using a large dataset like ImageNet for pre-training. Moreover, in terms of memory usage, model size, and inference time, Stripformer performs quite competitively. We believe that Stripformer is a friendly transformer-based model that can serve as a good basis for further advancing transformer-based architectures in image deblurring and more.

Acknowledgments. This work was supported in part by the Ministry of Science and Technology (MOST) under grants 109–2221-E-009–113- MY3, 111–2628-E-A49-025-MY3, 111–2634-F-007–002, 110–2634-F-002–050, 110–2634-F-006–022, 110–2622-E-004–001, and 111–2221-E-004–010. This work was funded in part by Qualcomm through a Taiwan University Research Collaboration Project and by MediaTek. We thank the National Center for High-performance Computing (NCHC) of National Applied Research Laboratories (NARLabs) in Taiwan for providing computational and storage resources.

References

1. Carion, N., Massa, F., Synnaeve, G., Usunier, N., Kirillov, A., Zagoruyko, S.: End-to-end object detection with transformers. In: Proceedings of the European Conference on Computer Vision (2020)
2. Chen, H., et al.: Pre-trained image processing transformer. In: Proceedings of the Conference on Computer Vision and Pattern Recognition (2021)
3. Chen, T., Kornblith, S., Norouzi, M., Hinton, G.: A simple framework for contrastive learning of visual representations. In: Proceedings of the Conference on Machine Learning (2020)
4. Chi, Z., Wang, Y., Yu, Y., Tang, J.: Test-time fast adaptation for dynamic scene deblurring via meta-auxiliary learning. In: Proceedings of the Conference on Computer Vision and Pattern Recognition (2021)
5. Cho, S.J., Ji, S.W., Hong, J.P., Jung, S.W., Ko, S.J.: Rethinking coarse-to-fine approach in single image deblurring. In: Proceedings of the Conference on Computer Vision (2021)
6. Cho, S., Lee, S.: Fast motion deblurring. In: ACM Trans. Graphic. (2009)
7. Chu, X., et al.: Twins: Revisiting the design of spatial attention in vision transformers. In: Proceedings of the Conference on Neural Information Processing Systems (2021)
8. Chu, X., et al.: Conditional positional encodings for vision transformers. In: arxiv preprint arXiv:2102.10882 (2021)

9. Dosovitskiy, A., et al.: An image is worth 16x16 words: Transformers for image recognition at scale. In: Proceedings of the Conference on Learning Representations (2021)
10. Fergus, R., Singh, B., Hertzmann, A., Roweis, S.T., Freeman, W.T.: Removing camera shake from a single photograph. ACM Trans. Graphic. **25**(3), 787–794 (2006)
11. Gao, H., Tao, X., Shen, X., Jia, J.: Dynamic scene deblurring with parameter selective sharing and nested skip connections. In: Proceedings of the Conference on Computer Vision and Pattern Recognition (2019)
12. Hou, Q., Zhang, L., Cheng, M.M., Feng, J.: Strip Pooling: Rethinking spatial pooling for scene parsing. In: Proceedings of the Conference on Computer Vision and Pattern Recognition (2020)
13. Hu, J., Shen, L., Sun, G.: Squeeze-and-excitation networks. In: Proc. Conf. Computer Vision and Pattern Recognition (2018)
14. Hu, X., et al.: Pyramid architecture search for real-time image deblurring. In: Proceedings of the Conference on Computer Vision (2021)
15. Huang, Z., Wang, X., Huang, L., Huang, C., Wei, Y., Liu, W.: Ccnet: Criss-cross attention for semantic segmentation. In: Proceedings of the Conference on Computer Vision (2019)
16. Joshi, N., Zitnick, C.L., Szeliski, R., Kriegman, D.J.: Image deblurring and denoising using color priors. In: Proceedings of the Conference on Computer Vision and Pattern Recognition (2009)
17. Kupyn, O., Martyniuk, T., Wu, J., Wang, Z.: Deblurgan-v2: Deblurring (orders-of-magnitude) faster and better. In: Proceedings of the Conference on Computer Vision (2019)
18. Li, J., Tan, W., Yan, B.: Perceptual variousness motion deblurring with light global context refinement. In: Proceedings of the Conference on Computer Vision (2021)
19. Liu, Z., et al.: Swin transformer: Hierarchical vision transformer using shifted windows. In: Proceedings of the Conference on Computer Vision (2021)
20. Nah, S., Kim, T.H., Lee, K.M.: Deep multi-scale convolutional neural network for dynamic scene deblurring. In: Proceedings of the Conference on Computer Vision and Pattern Recognition (2017)
21. Pan, J., Hu, Z., Su, Z., Yang, M.H.: Deblurring text images via l0-regularized intensity and gradient prior. In: Proceedings of the Conference on Computer Vision and Pattern Recognition (2014)
22. Pan, J., Sun, D., Pfister, H., Yang, M.H.: Deblurring images via dark channel prior. In: Proceedings of the Conference on Computer Vision and Pattern Recognition (2018)
23. Park, D., Kang, D.U., Kim, J., Chun, S.Y.: Multi-temporal recurrent neural networks for progressive non-uniform single image deblurring with incremental temporal training. In: Proceedings of the European Conference on Computer Vision (2020)
24. Parmar, N., Vaswani, A., Uszkoreit, J., Kaiser, Ł., Shazeer, N., Ku, A., Tran, D.: Image transformer. arXiv preprint arXiv:1802.05751 (2018)
25. Purohit, K., Rajagopalan, A.N.: Region-adaptive dense network for efficient motion deblurring. In: Proceedings of the Conference on Artificial Intelligence (2020)
26. Purohit, K., Suin, M., Rajagopalan, A.N., Boddeti, V.N.: Spatially-adaptive image restoration using distortion-guided networks. In: Proceedings of the Conference on Computer Vision (2021)
27. Ranftl, R., Bochkovskiy, A., Koltun, V.: Vision transformers for dense prediction. In: Proceedings of the Conference on Computer Vision (2021)

28. Rim, J., Lee, H., Won, J., Cho, S.: Real-world blur dataset for learning and bench-marking deblurring algorithms. In: Proceedings of the European Conference Computer Vision (2020)
29. Shen, Z., Wang, W., Shen, J., Ling, H., Xu, T., Shao, L.: Human-aware motion deblurring. In: Proceedings of the Conference on Computer Vision (2019)
30. Simonyan, K., Zisserman, A.: Very deep convolutional networks for large-scale image recognition. In: Proceedings of the Conference on Learning Representations (2015)
31. Suin, M., Purohit, K., Rajagopalan, A.N.: Spatially-attentive patch-hierarchical network for adaptive motion deblurring. In: Proceedings of the Conference on Computer Vision and Pattern Recognition (2020)
32. Sun, J., Cao, W., Xu, Z., Ponce, J.: Learning a convolutional neural network for non-uniform motion blur removal. In: Proceedings of the Conference on Computer Vision and Pattern Recognition (2015)
33. Tao, X., Gao, H., Shen, X., Wang, J., Jia, J.: Scale-recurrent network for deep image deblurring. In: Proceedings of the Conference on Computer Vision and Pattern Recognition (2018)
34. Vaswani, A., et al.: Attention is all you need. In: Proceedings of the Conference on Neural Information Processing Systems (2017)
35. Wang, X., Girshick, R., Gupta, A., He, K.: Non-local neural networks. In: Proceedings of the Conference on Computer Vision and Pattern Recognition (2018)
36. Wu, H., et al.: Contrastive learning for compact single image dehazing. In: Proceedings of the Conference on Computer Vision and Pattern Recognition (2021)
37. Yang, F., Yang, H., Fu, J., Lu, H., Guo, B.: Learning texture transformer network for image super-resolution. In: Proceedings of the Conference on Computer Vision and Pattern Recognition (2020)
38. Yuan, Y., Su, W., Ma, D.: Efficient dynamic scene deblurring using spatially variant deconvolution network with optical flow guided training. In: Proceedings of the Conference on Computer Vision and Pattern Recognition (2020)
39. Zamir, S.W., et al.: Multi-stage progressive image restoration. In: Proceedings of the Conference on Computer Vision and Pattern Recognition (2021)
40. Zeng, Y., Fu, J., Chao, H.: Learning joint spatial-temporal transformations for video inpainting. In: Proceedings of the European Conference on Computer Vision (2020)
41. Zhang, H., Goodfellow, I., Metaxas, D., Odena, A.: Self-attention generative adversarial networks. In: arXiv preprint arXiv:1805.08318 (2019)
42. Zhang, H., Dai, Y., Li, H., Koniusz, P.: Deep stacked hierarchical multi-patch network for image deblurring. In: Proceedings of the Conference on Computer Vision and Pattern Recognition (2019)
43. Zhang, K., et al.: Deblurring by realistic blurring. In: Proceedings of the Conference on Computer Vision and Pattern Recognition (2020)

Deep Fourier-Based Exposure Correction Network with Spatial-Frequency Interaction

Jie Huang[1], Yajing Liu[2], Feng Zhao[1(✉)], Keyu Yan[1], Jinghao Zhang[1], Yukun Huang[1], Man Zhou[1(✉)], and Zhiwei Xiong[1]

[1] University of Science and Technology of China, Hefei, China
{hj0117,keyu,jhaozhang,kevinh,manman}@mail.ustc.edu.cn,
{fzhao956,zwxiong}@ustc.edu.cn
[2] JD Logistics, JD.com, Beijing, China
{lyj123}@mail.ustc.edu.cn

Abstract. Images captured under incorrect exposures unavoidably suffer from mixed degradations of lightness and structures. Most existing deep learning-based exposure correction methods separately restore such degradations in the spatial domain. In this paper, we present a new perspective for exposure correction with spatial-frequency interaction. Specifically, we first revisit the frequency properties of different exposure images via Fourier transform where the amplitude component contains most lightness information and the phase component is relevant to structure information. To this end, we propose a deep Fourier-based Exposure Correction Network (FECNet) consisting of an amplitude sub-network and a phase sub-network to progressively reconstruct the representation of lightness and structure components. To facilitate learning these two representations, we introduce a Spatial-Frequency Interaction (SFI) block in two formats tailored to these two sub-networks, which interactively process the local spatial features and the global frequency information to encourage the complementary learning. Extensive experiments demonstrate that our method achieves superior results than other approaches with fewer parameters and can be extended to other image enhancement tasks, validating its potential in wide-range applications. Code will be available at https://github.com/KevinJ-Huang/FECNet.

Keywords: Exposure correction · Fourier transform · Spatial-frequency interaction

1 Introduction

With the wide-range applications of camera devices, images can be captured under scenes with varying exposures, which could result in unsatisfactory visual results including lightness and structure distortions. Thus, it is necessary to

---

J. Huang and Y. Liu—Equal contribution.

S. Avidan et al. (Eds.): ECCV 2022, LNCS 13679, pp. 163–180, 2022.
https://doi.org/10.1007/978-3-031-19800-7_10

164   J. Huang et al.

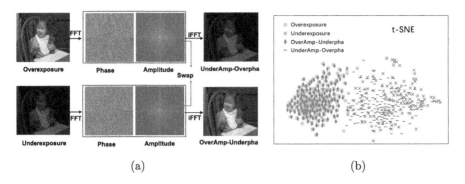

(a)   (b)

**Fig. 1. (a) We swap the amplitude and phase components of different expo-
sures of the same context.** The recombined result of the amplitude of underexposure
and the phase of overexposure (UnderAmp-Overpha) has similar lightness appearance
with underexposure, while the recombined result of the amplitude of overexposure and
the phase of underexposure (OverAmp-Underpha) has similar lightness appearance
with overexposure. **(b) The t-SNE [28] for images of overexposure, underexposure, UnderAmp-Overpha, and OverAmp-Underpha.** The distributions of
images in UnderAmp-Overpha and Underexposure are matched, while the distributions of images in OverAmp-Underpha and Overexposure are matched, which indicate
that the swapped amplitude components include the most lightness information.

correct such exposures of these images, which not only improves their visual
qualities but also benefits other sub-sequential high-level vision tasks such as
image detection and segmentation [40,45].

The mixed degradations of both lightness and structure components may lead
to difficulties in conducting exposure correction [26], which may cause structure
distortions and ineffective lightness adjustments [2,25]. To solve this problem,
since different exposures share similar structure representations but different
lightness depictions [22], it is natural to decompose and restore the lightness
and structure components of the input image, respectively. Retinex theory-based
methods [16,41,50] decompose images into illumination and reflectance components, and then separately recover the lightness and structure information.
Multi-scale decomposition-based approaches [2,23,25] intend to decompose and
recover the coarse-scale lightness and fine-scale structures in a progressive manner. With the advanced design of deep neural networks, recent techniques have
significantly improved the visual quality. However, most of them rarely explore
the potential solutions in the frequency domain, which is quite crucial for improving the image quality [13,20].

In this work, we introduce a novel Fourier-based perspective to conduct exposure correction, which facilitates utilizing and restoring the frequency-domain
information. From [42], the amplitude and phase components of Fourier space
correspond to the style and semantic information of an image. This property can
be extended in exposure correction, i.e., the amplitude component of an image
reflects the lightness representation, while the phase component corresponds to
structures and is less related to lightness. As shown in Fig. 1, we first swap the
amplitude and phase components of different exposures of the same context.

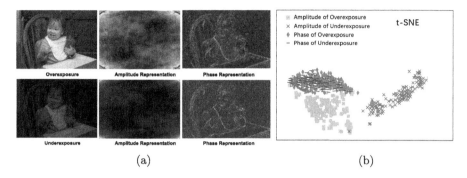

Fig. 2. (a) **The visualization for the amplitude and phase components of the same context.** We apply the iFFT to the phase and amplitude to compare them in the spatial domain. The amplitude representations differ significantly between different exposures, while the phase representations are very similar across exposures and present structure representation. (b) **The t-SNE of amplitude and phase of different exposures.** The distributions of phase representations across different exposures are matched, while distributions of amplitude representations across different exposures vary greatly. It means that the phase component includes the most structure information and is less affected by lightness.

The recombined result of the amplitude of underexposure and the phase of overexposure has similar lightness appearance with underexposure, while the other behaves conversely. This implies that the swapped amplitude components include the most lightness information, and the phase component may correspond to the structure representation and is less affected by lightness.

To validate this, as shown in Fig. 2, we apply the inverse Fast Fourier Transform (iFFT) [31] to the phase and amplitude components to visualize them in the spatial domain. The appearance of the phase representation is more similar to the structure representation, and the distribution of the phase components is less affected by lightness. To this end, the phase component is more related to structures that are less affected by lightness in the spatial domain. Therefore, following existing works that separately restore lightness and structure degradations, we intend to restore the amplitude and phase components progressively.

Based on the above analysis, we propose a Fourier-based Exposure Correction Network (FECNet), as shown in Fig. 3. It consists of an amplitude sub-network and a phase sub-network that are arranged sequentially. Specifically, the amplitude sub-network learns to restore the amplitude representation to improve the lightness appearance, while the phase sub-network learns to reconstruct the phase representation that refines the structures. To guide the learning of these two sub-networks, in addition to the constraint of the ground truth, we supervise them with corresponding amplitude and phase components of the ground truth.

To further facilitate the representation learning of the amplitude and phase, we introduce a Spatial-Frequency Interaction (SFI) block (see Fig. 5). It is tailored in two formats (amplitude and phase) with two sub-networks as the basic units to learn the corresponding representation, and the SFI block of each format is composed of a frequency branch and a spatial branch to complement the global and local information. On the one hand, for the amplitude or phase sub-network, the amplitude/phase format of SFI processes the corresponding amplitude/phase component in the Fourier space and bypasses the other component. On the other hand, since the Fourier transform allows the image-wide receptive field to cover the whole image [11,21], the frequency-domain representation focuses on global attributions. Meanwhile, the local attribution can be learned in the spatial branch by normal convolutions. To this end, we interact with these two branches to obtain the complementary information, which benefits the learning of corresponding representations.

Moreover, our proposed FECNet is lightweight and can be extended to other enhancement tasks like low-light image enhancement and retouching, showing its potential in wide-range applications. In summary, our contributions include:

1. We introduce a new perspective for exposure correction by restoring the representation of different components in the frequency domain. Particularly, we propose a Fourier-based Exposure Correction Network (FECNet) consisting of an amplitude sub-network and a phase sub-network, which restores the amplitude and phase representations that correspond to improving lightness and refining structures progressively.
2. Tailored with the learning of the amplitude and phase sub-networks, we design a Spatial-Frequency Interaction (SFI) block in two formats that correspond to the two sub-networks as their basic units. The interaction of spatial and frequency information helps integrate the global and local representations that provide complementary information.
3. Our FECNet is lightweight, and we validate its effectiveness on several datasets. Furthermore, we extend our method to other enhancement tasks, including low-light enhancement and retouching, which demonstrate its superiority ability in wide-range applications.

2   Related Work

2.1   Exposure Correction

Exposure correction has been studied for a long time. Several conventional methods apply histogram adjustment for correcting the lightness and contrast [1,33,36,47]. Another line of works is based on the Retinex theory [22], which improves the lightness through enhancing the illumination component, and regularizes the reflectance component to recover the texture [6,16,24,35,48].

In recent years, deep learning-based methods have been developed for exposure correction [9,26,27,39,44]. Most exposure correction works are dedicated to enhancing underexposure images. Based on the Retinex theory, RetinexNet [41] and KinD [50] decompose the image into illumination and reflectance components and then restore them in a data-driven manner. As another form of component decomposition, DRBN [43] decomposes features into different band representations and then recursively recovers them. More recently, targeting at correcting both underexposure and overexposure images, MSEC [2] proposes to correct varieties of exposures with a pyramid structure to restore different-scale components in a coarse-to-fine manner. CMEC [30] employs an encoder to map different exposures to an exposure-invariant space with the assistance of a transformer for exposure correction. However, existing methods rarely consider correcting exposures by frequency-domain representations. Compared with these methods, our algorithm focuses on processing information in the Fourier space to recover frequency representations, which is a new perspective in this area.

2.2   Fourier Transform in Neural Networks

Recently, information processing in the Fourier space of frequency domain has attracted increasing attentions [10,11,34,37,42], which is capable of capturing global frequency representation effectively [21]. A line of works leverages the Fourier transform to improve the generalization of neural networks. For example, FDA [46] develops a data augmentation strategy by swapping the amplitude and phase components in the Fourier space across images, enabling the network to learn robust representations for image segmentation. Similarly, Xu *et al.* [42] proposed a Fourier-based augmentation strategy with the combing of a mix-up for generalized image classification. Another line of works employs the Fourier transform to improve the representation ability of neural networks. For instance, GFNet [34] attempts to transform features to the Fourier space before fully-connected layers to improve the network stability. FFC [10] introduces paired spatial-frequency transforms and devises several new layers in the Fourier space. Besides, a few works adopt Fourier-based loss functions for image restoration [13] and image translation [20], achieving pleasant visual results. Motivated by the success of these works, we propose a deep Fourier-based exposure correction network, which learns to recover different components of frequency representations.

3   Method

3.1   Motivation and Background

Images captured under improper exposures often suffer from unsatisfactory visual problems, including lightness and structure distortions. Previous works rarely restore these distortions in the frequency domain, which has been proved crucial for improving the visual qualities [13]. To this end, we design a deep Fourier-based exposure correction network to capture and restore the frequency representations effectively.

Firstly, we revisit the operation and property of the Fourier transform. Given a single channel image x with the shape of $H \times W$, the Fourier transform $\mathcal{F}$ converts to the Fourier space as a complex component X, which is expressed as:

$$\mathcal{F}(x)(u,v) = X(u,v) = \frac{1}{\sqrt{HW}} \sum_{h=0}^{H-1} \sum_{w=0}^{W-1} x(h,w) e^{-j2\pi(\frac{h}{H}u + \frac{w}{W}v)}, \tag{1}$$

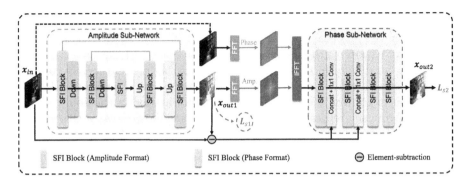

Fig. 3. The overview of our proposed FECNet consisting of an amplitude sub-network that restores the amplitude representation and a phase sub-network that restores the phase representation. The phase sub-network takes the recombined results of $\mathcal{F}^{-1}(\mathcal{A}(X_{out1}), \mathcal{P}(X_{in}))$ as the input, with the lightness changing residual of the amplitude sub-network to guide its learning. Both sub-networks employ the corresponding amplitude and phase components of the ground truth as the supervision signal, and the two formats of the SFI block are set as their basic units correspondingly.

and $\mathcal{F}^{-1}$ denotes the inverse Fourier transform. Since an image or feature may contain multiple channels, we separately apply Fourier transform to each channel in our work with the FFT [31].

In the Fourier space, each complex component $X(u, v)$ can be represented by the amplitude component $\mathcal{A}(X(u, v))$ and the phase component $\mathcal{P}(X(u, v))$, which provides an intuitive analysis of the frequency components [13]. These two components are expressed as:

$$\mathcal{A}(X(u,v)) = \sqrt{R^2(X(u,v)) + I^2(X(u,v))},$$
$$\mathcal{P}(X(u,v)) = arctan[\frac{I(X(u,v))}{R(X(u,v))}],$$

(2)

where $R(x)$ and $I(x)$ represent the real and imaginary parts of $X(u, v)$.

According to the Fourier theory, the amplitude component $\mathcal{A}$ reflects the style information of an image in the frequency domain, while the phase component $\mathcal{P}$ represents the semantic information [42,46]. For exposure correction, we explore whether $\mathcal{A}$ and $\mathcal{P}$ could correspond to the frequency-domain representations of lightness and structure components. To visualize the amplitude and phase components, we swap the amplitude and phase components of different exposures of the same context, then we observe the phenomenon as shown in Fig. 1. Denoting the underexposure and overexposure image as x_{under} and x_{over}, and their Fourier representations as X_{under} and X_{over}, respectively. The recombined result $\mathcal{F}^{-1}(\mathcal{A}(X_{under}), \mathcal{P}(X_{over}))$ has similar lightness appearance with x_{under}, while $\mathcal{F}^{-1}(\mathcal{A}(X_{over}), \mathcal{P}(X_{under}))$ behaves conversely. Furthermore, we convert the amplitude (phase) components of x_{under} and x_{over} to spatial domain by replacing the amplitude (phase) components with a constant c, and we observe the phenomenon in Fig. 2. The appearance of the converted phase

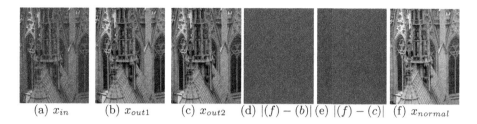

(a) x_{in} (b) x_{out1} (c) x_{out2} (d) $|(f) - (b)|$ (e) $|(f) - (c)|$ (f) x_{normal}

Fig. 4. Visualization of different components in FECNet. As can be seen, with the amplitude sub-network, the overall lightness representations are improved. After the processing of the phase sub-network, the structures are refined with lower residual error. $|\cdot|$ denotes the "absolute" operation. Darker areas in the residual map denote lower errors.

representation looks like more similar to structures than the converted amplitude one. Besides, the difference between the converted result $\mathcal{F}^{-1}(c, \mathcal{P}(X_{under}))$ and $\mathcal{F}^{-1}(c, \mathcal{P}(X_{over}))$ is small, while the difference between $\mathcal{F}^{-1}(\mathcal{A}(X_{under}), c)$ and $\mathcal{F}^{-1}(\mathcal{A}(X_{over}), c)$ is larger. It proves the phase component responds more to the structure information and is less affected by the lightness.

Based on the above observations, we can draw the conclusion that the amplitude component of an image reflects the lightness representation, while the phase component corresponds to the structures and is less affected by lightness. Following existing works that respectively restore degradations of lightness and structures, we restore the amplitude and phase components progressively, which facilitate the recovering the frequency representations of lightness and structures that benefit improving the image quality.

3.2 Deep Fourier-Based Exposure Correction Network

Based on the above analysis, we design a simple but effective FECNet net as shown in Fig. 3. The entire network consists of two sub-networks: an amplitude sub-network and a phase sub-network, progressively restoring the amplitude and phase representations. Specifically, both sub-networks employ the SFI block as the basic unit, which will be described in Sect. 3.3.

We design an encoder-decoder format for the amplitude sub-network, consisting of five SFI blocks of its amplitude format. Let us denote x_{in} and x_{out1} as the input and output of the amplitude sub-network, x_{normal} represents the ground truth normal exposure image, and their representations in Fourier space are denoted as X_{in}, X_{out1} and X_{normal}, respectively. To guarantee this sub-network learns the amplitude representation, it is supervised by the recombined component $\mathcal{F}^{-1}(\mathcal{A}(X_{normal}), \mathcal{P}(X_{in}))$, as well as the amplitude component of the ground truth $\mathcal{A}(X_{normal})$. The loss function for this sub-network $\mathcal{L}_{s1}$ is expressed as:

$$L_{s1} = ||x_{out1} - \mathcal{F}^{-1}(\mathcal{A}(X_{normal}), \mathcal{P}(X_{in}))||_1 + \alpha||\mathcal{A}(X_{out1}) - \mathcal{A}(X_{normal})||_1, \quad (3)$$

where $||\cdot||_1$ denotes the mean absolutely error, α is the weight factor and we set it as 0.2.

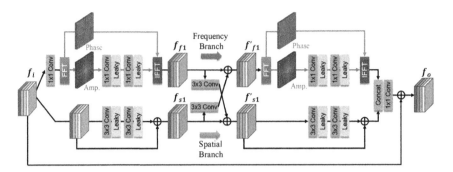

Fig. 5. The illustration of the amplitude format of the SFI block, which consists of a frequency branch and a spatial branch. The frequency branch processes the amplitude component and bypasses the phase component, while the spatial one utilizes a residual block. There exist interactions across representations of these two branches for complementary information. The phase format of the SFI block is similar except for the frequency branch, and we illustrate it in the supplementary material.

While for the phase sub-network, we formulate it sequentially with four SFI blocks of its phase format. Specifically, we use the recombined component $\mathcal{F}^{-1}(\mathcal{A}(X_{out1}), \mathcal{P}(X_{in}))$ as the input of this sub-network instead of x_{out1}, avoiding introduce the altered phase component [46]. In addition, since the distortion of structures are relevant to the lightness changing [22,24], and the residual of the amplitude sub-network can represent the lightness changing, we utilize the residual between x_{out1} and x_{in} to guide the learning of this sub-network. It is implemented by concatenating this residual with the features in the phase sub-network, following by a 1×1 convolution to integrate them. Denoting the output of the phase sub-network as x_{out2}, we set the loss function L_{s2} for this sub-network as:

$$L_{s2} = ||x_{out2} - x_{normal}||_1 + \beta ||\mathcal{P}(X_{out2}) - \mathcal{P}(X_{normal})||_1, \qquad (4)$$

where β is the weight factor and we set it as 0.1. The phase sub-network can learn the recovery of the phase representation, and x_{out2} is the final output of FECNet. In this way, the FECNet is able to conduct exposure correction in a coarse to fine manner as shown in Fig. 4.

The overall network comprised of these two sub-networks is training in an end-to-end manner, and the overall loss L_{total} is the combination of L_{s1} and L_{s2}, which is formulated as:

$$L_{total} = L_{s2} + \lambda L_{s1}, \qquad (5)$$

where λ is the weight factor and is empirically set as 0.5.

3.3   Spatial-Frequency Interaction Block

To further facilitate learning the amplitude and phase representations, we propose the SFC block in two formats as the basic unit of the two sub-networks correspondingly. According to Fourier theory [21], processing information in Fourier

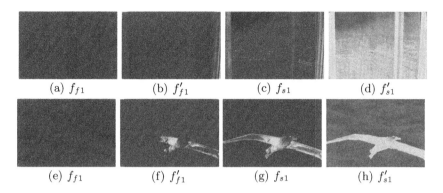

(a) f_{f1} (b) f'_{f1} (c) f_{s1} (d) f'_{s1}

(e) f_{f1} (f) f'_{f1} (g) f_{s1} (h) f'_{s1}

Fig. 6. Feature visualization of different representations in the SFI block. As can be seen, since features after interaction can obtain complementary representations from each other, features with and without interaction across the frequency branch and spatial branch are quite different. f_{f1} is more spatial invariant and f_{s1} keeps more spatial information, while f'_{f1} obtains the spatial information and the details in f'_{s1} are enhanced.

space is capable of capturing the global frequency representation in the frequency domain. In contrast, the normal convolution focuses on learning local representations in the spatial domain. In this way, we propose the interactive block to combine these two representations, which can learn more representative features.

We illustrate the amplitude format of the SFI block as shown in Fig. 5. Specifically, it comprises a spatial branch and a frequency branch for processing spatial and frequency representations. Denoting f_i as the input features of SFI block, the spatial branch first adopts a residual block with 3×3 convolution layers to process information in the spatial domain and obtain f_{s1}. While the frequency branch uses a 1×1 convolution to process f_i first that obtains f_{f0}, and then adopts Fourier transform to convert it to the Fourier space as F_{f0} by Eq. 1. To process frequency-domain representation F_{f0}, we adopt the operation $Op(\cdot)$ that consists of 1×1 convolution layers on its amplitude component, and then recompose the operated result with the phase component that obtain f_{f1}, which is expressed as:

$$f_{f1} = \mathcal{F}^{-1}(Op(\mathcal{A}(F_{f0})), \mathcal{P}(F_{f0})). \tag{6}$$

Thus, f_{f1} is the processed result of the frequency-domain representation. Next, we interact the features from spatial branch f_{s1} and frequency branch f_{f1} as:

$$\begin{aligned} f'_{s1} &= f_{s1} + W_1(f_{f1}), \\ f'_{f1} &= f_{f1} + W_2(f_{s1}), \end{aligned} \tag{7}$$

where both $W_1(\cdot)$ and $W_2(\cdot)$ denote the 3×3 convolution operation, f'_{s1} and f'_{f1} are the output of the interacted spatial branch and frequency branch. As illustrated in Fig. 6, both f'_{s1} and f'_{f1} get the complementary representation, which benefits for these two branches to obtain more representational features. The following spatial and frequency branches are formulated in the same way as above and output the results f_{s2} and f_{f2}, respectively.

Table 1. Quantitative results of different methods on the ME and SICE datasets in terms of PSNR and SSIM. #Param denotes the number of parameters.

Method	ME						SICE						#Param
	Under		Over		Average		Under		Over		Average		
	PSNR	SSIM	PSNR	SSIM	PSNR	SSIM	PSNR	SSIM	PSNR	SSIM	PSNR	SSIM	
CLAHE [36]	16.77	0.6211	14.45	0.5842	15.38	0.5990	12.69	0.5037	10.21	0.4847	11.45	0.4942	–
RetinexNet [41]	12.13	0.6209	10.47	0.5953	11.14	0.6048	12.94	0.5171	12.87	0.5252	12.90	0.5212	0.84 M
Zero-DCE [15]	14.55	0.5887	10.40	0.5142	12.06	0.5441	16.92	0.6330	7.11	0.4292	12.02	0.5311	0.079 M
DPED [19]	13.14	0.5812	20.06	0.6826	15.91	0.6219	16.83	0.6133	7.99	0.4300	12.41	0.5217	0.39 M
DRBN [43]	19.74	0.8290	19.37	0.8321	19.52	0.8309	17.96	**0.6767**	17.33	0.6828	17.65	0.6798	0.53 M
SID [8]	19.37	0.8103	18.83	0.8055	19.04	0.8074	19.51	0.6635	16.79	0.6444	18.15	0.6540	7.40 M
RUAS [38]	13.43	0.6807	6.39	0.4655	9.20	0.5515	16.63	0.5589	4.54	0.3196	10.59	0.4393	**0.003 M**
MSEC [2]	20.52	0.8129	19.79	0.8156	20.35	0.8210	19.62	0.6512	17.59	0.6560	18.58	0.6536	7.04 M
CMEC [30]	22.23	0.8140	22.75	0.8336	22.54	0.8257	17.68	0.6592	18.17	0.6811	17.93	0.6702	5.40 M
FECNet (Ours)	**22.96**	**0.8598**	**23.22**	**0.8748**	**23.12**	**0.8688**	**22.01**	0.6737	**19.91**	**0.6961**	**20.96**	**0.6849**	0.15 M

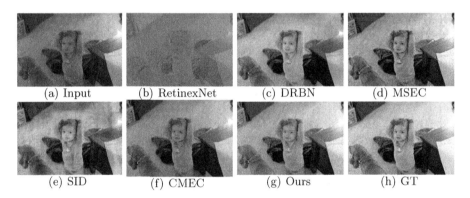

(a) Input　(b) RetinexNet　(c) DRBN　(d) MSEC

(e) SID　(f) CMEC　(g) Ours　(h) GT

Fig. 7. Visualization results on the ME dataset of underexposure correction. There exist color and lightness shift as well as artifact generation problems in other methods, while our method can simultaneously achieve good context and lightness recovery.

Finally, we concatenate f_{s2} and f_{f2} and then apply a 1×1 convolution operation to integrate them as f_o, which is the output of SFI block. Similarly, in the phase format of the SFI block, we replace the operation on the amplitude component in Eq. 6 with the phase component, while other parts keep unchanged.

4　Experiment

4.1　Settings

Datasets. We train our network on two representative multiple exposure datasets, including the multiple exposure (ME) dataset proposed in MSEC [2] and SICE dataset [7]. The ME dataset contains exposure images of 5 exposure levels, including 17675 images for training, 750 images for validation, and 5905 images for testing. For the SICE dataset, we derive the middle-level exposure subset as the ground truth and the corresponding second and last-second exposure subsets are set as underexposed and overexposed images, respectively.

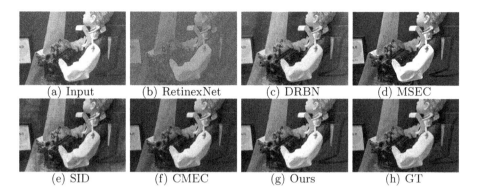

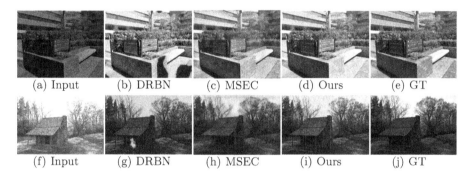

Fig. 8. Visualization results on the ME dataset of overexposure correction. As can be seen, the context and lightness can be well recovered in our method.

Fig. 9. Visualization results on the SICE dataset of (top) underexposure correction and (bottom) overexposure correction.

We adopt 1000 images for training, 24 images for validation and 60 images for testing respectively.

Implementation Details. The implement of our proposed method is based on PyTorch framework with one NVIDIA 3090 GPU. During the training, we adopt the Adam optimizer with the patch size of 384×384 and batch size of 4. For the ME and SICE datasets, the total number of epochs is set as 120 and 240, respectively. The initial learning rate of our FECNet is $1e^{-4}$, which decays by a factor value of 0.5 every 40 epochs and 80 epochs for the ME and SICE datasets. We adopt the commonly used metrics PSNR and SSIM for evaluation.

Table 2. Ablation study of investigating different settings of FECNet on the SICE dataset.

Option	(a)	(b)	(c)	(d)	(e)	(f)	FECNet
PSNR	19.98	20.03	19.35	20.78	20.67	20.77	20.96
SSIM	0.6698	0.6712	0.6643	0.6795	0.6773	0.6809	0.6849

Table 3. Ablation study of investigating the loss functions on the SICE dataset. (a) denotes removing the second term of L_{s1} on the base of L_{total}.

Options	Baseline	L_{s2}	Baseline+L_{s1}	(a)	L_{total}
PSNR/SSIM	20.01/0.6682	20.03/0.6713	20.83/0.6827	20.43/0.6785	20.96/0.6849

Table 4. Ablation study of investigating the SFI block on the SICE dataset. 2-SPB represents both branches are set to the spatial branches, and 2-FRB represents both branches are set to the frequency branches.

Option	2-SPB	2-FRB	w/o Interaction	SFI block
PSNR/SSIM	18.57/0.6593	18.64/0.6602	19.82/0.6676	20.96/0.6849

4.2 Performance Evaluation

In this paper, we compare our algorithm with several state-of-the-art exposure correction methods, including MSEC [2], DRBN [43], SID [8], RetinexNet [41], Zero-DCE [15], CMEC [30] and RUAS [38]. We provide more comparison results with other methods in the supplementary material.

Quantitative Evaluation. The quantitative results are shown in Table 1. For the ME dataset, following MSEC, we average the results of the exposures of the first two levels and the remaining levels of exposures as the underexposure and overexposure results, respectively. As can be observed, our method achieves the best performance among these methods. Specifically, MSEC significantly outperforms other methods except ours due to its well-designed architecture, while our FECNet has superior results than MSEC using its 2.1% network parameters, demonstrating the effectiveness and efficiency of our methods.

Qualitative Evaluation. In addition, we provide the visualization results of the ME dataset in Fig. 7 and Fig. 8, and the results of the SICE dataset in Fig. 9, respectively. It can be seen that our FECNet produces the more pleasing results with corrected lightness and color appearance while maintaining the detailed structures. We provide more visualization results in the supplementary material.

4.3 Ablation Studies

In this section, we conduct the experiments to demonstrate the effectiveness of our method. More ablation studies are provided in supplementary materials.

Investigation of FECNet. To demonstrate the effectiveness of the overall setting of FECNet, we set several settings as ablations and present the results in Table 2. Particularly, (a) denotes removing the amplitude sub-network in FEC-Net; (b) represents removing the phase sub-network in FECNet; (c) denotes recovering the phase representation first and then restoring the amplitude representation; (d) represents swapping the two formats of SFI block in the two sub-networks; (e) denotes replacing the input of the phase sub-network with

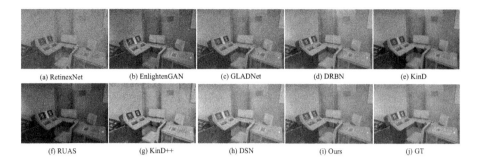

Fig. 10. Visualization results on the LOL dataset.

Table 5. Quantitative results of different methods on the LOL dataset in terms of PSNR and SSIM. #Param denotes the number of parameters.

Method	LIME	RetinexNet	MBLLEN	EnGAN	GLADNet	KinD	DRBN	RUAS	KinD++	DSN	FECNet (Ours)
PSNR	17.18	16.77	17.56	17.48	19.72	20.38	18.65	16.41	21.80	22.04	**23.44**
SSIM	0.5621	0.4249	0.7293	0.6737	0.6803	0.8248	0.8008	0.5001	0.8285	0.8334	**0.8383**
#Param	–	0.84 M	0.45 M	8.37 M	1.13 M	8.54 M	0.58 M	**0.003 M**	8.23 M	4.42 M	0.15 M

the output of the amplitude sub-network; (f) represents removing the lightness residual guidance for the phase sub-network.

As can be seen, both amplitude and phase sub-networks are effective for exposure correction, and the sequential order of arranging them are important, demonstrating the reasonableness of recovering the amplitude component first and then refine the phase component. In addition, the two formats of SFI block are proved to be coupled with these two sub-networks. For the input of the phase sub-network, the recombination with the phase component of the original input is more effective than the amplitude sub-network output. The residual map of the amplitude sub-net also helps improve performance.

Investigation of Losses. To validate the effectiveness of loss functions, we conduct experiments with different losses. The baseline set the L_1 loss on the final output, and we present results in Table 3. As can be seen, without the constraint of L_{s1}, the performance drops significantly, while the amplitude constraint and phase constraint in L_{s1} and L_{s2} are also proved to be effective, demonstrating the reasonableness of the supervision manner.

Investigation of SFI Block. We validate the effectiveness of the design of the SFI block in Table 4. As can be seen, both replacing the spatial branch with frequency branch or replacing the frequency branch with spatial branch results in a significant performance drop. While interacting these two branches can further improve performance remarkably, demonstrating the effectiveness of integrating these two complementary representations.

Table 6. Quantitative results of different methods on the MIT-FiveK dataset in terms of PSNR and SSIM. #Param denotes the number of parameters.

Method	White-Box	Distort-Recover	HDRNet	DUPE	DeepLPF	CSRNet	DSN	FECNet (Ours)
PSNR	18.59	19.54	22.65	20.22	23.21	23.69	23.84	**24.18**
SSIM	0.7973	0.7998	0.8802	0.8287	0.8863	0.8951	0.9002	**0.9030**
#Param	8.17 M	247.25 M	0.46 M	0.95 M	0.80 M	**0.034 M**	4.42 M	0.15 M

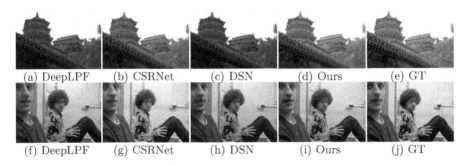

(a) DeepLPF   (b) CSRNet   (c) DSN   (d) Ours   (e) GT

(f) DeepLPF   (g) CSRNet   (h) DSN   (i) Ours   (j) GT

Fig. 11. Visualization results on the MIT-FiveK dataset. Images processed by other methods exist color and lightness shift and the details cannot be well recovered, while our method can obtain better visual qualities.

4.4   Extensions on Other Image Enhancement Tasks

To demonstrate the potential of our FECNet, we extend it to other image enhancement tasks, including low-light image enhancement and image retouching.

Extension on Low-Light Image Enhancement. Low-light image enhancement mainly focuses on lighting the darkness of a scene and removing the amplified noise. We adopt LOL dataset [41] to train and evaluate different methods, consisting of 485 images for training and 15 images for testing. Several low-light image enhancement methods are selected for comparison: LIME [16], RetinexNet [41], MBLLEN [12], DRBN [43], KinD [50], GLADNet [3], EnGAN [4], RUAS [38], KinD++ [49] and DSN [51]. The quantitative and qualitative results are shown in Table 5 and Fig. 10, respectively. As can be seen, our FECNet achieves the best performance both quantitatively and qualitatively.

Extension on Image Retouching. Image retouching aims to improve the color and lightness of an image to the expert manipulated effect. In this task, we apply the MIT-FiveK dataset [5] that is adopted by CSRNet [17], which contains 4500 images for training and 500 images for testing. Specifically, we compare our FECNet with several methods, including CSRNet [17], HDRNet [14] DUPE [39], Distort-Recover [32], White-box [18], DeepLPF [29] and DSN [51]. We give the quantitative evaluation in Table 6, and present the visualization results in Fig. 11. It can be seen that the generated results of our FECNet achieves the best performance with high quantitative performance and visual effects.

5 Conclusion

In this paper, we develop a new perspective for exposure correction with spatial-frequency information interaction in the spatial and frequency domain. We propose a deep Fourier-based Exposure Correction network (FECNet), which consists of two sub-networks: amplitude sub-network and phase sub-network. Specifically, the former aims to restore the amplitude, thus improving the lightness, while the latter is responsible for phase reconstruction, corresponding to refining structures. We further design a Spatial-Frequency Interaction (SFI) block as the basic unit of the FECNet to facilitate the learning of these two components with complementary representations. Extensive experimental results show that our method achieves superior performance for exposure correction. Moreover, the proposed approach can be extended to other image enhancement tasks, demonstrating its potential usage in wide-range applications. Although there exists color shift problem in some cases, we believe that the dynamic mechanism could be leveraged to relieve this issue. Considering that the mainstream of related works is still based on the spatial domain, we hope that the validity of our work will provide some insights into this community.

Acknowledgments.. This work was supported by the Anhui Provincial Natural Science Foundation under Grant 2108085UD12. We acknowledge the support of GPU cluster built by MCC Lab of Information Science and Technology Institution, USTC.

References

1. Abdullah-Al-Wadud, M., Kabir, M.H., Akber Dewan, M.A., Chae, O.: A dynamic histogram equalization for image contrast enhancement. IEEE Trans. Consum. Electron. **53**(2), 593–600 (2007)
2. Afifi, M., Derpanis, K.G., Ommer, B., Brown, M.S.: Learning multi-scale photo exposure correction. In: Proceedings of the IEEE Conference on Computer Vision and Pattern Recognition (CVPR) (2021)
3. Wang et al., W.: GladNet: low-light enhancement network with global awareness. In: Proceedings of the IEEE Conference on Automatic Face and Gesture Recognition (FG) (2018)
4. Jiang, Y., et al.: EnlightenGAN: deep light enhancement without paired supervision. IEEE Trans. Image Process. (TIP) **30**, 2340–2349 (2021)
5. Bychkovsky, V., Paris, S., Chan, E., Durand, F.: Learning photographic global tonal adjustment with a database of input output image pairs. In: Proceedings of the IEEE Conference on Computer Vision and Pattern Recognition (CVPR) (2011)
6. Cai, B., Xu, X., Guo, K., Jia, K., Hu, B., Tao, D.: A joint intrinsic-extrinsic prior model for retinex. In: Proceedings of the IEEE/CVF International Conference on Computer Vision (ICCV), pp. 4000–4009 (2017)
7. Cai, J., Gu, S., Zhang, L.: Learning a deep single image contrast enhancer from multi-exposure images. IEEE Trans. Image Process. (TIP) **27**(4), 2049–2062 (2018)
8. Chen, C., Chen, Q., Xu, J., Koltun, V.: Learning to see in the dark. arXiv preprint arXiv:1805.01934 (2018)

9. Chen, Y.S., Wang, Y.C., Kao, M.H., Chuang, Y.Y.: Deep photo enhancer: unpaired learning for image enhancement from photographs with GANs. In: Proceedings of the IEEE Conference on Computer Vision and Pattern Recognition (CVPR), pp. 6306–6314 (2018)

10. Chi, L., Jiang, B., Mu, Y.: Fast Fourier convolution. In: Advances in Neural Information Processing Systems (NIPS), vol. 33, pp. 4479–4488 (2020)

11. Chi, L., Tian, G., Mu, Y., Xie, L., Tian, Q.: Fast non-local neural networks with spectral residual learning. In: Proceedings of the 27th ACM International Conference on Multimedia (MM), pp. 2142–2151 (2019)

12. Feifan Lv, Feng Lu, J.W.C.L.: Mbllen: low-light image/video enhancement using CNNs. In: Proceedings of the The British Machine Vision Conference (BMVC) (2018)

13. Fuoli, D., Van Gool, L., Timofte, R.: Fourier space losses for efficient perceptual image super-resolution. In: Proceedings of the IEEE/CVF International Conference on Computer Vision (ICCV), pp. 2360–2369 (2021)

14. Gharbi, M., Chen, J., Barron, J.T., Hasinoff, S.W., Durand, F.: Deep bilateral learning for real-time image enhancement. ACM Trans. Graphics (TOG) **36**(4), 118 (2017)

15. Guo, C.G., et al.: Zero-reference deep curve estimation for low-light image enhancement. In: Proceedings of the IEEE Conference on Computer Vision and Pattern Recognition (CVPR), pp. 1780–1789 (2020)

16. Guo, X., Li, Y., Ling, H.: Lime: low-light image enhancement via illumination map estimation. IEEE Trans. Image Process. (TIP) **26**(2), 982–993 (2016)

17. He, J., Liu, Y., Qiao, Yu., Dong, C.: Conditional sequential modulation for efficient global image retouching. In: Vedaldi, A., Bischof, H., Brox, T., Frahm, J.-M. (eds.) ECCV 2020. LNCS, vol. 12358, pp. 679–695. Springer, Cham (2020). https://doi.org/10.1007/978-3-030-58601-0_40

18. Hu, Y., He, H., Xu, C., Wang, B., Lin, S.: Exposure: a white-box photo postprocessing framework. ACM Trans. Graphics (TOG) **37**(2), 1–17 (2018)

19. Ignatov, A., Kobyshev, N., Timofte, R., Vanhoey, K., Van Gool, L.: DSLR-quality photos on mobile devices with deep convolutional networks. In: Proceedings of the IEEE/CVF International Conference on Computer Vision (ICCV), pp. 3277–3285 (2017)

20. Jiang, L., Dai, B., Wu, W., Loy, C.C.: Focal frequency loss for image reconstruction and synthesis. In: Proceedings of the IEEE Conference on Computer Vision and Pattern Recognition (CVPR), pp. 13919–13929 (2021)

21. Katznelson, Y.: An Introduction to Harmonic Analysis. Cambridge University Press, Cambridge (2004)

22. Land, E.H.: The retinex theory of color vision. Sci. Am. **237**(6), 108–129 (1977)

23. Li, J., Li, J., Fang, F., Li, F., Zhang, G.: Luminance-aware pyramid network for low-light image enhancement. IEEE Trans. Multimedia (TMM) **23**, 3153–3165 (2020)

24. Li, M., Liu, J., Yang, W., Sun, X., Guo, Z.: Structure-revealing low-light image enhancement via robust retinex model. IEEE Trans. Image Process. (TIP) **27**(6), 2828–2841 (2018)

25. Lim, S., Kim, W.: DSLR: deep stacked Laplacian restorer for low-light image enhancement. IEEE Trans. Multimedia (TMM) **23**, 4272–4284 (2020)

26. Liu, J., Xu, D., Yang, W., Fan, M., Huang, H.: Benchmarking low-light image enhancement and beyond. Int. J. Comput. Vision **129**(4), 1153–1184 (2021). https://doi.org/10.1007/s11263-020-01418-8

27. Lv, F., Li, Y., Lu, F.: Attention guided low-light image enhancement with a large scale low-light simulation dataset. Int. J. Comput. Vis. (IJCV) **129**, 2175–2193 (2021). https://doi.org/10.1007/s11263-021-01466-8

28. Van der Maaten, L., Hinton, G.: Visualizing data using t-SNE. J. Mach. Learn. Res. (JMLR) **9**(11), 2579–2605 (2008)

29. Moran, S., Marza, P., McDonagh, S., Parisot, S., Slabaugh, G.: DeepLPF: deep local parametric filters for image enhancement. In: Proceedings of the IEEE Conference on Computer Vision and Pattern Recognition (CVPR) (2020)

30. Nsamp, N.E., Hu, Z., Wang, Q.: Learning exposure correction via consistency modeling. In: Proceedings of the British Machine Vision Conference (BMVC), pp. 1–12 (2018)

31. Prince, E.: The fast Fourier transform. In: Mathematical Techniques in Crystallography and Materials Science, pp. 140–156. Springer, Heidelberg (1994). https://doi.org/10.1007/978-3-642-97576-9_10

32. Park, J., Lee, J.Y., Yoo, D., Kweon, I.S.: Distort-and-recover: color enhancement using deep reinforcement learning. In: Proceedings of the IEEE Conference on Computer Vision and Pattern Recognition (CVPR), pp. 5928–5936 (2018)

33. Pizer, S.M., et al.: Adaptive histogram equalization and its variations. Comput. Vis. Graphics Image Process. **39**(3), 355–368 (1987)

34. Rao, Y., Zhao, W., Zhu, Z., Lu, J., Zhou, J.: Global filter networks for image classification. In: Advances in Neural Information Processing Systems (NIPS), vol. 34 (2021)

35. Ren, X., Yang, W., Cheng, W.H., Liu, J.: Lr3m: robust low-light enhancement via low-rank regularized Retinex model. IEEE Trans. Image Process. (TIP) **29**, 5862–5876 (2020)

36. Reza, A.M.: Realization of the contrast limited adaptive histogram equalization (CLAHE) for real-time image enhancement. J. VLSI Signal Process. Syst. Signal, Image Video Technol. **38**(1), 35–44 (2004). https://doi.org/10.1023/B:VLSI.0000028532.53893.82

37. Rippel, O., Snoek, J., Adams, R.P.: Spectral representations for convolutional neural networks. In: Advances in Neural Information Processing Systems (NIPS), vol. 28 (2015)

38. Risheng, L., Long, M., Jiaao, Z., Xin, F., Zhongxuan, L.: Retinex-inspired unrolling with cooperative prior architecture search for low-light image enhancement. In: Proceedings of the Proceedings of the IEEE Conference on Computer Vision and Pattern Recognition (CVPR) (2021)

39. Wang, R., Zhang, Q., Fu, C.W., Shen, X., Zheng, W.S., Jia, J.: Underexposed photo enhancement using deep illumination estimation. In: Proceedings of the IEEE Conference on Computer Vision and Pattern Recognition (CVPR), pp. 6849–6857 (2019)

40. Wang, W., Yang, W., Liu, J.: Hla-face: joint high-low adaptation for low light face detection. In: Proceedings of the IEEE Conference on Computer Vision and Pattern Recognition (CVPR) (2021)

41. Wei, C., Wang, W., Yang, W., Liu, J.: Deep Retinex decomposition for low-light enhancement. In: Proceedings of the British Machine Vision Conference (BMVC), pp. 155–165 (2018)

42. Xu, Q., Zhang, R., Zhang, Y., Wang, Y., Tian, Q.: A Fourier-based framework for domain generalization. In: Proceedings of the IEEE Conference on Computer Vision and Pattern Recognition (CVPR), pp. 14383–14392 (2021)

43. Yang, W., Wang, S., Fang, Y., Wang, Y., Liu, J.: From fidelity to perceptual quality: a semi-supervised approach for low-light image enhancement. In: Proceedings of the IEEE Conference on Computer Vision and Pattern Recognition (CVPR), pp. 3063–3072 (2020)
44. Yang, W., Wang, W., Huang, H., Wang, S., Liu, J.: Sparse gradient regularized deep retinex network for robust low-light image enhancement. IEEE Trans. Image Process. (TIP) **30**, 2072–2086 (2021)
45. Yang, W., et al.: Advancing image understanding in poor visibility environments: a collective benchmark study. IEEE Trans. Image Process. (TIP) **29**, 5737–5752 (2020)
46. Yang, Y., Soatto, S.: FDA: Fourier domain adaptation for semantic segmentation. In: Proceedings of the IEEE Conference on Computer Vision and Pattern Recognition (CVPR), pp. 4085–4095 (2020)
47. Ying, Z., Li, G., Ren, Y., Wang, R., Wang, W.: A new image contrast enhancement algorithm using exposure fusion framework. In: Felsberg, M., Heyden, A., Krüger, N. (eds.) CAIP 2017. LNCS, vol. 10425, pp. 36–46. Springer, Cham (2017). https://doi.org/10.1007/978-3-319-64698-5_4
48. Zhang, Q., Yuan, G., Xiao, C., Zhu, L., Zheng, W.S.: High-quality exposure correction of underexposed photos. In: ACM International Conference on Multimedia (ACM MM), pp. 582–590 (2018)
49. Zhang, Y., Guo, X., Ma, J., Liu, W., Zhang, J.: Beyond brightening low-light images. Int. J. Comput. Vis. (IJCV) **129**, 1013–1037 (2021)
50. Zhang, Y., Zhang, J., Guo, X.: Kindling the darkness: a practical low-light image enhancer. In: ACM International Conference on Multimedia (ACM MM), pp. 1632–1640 (2019)
51. Zhao, L., Lu, S.P., Chen, T., Yang, Z., Shamir, A.: Deep symmetric network for underexposed image enhancement with recurrent attentional learning. In: Proceedings of the IEEE/CVF International Conference on Computer Vision (ICCV), pp. 12075–12084 (2021)

Frequency and Spatial Dual Guidance for Image Dehazing

Hu Yu, Naishan Zheng, Man Zhou, Jie Huang, Zeyu Xiao, and Feng Zhao[✉]

University of Science and Technology of China, Hefei, China
{yuhu520,nszheng,manman,hj0117,zeyuxiao}@mail.ustc.edu.cn,
fzhao956@ustc.edu.cn

Abstract. In this paper, we propose a novel image dehazing framework with frequency and spatial dual guidance. In contrast to most existing deep learning-based image dehazing methods that primarily exploit the spatial information and neglect the distinguished frequency information, we introduce a new perspective to address image dehazing by jointly exploring the information in the frequency and spatial domains. To implement frequency and spatial dual guidance, we delicately develop two core designs: amplitude guided phase module in the frequency domain and global guided local module in the spatial domain. Specifically, the former processes the global frequency information via deep Fourier transform and reconstructs the phase spectrum under the guidance of the amplitude spectrum, while the latter integrates the above global frequency information to facilitate the local feature learning in the spatial domain. Extensive experiments on synthetic and real-world datasets demonstrate that our method outperforms the state-of-the-art approaches both visually and quantitatively. Our code is released publicly at https://github.com/yuhuUSTC/FSDGN.

Keywords: Image dehazing · Frequency and spatial dual-guidance · Amplitude and phase

1 Introduction

Haze is a common atmospheric phenomenon, which is composed of tiny water droplets or ice crystals suspended in the air near the ground. Images captured in hazy environments usually have noticeable visual quality degradation in object appearance and contrast. The goal of image dehazing is to restore a clean scene from a hazy image. The performance of high-level computer vision tasks such as object detection [10,27] and scene understanding [43,44] are considerably influenced by the input images captured in hazy scenes. Thus, throughout the last decade, restoring clear photographs from hazy ones has been a focus of research in the computational photography and vision communities.

Estimating the clean image from a single hazy input is an ill-posed and challenging problem. Conventional approaches rely on the physical scattering

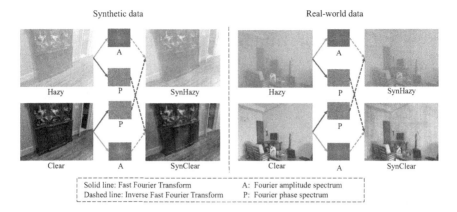

Fig. 1. Visualization on the relationship between the haze degradation and the characteristics of amplitude spectrum and phase spectrum in the frequency domain. We denote the image with clear image amplitude and hazy image phase as **SynClear**, and the image with hazy image amplitude and clear image phase as **SynHazy**.

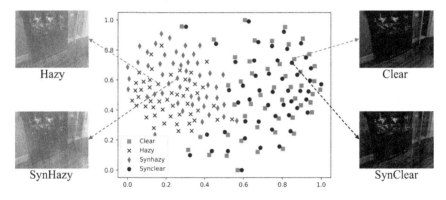

Fig. 2. The t-SNE map of hazy, clear, **SynHazy**, and **SynClear** images. Obviously, clear and **SynClear** images are tightly connected and coupled, indicating more similar distributions. Similarly, hazy and **SynHazy** images are clustered together. (Color figure online)

model [35] and regularize the solution space using a variety of crisp image priors [5,15,16,19]. However, these hand-crafted image priors are created based on specific observations, which may not be reliable to model the intrinsic features of images or estimate the transmission map in the physical scattering model.

Inspired by the success of deep learning, numerous deep learning-based approaches [6,13,18,26,30,32,37,41,49] have been developed recently to learn the translation from hazy image to clear image in an end-to-end manner. Although these methods have made remarkable progress in image dehazing tasks, they have a main limitation: they primarily exploit the spatial information and neglect the distinguished frequency information. Compared to spatial domain processing, the difference between hazy and clear image pairs in the frequency domain is physically definite. Thus, finding the correlation between haze degradation and frequency is of great importance for understanding the dehazing problem.

In this paper, we reveal the relationship between the haze degradation and the characteristics of the amplitude and phase spectrums in the frequency domain (see Fig. 1). Specifically, we first transform a spatial domain image to frequency-domain amplitude and phase spectrums by fast Fourier transform, and then exchange the amplitude and phase spectrums of hazy and clear image pairs. Finally, the exchanged spectrums are transformed back to get **Synclear** and **SynHazy** images by inverse fast Fourier transform. From Fig. 1, we can see that: (1) Clear and **SynClear** images have the same amplitude spectrum but different phase spectrums, and they look similar; (2) Clear and **SynHazy** images have the same phase spectrum but different amplitude spectrums, and they look different. This observation leads to the conclusion that: (1) the degradation property induced by haze is mainly manifested in the amplitude spectrum; and (2) the difference between phase spectrums of hazy and clear image pairs is small.

To further explain and testify this conclusion, we show the t-SNE map of 50 groups of hazy, clear, **SynClear**, and **SynHazy** images in Fig. 2. It is apparent that clear and **SynClear** images are clustered together, indicating highly similar distributions. This also applies to hazy and **SynHazy** images.

Based on the above observation and conclusion, we propose a novel Frequency and Spatial Dual-Guidance Network (FSDGN) for single-image dehazing. From a new perspective, we address image dehazing by jointly exploring the information in the frequency and spatial domains. To implement the frequency and spatial dual guidance, we delicately develop two core designs, i.e., Amplitude Guided Phase (AGP) module in the frequency domain and Global Guided Local (GGL) module in the spatial domain. Specifically, the AGP module processes the global frequency information via deep Fourier transform and reconstruct the phase spectrum under the guidance of the amplitude spectrum, while the GGL module integrates the above global frequency information to facilitate the local feature learning in the spatial domain. Thanks to the frequency property observation and our finely constructed modules, our method achieves state-of-the-art (SOTA) performance efficiently. In Fig. 3, several SOTA models are shown in terms of performance, parameters, and FLOPs.

In conclusion, the main contributions of our work are as follows:

- We reveal the correlation between haze degradation and the statistical properties of amplitude and phase spectrums, and integrate the frequency and spatial information for image dehazing.
- We propose a novel Frequency and Spatial Dual-Guidance Network for effectively generating high-quality haze-free images by completely utilizing dual guidance in both the frequency and spatial domains. To the best of our knowledge, we are the first to introduce amplitude and phase spectrums for the image dehazing task.
- We propose the tailor designed GGL and AGP modules for the spatial-domain and frequency-domain guidance, respectively.
- Extensive experiments demonstrate that our method outperforms state-of-the-art approaches with fewer parameters and FLOPs.

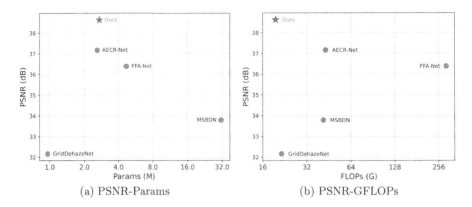

(a) PSNR-Params   (b) PSNR-GFLOPs

Fig. 3. Trade-off between PSNR, number of parameters, and FLOPs. FLOPs are calculated with an input size 256 × 256.

2 Related Work

Single Image Dehazing. In recent years, we have witnessed significant advances in single image dehazing. Existing methods can be roughly categorized into two classes: physical-based methods and deep learning-based methods.

Physical-based methods depend on the physical model [35] and the handcraft priors from empirical observations, such as dark channel prior [19], color line prior [16], color attenuation prior [57], sparse gradient prior [8], maximum reflectance prior [55], and non-local prior [5]. However, the density of haze can be affected by various factors including temperature, altitude, and humidity, which make the haze formation at individual spatial locations space-variant and non-homogeneous. Therefore, the haze usually cannot be accurately characterized by merely a single transmission map.

Different from the physical-based methods, deep learning-based methods employ convolution neural networks to learn the image prior [6,26,31,33,40,54] or directly learn hazy-to-clear translation [12–14,17,22,32,37,38,41,47,49,51, 56]. For example, AOD-Net [26] produces the recovered images by reformulating the physical scattering model. MSBDN [13] proposes a boosted decoder to progressively restore the haze-free images. Ye et al. [51] developed perceiving and modeling density for uneven haze distribution to increase its generalization ability on real-world hazy images. AECR-Net [49] introduces the contrastive regularization to exploit both the information of hazy images and clear images as negative and positive samples, respectively. The above techniques have shown outstanding performance on image dehazing. However, they only utilize the information in the spatial domain, which cannot sufficiently model the characteristics of haze degradation. It is necessary to mention that DW-GAN [17] also employs the frequency information, but it works in the wavelet domain and exploits the low-high frequency property. Instead, our method works in the Fourier domain and reveals the relationship between amplitude-phase and haze degradation.

Applications of Fourier Transform. In recent years, some algorithms [7,11,34,39,46,50,58] have been proposed to extract the information from the frequency domain to address different tasks. For instance, DeepRFT [34] applies the convolution operations to the real and imaginary parts of the spectrum in the frequency domain to restore the blurry images. FDIT [7] decomposes the images into low-frequency and high-frequency components to enhance the image generation process. However, existing frequency-based methods neglect to build the relationship between the frequency property and the image degradation. Different from these existing techniques, we further discover the correlation between haze degradation and the characteristics of amplitude and phase spectrums in the frequency domain and tailor design the AGP module to exploit this observation.

3   Method

3.1   Motivation

Our main inspiration comes from observing the relationship between haze degradation and the characteristics of Fourier amplitude and phase spectrums in the frequency domain. As shown in Fig. 1 and analyzed above, we get the conclusion that the degradation property mainly manifests in the amplitude spectrum, while the phase spectrum just has a slight difference between hazy image and corresponding clear image. Moreover, the illumination contrast of an image is represented by the amplitude spectrum, while the texture structure information is represented by the phase spectrum [36,45]. Therefore, our conclusion is also consistent with this theory, for the reason that haze mainly affects the illumination contrast of an image, while the structural information is immune to haze degradation. In addition, the artifacts in **SynClear** image show that slight difference exists between the phase spectrums of clear and hazy image pairs and it is related to the global distribution of haze. Thus, the amplitude spectrum's learned residual can be utilized as a guide to restore the phase spectrum. According to these observations, we design the Amplitude Guided Phase (AGP) module to deal with amplitude and phase spectrums and exploit the spectrum's learned residual to guide phase restoration in the frequency domain.

Our second insight is the discrepancy between global and local modeling for image dehazing in the spatial domain. We explain their difference through the limited receptive field of CNN-based network. Receptive field can be defined as the region around a pixel that contributes to the output at that pixel [4,25]. Due to the convolution operator's intrinsic limitations, the network has a limited receptive field, particularly in the early layers. Consequently, existing CNN-based methods fail to accurately model the long-range dependency of an image and the context for comprehending the haze's global distribution. Specifically for image dehazing, when the dense haze block gets larger than the receptive field, the pixels that fall into the haze block can't get enough information to remove the haze. Undoubtedly, understanding the content globally is essential for reconstructing a high-quality clear image from its hazy counterpart. Based on this insight, we

design the Global Guided Local (GGL) module to enable local modeling part
with global information.

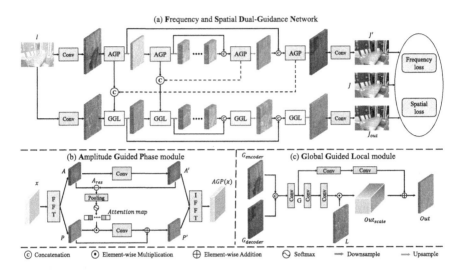

Fig. 4. Overview of the proposed network architecture for image dehazing. (a) The
whole framework consists of a frequency branch and a spatial branch with the proposed
(b) AGP module in the frequency domain and (c) GGL module in the spatial domain.

3.2 Frequency and Spatial Dual-Guidance Network

The two-branch-designed network has been successfully applied in various image
restoration methods [9,53]. Because each branch concentrates on its own information processing procedure, it might extract distinct representations of the
same input. Further, if we can use such distinct information wisely and introduce proper guidance between these two branches, comprehensive information
from two branches can significantly boost the performance of image dehazing.
Based on this idea, we design our two-branch neural network.

Our proposed network is based on the U-Net [42] architecture. As shown
in Fig. 4, the network includes two branches, a frequency/global branch and a
spatial/local branch. For an input hazy image I, frequency branch outputs J',
spatial branch outputs the final dehazed image J_{out} and J is the corresponding
ground-truth image. Specifically, for the frequency branch, the feature passes the
delicately designed Amplitude Guided Phase (AGP) module. The AGP module
performs in the frequency domain, which is global information. Besides, in order
to fully exploit the restored global information and introduce global guidance
for local feature learning, we introduce Global Guided Local (GGL) module to
provide global information for the learning of local features at every stage of the
U-Net architecture. Besides the specially designed modules mentioned above, we
also use dense connection [23] and skip connection [20] in our network.

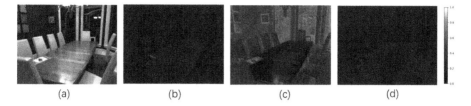

(a)   (b)   (c)   (d)

Fig. 5. Features from the same stage of global branch and local branch. (a) Clear image, (b) feature without applying GGL and AGP modules (local feature), (c) feature (b) + AGP module (global feature), and (d) feature (b) + GGL module (local feature with global feature guidance). (Color figure online)

3.3 Amplitude Guided Phase Module

Phase conveys more information regarding image structure than amplitude does and is highly immune to noise and contrast distortions [36,45]. Along with this theory, we further find that the degradation caused by haze mainly manifests in the amplitude spectrum, and the phase spectrum is affected slightly. In other words, haze primarily changes the illumination contrast of an image, and the structure of an image is influenced mildly due to reduced visibility of the whole image. Based on our discovery, we propose the Amplitude Guided Phase (AGP) module. Let x and $AGP(x)$ denote the input and output of the AGP module. AGP module first transforms the spatial domain feature x to its frequency domain Fourier transformation $\mathcal{F}(x)$, formulated as follows:

$$\mathcal{F}(x)(u,v) = \sum_{h=0}^{H-1}\sum_{w=0}^{W-1} x(h,w)e^{-j2\pi\left(\frac{h}{H}u+\frac{w}{W}v\right)}. \tag{1}$$

The frequency-domain feature $\mathcal{F}(x)$ is denoted as $\mathcal{F}(x) = \mathcal{R}(x) + j\mathcal{I}(x)$, where $\mathcal{R}(x)$ and $\mathcal{I}(x)$ represent the real and imaginary part of $\mathcal{F}(x)$. Then the real and imaginary parts are converted to amplitude and phase spectrums, which can be formulated as:

$$\begin{aligned}
\mathcal{A}(x)(u,v) &= \left[\mathcal{R}^2(x)(u,v) + \mathcal{I}^2(x)(u,v)\right]^{1/2}, \\
\mathcal{P}(x)(u,v) &= \arctan\left[\frac{\mathcal{I}(x)(u,v)}{\mathcal{R}(x)(u,v)}\right],
\end{aligned} \tag{2}$$

where $\mathcal{A}(x)$ is the amplitude spectrum, $\mathcal{P}(x)$ is the phase spectrum. Given that amplitude is severely distorted, we first restore the amplitude using a 1×1 convolution. Then, the residual $\mathcal{A}_{res}(x)$ of the restored amplitude $\mathcal{A}'(x)$ and the raw amplitude $\mathcal{A}(x)$ is expressed as follows:

$$\begin{aligned}
\mathcal{A}'(x)(u,v) &= \mathcal{A}(x)(u,v) \otimes k_1, \\
\mathcal{A}_{res}(x)(u,v) &= \mathcal{A}'(x)(u,v) - \mathcal{A}(x)(u,v),
\end{aligned} \tag{3}$$

here, $\otimes$ denotes the convolution operator. In this paper, we denote k_s as the convolution filter with kernel size of $s \times s$ pixel for simplicity. Further, we apply the attention map $Atten(x)$ of residual amplitude $\mathcal{A}_{res}(x)$ to compensate for the slight phase change, formulated by:

$$
\begin{aligned}
Atten(x)(u,v) &= Softmax\left[GAP\left(\mathcal{A}_{res}(x)(u,v)\right)\right], \\
\mathcal{P}^{'}(x)(u,v) &= \left[Atten(x)(u,v) \odot \mathcal{P}(x)(u,v)\right] \otimes k_1 + \mathcal{P}(x)(u,v),
\end{aligned}
\tag{4}
$$

where, GAP means the global average pooling and $\odot$ denotes the element-wise product operation. After the recovery in amplitude and phase, we turn them back to real and imaginary parts by:

$$
\begin{aligned}
\mathcal{R}^{'}(x)(u,v) &= \mathcal{A}^{'}(x)(u,v)\cos\mathcal{P}^{'}(x)(u,v), \\
\mathcal{I}^{'}(x)(u,v) &= \mathcal{A}^{'}(x)(u,v)\sin\mathcal{P}^{'}(x)(u,v).
\end{aligned}
\tag{5}
$$

Finally, we transform the frequency domain feature $\mathcal{F}^{'}(x) = \mathcal{R}^{'}(x) + j\mathcal{I}^{'}(x)$ back to the spatial domain feature $AGP(x)$ by inverse Fourier transform. Besides the frequency transformation, we keep a 3×3 convolution branch in the spatial domain to stabilize the training of the AGP module.

In Fig. 5, we show features produced under different settings. The local branch b generates artifacts and fails to model the global architecture, but with finer details in some regions. Compared with feature b, global feature c models the low-frequency representations (illumination, color and contrast) and generates globally visual pleasing results with the consistent overall structure of the scene. This well proves the validity and importance of our AGP module.

3.4   Global Guided Local Module

In order to gain global context modeling ability, some image restoration methods employ transformer/non-local [29,52]. But the considerable computational complexity of aforementioned global modeling strategy usually hampers its efficient usage. In contrast, we possess a global context modeling ability by exploiting frequency characteristics.

Due to the limited receptive field in the early layers of the local branch, the network fails to capture long-range dependency and has no enough information to remove the haze in local regions. Therefore, we propose Global Guided Local (GGL) module. In the GGL module, we incorporate the features from the same stage in the encoder and decoder of the global branch to guide the local feature in the corresponding encoder stage of the local branch. Similar to SFT [48], we inject the local feature with the scaling and shifting of global feature. Concretely, we first concatenate the two global features $G^n_{encoder}$ and $G^n_{decoder}$ from the n-th stage of the encoder and decoder and perform a simple convolution to get G^n.

$$
G^n = Cat\left(G^n_{encoder}, G^n_{decoder}\right) \otimes k_3,
\tag{6}
$$

where, Cat denotes the concatenation operation. Then, we use the global feature G^n to guide the local feature L^n from the n-th stage of the encoder in the spatial branch. We first inject the local feature L^n with the scaling operation of G^n to get Out^n_{scale} as:

$$
Out^n_{scale} = (G^n \otimes k_1 \otimes k_1) \odot L^n.
\tag{7}
$$

Then, with the obtained Out^n_{scale}, We introduce the shifting operation of G^n to get the output of the n-th GGL module as:

$$Out^n = (G^n \otimes k_1 \otimes k_1) + Out^n_{scale}. \tag{8}$$

In this way, our method not only focuses on details by the stack of convolution but also introduces global information to enrich the global context structure.

In Fig. 5, feature (d) is produced by introducing global information guidance to local feature (b). Obviously, after the GGL module, feature (d) is not only well structured but also have fine details and less artifacts. This means that feature (d) combines the strong point of local feature (b) and global feature (c), as we ideally expected.

3.5   Frequency and Spatial Dual Supervision Losses

The training loss of our FSDGN is comprised of both spatial and frequency domain losses. In addition to the spatial domain Charbonnier loss [24] $\mathcal{L}_{cha}$, the frequency domain loss $\mathcal{L}_{fre}$ consists of $\mathcal{L}_{amp}$ and $\mathcal{L}_{pha}$ for supervision from the ground-truth amplitude and phase spectrums during training.

$$\mathcal{L}_{cha} = \sqrt{\left(J_{out}\left(x\right) - J\left(x\right)\right)^2 + \varepsilon} + \sqrt{\left(J'\left(x\right) - J\left(x\right)\right)^2 + \varepsilon}, \tag{9}$$

$$\mathcal{L}_{amp} = \frac{2}{UV} \sum_{u=0}^{U/2-1} \sum_{v=0}^{V-1} \left(\left\| \left|A_{out}\right|_{u,v} - \left|A\right|_{u,v} \right\|_1 + \left\| \left|A'\right|_{u,v} - \left|A\right|_{u,v} \right\|_1 \right), \tag{10}$$

$$\mathcal{L}_{pha} = \frac{2}{UV} \sum_{u=0}^{U/2-1} \sum_{v=0}^{V-1} \left(\left\| \left|P_{out}\right|_{u,v} - \left|P\right|_{u,v} \right\|_1 + \left\| \left|P'\right|_{u,v} - \left|P\right|_{u,v} \right\|_1 \right). \tag{11}$$

Note, in our implementation, $\varepsilon = 1 \times e^{-12}$ and the summation for u is only performed up to $U/2 - 1$, since 50% of all frequency components are redundant. Thus, the total loss L of our network is denoted as:

$$\mathcal{L} = \mathcal{L}_{cha} + \beta \left(\mathcal{L}_{amp} + \mathcal{L}_{pha}\right), \tag{12}$$

where β is weight factor and set to 0.1 empirically.

4   Experiments

In this section, we first introduce the datasets and implement details of our experiment. Then, we make a comprehensive comparison with existing methods quantitatively and visually. Experiments on the public synthetic dataset RESIDE [28] and two different type real-word datasets demonstrate the superiority of the proposed FSDGN. Furthermore, extensive ablation studies and statistical analysis are conducted to justify the effectiveness of the core modules of FSDGN.

4.1   Experiment Setup

Datasets. We evaluate the proposed method on synthetic and real-world datasets. For synthetic scenes, we employ RESIDE [28] dataset. The subset Indoor Training Set (ITS) of RESIDE contains a total of 13990 hazy indoor images, generated from 1399 clear images. The subset Synthetic Objective Testing Set (SOTS) of RESIDE consists of 500 indoor hazy images and 500 outdoor ones. We apply ITS and SOTS indoor as our training and testing sets. In addition, we adopt two real-world datasets: Dense-Haze [1] and NH-HAZE [2], to evaluate the robustness of our method in the real-world scenarios. Dense-Haze consists of dense and homogeneous hazy scenes, whereas NH-HAZE consists of nonhomogeneous hazy scenes. Both of the two datasets consist of 55 paired images.

Implementation Details. Our FSDGN is implemented by PyTorch with an NVIDIA RTX 2080Ti. We use ADAM as the optimizers with $\beta_1 = 0.9$, and $\beta_2 = 0.999$, and the initial learning rate is set to 2×10^{-4}. The learning rate is adjusted by the cosine annealing strategy [21]. In the training stage, we empirically set the total number of iteration to 600k. The batch and patch sizes are set to 16 and 256×256, respectively.

Table 1. Quantitative comparison with SOTA methods on synthetic and real-world dehazing datasets.

Method	SOTS [28]		Dense-Haze [1]		NH-HAZE [2]		Param (M)	GFLOPs
	PSNR	SSIM	PSNR	SSIM	PSNR	SSIM		
DCP [19]	15.09	0.7649	10.06	0.3856	10.57	0.5196	–	–
DehazeNet [6]	20.64	0.7995	13.84	0.4252	16.62	0.5238	0.01M	–
AOD-Net [26]	19.82	0.8178	13.14	0.4144	15.40	0.5693	0.002M	0.1
GridDehazeNet [32]	32.16	0.9836	13.31	0.3681	13.80	0.5370	0.96M	21.5
FFA-Net [37]	36.39	0.9886	14.39	0.4524	19.87	0.6915	4.68M	288.1
MSBDN [13]	33.79	0.9840	15.37	0.4858	19.23	0.7056	31.35M	41.5
KDDN [22]	34.72	0.9845	14.28	0.4074	17.39	0.5897	5.99M	–
AECR-Net [49]	37.17	0.9901	15.80	0.4660	19.88	0.7173	2.61M	43.0
Ours	**38.63**	**0.9903**	**16.91**	**0.5806**	**19.99**	**0.7306**	2.73M	19.6

4.2   Comparison with State-of-the-Art Methods

We compare our FSDGN with the SOTA methods qualitatively and quantitatively, including one prior-based algorithm (DCP [19]) and six deep learning-based methods (DehazeNet [6], AOD-Net [26], GridDehazeNet [32], FFA-Net [37], MSBDN [13] and AECR-Net [49]). The results are produced by using publicly available source codes with recommended parameters. To evaluate the performance of our method, we employ two widely used metrics for quantitative comparisons, including the Peak Signal to Noise Ratio (PSNR) and the Structural Similarity index (SSIM).

Results on Synthetic Dataset. Table 1 compares the quantitative results of different methods on SOTS dataset [27], which indicates our FSDGN achieves the best performance with 38.36dB PSNR and 0.9903 SSIM. To further demonstrate the effectiveness of our method, we also show the visual comparison with other techniques on the typical hazy images sampled from the SOTS dataset in Fig. 6. Compared with the ground truths, it is evident that the results of DCP, AODNet and DehazeNet not only fail to remove the dense haze but also suffer from severe color distortion (see the table and wall in Fig. 6(b)-(d)). Different from these three techniques, GridDehazeNet [32], FFA-Net [37], MSBDN [13] and AECR-Net [49] perform the hazy-to-clear image translation in an end-to-end manner. Undeniably, they mitigate the color distortion problem and achieve the restored images with higher PSNR and SSIM. However, they cannot completely remove the haze in their results (*e.g.* the red square in Fig. 6(e), the wall in Fig. 6(f) and the gap between chairs in Fig. 6(g)), and produce color shift (see the desktop in Fig. 6(h)). In contrast, our FSDGN generates the highest-fidelity dehazed results that also look perceptually close to the reference ground truths.

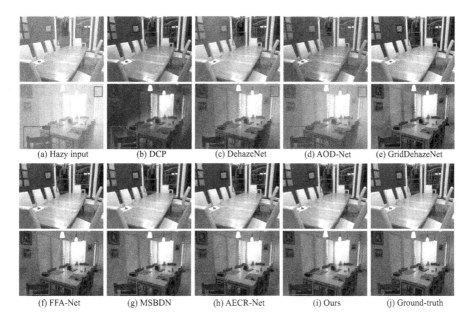

(a) Hazy input   (b) DCP   (c) DehazeNet   (d) AOD-Net   (e) GridDehazeNet

(f) FFA-Net   (g) MSBDN   (h) AECR-Net   (i) Ours   (j) Ground-truth

Fig. 6. Comparison of visual results on SOTS [28] dataset. Red boxes indicate the obvious differences. Zoom in for best view. (Color figure online)

Results on Real-World Datasets. We further compare our FSDGN with SOTA methods on the two real-world datasets: Dense-Haze [1] and NH-HAZE [2] datasets. Due to the dense and nonhomogeneous distribution of haze in real-world, removing the real-world haze is more complex and challenging. As described in Table 1, the proposed FSDGN achieves the best performance on

Fig. 7. Comparison of visual results on Dense-Haze [1] dataset. Zoom in for best view.

Fig. 8. Comparison of visual results on NH-HAZE [2] dataset. Zoom in for best view.

both datasets, outperforming the second-highest performance AECR-Net [49] with 1.11dB PSNR and 0.1146 SSIM on the Dense-Haze dataset and 0.11dB PSNR and 0.0233 SSIM on the NH-HAZE dataset. Figure 7 and Fig. 8 illustrate the results of the real-world haze images sampled from the Dense-Haze and NH-HAZE datasets, respectively. The compared methods generate either color distortion or haze-remained results. Concretely, DCP [19], AOD-Net [26], Grid-DehazeNet [32], FFA-Net [37] and AECR-Net [49] produce the serious color deviation and texture loss in the restored images. Besides, apparent thick haze residual is remained in the results of DCP [19], DehazeNet [6], GridDehazeNet [32] and MSBDN [13]. In contrast, our model generates the natural and visually desirable results.

Note that we don't compare the results on Real-world datasets with workshop methods. For the reason that workshop methods achieve high performance at the cost of huge parameters. For example, the model size of DW-GAN [17] is 51.51M, much larger than ours. The champion model iPAL-AtJ on NTIRE 2019 Challenge [3] has a parameter of 46.17M.

Table 2. Ablation study on our FSDGN. AllG* represents the model consisting of two global branches without spatial guidance.

Label	AllL	GGL	AGP	AllG*	$\mathcal{L}_{fre}$	PSNR (dB)	SSIM	Params (M)
a	✓					37.41	0.9889	2.573
b	✓	✓				38.02	0.9899	2.580
c	✓		✓			38.34	0.9901	2.725
d				✓		37.56	0.9893	2.876
e		✓		✓		38.19	0.9901	2.883
f	✓	✓	✓			38.51	0.9902	2.731
g	✓	✓	✓		✓	38.63	0.9903	2.731

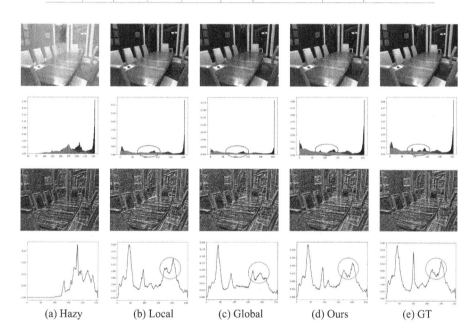

(a) Hazy   (b) Local   (c) Global   (d) Ours   (e) GT

Fig. 9. Visualization of output images, histogram of color images, texture images, and histogram of gray images. (a) Input hazy image, (b) output of the local branch (without spatial guidance), (c) output of the global branch (with additional AGP module compared to the local branch), (d) output of our model (with AGP and GGL modules), and (e) ground-truth clear image. (Color figure online)

4.3   Ablation Studies

In this section, we perform several ablation studies to analysis the effectiveness of the proposed method. In order to verify the effect of two global branches, we further introduce the AllG model, which applies the AGP module in both branches and involves no local features. Different models are denoted as follows: (a) **AllL**: The same as our FSDGN except for the AGP and GGL module.

Namely, two spatial branches without spatial guidance and frequency loss. (b) **AllL+GGL**: Two spatial branches, with spatial guidance. (c) **AllL+AGP**: A spatial branch and a frequency branch. (d) **AllG**: Two global branches, without spatial guidance. (e) **AllG+GGL**: Two global branches, with spatial guidance. (f) **AllL+GGL+AGP**: A global branch and a local branch, with spatial guidance. (g) **(Ours)AllL+GGL+AGP**+$\mathcal{L}_{fre}$: Our final setting in this method. The performance of these models are summarized in Table 2.

Effectiveness of the AGP Module. Compared to the AllL model, the AllL+AGP model possesses a significant performance improvement of 0.93 PSNR with negligible parameters increasing. This indicates that the AGP module is an indispensable component of our network, representing the global information and, more importantly, correlating with the haze degradation.

Effectiveness of the GGL Module. Compared to the AllL model, the AllL+GGL model improves the performance from 37.41 to 38.02 PSNR. In addition, the improvement of the model from AllG to AllG+GGL increases the PSNR by 0.63 dB.

More Comparisons. AllL and AllG models extract all local information and global information, respectively. Experiments show that combining the global and local information is superior to using just one. Besides, the comparison between model f and g demonstrates that the introduction of the frequency loss $\mathcal{L}_{fre}$ is beneficial for performance improvement.

To further explain and prove the superiority of our proposed modules, we present the statistical distributions in Fig. 9. Specifically, the first row is the hazy image, the output of different models, and the ground truth, respectively. The second row is the histogram of the above images, which represents the illumination and color distribution. The third row describes the textures of the first row produced by the LBP operator, and the bottom row is the histogram of the corresponding gray image, indicating the texture, light, and contrast changes. Undeniably both the local and global branch outputs remove the haze and preserve textures well with the visually pleasing image. However, it is easy to find the discrepancies in their histograms compared with the ground truth. It is evident that our FSDGN achieves a more similar distribution to the ground truth compared with the global or local branch (*e.g.* the red circles in the second row and the green circles in the bottom row of Fig. 9).

5   Conclusion

In this paper, we revisit the haze degradation in the frequency domain via Fourier transform. Based on the frequency analysis, we propose a novel image dehazing framework, termed as Frequency and Spatial Dual-Guidance Network, to explore potentials in the frequency and spatial dual domains. Specifically, we introduce two core designs to equip the proposed network, i.e., the Global Guided Local module and Amplitude Guided Phase module for the spatial-domain and frequency-domain guidance, respectively. Extensive experiments validate that the proposed method achieves state-of-the-art performance on both synthetic and real hazy images in an efficient way.

Acknowledgements. This work was supported by the JKW Research Funds under Grant 20-163-14-LZ-001-004-01 and the University Synergy Innovation Program of Anhui Province under Grant GXXT-2019-025. We acknowledge the support of GPU cluster built by MCC Lab of Information Science and Technology Institution, USTC. We also thank the technical support from Jie Huang.

References

1. Ancuti, C.O., Ancuti, C., Sbert, M., Timofte, R.: Dense haze: a benchmark for image dehazing with dense-haze and haze-free images. In: Proceedings of the IEEE International Conference on Image Processing, pp. 1014–1018 (2019)
2. Ancuti, C.O., Ancuti, C., Timofte, R.: NH-HAZE: an image dehazing benchmark with non-homogeneous hazy and haze-free images. In: Proceedings of the IEEE/CVF Conference on Computer Vision and Pattern Recognition Workshops, pp. 444–445 (2020)
3. Ancuti, C.O., Ancuti, C., Timofte, R., Van Gool, L., Zhang, L., Yang, M.H.: Ntire 2019 image dehazing challenge report. In: Proceedings of the IEEE/CVF Conference on Computer Vision and Pattern Recognition Workshops, pp. 1–13 (2019)
4. Araujo, A., Norris, W., Sim, J.: Computing receptive fields of convolutional neural networks. Distill **4**(11), e21 (2019)
5. Berman, D., Avidan, S., et al.: Non-local image dehazing. In: Proceedings of the IEEE Conference on Computer Vision and Pattern Recognition, pp. 1674–1682 (2016)
6. Cai, B., Xu, X., Jia, K., Qing, C., Tao, D.: DehazeNet: an end-to-end system for single image haze removal. IEEE Trans. Image Process. **25**(11), 5187–5198 (2016)
7. Cai, M., Zhang, H., Huang, H., Geng, Q., Li, Y., Huang, G.: Frequency domain image translation: More photo-realistic, better identity-preserving. In: Proceedings of the IEEE/CVF International Conference on Computer Vision, pp. 13930–13940 (2021)
8. Chen, C., Do, M.N., Wang, J.: Robust image and video dehazing with visual artifact suppression via gradient residual minimization. In: Leibe, B., Matas, J., Sebe, N., Welling, M. (eds.) ECCV 2016. LNCS, vol. 9906, pp. 576–591. Springer, Cham (2016). https://doi.org/10.1007/978-3-319-46475-6_36
9. Chen, L., Lu, X., Zhang, J., Chu, X., Chen, C.: HINet: half instance normalization network for image restoration. In: Proceedings of the IEEE/CVF Conference on Computer Vision and Pattern Recognition, pp. 182–192 (2021)
10. Chen, Y., Li, W., Sakaridis, C., Dai, D., Van Gool, L.: Domain adaptive faster R-CNN for object detection in the wild. In: Proceedings of the IEEE Conference on Computer Vision and Pattern Recognition, pp. 3339–3348 (2018)
11. Chi, L., Tian, G., Mu, Y., Xie, L., Tian, Q.: Fast non-local neural networks with spectral residual learning. In: Proceedings of the 27th ACM International Conference on Multimedia, pp. 2142–2151 (2019)
12. Deng, Q., Huang, Z., Tsai, C.-C., Lin, C.-W.: HardGAN: a haze-aware representation distillation gan for single image dehazing. In: Vedaldi, A., Bischof, H., Brox, T., Frahm, J.-M. (eds.) ECCV 2020. LNCS, vol. 12351, pp. 722–738. Springer, Cham (2020). https://doi.org/10.1007/978-3-030-58539-6_43

13. Dong, H.,et al.: Multi-scale boosted dehazing network with dense feature fusion. In: Proceedings of the IEEE/CVF Conference on Computer Vision and Pattern Recognition, pp. 2157–2167 (2020)
14. Dong, J., Pan, J.: Physics-based feature dehazing networks. In: Vedaldi, A., Bischof, H., Brox, T., Frahm, J.-M. (eds.) ECCV 2020. LNCS, vol. 12375, pp. 188–204. Springer, Cham (2020). https://doi.org/10.1007/978-3-030-58577-8_12
15. Fattal, R.: Single image dehazing. ACM Trans. Graphics (TOG) **27**(3), 1–9 (2008)
16. Fattal, R.: Dehazing using color-lines. ACM Trans. Graphics (TOG) **34**(1), 1–14 (2014)
17. Fu, M., Liu, H., Yu, Y., Chen, J., Wang, K.: DW-GAN: a discrete wavelet transform GAN for nonhomogeneous dehazing. In: Proceedings of the IEEE/CVF Conference on Computer Vision and Pattern Recognition, pp. 203–212 (2021)
18. Guo, T., Li, X., Cherukuri, V., Monga, V.: Dense scene information estimation network for dehazing. In: Proceedings of the IEEE/CVF Conference on Computer Vision and Pattern Recognition Workshops (2019)
19. He, K., Sun, J., Tang, X.: Single image haze removal using dark channel prior. IEEE Trans. Pattern Anal. Mach. Intell. **33**(12), 2341–2353 (2010)
20. He, K., Zhang, X., Ren, S., Sun, J.: Deep residual learning for image recognition. In: Proceedings of the IEEE Conference on Computer Vision and Pattern Recognition, pp. 770–778 (2016)
21. He, T., Zhang, Z., Zhang, H., Zhang, Z., Xie, J., Li, M.: Bag of tricks for image classification with convolutional neural networks. In: Proceedings of the IEEE/CVF Conference on Computer Vision and Pattern Recognition, pp. 558–567 (2019)
22. Hong, M., Xie, Y., Li, C., Qu, Y.: Distilling image dehazing with heterogeneous task imitation. In: Proceedings of the IEEE/CVF Conference on Computer Vision and Pattern Recognition, pp. 3462–3471 (2020)
23. Huang, G., Liu, Z., Van Der Maaten, L., Weinberger, K.Q.: Densely connected convolutional networks. In: Proceedings of the IEEE Conference on Computer Vision and Pattern Recognition, pp. 4700–4708 (2017)
24. Lai, W.S., Huang, J.B., Ahuja, N., Yang, M.H.: Deep laplacian pyramid networks for fast and accurate super-resolution. In: Proceedings of the IEEE Conference on Computer Vision and Pattern Recognition, pp. 624–632 (2017)
25. Le, H., Borji, A.: What are the receptive, effective receptive, and projective fields of neurons in convolutional neural networks? arXiv preprint arXiv:1705.07049 (2017)
26. Li, B., Peng, X., Wang, Z., Xu, J., Feng, D.: AOD-Net: All-in-one dehazing network. In: Proceedings of the IEEE International Conference on Computer Vision, pp. 4770–4778 (2017)
27. Li, B., Peng, X., Wang, Z., Xu, J., Feng, D.: End-to-end united video dehazing and detection. In: Proceedings of the AAAI Conference on Artificial Intelligence, vol. 32 (2018)
28. Li, B., et al.: Benchmarking single-image dehazing and beyond. IEEE Trans. Image Process. **28**(1), 492–505 (2018)
29. Liang, J., Cao, J., Sun, G., Zhang, K., Van Gool, L., Timofte, R.: SwinIR: image restoration using swin transformer. In: Proceedings of the IEEE/CVF International Conference on Computer Vision, pp. 1833–1844 (2021)
30. Liu, J., Wu, H., Xie, Y., Qu, Y., Ma, L.: Trident dehazing network. In: Proceedings of the IEEE/CVF Conference on Computer Vision and Pattern Recognition Workshops, pp. 430–431 (2020)
31. Liu, R., Fan, X., Hou, M., Jiang, Z., Luo, Z., Zhang, L.: Learning aggregated transmission propagation networks for haze removal and beyond. IEEE Trans. Neural Networks Learn. Syst. **30**(10), 2973–2986 (2018)

32. Liu, X., Ma, Y., Shi, Z., Chen, J.: GridDehazeNet: attention-based multi-scale network for image dehazing. In: Proceedings of the IEEE/CVF International Conference on Computer Vision, pp. 7314–7323 (2019)

33. Liu, Y., Pan, J., Ren, J., Su, Z.: Learning deep priors for image dehazing. In: Proceedings of the IEEE/CVF International Conference on Computer Vision, pp. 2492–2500 (2019)

34. Mao, X., Liu, Y., Shen, W., Li, Q., Wang, Y.: Deep residual Fourier transformation for single image deblurring. arXiv preprint arXiv:2111.11745 (2021)

35. McCartney, E.J.: Optics of the atmosphere: scattering by molecules and particles. New York (1976)

36. Oppenheim, A.V., Lim, J.S.: The importance of phase in signals. Proc. IEEE **69**(5), 529–541 (1981)

37. Qin, X., Wang, Z., Bai, Y., Xie, X., Jia, H.: FFA-Net: Feature fusion attention network for single image dehazing. In: Proceedings of the AAAI Conference on Artificial Intelligence, vol. 34, pp. 11908–11915 (2020)

38. Qu, Y., Chen, Y., Huang, J., Xie, Y.: Enhanced pix2pix dehazing network. In: Proceedings of the IEEE/CVF Conference on Computer Vision and Pattern Recognition, pp. 8160–8168 (2019)

39. Rao, Y., Zhao, W., Zhu, Z., Lu, J., Zhou, J.: Global filter networks for image classification. In: Advances in Neural Information Processing Systems, vol. 34 (2021)

40. Ren, W., Liu, S., Zhang, H., Pan, J., Cao, X., Yang, M.-H.: Single image dehazing via multi-scale convolutional neural networks. In: Leibe, B., Matas, J., Sebe, N., Welling, M. (eds.) ECCV 2016. LNCS, vol. 9906, pp. 154–169. Springer, Cham (2016). https://doi.org/10.1007/978-3-319-46475-6_10

41. Ren, W., et al.: Gated fusion network for single image dehazing. In: Proceedings of the IEEE Conference on Computer Vision and Pattern Recognition, pp. 3253–3261 (2018)

42. Ronneberger, O., Fischer, P., Brox, T.: U-Net: convolutional networks for biomedical image segmentation. In: Navab, N., Hornegger, J., Wells, W.M., Frangi, A.F. (eds.) MICCAI 2015. LNCS, vol. 9351, pp. 234–241. Springer, Cham (2015). https://doi.org/10.1007/978-3-319-24574-4_28

43. Sakaridis, C., Dai, D., Hecker, S., Van Gool, L.: Model adaptation with synthetic and real data for semantic dense foggy scene understanding. In: Ferrari, V., Hebert, M., Sminchisescu, C., Weiss, Y. (eds.) ECCV 2018. LNCS, vol. 11217, pp. 707–724. Springer, Cham (2018). https://doi.org/10.1007/978-3-030-01261-8_42

44. Sakaridis, C., Dai, D., Van Gool, L.: Semantic foggy scene understanding with synthetic data. Int. J. Comput. Vision **126**(9), 973–992 (2018)

45. Skarbnik, N., Zeevi, Y.Y., Sagiv, C.: The importance of phase in image processing. Technion-Israel Institute of Technology, Faculty of Electrical Engineering (2009)

46. Suvorov, R., et al.: Resolution-robust large mask inpainting with Fourier convolutions. In: Proceedings of the IEEE/CVF Winter Conference on Applications of Computer Vision, pp. 2149–2159 (2022)

47. Wang, C., et al.: EAA-Net: a novel edge assisted attention network for single image dehazing. Knowl.-Based Syst. **228**, 107279 (2021)

48. Wang, X., Yu, K., Dong, C., Loy, C.C.: Recovering realistic texture in image super-resolution by deep spatial feature transform. In: Proceedings of the IEEE Conference on Computer Vision and Pattern Recognition, pp. 606–615 (2018)

49. Wu, H., et al.: Contrastive learning for compact single image dehazing. In: Proceedings of the IEEE/CVF Conference on Computer Vision and Pattern Recognition, pp. 10551–10560 (2021)

50. Yang, Y., Soatto, S.: FDA: Fourier domain adaptation for semantic segmentation. In: Proceedings of the IEEE/CVF Conference on Computer Vision and Pattern Recognition, pp. 4085–4095 (2020)
51. Ye, T., et al.: Perceiving and modeling density is all you need for image dehazing. arXiv preprint arXiv:2111.09733 (2021)
52. Yi, P., Wang, Z., Jiang, K., Jiang, J., Ma, J.: Progressive fusion video super-resolution network via exploiting non-local spatio-temporal correlations. In: Proceedings of the IEEE/CVF International Conference on Computer Vision, pp. 3106–3115 (2019)
53. Zamir, S.W., et al.: Multi-stage progressive image restoration. In: Proceedings of the IEEE/CVF Conference on Computer Vision and Pattern Recognition, pp. 14821–14831 (2021)
54. Zhang, H., Patel, V.M.: Densely connected pyramid dehazing network. In: Proceedings of the IEEE Conference on Computer Vision and Pattern Recognition, pp. 3194–3203 (2018)
55. Zhang, J., Cao, Y., Fang, S., Kang, Y., Wen Chen, C.: Fast haze removal for nighttime image using maximum reflectance prior. In: Proceedings of the IEEE Conference on Computer Vision and Pattern Recognition, pp. 7418–7426 (2017)
56. Zheng, Z., et al.: Ultra-high-definition image dehazing via multi-guided bilateral learning. In: Proceedings of the IEEE/CVF Conference on Computer Vision and Pattern Recognition, pp. 16180–16189. IEEE (2021)
57. Zhu, Q., Mai, J., Shao, L.: Single image dehazing using color attenuation prior. In: BMVC. Citeseer (2014)
58. Zou, W., Jiang, M., Zhang, Y., Chen, L., Lu, Z., Wu, Y.: SDWNet: a straight dilated network with wavelet transformation for image deblurring. In: Proceedings of the IEEE/CVF International Conference on Computer Vision, pp. 1895–1904 (2021)

Towards Real-World HDRTV Reconstruction: A Data Synthesis-Based Approach

Zhen Cheng[1], Tao Wang[2], Yong Li[2], Fenglong Song[2(✉)], Chang Chen[2], and Zhiwei Xiong[1(✉)]

[1] University of Science and Technology of China, Hefei, China
mywander@mail.ustc.edu.cn, zwxiong@ustc.edu.cn
[2] Huawei Noah's Ark Lab, Shenzhen, China
{wangtao10,liyong156,songfenglong,chenchang25}@huawei.com

Abstract. Existing deep learning based HDRTV reconstruction methods assume one kind of tone mapping operators (TMOs) as the degradation procedure to synthesize SDRTV-HDRTV pairs for supervised training. In this paper, we argue that, although traditional TMOs exploit efficient dynamic range compression priors, they have several drawbacks on modeling the realistic degradation: information over-preservation, color bias and possible artifacts, making the trained reconstruction networks hard to generalize well to real-world cases. To solve this problem, we propose a learning-based data synthesis approach to learn the properties of real-world SDRTVs by integrating several tone mapping priors into both network structures and loss functions. In specific, we design a conditioned two-stream network with prior tone mapping results as a guidance to synthesize SDRTVs by both global and local transformations. To train the data synthesis network, we form a novel self-supervised content loss to constraint different aspects of the synthesized SDRTVs at regions with different brightness distributions and an adversarial loss to emphasize the details to be more realistic. To validate the effectiveness of our approach, we synthesize SDRTV-HDRTV pairs with our method and use them to train several HDRTV reconstruction networks. Then we collect two inference datasets containing both labeled and unlabeled real-world SDRTVs, respectively. Experimental results demonstrate that, the networks trained with our synthesized data generalize significantly better to these two real-world datasets than existing solutions.

Keywords: Real-world HDRTV reconstruction · Data synthesis · Tone mapping operators

---

Z. Cheng and T. Wang—Equal contribution. This work was done when Zhen Cheng was an intern in Huawei Noah's Ark Lab.

Supplementary Information The online version contains supplementary material available at https://doi.org/10.1007/978-3-031-19800-7_12.

1 Introduction

Recent years have seen the huge progress on ultra high-definition (UHD) display devices such as OLED [14], which can display high dynamic range television sources (HDRTVs) with high dynamic range (HDR, *e.g.*, 10 bit quantization) and wide color gamut (WCG, *e.g.*, BT.2020 [19]). However, while such HDR display devices (named HDR-TVs) become more popular, most available images/videos are still standard dynamic range television sources (SDRTVs).

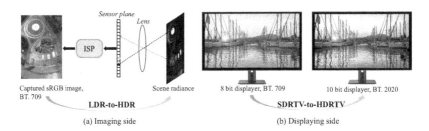

Fig. 1. Illustration of the difference between the tasks LDR-to-HDR (at the imaging side) and SDRTV-to-HDRTV (at the displaying side).

To this end, previous researches [4,12,13,26,31,34,43,44] focus on recovering the linear and scene radiance maps from the captured sRGB sources, forming the LDR-to-HDR problem defined at the imaging side, as shown in Fig. 1(a). Then the scene radiance maps are transformed to HDRTVs via complicated post-processing [9,24,25]. However, such post-processing has been not well-defined for the standards of HDRTVs, resulting in severe color bias and artifacts [9,25]. Recently, researchers introduced deep learning techniques to straightforwardly reconstruct HDRTVs from their corresponding SDRTVs [9,24,25,54], forming the problem SDRTV-to-HDRTV at the displaying side (Fig. 1(b)). Such solutions need to train convolutional neural networks (CNNs) relying on SDRTV-HDRTV pairs. Hence, the acquisition of such paired data becomes a vital problem.

There exists two possible ways to get SDRTV-HDRTV pairs: acquisition by cameras and synthesis by algorithms. The former acquires SDRTV-HDRTV pairs via asynchronous camera shots like those in super-resolution [5,7]. However, such approach faces difficulties to get large datasets for network training due to its high sensitivity to motion and light condition changes. The latter solution can be further divided into two categories: camera pipeline based and tone mapping operator (TMO) based. Camera pipeline based approaches get the scene radiance map first and then process it to SDRTV and HDRTV via different processing pipelines. However, mostly the processing from light radiance to HDRTV is unknown, which makes the solution unavailable [9]. In consequence, existing SDRTV-to-HDRTV methods rely on TMOs [10,16,27,29,33,40,42] that compress the dynamic range via global or local transformations as the degradation procedure to synthesize the SDRTV data.

However, through detailed analysis, we observe that, because TMOs aim at preserving the information from HDRTVs as much as possible, they may inherit

Youtube [1]   UTMNet [47]   GT   Youtube [1]   UTMNet [47]   GT
          (a) SDRTVs   (b) HDRTVs

Fig. 2. (a) Drawbacks on SDRTV data synthesis of two representative TMOs [1,47]. From top to bottom: information over-preservation, color bias and artifacts. (b) Reconstruction artifacts on real-world HDRTVs of the networks (HDRTVNet [9]) trained with data synthesized by these two TMOs. (Color figure online)

too much information such as extreme-light details from HDRTVs, which often do not appear in real-world SDRTVs. Such information over-preservation, as shown in Fig. 2(a), is the main drawback of TMOs as SDRTV data synthesis solutions. Moreover, most TMOs will also introduce color bias due to inaccurate gamut mapping and obvious artifacts such as wrong structures. Accordingly, the HDRTV reconstruction networks trained by TMO-synthesized SDRTV-HDRTV pairs are hard to generalize well to real-world cases as shown in Fig. 2(b).

To solve this problem, we propose an learning-based SDRTV data synthesis approach to synthesize realistic SDRTV-HDRTV pairs. Inspired by real-world degradation learning with the help of predefined degradations in super-resolution [8,35,52], we exploit the tone mapping priors in our method for both network structures and loss functions.

In specific, we model the SDRTV data synthesis with two streams, *i.e.*, a global mapping stream and a local adjustment one and use some representative tone mapping results to generate global guidance information for better HDRTV-to-SDRTV conversion. To train the network, we utilize different tone mapping results as the supervisor for regions with different light conditions, forming a novel unsupervised content loss to constraint different aspects of the synthesized SDRTVs. We also introduce an adversarial loss to emphasize the synthesized SDRTVs to be more realistic.

To validate the effectiveness of our approach, we synthesize SDRTV-HDRTV pairs using our method and use them to train several HDRTV reconstruction networks. For inference, we collect two inference datasets containing labeled SDRTVs captured by a smartphone and unlabeled SDRTVs from public datasets [25]. Quantitative and qualitative experimental results on these two inference datasets demonstrate that, the networks trained with our synthesized data can achieve significantly better performance than those with other data synthesis approaches.

2   Related Work

SDRTV-to-HDRTV Methods. SDRTV-to-HDRTV is a highly ill-posed problem since the complicated degradation from HDRTVs to SDRTVs. While

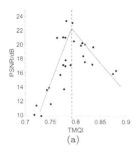 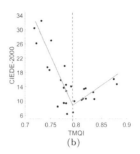

(a)   (b)

Fig. 3. The scatters showing statistical relationships between PSNR (a) and CIEDE-2000 [45] (b) *w.r.t* TMQI [53], respectively. We use solid lines and dotted lines to represent the trend and the turning point of trend changes, respectively. These metrics are evaluated and averaged on our collected RealHDRTV dataset.

early researches aim at restoring HDR radiance map from a low dynamic range (LDR) input, which is called inverse tone mapping [4,12,13,26,31,34,43,44], they only consider HDR reconstruction at the imaging side and ignore the color gamut transform. Recently, SDRTV-to-HDRTV with deep learning techniques relying on synthesized SDRTV data becomes popular [9,24,25]. In this paper, we focus on the solution of data synthesis for real-world HDRTV reconstruction.

Tone Mapping Operators. TMOs aim at compressing the dynamic range of HDR sources but preserve image details as much as possible. Traditional TMOs always involve some useful tone mapping priors such as the Weber-Fechner law [11] and the Retinex Theory [28] to make either global mappings [1,16,42] or local mappings [10,27,29,33,40]. Recently, learning-based TMOs become popular due to their remarkable performance. They rely on ranking traditional TMOs [6,38,39,41,56] as labels for fully supervision or unpaired datasets for adversarial learning [47]. In this paper, we argue that TMOs have several drawbacks for realistic HDRTV data synthesis. Accordingly, we propose a learning-based method integrating tone mapping priors to solve these drawbacks.

3   Motivation

As we all know, the core target of TMOs is to preserve as much information as possible from the HDR sources. However, the essential of the degradation from HDRTVs to SDRTVs is to lose information selectively, *i.e.*, drop out details at extreme-light regions. Thus sometimes a contradiction will occur when we use TMOs to model the degradation. To get a deep-in understanding of this problem, we make an evaluation on 31 TMOs (detailed in the supplementary material) with our RealHDRTV dataset (detailed in Sect. 5.1).

Specifically, we use TMQI [53] (higher is better), which is mostly used for the evaluations of TMOs, to evaluate the amount of information an SDRTV preserves from the corresponding HDRTV. Meanwhile, we use PSNR (higher is

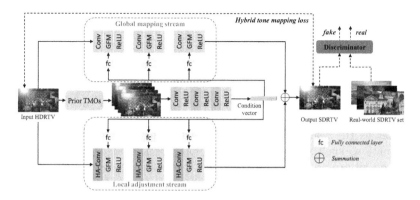

Fig. 4. Our proposed SDRTV data synthesis approach. We integrate several tone mapping priors into this framework, resulting a two-stream data synthesis network conditioned by prior tone mapping results and a novel content loss function formulated by tone mapping priors.

better) and CIEDE-2000 [45] (lower is better) to evaluate the distance between a synthesized SDRTV and the ground truth real-world one. We draw the evaluation results averaged over the RealHDRTV dataset to two scatters in Fig. 3 where each point represents a TMO.

Interestingly, we can see that, on our RealHDRTV dataset, when the TMQI of a TMO exceeds a threshold at about 0.8, the distance between synthesized and real-world data turns to increase. It indicates that the information preserved by this TMO may be too much compared with realistic SDRTVs. We can also observe such information over-preservation in Fig. 2(a). Such drawback may lead the trained HDRTV reconstruction networks fail to hallucinate the extreme-light details in real-world cases as shown in Fig. 2(b).

Moreover, most TMOs transform the color gamut by simple transformation matrix [20] or color channel rescaling [47], resulting obvious color bias, let alone possible artifacts such as halo, wrong structures and color banding occur for most TMOs [47]. The data synthesized by TMOs will lead the trained reconstruction network to generate artifacts in real-world cases as shown in Fig. 2(b).

Motivated by these drawbacks of TMOs on realistic SDRTV data synthesis, we propose a learning-based approach to synthesize training data for better HDRTV reconstruction in real-world cases.

4 Learning-Based SDRTV Data Synthesis

Figure 4 illustrates the framework of our data synthesis method. Inspired by learning real-world degradation with the help of predefined downsampling methods in the field of image super-resolution [8,35,52], we involve the prior knowledge for designing TMOs to our framework. Although these priors themselves cannot be used for straightforward degradation modeling, some of them can provide regional constraints or global guidance to benefit our learning. Thus, we integrate several tone mapping priors into both network structures and loss functions.

4.1   Conditioned Two-Stream Network

Given an input HDRTV $H \in \mathbb{R}^{X \times Y \times 3}$ where X and Y denote the image size, our network N aims to convert it into an SDRTV $S \in \mathbb{R}^{X \times Y \times 3}$ whose properties are similar as the real-world SDRTVs. Considering that we need both global transformations such as color gamut mapping and local adjustments such as selective detail preservation at extreme-light regions, our network N includes a global mapping stream N_g and a local adjustment stream N_l as shown in Fig. 4.

The global stream N_g is composed of three 1×1 convolutions which performs similarly as global TMOs with 3DLUTs [1] or S-curves [16, 42]. Such network has been validated effective for global color [9] and style [17] transformations. The other stream N_l is composed of three highlight-aware convolution blocks (HA-conv, detailed in the supplementary material), which shows superior performance on the task sensitive to extreme-light regions such as SVBRDF estimation [15]. For simplicity of the data synthesis network, we straightforwardly add the results of global and the local stream together to get the final synthesized SDRTVs.

Moreover, to benefit the learning, we involve the prior knowledge of existing TMOs into these two streams. For each input HDRTV H, we obtain a number of tone mapped versions $\{S_i | i = 1, 2, \cdots, K\}$ as the condition to guide the data synthesis. Specifically, we concatenate these condition images and feed them into a condition network N_c. The condition network is composed of three convolution layers with large kernel sizes and strides followed by a global average pooling layer. The pooling layer will output a 1D condition vector $v_c \in \mathbb{R}^{B \times C_{cond}}$ where B and C_{cond} denote the batch size and the channel number, respectively.

Because the condition vector embeds sufficient global information of the prior tone mapping results, it is then used to modulate the main branch of the two stream network N. For the output feature maps $F \in \mathbb{R}^{B \times C_{feat} \times X \times Y}$ of each layer/block in the global/local stream where C_{feat} denotes the channel number, we use a fully connected layer to transform v_c to scale factors $\omega_1 \in \mathbb{R}^{B \times C_{feat}}$ and shift factors $\omega_2 \in \mathbb{R}^{B \times C_{feat}}$ and modulate the feature maps F via global feature modulation (GFM) [17], which can be described as:

$$F_{mod} = F * \omega_1 + \omega_2. \tag{1}$$

Note that we do not share the fully connected layers used for N_g and N_l, they can provide different guidances for different transformation granularities.

4.2   Hybrid Tone Mapping Prior Loss

As analyzed in Sect. 3, the synthesized SDRTVs should have several aspects: globally compressed dynamic range, accurate color gamut and lost details at extreme-light regions. However, there are no paired HDRTV-SDRTV datasets and the acquisition of large-scale and high-quality datasets for training with imaging devices is also difficult. Therefore, we follow these region-aware aspects and divide the whole image into several regions according to their brightness distributions. After that, we transform the input HDRTVs with existing TMOs to get weak supervisors for different regions, forming a novel content loss function, namely hybrid tone mapping prior (HTMP) loss ($\mathcal{L}_{htmp}$).

Region Division. At the very first, we divide the input HDRTV H into three regions, $i.e.$, the high-, mid- and low-light regions. Specifically, we get the light radiance L by linearizing H with a PQ EOTF [21] and segment the radiance map into three regions by two truncation points α and β, which are the a-th and b-th percentiles of the radiance map's histogram, respectively. The resulting region division masks are calculated as:

$$M_{high} = I(L > a), M_{low} = I(L < b), M_{mid} = \mathbf{1} - M_{high} - M_{low}, \qquad (2)$$

where $I(\cdot)$ denotes the indicative function and $\mathbf{1}$ is a all-one map.

High-Light Loss. For the high-light regions, the output SDRTV should be saturated. Thus we use a all-one map as the supervisor at this region as:

$$\mathcal{L}_{high} = \|M_{high} \odot (\mathbf{1} - N(H))\|_1, \qquad (3)$$

where $\odot$ means element-wise production. Note that, although the supervisor at the high-light regions is a all-one map, due to the fact that CNNs have denoising and smoothing effects [46], the resultant SDRTVs will become smooth here.

Low-Light Loss. For the low-light regions, the output SDRTV should linearly compress the radiance due to its lower bit width. Thus we use the results of a simple TMO Linear [51] $l.$ as the supervisor:

$$\mathcal{L}_{low} = \|M_{low} \odot (l(H) - N(H))\|_1. \qquad (4)$$

Mid-Light Loss. For the mid-light regions, we need to consider both global dynamic range compression and accurate color gamut. However, there is no proper TMO for both properties. Thus we combine two TMOs to achieve this goal. In specific, we firstly use a μ-law function [23] $\mu(\cdot)$ after global color gamut mapping [20] $CGM(\cdot)$. Since the μ-law function is a logarithm curve, which is similar to the compressive response to light in the human visual system, $i.e.$, the Weber-Fechner law [11], it can provide a visually pleasant global transformation for dynamic range compression and preserve low-light details by stretching the brightness. Meanwhile, such stretching will lead to under-saturated color, so we then introduce another TMO Youtube [1] $y(\cdot)$, which uses 3D lookup tables predefined by Youtube tools for online film showcase. Youtube can provide vivid but sometimes over-saturated color. Moreover, due to its point-wise processing nature, Youtube will generate discontinuous textures near the high-light regions. Because the μ-law function and Youtube are complementary to each other, we use an invert μ-law function, $i.e.$, $\mu^{-1}(\cdot)$ with the normalized linear radiance as input to generate a weighting matrix $W = \mu^{-1}(\frac{L-\beta}{\alpha-\beta})$. So the loss function at the mid-light regions can be described as:

$$\mathcal{L}_{mid} = \|M_{mid} \odot (W \odot \mu(CGM(H)) + (1 - W) \odot y(H)) - N(H)\|_1. \qquad (5)$$

Finally, we add the above three loss functions, forming our HTMP loss via $\mathcal{L}_{htmp} = \mathcal{L}_{high} + \mathcal{L}_{mid} + \mathcal{L}_{low}$. We also illustrate a flowchart of our HTMP loss for a more intuitive understanding in the supplementary material.

4.3　Adversarial Loss

With the content loss $\mathcal{L}_{htmp}$, the network has had the ability to model the region-aware properties of realistic SDRTVs. To further emphasize the synthesized SDRTVs to be more realistic, we introduce an additional adversarial loss with a discriminator following the GAN-based low-level researches [30]. Specifically, we collect a large real-world SDRTV dataset $\mathcal{S}$ containing 3603 4K SDRTVs from public datasets [25]. We split the dataset into train and inference subsets $\mathcal{S}_{train}$ and $\mathcal{S}_{test}$ while the latter contains 25 SDRTVs. The dataset $\mathcal{S}$ contains SDRTVs captured in different environments and with different devices.

During the adversarial training, we utilize the least square GAN approach [37] with a 70×70 PatchGAN [18,30,32,57] and the overall loss function for the generator network N is $\mathcal{L}_N = \mathcal{L}_{htmp} + \lambda \mathcal{L}_{adv}$, where λ is a weighting factor. More implementation details can be found in the supplementary material.

5　Experimental Results

5.1　Experimental Settings

For the training of our SDRTV data synthesis network N, we collect a dataset $\mathcal{H}$ containing 3679 HDRTVs (BT.2020 with PQ EOTF [20]) from public datasets [25] as the input of network N. To validate the effectiveness of our the trained data synthesis network, we firstly train several HDRTV reconstruction networks using the SDRTV-HDRTV pairs synthesized by our well-trained N. Then we inference these networks on two real-world SDRTV datasets to see the generalization ability of trained networks.

Datasets. With the unlabeled inference dataset $\mathcal{S}_{test}$ introduced in Sect. 4.3, we can only make visual comparisons and user study to validate the quality of reconstructed HDRTVs. In order to make full-reference evaluations, we also capture a dataset, named RealHDRTV, containing SDRTV-HDRTV pairs. Specifically, we capture 93 SDRTV-HDRTV pairs with 8K resolutions using a smartphone camera with the "SDR" and "HDR10" modes. To avoid possible misalignment, we use a professional steady tripod and only capture indoor or controlled static scenes. After the acquisition, we cut out regions with obvious motions (10+ pixels) and light condition changes, crop them into 4K image pairs and use a global 2D translation to align the cropped image pairs [7]. Finally, we remove the pairs which are still with obvious misalignment and get 97 4K SDRTV-HDRTV pairs with misalignment no more than 1 pixel as our labeled inference dataset. We've release the RealHDRTV dataset in https://github.com/huawei-noah/benchmark. More details about the dataset acquisition and post-processing can be found in the supplementary material.

Data Synthesis Baselines. As for baseline SDRTV synthesis methods, we use three traditional TMOs, *i.e.*, Youtube [1], Hable [16] and Raman [40] because they are often used for film showcase in different online video platforms. We then collect other 27 traditional TMOs (detailed in the supplementary material) and rank the 30 TMOs using TMQI [53] and choose the best one as a new baseline named Rank following [6,38,39,41]. In addition, the state-of-the-art learning-based TMO, named UTMNet [47] is also involved here for SDRTV synthesis.

HDRTV Reconstruction Networks. We use the public HDRTV dataset HDRTV1K [9] as the input of both our well-trained network N and other five baselines to synthesize SDRTV-HDRTV pairs. As a result, we get 6 datasets named after their synthesis methods to train HDRTV reconstruction networks. Specifically, we choose four state-of-the-art networks (JSI-Net [25], CSRNet [17], SpatialA3DLUT [48], and HDRTVNet-AGCM [9]). To compare with existing unpaired learning-based reconstruction methods, we also involve CycleGAN [57] as another reconstruction network. Note that because CycleGAN has no explicit modeling of the unique relationships between SDRTVs and HDRTVs, we do not involve it as a data synthesis baseline. The implementation details of these networks can be found in the supplementary material.

Evaluation Metrics. With the labeled dataset, *i.e.*, our RealHDRTV dataset, we evaluate the reconstructed HDRTVs using several metrics for fidelity, perceptual quality and color difference. For fidelity, we use PSNR, mPSNR [3], SSIM [49], and MS-SSIM [50]. For perceptual quality, we use HDR-VDP-3 [36] and SR-SIM [55] because they are highly correlated to the human perceptions for HDRTVs [2]. For color difference, we utilize $\triangle E_{ITP}$ [22] which is designed for the color gamut BT.2020. For visualization, we visualize HDRTVs without any post-processing following [9] to keep the details in extreme-light regions.

5.2   Generalize to Labeled Real-World SDRTVs

Quantitative Results. Quantitative results on the generalization to our RealHDRTV dataset are shown in Table 1. As we can see, for each network, the version trained by paired data synthesized by our method works the best in terms of every evaluation metric and achieves significant gains over the baseline methods. Taking HDRTVNet-AGCM [9], the state-of-the-art HDRTV reconstruction network, as an example, compared with the best-performed TMO Hable [16], our method gains 2.60 dB, 0.014 and 6.7 in terms of PSNR, SR-SIM and $\triangle E_{ITP}$, respectively. Such results validate that, with our synthesized training data, the networks can generalize well to the real-world SDRTVs. Note that there are still small misalignment between SDRTVs and HDRTVs within this dataset, the absolute full-reference metrics will be not as high as those well-aligned ones, but the metric difference can still reflect the superiority of our method.

Qualitative Results. We also show some visual examples in Fig. 5, we can see that, with CycleGAN, the reconstructed HDRTVs suffer from severe color bias and lose details at extreme light regions, which is consistent with the results shown in Table 1. Although the cycle consistency has been proved useful for

Table 1. Evaluation results of the HDRTV reconstruction results on the RealHDRTV dataset via various networks trained on datasets synthesized by different SDRTV data synthesis methods.

Network	TrainData	PSNR↑	mPSNR↑	SSIM↑	MS-SSIM↑	HDR-VDP3↑	SR-SIM↑	$\triangle E_{ITP}$↓
JSI-Net [25]	Raman [40]	18.91	13.23	0.708	0.719	3.54	0.736	74.2
	Rank	17.75	11.42	0.680	0.668	4.16	0.723	81.9
	UTMNet [47]	15.68	8.09	0.598	0.737	4.26	0.753	107.3
	Youtube [1]	25.47	18.56	0.842	0.923	6.32	0.942	33.6
	Hable [16]	25.45	19.60	0.851	0.918	5.71	0.926	33.8
	Ours	**27.80**	**22.92**	**0.878**	**0.933**	**6.38**	**0.943**	**27.2**
CSRNet [17]	Raman [40]	15.16	9.04	0.628	0.868	5.16	0.843	131.3
	Rank	19.41	13.43	0.749	0.912	6.28	0.929	84.0
	UTMNet [47]	12.37	5.40	0.433	0.829	4.63	0.815	172.2
	Youtube [1]	25.29	18.30	0.834	0.923	6.36	0.945	34.2
	Hable [16]	25.34	19.45	0.847	0.925	6.35	0.942	33.8
	Ours	**27.73**	**22.65**	**0.874**	**0.935**	**6.43**	**0.950**	**27.2**
Spatial-A3DLUT [48]	Raman [40]	15.35	10.77	0.726	0.882	5.61	0.852	117.4
	Rank	22.68	16.74	0.829	0.920	5.90	0.931	50.1
	UTMNet [47]	18.55	13.51	0.805	0.924	6.04	0.910	84.2
	Youtube [1]	25.27	18.23	0.832	0.921	6.34	0.943	34.2
	Hable [16]	25.48	19.40	0.846	0.924	6.35	0.942	33.5
	Ours	**27.56**	**22.44**	**0.871**	**0.933**	**6.37**	**0.945**	**27.7**
HDRTVNet-AGCM [9]	Raman [40]	19.35	13.61	0.749	0.902	5.90	0.904	88.6
	Rank	19.73	14.06	0.778	0.917	6.16	0.936	77.5
	UTMNet [47]	16.34	10.43	0.649	0.887	5.39	0.868	112.4
	Youtube [1]	25.26	18.29	0.833	0.922	6.36	0.945	34.1
	Hable [16]	25.44	19.48	0.847	0.925	6.36	0.943	33.6
	Ours	**28.04**	**22.82**	**0.876**	**0.938**	**6.47**	**0.957**	**26.9**
CycleGAN [57]	—	10.70	8.90	0.743	0.891	5.59	0.862	203.7

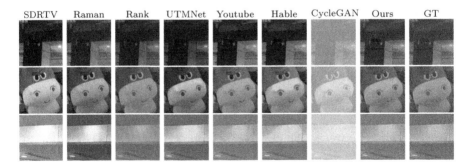

SDRTV   Raman   Rank   UTMNet   Youtube   Hable   CycleGAN   Ours   GT

Fig. 5. Visual comparisons on real-world SDRTV-HDRTV pairs and the HDRTVs reconstructed by HDRTVNet-AGCM [9] trained with different data synthesis methods. The images are from our RealHDRTV dataset. Zoom in the figure for a better visual experience.

style transfer [57], the real-world HDRTV reconstruction does not work well with such constraint. In contrast, by exploiting several tone mapping priors as both constraints and guidance, our method can perform pretty well in real-world cases. While the networks trained with data synthesized by other methods show

Table 2. The preference matrix from the user study on the unlabeled real-world dataset $\mathcal{S}_{test}$.

	Hable	Youtube	Ours	**Total**
Hable	–	125	70	**195**
Youtube	150	–	83	**233**
Ours	205	192	–	***397***

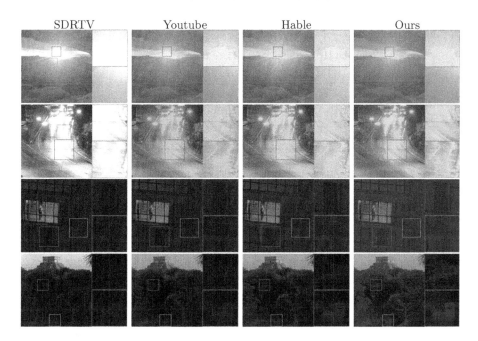

Fig. 6. Visual comparisons on the HDRTVs reconstructed by HDRTVNet-AGCM [9] trained with data synthesized by Youtube [1], Hable [16] and Ours. The input SDRTVs are from the dataset $\mathcal{S}_{test}$. Zoom in the figure for a better visual experience.

weak ability to recover the low-light region and expand the accurate color gamut, the network trained by our dataset show significant advantage over them and produce results much more close to the ground truth.

5.3 Generalize to Unlabeled Real-World SDRTVs

We also reveal the generalization ability of the networks trained with our synthesized dataset in a more open situation, we compare the performance of three versions (Hable, Youtube, and Ours) of the network HDRTVNet-AGCM on the unlabeled inference dataset $\mathcal{S}_{test}$ collected from public datasets [25].

User Study. We conduct a user study on the reconstructed HDRTVs with 11 professional photographers for subjective evaluation. Each participant is asked to

Table 3. Evaluation metrics on fidelity and color difference between the SDRTVs synthesized by several methods and the ground truth ones on our RealHDRTV dataset.

	PSNR↑	SSIM ↑	CIEDE ↓	TMQI ↑
Clip	13.82	0.719	18.68	0.7477
Linear [51]	16.46	0.758	15.15	0.7353
Reinhard [42]	19.94	0.776	10.65	0.8194
Raman [40]	20.97	0.627	9.52	0.7759
Kuang [27]	20.92	0.717	9.35	0.7804
Youtube [1]	22.99	0.824	6.83	0.7940
Hable [16]	23.27	0.840	6.38	0.7822
Liang [33]	16.21	0.676	14.81	0.8807
Rank [41]	16.57	0.692	14.32	**0.8850**
UTMNet [47]	15.77	0.681	16.14	0.8747
Ours	**24.54**	**0.844**	**5.80**	0.7988

make pairwise comparisons on 3 results of each image displayed on an HDR-TV (EIZO ColorEdge CG319X with a peak brightness of 1000 nits) in a darkroom. The detailed settings can be found in the supplementary material. We show the preference matrix in Table 2. We can see that, when comparing our method with the best-performed TMOs, *i.e.*, Hable and Youtube, 74.5% and 69.8% of users prefer our results, respectively.

Qualitative Results. We also show some examples for visual comparison in Fig. 6. We can find that while the networks trained by Youtube's and Hable's data has less awareness of high-light (the top two) and low-light (the bottom two) regions, the network trained by our data can enrich the details as well as preserve continuous structures.

To sum up, while the training datasets for both our data synthesis network and the HDRTV reconstruction networks have no overlap with our RealHDRTV and $\mathcal{S}_{test}$ datasets, the networks trained by our data show notable performance gains in both numerical and visual comparisons as well as the user study. It indicates that, our approach can serve as a better solution for paired SDRTV-HDRTV synthesis towards real-world HDRTV reconstruction.

5.4 The Quality of Synthesized SDRTVs

In addition to the generalization evaluations of networks trained by our data, we also evaluate the quality of synthesized SDRTVs. Specifically, we feed the HDRTVs in our RealHDRTV dataset into our well-trained data synthesis network and evaluate the distance and difference between our synthesized SDRTVs and the real-world ones. We evaluate the distances in terms of fidelity metrics

PSNR and SSIM [49] and color difference for color gamut BT.709, *i.e.*, CIEDE-2000 [45]. Following the experiment in Sect. 3, we also calculate TMQI [53] to evaluate the ability of information preservation from HDRTVs. Besides the baselines compared in Sects. 5.2 and 5.3, we involve more representative TMOs for the comparison as shown in Table 3.

We can observe that, although the state-of-the-art TMOs like Liang [33] and UTMNet [47] have significantly high TMQI values, the SDRTVs generated by them are far away from the ground truth SDRTVs. On the contrary, the SDRTVs generated by our method shows much better fidelity and color accuracy by 1.27 dB gain of PSNR and 0.58 drop of CIEDE-2000 compared with the best performed TMO Hable [16]. Such results are consistent with what we observe in Fig. 3 and interestingly, we find that our average TMQI value is pretty close to the turning point in the scatters, *i.e.*, about 0.8 for this dataset. It reveals our success on avoiding information over-preservation.

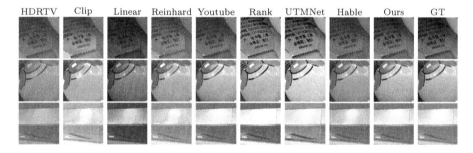

Fig. 7. Visual comparisons on SDRTVs synthesized by different representative synthesis methods together with the input HDRTVs and ground truth SDRTVs. The images are from our RealHDRTV dataset. Zoom in the figure for a better visual experience.

We also show some visual examples in Fig. 7. We can see that, compared with the ground truth SDRTVs, the information over-preservation (*e.g.*, Clip and Rank for the top example), color bias (*e.g.*, Hable and UTMNet for the middle example) and artifacts (*e.g.*, Reinhard and Linear in the bottom example) are very obvious. Meanwhile, our method can selectively preserve the information from the HDRTVs, transform color gamut accurately and avoid the artifacts.

5.5   Ablation

With the evaluations on synthesized SDRTVs, we'd like to show some ablation studies about the network structures and loss functions, particularly the effects on the tone mapping priors we utilize in our framework. We compare the values of PSNR and CIEDE-2000 [45] calculated on the synthesized SDRTVs by different variants in Table 4 and show visual comparisons in the supplementary material.

Network Design. We conduct several experiments to validate the effectiveness of tone mapping priors used for network designs. Specifically, we remove the condition network or use the input HDRTV itself to replace the condition tone mapping results to keep the parameter numbers the same. We can see in Table 4 that the condition network as well as the condition tone mapping results make very important contributions to more accurate real-world data synthesis. As Fig. 7 shows that, the condition TMOs, *i.e.*, Clip, Linear, Reinhard and Youtube we use here shows different performance advantages at different regions. For example, Linear performs very well at losing low-light details. Meanwhile, our method apparently take merits of these conditions, which validates the importance of them again. In addition, the ablation results on only the global or local stream validate the effectiveness of combining them, the visual results in the supplementary material also validate the advantages of these two streams on global and local mappings, respectively.

Table 4. Ablation study on the RealHDRTV dataset.

Loss		Network			PSNR	CIEDE
$\mathcal{L}_{htmp}$	$\mathcal{L}_{adv}$	N_c	N_l	N_g		
✓	✓	✓	✓	✓	**24.54**	**5.80**
×	✓	✓	✓	✓	11.74	27.01
✓	×	✓	✓	✓	24.24	6.00
S-Linear	✓	✓	✓	✓	16.35	15.33
S-μ-law	✓	✓	✓	✓	18.18	12.42
S-Youtube	✓	✓	✓	✓	23.32	6.64
✓	✓	×	✓	✓	24.08	6.03
✓	✓	*Self*	✓	✓	24.15	5.97
✓	✓	✓	×	✓	24.33	5.99
✓	✓	✓	✓	×	24.44	5.83

Loss Function. As we can see in the table, if we only use $\mathcal{L}_{adv}$ to train the network, the network will synthesize SDRTVs far away from the real-world ones due to the lack of content and structure constraints. However, it does not mean that $\mathcal{L}_{adv}$ is useless, we can see that with the help of $\mathcal{L}_{adv}$, the network with only $\mathcal{L}_{htmp}$ achieves a notable performance gain. In addition, to show the impacts on the involved TMOs for $\mathcal{L}_{htmp}$, we use simple L_1 loss function between the tone mapping results of each TMO as the content loss to replace $\mathcal{L}_{htmp}$. As we can see in the table, with either TMO as the supervisor, the network performance will be inferior than our $\mathcal{L}_{htmp}$. Such results validate the effectiveness of our region-aware content loss. We also show a visual example in the supplementary material to illustrate their complementarity.

6   Conclusion

In this paper, we propose a data synthesis approach to synthesize realistic SDRTV-HDRTV pairs for the training of HDRTV reconstruction networks to benefit their generalization ability on real-world cases. Through statistical and visual analysis, we observe that, existing TMOs suffer from several drawbacks on the modeling of HDRTV-to-SDRTV including information over-preservation, color bias and artifacts. To solve this problem, we propose a learning-based SDRTV data synthesis to learn the aspects of real-world SDRTVs. We integrate several tone mapping priors into both network structures and loss functions to benefit the learning. Experimental results on our collected labeled and unlabeled datasets validate that, the HDRTV reconstruction networks trained by our synthesized dataset can generalize significantly better than other methods. In addition, we believe that integrating degradation priors into degradation learning framework may also be promoted to benefit other low-level vision tasks.

Acknowledgments. We acknowledge funding from National Key R&D Program of China under Grant 2017YFA0700800, and National Natural Science Foundation of China under Grants 62131003 and 62021001.

References

1. https://www.youtube.com
2. Athar, S., Costa, T., Zeng, K., Wang, Z.: Perceptual quality assessment of UHD-HDR-WCG videos. In: 2019 IEEE International Conference on Image Processing (ICIP), pp. 1740–1744. IEEE (2019)
3. Banterle, F., Artusi, A., Debattista, K., Chalmers, A.: Advanced high dynamic range imaging. AK Peters/CRC Press (2017)
4. Banterle, F., Ledda, P., Debattista, K., Chalmers, A.: Inverse tone mapping. In: Proceedings of the 4th international conference on Computer graphics and interactive techniques in Australasia and Southeast Asia, pp. 349–356 (2006)
5. Cai, J., Zeng, H., Yong, H., Cao, Z., Zhang, L.: Toward real-world single image super-resolution: a new benchmark and a new model. In: ICCV, pp. 3086–3095 (2019)
6. Cao, X., Lai, K., Yanushkevich, S.N., Smith, M.: Adversarial and adaptive tone mapping operator for high dynamic range images. In: 2020 IEEE Symposium Series on Computational Intelligence, pp. 1814–1821. IEEE (2020)
7. Chen, C., Xiong, Z., Tian, X., Zha, Z.J., Wu, F.: Camera lens super-resolution. In: CVPR, pp. 1652–1660 (2019)
8. Chen, S., et al.: Unsupervised image super-resolution with an indirect supervised path. In: CVPRW (2020)
9. Chen, X., Zhang, Z., Ren, J.S., Tian, L., Qiao, Y., Dong, C.: A new journey from SDRTV to HDRTV. In: ICCV, pp. 4500–4509 (2021)
10. Chiu, K., et al.: Spatially nonuniform scaling functions for high contrast images. In: Graphics Interface. Canadian Information Processing Society (1993)
11. Drago, F., Myszkowski, K., Annen, T., Chiba, N.: Adaptive logarithmic mapping for displaying high contrast scenes. In: Computer graphics forum, vol. 22, pp. 419–426. Wiley Online Library (2003)

12. Eilertsen, G., Kronander, J., Denes, G., Mantiuk, R.K., Unger, J.: HDR image reconstruction from a single exposure using deep CNNs. ACM Trans. Graph. **36**(6), 1–15 (2017)
13. Endo, Y., Kanamori, Y., Mitani, J.: Deep reverse tone mapping. ACM Trans. Graph. **36**(6), 1–10 (2017). https://doi.org/10.1145/3130800.3130834
14. Geffroy, B., Le Roy, P., Prat, C.: Organic light-emitting diode (oled) technology: materials, devices and display technologies. Polym. Int. **55**(6), 572–582 (2006)
15. Guo, J., et al.: Highlight-aware two-stream network for single-image SVBRDF acquisition. ACM Trans. Graph. **40**(4), 1–14 (2021)
16. Hable, J.: Uncharted 2: HDR lighting. In: Game Developers Conference, p. 56 (2010)
17. He, J., Liu, Y., Qiao, Yu., Dong, C.: Conditional sequential modulation for efficient global image retouching. In: Vedaldi, A., Bischof, H., Brox, T., Frahm, J.-M. (eds.) ECCV 2020. LNCS, vol. 12358, pp. 679–695. Springer, Cham (2020). https://doi.org/10.1007/978-3-030-58601-0_40
18. Isola, P., Zhu, J.Y., Zhou, T., Efros, A.A.: Image-to-image translation with conditional adversarial networks. In: CVPR, pp. 1125–1134 (2017)
19. ITU-R: Parameter values for ultra-high definition television systems for production and international programme exchange. Recommendation ITU-R BT. 2020–2 (2015)
20. ITU-R: Colour gamut conversion from recommendation ITU-R BT.2020 to recommendation ITU-R BT.709. Recommendation ITU-R BT. 2407–0 (2017)
21. ITU-R: Image parameter values for high dynamic range television for use in production and international programme exchange. Recommendation ITU-R BT. 2100–2 (2018)
22. ITU-R: Objective metric for the assessment of the potential visibility of colour differences in television. Recommendation ITU-R BT. 2124–0 (2019)
23. Kalantari, N.K., Ramamoorthi, R., et al.: Deep high dynamic range imaging of dynamic scenes. ACM Trans. Graph. **36**(4), 1–144 (2017)
24. Kim, S.Y., Oh, J., Kim, M.: Deep SR-ITM: joint learning of super-resolution and inverse tone-mapping for 4K UHD HDR applications. In: ICCV, pp. 3116–3125 (2019)
25. Kim, S.Y., Oh, J., Kim, M.: JSI-GAN: Gan-based joint super-resolution and inverse tone-mapping with pixel-wise task-specific filters for UHD HDR video. In: AAAI, vol. 34, pp. 11287–11295 (2020)
26. Kovaleski, R.P., Oliveira, M.M.: High-quality brightness enhancement functions for real-time reverse tone mapping. Vis. Comput. **25**(5), 539–547 (2009)
27. Kuang, J., Johnson, G.M., Fairchild, M.D.: icam06: a refined image appearance model for HDR image rendering. J. Vis. Commun. Image Represent. **18**(5), 406–414 (2007)
28. Land, E.H., McCann, J.J.: Lightness and retinex theory. Josa **61**(1), 1–11 (1971)
29. Larson, G.W., Rushmeier, H., Piatko, C.: A visibility matching tone reproduction operator for high dynamic range scenes. IEEE Trans. Visual Comput. Graphics **3**(4), 291–306 (1997)
30. Ledig, C., et al.: Photo-realistic single image super-resolution using a generative adversarial network. In: Proceedings of the IEEE Conference on Computer Vision and Pattern Recognition, pp. 4681–4690 (2017)
31. Lee, S., An, G.H., Kang, S.-J.: Deep recursive HDRI: inverse tone mapping using generative adversarial networks. In: Ferrari, V., Hebert, M., Sminchisescu, C., Weiss, Y. (eds.) ECCV 2018. LNCS, vol. 11206, pp. 613–628. Springer, Cham (2018). https://doi.org/10.1007/978-3-030-01216-8_37

32. Li, C., Wand, M.: Precomputed real-time texture synthesis with Markovian generative adversarial networks. In: Leibe, B., Matas, J., Sebe, N., Welling, M. (eds.) ECCV 2016. LNCS, vol. 9907, pp. 702–716. Springer, Cham (2016). https://doi.org/10.1007/978-3-319-46487-9_43

33. Liang, Z., Xu, J., Zhang, D., Cao, Z., Zhang, L.: A hybrid l1–l0 layer decomposition model for tone mapping. In: CVPR, pp. 4758–4766 (2018). https://doi.org/10.1109/CVPR.2018.00500

34. Liu, Y.L., Lai, W.S., Chen, Y.S., Kao, Y.L., Yang, M.H., Chuang, Y.Y., Huang, J.B.: Single-image HDR reconstruction by learning to reverse the camera pipeline. In: CVPR, pp. 1651–1660 (2020)

35. Maeda, S.: Unpaired image super-resolution using pseudo-supervision. In: CVPR, pp. 291–300 (2020)

36. Mantiuk, R., Kim, K.J., Rempel, A.G., Heidrich, W.: HDR-VDP-2: a calibrated visual metric for visibility and quality predictions in all luminance conditions. ACM Trans. Graph. **30**(4), 1–14 (2011)

37. Mao, X., Li, Q., Xie, H., Lau, R.Y., Wang, Z., Smolley, S,P.: Least squares generative adversarial networks. In: ICCV, pp. 2794–2802 (2017)

38. Montulet, R., Briassouli, A., Maastricht, N.: Deep learning for robust end-to-end tone mapping. In: BMVC, p. 194 (2019)

39. Patel, V.A., Shah, P., Raman, S.: A generative adversarial network for tone mapping HDR images. In: Rameshan, R., Arora, C., Dutta Roy, S. (eds.) NCVPRIPG 2017. CCIS, vol. 841, pp. 220–231. Springer, Singapore (2018). https://doi.org/10.1007/978-981-13-0020-2_20

40. Raman, S., Chaudhuri, S.: Bilateral filter based compositing for variable exposure photography. In: Eurographics, pp. 1–4 (2009)

41. Rana, A., Singh, P., Valenzise, G., Dufaux, F., Komodakis, N., Smolic, A.: Deep tone mapping operator for high dynamic range images. IEEE Trans. Image Process. **29**, 1285–1298 (2019)

42. Reinhard, E., Stark, M., Shirley, P., Ferwerda, J.: Photographic tone reproduction for digital images. In: Proceedings of the 29th Annual Conference on Computer Graphics and Interactive Techniques, pp. 267–276 (2002)

43. Rempel, A.G., et al.: LDR2HDR: on-the-fly reverse tone mapping of legacy video and photographs. ACM Trans. Graph. **26**(3), 39-es (2007)

44. Santos, M.S., Ren, T.I., Kalantari, N.K.: Single image HDR reconstruction using a CNN with masked features and perceptual loss. ACM Trans. Graph. **39**(4), 80–1 (2020)

45. Sharma, G., Wu, W., Dalal, E.N.: The ciede2000 color-difference formula: implementation notes, supplementary test data, and mathematical observations. Color Res. Appl. **30**(1), 21–30 (2005)

46. Ulyanov, D., Vedaldi, A., Lempitsky, V.: Deep image prior. In: Proceedings of the IEEE conference on computer vision and pattern recognition, pp. 9446–9454 (2018)

47. Vinker, Y., Huberman-Spiegelglas, I., Fattal, R.: Unpaired learning for high dynamic range image tone mapping. In: ICCV, pp. 14657–14666 (2021)

48. Wang, T., et al.: Real-time image enhancer via learnable spatial-aware 3D lookup tables. In: ICCV, pp. 2471–2480 (2021)

49. Wang, Z., Bovik, A.C., Sheikh, H.R., Simoncelli, E.P.: Image quality assessment: from error visibility to structural similarity. IEEE Trans. Image Process. **13**(4), 600–612 (2004)

50. Wang, Z., Simoncelli, E.P., Bovik, A.C.: Multiscale structural similarity for image quality assessment. In: The Thrity-Seventh Asilomar Conference on Signals, Systems & Computers, 2003. vol. 2, pp. 1398–1402. IEEE (2003)

51. Ward, G.: A contrast-based scalefactor for luminance display. Graphics Gems **4**, 415–21 (1994)
52. Wei, Y., Gu, S., Li, Y., Timofte, R., Jin, L., Song, H.: Unsupervised real-world image super resolution via domain-distance aware training. In: CVPR, pp. 13385–13394 (2021)
53. Yeganeh, H., Wang, Z.: Objective quality assessment of tone-mapped images. IEEE Trans. Image Process. **22**(2), 657–667 (2012)
54. Zeng, H., Zhang, X., Yu, Z., Wang, Y.: SR-ITM-GAN: Learning 4K UHD HDR with a generative adversarial network. IEEE Access **8**, 182815–182827 (2020)
55. Zhang, L., Li, H.: SR-SIM: a fast and high performance IQA index based on spectral residual. In: ICIP, pp. 1473–1476. IEEE (2012)
56. Zhang, N., Wang, C., Zhao, Y., Wang, R.: Deep tone mapping network in HSV color space. In: VCIP, pp. 1–4. IEEE (2019)
57. Zhu, J.Y., Park, T., Isola, P., Efros, A.A.: Unpaired image-to-image translation using cycle-consistent adversarial networks. In: ICCV, pp. 2223–2232 (2017)

Learning Discriminative Shrinkage Deep Networks for Image Deconvolution

Pin-Hung Kuo[1]([✉]), Jinshan Pan[2], Shao-Yi Chien[1], and Ming-Hsuan Yang[3,4,5]

[1] Graduate Institute of Electronics Engineering, National Taiwan University, Taipei, Taiwan
setsunil@media.ee.ntu.edu.tw
[2] Nanjing University of Science and Technology, Nanjing, China
[3] Google Research, Nanjing, China
[4] University of California, Merced, USA
[5] Yonsei University, Seoul, South Korea

Abstract. Most existing methods usually formulate the non-blind deconvolution problem into a maximum-a-posteriori framework and address it by manually designing a variety of regularization terms and data terms of the latent clear images. However, explicitly designing these two terms is quite challenging and usually leads to complex optimization problems which are difficult to solve. This paper proposes an effective non-blind deconvolution approach by learning discriminative shrinkage functions to model these terms implicitly. Most existing methods use deep convolutional neural networks (CNNs) or radial basis functions to learn the regularization term simply. In contrast, we formulate both the data term and regularization term and split the deconvolution model into data-related and regularization-related sub-problems according to the alternating direction method of multipliers. We explore the properties of the Maxout function and develop a deep CNN model with Maxout layers to learn discriminative shrinkage functions, which directly approximates the solutions of these two sub-problems. Moreover, the fast-Fourier-transform-based image restoration usually leads to ringing artifacts. At the same time, the conjugate-gradient-based approach is time-consuming; we develop the Conjugate Gradient Network to restore the latent clear images effectively and efficiently. Experimental results show that the proposed method performs favorably against the state-of-the-art methods in terms of efficiency and accuracy. Source codes, models, and more results are available at https://github.com/setsunil/DSDNet.

1 Introduction

The single image deconvolution, or deblurring, aims to restore a clear and sharp image from a single blurry input image. Blind image deblurring has attracted

---

Supplementary Information The online version contains supplementary material available at https://doi.org/10.1007/978-3-031-19800-7_13.

S. Avidan et al. (Eds.): ECCV 2022, LNCS 13679, pp. 217–234, 2022.
https://doi.org/10.1007/978-3-031-19800-7_13

interest from many researchers [24,31,43,49]. With the rapid development of deep learning, tremendous progress has been made in blind image deblurring recently [13,26,59,62,74]. Since the kernel is available via blind methods, how to utilize these kernels well is still an important issue. Therefore, non-blind deconvolution has never lost the attention of researchers over the past decades [8, 10,14,50]. Due to the deconvolution problem's ill-posedness, numerous methods explore the statistical properties of clear images as the image priors (e.g., hyper-Laplacian prior [23,30]) to make this problem tractable. Although using the hand-crafted image priors facilitates ringing artifacts removal, the fine details are not restored well, as these limited priors may not model the inherent properties of various latent images sufficiently.

To overcome this problem, discriminative image priors are learned from training examples [9,48,56,58]. These methods usually leverage radial basis functions (RBFs) as the shrinkage functions of the image prior. However, the RBFs contain many parameters, leading to complex optimization problems.

Deep convolutional neural network (CNN) has been developed to learn more effective regularization terms for the deconvolution problem [70]. These methods are motivated by [56] and directly estimate the solution to the regularization-related sub-problem by deep CNN models. As analyzed by [56], we can obtain the solution to the regularization-related sub-problem by combining the shrinkage functions. However, as the shrinkage functions are complex (e.g., non-Monotonic), simply using the convolution operation followed by the common activation functions, e.g., ReLU, cannot model the property of the shrinkage functions. Given the effectiveness of the deep features, it is of great interest to learn discriminative shrinkage functions. Therefore, if we can learn more complex shrinkage functions corresponding to the deep features, they shall surpass the hand-crafted ones in solving the regularization-related sub-problem.

We note that image restoration involves an image deconvolution step, usually taking advantage of fast Fourier transform (FFT) [43,56,73] or the Conjugate Gradient (CG) method [2,10,28]. However, the FFT-based approaches usually lead to ringing artifacts, while the CG-based ones are time-consuming. Besides, these two methods suffer from information loss: for FFT, we lose little information when we discard the imaginary parts in the inverse real FFT; for the CG method, the iterations we execute are usually far less than the upper bound. Therefore, developing an effective yet efficient image restoration method is also necessary.

In this paper, we develop a simple and effective model to discriminatively learn the shrinkage functions for non-blind deconvolution, which is called Discriminative Shrinkage Deep Network (DSDNet). We formulate the data and regularization terms as learnable and split the image deconvolution model into the data-related and regularization-related sub-problems. As shrinkage functions can solve both sub-problems, and the learnable Maxout functions can efficiently approximate any complex functions, we directly learn the shrinkage functions of sub-problems via a deep CNN model with Maxout layers [16]. To effectively and efficiently generate clear images from the output of the learned functions, we develop a fully convolutional Conjugate Gradient Network (CGNet) motivated by the mathematical concept of the CG method. Finally, to solve the problem, we formulate our method into an end-to-end network based on the Alternating Direction Method of Multipliers (ADMM) [44]. Experimental results show that the proposed method performs favorably against the state-of-the-art ones.

The main contributions of this work are:

– We propose a simple yet effective non-blind deconvolution model to directly learn discriminative shrinkage functions to implicitly model the data and regularization terms for image deconvolution.
– We develop an efficient and effective CGNet to restore clear images without the problems of CG and FFT.
– The architecture of DSDNet is designed elaborately, which makes it flexible in model size and easy to be trained. Even the smallest DSDNet performs favorably against the state-of-the-art methods in speed and accuracy.

2   Related Work

Because numerous image deconvolution methods have been proposed, we discuss those most relevant to this work.

Statistical Image Prior-Based Methods. Since non-blind deconvolution is an ill-posed problem, conventional methods usually develop image priors based on the statistical properties of clear images. Representative methods include total variation [6,46,52,65], hyper-Laplacian prior [23,28], and patch-based prior [17,61,75], to name a few. However, these hand-crafted priors may not model the inherent properties of the latent image well; thus, these methods do not effectively restore realistic images.

Learning-Based Methods. To overcome the above limitations of the hand-crafted priors, researchers have proposed learning-based approaches, e.g., Markov random fields [51,54], Gaussian mixture models [75], conditional random fields [19,55,57,63], and radial basis functions [9,56].

The learning-based non-blind deconvolution also gets deeper with the development of neural networks. Many methods use deep CNNs to model the regularization term and solve image restoration problems by unrolling existing optimization algorithms. For example, Iterative Shrinkage-Thresholding algorithm [67,69], Douglas-Rachford method [1], Half-Quadratic Splitting algorithm [4,7,21,22,32,33,70,71], gradient descend [15,47] and ADMM [68]. These methods use deep CNN models to estimate the solution to the regularization-related sub-problem. As demonstrated by [56], the solutions are the combinations of the shrinkage functions. Simply using deep CNN models does not model the shrinkage functions well since most activation functions are too simple. Besides, most of them focus on the regularization terms yet ignore the importance of data terms. In addition, the image restoration step in these methods usually depends

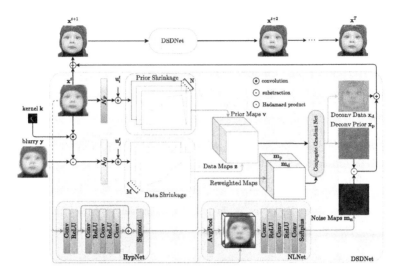

Fig. 1. Overview of the proposed method. The blue blocks and lines are the layers and flow of the regularization terms; the yellow ones are that of data terms. The HypNet is responsible for the reweighted maps the NLNet learns to control the weights of regularization and data terms according to the local noise level. (Color figure online)

on an FFT-based solution. However, using FFT may lead to results with ringing artifacts. Even though the edge taper [25] alleviates artifacts, they are still inevitable in many scenes.

To overcome these problems, we leverage Maxout layers to learn discriminative shrinkage functions for regularization and data terms and develop the CGNet to restore images better. Furthermore, we adopt average pooling for noise level estimation and residual block for re-weights computation. In other words, we design each component according to the mathematical characteristics rather than stacking as many convolutional layers as possible, as in most previous works.

Blind Deblurring Methods. Numerous end-to-end deep networks [26,40,60, 62] have been developed to restore clear images from blurry images directly. However, as demonstrated in [10], when the blur kernels are given, these methods do not perform well compared to the non-blind deconvolution methods. As non-blind deconvolution is vital for image restoration, we focus on this problem and develop a simple and effective approach to restoring high-quality images.

3   Revisiting Deep Unrolling-Based Methods

We first revisit deep unrolling-based methods for image deconvolution to motivate our work. Mathematically, the degradation process of the image blur is usually formulated as:

$$y = k * x + n, \tag{1}$$

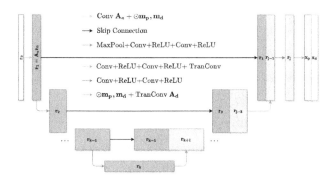

Fig. 2. Network architecture of the proposed CGNet. The residual vector $\mathbf{r_0} = \mathbf{b} - \mathbf{A}\mathbf{x}^t$ is the input feature map, the operation $\mathbf{A}$, the convolution $\mathbf{A_e}$ and the transposed convolution $\mathbf{A_d}$ are composed of the input filters $\mathbf{F}_i$, $\mathbf{G}_j$ and $\mathbf{H}$. The reweighted maps $\mathbf{m_p}$, $\mathbf{m_d}$ are multiplied between $\mathbf{A_e}$ and $\mathbf{A_d}$ as the IRLS.

where $*$ denotes the convolution operator; y, k, x and n denote the blurry image, the blur kernel, the latent image and noise, respectively. With the known kernel k, we usually use formulate the deconvolution as a maximum-a-posteriori (MAP) problem:

$$x = \arg\max_{x} p(x|y, k) = \arg\max_{x} p(y|x, k)p(x), \qquad (2)$$

where $p(y|x, k)$ is the likelihood of the observation (blurry) y, while $p(x)$ denotes an image prior of the latent image x. This equation is equivalent to

$$\min_{x} R(x) + D(y - k * x), \qquad (3)$$

where $R(x)$ and $D(y - k * x)$ denote the regularization term and data term. In addition, the data term is usually modeled in the form of ℓ_2-norm, then (3) can be rewritten as

$$\min_{\mathbf{x}} \frac{1}{2} \|\mathbf{y} - \mathbf{H}\mathbf{x}\|_2^2 + R(\mathbf{x}), \qquad (4)$$

where $\mathbf{x}$, $\mathbf{y}$ denote the vector forms of x and y, respectively; $\mathbf{H}$ denotes the Toeplitz matrix of the blur kernel k. The ADMM method for image deconvolution is usually achieved by solving:

$$\min_{\mathbf{x},\mathbf{u}} \frac{1}{2} \|\mathbf{y} - \mathbf{H}\mathbf{x}\|_2^2 + R(\mathbf{v}) + \mathbf{u}^\top (\mathbf{v} - \mathbf{x}) + \frac{\rho}{2} \|\mathbf{v} - \mathbf{x}\|_2^2, \qquad (5)$$

where $\mathbf{v}$ is an auxiliary variable, $\mathbf{u}$ is a Lagrangian multiplier, ρ is a weight parameter.

The solution of (5) can be obtained by alternatively solving:

$$\mathbf{x}^{t+1} = \min_{\mathbf{x}} \|\mathbf{y} - \mathbf{Hx}\|_2^2 + \rho\|\mathbf{v}^t - \mathbf{x} + \frac{\mathbf{u}^t}{\rho}\|_2^2, \tag{6a}$$

$$\mathbf{v}^{t+1} = \min_{\mathbf{v}} \frac{\rho}{2}\|\mathbf{v} - \mathbf{x}^{t+1} + \frac{\mathbf{u}^t}{\rho}\|_2^2 + R(\mathbf{v}), \tag{6b}$$

$$\mathbf{u}^{t+1} = \mathbf{u}^t + \rho(\mathbf{v}^{t+1} - \mathbf{x}^{t+1}). \tag{6c}$$

Existing methods [70,72,73] usually solve (6a) via fast Fourier transform (FFT) or Conjugate Gradient methods. For (6b), its solution can be represented as a proximal operator:

$$\mathbf{prox}_{\lambda R}(\mathbf{x}^{t+1} - \mathbf{u}'^t) = \arg\min_{\mathbf{v}} \frac{1}{2}\|\mathbf{v} - \mathbf{x}^{t+1} + \mathbf{u}'^t\|_2^2 + \lambda R(\mathbf{v}), \tag{7}$$

where $\lambda = 1/\rho$. With $\mathbf{u}'^t = \lambda\mathbf{u}^t$, the multiplier in the (6) and (7) can be absorbed [44]. As demonstrated in [56], (7) can be approximated by shrinkage functions. Existing methods usually use deep CNN model to approximate the solution of (7). However, simply using the convolution operation followed by the fixed activation functions (e.g., ReLU) cannot model the shrinkage functions well as they are far more complex (e.g., non-monotonic) [56]. To better approximate the solution of (6b), we develop a deep CNN model with the Maxout function [16], which can effectively approximate proximal functions. In addition, we note that using FFT to solve (6a) does not obtain better results than the CG method demonstrated by [28,29]. However, the CG method is time-consuming and unstable in deep networks (see Sect. 5.4 for more detail). To overcome this problem, we learn a differentiable CG network to restore a clear image more efficiently and effectively.

4   Proposed Method

Different from existing methods that simply learn the regularization term or the data term [4,32,70], we formulate both the data term and the regularization term as the learnable ones:

$$\min_{\mathbf{u},\mathbf{v},\mathbf{x},\mathbf{z}} \sum_{i=1}^{N} R_i(\mathbf{v}_i) + \sum_{j=1+N}^{M+N} R_j(\mathbf{z}_j)$$

$$s.t. \quad \mathbf{F}_i\mathbf{x} = \mathbf{v}_i, \quad \mathbf{G}_j(\mathbf{y} - \mathbf{Hx}) = \mathbf{z}_j, \tag{8}$$

where R_i denotes the i-th learnable function; $\mathbf{v}_i$ and $\mathbf{z}_j$ are auxiliary variables that correspond to the regularization and data terms; $\mathbf{F}_i$ and $\mathbf{G}_j$ are the i-th and j-th learnable filters for regularization and data, respectively.

By introducing the Lagrangian multipliers $\mathbf{u}_i$ and $\mathbf{u}_j$ corresponding to the regularization and data terms, we can solve (8) using the ADMM method by:

$$\mathbf{v}_i^{t+1} = \mathbf{prox}_{\lambda_i R_i}(\mathbf{F}_i \mathbf{x}^t + \mathbf{u}_i^t), \tag{9a}$$

$$\mathbf{z}_j^{t+1} = \mathbf{prox}_{\lambda_j R_j}(\mathbf{G}_j(\mathbf{y} - \mathbf{H}\mathbf{x}^t) + \mathbf{u}_j^t), \tag{9b}$$

$$\left(\sum_{i=1}^{N} \rho_i \mathbf{F}_i^\top \mathbf{F}_i + \sum_{j=N+1}^{N+M} \rho_j \mathbf{H}^\top \mathbf{G}_j^\top \mathbf{G}_j \mathbf{H} \right) \mathbf{x}^{t+1}$$

$$= \left(\sum_{i=1}^{N} \rho_i \mathbf{F}_i^\top (\mathbf{v}_i^{t+1} - \mathbf{u}_i^t) + \sum_{j=N+1}^{N+M} \rho_j \mathbf{H}^\top \mathbf{G}_j^\top (\mathbf{G}_j \mathbf{y} - \mathbf{z}_j^{t+1} + \mathbf{u}_j^t) \right) \tag{9c}$$

$$\mathbf{u}_i^{t+1} = \mathbf{u}_i^t + \mathbf{F}_i \mathbf{x}^{t+1} - \mathbf{v}_i^{t+1}, \tag{9d}$$

$$\mathbf{u}_j^{t+1} = \mathbf{u}_j^t + \mathbf{G}_j(\mathbf{y} - \mathbf{H}\mathbf{x}^{t+1}) - \mathbf{z}_j^{t+1}. \tag{9e}$$

In the following, we will develop deep CNN models with a Maxout layer to approximate the functions of (9a) and (9b). Moreover, we design a simple and effective deep CG network to solve (9c).

4.1 Network Architecture

This section describes how to design our deep CNN models to effectively solve(9a)–(9c).

Learning Filters $\mathbf{F}_i$ and $\mathbf{G}_j$. To learn filters $\mathbf{F}_i$ and $\mathbf{G}_j$, we develop two networks ($\mathcal{N}_F$ and $\mathcal{N}_G$), each containing one convolutional layer. The convolutional layer of $\mathcal{N}_F$ has N filters of 7×7 pixels, and the convolutional layer of $\mathcal{N}_G$ contains M filters of the same size. The $\mathcal{N}_F$ and $\mathcal{N}_G$ are applied to $\mathbf{x}^t$ and $\mathbf{y} - \mathbf{H}\mathbf{x}^t$ to learn the filters $\mathbf{F}_i$ and $\mathbf{G}_j$, respectively.

Learning Discriminative Shrinkage Functions for (9a) **and** (9b). To better learn the unknown discriminative shrinkage functions of (9a) and (9b), we take advantage of Maxout layers [16]. Specifically, the convolutional Maxout layer consists of two Maxout units. Each Maxout unit contains one convolutional layer followed by a channel-wise Max-pooling layer. Given an input feature map $\mathbf{X} \in \mathbb{R}^{H \times W \times C}$ and the output feature map $\mathbf{X}^\mathbf{o} \in \mathbb{R}^{H \times W \times KC}$ of the convolutional layer, a Maxout unit is achieved by:

$$o_{h,w,c}(\mathbf{X}) = \max_{j \in [0,K)} x_{h,w,c \times K+j}^o, \tag{10}$$

where $h \in [0, H)$, $w \in [0, W)$ and $c \in [0, C)$; the $x_{h,w,c}^o$ is the element of $\mathbf{X}^\mathbf{o}$ at the position (h, w, c), and the $o_{h,w,c}$ is the function to output the (h, w, c)-th element of the output tensor $\mathbf{O}$. In our implementation, we have $\mathbf{O} \in \mathbb{R}^{H \times W \times C}$ is of the same size as the input $\mathbf{X}$ and $K = 4$.

With two Maxout units, we acquire two output features, $\mathbf{O}_1$ and $\mathbf{O}_2$; the final output tensor of the Maxout layer is their difference, $\mathbf{O}_1 - \mathbf{O}_2$. We note that Maxout networks are universal approximators that can effectively approximate functions. Thus, we use it to obtain the solutions of (9a) and (9b).

Learning a Differentiable CG Network for (9c). As stated in Sect. 3, although using FFT with boundary processing operations (e.g., edge taper and Laplacian smoothing [35]) can efficiently solve (9c), the results are not better than the CG-based solver, which can be observed in Table 5. However, using a CG-based solver is time-consuming. To generate latent clear images better, we develop a differentiable CG network to solve (9c). The CG method is used to solve the linear equation:

$$\mathbf{A}\mathbf{x}^{t+1} = \mathbf{b}, \tag{11}$$

where $\mathbf{A}$ corresponds to the first term in (9c) and $\mathbf{b}$ to the last term in (9c). Given $\mathbf{x} \in \mathbb{R}^d$, the CG method recursively computes conjugate vectors $\mathbf{p}_l$ and find the difference between desired $\mathbf{x}^{t+1}$ and initial input $\mathbf{x}^t$ as

$$\mathbf{x}^{t+1} - \mathbf{x}^t = \mathbf{s_L} = \sum_{l=0}^{L} \alpha_l \mathbf{p}_l,$$

where L is the iteration number upper-bounded by d, and α_l is the weight calculated with $\mathbf{p}_l$.

However, if the size of matrix $\mathbf{A}$ is large, using CG to solve (11) needs high computational costs. To overcome this problem, we develop a differentiable CG network based on a U-Net to compute the $\mathbf{s_L}$. The network design is motivated by the following reasons:

– As one of Krylov subspace methods [2], the solution $\mathbf{s_L}$ can be found in the Krylov subspace $\mathcal{K}_L(\mathbf{A}, \mathbf{r_0}) = \mathrm{span}\{\mathbf{r_0}, \mathbf{A}\mathbf{r_0}, \dots, \mathbf{A}^{L-1}\mathbf{r_0}\}$, where $\mathbf{r_0} = \mathbf{b} - \mathbf{A}\mathbf{x}^t$ is the residual vector. In other words, the CG method is a function of $\mathbf{A}$ and $\mathbf{r_0}$. Our CGNet takes $\mathbf{r_0}$ as input and $\mathbf{A}$ as parts of the network. Its output is $\mathbf{s_L}$, which behaves as the CG method.
– For a typical deconvolution problem, $\mathbf{A}$ is composed of convolution $\mathbf{A_e}$ and transpose convolution $\mathbf{A_d}$ pairs as the first term in (9c). $\mathbf{A_e}$ stands for the operation of $\mathbf{G}_j\mathbf{H}$ and $\mathbf{F}_i$, and $\mathbf{A_d}$ for $\mathbf{H}^\top\mathbf{G}_j^\top$ and $\mathbf{F}_i^\top$. This observation can be intuitively connected to an encoder-decoder architecture, so we integrate $\mathbf{A_e}$ into the encoder and $\mathbf{A_d}$ into the decoder.
– The Conjugate Gradient method is sensitive to noise [34,53]. With an encoder-decoder architecture, U-Net is robust to noise.
– As the Conjugate Gradient method is a recursive algorithm, U-Net computes feature maps in a recursive fashion.

In the practical CG iterations, $\mathbf{A_e}$ and $\mathbf{A_d}$ are usually updated with iterative reweighted least squares (IRLS) to utilize the sparsity of priors [29]. We design a simple HypNet to estimate these weights. The network architecture of the HypNet is shown in Fig. 1. In addition, we note that the values of ρ_i and ρ_j in (9c) depend on the noise level. We design a simple NLNet to estimate the noise map $\mathbf{m_n}$, which plays a role similar to ρ_i and ρ_j (see Fig. 1). In contrast to most conventional methods, the NLNet computes the weight for each pixel, which is locally adaptive.

5   Experimental Results

5.1   Datasets and Implementation Details

Training Dataset. Similar to [10,11], the training data is composed of 4,744 images from the Waterloo Exploration dataset [36] and 400 images from the Berkeley segmentation dataset (BSD) [38]. To synthesize blurry images, we first generate 33,333 blur kernels by [55], where the sizes of these generated blur kernels range from 13×13 pixels to 35×35 pixels. We first crop image patches of 128×128 pixels from each image, and then we randomly use generated blur kernels to generate blurry images. Each blurry image is randomly added Gaussian noise with noise levels from 1% to 5%.

Test Datasets. We evaluate our method on both synthetic datasets and real ones. For the synthetic case, we use the 100 images from BSD100 and 100 kernels by [55] to generate blurry images, similar to training data. We also use the SET5 [3] dataset with the kernels generated by [5] as our test dataset. In addition, we use the datasets by LEVIN [30] and LAI [27] for evaluation.

For the real-world dataset, we evaluate our model on the data of PAN [43], where 23 blurry images and 23 kernels estimated by their method are contained.

Table 1. Configuration of four models. T is the number of stages, i.e., how many duplicates are in the whole model. M and N denote the number of filters $\mathbf{F}_i$ and $\mathbf{G}_i$, respectively. The PSNR (dB) and execution time are tested on SET5.

	Feather	Light	Heavy	Full
T	2	3	3	4
M, N	24	24	49	49
PSNR	32.51	32.78	33.11	33.43
Second	1.893	2.191	2.672	3.065

Implementation Details. We train the networks using the ADAM [20] optimizer with default parameter settings. The batch size is 8. The total training iterations is 1 million, and the learning rate is from 1×10^{-4} to 1×10^{-7}. We gradually decay the learning rate to 1×10^{-7} every 250,000 iterations and reset it to 1×10^{-4}, 5×10^{-5} and 2.5×10^{-5} at the iteration of 250,001, 500,001 and 750,001, respectively. To constrain the network training, we apply the commonly used ℓ_1-norm loss to the ground truth and the network output $\mathbf{x}^T$. The data augmentation (including $\pm 90°$ and $180°$ rotations, vertical and horizontal flipping) is used. In this paper, we train 4 models of different sizes, i.e., Feather, Light, Heavy and Full, whose configurations and simple results on SET5 are shown in Table 1.

It is worth noting that all the stages contain their own parameters and are end-to-end trained rather than share weights [71] or progressively trained [70]. We implement the networks in Pytorch [45] and train on one NVIDIA RTX 3090 GPU.

Table 2. Average PSNR(dB)/SSIM of the deblurring results with Gaussian noise using different methods. We highlight the best and second best results. Our Full DSDNet wins first place, while our Light one also performs favorably against these state-of-the-art methods.

Dataset	noise	IRCNN [73] PSNR / SSIM	SFARL [48] PSNR / SSIM	ADM_UDM [21] PSNR / SSIM	CPCR [12] PSNR / SSIM	KerUNC [41] PSNR / SSIM	VEM [42] PSNR / SSIM	DWDN [10] PSNR / SSIM	SVMAP [11] PSNR / SSIM	DRUNet [72] PSNR / SSIM	DSDNet(Light) PSNR / SSIM	DSDNet(Full) PSNR / SSIM
Levin [30]	1%	30.61 / 0.883	25.41 / 0.600	31.48 / 0.922	28.43 / 0.858	32.02 / 0.928	32.05 / 0.927	34.89 / 0.957	35.24 / 0.962	31.94 / 0.922	35.48 / 0.960	36.62 / 0.965
	3%	29.70 / 0.864	16.82 / 0.255	28.61 / 0.812	25.61 / 0.765	21.72 / 0.416	29.47 / 0.867	31.94 / 0.916	31.20 / 0.893	30.86 / 0.905	32.13 / 0.918	32.89 / 0.925
	5%	28.98 / 0.854	13.07 / 0.157	27.83 / 0.827	23.68 / 0.703	18.25 / 0.272	27.79 / 0.819	30.21 / 0.883	30.12 / 0.876	29.79 / 0.880	30.24 / 0.883	30.94 / 0.893
BSD100 [38]	1%	29.20 / 0.817	24.21 / 0.568	29.39 / 0.836	28.77 / 0.829	29.23 / 0.829	29.54 / 0.848	31.10 / 0.881	31.52 / 0.888	30.36 / 0.872	31.50 / 0.892	32.01 / 0.898
	3%	27.54 / 0.762	15.80 / 0.245	26.92 / 0.722	25.96 / 0.712	22.10 / 0.430	27.09 / 0.746	28.47 / 0.797	27.94 / 0.762	28.10 / 0.798	28.73 / 0.812	29.08 / 0.820
	5%	27.04 / 0.756	12.56 / 0.146	26.04 / 0.697	25.75 / 0.688	18.99 / 0.297	26.11 / 0.698	27.50 / 0.762	27.59 / 0.763	27.19 / 0.767	27.64 / 0.774	27.96 / 0.782
Set5 [3]	1%	30.15 / 0.853	26.21 / 0.632	30.52 / 0.868	30.59 / 0.875	30.45 / 0.864	31.00 / 0.875	32.18 / 0.893	32.31 / 0.892	30.84 / 0.881	32.78 / 0.899	33.43 / 0.905
	3%	28.66 / 0.813	15.50 / 0.211	27.64 / 0.709	27.94 / 0.799	21.39 / 0.376	28.40 / 0.804	29.54 / 0.838	28.78 / 0.812	29.21 / 0.841	29.04 / 0.843	30.40 / 0.851
	5%	27.55 / 0.789	11.91 / 0.122	26.75 / 0.756	26.64 / 0.754	17.74 / 0.241	26.46 / 0.732	28.13 / 0.806	28.02 / 0.793	27.85 / 0.805	28.46 / 0.804	28.89 / 0.814

Table 3. Evaluation on the dataset LAI [27]. The best and second best results are highlighted as Table 2. The SATURATION results of SVMAP [11] are obtained by the model specifically trained for saturation scenes.

Subset	IRCNN [73] PSNR / SSIM	ADM_UDM [21] PSNR / SSIM	KerUNC [41] PSNR / SSIM	VEM [42] PSNR / SSIM	DWDN [10] PSNR / SSIM	SVMAP [11] PSNR / SSIM	DRUNet [72] PSNR / SSIM	DSDNet PSNR / SSIM
MANMADE	20.47 / 0.604	22.43 / 0.724	22.19 / 0.725	22.71 / 0.780	24.02 / 0.836	23.75 / 0.776	20.62 /0.613	25.44 / 0.859
NATURAL	23.26 / 0.636	25.04 / 0.733	25.42 / 0.757	25.29 / 0.752	25.91 / 0.814	26.23 / 0.778	23.25 /0.630	27.01 / 0.837
PEOPLE	28.04 / 0.843	28.81 / 0.866	28.80 / 0.848	27.19 / 0.723	30.02 / 0.905	30.88 / 0.899	28.04 /0.838	30.95 / 0.908
SATURATION	16.99 / 0.642	17.57 / 0.627	17.70 / 0.640	17.65 / 0.600	17.90 / 0.695	18.75 / 0.733	17.14 /0.658	18.38 / 0.734
TEXT	21.37 / 0.828	25.13 / 0.883	23.32 / 0.855	24.92 / 0.853	25.40 / 0.877	25.60 / 0.894	21.79 /0.829	28.13 / 0.920
Overall	22.03 / 0.710	23.80 / 0.767	23.49 / 0.765	23.55 / 0.742	24.65 / 0.825	25.04 / 0.816	22.17 /0.714	25.98 / 0.852

5.2 Quantitative Evaluation

We compare the proposed DSDNet with the state-of-the-art methods including IRCNN [73], SARFL [48], ADM_UDM [21], CPCR [12], KerUNC [41], VEM [42], DWDN [10], SVMAP [9] and DRUNet [72]. These methods are fine-tuned using the same training dataset as Sect. 5.1 and choose the better ones from the fine-tuned and the original models for comparison.

PSNR and SSIM [66] are used for quantitative evaluation. All the quantitative evaluations are conducted without border cropping for fair comparisons.

Table 2 shows quantitative evaluation results on the synthetic datasets. The proposed method generates results with higher PSNR and SSIM values. In addition, we note that the proposed light-weighted model generates favorable results against the state-of-the-art, showing the effectiveness of the proposed algorithm. Due to the space limit, we only present the evaluation results of the Full DSDNet hereafter.

We then evaluate our method on the LAI [27] dataset. Because it contains MANMADE, NATURAL, PEOPLE, SATURATION, and TEXT subsets, we present the evaluation accordingly. Table 3 shows that our method performs better than the evaluated methods. Similar to Table 2, our method also achieves the highest PSNR and SSIM in most tests, except for the SATURATION subset. We note that Dong et al. [11] specifically train a model for saturation scenes; thus, this method performs slightly better. However, our model is only trained with common scenes but comparable in terms of PSNR on the SATURATION images. Moreover, the SSIM values of our method are better than SVMAP [11], demonstrating the efficiency and robustness of our approach.

Table 4. Quantitative evaluation of real cases PAN [43]. Non-reference image quality metrics BRISQUE [39] and PIQE [64] are used.

	IRCNN [73]	ADM_UDM [21]	KerUNC [41]	VEM [42]	DWDN [10]	SVMAP [11]	DRUNet [72]	DSDNet
BRISQUE	43.484	36.598	37.816	33.663	34.027	35.508	46.774	33.129
PIQE	78.700	67.605	65.674	44.942	51.348	56.032	81.074	49.788

We also quantitatively evaluate our method on real-world blurry images and estimated kernels from PAN [43]. Since the ground truth images are unavailable, we use the no-reference BRISQUE [39] and PIQE [65] metrics for evaluation. Our model achieves the best score in BRISQUE and second place in PIQE, as shown in Table 4. As BRISQUE is a metric based on subject scoring, Table 4 shows that our model generates more subjectively satisfying results than other state-of-the-art methods.

5.3   Qualitative Evaluation

We show visual comparisons of a synthesized and a real-world case in Figs. 3, 4, respectively.

Figure 3 shows the results of MANMADE from the dataset LAI [27]. The evaluated methods generate blur results. In contrast, our method reconstructs better images (e.g., the wood texture is better restored, as shown in both red and green boxes).

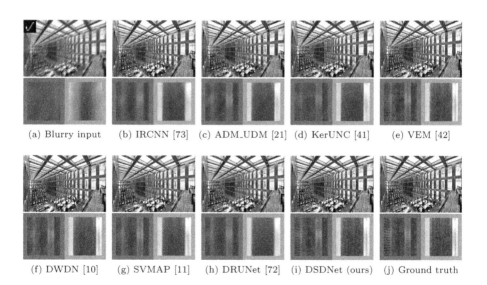

(a) Blurry input   (b) IRCNN [73]   (c) ADM_UDM [21]   (d) KerUNC [41]   (e) VEM [42]

(f) DWDN [10]   (g) SVMAP [11]   (h) DRUNet [72]   (i) DSDNet (ours)   (j) Ground truth

Fig. 3. A synthetic case comes from LAI [27]. Our method restores clearer images with finer details (e.g., the wood texture).

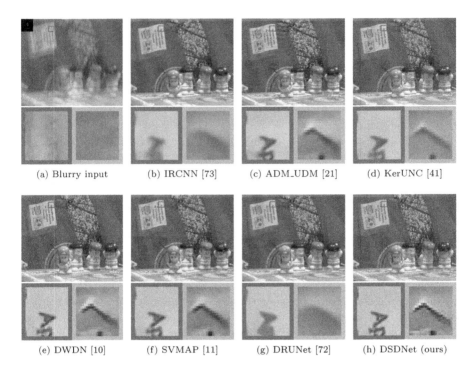

(a) Blurry input   (b) IRCNN [73]   (c) ADM_UDM [21]   (d) KerUNC [41]

(e) DWDN [10]   (f) SVMAP [11]   (g) DRUNet [72]   (h) DSDNet (ours)

Fig. 4. A real-world case whose kernel is estimated by [43]. Our method generates a better image with clearer text and a sharper eyebrow. In the olive background, our method produces the sharpest result without noise.

Figure 4 shows the deblurred results of a pair of real-world blurry images and estimated kernel [43]. Our method restores the text to sharpness in the red boxes and the blackest and sharpest eyebrow in the green boxes. In contrast, other methods cannot restore the text well and mix the eyebrow with the skin color. Furthermore, they also generate artifacts and noise in the olive background.

5.4 Ablation Study

In this section, we design experiments to show the efficiency of the proposed discriminative shrinkage functions and the differentiable CGNet. Table 5 shows the ablation results w.r.t. different baselines. In this study, we train 7 models based on the architecture of the Heavy DSDNet. We compare the number of floating point operations (FLOPs) and the parameters in this study.

To validate the effects of the $\mathbf{F}_i$ and $\mathbf{G}_j$, we train a model without estimating these two filters, denoted by "w/o $\mathbf{F},\mathbf{G}$". Without the feature maps coming from them, we can only learn the shrinkage functions from RGB inputs. Table 5 shows that the PSNR value of the results by the baseline method without $\mathbf{F}_i$ and $\mathbf{G}_j$ is at least 6.45 dB lower than that of our approach.

Table 5. Ablation study on SET5. "w/o **F**, **G**" is out of the convolutional layers before the Maxout layers; "ReLU" and "RBF" replace the Maxout layers with ReLU and RBF layers, respectively; "CG" performs conventional Conjugate Gradient method for deconvolution rather than CGNet, "FFT" performs FFT deconvolution with edge taper [25], and the superscript † means the input is denoised by DRUNet [72] first.

	w/o **F**, **G**	ReLU	RBF	CG	CG†	FFT	FFT†	DSDNet
PSNR(dB)	26.66		32.78	32.98	29.07	32.39	31.30	32.03	33.11
FLOPs(G)	136.26		464.94	468.03	470.73	559.97	288.89	391.57	466.32
Parameters(M)	1.04		237.85	237.85	0.31	32.95	0.27	32.09	237.87
Gain(dB)	−6.45		−0.33	−0.13	−4.04	−0.72	−1.81	−1.08	−/−

We also evaluate the effect of the Maxout layers by replacing them with ReLU. Table 5 shows that the method using ReLU does not generate better results than the proposed method, suggesting the effectiveness of the Maxout layers.

As RBFs are usually used to approximate shrinkage functions, one may wonder whether using them generates better results or not. To answer this question, we replace the Maxout layers with the commonly-used Gaussian RBFs. Table 5 shows that the PSNR value of the method using RBFs is at least 0.13 dB lower than that of our method, indicating the effectiveness of the proposed method.

Finally, to demonstrate the efficiency of the proposed CGNet, we train 2 models with the conventional CG method and 2 models with FFT deconvolution. The CG method is unstable with respect to even small perturbations [18,37]. Each optimization step in training and the existence of noise may cause the divergence of the CG method. Hence we have to reduce the learning rate and apply gradient clipping to avoid the gradient exploding during the training. However, it still performs poorly even if the training can be finished. To make the training more feasible, we denoise the inputs first by DRUNet [72], and this model is denoted as "CG†". The training of "CG†" is smoother, the learning rate can be set as that of the DSDNet, and the performance is much better than generic "CG". With another model to denoise, the computational cost is about 26% more FLOPs, and it takes more than twice the time for training compared to the DSDNet.

Similar to CG ones, we also provide results of deconvolution via FFT with the artifact processing operation by [25], i.e., "FFT" and "FFT†". Although FFT ones are much faster than CG ones, the gap between "CG†" and "FFT†" is considerable, as mentioned in Sect. 3. As for the test time on SET5, "CG" is 5.6001 s, "CG†" is 5.8252 s, "FFT" is 3.6941 s, "FFT†" is 4.0330 s, and DSDNet is 2.6717 s. These result show the efficiency of the proposed CGNet. We include the ablation study on HypNet and NLNet in the supplementary material.

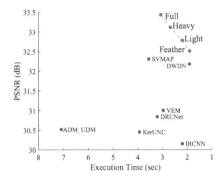

Fig. 5. Speed and accuracy trade-off. The results are evaluated on the SET5 dataset with 1% Gaussian noise. Results of this work are shown in red points; the fastest Feather DSDNet still performs favorably against the state-of-the-art methods (blue points) in PSNR.

5.5   Execution Time Analysis

We analyze the execution time of the proposed methods and state-of-the-art ones. All the execution times are evaluated on one nVidia RTX 2080Ti GPU. Figure 5 shows that our models are faster and more accurate than the state-of-the-art methods. Among these methods, our Feather model is a little bit faster than DWDN by 0.0052 s yet outperforms all other methods in PSNR.

5.6   Limitations

Although better performance on various datasets has been achieved, our method has some limitations. Our model cannot deal with blurry images containing significant saturation regions, which may lead to overflow. More analysis can be found in the supplementary material.

6   Conclusion

In this paper, we present a fully learnable MAP model for non-blind deconvolution. We formulate the data and regularization terms as the learnable ones and split the deconvolution model into data-related and regularization-related sub-problems in the ADMM framework. Maxout layers are used to learn the discriminative shrinkage functions, which directly approximate the solutions of these two sub-problems. We have further developed a CGNet to restore the images effectively and efficiently. With a reasonable design, the size of our model is flexibly adjustable while keeping competitive in performance. Extensive evaluations on the benchmark datasets demonstrate that the proposed model performs favorably against the state-of-the-art non-blind deconvolution methods in terms of quantitative metrics, visual quality, and computational efficiency.

References

1. Aljadaany, R., Pal, D.K., Savvides, M.: Douglas-rachford networks: learning both the image prior and data fidelity terms for blind image deconvolution. In: CVPR, pp. 10235–10244 (2019)
2. Barrett, R., et al.: Templates for the Solution of Linear Systems: Building Blocks for Iterative Methods. SIAM (1994)
3. Bevilacqua, M., Roumy, A., Guillemot, C., Alberi-Morel, M.L.: Low-complexity single-image super-resolution based on nonnegative neighbor embedding. In: BMVC (2012)
4. Bigdeli, S.A., Zwicker, M., Favaro, P., Jin, M.: Deep mean-shift priors for image restoration. In: NeurIPS (2017)
5. Chakrabarti, A.: A neural approach to blind motion deblurring. In: Leibe, B., Matas, J., Sebe, N., Welling, M. (eds.) ECCV 2016. LNCS, vol. 9907, pp. 221–235. Springer, Cham (2016). https://doi.org/10.1007/978-3-319-46487-9_14
6. Chan, T.F., Wong, C.K.: Total variation blind deconvolution. IEEE TIP $7(3)$, 370–375 (1998)
7. Chen, L., Zhang, J., Pan, J., Lin, S., Fang, F., Ren, J.S.: Learning a non-blind deblurring network for night blurry images. In: CVPR, pp. 10542–10550 (2021)
8. Cho, S., Wang, J., Lee, S.: Handling outliers in non-blind image deconvolution. In: ICCV, pp. 495–502 (2011)
9. Dong, J., Pan, J., Sun, D., Su, Z., Yang, M.-H.: Learning data terms for non-blind deblurring. In: Ferrari, V., Hebert, M., Sminchisescu, C., Weiss, Y. (eds.) ECCV 2018. LNCS, vol. 11215, pp. 777–792. Springer, Cham (2018). https://doi.org/10.1007/978-3-030-01252-6_46
10. Dong, J., Roth, S., Schiele, B.: Deep wiener deconvolution: Wiener meets deep learning for image deblurring. In: NeurIPS (2020)
11. Dong, J., Roth, S., Schiele, B.: Learning spatially-variant map models for non-blind image deblurring. In: CVPR, pp. 4886–4895 (2021)
12. Eboli, T., Sun, J., Ponce, J.: End-to-end interpretable learning of non-blind image deblurring. In: Vedaldi, A., Bischof, H., Brox, T., Frahm, J.-M. (eds.) ECCV 2020. LNCS, vol. 12362, pp. 314–331. Springer, Cham (2020). https://doi.org/10.1007/978-3-030-58520-4_19
13. Gao, H., Tao, X., Shen, X., Jia, J.: Dynamic scene deblurring with parameter selective sharing and nested skip connections. In: CVPR, pp. 3848–3856 (2019)
14. Geman, D., Reynolds, G.: Constrained restoration and the recovery of discontinuities. IEEE TPAMI $14(3)$, 367–383 (1992)
15. Gong, D., Zhang, Z., Shi, Q., van den Hengel, A., Shen, C., Zhang, Y.: Learning deep gradient descent optimization for image deconvolution. IEEE Trans. Neural Netw. Learn. Syst. $31(12)$, 5468–5482 (2020)
16. Goodfellow, I., Warde-Farley, D., Mirza, M., Courville, A., Bengio, Y.: Maxout networks. In: ICML, pp. 1319–1327 (2013)
17. Gu, S., Zhang, L., Zuo, W., Feng, X.: Weighted nuclear norm minimization with application to image denoising. In: CVPR, pp. 2862–2869 (2014)
18. Hadamard, J.: Lectures on Cauchy's Problem in Linear Partial Differential Equations. Courier Corporation (2003)
19. Jancsary, J., Nowozin, S., Rother, C.: Loss-specific training of non-parametric image restoration models: a new state of the art. In: Fitzgibbon, A., Lazebnik, S., Perona, P., Sato, Y., Schmid, C. (eds.) ECCV 2012. LNCS, vol. 7578, pp. 112–125. Springer, Heidelberg (2012). https://doi.org/10.1007/978-3-642-33786-4_9

20. Kingma, D.P., Ba, J.: Adam: A method for stochastic optimization. arXiv preprint arXiv:1412.6980 (2014)
21. Ko, H.C., Chang, J.Y., Ding, J.J.: Deep priors inside an unrolled and adaptive deconvolution model. In: ACCV (2020)
22. Kong, S., Wang, W., Feng, X., Jia, X.: Deep red unfolding network for image restoration. IEEE TIP **31**, 852–867 (2021)
23. Krishnan, D., Fergus, R.: Fast image deconvolution using hyper-Laplacian priors. In: NeurIPS, pp. 1033–1041 (2009)
24. Krishnan, D., Tay, T., Fergus, R.: Blind deconvolution using a normalized sparsity measure. In: CVPR, pp. 233–240 (2011)
25. Kruse, J., Rother, C., Schmidt, U.: Learning to push the limits of efficient FFT-based image deconvolution. In: ICCV, pp. 4586–4594 (2017)
26. Kupyn, O., Budzan, V., Mykhailych, M., Mishkin, D., Matas, J.: Deblurgan: Blind motion deblurring using conditional adversarial networks. In: CVPR, pp. 8183–8192 (2018)
27. Lai, W.S., Huang, J.B., Hu, Z., Ahuja, N., Yang, M.H.: A comparative study for single image blind deblurring. In: CVPR, pp. 1701–1709 (2016)
28. Levin, A., Fergus, R., Durand, F., Freeman, W.T.: Image and depth from a conventional camera with a coded aperture. ACM TOG. **26**(3), 70-es (2007)
29. Levin, A., Weiss, Y.: User assisted separation of reflections from a single image using a sparsity prior. IEEE TPAMI **29**(9), 1647–1654 (2007)
30. Levin, A., Weiss, Y., Durand, F., Freeman, W.T.: Understanding and evaluating blind deconvolution algorithms. In: CVPR, pp. 1964–1971 (2009)
31. Levin, A., Weiss, Y., Durand, F., Freeman, W.T.: Understanding blind deconvolution algorithms. IEEE TPAMI **33**(12), 2354–2367 (2011)
32. Li, L., Pan, J., Lai, W.S., Gao, C., Sang, N., Yang, M.H.: Blind image deblurring via deep discriminative priors. IJCV **127**(8), 1025–1043 (2019)
33. Li, Y., Tofighi, M., Geng, J., Monga, V., Eldar, Y.C.: Deep algorithm unrolling for blind image deblurring. arXiv preprint arXiv:1902.03493 (2019)
34. Liu, C.S.: Modifications of steepest descent method and conjugate gradient method against noise for ill-posed linear systems. Commun. Numer. Anal. **2012**, 5 (2012)
35. Liu, R., Jia, J.: Reducing boundary artifacts in image deconvolution. In: ICIP, pp. 505–508 (2008)
36. Ma, K., et al.: Waterloo exploration database: new challenges for image quality assessment models. IEEE TIP **26**(2), 1004–1016 (2016)
37. Marin, L., Háo, D.N., Lesnic, D.: Conjugate gradient-boundary element method for a Cauchy problem in the lamé system. WIT Trans. Modell. Simul. **27**, 10 (2001)
38. Martin, D., Fowlkes, C., Tal, D., Malik, J.: A database of human segmented natural images and its application to evaluating segmentation algorithms and measuring ecological statistics. In: ICCV, pp. 416–423 (2001)
39. Mittal, A., Moorthy, A.K., Bovik, A.C.: No-reference image quality assessment in the spatial domain. IEEE TIP **21**(12), 4695–4708 (2012). https://doi.org/10.1109/TIP.2012.2214050
40. Nah, S., Hyun Kim, T., Mu Lee, K.: Deep multi-scale convolutional neural network for dynamic scene deblurring. In: CVPR, pp. 3883–3891 (2017)
41. Nan, Y., Ji, H.: Deep learning for handling kernel/model uncertainty in image deconvolution. In: CVPR, pp. 2388–2397 (2020)
42. Nan, Y., Quan, Y., Ji, H.: Variational-em-based deep learning for noise-blind image deblurring. In: CVPR, pp. 3626–3635 (2020)
43. Pan, J., Sun, D., Pfister, H., Yang, M.H.: Blind image deblurring using dark channel prior. In: CVPR, pp. 1628–1636 (2016)

44. Parikh, N., Boyd, S.: Proximal algorithms. Found. Trends Optim. **1**(3), 127–239 (2014)
45. Paszke, A., et al.: Pytorch: an imperative style, high-performance deep learning library. In: Wallach, H., Larochelle, H., Beygelzimer, A., d' Alché-Buc, F., Fox, E., Garnett, R. (eds.) NeurIPS, pp. 8024–8035. Curran Associates, Inc. (2019). https://papers.neurips.cc/paper/9015-pytorch-an-imperative-style-high-performance-deep-learning-library.pdf
46. Perrone, D., Favaro, P.: Total variation blind deconvolution: the devil is in the details. In: CVPR, pp. 2909–2916 (2014)
47. Qiu, H., Hammernik, K., Qin, C., Rueckert, D.: GraDIRN: learning iterative gradient descent-based energy minimization for deformable image registration. arXiv preprint arXiv:2112.03915 (2021)
48. Ren, D., Zuo, W., Zhang, D., Zhang, L., Yang, M.H.: Simultaneous fidelity and regularization learning for image restoration. IEEE TPAMI **43**, 284–299 (2019)
49. Ren, W., Cao, X., Pan, J., Guo, X., Zuo, W., Yang, M.H.: Image deblurring via enhanced low-rank prior. IEEE TIP **25**(7), 3426–3437 (2016)
50. Richardson, W.H.: Bayesian-based iterative method of image restoration. JoSA **62**(1), 55–59 (1972)
51. Roth, S., Black, M.J.: Fields of experts: a framework for learning image priors. In: CVPR, pp. 860–867 (2005)
52. Rudin, L.I., Osher, S.: Total variation based image restoration with free local constraints. In: ICIP, vol. 1, pp. 31–35 (1994)
53. Ryabtsev, A.: The error accumulation in the conjugate gradient method for degenerate problem. arXiv preprint arXiv:2004.10242 (2020)
54. Samuel, K.G., Tappen, M.F.: Learning optimized map estimates in continuously-valued MRF models. In: CVPR, pp. 477–484 (2009)
55. Schmidt, U., Jancsary, J., Nowozin, S., Roth, S., Rother, C.: Cascades of regression tree fields for image restoration. IEEE TPAMI **38**(4), 677–689 (2015)
56. Schmidt, U., Roth, S.: Shrinkage fields for effective image restoration. In: CVPR, pp. 2774–2781 (2014)
57. Schmidt, U., Rother, C., Nowozin, S., Jancsary, J., Roth, S.: Discriminative non-blind deblurring. In: CVPR, pp. 604–611 (2013)
58. Schuler, C.J., Christopher Burger, H., Harmeling, S., Scholkopf, B.: A machine learning approach for non-blind image deconvolution. In: CVPR, pp. 1067–1074 (2013)
59. Suin, M., Purohit, K., Rajagopalan, A.: Spatially-attentive patch-hierarchical network for adaptive motion deblurring. In: CVPR, pp. 3606–3615 (2020)
60. Sun, J., Cao, W., Xu, Z., Ponce, J.: Learning a convolutional neural network for non-uniform motion blur removal. In: CVPR, pp. 769–777 (2015)
61. Sun, L., Cho, S., Wang, J., Hays, J.: Edge-based blur kernel estimation using patch priors. In: ICCP, pp. 1–8 (2013)
62. Tao, X., Gao, H., Shen, X., Wang, J., Jia, J.: Scale-recurrent network for deep image deblurring. In: CVPR, pp. 8174–8182 (2018)
63. Tappen, M.F., Liu, C., Adelson, E.H., Freeman, W.T.: Learning gaussian conditional random fields for low-level vision. In: CVPR, pp. 1–8 (2007)
64. Venkatanath, N., Praneeth, D., Bh, M.C., Channappayya, S.S., Medasani, S.S.: Blind image quality evaluation using perception based features. In: National Conference on Communications (NCC), pp. 1–6 (2015)
65. Wang, Y., Yang, J., Yin, W., Zhang, Y.: A new alternating minimization algorithm for total variation image reconstruction. SIAM J. Imag. Sci. **1**(3), 248–272 (2008)

66. Wang, Z., Bovik, A.C., Sheikh, H.R., Simoncelli, E.P.: Image quality assessment: from error visibility to structural similarity. IEEE TIP **13**(4), 600–612 (2004)
67. Xiang, J., Dong, Y., Yang, Y.: FISTA-net: Learning a fast iterative shrinkage thresholding network for inverse problems in imaging. IEEE TMI **40**, 1329–1339 (2021)
68. Yang, Y., Sun, J., Li, H., Xu, Z.: Deep ADMM-net for compressive sensing MRI. In: NeurIPS, pp. 10–18 (2016)
69. Zhang, J., Ghanem, B.: ISTA-net: interpretable optimization-inspired deep network for image compressive sensing. In: CVPR, pp. 1828–1837 (2018)
70. Zhang, J., shan Pan, J., Lai, W.S., Lau, R.W.H., Yang, M.H.: Learning fully convolutional networks for iterative non-blind deconvolution. In: CVPR, pp. 6969–6977 (2017)
71. Zhang, K., Gool, L.V., Timofte, R.: Deep unfolding network for image super-resolution. In: CVPR, pp. 3217–3226 (2020)
72. Zhang, K., Li, Y., Zuo, W., Zhang, L., Van Gool, L., Timofte, R.: Plug-and-play image restoration with deep denoiser prior. IEEE TPAMI. **44**, 6360–6376 (2021)
73. Zhang, K., Zuo, W., Gu, S., Zhang, L.: Learning deep CNN denoiser prior for image restoration. In: CVPR, pp. 3929–3938 (2017)
74. Zhang, K., Zuo, W., Zhang, L.: Deep plug-and-play super-resolution for arbitrary blur kernels. In: CVPR, pp. 1671–1681 (2019)
75. Zoran, D., Weiss, Y.: From learning models of natural image patches to whole image restoration. In: ICCV, pp. 479–486 (2011)

KXNet: A Model-Driven Deep Neural Network for Blind Super-Resolution

Jiahong Fu[1], Hong Wang[2], Qi Xie[1(✉)], Qian Zhao[1], Deyu Meng[1,3], and Zongben Xu[1,3]

[1] Xi'an Jiaotong University, Shaanxi, People's Republic of China
jiahongfu@stu.xjtu.edu.cn,
{xie.qi,timmy.zhaoqian,dymeng}@mail.xjtu.edu.cn
[2] Tencent Jarvis Lab, Shenzhen, People's Republic of China
hazelhwang@tencent.com
[3] Pazhou Lab, Guangzhou, People's Republic of China

Abstract. Although current deep learning-based methods have gained promising performance in the blind single image super-resolution (SISR) task, most of them mainly focus on heuristically constructing diverse network architectures and put less emphasis on the explicit embedding of the physical generation mechanism between blur kernels and high-resolution (HR) images. To alleviate this issue, we propose a model-driven deep neural network, called KXNet, for blind SISR. Specifically, to solve the classical SISR model, we propose a simple-yet-effective iterative algorithm. Then by unfolding the involved iterative steps into the corresponding network module, we naturally construct the KXNet. The main specificity of the proposed KXNet is that the entire learning process is fully and explicitly integrated with the inherent physical mechanism underlying this SISR task. Thus, the learned blur kernel has clear physical patterns and the mutually iterative process between blur kernel and HR image can soundly guide the KXNet to be evolved in the right direction. Extensive experiments on synthetic and real data finely demonstrate the superior accuracy and generality of our method beyond the current representative state-of-the-art blind SISR methods. Code is available at: https://github.com/jiahong-fu/KXNet.

Keywords: Blind single image super-resolution · Physical generation mechanism · Model-driven · Kernel estimation · Mutual learning

1 Introduction

Single image super-resolution (SISR) has been widely adopted in various vision applications, *e.g.* video surveillance, medical imaging, and video enhancement. For this SISR task, the main goal is to reconstruct the high-resolution (HR) image with high visual quality from an observed low-resolution (LR) image.

Supplementary Information The online version contains supplementary material available at https://doi.org/10.1007/978-3-031-19800-7_14.

Specifically, in traditional SISR framework, the degradation process for an LR image Y can be mathematically expressed as [11,12]:

$$Y = (X \otimes K) \downarrow_s + N, \tag{1}$$

where X is the to-be-estimated HR image; K is a blur kernel; $\otimes$ denotes two-dimensional (2D) convolution operation; $\downarrow_s$ represents the standard s-fold down-sampler, $i.e.$, only keeping the upper-left pixel for each distinct $s \times s$ patch [53]; N denotes the Additive White Gaussian Noise (AWGN) with noise level σ. Clearly, estimating X and K from Y is an ill-posed inversion problem.

With the rapid development of deep neural networks (DNNs), in recent years, many deep learning (DL)-methods have been proposed for this SISR task [19, 21,22,24,31,59,60]. Albeit achieving promising performance in some scenes, the assumption that the blur kernel K is known, such as bicubic [7,19,24,59,60], would make these methods tend to fail in real applications where the practical degradation process is always complicated. To alleviate this issue, researchers have focused on the more challenging blind super-resolution (SR) task where the blur kernel K is unknown. Currently, blind SR methods can be mainly divided into two categories: traditional-model-based ones and DL-based ones.

Specifically, conventional blind SR works [6,27] aim to formulate the hand-crafted prior knowledge of blur kernel K and HR image X, into an optimization algorithm to constrain the solution space of the ill-posed SISR problem. Due to the involved iterative computations, these methods are generally time-consuming. Besides, the manually-designed priors cannot always sufficiently represent the complicated and diverse images in real scenarios.

Recently, to flexibly deal with multi-degradation situations, some DL-based blind SR methods [3,23,58] have been proposed, which are composed of two successive steps, $i.e.$, blur kernel estimation and non-blind super-resolver. Since these two steps are independently handled, the estimated blur kernel and the recovered HR image are possibly not compatible well. To further boost the performance, some works [14,25,43,44,54] directly utilized off-the-shelf network modules to recover HR images in an end-to-end manner without fully embedding the physical generation mechanism underlying this SISR task.

Very recently, the end-to-end deep unfolding framework has achieved good performance in this SISR task [5,16,25,53]. Typically, by alternately updating the blur kernel K and the HR image X, the blind SR work [25] heuristically constructs an optimization-inspired SR network. However, there are two main limitations: 1) the inherent physical generation mechanism in Eq. (1) is still not fully and explicitly embedded into the iterative computations of K and X, and every network module has relatively weak physical meanings; 2) most of these deep unfolding-based methods cannot finely extract blur kernels with clear physical patterns, which is caused by weak interpretable operations on blur kernels, such as concatenation and stretching [25] and spatial feature transform (SFT) layer [14]. Hence, there is still room for further performance improvement.

To alleviate these issues, we propose a novel deep unfolding blind SR network that explicitly embeds the physical mechanism in Eq. (1) into the mutual learning

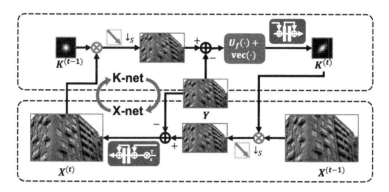

Fig. 1. Illustration of the proposed KXnet where K-net for blur kernel estimation and X-net for HR image estimation are constructed based on the physical generation mechanism in Eq. (1).

between blur kernel and HR image in a sufficient manner. Under the explicit guidance of the degradation process Eq. (1), the updating of K and X finely proceeds, and the learned blur kernel presents clear structural patterns with specific physical meanings. In summary, our contributions are mainly three-fold:

- We propose a novel model-driven deep unfolding blind super-resolution network (called KXNet) to jointly estimate the blur kernel K and the HR image X, which is explicitly integrated with the physical generation mechanism in Eq. (1), as shown in Fig. 1. Specifically, we propose an iterative algorithm to solve the classical degradation model Eq. (1) and then construct the KXNet by unfolding the iterative steps into the corresponding network modules. Naturally, the mutually iterative learning process between blur kernel and HR image fully complies with the inherent physical generation mechanism, and every network module in KXNet has clear physical interpretability.
- Instead of heuristic operations (*e.g.* concatenation and affine transformation) on blur kernel in most of the current SR methods, the learning and estimation of blur kernel in our method is proceeding under the guidance of Eq. (1) and thus has clearer physical meanings. As shown in Fig. 1, the K-net is finely corresponding to the iterative steps for updating blur kernel and thus the extracted blur kernel K has reasonable and clear physical structures. Besides, attributed to the intrinsic embedding of the physical generation mechanism, we maintain the essential convolution computation between blur kernel and HR image, which is expected to achieve better SR performance.
- Extensive experiments executed on synthetic and real data comprehensively demonstrate the superiority of the proposed KXNet in SR performance and model generalizability beyond the current state-of-the-art (SOTA) methods. Besides, more analysis and network visualization validate the rationality and effectiveness of our method, and the extracted blur kernels with clear structures would be helpful for other vision tasks in real applications.

2   Related Work

2.1   Non-Blind Single Image Super-Resolution

In recent years, deep learning (DL) has achieved great progress in SISR task. Current SISR methods mainly focus on utilizing deep neural networks to learn the mapping function from a low-resolution (LR) image to the corresponding high-resolution (HR) image via paired training data. Since it is very time-consuming and labor-intensive to pre-collect massive paired LR-HR images, many researchers adopt the manually-designed degradation processes to generate the LR images, such as the classical bicubic interpolation (K in Eq. (1) is set as the bicubic kernel). This setting has been widely adopted from the early SRCNN [7] to the recent various SISR methods [22,24,31,59]. These methods aim to design diverse network modules to improve the SISR performance.

Considering that in real scenes, the degradation process is always complicated, there are some works [48,53,57] dealing with multiple degradation forms. For example, SRMD [57] takes different degradation feature maps as additional inputs for the SR task. Very recently, Zhang [53] constructs an optimization-inspired non-blind SISR network for handling the multiple degradation scenes.

2.2   Blind Single Image Super-Resolution

To better represent the real degradation process and improve the SR performance in real-world, blind single image super-resolution has been attracting the attention of researchers in this field. In this case, the goal is to jointly estimate the unknown blur kernel K and the expected HR image X. Currently, against this task, the existing methods can be mainly categorized into two groups: two-step methods and end-to-end methods.

Two-step Blind Super-Resolution. In this research line, researchers first estimate the blur kernel based on different prior knowledge [23,32,34,49]. For example, Michaeli [30] utilizes the inter-scale recurrence property of an image to help extract the blur kernel. Then by inserting the estimated blur kernel into non-blind SR methods [58], the corresponding SR results can be restored. Recently, Kligler [3] have proposed an unsupervised KernelGAN to estimate the blur kernel based on the recurrence property of the image patch, then utilized the extracted kernel to help reconstruct SR images. Similarly, Liang [23] have proposed a flow-based architecture to capture the prior knowledge of the blur kernel which can be used for the subsequent non-blind SR task. Most of these two-step methods have not fully considered the iterative and mutual learning between blur kernels and HR images.

End-to-End Blind Super-Resolution. Very recently, some works begin to emphasize how to merge the kernel estimation process with the non-blind SR process and thus design an end-to-end blind SR framework. Gu [14] firstly designed a single network architecture that contains a kernel estimation module and a non-blind SR module. However, this method needs to separately train multiple modules. To alleviate this issue, Luo [25,26] proposed a complete end-to-end network that can be trained in an end-to-end manner. Wang [43] proposed an unsupervised degradation representation learning scheme and then utilized it to help accomplish the blind SR task. Zhang [54] and Wang [44] design a "high-order" degradation model to simulate the image degradation process.

Albeit achieving promising performance in some scenarios, most of these methods have the following limitations: 1) The estimated degradation form has relatively weak physical meanings or cannot fully reflect blur kernels with clear and structural patterns; 2) The degradation representation is heuristically used, such as simple concatenation with LR image, without explicitly reflecting the inherent convolution operation between blur kernel and image; 3) The intrinsic physical generation mechanism in Eq. (1) has not been fully embedded into network design. To alleviate these issues, we adopt the deep unfolding technique [42,46], with several novel designs, for better embedding the inherent mechanism into network structure and improving the performance in blind SR restoration.

3   Blind Single Image Super-Resolution Model

In this section, for the blind SISR task, we formulate the corresponding mathematical model and propose an optimization algorithm.

3.1   Model Formulation

From Eq. (1), given an observed LR image $\boldsymbol{Y} \in \mathbb{R}^{h \times w}$, our goal is to estimate the two unknown variables, $i.e.$, blur kernel $\boldsymbol{K} \in \mathbb{R}^{p \times p}$ and HR image $\boldsymbol{X} \in \mathbb{R}^{H \times W}$. Correspondingly, we can formulate the following optimization problem as:

$$\min_{\boldsymbol{K},\boldsymbol{X}} \left\| \boldsymbol{Y} - (\boldsymbol{X} \otimes \boldsymbol{K}) \downarrow_{\mathbf{s}} \right\|_F^2 + \lambda_1 \phi_1(\boldsymbol{K}) + \lambda_2 \phi_2(\boldsymbol{X})$$
$$s.t.\ \boldsymbol{K}_j \geq 0, \sum_j \boldsymbol{K}_j = 1, \forall j, \tag{2}$$

where $\phi_1(\boldsymbol{K})$ and $\phi_2(\boldsymbol{X})$ represent the regularizers for delivering the prior knowledge of blur kernel and HR image, respectively; λ_1 and λ_2 are trade-off regularization parameters. Similar to [33,34,37], we introduce the non-negative and equality constraints for every element $\boldsymbol{K}_j$ in blur kernel $\boldsymbol{K}$. Specifically, the data fidelity term ($i.e.$, the first term in the objective function of Eq. (2)) represents the physical generation mechanism, which would provide the explicit guidance during the iterative updating of $\boldsymbol{K}$ and $\boldsymbol{X}$, and the prior terms $\phi_1(\boldsymbol{K})$ and $\phi_2(\boldsymbol{X})$ enforce the expected structures of the solution for this ill-posed problem.

Instead of adopting hand-crafted prior functions as in conventional optimization-based SR methods, we utilize a data-driven strategy to flexibly extract the implicit prior knowledge underlying $\boldsymbol{X}$ and $\boldsymbol{K}$ from data via DNNs in an end-to-end manner. This operation has been fully validated to be effective in many diverse vision tasks by extensive studies [42,46,55]. The details for learning $\phi_1(\boldsymbol{K})$ and $\phi_2(\boldsymbol{X})$ are given in Sect. 4.

3.2 Model Optimization

For this blind SISR task, our goal is to build a deep unfolding network where network modules are possibly corresponding to iterative steps involved in an optimization algorithm so as to make the network interpretable and easily controllable. Thus, it is necessary to derive an iterative algorithm for solving the SR problem in Eq. (2).

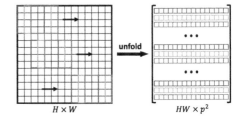

Fig. 2. Illustration of the operator $U_f(\cdot)$.

To this end, we adopt a proximal gradient technique [2,13] to alternatively update the blur kernel $\boldsymbol{K}$ and HR image $\boldsymbol{X}$. Then, the derived optimization algorithm contains only simple operators which makes it possible to be easily unfolded into network modules, as shown in following.

Updating blur kernel $\boldsymbol{K}$: The blur kernel $\boldsymbol{K}$ can be optimized by solving the quadratic approximation [2] of the problem Eq. (2) with respect to the variable $\boldsymbol{K}$, expressed as:

$$
\min_{\boldsymbol{K}} \left\| \boldsymbol{K} - \left(\boldsymbol{K}^{(t-1)} - \delta_1 \nabla f\left(\boldsymbol{K}^{(t-1)}\right)\right)\right\|_F^2 + \lambda_1 \delta_1 \phi_1(\boldsymbol{K})
$$
$$
s.t. \ \boldsymbol{K}_j \geq 0, \sum_j \boldsymbol{K}_j = 1, \forall j, \tag{3}
$$

where $\boldsymbol{K}^{(t-1)}$ denotes the updating result after the last iteration; δ_1 denotes the stepsize parameter; $f(\boldsymbol{K}^{(t-1)}) = \left\| \boldsymbol{Y} - \left(\boldsymbol{X}^{(t-1)} \otimes \boldsymbol{K}^{(t-1)}\right)\downarrow_s\right\|_F^2$. For a general regularizer $\phi_1(\cdot)$, the solution of Eq. (3) can be easily expressed as [8]:

$$
\boldsymbol{K}^{(t)} = \mathrm{prox}_{\lambda_1 \delta_1}\left(\boldsymbol{K}^{(t-1)} - \delta_1 \nabla f\left(\boldsymbol{K}^{(t-1)}\right)\right), \tag{4}
$$

where the specific form of $\nabla f\left(\boldsymbol{K}^{(t-1)}\right)$ is complicated. For ease of calculation, by transforming the convolutional operation in $f(\boldsymbol{K}^{(t-1)})$ into matrix multiplication, we can derive that:

$$
f\left(\boldsymbol{k}^{(t-1)}\right) = \mathrm{vec}\left(\left\| \boldsymbol{Y} - \left(\boldsymbol{X}^{(t-1)} \otimes \boldsymbol{K}^{(t-1)}\right)\downarrow_s\right\|_F^2\right)
$$
$$
= \left\| \boldsymbol{y} - D_s U_f\left(\boldsymbol{X}^{(t-1)}\right)\boldsymbol{k}^{(t-1)}\right\|_F^2, \tag{5}
$$

where $\boldsymbol{y} = \mathrm{vec}\,(\boldsymbol{Y})$ and $\boldsymbol{k} = \mathrm{vec}\,(\boldsymbol{K})$ denote the vectorizations of $\boldsymbol{Y}$ and $\boldsymbol{K}$, respectively; $\boldsymbol{y} \in \mathbb{R}^{hw \times 1}; \boldsymbol{k} \in \mathbb{R}^{p^2 \times 1}; U_f\left(\boldsymbol{X}^{(t-1)}\right) \in \mathbb{R}^{HW \times p^2}$ are the unfolded result of $\boldsymbol{X}^{(t-1)}$ (see Fig. 2); D_s denotes the downsampling operator which is corresponding to the operator $\downarrow_s$, and achieves the transformation from the size HW to the size hw. Thus, the result $D_s U_f\left(\boldsymbol{X}^{(t-1)}\right)^1$ has the size with $hw \times p^2$ and $\nabla f(\boldsymbol{k}^{(t-1)})$ is derived as:

---

[1] More derivations are provided in the supplementary material.

$$\nabla f\left(\boldsymbol{k}^{(t-1)}\right) = \left(D_s U_f\left(\boldsymbol{X}^{(t-1)}\right)\right)^{\mathrm{T}} \mathrm{vec}\left(\boldsymbol{Y} - \left(\boldsymbol{X}^{(t-1)} \otimes \boldsymbol{K}^{(t-1)}\right) \downarrow_{\mathbf{s}}\right), \tag{6}$$

where $\nabla f(\boldsymbol{k}^{(t-1)}) \in \mathbb{R}^{p^2 \times 1}$; $\nabla f(\boldsymbol{K}^{(t-1)}) = \mathrm{vec}^{-1}\left(\nabla f(\boldsymbol{k}^{(t-1)})\right)$; $\mathrm{vec}^{-1}(\cdot)$ is the reverse vectorization; $\mathrm{prox}_{\lambda_1 \delta_1}(\cdot)$ is the proximal operator dependent on the regularization term $\phi_1(\cdot)$ with respect to $\boldsymbol{K}$. Different from the traditional methods with hand-crafted regularization terms, we rely on the powerful fitting capability of residual networks to automatically learn the implicit proximal operator $\mathrm{prox}_{\lambda_1 \delta_1}(\cdot)$ via training data. Such operations have achieved great success in other deep unfolding works [42,46]. The details are described in Sect. 4.

Updating HR image X: Similarly, the quadratic approximation of the problem in Eq. (2) with respect to $\boldsymbol{X}$ can be derived as:

$$\min_{\boldsymbol{X}} \left\| \boldsymbol{X} - \left(\boldsymbol{X}^{(t-1)} - \delta_2 \nabla h\left(\boldsymbol{X}^{(t-1)}\right)\right) \right\|_F^2 + \lambda_2 \delta_2 \phi_2(\boldsymbol{X}), \tag{7}$$

where $h\left(\boldsymbol{X}^{(t-1)}\right) = \left\| \boldsymbol{Y} - \left(\boldsymbol{X}^{(t-1)} \otimes \boldsymbol{K}^{(t)}\right) \downarrow_{\mathbf{s}} \right\|_F^2$; With $\nabla h\left(\boldsymbol{X}^{(t-1)}\right) = \boldsymbol{K}^{(t)} \otimes_{\mathbf{s}}^{\mathrm{T}} \left(\boldsymbol{Y} - \left(\boldsymbol{X}^{(t-1)} \otimes \boldsymbol{K}^{(t)}\right) \downarrow_{\mathbf{s}}\right)$, we can deduce the updating rule for $\boldsymbol{X}$ as:

$$\boldsymbol{X}^{(t)} = \mathrm{prox}_{\lambda_2 \delta_2}\left(\boldsymbol{X}^{(t-1)} - \delta_2 \boldsymbol{K}^{(t)} \otimes_{\mathbf{s}}^{\mathrm{T}} \left(\boldsymbol{Y} - (\boldsymbol{X}^{(t-1)} \otimes \boldsymbol{K}^{(t)}) \downarrow_{\mathbf{s}}\right)\right), \tag{8}$$

where $\mathrm{prox}_{\lambda_2 \delta_2}(\cdot)$ is the proximal operator dependent on the regularization term $\phi_2(\cdot)$ about $\boldsymbol{X}$; $\otimes_{\mathbf{s}}^{\mathrm{T}}$ denotes the transposed convolution operation with stride as $\mathbf{s}$. Similar to $\mathrm{prox}_{\lambda_1 \delta_1}(\cdot)$, we adopt deep network to flexibly learn the $\mathrm{prox}_{\lambda_2 \delta_2}(\cdot)$.

As seen, the proposed optimization algorithm is composed of the iterative rules Eq. (4) and Eq. (8). By unfolding every iterative step into the corresponding network module, we can naturally build the deep unfolding network architecture for solving the blind SISR task as given in Eq. (2).

4   Blind Super-Resolution Unfolding Network

Recently, deep unfolding techniques have achieved great progress in various computer vision fields [39–41,50,51], such as spectral image fusion [46,47], deraining [42], and non-blind super-resolution [53]. Inspired by these methods, in this section, we aim to build an end-to-end deep unfolding network for blind super-resolution problem by unfolding each iterative step involved in Eq. (4) and Eq. (8) as the corresponding network module.

As shown in Fig. 3a, the proposed network consists of T stages, which correspond to T iterations of the proposed optimization algorithm for solving the problem in Eq. (2). At each stage, as illustrated in Fig. 3b, the network is subsequently composed of K-net and X-net. In specific, the K-net takes the LR image $\boldsymbol{Y}$, the estimated blur kernel $\boldsymbol{K}^{(t-1)}$ and the estimated HR image $\boldsymbol{X}^{(t-1)}$ as inputs and outputs the updated $\boldsymbol{K}^{(t)}$. Then, X-net takes $\boldsymbol{Y}$, $\boldsymbol{K}^{(t)}$, and $\boldsymbol{X}^{(t-1)}$ as inputs, and outputs the updated $\boldsymbol{X}^{(t)}$. This alternative iterative process complies with the proposed algorithm.

242   J. Fu et al.

(a) The algorithm processes of the entire KXNet.

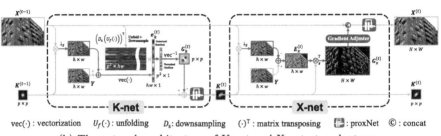

$\text{vec}(\cdot)$: vectorization $U_f(\cdot)$: unfolding D_s: downsampling $(\cdot)^{\mathrm{T}}$: matrix transposing   ⊞ : proxNet   ⓒ : concat

(b) The network architecture of K-net and X-net at each stage.

Fig. 3. (a) The overall architecture of the proposed KXNet contains T stages. It inputs the initialized HR image $X^{(0)}$ and initialized blur kernel $K^{(0)}$, and outputs the HR image X and the blur kernel K. (b) The network architecture at the tth stage, which consists of K-net and X-net for updating the blur kernel K and HR image X, respectively.

4.1   Network Module Design

By step-by-step decomposing the iterative rules of Eq. (4) and Eq. (8) into substeps and then unfolding them as the fundamental network modules, we can easily construct the entire deep unfolding framework. However, the key problem is how to deal with the implicit proximal operators $\mathrm{prox}_{\lambda_1\delta_1}(\cdot)$ and $\mathrm{prox}_{\lambda_2\delta_2}(\cdot)$. As stated in Sect. 3.2, following the current other unfolding-based networks [42, 46], we can utilize ResNet [15] to construct $\mathrm{prox}_{\lambda_1\delta_1}(\cdot)$ and $\mathrm{prox}_{\lambda_2\delta_2}(\cdot)$. Thus, at the tth stage, the network is built as:

$$\text{K-net:} \begin{cases} e_k^{(t)} = \mathrm{vec}\left(Y - \left(X^{(t-1)} \otimes K^{(t-1)}\right) \downarrow_s\right) \\ G_k^{(t)} = \mathrm{vec}^{-1}\left(\left(D_s U_f\left(X^{(t-1)}\right)\right)^{\mathrm{T}} e_k^{(t)}\right) \\ K^{(t)} = \mathrm{proxNet}_{\theta_k^{(t)}}\left(K^{(t-1)} - \delta_1\left(G_k^{(t)}\right)\right), \end{cases} \tag{9}$$

$$\text{X-net:} \begin{cases} E_x^{(t)} = Y - (X^{(t-1)} \otimes K^{(t)}) \downarrow_s \\ G_x^{(t)} = K^{(t)} \otimes_s^{\mathrm{T}} E_x^{(t)} \\ \hat{G}_x^{(t)} = \mathrm{adjuster}\left(G_x^{(t)}\right) \\ X^{(t)} = \mathrm{proxNet}_{\theta_x^{(t)}}\left(X^{(t-1)}, \hat{G}_x^{(t)}\right), \end{cases} \tag{10}$$

where $\mathrm{proxNet}_{\theta_k^{(t)}}$ and $\mathrm{proxNet}_{\theta_x^{(t)}}$ are two shallow ResNets with the parameters $\theta_k^{(t)}$ and $\theta_x^{(t)}$ at the t-th stage, respectively; adjuster$(\cdot)$ is an operation for boosting the gradient, whose details are discussed later. All these network parameters can be automatically learned from training data in an end-to-end manner. Note that the proximal gradient descent algorithm usually needs lots of iterations for convergence, which will lead to too many network stages when adopting the unfolding technique. To avoid this issue, as shown in the last equation of Eq. (10), instead of directly adopting the subtraction between $\boldsymbol{X}^{(t-1)}$ and $\hat{\boldsymbol{G}}_x^{(t)}$, we concatenate $\boldsymbol{X}^{(t-1)}$ and $\hat{\boldsymbol{G}}_x^{(t)}$ as the input of the proximal network $\mathrm{proxNet}_{\theta_x^{(t)}}(\cdot)$, which introduces more flexibility to the combination of $\boldsymbol{X}^{(t-1)}$ and $\hat{\boldsymbol{G}}_x^{(t)}$.

Remark for K-net. The proposed KXNet has clear physical interpretability. Different from the current most deep blind SR methods which heuristically adopt the concatenation or affine transformation operators on $\boldsymbol{K}^{(t-1)}$ to help the learning of HR images, the proposed K-net is constructed based on the iterative rule in Eq. (4) and every network sub-module has its specific physical meanings as shown in Fig. 3b. Specifically, following the degradation model, $\boldsymbol{X}^{(t-1)}$ is convolved with $\boldsymbol{K}^{(t-1)}$ followed by the downsampling operator. Then by subtracting the result from $\boldsymbol{Y}$, we get the residual information $e_k^{(t)}$, which is actually the key information for updating the current estimation. Then, we regard $e_k^{(t)}$ as a weight and adopt it to perform a weighted summation on the corresponded patches in $\boldsymbol{X}^{(t-1)}$ (i.e., row vectors in $D_s U_f(\boldsymbol{X}^{(t-1)}) \in \mathbb{R}^{hw \times p^2}$, as shown in Fig. 3b), and get $\boldsymbol{G}_k^{(t)}$ for updating $\boldsymbol{K}^{(t-1)}$. Actually, this is consistent with the relationship between $\boldsymbol{K}^{(t-1)}$ and $\boldsymbol{X}^{(t-1)}$, since convolution operation is executed based on the patch with $p \times p$.

Gradient Adjuster. For X-net, an adjuster is adopted to the gradient $\boldsymbol{G}_x^{(t)}$ as shown in the third equation of Eq. (10). Specifically, the transposed convolution $\boldsymbol{G}_x^{(t)}$ in X-net can easily cause "uneven overlap", putting more of the metaphorical paint in some places than others [9,36], which is unfriendly to the reconstruction of HR images. To alleviate the unevenness issue, we introduce the operator $\boldsymbol{K}^{(t)} \otimes_s^{\mathrm{T}} \mathbf{1}$ and the adjusted gradient $\hat{\boldsymbol{G}}_x^{(t)}$ is[2]:

$$\hat{\boldsymbol{G}}_x^{(t)} = \frac{\boldsymbol{G}_x^{(t)}}{\boldsymbol{K}^{(t)} \otimes_s^{\mathrm{T}} \mathbf{1}}, \tag{11}$$

where $\mathbf{1} \in \mathbb{R}^{h \times w}$ is a matrix with all elements as 1.

4.2   Network Training

To train the proposed deep unfolding blind SR network, we utilize the L_1 loss [61] to supervise the predicted blur kernel $\boldsymbol{K}^{(t)}$ and the estimated HR image $\boldsymbol{X}^{(t)}$ at each stage. Correspondingly, the total objective function is:

$$L = \sum_{t=1}^{T} \alpha_t \|\boldsymbol{K} - \boldsymbol{K}^{(t)}\|_1 + \sum_{t=1}^{T} \beta_t \|\boldsymbol{X} - \boldsymbol{X}^{(t)}\|_1, \tag{12}$$

---

[2] More analysis is provided in the supplementary material.

where $\boldsymbol{K}^{(t)}$ and $\boldsymbol{X}^{(t)}$ are obtained based on the updating process in Eq. (9) and Eq. (10) at the tth stage, respectively; α_t and β_t are trade-off parameters[3]. $\boldsymbol{X}^{(0)}$ is initialized as the bicubic upsampling of the LR image $\boldsymbol{Y}$, and $\boldsymbol{K}^{(0)}$ is initialized as a standard Gaussian kernel.

5 Experimental Results

5.1 Details Descriptions

Synthesized Datasets. Following [14,25,43], we collect 800 HR images from DIV2K [1] and 2650 HR images from Flickr2K [38] to synthesize the training data, and adopt the four commonly-used benchmark datasets, *i.e.*, Set5 [4], Set14 [52], BSD100 [28], and Urban100 [17], to synthesize the testing data. During the synthesis process of training and testing pairs, we adopt the degradation process in Eq. (1) with two different degradation settings: 1) isotropic Gaussian blur kernel with noise free; 2) anisotropic Gaussian blur kernel with noise [10,23,35, 53], and set the s-fold downsampler as in [3,23,53]. Note that as stated in [35,53], the later setting is very close to the real SISR scenario.

In setting 1), for training set, following [14,25,43], the blur kernel size $p \times p$ is set as 21×21 for all scales $\mathbf{s} \in \{2,3,4\}$ and the corresponding kernel width for different scales ($\times 2$, $\times 3$, and $\times 4$ SR) is uniformly sampled from the ranges $[0.2,2.0]$, $[0.2,3.0]$, and $[0.2,4.0]$, respectively. For testing set, the blur kernel is set as *Gaussian8* [14], which uniformly samples 8 kernels from the ranges $[0.8,1.6]$, $[1.35,2.40]$, and $[1.8,3.2]$ for the scale factors 2, 3, and 4, respectively.

In setting 2), for trainings set, we set the kernel size p as $11/15/21$ for $\times 2/3/4$ SR, respectively. Specifically, the kernel width at each axis are obtained by randomly rotating the widths λ_1 and λ_2 with an angle $\theta \sim U[-\pi,\pi]$, where λ_1 and λ_2 are uniformly distributed in $U(0.6, 5.0)$. Besides, the range of noise level σ is set to $[0, 25]$. For testing set, we separately set the kernel width as $\lambda_1 = 0.8, \lambda_2 = 1.6$ and $\lambda_1 = 2.0, \lambda_2 = 4.0$, and rotate them by $\theta \in \{0, \frac{\pi}{4}, \frac{\pi}{2}, \frac{3\pi}{4}\}$, respectively. This means every HR testing image is degraded by 8 different blur kernels.

Real Dataset. To verify the performance of the proposed method in real scenarios, we use the dataset RealSRSet [54] for generalization evaluation, which includes 20 real LR images collected from various sources [18,28,29,56].

Training Details. Based on the PyTorch framework executed on two RTX20-80Ti GPUs, we adopt the Adam solver [20] with the parameters as $\beta_1 = 0.9$ and $\beta_2 = 0.99$ to optimize the proposed network with the batch size and patch size set as 12 and 64×64, respectively. The learning rate is initialized as 2×10^{-4} and decays by multiplying a factor of 0.5 at every 2×10^5 iteration. The training process ends when the learning rate decreases to 1.25×10^{-5}.

Comparison Methods. We comprehensively substantiate the superiority of our method by comparing it with several recent SOTA methods, including the non-blind SISR method RCAN [59], and blind SISR methods, including IKC [14],

---

[3] We set $\alpha_t = \beta_t = 0.1$ at middle stages, $\alpha_T = \beta_T = 1$ at the last stage, and $T = 19$.

Table 1. Average PSNR/SSIM of all the comparing methods (**Setting 1**).

Method	Scale	Urban100 [17]		BSD100 [28]		Set14 [52]		Set5 [4]	
		PSNR	SSIM	PSNR	SSIM	PSNR	SSIM	PSNR	SSIM
Bicubic	x2	24.23	0.7430	27.02	0.7472	27.13	0.7797	29.42	0.8666
RCAN [59]		24.69	0.7727	27.40	0.7710	27.54	0.8804	29.81	0.8797
IKC [14]		29.22	0.8752	30.51	0.8540	31.69	0.8789	34.31	0.9287
DASR [43]		30.63	0.9079	31.76	0.8901	32.93	0.9029	37.22	0.9515
DAN [25]		31.31	0.9165	31.93	0.8906	33.31	0.9085	37.54	0.9546
KXNet (ours)		**31.48**	**0.9192**	**32.03**	**0.8941**	**33.36**	**0.9091**	**37.58**	**0.9552**
Bicubic	x3	22.07	0.6216	24.93	0.6360	24.58	0.6671	26.19	0.7716
RCAN [59]		22.18	0.6366	25.06	0.6501	24.73	0.6800	26.37	0.7840
IKC [14]		26.85	0.8087	28.29	0.7724	29.41	0.8106	32.90	0.8997
DASR [43]		27.28	0.8307	28.85	0.7932	29.94	0.8266	33.78	0.9200
DAN [25]		27.94	0.8450	29.04	0.8001	30.24	**0.8350**	34.18	0.9237
KXNet (ours)		**28.00**	**0.8457**	**29.06**	**0.8010**	**30.27**	0.8340	**34.22**	**0.9238**
Bicubic	x4	20.96	0.5544	23.84	0.5780	23.25	0.6036	24.43	0.7045
RCAN [59]		20.96	0.5608	23.89	0.5865	23.30	0.6109	24.52	0.7148
IKC [14]		24.42	0.7112	26.55	0.6867	26.88	0.7301	29.83	0.8375
DASR [43]		25.49	0.7621	27.40	0.7238	28.26	0.7668	31.68	0.8854
DAN [25]		25.95	0.7787	27.53	0.7311	28.55	0.7749	**31.96**	0.8898
KXNet (ours)		**26.18**	**0.7873**	**27.59**	**0.7330**	**28.67**	**0.7782**	31.94	**0.8912**

GT   Zoomed LR   IKC [14]   DASR [43]   DAN [25]   **KXNet**(ours)

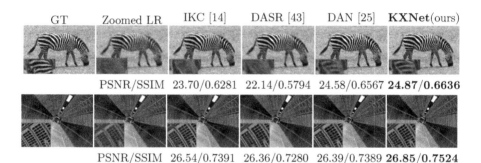

PSNR/SSIM   23.70/0.6281   22.14/0.5794   24.58/0.6567 **24.87/0.6636**

PSNR/SSIM   26.54/0.7391   26.36/0.7280   26.39/0.7389 **26.85/0.7524**

Fig. 4. Performance comparison on *img 14* in Set14 [52] and *img 078* in Urban100 [17]. The scale factor is 4 and noise level is 5.

DASR [43], and DAN [25]. For a fair comparison, we have retrained IKC, DASR, and DAN based on the aforementioned two settings with the public codes.

Performance Evaluation. For synthetic data, we adopt the PSNR and SSIM [45] computed on Y channel in YCbCr space. While for RealSRSet, we only provide the visual results since there is no ground-truth (GT) image.

5.2 Experiments on Synthetic Data

Table 1 reports the average PSNR and SSIM of all the comparison methods on four benchmark datasets with the first simple synthesis setting. From it, we can easily find that the proposed KXNet is superior or at least comparable to

Table 2. Average PSNR/SSIM of all the comparing methods (**Setting 2**).

Method	Scale	Urban100 [17]		BSD100 [28]		Set14 [52]		Set5 [4]		Noise
		PSNR	SSIM	PSNR	SSIM	PSNR	SSIM	PSNR	SSIM	Level
Bicubic	x2	23.00	0.6656	25.85	0.6769	25.74	0.7085	27.68	0.8047	0
RCAN [59]		23.22	0.6791	26.03	0.6896	25.92	0.7217	27.85	0.8095	
IKC [14]		27.46	0.8401	29.85	0.8390	30.69	0.8614	33.99	0.9229	
DASR [43]		26.65	0.8106	28.84	0.7965	29.44	0.8224	32.50	0.8961	
DAN [25]		27.93	0.8497	30.09	0.8410	31.03	0.8647	34.40	0.9291	
KXNet (ours)		**28.33**	**0.8627**	**30.21**	**0.8456**	**31.14**	**0.8672**	**34.59**	**0.9315**	
Bicubic	x3	21.80	0.6084	24.68	0.6254	24.28	0.6546	25.78	0.7555	
RCAN [59]		21.38	0.6042	24.47	0.6299	24.07	0.6606	25.63	0.7572	
IKC [14]		25.36	0.7626	27.56	0.7475	28.19	0.7805	31.60	0.8853	
DASR [43]		25.20	0.7575	27.39	0.7379	27.96	0.7727	30.91	0.8723	
DAN [25]		25.82	0.7855	27.88	0.7603	28.69	0.7969	31.70	0.8940	
KXNet (ours)		**26.37**	**0.8035**	**28.15**	**0.7672**	**29.04**	**0.8036**	**32.53**	**0.9034**	
Bicubic	x4	20.88	0.5602	23.75	0.5827	23.17	0.6082	24.35	0.7086	
RCAN [59]		19.84	0.5307	23.10	0.5729	22.38	0.5967	23.72	0.6973	
IKC [14]		24.33	0.7241	26.49	0.6968	27.04	0.7398	29.60	0.8503	
DASR [43]		24.20	0.7150	26.43	0.6903	26.89	0.7306	29.53	0.8455	
DAN [25]		24.91	0.7491	26.92	0.7168	27.69	0.7600	30.53	0.8746	
KXNet (ours)		**25.30**	**0.7647**	**27.08**	**0.7221**	**27.98**	**0.7659**	**30.99**	**0.8815**	
Bicubic	x2	22.19	0.5159	24.44	0.5150	24.38	0.5497	25.72	0.6241	15
RCAN [59]		21.28	0.3884	22.98	0.3822	22.96	0.4155	23.76	0.4706	
IKC [14]		24.69	0.7208	26.49	0.6828	26.93	0.7244	29.21	0.8260	
DASR [43]		24.84	0.7273	26.63	0.6841	27.22	0.7283	29.44	0.8322	
DAN [25]		25.32	0.7447	26.84	0.6932	27.56	0.7392	29.91	0.8430	
KXNet(ours)		**25.45**	**0.7500**	**26.87**	**0.6959**	**27.59**	**0.7422**	**29.93**	**0.8449**	
Bicubic	x3	21.18	0.4891	23.55	0.4961	23.28	0.5289	24.42	0.6119	
RCAN [59]		20.22	0.3693	22.20	0.3726	21.99	0.4053	22.85	0.4745	
IKC [14]		24.21	0.7019	25.93	0.6564	26.42	0.7018	28.61	0.8135	
DASR [43]		23.93	0.6890	25.82	0.6484	26.27	0.6940	28.27	0.8047	
DAN [25]		24.17	0.7013	25.93	0.6551	26.46	0.7014	28.52	0.8130	
KXNet(ours)		**24.42**	**0.7135**	**25.99**	**0.6585**	**26.56**	**0.7063**	**28.64**	**0.8178**	
Bicubic	x4	20.38	0.4690	22.83	0.4841	22.39	0.5120	23.33	0.5977	
RCAN [59]		19.23	0.3515	21.47	0.3686	21.05	0.3960	21.77	0.4689	
IKC [14]		23.35	0.6665	25.21	0.6238	25.58	0.6712	27.45	0.7867	
DASR [43]		23.26	0.6620	25.20	0.6223	25.55	0.6683	27.32	0.7842	
DAN [25]		23.48	0.6742	25.25	0.6283	25.72	0.6760	27.55	0.7938	
KXNet (ours)		**23.67**	**0.6844**	**25.30**	**0.6296**	**25.78**	**0.6792**	**27.66**	**0.7977**	

other comparison methods under different scales. This is mainly attributed to its proper and full embedding of physical generation mechanism which finely helps the KXNet to be trained in the right direction.

Table 2 provides the quantitative comparison where testing sets are synthesized under the second complicated setting. Clearly, even in this hard case, our proposed KXNet still achieves the most competing performance and consistently outperforms other comparison methods on the four benchmark datasets with different SR scales. This comprehensively substantiates the generality of the proposed method and it potential usefulness in real-world scenarios.

Figure 4 visually displays the SR results on *img014* from Set14 and *img078* from Urban100 where the corresponding LR images are synthesized based on the second settings. As seen, almost all the blind comparison methods cannot finely reconstruct the image details. However, our KXNet achieves superior SR performance and the SR images contain more useful textures and sharper edges.

5.3 More Analysis and Verification

Number of Iterations for KXNet. To explore the effectiveness of KXNet, we investigate the effect of the number of iterations on the performance of KXNet. In Table 3, $S = 0$ means that the initialization $X^{(0)}$ and $K^{(0)}$ are directly used as the recovery result. Taking $S = 0$ as a baseline, we can clearly see that when $S = 5$, our method has been able to achieve a significant recovery performance which strongly validates the effectiveness of K-net and X-net. Beside, since larger stages would make gradient propagation more difficult, the case $S = 21$ has the same PSNR to the case $S = 19$. Thus, we set $S = 19$ for this work.

Non-Blind Super-Resolution. We provide ground truth (GT) kernel to verify the effectiveness of KXNet and other method on Set14 [52]. Providing blur kernel for KXNet and DAN, namely KXNet(GT kernel) and DAN(GT kernel), the PSNR of the results are 32.85 and 32.67, respectively. While the baseline KXNet with unknown blur kernel is 31.97. This means that when we provide X-net with an accurate blur kernel, the restoration accuracy can be further improved while illustrating the rationality and superiority of X-net for image restoration.

Stage Visualization. Owning to the full embedding of the physical generation mechanism, the proposed KXNet can facilitate us to easily understand the iterative process via stage visualization. As shown in Fig. 5(a), it presents the estimated SR images and the predicted blur kernel at different stages, where

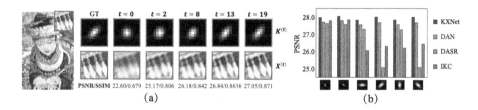

(a)   (b)

Fig. 5. (a) The estimated SR image and the extracted blur kernel at different iterative stages of KXNet. (b) Performance comparison under different blur kernel settings on Set14 [52] (scale = 4, noise = 0).

Table 3. Effect of stage number S on the performance of KXNet on Set14.

Stage No	S = 0	S = 5	S = 10	S = 17	S = 19	S = 21
PSNR	25.74	29.91	30.57	30.96	31.14	31.14
SSIM	0.7085	0.8400	0.8556	0.8631	0.8672	0.8665
Params (M)	-	1.72	3.42	5.82	6.50	7.18
Speed (seconds)	-	0.51	0.54	0.58	0.59	0.64

248   J. Fu et al.

the blur kernel is simply initialized as standard Gaussian kernel. Clearly, with the increasing of the iterative stages, the extracted blur kernel has a better and clearer pattern, which is getting closer to the GT kernel. Correspondingly, the SR image is gradually ameliorated and achieves higher PSNR/SSIM scores. This interpretable learning process is the inherent characteristic of the proposed KXNet which is finely guided by the mutual promotion between K-net and X-net.

Robustness to Blur Kernel. To comprehensively validate the effectiveness of the proposed method and its advantage over blur kernel extraction, we compare the SR performance of different methods on synthesized Set14 [52] with different blur kernel widths. As displayed in Fig. 5(b), as the structures of the testing blur kernels become more complex, the performance of most comparison methods has severely deteriorated. However, the proposed KXNet can consistently achieve the most competing PSNR scores and the fluctuation is very small. This result fully shows that our method has better robustness to the types of blur kernels and it has better potential to deal with general and real scenes.

5.4 Inference Speed

Based on Set5 under setting2 (scale = 2, noise = 0), we evaluate the inference time computed on an P100 GPU. For every image, the average testing time for IKC [14], DAN [25], and our proposed KXNet are shown in Table 4. Clearly, compared to these representative SOTA methods, our method has high inference speed and better computation efficiency, which is meaningful for real applications.

Table 4. Average inference speed of different methods on Set5.

Methods	IKC [14]	DAN [25]	KXNet
Times (s)	2.15	0.52	0.38

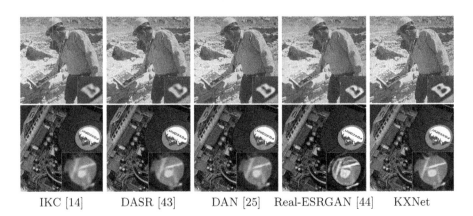

IKC [14]   DASR [43]   DAN [25]   Real-ESRGAN [44]   KXNet

Fig. 6. Visual comparison on RealSRSet with scale factor as 4.

5.5 Experiments on Real Images

We further evaluate the effectiveness of our method for real-world image restoration on RealSRSet [54]. As shown in Fig. 6, the proposed KXNet can recover clearer edges and generate more useful information.

6 Conclusion

In this paper, we have proposed an end-to-end blind super-resolution network for SISR, named as KXNet. In specific, we analyze the classical degradation process of low-resolution (LR) images and utilize the proximal gradient technique to derive an optimization algorithm. By unfolding the iterative steps into network modules, we easily construct the entire framework which is composed of K-net and X-net, and the explicit physical generation mechanism of blur kernels and high-resolution (HR) images are fully incorporated into the entire learning process. Besides, the proposed KXNet has better potential to finely extract different types of blur kernels which should be useful for other related tasks. All these advantages have been fully substantiated by comprehensive experiments executed on synthesized and real-world data under different degradation settings. This also finely validates the effectiveness and generality of the proposed KXNet.

Acknowledgment. This research was supported by NSFC project under contracts U21A6005, 61721002, U1811461, 62076196, The Major Key Project of PCL under contract PCL2021A12, and the Macao Science and Technology Development Fund under Grant 061/2020/A2.

References

1. Agustsson, E., Timofte, R.: NTIRE 2017 challenge on single image super-resolution: Dataset and study. In: Proceedings of the IEEE Conference on Computer Vision and Pattern Recognition Workshops, pp. 126–135 (2017)
2. Beck, A., Teboulle, M.: A fast iterative shrinkage-thresholding algorithm for linear inverse problems. SIAM J. Imag. Sci. **2**(1), 183–202 (2009)
3. Bell-Kligler, S., Shocher, A., Irani, M.: Blind super-resolution kernel estimation using an internal-GAN. Adv. Neural Inf. Process. Syst. **32**, 1–10 (2019)
4. Bevilacqua, M., Roumy, A., Guillemot, C., Alberi-Morel, M.L.: Low-complexity single-image super-resolution based on nonnegative neighbor embedding. In: Proceedings of the British Machine Vision Conference, pp. 135.1–135.10. BMVA press (2012)
5. Brifman, A., Romano, Y., Elad, M.: Unified single-image and video super-resolution via denoising algorithms. IEEE Trans. Image Process. **28**(12), 6063–6076 (2019)
6. Dai, S., Han, M., Xu, W., Wu, Y., Gong, Y., Katsaggelos, A.K.: SoftCuts: a soft edge smoothness prior for color image super-resolution. IEEE Trans. Image Process. **18**(5), 969–981 (2009)
7. Dong, C., Loy, C.C., He, K., Tang, X.: Image super-resolution using deep convolutional networks. IEEE Trans. Pattern Anal. Mach. Intell. **38**(2), 295–307 (2015)

8. Donoho, D.L.: De-noising by soft-thresholding. IEEE Trans. Inf. Theory **41**(3), 613–627 (1995)
9. Dumoulin, V., Visin, F.: A guide to convolution arithmetic for deep learning. arXiv preprint arXiv:1603.07285 (2016)
10. Efrat, N., Glasner, D., Apartsin, A., Nadler, B., Levin, A.: Accurate blur models vs. image priors in single image super-resolution. In: Proceedings of the IEEE International Conference on Computer Vision, pp. 2832–2839 (2013)
11. Elad, M., Feuer, A.: Restoration of a single superresolution image from several blurred, noisy, and undersampled measured images. IEEE Trans. Image Process. **6**(12), 1646–1658 (1997)
12. Farsiu, S., Robinson, D., Elad, M., Milanfar, P.: Advances and challenges in super-resolution. Int. J. Imaging Syst. Technol. **14**(2), 47–57 (2004)
13. Gregor, K., LeCun, Y.: Learning fast approximations of sparse coding. In: Proceedings of the 27th International Conference on International Conference on Machine Learning, pp. 399–406 (2010)
14. Gu, J., Lu, H., Zuo, W., Dong, C.: Blind super-resolution with iterative kernel correction. In: Proceedings of the IEEE/CVF Conference on Computer Vision and Pattern Recognition, pp. 1604–1613 (2019)
15. He, K., Zhang, X., Ren, S., Sun, J.: Deep residual learning for image recognition. In: Proceedings of the IEEE Conference on Computer Vision and Pattern Recognition, pp. 770–778 (2016)
16. Heide, F., et al.: Proximal: efficient image optimization using proximal algorithms. ACM Trans. Graph. (TOG) **35**(4), 1–15 (2016)
17. Huang, J.B., Singh, A., Ahuja, N.: Single image super-resolution from transformed self-exemplars. In: Proceedings of the IEEE Conference on Computer Vision and Pattern Recognition, pp. 5197–5206 (2015)
18. Ignatov, A., Kobyshev, N., Timofte, R., Vanhoey, K., Van Gool, L.: DSLR-quality photos on mobile devices with deep convolutional networks. In: Proceedings of the IEEE International Conference on Computer Vision, pp. 3277–3285 (2017)
19. Kim, J., Lee, J.K., Lee, K.M.: Deeply-recursive convolutional network for image super-resolution. In: Proceedings of the IEEE Conference on Computer Vision and Pattern Recognition, pp. 1637–1645 (2016)
20. Kingma, D.P., Ba, J.: ADAM: a method for stochastic optimization. arXiv preprint arXiv:1412.6980 (2014)
21. Lai, W.S., Huang, J.B., Ahuja, N., Yang, M.H.: Deep Laplacian pyramid networks for fast and accurate super-resolution. In: Proceedings of the IEEE Conference on Computer Vision and Pattern Recognition, pp. 624–632 (2017)
22. Liang, J., Cao, J., Sun, G., Zhang, K., Van Gool, L., Timofte, R.: SwinIR: Image restoration using Swin transformer. In: Proceedings of the IEEE/CVF International Conference on Computer Vision, pp. 1833–1844 (2021)
23. Liang, J., Zhang, K., Gu, S., Van Gool, L., Timofte, R.: Flow-based kernel prior with application to blind super-resolution. In: Proceedings of the IEEE/CVF Conference on Computer Vision and Pattern Recognition, pp. 10601–10610 (2021)
24. Lim, B., Son, S., Kim, H., Nah, S., Mu Lee, K.: Enhanced deep residual networks for single image super-resolution. In: Proceedings of the IEEE Conference on Computer Vision and Pattern Recognition Workshops, pp. 136–144 (2017)
25. Luo, Z., Huang, Y., Li, S., Wang, L., Tan, T.: Unfolding the alternating optimization for blind super resolution. Adv. Neural Inf. Process. Syst. (NeurIPS). **33**, 5632–5643 (2020)
26. Luo, Z., Huang, Y., Li, S., Wang, L., Tan, T.: End-to-end alternating optimization for blind super resolution. arXiv preprint arXiv:2105.06878 (2021)

27. Marquina, A., Osher, S.J.: Image super-resolution by TV-regularization and Breg-man iteration. J. Sci. Comput. **37**(3), 367–382 (2008)

28. Martin, D., Fowlkes, C., Tal, D., Malik, J.: A database of human segmented natural images and its application to evaluating segmentation algorithms and measuring ecological statistics. In: Proceedings Eighth IEEE International Conference on Computer Vision. ICCV 2001, vol. 2, pp. 416–423. IEEE (2001)

29. Matsui, Y., et al.: Sketch-based manga retrieval using manga109 dataset. Multimed. Tools App. **76**(20), 21811–21838 (2017)

30. Michaeli, T., Irani, M.: Nonparametric blind super-resolution. In: Proceedings of the IEEE International Conference on Computer Vision, pp. 945–952 (2013)

31. Niu, B., Wen, W., Ren, W., Zhang, X., Yang, L., Wang, S., Zhang, K., Cao, X., Shen, H.: Single image super-resolution via a holistic attention network. In: Vedaldi, A., Bischof, H., Brox, T., Frahm, J.-M. (eds.) ECCV 2020. LNCS, vol. 12357, pp. 191–207. Springer, Cham (2020). https://doi.org/10.1007/978-3-030-58610-2_12

32. Pan, J., Sun, D., Pfister, H., Yang, M.H.: Blind image deblurring using dark channel prior. In: Proceedings of the IEEE Conference on Computer Vision and Pattern Recognition, pp. 1628–1636 (2016)

33. Perrone, D., Favaro, P.: Total variation blind deconvolution: the devil is in the details. In: Proceedings of the IEEE Conference on Computer Vision and Pattern Recognition, pp. 2909–2916 (2014)

34. Ren, D., Zhang, K., Wang, Q., Hu, Q., Zuo, W.: Neural blind deconvolution using deep priors. In: Proceedings of the IEEE/CVF Conference on Computer Vision and Pattern Recognition, pp. 3341–3350 (2020)

35. Riegler, G., Schulter, S., Ruther, M., Bischof, H.: Conditioned regression models for non-blind single image super-resolution. In: Proceedings of the IEEE International Conference on Computer Vision, pp. 522–530 (2015)

36. Shi, W., et al.: Is the deconvolution layer the same as a convolutional layer? arXiv preprint arXiv:1609.07009 (2016)

37. Sun, L., Cho, S., Wang, J., Hays, J.: Edge-based blur kernel estimation using patch priors. In: IEEE International Conference on Computational Photography (ICCP), pp. 1–8. IEEE (2013)

38. Timofte, R., Agustsson, E., Van Gool, L., Yang, M.H., Zhang, L.: NTIRE 2017 challenge on single image super-resolution: methods and results. In: Proceedings of the IEEE Conference on Computer Vision and Pattern Recognition Workshops, pp. 114–125 (2017)

39. Wang, H., Li, Y., He, N., Ma, K., Meng, D., Zheng, Y.: DICDNet: deep interpretable convolutional dictionary network for metal artifact reduction in CT images. IEEE Trans. Med. Imaging **41**(4), 869–880 (2021)

40. Wang, H., et al.: InDuDoNet: an interpretable dual domain network for CT metal artifact reduction. In: de Bruijne, M., et al. (eds.) MICCAI 2021. LNCS, vol. 12906, pp. 107–118. Springer, Cham (2021). https://doi.org/10.1007/978-3-030-87231-1_11

41. Wang, H., Xie, Q., Zhao, Q., Liang, Y., Meng, D.: RCDNet: an interpretable rain convolutional dictionary network for single image deraining. arXiv preprint arXiv:2107.06808 (2021)

42. Wang, H., Xie, Q., Zhao, Q., Meng, D.: A model-driven deep neural network for single image rain removal. In: Proceedings of the IEEE/CVF Conference on Computer Vision and Pattern Recognition, pp. 3103–3112 (2020)

43. Wang, L., et al.: Unsupervised degradation representation learning for blind super-resolution. In: Proceedings of the IEEE/CVF Conference on Computer Vision and Pattern Recognition, pp. 10581–10590 (2021)

44. Wang, X., Xie, L., Dong, C., Shan, Y.: Real-ESRGAN: training real-world blind super-resolution with pure synthetic data. In: Proceedings of the IEEE/CVF International Conference on Computer Vision, pp. 1905–1914 (2021)
45. Wang, Z., Bovik, A.C., Sheikh, H.R., Simoncelli, E.P.: Image quality assessment: from error visibility to structural similarity. IEEE Trans. Image Process. **13**(4), 600–612 (2004)
46. Xie, Q., Zhou, M., Zhao, Q., Meng, D., Zuo, W., Xu, Z.: Multispectral and hyperspectral image fusion by MS/HS fusion net. In: Proceedings of the IEEE/CVF Conference on Computer Vision and Pattern Recognition, pp. 1585–1594 (2019)
47. Xie, Q., Zhou, M., Zhao, Q., Xu, Z., Meng, D.: MHF-Net: an interpretable deep network for multispectral and hyperspectral image fusion. IEEE Trans. Pattern Anal. Mach. Intell. (2020)
48. Xu, Y.S., Tseng, S.Y.R., Tseng, Y., Kuo, H.K., Tsai, Y.M.: Unified dynamic convolutional network for super-resolution with variational degradations. In: Proceedings of the IEEE/CVF Conference on Computer Vision and Pattern Recognition, pp. 12496–12505 (2020)
49. Yan, Y., Ren, W., Guo, Y., Wang, R., Cao, X.: Image deblurring via extreme channels prior. In: Proceedings of the IEEE Conference on Computer Vision and Pattern Recognition, pp. 4003–4011 (2017)
50. Yang, D., Sun, J.: Proximal dehaze-net: a prior learning-based deep network for single image dehazing. In: Ferrari, V., Hebert, M., Sminchisescu, C., Weiss, Y. (eds.) ECCV 2018. LNCS, vol. 11211, pp. 729–746. Springer, Cham (2018). https://doi.org/10.1007/978-3-030-01234-2_43
51. Yang, Y., Sun, J., Li, H., Xu, Z.: Deep ADMM-Net for compressive sensing MRI. In: Proceedings of the 30th International Conference on Neural Information Processing Systems, pp. 10–18 (2016)
52. Zeyde, R., Elad, M., Protter, M.: On single image scale-up using sparse-representations. In: Boissonnat, J.-D., et al. (eds.) Curves and Surfaces 2010. LNCS, vol. 6920, pp. 711–730. Springer, Heidelberg (2012). https://doi.org/10.1007/978-3-642-27413-8_47
53. Zhang, K., Gool, L.V., Timofte, R.: Deep unfolding network for image super-resolution. In: Proceedings of the IEEE/CVF Conference on Computer Vision and Pattern Recognition, pp. 3217–3226 (2020)
54. Zhang, K., Liang, J., Van Gool, L., Timofte, R.: Designing a practical degradation model for deep blind image super-resolution. In: Proceedings of the IEEE/CVF International Conference on Computer Vision, pp. 4791–4800 (2021)
55. Zhang, K., Zuo, W., Gu, S., Zhang, L.: Learning deep CNN denoiser prior for image restoration. In: Proceedings of the IEEE Conference on Computer Vision and Pattern Recognition, pp. 3929–3938 (2017)
56. Zhang, K., Zuo, W., Zhang, L.: FFDNet: toward a fast and flexible solution for CNN-based image denoising. IEEE Trans. Image Process. **27**(9), 4608–4622 (2018)
57. Zhang, K., Zuo, W., Zhang, L.: Learning a single convolutional super-resolution network for multiple degradations. In: Proceedings of the IEEE Conference on Computer Vision and Pattern Recognition, pp. 3262–3271 (2018)
58. Zhang, K., Zuo, W., Zhang, L.: Deep plug-and-play super-resolution for arbitrary blur kernels. In: Proceedings of the IEEE/CVF Conference on Computer Vision and Pattern Recognition, pp. 1671–1681 (2019)
59. Zhang, Y., Li, K., Li, K., Wang, L., Zhong, B., Fu, Y.: Image super-resolution using very deep residual channel attention networks. In: Ferrari, V., Hebert, M., Sminchisescu, C., Weiss, Y. (eds.) ECCV 2018. LNCS, vol. 11211, pp. 294–310. Springer, Cham (2018). https://doi.org/10.1007/978-3-030-01234-2_18

60. Zhang, Y., Tian, Y., Kong, Y., Zhong, B., Fu, Y.: Residual dense network for image super-resolution. In: Proceedings of the IEEE Conference on Computer Vision and Pattern Recognition, pp. 2472–2481 (2018)
61. Zhao, H., Gallo, O., Frosio, I., Kautz, J.: Loss functions for image restoration with neural networks. IEEE Trans. Comput. Imaging **3**(1), 47–57 (2016)

ARM: Any-Time Super-Resolution Method

Bohong Chen[1], Mingbao Lin[3], Kekai Sheng[3], Mengdan Zhang[3], Peixian Chen[3], Ke Li[3], Liujuan Cao[1(✉)], and Rongrong Ji[1,2,4]

[1] School of Informatics, Xiamen University, Xiamen, China
bhchen@stu.xmu.edu.cn, {caoliujuan,rrji}@xmu.edu.cn
[2] Institute of Artificial Intelligence, Xiamen University, Xiamen, China
[3] Tencent Youtu Lab., Shanghai, China
{saulsheng,davinazhang,peixianchen,tristanli}@tencent.com
[4] Institute of Energy Research, Jiangxi Academy of Sciences, Nanchang, China

Abstract. This paper proposes an Any-time super-Resolution Method (ARM) to tackle the over-parameterized single image super-resolution (SISR) models. Our ARM is motivated by three observations: (1) The performance of different image patches varies with SISR networks of different sizes. (2) There is a tradeoff between computation overhead and performance of the reconstructed image. (3) Given an input image, its edge information can be an effective option to estimate its PSNR. Subsequently, we train an ARM supernet containing SISR subnets of different sizes to deal with image patches of various complexity. To that effect, we construct an Edge-to-PSNR lookup table that maps the edge score of an image patch to the PSNR performance for each subnet, together with a set of computation costs for the subnets. In the inference, the image patches are individually distributed to different subnets for a better computation-performance tradeoff. Moreover, each SISR subnet shares weights of the ARM supernet, thus no extra parameters are introduced. The setting of multiple subnets can well adapt the computational cost of SISR model to the dynamically available hardware resources, allowing the SISR task to be in service at any time. Extensive experiments on resolution datasets of different sizes with popular SISR networks as backbones verify the effectiveness and the versatility of our ARM. The source code is available at https://github.com/chenbong/ARM-Net.

Keywords: Super-resolution · Dynamic network · Supernet

1 Introduction

Recent years have witnessed the rising popularity of convolutional neural networks (CNNs) in the classic single image super-resolution (SISR) task that

Supplementary Information The online version contains supplementary material available at https://doi.org/10.1007/978-3-031-19800-7_15.

S. Avidan et al. (Eds.): ECCV 2022, LNCS 13679, pp. 254–270, 2022.
https://doi.org/10.1007/978-3-031-19800-7_15

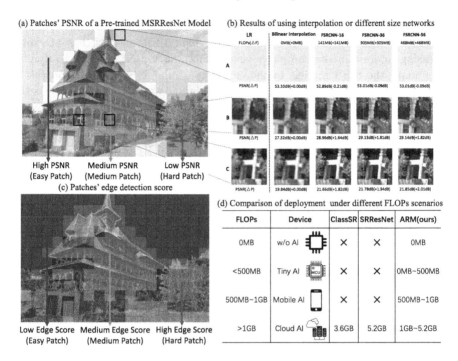

Fig. 1. Our observations in this paper. (a) Image patchs are categorized to three groups of "easy" (green), "moderate" (yellow) and "difficult" (red) according to their PSNR via a pre-trained MSRResNet [28]. (b) Three groups prefer different super-resolution procedures: The "easy" patch benefits from the simple interpolation, the "moderate" patch benefits from a medium-sized SISR model, while "difficult" patch benefits from a large-sized SISR model. (c) Visualization of edge information. (d) Using SRResNet as a backbone, our ARM can support arbitrary size of FLOPs overhead without retraining.

refers to constructing a high-resolution (HR) image from a given low-resolution (LR) version [5,16,20,24,36,37]. SISR has a wide application in daily life such as facial recognition on low-resolution images, real-time video upscaling resolution on mobile devices, video quality enhancement on televisions, *etc.*. For the sake of real-time experience, the SISR systems are required to be in service at any time. However, the platforms to conduct SISR task are featured with: (1) The memory storage and computation ability are very limited. (2) The configured resources vary across different hardware devices. (3) The availability of hardware resources on the same device even changes greatly over different times.

Unfortunately, newly developed SISR models tend to have more learnable parameters as well as more floating-point operations (FLOPs). For example, the earliest CNN-based SISR model, SRCNN [4], has only 3 convolutional layers with 57k parameters. Later, VDSR [13] increases the number of parameters to 2.5M. After that, RCAN [38] increases its parameters to over 15M. where a total of 66,015G FLOPs are required to process one single $1{,}920 \times 1{,}080$ image. Consequently, existing SISR models can be barely deployed on the resource-hungry platforms. Therefore, how to design an efficient SISR network has attracted increasing interest in the computer vision community. Besides, how to dynamically adapt the SISR models to the currently available hardware resources for a real-time deployment also arouses the community's wide attention. To this end, we investigate the computational redundancy in modern SISR networks and some observations are excavated as shown in Fig. 1.

First, we observe that the performance of different image patches varies with SISR networks of different sizes. In Fig. 1(a), we categorize the image patches into three categories of "easy" (green), "moderate" (yellow), and "difficult" (red) according to their PSNR scores from the pre-trained MSRResNet [28]. Generally, we observe a higher PSNR for an "easy" patch, and vice versa. Then, we randomly pick up one patch from each of the three categories and super-resolution them up with the bilinear interpolation and FSRCNN network [6] with different widths (i.e., the number of output channels) of 16/36/56. Visualization is shown in Fig. 1(b). We find that for "easy" patch, the bilinear interpolation leads to the best results while FSRCNN not only requires more computation, but degrades the performance. In contrast, a wider FSRCNN benefits the "hard" patch. This observation indicates that traditional SISR models suffer spatial redundancy from the input and it is necessary to deal with each patch based on its complexity for saving computation cost.

Second, for some image patches such as these from the "moderate" category, a medium-sized FSRCNN-36 can well complete the SR task while a larger FSRCNN-56 results in much heavier computation (+53% FLOPs) with a very limited performance gain (+0.01 PSNR). This observation indicates a trade-off between computation overhead and performance of the reconstructed image. How to maintain the performance with a smaller computation burden deserves studying. Finally, we find that "hard" patches often contain more edge information. To verify this, we perform edge detection [3,23] on each patch in Fig. 1 (c) and find a strong Spearman correlation coefficient between PSNR and negative edge score (see Fig. 4 **Left**). This observation implies that edge information can be an effective option to estimate PSNR of each patch with a cheaper computation cost since edge information can be obtained in an economical manner.

Inspired by the above observations, we propose an Any-time super-Resolution Method, referred to as ARM. Different from traditional CNNs-based SISR model with a fixed inference graph, our ARM dynamically selects different subnets for image super-resolution according to the complexity of input patches, and also dynamically adapts the computational overhead to the currently available hardware resources in inference. Specifically, we first use a backbone network as the supernet, and train several weight-shared subnets of different sizes within the supernet. The weight-sharing mechanism avoids introducing extra parameters, leading to a light-weight SISR supernet. Then, for each subnet, we construct an Edge-to-PSNR lookup table that maps the edge score of each patch to its estimated PSNR value. Finally, we propose to choose the subnet for reconstructing a HR image patch with a larger output of PSNR prediction but a smaller computation cost to reach a computation-performance tradeoff. We conduct extensive experiments on three large resolution datasets and results show that our ARM outperforms previous adaptive-based super-resolution ClassSR [15] with a computation-performance tradeoff. Moreover, comparing to ClassSR, with a better performance, our ARM reduces parameters by 78%, 54% and 52% when using FSRCNN [6], CARN [2], and SRResNet [16] as the supernet backbones.

Earlier studies [15,30] also explore the spatial redundancy of image patches in SISR networks. They set up multiple independent branches to handle patches with different complexity. However, these operations increase the model parameters and can not adapt to the available hardware resources since the inference graph is static for a fixed image patch. On the one hand, our ARM implements super-resolution in an economical manner since different image patches are fed to different small-size subnets of the supernet without introducing extra parameters. On the other hand, our ARM enables a fast subnet switch for inference once the available hardware resources change. The main difference between the proposed ARM and the previous approach is shown in Fig. 1 (d), where the proposed ARM can theoretically support arbitrary computational overhead without retraining. Thus the SISR task can be in service at any time.

2   Related Work

Interpolation-based SISR. Image interpolation is built on the assumption of image continuity. Usually, it uses nearby pixels to estimate unknown pixels in high-resolution images by a fixed interpolation algorithm. Classical interpolation algorithms include nearest neighbor interpolation, bilinear interpolation, bicubic interpolation and their variants [7,25]. The interpolation-based super-resolution benefits in cheap computation, but disadvantages in detail loss in the reconstructed images with complex textures.

Region-irrelevant CNNs-based SISR. SRCNN [4] is the first work to build a three-layer convolutional network for high-resolution image reconstruction. Since then, the successors [13,16,26] enhance the performance of SISR task by deepening the networks as well as introducing skip connections such as residual blocks and dense blocks. EDSR [20] reveals that the batch normalization (BN) layer destroys the scale information of the input images, which the super-resolution is sensitive to. Thus, it advocates removing BN layers in SISR task. The increasing model complexity also arouses the community to design light-weight SISR models [2,6,33]. TPSR [17] builds a network with the aid of network architecture search. Zhan *et al.* [37] combined NAS with parameter pruning to obtain a real-time SR model for mobile devices. Many researches [19,22,31] are indicated to representing the full-precision SISR models with a lower-bit format. Also, the knowledge distillation is often considered to strengthen the quality of reconstructed images from light-weight models [9,11,18,29] Overall, these CNN models for SISR are often region-irrelevant, that is, the computational graph is never being adjusted to adapt to the input images. On the contrary, our ARM picks up different subnets according to the complexity of input image patches, leading to a better tradeoff between model performance and computation.

Region-aware CNNs-based SISR. Recently, several works have realized the redundancy of input images on spatial regions in the SISR task. SMSR [27] introduces sparse masks upon spaces and channels within each block and then performs sparse convolution to reduce the computational burden. FAD [30] discovers that high-frequency regions contain more information and require a computationally intensive branch. It adds multiple convolutional branches of different sizes and each feature map region is fed to one branch according to its region frequency. ClassSR [15] classifies the image patches into three groups according to the patch difficulty. The image patches are respectively sent to the stand-alone trained backbone networks with different widths to realize super-resolution.

Despite the progress, the introductions of masks and additional network branches inevitably cause more parameters in these SISR models. Moreover, they fail to perform SISR task once the supportive hardware resources are insufficient. On the contrary, our ARM innovates in its subnet weights sharing with the supernet. Thus, no additional parameters are introduced. With multiple subnets, our SISR can well adapt to the hardware by a fast switch to perform the subnet capable of being run on the available resources.

Resource-aware Supernet. In order to achieve dynamic adjustment of computational overhead during inference, many studies [21,32,34,35] devise a supernet training paradigm with weight-shared subnets of multiple sizes. They uniformly sample different-size subnets for network training. Compared with these resource-aware supernet training methods, our proposed ARM follows a similar supernet training paradigm but differs in the subnet selection that considers a tradeoff between computation and performance.

3   Method

3.1   Preliminary

Our ARM network is a CNN-based SISR supernet $\mathcal{N}_{W[0:1.0]}$ with its weights denoted as $W[0:1.0]$, where 1.0 indicates a width multiplier of each convolutional layer. For example, a subnet can be represented as $\mathcal{N}_{W[0:0.5]}$ if its width of each convolutional layer is half of that in the supernet. By setting the width multiplier to different values, we can obtain a SISR subnet set $\{\mathcal{N}_{W[0:\alpha^j]}\}_{j=1}^{M}$ where $\alpha^j \in (0,1]$ is the width multiplier of the j-th subnet and M is the number of subnets. Note that, $W[0:\alpha^j]$ is a subset of $W[0:1.0]$, *i.e.*, $W[0:\alpha^j] \in W[0:1.0]$. Therefore, each SISR subnet shares parts of weights in the SISR supernet.

For the traditional SISR task, a training set $\{X,Y\}$ can be available in advance, where $X = \{x_i\}_{i=1...N}$ are the low-resolution (LR) images, $Y = \{y_i\}_{i=1...N}$ are the high-resolution (HR) images, and N is the number of training samples. Our goal in this paper is to optimize the overall performance of each subnet with LR images X as its inputs to fit the HR images Y. The formal optimization objective can be formulated as:

$$\min_{W} \sum_{j=1}^{M} \frac{1}{N} \|\mathcal{N}_{W[0:\alpha^j]}(X) - Y\|_1, \qquad (1)$$

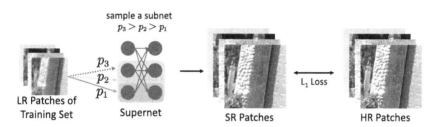

Fig. 2. Training of our ARM supernet. In each training iteration, one subnet is sampled to process a batch of low-resolution image patches with ℓ_1 loss.

where $\| \cdot \|_1$ denotes the commonly-used ℓ_1-norm in the SISR task[1]. Note that, to update the subnets is to update the supernet in essence since weights of each subnet are a subset of the supernet weights. Any existing SISR network can serve as the backbone of our supernet $\mathcal{N}_{W[0:1.0]}$. Figure 2 illustrates the training paradigm of our ARM supernet for an any-time SISR task. More details are given in the following context.

3.2 ARM Supernet Training

The optimization of Eq. (1) requires all subnets to involve in the network training, which causes a heavy training consumption. Instead, we propose to iteratively optimize each subnet based on a divide-and-conquer manner by performing optimization for a particular subnet $\mathcal{N}_{W[0:\alpha^j]}$ in each iteration. In this case, the suboptimization problem becomes:

$$\min_{W} \frac{1}{N'} \|\mathcal{N}_{W[0:\alpha^j]}(X') - Y'\|_1, \qquad (2)$$

where $X' = \{x'_i\}_{i=1...N'} \in X$ and $Y' = \{y_i\}_{i=1...N} \in Y$ are respectively the LR image batch and HR image batch in the current training iteration[2]. The rationale behind our divide-and-conquer optimization is that the overall objective is

---

[1] To stress the superiority of our method, we only consider ℓ_1-norm loss in this paper. Other training losses [8,12] for SISR can be combined to further enhance the results.

[2] In our supernet training, X' and Y' are indeed batches of local image patches from the X and Y. Details are given in Sect. 4.1. For brevity, herein we simply regard them as image batches.

minimized if and only if each stand-alone subnet in Eq. (1) is well optimized. Thus, we choose to decouple the overall objective and optimize individual subnets respectively, which also leads to the minimization of Eq. (1).

So far, the core of our supernet training becomes how to choose a subnet for optimization in each training iteration. Traditional supernet training in image classification tasks [34,35] usually adopts the uniform sampling where the subnets of different sizes are endowed with the same sampling probability. Though applicable well in the high-level classification, we find the sampling strategy could impair SISR task (see the numerical values in Sect. 4.4). Empirically, in the supernet training: i) smaller subnets tend to overfit the inputs and require less training, ii) larger subnets tend to underfit the inputs, therefore require more training. Consequently, we believe that the performance impairment of uniform subnet sampling is due to the different degree of training required by different size subnets.

Therefore, we propose a computation-aware subnet sampling method where subnets with heavier computation burden are endowed with a higher training priority. Concretely, the sampling probability of the j-th subnet is defined as:

$$p^j = \left(\frac{FLOPs(\mathcal{N}_{W[0:\alpha^j]})^2)}{\sum_{k=1}^{M} FLOPs(\mathcal{N}_{W[0:\alpha^k]})^2)} \right), \tag{3}$$

where $FLOPs(\cdot)$ calculates the FLOPs consumption of its input subnet.

To sum up, in the forward propagation, we sample a subnet with its probability of Eq. (3) to perform loss optimization of Eq. (2). In the backward propagation, we only update weights of the sampled subnet. Consequently, after training, we obtain a supernet $\mathcal{N}_{[0:1.0]}$ containing M high-performing subnets $\{\mathcal{N}_{W[0:\alpha^j]}\}_{j=1}^{M}$. It is a remarkable fact that our ARM supernet does not introduce additional parameterized modules for its weight-sharing mechanism. In addition to the ARM supernet, we have added an interpolation branch, i.e. using interpolation directly for super-resolution, denoted as a special subnet $\mathcal{N}_{W[0:\alpha^0]}$, where $\alpha^0 = 0$. This interpolation branch can be run on the device with very low computational performance, i.e., the "w/o AI" device in Fig. 1 (d). Thus the $M + 1$ subnets in our ARM supernet can be further expressed uniformly as $\{\mathcal{N}_{W[0:\alpha^j]}\}_{j=0}^{M}$. Besides, our ARM eliminates the spatial redundancy of the inputs by adapting the complexity of image patches to different subnets for a computationally economical inference, as detailed below.

3.3   ARM Supernet Inference

Figure 3 outlines the pipeline of our ARM supernet inference. In short, we first split a complete LR image into several local patches of the same size, and performs the edge detection on these LR patches to calculate their edge scores. Then, the PSNR performance of each patch is estimated by our pre-built Edge-to-PSNR lookup table. For each subnet, we further pre-calculate its computation cost, and propose to choose the subnet for SR inference with a larger

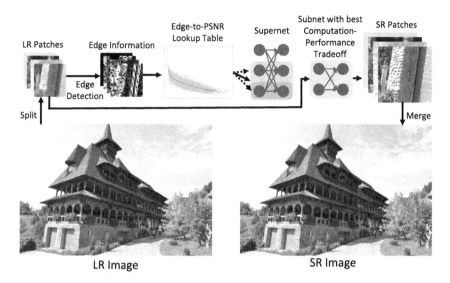

Fig. 3. Inference of our ARM supernet. We first detect the edge information of the local LR image patches, PSNR performance of which is then estimated by the pre-built Edge-to-PSNR lookup tables. The subnet with a best computation-performance tradeoff is then selected to construct HR version of the input LR image patches.

PSNR output but a smaller computation cost in order to pursue a computation-performance tradeoff. Finally, the SR patches are merged to recover the complete SR image.

Edge Score. Recall that in Sect. 1, we observe a strong correlation between the image edge and the PSNR performance, which is also verified in Fig. 4 **Left**. To measure the edge information, we first generate the edge patches using the laplacian edge detection operator [23] that allows observing the features of a patch for a significant change in the gray level. A large pixel value indicates richer edge information. Thus, we define the mean value of all pixels in a gray edge patch as the edge score to reflect the overall information in an edge patch.

Edge-to-PSNR Lookup Table. In contrast to a heavy network inference to derive the PSNR of each patch, the edge-psnr correlation inspires us to construct a set of Edge-to-PSNR lookup tables $T = \{t^j\}_{j=0}^{M}$ where the j-th lookup table t^j maps the patch's the edge score to the estimated PSNR performance for the corresponding subnet $\mathcal{N}_{W[0:\alpha^j]}$.

To be more specific, we first compute the edge score set for all the LR patches from the validation set of DIV2K [1], denoted as $E = \{e_i\}_{i=1}^{O}$ where e_i is the edge score of the i-th patch and O is the patch size. We split the edge score interval $[\min(E), \max(E)]$ equally into a total of K subintervals $S = \{s_k\}_{k=1}^{K}$, where $\min(\cdot)$ and $\max(\cdot)$ return the minimum and maximum of the input edge

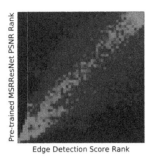 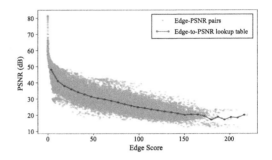

Fig. 4. Left: A strong Spearman correlation coefficient (0.85) between PSNR and negative edge score. **Right:** Edge-PSNR pairs and the Edge-to-PSNR lookup table.

score set. As a result, we know that the scope of the k-th subinterval falls into:

$$s_k = [\min(E) + \frac{\max(E) - \min(E)}{K} \cdot (k-1), \ \min(E) + \frac{\max(E) - \min(E)}{K} \cdot k].$$

After the supernet training, these LR patches are further fed to the trained subnet $\mathcal{N}_{W[0:\alpha^j]}$ to obtain their reconstructed HR patches. Then, the PSNR values between SR patches and HR patches are computed, denoted as $P^j = \{p_i^j\}_{i=1}^O$. Based on the subinterval splittings, we calculate the average PSNR within the k-th subinterval for the subnet $\mathcal{N}_{W[0:\alpha^j]}$ as:

$$\bar{p}_k^j = \frac{\sum_{i=1}^O \mathcal{I}(e_i \in s_k) \cdot p_i^j}{\sum_{i=1}^O \mathcal{I}(e_i \in s_k)}, \tag{4}$$

where $\mathcal{I}(\cdot)$ is an indicator which returns 1 if the input is true, and 0 otherwise.

Subsequently, our j-th Edge-to-PSNR lookup table t^j is defined as: $S \to \bar{P}^j = \{\bar{p}_k^j\}_{k=1}^K$. For an illustrative example, we use FSRCNN [6] as our supernet backbone and three subnets with $\alpha_1 = 0.29$, $\alpha_2 = 0.64$ and $\alpha_3 = 1.0$ are trained on DIV2K dataset [1]. In Fig. 4 **Right**, we plot the statistical results of the first subnet $\mathcal{N}_{W[0:\alpha_1]}$ including edge-psnr pairs of $\{(e_i, p_i^1)\}_{i=1}^O$ and Edge-to-PSNR lookup table t_1. Generally, our lookup table can well fit the distribution of edge-psnr pairs, thus it can be used to estimate the PSNR performance.

Computation-Performance Tradeoff. Given a new LR image patch during inference, we derive its edge score $\hat{e}$ first, and it is easy to know that this patch falls into the $\hat{k}$-th subinterval where $\hat{k} = \lfloor \frac{(\hat{e} - \min(E)) \cdot K}{\max(E) - \min(E)} + 1 \rfloor$, in which $\lfloor \cdot \rfloor$ is a floor function. With the pre-built lookup tables, we can easily obtain the estimated PSNR $\bar{p}_k^j$ for the subnet $\mathcal{N}_{W[0:\alpha^j]}$. It is natural to choose the subnet with the best predicted PSNR to reconstruct the HR version of a given LR image patch. In this case, the selected subnet index is: $\arg\max_j \bar{p}_k^j$.

However, our observation in Sect. 1 indicates a tradeoff between the computation and performance. A larger subnet may result in a slightly better performance, but a much heavier increase in computation. Given this, we further propose to take into consideration the computation burden of each subnet. To that effect, we further maintain a set of computation costs $C = \{c^j\}_{j=0}^M$ where c^j denotes the computation of the j-th subnet $\mathcal{N}_{W[0:\alpha_j]}$. Then, we propose a computation-performance tradeoff function based on the estimated PSNR performance as well as the computation cost c^j to pick up a subnet for SISR as:

$$\hat{j} = \arg\max_j \; \eta \cdot \bar{p}_{\hat{k}}^j - c^j, \tag{5}$$

where η is a hyper-parameter to balance the numerical difference between computation cost and PSNR estimation during inference stage. Its influence will be studied in supplementary materials. As result, the subnet $\mathcal{N}_{W[0:\alpha_{\hat{j}}]}$ is used to deal with the input patch. And we accomplish the goal to deal with each image patch according to its complexity, as observed in Sect. 1.

We would like to stress that the lookup tables $T = \{t^j\}_{j=0}^M$ and the computation cost set $C = \{c^j\}_{j=0}^M$ are built offline and once-for-all. In the online inference stage, the PSNR values of new image patches can be quickly fetched from the pre-built lookup tables according to their edge information which also can be quickly derived by off-the-shelf efficient edge detection operator [3,23]. Thus, our ARM supernet does not increase any computation burden for the SISR task. Moreover, the setting of multiple subnets within a supernet enables a fast subnet switch for inference once the available hardware resources change. Therefore, our ARM can be in service at any time.

4   Experiments

4.1   Settings

Training. Without loss of generality, we construct the ARM supernets on three typical types of SISR backbones of different sizes, including FSRCNN-56 [6] (small), CARN-64 [2] (medium), and SRResNet-64 [16] (large), where 56, 64, and 64 are the width of the corresponding supernets. We set three subnets in each supernet, and the width multipliers (α_j) of them are (0.29, 0.46, 1.0) for FSRCNN, (0.56, 0.81, 1.0) for CARN and SRResNet, which are the same model configurations of ClassSR [15] for fair comparison. Moreover, the images of the training set will be pre-processed into small patches in the same way as ClassSR [15] before our ARM supernet training. Also, the training set of DIV2K (index 0001–0800) [1] is used to train our ARM supernet. During training, the data augmentation includes random rotation and random flipping. The training process lasts 20 epochs with a batch size of 16. The ADAM optimizer [14] is applied with $\beta_1 = 0.9$ and $\beta_2 = 0.999$. The training costs for FSRCNN, CARN and SRResNet are 4, 22 and 24 GPU hours on a single NVIDIA V100 GPU, respectively. For more details, please refer to our code.

Benchmark and Evaluation Metric. We apply the Peak signal-to-noise ratio (PSNR) as the metric to evaluate SR performance of all methods on four test sets: F2K, Test2K, Test4K, and Test8K. F2K consists of the first 100 images (index 000001–000100) of Flickr2K [20] dataset. Test2K, Test4K, and Test8K datasets are constructed from DIV8K [10] following the previous work [15]. Other evaluation settings are also the same as the standard protocols in [15]. Unless otherwise stated, the FLOPs in this paper are calculated as the average FLOPs for all 32×32 LR patches with ×4 super-resolution across the whole test set.

4.2 Main Results

As listed in Tables 1 and 2, our ARM network achieves better results with less computation than the three SISR backbones. Overall, as we can observe in Fig. 5: compared to the backbones, the width of the ARM network can be dynamically adjusted to achieve the computation-performance tradeoff.

Table 1. The comparison of various methods and our ARM on F2K and Test2K.

Model	Params	F2K	FLOPs	Test2K	FLOPs
FSRCNN [6]	25K (100%)	27.91 (+0.00)	468M (100%)	25.61 (+0.00)	468M (100%)
ClassSR [15]	113K (452%)	27.93 (+0.02)	297M (63%)	25.61 (+0.00)	311M (66%)
ARM-L	25K (100%)	27.98 (+0.07)	380M (82%)	25.64 (+0.03)	366M (78%)
ARM-M		27.91 (+0.00)	276M (59%)	25.61 (+0.00)	289M (62%)
ARM-S		27.65 (−0.26)	184M (39%)	25.59 (−0.02)	245M (52%)
CARN [2]	295K (100%)	28.68 (+0.00)	1.15G (100%)	25.95 (+0.00)	1.15G (100%)
ClassSR [15]	645K (219%)	28.67 (−0.01)	766M (65%)	26.01 (+0.06)	841M (71%)
ARM-L	295K (100%)	28.76 (+0.08)	1046M (89%)	26.04 (+0.09)	945M (80%)
ARM-M		28.68 (+0.00)	819M (69%)	26.02 (+0.07)	831M (71%)
ARM-S		28.57 (−0.11)	676M (57%)	25.95 (+0.00)	645M (55%)
SRResNet [16]	1.5M (100%)	29.01 (+0.00)	5.20G (100%)	26.19 (+0.00)	5.20G (100%)
ClassSR [15]	3.1M (207%)	29.02 (+0.01)	3.43G (66%)	26.20 (+0.01)	3.62G (70%)
ARM-L	1.5M (100%)	29.03 (+0.02)	4.23G (81%)	26.21 (+0.02)	4.00G (77%)
ARM-M		29.01 (+0.00)	3.59G (69%)	26.20 (+0.01)	3.48G (67%)
ARM-S		28.97 (−0.04)	2.74G (53%)	26.18 (−0.01)	2.87G (55%)

Since our method is the most similar to ClassSR, for fair comparisons, our experimental settings are basically the same as ClassSR. The results verify that ARM achieves comparable or better results than ClassSR in most cases. On the three backbones, ARM outperforms ClassSR in terms of computation-performance tradeoff on both the Test2K and Test8K datasets. Figure 6 also indicate that our ARM can better reconstruct the HR images.

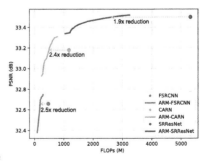

Fig. 5. ARM networks use the same parameters as the backbones, but offer adjustable computations and thus better FLOPs-PSNR tadeoffs.

Table 2. The comparison of various methods and our ARM on Test4K and Test8K.

Model	Params	Test4K	FLOPs	Test8K	FLOPs
FSRCNN [6]	25K (100%)	26.90 (+0.00)	468M (100%)	32.66 (+0.00)	468M (100%)
ClassSR [15]	113K (452%)	26.91 (+0.01)	286M (61%)	32.73 (+0.07)	238M (51%)
ARM-L	25K (100%)	26.93 (+0.03)	341M (73%)	32.75 (+0.09)	290M (62%)
ARM-M		26.90 (+0.00)	282M (60%)	32.73 (+0.07)	249M (53%)
ARM-S		26.87 (−0.03)	230M (50%)	32.66 (+0.00)	187M (40%)
CARN [2]	295K (100%)	27.34 (+0.00)	1.15G (100%)	33.18 (+0.00)	1.15G (100%)
ClassSR [15]	645K (219%)	27.42 (+0.08)	742M (64%)	33.24 (+0.06)	608M (53%)
ARM-L	295K (100%)	27.45 (+0.11)	825M (70%)	33.31 (+0.13)	784M (66%)
ARM-M		27.42 (+0.08)	743M (64%)	32.27 (+0.09)	612M (53%)
ARM-S		27.34 (+0.00)	593M (50%)	33.18 (+0.00)	489M (42%)
SRResNet [16]	1.5M (100%)	27.65 (+0.00)	5.20G (100%)	33.50 (+0.00)	5.20G (100%)
ClassSR [15]	3.1M (207%)	27.66 (+0.01)	3.30G (63%)	33.50 (+0.00)	2.70G (52%)
ARM-L	1.5M (100%)	27.66 (+0.01)	3.41G (66%)	33.52 (+0.02)	3.24G (62%)
ARM-M		27.65 (+0.00)	3.24G (62%)	33.50 (+0.00)	2.47G (48%)
ARM-S		27.63 (−0.02)	2.77G (53%)	33.46 (−0.04)	1.83G (35%)

4.3 Computation Cost Analysis

In the training phase, ARM differs from a normal backbone network only in the way the subnets of each batch are selected. Therefore, there is no additional computational and parameter storage overhead for training ARM networks. However, ClassSR has more parameters to be updated due to the higher number of parameters, thus incurring additional computational and parameter storage overheads. After the training, ARM needs to use the validation set of DIV2K (index 801–900) for inference to construct the Edge-to-PSNR lookup tables T, this step will incur additional inference overhead and CPT function storage parameters storage overhead. Luckily, since only forward and not backward gradient updates are required, this step is quick, taking only a few minutes, and it can be done offline only once. Actually, the Edge-to-PSNR lookup tables T take only $M \times K$ parameters, where M is the number of subnets of different widths and K is the number of subintervals (see Sect. 3.2). In this paper, we take $K = 30$. Thus for $M = 3$ subnets, only 90 additional parameters are needed, which is almost negligible compared to the large amount of parameters in the original network.

In the inference, the input patch needs to be edge detected. The FLOPs for edge detection are about 0.02M, which is also almost negligible compared to 468M FLOPs for FSRCNN, 1.15G FLOPs for CARN and 5.20G FLOPs for SRResNet. Thus, our inference is very efficient.

Fig. 6. Quantitative comparison of ARM networks with backbone networks, and SOTA dynamic SISR method [15] with ×4 super-resolution. These two examples are image "1294" (above) from Test2K and image "1321" (below) from Test4K, respectively. ARM produce a higher PSNR compared to backbone networks and SOTA methods.

4.4 Ablation Study

Edge-to-PSNR Lookup Tables. To verify the effectiveness of subnet selection via the Edge-to-PSNR lookup tables, we compared the computation-performance tradeoff of different strategies on the same pre-trained ARM-FSRCNN supernet: using the Edge-to-PSNR lookup tables, manually setting the edge score threshold, and using each size of subnet. For an ARM network with one interpolation branch and three different sizes networks, each patch has four choices and needs to be classified into four categories according to the edge score during inference. There are many optional strategies to divide the patches. For simplicity, we apply the most intuitive one by calculating the edge scores of all patches on the validation set of DIV2K and sorting them to obtain thresholds that allow the validation set to be averaged into four categories. The thresholds are then used in the test set. We also test the performance of different width subnets of the ARM supernet. As illustrated in Fig. 7 **Left**, the subnet selection with the Edge-to-PSNR lookup tables outperforms both the manual setting of thresholds (▲ in Fig. 7 **Left**) and the three separate subnets (♦ in Fig. 7 **Left**). The results

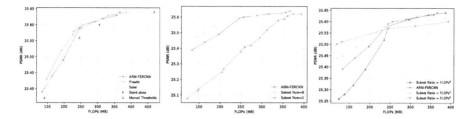

Fig. 7. Left: Effectiveness of lookup tables and several edge detection operators. **Middle:** Different numbers of subnets.**Right:** Various subnet sampling ratios.

ensure that using the Edge-to-PSNR lookup tables is indeed more effective in selecting subnets according to the specificity of the patch.

Edge Detection Operators. Recall that in Sect. 3.3, ARM use the edge detection operator to obtain the edge score of patches, and ARM uses the laplacian as the edge detection operator by default. Here, we conduct ablation experiments on the types of edge detection operators. Specifically, besides the default laplacian operator, we also tried the Sobel and Prewitt operators. The results are shown as Fig. 7. Different operators achieve good FLOPs-PSNR tradeoff, and it indicates that our ARM is robust to different edge detection operators.

The Number of Subnets. As shown in Fig. 7 **Middle**, a larger number of subnets results in a better tradeoff, especially under lower computation resources. Hence, setting the number of subnets to 3 is not optimal. However, for a fair comparison with ClassSR, we still set the number of subnets to 3.

Subnet Sampling. As we point out in Sect. 3.2, uniform sampling can lead to performance degradation. In the main experiment, the sampling probabilities of different sized subnets are set to be proportional to the n-th power of subnet FLOPs, which can be denoted as FLOPs^n: $p^j = \left(\frac{FLOPs(\mathcal{N}_{W_{[0:\alpha^j]}})^n}{\sum_{k=1}^{M} FLOPs(\mathcal{N}_{W_{[0:\alpha^k]}})^n} \right)$, where M is the number of subnets of different widths. The sampling probabilities of different sized subnets of ARM are set to FLOPs^2 by default. We experiment with different sampling ratios such as FLOPs^0, *a.k.a.* uniform sampling, FLOPs^1, FLOPs^2 and so on. The results are shown in Fig. 7 **Right**. When using uniform sampling, the smaller networks are entitled with enough chances to be selected for training. Then the performance under smaller FLOPs will be better, but the performance at larger FLOPs is degraded. As the sampling probability of large subnets gradually increases, *e.g.*, FLOPs^1, FLOPs^2 and FLOPs^3 in Fig. 7 **Right**, the performance at large FLOPs gradually improves. On the contrary, the performance at small FLOPs gradually decreases. In our experiments, we focus more on the performance of the ARM at larger FLOPs. As shown in Fig. 7 **Right**, FLOPs^3 has limited performance improvement over FLOPs^2 on large FLOPs, but much lower performance on small FLOPs. Thus, in this paper, we set the sampling probability of the subnets to FLOPs^2 by default.

5   Conclusion

In this paper, we introduce an ARM supernet method towards any-time super-resolution. Several weight-shared subnets are trained separately to deal with images patches of different complexities for saving computation cost. We observe that the edge information can be an effective option to estimate the PSNR performance of an image patch. Subsequently, we build an Edge-to-PSNR lookup table for each subnet to pursue a fast performance estimation. On the basis of lookup tables, we further propose a computation-performance tradeoff function to pick up a subnet for constructing a HR version of the given LR image patch. This leads to a supreme performance of our ARM in SISR task, as well as significant reduction on computation cost.

Acknowledgments. This work was supported by the National Science Fund for Distinguished Young Scholars (No. 62025603), the National Natural Science Foundation of China (No. U21B2037, No. 62176222, No. 62176223, No. 62176226, No. 62072386, No. 62072387, No. 62072389, and No. 62002305), Guangdong Basic and Applied Basic Research Foundation (No. 2019B1515120049), and the Natural Science Foundation of Fujian Province of China (No. 2021J01002).

References

1. Agustsson, E., Timofte, R.: Ntire 2017 challenge on single image super-resolution: Dataset and study. In: Proceedings of the IEEE/CVF Conference on Computer Vision and Pattern Recognition Workshops (CVPRW), pp. 1122–1131 (2017)
2. Ahn, N., Kang, B., Sohn, K.-A.: Fast, accurate, and lightweight super-resolution with cascading residual network. In: Ferrari, V., Hebert, M., Sminchisescu, C., Weiss, Y. (eds.) ECCV 2018. LNCS, vol. 11214, pp. 256–272. Springer, Cham (2018). https://doi.org/10.1007/978-3-030-01249-6_16
3. Canny, J.: A computational approach to edge detection. IEEE Trans. Pattern Anal. Mach. Intell. (TPAMI). **6**, 679–698 (1986)
4. Dong, C., Loy, C.C., He, K., Tang, X.: Image super-resolution using deep convolutional networks. IEEE Trans. Pattern Anal. Mach. Intell. (TPAMI). **38**, 295–307 (2015)
5. Dong, C., Loy, C.C., He, K., Tang, X.: Image super-resolution using deep convolutional networks. IEEE Trans. Pattern Anal. Mach. Intell. (TPAMI). **38**, 295–307 (2016)
6. Dong, C., Loy, C.C., Tang, X.: Accelerating the super-resolution convolutional neural network. In: Leibe, B., Matas, J., Sebe, N., Welling, M. (eds.) ECCV 2016. LNCS, vol. 9906, pp. 391–407. Springer, Cham (2016). https://doi.org/10.1007/978-3-319-46475-6_25
7. Fekri, F., Mersereau, R.M., Schafer, R.W.: A generalized interpolative VQ method for jointly optimal quantization and interpolation of images. In: Proceedings of the IEEE International Conference on Acoustics, Speech and SP (ICASSP), vol. 5, pp. 2657–2660 (1998)
8. Fuoli, D., Van Gool, L., Timofte, R.: Fourier space losses for efficient perceptual image super-resolution. In: Proceedings of the IEEE/CVF International Conference on Computer Vision (ICCV), pp. 2360–2369 (2021)

9. Gao, Q., Zhao, Y., Li, G., Tong, T.: Image super-resolution using knowledge distillation. In: Proceedings of the Asian Conference on Computer Vision (ACCV), pp. 527–541 (2018)

10. Gu, S., Lugmayr, A., Danelljan, M., Fritsche, M., Lamour, J., Timofte, R.: Div8k: diverse 8k resolution image dataset. In: Proceedings of the IEEE/CVF International Conference on Computer Vision Workshops (ICCVW), pp. 3512–3516 (2019)

11. He, Z., Dai, T., Lu, J., Jiang, Y., Xia, S.T.: FAKD: Feature-affinity based knowledge distillation for efficient image super-resolution. In: Proceedings of the International Conference on Image Processing (ICIP), pp. 518–522 (2020)

12. Johnson, J., Alahi, A., Fei-Fei, L.: Perceptual losses for real-time style transfer and super-resolution. In: Leibe, B., Matas, J., Sebe, N., Welling, M. (eds.) ECCV 2016. LNCS, vol. 9906, pp. 694–711. Springer, Cham (2016). https://doi.org/10.1007/978-3-319-46475-6_43

13. Kim, J., Lee, J.K., Lee, K.M.: Accurate image super-resolution using very deep convolutional networks. In: Proceedings of the IEEE/CVF Conference on Computer Vision and Pattern Recognition (CVPR), pp. 1646–1654 (2016)

14. Kingma, D.P., Ba, J.: Adam: a method for stochastic optimization. In: Proceedings of the International Conference on Learning Representations (ICLR) (2015)

15. Kong, X., Zhao, H., Qiao, Y., Dong, C.: Classsr: A general framework to accelerate super-resolution networks by data characteristic. In: Proceedings of the IEEE/CVF International Conference on Computer Vision (ICCV), pp. 12016–12025 (2021)

16. Ledig, C., et al.: Photo-realistic single image super-resolution using a generative adversarial network. In: Proceedings of the IEEE/CVF Conference on Computer Vision and Pattern Recognition (CVPR), pp. 4681–4690 (2017)

17. Lee, R., et al.: Journey towards tiny perceptual super-resolution. In: Vedaldi, A., Bischof, H., Brox, T., Frahm, J.-M. (eds.) ECCV 2020. LNCS, vol. 12371, pp. 85–102. Springer, Cham (2020). https://doi.org/10.1007/978-3-030-58574-7_6

18. Lee, W., Lee, J., Kim, D., Ham, B.: Learning with privileged information for efficient image super-resolution. In: Vedaldi, A., Bischof, H., Brox, T., Frahm, J.-M. (eds.) ECCV 2020. LNCS, vol. 12369, pp. 465–482. Springer, Cham (2020). https://doi.org/10.1007/978-3-030-58586-0_28

19. Li, H., et al.: PAMS: quantized super-resolution via parameterized max scale. In: Vedaldi, A., Bischof, H., Brox, T., Frahm, J.-M. (eds.) ECCV 2020. LNCS, vol. 12370, pp. 564–580. Springer, Cham (2020). https://doi.org/10.1007/978-3-030-58595-2_34

20. Lim, B., Son, S., Kim, H., Nah, S., Mu Lee, K.: Enhanced deep residual networks for single image super-resolution. In: Proceedings of the IEEE/CVF Conference on Computer Vision and Pattern Recognition Workshops (CVPRW), pp. 136–144 (2017)

21. Lou, W., Xun, L., Sabet, A., Bi, J., Hare, J., Merrett, G.V.: Dynamic-OFA: Runtime DNN architecture switching for performance scaling on heterogeneous embedded platforms. In: Proceedings of the IEEE/CVF Conference on Computer Vision and Pattern Recognition (CVPR), pp. 3110–3118 (2021)

22. Ma, Y., Xiong, H., Hu, Z., Ma, L.: Efficient super resolution using binarized neural network. In: Proceedings of the IEEE/CVF Conference on Computer Vision and Pattern Recognition Workshops (CVPRW) (2019)

23. Marr, D., Hildreth, E.: Theory of edge detection. Proc. R. Soc. London Ser. B. **207**, 187–217 (1980)

24. Song, D., Wang, Y., Chen, H., Xu, C., Xu, C., Tao, D.: AdderSR: towards energy efficient image super-resolution. In: Proceedings of the IEEE/CVF Conference on Computer Vision and Pattern Recognition (CVPR), pp. 15648–15657 (2021)

25. Thurnhofer, S., Mitra, S.K.: Edge-enhanced image zooming. Opt. Eng. **35**, 1862–1870 (1996)

26. Tong, T., Li, G., Liu, X., Gao, Q.: Image super-resolution using dense skip connections. In: Proceedings of the IEEE/CVF International Conference on Computer Vision (ICCV), pp. 4799–4807 (2017)

27. Wang, L., et al.: Exploring sparsity in image super-resolution for efficient inference. In: Proceedings of the IEEE/CVF Conference on Computer Vision and Pattern Recognition (CVPR), pp. 4917–4926 (2021)

28. Wang, X., Yu, K., Dong, C., Loy, C.C.: Recovering realistic texture in image super-resolution by deep spatial feature transform. In: Proceedings of the IEEE/CVF Conference on Computer Vision and Pattern Recognition (CVPR), pp. 606–615 (2018)

29. Wang, Y., et al.: Towards compact single image super-resolution via contrastive self-distillation. In: Proceedings of the International Joint Conference on Artificial Intelligence (IJCAI) (2021)

30. Xie, W., Song, D., Xu, C., Xu, C., Zhang, H., Wang, Y.: Learning frequency-aware dynamic network for efficient super-resolution. In: Proceedings of the IEEE/CVF International Conference on Computer Vision (ICCV), pp. 4308–4317 (2021)

31. Xin, J., Wang, N., Jiang, X., Li, J., Huang, H., Gao, X.: Binarized neural network for single image super resolution. In: Vedaldi, A., Bischof, H., Brox, T., Frahm, J.-M. (eds.) ECCV 2020. LNCS, vol. 12349, pp. 91–107. Springer, Cham (2020). https://doi.org/10.1007/978-3-030-58548-8_6

32. Yang, T., et al.: MutualNet: Adaptive convnet via mutual learning from different model configurations. IEEE Trans. Pattern Anal. Machine Intell. (TPAMI) (2021)

33. Yu, J., et al.: Wide activation for efficient and accurate image super-resolution. In: Proceedings of the IEEE/CVF Conference on Computer Vision and Pattern Recognition (CVPR) (2018)

34. Yu, J., Huang, T.S.: Universally slimmable networks and improved training techniques. In: Proceedings of the IEEE/CVF International Conference on Computer Vision (ICCV), pp. 1803–1811 (2019)

35. Yu, J., Yang, L., Xu, N., Yang, J., Huang, T.: Slimmable neural networks. In: Proceedings of the International Conference on Learning Representations (ICLR) (2019)

36. Yu, K., Wang, X., Dong, C., Tang, X., Loy, C.C.: Path-restore: learning network path selection for image restoration. IEEE Trans. Pattern Anal. Mach. Intell. (TPAMI) (2021)

37. Zhan, Z., et al.: Achieving on-mobile real-time super-resolution with neural architecture and pruning search. In: Proceedings of the IEEE/CVF International Conference on Computer Vision (ICCV), pp. 4821–4831 (2021)

38. Zhang, Y., Li, K., Li, K., Wang, L., Zhong, B., Fu, Y.: Image super-resolution using very deep residual channel attention networks. In: Ferrari, V., Hebert, M., Sminchisescu, C., Weiss, Y. (eds.) ECCV 2018. LNCS, vol. 11211, pp. 294–310. Springer, Cham (2018). https://doi.org/10.1007/978-3-030-01234-2_18

Attention-Aware Learning for Hyperparameter Prediction in Image Processing Pipelines

Haina Qin[1,2], Longfei Han[3], Juan Wang[1], Congxuan Zhang[4], Yanwei Li[5], Bing Li[1,2(✉)], and Weiming Hu[1,2]

[1] NLPR, Institute of Automation, Chinese Academy of Sciences, Beijing, China
{qinhaina2020,jun_wang}@ia.ac.cn,
{bli,wmhu}@nlpr.ia.ac.cn
[2] School of Artificial Intelligence, University of Chinese Academy of Sciences, Beijing, China
[3] Beijing Technology and Business University, Beijing, China
longfeihan@btbu.edu.cn
[4] Nanchang Hangkong University, Nanchang, China
[5] Zeku Technology, Shanghai, China

Abstract. Between the imaging sensor and the image applications, the hardware image signal processing (ISP) pipelines reconstruct an RGB image from the sensor signal and feed it into downstream tasks. The processing blocks in ISPs depend on a set of tunable hyperparameters that have a complex interaction with the output. Manual setting by image experts is the traditional way of hyperparameter tuning, which is time-consuming and biased towards human perception. Recently, ISP has been optimized by the feedback of the downstream tasks based on different optimization algorithms. Unfortunately, these methods should keep parameters fixed during the inference stage for arbitrary input without considering that each image should have specific parameters based on its feature. To this end, we propose an attention-aware learning method that integrates the parameter prediction network into ISP tuning and utilizes the multi-attention mechanism to generate the attentive mapping between the input RAW image and the parameter space. The proposed method integrates downstream tasks end-to-end, predicting specific parameters for each image. We validate the proposed method on object detection, image segmentation, and human viewing tasks.

Keywords: ISP · Hyperparameter prediction

1 Introduction

Hardware ISPs are low-level image processing pipelines that convert RAW sensor data into images suitable for human viewing and downstream tasks. Hardware

---

Supplementary Information The online version contains supplementary material available at https://doi.org/10.1007/978-3-031-19800-7_16.

ISPs introduce several processing blocks that are less programmable and operate efficiently at real-time applications [8,43]. ISPs are widely used in a variety of devices like cameras [3], smartphones, self-driving vehicles, and surveillance [30].

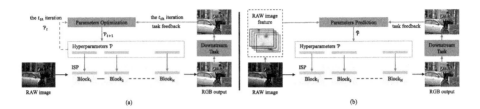

Fig. 1. Illustrations of different ISP tuning methods. (a) Previous methods leverage a mapping between the parameter space and high-level evaluation metrics based on differentiable approximations or hardware ISP. (b) Our proposed framework firstly constructs an attention-aware prediction network between RAW sensor data and parameter space, and then follows the previous work to create the mapping function between the parameter space and high-level evaluation metrics

Existing processing blocks in hardware ISPs are configurable and sensitive with a set of user-tunable hyperparameters. These hyperparameters affect not only the output images but also the downstream tasks [13,31]. It is important and still challenging to find optimal ISP hyperparameters for different specific tasks. In general, the industries rely on image experts to manually tune the parameters on a small typical dataset [1]. This artificial process is time-consuming and biased toward human perception, and especially hard to subjectively find task-specific optimal hyperparameters for various downstream tasks, such as object detection and image segmentation [38,39].

Hence, the potential of automated loss-based ISP hyperparameter optimization [35,40] comes into sight. A full grid search is not an alternative way due to the large parameter space. Instead, several recent works reproduce the entire ISP transformation with software approximations [17,20], then implement derivative-free methods [27] or gradient methods based on differentiable approximation [15,33,36]. These methods leverage a relationship between high-level evaluation metrics and the parameter space but ignore the mapping from the input RAW images to the parameter space. In addition, some methods try to directly optimize the hardware ISP with evolution strategy [11] in an end-to-end way [26]. They chose reasonably reduced search spaces and let the evolutionary algorithms do the exploration. However, during the inference stage, these methods should set fixed hyperparameters tuned in the training stage, which leads to being eclectic, not discriminative for a wide variety of input images.

In this work, we tune the ISP based on the statistical relationship among the input image, the parameter space, and the high-level evaluation metrics of downstream tasks. The optimal ISP settings should have high relevance with raw sensor data (low-level pixel-wise information [23], such as texture, exposure) and the scenario of downstream tasks (high-level semantic information, such as object location and object categories [9]). So we decouple the ISP pipelines into two modules: attention-aware prediction network and differentiable proxy network. The first module aims to construct a mapping function from RAW sensor data to parameters space, and the second one tries to reveal the relationship between the parameter space and high-level evaluation metrics, as shown in Fig. 1.

To construct a mapping function from RAW sensor data to parameters space, we propose an attention-aware prediction network for ISP hyperparameter prediction, which is able to learn the natural information from the RAW low-level feature through Parameter Prediction Path. Further on, it is important to attach weights [24] to specific locations, which makes different hyperparameters distinctively contribute to the input image. Hence, we introduce a multi-scale attention mechanism, named Multi-Attention Path, into the parameter prediction path, which aims to better represent the discrimination of different processing blocks. Multi-attention path enables the network exchange and aggregates the multi-scale information, and highlights the activation map for each hyperparameter of ISP by adaptively selecting multi-scale features. Meanwhile, to reveal the relationship between the parameter space and high-level evaluation metrics, we use a differentiable proxy network to mimic hardware ISP and use the output of the proxy network as the input for downstream tasks.

In our proposed framework, two differentiable networks, attention-aware prediction network and differentiable proxy network based on fully convolutional network(FCN) [36], are constructed and optimized end-to-end by using feedback from the high-level downstream task, and the predicted parameters of ISP are task-specific. We validate the proposed method in a variety of applications, including object detection, image segmentation, and human viewing. For these applications, we demonstrate that our method has better results compared with manual tuning methods and existing numerical optimization methods.

The contributions of this paper can be summarized as follows:

- We propose a novel framework for hyperparameter prediction in ISP that directly infers parameters based on RAW images while integrating downstream tasks in an end-to-end manner. For inference, our method can give distinctive results for each image suitable to the downstream task.
- We introduce a Multi-Attention structure for the parameter prediction network. It enables the network exchange and aggregate the multi-scale information, and highlight the activation map for hyperparameter of ISP.
- We validate the effectiveness of ISP hyperparameter prediction on 2D object detection, image segmentation, and human observation tasks. In these applications, our method approach outperforms existing numerical optimization methods and expert tuning.

Limitations: In the objective evaluation, such as object detection and image segmentation, the performance of the proposed method is compared with recent existing methods based on synthetic ISPs. However, the synthetic ISPs used have similar processing pipelines but not exactly the same. Further on, the subjective evaluation is compared with expert tuning methods, which bias towards human visual perception. Therefore, it is important to build a standard Synthetic ISP and standard subjective evaluation metrics. We believe that the release of relevant standard modules will be critical for future works on ISP tuning.

2   Related Work

There are several image processing components in the ISP pipelines. In traditional ISP, a specific algorithm is developed for each associated ISP component. Such a divide-and-conquer strategy decomposes the complex ISP design problem into many sub-tasks. These sub-problems are always formed by tens to hundreds of handcrafted parameters and tuned towards to perception of imaging experts.

Recently, to tackle this challenging optimization problem, several automatic ISP tuning methods optimize the hyperparameters with downstream task feedback [4,5,44]. The impact of ISP hyperparameter on the performance of a downstream task is well explored in [2,7,39,41]. Tseng *et al.* [36] optimizes ISP for object detection and classification using IoU. Mosleh *el al.* [26] utilizes object detection and object segmentation with mAP and PQ. Wu *et al.* [38] optimizes a simple ISP with an object detection task.

With the high-level feedback information, recent works always leverage a differentiable mapping between the parameter space and high-level evaluation metrics. Some existing optimization methods explore the optimal parameters from reasonably large reduced search spaces via an implicit end-to-end loss. For instance, Pfister *et al.* [29] proposes to optimize sparsity regularization for denoising. Nishimura *et al.* [27] optimizes software ISP model with a 0-th order Nelder-Mead method. However, it can only be used to optimize one ISP component at a time. Mosleh *et al.* [26,32] directly optimizes hardware ISP by a novel CMA-ES strategy [12] with max-rank-based multi-objective scalarization and initial search space reduction. Robidoux *et al.* The other methods try to reproduce the entire ISP transformation with a CNN-based differentiable proxy [10,15,42]. For instance, Tseng *et al.* [36] trained an approximate CNN proxy model to mimic hardware ISP and optimized the differentiable CNN model with Stochastic Gradient Descent. Kim *et al.* [19] utilize the objective function of multi-output regression for modeling the relation between ISP parameter and IQM score. Onzon *et al.* [28] propose a neural network for exposure selection that is jointly end-to-end with an object detector and ISP pipeline. However, these methods should set fixed hyperparameters during the inference, which lack diversity and discrimination for various input RAW images.

Therefore, we believe that ISP tuning should require more knowledge to reveal the relationship among the raw image, parameter space, and the high-level evaluation metrics. The difference between our approach and the others is that we both construct an attention-aware prediction network and the differentiable proxy network. We not only train an ISP proxy to approximate the entire ISP as a RAW-to-output RGB image transfer function, but we also construct the parameter prediction network to explicitly joint optimized the trainable ISP with the downstream vision tasks.

3   Image Processing Pipelines

ISPs are low-level pipelines composed of many processing stages, generally converting RAW sensor pixels into human-viewing images. We briefly review the most common ISP modules and their associated parameters. The ISP whose parameters are optimized in this paper contains the following typical stages [6]:

(1) Optics and Sensor: The scene radiation is focused on the sensor through an assembly of lenses. The color filter array on the camera filters the light into three sensor-specific RGB primaries, and the RAW pixel output of the sensor is linearly related to the irradiance falling on the sensor.

(2) Noise Reduction: Denoising is applied after the A/D conversion, which is done by blurring the image. Blurring will reduce noise but also remove details.

(3) DigitalGain and White Balance: After removing the black level bias and correcting defective pixels, the imaging sensor signal is amplified and digitized. The pixel values are color-corrected and gain-adjusted according to the white-balance matrices for common or automatically estimated illuminations.

(4) Demosaicking: Convert the color filter array over pixel sensors to RGB values for each pixel by performing interpolation.

(5) Color Space Transform: Map the white-balanced raw-RGB values to CIE XYZ using a 3×3 color space transform matrix, where CIE XYZ is a canonical color space definition.

(6) Sharpening: Compensate the outline of the image, enhance the edges and the part of the grayscale jump, make the image details enhanced.

(7) Color and Tone Correction: This is the stage to improve overall image appearance, including applying gamma curves and adjusting image contrast by histogram operations.

(8) Compression: Pixels values compressed to JPEG and storage.

Our ISP model f_{ISP} takes RAW Pixel values as input and models stages (2) to (8). This ISP converts the RAW image $\mathbf{I}$ into an RGB image $\mathbf{O}_{\mathrm{ISP}}$.

$$\mathbf{O}_{\mathrm{ISP}} = f_{\mathrm{ISP}}(\mathbf{I}; \mathcal{P}), \ \mathcal{P} \in \mathbb{R}_{[0,1]}^{N} \tag{1}$$

where $\mathbf{I} \in \mathbb{R}^{W \times H}$, $\mathbf{O}_{\mathrm{ISP}} \in \mathbb{R}^{W \times H \times 3}$. The conversion is modulated by the values of N continuous hyperparameters $\mathcal{P}$ with a range of values normalized to $[0, 1]$. For the discrete parameters in ISP, mapping them to continuous values within the range of values facilitates prediction [26].

4   Method

4.1   Framework

For a RAW image $\mathbf{I}$ from an imaging sensor, our aim is to predict N parameters $\mathcal{P} = \{p_1, p_2, \ldots, p_N\}$ for the target ISP. The original image $\mathbf{I}$ generates an RGB output image $\mathbf{O}_{\mathrm{ISP}} = f_{\mathrm{ISP}}(\mathbf{I}; \mathcal{P})$ after the ISP processing under the parameter

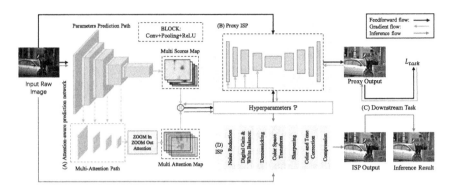

Fig. 2. Proposed attention-aware Learning framework and proxy architecture. (a) Attention-aware prediction network, each block consists of 3×3 conv, max pooling, and ReLU unit ; (b) Training ISP differentiable CNN proxy for mimic the hardware ISP; (c) Fixing learned parameters of the CNN-based ISP and the downstream task model, and optimizing input parameters itself given a high-level loss function. (d) Runtime execution using Hardware ISP architecture with predicted parameters

$\mathcal{P}$ setting, and $\mathbf{O}_{\mathrm{ISP}}$ is used as the RGB image input for the downstream task. In this paper, we focus on downstream tasks that conform to human viewing preferences and visual analysis tasks.

Our approach is to learn an approximation function $\hat{\mathcal{P}} = f_{\mathrm{pred}}(\mathbf{I}; \mathbf{W})$ that directly utilizes the raw sensor data to predict the parameter $\mathcal{P}$, where $\mathbf{W}$ denotes the trainable weights. Then we utilize the feedback from the downstream task, making $\mathbf{O}_{\mathrm{ISP}} = f_{\mathrm{ISP}}(\mathbf{I}; \hat{\mathcal{P}})$ favorable for it. The performance of f_{pred} is determined by the parameters $\mathbf{W}$ of the network, and then $\mathbf{W}$ is learned by minimizing the high-level loss function.

$$L_{\mathrm{task}}(\mathbf{O}_{\mathrm{ISP}}) = L_{\mathrm{task}}(f_{\mathrm{ISP}}(\mathbf{I}; \hat{\mathcal{P}})) = L_{\mathrm{task}}(f_{\mathrm{ISP}}(\mathbf{I}; f_{\mathrm{pred}}(\mathbf{I}; \mathbf{W}))) \qquad (2)$$

where L_{task} is defined as the loss function for the downstream task, e.g., $\mathcal{L}_2$ loss with the reference image is used for conforming to human viewing preferences, and loss with a combination of classification and location regression is used for the object detection task. Since ISPs are non-differentiable black-box units, in order to utilize feedback from downstream tasks for parameter prediction network, a differentiable proxy network [36] based on FCN is built. The black-box ISPs are modeled as shown in Eq. 1. The proxy ISP $f_{\mathrm{PROXY}}(\mathbf{I}, \mathcal{P}; \mathbf{W}_{\mathrm{proxy}})$ consists of an fully connected network, taking $\mathbf{I}$ and hyperparameters $\mathcal{P}$ as inputs, and $\mathbf{W}_{\mathrm{proxy}}$ as f_{PROXY} learnable CNN weights. The proxy should achieve such a goal: $\mathbf{O}_{\mathrm{PROXY}} \approx \mathbf{O}_{\mathrm{ISP}}$. The optimal weights $\mathcal{W}^*_{\mathrm{proxy}}$ are optimized by minimizing the loss function and then froze for training the prediction network:

$$L_{\mathrm{proxy}} = ||f_{\mathrm{PROXY}}(\mathbf{I}, \mathcal{P}; \mathbf{W}_{\mathrm{proxy}}) - f_{\mathrm{ISP}}(\mathbf{I}; \mathcal{P})||. \qquad (3)$$

After f_{pred} predicts the parameters $\hat{\mathcal{P}}$ of $\mathbf{I}$, $\hat{\mathcal{P}}$ with $\mathbf{I}$ are fed to the proxy ISP f_{PROXY} to produce an output image which is used as input for the downstream task. Since the proxy function f_{PROXY} is differentiable for $\mathbf{W}$, we can achieve an end-to-end learning process to jointly optimize the whole framework. The process of optimizing $\mathbf{W}$ on M images can be performed on the parameter prediction network f_{pred} and FCN-based proxy network using the supervised information from downstream tasks.

$$\mathbf{W}^*_{\text{task}} = \underset{\{\mathbf{W}\}}{argmin} \sum_{i=1}^{M} L_{\text{task}}(f_{\text{PROXY}}(\mathbf{I}_i, f_{\text{pred}}(\mathbf{I}_i; \mathbf{W}); \mathbf{W}^*_{\text{proxy}})). \qquad (4)$$

In the inference stage, the parameter prediction network f_{pred} can estimate the optimal parameters $\mathcal{P}^*_{\text{task}}$ for the downstream task based on the raw data $\mathbf{I}$.

$$\mathcal{P}^*_{\text{task}} = f_{\text{pred}}(\mathbf{I}; \mathbf{W}^*_{\text{task}}). \qquad (5)$$

Further on, aiming to discriminate the effects of the parameters on input images, we design a novel structure based on a multi-scale attention structure. Figure 2 illustrates our network structure.

4.2   Attention-aware Parameter Prediction Network

Parameter Prediction Path. The semantic information contained in the RAW Image largely determines the parameter fetching, so we design a parameter prediction network that generates a prediction path with multiple encoders to implement the encoding from the RAW Image to the target parameters, which is illustrated in Fig. 2. For the input Bayer array, we split the input data into three channels with RGB values respectively. Then, the formatted input is fed into a fully convolutional neural network. Followed by several convolutional blocks, the spatial resolution of the feature map is smaller than the size of the input RAW Image, and the number of channels is the number N of parameters $\mathcal{P}$. The output feature maps are finally passed to a weighted pooling layer for local-to-global aggregation:

$$p_i = \sum_{j=1}^{m} c_i(R_j)g_i(R_j), \ i = 1, \ldots, N \qquad (6)$$

where $\mathcal{R} = \{R_1, R_2, \ldots, R_m\}$ is a set of overlapping perceptual field regions of the original image $\mathbf{I}$, m is the number of R. Meanwhile, different local regions will generate different local parameter prediction $g_i(R_j)$ because they have different semantic information. The $c_i(R_j)$ represents the degree of attention of the parameter p_i for the local region R_j, which will be expressed in detail in Multi-Attention Path.

For predicting the value $g_i(R_j)$ of the parameter p_i on the local region R, we utilize five encoders for extracting the higher-level features from the image. In Parameter Prediction Path, different local regions in the image are progressively abstracted into high-level representations. Each encoder contains a 3×3 convolution followed by a ReLU unit and a 2×2 maximum pooling operation for span-2 downsampling. During each encoder, the number of feature channels is doubled. Subsequent convolution kernels with $1 \times 1 \times N$ are used to downsample the feature maps while generating parameter estimation maps for N channels.

Multi-Attention Path. We believe that the parameter prediction network should highly focus on the semantically informative parts while ignoring the semantically ambiguous regions on the input image. For this purpose, we added the attention path to the network, shown in Eq. 6. For the specific local region R, the value of the function $c_i(R)$ will reflect the effectiveness of the parameter p_i to the image region R. If the semantic information on R is informative for the setting of the parameter p_i, the value of $c_i(R)$ will be large, which will make the prediction p_i on R, $g_i(R)$ have a greater influence.

Since different parameters p of ISP processing blocks have different functions, the attentive regions are not the same for different p. Here, we combine the multi-scale features from the parameter prediction path to generate Multi-level attention, and Fig. 2 shows the structure. Specifically, we add one channel to each encoder. The feature maps on these five channels are named Multi-Level features $\{F_1, F_2, F_3, F_4, F_5\}$, which contains different levels of semantic information of the input image. Then, we introduce a zoom-in-zoom-out attention module, which utilizes interpolation (UpSampling) and max-pooling (DownSampling) operations to keep the same size as F_3, and concatenates the feature maps separately. Finally, the multi-scale features are downsampled twice, and undergo convolution of 3×3 and 1×1xN to generate the Multi-Attention Path. The size is the same as the size of the parameter prediction path outputs, and the number of channels for both maps is the number of parameters N. The i_{th} channel are corresponding to the parameter p_i.

The prediction path $G(R)$ generates the following set of parameter predictions, which correspond to local regions R for different parameters p:

$$G(R) = \{g_1(R), g_2(R), \ldots g_N(R)\} \tag{7}$$

At the same time, the multi-attention path $C(R)$ can predict the attention of the local region R_j for different parameters p:

$$C(R) = \{c_1(R), c_2(R), \ldots c_N(R)\} \tag{8}$$

Finally, as in the Eq. 6, the results of the parameter prediction path and multi-attention path are integrated to generate the global prediction results for all parameters. In this process, each parameter can automatically select and fuse the attention at different levels to obtain targeted regions.

5   Experiments

5.1   Settings

We validate the proposed ISP hyperparameter prediction method on the following downstream tasks and datasets:

(1) 2D object detection using [31] on MS COCO [22]. Using a synthetic (simulated) ISP processing simulated RAW as the upstream module for the

Fig. 3. Image understanding evaluation: Object Detection on COCO (left), Image Segmentation on COCO (right). Default ISP hyperparameters (top), expert-tuned hyperparameters (middle), and our method (bottom). Our prediction achieve better performance for downstream tasks

task. The processing blocks of the ISP are described in Sect. 3 with 20 ISP hyperparameters.

(2) Instance segmentation using [13] on COCO, which has the same ISP settings as the 2D object detection task.

(3) Perceptual image quality for human viewing. The dataset was collected by SONY IMX766 CMOS sensor. The reference images are obtained by Qualcomm Spectra 580 ISP processing, with 32 expert-tuned ISP hyperparameters. The synthetic ISP processing 4096×3072 RAW data from the sensor is the upstream module for the task.

In the training stage, the RAW image is the input to the model and generates the corresponding predicted hyperparameters. The predicted parameters and the RAW image are used as input to the proxy ISP, which later outputs the RGB image. The proxy ISP has fixed network weights as described in Sect. 4.1. We train the parameter prediction network from scratch using the loss of the downstream task and the RMSprop optimizer. For the object detection and image segmentation tasks, we use the loss with a combination of classification and location regression; for the human viewing optimization task, we use the $\mathcal{L}_2$ loss between the RGB output and the reference image. The learning rate is initially set to 10^{-4} and reduced to 10^{-6} after 200 epochs. The training was performed for 400 epochs. More details of the training procedure are described in the supplementary material.

In the evaluation stage, we use the RAW image from the test set as model input to predict the hyperparameters for each RAW image. The RAW image and hyperparameter pairs are processed into the ISP to obtain the RGB output.

For the object detection and image segmentation tasks, the RGB outputs are used as input, and the evaluation metric uses mean average precision(mAP) [22]. The PSNR and SSIM between the RGB outputs and the corresponding reference images are used as evaluation metrics for the human viewing optimization task.

5.2 ISP Hyperparameter Prediction for Object Detection

Table 1. Synthetic ISP optimization for Object Detection on COCO. It is important to point out that our ISP has similar processing pipelines compared with the ISPs used in other methods. So we borrow the results from [26]

	ISP Model	$mAP_{0.5}$	$mAP_{0.75}$	$mAP_{0.5:0.95}$
Default Parameters	Synthetic ISP [26]	0.15	–	–
blockwise-tuned for Object Detection		0.20	–	–
Expert-tuned for Image Quality		0.35	–	–
Hardware-tuned for Object Detection		0.39	–	–
Default Parameters	Synthetic ISP Sec. 3	0.34	0.22	0.21
Expert-tuned for Image Quality		0.56	0.40	0.37
Predicted Parameters (Ours)		**0.61**	**0.44**	**0.41**

In this task, we use an existing sRGB dataset and a synthetic ISP to evaluate our hyperparametric prediction method. Since the input of the ISP is RAW data, we processed sRGB images with RAW data simulation [18]. For the task of object detection using [31] on the MS COCO dataset [22], we trained and tested our hyperparameters prediction results. The results in Table 1 demonstrate that our method has a greater improvement in the default parameters than the recent methods and has the best final results. While the images produced by our expert-tuned ISP are more consistent with human perception (see Fig. 3), the images produced by our predicted parameters result in better performance for object detection tasks. These images have emphasized texture details and color features that are more in line with the preferences of the object detection compared to the expert-tuned images.

5.3 ISP Hyperparameter Prediction for Image Segmentation

For the image segmentation task, we trained the prediction network end-to-end with [13] a downstream task and validated the results on synthetic ISP and simulated RAW COCO datasets. The results in Table 2 are shown that our method has more significant improvement than other methods, and better final results, especially better than the default parameters(baseline), Fig. 3 demonstrates an example of our method with default parameters and expert-tuned parameters for instance segmentation. It can be seen that our predicted parameters can adjust

Table 2. Synthetic ISP optimization for Image Segmentation on COCO. It is important to point out that our ISP has similar processing pipelines compared with the ISPs used in other methods. So we borrow the results from [26]

	ISP Model	$mAP_{0.5}$	$mAP_{0.75}$	$mAP_{0.5:0.95}$
Default Parameters	Synthetic ISP [26]	0.12	–	–
Expert-tuned for Image Quality		0.26	–	–
Hardware-tuned for Segmentation		0.32	–	–
Default Parameters	Synthetic ISP Sec. 3	0.22	0.13	0.12
Expert-tuned for Image Quality		0.46	0.28	0.27
Predicted Parameters (Ours)		**0.52**	**0.33**	**0.31**

the texture and color of the image to match the preferences of the image segmentation task. The parameters predicted by our model for each image achieve an improvement of 0.3 $mAP_{0.5}$ compared to the default parameters. Also, compared to the imaging experts tuned parameters for the task, the parameters predicted by our model can achieve a $mAP_{0.5}$ improvement of 0.1.

5.4   ISP Hyperparameter Prediction for Human Viewing

Fig. 4. Comparison of Expert-tuned hyperparameters and our method. These images are processed by a synthetic ISP described in Sect. 3 to match the image quality of the reference images generated by the Qualcomm Spectra580 ISP

Unlike visual analysis tasks, subjective image quality is an attribute that describes a preference for a particular image rendering [25]. This particular image rendering should consider the visibility of the distortions in an image, such as colour shifts, blurriness, noise, and blockiness [34]. Our goal is to predict the hyperparameters on the synthetic ISP corresponding to the RAW image such that the distance between the output of the synthetic ISP and the reference image is minimized.

In this task, we train the hyperparameter prediction network using the $\mathcal{L}_2$ distance between the RGB output and the reference image as the loss function described in the previous section. The proposed method predicts the hyperparameters of the synthetic ISP corresponding to the RAW image. We collected a new dataset for training and testing the performance of the proposed method on this task. To sufficiently validate the model, this dataset contains images from 108 different scenes. The RAW image is acquired by the IMX766 sensor, and the corresponding reference image is generated by the Spectra 580 ISP, where the hyperparameters of the ISP are set manually by our imaging experts. We compared with the expert-tuned synthetic ISP output and the default hyperparameter settings, and the results are shown in Fig. 5 (a). Compared with the expert-tuned parameters, we have better PSNR and SSIM results between the reference image and the RGB output produced by the predicted parameters. This indicates that our predicted parameters are more consistent with human preferences. Figure 4 shows our results on the human viewing task. It can be seen that our predicted parameters produce images with clearer texture details, better noise control, and human-adapted color features than the expert-tuned.

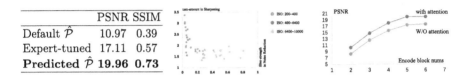

	PSNR	SSIM
Default $\hat{\mathcal{P}}$	10.97	0.39
Expert-tuned	17.11	0.57
Predicted $\hat{\mathcal{P}}$	**19.96**	**0.73**

Fig. 5. (a)Left: ISP tuning for Perceptual image quality using expert-tuned and the proposed methods. (b)Middle: The scatter plot of the predicted hyperparameters on different ISO ranges. (c)Right: The PSNR perfomance versus the number of encoding blocks on the human viewing dataset

5.5 Ablation Study

Parameter Prediction Path. In general, the industries rely on image experts to manually tune the parameters on a small typical dataset. The automatic ISP methods set fixed hyperparameters tuned with downstream tasks in an end-to-end way. In contrast, the proposed method can predict specific parameters for each input image. We verify that this prediction method for RAW images has better results than fixed parameters in this ablation study.

To demonstrate the diversity of the predicted parameters across images, we chose several images based on different ISO ranges and plot scatter plots with two parameters in the Noise Reduction module and the Sharpening module, as shown in Fig. 5 (b). It shows that our method can self-adaptively optimize the parameters on different lighting conditions. For noisy images in low light conditions (high ISO), the predicted parameter is preferred to increase the noise reduction level (filter strength) on the BM3D module. The results in Fig. 5 (a) show that distinctive prediction parameters provide better performance than fixed expert-tuned parameters. We also evaluate the performance and efficiency

Table 3. Ablation study of evaluate the visual analysis results based on fixed parameters and diverse predicted parameters. And effectiveness analysis on proposed multi-attention path. The first column is the results for object detection, and the second is the results for image segmentation

	Detection			Segmentation		
	mAP 0.5	mAP 0.75	mAP 0.5:0.95	mAP 0.5	mAP 0.75	mAP 0.5:0.95
Predicted $\hat{\mathcal{P}}$ (Fixed)	0.57	0.40	0.38	0.48	0.29	0.27
Predicted $\hat{\mathcal{P}}$ (W/O Attention)	0.57	0.41	0.38	0.47	0.30	0.28
Predicted $\hat{\mathcal{P}}$ (Single Attention)	0.58	0.43	0.40	0.50	0.31	0.30
Predicted $\hat{\mathcal{P}}$ (Self-attention [37])	0.57	0.42	0.38	0.48	0.30	0.28
Diverse Predicted $\hat{\mathcal{P}}$ (Ours)	**0.61**	**0.44**	**0.41**	**0.52**	**0.33**	**0.31**

of our network architecture design. We test the network performance by changing the number of encoding blocks on the human viewing dataset. On this basis we further validate our attention module, shown in Fig. 5 (c). Meanwhile, compared with the previous methods [26,35] which required hundreds of loops in the ISP tuning process, our method is more efficient, a 4096×3072 RAW image with a 2x down-sample can be processed in 0.5s by our method (on an NVIDIA RTX3090) and 129.39 GFLOPS.

Also, we selected 300 representative images from the COCO [22] training set and predict parameters by the proposed method. The mode of the discrete predicted parameters and the mean of the continuous parameters as the fixed hyperparameters, and fed into the synthetic ISP with the corresponding raw image to generate sRGB output for detection and segmentation tasks. Table 3 demonstrate the value of diverse parameters for different images; averaging and fixing the diverse parameters is a compromise process. It is important and challenging to find optimal ISP hyperparameters for specific tasks.

Multi-Attention Path. In Multi-Attention Path, the scoring map for each parameter is multiplied by its corresponding attention map. The prediction results reflect the distinctive contributions of image patches to multi-target parameters. Figure 6 shows the attention maps created by our feature attention-based network. The Sharpening module (second row, prediction $\hat{\mathcal{P}}_1$) does not significantly affect texture-flat areas so that the attention map activates the features in texture-rich areas in the image. The Noise Reduction module (third row, prediction $\hat{\mathcal{P}}_2$) is prone to remove noise in the background areas so that the background with details in the image are activated via the attention map. For $\hat{\mathcal{P}}_N$ (bottom row) in the WB module, a wider range of color features are activated as reference areas for color prediction.

To verify the effectiveness of multi-attention, we replace the Multi-attention Path with Single-Attention Path (the same attention map is used for all parameters predictions). We also test the results by removing the attention path and only using Parameters Prediction Path for parameter prediction. It can be seen from Table 3 that the methods with attention path have better performance than those without attention module. The results indicate that it is a benefit for learning the mapping between the raw input image and the parameter space by

284 H. Qin et al.

highlighting high-value image regions. Meanwhile, the performance of uniform single-attention for multi parameters is not well performed than Multi-Attention scheme, which indicates that the effectiveness of the proposed multi-attention path. In addition, in contrast to existing common designs, the attention structure is specifically designed for ISP parameters prediction tasks, highlighting different image details for various parameters predictions. To compare the multi-attention structure with other common designs, we replace the multi-attention structure by combining Parameters Prediction Path with Self-attention [37]. Experimental results show that the multi-attention structure that can combine features at different scales and generate attention maps is more suitable for ISP hyperparameters prediction tasks and better performance.

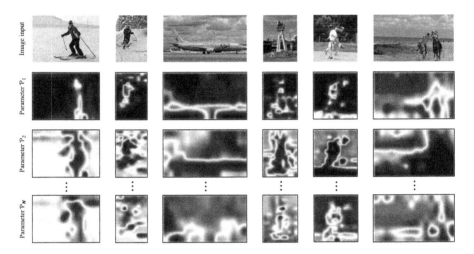

Fig. 6. Examples of attention map outputs by our network. It shows three attention maps corresponding to different parameters for each image. $\hat{\mathcal{P}}_1$ is in the sharpening module, $\hat{\mathcal{P}}_2$ is in the noise reduction module, and $\hat{\mathcal{P}}_N$ is in the WB module

6 Conclusions and Future Work

In this paper, we propose a novel ISP tuning framework named attention-aware learning for hyperparameter prediction, compared with the existing CNN methods to simulate commercial ISPs, our method try to mimic the expert-tuning procedure via predicting the parameters for all ISP modules. It simultaneously constructs the mapping functions between RAW input & parameter space and the parameter space & high-level metrics. Considering that different hyperparameters make a distinctive contribution to the input image, we design a novel multi-attention structure for jointly predicting the hyperparamter. Experimental results demonstrate that the proposed method can improve the performance of models.

The presented method needs to predict the hyperparameters directly while the ISP processes the image and maintains the efficiency of ISP. The efficiency of the proposed method is a crucial issue for deployment to ISPs for application. The next step is to make the model lightweight through algorithms compression and acceleration, including pruning policy [14,21] and quantization policy [16], can be an avenue of future research. Running the method efficiently on ISPs is one of our future works.

Acknowledgments. This work was supported by the National Key Research and Development Program of China (Grant No. 2020AAA0105802), the Natural Science Foundation of China (Grant No. 62036011,62192782, 61721004,62122086, 61906192, U1936204), the Key Research Program of Frontier Sciences, CAS, Grant No. QYZDJ-SSW-JSC040, Beijing Natural Science Foundation (No. 4222003).

References

1. IEEE standard for camera phone image quality. IEEE Std 1858–2016 (Incorporating IEEE Std 1858–2016/Cor 1–2017), pp. 1–146 (2017). https://doi.org/10.1109/IEEESTD.2017.7921676
2. Bardenet, R., Brendel, M., Kégl, B., Sebag, M.: Collaborative hyperparameter tuning. In: International conference on machine learning, pp. 199–207 (2013)
3. van Beek, P., Wu, C.T.R., Chaudhury, B., Gardos, T.R.: Boosting computer vision performance by enhancing camera ISP. Electronic Imaging **2021**(17), 1–174 (2021)
4. Bergstra, J., Bardenet, R., Bengio, Y., Kégl, B.: Algorithms for hyper-parameter optimization. In: Advances in Neural Information Processing Systems 24 (2011)
5. Bergstra, J., Yamins, D., Cox, D.: Making a science of model search: hyperparameter optimization in hundreds of dimensions for vision architectures. In: International Conference on Machine Learning, pp. 115–123 (2013)
6. Brown, M.S., Kim, S.: Understanding the in-camera image processing pipeline for computer vision. In: IEEE International Conference on Computer Vision, vol. 3 (2019)
7. Buckler, M., Jayasuriya, S., Sampson, A.: Reconfiguring the imaging pipeline for computer vision. In: Proceedings of the IEEE International Conference on Computer Vision, pp. 975–984 (2017)
8. Cao, Y., Wu, X., Qi, S., Liu, X., Wu, Z., Zuo, W.: Pseudo-ISP: learning pseudo in-camera signal processing pipeline from a color image denoiser. arXiv preprint arXiv:2103.10234 (2021)
9. Carion, N., Massa, F., Synnaeve, G., Usunier, N., Kirillov, A., Zagoruyko, S.: End-to-end object detection with transformers. In: Vedaldi, A., Bischof, H., Brox, T., Frahm, J.-M. (eds.) ECCV 2020. LNCS, vol. 12346, pp. 213–229. Springer, Cham (2020). https://doi.org/10.1007/978-3-030-58452-8_13
10. Chen, C., Chen, Q., Xu, J., Koltun, V.: Learning to see in the dark. In: Proceedings of the IEEE Conference on Computer Vision and Pattern Recognition, pp. 3291–3300 (2018)
11. Cheung, E.C., Wong, J., Chan, J., Pan, J.: Optimization-based automatic parameter tuning for stereo vision. In: 2015 IEEE International Conference on Automation Science and Engineering (CASE), pp. 855–861 (2015)

12. Hansen, N., Müller, S.D., Koumoutsakos, P.: Reducing the time complexity of the derandomized evolution strategy with covariance matrix adaptation (CMA-ES). Evol. Comput. **11**(1), 1–18 (2003)
13. He, K., Gkioxari, G., Dollár, P., Girshick, R.: Mask R-CNN. In: Proceedings of the IEEE international conference on computer vision, pp. 2961–2969 (2017)
14. He, Y., Zhang, X., Sun, J.: Channel pruning for accelerating very deep neural networks. In: Proceedings of the IEEE International Conference on Computer Vision, pp. 1389–1397 (2017)
15. Ignatov, A., Van Gool, L., Timofte, R.: Replacing mobile camera ISP with a single deep learning model. In: Proceedings of the IEEE/CVF Conference on Computer Vision and Pattern Recognition Workshops, pp. 536–537 (2020)
16. Jacob, B., et al.: Quantization and training of neural networks for efficient integer-arithmetic-only inference. In: Proceedings of the IEEE Conference on Computer Vision and Pattern Recognition, pp. 2704–2713 (2018)
17. Karaimer, H.C., Brown, M.S.: A software platform for manipulating the camera imaging pipeline. In: Leibe, B., Matas, J., Sebe, N., Welling, M. (eds.) ECCV 2016. LNCS, vol. 9905, pp. 429–444. Springer, Cham (2016). https://doi.org/10.1007/978-3-319-46448-0_26
18. Kim, S.J., Lin, H.T., Lu, Z., Süsstrunk, S., Lin, S., Brown, M.S.: A new in-camera imaging model for color computer vision and its application. IEEE Trans. Pattern Anal. Mach. Intell. **34**(12), 2289–2302 (2012)
19. Kim, Y., Lee, J., Kim, S.S., Yang, C., Kim, T., Yim, J.: DNN-based ISP parameter inference algorithm for automatic image quality optimization. Electronic Imaging **2020**(9), 1–315 (2020)
20. Liang, Z., Cai, J., Cao, Z., Zhang, L.: CameraNet: a two-stage framework for effective camera ISP learning. IEEE Trans. Image Process. **30**, 2248–2262 (2021)
21. Lin, J., Rao, Y., Lu, J., Zhou, J.: Runtime neural pruning. In: Advances in neural information processing systems 30 (2017)
22. Lin, T.-Y., et al.: Microsoft COCO: common objects in context. In: Fleet, D., Pajdla, T., Schiele, B., Tuytelaars, T. (eds.) ECCV 2014. LNCS, vol. 8693, pp. 740–755. Springer, Cham (2014). https://doi.org/10.1007/978-3-319-10602-1_48
23. Liu, D., Wen, B., Jiao, J., Liu, X., Wang, Z., Huang, T.S.: Connecting image denoising and high-level vision tasks via deep learning. IEEE Trans. Image Process. **29**, 3695–3706 (2020)
24. Majumdar, P., Singh, R., Vatsa, M.: Attention aware debiasing for unbiased model prediction. In: Proceedings of the IEEE/CVF International Conference on Computer Vision, pp. 4133–4141 (2021)
25. Mantiuk, R.K., Tomaszewska, A., Mantiuk, R.: Comparison of four subjective methods for image quality assessment. In: Computer graphics forum, vol. 31, pp. 2478–2491. Wiley Online Library (2012)
26. Mosleh, A., Sharma, A., Onzon, E., Mannan, F., Robidoux, N., Heide, F.: Hardware-in-the-loop end-to-end optimization of camera image processing pipelines. In: Proceedings of the IEEE/CVF Conference on Computer Vision and Pattern Recognition, pp. 7529–7538 (2020)
27. Nishimura, J., Gerasimow, T., Sushma, R., Sutic, A., Wu, C.T., Michael, G.: Automatic ISP image quality tuning using nonlinear optimization. In: 2018 25th IEEE International Conference on Image Processing, pp. 2471–2475. IEEE (2018)
28. Onzon, E., Mannan, F., Heide, F.: Neural auto-exposure for high-dynamic range object detection. In: Proceedings of the IEEE/CVF Conference on Computer Vision and Pattern Recognition, pp. 7710–7720 (2021)

29. Pfister, L., Bresler, Y.: Learning filter bank sparsifying transforms. IEEE Trans. Signal Process. **67**(2), 504–519 (2018)
30. Phan, B., Mannan, F., Heide, F.: Adversarial imaging pipelines. In: Proceedings of the IEEE/CVF Conference on Computer Vision and Pattern Recognition, pp. 16051–16061 (2021)
31. Redmon, J., Farhadi, A.: Yolov3: an incremental improvement. arXiv preprint arXiv:1804.02767 (2018)
32. Robidoux, N., Capel, L.E.G., Seo, D., Sharma, A., Ariza, F., Heide, F.: End-to-end high dynamic range camera pipeline optimization. In: Proceedings of the IEEE/CVF Conference on Computer Vision and Pattern Recognition, pp. 6297–6307 (2021)
33. Schwartz, E., Giryes, R., Bronstein, A.M.: DeepISP: toward learning an end-to-end image processing pipeline. IEEE Trans. Image Process. **28**(2), 912–923 (2018)
34. Thung, K.H., Raveendran, P.: A survey of image quality measures. In: IEEE international conference for technical postgraduates, pp. 1–4 (2009)
35. Tseng, E., et al.: Differentiable compound optics and processing pipeline optimization for end-to-end camera design. ACM Trans. Graph. **40**(2), 1–19 (2021)
36. Tseng, E., et al.: Hyperparameter optimization in black-box image processing using differentiable proxies. ACM Trans. Graph. **38**(4), 1–27 (2019)
37. Vaswani, A., et al.: Attention is all you need. In: Advances in neural information processing systems 30 (2017)
38. Wu, C.T., et al.: VisionISP: repurposing the image signal processor for computer vision applications. In: IEEE International Conference on Image Processing, pp. 4624–4628. IEEE (2019)
39. Yahiaoui, L., Hughes, C., Horgan, J., Deegan, B., Denny, P., Yogamani, S.: Optimization of ISP parameters for object detection algorithms. Electronic Imaging **2019**(15), 1–44 (2019)
40. Yang, C., et al.: Effective ISP tuning framework based on user preference feedback. Electronic Imaging **2020**(9), 1–316 (2020)
41. Yogatama, D., Mann, G.: Efficient transfer learning method for automatic hyperparameter tuning. In: Artificial intelligence and statistics, pp. 1077–1085. PMLR (2014)
42. Yu, K., Li, Z., Peng, Y., Loy, C.C., Gu, J.: ReconfigISP: reconfigurable camera image processing pipeline. arXiv preprint arXiv:2109.04760 (2021)
43. Zamir, S.W., et al.: CycleISP: real image restoration via improved data synthesis. In: Proceedings of the IEEE/CVF Conference on Computer Vision and Pattern Recognition, pp. 2696–2705 (2020)
44. Zoph, B., Vasudevan, V., Shlens, J., Le, Q.V.: Learning transferable architectures for scalable image recognition. In: Proceedings of the IEEE conference on computer vision and pattern recognition, pp. 8697–8710 (2018)

RealFlow: EM-Based Realistic Optical Flow Dataset Generation from Videos

Yunhui Han[1], Kunming Luo[2], Ao Luo[2], Jiangyu Liu[2], Haoqiang Fan[2], Guiming Luo[1], and Shuaicheng Liu[2,3(✉)]

[1] School of Software, Tsinghua University, Beijing 100084, China
hanyh19@mails.tsinghua.edu.cn, gluo@tsinghua.edu.cn
[2] Megvii Technology, Beijing, China
{luokunming,luoao02,liujiangyu,fhq}@megvii.com
[3] University of Electronic Science and Technology of China, Chengdu, China
liushuaicheng@uestc.edu.cn

Abstract. Obtaining the ground truth labels from a video is challenging since the manual annotation of pixel-wise flow labels is prohibitively expensive and laborious. Besides, existing approaches try to adapt the trained model on synthetic datasets to authentic videos, which inevitably suffers from domain discrepancy and hinders the performance for real-world applications. To solve these problems, we propose RealFlow, an Expectation-Maximization based framework that can create large-scale optical flow datasets directly from any unlabeled realistic videos. Specifically, we first estimate optical flow between a pair of video frames, and then synthesize a new image from this pair based on the predicted flow. Thus the new image pairs and their corresponding flows can be regarded as a new training set. Besides, we design a Realistic Image Pair Rendering (RIPR) module that adopts softmax splatting and bi-directional hole filling techniques to alleviate the artifacts of the image synthesis. In the E-step, RIPR renders new images to create a large quantity of training data. In the M-step, we utilize the generated training data to train an optical flow network, which can be used to estimate optical flows in the next E-step. During the iterative learning steps, the capability of the flow network is gradually improved, so is the accuracy of the flow, as well as the quality of the synthesized dataset. Experimental results show that RealFlow outperforms previous dataset generation methods by a considerably large margin. Moreover, based on the generated dataset, our approach achieves state-of-the-art performance on two standard benchmarks compared with both supervised and unsupervised optical flow methods. Our code and dataset are available at https://github.com/megvii-research/RealFlow.

Supplementary Information The online version contains supplementary material available at https://doi.org/10.1007/978-3-031-19800-7_17.

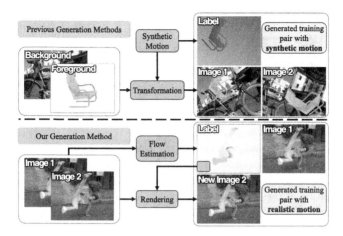

Fig. 1. Illustration of our motivation. Top: previous methods use synthetic motion to produce training pairs. Bottom: we propose to construct training pairs with realistic motion labels from the real-world video sequence. We estimate optical flow between two frames as the training label and synthesize a 'New Image 2'. Both the new view and flow labels are refined iteratively in the EM-based framework for mutual improvements

1 Introduction

Deep optical flow methods [46,47] adopt large-scale datasets to train networks, which have achieved good computational efficiency and state-of-the-art performances in public benchmarks [3,34]. One key ingredient of these deep learning methods is the training dataset. We summarize **four** key characteristics of flow datasets that have significant impacts on the success of deep learning algorithms: **1)** the *quantity* of labeled pairs; **2)** the *quality* of flow labels; **3)** the *image realism*; and **4)** the *motion realism*. We refer to the first two as the label criteria and the latter two as the realism criteria.

However, we find it is difficult for existing flow datasets to be satisfactory in all aspects. For example, FlyingThings [31] synthesizes the flows by moving a foreground object on top of a background image. Sintel [3] is purely rendered from virtual 3D graphic animations. AutoFlow [44] presents a learning approach searching for hyperparameters to render synthetic training pairs. As a result, these methods can produce large amounts of training data with accurate flow labels, satisfying the label criteria. However, they failed to meet the demand of realism criteria, as both the scene objects and their motions are synthesized. If flow networks are trained on these datasets, they may suffer from the domain gap between the synthetic and authentic scenes [18], resulting in sub-optimal performance on real-world images.

To achieve realism, some methods propose to manually annotate flow labels using realistic videos [2,21]. Although these methods can naturally satisfy the realism criteria, the process of manual labeling is time-consuming, and neither

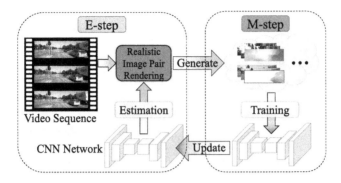

Fig. 2. Illustration of the EM-based framework. In the E-step, we estimate flow labels and synthesize new views to generate training data. In the M-step, we use the training data to train a network, which can update flow labels for the next E-step.

the quality nor the quantity can be guaranteed, potentially at odds with the requirements for label criteria. Recently, Aleotti *et al.* [1] propose to create training pairs from a single image. It randomly generates transformations as the flow labels, based on which the image is warped to produce the other image, yielding a pair of images together with the flow labels. In this way, the label criteria are satisfied. However, the realism criteria can only be satisfied partially. Because, the synthesized images sometimes contain artifacts, and more importantly, the generated motions cannot resemble realistic object motion behaviors of real-world scenarios.

To address these issues, we propose RealFlow, an iterative learning framework to simultaneously generate the training pairs from realistic video frames and obtain an enhanced flow network with the generated flow data, which can satisfy both the label and realism criteria. Figure 1 shows an illustration of our RealFlow in comparison with existing methods. Previous work [5,44] (Fig. 1 top) synthesizes the flows (motions) by pasting foreground objects on top of backgrounds at different positions, where the motions are manually generated. In our approach (Fig. 1 bottom), we first estimate the optical flows F between frame pairs (I_1 and I_2) from existing videos, and then exploit the predicted flows as labels to synthesize I_2', a set of new images of the 'frame 2'. After that, we abandon the original I_2, and use the I_1 and I_2' as image pairs, together with the estimated F as the flow labels to compose a sample (I_1, I_2', F) of the new optical flow dataset. Note that the flow labels are naturally accurate for warping I_1 to I_2', since the pixels in I_2' are synthesized based on the F and I_1.

This strategy faces two challenges: 1) image synthesis may introduce artifacts, *e.g.*, disparity occlusions; 2) the motion realism is affected by the quality of estimated flows. For the first challenge, we design Realistic Image Pair Rendering (RIPR) method to robustly render a new image I_2'. Specifically, we employ softmax splatting and bi-directional hole filling techniques, based on the flow and depth maps predicted from the image pairs I_1 and I_2, to generate the new images, where most of the artifacts can be effectively alleviated. For the second one, we design an Expectation-Maximization (EM) based learning framework, as illustrated in Fig. 2. Specifically, during the E-step, RIPR renders new images to create the training samples, and during M-step, we use the generated data to train the optical flow network that will estimate optical flows for the next E-step. During the iterative learning steps, the capability of the flow network is gradually improved, so is the accuracy of the flow, as well as the quality of synthesized dataset. Upon the convergence of our EM-based framework, we can obtain a new flow dataset generated from the input videos and a high-precision optical flow network benefiting from the new training data.

By applying RealFlow, huge amounts of videos can be used to generate training datasets, which allows supervised optical flow networks to be generalized to any scene. In summary, our main contributions are:

- We propose **RealFLow**, an EM-based iterative refinement framework, to effectively generate large-scale optical flow datasets with realistic scene motions and reliable flow labels from real-world videos.
- We present Realistic Image Pair Rendering (**RIPR**) method for high-quality new view synthesis, overcoming issues such as occlusions and holes.
- RealFlow leads to a significant performance improvement compared against prior dataset generation methods. We generate a large real-world dataset, with which we set new records on the public benchmarks using widely-used optical flow estimation methods.

2   Related Work

Supervised Optical Flow Network. FlowNet [5] is the first work to estimate optical flow by training a convolutional network on synthetic dataset. Following FlowNet, early approaches [9–11,38] improve the flow accuracy with the advanced modules and network architectures. Recent works [16,27,28] propose graph and attention-based global motion refinement approaches in the recurrent framework [47], making large progress on supervised learning. However, for the existing supervised networks, the domain gap between synthetic datasets and realistic datasets is non-negligible and inevitably degrades the performance. Our work aims to generate datasets from realistic videos to solve this problem.

Unsupervised Optical Flow Network. The advantage of unsupervised methods is that no annotations are required for the training [15,40]. Existing works [19,23–25,39,52] present multiple unsupervised losses and image alignment constraints to achieve competitive results. However, there are many challenges for unsupervised methods, including but not limited to, occlusions [13,26,48], lack of textures [12], and illumination variations [33], all of which break the basic hypothesis of brightness constancy assumption. Therefore, supervised networks achieve better performance than unsupervised ones.

Dataset Generation for Optical Flow. Middlebury [2] records objects with fluorescent texture under UV light illumination to obtain flow labels from real-world scenes. Liu. *et al.* [21] propose a human-in-loop methodology to annotate

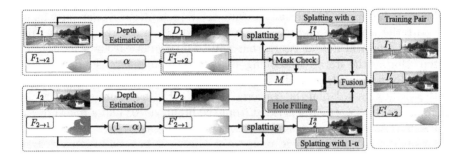

Fig. 3. Illustration of Realistic Image Pair Rendering (RIPR). Given two frames I_1 and I_2 from real-world videos and their estimated flow fields $F_{1\to2}$ and $F_{2\to1}$, we first obtain the depth D_1 and D_2 by the monocular depth network [36]. Then, we modify the flow maps to $F'_{1\to2}$ and $F'_{2\to1}$ and use $F'_{1\to2}$ to check the hole mask M. Finally, splatting method is used to generate new views I_1^s and I_2^s, which are further fused to render 'new image 2' I'_2. The (I_1, I'_2, F) serves as the new generated training pair

ground-truth motion for arbitrary real-world videos. KITTI [7,34] is a popular autonomous driving dataset, which provides sophisticated training data through complex device setups. However, the quantity of the above real-world datasets is small, which is insufficient for deep supervised learning. Flyingchairs [5] makes the first attempt to show that synthesized training pairs can be used for supervised learning. Flyingthings [31] further improves the quantity. Virtual KITTI [6] uses Unity game engine to create a large driving dataset. AutoFlow [44] presents a learning approach to search the hyperparameter for rendering training data. However, these datasets are all synthetic. There is a constant shift from synthetic scene towards real-world scene. SlowFlow [14] attempts to collect large-scale dataset using a high-speed video camera, but the flow labels are not totally reliable. Efforts to tackle the above problem is Depthstillation [1], which synthesizes a new image from a single real image. The motion labels are the sampled parametric transformations for the foreground and background. However, the sampled motions are not real, and the synthesis sometimes introduces artifacts. In contrast, our method obtains reliable flow labels from real videos and synthesizes the new view from two frames instead of a single image.

3   Method

3.1   RealFlow Framework

The pipeline of the proposed RealFlow framework is illustrated in Fig. 2. Given a set of real-world videos, our goal is to generate a large-scale training dataset and learn an optical flow estimation network at the same time. The key idea behind RealFlow is that a better training dataset can help learn a better optical flow network and inversely, a better network can provide better flow predictions for dataset generation. Therefore, we integrate the dataset generation procedure and optical flow network training procedure as a generative model, which can be iteratively optimized by Expectation-Maximization (EM) algorithm [32].

As illustrated in Fig. 2, RealFlow is an iterative framework that contains two main steps: E-step and M-step. In iteration t, we first conduct the E-step to generate a training dataset $X^t = \{x^t\}$. Given a consecutive image pair (I_1, I_2) sampled from the input videos, the training data generation procedure can be formulated as follows:

$$x^t = \mathcal{R}(I_1, I_2, \Theta^{t-1}), \tag{1}$$

where Θ^{t-1} is the learned optical flow network Θ in previous iteration $t - 1$, x^t is the generated training sample, and $\mathcal{R}$ represents our training pair rendering method Realistic Image Pair Rendering (RIPR), illustrated in Sect. 3.2.

Then, in M-step, we use the newly generated dataset X^t to train and update the optical flow estimation network in a fully supervised manner:

$$\Theta^t = \arg\min_{\Theta} \mathcal{L}(X^t, \Theta), \tag{2}$$

where $\mathcal{L}$ is the learning objective of the optical flow network. Finally, an optical flow dataset and a high-precision optical flow network can be obtained by RealFlow with several EM iterations.

3.2   Realistic Image Pair Rendering

The pipeline of the proposed RIPR method is shown in Fig. 3. Given a pair of consecutive images (I_1, I_2) and an optical flow estimation network Θ, our goal is to generate an image pair with its flow label for network training. The main idea is to render a new image I_2' based on the image pair (I_1, I_2) and an estimated flow F between (I_1, I_2), so that F can be used as the training label of the new image pair (I_1, I_2'). Specifically, the reference image I_1 is first forward-warped to the target view I_2'. Then, in order to ensure the realism of the synthesized view I_2', we need to remove the occlusions and holes caused by dynamic moving objects as well as depth disparities. Figure 4 illustrates an example.

Here, we use the **Splatting** method to identify foreground and background for these occlusion regions based on a monocular depth network [36]. Moreover, we design a **Bi-directional Hole Filling (BHF)** method to fill these hole regions using backward flow and image content from I_2. Finally, after the target view generation, the reference image, synthesized new view, and the estimated flow (I_1, I_2', F) are chosen as a training pair for dataset construction.

As detailed in Fig. 3, we first estimate the forward flow, backward flow, and the depth of I_1 and I_2 as follows:

$$F_{1\rightarrow2} = \Theta(I_1, I_2), \qquad\qquad F_{2\rightarrow1} = \Theta(I_2, I_1), \tag{3}$$
$$D_1 = \Psi(I_1), \qquad\qquad\qquad D_2 = \Psi(I_2), \tag{4}$$

where $F_{1\rightarrow2}$ and $F_{2\rightarrow1}$ are the estimated forward and backward flow, and D_1 and D_2 are the estimated depth results by the monocular depth network Ψ. Note

Fig. 4. Examples of the splatting results (top) and the hole filling results (bottom). For the splatting, summation is a conventional approach that produces brightness inconsistency results. Softmax leads to transparent artifacts. Max splatting renders a natural image. After hole filling by our proposed BHF, a new view image with few artifacts can be generated

that D_1 and D_2 are the inverse depth maps so that the pixel with larger value is closer to the camera.

In order to increase the diversity of the generated dataset, we use a factor α to add a disturbance to the estimated flow, so that the generated view is not exactly the original I_2 but a new view controlled by the factor α. Thus we obtain new flow fields by the follows:

$$F'_{1\to 2} = \alpha F_{1\to 2}, \quad F'_{2\to 1} = (1-\alpha)F_{2\to 1}. \tag{5}$$

Then, we use flow fields $F'_{1\to 2}$ and $F'_{2\to 1}$ to render the new view by splatting method, which can be represented as:

$$I_1^s = \mathcal{S}(I_1, F'_{1\to 2}, D_1), \quad I_2^s = \mathcal{S}(I_2, F'_{2\to 1}, D_2), \tag{6}$$

where $\mathcal{S}$ represents the splatting method, I_1^s and I_2^s are the same view rendered from different directions. Note that the occlusion problem is addressed after the splatting operation which we will introduce later. Finally, the result view can be generated by our BHF method, which is formulated as:

$$I_2' = \mathcal{B}(I_1^s, F'_{1\to 2}, I_2^s), \tag{7}$$

where $\mathcal{B}$ represents our BHF method, I_2' is the new image and $(I_1, I_2', F'_{1\to 2})$ is the training pair generated of RIPR.

Splatting. Splatting can be used to forward-warp the reference image I_1 into a new view I_s according to a given flow field $F'_{1\to 2}$. As shown in Fig. 4 (top), the conventional sum operation for splatting often produces brightness inconsistency results. The softmax splatting method [35] is proposed to ease this problem.

Assuming q is a coordinate in I_1, and p is a coordinate in the target view. The softmax splatting operation can be formulated as follows:

$$\text{let } u = p - (q + F'_{1\to2}(q)), \tag{8}$$

$$b(u) = \max(0, 1 - |u_x|) \cdot \max(0, 1 - |u_y|), \tag{9}$$

$$I_s(p) = \frac{\sum_q \exp D_1(q) \cdot I_1(q) \cdot b(u)}{\sum_q \exp D_1(q) \cdot b(u)}, \tag{10}$$

where $b(u)$ is the bilinear kernel, D_1 is the depth map of I_1 and I_s is the forward-warp result. By applying Eq. 10, background pixels that are occluded in the target view can be compressed by incorporating the depth map and the softmax operation, compared with the original sum splatting operation as illustrated in Fig. 4 (top). However, Softmax splatting in Eq. 10 may still cause unnatural results in occlusion regions. To this end, we propose to use max splatting as an alternative option of the splatting method:

$$\text{let } k = \begin{cases} 1, & \text{if } |q + F'_{1\to2}(q) - p| \leq \frac{\sqrt{2}}{2} \\ 0, & \text{otherwise,} \end{cases} \tag{11}$$

$$I_s(p) = I_1(r), \text{ where } r = \arg\max_q D(q) \cdot k, \tag{12}$$

where k is the nearest kernel. Equation 12 means that when multiple pixels are located to position p, we only assign the pixel with the largest depth value to the target view. As such, the resulting image is more natural compared with the softmax version as shown in Fig. 4 (top). However, we find that the dataset generated by softmax splatting performs better than the max version in our experiments. Detailed analysis will be discussed in our experiment Sect. 6.

Bi-directional Hole Filling. Apart from occlusions, there is another problem called holes, which are produced when no pixels from original image are projected to these regions. Previous method [1] adopted an inpainting model to solve this problem, which often introduces artifacts that reduce the quality of the generated dataset. Here, we design a bi-directional hole filling method to handle these empty regions. As in Eq. 7, the input of BHF is the forward flow $F'_{1\to2}$, and the target views I_1^s and I_2^s generated by splatting with forward and backward flows, respectively. We first check a hole mask M from $F'_{1\to2}$ using the range map check method [48], which is formulated as follows:

$$M(p) = \min\left(1, \sum_q b(u)\right), \tag{13}$$

where $b(u)$ is the bilinear kernel described in Eq. 9. In the hole mask M, the hole pixels are labeled as 0 and others as 1. Then, we can generate a novel view image I_2' by fusing I_1^s and I_2^s as follows:

$$I_2' = I_1^s + (1 - M) \cdot I_2^s, \tag{14}$$

which means that the hole regions in I_1^s are filled with regions in I_2^s. By applying our BHF, realistic images can be generated, which is shown in Fig. 4 (bottom).

Fig. 5. Example training pairs from our generated RF-AB and RF-DAVIS. The first sample contains large motion and complex scenes.

4   Experiments

4.1   Datasets

Flying Chairs [5] and **Flying Things** [50]: These two synthetic datasets are generated by randomly moving foreground objects on top of a background image. State-of-the-art supervised networks usually train on Chairs and Things.

Virtual KITTI [6]: Virtual KITTI is a synthetic dataset, which contains videos generated from different virtual urban environments.

DAVIS [4]: DVAIS dataset consists of high-quality video sequences under various kinds of scenes. No optical flow label is provided. We use 10,581 images from DAVIS challenge 2019 to generate **RF-DAVIS**.

ALOV [41] *and BDD100K* [51]: ALOV and BDD100K datasets are large-scale real-world video databases. We capture 75,581 image pairs from ALOV dataset and 86,128 image pairs from BDD100K dataset. There is no flow label for these image pairs, so we use RealFlow to create a large diverse real-world dataset with flow label, named **RF-AB**.

KITTI [7,34]: KITTI2012 and KITTI2015 are benchmarks for optical flow estimation. There are multi-view extensions (4,000 training and 3,989 testing) datasets with no ground truth. We use the multi-view extension videos (training and testing) of KITTI 2015 to generate **RF-Ktrain** and **RF-Ktest** datasets.

Sintel [3]: Sintel is a synthetic flow benchmark derived from 3D animated film, which contains 1,041 training pairs and 564 test pairs. We use the images from the training set to generate our **RF-Sintel**.

4.2   Implementation Details

Our RIPR consists of a depth estimation module, a flow estimation module, a splatting module, and a hole filling module. For the flow estimation module,

Table 1. Comparison with previous dataset generation method [1]. We use the same source images to generate dataset and train the same network for comparison. The best results are marked in red.

Model	Dataset	KITTI12		KITTI15	
		EPE	F1	EPE	F1
RAFT	dDAVIS [1]	1.78	6.85%	3.80	13.22%
RAFT	RF-DAVIS	1.64	5.91%	3.54	9.23%
RAFT	dKITTI [1]	1.76	5.91%	4.01	13.35%
RAFT	RF-Ktest	1.32	5.41%	2.31	8.65%

Table 2. Comparison with Unsupervised Methods. The best results are marked in red and the second best are in blue, '-' indicates no results. End-point error (epe) is used as the evaluation metric.

Method	KITTI12	KITTI15	Sintel C.	Sintel F.
ARFlow [22]	1.44	2.85	2.79	3.87
SimFlow [12]	–	5.19	2.86	3.57
UFlow [17]	1.68	2.71	2.50	3.39
UpFlow [29]	1.27	2.45	2.33	2.67
SMURF [42]	–	2.00	1.71	2.58
IRRPWC(C+T) [10]	3.49	10.21	1.87	3.39
IRRPWC(C+T)+UpFlow	1.87	2.62	1.79	3.31
Ours(IRRPWC)	1.83	2.39	1.74	3.20
RAFT(C+T) [47]	2.15	5.04	1.43	2.71
Ours(RAFT)	1.20	2.16	1.34	2.38

we select RAFT [47] which represents state-of-the-art architecture for supervised optical flow. We train the RAFT using official implementation without any modifications. We initialized the RealFlow framework using RAFT pre-trained on FlyingChairs and FlyingThings unless otherwise specified. For the depth estimation module, we select DPT [36] monocular depth network, which represents the state-of-the-art architecture. For the splatting module, softmax splatting [35] is used due to the better performance. For the hole filling, our BHF uses the bidirectional flow estimated from RAFT. We will show the performance of our RIPR method affected by the different settings of above modules in Sect. 4.4.

4.3   Comparison with Existing Methods

In this section, we evaluate the effectiveness of RealFlow generation framework on the public benchmarks.

Comparison with Dataset Generation Methods. Due to the scarcity of real-world dataset generation methods for optical flow, we only select the

298   Y. Han et al.

Table 3. Comparison of our method with supervised methods on KITTI2015 train set and test set. '-' indicates no results reported.

method	KITTI15 (train)		KITTI15 (test)
	EPE	F1	F1
PWC-Net [45]	2.16	9.80%	9.60%
LiteFlowNet [9]	1.62	5.58%	9.38%
IRR-PWC [10]	1.63	5.32%	7.65%
RAFT [47]	0.63	1.50%	5.10%
RAFT-RVC [43]	–	–	5.56%
AutoFlow [44]	–	–	4.78%
Ours	0.58	1.35%	4.63%

Depthstillation method [1] for comparison. Depthstillation generated optical flow dataset dDAVIS and dKITTI from DAVIS and KITTI multi-view test. For fair comparison, we also choose the DAVIS and KITTI multi-view test videos to generate our RF-DAVIS and RF-Ktest. Figure 5 shows our rendered training pairs. We evaluate our method on KITTI12-training and KITTI15-training sets. Quantitative results are shown in Table 1, where our method outperforms Depthstillation [1], proving the importance of realism of object motion behavior.

Comparison with Unsupervised Methods. When supervised optical flow networks are trained on synthetic datasets, they are hard to be generalized to real-world data due to the domain gap and motion discrepancy between synthetic and authentic datasets. To some extent, the effectiveness of our method depends on domain adaptation. Given the rich literature of unsupervised methods, we compare our method with them to exclude the influence of the domain. We train the RAFT [47] on RF-Ktrain and RF-Sintel by RealFlow framework. As shown in Table 2, RealFlow outperforms all the unsupervised methods on Sintel-training. We obtain a competitive result on KITTI15-training which surpass all the unsupervised methods except SMURF [42]. One reason is that SMURF adopted multiple frames for training, while RealFlow only uses two frames.

Since our method is based on a model pre-trained on C+T (FlyChairs and FlyThings) in a supervised manner, we also provide the results of unsupervised methods that are pre-trained with groundtruth on C+T for a fair comparison. Because we cannot implement SMURF, we use IRRPWC [10] structure and UpFlow [29] for comparison. Specifically, we use IRRPWC pre-trained on C+T as a baseline, which is 'IRRPWC(C+T)' in Table 2. Then we train IRRPWC from the C+T pre-trained weights using unsupervised protocol provided by UpFlow on KITTI 2015 multi-view videos and Sintel sequences and do evaluation on KITTI 2012/2015 train and Sintel train data sets, which is 'IRRPWC(C+T)+UpFlow'. Finally, we perform our method using IRRPWC(C+T), which is 'Ours(IRRPWC)'. As a result, Our method can achieve better performance than unsupervised method trained from C+T pre-trained weights.

Table 4. Comparison with large datasets. '-' indicates no results. End-point error (epe) is used as the evaluation metric.

Model	Dataset	KITTI12	KITTI15	Sintel C.	Sintel F.
RAFT	C+T [47]	2.15	5.04	1.43	2.71
RAFT	AutoFlow [44]	–	4.23	1.95	2.57
RAFT	dCOCO [1]	1.82	3.81	2.63	3.90
RAFT	RF-AB	1.80	3.48	1.80	3.28

Comparison with Supervised Methods. To further prove the effectiveness of RealFlow, we use KITTI15-training to fine-tune the RAFT model pre-trained by our RF-Ktrain. Note that RF-Ktrain is generated without any sequence that contains the frames in KITTI test set. The evaluation results on KITTI15-training and KITTI15-testing are shown in Table 3. We achieve state-of-art performance on KITTI 2015 test benchmark compared to previous supervised methods.

Comparison on Large Datasets. To make our trained networks general, we collect a large-scale realistic dataset named RF-AB. We train the RAFT from scratch using our RF-AB as official implementation. Because of the scarcity of real-world evaluation benchmarks, we only evaluate our dataset on KITTI and Sintel. As summarized in Table 4, RAFT trained on RF-AB is more accurate than on other datasets when evaluated on KITTI12-training and KITTI15-training, which demonstrates the generalization ability of our method on real-world scenes. We also obtain comparable results on Sintel, which only surpass dCOCO [1]. RF-AB and dCOCO are both real-world datasets. The networks trained on them are hardly adapted to Sintel (synthetic data). So their performance is worse than C+T and Autoflow. Moreover, AutoFlow [44] learns the hyperparameters to render training data using the average end-point error (AEPE) on Sintel as the learning metric. FlyChairs and FlyingThings are also rendered to match the displacement distribution of Sintel. Mayer *et al.* [30] shows that matching the displacement statistics of the test data is important.

Impact on Different Optical Flow Networks. In Table 5, we also provide experiment results to prove that our method can improve other supervised networks on real-world scenes not only on specific architecture such as RAFT. For fair comparison, we trained IRR-PWC [10] and GMA [16] on RF-AB and RF-Sintel with the official settings. Table 5 shows that RAFT and GMA trained on RF-AB outperform the original variants trained on C+T when testing on real-world data KITTI. Moreover, there is a significant improvement on IRR-PWC which is effective as trained RAFT on C+T. This fact proves that a better dataset is crucial to a supervised network.

4.4   Ablation Study

In this section, we conduct a series of ablation studies to analyze the impact of different module choices of the RIPR method. We measure all the factors using

Table 5. Impact on different optical flow networks. The value in the bracket means the percentage of improvement. End-point error (epe) is used as the evaluation metric.

Model	Dataset	KITTI12	KITTI15	Sintel C.	Sintel F.
IRR-PWC [10]	C+T	3.49	10.21	1.87	3.39
IRR-PWC	RF-AB	2.13	5.09	3.68	4.72
IRR-PWC	RF-Sintel	2.67	7.06	1.74	3.20
GMA [16]	C+T	1.99	4.69	1.30	2.73
GMA	RF-AB	1.82	3.64	1.93	3.45
GMA	RF-Sintel	1.74	4.39	1.23	2.32
RAFT [47]	C+T	2.15	5.04	1.43	2.71
RAFT	RF-AB	1.80	3.48	1.80	3.28
RAFT	RF-Sintel	1.76	4.36	1.34	2.38

RF-Ktrain to train RAFT and evaluate on KITTI12-training and KITTI15-training. Because there are multiple combinations of these factors, we only test a specific component of our approach in isolation. As shown in Table 6, default settings are underlined and detail experiment settings will be discussed below.

Render. We conduct an experiment named 'Render Off' where we use original image pairs and their estimated flows to train the network. When applying our RIPR method, as the 'Render On' in Table 6, the accuracy of the network can be improved significantly. Moreover, our rendering method is also related to the video interpolation methods [8,49]. We replace our rendering method with QVI [49] for fair comparison. Note that 'QVI(RAFT)' uses RAFT pre-trained on C+T for optical flow estimation, which is the same model as the initial model of RealFlow. As a result, our method outperforms QVI for optical flow dataset generation because the frame synthesis process in QVI may cause the content of the generated frame to not match the optical flow label.

Depth. To measure the effectiveness of the depth estimation in the splatting method, we conduct three different experiments: DPT [36], Midas [37], and 'Occ-bi'. The 'Occ-bi' means that the depth map is replaced by the occlusion map produced by the bi-directional flow check method [33]. DPT is a state-of-art method that outperforms Midas in the task of monocular depth estimation. From Table 6, we can notice that with more accurate depth estimation results, our RealFlow can generate better dataset for optical flow learning, which proves that depth is a crucial cue in our framework.

Splatting. We compared two versions of splatting: Max and Softmax [35]. Max splatting leads to the right rendering result of visual appearance. However, we find that Softmax splatting outperforms Max splatting as in Table 6. The reason

Table 6. Ablation experiments. Settings used in our final framework are underlined. Here we only perform one EM iteration for these experiments due to the limitation of computational resources.

Experiment	Method	KITTI12		KITTI15	
		EPE	F1	EPE	F1
Render	Off	1.80	7.78%	3.93	14.38%
	QVI [49]	2.84	10.7%	7.27	20.36%
	QVI(RAFT)	4.03	14.0%	9.03	24.70%
	<u>On</u>	1.44	5.90%	2.79	10.66%
Depth	Occ-bi	1.51	6.22%	3.01	11.12%
	MiDas [37]	1.49	6.25%	2.90	11.18%
	<u>DPT</u> [36]	1.44	5.90%	2.79	10.66%
Splatting	Max	1.62	5.90%	3.03	11.04%
	<u>Softmax</u> [35]	1.44	5.90%	2.79	10.66%
Hole Filling	w/o Filling	1.45	6.06%	2.95	10.80%
	RFR [20]	1.53	6.07%	2.95	11.23%
	<u>BHF</u>	1.44	5.90%	2.79	10.66%
Range of α	[1]	1.57	6.34%	3.38	12.30%
	[−2,2]	1.45	5.92%	2.83	10.90%
	<u>[0,2]</u>	1.44	5.90%	2.79	10.66%

is that max splatting may cause tearing of texture when the depth is incorrect, while softmax splatting can alleviate this problem by generating a translucent fusion result. Please refer to supplementary materials for more details.

Hole Filling. The optical flow network learns a per-pixel matching of two images. The hole in the newly generated image means that there is no pixel matched to the reference image. Although it happens, the context information can also help the network. For fair comparison, we use the RFR [20] fine-tuned on KITTI dataset for inpainting these holes. As summarized in Table 6, our designed BHF method achieves the best results. We also conduct an experiment without hole filling which leads to a moderate improvement over RFR. It suggests that a worse hole filling result may introduce negative effects.

Range of α. To increase the diversity of our generated dataset, we add a disturbance to our RealFlow by α, which is introduced in Sect. 3.1. We use three different settings in Table 6 'Range of α'. '[1]' means that α is always set as 1. The other two settings mean that we randomly sample a value within that range. As can be seen, factor α sampled from range [0, 2] achieves better result.

Table 7. Iteration times. The best iteration time is underlined. Our RealFlow can converge to similar results with different initialization settings.

Model	Initialize Dataset	Iteration Times	KITTI12 EPE	KITTI12 F1	KITTI15 EPE	KITTI15 F1
RAFT	C+T	init	2.15	9.29%	5.04	17.4%
		Iter.1	1.44	5.90%	2.79	10.7%
		Iter.1*4	1.45	5.59%	2.86	10.4%
		Iter.2	1.31	5.28%	2.36	8.46%
		Iter.3	1.28	5.02%	2.20	8.27%
		Iter.4	1.27	5.17%	2.16	8.45%
RAFT	VKITTI	init	1.81	5.04%	3.13	8.63%
		Iter.1	1.26	4.47%	2.11	7.50%
GMA	C+T	init	1.99	9.28%	4.69	17.1%
		Iter.1	1.46	5.56%	2.79	10.2%

EM Iteration Times. In RealFlow framework, the generated dataset and the optical flow network are gradually improved after iterations. However, a certain upper limit exists in RealFlow and it will converge after several iterations. As summarized in Table 7, after 4 iterations, RealFlow converges and the result cannot be further improved. 'Iter.1*4' means that the network is trained 4 times longer (more training steps) with the data of 'Iter.1'. As can be seen, simply training 4 times longer cannot bring improvement compared with 4 EM iterations of RealFlow (see 'Iter.4'), which demonstrates the effectiveness of our approach.

Initial Model. It is well-known that the initialization is important for EM algorithm. In Table 7, we implement RAFT pre-trained on Virtual KITTI (VKITTI) and GMA pre-trained on C+T as the initial model of RealFlow. As can be seen, the performance can be improved after learning with our RealFlow.

5   Conclusions

In this work, we have presented RealFlow, an EM-based framework for optical flow dataset generation on realistic videos. We have proposed a Realistic Image Pair Rendering (RIPR) method to render a new view from a pair of images, according to the estimated optical flow. We have trained optical flow networks on the synthesized dataset. Experiment results show that the trained networks and the generated datasets can be improved iteratively, yielding a large-scale high-quality flow dataset as well as a high-precision optical flow network. Experiments show that the performance of existing methods can be largely improved on widely-used benchmarks while using our RealFlow dataset for training.

Acknowledgement. This work was supported by the National Natural Science Foundation of China (NSFC) No.62173203, No.61872067 and No.61720106004.

References

1. Aleotti, F., Poggi, M., Mattoccia, S.: Learning optical flow from still images. In: Proceedings CVPR, pp. 15201–15211 (2021)
2. Baker, S., Scharstein, D., Lewis, J., Roth, S., Black, M.J., Szeliski, R.: A database and evaluation methodology for optical flow. Int. J. Comput. Vision **92**(1), 1–31 (2011)
3. Butler, D.J., Wulff, J., Stanley, G.B., Black, M.J.: A naturalistic open source movie for optical flow evaluation. In: Fitzgibbon, A., Lazebnik, S., Perona, P., Sato, Y., Schmid, C. (eds.) ECCV 2012. LNCS, vol. 7577, pp. 611–625. Springer, Heidelberg (2012). https://doi.org/10.1007/978-3-642-33783-3_44
4. Caelles, S., Pont-Tuset, J., Perazzi, F., Montes, A., Maninis, K.K., Van Gool, L.: The 2019 davis challenge on vos: unsupervised multi-object segmentation. arXiv:1905.00737 (2019)
5. Dosovitskiy, A., et al.: Flownet: learning optical flow with convolutional networks. In: Proceedings ICCV, pp. 2758–2766 (2015)
6. Gaidon, A., Wang, Q., Cabon, Y., Vig, E.: Virtual worlds as proxy for multi-object tracking analysis. In: Proceedings CVPR, pp. 4340–4349 (2016)
7. Geiger, A., Lenz, P., Urtasun, R.: Are we ready for autonomous driving? the kitti vision benchmark suite. In: Proceedings CVPR, pp. 3354–3361 (2012)
8. Huang, Z., Zhang, T., Heng, W., Shi, B., Zhou, S.: Real-time intermediate flow estimation for video frame interpolation. In: Proceedings ECCV (2022)
9. Hui, T.W., Tang, X., Loy, C.C.: Liteflownet: a lightweight convolutional neural network for optical flow estimation. In: Proceedings CVPR, pp. 8981–8989 (2018)
10. Hur, J., Roth, S.: Iterative residual refinement for joint optical flow and occlusion estimation. In: Proceedings CVPR, pp. 5754–5763 (2019)
11. Ilg, E., Mayer, N., Saikia, T., Keuper, M., Dosovitskiy, A., Brox, T.: Flownet 2.0: evolution of optical flow estimation with deep networks. In: Proceedings CVPR, pp. 2462–2470 (2017)
12. Im, W., Kim, T.-K., Yoon, S.-E.: Unsupervised learning of optical flow with deep feature similarity. In: Vedaldi, A., Bischof, H., Brox, T., Frahm, J.-M. (eds.) ECCV 2020. LNCS, vol. 12369, pp. 172–188. Springer, Cham (2020). https://doi.org/10.1007/978-3-030-58586-0_11
13. Janai, J., Güney, F., Ranjan, A., Black, M., Geiger, A.: Unsupervised learning of multi-frame optical flow with occlusions. In: Ferrari, V., Hebert, M., Sminchisescu, C., Weiss, Y. (eds.) ECCV 2018. LNCS, vol. 11220, pp. 713–731. Springer, Cham (2018). https://doi.org/10.1007/978-3-030-01270-0_42
14. Janai, J., Guney, F., Wulff, J., Black, M.J., Geiger, A.: Slow flow: exploiting high-speed cameras for accurate and diverse optical flow reference data. In: Proceedings CVPR, pp. 3597–3607 (2017)
15. Yu, J.J., Harley, A.W., Derpanis, K.G.: Back to basics: unsupervised learning of optical flow via brightness constancy and motion smoothness. In: Hua, G., Jégou, H. (eds.) ECCV 2016. LNCS, vol. 9915, pp. 3–10. Springer, Cham (2016). https://doi.org/10.1007/978-3-319-49409-8_1
16. Jiang, S., Campbell, D., Lu, Y., Li, H., Hartley, R.: Learning to estimate hidden motions with global motion aggregation. In: Proceedings ICCV, pp. 9772–9781 (2021)

17. Jonschkowski, R., Stone, A., Barron, J.T., Gordon, A., Konolige, K., Angelova, A.: What matters in unsupervised optical flow. In: Vedaldi, A., Bischof, H., Brox, T., Frahm, J.-M. (eds.) ECCV 2020. LNCS, vol. 12347, pp. 557–572. Springer, Cham (2020). https://doi.org/10.1007/978-3-030-58536-5_33

18. Lai, W.S., Huang, J.B., Yang, M.H.: Semi-supervised learning for optical flow with generative adversarial networks. In: Proceedings NeurIPS, pp. 353–363 (2017)

19. Li, H., Luo, K., Liu, S.: Gyroflow: gyroscope-guided unsupervised optical flow learning. In: Proceedings ICCV, pp. 12869–12878 (2021)

20. Li, J., Wang, N., Zhang, L., Du, B., Tao, D.: Recurrent feature reasoning for image inpainting. In: Proceedings CVPR, pp. 7760–7768 (2020)

21. Liu, C., Freeman, W.T., Adelson, E.H., Weiss, Y.: Human-assisted motion annotation. In: Proceedings CVPR, pp. 1–8 (2008)

22. Liu, L., et al.: Learning by analogy: reliable supervision from transformations for unsupervised optical flow estimation. In: Proceedings CVPR, pp. 6489–6498 (2020)

23. Liu, P., King, I., Lyu, M., Xu, J.: Ddflow:learning optical flow with unlabeled data distillation. In: Proceedings AAAI, pp. 8770–8777 (2019)

24. Liu, P., Lyu, M., King, I., Xu, J.: Selflow:self-supervised learning of optical flow. In: Proceedings CVPR, pp. 4571–4580 (2019)

25. Liu, S., Luo, K., Luo, A., Wang, C., Meng, F., Zeng, B.: Asflow: unsupervised optical flow learning with adaptive pyramid sampling. IEEE Trans. Circuits Syst. Video Technol. **32**(7), 4282–4295 (2021)

26. Liu, S., Luo, K., Ye, N., Wang, C., Wang, J., Zeng, B.: Oiflow: Occlusion-inpainting optical flow estimation by unsupervised learning. IEEE Trans. on Image Processing **30**, 6420–6433 (2021)

27. Luo, A., Yang, F., Li, X., Liu, S.: Learning optical flow with kernel patch attention. In: Proceedings CVPR, pp. 8906–8915 (2022)

28. Luo, A., Yang, F., Luo, K., Li, X., Fan, H., Liu, S.: Learning optical flow with adaptive graph reasoning. In: Proceedings AAAI, pp. 1890–1898 (2022)

29. Luo, K., Wang, C., Liu, S., Fan, H., Wang, J., Sun, J.: Upflow: upsampling pyramid for unsupervised optical flow learning. In: Proceedings CVPR, pp. 1045–1054 (2021)

30. Mayer, N., et al.: What makes good synthetic training data for learning disparity and optical flow estimation? Int. J. Comput. Vision **126**(9), 942–960 (2018)

31. Mayer, N., et al.: A large dataset to train convolutional networks for disparity, optical flow, and scene flow estimation. In: Proceedings CVPR, pp. 4040–4048 (2016)

32. McLachlan, G.J., Krishnan, T.: The EM algorithm and extensions, vol. 382. John Wiley & Sons (2007)

33. Meister, S., Hur, J., Roth, S.: Unflow: unsupervised learning of optical flow with a bidirectional census loss. In: Proceedings AAAI (2018)

34. Menze, M., Geiger, A.: Object scene flow for autonomous vehicles. In: Proceedings CVPR, pp. 3061–3070 (2015)

35. Niklaus, S., Liu, F.: Softmax splatting for video frame interpolation. In: Proceedings CVPR, pp. 5437–5446 (2020)

36. Ranftl, R., Bochkovskiy, A., Koltun, V.: Vision transformers for dense prediction. In: Proceedings ICCV, pp. 12179–12188 (2021)

37. Ranftl, R., Lasinger, K., Hafner, D., Schindler, K., Koltun, V.: Towards robust monocular depth estimation: mixing datasets for zero-shot cross-dataset transfer. IEEE Trans. Pattern Anal. Mach. Intell. **44**(3), 1623–1637 (2022)

38. Ranjan, A., Black, M.J.: Optical flow estimation using a spatial pyramid network. In: Proceedings CVPR, pp. 4161–4170 (2017)

39. Ren, Z., et al.: Stflow: self-taught optical flow estimation using pseudo labels. IEEE Trans. Image Process. **29**, 9113–9124 (2020)
40. Ren, Z., Yan, J., Ni, B., Liu, B., Yang, X., Zha, H.: Unsupervised deep learning for optical flow estimation. In: Proceedings AAAI, pp. 1495–1501 (2017)
41. Smeulders, A.W., Chu, D.M., Cucchiara, R., Calderara, S., Dehghan, A., Shah, M.: Visual tracking: an experimental survey. IEEE Trans. Pattern Anal. Mach. Intell. **36**(7), 1442–1468 (2013)
42. Stone, A., Maurer, D., Ayvaci, A., Angelova, A., Jonschkowski, R.: Smurf: self-teaching multi-frame unsupervised raft with full-image warping. In: Proceedings CVPR, pp. 3887–3896 (2021)
43. Sun, D., et al.: Tf-raft: a tensorflow implementation of raft. In: ECCV Robust Vision Challenge Workshop (2020)
44. Sun, D., et al.: Autoflow: learning a better training set for optical flow. In: Proceedings CVPR, pp. 10093–10102 (2021)
45. Sun, D., Yang, X., Liu, M.Y., Kautz, J.: PWC-Net: CNNs for optical flow using pyramid, warping, and cost volume. In: Proceedings CVPR, pp. 8934–8943 (2018)
46. Sun, D., Yang, X., Liu, M.Y., Kautz, J.: Models matter, so does training: an empirical study of cnns for optical flow estimation. IEEE Trans. Pattern Anal. Mach. Intell. **42**(6), 1408–1423 (2020)
47. Teed, Z., Deng, J.: RAFT: recurrent all-pairs field transforms for optical flow. In: Vedaldi, A., Bischof, H., Brox, T., Frahm, J.-M. (eds.) ECCV 2020. LNCS, vol. 12347, pp. 402–419. Springer, Cham (2020). https://doi.org/10.1007/978-3-030-58536-5_24
48. Wang, Y., Yang, Y., Yang, Z., Zhao, L., Wang, P., Xu, W.: Occlusion aware unsupervised learning of optical flow. In: Proceedings CVPR, pp. 4884–4893 (2018)
49. Xu, X., Siyao, L., Sun et al., W.: Quadratic video interpolation. In: Proceedings NeurIPS 32 (2019)
50. Yang, G., Song, X., Huang, C., Deng, Z., Shi, J., Zhou, B.: Drivingstereo: a large-scale dataset for stereo matching in autonomous driving scenarios. In: Proceedings CVPR, pp. 899–908 (2019)
51. Yu, F., et al.: BDD100K: a diverse driving dataset for heterogeneous multitask learning. In: Proceedings CVPR, pp. 2636–2645 (2020)
52. Zhong, Y., Ji, P., Wang, J., Dai, Y., Li, H.: Unsupervised deep epipolar flow for stationary or dynamic scenes. In: Proceedings CVPR, pp. 12095–12104 (2019)

Memory-Augmented Model-Driven Network for Pansharpening

Keyu Yan[1,2], Man Zhou[1,2(✉)], Li Zhang[1,2], and Chengjun Xie[1(✉)]

[1] Hefei Institute of Physical Science, Chinese Academy of Sciences, Hefei, China
{keyu,manman,zanly20}@mail.ustc.edu.cn, cjxie@iim.ac.cn
[2] University of Science and Technology of China, Hefei, China

Abstract. In this paper, we propose a novel memory-augmented model-driven deep unfolding network for pan-sharpening. First, we devise the maximal a posterior estimation (MAP) model with two well-designed priors on the latent multi-spectral (MS) image, i.e., global and local implicit priors to explore the intrinsic knowledge across the modalities of MS and panchromatic (PAN) images. Second, we design an effective alternating minimization algorithm to solve this MAP model, and then unfold the proposed algorithm into a deep network, where each stage corresponds to one iteration. Third, to facilitate the signal flow across adjacent iterations, the persistent memory mechanism is introduced to augment the information representation by exploiting the Long short-term memory unit in the image and feature spaces. With this method, both the interpretability and representation ability of the deep network are improved. Extensive experiments demonstrate the superiority of our method to the existing state-of-the-art approaches. The source code is released at https://github.com/Keyu-Yan/MMNet.

Keywords: Pan-sharpening · Maximal a posterior estimation model · Deep unfolding method · Memory mechanism

1 Introduction

Nowadays, Many researchers are concerned on pan-sharpening since it is a critical image processing technology in the domain of remote sensing. Current remote satellites are often outfitted with two types of imaging sensors: multi-spectral and panchromatic sensors, which separately produce low-spatial resolution multi-spectral (LRMS) and panchromatic (PAN) images. Nonetheless, due to technological limits of imaging equipment, providing high-spatial resolution multi-spectral (HRMS) images, which is needed in practice, is difficult. Pan-sharpening attempts to construct the HRMS version by fusing the LRMS image and PAN image.

K. Yan and M. Zhou—Contributed equally.

Supplementary Information The online version contains supplementary material available at https://doi.org/10.1007/978-3-031-19800-7_18.

S. Avidan et al. (Eds.): ECCV 2022, LNCS 13679, pp. 306–322, 2022.
https://doi.org/10.1007/978-3-031-19800-7_18

The main challenge of the Pan-sharpening task is how to recover more spatial features and keep more comprehensive spectral information. In the past decades, many traditional techniques, such as component substitution (CS), multi-resolution analysis (MRA), and variational optimization (VO) methodologies, have been put forth. When processing complex scenes, the limited representational capacity of traditional approaches yields disappointing results. Recently, Pan-sharpening techniques based on deep learning (DL) [18,34] have seen considerable success. However, the majority of DL-based approaches currently in use simply concentrate on constructing deeper and more sophisticated network topologies in a black-box fashion without considering the rationality of models, and ignore the inherent information that exists between various modalities.

To increase the interpretability, some model-driven CNN models with clear physical meaning have emerged. The basic idea is to adopt prior knowledge to formulate optimization problems for computer vision tasks such as denoising [4], image compressive [41], then unfold the optimization algorithms into deep neural modules. Motivated by such designs [8,10], Xu et al. [37] propose the first deep unfolding network for Pan-sharpening. It formulates Pan-sharpening as two separate optimization problems and each stage in the implementation corresponds to one iteration in optimization. However, the potential of cross-stages has not been fully explored and feature transformation between adjacent stages with reduced channel numbers leads to information loss, which further hinders their performance improvements.

We present a novel interpretable memory-augmented model-driven network for Pan-sharpening to address the aforementioned issues. To be more specific, we first build a variational model from a maximal a posterior (MAP) framework to define the Pan-sharpening problem with two well-designed priors, namely, local and global implicit priors. The local implicit prior implicitly models the relationship between the HRMS and the PAN image from a local perspective, and so can assist in capturing the local relevant information between the HRMS and the PAN image. The global implicit prior addresses the non-local auto-regression property between the two images from a global perspective, allowing for effective use of the global correlation between the two images. Because the scene in the HRMS and PAN images is nearly identical, both images include repetitively similar patterns, which corresponds to the motivation of the developed non-local auto-regression prior. Second, we present an alternating minimization algorithm to unfold the variational model with cascading stages. Each stage has three interrelated sub-problems, and each module corresponds to an iterative algorithm operator. Figure 1 shows a specific flowchart with colored sub-problems. To facilitate signal flow between iterative stages, persistent memory enhances information representation by using the long-short term unit. In the three sub-problems, each iterative module's output feature maps are picked and combined for the next iterative step, promoting information fusion and decreasing information loss. With this method, both the interpretability and representation ability of the deep network are improved.

Our main contributions are summarized in the following three aspects:

1. By extending the iterative algorithm into a multistage solution that combines the benefits of both model-based and data-driven deep learning techniques, we present a novel interpretable memory-augmented model-driven network (MMNet) for Pan-sharpening. The interpretation of the deep model is enhanced by such a design.
2. To address the significant information loss problem in the signal flow, we suggest a new memory mechanism which is orthogonal to signal flow and develop a non-local cross-modality module. Such a design enhances the deep model's capacity for representation.
3. Extensive experiments over three satellite datasets demonstrate that our proposed network outperforms other state-of-the-art algorithms both qualitatively and quantitatively.

2 Related Work

2.1 Traditional Methods

By observing the existing Pan-sharpening methods, we can roughly divide the traditional methods into three main categories: CS-based methods, MRA-based methods and VO-based methods.

The CS-based approaches separate spatial and spectral information from the LRMS image and replace spatial information with a PAN image. Intensity hue-saturation (IHS) fusion [5], the principal component analysis (PCA) methods [21,32], Brovey transforms [14], and the Gram-Schmidt (GS) orthogonalization method [22] are common CS-based approaches. These CS-based approaches are rapid since LRMS images simply need spectral treatment to remove and replace spatial components, but the resultant HRMS show severe spectral distortion.

The MRA-based methods inject high-frequency features of PAN derived by multi-resolution decomposition techniques into upsampled multi-spectral images. Decimated wavelet transform (DWT) [26], high-pass filter fusion (HPF) [31], Laplacian pyramid (LP) [34], the smoothing filter-based intensity modulation (SFIM) [25] and atrous wavelet transform (ATWT) [28] are typical MRA-based methods that reduce spectral distortion and improve resolution, but they rely heavily on multi-resolution technique, which can cause local spatial artifacts.

Recent years, the VO-based methods are concerned because of the fine fusion effect on ill-posed problems. P+XS pan-sharpening approach [2] firstly assumes that PAN image is derived from the linear combination of various bands of HRMS, whereas the LRMS image is from the blurred HRMS. However, the conditions for the assumption linear combinatorial relationship are untenable. To avoid original drawbacks, constraints such as dynamic gradient sparsity property (SIRF) [6], local gradient constraint (LGC) [9], and group low-rank constraint for texture similarity (ADMM) [33] were introduced. These various constraints requiring the manual setting of parameters can only inadequately reflect the limited structural relations of the images, which can also result in degradation.

2.2   Deep Learning Based Methods

With the excellent capabilities for nonlinear mapping learning and feature extraction, (DL)-based methods have rapidly been widely used for Pan-sharpening. PNN [27] tries to use three convolutional units to directly map the relationship between PAN, LRMS and HRMS images. Inspired by PNN, a large number of pan-sharpening studies based on deep learning have emerged. For example, PAN-Net [38] adopts the residual learning module in Resnet [16], MSDCNN [39] adds multi-scale modules on the basis of residual connection, and SRPPNN [3] refers to the design idea of SRCNN [7] in the field of image super-resolution. Fu *et al.* [11] introduced grouped multi-scale dilated convolutions to obtain multi-scale contextual features. The above networks roughly stack the existing CNN frameworks, but they don't effectively utilize the spatial and spectral information of PAN and LRMS images, resulting in large redundancy in structural design.

Recently, some model-driven CNN models with clear physical meaning emerged. The basic idea is to use prior knowledge to formulate optimization problems for computer vision tasks, then unfold the optimization algorithms and replace the steps in the algorithm with deep neural networks. For example, Lefkimmiatis [23] unrolled the proximal gradient method and used a limited number of the iterations to construct the denoising network. Zhang *et al.* [41] transformed the iterative shrinkage-thresholding algorithm into a deep network form for image compressive sensing. Recently, based on the observation models for LRMS and PAN images, Xie *et al.* [36] and Xu *et al.* [37] propose the model-based deep learning network MHNet and GPPNN for Pan-sharpening,

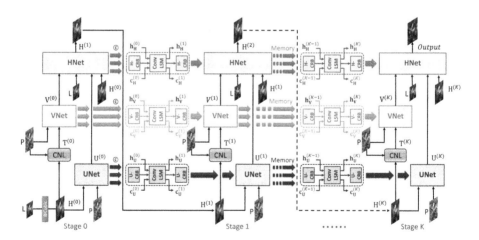

Fig. 1. The overall architecture of our proposed MMNet, consisting of information flow and memory flow. For information flow, LRMS is firstly up-sampled and then performs the stage-wise iteration updating in the overall K stages. CNL aims to explore the cross-modalities information to transfer the detailed structures of PAN to generate the immediate output N. The persistent memory mechanism (memory flow) is introduced to augment the information representation. (Best viewed in color.) (Color figure online)

respectively. Unfortunately, the cross-stages with reduced channel numbers lead to the loss of information, which hinders their performance improvements.

3   Proposed Approach

3.1   Model Formulation

In general, Pan-sharpening aims to obtain the HRMS image $\mathbf{H}$ from its degradation observation $\mathbf{L} = (\mathbf{H} \otimes \mathbf{K}) \downarrow_s + \mathbf{n_s}$, where $\mathbf{K}$ and $\downarrow_s$ denote blurring kernel and down-sampling operation, and $\mathbf{n_s}$ is usually assumed to be additive white Gaussian noise (AWGN) [36,37]. In formula, the degradation process by using the maximum a posterior (MAP) principle can be reformulated as (A detailed derivation process of the MAP model is provided in the supplementary material):

$$\max_{\mathbf{H}} \frac{1}{2} ||\mathbf{L} - \mathbf{DKH}||_2^2 + \eta \Omega_l(\mathbf{H}|\mathbf{P}) + \lambda \Omega_{NL}(\mathbf{H}|\mathbf{P}), \tag{1}$$

where $\mathbf{D}$ matrix denotes $\downarrow_s$, $\Omega_l(.)$ and $\Omega_{NL}(.)$ are the local and global implicit prior associated with $\mathbf{H}$. We solve the optimization problem using half-quadratic splitting (HQS) algorithm [12,17,20]. By introducing two auxiliary variables $\mathbf{U}$ and $\mathbf{V}$, Eq. 1 can be reformulated as a non-constrained optimization problem:

$$\min_{\mathbf{H},\mathbf{U},\mathbf{V}} \frac{1}{2} ||\mathbf{L} - \mathbf{DKH}||_2^2 + \frac{\eta_1}{2} ||\mathbf{U} - \mathbf{H}||_2^2 + \eta \Omega_l(\mathbf{U}|\mathbf{P})$$

$$+ \frac{\lambda_1}{2} ||\mathbf{V} - \mathbf{H}||_2^2 + \lambda \Omega_{NL}(\mathbf{V}|\mathbf{P}), \tag{2}$$

where η_1 and λ_1 are penalty parameters. When η_1 and λ_1 approach infinity, Eq. 2 converges to Eq. 1. Minimizing Eq. 2 involves updating $\mathbf{U}$, $\mathbf{V}$, and $\mathbf{H}$ alternately.

Updating U. Given the estimated HRMS image $\mathbf{H}^{(k)}$ at iteration k, the auxiliary variable $\mathbf{U}$ can be updated as:

$$\mathbf{U}^{(k)} = \arg\min_{\mathbf{U}} \frac{\eta_1}{2} \left|\left|\mathbf{U} - \mathbf{H}^{(k)}\right|\right|_2^2 + \eta_2 \Omega_l(\mathbf{U}|\mathbf{P}). \tag{3}$$

By applying the proximal gradient method [30] to Eq. (3), we can derive

$$\mathbf{U}^{(k)} = \text{prox}_{\Omega_l(.)}(\mathbf{U}^{(k-1)} - \delta_1 \nabla f_1(\mathbf{U}^{(k-1)})), \tag{4}$$

where $\text{prox}_{\Omega_l}(\cdot)$ is the proximal operator corresponding to the implicit local prior $\Omega_l(\cdot)$, δ_1 denotes the updating step size, and the gradient $\nabla f_1(\mathbf{U}^{(k-1)})$ is

$$\nabla f_1(\mathbf{U}^{(k-1)}) = \mathbf{U}^{(k-1)} - \mathbf{H}^{(k)}. \tag{5}$$

Updating V. Given $\mathbf{H}^{(k)}$, $\mathbf{V}$ can be updated as:

$$\mathbf{V}^{(k)} = \arg\min_{\mathbf{V}} \frac{\lambda_1}{2} \left\|\mathbf{V} - \mathbf{H}^{(k)}\right\|_2^2 + \lambda\Omega_{NL}(\mathbf{V}|\mathbf{P}). \tag{6}$$

Similarly, we can obtain

$$\mathbf{V}^{(k)} = \text{prox}_{\Omega_{NL}(.)}(\mathbf{V}^{(k-1)} - \delta_2\nabla f_2(\mathbf{V}^{(k-1)})), \tag{7}$$

where $\text{prox}_{\Omega_{NL}}(\cdot)$ is the proximal operator corresponding to the non-local prior term $\Omega_{NL}(\cdot)$, δ_2 indicates the updating step size, and the gradient $\nabla f_2(\mathbf{V}^{(k-1)})$ is computed as

$$\nabla f_2(\mathbf{V}^{(k-1)}) = \mathbf{V}^{(k-1)} - \mathbf{H}^{(k)}. \tag{8}$$

Updating H. Given $\mathbf{U}^{(k)}$ and $\mathbf{V}^{(k)}$, $\mathbf{H}$ is updated as:

$$\mathbf{H}^{(k+1)} = \arg\min_{\mathbf{H}} \frac{1}{2} \|\mathbf{L} - \mathbf{DKH}\|_2^2 + \frac{\eta_1}{2} \left\|\mathbf{U}^{(k)} - \mathbf{H}\right\|_2^2$$
$$+ \frac{\lambda_1}{2} \left\|\mathbf{V}^{(k)} - \mathbf{H}\right\|_2^2. \tag{9}$$

Although we can derive the closed form update of $\mathbf{H}$ from Eq. 9, the updating equation requires computing the inverse of a large matrix, which is computationally inefficient. To solve this problem, we continue to update $\mathbf{U}$ and $\mathbf{V}$ according to the established updating rules, and we update $\mathbf{H}$ using the gradient decent method. Consequently, the updated equation for $\mathbf{H}$ is

$$\mathbf{H}^{(k+1)} = \mathbf{H}^{(k)} - \delta_3\nabla f_3(\mathbf{H}^{(k)}), \tag{10}$$

where δ_3 is the step size, and the gradient $\nabla f_3(\mathbf{H}^{(k)})$ is

$$\nabla f_3(\mathbf{H}^{(k)}) = (\mathbf{DK})^T(\mathbf{DKH}^{(k)} - \mathbf{L}) + \eta_1(\mathbf{H}^{(k)} - \mathbf{U}^{(k)})$$
$$+ \lambda_1(\mathbf{H}^{(k)} - \mathbf{V}^{(k)}), \tag{11}$$

where T is the matrix transpose operation.

3.2   Memory-Augmented Model-Driven Network

Based on the iterative algorithm, we construct a model-driven deep neural network for Pan-sharpening as shown in Fig. 1. This network is an implementation of the algorithm for solving Eq. (1). Since the regularization terms $\Omega_l(\cdot)$ and $\Omega_{NL}(\cdot)$ are not explicitly defined, the two proximal operators $\text{prox}_{\Omega_l}(\cdot)$ and $\text{prox}_{\Omega_{NL}}(\cdot)$ cannot be explicitly inferred in the proposed algorithm. Thus, we employ deep CNNs to learn the two proximal operators for updating $\mathbf{U}$ and $\mathbf{V}$.

However, there are still several problems of deep unfolding network need to be resolved. First, cross-stages, or short-term memory, hasn't been fully explored.

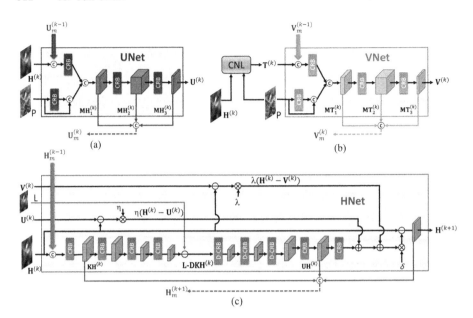

Fig. 2. The detailed structures of each sub-problems of U, V and H.

Further limiting their advancements is the fact that the feature transformation with channel number reduction obscured the severe information loss between adjacent stages, which is acknowledged as the rarely realized long-term dependency. We integrate the memory mechanism into the UNet, VNet and HNet shown in Fig. 2 in order to facilitate the signal flow between iterative stages. To be more precise, each iterative module's output intermediate images and different-layer feature maps are chosen, integrated for additional transformation, and then inserted into the following iterative stage for information interaction across stages, minimizing information loss. Next, we'll go into more detail about the upgraded versions of three sub-networks with embedded memory mechanism.

UNet. To increase the model capability, the memory of previous information at previous stages is introduced to the expressed module corresponding to $\mathrm{prox}_{\Omega_l}(\cdot)$. As illustrated in Fig. 2 (a), the UNet is designed with the basic CRB unit which consists of the pure convolution layer and the effective residual blocks. Taking the k-th iteration for example, the computation flow of UNet is defined as

$$\mathbf{P}_1^{(k-1)} = \mathrm{Cat}(\mathrm{CRB}(\mathbf{P}), \mathbf{P}), \tag{12}$$

$$\mathbf{H}_1^{(k-1)} = \mathrm{Cat}(\mathrm{CRB}(\mathbf{H}^{(k-1)}), \mathbf{U}_m^{(k-1)}), \tag{13}$$

$$\mathbf{MH}_1^{(k-1)} = \mathrm{Cat}(\mathbf{H}_1^{(k-1)}, \mathbf{P}_1^{(k-1)}), \tag{14}$$

$$\mathbf{MH}_2^{(k-1)} = \mathrm{CRB}(\mathbf{MH}_1^{(k-1)}), \tag{15}$$

$$\mathbf{U}^{(k)} = \mathrm{CRB}(\mathbf{MH}_2^{(k-1)}), \tag{16}$$

where $\mathrm{Cat}(\cdot)$ represents the concatenation operation along the channel dimension and $\mathbf{U}_m^{(k-1)}$ is the high-throughput information from previous stage to reduce the information loss. The updated memory $\mathbf{U}^{(k)}$ can be obtained by exploiting ConvLSTM unit to transform the different-layer's features $\mathbf{MH}_1^{(k-1)}$, $\mathbf{MH}_2^{(k-1)}$ and $\mathbf{U}^{(k)}$ as

$$\mathbf{MHU} = \mathrm{CRB}(\mathrm{Cat}(\mathbf{MH}_1^{(k-1)}, \mathbf{MH}_2^{(k-1)}, \mathbf{MH}_3^{(k-1)})), \tag{17}$$

$$\mathbf{h}_{\mathbf{U}}^{(k)}, \mathbf{c}_{\mathbf{U}}^{(k)} = \mathrm{ConvLSTM}(\mathbf{MHU}, \mathbf{h}_{\mathbf{U}}^{(k-1)}, \mathbf{c}_{\mathbf{U}}^{(k-1)}), \tag{18}$$

$$\mathbf{U}_m^{(k)} = \mathrm{CRB}(\mathbf{h}_{\mathbf{U}}^{(k)}), \tag{19}$$

where $\mathbf{h}_{\mathbf{U}}^{(k-1)}$ and $\mathbf{c}_{\mathbf{U}}^{(k-1)}$ denotes the hidden state and cell state in $ConvLSTM$ to augment the long-range cross stage information dependency. Furthermore, $\mathbf{h}_{\mathbf{U}}^{(k)}$ is directly fed into the CRB to generate the updated memory $\mathbf{U}_m^{(k)}$. The transition process of ConvLSTM is unfolded as

$$\mathbf{i}^{(k)} = \sigma(\mathbf{W}_{si} * \mathbf{MHU} + \mathbf{W}_{hi} * \mathbf{h}_{\mathbf{U}}^{(k-1)} + \mathbf{b}_i), \tag{20}$$

$$\mathbf{f}^{(k)} = \sigma(\mathbf{W}_{sf} * \mathbf{MHU} + \mathbf{W}_{hf} * \mathbf{h}_{\mathbf{U}}^{(k-1)} + \mathbf{b}_f), \tag{21}$$

$$\mathbf{c}^{(k)} = \mathbf{f}^{(k)} \odot \mathbf{c}_{\mathbf{U}}^{(k-1)} + \mathbf{i}^{(k)} \odot tanh(\mathbf{W}_{sc} * \mathbf{MHU}, \tag{22}$$
$$+ \mathbf{W}_{hc} * \mathbf{h}_{\mathbf{U}}^{(k-1)} + \mathbf{b}_c),$$

$$\mathbf{o}^{(k)} = \sigma(\mathbf{W}_{so} * \mathbf{MHU} + \mathbf{W}_{ho} * \mathbf{h}_{\mathbf{U}}^{(k-1)} + \mathbf{b}_o), \tag{23}$$

$$\mathbf{h}_{\mathbf{U}}^{(k)} = \mathbf{o}^{(k)} \odot tanh(\mathbf{c}_{\mathbf{U}}^{(k)}), \tag{24}$$

where $*$ and $\odot$ denote the convolution operation and Hadamard product, respectively. $\mathbf{c}_{\mathbf{U}}^{(k)}$ and $\mathbf{h}_{\mathbf{U}}^{(k)}$ represent the cell state and hidden state, respectively. σ and $tanh$ denote the sigmoid and tanh function, respectively. In this way, not only the information loss of feature channel reduction is alleviated, but also the long-term cross-stage information dependency can be enhanced.

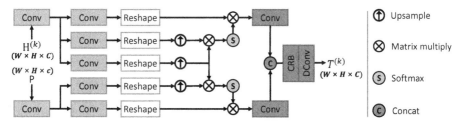

Fig. 3. The cross-modality non-local operation module. It takes the updated $\mathbf{H}^{(k)}$ and $\mathbf{P}$ as input and generates the refined image $\mathbf{T}^{(k)}$.

VNet. In Eq. 7, global implicit prior aims to measure the non-local cross-modality similarity and then aggregates the semantically-related and structure-consistent content from long-range patches in HRMS images and across the modalities of HRMS and PAN images. To this end, we devise a novel cross-modality non-local operation module (denoted as CNL). Figure 3 illustrates the CNL module, which receives the updated HRMS image $\mathbf{H}^{(k)}$ and PAN image $\mathbf{P}$ as input and generates the refined image $\mathbf{T}^{(k)}$.

With the output of CNL module $\mathbf{T}^{(k)}$, the previous output $\mathbf{V}^{(k-1)}$ and the accumulated memory state $\mathbf{V}_m^{(k-1)}$, we can obtain the updated $\mathbf{V}^{(k)}$ as shown in Fig. 2 (b). It can be clearly seen that the VNet has a similar architecture with that of UNet, which is consistent with their similar updating rules. Additionally, the memory transmission of VNet is also the same as that of UNet.

HNet. To transform the update process of $\mathbf{H}^{(k+1)}$ in Eq. 10 into a network. Firstly, we need to implement the two operations, i.e., $Down \downarrow_s$ and $Up \uparrow_s$, using the network. Specifically, $Down \downarrow_s$ is implemented by a CRB module with spatial identify transformation, and an additional s-strides followed CRB module with spatial resolution reduction:

$$\mathbf{KH}^{(k)} = \text{CRB}(\text{Cat}(\mathbf{H}^{(k)}, \mathbf{H}_m^{(k)})), \tag{25}$$

$$\mathbf{DKH}^{(k)} = \text{CRB}^{(s)} \downarrow (\mathbf{KH}^{(k)}), \tag{26}$$

where $\text{CRB}^{(s)} \downarrow$ aims to perform the s times down-sampling. The latter operation $Up \uparrow_s$ is implemented by a deconvolution layer containing the s-strides CRB module with spatial resolution expansion and a CRB module with spatial identify transformation:

$$\mathbf{UH}^{(k)} = \text{CRB}^{(s)} \uparrow (\mathbf{L} - \mathbf{DKH}^{(k)}), \tag{27}$$

where $\text{CRB}^{(s)} \uparrow$ aims to perform the s times up-sampling. Further, in context of Eqs. 10, 26 and 27, the updated $\mathbf{H}^{(k+1)}$ and the updated memory $\mathbf{H}_m^{(k+1)}$ can be obtained as follows:

$$\mathbf{MH}^{(k+1)} = \text{CRB}(\text{Cat}(\mathbf{KH}^{(k)}, \mathbf{UH}^{(k)}, \mathbf{H}^{(k+1)})), \tag{28}$$

$$\mathbf{h_H}^{(k+1)}, \mathbf{c_H}^{(k+1)} = \text{ConvLSTM}(\mathbf{MH}^{(k+1)}, \mathbf{h_H}^{(k)}, \mathbf{c_H}^{(k)}), \tag{29}$$

$$\mathbf{H}_m^{(k+1)} = \text{CRB}(\mathbf{h_H}^{(k+1)}), \tag{30}$$

where ConvLSTM performs similar functions as aforementioned. The features $\mathbf{KH}^{(k)}$, $\mathbf{UH}^{(k)}$ and $\mathbf{H}^{(k+1)}$ are obtained by different locations, thus possessing more adequate information and alleviate the information loss. Finally, with the updated $\mathbf{V}^{(k)}$, $\mathbf{U}^{(k)}$ and the accumulated memory state $\mathbf{H}_m^{(k)}$, we can obtain the updated $\mathbf{H}^{(k+1)}$ as illustrated in Fig. 2 (c).

3.3 Network Training

The distance between the estimated HRMS image from our proposed MMNet and the ground truth HRMS image is defined as the training loss for each training pair. Mean squared error (MSE) loss is the most commonly used loss function for calculating distance. MSE loss, on the other hand, usually produces over-smoothed results. Therefore, we construct our training objective function using the mean absolute error (MAE) loss, which is defined as

$$\mathcal{L} = \sum_{i=1}^{N} \left\| \mathbf{H}_i^{(K+1)} - \mathbf{H}_{gt,i} \right\|_1, \qquad (31)$$

where $\mathbf{H}_i^{(K+1)}$ denote the i-th estimated HRMS image, $\mathbf{H}_{gt,i}$ is i-th ground truth HRMS image and N is the number of training pairs.

4   Experiments

4.1   Datasets and Evaluation Metrics

We use the Wald protocol tool [35] to produce the training set since ground-truth pan-sharpened images are not available. To be more precise, the PAN image $\mathbf{P} \in R^{rM \times rN}$ and the MS image $\mathbf{H} \in R^{M \times N \times C}$ are both down-sampled with a ratio of r and then are represented by $\mathbf{L} \in R^{M/r \times N/r \times C}$ and $\mathbf{p} \in R^{M \times N}$, respectively. The LRMS image is thus considered to be $\mathbf{L}$, the PAN image to be $\mathbf{p}$, and the ground truth HRMS picture to be $\mathbf{H}$. In our experiment, the WorldViewII, WorldViewIII, and GaoFen2 satellites' remote sensing images are used for evaluation. There are hundreds of image pairs in each database, which are split into training, validation, and testing sets using the 7:2:1 ratio. Each training pair in the training set consists of one PAN image measuring 128 by 128 pixels, one LRMS patch measuring 32 by 32 pixels, and one ground truth HRMS patch measuring 128 by 128 pixels.

We use the the the peak signal-to-noise ratio (PSNR), the structural similarity (SSIM), the relative dimensionless global error in synthesis (ERGAS) [1], the spectral angle mapper (SAM) [40], the correlation coefficient (SCC), and the Q index [34] to measure how well all the methods work on the test data compared to the ground truth.

In order to assess the generalizability of our approach, we generate an additional real-world, full-resolution dataset of 200 samples over the chosen GaoFen2 satellite for evaluation. Specifically, the additional dataset is created using the full-resolution setting, which produces the MS and PAN images in the way described above without downsampling. As a result, the MS image is $128 \times 128 \times 4$ and the PAN image is $32 \times 32 \times 1$. Since a ground-truth HRMS image is not available, we adopt three widely-used non-reference image quality assessment (IQA) metrics for evaluation: the spectral distortion index D_λ, the spatial distortion index D_S, and the quality without reference (QNR).

4.2   Implementation Details

In our experiments, all our designed networks are implemented in PyTorch [29] framework and trained on the PC with a single NVIDIA GeForce GTX 3060

GPU. In the training phase, these networks are optimized by the Adam optimizer [19] over 1000 epochs with a mini-batch size of 4. The learning rate is initialized with 8×10^{-4}. When reaching 200 epochs, the learning rate is decayed by multiplying 0.5. Furthermore, all the hidden and cell states of ConvLSTM are initialized as zero and the input $\mathbf{H}^{(0)}$ of our unfolding network is obtained by applying Bibubic up-sampling over LRMS image $\mathbf{L}$.

4.3   Comparison with SOTA Methods

To verify the effectiveness of our proposed method on the Pan-sharpening task, we conduct several experiments on the benchmark datasets compared with several representative pan-sharpening methods: 1) five commonly-recognized state-of-the-art deep-learning based methods, including PNN [27], PANNET [38], MSDCNN [39], SRPPNN [3], and GPPNN [37]; 2) five promising traditional methods, including SFIM [25], Brovey [13], GS [22], IHS [15], and GFPCA [24].

Quantitative and Qualitative Results. The average quantitative performance between our method and aforementioned competitive algorithms on the three satellite datasets are tabulated in Table 1. It is clearly figured out that deep DL-based methods surpass the traditional methods and our proposed method can significantly outperform other state-of-the-art competing methods in terms of all the metrics. The qualitative comparison of the visual results over the representative sample from the WorldView-II dataset is in Fig. 4. To highlight the differences in detail, we select the Red, Green and Blue bands of the generated HRMS images to better visualize the qualitative comparison. As can be seen, our method can obtain a better visual effect since it accurately enhances the spatial details and preserves the spectral information, which is consistent with quantitative results shown in Table 1. More experimental results on the three datasets are included in the y material.

Table 1. Quantitative comparison with the state-of-the-art methods. The best results are highlighted by **bold**. The ↑ or ↓ indicates higher or lower values correspond to better results.

Method	WordView II				GaoFen2				WorldView III			
	PSNR ↑	SSIM↑	SAM↓	ERGAS↓	PSNR ↑	SSIM↑	SAM↓	ERGAS↓	PSNR ↑	SSIM↑	SAM↓	ERGAS↓
SFIM	34.1297	0.8975	0.0439	2.3449	36.9060	0.8882	0.0318	1.7398	21.8212	0.5457	0.1208	8.9730
Brovey	35.8646	0.9216	0.0403	1.8238	37.7974	0.9026	0.0218	1.3720	22.506	0.5466	0.1159	8.2331
GS	35.6376	0.9176	0.0423	1.8774	37.2260	0.9034	0.0309	1.6736	22.5608	0.5470	0.1217	8.2433
IHS	35.2962	0.9027	0.0461	2.0278	38.1754	0.9100	0.0243	1.5336	22.5579	0.5354	0.1266	8.3616
GFPCA	34.5581	0.9038	0.0488	2.1411	37.9443	0.9204	0.0314	1.5604	22.3344	0.4826	0.1294	8.3964
PNN	40.7550	0.9624	0.0259	1.0646	43.1208	0.9704	0.0172	0.8528	29.9418	0.9121	0.0824	3.3206
PANNet	40.8176	0.9626	0.0257	1.0557	43.0659	0.9685	0.0178	0.8577	29.684	0.9072	0.0851	3.4263
MSDCNN	41.3355	0.9664	0.0242	0.9940	45.6874	0.9827	0.0135	0.6389	30.3038	0.9184	0.0782	3.1884
SRPPNN	41.4538	0.9679	0.0233	0.9899	47.1998	0.9877	0.0106	0.5586	30.4346	0.9202	0.0770	3.1553
GPPNN	41.1622	0.9684	0.0244	1.0315	44.2145	0.9815	0.0137	0.7361	30.1785	0.9175	0.0776	3.2596
Ours	**41.8577**	**0.9697**	**0.0229**	**0.9420**	**47.2668**	**0.9890**	**0.0102**	**0.5472**	**30.5451**	**0.9214**	**0.0769**	**3.1032**

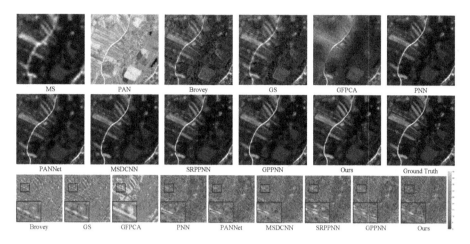

Fig. 4. Visual comparisons of the fused HRMS image for all the methods on one WorldView-II dataset. Images in the last row visualizes the MSE between the pansharpened results and the ground truth.

Effect on Full-Resolution Scenes. To assess the performance of our network in the full resolution case, we apply a pre-trained model built on GaoFen2 data to the unseen GaoFen2 satellite datasets are constructed using the full-resolution setting in the preceding Sect. 4.1. The experimental results of the all the methods are summarized in Table 2. Additionally, we also show visual comparisons for all the methods on a full-resolution sample in Fig. 5, from which we can observe that our proposed network obtains better visual fused effect both spatially and spectrally than other competing approaches.

Complexity Analysis. Comparisons on parameter numbers, actual inference speed on GPU and model performance (as measured by PSNR) are provided in Fig. 6. The most comparable solution to ours, GPPNN [37], is organized around the model-based unfolding principle and has comparable model parameters and flops reductions but inferior performance. This is due to the cross-stages with reduced channel numbers leading to the information loss and each stage of the model without fully exploring the potential of different modalities.

4.4 Ablation Study

Ablation studies are implemented on the WorldView-II dataset to explore the contribution of different hyper-parameters and model components to the performance of our proposed model.

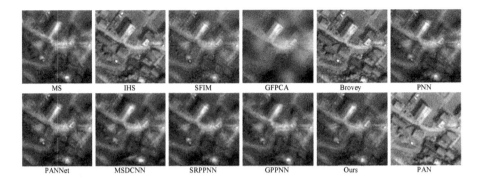

Fig. 5. Visual comparisons of the fused HRMS image on a full resolution sample.

Table 2. The average quantitative results on the GaoFen2 datasets in the full resolution case (boldface highlights the best).

Metrics	SFIM	GS	Brovey	IHS	GFPCA	PNN	PANNET	MSDCNN	SRPPNN	GPPNN	Ours
$D_\lambda \downarrow$	0.0822	0.0696	0.1378	0.0770	0.0914	0.0746	0.0737	0.0734	0.0767	0.0782	**0.0695**
$D_s \downarrow$	**0.1087**	0.2456	0.2605	0.2985	0.1635	0.1164	0.1224	0.1151	0.1162	0.1253	0.1139
$QNR \uparrow$	0.8214	0.7025	0.6390	0.6485	0.7615	0.8191	0.8143	0.8251	0.8173	0.8073	**0.8235**

Number of Stages. To investigate the impact of the number of unfolded stages on the performance, we experiment the proposed MMNet with varying numbers of stages K. Observing the results from Table 3, the model's performance has obtained considerable improvement as the number of stages increases until reaching to 4. When further increasing the K, the results show a decreasing trend, which may be caused by the difficulty of gradient propagation. We set $K = 4$ as the default stage number based on this experiment to balance the performance and computational complexity.

Table 3. The average results of MMNet with different number of stages.

Stage Number (K)	PSNR↑	SSIM↑	SAM↓	ERGAS↓	SCC↑	Q ↑	$D_\lambda \downarrow$	$D_S \downarrow$	QNR ↑
1	41.2772	0.9653	0.0249	1.0114	0.9664	0.7556	0.0616	0.1145	0.8319
2	41.4274	0.9673	0.0242	0.9834	0.9696	0.7650	0.0595	0.1106	0.8375
3	41.8058	0.9697	0.0224	0.9306	0.9737	0.7698	0.0622	0.1128	0.8329
4	**41.8577**	**0.9697**	**0.0229**	**0.9420**	**0.9745**	**0.7740**	**0.0629**	**0.1154**	**0.8299**
5	41.7545	0.9690	0.0226	0.9431	0.9729	0.7699	0.0600	0.1166	0.8315
6	41.4274	0.9673	0.0242	0.9834	0.9696	0.7650	0.0595	0.1106	0.8375

Effects of Different Components. To investigate the contribution of the devised modules in our network, we take the model with $K = 4$ as the baseline and then conduct the comparison by observing the difference before and after deleting the components. The corresponding quantitative comparison reported

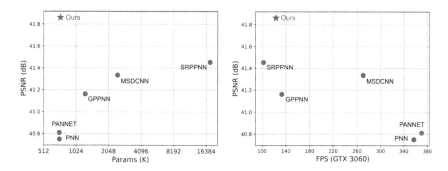

Fig. 6. Comparisons of model performance, number of parameters and FPS.

in Table 4, where SM represents memorizing information from a single layer and MM represents memorizing information from different-layer information at three locations. As can be observed, adding CNL and the memorized information from different locations will significantly improve the model performance.

Table 4. The results of MMNet with different components.

CNL	SM	MM	PSNR↑	SSIM↑	SAM↓	ERGAS↓	SCC↑	Q↑	D_λ ↓	D_S ↓	QNR↑
			41.4325	0.9668	0.0240	0.9933	0.9722	0.7579	0.0647	0.1178	0.8251
✓			41.6287	0.9683	0.0237	0.9653	0.9727	0.7673	0.0641	0.1154	0.8287
	✓		41.6476	0.9680	0.0237	0.9648	0.9729	0.7686	0.0639	0.1171	0.8277
		✓	41.7665	0.9697	0.0233	0.9437	0.9742	0.7731	0.0636	0.1168	0.8279
✓	✓		41.7199	0.9688	0.0235	0.9461	0.9734	0.7707	0.0618	0.1174	0.8289
✓		✓	**41.8577**	**0.9697**	**0.0229**	**0.9420**	**0.9745**	**0.7740**	**0.0629**	**0.1154**	**0.8299**

5 Conclusions

In this work, we propose a Memory-augmented Model-driven Network (MMNet) with interpretable structures for Pan-sharpening by unfolding the iterative algorithm into a multistage implementation. To augment the information representation across iterative stages, the persistent memory module is introduced. In this way, both the interpretability and representation ability of the deep network are improved. Extensive experiments demonstrate the superiority of the proposed method against other state-of-the-art models qualitatively and quantitatively. Additionally, compared to the other state-of-the-art models, MMNet also has competitive model parameters and running time.

References

1. Alparone, L., Wald, L., Chanussot, J., Thomas, C., Gamba, P., Bruce, L.M.: Comparison of pansharpening algorithms: outcome of the 2006 grs-s data fusion contest. IEEE Trans. Geosci. Remote Sens. **45**(10), 3012–3021 (2007)

2. Ballester, C., Caselles, V., Igual, L., Verdera, J., Rougé, B.: A variational model for P+XS image fusion. Int. J. Comput. Vision **69**(1), 43–58 (2006)

3. Cai, J., Huang, B.: Super-resolution-guided progressive pansharpening based on a deep convolutional neural network. IEEE Transactions on Geoscience and Remote Sensing (2020)

4. Cao, X., Fu, X., Xu, C., Meng, D.: Deep spatial-spectral global reasoning network for hyperspectral image denoising. IEEE Trans. Geosci. Remote Sens. **60**, 1–14 (2022)

5. Carper, W., Lillesand, T., Kiefer, R.: The use of intensity-hue-saturation transformations for merging spot panchromatic and multispectral image data. Photogramm. Eng. Remote. Sens. **56**(4), 459–467 (1990)

6. Chen, C., Li, Y., Liu, W., Huang, J.: SIRF: simultaneous satellite image registration and fusion in a unified framework. IEEE Trans. Image Process. **24**(11), 4213–4224 (2015)

7. Dong, C., Loy, C.C., He, K., Tang, X.: Image super-resolution using deep convolutional networks. IEEE Image Prior Migr. Pattern Anal. Mach. Intell. **38**(2), 295–307 (2015)

8. Dong, W., Wang, P., Yin, W., Shi, G., Wu, F., Lu, X.: Denoising prior driven deep neural network for image restoration. IEEE TPAMI **41**(10), 2305–2318 (2018)

9. Fu, X., Lin, Z., Huang, Y., Ding, X.: A variational pan-sharpening with local gradient constraints. In: Proceedings of the IEEE/CVF Conference on Computer Vision and Pattern Recognition, pp. 10265–10274 (2019)

10. Fu, X., Wang, M., Cao, X., Ding, X., Zha, Z.J.: A model-driven deep unfolding method for jpeg artifacts removal. IEEE Transactions on Neural Networks and Learning Systems, pp. 1–15 (2021)

11. Fu, X., Wang, W., Huang, Y., Ding, X., Paisley, J.: Deep multiscale detail networks for multiband spectral image sharpening. IEEE Trans. Neural Netw. Learn. Syst. **32**(5), 2090–2104 (2021)

12. Geman, D., Yang, C.: Nonlinear image recovery with half-quadratic regularization. IEEE Trans. Image Process. **4**(7), 932–946 (1995)

13. Gillespie, A.R., Kahle, A.B., Walker, R.E.: Color enhancement of highly correlated images. ii. channel ratio and "chromaticity" transformation techniques - sciencedirect. Remote Sens. Environ. **22**(3), 343–365 (1987)

14. Gillespie, A.R., Kahle, A.B., Walker, R.E.: Color enhancement of highly correlated images. ii. channel ratio and "chromaticity" transformation techniques. Remote Sens. Environ. **22**(3), 343–365 (1987)

15. Haydn, R., Dalke, G.W., Henkel, J., Bare, J.E.: Application of the ihs color transform to the processing of multisensor data and image enhancement. Nat. Acad. Sci. U.S.A **79**(13), 571–577 (1982)

16. He, K., Zhang, X., Ren, S., Sun, J.: Deep residual learning for image recognition. In: IEEE Conference on Computer Vision and Pattern Recognition, pp. 770–778 (2016)

17. He, R., Zheng, W.S., Tan, T., Sun, Z.: Half-quadratic-based iterative minimization for robust sparse representation. IEEE Trans. Pattern Anal. Mach. Intell. **36**(2), 261–275 (2014)

18. Hu, J., Hong, D., Wang, Y., Zhu, X.: A comparative review of manifold learning techniques for hyperspectral and polarimetric SAR image fusion. Remote Sens. **11**, 681 (2019)

19. Kingma, D.P., Ba, J.: Adam: a method for stochastic optimization (2017)

20. Krishnan, D., Fergus, R.: Fast image deconvolution using hyper-Laplacian priors. Adv. Neural. Inf. Process. Syst. **22**, 1033–1041 (2009)

21. Kwarteng, P., Chavez, A.: Extracting spectral contrast in landsat thematic mapper image data using selective principal component analysis. Photogramm. Eng. Remote. Sens. **55**(339–348), 1 (1989)
22. Laben, C.A., Brower, B.V.: Process for enhancing the spatial resolution of multispectral imagery using pan-sharpening (2000), uS Patent 6,011,875
23. Lefkimmiatis, S.: Non-local color image denoising with convolutional neural networks. In: CVPR (2017)
24. Liao, W., Xin, H., Coillie, F.V., Thoonen, G., Philips, W.: Two-stage fusion of thermal hyperspectral and visible RGB image by PCA and guided filter. In: Workshop on Hyperspectral Image and Signal Processing: Evolution in Remote Sensing (2017)
25. Liu, J.G.: Smoothing filter-based intensity modulation: a spectral preserve image fusion technique for improving spatial details. Int. J. Remote Sens. **21**(18), 3461–3472 (2000)
26. Mallat, S.: A theory for multiresolution signal decomposition: the wavelet representation. IEEE Trans. Pattern Anal. Mach. Intell. **11**(7), 674–693 (1989)
27. Masi, G., Cozzolino, D., Verdoliva, L., Scarpa, G.: Pansharpening by convolutional neural networks. Remote Sens. **8**(7), 594 (2016)
28. Nunez, J., Otazu, X., Fors, O., Prades, A., Pala, V., Arbiol, R.: Multiresolution-based image fusion with additive wavelet decomposition. IEEE Trans. Geosci. Remote Sens. **37**(3), 1204–1211 (1999)
29. Paszke, A., Gross, S., Massa, F., Lerer, A., Chintala, S.: PyTorch: an imperative style, high-performance deep learning library (2019)
30. Rockafellar, R.T.: Monotone operators and the proximal point algorithm. SIAM J. Control. Optim. **14**(5), 877–898 (1976)
31. Schowengerdt, R.A.: Reconstruction of multispatial, multispectral image data using spatial frequency content. Photogramm. Eng. Remote. Sens. **46**(10), 1325–1334 (1980)
32. Shah, V.P., Younan, N.H., King, R.L.: An efficient pan-sharpening method via a combined adaptive PCA approach and contourlets. IEEE Image Prior Migr. Geosci. Remote Sens. **46**(5), 1323–1335 (2008)
33. Tian, X., Chen, Y., Yang, C., Ma, J.: Variational pansharpening by exploiting cartoon-texture similarities. IEEE Transactions on Geoscience and Remote Sensing, pp. 1–16 (2021)
34. Vivone, G., et al.: A critical comparison among pansharpening algorithms. IEEE Trans. Geosci. Remote Sens. **53**(5), 2565–2586 (2014)
35. Wald, L., Ranchin, T., Mangolini, M.: Fusion of satellite images of different spatial resolutions: assessing the quality of resulting images. Photogrammet. Eng. Remote Sens. **63**, 691–699 (1997)
36. Xie, Q., Zhou, M., Zhao, Q., Meng, D., Zuo, W., Xu, Z.: Multispectral and hyperspectral image fusion by MS/HS fusion net. In: CVPR, pp. 1585–1594 (2019)
37. Xu, S., Zhang, J., Zhao, Z., Sun, K., Liu, J., Zhang, C.: Deep gradient projection networks for pan-sharpening. In: CVPR, pp. 1366–1375 (2021)
38. Yang, J., Fu, X., Hu, Y., Huang, Y., Ding, X., Paisley, J.: PanNet: a deep network architecture for pan-sharpening. In: IEEE International Conference on Computer Vision, pp. 5449–5457 (2017)
39. Yuan, Q., Wei, Y., Meng, X., Shen, H., Zhang, L.: A multiscale and multidepth convolutional neural network for remote sensing imagery pan-sharpening. IEEE J. Selected Top. Appl. Earth Observ. Remote Sens. **11**(3), 978–989 (2018)

40. Yuhas, R.H., Goetz, A.F.H., Boardman, J.W.: Discrimination among semi-arid landscape endmembers using the spectral angle mapper (sam) algorithm. In: Proceedings Summaries Annual JPL Airborne Geoscience Workshop, pp. 147–149 (1992)
41. Zhang, J., Ghanem, B.: ISTA-Net: interpretable optimization-inspired deep network for image compressive sensing. In: CVPR, pp. 1828–1837 (2018)

All You Need Is RAW: Defending Against Adversarial Attacks with Camera Image Pipelines

Yuxuan Zhang, Bo Dong, and Felix Heide$^{(\boxtimes)}$

Princeton University, Princeton, USA
`fheide@cs.princeton.edu`

Abstract. Existing neural networks for computer vision tasks are vulnerable to adversarial attacks: adding imperceptible perturbations to the input images can fool these models into making a false prediction on an image that was correctly predicted without the perturbation. Various defense methods have proposed image-to-image mapping methods, either including these perturbations in the training process or removing them in a preprocessing step. In doing so, existing methods often ignore that the natural RGB images in today's datasets are not captured but, in fact, recovered from RAW color filter array captures that are subject to various degradations in the capture. In this work, we exploit this RAW data distribution as an empirical prior for adversarial defense. Specifically, we propose a model-agnostic adversarial defensive method, which maps the input RGB images to Bayer RAW space and back to output RGB using a learned camera image signal processing (ISP) pipeline to eliminate potential adversarial patterns. The proposed method acts as an off-the-shelf preprocessing module and, unlike model-specific adversarial training methods, does not require adversarial images to train. As a result, the method generalizes to unseen tasks without additional retraining. Experiments on large-scale datasets, *e.g.*, ImageNet, COCO, for different vision tasks, *e.g.*, classification, semantic segmentation, object detection, validate that the method significantly outperforms existing methods across task domains.

Keywords: Adversarial defense · Low-level imaging · Neural image processing

1 Introduction

The most successful methods for a wide range of computer vision tasks rely on deep neural networks [10,29,30,34,88] (DNNs), including classification, detection, segmentation, scene understanding, scene reconstruction, and generative tasks. Although we rely on the predictions of DNNs for safety-critical applications in robotics, self-driving vehicles, medical diagnostics, and video security,

Supplementary Information The online version contains supplementary material available at https://doi.org/10.1007/978-3-031-19800-7_19.

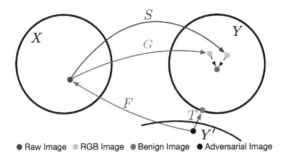

Fig. 1. Existing defense approaches learn an RGB-to-RGB projection from an adversarial distribution (Y') to its natural RGB distribution (Y): $T : Y' \rightarrow Y$. In contrast, our approach learns a mapping via the intermediate natural RAW distribution (X), which is achieved by utilizing three specially designed operators: $F : Y' \rightarrow X$, $G : X \rightarrow Y$, and $S : X \rightarrow Y$.

existing networks have been shown to be vulnerable to adversarial attacks [72]: small perturbations to images that are imperceptible to the human vision system can deceive DNNs to make incorrect predictions [50,54,61,71,76]. As such, defending against adversarial attacks [4,49,50,58,83] can help resolve failure cases in safety-critical applications and provide insights into the generalization capabilities of training procedures and network architectures.

Existing defense methods fall into two approaches: they either introduce adversarial examples to the training dataset, resulting in new model weights, or transform the inputs, aiming to remove the adversarial pattern, before feeding them into the unmodified target models. Specifically, the first line of defense methods generates adversarial examples by iteratively training a target model while finding and adding remaining adversarial images as training samples in each iteration [23,78,79,79,86]. Although the set of successful adversarial examples shrinks over time, iteratively generating them is extremely costly in training time, and different adversarial images must be included for defending against different attack algorithms. Moreover, the adversarial examples cannot be captured in a single training set as they are model-specific and domain-specific, meaning they must be re-generated when used for different models or on other domains.

Defense methods that transform the input image aim to overcome the limitations of adversarial training approaches. Considering adversarial perturbations as noise, these methods "denoise" the inputs before feeding them into unmodified target models. The preprocessing module can either employ image-to-image models such as auto-encoders or generative adversarial methods [37,48,65] or rely on conventional image-processing operations [15,18,26,44]. Compared to adversarial training methods, these methods are model-agnostic and require no adversarial images for training.

All methods in this approach have in *common that they rely on RGB image data as input and output.* That is, they aim to recover the distribution of natural RGB images and project the adversarial image input to the closest match in this distribution, using a direct image-to-image mapping network. As such, existing methods often ignore the fact that images in natural image datasets are the result of several processing steps applied to the raw captured images. In particular, training datasets are produced by interpolating sub-sampled, color filtered (*e.g.*, using Bayer filter) raw data, followed by a rich low-level processing pipeline, including readout and photon noise denoising. As a result, the raw per-pixel photon counts are heavily subsampled, degraded, and processed in an RGB image. We rely on the *RAW data distribution, before becoming RGB images, as a prior in the proposed adversarial defense method*, which is empirically described in large datasets of RAW camera captures. Specifically, instead of directly learning a mapping between adversarially perturbed input RGBs and "clean" output RGBs, we learn a mapping via the intermediate RAW color filter array domain. In this mapping, we rely on learned ISP pipelines as low-level camera image processing blocks to map from RAW to RGB. The resulting method is entirely model-agnostic, requires no adversarial examples to train, and acts as an off-the-shelf preprocessing module that can be transferred to any task on any domain. We validate our method on large-scale datasets (ImageNet, COCO) for different vision tasks (classification, semantic segmentation, object detection) and also perform extensive ablation studies to assess the robustness of the proposed method to various attack methods, model architecture choices, and hyper-parameters choices. Code and data to reproduce the findings in this work are available here.

Specifically, we make the following contributions:

- We propose the first adversarial defense method that exploits the natural distribution of RAW domain images.
- The proposed method avoids the generation of adversarial training images and can be used as an off-the-shelf preprocessing module for diverse tasks.
- We analyze how the natural RAW image distribution helps defend against adversarial attacks, and we validate that the method achieves *state-of-the-art* defense accuracy for input transformation defenses, outperforming existing approaches.

2   Related Work

2.1   Camera Image Signal Processing (ISP) Pipeline

A camera image signal processing (ISP) pipeline converts RAW measurements from a digital camera sensor to high-quality images suitable for human viewing or downstream analytic tasks. To this end, a typical ISP pipeline encompasses a sequence of modules [38], each addressing a portion of this image reconstruction problem. In a hardware ISP, these modules are proprietary compute units, and their behaviors are unknown to the user. More importantly, the modules are not differentiable [53,74]. Two lines of work rely on deep-learning-based approaches to cope with the significant drawback.

The first flavor of methods directly replaces the hardware ISP with a deep-learning-based model to target different application scenarios, such as low-light enhancement [8,9], super-resolution [84,85,89], smartphone camera enhancement [14,33,66], and ISP replacement [43]. Nevertheless, the deep-learning-based models used by these works contain a massive number of parameters and are computationally expensive. Hence, their application is limited to offline tasks. In contrast, another thread of works focused on searching for the best hardware ISP hyperparameters for different downstream tasks by using deep-learning-based approaches. Specifically, Tseng et al. [74] proposed differentiable proxy functions to model arbitrary ISP pipelines and used them to find the best hardware ISP hyperparameters for different downstream tasks. Yu et al. [87] proposed ReconfigISP, which uses different proxy functions for each module of a hardware ISP instead of the entire ISP pipeline. Mosleh et al. [53] proposed a hardware-in-the-loop method to optimize hyperparameters of a hardware ISP directly.

2.2   Adversarial Attack Methods

Adversarial attacks have drawn significant attention from the deep-learning community. Based on the level of access to target networks, adversarial attacks can be broadly categorized into white-box attacks and black-box attacks.

Among white-box attacks, one important direction is gradient-based attacks [24,40,50]. These approaches generate adversarial samples based on the gradient of the loss function with respect to input images. Another flavor of attacks is based on solving optimization problems to generate adversarial samples [6,71]. In the black-box setting, only benign images and their class labels are given, meaning attackers can only query the target model. With the free query, Black-box attacks rely on adversarial transferability to train substitute models [31,57,59,69] or directly estimate the target model gradients [12,13,77] to generate adversarial examples. To avoid the transferability and the overhead of gathering data to train a substitute model, several works proposed local-search-based black-box attacks to generate adversarial samples directly in the input domain [5,42,55].

In the physical world, adversarial samples are captured by cameras providing image inputs to target networks. A variety of strategies have been developed to guard the effectiveness of the adversarial patterns in the wild [2,17,21,35]. These methods typically assume that the camera acquisition and subsequent hardware processing do not alter the adversarial patterns. Phan et al. [60] have recently realized attacks on individual camera types by exploiting slight differences in their hardware ISPs and optical systems.

2.3   Defense Methods

In response to adversarial attack methods, there have been significant efforts in constructing defenses to counter those attacks. These include adversarial training [50], input transformation [3,19], defensive distillation [58], dynamic models [80], loss modifications [56], model ensemble [67] and robust architecture [27]. We next analyze the two representative categories of defense methods.

Adversarial Training (AT): The idea of AT is the following: in each training loop, we augment training data with adversarial examples generated by different attacks. AT is known to "overfit" to the attacks "seen" during training and has

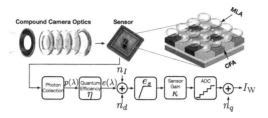

Fig. 2. Overview of the RAW imaging pipeline model. The scene light field is captured by compound camera optics, and then it is gathered by a microlens array layer before being captured on the color filter array. The color-filtered photons are converted into electrons based on quantum efficiency before adding dark current and noise. Next, the converted electrons are clipped based on the maximum well capacity, e_s, and scaled by a sensor gain factor κ. Finally, an ADC converts the analog signal into a digital readout with quantization noise n_q, I_W.

been demonstrated to be vastly effective in defending those attacks. However, AT does not generalize well to "unseen" attacks [70]. Furthermore, iteratively generating adversarial images is time-consuming, causing 3–30 times longer than standard training before the model converges [68]. Multiple methods have been proposed to reduce the training time, making AT on large datasets (*e.g.*, ImageNet) possible [23,78,79,90]. Even so, for each specific model, the approach still requires an extra adversarial training process and suffers from cross-domain attacks. Besides the target model, it is also worth noting that adversarial examples can be used to train the input preprocessing models. [44].

Input Transformation (IT): IT, as an image pre-processing approach, aims to remove adversarial patterns to counter attacks. A considerable number of IT methods have been proposed, such as JPEG compression [15,19,47], randomization [81], image quilting [26], pixel deflection [62], and deep-learning-based approaches [37,48,65]. These IT methods can seamlessly work with different downstream models and tasks. More importantly, IT methods can be easily combined with other model-specific defense methods to offer a stronger defense.

Our work falls into the IT category. Unlike existing IT methods to focus on the preprocessing in the RGB distribution, the proposed approach leverages the intermediate natural RAW distribution to remove adversarial patterns.

3   Sensor Image Formation

In this section, we review how a RAW image is formed. When light from the scene enters a camera aperture, it first passes through compound camera optics which focus the light on an image sensor (*e.g.*, CCD and CMOS), where the photons are color-filtered and converted to electrons. Finally, the electrons are converted to digital values, comprising a RAW image. We refer the reader to Karaimer and Brown [38] for a detailed review.

Compound Camera Optics: A compound lens consisting of a sequence of optics is designed to correct optical aberrations. When scene radiance, I_{SCENE} (in the form of a light field) enters a compound lens, the radiance is modulated by the complex optical pipeline and generates the image I_O. Compound optics can be modeled by spatially-varying point spread functions (PSFs) [73].

Color Image Sensor Model: A conventional color image sensor has three layers. On the top is a micro-lens array (MLA) layer; the bottom is a matrix of small potential wells; a color filter array (CFA) layer sits in the middle. When I_O falls on a color image sensor, photons first pass through the MLA to improve light collection. Next, light passes through the CFA layer, resulting in a mosaic pattern of the three stimulus RGB colors. Finally, the bottom layer collects the color-filtered light and outputs a single channel RAW image, I_W.

The detailed process is illustrated in Fig. 2. In particular, at the bottom layer, a potential well counts photons arriving at its location (x, y) and converts the accumulated photons to electrons, and the conversion process is specified by the detector quantum efficiency. During this process, electrons can fluctuate randomly which we summarize as electron noise. Two common types of electron noise are the dark noise n_d, which is independent of light; and dark current n_I, which depends on the sensor temperature. These follow normal and Poisson distributions, respectively [73]. Next, the converted electrons are clipped based on the maximum well capacity, e_s, and scaled by a sensor gain factor κ. Finally, the modulated electrons are converted to digital values by an analog-to-digital converter (ADC), which quantizes the input and introduces a small amount of noise, n_q.

Mathematically, a pixel of a RAW image, I_W, at position (x, y) can be defined as

$$I_W(x, y) = b + n_q + \kappa \min(e_s, n_d + n_I + \sum_\lambda e(x, y, \lambda)), \tag{1}$$

where b is the black level, level of brightness with no light; $e(x, y, \lambda)$ is the number of electrons arrived at a well at position (x, y) for wavelength λ.

This image formation model reveals that besides the natural scene being captured, RAW images heavily depend on the *specific stochastic nature of the optics, color filtering, sensing, and readout components*. The proposed method exploits these statistics.

4   Raw Image Domain Defense

In this section, we describe the proposed defense method, which exploits the distribution of RAW measurements as a prior to project adversarially perturbed RGB images to benign ones. Given an adversarial input, existing defense approaches learn an RGB-to-RGB projection from the adversarially perturbed distribution of RGB images, Y', to the closest point in corresponding RGB natural distribution, Y. We use the operator $T : Y' \rightarrow Y$ for this projection operation. As this RGB distribution Y empirically samples from the ISP outputs of diverse existing cameras, it also ingests diverse reconstruction artifacts,

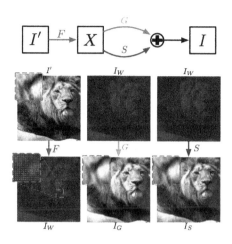

Fig. 3. Overview of the proposed defense approach; see text. We note that the resolution of the RAW image (RGGB) is twice larger than that of the RGB image. We linearly scaled the RAW image in this figure for better visualization. (Color figure online)

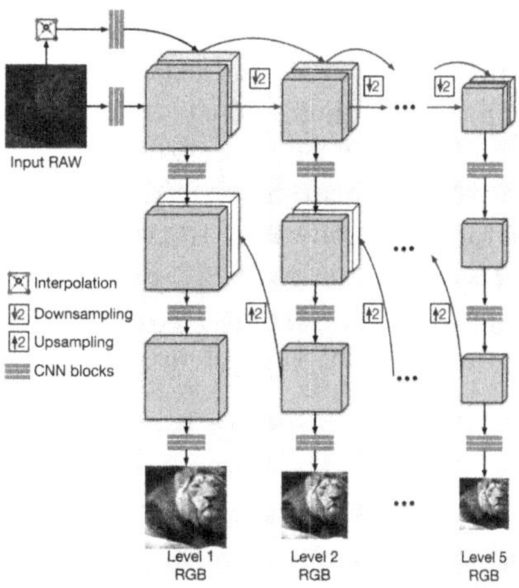

Fig. 4. The architecture of the G operator is adopted and modified from PyNet [32]. The finer operator level exploits upsampled coarser-level features to reconstruct the RGB output. The model is trained sequentially in a coarse-to-fine manner.

making it impossible to exploit photon-flux-specific cues, e.g., photon shot noise, optical aberrations, or camera-specific readout characteristics – image processing pipelines are designed to remove such RAW cues.

Departing from existing methods, as illustrated in Fig. 1, we learn a mapping from Y' to Y via an intermediate RAW distribution, X, which incorporates these RAW statistics of natural images, such as sensor photon counts, multispectral color filter array distributions and optical aberrations. To this end, the approach leverages three specially designed operators: $F : Y' \rightarrow X$, $G : X \rightarrow Y$, and $S : X \rightarrow Y$. Specifically, the F operator is a learned model, which maps an adversarial sample from its adversarial distribution to its corresponding RAW sample in the natural image distribution of RAW images. Operator G is another learned network that performs an ISP reconstruction task, *i.e.*, it converts a RAW image to an RGB image. In theory, our goal can be achieved with these two operators by concatenating both $G(F(\cdot)) : Y' \rightarrow X \rightarrow Y$. However, as these two operators are differentiable models, the potential adversary may still be able to attack the model if, under stronger attack assumptions, he has full access to the weight of preprocessing modules. To address this issue, we rely on an additional operator S, a conventional ISP, to our approach, which is implemented as a sequence of cascaded software-based sub-modules. In contrast to the operator F, the operator S is non-differentiable. The operators F and G are trained separately without end-to-end fine-tuning. Notably, the proposed defense scheme is *entirely model-agnostic* as it does not require any knowledge of potential adversarial attacks.

For defending against an attack, as shown in Fig. 3, the proposed approach first uses the F operator to map an input adversarial image, I', to its intermediate RAW measurements, I_W. Then, I_W is processed separately by the G and S operators to convert it to two images in the natural RGB distribution, denoted as I_G and I_S, respectively. Finally, our method outputs a benign image, I, in the natural RGB distribution, by combining I_G and I_S in a weighted-sum manner. Mathematically, the defense process is defined as

$$I = \omega G(F(I')) + (1 - \omega)S(F(I')), \tag{2}$$

where ω is a hyper-parameter for weighting the contributions from the two operators G and S. In the following sections, we introduce each operator in detail.

4.1 F Operator: Image-to-RAW Mapping

We use a small learned encoder-decoder network as the F operator to map an RGB image to its intermediate RAW measurements. The details of network architecture are given in the Supplementary Material.

We train this module in a supervised manner with two $\mathcal{L}_2$ losses. Both $\mathcal{L}_2$ losses are calculated between the ground truth (GT) RAW and estimated RAW images. The only difference between the two losses is the input RGB image corresponding to the estimated RAW. One is using the original input RGB image, while the other is generated by adding Gaussian noise to the original input RGB image. In doing so, F is trained with the ability to convert both benign and slightly perturbed RGB images to their corresponding RAW distributions. We note that the added Gaussian distribution is *different from the correlated noise generated by various adversarial attacks*. Mathematically, given a benign RGB image, I, and its corresponding GT RAW measurements, GT_W, the loss function is defined as

$$\mathcal{L}_F = ||F(I), GT_W||_2 + ||F(I + \alpha\varepsilon), GT_W||_2, \tag{3}$$
$$\varepsilon \sim \mathcal{N}(\mu, \sigma), \tag{4}$$

where ε is a Gaussian noise with mean, μ, and standard deviation, σ; α is a random number in the range between 0 and 1, weighting the amount of noise added. We empirically set μ and σ to 0 and 1, respectively.

4.2 G Operator: Learned ISP

The G operator is represented by a neural network that converts the I_w generated by the F operator to an RGB image. During this process, we aim to guide local adjustment by global contextual information. This motivates us to devise a pyramidal convolutional neural network to fuse global and local features. To this end, we propose a variant of PyNet [32] consisting of five levels; see Fig. 4.

Here, the $1st$ level is the finest, and the $5th$ level is the coarsest. The finer levels use upsampled features from the coarser levels by concatenating them. We modify PyNet by adding an interpolation layer before the input of each level, interpolating the downsampled RAW Bayer pattern. This facilitates learning as the network only needs to learn the residuals between interpolated RGB and ground truth RGB.

The loss function for this model consists of three components: perceptual, structural similarity, and $\mathcal{L}_2$ loss. Given an input RAW image, I_W, and the corresponding GT RGB image GT_I, the loss function can be defined as

$$\mathcal{L}_G^i = \beta^i \mathcal{L}_{Perc}(G(I_W), GT_I) + \gamma^i \mathcal{L}_{SSIM}((G(I_W), GT_I)) \\ + \mathcal{L}_2(G(I_W), GT_I) \quad \text{for} \quad i \in [1, 5], \tag{5}$$

where i represents the training level. As the model is trained in a coarse-to-fine manner, different losses are used for each level i. $\mathcal{L}_{Perc}$, $\mathcal{L}_{SSIM}$, and $\mathcal{L}_2$ represent the perceptual loss calculated with VGG architecture, structural similarity loss, and $\mathcal{L}_2$ loss, respectively; β^i and γ^i are the two hyperparameter weights, which are set empirically. The model is trained sequentially in a coarse-to-fine manner, i.e., from $i = 5$ to $i = 1$.

4.3 S Operator: Conventional ISP

The S operator has the same functionality as the G operator, converting a RAW image to an RGB image. Unlike the G operator, the S operator offers the functionalities of a conventional hardware ISP pipeline using a sequence of cascaded sub-modules, which is non-differentiable.

While we may use the ISP pipeline of any digital camera we can extract raw and post-ISP data from, we employ a software-based ISP pipeline consisting of the following components: Bayer demosaicing, color balancing, white balancing, contrast improvement, and colorspace conversion sub-modules. Using on the Zurich-Raw-to-RGB dataset [33], we manually tune the hyperparameters of all sub-modules. We refer the reader to the Supplementary Material for a detailed description.

4.4 Operator Training

We use the Zurich-Raw-to-RGB dataset [33] to train the F and G operators. The Zurich-Raw-to-RGB dataset consists of 20,000 RAW-RGB image pairs, captured using a Huawei P20 smartphone with a 12.3 MP Sony Exmor IMX380 sensor and a Canon 5D Mark IV DSLR. Both of the F and G operators are trained in PyTorch with Adam optimizer on NVIDIA A100 GPUs. We set the learning rate to 1e−4 and 5e−5 for training the F and G operators, respectively. We use the following hyperparameters settings: $\omega = 0.7$ in Eq. 2; $\mu = 0$ and $\sigma = 1$ for the Gaussian component in Eq. 4; In Eq. 5, β^i is set to 1 for $i \in [1, 3]$ and 0 for $i \in [4, 5]$; γ^i is set to 1 for $i = 1$ and 0 for $i \in [2, 5]$.

5   Experiments and Analysis

Table 1. Quantitative Comparisons on ImageNet We evaluate Top-1 Accuracy on ImageNet and compare the proposed method to existing input-transformation methods. The best Top-1 accuracies are marked in bold. Our defense method offers the best performance in all settings, except for the DeepFool attack.

	FSGM		PGD		BIM		DeepFool		C&W		NewtonFool	BPDA
	2/255 ↑	4/255 ↑	2/255 ↑	4/255 ↑	2/255 ↑	4/255 ↑	L_∞ ↑	L_2 ↑	L_∞ ↑	L_2 ↑	L_∞ ↑	L_∞ ↑
ResNet-101												
JPEG-defense[19]	33.14	20.71	45.19	21.74	36.78	8.5	53.16	45.69	59.06	52.01	24.65	0.08
TVM[26]	43.75	40.02	45.46	44.35	44.86	41.93	47.69	39.89	45.51	40.44	22.6	6.39
Randomized resizing & Padding [81]	45.21	34.97	45.38	27.75	40.04	18.04	73.06	62.47	66.53	59.87	27.93	2.66
HGD [45]	54.75	43.85	55.26	50.05	56.74	48.61	64.34	58.13	59.98	52.88	27.70	0.03
Pixel-Deflection [62]	54.56	35.14	60.68	34.86	58.71	41.91	**75.97**	**64.13**	66.29	60.91	28.81	1.87
ComDefend [37]	48.21	36.51	53.28	48.38	51.39	42.01	63.68	55.62	58.53	50.38	26.46	0.03
Proposed Method	**66.02**	**58.85**	**68.34**	**66.17**	**66.91**	**63.01**	72.04	63.52	**71.40**	**67.33**	**40.96**	**38.85**
InceptionV3												
JPEG-Defense [19]	31.97	20.25	43.34	21.15	34.68	8.55	51.20	43.49	55.00	50.39	24.06	0.12
TVM [26]	42.47	37.23	42.75	41.61	42.80	39.71	45.21	37.39	43.27	37.51	23.05	4.58
Randomized Resizing & Padding [81]	41.86	34.49	43.41	25.60	39.42	16.62	70.24	58.65	63.24	55.62	27.55	2.09
HGD [45]	52.83	40.99	50.35	47.62	56.02	47.78	60.33	56.61	59.55	52.0	26.84	0.03
Pixel-deflection [62]	51.42	34.27	56.13	32.49	56.18	39.13	**71.16**	**61.58**	61.94	57.58	28.01	1.56
ComDefend [37]	47.00	35.34	49.99	46.15	48.74	39.58	60.01	52.47	55.85	47.70	25.44	0.03
Proposed Method	**63.03**	**56.34**	**65.69**	**63.03**	**64.77**	**59.49**	69.25	60.04	**66.97**	**64.69**	**38.01**	**36.43**

The proposed method acts as an off-the-shelf input preprocessing module, requiring no additional training to be transferred to different tasks. To validate the effectiveness and generalization capabilities of the proposed defense approach, we evaluate the method on three different vision tasks, *i.e.*, classification, semantic segmentation, and 2D object detection, with corresponding adversarial attacks.

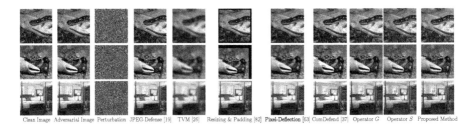

Clean Image   Adversarial Image   Perturbation   JPEG-Defense [19]   TVM [26]   Resizing & Padding [82]   **Pixel-Deflection** [63]   ComDefend [37]   Operator G Operator S Proposed Method

Fig. 5. Qualitative outputs of the proposed method along with both G and S operators and state-of-the-art defense methods on the ImageNet dataset; see text.

Table 2. Quantitative Comparison to SOTA Input-Transformation Defense Methods on the COCO dataset. We evaluate all methods for mean IoU (mIoU) and mark the best mIoU in bold. Our defense method achieves the best performance in all settings.

	FSGM		PGD		BIM		DAG	
	$L_\infty = 2/255$ ↑	$L_\infty = 4/255$ ↑	$L_\infty = 2/255$ ↑	$L_\infty = 4/255$ ↑	$L_\infty = 2/255$ ↑	$L_\infty = 4/255$ ↑	$L_\infty = 2/255$ ↑	$L_\infty = 4/255$ ↑
JPEG-Defense [19]	37.41	32.27	24.53	6.21	25.74	10.18	14.12	5.66
TVM [26]	42.64	41.53	45.55	42.24	44.51	38.44	31.88	25.56
HGD [45]	43.39	40.82	44.54	40.88	40.03	39.95	28.61	22.36
Pixel-Deflection [62]	44.13	41.88	46.38	42.32	44.78	37.22	30.73	24.61
ComDefend [37]	45.57	39.23	44.85	41.14	42.71	36.12	28.94	23.36
Proposed Method	**52.35**	**48.04**	**53.41**	**49.59**	**54.86**	**50.51**	**40.35**	**37.88**

5.1 Experimental Setup

Adversarial Attack Methods: We evaluate our method by defending against the following attacks: FGSM [25], BIM [41], PGD [51] , C&W [7], NewtonFool [36], and DeepFool [52]. For classification, we use the widely used Foolbox benchmarking suite [63] to implement these attack methods. Since Foolbox does not directly support semantic segmentation and object detection attacks, we use the lightweight TorchAttacks library [39] for generating adversarial examples with FGSM, PGD, and BIM attacks. We also evaluate against the DAG [82] attack, a dedicated attack approach for semantic segmentation and object detection tasks. Moreover, we further evaluate against BPDA [1], an attack method specifically

Table 3. Quantitative Comparison to SOTA Input-Transformation Defense Methods on the ADE20K dataset. We evaluate all methods for mean IoU (mIoU) and mark the best mIoU in bold. Our defense method achieves the best performance in all settings.

	FSGM		PGD		BIM		DAG	
	$L_\infty = 2/255$ ↑	$L_\infty = 4/255$ ↑	$L_\infty = 2/255$ ↑	$L_\infty = 4/255$ ↑	$L_\infty = 2/255$ ↑	$L_\infty = 4/255$ ↑	$L_\infty = 2/255$ ↑	$L_\infty = 4/255$ ↑
JPEG-Defense[19]	22.18	17.61	23.40	8.37	20.39	6.55	7.09	4.35
TVM [26]	26.72	24.79	23.91	21.07	20.60	18.53	16.12	14.28
HGD [45]	31.15	26.23	29.44	25.78	24.42	23.08	20.17	19.75
Pixel-Deflection [62]	29.40	25.36	30.28	26.59	28.94	21.30	18.82	17.55
ComDefend [37]	30.62	25.89	28.74	27.69	27.08	21.39	20.83	19.42
Proposed Method	**37.83**	**35.15**	**39.22**	**36.20**	**38.63**	**35.18**	**25.09**	**22.47**

Table 4. Quantitative Comparison to SOTA Input-Transformation Defenses on the Pascal VOC dataset. We evaluate all compared methods on mean average precision (mAP) on the Pascal VOC dataset. The best mAPs are marked in bold. Our defense method achieves the best performance in all settings.

	FSGM		PGD		BIM		DAG	
	$L_\infty = 2/255$ ↑	$L_\infty = 4/255$ ↑	$L_\infty = 2/255$ ↑	$L_\infty = 4/255$ ↑	$L_\infty = 2/255$ ↑	$L_\infty = 4/255$ ↑	$L_\infty = 2/255$ ↑	$L_\infty = 4/255$ ↑
JPEG-Defense[19]	39.02	35.88	37.96	33.51	38.85	34.69	30.72	25.07
TVM[26]	48.11	39.66	47.1	44.38	48.94	41.76	39.20	33.18
HGD [45]	50.68	40.06	51.24	45.92	46.80	39.74	41.15	37.23
Pixel-deflection[62]	53.77	44.82	54.45	47.22	55.32	48.32	46.52	39.87
ComDefend[37]	50.18	42.93	50.46	43.08	52.32	44.2	44.68	37.22
Proposed method	**61.68**	**59.37**	**64.71**	**60.23**	**66.52**	**61.82**	**57.83**	**54.12**

designed for circumventing input transformation defenses that rely on obfuscated gradients. Defending against BPDA with our method, however, requires a slight modification at inference time; see Supplementary Material for details. We note that all applied attacks are untargeted. Definitions of all attack methods are provided in the Supplementary Material.

Baseline Defense Approaches: We compare to the following input transformation defense methods: JPEG compression [19], randomized resizing & padding[81], image quilting [26], TVM [26], HGD [45], pixel deflection [62], and Comdefend [37]. We evaluate all baseline methods on the three vision tasks, except that the randomized resizing & padding is omitted in semantic segmentation and object detection tasks as it destroys the semantic structure. We directly adopt the open-source PyTorch implementation for all baseline methods. We use the same training dataset as the one used to train our method for those methods that required training. It is worth noting that all baseline methods do not require adversarial examples for training.

Evaluation Dataset and Metrics: For classification, we use the ImageNet validation set and evaluate the Top-1 classification accuracy of all competing defense approaches. For semantic segmentation and object detection, we evaluate on the MS COCO [46], ADE20K [91] and Pascal VOC [20] datasets. The effectiveness of all methods for segmentation and detection is measured by mean Intersection over Union (mIoU) and mean Average Precision (mAP), respectively.

5.2   Assessment

Classification: We apply a given attack method with ResNet101 and InceptionV3 to generate adversarial samples. For FGSM, BIM, and PGD, we set two different maximum perturbation levels in L_∞ distance, namely $2/255$ and $4/255$. The maximum number of iterations is set to 100 for both BIM and PGD. For C&W, NewtonFool, and DeepFool attacks, we generate both L_∞ distance based attacks and L_2 distance-based attacks; we choose 100 update steps for C&W and NewtonFool, and 50 for DeepFool; DeepFool requires the number of candidate classes which is set to 10 in our experiments.

The Top-1 classification accuracies of all methods are reported in Table 1. Our approach outperforms the baseline methods with a large margin under all experimental settings except those with DeepFool attacks. Notably, under DeepFool attacks, the differences between the best performer pixel-deflection and ours are marginal. Moreover, for PGD and BIM attacks, our defense method offers the lowest relative performance degradation when the more vigorous attack is performed (*i.e.*, maximum perturbation increases from $2/255$ to $4/255$). Figure 5 qualitatively underlines the motivation of combining the G and S operators. The G operator learns to mitigate the adversarial pattern, *i.e.*, it recovers a latent image in the presence of severe measurement uncertainty. In contrast, the S operator can faithfully reconstruct high-frequency details. Note that our method is able to generalize well to images from the ImageNet dataset, which typically depict single objects, although it is trained on the Zurich-Raw-to-RGB dataset, consisting of street scenes.

Semantic Segmentation: In this task, we conduct experiments with two different types of attacks: commonly used adversarial attacks and attacks specially designed for attacking semantic segmentation models. For the former, FGSM, BIM, and PGD are used, and we employ DAG [82], a dedicated semantic segmentation attack, for the latter. All attacks are based on pre-trained DeepLabV3 models [11]. Two different maximum perturbation levels in L_∞ are used (*i.e.*, 2/255 and 4/255). The corresponding experimental results are reported in Table 2 and 3. The proposed approach significantly outperforms all baseline methods in all experimental settings. Note that no additional training is required to apply the proposed approach, validating the generalization capabilities of the method.

2D Object Detection: The experimental settings are the same as the ones used for semantic segmentation experiments, except that we use a pre-trained Faster R-CNN [64]. We report the mAP on the Pascal VOC dataset under different experimental settings in Table 4. The proposed defense method offers the best defense performance in all experimental settings, indicating that our approach generalizes well to unseen tasks.

5.3   RAW Distribution Analysis

In this section, we provide additional analysis on the function of the RAW distribution as an intermediate mapping space. Fundamentally, we share the motivation from existing work that successfully exploits RAW data for imaging and vision tasks, including end-to-end image processing and camera design [16,75]. RGB images are generated by processing RAW sensor measurements (see Sect. 3) with an image processing pipeline. This process removes statistical information embedded in the sensor measurements by aberrations in the optics, readout noise, color filtering, exposure, and scene illumination. While existing work directly uses RAW inputs to preserve this information, we exploit it in the form of an *empirical intermediate image distribution*. Specifically, we devise a mapping via RAW space, thereby using RAW data to train network mapping modules, which we validate further below. As a result, we allow the method to remove adversarial patterns not only by relying on RGB image priors but also RAW image priors. We *validate the role of RAW data* in our method in Table 5, discussed in the following, resulting in a large Top-1 accuracy drop (*i.e.*, more than 12%), when swapping the real RAW distribution to a synthesized one. This is further corroborated in Table 6, which we also discuss following, where the defense breaks down from 71% to 53%, when gradually moving from RAW to RGB as intermediate image space. These experiments validate that *the "rawer" the intermediate image space is, the better the defense performs.*

Effect of Intermediate Mapping Space: We use the RAW image distribution as the intermediate mapping space in our method. We next map to other intermediate stages in the processing pipeline, such as demosaicing stage, color balance stage, and white balance stage. Specifically, we assess how using different stage values as intermediate mapping space affects the defense performance (*i.e.*, we ablate on the intermediate mapping space used). As reported in Table 6, we observe that the defense performance gradually decreases as we map via a less RAW intermediate space.

Real RAW Versus Synthetic RAW: We further ablate on the dataset used to train our model. Specifically, we trained F and G operators on the Zurich-Raw-to-RGB dataset, HDR-RAW-RGB [28] and MIT-RAW-RGB [22] respectively, and assess how the defense performance changes. Similar to the Zurich-Raw-to-RGB dataset, the RAW images in the HDR-RAW-RGB dataset are captured by a real camera; however, the ones offered by MIT-RAW-RGB are purely synthesized by reformatting downsampled RGB images into Bayer patterns with handcrafted Gaussian noise. We note that, as such, the MIT-RAW-RGB dataset does not include the RAW distribution cues. Experimental results are reported in Table 5. As observed, both RAW distributions of Zurich-Raw-to-RGB and HDR-RAW-RGB allow us to learn effective adversarial defenses, while a sharp performance degradation occurs when shifting from real RAW distribution to the synthesized one due to the lack of natural RAW distribution cues.

Table 5. Quantitative Ablation Study on RAW Training Datasets. We train F and G operators on three different RAW-RGB datasets and report the Top-1 defense accuracy on the ImageNet dataset. The RAW images in the Zurich-Raw-to-RGB and HDR-RAW-RGB are captured by real cameras, while the ones in MIT-RAW-RGB are synthesized. We see a sharp performance drop when swapping the real RAW training data to synthetic data due to the lack of natural RAW distribution cues.

	FSGM	PGD	C&W	NewtonFool	DeepFool
Zurich-Raw-to-RGB[33]	58.85	66.17	71.40	40.96	72.04
HDR-RAW-RGB[28]	55.57	64.12	71.65	42.36	70.77
MIT-RAW-RGB[22]	40.52	47.29	55.13	28.52	58.49

Table 6. Effect of Different Intermediate Mapping Spaces. We report the Top-1 adversarial defense accuracy on the ImageNet dataset when mapping to different intermediate mapping spaces that are the steps of the image processing pipeline. The performance drops as the intermediate image space moves from RAW to the RGB output space. This validates the importance of exploiting the RAW space in the proposed defense.

	FSGM	PGD	C&W	NewtonFool	DeepFool
Raw capture	57.33	65.02	70.86	40.65	70.23
Demosaic stage	52.93	59.83	63.29	36.76	64.81
Color balance stage	48.38	55.41	57.92	33.92	59.37
White blance stage	47.35	54.02	56.23	33.01	57.08
contrast Improvement stage	45.2	52.18	54.18	31.84	55.64
Agamma adjustment stage	44.4	50.91	53.08	30.57	54.19

5.4 Robustness to Hyperparameter and Operator Deviations

Hyper-parameter ω: We introduce a hyperparameter ω for weighting the contributions of the two operators G and S. Here, we evaluate how varying values

Table 7. Effect of hyperparameter ω. We evaluate the impact of the method hyperparameter ω on the effectiveness of the proposed defense method.

Hyper-parameter ω =	0	0.1	0.2	0.3	0.4	0.5	0.6	0.7	0.8	0.9	1
Against FSGM Attack	64.25	64.41	64.83	65.27	65.58	65.87	65.93	**66.02**	65.75	65.53	65.39
Against C&W Attack	69.16	69.44	69.93	70.26	70.81	70.96	71.35	71.40	**72.70**	71.28	71.07
Against DeepFool Attack	69.55	69.84	71.19	71.51	71.88	72.35	**72.63**	72.04	71.75	71.69	71.04

Table 8. Robustness to Deviations of F **and** G. We evaluate the defense accuracy when mixing operator from different training epochs.

	F-300	F-320	F-340	F-360	F-380	F-400
G-300	66.02	66.08	65.93	66.05	66.03	66.05
G-330	66.11	66.04	65.97	66.01	65.99	66.04
G-360	65.98	66.04	66.02	65.89	66.08	69.01
G-390	65.98	65.95	66.00	66.04	65.99	65.94

Table 9. Robustness to Deviations of F. We perturb the output of operator F with Gaussian noise of different standard deviations and report the defense accuracy.

Gausian noise σ	0 (no noise)	0.01	0.05	0.1	0.3	0.5
Against FSGM attack	66.02	66.01	65.98	65.90	65.73	65.64
Against PGD attack	68.34	68.30	68.22	68.10	68.03	67.83

of ω affect the overall defense accuracy. As reported in Table 7, we find that, while each attack has a different optimal value of ω, the range 0.6–0.8 provides a good trade-off, and we use 0.7 in our experiments.

Deviations of Operators F **and** G: The operators F and G are trained separately and used jointly at inference time. We evaluate how deviations in each operator affect the overall performance in two experiments. First, we mix the operators F and G from different training checkpoints and evaluate the effect on the defense accuracy. Table 8 reports that the checkpoint combinations do not result in a failure but only slight deviations of the defense performance. Second, we add varying levels of Gaussian noise $G(0, \sigma)$ to the output of operator F and evaluate how such deviation affects the following steps and the overall defense accuracy. Table 9 reports that the perturbations are not amplified in the following steps, and the defense accuracy only fluctuates slightly. The experiments show that the ISP operators G and S themselves are robust to slight deviation in each component.

6   Conclusion

We exploit RAW image data as an empirical latent space in the proposed adversarial defense method. Departing from existing defense methods that aim to directly map an adversarially perturbed image to the closest benign image, we exploit large-scale natural image datasets as an empirical prior for sensor captures – before they end up in existing datasets after their transformation through conventional image processing pipelines. This empirical prior allows us to rely on low-level image processing pipelines to design the mappings between the benign and perturbed image distributions. We extensively validate the effectiveness of the method on existing classification and segmentation datasets. The method is entirely model-agnostic, requires no adversarial examples to train, and acts as an off-the-shelf preprocessing module that can be transferred to diverse vision tasks. We also provide insight into the working principles of the approach, confirming the role of the RAW image space in the proposed method. In the future, we plan to explore RAW natural image statistics as an unsupervised prior for image reconstruction and generative neural rendering tasks.

Acknowledgement. Felix Heide was supported by an NSF CAREER Award (2047359), a Sony Young Faculty Award, Amazon Research Award, and a Project X Innovation Award.

References

1. Athalye, A., Carlini, N., Wagner, D.: Obfuscated gradients give a false sense of security: Circumventing defenses to adversarial examples. In: International Conference on Machine Learning, pp. 274–283. PMLR (2018)
2. Athalye, A., Engstrom, L., Ilyas, A., Kwok, K.: Synthesizing robust adversarial examples. In: International Conference on Machine Learning, pp. 284–293. PMLR (2018)
3. Bahat, Y., Irani, M., Shakhnarovich, G.: Natural and adversarial error detection using invariance to image transformations. arXiv preprint arXiv:1902.00236 (2019)
4. Borkar, T., Heide, F., Karam, L.: Defending against universal attacks through selective feature regeneration. In: Proceedings of the IEEE/CVF Conference on Computer Vision and Pattern Recognition, pp. 709–719 (2020)
5. Brendel, W., Rauber, J., Bethge, M.: Decision-based adversarial attacks: Reliable attacks against black-box machine learning models. In: International Conference on Learning Representations (2018)
6. Carlini, N., Wagner, D.: Towards evaluating the robustness of neural networks. In: IEEE Symposium on Security and Privacy (2017)
7. Carlini, N., Wagner, D.: Towards evaluating the robustness of neural networks (2017)
8. Chen, C., Chen, Q., Do, M.N., Koltun, V.: Seeing motion in the dark. In: 2019 IEEE/CVF International Conference on Computer Vision, ICCV 2019, Seoul, Korea (South), 27 Oct –2 Nov 2019. pp. 3184–3193. IEEE (2019). https://doi.org/10.1109/ICCV.2019.00328
9. Chen, C., Chen, Q., Xu, J., Koltun, V.: Learning to see in the dark. In: 2018 IEEE Conference on Computer Vision and Pattern Recognition, CVPR 2018, Salt Lake City, UT, USA, 18–22 June 2018, pp. 3291–3300. Computer Vision Foundation/IEEE Computer Society (2018). https://doi.org/10.1109/CVPR.2018.00347,https://openaccess.thecvf.com/content_cvpr_2018/html/Chen_Learning_to_See_CVPR_2018_paper.html
10. Chen, L.C., Papandreou, G., Kokkinos, I., Murphy, K., Yuille, A.L.: Deeplab: Semantic image segmentation with deep convolutional nets, atrous convolution, and fully connected crfs. IEEE Trans. Pattern Anal. Mach. Intell. **40**(4), 834–848 (2017)
11. Chen, L.C., Papandreou, G., Schroff, F., Adam, H.: Rethinking atrous convolution for semantic image segmentation (2017)

12. Chen, P.Y., Zhang, H., Sharma, Y., Yi, J., Hsieh, C.J.: Zoo: Zeroth order optimization based black-box attacks to deep neural networks without training substitute models. In: Proceedings of the 10th ACM Workshop on Artificial Intelligence and Security, pp. 15–26 (2017)

13. Cheng, M., Le, T., Chen, P.Y., Yi, J., Zhang, H., Hsieh, C.J.: Query-efficient hard-label black-box attack: An optimization-based approach. arXiv preprint arXiv:1807.04457 (2018)

14. Dai, L., Liu, X., Li, C., Chen, J.: AWNet: Attentive wavelet network for image ISP. In: Bartoli, A., Fusiello, A. (eds.) ECCV 2020. LNCS, vol. 12537, pp. 185–201. Springer, Cham (2020). https://doi.org/10.1007/978-3-030-67070-2_11

15. Das, N., Shanbhogue, M., Chen, S.T., Hohman, F., Chen, L., Kounavis, M.E., Chau, D.H.: Keeping the bad guys out: Protecting and vaccinating deep learning with jpeg compression. arXiv preprint arXiv:1705.02900 (2017)

16. Diamond, S., Sitzmann, V., Julca-Aguilar, F., Boyd, S., Wetzstein, G., Heide, F.: Dirty pixels: Towards end-to-end image processing and perception. ACM Trans. Graph. (SIGGRAPH) (2021)

17. Duan, R., Ma, X., Wang, Y., Bailey, J., Qin, A.K., Yang, Y.: Adversarial camouflage: Hiding physical-world attacks with natural styles. In: Proceedings of the IEEE/CVF Conference on Computer Vision and Pattern Recognition, pp. 1000–1008 (2020)

18. Dziugaite, G.K., Ghahramani, Z., Roy, D.M.: A study of the effect of jpg compression on adversarial images (2016)

19. Dziugaite, G.K., Ghahramani, Z., Roy, D.M.: A study of the effect of JPG compression on adversarial images. CoRR abs/ arXIv: 1608.00853 (2016)

20. Everingham, M., Van Gool, L., Williams, C.K., Winn, J., Zisserman, A.: The pascal visual object classes (voc) challenge. Int. J. Comput. Vision **88**(2), 303–338 (2010)

21. Eykholt, K., et al.: Robust physical-world attacks on deep learning visual classification. In: Proceedings of the IEEE Conference on Computer Vision and Pattern Recognition, pp. 1625–1634 (2018)

22. Gharbi, M., Chaurasia, G., Paris, S., Durand, F.: Deep joint demosaicking and denoising. ACM Trans. Graph. (TOG) **35**(6), 191 (2016)

23. Gong, C., Ren, T., Ye, M., Liu, Q.: Maxup: Lightweight adversarial training with data augmentation improves neural network training. In: Proceedings of the IEEE/CVF Conference on Computer Vision and Pattern Recognition (CVPR), pp. 2474–2483 (June 2021)

24. Goodfellow, I.J., Shlens, J., Szegedy, C.: Explaining and harnessing adversarial examples. CoRR abs/ arXiv: 1412.6572 (2015)

25. Goodfellow, I.J., Shlens, J., Szegedy, C.: Explaining and harnessing adversarial examples (2015)

26. Guo, C., Rana, M., Cisse, M., Van Der Maaten, L.: Countering adversarial images using input transformations. In: ICLR (2018)

27. Guo, M., Yang, Y., Xu, R., Liu, Z., Lin, D.: When nas meets robustness: In search of robust architectures against adversarial attacks. In: Proceedings of the IEEE/CVF Conference on Computer Vision and Pattern Recognition, pp. 631–640 (2020)

28. Hasinoff, S.W., Sharlet, D., Geiss, R., Adams, A., Barron, J.T., Kainz, F., Chen, J., Levoy, M.: Burst photography for high dynamic range and low-light imaging on mobile cameras. ACM Trans. Graph. (ToG) **35**(6), 1–12 (2016)

29. He, K., Gkioxari, G., Dollár, P., Girshick, R.: Mask r-cnn. In: Proceedings of the IEEE International Conference on Computer Vision, pp. 2961–2969 (2017)

30. He, K., Zhang, X., Ren, S., Sun, J.: Deep residual learning for image recognition. In: Proceedings of the IEEE Conference on Computer Vision and Pattern Recognition, pp. 770–778 (2016)
31. Hu, W., Tan, Y.: Generating adversarial malware examples for black-box attacks based on gan. ArXiv abs/ arXiv: 1702.05983 (2017)
32. Ignatov, A., Gool, L.V., Timofte, R.: Replacing mobile camera isp with a single deep learning model (2020)
33. Ignatov, A.D., Gool, L.V., Timofte, R.: Replacing mobile camera isp with a single deep learning model. 2020 IEEE/CVF Conference on Computer Vision and Pattern Recognition Workshops (CVPRW), pp. 2275–2285 (2020)
34. Isola, P., Zhu, J.Y., Zhou, T., Efros, A.A.: Image-to-image translation with conditional adversarial networks. In: Proceedings of the IEEE Conference on Computer Vision and Pattern Recognition (CVPR), (July 2017)
35. Jan, S.T., Messou, J., Lin, Y.C., Huang, J.B., Wang, G.: Connecting the digital and physical world: Improving the robustness of adversarial attacks. In: Proceedings of the AAAI Conference on Artificial Intelligence, vol. 33, pp. 962–969 (2019)
36. Jang, U., Wu, X., Jha, S.: Objective metrics and gradient descent algorithms for adversarial examples in machine learning. In: Proceedings of the 33rd Annual Computer Security Applications Conference, pp. 262–277 (2017)
37. Jia, X., Wei, X., Cao, X., Foroosh, H.: Comdefend: An efficient image compression model to defend adversarial examples. In: Proceedings of the IEEE/CVF Conference on Computer Vision and Pattern Recognition, pp. 6084–6092 (2019)
38. Karaimer, H.C., Brown, M.S.: A software platform for manipulating the camera imaging pipeline. In: Leibe, B., Matas, J., Sebe, N., Welling, M. (eds.) ECCV 2016. LNCS, vol. 9905, pp. 429–444. Springer, Cham (2016). https://doi.org/10.1007/978-3-319-46448-0_26
39. Kim, H.: Torchattacks: A pytorch repository for adversarial attacks (2021)
40. Kurakin, A., Goodfellow, I., Bengio, S.: Adversarial examples in the physical world. arXiv preprint arXiv:1607.02533 (2016)
41. Kurakin, A., Goodfellow, I., Bengio, S.: Adversarial examples in the physical world (2017)
42. Li, Y., Li, L., Wang, L., Zhang, T., Gong, B.: Nattack: Learning the distributions of adversarial examples for an improved black-box attack on deep neural networks. arXiv preprint arXiv:1905.00441 (2019)
43. Liang, Z., Cai, J., Cao, Z., Zhang, L.: Cameranet: A two-stage framework for effective camera isp learning. IEEE Trans. Image Process. **30**, 2248–2262 (2021). https://doi.org/10.1109/TIP.2021.3051486
44. Liao, F., Liang, M., Dong, Y., Pang, T., Hu, X., Zhu, J.: Defense against adversarial attacks using high-level representation guided denoiser. In: Proceedings of the IEEE/CVF International Conference on Computer Vision, pp. 1778–1787 (2018)
45. Liao, F., Liang, M., Dong, Y., Pang, T., Hu, X., Zhu, J.: Defense against adversarial attacks using high-level representation guided denoiser. In: Proceedings of the IEEE Conference on Computer Vision and Pattern Recognition, pp. 1778–1787 (2018)
46. Lin, T.Y., et al.: Microsoft coco: Common objects in context (2015)
47. Liu, Z., Liu, Q., Liu, T., Wang, Y., Wen, W.: Feature Distillation: DNN-oriented JPEG compression against adversarial examples. In: International Joint Conference on Artificial Intelligence (2018)
48. Liu, Z., et al.: Feature distillation: Dnn-oriented jpeg compression against adversarial examples. In: 2019 IEEE/CVF Conference on Computer Vision and Pattern Recognition (CVPR), pp. 860–868. IEEE (2019)

49. Lu, J., Issaranon, T., Forsyth, D.: Safetynet: Detecting and rejecting adversarial examples robustly. In: Proceedings of the IEEE International Conference on Computer Vision, pp. 446–454 (2017)
50. Madry, A., Makelov, A., Schmidt, L., Tsipras, D., Vladu, A.: Towards deep learning models resistant to adversarial attacks. arXiv preprint arXiv:1706.06083 (2017)
51. Madry, A., Makelov, A., Schmidt, L., Tsipras, D., Vladu, A.: Towards deep learning models resistant to adversarial attacks (2019)
52. Moosavi-Dezfooli, S.M., Fawzi, A., Frossard, P.: Deepfool: a simple and accurate method to fool deep neural networks (2016)
53. Mosleh, A., Sharma, A., Onzon, E., Mannan, F., Robidoux, N., Heide, F.: Hardware-in-the-loop end-to-end optimization of camera image processing pipelines. In: IEEE Conference on Computer Vision and Pattern Recognition (CVPR) (June 2020)
54. Nakkiran, P.: Adversarial robustness may be at odds with simplicity. arXiv preprint arXiv:1901.00532 (2019)
55. Narodytska, N., Kasiviswanathan, S.: Simple black-box adversarial attacks on deep neural networks. In: 2017 IEEE Conference on Computer Vision and Pattern Recognition Workshops (CVPRW), pp. 1310–1318 (2017). https://doi.org/10.1109/CVPRW.2017.172
56. Pang, T., Xu, K., Dong, Y., Du, C., Chen, N., Zhu, J.: Rethinking softmax cross-entropy loss for adversarial robustness. In: ICLR (2020)
57. Papernot, N., McDaniel, P., Goodfellow, I., Jha, S., Celik, Z.B., Swami, A.: Practical black-box attacks against machine learning. In: Proceedings of the 2017 ACM on Asia Conference on Computer and Communications Security, ASIA CCS 2017, pp. 506–519. Association for Computing Machinery, New York, NY, USA (2017). https://doi.org/10.1145/3052973.3053009
58. Papernot, N., McDaniel, P., Wu, X., Jha, S., Swami, A.: Distillation as a defense to adversarial perturbations against deep neural networks. In: 2016 IEEE Symposium on Security and Privacy (SP), pp. 582–597. IEEE (2016)
59. Papernot, N., McDaniel, P.D., Goodfellow, I.J.: Transferability in machine learning: from phenomena to black-box attacks using adversarial samples. CoRR abs/arXiv: 1605.07277 (2016)
60. Phan, B., Mannan, F., Heide, F.: Adversarial imaging pipelines. In: Proceedings of the IEEE/CVF Conference on Computer Vision and Pattern Recognition, pp. 16051–16061 (2021)
61. Poursaeed, O., Katsman, I., Gao, B., Belongie, S.: Generative adversarial perturbations. In: Proceedings of the IEEE Conference on Computer Vision and Pattern Recognition, pp. 4422–4431 (2018)
62. Prakash, A., Moran, N., Garber, S., DiLillo, A., Storer, J.: Deflecting adversarial attacks with pixel deflection. In: 2018 IEEE/CVF Conference on Computer Vision and Pattern Recognition (CVPR), IEEE (2018)
63. Rauber, J., Brendel, W., Bethge, M.: Foolbox: A python toolbox to benchmark the robustness of machine learning models (2018)
64. Ren, S., He, K., Girshick, R., Sun, J.: Faster r-cnn: Towards real-time object detection with region proposal networks (2016)
65. Samangouei, P., Kabkab, M., Chellappa, R.: Defense-gan: Protecting classifiers against adversarial attacks using generative models. In: ICLR (2018)
66. Schwartz, E., Giryes, R., Bronstein, A.M.: Deepisp: Toward learning an end-to-end image processing pipeline, vol. 28(2), pp. 912–923 (Feb 2019). https://doi.org/10.1109/TIP.2018.2872858

67. Sen, S., Ravindran, B., Raghunathan, A.: Empir: Ensembles of mixed precision deep networks for increased robustness against adversarial attacks. In: ICLR (2020)
68. Shafahi, A., et al.: Adversarial training for free! In: Proceedings of the 33rd International Conference on Neural Information Processing Systems, pp. 3358–3369 (2019)
69. Shi, Y., Wang, S., Han, Y.: Curls & whey: Boosting black-box adversarial attacks. In: 2019 IEEE/CVF Conference on Computer Vision and Pattern Recognition (CVPR), pp. 6512–6520 (2019)
70. Stutz, D., Hein, M., Schiele, B.: Confidence-calibrated adversarial training: Generalizing to unseen attacks. In: International Conference on Machine Learning, pp. 9155–9166. PMLR (2020)
71. Szegedy, C., et al.: Intriguing properties of neural networks. arXiv preprint arXiv:1312.6199 (2013)
72. Szegedy, C., et al.: Intriguing properties of neural networks (2014)
73. Tseng, E., et al.: Differentiable compound optics and processing pipeline optimization for end-to-end camera design. ACM Trans. Graph. (TOG) 40(4) (2021)
74. Tseng, E., et al.: Hyperparameter optimization in black-box image processing using differentiable proxies, vol. 38(4) (Jul 2019). https://doi.org/10.1145/3306346.3322996
75. Tseng, E., et al.: Hyperparameter optimization in black-box image processing using differentiable proxies. ACM Trans. Graph. **38**(4), 1–27 (2019)
76. Tsipras, D., Santurkar, S., Engstrom, L., Turner, A., Madry, A.: Robustness may be at odds with accuracy. In: International Conference on Learning Representations, vol. 2019 (2019)
77. Tu, C.C., et al.: Autozoom: Autoencoder-based zeroth order optimization method for attacking black-box neural networks. In: Proceedings of the AAAI Conference on Artificial Intelligence, vol. 33, pp. 742–749 (2019)
78. Wang, J., Zhang, H.: Bilateral adversarial training: Towards fast training of more robust models against adversarial attacks. In: Proceedings of the IEEE/CVF International Conference on Computer Vision, pp. 6629–6638 (2019)
79. Wong, E., Rice, L., Kolter, J.Z.: Fast is better than free: Revisiting adversarial training. In: ICLR (2020)
80. Wu, Y.H., Yuan, C.H., Wu, S.H.: Adversarial robustness via runtime masking and cleansing. In: International Conference on Machine Learning, pp. 10399–10409. PMLR (2020)
81. Xie, C., Wang, J., Zhang, Z., Ren, Z., Yuille, A.: Mitigating adversarial effects through randomization. arXiv preprint arXiv:1711.01991 (2017)
82. Xie, C., Wang, J., Zhang, Z., Zhou, Y., Xie, L., Yuille, A.: Adversarial examples for semantic segmentation and object detection (2017)
83. Xie, C., Wu, Y., Maaten, L.v.d., Yuille, A.L., He, K.: Feature denoising for improving adversarial robustness. In: Proceedings of the IEEE Conference on Computer Vision and Pattern Recognition, pp. 501–509 (2019)
84. Xu, X., Ma, Y., Sun, W.: Towards real scene super-resolution with raw images. In: 2019 IEEE/CVF Conference on Computer Vision and Pattern Recognition (CVPR), pp. 1723–1731 (2019). https://doi.org/10.1109/CVPR.2019.00182
85. Xu, X., Ma, Y., Sun, W., Yang, M.H.: Exploiting raw images for real-scene super-resolution. arXiv preprint arXiv:2102.01579 (2021)
86. Yin, X., Kolouri, S., Rohde, G.K.: Gat: Generative adversarial training for adversarial example detection and robust classification. In: International Conference on Learning Representations (2019)

87. Yu, K., Li, Z., Peng, Y., Loy, C.C., Gu, J.: Reconfigisp: Reconfigurable camera image processing pipeline. arXiv: 2109.04760 (2021)
88. Zhang, R., Isola, P., Efros, A.A.: Colorful image colorization. In: Leibe, B., Matas, J., Sebe, N., Welling, M. (eds.) ECCV 2016. LNCS, vol. 9907, pp. 649–666. Springer, Cham (2016). https://doi.org/10.1007/978-3-319-46487-9_40
89. Zhang, X., Chen, Q., Ng, R., Koltun, V.: Zoom to learn, learn to zoom. In: Proceedings of the IEEE/CVF Conference on Computer Vision and Pattern Recognition, pp. 3762–3770 (2019)
90. Zheng, H., Zhang, Z., Gu, J., Lee, H., Prakash, A.: Efficient adversarial training with transferable adversarial examples. In: Proceedings of the IEEE/CVF Conference on Computer Vision and Pattern Recognition, pp. 1181–1190 (2020)
91. Zhou, B., Zhao, H., Puig, X., Fidler, S., Barriuso, A., Torralba, A.: Scene parsing through ade20k dataset. In: Proceedings of the IEEE Conference on Computer Vision and Pattern Recognition, pp. 633–641 (2017)

Ghost-free High Dynamic Range Imaging with Context-Aware Transformer

Zhen Liu[1(✉)], Yinglong Wang[2], Bing Zeng[3], and Shuaicheng Liu[1,3(✉)]

[1] Megvii Technology, Beijing, China
liuzhen03@megvii.com
[2] Noah's Ark Lab, Huawei Technologies, Shenzhen, China
[3] University of Electronic Science and Technology of China, Chengdu, China
{zengbing,liushuaicheng}@uestc.edu.cn

Abstract. High dynamic range (HDR) deghosting algorithms aim to generate ghost-free HDR images with realistic details. Restricted by the locality of the receptive field, existing CNN-based methods are typically prone to producing ghosting artifacts and intensity distortions in the presence of large motion and severe saturation. In this paper, we propose a novel Context-Aware Vision Transformer (CA-ViT) for ghost-free high dynamic range imaging. The CA-ViT is designed as a dual-branch architecture, which can jointly capture both global and local dependencies. Specifically, the global branch employs a window-based Transformer encoder to model long-range object movements and intensity variations to solve ghosting. For the local branch, we design a local context extractor (LCE) to capture short-range image features and use the channel attention mechanism to select informative local details across the extracted features to complement the global branch. By incorporating the CA-ViT as basic components, we further build the HDR-Transformer, a hierarchical network to reconstruct high-quality ghost-free HDR images. Extensive experiments on three benchmark datasets show that our approach outperforms state-of-the-art methods qualitatively and quantitatively with considerably reduced computational budgets. Codes are available at https://github.com/megvii-research/HDR-Transformer.

Keywords: High dynamic range deghosting · Context-aware vision transformer

1 Introduction

Multi-frame high dynamic range (HDR) imaging aims to generate images with a wider dynamic range and more realistic details by merging several low dynamic range (LDR) images with varying exposures, which can be well fused to an HDR

Z. Liu and Y. Wang—-Joint First Author.

Supplementary Information The online version contains supplementary material available at https://doi.org/10.1007/978-3-031-19800-7_20.

image if they are aligned perfectly [20,21,23,31,32,41]. In practice, however, this ideal situation is often undermined by camera motions and foreground dynamic objects, yielding unfavorable *ghosting artifacts* in the reconstructed HDR results. Various methods, commonly referred to as *HDR deghosting algorithms*, have thus been proposed to acquire high-quality ghost-free HDR images.

Traditionally, several methods propose to remove ghosting artifacts by aligning the input LDR images [2,10,14,42] or rejecting misaligned pixels [7,8,11,15, 27] before the image fusion. However, accurate alignment is challenging, and the overall HDR effect is diminished when useful information is dropped by imprecise pixel rejection. Therefore, CNN-based learning algorithms have been introduced to solve ghosting artifact by exploring deep features in data-driven manners.

Existing CNN-based deghosting methods can be mainly classified into two categories. In the first category, LDR images are pre-aligned using homography [9] or optical flow [1], and then multi-frame fusion and HDR reconstruction are performed using a CNN [13,28,29,37]. However, homography cannot align dynamic objects in the foreground, and optical flow is unreliable in the presence of occlusions and saturations. Hence, the second category proposes end-to-end networks with implicit alignment modules [4,19,39] or novel learning strategies [25,30] to handle ghosting artifacts, achieving state-of-the-art performance. Nonetheless, the restraints appear when confronted with long-range object movements and heavy intensity variations. Figure 1 shows a representative scene where large motions and severe saturations occur, producing unexpected ghosting and distortion artifacts in the results of previous CNN-based methods. The reason lies in the intrinsic locality restriction of convolution. CNN needs to stack deep layers to obtain a large receptive field and is thus ineffective to model long-range dependency (e.g., ghosting artifacts caused by large motion) [24]. Moreover, convolutions are content-independent as the same kernels are shared within the whole image, ignoring the long-range intensity variations of different image regions [16]. Therefore, exploring content-dependent algorithms with long-range modeling capability is demanding for further performance improvement.

Vision Transformer (ViT) [6] has recently received increasing research interest due to its superior long-range modeling capability. However, our experimental results indicate two major issues that hinder its applications on HDR deghosting. On the one hand, Transformers lack the inductive biases inherent to CNN and therefore do not generalize well when trained on insufficient amounts of data [6,16], despite the fact that available datasets for HDR deghosting are limited as gathering huge numbers of realistic labeled samples is prohibitively expensive. On the other hand, the neighbor pixel relationships of both intra-frame and inter-frame are critical for recovering local details across multiple frames, while the pure Transformer is ineffective for extracting such local context.

To this end, we propose a novel Context-Aware Vision Transformer (CA-ViT), which is formulated to concurrently capture both global and local dependencies with a dual-branch architecture. For the global branch, we employ a window-based multi-head Transformer encoder to capture long-range contexts. For the local branch, we design a local context extractor (LCE), which extracts the local feature maps through a convolutional block and selects the most useful features across multiple frames by channel attention mechanism. The proposed CA-ViT, therefore, makes local and global contexts work in a complementary manner. By incorporating with the CA-ViT, we propose a novel Transformer-based framework (termed as HDR-Transformer) for ghost-free HDR imaging.

LDRs   Our tonemapped HDR image   LDR patches

Sen et al.   Hu et al.   Kalantari et al.   DeepHDR   AHDRNet   HDR-GAN   Ours   GT
Example (Building) from Kalantari et al. 2017's dataset

Fig. 1. Visual comparisons with the state-of-the-art methods [10,13,25,33,37,39] on Kalantari *et al.* [13]'s dataset. As shown, the patch-match based methods [10,33] and the CNN-based methods [13,25,37,39] fail to remove the long-range ghosts caused by large motion and hallucinate reasonable local details in saturated regions. On the contrary, the proposed HDR-Transformer can effectively remove the ghosting artifacts and produce visual consistent local details.

Specifically, the proposed HDR-Transformer mainly consists of a feature extraction network and an HDR reconstruction network. The feature extraction network extracts shallow features and fuses them coarsely through a spatial attention module. The early convolutional layers can stabilize the training process of the vision Transformer and the spatial attention module helps to suppress undesired misalignment. The HDR reconstruction network takes the proposed CA-ViT as basic components and is constituted hierarchically. The CA-ViTs model both long-range ghosting artifacts and local pixel relationship, thus helping to reconstruct ghost-free high-quality HDR images (an example is shown in Fig. 1) without the need of stacking very deep convolution blocks. In summary, the main contributions of this paper can be concluded as follows:

– We propose a new vision Transformer, called CA-ViT, which can fully exploit both global and local image context dependencies, showing significant performance improvements over prior counterparts.

- We present a novel HDR-Transformer that is capable of removing ghosting artifacts and reconstructing high-quality HDR images with lower computational costs. To our best knowledge, this is the first Transformer-based framework for HDR deghosting.
- We conduct extensive experiments on three representative benchmark HDR datasets, which demonstrates the effectiveness of HDR-Transformer against existing state-of-the-art methods.

2   Related Work

2.1   HDR Deghosting Algorithms

We summarize existing HDR deghosting algorithms into three categories, i.e., motion rejection methods, image registration methods, and CNN-based methods.

Motion Rejection Methods. Methods based on motion rejection proposed first to register the LDR images globally and then reject the pixels which are detected as misaligned. Grosch *et al.* generated an error map based on the alignment color differences to reject mismatched pixels [8]. Pece *et al.* detected motion areas using a median threshold bitmap for input LDR images [27]. Jacobs *et al.* identified misaligned locations using weighted intensity variance analysis [11]. Zhang *et al.* [41] and Khan *et al.* [15] proposed to calculate gradient-domain weight maps and probability maps for the LDR input images, respectively. Additionally, Oh *et al.* presented a rank minimization method for the purpose of detecting ghosting regions [26]. These methods frequently produce unpleasing HDR results due to the loss of useful information while rejecting pixels.

Motion Registration Methods. Motion registration methods rely on aligning the non-reference LDR images to the reference one before merging them. Begoni *et al.* proposed using optical flow to predict motion vectors [2]. Kang *et al.* transferred the LDR picture intensities to the luminance domain based on the exposure time and then estimated optical flow to account for motion [14]. Zimmer *et al.* reconstructed the HDR image by first registering the LDR images with optical flow [42]. Sen *et al.* presented a patch-based energy minimization method that simultaneously optimizes alignment and HDR reconstruction [33]. Hu *et al.* proposed to optimize the image alignment using brightness and gradient consistencies on the transformed domain [10]. Motion registration methods are more robust than motion rejection methods. However, when large motions occur, this approach generates visible ghosting artifacts.

CNN-Based Methods. Several CNN-based methods have been recently proposed. Kalantari *et al.* proposed the first CNN-based method for multi-frame HDR imaging of dynamic scenes. They employed a CNN to blend the LDR images after aligning them with optical flow [13]. Wu *et al.* developed the first non-flow-based framework by formulating HDR imaging as an image translation problem [37]. Instead of using explicit alignment, Yan *et al.* adopted a spatial attention module to address ghosting artifacts [39]. Prabhakar *et al.* proposed an efficient method to generate HDR images with bilateral guided upsampler [28] and further explored zero and few-shot learning for HDR Deghosting [30]. Lately, Niu *et al.* proposed the first GAN-based framework for multi-frame HDR imaging [25]. The approaches based on CNNs demonstrate superior capabilities and achieve state-of-the-art performance. However, ghosting artifacts can still be observed when confronted with large motion and extreme saturation.

2.2 Vision Transformers

Transformers have achieved huge success in the field of natural language processing [5,36], where the multi-head self-attention mechanism is employed to capture long-range correlations between word token embeddings. Recently, ViT [6] has shown that a pure Transformer can be applied directly to sequences of non-overlapping image patches and performs very well on image classification tasks. Liu *et al.* developed Swin Transformer, a hierarchical structure where cross-window contexts are captured through the shift-window scheme [18]. Chen *et al.* built IPT, a pretrained Transformer model for low-level computer vision tasks [3]. Liang *et al.* extended the Swin Transformer for image restoration and proposed SwinIR, achieving state-of-the-art performance on image super-resolution and denoising [16]. Unlike CNN-based methods, our approach is inspired by [16,18] and built on Transformers.

3   Method

3.1   CA-ViT

Unlike prior vision Transformers that adopt the pure Transformer encoder, we propose a dual-branch context-aware vision Transformer (CA-ViT), which explores both the global and local image information. As depicted in Fig. 2 (a), the proposed CA-ViT is constructed with a global Transformer encoder branch and a local context extractor branch.

Global Transformer Encoder. For the global branch, we employ a window-based multi-head Transformer encoder [6] to capture long-range information. The Transformer encoder consists of a multi-head self-attention (MSA) module and a multi-layer perceptron (MLP) with residual connection.

Considering the input token embeddings $E \in \mathbb{R}^{H \times W \times D}$, the global context branch can be formulated as:

$$E = MSA(LN(E)) + E,$$
$$CTX_{global} = MLP(LN(E)) + E, \tag{1}$$

where LN denotes LayerNorm, and CTX_{global} denotes the global contexts captured by the Transformer encoder.

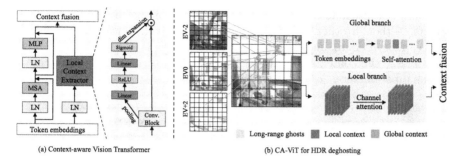

(a) Context-aware Vision Transformer   (b) CA-ViT for HDR deghosting

Fig. 2. Illustration of the proposed CA-ViT. As shown in Fig. 2(a), the CA-ViT is designed as a dual-branch architecture where the global branch models long-range dependency among image contexts through a multi-head Transformer encoder, and the local branch explores both intra-frame local details and inner-frame feature relationship through a local context extractor. Figure 2(b) depicts the key insight of our HDR deghosting approach with CA-ViT. To remove the residual ghosting artifacts caused by large motions of the hand (marked with blue), long-range contexts (marked with red), which are required to hallucinate reasonable content in the ghosting area, are modeled by the self-attention in the global branch. Meanwhile, the well-exposed non-occluded local regions (marked with green) can be effectively extracted with convolutional layers and fused by the channel attention in the local branch. (Color figure online)

Local Feature Extractor. For the local branch, we design a local context extractor (LCE) to extract local information CTX_{local} from adjacent pixels and select cross-channel features for fusion, which is defined as:

$$CTX_{local} = LCE(LN(E)). \tag{2}$$

Specifically, for the token embeddings E normalized with an LN layer, we first reshape them into $H \times W \times D$ features and use a convolution block to extract local feature maps f_{local}. The local features are then average pooled to a shape of $1 \times 1 \times D$, and the channel-wise weights ω are calculated from two linear layers followed by a ReLU and a sigmoid activation layer, respectively. Afterward, the useful feature maps are selected through a channel-wise calibration from the original local features f_{local}, i.e.,

$$\begin{aligned} f_{local} &= Conv(LN(E)), \\ \omega &= \sigma_2(FC(\sigma_1(FC(f_{local})))), \\ CTX_{local} &= \omega \odot f_{local}, \end{aligned} \tag{3}$$

where σ_1 and σ_2 denote the ReLU and sigmoid layer, and FC denotes the linear layer. As a result, the local context branch not only adds the locality into the Transformer encoder, but also identifies the most informative local features across multiple frames for feature fusion.

Finally, a context fusion layer is employed to combine the global and local contexts. Although other transformation functions (e.g., linear or convolution layer) can be used to implement the context fusion layer, in this paper, we simply merge the contexts by element-wise addition to reduce the influence of additional parameters.

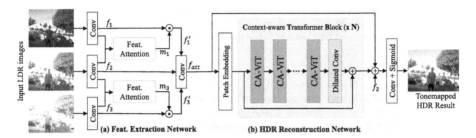

Fig. 3. The network architecture of HDR-Transformer. The pipeline consists of two stages: (a) The feature extraction network first extracts the coarse features through a spatial attention module. (b) The extracted features are then fed into the HDR reconstruction network to recover the HDR results. The HDR reconstruction network consists of several Context-aware Transformer Blocks (CTBs), which take the proposed CA-ViT as basic components.

3.2   HDR Deghosting

The task of deep HDR deghosting aims to reconstruct a ghost-free HDR image through deep neural networks. Following most of the previous works [13,37,39], we consider 3 LDR images (i.e., $I_i, i = 1, 2, 3$) as input and refer to the middle frame I_2 as the reference image. To better utilize the input data, the LDR images $\{I_i\}$ are first mapped to the HDR domain using the gamma correction, generating the gamma-corrected images $\{\check{I}_i\}$:

$$\check{I}_i = \frac{(I_i)^{\gamma}}{t_i}, \quad i = 1, 2, 3, \tag{4}$$

where t_i denotes the exposure time of I_i, and γ is the gamma correction parameter, which is set to 2.2 in this paper. We then concatenate the original LDR images $\{I_i\}$ and the corresponding gamma-corrected images $\{\check{I}_i\}$ into a 6-channels input $\{X_i\}$. This strategy is suggested in [13] as the LDR images help to detect the noisy or saturated regions, while the gamma-corrected images are helpful for detecting misalignments. Finally, the network $\Phi(\cdot)$ is defined as:

$$I^{\hat{H}} = \Phi(X_i; \theta), \quad i = 1, 2, 3, \tag{5}$$

where $I^{\hat{H}}$ denotes the reconstructed HDR image, and θ is the network parameters to be optimized.

Instead of stacking very deep CNN layers to obtain a large receptive field as existing CNN-based approaches, we propose the HDR-Transformer to handle

HDR deghosting. Our key insight is that, with the specifically-designed dual-branch CA-ViT, the long-range ghosting can be well modeled in the global branch, and the local branch helps to recover fine-grained details. We describe the architecture of the proposed HDR-Transformer in the next section.

3.3 Overall Architecture of HDR-Transformer

As illustrated in Fig. 3, the overall structure of our proposed HDR-Transformer mainly consists of two components, i.e., feature extraction network (Fig. 3(a)) and HDR reconstruction network (Fig. 3(b)). Given three input images, we first extract the spatial features through a spatial attention module. The extracted coarser features are then embedded and fed into the Transformer-based HDR reconstruction network, generating the reconstructed ghost-free HDR image.

Feature Extraction Network. The early convolution layers help to stabilize the training process of Vision Transformers [38]. For the input images $X_i \in \mathbb{R}^{H \times W \times 6}$, $i = 1, 2, 3$, we first extract the shallow features $f_i \in \mathbb{R}^{H \times W \times C}$ by three separate convolution layers, where C is the number of channels. Then, we concatenate each non-reference feature (i.e., f_1 and f_3) with the reference feature f_2 and calculate the attention maps m_i through a spatial attention module $\mathcal{A}$:

$$m_i = \mathcal{A}(f_i, f_2), \quad i = 1, 3, \tag{6}$$

The attention features f_i' are computed by multiplying the attention maps m_i by the non-reference features f_i, i.e.,

$$f_i' = f_i \odot m_i, \quad i = 1, 3, \tag{7}$$

where $\odot$ denotes the element-wise multiplication. The spatial attention module has been proved to effectively reduce undesired contents caused by foreground object movements [19,39]. The convolution layers in the attention module can also increase the inductive biases for the subsequent Transformer layers.

HDR Reconstruction Network. As shown in Fig. 3, the HDR reconstruction network is mainly composed of several context-aware Transformer blocks (CTBs). The input of the first CTB $f_{att} \in \mathbb{R}^{H \times W \times D}$ is obtained from f_1', f_2, and f_3' and embedded into token embeddings, where D denotes the embed dimension. The HDR result is reconstructed by N subsequent CTBs and a following convolution block. We also adopt the global skip connection to stabilize the optimization process.

Context-Aware Transformer Block. As illustrated in Fig. 2 (b), when suffering occlusion caused by large object movements and heavy saturation, long-range context is required for removing the corresponding ghosting regions and hallucinating reasonable content, while the non-occluded areas can be fused well by the convolutional layers. To this end, we develop the context-aware Transformer block (CTB) by taking the proposed CA-ViT as the basic component.

For clarity, each CTB contains M CA-ViTs. For the n-th CTB with the input of $F_{n,0}$, the output of the m-th CA-ViT can be formulated as:

$$F_{n,m} = C_{n,m}(F_{n,m-1}), \quad m = 1, 2, ..., M, \tag{8}$$

where $C_{n,m}(\cdot)$ denotes the corresponding CA-ViT. Then, we feed the output of the M-th CA-ViT into a dilated convolution layer. The dilated convolutional layer is employed to increase the receptive field of the context range. We also adopt the residual connection in each CTB for better convergence. Consequently, the output of the n-th CTB is formulated as:

$$F_n = DConv(F_{n,M}) + F_{n,0}, \tag{9}$$

where $DConv(\cdot)$ denotes the dilated convolutional layer, and M and N are empirically set to 6 and 3, respectively.

3.4   Loss Function

As HDR images are typically viewed after tonemapping, we compute the loss in the tonemapped domain using the commonly used μ-law function:

$$\mathcal{T}(x) = \frac{\log(1 + \mu x)}{\log(1 + \mu)}, \tag{10}$$

where $\mathcal{T}(x)$ is the tonemapped HDR image, and we set μ to 5000. Unlike previous methods [13,37,39] that only adopt the pixel-wise loss (e.g., l_1 or l_2 error), we utilize l_1 loss and perceptual loss to optimize the proposed HDR-Transformer. Given the estimated HDR image $I^{\hat{H}}$ and the ground truth HDR image I^H, the l_1 loss term is defined as:

$$\mathcal{L}_r = \| \mathcal{T}(I^H) - \mathcal{T}(I^{\hat{H}}) \|_1, \tag{11}$$

The perceptual loss [12] is widely used in image inpainting [17] for better visual quality improvements. We also apply the perceptual loss to enhance the quality of the reconstructed HDR images:

$$\mathcal{L}_p = \sum_j \| \Psi_j(\mathcal{T}(I^H)) - \Psi_j(\mathcal{T}(I^{\hat{H}})) \|_1, \tag{12}$$

where $\Psi(\cdot)$ denotes the activation feature maps extracted from a pre-trained VGG-16 network [34], and j denotes the j-th layer. We analyze the effectiveness of the perceptual loss in our ablation study (Sect. 4.3). Eventually, our training loss function $\mathcal{L}$ is formulated as:

$$\mathcal{L} = \mathcal{L}_r + \lambda_p \mathcal{L}_p, \tag{13}$$

where λ_p is the hyper-parameter and we set it to 0.01.

4   Experiments

4.1   Dataset and Implementation Details.

Datasets. Following previous methods [25,37,39,40], we train our network on the widely used Kalantari *et al.*'s dataset [13], which consists of 74 samples for training and 15 samples for testing. Each sample from Kalantari *et al.*'s dataset comprises three LDR images with exposure values of $\langle -2, 0, +2 \rangle$ or $\langle -3, 0, +3 \rangle$, as well as a ground truth HDR image. During the training, we first crop patches of size 128×128 with a stride of 64 from the training set. We then apply rotation and flipping augmentation to increase the training size. We quantitatively and qualitatively evaluate our method on Kalantari *et al.*'s testing set. We also conduct evaluations on Sen *et al.* [33]'s and Tursun *et al.* [35]'s datasets to verify the generalization ability of our method.

Evaluation Metrics. We use PSNR and SSIM as evaluation metrics. To be more precise, we calculate PSNR-l, PSNR-μ, SSIM-l, and SSIM-μ scores between the reconstructed HDR images and their corresponding ground truth. The '-l' and '-μ' denote the linear and tonemapped domain values, respectively. Given that HDR images are typically displayed on LDR displays, metrics in the tonemapped domain more accurately reflect the quality of the reconstructed HDR images. Additionally, we conduct evaluations using the HDR-VDP-2 [22], which is developed specifically for evaluating the quality of HDR images.

Implementation Details. Our HDR-Transformer is implemented by PyTorch. We use the ADAM optimizer with an initial learning rate of 2e-4 and set β_1 to 0.9, β_2 to 0.999, and ϵ to 1e-8, respectively. We train the network from scratch with a batch size of 16 and 100 epochs enables it to converge. The whole training is conducted on four NVIDIA 2080Ti GPUs and costs about two days.

4.2   Comparison with State-of-the-Art Methods

Results on Kalantari *et al.*'s Dataset. We first compare the results of the proposed HDR-Transformer with several state-of-the-art methods, which

Table 1. Quantitative comparison between previous methods and ours on Kalantari *et al.*'s [13] test set. We use PSNR, SSIM, and HDR-VDP-2 as evaluation metrics. The '-μ' and '-l' refers to values calculated on the tonemapped domain and the linear domain, respectively. All values are the average over 15 testing images and higher better. The best results are highlighted and the second best are underlined.

Metrics	Methods								
	Sen12 [33]	Hu13 [10]	Kalantari17 [13]	DeepHDR [37]	AHDRNet [39]	NHDRRNet [40]	HDR-GAN [25]	SwinIR [16]	HDR-Transformer Ours
PSNR-μ	40.80	35.79	42.67	41.65	43.63	42.41	_43.92_	43.42	**44.32**
PNRR-l	38.11	30.76	41.23	40.88	41.14	41.43	41.57	_41.68_	**42.18**
SSIM-μ	0.9808	0.9717	0.9888	0.9860	0.9900	0.9877	_0.9905_	0.9882	**0.9916**
SSIM-l	0.9721	0.9503	0.9846	0.9858	0.9702	0.9857	_0.9865_	0.9861	**0.9884**
HDR-VDP-2	59.38	57.05	65.05	64.90	64.61	61.21	_65.45_	64.52	**66.03**

LDRs   Our tonemapped HDR image   LDR patches

Sen et al.   Hu et al.   Kalantari et al.   DeepHDR   AHDRNet   HDR-GAN   Ours   GT

Example (Parking) from Kalantari et al. 2017's dataset

Fig. 4. More visual comparisons between the proposed method and state-of-the-art methods [10,13,25,33,37,39] on Kalantari *et al.*'s [13] dataset.

include two patch match based methods (Sen *et al.* [33] and Hu *et al.* [10]) and five CNN-based methods (Kalantari *et al.* [13], DeepHDR [37], AHDRNet [39], NHDRRNet [40], and HDR-GAN [25]). We also compare with a tiny version of SwinIR [16] as the original one fails to converge on the limited dataset. Among the deep learning-based methods, Kalantari *et al.* [13] adopt optical flow to align the input LDR images while DeepHDR [37] aligns the background using homography. In contrast, the left approaches and our HDR-Transformer don't require any pre-alignment. We report the quantitative and qualitative comparison results as this testing set contains ground truth HDR images.

Quantitative Results. Table 1 lists the quantitative results. For the sake of fairness, the results of prior works are borrowed from HDR-GAN [25], and all results are averaged over 15 testing samples from Kalantari *et al.*'s dataset. Several conclusions can be drawn from Table 1. Firstly, all deep learning-based algorithms have demonstrated significant performance advantages over patch match based methods. Secondly, the pure Transformer encoder adopted in SwinIR doesn't perform well for the aforementioned reasons. Thirdly, the proposed HDR-Transformer surpasses the recently published HDR-GAN [25] by up to 0.6dB and 0.4dB in terms of PSNR-l and PSNR-μ, respectively, demonstrating the effectiveness of our method.

Qualitative Results. For fair comparisons, all qualitative results are obtained using the codes provided by the authors and tonemapped using the same settings in Photomatix Pro. Figure 4 illustrates an intractable scene that contains saturations and large motion. The first row shows the input LDR images, our

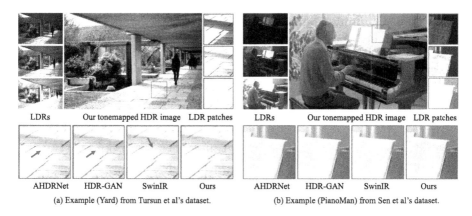

LDRs   Our tonemapped HDR image   LDR patches   LDRs   Our tonemapped HDR image   LDR patches

AHDRNet   HDR-GAN   SwinIR   Ours   AHDRNet   HDR-GAN   SwinIR   Ours

(a) Example (Yard) from Tursun et al's dataset.   (b) Example (PianoMan) from Sen et al's dataset.

Fig. 5. Comparison results on the datasets without ground truth. Scenes are obtained from the Tursun *et al.*'s [35] and the Sen *et al.*'s [33] datasets. Our approach generates better results in the saturated boundary and hallucinates more high-frequency details when suffering heavy intensity variation.

tonemapped HDR result, and the corresponding zoomed LDR patches from left to right. The second row lists the compared HDR results, where the two comparison locations are highlighted in red and blue, respectively. As can be seen, the red boxed area suffers heavy intensity variation within the three input LDR images and causes long-range saturation. Previous approaches remove the ghosting artifacts induced by slight head movements but fail to hallucinate the details of the saturation regions on the face, resulting in color distortions and inconsistent details. The blue boxed patches show a large motion region caused by the hand, patch match based methods fail to discover the correct regions, and CNN-based methods fail to handle the long-range motion, leading to ghosting artifacts in the reconstructed HDR image. On the contrary, The proposed HDR-Transformer reconstructs ghost-free results while hallucinating more visually pleasing details in these areas.

Results on the Datasets w/o Ground Truth. To validate the generalization ability of our method, we conduct evaluations on Sen *et al.* [33]'s and Tursun *et al.* [35]'s datasets. As illustrated in Fig. 5, we report the qualitative results as both datasets have no ground truth HDR images. As seen in Fig. 5 (a), When suffering long-range saturation, the CNN-based algorithms AHDRNet [39] and HDR-GAN [25] produce undesired distortions in saturated boundaries. The Transformer-based method SwinIR [16] performs better but still contains noticeable distortion as the inefficiency of local context modeling. On the contrary, the proposed HDR-Transformer generates more precise boundaries (best to compare with the corresponding LDR patches), demonstrating the context-aware modeling ability of our method. Figure 5 (b) shows a scene where the piano spectrum gets saturated. Previous methods lose the high-frequency details and produce blurry results, while our approach hallucinates more details than them.

Analysis of Computational Budgets. We also compare the inference times and model parameters with previous works. As shown in Table 2, the patch match based methods [10,33] take more than 60 s to fuse a 1.5MP LDR sequence. Among the CNN-based methods, Kalantari *et al.* [13] costs more time than the left non-flow based methods because of the time-consuming optical flow preprocess. DeepHDR [37] and NHDRRNet [40] consume fewer inference times but need huge amounts of parameters. AHDRNet [39] and HDR-GAN [25] have a better balance of performance and efficiency by taking advantage of their well-designed architectures. In contrast, HDR-Transformer outperforms the state-of-the-art method HDR-GAN [25] with only half computational budgets.

4.3   Ablation Study

To analyze the effectiveness of each component, we conduct comprehensive ablation studies on Kalantari *et al.* [13]'s dataset. We report the PSNR and HDR-VDP-2 scores for quantitative comparison.

Ablation on the Network Architecture. For the network design, we compare the proposed CA-ViT, the adopted spatial attention (SA) module, and the overall HDR-Transformer with the baseline model. Specifically, we design the following variants:

- **Baseline**. We take a tiny version of SwinIR [16], which is constituted with vanilla Transformer encoders, as our baseline model. The baseline model keeps comparable network parameters and the same training settings as our proposed HDR-Transformer.
- **+ CA-ViT**. This variant replaces the vanilla Transformer encoder used in the baseline model with the proposed Context-aware Vision Transformer.
- **+ SA**. In this variant, we add a spatial attention (SA) module to fuse the shallow features extracted from the three input LDR images.
- **+ CA-ViT + SA**. The overall network of the proposed HDR-Transformer.

Table 3 summarizes the quantitative results of our ablation study. The first row in Table 3 shows that directly applying the Transformer to HDR deghosting does not perform well. By comparing the first four rows, several conclusions can be drawn. On the one hand, the CA-ViT and SA both improve the performance,

Table 2. The inference times and parameters of different methods. Part of the values are from [40]. The '-' denotes the patch match based methods have no parameters.

Method	Sen12 [33]	Hu13 [10]	Kalantari17 [13]	DeepHDR [37]	AHDRNet [39]	NHDRRNet [40]	HDR-GAN [25]	HDR-Transformer Ours
Environment	CPU	CPU	CPU+GPU	GPU	GPU	GPU	GPU	GPU
Time (s)	61.81 s	79.77 s	29.14 s	0.24 s	0.30 s	0.31 s	0.29 s	0.15 s
Parameters (M)	–	–	0.3 M	20.4 M	1.24 M	38.1 M	2.56 M	1.22 M

Table 3. Quantitative results of the ablation studies. BL: the baseline model, CA-ViT: the proposed Context-aware Vision Transformer, SA: the spatial attention module, $\mathcal{L}_p$: the perceptual loss term.

BL	CA-ViT	SA	$\mathcal{L}_p$	PSNR-μ	PSNR-l	HDR-VDP-2
✓				43.42	41.68	64.52
✓	✓			44.03	41.99	65.94
✓		✓		43.77	41.78	65.30
✓	✓	✓		44.26	42.09	65.97
✓	✓	✓	✓	44.32	42.18	66.03

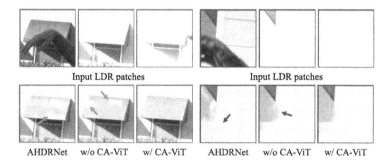

Fig. 6. Qualitative results of our ablation study on the proposed CA-ViT.

but the benefit from CA-ViT is more significant than SA. We conclude the reasons in two folds. Firstly, the inductive biases introduced by the convolution layers in the CA-ViT or SA help the Transformer be better optimized in limited data. Moreover, by incorporating the CA-ViT into each Transformer encoder, both the global and local contexts are explored, resulting in better capabilities of long-range ghosting removal and local details reconstruction. The qualitative results in Fig. 6 also demonstrate our conclusions. On the other hand, the performance is further improved by combining all the components, which proves the effectiveness of the HDR-Transformer's pipeline design.

Ablation on Losses. We also conduct experiments to verify the effectiveness of the perceptual loss by training the HDR-Transformer from scratch both with and without the perceptual loss term. Comparing the last two rows in Table 3, we can see that the adopted perceptual loss improves the performance of the proposed HDR-Transformer.

5 Conclusions

In this paper, we have proposed a dual-branch Context-aware Vision Transformer (CA-ViT), which overcomes the lack of locality in vanilla ViTs. We have extended the standard ViTs by incorporating a local feature extractor, and therefore both global and local image contexts are modeled concurrently. Furthermore, we have introduced the HDR-Transformer, a task-specific framework for ghost-free high dynamic range imaging. The HDR-Transformer incorporates the benefits of Transformers and CNNs, where the Transformer encoder and the local context extractor are used to model the long-range ghosting artifacts and short-range pixel relationship, respectively. Extensive experiments have demonstrated that the proposed method achieves state-of-the-art performance.

Acknowledgement. This work was supported by National Natural Science Foundation of China under grants No. (61872067, 62031009 and 61720106004).

References

1. Baker, S., Scharstein, D., Lewis, J., Roth, S., Black, M.J., Szeliski, R.: A database and evaluation methodology for optical flow. IJCV **92**(1), 1–31 (2011)
2. Bogoni, L.: Extending dynamic range of monochrome and color images through fusion. In: Proceedings of the ICPR, pp. 7–12 (2000)
3. Chen, H., et al.: Pre-trained image processing transformer. In: Proceedings of the CVPR, pp. 12299–12310 (2021)
4. Chung, H., Cho, N.I.: High dynamic range imaging of dynamic scenes with saturation compensation but without explicit motion compensation. In: Proceedings of the CVPR, pp. 2951–2961 (2022)
5. Devlin, J., Chang, M.W., Lee, K., Toutanova, K.: Bert: Pre-training of deep bidirectional transformers for language understanding. arXiv preprint arXiv:1810.04805 (2018)
6. Dosovitskiy, A., et al.: An image is worth 16×16 words: Transformers for image recognition at scale. arXiv preprint arXiv:2010.11929 (2020)
7. Gallo, O., Gelfandz, N., Chen, W.C., Tico, M., Pulli, K.: Artifact-free high dynamic range imaging. In: Proceedings of the ICCP, pp. 1–7 (2009)
8. Grosch, T.: Fast and robust high dynamic range image generation with camera and object movement. In: Proceedings of the VMV, pp. 277–284 (2006)
9. Hartley, R., Zisserman, A.: Multiple view geometry in computer vision. Cambridge University Press (2003)
10. Hu, J., Gallo, O., Pulli, K., Sun, X.: Hdr deghosting: How to deal with saturation? In: Proceedings of the CVPR, pp. 1163–1170 (2013)
11. Jacobs, K., Loscos, C., Ward, G.: Automatic high-dynamic range image generation for dynamic scenes. IEEE Comput. Graphics Appl. **28**(2), 84–93 (2008)
12. Johnson, J., Alahi, A., Fei-Fei, L.: Perceptual losses for real-time style transfer and super-resolution. In: Leibe, B., Matas, J., Sebe, N., Welling, M. (eds.) ECCV 2016. LNCS, vol. 9906, pp. 694–711. Springer, Cham (2016). https://doi.org/10.1007/978-3-319-46475-6_43
13. Kalantari, N.K., Ramamoorthi, R.: Deep high dynamic range imaging of dynamic scenes. ACM Trans. Graphics **36**(4), 144 (2017)
14. Kang, S.B., Uyttendaele, M., Winder, S., Szeliski, R.: High dynamic range video. ACM Trans. Graphics **22**(3), 319–325 (2003)
15. Khan, E.A., Akyuz, A.O., Reinhard, E.: Ghost removal in high dynamic range images. In: Proceedings of the ICIP, pp. 2005–2008 (2006)

16. Liang, J., Cao, J., Sun, G., Zhang, K., Van Gool, L., Timofte, R.: Swinir: Image restoration using swin transformer. In: Proceedings of the ICCVW, pp. 1833–1844 (2021)
17. Liu, G., Reda, F.A., Shih, K.J., Wang, T.-C., Tao, A., Catanzaro, B.: Image inpainting for irregular holes using partial convolutions. In: Ferrari, V., Hebert, M., Sminchisescu, C., Weiss, Y. (eds.) ECCV 2018. LNCS, vol. 11215, pp. 89–105. Springer, Cham (2018). https://doi.org/10.1007/978-3-030-01252-6_6
18. Liu, Z., et al.: Swin transformer: Hierarchical vision transformer using shifted windows. In: Proceedings of the ICCV, pp. 10012–10022 (2021)
19. Liu, Z., et al.: Adnet: Attention-guided deformable convolutional network for high dynamic range imaging. In: Proceedings of the CVPRW, pp. 463–470 (2021)
20. Ma, K., Duanmu, Z., Zhu, H., Fang, Y., Wang, Z.: Deep guided learning for fast multi-exposure image fusion. IEEE Trans. on Image Processing **29**, 2808–2819 (2019)
21. Ma, K., Li, H., Yong, H., Wang, Z., Meng, D., Zhang, L.: Robust multi-exposure image fusion: a structural patch decomposition approach. IEEE Trans. on Image Processing **26**(5), 2519–2532 (2017)
22. Mantiuk, R., Kim, K.J., Rempel, A.G., Heidrich, W.: Hdr-vdp-2: A calibrated visual metric for visibility and quality predictions in all luminance conditions. ACM Trans. Graphics **30**(4), 1–14 (2011)
23. Mertens, T., Kautz, J., Van Reeth, F.: Exposure fusion. In: Proceedings of the PG, pp. 382–390 (2007)
24. Naseer, M., Ranasinghe, K., Khan, S., Hayat, M., Khan, F.S., Yang, M.H.: Intriguing properties of vision transformers. arXiv preprint arXiv:2105.10497 (2021)
25. Niu, Y., Wu, J., Liu, W., Guo, W., Lau, R.W.: Hdr-gan: Hdr image reconstruction from multi-exposed ldr images with large motions. IEEE Trans. on Image Processing **30**, 3885–3896 (2021)
26. Oh, T.H., Lee, J.Y., Tai, Y.W., Kweon, I.S.: Robust high dynamic range imaging by rank minimization. IEEE Trans. Pattern Anal. Mach. Intell. **37**(6), 1219–1232 (2014)
27. Pece, F., Kautz, J.: Bitmap movement detection: Hdr for dynamic scenes. In: Proceedings of the CVMP, pp. 1–8 (2010)
28. Prabhakar, K.R., Agrawal, S., Singh, D.K., Ashwath, B., Babu, R.V.: Towards practical and efficient high-resolution HDR deghosting with CNN. In: Vedaldi, A., Bischof, H., Brox, T., Frahm, J.-M. (eds.) ECCV 2020. LNCS, vol. 12366, pp. 497–513. Springer, Cham (2020). https://doi.org/10.1007/978-3-030-58589-1_30
29. Prabhakar, K.R., Arora, R., Swaminathan, A., Singh, K.P., Babu, R.V.: A fast, scalable, and reliable deghosting method for extreme exposure fusion. In: Proceedings of the ICCP, pp. 1–8. IEEE (2019)
30. Prabhakar, K.R., Senthil, G., Agrawal, S., Babu, R.V., Gorthi, R.K.S.S.: Labeled from unlabeled: Exploiting unlabeled data for few-shot deep hdr deghosting. In: Proceedings of the CVPR, pp. 4875–4885 (2021)
31. Ram Prabhakar, K., Sai Srikar, V., Venkatesh Babu, R.: Deepfuse: A deep unsupervised approach for exposure fusion with extreme exposure image pairs. In: Proceedings of the ICCV, pp. 4714–4722 (2017)
32. Raman, S., Chaudhuri, S.: Reconstruction of high contrast images for dynamic scenes. Vis. Comput. **27**(12), 1099–1114 (2011)
33. Sen, P., Kalantari, N.K., Yaesoubi, M., Darabi, S., Goldman, D.B., Shechtman, E.: Robust patch-based hdr reconstruction of dynamic scenes. ACM Trans. Graphics **31**(6), 203 (2012)

34. Simonyan, K., Zisserman, A.: Very deep convolutional networks for large-scale image recognition. arXiv preprint arXiv:1409.1556 (2014)
35. Tursun, O.T., Akyüz, A.O., Erdem, A., Erdem, E.: An objective deghosting quality metric for hdr images. In: Proceedings of the CGF, pp. 139–152 (2016)
36. Vaswani, A., et al.: Attention is all you need. In: Proceedings of the NeurIPS, pp. 5998–6008 (2017)
37. Wu, S., Xu, J., Tai, Y.-W., Tang, C.-K.: Deep high dynamic range imaging with large foreground motions. In: Ferrari, V., Hebert, M., Sminchisescu, C., Weiss, Y. (eds.) ECCV 2018. LNCS, vol. 11206, pp. 120–135. Springer, Cham (2018). https://doi.org/10.1007/978-3-030-01216-8_8
38. Xiao, T., Singh, M., Mintun, E., Darrell, T., Dollár, P., Girshick, R.: Early convolutions help transformers see better. arXiv preprint arXiv:2106.14881 (2021)
39. Yan, Q., et al.: Attention-guided network for ghost-free high dynamic range imaging. In: Proceedings of the CVPR, pp. 1751–1760 (2019)
40. Yan, Q., et al.: Deep hdr imaging via a non-local network. IEEE Trans. on Image Processing **29**, 4308–4322 (2020)
41. Zhang, W., Cham, W.K.: Gradient-directed multiexposure composition. IEEE Trans. on Image Processing **21**(4), 2318–2323 (2011)
42. Zimmer, H., Bruhn, A., Weickert, J.: Freehand hdr imaging of moving scenes with simultaneous resolution enhancement. In: Proceedings of the CGF, pp. 405–414 (2011)

Style-Guided Shadow Removal

Jin Wan[1], Hui Yin[1(✉)], Zhenyao Wu[2], Xinyi Wu[2], Yanting Liu[3],
and Song Wang[2(✉)]

[1] Beijing Key Lab of Traffic Data Analysis and Mining, Beijing Jiaotong University,
Beijing, China
{jinwan,hyin}@bjtu.edu.cn
[2] Department of Computer Science and Engineering, University of South Carolina,
South Carolina, USA
{zhenyao,xinyiw}@email.sc.edu, songwang@cec.sc.edu
[3] Key Laboratory of Beijing for Railway Engineering, Beijing Jiaotong University,
Beijing, China
19112024@bjtu.edu.cn

Abstract. Shadow removal is an important topic in image restoration, and it can benefit many computer vision tasks. State-of-the-art shadow-removal methods typically employ deep learning by minimizing a pixel-level difference between the de-shadowed region and their corresponding (pseudo) shadow-free version. After shadow removal, the shadow and non-shadow regions may exhibit inconsistent appearance, leading to a visually disharmonious image. To address this problem, we propose a style-guided shadow removal network (SG-ShadowNet) for better image-style consistency after shadow removal. In SG-ShadowNet, we first learn the style representation of the non-shadow region via a simple region style estimator. Then we propose a novel effective normalization strategy with the region-level style to adjust the coarsely re-covered shadow region to be more harmonized with the rest of the image. Extensive experiments show that our proposed SG-ShadowNet outperforms all the existing competitive models and achieves a new state-of-the-art performance on ISTD+, SRD, and Video Shadow Removal benchmark datasets. Code is available at: https://github.com/jinwan1994/SG-ShadowNet.

Keywords: Shadow removal · Region style · Normalization

1 Introduction

Shadows are widespread in real-world images. In many computer-vision applications, shadows can be regarded as a kind of image degradation that undermines the information to be conveyed by the images and usually increases the difficulty of the downstream tasks [3,8,9,14,34,44,45]. In response to this problem, many shadow-removal approaches [7,10,12,15,21–23,29,32,40] have been developed in

Supplementary Information The online version contains supplementary material available at https://doi.org/10.1007/978-3-031-19800-7_21.

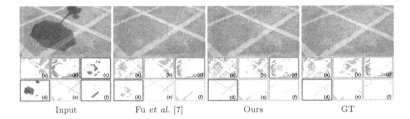

Input   Fu *et al.* [7]   Ours   GT

Fig. 1. De-shadowed images produced by the existing method of Fu *et al.* [7] and our proposed method. The color clustering results of each image are shown below it, by setting the number of clusters to 6, (a)∼(f). Compared with the clusters from Fu *et al.*, ours are more consistent with those from the shadow-free image, without separating out the shadow region, as shown by the cluster (d). (Color figure online)

recent years, aiming to restore images to shadow-free ones. Shadow removal is still considered to be a very challenging problem due to various and complex shadow formation environments [1,10,26,46].

Shadow removal has been well studied from different perspectives, such as feature extraction [4,5,32], multi-task learning [15,40], image generation [28,29,49], image decomposition [22,23], and auto-exposure fusion [7]. The shadow-removal performance has been significantly improved in recent years by employing various advanced deep neural networks [5,7,22,23,29]. However, most of existing methods try to minimize certain pixel-level differences between the de-shadowed region and their corresponding (pseudo) shadow-free version, without explicitly considering the style consistency of de-shadowed and non-shadow regions. As a results, the image appearance of the de-shadowed and non-shadow regions may be inharmonious after shadow removal. An example is shown in Fig. 1, where the shadow region, after shadow removal using an existing method [7], is still visually distinguishable from the rest of image. In Fig. 1, we also use the color-based clustering to show the harmony of the de-shadowed results since color is an important cue in describing the image style [41] and style consistency [25]. We can see that the six clusters obtained from the image de-shadowed by the existing method are more aligned with those obtained from the original image with shadow, while the six clusters obtained from the image de-shadowed by our proposed method are more aligned with those obtained from the corresponding ground-truth shadow-free image.

In this paper, we reformulate shadow removal as an intra-image style transfer problem by explicitly considering the style consistency between shadow regions and non-shadow regions after shadow removal. Based on this formulation, we propose a new style-guided shadow removal network, namely SG-ShadowNet, which consists of a coarse deshadow network (CDNet) and a style-guided re-deshadow network (SRNet) by taking the whole model scale into account. The former employs a simple U-net structure to obtain a coarse de-shadowed result. The latter estimates the style representation of non-shadow regions and then uses it to help further refine the shadow removal, which is achieved by a new learnable spatially region-aware prototypical normalization (SRPNorm) layer for aligning the pixel-wise mean and variance between the de-shadowed and non-shadow regions. SRNet can also perform shadow removal without CDNet and achieve comparable shadow removal performance. To evaluate the proposed SG-ShadowNet, we conduct extensive experiments on the ISTD+ and SRD datasets and assess the generalization ability of the proposed method on the Video Shadow Removal dataset. In summary, the contributions of this work are as follows:

– To the best of our knowledge, this paper is the first work to study the problem of shadow removal from the perspective of *intra-image style transfer* and tackle it by preserving the whole image harmonization through the region style guidance.
– We propose a novel SG-ShadowNet, with a newly designed SRPNorm layer, to remove shadows while maintaining the style consistency between de-shadowed and non-shadow regions.
– The proposed SG-ShadowNet achieves new state-of-the-art performances on three public datasets, and it also exhibits strong generalization ability with fewer parameters.

2   Related Work

Before the deep learning era, shadow removal is usually achieved by extracting hand-crafted features and leveraging physical models of shadows [12,33,35] with limited performance. In this section, we mainly review state-of-the-art deep-learning approaches for shadow removal. We also go over existing works on the usage of normalization layers.

Shadow Removal. Using deep learning, shadows can be removed by learning a complex mapping between shadow images/regions and the corresponding shadow-free images/regions with large-scale annotated training datasets [22,32].

The existing works formulate the shadow removal using different models, resulting in different algorithms. 1) From the feature extraction perspective, Qu *et al.* [32] proposed DeshadowNet to extract multi-context information and predict a shadow matte layer for removing shadows. Cun *et al.* [5] designed a dual hierarchically aggregation network (DHAN) to eliminate boundary artifacts by aggregating the dilated multi-context features and attentions. Most recently, Chen *et al.* [4] presented to remove shadows based on patch-level feature matching and transferring which cannot guarantee the global harmony of the whole image. 2) From the multi-task learning perspective, Wang *et al.* [40] employed a stacked conditional GAN to combine shadow detection and removal. Hu *et al.* [15] proposed to utilize direction-aware context to further improve the ability of shadow detection and removal. 3) From the image decomposition perspective, Le *et al.* [22,23] and [24] employed a physical shadow illumination model to decompose the shadow images into different learnable parameters for generating shadow-free images, which implicitly considers image harmonization very roughly without adequately exploring the underlying relationship between shadow and non-shadow regions. 4) From the image generation perspective, Mask-shadowGAN [16] and LG-ShadowNet [28] leveraged GAN-based models to perform unsupervised shadow removal by learning a map between shadow domain and non-shadow domain. Recently, Liu *et al.* [29] developed a shadow generation model with shadow mask to construct pseudo shadows and shadow-free image pairs for weakly-supervised shadow removal. 5) From the auto-exposure fusion perspective, Fu *et al.* [7] proposed an auto-exposure fusion network, which utilizes shadow-aware fusion network to adaptively fuse the estimated multiple over-exposure images to generate the shadow-free image.

As mentioned earlier, these methods do not explicitly consider the style consistency between shadow and non-shadow regions after shadow removal, and therefore may lead to an image disharmony. In this paper, we focus on addressing this problem by developing a new SG-ShadowNet with explicit consideration of the style consistency in the same image.

Normalization Layers. Normalization of the training data can improve the similarity of data distribution and facilitate the network optimization [36]. Normalizing the intermediate representation of deep networks can also improve the network prediction performance, which has led to many studies on the use of normalization layers in deep learning. Two kinds of normalization have been used for network layers: unconditional normalization [2,18,36,37,43] and conditional normalization [6,17,25,27,31,39,47]. The former does not use external data to provide affine parameters, which is irrelevant to our work. The latter normalizes the mean and deviation of feature maps and then uses external data to learn the affine transformation parameters to denormalize the feature map. Huang *et al.* [17] proposed an adaptive instance normalization (AdaIN) for real-time image stylization, which uses a pre-trained VGG network to extract the style representation of other images. This is not applicable to our task, because the style representation of the non-shadow region cannot be extracted by a pre-trained network. Ling *et al.* [25] proposed a region-aware adaptive instance normalization (RAIN) for image harmonization where the foreground feature is normalized with the channel-wise affine parameters predicted by the background feature in the same intermediate feature map. This inspires us to take the non-shadow region as external data to generate the style representation for adjusting the shadow region. Different from [25], 1) we adopt a coarse-to-fine network to mitigate the difficulty of style transfer directly from shadow to non-shadow version, 2) we employ a region style estimator to accurately learn the style representation of the non-shadow region which later provides guidance for shadow removal, and 3) we design a spatially region-aware normalization layer, which can estimate pixel-wise affine parameters to capture the spatial-variant property of shadows.

3   Methodology

3.1   Problem Formulation

In this work, we propose to reformulate the shadow removal as an intra-image style transfer problem, *i.e.*, the style representation learned from the non-shadow region is applied to the shadow removal of the shadow region, so that the de-shadowed region holds the similar style, such as color and lighting, as the non-shadow region. Specifically, we render the shadow region of the original shadow

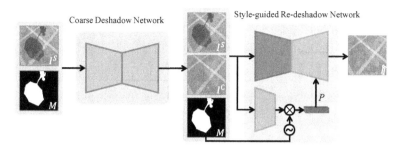

Fig. 2. An illustration of the proposed SG-ShadowNet. It sets the non-shadow proto-type P as prior information to adjust the shadow region of the coarsely de-shadowed results I^C, resulting in a visual consistent shadow-free image $\hat{I}$.

image I^S by using the style of the non-shadow region of the same image to achieve a de-shadowed image $\hat{I}$ with consistent visual styles. It can be formulated as:

$$\hat{I} = \psi(I^S, M|P), \tag{1}$$

where $\psi(\cdot, \cdot)$ represents a style transfer function, P denotes the non-shadow prototype, and M indicates the shadow mask (region) in I^S. Meanwhile, consid-ering the difficulty in stylizing directly from shadow to non-shadow version, we achieve the image stylization on a coarsely de-shadowed result I^C, by reformu-lating Eq. (1) as

$$\hat{I} = \psi(I^C, M|P) = \psi(\mathcal{G}(I^S, M), M|P), \tag{2}$$

where $\mathcal{G}(\cdot, \cdot)$ represents the coarse deshadow network which takes the original shadow image I^S and the corresponding shadow mask M as inputs.

Figure 2 shows the overall framework of the proposed shadow-removal net-work, which consists of two stages. In the first stage, a coarse deshadow network (CDNet) is utilized to obtain I^C for alleviating the difficulty of style transfer. We use the U-net structure in [13] as its backbone and remove all skip connections and half of the filters to reduce computational complexity. In the second stage, we propose a style-guided re-deshadow network (SRNet) in Sect. 3.2, which uses the estimated style representation of the non-shadow region to adaptively adjust the style of the shadow region in the same image. In addition, given that shad-ows present spatial-variant property, i.e., the color and illumination distortion across shadow region are variant, we propose a novel spatially region-aware pro-totypical normalization (SRPNorm) in Sect. 3.3 to adjust the coarsely re-covered shadow region in I^C to be more harmonious with the rest of the image. Note that we can also perform SRNet without CDNet by using I^S and M as inputs for shadow removal, and the results are shown in Table 4.

3.2 Style-Guided Re-deshadow Network

In this section, we elaborate on the style-guided re-deshadow network (SRNet), which is composed of a light-weight region style estimator and a re-deshadow

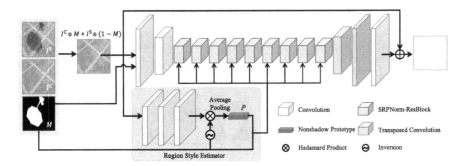

Fig. 3. An illustration of the proposed style-guided re-deshadow network.

network, as shown in Fig. 3. To accurately obtain the style representation of the realistic non-shadow region, we composite the coarsely predicted result I^C and the shadow image I^S using shadow mask M as one of the inputs of the region style estimator and the re-deshadow network, which can be calculated as

$$I^{\text{in}} = I^C \otimes M + I^S \otimes \bar{M} \tag{3}$$

where $\otimes$ is the Hadamard product, and $\bar{M} = 1 - M$ represents the mask of non-shadow region. The region style estimator takes I^{in} and $\bar{M}$ as inputs to get non-shadow prototype P. The re-deshadow network takes I^{in}, M and P as inputs to generate the final shadow-free image $\hat{I}$.

Region Style Estimator. To incorporate the style information of the non-shadow region, a newly designed region style estimator is proposed to learn the non-shadow prototype P for the re-deshadow network, which consists of three convolution layers and a global pooling layer. Note that: **1)** To avoid interference of non-shadow and shadow regions in the same image, we restrict the receptive field of the estimator by using 1×1 kernels for all the convolution layers. **2)** To obtain the accurate style representation of the non-shadow region, we perform the Hadamard product on the $\bar{M}$ and the unpooled features to ensure that the output prototype P is only related to the non-shadow region. The details of the estimator are depicted in Fig. 3 (bottom).

Re-deshadow Network. As shown in Fig. 3 (top), the architecture of the re-deshadow network follows the U-Net [28] and includes 9 residual blocks in the middle. One unique trait of the re-deshadow network is that we embed the proposed spatial region prototypical normalization (SRPNorm) in each residual block, called SRPNorm-ResBlock. The SRPNorm-ResBlock consists of two convolutions and two SRPNorm modules, as shown in Fig. 4.

3.3   Spatially Region-aware Prototypical Normalization (SRPNorm)

In each SRPNorm-ResBlock, the proposed SRPNorm module utilizes the non-shadow prototype $P \in \mathbb{R}^{1 \times 1 \times C}$ and the resized shadow mask $M \in \mathbb{R}^{H \times W \times 1}$ as conditional inputs to perform affine transformation on the input feature map

$F^{\text{in}} \in \mathbb{R}^{H \times W \times C}$, where H, W, C are the height, width, and channel number of the feature maps.

There are two options for the affine parameters here. One is to learn channel-wise affine parameters, *i.e.*, the pixels on each channel are affinely transformed with the same scale and bias. The other is to learn pixel-wise affine parameters, *i.e.*, each pixel has its own individually adapted scale and bias for affine transformation. Considering the spatial-variant property of the shadows, we adopt the latter to perform a pixel-wise affine transformation on shadow regions.

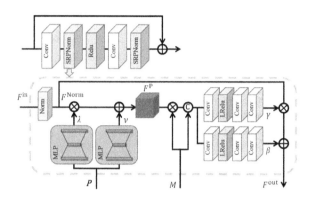

Fig. 4. An illustration of the proposed SRPNorm-ResBlock.

Specifically, we first perform a region normalization on F^{in} to obtain the normalized features F^{Norm}, which can be calculated by

$$
\begin{aligned}
F^{\text{Norm}}_{h,w,c} &= \frac{F^{\text{in}}_{h,w,c} \otimes M_{h,w} - \mu_{M,c}}{\sqrt{\delta^2_{M,c} + \epsilon}} + \frac{F^{\text{in}}_{h,w,c} \otimes \bar{M}_{h,w} - \mu_{\bar{M},c}}{\sqrt{\delta^2_{\bar{M},c} + \epsilon}}, \\
\mu_{M,c} &= \frac{1}{\sum_{h,w} M_{h,w}} \sum_{h,w} (F^{\text{in}}_{h,w,c} \otimes M_{h,w}), \\
\mu_{\bar{M},c} &= \frac{1}{\sum_{h,w} \bar{M}_{h,w}} \sum_{h,w} (F^{\text{in}}_{h,w,c} \otimes \bar{M}_{h,w}), \\
\delta_{M,c} &= \sqrt{\frac{1}{\sum_{h,w} M_{h,w}} \sum_{h,w} \left(M_{h,w} \otimes (F^{\text{in}}_{h,w,c} - \mu_{M,c})^2 \right)}, \\
\delta_{\bar{M},c} &= \sqrt{\frac{1}{\sum_{h,w} \bar{M}_{h,w}} \sum_{h,w} \left(\bar{M}_{h,w} \otimes (F^{\text{in}}_{h,w,c} - \mu_{\bar{M},c})^2 \right)},
\end{aligned}
\tag{4}
$$

where μ_M, δ_M and $\mu_{\bar{M}}$, $\delta_{\bar{M}}$ are channel-wise average and standard deviation of shadow and non-shadow regions in F^{in}. ϵ is set to 1e−5.

Since shadows present spatial-variant property, each pixel in the shadow region is subject to different affine parameters. We further utilize P to modulate F^{Norm} and compute the spatial prior information F^{P} of the non-shadow region. This is achieved by sending P to two MLPs and generating two channel-wise modulated parameters $\lambda_c(P)$ and $\nu_c(P)$ for F^{Norm}. F^{P} can be expressed by

$$F^{\text{P}}_{h,w,c} = \lambda_c(P) \otimes F^{\text{Norm}}_{h,w,c} + \nu_c(P). \tag{5}$$

Then we learn the pixel-wise affine parameters $\gamma_{h,w,c}(F^{\text{P}}, M)$ and $\beta_{h,w,c}(F^{\text{P}}, M)$ by using three convolution layers and taking F^{P} and M as input. Finally, we perform affine processing on the normalized features F^{Norm} based on the scale (γ) and bias (β) learned from non-shadow regions. The output of SRPNorm is defined as:

$$F^{\text{out}}_{h,w,c} = \gamma_{h,w,c}(F^{\text{P}}, M) \otimes F^{\text{Norm}}_{h,w,c} + \beta_{h,w,c}(F^{\text{P}}, M). \tag{6}$$

3.4   Loss Function

For the coarse deshadow network, the pixel-level reconstruction loss L_{r1} is used to optimize the distance between the ground truth shadow-free image I^{SF} and the coarsely de-shadowed image I^{C}:

$$L_{\text{r1}} = \|I^{\text{C}} - I^{\text{SF}}\|_1. \tag{7}$$

Moreover, we use area loss L_{a1} to strengthen the constraint of the shadow region as in previous work [29]. Formally, the area loss is defined as

$$L_{\text{a1}} = \|\phi(M) \otimes I^{\text{C}} - \phi(M) \otimes I^{\text{SF}}\|_1, \tag{8}$$

where $\phi(\cdot)$ denotes the image dilation function with a kernel size of 50 and $\otimes$ is the Hadamard product.

For the style-guided re-deshadow network (SRNet), the output of SRNet is the final de-shadowed result $\hat{I}$. We also calculate the reconstruction loss L_{r2} and the area loss L_{a2} between $\hat{I}$ and I^{SF} as

$$L_{\text{r2}} = \|\hat{I} - I^{\text{SF}}\|_1, $$
$$L_{\text{a2}} = \|\phi(M) \otimes \hat{I} - \phi(M) \otimes I^{\text{SF}}\|_1. \tag{9}$$

To ensure the spatial consistency of $\hat{I}$, we apply the spatial consistency loss [11]:

$$L_{\text{s}} = \frac{1}{K} \sum_{i=1}^{K} \sum_{j \in \Omega(i)} (|(Y_i, Y_j)| - |(V_i, V_j)|)^2, \tag{10}$$

where K denotes the number of local areas, $\Omega(i)$ represents four adjacent areas centered at area i, and Y and V are the average intensity values of the local areas of $\hat{I}$ and I^{SF}, respectively. Finally, we define the total loss function $\mathcal{L}$ as

$$\mathcal{L} = L_{\text{a1}} + L_{\text{r1}} + L_{\text{a2}} + L_{\text{r2}} + \zeta L_{\text{s}}, \tag{11}$$

where ζ denotes the weight term of spatial consistency loss and is empirically set to 10. In our experiments, we set the weights of reconstruction losses and area losses to 1 by following [29].

4 Experiments

4.1 Experimental Setup

Datasets. We train and evaluate the proposed method on the ISTD+ [22] and SRD [32] datasets and verify the generalization of our model on the Video Shadow Removal dataset [23]. **1)** The ISTD+ dataset has 1,870 triplets of shadow, shadow-free, and shadow mask images, where 1,330 triplets are used for training and the remaining 540 triplets are used for testing. We use the provided ground-truth shadow mask in the training phase, while for the test, the corresponding shadow mask of the test shadow image is calculated by a pretrained BDRAR shadow detector [50] that trained on the SBU [38] and ISTD+ datasets. The Balanced Error Rate of the model in the ISTD+ testing set is 2.4. **2)** SRD dataset contains 2,680 training pairs of shadow and shadow-free images and 408 testing pairs. Same as [7], we utilize Otsu's algorithm [30] to extract the shadow mask from the difference between shadow-free and shadow images during training, and we exploit the shadow masks detected by DHAN [5] for testing. **3)** Video Shadow Removal dataset consists of 8 videos captured in the static scene, *i.e.*, there are no moving objects in each video. As [23], we employ a threshold of 40 to get the moving shadow mask for evaluation which divides shadow and non-shadow pixels according to intensity difference. In addition, we utilize a pre-trained BDRAR [50] to generate shadow masks for testing.

Evaluation Metrics. We employ the root mean square error (RMSE[1]) in the LAB color space, and we adopt the learned perceptual image patch similarity (LPIPS) [48] to evaluate the perceptual quality of the de-shadowed results.

Implementation Details. We implement the proposed network using PyTorch with a single NVIDIA GeForce GTX 2080Ti GPU card. In our experiments, the coarse deshadow network (CDNet) and style-guided re-deshadow network (SRNet) are jointly trained to obtain the final shadow-free image. For data augmentation, we exploit random flipping and random cropping with a crop size of 400×400. During training, our model is optimized by Adam [20] with the first and the second momentum being set to 0.50 and 0.99, respectively, and the batch size is set to 1. The basic learning rate is set to 2×10^{-4} and halved every 50 epochs with 200 epochs in total.

4.2 Comparison with State-of-the-Arts

We compare our SG-ShadowNet with 14 state-of-the-art shadow removal algorithms, including unsupervised methods of Mask-ShadowGAN [40], LG-ShadowNet [28], and DC-shadowNet [19], weakly supervised methods of Gong & Cosker [10], Param+M+D-Net [23], and G2R-ShadowNet [29], and fully supervised methods of ST-CGAN [40], DeshadowNet [32], SP+M-Net [22], DSC [15], DHAN [5], CANet [4], Fu *et al.* [7], and SP+M+I-Net [24]. For a fair comparison, all results are taken from their original papers or generated by their official code.

---

[1] The RMSE is actually calculated by the mean absolute error (MAE) as [22].

Quantitative Evaluation. Tables 1 and 2 quantitatively show the test results of different shadow-removal methods on the ISTD+ and SRD datasets. Compared with unsupervised, weakly-supervised and supervised methods, SG-ShadowNet performs the best on both shadow regions and the whole image. Specifically, on the ISTD+ dataset, our method outperforms Fu *et al.* [7] by decreasing the RMSE of the shadow region and entire image by 9.2% and 19.0%, respectively. Our method also outperforms SP+M+I-Net [24] by a small margin in shadow regions. Meanwhile, our method obtains a lower LPIPS score than other existing methods, which verifies that our de-shadowed results show a more consistent style with the shadow-free images, and further proves the effectiveness of the style guidance strategy. On the SRD dataset, the public shadow masks generated by [5] are employed for evaluation. Our method outperforms the fully-

Table 1. Shadow removal results of the proposed method compared to state-of-the-art shadow removal methods on ISTD+ [22]. RMSE and LPIPS are the lower the better.

Scheme	Method	Shadow	Non-shadow	All	
		RMSE↓	RMSE↓	RMSE↓	LPIPS↓
Un-supervised	Mask-ShadowGAN [40]	9.9	3.8	4.8	0.095
	LG-ShadowNet [28]	9.7	3.4	4.4	0.103
	DC-ShadowNet [19]	10.4	3.6	4.7	0.170
Weakly- supervised	Gong & Cosker [10]	13.3	**2.6**	4.3	0.086
	Param+M+D-Net [23]	9.7	2.9	4.1	0.086
	G2R-ShadowNet [29]	8.8	2.9	3.9	0.096
Fully-supervised	ST-CGAN [40]	13.4	7.9	8.6	0.150
	SP+M-Net [22]	7.9	2.8	3.6	0.085
	Fu *et al.* [7]	6.5	3.8	4.2	0.106
	SP+M+I-Net [24]	6.0	3.1	3.6	0.092
	SG-ShadowNet (Ours)	**5.9**	2.9	**3.4**	**0.070**

Table 2. Shadow removal results of the proposed method compared to state-of-the-art shadow removal methods on SRD [32]. '*' indicates that the result is directly cited from the original paper.

Method	Shadow	Non-Shadow	All	
	RMSE↓	RMSE↓	RMSE↓	LPIPS↓
DeshadowNet [32]	11.78	4.84	6.64	0.165
DSC [15]	10.89	4.99	6.23	0.147
DHAN [5]	8.94	4.80	5.67	0.104
Fu *et al.* [7]	8.56	5.75	6.51	0.153
CANet* [4]	7.82	5.88	5.98	–
DC-ShadowNet [19]	8.26	3.68	4.94	0.167
SG-ShadowNet (Ours)	**7.53**	**2.97**	**4.23**	**0.099**

supervised Fu *et al.* [7] and unsupervised DC-ShadowNet [19] in shadow regions, reducing RMSE by 12.0% and 8.8%, respectively. It also decreases the RMSE from 7.82 to 7.53, compared to CANet [4]. Moreover, it can be seen from Table 3 that SG-ShadowNet has only 6.2M parameters, which is less than 4.4% and 3.2% of the shadow removal network parameters in [7] and [24], respectively.

Qualitative Evaluation. Figure 5 provides the visual comparisons of shadow-removal results produced by different methods. It can be easily observed that the existing methods suffer inconsistent appearance between the shadow and non-shadow regions after shadow removal. On the contrary, our SG-ShadowNet can produce visually more harmonious de-shadowed images.

4.3   Ablation Study

Effectiveness of SRPNorm. To investigate the effect of SRPNorm, we conduct the following ablations: 1) replacing all SRPNorms with other normalization layers (*i.e.*, BN [18], IN [37], RN [47], and RAIN [25]); 2) using SRPNorm to provide different style-guided affine parameters (channel- and pixel- wise) for the normalization layer; and 3) adding k SRPNorm into the innermost ResBlocks of the SRNet (SRPNorm-k) with different k values. The results are reported in the Table 4.

Table 3. Number of parameters and flops of SG-ShadowNet and other comparison methods, with input size of 256×256.

Method	#Params.	Flops
SP+M-Net [22]	141.2 M	39.8 G
G2R-ShadowNet [29]	22.8 M	113.9 G
Fu *et al.* [7]	142.2 M	104.8 G
SP+M+I-Net [24]	195.6 M	58.0 G
SG-ShadowNet(Ours)	6.2 M	39.7 G

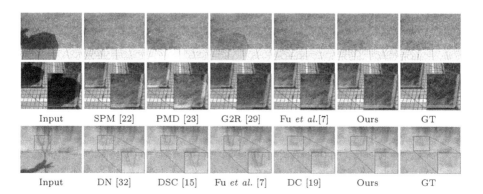

| Input | SPM [22] | PMD [23] | G2R [29] | Fu *et al.*[7] | Ours | GT |
| Input | DN [32] | DSC [15] | Fu *et al.* [7] | DC [19] | Ours | GT |

Fig. 5. Visualisation comparisons on the ISTD+ [22] (top two rows) and SRD [32] (bottom row) datasets.

We first apply the classic BN and IN as the normalization layer of the network. We can see that their performances are limited since they do not use additional conditions to de-normalize the features of shadow regions. Then we deploy RN and RAIN into our network. Although RN can use external conditions to de-normalize shadow and non-shadow regions separately, it strictly distinguishes the features of shadow and non-shadow regions, preventing the information of non-shadow regions from spreading to shadow regions. The RAIN, an enhanced version of RN, utilize the non-shadow region information within the feature maps to de-normalize features of shadow regions, where the information between shadow and non-shadow regions would interfere with each other in the middle feature maps, so it cannot accurately reflect the style of non-shadow regions. Moreover, RAIN adopts channel-wise normalization, $i.e.$, the same mean and variance are used to de-normalize the features of shadow regions. This obviously does not consider the spatial-variant property of shadows, which makes it unable to generalize well to the shadow removal task. As shown in Fig. 6, without the style guidance of the non-shadow region, the de-shadowed results of IN and RN show obvious color and lighting distinction with the original non-shadowed part of this image. In addition, the color of de-shadowed results from RAIN is not consistent with the neighbor regions since it's hard to accurately extract the

Table 4. Ablation study of the proposed SRPNorm on ISTD+ [22].

Model	Shadow	Non-Shadow	All	
	RMSE↓	RMSE↓	RMSE↓	LPIPS↓
BN [18]	7.5	3.8	4.0	0.099
IN [42]	7.3	2.9	3.7	0.076
RN [47]	6.7	3.0	3.6	0.073
RAIN [25]	6.6	2.9	3.5	0.074
SRPNorm w/o S	6.3	2.9	3.4	0.072
SRPNorm w/o P	6.7	2.9	3.5	0.073
SRPNorm w/o M	6.2	2.9	3.4	0.072
SRPNorm-3	6.3	2.9	3.5	0.071
SRPNorm-5	6.1	2.9	3.4	0.071
SRPNorm-7	6.0	2.9	3.4	0.070
SRPNorm-All	5.9	2.9	3.4	0.070

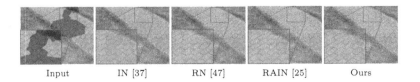

Input   IN [37]   RN [47]   RAIN [25]   Ours

Fig. 6. Visualisation comparisons of different normalization methods.

non-shadow region style. Obviously, our method achieves more visual consistent results than other normalization-based methods. The numerical performance on the ISTD+ dataset in Table 4 also verifies our observation.

Besides, SRPNorm can also provide channel-wise normalization (SRPNorm w/o S), $i.e.$, the results of Eq. (5) is the output of SRPNorm. It can be found in Table 4 that SRPNorm w/o S leads to a performance drop, which verifies the effectiveness of performing the pixel-wise (spatial) affine transformation on de-shadowed regions. Note that even if SRPNorm degenerates to a channel-wise normalization, it still outperforms the above-mentioned normalization methods, by benefiting from accurately extracting the style of the non-shadow region via the region style estimator. We also try to replace the non-shadow prototype in SRPNorm (SRPNorm w/o P) by only using the shadow mask as the prior information of SRPNorm. The decreased performance further verifies the effectiveness of the proposed style guidance from the non-shadow region. We then remove the shadow mask in Eq. (6) (SRPNorm w/o M) –we can see a slight drop in performance, which motivates us to focus on shadow regions during denormalization. Finally, we try to insert different numbers of SRPNorms into the innermost ResBlocks of SRnet. It is obvious that shadow-removal performance is improved with the increase of the number of SRPNorm-ResBlocks (involving more layers for style transfer), which shows the superiority of SPRNorm.

Table 5. Ablation study on the effectiveness of network architecture and loss functions on ISTD+ [22].

Model	Shadow	Non-Shadow	All	
	RMSE↓	RMSE↓	RMSE↓	LPIPS↓
w/o $CDNet$	6.5	2.9	3.5	0.076
w/o $SRNet$	7.0	2.9	3.5	0.072
w/o L_{a1}, L_{a2}	6.0	2.8	3.3	0.068
w/o L_s	6.2	3.0	3.5	0.073
SG-ShadowNet (Ours)	5.9	2.9	3.4	0.070

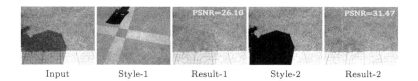

| Input | Style-1 | Result-1 | Style-2 | Result-2 |

Fig. 7. Visualisation comparisons of the intra- vs. inter- image region style guidance capability for shadow removal.

Effectiveness of Network Architecture and Loss Function. We also provide ablation experiments to verify the contribution of the designed network architecture and loss function. From the first two rows of Table 5, we can see

J. Wan et al.

that the coarse deshadow network and style-guided re-deshadow network well complement each other – the shadow-removal performance drops by removing any one of these two networks. Note that the shadow removal performance on ISTD+ achieved by SRNet alone, *i.e.*, a one-stage processing, is comparable to Fu *et al.* [7], which is an impressive result. The remaining rows of Table 5 show the effectiveness of the area loss and the spatial consistency loss, without which RMSE of the shadow region increases by 0.1 and 0.3, respectively.

Intra- vs. Inter-Image Style Transfer. With the region style estimator, we are able to perform style transfer not only with the region style of the desired image (*Style-2*), but also with the region style of an irrelevant reference image (*Style-1*). From Fig. 7, it is obvious that *Result-1* by performing the style transfer with the latter is less harmonious and exists detailed style-related (*i.e.*, color) traces, which verifies the superiority of intra-image style transfer for shadow removal.

4.4 Generalization Ability

To verify the generalization ability of our method, we compare it with several state-of-the-art methods, including SP+M-Net [22], Param+M+D-Net [23], Mask-ShadowGAN [16], LG-ShadowNet [28], G2R-ShadowNet [29], and DC-

Table 6. Shadow removal results on Video Shadow Removal dataset [23].

Method	RMSE↓	PSNR↓	SSIM↓
SP+M-Net [22]	22.2	–	–
Param+M+D-Net [23]	20.9	–	–
Mask-ShadowGAN [16]	19.6	19.47	0.850
LG-ShadowNet [28]	18.3	19.90	0.843
G2R-ShadowNet [29]	18.8	20.00	0.838
DC-ShadowNet [19]	18.9	19.92	0.848
SG-ShadowNet (Ours)	**16.5**	**21.65**	**0.852**

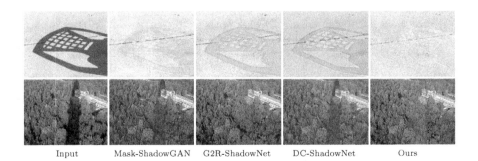

Input	Mask-ShadowGAN	G2R-ShadowNet	DC-ShadowNet	Ours

Fig. 8. Visual comparisons on the Video Shadow Removal dataset [23].

ShadowNet [19] on the Video Shadow Removal dataset [23]. All compared methods are pre-trained on ISTD+ [22] and tested directly on the video dataset.

From Table 6, we see that our method performs best on all evaluation metrics, and outperforms the fully-supervised method SP+M-Net with RMSE decreased by 25.7% in the shaded region, and also outperforms the recent weakly supervised G2R-ShadowNet and unsupervised DC-ShadowNet. By using the style of non-shadow regions in an image as guidance for shadow removal, our proposed SG-ShadowNet exhibits better generalization ability in unknown environments, which also can be seen in the comparison of the qualitative results in Fig. 8.

5   Conclusion

In this paper, we proposed a style-guided shadow removal network (SG-Shadow-Net) to achieve better image-style consistency after shadow removal. SG-Shadow-Net can accurately learn the style representation of the non-shadow region using the regional style estimator, and employ the proposed spatially region-aware prototypical normalization (SRPNorm) to render the non-shadow region style to the shadow region on a coarsely de-shadowed image. Experimental results showed that the proposed SG-ShadowNet achieves the new state-of-the-art shadow removal performance on the ISTD+, SRD, and Video Shadow Removal datasets.

Acknowledgement. This work was supported by the Fundamental Research Funds for the Central Universities (2020YJS031), National Nature Science Foundation of China (51827813, 61472029, U1803264), and Research and Development Program of Beijing Municipal Education Commission (KJZD20191000402).

References

1. Arbel, E., Hel-Or, H.: Shadow removal using intensity surfaces and texture anchor points. IEEE Trans. Pattern Anal. Mach. Intell. **33**(6), 1202–1216 (2011)
2. Ba, J.L., Kiros, J.R., Hinton, G.E.: Layer normalization. arXiv preprint arXiv:1607.06450 (2016)
3. Caelles, S., et al.: One-shot video object segmentation. In: IEEE Conference on Computer Vision and Pattern Recognitio, pp. 5320–5329 (2017)
4. Chen, Z., Long, C., Zhang, L., Xiao, C.: Canet: A context-aware network for shadow removal. In: International Conference on Computer Vision, pp. 4743–4752 (Oct 2021)
5. Cun, X., Pun, C.M., Shi, C.: Towards ghost-free shadow removal via dual hierarchical aggregation network and shadow matting gan. In: AAAI, pp. 10680–10687 (2020)
6. Dumoulin, V., Shlens, J., Kudlur, M.: A learned representation for artistic style. arXiv preprint arXiv:1610.07629 (2017)
7. Fu, L., et al.: Auto-exposure fusion for single-image shadow removal. In: IEEE Conference on Computer Vision and Pattern Recognition, pp. 10571–10580 (June 2021)

8. Girshick, R., Donahue, J., Darrell, T., Malik, J.: Rich feature hierarchies for accurate object detection and semantic segmentation. In: IEEE Conference on Computer Vision and Pattern Recognition (June 2014)

9. Girshick, R.B.: Fast rcnn. In: International Conference on Computer Vision, pp. 1440–1448 (2015)

10. Gong, H., Cosker, D.: Interactive shadow removal and ground truth for variable scene categories. In: British Machine Vision Conference (2014)

11. Guo, C., et al.: Zero-reference deep curve estimation for low-light image enhancement. In: Conference on Computer Vision and Pattern Recognition, pp. 1777–1786 (2020)

12. Guo, R., Dai, Q., Hoiem, D.: Paired regions for shadow detection and removal. IEEE Trans. Pattern Anal. Mach. Intell. **35**(12), 2956–2967 (2012)

13. Guo, S., Yan, Z., Zhang, K., Zuo, W., Zhang, L.: Toward convolutional blind denoising of real photographs. In: IEEE Conference on Computer Vision and Pattern Recognition, pp. 1712–1722 (2019)

14. He, K., Gkioxari, G., Dollar, P., Girshick, R.: Mask r-cnn. In: International Conference on Computer Vision (Oct 2017)

15. Hu, X., Fu, C.W., Zhu, L., Qin, J., Heng, P.A.: Direction-aware spatial context features for shadow detection and removal. IEEE Trans. Pattern Anal. Mach. Intell. (2019)

16. Hu, X., Jiang, Y., Fu, C.W., Heng, P.A.: Mask-shadowgan: Learning to remove shadows from unpaired data. In: International Conference on Computer Vision (2019)

17. Huang, X., Belongie, S.: Arbitrary style transfer in real-time with adaptive instance normalization. In: International Conference on Computer Vision (2017)

18. Ioffe, S., Szegedy, C.: Batch normalization: Accelerating deep network training by reducing internal covariate shift. In: Proceedings of the International Conference on Machine Learning, vol. 37, pp. 448–456 (2015)

19. Jin, Y., Sharma, A., Tan, R.T.: Dc-shadownet: Single-image hard and soft shadow removal using unsupervised domain-classifier guided network. In: International Conference on Computer Vision, pp. 5027–5036 (2021)

20. Kingma, D.P., Ba, J.: Adam: A method for stochastic optimization. arXiv preprint arXiv:1412.6980 (2015)

21. Le, H., Goncalves, B., Samaras, D., Lynch, H.: Weakly labeling the antarctic: The penguin colony case. In: IEEE Conference on Computer Vision and Pattern Recognition of Workshop, pp. 18–25 (2019)

22. Le, H., Samaras, D.: Shadow removal via shadow image decomposition. In: International Conference on Computer Vision (2019)

23. Le, H., Samaras, D.: From shadow segmentation to shadow removal. In: Vedaldi, A., Bischof, H., Brox, T., Frahm, J.-M. (eds.) ECCV 2020. LNCS, vol. 12356, pp. 264–281. Springer, Cham (2020). https://doi.org/10.1007/978-3-030-58621-8_16

24. Le, H., Samaras, D.: Physics-based shadow image decomposition for shadow removal. IEEE Trans. Pattern Anal. Mach. Intell. (2021)

25. Ling, J., Xue, H., Song, L., Xie, R., Gu, X.: Region-aware adaptive instance normalization for image harmonization. In: IEEE Conference on Computer Vision and Pattern Recognition, pp. 9361–9370 (June 2021)

26. Liu, F., Gleicher, M.: Texture-consistent shadow removal. In: Forsyth, D., Torr, P., Zisserman, A. (eds.) ECCV 2008. LNCS, vol. 5305, pp. 437–450. Springer, Heidelberg (2008). https://doi.org/10.1007/978-3-540-88693-8_32

27. Liu, H., Wan, Z., Huang, W., Song, Y., Han, X., Liao, J.: Pd-gan: Probabilistic diverse gan for image inpainting. In: IEEE Conference on Computer Vision and Pattern Recognition, pp. 9371–9381 (June 2021)

28. Liu, Z., Yin, H., Mi, Y., Pu, M., Wang, S.: Shadow removal by a lightness-guided network with training on unpaired data. IEEE Trans. Image Process. **30**, 1853–1865 (2021)

29. Liu, Z., Yin, H., Wu, X., Wu, Z., Mi, Y., Wang, S.: From shadow generation to shadow removal. In: IEEE Conference on Computer Vision and Pattern Recognition (2021)

30. Otsu, N.: A threshold selection method from gray-level histograms. IEEE Trans. Syst. Man Cybern. Syst. **9**(1), 62–66 (1979)

31. Park, T., Liu, M.Y., Wang, T.C., Zhu, J.Y.: Semantic image synthesis with spatially-adaptive normalization. In: IEEE Conference on Computer Vision and Pattern Recognition, pp. 2332–2341 (2019)

32. Qu, L., Tian, J., He, S., Tang, Y., Lau, R.W.: Deshadownet: A multi-context embedding deep network for shadow removal. In: IEEE Conference on Computer Vision and Pattern Recognition (2017)

33. Shechtman, E., Sunkavalli, L.-Q., Kalyan, S.-M., Wang, J.: Appearance harmonization for single image shadow removal. Euro. Assoc. Comput. Graph. **35**(7), 189–197 (2016)

34. Shelhamer, E., Long, J., Darrell, T.: Fully convolutional networks for semantic segmentation. IEEE Trans. Pattern Anal. Mach. Intell. **39**, 640–651 (2017)

35. Shor, Y., Lischinski, D.: The shadow meets the mask: Pyramid-based shadow removal. Comput. Graph. Forum 27, 577–586 (04 2008)

36. Singh, S., Krishnan, S.: Filter response normalization layer: Eliminating batch dependence in the training of deep neural networks. In: IEEE Conference on Computer Vision and Pattern Recognition (June 2020)

37. Ulyanov, D., Vedaldi, A., Lempitsky, V.S.: Instance normalization: The missing ingredient for fast stylization. arXiv preprint arXiv:1607.08022 (2016)

38. Vicente, T.F.Y., Hou, L., Yu, C.-P., Hoai, M., Samaras, D.: Large-scale training of shadow detectors with noisily-annotated shadow examples. In: Leibe, B., Matas, J., Sebe, N., Welling, M. (eds.) ECCV 2016. LNCS, vol. 9910, pp. 816–832. Springer, Cham (2016). https://doi.org/10.1007/978-3-319-46466-4_49

39. de Vries, H., Strub, F., Mary, J., Larochelle, H., Pietquin, O., Courville, A.C.: Modulating early visual processing by language. In: Advances in Neural Information Processing Systems (2017)

40. Wang, J., Li, X., Yang, J.: Stacked conditional generative adversarial networks for jointly learning shadow detection and shadow removal. In: IEEE Conference on Computer Vision and Pattern Recognition (2018)

41. Wang, P., Li, Y., Vasconcelos, N.: Rethinking and improving the robustness of image style transfer. In: IEEE Conference on Computer Vision and Pattern Recognition, pp. 124–133 (June 2021)

42. Wang, T., Hu, X., Wang, Q., Heng, P.A., Fu, C.W.: Instance shadow detection. In: IEEE Conference on Computer Vision and Pattern Recognition, pp. 1880–1889 (2020)

43. Wu, Y., He, K.: Group normalization. In: Ferrari, V., Hebert, M., Sminchisescu, C., Weiss, Y. (eds.) ECCV 2018. LNCS, vol. 11217, pp. 3–19. Springer, Cham (2018). https://doi.org/10.1007/978-3-030-01261-8_1

44. Wu, Z., Wu, X., Zhang, X., Wang, S., Ju, L.: Semantic stereo matching with pyramid cost volumes. In: International Conference on Computer Vision, pp. 7483–7492 (2019)

45. Xie, S., Tu, Z.: Holistically-nested edge detection. Int. J. Comput. Vis. **125**, 3–18 (2015)
46. Yang, Q., Tan, K.H., Ahuja, N.: Shadow removal using bilateral filtering. IEEE Trans. Image Process. **21**(10), 4361–4368 (2012)
47. Yu, T., et al.: Region normalization for image inpainting. In: AAAI, pp. 12733–12740 (2020)
48. Zhang, R., Isola, P., Efros, A.A., Shechtman, E., Wang, O.: The unreasonable effectiveness of deep features as a perceptual metric. In: IEEE Conference on Computer Vision and Pattern Recognition, pp. 586–595 (2018)
49. Zhang, S., Liang, R., Wang, M.: Shadowgan: Shadow synthesis for virtual objects with conditional adversarial networks. Comput. Visual Media **5**(1), 105–115 (2019)
50. Zhu, L., et al.: Bidirectional feature pyramid network with recurrent attention residual modules for shadow detection. In: Ferrari, V., Hebert, M., Sminchisescu, C., Weiss, Y. (eds.) ECCV 2018. LNCS, vol. 11210, pp. 122–137. Springer, Cham (2018). https://doi.org/10.1007/978-3-030-01231-1_8

D2C-SR: A Divergence to Convergence Approach for Real-World Image Super-Resolution

Youwei Li[1], Haibin Huang[2], Lanpeng Jia[3], Haoqiang Fan[1], and Shuaicheng Liu[1,4(✉)]

[1] Megvii Technology, Beijing, China
{liyouwei,fhq}@megvii.com
[2] Kuaishou Technology, Beijing, China
[3] Great Wall Motor Company Limited, Baoding, China
jialanpeng@gwm.cn
[4] University of Electronic Science and Technology of China, Chengdu, China
liushuaicheng@uestc.edu.cn

Abstract. In this paper, we present D2C-SR, a novel framework for the task of real-world image super-resolution. As an ill-posed problem, the key challenge in super-resolution related tasks is there can be multiple predictions for a given low-resolution input. Most classical deep learning based approaches ignored the fundamental fact and lack explicit modeling of the underlying high-frequency distribution which leads to blurred results. Recently, some methods of GAN-based or learning super-resolution space can generate simulated textures but do not promise the accuracy of the textures which have low quantitative performance. Rethinking both, we learn the distribution of underlying high-frequency details in a discrete form and propose a two-stage pipeline: divergence stage to convergence stage. At divergence stage, we propose a tree-based structure deep network as our divergence backbone. Divergence loss is proposed to encourage the generated results from the tree-based network to diverge into possible high-frequency representations, which is our way of discretely modeling the underlying high-frequency distribution. At convergence stage, we assign spatial weights to fuse these divergent predictions to obtain the final output with more accurate details. Our approach provides a convenient end-to-end manner to inference. We conduct evaluations on several real-world benchmarks, including a new proposed D2CRealSR dataset with x8 scaling factor. Our experiments demonstrate that D2C-SR achieves better accuracy and visual improvements against state-of-the-art methods, with a significantly less parameters number and our D2C structure can also be applied as a generalized structure to some other methods to obtain improvement. Our codes and dataset are available at https://github.com/megvii-research/D2C-SR.

Supplementary Information The online version contains supplementary material available at https://doi.org/10.1007/978-3-031-19800-7_22.

1   Introduction

Super-resolution (SR) is one of the fundamental problems in computer vision with its applications for several important image processing tasks. Despite decades of development in SR technologies, it remains challenging to recover high-quality and accurate details from low-resolution (LR) inputs due to its ill-posed nature.

In fact, given a LR image, there exist infinitely possible high-resolution (HR) predictions by adding different high-frequency information. This is the key challenge for the design of learning-based SR methods. Recently, deep neural network (DNN) based methods [13,15,19,20,32] have achieved tremendous success and outperformed most classical methods based on sparse coding [6,30] or local liner regression [23,29]. However, these early deep learning methods only rely on L_1 or L_2 reconstruction loss, which have a relatively high quantitative performance but can not reproduce rich texture details due to ill-posed nature. Later on, conditional GAN-based methods [7] are adapted into SR tasks, which provide methods for learning the distribution in a data-driven way and led to generate richer simulated textures. However, these methods still suffered from mode collapse and tend to generate implausible or inaccurate texture details. Thus, the quantitative performance of GAN-based methods are not satisfactory. After realizing the importance of modeling the underlying high-frequency distribution explicitly, some methods of learning SR space appear. SRFlow [14] introduced a normalizing flow-based method which tried to address the mode collapse problem and make a continuous Gaussian distribution to model all the high-frequency. Therefore, although SRFlow can sample to get a certain prediction, it does not promise the most accurate prediction. Furthermore, when adapting more complicated distribution, like large amount of real-world scenes, it would significantly increase the hardness of convergence during training. Some works [11,16,24,28] introduced ensemble-based SR approaches that trained a same network from different initialization or different down-sampling methods and merged the outputs into the SR results. Due to the lack of explicit modeling of the SR space, the different results produced by these methods are very dependent on the randomness of the initialization or artificially rules, and are therefore unstable and has a risk of degradation. In other words, they lack an explicit and stable way to make the results divergent. However, these works still give us meaningful inspiration. In this paper, some discussions are made based on this.

In this paper, we present D2C-SR, a novel divergence to convergence framework for real-world SR, by rethinking the ill-posed problem and the SR space approaches. D2C-SR follows the idea of explicitly learning the underlying distribution of high-frequency details. But unlike conditional GAN-based methods or SRFlow [14], our D2C-SR model the high-frequency details distribution using a discrete manner. Our key insight is that: most classical SR methods use a single output to fit all high-frequency details directly and 'regression to mean', therefore only obtains average and blurred outputs. While SRFlow [14] uses an continuous Gaussian distribution to fit all high-frequency details, but the fit is very difficult and does not guarantee stable and accurate high-frequency details. The GAN-based approaches have the same problem. Therefore, we adopt a trade-off approach by using a finite discrete distribution to fit the high-frequency details, thus ensuring a stable, controllable and accurate output relatively.

Specifically, at divergence stage, we first propose a tree-based structure network, where end branches are designed to learn random possible high-frequency details separately. To stabilize the divergence process, we also propose the divergence loss which can explicitly allows for divergence of the results produced by different branches. Meanwhile, we use the construction loss to ensure consistency with HR during the entire process. Due to there are multiple local minima in the network optimization process, we expect different branches to have access to different local minima through the appropriate strength of these restraints. Theoretically, if there are multiple branches and fit to the full range of high-frequency possibilities, the best HR image should be the fusion of the high-frequency details exactly. Hence, at convergence stage, we assign spatial weights to combine the divergent predictions to produce a more accurate result.

To fully evaluate the efficiency and generality of D2C-SR for real-world SISR, we conduct experiments on several benchmarks, including RealSR [4], DRealSR [27] and our new benchmark, D2CRealSR, with x8 upscaling factor. Experimental results show that our D2C-SR can achieve state-of-the-art performance and visual improvements with less parameters. In sum, the main contributions are as follows:

- We present D2C-SR, a novel framework with divergence and convergence stage for real-world SR. D2C-SR explicitly model the underlying distribution of high-frequency details in a discrete manner and provide a convenient end-to-end inference. For stable divergence, we also propose the divergence loss to generated multiple results with divergent high-frequency representations.
- A new real-world SR benchmark (D2CRealSR), which has a larger scaling factor (x8) compared to existing real-world SR benchmarks.
- D2C-SR sets up new state-of-the-art performance on many popular real-world SR benchmarks, including our new proposed D2CRealSR benchmark and, it can provide compatible performance with significantly less parameter number.
- Our D2C structure can also be applied as a generalized structure to some other methods to obtain improvement.

2   Related Work

2.1   DNN-Based SISR

Single Image Super-Resolution (SISR) is a long standing research topic due to its importance and ill-posed nature. Traditional learning-based methods adopts sparse coding [6, 21, 30] or local linear regression [22, 23, 29]. Deep learning (DL)-based methods have achieved dramatic advantages against conventional methods for SISR [1, 26]. It is first proposed by SRCNN [19] that employs a relatively shallow network and adopts the bicubic degradation for HR and LR pairs. Following which, various SISR approaches have been proposed, such as VDSR that adopts very deep network [19]; EDSR that modifies the ResNet for enhancement [13];

ESPCN that uses efficient sub-pixel CNN [18]; CDC that divides images into multiple regions [27], and VGG loss [19], GAN loss [7] that improve the perceptual visual quality [12,17,25]. Ensemble-based methods [11,16,24,28] train a same network from different initialization or different training pair generation but it lacks explicit modeling of SR space. In this work, we propose a tree-based network structure, for the purpose of multi-mode learning.

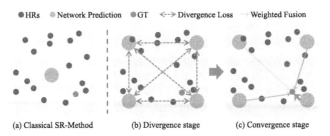

Fig. 1. Difference between our method and the classical methods in handling ill-posed problems. Blue and red dots in the box indicate possible HR texture details and the ideal details for a settled LR region. Classical methods only find the single average prediction. Our method can produce multiple divergent predictions at divergence stage and fuse to obtain more accurate predictions at convergence stage. (Color figure online)

2.2   Learning Super-Resolution Space

Single image super-resolution is ill-posed, where infinitely many high-resolution images can be downsampled to the same low-resolution images. Therefore learning a deterministic mapping may not be optimal. The problem can be converted to stochastic mapping, where multiple plausible high-resolution images are predicted given a single low-resolution input [2]. DeepSEE incorporates semantic maps for explorative facial super-resolution [3]. SRFlow adopts normalizing flow to learn the high-frequency distribution of facial datasets by using an continuous Gaussian distribution [14]. Unlike this, our method model the high-frequency distribution using a discrete manner. Thus the prediction of our method has better texture consistency with HR and the details are more accurate.

2.3   Real-World Super-Resolution and Datasets

Bicubic downsampling datasets are widely used but the gap between the simulation and the real degradation limits the performance in the real-world application [8]. Therefore, some works explore degradation of real scenarios by collecting real-world datasets, e.g., City100 [5], RealSR [4], SR-RAW [31] and DRealSR [27]. We propose the D2CRealSR dataset with larger scaling factor (x8) compared to the above datasets. Real-world degradation loses more details compared to simulated degradation [5], and the reduction of the prior makes recovery more difficult. Our method can handle these problems better than others.

3   Method

3.1   Overview

As shown in Fig. 2, D2C-SR consists of two sub-networks: a divergence network to learn the possible predictions and a convergence network to fuse the predictions to final result. In this section, we first describe divergence network in Sect. 3.2. Then, we introduce convergence network in Sect. 3.3. The network training strategy are described in Sect. 3.4. To facilitate the explanation, we also present in Fig. 1.

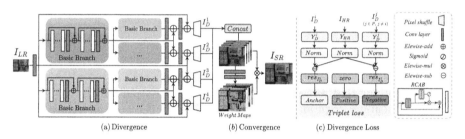

Fig. 2. Two stages in D2C architecture: (a) Divergence stage, (b) Convergence stage. Divergence network with tree-based structure outputs multi-predictions I_D^i with different high-frequency recovery. Convergence network obtains more accurate result by weighted combining divergence results. (c) Divergence loss.

3.2   Divergence Network

Divergence network produce multiple divergent predictions to address the ill-posed nature. We built a tree-based structure network to get the desired predictions. There are four main modules in the divergence network: shallow feature extraction, basic branch module, multi-branch deep residual structure and upscale module. We define the depth of the tree network is L, and each branch has C sub-branches. Each branch and its sub-branches are composed of a basic branch module and non-weight shared. Further, the basic branch module contains G residual groups, and each residual group contains B residual channel attention blocks, which refer to RCAN [32]. The divergence network first extracts the shallow features from the input LR image by the shallow feature extraction module, which is a simple Conv layer. Then, the input features are each fed into their own branch and sub-branches modules. The feature outputs of the end branches go through the multi-branch deep residual structure, then upscaled by the upscale module. So far, the divergence network generate P divergent predictions. These predictions are expressed as $I_D = \mathcal{F}(I_{LR}; \Theta_D)$, where Θ_D is the divergence network parameter and I_{LR} is the LR image. I_D^i denotes i-th prediction of divergence network.

Multi-branch Deep Residual Structure. We construct relatively deeper residuals and apply residuals structure to all branches of our tree-based divergence network. In addition to the residuals within the residual group and the residuals from the input features to the end branches, we also add the residuals from intermediate branches to their own sub-branches as shown in Fig. 2. Residual learning address the problem of long-term memory in deep SR network. Therefore, inspired by previous works [10, 12, 32], we utilize multi-branch deep residual structure to achieve more performance gain. We validate the effect of deep residual structure in Sect. 4.5.

Divergence Loss. Divergence loss used in divergence network, which composed of L_2 loss and modified triplet loss. The L_2 loss can be defined as

$$L_2^D = \sum_{i=1}^{P} \left\| I_D^i - I_{HR} \right\|_2 . \tag{1}$$

It is worth noting that we used L_2 loss on all branches separately instead of just averaging them out with an overall L_2 loss. Because it allows for a more independent divergence of each branch, which is beneficial for the divergence stage. In order to make the divergence network produce divergence results more stable, we adopt triplet loss between all pairs of different predictions from divergence network. Our goal is to make the distance between I_D^i and HR close and the distance between different members within I_D farther. However, using triplet loss directly on RGB images causes the network to focus more on other differentiated directions (e.g., RGB space and luminance) than texture features. Therefore, we perform a series of processes on the triplet inputs shown in Fig. 2. Firstly, we process I_D^i by $G(\cdot)$:

$$G(I_D^i) = \frac{Y_D^i - \mu_{Y_D^i}}{\sigma_{Y_D^i}}, \tag{2}$$

where Y_D^i is Y channel of I_D^i in YCbCr space, $\mu_{Y_D^i}$ and $\sigma_{Y_D^i}$ are mean and standard deviation of Y_D^i respectively. $G(\cdot)$ operation enables network to focus more on the differentiation of texture space rather than color and luminance space. Secondly, the triplet inputs are converted to the residual domain where texture differences can be better represented. We express the residual of I_D^i as

$$res_{I_D^i} = \left| G(I_D^i) - G(I_{HR}) \right|, \tag{3}$$

where $|\cdot|$ is absolute value function. The pixel value of the residual images can oscillate between positive and negative, and absolute value function can reduce the checkerboard phenomenon caused by triplet loss as shown in Fig 6. Overall, the formula for triplet loss is

$$trip(a, p, n) = Max[d(a, p) - d(a, n) + margin, 0], \tag{4}$$

where a, p and n are anchor, positive and negative, respectively. Therefore, we can represent our final triplet loss as

$$T_D = \frac{\sum_{i=1}^{P} \sum_{j=1, j \neq i}^{P} \beta_{ij} * trip(res_{I_D^i}, zero, res_{I_D^j})}{(P(P-1))}, \tag{5}$$

where $zero$ is zero map and it is the positive in residual domain. β is a attenuation coefficient which can be described as

$$\beta_{ij} = \theta^{l-1}, l \in [1, L], \tag{6}$$

where θ is parameter and $\theta \in (0, 1]$. The l is index of the tree depths where the common parent branch of I_D^i and I_D^j is located. We use β because that in a tree structure, differentiation should be progressive, i.e., branches with closer relatives should have relatively smaller degrees of divergence. Finally, our divergence loss is described as

$$L_D = L_2^D + \alpha * T_D, \tag{7}$$

where α is weight hyperparameter of T_D. Some detailed parameter settings will be introduced in Sect. 4.1.

3.3   Convergence Network

Combining the divergence results generated by the divergence network can produce more accurate results. We think that different areas on the predictions have different contribution weights for the final result. So we construct convergence network to merge divergent predictions weighted pixel-by-pixel, which can generate the result closer to the real HR image. Convergence network concatenates all the P predictions of the divergence network and outputs weight map for each prediction I_D^i. Weight maps can be expressed as $W = F(Concat(I_D); \Theta_C)$, where Θ_C is the convergence network model parameter. We denote W_i as the weight map of I_D^i. Every I_D^i are element-wise multiplied by respective weight map W_i, and then all of the results are summed to produce the final SR result. Accordingly, SR result can be defined as

$$I_{SR} = \sum_{i=1}^{P} \left(I_D^i \cdot W_i \right), \tag{8}$$

where I_{SR} represents final SR result.

Convergence Loss. The goal of convergence network is to merge I_D^i from divergence network. Therefore, loss function of convergence network is called convergence loss, which only consists of L_2 loss. We denote convergence loss as L_2^C, which can be expressed as

$$L_2^C = \|I_{SR} - I_{HR}\|_2. \tag{9}$$

How to generate I_{SR} has been introduced in Eq. 8. The goal of convergence loss is to make the generated SR image get closer to the ground-truth HR image.

3.4 Training Strategy

The two networks in our framework are trained separately. We firstly train the divergence network into a stable status where it can generate super-resolution divergence predictions. We then freeze the parameters of divergence network and train the convergence network by enabling the whole pipeline. More details will be discussed in Sect. 4.1.

Table 1. Performance comparison on RealSR [4], DRealSR [27] and our proposed D2CRealSR datasets. The best results are **highlighted**. '-' indicates either the available model is not supported for such a test, or not open-sourced.

Method	RealSR						DRealSR (train on RealSR)						D2CRealSR	
	x2		x3		x4		x2		x3		x4		x8	
	PSNR	SSIM	PSNR	SSIM	PSNR	SSIM	PSNR	SSIM	PSNR	SSIM	PSNR	SSIM	PSNR	SSIM
Bicubic	31.67	0.887	28.61	0.810	27.24	0.764	32.67	0.877	31.50	0.835	30.56	0.820	27.74	0.822
DRCN [11]	33.42	0.912	30.36	0.848	28.56	0.798	32.46	0.873	31.58	0.838	30.14	0.816	29.99	0.833
SRResNet [12]	33.17	0.918	30.65	0.862	28.99	0.825	32.85	0.890	31.25	0.841	29.98	0.822	30.01	0.864
EDSR [13]	33.88	0.920	30.86	0.867	29.09	0.827	32.86	0.891	31.20	0.843	30.21	0.817	30.23	0.868
RCAN [32]	33.83	0.923	30.90	0.864	29.21	0.824	32.93	0.889	31.76	0.847	30.37	0.825	30.26	0.868
ESRGAN [25]	33.80	0.922	30.72	0.866	29.15	0.826	32.70	0.889	31.25	0.842	30.18	0.821	30.06	0.865
SR-Flow [14]	-	-	-	-	24.20	0.710	-	-	-	-	24.97	0.730	23.11	0.600
LP-KPN [4]	33.49	0.917	30.60	0.865	29.05	**0.834**	32.77	-	31.79	-	30.75	-	-	-
CDC [27]	33.96	0.925	30.99	0.869	29.24	0.827	32.80	0.888	31.65	0.847	30.41	**0.827**	30.02	0.841
D2C-SR(Ours)	**34.40**	**0.926**	**31.33**	**0.871**	**29.72**	0.831	**33.42**	**0.892**	**31.80**	0.847	**30.80**	0.825	**30.55**	**0.871**

4 Experiment

4.1 Dataset and Implementation Details

D2CRealSR. Existing RealSR datasets generally include x2, x3 and x4 scaling factor only, but lack of larger scaling factor. We collect a new dataset on x8 scaling factor, which called D2CRealSR. We construct the LR and HR pairs by zooming the lens of DSLR cameras. D2CRealSR consists of 115 image pairs and 15 image pairs are selected randomly for testing set; the rest pairs construct the training set. We use SIFT method to register the image pairs iterative: we first register the image pairs roughly and crop the main central area, then we align the brightness of the central area of image pairs and register them once again. After, we crop off the edges of aligned image pairs. The image size of each pair is 3,456×2,304 after the alignment process.

Existing Datasets. We also conduct experiments on existing real-world SR datasets: RealSR and DRealSR. RealSR has 559 scenes captured from DSLR cameras and align the image pairs strictly. 459 scenes for training and 100 scenes for testing. The image sizes of RealSR image pairs are in the range of 700~3000 and 600~3500. DRealSR has 83, 84 and 93 image pairs in testing set, 884, 783 and 840 image pairs in training set for x2, x3, x4 scaling factors, respectively. Note that we found some of the image pairs in DRealSR are misaligned, which is caused by the depth of field. So we only validate our results on testing set of DRealSR to show the performance of the cross-dataset of our method.

Implementation Details. In the experiment, we set the number of branch layers as $L = 2$, the number of child branches $C = 2$. The basic branch module include $G = 2$ residual groups and $B = 4$ residual blocks in each group. We use Adam optimizer and set exponential decay rates as 0.9 and 0.999. The initial learning rate is set to 10^{-4} and then reduced to half every $2k$ epochs. For each training batch, we randomly extract 4 LR image patches with the size of 96 × 96. We implement D2C-SR method with the Pytorch framework and train the network using NVIDIA 2080Ti GPU.

4.2 Comparisons with Existing Methods

To evaluate our method, we train and test our model on our D2CRealSR with scaling factor x8 and an existing real-world SR dataset, RealSR with scaling factor x4, x3, x2. In addition, we validate on DRealSR tesing set for performance of cross-dataset. We compare our model with other state-of-the-art SISR methods, including DRCN [11], SRResNet [12], EDSR [13], RCAN [32], ESR-GAN [25], LP-KPN [4] and CDC [27]. The SISR results were evaluated on the Y channel in the YCbCr space using PSNR and SSIM. Among these SR methods, EDSR and RCAN are the classic SISR methods and DRCN is the open-source ensemble-based method. In addition, LP-KPN and CDC are designed to solve the real-world SR problem and they outperform on real-world SR benchmarks.

Quantitative Comparison. The evaluation results of the SR methods, including our model and the other 8 methods are demonstrated in Table 1. The best results are highlighted and our method are 0.48 dB higher than the second ranked CDC method on x4 RealSR. Our model outperforms by a large margin on all the benchmarks and achieve state-of-the-art performance.

Qualitative Comparison. Visualization results of SR methods and ours on RealSR and D2CRealSR datasets are shown in Fig. 3 and Fig. 4. It is observed that existing SR methods (e.g., RCAN, LP-KPN, CDC) tend to restore the details to be thicker, blurry, or unnatural. Meanwhile, in Canon-041, Nikon-050 and Sony-101, our method recovered sharper and more accurate edge textures. In Nikon-024, we recover more information on the letters. From the visual comparisons, our method has the ability to recover richer and more accurate details.

Visualization of D2C Processes. To further represent the progress of the D2C-SR, we visualize and compare the LR image, HR image, divergence intermediate results, and final results as well as the results of other comparison methods in Fig. 5. Classical SR methods directly use a single prediction to fit the distribution of all high-frequency details, thus obtain blurred outputs due to the ill-posed nature. Our two-stage approach explicitly learns the distribution of high-frequency details using a discrete manner, thus we can get rich and accurate texture details.

Comparison in Perceptual Metric. In recent years, the perceptual metric becomes another dimension to evaluate the image quality, and we also conduct a comparison on the perceptual metric in Table 2. Based on Sect. 3, we add vgg loss to train our model [12] to obtain a balance of multiple metrics. Experiments demonstrate that our method can achieve better performance on several evaluation measures, including the perceptual metric.

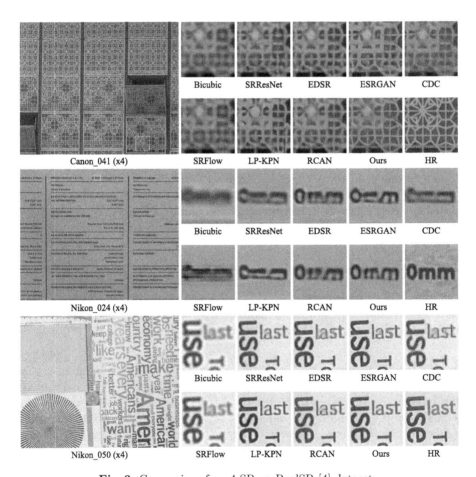

Fig. 3. Comparison for x4 SR on RealSR [4] dataset.

4.3   Applying the D2C Structure to Other Methods

In Table 3, we apply the D2C structure to other methods and compare the performance with the original method. To make a fair comparison and reduce the influences caused by different sizes of parameters, we reduce the number of feature channels or the basic modules such that the number of parameters of the D2C counterpart model is smaller than the original model. Our results show

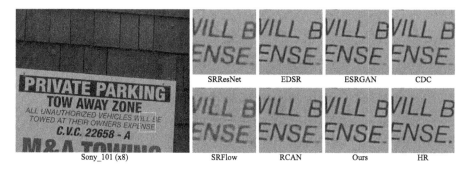

Fig. 4. Comparison for x8 SR on our captured D2CRealSR dataset.

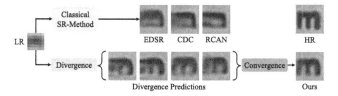

Fig. 5. Visualization of D2C processes and other methods (x4).

that multiple methods can achieve better performance with fewer number of parameters by applying the D2C structure.

4.4   Model Size Analyses

We show comparisons about model size and performance in Fig. 7. We list six sizes of models: 5.88M, 4.53M, 3.63M, 0.91M, 0.23M and 0.19M. These models are constructed by changing the number of residual groups G and the number of residual block B. Our 0.23M model can achieve a better effect than other methods. At this PSNR level, CDC uses 39.92M, and RCAN also uses 15M parameters. Our baseline model chieve higher performance using 5.88M parameters only. Our method have a better trade-off between model size and performance.

Table 2. Performance comparison in LPIPS on RealSR.

Method	x2			x3			x4		
	PSNR	SSIM	LPIPS	PSNR	SSIM	LPIPS	PSNR	SSIM	LPIPS
Bicubic	31.67	0.887	0.223	28.61	0.810	0.389	27.24	0.764	0.476
SRResNet [12]	33.17	0.918	0.158	30.65	0.862	0.228	28.99	0.825	0.281
EDSR [13]	33.88	0.920	0.145	30.86	0.867	0.219	29.09	0.827	0.278
RCAN [32]	33.83	0.923	0.147	30.90	0.864	0.225	29.21	0.824	0.287
CDC [27]	33.96	0.925	0.142	30.99	0.869	0.215	29.24	0.827	0.278
D2C-SR(Ours)	**34.39**	**0.926**	**0.136**	**31.31**	**0.870**	**0.214**	**29.67**	**0.830**	**0.270**

Table 3. Performance of applying our D2C structure to other methods on RealSR.

Method	x2		x3		x4		Parameters
	PSNR	SSIM	PSNR	SSIM	PSNR	SSIM	
SRResNet [12]	33.17	0.918	30.65	0.862	28.99	**0.825**	1.52M
D2C-SRResNet	**33.82**	**0.920**	**30.69**	**0.862**	**29.19**	0.822	**1.37M**
VDSR [10]	31.39	0.876	30.03	0.845	27.07	0.751	0.67M
D2C-VDSR	**34.08**	**0.920**	**30.29**	**0.858**	**28.21**	**0.793**	**0.67M**
RRDBNet [25]	33.44	0.919	30.29	0.858	28.34	0.813	16.7M
D2C-RRDBNet	**33.49**	**0.920**	**30.33**	**0.859**	**28.47**	**0.814**	**9.16M**
RDN [33]	33.97	0.922	30.90	0.864	29.23	0.824	6.02M
D2C-RDN	**34.03**	**0.922**	**30.93**	**0.865**	**29.32**	**0.825**	**5.59M**
EDSR [13]	33.88	0.920	30.86	0.867	29.09	0.827	43.1M
D2C-EDSR	**34.17**	**0.924**	**31.08**	**0.868**	**29.41**	**0.829**	**7.91M**
IMDN [9]	33.59	0.916	30.74	0.859	29.17	0.819	0.874M
D2C-IMDN	**33.95**	**0.920**	**30.98**	**0.862**	**29.45**	**0.824**	**0.738M**

(a) Without ABS   (b) With ABS

Fig. 6. Absolute value function (ABS) reduces the checkerboard phenomenon.

Table 4. Effect study on the width and depth of the tree-based network (x4).

	1	2	3	4
Width (C)	29.41	29.54	29.56	**29.58**
Depth (L)	29.30	29.54	29.63	**29.64**

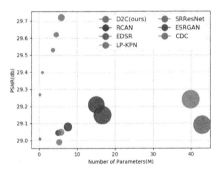

Fig. 7. Performance vs. parameters.

4.5 Ablation Studies

The Width and Depth of Tree-Based Network. Our divergence network is a tree-based architecture. We set different L and C to provide experimental evaluations on the width and depth of the tree. Because increasing the depth and width increases memory usage. So we do these experiments on a small baseline model, which has $G = 2$ residual groups and each group has $B = 1$ block. As show in Table 4, we increase the width and depth from 1 to 4 respectively on x4 scaling factor and show the changes in PSNR. By increasing the width or depth of the tree-based network, the performance of our D2C-SR improves.

Divergence Loss. As mentioned in Sect. 3.2, the divergence loss is used to enforce the outputs from different branches divergent. In Fig. 8, the visualization divergent results show that different branches produce different texture predictions. We verify the effectiveness of our divergence loss by removing the term of Eq. 5. As shown in Table 5 "w/o. divergence loss", the approach appears degraded. Because of the random nature of the model initialization, it is possible to lead to some degree of divergence in the results without using triplet loss and thus still gain some performance, it is still possible to gain some benefit from the effect of divergence. However, as mentioned in Sect. 1, it is not stable without the explicit divergence constraint, and thus may still bring degradation of performance. Further, we change the weight of the divergence loss and observe the changes that occur in different branches. As shown in Fig. 9, the results are relatively similar when divergence loss is not used. As the coefficients α increase, the differentiation of the different branches becomes more obvious. In this example, the results containing richer and more details appear. Theoretically, if α or the margin is too large it may lead to performance degradation, so we determine the α or the margin based on the model convergence.

Table 5. Effect of our divergence loss and multi-branch deep residual structure.

	x2		x3		x4	
	PSNR	SSIM	PSNR	SSIM	PSNR	SSIM
w/o. Divergence Loss	33.98	0.920	31.12	0.863	29.43	0.824
w/o. Multi Deep Res	34.28	0.925	31.28	0.870	29.68	0.830
D2C-SR(Ours)	**34.40**	**0.926**	**31.33**	**0.871**	**29.72**	**0.831**

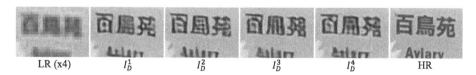

LR (x4) I_D^1 I_D^2 I_D^3 I_D^4 HR

Fig. 8. Visualization of the divergent predictions.

Multi-branch Deep Residual Structure. As mentioned in Sect. 3.2, we also disable the structure to verify its effectiveness. As shown in Table 5 "w/o. Multi Deep Res", the PSNR decreased without the multi-branch deep residual structure.

4.6 Visualization of Weight Maps

We assign spatial weights to the divergence results and use this weight for the fusion of the divergence results at the convergence stage. In Fig. 10, we visualize the weight maps using the heatmap. The visualization results show that predictions have some regional and texture correlation. We suggest that the weight generation depends mainly on the sharpness, edge style and texture preferences of the divergence results. We further measure the gap between the learned weight and the approximate ideal weight by finding the pixel that best matches the HR in the divergence results. The PSNR between the ideal fusion results and HR is 31.06 dB on RealSR x4, thus the gap is 1.34 dB (29.72 dB ours).

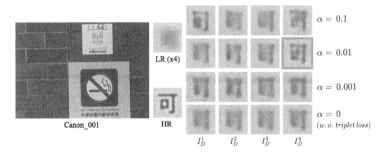

Fig. 9. Comparisons on different weighting coefficient α in our divergence loss.

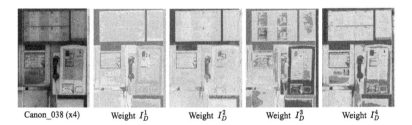

Fig. 10. Weight maps in convergence stage. Red indicates higher values. (Color figure online)

4.7 Simulated SISR and Real-World SISR

More works have focused on real-world SR because the great gap between simulated and real-world degradation hinders practical SR applications [4,27]. On the other hand, real-world degradation loses more information than bicubic compared with the HR, which also have been discussed in [5], and ill-posed problem becomes more apparent in real-world datasets. Therefore, the real-world datasets can better reflect the effectiveness of our method.

5   Conclusion

In this study, we revisit the problem of image super-resolution and provide a new two-stage approach: divergence stage for multiple predictions learning as well as convergence for predictions fusion. Considering the limitations of traditional SR methods and SR space methods, we adopt a trade-off approach by using a finite discrete distribution to fit the high-frequency details. This allows the network to be more efficient and achieves state-of-the-art performance with much less computational cost. Futher, our D2C framework is a promising direction for image processing tasks like image inpainting as well as image denoising, and it is worth further exploration.

Acknowledgement. This work was supported by the National Natural Science Foundation of China (NSFC) under grants No. 61872067 and No. 61720106004.

References

1. Anwar, S., Khan, S., Barnes, N.: A deep journey into super-resolution: a survey. ACM Comput. Surv. (CSUR) **53**(3), 1–34 (2020)
2. Bahat, Y., Michaeli, T.: Explorable super resolution. In: CVPR, pp. 2716–2725 (2020)
3. Buhler, M.C., Romero, A., Timofte, R.: DeepSEE: deep disentangled semantic explorative extreme super-resolution. In: ACCV (2020)
4. Cai, J., Zeng, H., Yong, H., Cao, Z., Zhang, L.: Toward real-world single image super-resolution: a new benchmark and a new model. In: CVPR, pp. 3086–3095 (2019)
5. Chen, C., Xiong, Z., Tian, X., Zha, Z.J., Wu, F.: Camera lens super-resolution. In: CVPR, pp. 1652–1660 (2019)
6. Dai, D., Timofte, R., Van Gool, L.: Jointly optimized regressors for image super-resolution. Comput. Graph. Forum **34**, 95–104 (2015)
7. Goodfellow, I.J., et al.: Y.: Generative adversarial networks. arXiv preprint arXiv:1406.2661 (2014)
8. Gu, J., Lu, H., Zuo, W., Dong, C.: Blind super-resolution with iterative kernel correction. In: CVPR, pp. 1604–1613 (2019)
9. Hui, Z., Gao, X., Yang, Y., Wang, X.: Lightweight image super-resolution with information multi-distillation network. In: Proceedings of the 27th ACM International Conference on Multimedia, pp. 2024–2032 (2019)
10. Kim, J., Kwon Lee, J., Mu Lee, K.: Accurate image super-resolution using very deep convolutional networks. In: CVPR, pp. 1646–1654 (2016)
11. Kim, J., Lee, J.K., Lee, K.M.: Deeply-recursive convolutional network for image super-resolution. In: CVPR, pp. 1637–1645 (2016)
12. Ledig, C., et al.: Photo-realistic single image super-resolution using a generative adversarial network. In: CVPR, pp. 4681–4690 (2017)
13. Lim, B., Son, S., Kim, H., Nah, S., Mu Lee, K.: Enhanced deep residual networks for single image super-resolution. In: CVPRW, pp. 136–144 (2017)
14. Lugmayr, A., Danelljan, M., Van Gool, L., Timofte, R.: SRFlow: learning the super-resolution space with normalizing flow. In: Vedaldi, A., Bischof, H., Brox, T., Frahm, J.-M. (eds.) ECCV 2020. LNCS, vol. 12350, pp. 715–732. Springer, Cham (2020). https://doi.org/10.1007/978-3-030-58558-7_42
15. Michelini, P.N., Liu, H., Zhu, D.: Multigrid backprojection super-resolution and deep filter visualization. In: AAAI, vol. 33, pp. 4642–4650 (2019)

16. Pan, Z., et al.: Real image super resolution via heterogeneous model ensemble using GP-NAS. In: Bartoli, A., Fusiello, A. (eds.) ECCV 2020. LNCS, vol. 12537, pp. 423–436. Springer, Cham (2020). https://doi.org/10.1007/978-3-030-67070-2_25

17. Sajjadi, M.S., Scholkopf, B., Hirsch, M.: EnhanceNet: single image super-resolution through automated texture synthesis. In: ICCV, pp. 4491–4500 (2017)

18. Shi, W., et al.: Real-time single image and video super-resolution using an efficient sub-pixel convolutional neural network. In: CVPR, pp. 1874–1883 (2016)

19. Simonyan, K., Zisserman, A.: Very deep convolutional networks for large-scale image recognition. arXiv preprint arXiv:1409.1556 (2014)

20. Song, D., Xu, C., Jia, X., Chen, Y., Xu, C., Wang, Y.: Efficient residual dense block search for image super-resolution. In: AAAI, vol. 34, pp. 12007–12014 (2020)

21. Sun, L., Hays, J.: Super-resolution from internet-scale scene matching. In: Proceedings of ICCP, pp. 1–12 (2012)

22. Timofte, R., De Smet, V., Van Gool, L.: Anchored neighborhood regression for fast example-based super-resolution. In: ICCV, pp. 1920–1927 (2013)

23. Timofte, R., De Smet, V., Van Gool, L.: A+: adjusted anchored neighborhood regression for fast super-resolution. In: Cremers, D., Reid, I., Saito, H., Yang, M.-H. (eds.) ACCV 2014. LNCS, vol. 9006, pp. 111–126. Springer, Cham (2015). https://doi.org/10.1007/978-3-319-16817-3_8

24. Wang, L., Huang, Z., Gong, Y., Pan, C.: Ensemble based deep networks for image super-resolution. Pattern Recogn. **68**, 191–198 (2017)

25. Wang, X., et al.: ESRGAN: enhanced super-resolution generative adversarial networks. In: Leal-Taixé, L., Roth, S. (eds.) ECCV 2018. LNCS, vol. 11133, pp. 63–79. Springer, Cham (2019). https://doi.org/10.1007/978-3-030-11021-5_5

26. Wang, Z., Chen, J., Hoi, S.C.: Deep learning for image super-resolution: a survey. IEEE Trans. Pattern Anal. Mach. Intell. **43**(10), 3365–3385 (2020)

27. Wei, P., et al.: Component divide-and-conquer for real-world image super-resolution. In: Vedaldi, A., Bischof, H., Brox, T., Frahm, J.-M. (eds.) ECCV 2020. LNCS, vol. 12353, pp. 101–117. Springer, Cham (2020). https://doi.org/10.1007/978-3-030-58598-3_7

28. Xiong, D., Gui, Q., Hou, W., Ding, M.: Gradient boosting for single image super-resolution. Inform. Sci. **454**, 328–343 (2018)

29. Yang, C.Y., Yang, M.H.: Fast direct super-resolution by simple functions. In: ICCV, pp. 561–568 (2013)

30. Yang, J., Wright, J., Huang, T., Ma, Y.: Image super-resolution as sparse representation of raw image patches. In: CVPR, pp. 1–8 (2008)

31. Zhang, X., Chen, Q., Ng, R., Koltun, V.: Zoom to learn, learn to zoom. In: CVPR, pp. 3762–3770 (2019)

32. Zhang, Y., Li, K., Li, K., Wang, L., Zhong, B., Fu, Y.: Image super-resolution using very deep residual channel attention networks. In: Ferrari, V., Hebert, M., Sminchisescu, C., Weiss, Y. (eds.) ECCV 2018. LNCS, vol. 11211, pp. 294–310. Springer, Cham (2018). https://doi.org/10.1007/978-3-030-01234-2_18

33. Zhang, Y., Tian, Y., Kong, Y., Zhong, B., Fu, Y.: Residual dense network for image super-resolution. In: CVPR, pp. 2472–2481 (2018)

GRIT-VLP: Grouped Mini-batch Sampling for Efficient Vision and Language Pre-training

Jaeseok Byun[1], Taebaek Hwang[2], Jianlong Fu[3], and Taesup Moon[1(✉)]

[1] Department of ECE/ASRI/IPAI, Seoul National University, Seoul, South Korea
tsmoon@snu.ac.kr
[2] Department of ECE, Sungkyunkwan University, Seoul, South Korea
[3] Microsoft Research Asia, Beijing, China

Abstract. Most of the currently existing vision and language pre-training (VLP) methods have mainly focused on how to extract and align vision and text features. In contrast to the mainstream VLP methods, we highlight that two routinely applied steps during pre-training have crucial impact on the performance of the pre-trained model: *in-batch* hard negative sampling for image-text matching (ITM) and assigning the large masking probability for the masked language modeling (MLM). After empirically showing the unexpected effectiveness of above two steps, we systematically devise our GRIT-VLP, which adaptively samples mini-batches for more effective mining of hard negative samples for ITM while maintaining the computational cost for pre-training. Our method consists of three components: 1) GRouped mIni-baTch sampling (GRIT) strategy that collects similar examples in a mini-batch, 2) ITC consistency loss for improving the mining ability, and 3) enlarged masking probability for MLM. Consequently, we show our GRIT-VLP achieves a new state-of-the-art performance on various downstream tasks with much less computational cost. Furthermore, we demonstrate that our model is essentially in par with ALBEF, the previous state-of-the-art, only with one-third of training epochs on the same training data. Code is available at https://github.com/jaeseokbyun/GRIT-VLP.

Keywords: Efficient vision and language pre-training · Hard negative sampling · Batch-sampling strategy · Shuffling

J. Byun and T. Hwang—Equal contribution. This work was performed when Jaeseok Byun did an internship at Microsoft Research Asia.

Supplementary Information The online version contains supplementary material available at https://doi.org/10.1007/978-3-031-19800-7_23.

1   Introduction

Recently, the pre-training and fine-tuning approach of the Transformer [35] based models have made exciting progress in natural-language-processing (NLP) [6] and vision tasks [8]. Particularly, despite the huge computational cost, vision and language pre-training (VLP) [4,9,13,17,20–22,27,31,33], which aims to learn cross-modal representations from large-scale image-text pairs, enabled to achieve the state-of-the-art results in various vision and language downstream tasks, *e.g.*, image-text retrieval (IRTR), natural language for visual reasoning (NLVR) [32], and visual question answering (VQA) [1], etc. For the joint understanding of image and text, a multi-modal encoder used in VLP is typically trained with the self-supervised learning objectives, such as image-text matching (ITM) and masked language modeling (MLM).

Majority of the existing VLP methods have focused on how to make the vision features to align with those of the text. The first popular approach [4, 22,24,33] is to utilize the salient region-based features extracted from a pre-trained object detector. However, these region feature based VLP methods suffer from severe computational inefficiency and heavy dependency on the pre-trained object detectors. In order to overcome such drawbacks, recent approaches have replaced the object detectors with CNN backbones [13,14] or linear embedding inspired by the recently developed Vision Transformer (ViT) [8], which enables efficient end-to-end training of the vision-language representation learning.

Recently, ALBEF [20] was proposed as another attempt to lift the dependency on the object detectors. They designed a novel VLP architecture to integrate the uni-modal encoder for each modality (*i.e.,* an object-detector-free vision encoder and a text encoder) by employing a multi-modal Transformer encoder that fuses features from them. Additionally, ALBEF employed the image-text contrastive (ITC) loss for uni-modal encoders to *pre-align* the features before fusing, the *in-batch* hard negative sampling strategy for the ITM, and a momentum distillation to further improve the performance. As a result, it achieved the state-of-the-art performance for the multiple vision and language downstream tasks.

While the main emphasis of [20] was on the pre-aligning stage via ITC, we double-check that proposition and carry out careful ablation analyses on ALBEF and identify that the two routinely applied sampling steps in fact have crucial impacts on the final downstream performance. Firstly, the *hard negative sampling* for the ITM task, of which effect was described as marginal compared to the pre-aligning in [20, Section 6], in fact turns out to be an essential component, even more than the ITC itself, for efficient VLP. Namely, when training for the ITM task, rather than using the randomly selected negatives as shown in Fig. 1(a) (for the text and image anchor, respectively), selecting *hard* negative samples as in Fig. 1(b), which is sampled from the given *mini-batch* by using the contrastive image-text similarity scores already computed for the ITC, becomes much more useful for promoting a more fine-grained representation learning. Secondly, the *mask sampling probability* for the MLM task, which typically is naively set to 15%, also is shown to have a significant impact on the VLP per-

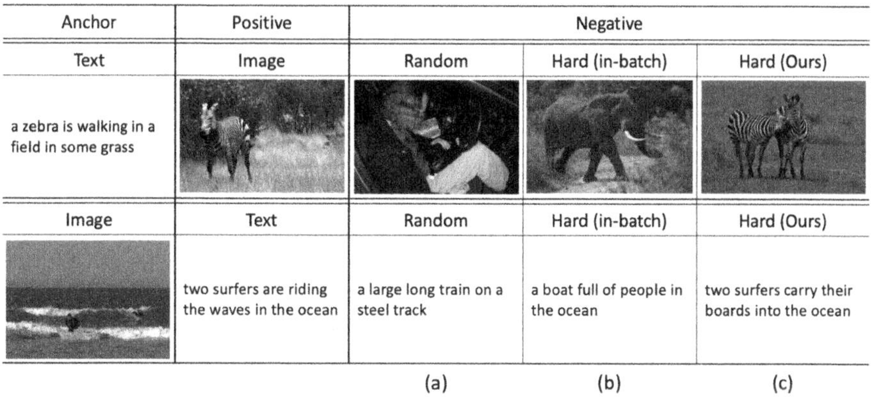

Anchor	Positive	Negative		
Text	Image	Random	Hard (in-batch)	Hard (Ours)
a zebra is walking in a field in some grass				
Image	Text	Random	Hard (in-batch)	Hard (Ours)
	two surfers are riding the waves in the ocean	a large long train on a steel track	a boat full of people in the ocean	two surfers carry their boards into the ocean
		(a)	(b)	(c)

Fig. 1. A comparison of negative samples for ITM task selected by (a) Random, (b) *In-batch* sampling by ALBEF [20], and (c) Our GRIT strategy.

formance. Namely, when the probability is enlarged up to 50%, the multi-modal encoder is enforced to use more visual context features for predicting the masked token, hence, a more consolidated multi-modal representations could be learned. A recent concurrent work [37] also suggests the enlarging of the masking probability for MLM; however, their focus was on the NLP domain, thus, they have not investigated the impact of enlarging the probability on the multi-modal encoder.

Motivated by above analyses, in this paper, we make the following three modifications on ALBEF to significantly improve the downstream performance and computational efficiency of VLP. First, we devise GRIT (GRouped mIni-baTch sampling) strategy that enables to select much more informative hard negative samples (as shown in Fig. 1(c)) than those in [20] (Fig. 1(b)), *without* introducing any significant memory and computational overhead. Note such improvement is far from being straightforward since a naive extension of previous approaches would require either additional GPU memory (when simply enlarging the batch size) or forward pass computation (when utilizing additional queues as in [12,36,40]). We elaborate on this point more in details in a later section. Second, we devise a consistency loss between the image-text similarity scores used for ITC such that the contrastive learning and pre-aligning become more effective and, as a result, enables our GRIT to sample more exquisite negative samples. Third, we use enlarged mask sampling probability (50%) for MLM such that the visual features can be further integrated with the text features when solving the downstream tasks.

Our final method that combines above modifications is dubbed as GRIT-VLP, and we show that it can significantly improve the efficiency of VLP compared to ALBEF. Namely, trained on the exact same training data, GRIT-VLP significantly outperforms ALBEF on all of the downstream tasks we tested with 33% fewer number of epochs, 21% less training time per epoch. Furthermore, our thorough analyses show that GRIT-VLP is model agnostic and can be easily applied to existing VLP with different model architectures and objectives, which demonstrates the potential of our method being an essential tool for VLP.

2 Preliminaries and Related Work

[**Vision-language pre-training**] Existing VLP methods, which can be categorized into three frameworks, have mainly focused on the development of objectives and architectures to learn multi-modal representations. The first approach is to adopt dual uni-modal encoders which are composed of separate image and text encoder. CLIP [27] and ALIGN [15] pre-trained with contrastive learning have been shown to be effective for IRTR, without object detectors. However, they suffer from the performance degradation in other downstream tasks (*e.g.*, VQA, NLVR). The second approach [19,22,24,31,33] mainly utilizes a single multi-modal encoder where concatenated text and image representations are used as input. In contrast to the former approach, these works consistently show promising results on various downstream tasks. However, these methods heavily depend on the pre-trained object detectors which are computationally inefficient. Thus, recent works [13,14,17,44] have struggled to replace object detectors with more efficient ones. The last category [20,45] offsets the shortcomings of the previous approaches by combining them, and achieves state-of-the-art performance. ALBEF [20] combines them by adding pre-alignmenet before fusing. Our method is built upon this ALBEF [20], but, deviating from the mainstream of VLP, our attention is on the *sampling strategy* for efficient pre-training.

[**Hard negative mining**] Most prior works on negative mining [11,29,38,42,43] point out that hard negatives can help a training model to converge faster. Recent approaches [3,5,28,39,46] mainly focus on the unsupervised contrastive learning setting where true dissimilarity of pairs are not available. However, these methods can not be applied to the VLP methods (second, third categories in the previous paragraph) due to the inherent architecture and input of multi-modal encoder.

2.1 ALign BEfore Fuse (ALBEF) [20]

Since ALBEF is the base model on which we build our method, we review it in details here. It consists of an image encoder f_v, a text encoder f_t, and a multi-modal encoder h, all of which are based on the Transformer architecture. Each input image V and sentence T is encoded into respective embedding sequences: $f_v(V) = \{v^{cls}, v^1, v^2, ..., v^{S_V}\}$ and $f_t(T) = \{t^{cls}, t^1, t^2, ..., t^{S_T}\}$, in which v^{cls} and t^{cls} denote the embedding of the [CLS] token for each modality, and S_V and S_T denote the sequence length of image and text, respectively. Then, vision and text representations are fused by a cross-attention module in the multi-modal encoder which requires both vision and text features as input (*i.e.*, $h(f_v(V), f_t(T)) =$

$\{w^{cls}, w^1, w^2, ..., w^{S_T}\}$). The three pre-training objectives of ALBEF are briefly introduced below[1].

(a) **Image-text contrastive learning (ITC)** focuses on the pre-alignment of uni-modal representations before fusing them with a multi-modal encoder. Like conventional contrastive learning, it promotes positive image-text pairs to have similar representations and negative ones to be dissimilar. Inspired by MoCo [12], ALBEF utilizes two *queues* for storing recent [CLS] embeddings from the unimodal encoders, *i.e.*, v^{cls} and t^{cls}, and use them as extra negatives for the contrastive learning. More specifically, a similarity between V and T is defined as $s(V,T) = g_v(v^{cls})^T g_t(t^{cls})$ in which $g_v(\cdot)$ and $g_t(\cdot)$ are linear projections for mapping [CLS] embeddings to the normalized lower dimensional features. Then, for each V and T, the normalized image-to-text and text-to-image similarities for $j = 1, \ldots, N$ are defined as:

$$p_j^{v2t}(V) = \frac{\exp(s(V,T_j)/\tau)}{\sum_{j=1}^{N}\exp(s(V,T_j)/\tau)}, \quad p_j^{t2v}(T) = \frac{\exp(s(V_j,T)/\tau)}{\sum_{j=1}^{N}\exp(s(V_j,T)/\tau)}, \quad (1)$$

in which τ is a learnable temperature, and N is the size of the queue. The ITC loss is then defined as:

$$\mathcal{L}_{\text{ITC}} = \frac{1}{2}\mathbb{E}_{(V,T)\sim D}[\text{CE}(\boldsymbol{y}^{v2t}(V), \boldsymbol{p}^{v2t}(V)) + \text{CE}(\boldsymbol{y}^{t2v}(T), \boldsymbol{p}^{t2v}(T))], \quad (2)$$

in which $\boldsymbol{y}^{v2t}(V)$ and $\boldsymbol{y}^{t2v}(T)$ denotes the ground-truth one-hot vector for the true pair sample for V and T, respectively. Now, in the pre-training, we do *not* use the queues for ITC but use the *in-batch* version, *i.e.*, N in (1) is the size of the mini-batch, to implement a lightweight version in terms of memory/computation.

(b) **Image-text matching (ITM)** is a binary classification task that predicts whether a pair of image and text, (V,T), is matched or not. The prediction probability of the classifier, $\boldsymbol{p}^{\text{ITM}}(V,T)$, is obtained by using the joint embedding feature of [CLS] token (w^{cls}) from the multi-modal encoder. Then, the ITM loss is defined as

$$\mathcal{L}_{\text{ITM}} = \mathbb{E}_{(V,T)\sim D}[\text{CE}(\boldsymbol{y}^{\text{ITM}}, \boldsymbol{p}^{\text{ITM}}(V,T))]. \quad (3)$$

in which $\boldsymbol{y}^{ITM}$ is the ground truth one-hot vector, and $\text{CE}(\cdot, \cdot)$ stands for the cross-entropy between the two probability vectors. The effectiveness of ITM is determined by the quality of the negative pair, and, as outlined in the Introduction, ALBEF proposes the *in-batch* hard negative sampling (ITM$_{\text{hard}}$) by utilizing $\boldsymbol{p}^{v2t}(V)$ and $\boldsymbol{p}^{t2v}(T)$ defined in (1) for sampling text and image that has high similarity for given V and T, respectively, as a negative sample pair.

(c) **Masked language modeling (MLM)** is a task to predict the randomly masked tokens in a text based on both contextual text and visual information. ALBEF uses the masking probability of 15% following [6], and by denoting the

---

[1] Note the Momentum Distillation (MD), which utilizes the soft outputs from an additional momentum model is omitted, since we do NOT use the momentum model.

randomly masked text as $\tilde{T}$ and the prediction probability for the masked tokens as $\boldsymbol{p}^{\mathrm{mask}}(V, \tilde{T})$, the loss function of MLM becomes

$$\mathcal{L}_{\mathrm{MLM}} = \mathbb{E}_{(V,\tilde{T}) \sim D}[\mathrm{CE}(\tilde{\boldsymbol{y}}, \boldsymbol{p}^{\mathrm{mask}}(V, \tilde{T}))], \tag{4}$$

in which $\tilde{\boldsymbol{y}}$ is a ground truth one-hot vector for the masked token.

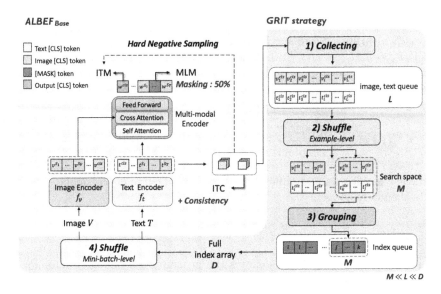

Fig. 2. The ALBEF$_{\mathrm{Base}}$ architecture and the overall process of GRIT-VLP.

3   Ablation Analyses on ALBEF

As mentioned in the Introduction, we carry out careful analyses on ALBEF to verify the true effect of the training objectives described in the previous section. To that end, we set the base model as "ALBEF$_{\mathrm{Base}}$", which mostly follows the model architecture and pre-training objectives of ALBEF, but does *not* use the additional momentum encoder and momentum distillation[2]. Highlighting the training objectives, we can also denote "ALBEF$_{\mathrm{Base}}$" by MLM+ITM$_{\mathrm{hard}}$+ITC, and we ablate each of those components and evaluate the performance of the model variants on two downstream tasks (IRTR, NLVR). All models are pre-trained with 4M dataset, and evaluated with MS-COCO [23] and NLVR2 dataset [32]. Details on the tasks, datasets and additional results are described in Sect. 5 and the Supplementary Material (S.M.).

---

[2] We defer describing the detailed model architecture to Sect. 5.1.

[**Hard negative sampling on ITM**] Table 1 compares the downstream task performance of models that have the fixed MLM objective (with masking probability 15%) but varying ITM and ITC objectives of $ALBEF_{Base}$. In the table, "MLM+ITM_{hard}" stands for the case in which only ITM_{hard} is carried out without the ITC objective—this case is missing in the analysis of the original ALBEF paper [20, Table 1], but we believe it is necessary for showing the effect of ITM_{hard} alone without the pre-algining effect of ITC. The subtlety here is that, since ITM_{hard} utilizes the image-text similarity scores from ITC (1) for selecting the *in-batch* hard negative samples, we use the scores obtained from the uni-modal encoders of ALBEF (without the multi-modal encoder) that are *pre-trained* only with the ITC loss. Moreover, "ITM_{rand}" in Table 1 stands for the ITM loss with randomly selected negative samples.

Table 1. Ablation study on ITM_{hard} and ITC for $ALBEF_{Base}$.

Epochs	Training tasks	TR		(COCO)	IR			NLVR	
		R@1	R@5	R@10	R@1	R@5	R@10	(val)	(test)
10	MLM + ITM_{rand}	61.6	86.1	92.5	47.8	75.4	84.8	77.02	78.44
	MLM + ITM_{rand} + ITC	66.8	88.8	94.5	51.1	78.4	86.8	76.59	78.69
	MLM + ITM_{hard}	68.6	89.4	94.9	52.1	79.0	87.1	79.18	79.32
	$ALBEF_{Base}$	72.3	91.3	96.0	55.1	81.0	88.5	79.21	79.78
20	MLM + ITM_{rand}	66.5	88.3	94.0	51.3	78.3	86.5	78.02	79.43
	MLM + ITM_{rand} + ITC	69.6	90.9	95.3	53.8	80.0	87.8	77.61	79.43
	MLM + ITM_{hard}	72.0	91.5	**96.6**	57.5	81.2	88.4	**80.44**	**80.83**
	$ALBEF_{Base}$	**73.8**	**92.3**	96.5	**57.7**	**82.5**	**89.6**	79.22	80.37

The original ALBEF essentially focuses on the effect of ITC by mainly comparing "MLM+ITM_{rand}" and "MLM+ITM_{rand}+ITC" and argues that "ITM_{hard}" only gives a marginal improvement when it replaces ITM_{rand}. However, we observe a different story in Table 1. Namely, even without the pre-alignment of the representations via ITC, "MLM+ITM_{hard}" gives a significant performance boost over "MLM+ITM_{rand}", which is substantially larger than the improvement we get by "MLM+ITM_{rand}+ITC". Moreover, even with a shorter 10 epochs, "MLM+ITM_{hard}" performs competitively or superior to "MLM+ITM_{rand}+ITC" trained for a longer 20 epochs. While the best performance is still obtained by using ITM_{hard} and ITC together, *i.e.*, $ALBEF_{Base}$, this result strongly motivates that further improving ITM_{hard} could be central in attaining efficient VLP.

[**Mask sampling probability for MLM**] Table 2 now focuses on MLM by varying the masking probability with fixed ITM and ITC. Namely, the original $ALBEF_{Base}$ trains with the masking probability of 15%, and we also test the model with the probability 50%, dubbed as $ALBEF_{Base_{50}}$. In the table, we observe that this simple change brings surprising performance gain; $ALBEF_{Base_{50}}$ always outperforms $ALBEF_{Base}$ for the same epoch and becomes comparable to $ALBEF_{Base}$ even when trained with significantly smaller number of epochs. This result clearly motivates using enlarged masking probability for MLM for VLP.

3.1   Motivation

The result in Table 1 suggests that improving the hard negative sampling strategy for ITM could bring further performance gain for VLP. An obvious way for such improvement is to enlarge the search space from which the negative samples are selected, hence, the sample that contains the nuanced difference with respect to the positive sample as in Fig. 1(c) can be obtained. However, we note that such enlargement in a memory- and computation-efficient way is far from being straightforward, described as below.

Table 2. Ablation study on the masking probability for MLM for ALBEF$_{\text{Base}}$.

Epochs	Training tasks	TR		(COCO)	IR			NLVR	
		R@1	R@5	R@10	R@1	R@5	R@10	(val)	(test)
10	ALBEF$_{\text{Base}}$	72.3	91.3	96.0	55.1	81.0	88.5	79.21	79.78
	ALBEF$_{\text{Base}_{50}}$	**73.4**	**92.5**	**96.4**	**57.2**	**82.3**	**89.4**	**79.42**	**79.87**
20	ALBEF$_{\text{Base}}$	73.8	92.3	96.5	57.7	82.5	89.6	79.22	80.37
	ALBEF$_{\text{Base}_{50}}$	**75.6**	**93.2**	**96.7**	**58.8**	**83.2**	**90.1**	**80.41**	**80.54**

The most naive way to enlarge the search space is to enlarge the size of the mini-batch during training. While conceptually simple, it clearly is limited by the GPU memory and high computational cost. An alternative is to utilize the additional queues to store the compressed representations of the samples (*i.e.*, the [CLS] tokens $[v^{cls}, t^{cls}]$ from the uni-modal encoders), like MoCo [12] or MemoryBank [40], and include those representations in the search space for mining the hard negatives. While this queue-based solution is highly effective in the ordinary contrastive learning, it causes additional complication for VLP using the ITM loss. Namely, as described in Sect. 3, the ITM loss is calculated with the [CLS] token from the multi-modal encoder (w^{cls}), which needs the *entire* sequence embeddings ($f_v(V)$, $f_t(T)$) to compute. Therefore, to employ the queue-based solution for ITM$_{\text{hard}}$, one should select between the following two options. One is to store the entire embedding sequences for both modalities in the queues, which is severely memory-inefficient due to the long sequence lengths (typically, $S_T : 30$ and $S_V : 200$). The other is to only store $[v^{cls}, t^{cls}]$ tokens from each modality to compute (1) and (2) for ITC, but carry out the additional forward passes for the samples that are not in the current mini-batch to compute w^{cls} and the ITM loss. Clearly, the second option would suffer from the additional computation cost required for the forward passes.

To overcome the limitations of the above naive solutions, we propose a new method that can enlarge the search space and select more informative negative samples for ITM *without* any significant overheads on the memory/computation.

4 Main Method: GRIT-VLP

4.1 GRouped mIni-baTch Sampling (GRIT)

In this section, we describe our main contribution, the GRouped mIni-baTch sampling (GRIT) strategy. The basic idea is to compose each mini-batch of size N with highly similar example groups such that the informative, hard negative samples are likely to be chosen by the *in-batch* sampling of ALBEF. In order to do that without significant memory/computation overhead, as described in Fig. 2 and Algorithm 1 in S.M, GRIT utilizes two additional queues of size L that store the [CLS] tokens from the uni-modal encoders, an index queue I of size M, and a full index array G of size D (the whole data size). The ordering of the sizes is $N \ll M \ll L \ll D$. Then, the procedure of constructing *grouped* mini-batches for the next epoch is performed concurrently with the loss calculation for pre-training at each epoch, and these grouped mini-batches are used for the ordinary mini-batch training in the following epoch.

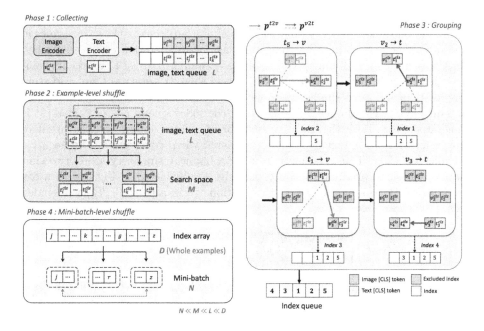

Fig. 3. Grouped mini-batch sampling (GRIT) strategy.

A subtle challenge of above simultaneous creation process for the grouped mini-batches is that it removes the randomness of the mini-batches, which is an essential ingredient for the *stochastic* gradient descent based learning. Therefore, we add two-level shuffling phases for preserving the randomness among the grouped mini-batches. As a result, our GRIT is composed of the following four phases: 1) collecting, 2) example-level shuffling 3) grouping, and 4) mini-batch-level shuffling. We note the first three phases are repeated whenever the queue of size L is filled, and the last phase is repeated once every epoch.

[**Phase 1: Collecting**] To construct mini-batches containing similar samples, we first store the [CLS] tokens $[v^{cls}, t^{cls}]$ (from uni-modal encoders) in the two additional queues of size L, which is much larger than the size of mini-batches (N), until filled as shown in Fig. 3.

[**Phase 2: Example-level shuffle**] Once the queues are filled, all the samples in the queues are randomly shuffled at the example-level, to secure the randomness mentioned above. After shuffling, each queue is divided into $\frac{L}{M}$ sub-queues of size M, which is the size of the enlarged search space for the hard negative samples for ITM. Then, the samples in each sub-queue are grouped based on similarity via the grouping phase below, which is sequentially performed for each sub-queue.

[**Phase 3: Grouping**] From the $[v^{cls}, t^{cls}]$ stored in the sub-queue, we can compute the image-to-text and text-to-image similarity scores, similarly as in (1), among the examples in the sub-queue. Accordingly, for each pair (V, T), those scores can be denoted by $q^{v2t}(V) \in \Delta^M$ and $q^{t2v}(T) \in \Delta^M$, respectively.

Based on the computed similarities, we aim group *similar* (V, T) examples in the sub-queue to each mini-batch as much as possible. To that end, as described in Algorithm 2 in S.M, our grouping phase is summarized as: 1) randomly sample the first pair (V_1, T_1) from the sub-queue, then 2) iteratively find and store the index of the most similar example one by one until all examples inside the sub-queue are visited once, and finally, 3) the index queue $I \in \{1, \ldots, M\}^M$ is generated. Note both the negative text for an anchor image and the negative image for an anchor text should be considered when constructing the negative samples for ITM. Thus, rather than using a one-way similarity score, two similarity scores are used alternatively; namely, as illustrated in Fig. 3 with a toy example of $M = 5$, at the $(i + 1)$-th iteration, given a pair (V_k, T_k) with index k, I_{i+1} is chosen as

$$I_{i+1} = \begin{cases} \text{argmax}_{j \notin I} q_j^{t2v}(T_k) & \text{if } I_i \text{ is chosen with } q^{v2t} \\ \text{argmax}_{j \notin I} q_j^{v2t}(V_k) & \text{if } I_i \text{ is chosen with } q^{t2v}. \end{cases} \quad (5)$$

Thus, during above *grouping* process for the sub-queue, half of the pairs are selected based on $(V \rightarrow T)$ direction, and the other half based on $(T \rightarrow V)$ direction. Whenever the index queue I is full, we convert the indices into the original data indices in $\{1, \ldots, D\}$ and append those to the full index array G.

[**Phase 4: Mini-batch-level shuffle**] After each epoch, the full index array G, which is a permutation of $\{1, \ldots, D\}$, is generated. Then, G is divided into multiple mini-batch-sized arrays, and these arrays are shuffled. Note this shuffling is done at the mini-batch level, not at the example level. Finally, these shuffled mini-batches are used for both training and GRIT for the next epoch.

Remark 1. We note the shuffling phases *Phase 2/4* in GRIT are important to secure the randomness among the mini-batches. Namely, since GRIT generates the indices during the previous epoch, it omits the conventional data re-shuffling performed at the start of each epoch. Hence, although the order of indices is continuously changed to some extent in *Phase 3*, such re-ordering happens only at the level of sub-queue of size M, hence the scope of shuffling is significantly limited. In Table 4 (Sect. 5), we verify that the performance of GRIT without shuffling is significantly degraded, justifying the proposed shuffling phases.

Remark 2. The naive implementation of GRIT would be to proceed *Phase 1/3* and training *separately*, not concurrently. To be specific, at the beginning of each epoch, the conventional re-shuffling of the whole data is done, followed by additional forward passes on the uni-modal encoders, and *Phase 1/3* are performed to generate grouped mini-batch indices. Then, the training begins with the generated indices. Since this naive version requires additional forward passes, it clearly has high computational cost and requires longer training time.

4.2   ITC Consistency Loss and Increased Masking Probability for MLM

GRIT encourages similar examples to be grouped within each mini-batch, hence, the ITM_{hard} can become more effective since the mini-batch may contain informative, hard negative samples. However, when GRIT is combined with ITC, one potential drawback is that the representations for similar samples would move away from each other unexpectedly, since all negatives will be equally penalized during the contrastive learning regardless of the similarity.

To address this issue, we add a consistency loss that can reflect the similarity among samples. Namely, when an image V and a text T form a positive pair (V, T), it is natural to assume that they share a similar semantic. Hence, we would expect the similarity scores $p^{v2t}(V)$ and $p^{t2v}(T)$ to be similar to each other. To this end, we define the soft pseudo-target $\tilde{p}^{t2v}(T)$ as $sg(p^{t2v}(T))$ and $\tilde{p}^{v2t}(V)$ as $sg(p^{v2t}(V))$ for $p^{v2t}(V)$ and $p^{t2v}(T)$, respectively, in which $sg(\cdot)$ is the stop-gradient operator. Then, our ITC with consistency loss is defined as

$$\mathcal{L}_{\text{ITC}_{\text{cons}}} = \mathcal{L}_{\text{ITC}} + \frac{\lambda_{\text{cons}}}{2} \mathbb{E}_{(V,T)\sim D}[KL(\tilde{p}^{v2t}(V) \,||\, p^{t2v}(T))) + KL(\tilde{p}^{t2v}(T) \,||\, p^{v2t}(V))],$$
(6)

in which λ_{cons} is the regularization parameter. We expect this loss refines similarity scores which affect the quality of the grouping phase of GRIT. We set λ_{cons} as 0.2 for all cases for simplicity.

Finally, our model, dubbed as GRIT-VLP and illustrated in Fig 2, is obtained as follows. We use $\text{ALBEF}_{\text{Base}}$ as our base model architecture, and combine our GRIT, ITC consistency loss, and masking probability of 50% for MLM. Consequently, the pre-training objective of GRIT-VLP is

$$\mathcal{L} = \mathcal{L}_{\text{ITM}_{\text{hard}}} + \mathcal{L}_{\text{MLM}_{50}} + \mathcal{L}_{\text{ITC}_{\text{cons}}},$$
(7)

in which the mini-batches are generated by the GRIT strategy. The pseudo-code for GRIT-VLP is given in Alg.1/2 in the S.M.

5   Experimental Results

5.1   Data and Experimental Settings

[**Training data**] Following ALBEF [20] and UNITER [4], we use four datasets (MS-COCO [23], Visual Genome [18], Conceptual Captions [30] and SBU Captions [25]) for training, which consist of 4M unique images and 5M image-text pairs.

[**Implementation details**] Here, we give the concrete model architecture of ALBEF$_{\text{Base}}$. We use a 12-layer vision transformer ViT-B/16 [8] with 86M parameters as the image encoder f_v and initialize it with the weights pre-trained on ImageNet-1k [34]. A 6-layer Transformer [35] is used for both the text encoder f_t and the multi-modal encoder h, which are initialized with the first 6 layers and the last 6 layers of BERT-base with 123.7M parameters [6], respectively. We use the same data augmentation technique of ALBEF, and our model is trained for 20 epochs. All experiments are performed on 4 NVIDIA A100 GPUs. Furthermore, unless otherwise noted, we set $N = 96$, $M = 960$, and $L = 48,000$. For all other hyper-parameter settings, we follow ALBEF [20]. More details on the dataset, software platform, training procedures, and hyper-parameters are in the S.M.

5.2   Downstream Vision and Language Tasks

After the pre-training step, our model is fine-tuned on three well-established downstream vision and language tasks, including image-text retrieval (IRTR), visual question answering (VQA2 [10]), and natural language for visual reasoning (NLVR2 [32]). For IRTR, we use MS-COCO [23] and Flickr30K (F30K) [26] resplited by [16]. We do not include SNLI-VE [41] in the evaluation, since the data set is known to be noisy according to [7]. We mostly follow the fine-tuning and evaluation process of ALBEF [20] except for using the momentum distillation. We compare our method with various VLP methods trained on the same 4M training set. More details on the downstream tasks including evaluation setting are given in S.M.

5.3   Comparison with the State-of-the-art VLP Methods

Since we mainly build our method upon ALBEF, the previous state-of-the-art, we mainly compare our method with it. Table 3 reports the results of GRIT-VLP with $N = 128$ and $M = 1920$ on IRTR, VQA, and NLVR2. In S.M, we present additional results on these hyper-parameters showing the robustness of our method with respect to N.

On all downstream tasks (IRTR, VQA, NLVR2), GRIT-VLP outperforms other methods trained on the same 4M dataset, including the previous best model ALBEF (4M) by a large margin (+4% TR/R@1 on MS-COCO, +1.1% on NLVR test-P). Moreover, GRIT-VLP is even competitive with ALBEF (14M) on some

Table 3. Comparison with various methods on downstream vision-language tasks. **Bold** denotes the best result among models trained with 4M dataset.

Method	#Pre-train Images	Flickr R@ 1		COCO R@1		VQA		NLVR2	
		TR	IR	TR	IR	test-dev	test-std	dev	test-P
UNITER [4]	4M	87.3	75.6	65.7	52.9	72.70	72.91	77.18	77.85
VILLA [9]	4M	87.9	76.3	–	–	73.59	73.67	78.39	79.30
OSCAR [22]	4M	–	–	70.0	54.0	73.16	73.44	78.07	78.36
ViLT [17]	4M	83.5	64.4	61.5	42.7	71.26	–	75.70	76.13
ALBEF [20]	4M	94.3	82.8	73.1	56.8	74.54	74.70	80.24	80.50
GRIT-VLP$_{E-10}$	4M	94.7	82.0	74.9	58.1	74.72	74.74	79.98	80.11
GRIT-VLP	4M	**96.0**	**83.8**	**77.1**	**59.5**	**75.11**	**75.26**	**80.73**	**81.60**
ALBEF	14M	95.9	85.6	77.6	60.7	75.84	76.04	82.55	83.14

metrics, while being trained on a much smaller dataset. Furthermore, "GRIT-VLP$_{E-10}$", denoting GRIT-VLP trained for only 10 epochs, achieves competitive performance compared to ALBEF (4M) trained with 30 epochs, highlighting the efficiency of our method. We believe the performance gains in Table 3 clearly highlights effectiveness of GRIT-VLP.

Table 4. Ablation study on the proposed method.

GRIT		λ_{cons}	Masking	TR		(COCO)	IR			NLVR	VQA	Time
Collecting	Shuffle		Prob(%)	R@1	R@5	R@10	R@1	R@5	R@10	(test)	(test-std)	per epoch
✗	✗	0	15	73.8	92.3	96.5	57.7	82.5	89.6	80.37	74.70	2h 27 m
✗	✗	0	50	75.6	93.2	96.7	58.8	83.2	**90.1**	80.54	75.07	2h 27 m
✓	✓	0	50	76.4	93.6	96.7	**59.6**	83.3	**90.1**	81.32	75.14	2h 30 m
✓(naive)	✗	0	50	76.8	93.6	96.8	**59.6**	**83.4**	90.0	80.63	75.16	3 h
✓	✗	0	50	74.7	93.2	96.6	58.6	82.8	89.7	80.50	75.06	2h 30 m
✓	✓	0.2	15	76.2	93.4	96.8	59.0	83.1	**90.1**	81.21	74.98	2h 30 m
✓	✓	0.2	50	**77.1**	**93.8**	**97.0**	59.5	**83.4**	90.0	**81.43**	**75.30**	2h 30 m

5.4 Ablation Studies on the Proposed Method

Table 4 shows the effectiveness of each proposed component: GRIT, ITC consistency loss, and enlarged masking probability ($15\% \rightarrow 50\%$) for MLM. First two rows indicate ALBEF$_{Base}$ and ALBEF$_{Base_{50}}$ analyzed in Sect. 3, respectively. By integrating the ALBEF$_{Base_{50}}$ with GRIT-variants (row 3, 4), we can verify that the performance is significantly improved. However, in the case of "naive" implementation version of GRIT described in Sect. 4 (row 4), the training time is significantly increased as expected. We believe that competitive results of row 3 and 4 clearly demonstrate the need of all components of GRIT. Moreover, if the both shufflings are removed from GRIT while collecting the mini-batches using the previous epoch (row 5), its performance is severely degraded due to the vanishing randomness. The last row denotes our final GRIT-VLP (ALBEF$_{Base_{50}}$

+ GRIT + consistency); by adding the consistency loss from row 3, we verify that the overall performance is increased. Furthermore, the gains of the last two rows compared to the first two rows show the combined effect of "GRIT + consistency" at two different mask sampling probabilities.

Table 5. Effect of GRIT on ITC

Training tasks	TR		(COCO)	IR		
	R@1	R@5	R@10	R@1	R@5	R@10
ITC	59.7	84.8	91.9	43.2	72.2	82.0
Queue-based ITC	60.3	85.2	92.2	43.5	72.3	82.3
ITC + GRIT	63.0	87.1	**93.2**	45.2	72.9	82.1
ITC$_{cons}$ + GRIT	**64.3**	**87.4**	**93.2**	**46.3**	**73.7**	**82.6**

Table 6. Results on top of TCL [45]

Method	TR		(COCO)	IR			NLVR2	VQA
	R@1	R@5	R@10	R@1	R@5	R@10	(test-P)	(test-std)
TCL	75.6	92.8	96.7	59.0	83.2	89.9	81.33	74.92
TCL+ours	**77.3**	**94.1**	**97.2**	**60.2**	**83.7**	**90.0**	**81.52**	**75.36**

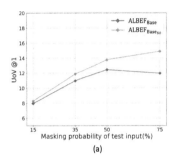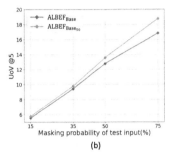

(a)   (b)

Fig. 4. UoV results on COCO validation dataset.

5.5   Experiments on the Model-Agnostic Property

To investigate the model-agnostic property of GRIT, we report the results when our method is integrated with different network architectures and objectives.

[**Small model, ITC**] Table 5 compares the IRTR results with several variants that are pre-trained and fine-tuned with only ITC loss and dual uni-modal encoders of ALBEF (without multi-modal encoder). "Queue-based ITC" denotes a model pre-trained with ITC and queues for leveraging the stored features from the momentum encoder (row 2), and the other two models denote models that adopt our approach. While the performance gain of the Queue-based ITC is marginal, our GRIT brings a significant gain when combined with ITC. Finally, ITC$_{cons}$+GRIT achieves the best result, demonstrating the standalone effectiveness of GRIT and consistency loss on ITC. We believe this result shows that our method has a potential to be easily integrated with existing contrastive learning based models.

[**Large model, more objectives**] In Table 6, we additionally measure the gains of the recently proposed TCL [45] when it is combined with "ours" (GRIT and enlarged masking probability). TCL introduces additional objectives and adopts almost the same but larger network architecture (additional momentum model) than ours. We omit the consistency loss since TCL already uses MD which has a similar role to it. Although the learning objectives and model sizes are different, we verify that the combination of our method and TCL again brings significant gains in Table 6, which clearly shows the model-agnostic property of our method. Details about this combined approach can be found in S.M.

5.6 Analysis on the Masking Probabilities

We believe the enlarged masking probability for MLM enables more usage of the visual features for predicting the masked token, resulting in a more effective multi-modal representation learning. To demonstrate this point, we introduce a *Usage of Vision* (UoV) metric like [2], which is defined as the difference between MLM accuracy of a pre-trained model with and without the image input (*Accuracy - Accuracy w/o image*). When evaluating the MLM *Accuracy* and *Accuracy w/o image* of the pre-trained model, test input sentences are masked with the same specific masking probability, and exactly the same tokens are masked for a fair comparison. Then, a high UoV value means that the pre-trained model is highly affected by visual information since it implies that the vision information is important for the model to correctly predict the masked token.

In Fig. 4, two pre-trained networks (ALBEF$_{Base}$, ALBEF$_{Base_{50}}$) are evaluated with test input sentences masked with various masking probability. We calculate the UoV@1 and UoV@5 by considering the top-1 and top-5 MLM accuracy, respectively. Figure 4 shows that ALBEF$_{Base_{50}}$ model always obtain higher UoV demonstrating the high usage of vision information. In particular, when the textual context almost disappears (75%), the difference in UoV becomes outright. As a result, we verify that enlarging the masking probability enriches the usage of visual information, which facilitates the alignment of image and text.

6   Concluding Remarks

We proposed GRIT-VLP, which effectively samples mini-batches for mining hard negatives while maintaining the computational overhead. We showed our method achieves state-of-the-art performance on various downstream tasks with much less computational overhead and can be easily integrated with existing VLP.

Acknowledgment. This work was supported in part by New Faculty Startup Fund from Seoul National University, NRF Mid Career Research Program [NRF-2021R1A2C2007884], IITP grants funded by the Korean government [No. 2021-0-01696], [No. 2021-0-01343, Artificial Intelligence Graduate School Program (Seoul National University)], [No. 2021-0-02068, Artificial Intelligence Innovation Hub (Artificial Intelligence Institute, Seoul National University)], [No.2022-0-00959] and SNU-NAVER Hyperscale AI Center.

References

1. Antol, S., et al.: VQA: visual question answering. In: ICCV (2015)
2. Bitton, Y., Stanovsky, G., Elhadad, M., Schwartz, R.: Data efficient masked language modeling for vision and language. arXiv preprint arXiv:2109.02040 (2021)
3. Chen, T.S., Hung, W.C., Tseng, H.Y., Chien, S.Y., Yang, M.H.: Incremental false negative detection for contrastive learning. arXiv preprint arXiv:2106.03719 (2021)
4. Chen, Y.-C., et al.: UNITER: UNiversal image-TExt representation learning. In: Vedaldi, A., Bischof, H., Brox, T., Frahm, J.-M. (eds.) ECCV 2020. LNCS, vol. 12375, pp. 104–120. Springer, Cham (2020). https://doi.org/10.1007/978-3-030-58577-8_7
5. Chuang, C.Y., Robinson, J., Lin, Y.C., Torralba, A., Jegelka, S.: Debiased contrastive learning. In: NeurIPS (2020)
6. Devlin, J., Chang, M.W., Lee, K., Toutanova, K.: BERT: Pre-training of deep bidirectional transformers for language understanding. arXiv preprint arXiv:1810.04805 (2018)
7. Do, V., Camburu, O.M., Akata, Z., Lukasiewicz, T.: e-SNLI-VE: Corrected visual-textual entailment with natural language explanations. arXiv preprint arXiv:2004.03744 (2020)
8. Dosovitskiy, A., et al.: An image is worth 16x16 words: Transformers for image recognition at scale. arXiv preprint arXiv:2010.11929 (2020)
9. Gan, Z., Chen, Y.C., Li, L., Zhu, C., Cheng, Y., Liu, J.: Large-scale adversarial training for vision-and-language representation learning. In: NeurIPS (2020)
10. Goyal, Y., Khot, T., Summers-Stay, D., Batra, D., Parikh, D.: Making the V in VQA matter: elevating the role of image understanding in visual question answering. In: CVPR (2017)
11. Harwood, B., Kumar BG, V., Carneiro, G., Reid, I., Drummond, T.: Smart mining for deep metric learning. In: ICCV (2017)
12. He, K., Fan, H., Wu, Y., Xie, S., Girshick, R.: Momentum contrast for unsupervised visual representation learning. In: CVPR (2020)
13. Huang, Z., Zeng, Z., Huang, Y., Liu, B., Fu, D., Fu, J.: Seeing out of the box: End-to-end pre-training for vision-language representation learning. In: CVPR (2021)
14. Huang, Z., Zeng, Z., Liu, B., Fu, D., Fu, J.: Pixel-BERT: Aligning image pixels with text by deep multi-modal transformers. arXiv preprint arXiv:2004.00849 (2020)
15. Jia, C., et al.: Scaling up visual and vision-language representation learning with noisy text supervision. arXiv preprint arXiv:2102.05918 (2021)
16. Karpathy, A., Fei-Fei, L.: Deep visual-semantic alignments for generating image descriptions. In: CVPR (2015)
17. Kim, W., Son, B., Kim, I.: VILT: Vision-and-language transformer without convolution or region supervision. arXiv preprint arXiv:2102.03334 (2021)
18. Krishna, R., et al.: Visual Genome: Connecting Language and vision using crowd-sourced dense image annotations. IJCV **123**, 32–73 (2017)
19. Li, G., Duan, N., Fang, Y., Gong, M., Jiang, D.: Unicoder-VL: A universal encoder for vision and language by cross-modal pre-training. In: AAAI (2020)
20. Li, J., Selvaraju, R., Gotmare, A., Joty, S., Xiong, C., Hoi, S.C.H.: Align before fuse: Vision and language representation learning with momentum distillation. In: NeurIPS (2021)
21. Li, L.H., Yatskar, M., Yin, D., Hsieh, C.J., Chang, K.W.: VisualBERT: A simple and performant baseline for vision and language. arXiv preprint arXiv:1908.03557 (2019)

22. Li, X., et al.: OSCAR: Object-semantics aligned pre-training for vision-language tasks. In: Vedaldi, A., Bischof, H., Brox, T., Frahm, J.-M. (eds.) ECCV 2020. LNCS, vol. 12375, pp. 121–137. Springer, Cham (2020). https://doi.org/10.1007/978-3-030-58577-8_8

23. Lin, T.-Y., et al.: Microsoft COCO: Common objects in context. In: Fleet, D., Pajdla, T., Schiele, B., Tuytelaars, T. (eds.) ECCV 2014. LNCS, vol. 8693, pp. 740–755. Springer, Cham (2014). https://doi.org/10.1007/978-3-319-10602-1_48

24. Lu, J., Batra, D., Parikh, D., Lee, S.: ViLBERT: Pretraining task-agnostic visiolinguistic representations for vision-and-language tasks. arXiv preprint arXiv:1908.02265 (2019)

25. Ordonez, V., Kulkarni, G., Berg, T.: Im2text: Describing images using 1 million captioned photographs. In: NeurIPS (2011)

26. Plummer, B.A., Wang, L., Cervantes, C.M., Caicedo, J.C., Hockenmaier, J., Lazebnik, S.: Flickr30k entities: Collecting region-to-phrase correspondences for richer image-to-sentence models. In: ICCV (2015)

27. Radford, A., et al.: Learning transferable visual models from natural language supervision. arXiv preprint arXiv:2103.00020 (2021)

28. Robinson, J., Chuang, C.Y., Sra, S., Jegelka, S.: Contrastive learning with hard negative samples. arXiv preprint arXiv:2010.04592 (2020)

29. Schroff, F., Kalenichenko, D., Philbin, J.: FaceNet: A unified embedding for face recognition and clustering. In: CVPR (2015)

30. Sharma, P., Ding, N., Goodman, S., Soricut, R.: Conceptual captions: A cleaned, hypernymed, image alt-text dataset for automatic image captioning. In: ACL (2018)

31. Su, W., et al.: VL-BERT: Pre-training of generic visual-linguistic representations. arXiv preprint arXiv:1908.08530 (2019)

32. Suhr, A., Zhou, S., Zhang, A., Zhang, I., Bai, H., Artzi, Y.: A corpus for reasoning about natural language grounded in photographs. arXiv preprint arXiv:1811.00491 (2018)

33. Tan, H., Bansal, M.: LXMERT: Learning cross-modality encoder representations from transformers. arXiv preprint arXiv:1908.07490 (2019)

34. Touvron, H., Cord, M., Douze, M., Massa, F., Sablayrolles, A., Jégou, H.: Training data-efficient image transformers & distillation through attention. In: ICML (2021)

35. Vaswani, A., et al.: Attention is all you need. In: NeurIPS (2017)

36. Wang, X., Zhang, H., Huang, W., Scott, M.R.: Cross-batch memory for embedding learning. In: CVPR (2020)

37. Wettig, A., Gao, T., Zhong, Z., Chen, D.: Should you mask 15% in masked language modeling? arXiv preprint arXiv:2202.08005 (2022)

38. Wu, C.Y., Manmatha, R., Smola, A.J., Krahenbuhl, P.: Sampling matters in deep embedding learning. In: ICCV (2017)

39. Wu, M., Mosse, M., Zhuang, C., Yamins, D., Goodman, N.: Conditional negative sampling for contrastive learning of visual representations. arXiv preprint arXiv:2010.02037 (2020)

40. Wu, Z., Xiong, Y., Yu, S.X., Lin, D.: Unsupervised feature learning via non-parametric instance discrimination. In: CVPR (2018)

41. Xie, N., Lai, F., Doran, D., Kadav, A.: Visual entailment: A novel task for fine-grained image understanding. arXiv preprint arXiv:1901.06706 (2019)

42. Xuan, H., Stylianou, A., Liu, X., Pless, R.: Hard negative examples are hard, but useful. In: Vedaldi, A., Bischof, H., Brox, T., Frahm, J.-M. (eds.) ECCV 2020. LNCS, vol. 12359, pp. 126–142. Springer, Cham (2020). https://doi.org/10.1007/978-3-030-58568-6_8

43. Xuan, H., Stylianou, A., Pless, R.: Improved embeddings with easy positive triplet mining. In: WACV (2020)
44. Xue, H., et al.: Probing inter-modality: Visual parsing with self-attention for vision-and-language pre-training. In: NeurIPS (2021)
45. Yang, J., et al.: Vision-language pre-training with triple contrastive learning. In: CVPR (2022)
46. Zolfaghari, M., Zhu, Y., Gehler, P., Brox, T.: CrossCLR: Cross-modal contrastive learning for multi-modal video representations. In: ICCV (2021)

Efficient Video Deblurring Guided by Motion Magnitude

Yusheng Wang[1]([✉]), Yunfan Lu[2], Ye Gao[4], Lin Wang[2,3], Zhihang Zhong[1], Yinqiang Zheng[1], and Atsushi Yamashita[1]

[1] The University of Tokyo, Bunkyo, Japan
{wang,yamashita}@robot.t.u-tokyo.ac.jp, zhong@is.s.u-tokyo.ac.jp,
yamashita@robot.t.u-tokyo.ac.jp
[2] AI Thrust, Information Hub, HKUST Guangzhou, Guangzhou, China
{yunfanlu,linwang}@ust.hk
[3] Department of Computer Science and Engineering, HKUST, Hong Kong, China
[4] Tokyo Research Center, Meguro, Japan
gaoye1984@yahoo.co.jp

Abstract. Video deblurring is a highly under-constrained problem due to the spatially and temporally varying blur. An intuitive approach for video deblurring includes two steps: a) detecting the blurry region in the current frame; b) utilizing the information from clear regions in adjacent frames for current frame deblurring. To realize this process, our idea is to detect the pixel-wise blur level of each frame and combine it with video deblurring. To this end, we propose a novel framework that utilizes the motion magnitude prior (MMP) as guidance for efficient deep video deblurring. Specifically, as the pixel movement along its trajectory during the exposure time is positively correlated to the level of motion blur, we first use the average magnitude of optical flow from the high-frequency sharp frames to generate the synthetic blurry frames and their corresponding pixel-wise motion magnitude maps. We then build a dataset including the blurry frame and MMP pairs. The MMP is then learned by a compact CNN by regression. The MMP consists of both spatial and temporal blur level information, which can be further integrated into an efficient recurrent neural network (RNN) for video deblurring. We conduct intensive experiments to validate the effectiveness of the proposed methods on the public datasets. Our codes are available at https://github.com/sollynoay/MMP-RNN.

Keywords: Blur estimation · Motion magnitude · Video deblurring

Supplementary Information The online version contains supplementary material available at https://doi.org/10.1007/978-3-031-19800-7_24.

S. Avidan et al. (Eds.): ECCV 2022, LNCS 13679, pp. 413–429, 2022.
https://doi.org/10.1007/978-3-031-19800-7_24

1 Introduction

Video deblurring is a classical yet challenging problem that aims to restore consecutive frames from the spatially and temporally varying blur. The problem is highly ill-posed because of the presence of camera shakes, object motions, and depth variations during the exposure interval. Recent methods using deep convolutional networks (CNNs) have shown a significant improvement in video deblurring performance. Among them, alignment-based methods usually align the adjacent frames explicitly to the current frame and reconstruct a sharp frame simultaneously or by multiple stages [15,19,28,35,44]. Such methods show stable performance for video deblurring; however, the alignment or warping processes require accurate flow estimation, which is difficult for blurry frames, and usually the computational cost is relatively high. Recurrent neural network (RNN)-based methods achieve deblurring by passing information between adjacent frames [13,18,43]; such methods usually have lower computation costs but with lower restoration quality compared with the alignment-based methods.

So far, many deblurring methods have utilized priors to improve the restoration quality. The priors usually come from optical flows or image segmentation. Inter-frame optical flow-based methods [15,19] directly borrow pixel information from the adjacent frames to improve the quality of the current frame. By contrast, intra-frame optical flow estimates the pixel movement during the exposure time of a blurry frame. Intra-frame optical flow-based methods [1,8] estimate the flow during the exposure time, and usually restore the sharp frame by energy minimization optimization. Image segmentation-based methods [2,4,22,25,37] utilize motion, semantic or background and foreground information to estimate the prior for deblurring.

However, previous priors for video deblurring suffer from one or more of the following problems. First, image segmentation and inter-frame optical flow estimation on blurry images are error-prone. And it is necessary to estimate the prior and implement video deblurring simultaneously via complex energy functions [12,21,22]. Second, inter-frame optical flow estimation requires heavy computational cost. For instance, the state-of-the-art (SoTA) methods, PWC-Net requires 181.68 GAMCs [30] and RAFT small model (20 iterations) requires 727.99 GMACs [34] on the 720P (1280×720) frames. However, a typical efficient video deblurring method is supposed to have 50~300 GMACs. Third, motion blur is directly correlated to the intra-frame optical flow. Although it is possible to directly estimate the intra-frame optical flow from a single image [1,8], the restored results suffer from artifacts.

An intuitive way for video deblurring is to detect the blurry region in the image first and then utilize information of clear pixels from adjacent frames. The detection of blurry region task can be considered as a blur estimation problem, which separates the image into binarized sharp and blurry regions, or directly tells the blur level of each pixel. Previous blur estimation methods, *e.g.*, [5,26], usually binarize the image into sharp and blurry regions and manually label the regions as it is difficult to determine the blur level of each pixel automatically.

However, the labelling process may be inaccurate and usually requires much human effort.

In this work, we propose a motion magnitude prior (MMP) to represent the blur level of a pixel which can determine the pixel-wise blur level without manually labelling. Recent works use high frequency sharp frames to generate a synthetic blurry frame [17]. Inspired by this, the pixel movement during the exposure time of a blurry frame, i.e., the MMP, can be estimated from the average magnitude of bi-directional optical flow from the high-frequency sharp frames. The value of MMP positively correlated to the level of motion blur. We propose a compact CNN to learn the MMP.

The proposed MMP can directly indicate the *spatial distribution* of blur level in one image. Besides, if the overall value of MMP is low, the image is sharp, and vice versa. *Temporal information* is also included in the prior. The CNN can be further merged into a *spatio-temporal network* (RNN) for video deblurring. For convenience, we use an efficient RNN with residual dense blocks (RDBs) [41,42] as our backbone video deblurring network (Sec. 3.2). For the utilization of MMP, we design three components: a) for the intra-frame utilization, we propose a motion magnitude attentive module (MMAM) to inject the MMP into the network; b) for the inter-frame utilization, different from other RNN-based methods [13,18,43] which only pass the deblurred features to the next frame, we also pass the features before deblurring to the next frame. The blurry frame with pixels of different blur level is weighted by the MMAM, as such, pixels under low blur level can be directly utilized by the next frame; c) for loss-level utilization, since the motion magnitude of network output can reflect the deblur performance. That is, the sharper the image is, the lower the average score is. Therefore, we can also use the prior as a loss term to further improve the optimization. Figure 1 is an example of the learned MMP from the network and the estimation result. High quality results can be generated from the proposed framework.

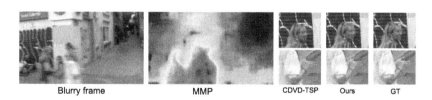

Blurry frame   MMP   CDVD-TSP   Ours   GT

Fig. 1. The blurry frame and the estimated MMP with results compared to the SoTA method [19].

In summary, our contributions are three folds. (I) We propose a novel motion magnitude prior for blurry image and its lightweight generation method. To the best of our knowledge, this is the first work to apply motion magnitude prior for the video deblurring task. (II) We propose a motion magnitude prior guided network, which utilizes the prior at intra-frame level, inter-frame level and loss level. (III) Our proposed method achieves competitive results with SoTA methods while with relatively lower computational cost.

2   Related Works

2.1   Prior for Deblurring

As mentioned above, image segmentation, inter-frame optical flow and intra-frame optical flow have been frequently used as priors in the deblurring tasks.

Image Segmentation. In early studies, segmentation priors have been proposed for dynamic scene deblur. Cho *et al.* [4] segmented the images into multiple regions of homogeneous motions while Bar *et al.* [2] segmented the images into foreground and background layers. Based on [2], Wulff *et al.* [37] focused on estimating the parameters for both foreground and background motions. Using segmentation priors can handle the dynamic scenes; however, with simple models, it is difficult to segment the non-parametrically varying complex motions. Ren *et al.* [22] exploited semantic segmentation which significantly improves the optical flow estimation for the deblurring tasks. Shen *et al.* [25] proposed a human-aware deblurring method by combining human segmentation and learning-based deblurring. Although these methods on the basis of physical models show promising results, the deblurring performance is highly related to the blur kernel estimation results. That is, inaccurate estimation of blur kernels results in severe artifacts.

Inter-frame Optical Flow. The inter-frame optical flows are usually directly estimated on blurry frames, and are used to warp the adjacent frames to the center frame before inputting to the network [15,19,28]. The flow from blurry frame is inaccurate. To solve the problem, Pan *et al.* [19] proposed a method to estimate optical flow from the intermediate latent frames using a deep CNN and restore the latent frames based on the optical flow estimations. A temporal sharpness prior is applied to constrain the CNN model to help the latent frame restoration. However, calculating inter-frame optical flow requires heavy computation and the temporal sharpness prior cannot deal with all frames with no sharp pixels.

Intra-frame Optical Flow. With deep learning, it is even possible to directly estimate intra-frame optical flows from a blurry frame [1,8,31], followed by energy function optimizations to estimate the blur kernels. However, the optimizations are usually difficult to solve and require a huge computational cost. The restored images also suffer from artifacts. Moreover, the definition of intra-frame is ambiguous as, during the exposure time, the movement of one pixel may be non-linear, which cannot be represented by a 2D vector.

Others. Statistical priors and extreme channel priors have shown their feasibility in single image deblurring [20,24,38,39]. Such methods are valid under certain circumstances, but are sensitive to noise and still require accurate estimation of the blur kernels. Differently, we propose a motion magnitude prior learned by a compact network. The prior shows pixel-wise blur level of the blurry image and can be easily applied to the video deblurring framework. It can detect which part of the image is blurry and to what extent it is blurred.

2.2 Blur Estimation

Blur estimation has been studied for the non-uniform blur. It is similar to image segmentation prior by specifically segmenting the image into blur and non-blur regions. In [5], horizontal motion or defocus blurs were estimated and the image is deconvolved for deblurring. Shi *et al.* [26] studied the effective local blur features to differentiate between blur and sharp regions which can be applied to the blur region segmentation, deblurring and blur magnification. The images are usually separated into blur and non-sharp regions; however, it is difficult to separate an image under a binarized way for dynamic scenes. Instead of classifying the pixels into blurry and sharp regions, we use a continuous way to represent the blur maps by estimating the motion magnitude of each pixel.

2.3 DNN-Based Deblurring

For single image deblurring, SoTA methods apply self-recurrent module on the multi-scale, multi-patch, or multi-stage to solve the problem [7,17,29,33,40]. Despite the high performance, they usually require a large computational cost. For video deblurring, the problem is less ill-posed and can be solved with less computational cost. The learning-based video deblurring methods can be grouped into alignment-based methods [15,19,28,35,44] and RNN-based methods [13,18,43]. The former usually explicitly aligns the adjacent frames to the center frame for deblurring. This can be achieved by directly warping the adjacent frames to the center frame [28], warping the intermediate latent frames, or both [15,19]. Wang *et al.* [35] implemented the deformable CNN [6] to realize the alignment process. Zhou *et al.* [44] proposed a spatio-temporal filter adaptive network (STFAN) for alignment and deblurring in a single network. Son et al. blur-invariant motion estimation learning to avoid the inaccuracy caused by optical flow estimation on blurry frames [27]. Although the alignment-based methods can achieve relatively high performance, the alignment process is usually computationally inefficient. In addition, the alignment has to be accurate, otherwise it may degrade the performance of deblurring. To ensure high quality results, multi-stage strategies were applied by iteratively implementing the alignment-deblurring process, which may lead to huge computational cost [15,19].

On the other hand, RNN-based methods transfer information between the RNN cells and usually have lower computational cost. Kim *et al.* [13] propose an RNN for video deblurring by dynamically blending features from previous frames. Nah *et al.* [17] iteratively updated the hidden state with one RNN cell before the final output. Zhong *et al.* [43] proposed an RNN network using RDB backbone with globally fusion of high-level features from adjacent frames and applied attention mechanism to efficiently utilize inter-frame information. In this paper, we propose an RNN with RDBs by utilizing the MMP. We use a compact CNN to estimate the MMP to reduce the computational cost. The MMP consists of spatial and temporal information, which can improve the effectiveness of information delivery between RNN cells. Our proposed method outperforms the SoTA performance.

3   The Proposed Approach

3.1   Motion Magnitude Prior

Motion Magnitude Prior from Optical Flow. In this section, we introduce preparing the ground truth of motion magnitude prior (MMP). For the learning-based deblurring methods, the datasets for training and validation are usually synthesized by high-frequency sharp frames [17,28,35]. It is based on the fact that images tend to be blurry after accumulating multiple sharp images with slight misalignment caused by motion [9]. The blur level of each pixel in the blurry frame is positively correlated to the motion magnitude of the pixel during exposure time. Although directly measuring the motion magnitude of one pixel is difficult, it is possible to be calculated by latent sharp frames during exposure time. Inspired by this, we generate blurry frame and blur level map pairs based on high-frequency sharp image sequence, as shown in Fig. 2. Denoting the blurry image as B and sampled sharp image as $\{S_1, S_2, \ldots, S_N\}$, the blurry image simulation process can be represented as follows.

$$B = c \left(\frac{1}{N} \sum_{i=1}^{N} S_i \right),$$

(1)

where $c(.)$ refers to the camera response function (CRF) [32]. During exposure time, we sample N sharp images to generate a blurry image. To measure the movement of pixels, we calculate the optical flow between the sharp frames. We use bi-directional flows to represent the pixel movement of one sharp frame. For instance, as shown in Fig. 2, for frame 1, we calculate the optical flow FL_{21} and FL_{23} to represent the pixel movement condition. For each pixel (m, n), the optical flow between frame i and j in x and y direction can be represented as $u_{i,j}(m, n)$ and $v_{i,j}(m, n)$, respectively. We denote the motion magnitude M for frame i as follows.

$$M_i(m, n) = \frac{\sqrt{u_{i,i-1}^2(m, n) + v_{i,i-1}^2(m, n)} + \sqrt{u_{i,i+1}^2(m, n) + v_{i,i+1}^2(m, n)}}{2}.$$

(2)

For frame 1 and frame N, we only use FL_{12} and $FL_{N,N-1}$ for calculation, respectively. Then, to acquire the pixel-wise motion magnitude for the synthetic blurry frame, we calculate the average movement during exposure time.

$$\bar{M} = \frac{1}{KN} \sum_{i=1}^{N} M_i, \tag{3}$$

where $\bar{M}$ refers to the motion magnitude or blur level map for the blurry frame. K is used to normalize the value at each position in MMP to 0~1. K is determined by the maximum value of the MMP before normalization in the training dataset which was set to 15.

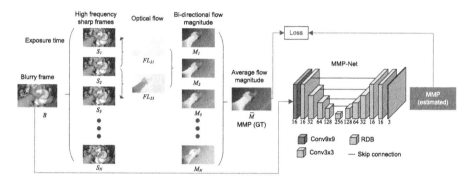

Fig. 2. Motion magnitude prior. High frequency sharp frames are used to generate synthetic blurry frames. Meanwhile, we estimate the bi-directional optical flows for each frame and calculate the average magnitude of bi-directional optical flows. Then, we take the average of the motion magnitude maps of all the latent frames. Finally, we use a modified UNet-like structure to learn the motion magnitude prior by regression.

The Learning of Motion Magnitude Prior. In this paper, we use the GOPRO raw dataset [17] to generate blurry image and MMP pairs. The GOPRO benchmark dataset used $7 \sim 13$ successive sharp frames in raw dataset to generate one blurry frame. We also use 7~13 to generate the blurry image and MMP pairs. We use the SoTA optical flow method RAFT [34] to estimate the optical flow. We propose a compact network to learn the blur level map by regression. We apply a modified UNet [23], as shown in Fig. 2. At the beginning, we use a 9 × 9 convolution layer to enlarge the reception field. The features are downsampled and reconstructed with a UNet-like structure. Then, a residual dense block (RDB) is used to refine the result. To process a 720P (1280 × 720) frame, the computational cost is only 38.81 GMACs with a model size of 0.85M parameters. At last, we can estimate the MMP for each frame using the compact network. In this paper, we apply the MMP as guidance to the video deblurring network. We will describe it in the following section.

3.2 Motion Magnitude Prior-Guided Deblurring Network

In this section, we describe using MMP as guidance to video deblurring network.

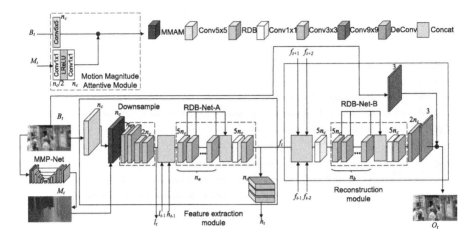

Fig. 3. The structure of MMP-RNN. Both center frame I_t and corresponding blur prior B_t estimated by MMP-Net are passed into RNN cell. We transmit both non-deblurred feature l and deblurred feature h from the previous frame to the next frame. Deblurred features f from the current frame and the adjacent frames are fused globally in decoder to generate final output image.

Network Structure. The structure of MMP-RNN is shown in Fig. 3. n_c refers to the channel dimension. The center frame B_t is first inputted into MMP-Net to estimate the MMP M_t. Then, B_t and M_t are passed to RNN cell to extract features. Non-deblurred features l_{t-1} and deblurred features h_{t-1} from the previous frame are delivered to feature extraction module (FEM). In this paper, we also use the deblurred features from adjacent frames globally to reconstruct output images. Features f_{t-2}, f_{t-1} from the past frames and f_{t+1}, f_{t+2} from the future frames with the current frame features f_t are inputted to reconstruction module (RM) for image reconstruction. We denote the output result as O_t. RDBs have high performances in low-level tasks which efficiently preserve features and save the computational cost [41–43]. In this work, we use RDBs as the backbone for downsampling, feature extraction and implicit alignment.

The FEM receives center frame B_t and corresponding MMP M_t with features l_{t-1} and h_{t-1} from the past frames to extract features of current frame. The structure of FEM is shown in Fig. 3. The Motion Magnitude Attentive Module (MMAM) is used to fuse the information of B_t and M_t. Here, we pass the non-deblurred features l_t to the next FEM and receive l_{t-1} from the previous FEM. The non-deblurred features and deblurred features are then concatenated and passed through RDB-Net-A with n_a RDBs. At last, deblurred features h_t are passed to the next FEM and f_t are used for image reconstruction.

RM is designed to globally aggregate high-level features for image reconstruction. We concatenate the features $\{f_{t-2}, \ldots, f_{t+2}\}$ and squeeze them in channel direction using 1×1 convolution operation. We use n_b RDBs in RDB-Net-B to implicitly align the features from different frames and then apply convolution transpose operation to reconstruct the image. A global skip connection is added to directly pass I_t to the output after 9×9 convolution operation. This can better preserve the information of the center frame.

Motion Magnitude Attentive Module. Both the blurry and sharp pixels are important to our task. The blurry pixels are the region to be concentrated for deblurring and the sharp pixels can be utilized for deblurring of adjacent frames. Especially for sharp pixels, the value of MMP is close to 0, directly multiplying MMP to image features may lose information of sharp features. To better utilize MMP, we use MMAM to integrate it with image features. The structure of MMAM layer is shown in Fig. 3. The MMP is passed through two 1 $\times$ 1 convolution layers to optimize MMP and adjust the dimension. The MMP is transformed to tensor γ. The operation to integrate γ and the feature from B, x can be represented as $x^{out} = \gamma \otimes x^{in}$, where $\otimes$ refers to element-wise multiplication. The whole operation can better integrate the MMP information with the blurry image.

Feature Transmission. We transmit two kinds of features l and h between FEM of the adjacent frames. The non-deblurred feature l_t consists of the information only from the center frame before integration. By contrast, h_t possesses features from the previous frame. The features are integrated in the network as follows.

$$a_t = CAT(l_t, l_{t-1}, h_{t-1}), \tag{4}$$

where CAT refers to concatenation operation. The RNN-based methods implicitly fusing information from previous frames which may sometimes cause lower performance compared to alignment-based methods. Passing non-deblurred features only consisting of the current frame with its blur level information can improve the overall performance of the network.

Motion Magnitude Loss. The proposed MMP-Net can estimate pixel-wise motion magnitude of the image. If O_t is an ideal sharp image, inputting O_t into MMP-Net should get a prior with all zeros. In this work, we propose a loss function based on the idea as follows.

$$\mathcal{L}_{MM} = \frac{1}{mn} \sum_{i=0}^{m-1} \sum_{j=0}^{n-1} M_{i,j}(O_t), \tag{5}$$

where $M(O_t)$ refers to the MMP of the output image O_t. Theoretically, by minimizing the average motion magnitude of O_t, it can generate ideal sharp image.

We also consider two kinds of content loss functions for training. We use a modified Charbonnier loss ($\mathcal{L}_{char}$) [3] and gradient loss ($\mathcal{L}_{grad}$) as content loss.

$$\mathcal{L}_{char} = \frac{1}{mn} \sum_{i=0}^{m-1} \sum_{j=0}^{n-1} \sqrt{\sum_{ch}^{r,g,b} (I_{i,j,ch} - O_{i,j,ch}) + \epsilon^2}, \tag{6}$$

422   Y. Wang et al.

where ϵ is a small value which is set to 0.001. m and n are the width and height of the image. I refers to the ground truth and O is the estimated image.

$$\mathcal{L}_{grad} = \frac{1}{mn} \sum_{i=0}^{m-1} \sum_{j=0}^{n-1} (G_{i,j} - \hat{G}_{i,j})^2, \tag{7}$$

where G and $\hat{G}$ refers to the image gradient of I and O, respectively. Then, the total loss is written as follows.

$$\mathcal{L} = \mathcal{L}_{char} + \lambda_1 \mathcal{L}_{grad} + \lambda_2 \mathcal{L}_{MM}, \tag{8}$$

where the weight λ_1 and λ_2 are set to 0.5 and 1.0 in our experiments.

4 Experiment

4.1 MMP-Net

Dataset Generation. To learn the deep image prior, we utilize GOPRO dataset [17]. The raw GOPRO dataset consists of 33 high-frequency video sequences with 34,874 images in total. In GOPRO benchmark dataset, the sharp images are used to generate synthetic dataset with 22 sequences for training and 11 sequences for evaluation with 2,103 training samples and 1,111 evaluation samples. We use the same data separation as GOPRO benchmark dataset to build the MMP dataset to avoid information leakage during video deblurring. We use 7~11 consecutive sharp frames to generate one blurry frame and corresponding MMP. We generate 22,499 training samples (22 sequences) and use the original GOPRO test dataset. We trim the training dataset by 50% during training.

Implementation Details. We train the model for 400 epochs with a mini-batch of size 8 using ADAM optimizer [14] with initial learning rate 0.0003. The learning rate decades by half after 200 epochs. The patch size is set to 512×512 for training and validation. The loss $\mathcal{L}_1 = \frac{1}{mn} \sum_{i=0}^{m-1} \sum_{j=0}^{n-1} |M_{i,j} - \hat{M}_{i,j}|$ is used for MMP training and as a metric for test. Here, $M_{i,j}$ refers to the value of estimated MMP at position i, j and $\hat{M}$ refers to the GT.

Table 1. The training result of MMP-Net.

	Train	Test (512 patch)	Test (Full image)
$\mathcal{L}_1$	0.0137	0.0169	0.0192

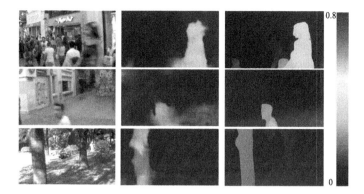

Fig. 4. Examples of motion magnitude estimation on GOPRO test dataset. Each column refers to the input blurry frames, the estimated results, and GT, respectively.

Fig. 5. Examples of test results on HIDE dataset [25]. The model was trained on GOPRO dataset and tested on HIDE dataset. Each column refer to the input blurry images, estimated results, and the estimated results overlaid to the input images. It indicates that the proposed method can successfully detect salient blurry region on other datasets.

Results. The training results are listed in Table 1. We visualize our results on GOPRO test dataset in Fig. 4. To prove the generality of the proposed method, we also test the GOPRO trained model to HIDE dataset [25]. HIDE dataset contains blurry images of human. As shown in Fig. 5, our proposed method can also detect the blur caused by human motion on other dataset.

4.2   Video Deblurring

Datasets. We test the proposed video deblurring method on two public datasets, GORPRO benchmark dataset [17] and beam-splitter datasets (BSD) [43]. BSD is a dataset of images from real world by controlling the length of exposure time and strength of exposure intensity during video shooting using beam-splitter system [11]. It can better evaluate deblurring performance in real scenarios. We use the 2ms-16mes BSD that the exposure time for sharp and blurry frames are 2 ms and 16 ms, respectively. The training and validation sets have 60 and 20 video sequences with 100 frames respectively, and the test set has 20 video sequences with 150 frames. The size of the frames is 640×480.

Implementation Details. We train the model using ADAM optimizer with a learning rate of 0.0005. We adopt cosine annealing schedule [16] to adjust learning rate during training. We sample 10-frame 256×256 RGB patch sequences from the dataset to construct a mini-batch of size 8 with random vertical and horizontal flips as well as $90°$ rotation for data augmentation for training. We train 1,000 epochs for GOPRO and 500 epochs for BSD, respectively. It is worth mentioning that we try to train the other methods using publicly available codes by ourselves and keep the same hyper-parameters if possible. For CDVD-TSP, we use the available test images for GOPRO and keep the training strategy used in [19] for BSD.

Table 2. Quantitative results on GOPRO.

Model	PSNR	SSIM	GMACs	Param	Time (s)
SRN [33]	29.94	0.8953	1527.01	10.25	0.173
DBN [28]	28.55	0.8595	784.75	15.31	0.128
IFIRNN ($c2h3$) [18]	29.69	0.8867	217.89	1.64	0.034
ESTRNN ($C_{70}B_7$) [43]	29.93	0.8903	115.19	1.17	0.021
ESTRNN ($C_{90}B_{10}$) [42]	31.02	0.9109	215.26	2.38	0.035
CDVD-TSP [19]	31.67	0.9279	5122.25	16.19	0.729
MMP-RNN ($A_3B_4C_{16}F_5$)	30.48	0.9021	136.42	1.97	0.032
MMP-RNN ($A_7B_8C_{16}F_8$)	31.71	0.9225	204.19	3.05	0.045
MMP-RNN ($A_9B_{10}C_{18}F_8$)	**32.64**	**0.9359**	264.52	4.05	0.059

Benchmark Results. The results of our method with SoTA lightweight image [33] and video deblurring methods on GOPRO is shown in Table 2. We use $A_\#B_\#C_\#F_\#$ to represent n_a, n_b, n_c and the length of the input image sequence in our model. We evaluate the image quality in terms of PSNR [10] and SSIM. We also measure the computational cost for each model when processing one 720P frame in terms of GMACs. Running time (s) of one 720P frame is also listed. For IFIRNN, $c2$ refers to the dual cell model and $h3$ refers to 'three times' of hidden state iteration. Our $A_7B_8C_{16}F_8$ model outperforms the other methods with only 204.19 GMACs. The visual comparison of the results are shown in Fig. 6.

The results on BSD of the proposed method with other SoTA methods are shown in Table 3. Here, we use the $A_8B_9C_{18}F_8$ model. The visualization results of the video deblurring on BSD are shown in Fig. 7. Our method outperforms SoTA methods with less computational cost.

Fig. 6. Visualization results of GoPRO. (a) Blurry frame. (b) the estimated MMP. (c) Overlaying (b) on (a). (d) Result from MMP-RNN. From (e) to (l) are, blurry input, DBN, IFIRNN, ESTRNN, proposed method w/o MMP, MMP-RNN, and the sharp frame, respectively.

4.3 Ablation Study

Network Structure. We conduct ablation tests on the proposed method with $A_9B_{10}C_{18}$ model on GOPRO and $A_8B_9C_{18}$ model on BSD. We focus on three parts, the MMAM, motion magnitude loss and the transmission of non-deblurred features as shown in Table 4. On GOPRO, the MMAM with MMP can improve PSNR by 0.31 dB. Together with motion magnitude loss, the prior can improve the score by 0.39 dB. If we remove all the components, the PSNR may drop by 0.58, which can indicate the effectiveness of the proposed method. As for BSD, the PSNR significantly increased by 0.63 dB after fusing prior using MMAM. The motion magnitude loss can improve PSNR by 0.09 dB.

Influence of Prior. We also did ablation tests with different types of priors using $A_3B_4C_{80}F_5$ model on GOPRO. As shown in Table 5, we tried the ground

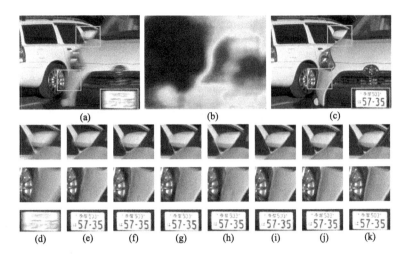

Fig. 7. Visualization results of BSD. a) Blurry frame. (b) the estimated MMP. (c) Result from MMP-RNN. From (d) to (k) are, blurry input, DBN, IFIRNN, ESTRNN, proposed method w/o MMP, MMP-RNN, and the sharp frame, respectively.

Table 3. Quantitative results on BSD 2ms-16ms.

Model	PSNR	SSIM	GMACs
DBN [28]	31.33	0.9132	784.75
IFIRNN ($c2h3$) [18]	31.59	0.9209	217.89
ESTRNN ($C_{90}B_{10}$) [43]	31.80	0.9245	215.26
CDVD-TSP [19]	32.06	0.9268	5122.25
MMP-RNN ($A_8B_9C_{18}F_8$)	32.79	0.9365	247.41
MMP-RNN ($A_9B_{10}C_{18}F_8$)	**32.81**	**0.9369**	264.52

Table 4. Ablation tests. NDF refers the transmission of non-deblurred features.

Model			GOPRO		BSD	
MMAM	$\mathcal{L}_{MM}$	NDF	PSNR	GMACs	PSNR	GMACs
✓	✓	✓	**32.64**	264.52	**32.79**	247.41
✗	✓	✓	32.33	225.34	32.16	208.23
✗	✗	✓	32.25	225.34	32.07	208.23
✗	✗	✗	32.06	227.21	32.03	210.09

Table 5. Influence of different types of prior. I. Ground truth, II.Ground truth of flow magnitude of center frame, III. Normalizing each ground truth map to 0~1, IV. Replacing the MMP and MMAM by spatial-self-attention [36]. V. None, VI. Estimated from MMP-Net.

Prior type	I	II	III	IV	V	VI
PSNR	**30.54**	30.47	30.41	30.37	30.17	30.48

truth MMP, the ground truth of flow magnitude of the center frame (from FL_{c1} and FL_{cN}, where c refers to the center frame), the normalized ground truth map ($M/\max(M)$), without MMP and the MMP from MMP-Net. We noticed that the ground truth as an upper boundary can increase the score by 0.37 dB. The MMP from MMP-Net can increase the PSNR by 0.31 dB. On the other hand, using the flow magnitude of the center frame will decrease the PSNR by 0.07 dB. The contour of the center frame magnitude only corresponds to the center frame, the attentive field cannot cover the whole blurry object. Normalizing the MMP by the maximum value of each MMP may lose temporal information, especially for some sharp images, the whole MMP value may be close to 1, which may influence the performance. We also compare the proposed method to spatial-self-attention [36]. Our proposed method use a supervised approach to tell the network where to concentrate and the results outperform vanilla spatial-self-attention.

5 Conclusion

In this paper, we proposed a motion magnitude prior for deblurring tasks. We built a dataset of blurry image and motion magnitude prior pairs and used a compact network to learn by regression. We applied the prior to video deblurring task, combining the prior with an efficient RNN. The prior is fused by motion magnitude attentive module and motion magnitude loss. We also transmitted the features before deblurring with features after deblurring between RNN cells to improve efficiency. We tested the proposed method on GOPRO and BSD, which achieved better performance on video deblurring tasks compared to SoTA methods on image quality and computational cost.

Acknowledgements. This paper is supported by JSPS KAKENHI Grant Numbers 22H00529 and 20H05951.

References

1. Argaw, D.M., Kim, J., Rameau, F., Cho, J.W., Kweon, I.S.: Optical flow estimation from a single motion-blurred image. In: AAAI, pp. 891–900 (2021)
2. Bar, L., Berkels, B., Rumpf, M., Sapiro, G.: A variational framework for simultaneous motion estimation and restoration of motion-blurred video. In: ICCV, pp. 1–8 (2007)
3. Charbonnier, P., Blanc-Feraud, L., Aubert, G., Barlaud, M.: Two deterministic half-quadratic regularization algorithms for computed imaging. In: ICIP, pp. 168–172 (1994)
4. Cho, S., Matsushita, Y., Lee, S.: Removing non-uniform motion blur from images. In: ICCV, pp. 1–8 (2007)
5. Couzinié-Devy, F., Sun, J., Alahari, K., Ponce, J.: Learning to estimate and remove non-uniform image blur. In: CVPR, pp. 1075–1082 (2013)
6. Dai, J., et al.: Deformable convolutional networks. In: ICCV, pp. 764–773 (2017)

7. Gao, H., Tao, X., Shen, X., Jia, J.: Dynamic scene deblurring with parameter selective sharing and nested skip connections. In: CVPR, pp. 3848–3856 (2019)

8. Gong, D., et al.: From motion blur to motion flow: a deep learning solution for removing heterogeneous motion blur. In: CVPR, pp. 3806–3815 (2017)

9. Hirsch, M., Schuler, C.J., Harmeling, S., Schölkopf, B.: Fast removal of non-uniform camera shake. In: ICCV, pp. 463–470 (2011)

10. Horé, A., Ziou, D.: Image quality metrics: PSNR vs. SSIM. In: ICPR, pp. 2366–2369 (2010)

11. Jiang, H., Zheng, Y.: Learning to see moving objects in the dark. In: ICCV, pp. 7324–7333 (2019)

12. Kim, T.H., Lee, K.M.: Generalized video deblurring for dynamic scenes. In: CVPR, pp. 5426–5434 (2015)

13. Kim, T.H., Lee, K.M., Scholkopf, B., Hirsch, M.: Online video deblurring via dynamic temporal blending network. In: ICCV, pp. 4038–4047 (2017)

14. Kingma, D.P., Ba, J.: Adam: a method for stochastic optimization. In: ICLR (2015)

15. Li, D., et al.: ARVo: learning all-range volumetric correspondence for video deblurring. In: CVPR, pp. 7721–7731, June 2021

16. Loshchilov, I., Hutter, F.: SGDR: stochastic gradient descent with warm restarts. In: ICLR (2017)

17. Nah, S., Kim, T.H., Lee, K.M.: Deep multi-scale convolutional neural network for dynamic scene deblurring. In: CVPR, pp. 3883–3891 (2017)

18. Nah, S., Son, S., Lee, K.M.: Recurrent neural networks with intra-frame iterations for video deblurring. In: CVPR, pp. 8102–8111 (2019)

19. Pan, J., Bai, H., Tang, J.: Cascaded deep video deblurring using temporal sharpness prior. In: CVPR, pp. 3043–3051 (2020)

20. Pan, J., Sun, D., Pfister, H., Yang, M.: Blind image deblurring using dark channel prior. In: CVPR, pp. 1628–1636 (2016)

21. Portz, T., Zhang, L., Jiang, H.: Optical flow in the presence of spatially-varying motion blur. In: CVPR, pp. 1752–1759 (2012)

22. Ren, W., Pan, J., Cao, X., Yang, M.H.: Video deblurring via semantic segmentation and pixel-wise non-linear kernel. In: ICCV, pp. 1077–1085 (2017)

23. Ronneberger, O., Fischer, P., Brox, T.: U-Net: convolutional networks for biomedical image segmentation. In: Navab, N., Hornegger, J., Wells, W.M., Frangi, A.F. (eds.) MICCAI 2015. LNCS, vol. 9351, pp. 234–241. Springer, Cham (2015). https://doi.org/10.1007/978-3-319-24574-4_28

24. Shan, Q., Jia, J., Agarwala, A.: High-quality motion deblurring from a single image. ACM Trans. Graph. **27**(3), 1–10 (2008)

25. Shen, Z., Wang, W., Shen, J., Ling, H., Xu, T., Shao, L.: Human-aware motion deblurring. In: ICCV (2019)

26. Shi, J., Xu, L., Jia, J.: Discriminative blur detection features. In: CVPR, pp. 2965–2972 (2014)

27. Son, H., Lee, J., Lee, J., Cho, S., Lee, S.: Recurrent Video Deblurring with Blur-invariant Motion Estimation and Pixel volumes. ACM Trans. Graph (2021)

28. Su, S., Delbracio, M., Wang, J., Sapiro, G., Heidrich, W., Wang, O.: Deep video deblurring for hand-held cameras. In: CVPR, pp. 237–246 (2017)

29. Suin, M., Purohit, K., Rajagopalan, A.N.: Spatially-attentive patch-hierarchical network for adaptive motion deblurring. In: CVPR, pp. 3606–3615 (2020)

30. Sun, D., Yang, X., Liu, M.Y., Kautz, J.: PWC-Net: CNNs for optical flow using pyramid, warping, and cost volume. In: CVPR (2018)

31. Sun, J., Cao, W., Xu, Z., Ponce, J.: Learning a convolutional neural network for non-uniform motion blur removal. In: CVPR, pp. 769–777 (2015)

32. Tai, Y.W., Chen, X., Kim, S., Kim, S.J., Li, F., Yang, J., Yu, J., Matsushita, Y., Brown, M.S.: Nonlinear camera response functions and image deblurring: theoretical analysis and practice. IEEE Trans. Pattern Anal. Mach. Intell. **35**(10), 2498–2512 (2013)

33. Tao, X., Gao, H., Shen, X., Wang, J., Jia, J.: Scale-recurrent network for deep image deblurring. In: CVPR, pp. 8174–8182 (2018)

34. Teed, Z., Deng, J.: RAFT: recurrent all-pairs field transforms for optical flow. In: Vedaldi, A., Bischof, H., Brox, T., Frahm, J.-M. (eds.) ECCV 2020. LNCS, vol. 12347, pp. 402–419. Springer, Cham (2020). https://doi.org/10.1007/978-3-030-58536-5_24

35. Wang, X., Chan, K.C., Yu, K., Dong, C., Loy, C.C.: EDVR: video restoration with enhanced deformable convolutional networks. In: CVPRW (2019)

36. Woo, S., Park, J., Lee, J.-Y., Kweon, I.S.: CBAM: convolutional block attention module. In: Ferrari, V., Hebert, M., Sminchisescu, C., Weiss, Y. (eds.) ECCV 2018. LNCS, vol. 11211, pp. 3–19. Springer, Cham (2018). https://doi.org/10.1007/978-3-030-01234-2_1

37. Wulff, J., Black, M.J.: Modeling blurred video with layers. In: Fleet, D., Pajdla, T., Schiele, B., Tuytelaars, T. (eds.) ECCV 2014. LNCS, vol. 8694, pp. 236–252. Springer, Cham (2014). https://doi.org/10.1007/978-3-319-10599-4_16

38. Xu, L., Zheng, S., Jia, J.: Unnatural l0 sparse representation for natural image deblurring. In: CVPR, pp. 1107–1114 (2013)

39. Yan, Y., Ren, W., Guo, Y., Wang, R., Cao, X.: Image deblurring via extreme channels prior. In: CVPR, pp. 6978–6986 (2017)

40. Zamir, S.W., et al.: Multi-stage progressive image restoration. In: CVPR (2021)

41. Zhang, Y., Tian, Y., Kong, Y., Zhong, B., Fu, Y.: Residual dense network for image super-resolution. In: CVPR, pp. 2472–2481 (2018)

42. Zhang, Y., Tian, Y., Kong, Y., Zhong, B., Fu, Y.: Residual dense network for image restoration. IEEE Trans. Pattern Anal. Mach. Intell. (2020)

43. Zhong, Z., Gao, Y., Zheng, Y., Zheng, B.: Efficient spatio-temporal recurrent neural network for video deblurring. In: Vedaldi, A., Bischof, H., Brox, T., Frahm, J.-M. (eds.) ECCV 2020. LNCS, vol. 12351, pp. 191–207. Springer, Cham (2020). https://doi.org/10.1007/978-3-030-58539-6_12

44. Zhou, S., Zhang, J., Pan, J., Xie, H., Zuo, W., Ren, J.: Spatio-temporal filter adaptive network for video deblurring. In: ICCV, pp. 2482–2491 (2019)

Single Frame Atmospheric Turbulence Mitigation: A Benchmark Study and a New Physics-Inspired Transformer Model

Zhiyuan Mao[1]([✉]), Ajay Jaiswal[2], Zhangyang Wang[2], and Stanley H. Chan[1]

[1] Purdue University, West Lafayette, IN 47907, USA
mao114@purdue.edu
[2] University of Texas at Austin, Austin, TX 78712, USA

Abstract. Image restoration algorithms for atmospheric turbulence are known to be much more challenging to design than traditional ones such as blur or noise because the distortion caused by the turbulence is an entanglement of spatially varying blur, geometric distortion, and sensor noise. Existing CNN-based restoration methods built upon convolutional kernels with static weights are insufficient to handle the spatially dynamical atmospheric turbulence effect. To address this problem, in this paper, we propose a physics-inspired transformer model for imaging through atmospheric turbulence. The proposed network utilizes the power of transformer blocks to jointly extract a dynamical turbulence distortion map and restore a turbulence-free image. In addition, recognizing the lack of a comprehensive dataset, we collect and present two new real-world turbulence datasets that allow for evaluation with both classical objective metrics (e.g., PSNR and SSIM) and a new task-driven metric using text recognition accuracy. The code and datasets are available at github.com/VITA-Group/TurbNet.

Keywords: Atmospheric turbulence mitigation · Image restoration

1 Introduction

In long-range imaging systems, atmospheric turbulence is one of the main sources of distortions that causes geometric displacements of the pixels and blurs. If unprocessed, the distorted images can have significant impacts on all downstream computer vision tasks such as detection, tracking, and biometric applications. The atmospheric turbulence effects are substantially harder to model and mitigate compared to the commonly seen image degradations such as deconvolution, as the turbulence is an entanglement of pixel displacement, blur, and noise. As a result, a dedicated image restoration pipeline is an essential element for long-range computer vision problems.

Z. Mao and A. Jaiswal—Equal contribution.

© The Author(s), under exclusive license to Springer Nature Switzerland AG 2022
S. Avidan et al. (Eds.): ECCV 2022, LNCS 13679, pp. 430–446, 2022.
https://doi.org/10.1007/978-3-031-19800-7_25

Image processing algorithms for mitigating the atmospheric turbulence effect have been studied for decades [1,10,12,14,18,20,21,23,36,40]. However, many of them have limitations that prohibit them from being launched to practical systems: 1) Many of the existing algorithms [1,1,10,12,21,40] are based on the principle of *lucky imaging* that requires multiple input frames. These methods often have a strong assumption that both the camera and the moving objects are static, which can easily become invalid in many real applications. 2) The conventional algorithms are often computationally expensive, making them unsuitable for processing large-scale datasets to meet the need of the latest computer vision systems. 3) Existing deep learning solutions [14,23,36] are not utilizing the physics of the turbulence. Many of them are also tailored to recovering faces instead of generic scenes. The generalization is therefore a question. 4) The algorithms may not be properly evaluated due to the absence of a widely accepted real large-scale benchmarking dataset.

To articulate the aforementioned challenges, in this paper we make three contributions:

1. We present a comprehensive benchmark evaluation of deep-learning based image restoration algorithms through atmospheric turbulence. We tune a sophisticated physics-grounded simulator to generate a large-scale dataset, covering a broad variety of atmospheric turbulence effects. The highly realistic and diverse dataset leads to exposing shortages of current turbulence mitigation algorithms.
2. Realizing the existing algorithms' limitations, we introduce a novel physics-inspired turbulence restoration model, termed *TurbNet*. Built on a transformer backbone, *TurbNet* features a modularized design that targets modeling the spatial adaptivity and long-range dynamics of turbulence effects, plus a self-supervised consistency loss.
3. We present a variety of evaluation regimes and collect two large-scale real-world turbulence *testing* datasets, one using the heat chamber for classical objective evaluation (e.g., PSNR and SSIM), and one using real long-range camera for optical text recognition as a semantic "proxy" task. Both of the new testing sets will be released.

2   Related Works

Turbulence Mitigation Methods. The atmospheric turbulence mitigation methods have been studied by the optics and vision community for decades. To reconstruct a turbulence degraded image, conventional algorithms [1,8–10,12,21, 34,40] often adopt the multi-frame image reconstruction strategy. The key idea is called "lucky imaging", where the geometric distortion is first removed using image registration or optical flow techniques. Sharper regions are then extracted from the aligned frames to form a lucky frame. A final blind deconvolution is usually needed to remove any residue blur. These methods are usually very computationally expensive. The time required to reconstruct a 256×256 image may range from a few seconds to tens of minutes. Despite the slow speed that prohibits them from being applied in real-world applications, the performance of conventional methods is often consistent across different image contents.

Recent deep learning methods adopt more dynamic strategies. Li et al. [18] propose to treat the distortion removal as an unsupervised training step. While it can effectively remove the geometric distortions induced by atmospheric turbulence, its computational cost is comparable to conventional methods, as it needs to repeat the training step for each input image. There are also several works that focus on specific types of images, such as face restoration [14,23,36]. They are usually based on a simplified assumption on atmospheric turbulence where they assume the blur to be spatially invariant. Such assumption cannot extend to general scene reconstruction, where the observed blur can be highly spatially varying due to a wide field of view.

There also exists general image processing methods, such as [37,38]. They have demonstrated impressive performance on restoration tasks, including denoising, deblurring, dehazing, etc. However, whether they can be extended to turbulence mitigation remains unclear as turbulence evolves more complicated distortions.

Available Datasets. Despite recent advances in turbulence mitigation algorithms, there is a very limited amount of publicly available datasets for atmospheric turbulence. The most widely used testing data are two images, the *Chimney* and *Building* sequences released in [10]. Besides, authors of [1,18,21] have released their own testing dataset, each of which often consists of less than 20 images. These data are then seldom used outside the original publications. Additionally, the scale of these datasets is not suitable for evaluating modern learning-based methods.

Due to the nature of the problem, it is very difficult to obtain aligned clean and corrupted image pairs. Existing algorithms are all trained with synthetic data. The computationally least expensive synthesis technique is based on the random pixel displacement + blur model [13,15]. In the optics community, there are techniques based on ray-tracing and wave-propagation [7,25,27]. A more recent physics-based simulation technique based on the collapsed phase-over-aperture model and the phase-to-space transform is proposed in [3,22]. Our data synthesis scheme is based on the *P2S* model provided by authors of [22].

3   Restoration Model

3.1   Problem Setting and Motivation

Consider a clean image $\mathbf{I}$ in the object plane that travels through the turbulence to the image plane. Following the classical split-step wave-propagation equation, the resulting image $\widetilde{\mathbf{I}}$ is constructed through a sequence of operations in the phase domain:

$$\mathbf{I} \rightarrow \text{Fresnel} \rightarrow \text{Kolmogorov} \rightarrow \cdots \text{Fresnel} \rightarrow \text{Kolmogorov} \rightarrow \widetilde{\mathbf{I}}, \qquad (1)$$

where "Fresnel" represents the wave propagation step by the Fresnel diffraction, and "Kolmogorov" represents the phase distortion due to the Kolmogorov power spectral density [11].

Certainly, Eq. 1 is implementable as a forward equation (i.e. for simulation) but it is nearly impossible to be used for solving an inverse problem. To mitigate this modeling difficulty, one computationally efficient approach is to approximate the turbulence as a composition of two processes:

$$\widetilde{\mathbf{I}} = \left(\underbrace{\mathcal{H}}_{\text{blur}} \circ \underbrace{\mathcal{G}}_{\text{geometric}} \right)(\mathbf{I}) + \mathbf{N}, \tag{2}$$

where $\mathcal{H}$ is a convolution matrix representing the spatially *varying* blur, and $\mathcal{G}$ is a mapping representing the geometric pixel displacement (known as the tilt). The variable $\mathbf{N}$ denotes the additive noise / model residue in approximating Eq. 1 with a simplified model. The operation "∘" means the functional composition. That is, we first apply $\mathcal{G}$ to $\mathbf{I}$ and then apply $\mathcal{H}$ to the resulting image.

We emphasize that Eqn. 2 is only a mathematically convenient way to derive an approximated solution for the inverse problem but not the true model. The slackness falls into the fact that the pixel displacement in $\mathcal{G}$ across the field of view are correlated, so do the blurs in $\mathcal{H}$. The specific correlation can be referred to the model construction in the phase space, for example [3]. In the literature, Eqn. 2 the shortcoming of this model is recognized, although some successful algorithms can still be derived [1,40].

The simultaneous presence of $\mathcal{H}$ and $\mathcal{G}$ in Eqn. 2 makes the problem hard. If there is only $\mathcal{H}$, the problem is a simple deblurring. If there is only $\mathcal{G}$, the problem is a simple geometric unwrapping. Generic deep-learning models such as [23,36] adopt network architectures for classical restoration problems based on conventional CNNs, which are developed for one type of distortion. Effective, their models treat the problem as

$$\widetilde{\mathbf{I}} = \mathcal{T}(\mathbf{I}) + \mathbf{N}, \tag{3}$$

where $\mathcal{T} = \mathcal{G} \circ \mathcal{H}$ is the overall turbulence operator. Without looking into how $\mathcal{T}$ is constructed, existing methods directly train a generic restoration network by feeding it with noisy-clean training pairs. Since there is no physics involved in this generic procedure, the generalization is often poor.

Contrary to previous methods, in this paper, we propose to jointly estimate the physical degradation model $\mathcal{T}$ of turbulence along with reconstruction of clean image from the degraded input $\widetilde{\mathbf{I}}$. Such formulation explicitly forces our model to focus on learning a generic turbulence degradation operator independent of image contents, along with the reconstruction operation to generate clean output. Moreover, our network training is assisted by high-quality, large-scale, and physics-motivated synthetic training data to better learn the key characteristics of the atmospheric turbulence effect. The detailed model architecture will be presented in the following subsection.

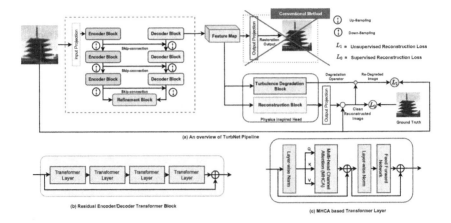

Fig. 1. Architecture of the proposed method. (a) The overall architecture consists: (i) a transformer to pull the spatially dynamical features from the scene; (ii) instead of directly constructing the image, we introduce a physics-inspired model to estimate the turbulence while reconstructing the image. (b) The structure of the residual encoder/decoder transformer block. (c) The details of each transformer layer.

3.2 Model Architecture

Turbulence and limitation of CNNs: CNNs have been *de facto* choice by most of the previous image restoration algorithms, yet they are limited by two primary issues: 1) The convolutional filters cannot adapt to image content during inference due to their static weights. 2) The local receptive fields cannot model the long-range pixel dependencies. A key characteristic of the atmospheric turbulence effect is the "lucky effect" [6], meaning that **image regions** or **frames** with less degradation will randomly occur due to the distortions being spatially varying. Previous restoration methods treat turbulence restoration as a regression problem using CNNs but ignore the fact that turbulence is highly location adaptive and should not be represented as static fixed kernel applied to all locations. It is not difficult to see that applying static weight convolutions to regions with drastically different distortions will lead to sub-optimal performance.

The *self-attention* mechanism proposed in recent work [5,30,31] can be a powerful alternative, as it can capture context-dependent global interactions by aggregating information across image regions. Leveraging the capability of multi-head self-attention, we propose the ***TurbNet***, a transformer-based end-to-end network for restoring turbulence degraded images. Transformer-based architecture allows the creation of input-adaptive and location-adaptive filtering effect using *key, query,* and *weight*, where *key* and *query* decide content-adaptivity while *weight* brings location-adaptivity. Our design, as shown in Fig. 1, is composed of several key building blocks:

Transformer Backbone: Our proposed network consists of a transformer-based backbone that has the flexibility of constructing an input-adaptive and location-adaptive unique kernel to model spatially- and instance-varying turbulence effect. Inspired by the success of [26,32,37] in various common image restoration tasks (e.g., denoising, deblurring, etc.), TurbNet adopts a U-shape encoder-decoder architecture due to its hierarchical multi-scale representation while remaining computationally efficient. As shown in Fig. 1 (b), the residual connection across the encoder-decoder provides an identity-based connection facilitating aggregation of different layers of features. Our backbone consists of three modules: input projection, deep encoder and decoder module. Input project module uses convolution layers to extract low frequency information and induces dose of convolutional inductive bias in early stage and improves representation learning ability of transformer blocks [33]. Deep encoder and decoder modules are mainly composed of a sequential cascade of Multi-head channel attention (MHCA) based transformer layers. Compared to prevalent CNN-based turbulence mitigation models, this design allows content-based interactions between image content and attention weights, which can be interpreted as spatially varying convolution [4].

The primary challenge of applying conventional transformer blocks for image restoration task comes from the quadratic growth of key-query dot product interactions, i.e., $\mathcal{O}(W^2 H^2)$, for images with $W \times H$ pixels. To alleviate this issue, we adopt the idea of applying self-attention across channels instead of spatial dimension [37], and compute cross-covarience across channels generating attention map. Given *query* ($\mathbf{Q}$), *key* ($\mathbf{K}$), and *value* ($\mathbf{V}$), we reshape $\mathbf{Q}$ and $\mathbf{K}$ such that their dot-product generates a transposed-attention map $\mathbf{A} \in \mathbb{R}^{C \times C}$, instead of conventional $\mathbb{R}^{HW \times HW}$ [5]. Overall, the MHCA can be summarized as:

$$\mathbf{X}' = \mathbf{W_p} \, \mathrm{Attention}(\mathbf{Q}, \mathbf{K}, \mathbf{V}) + \mathbf{X} \qquad (4)$$

$$\mathrm{Attention}(\mathbf{Q}, \mathbf{K}, \mathbf{V}) = \mathbf{V} \cdot \mathrm{softmax}\left\{ \frac{\mathbf{K} \cdot \mathbf{Q}}{\alpha} \right\} \qquad (5)$$

where $\mathbf{X}'$ and $\mathbf{X}$ are input and output feature maps, $\mathbf{W_p}^{(\cdot)}$ is the 1×1 point-wise convolution, and α is a learnable scaling parameter to control the magnitude of $(\mathbf{K} \cdot \mathbf{Q})$ before applying softmax.

Image Reconstruction Block: To further enhance deep features generated by the transformer backbone, TurbNet uses the reconstruction block. The primary job of the reconstruction block is to take deep features corresponding to turbulence degraded input image $\widetilde{\mathbf{I}}$ by the transformer backbone, further enrich it at high spatial resolution by encoding information from spatially neighboring pixel positions. Next, the enriched features pass through an output projection module with 3×3 convolution layers to project it back low dimension feature map corresponding to the reconstructed clean image $\mathbf{J}$. The design of the reconstruction block is very similar to the encoder block having MHCA, with an introduction of Locally-Enhanced Feed Forward Network (LoFFN) [32].

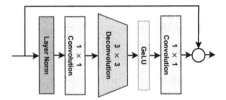

Fig. 2. Locally-Enhanced Feed Forward Network (LoFFN) used in the image reconstruction block and the turbulence degradation block.

Precisely, the work of Reconstruction module can be summarized as:

$$\underbrace{\mathbf{F}_{\tilde{\mathbf{I}}}}_{\substack{\text{Deep Features of degraded} \\ \text{Input Image } \tilde{\mathbf{I}}}} \rightarrow \text{Reconstruction Module} \rightarrow \underbrace{\mathbf{J}_{\tilde{\mathbf{I}}}}_{\substack{\text{Reconstructed Clean} \\ \text{Output Image}}} \quad (6)$$

Turbulence Degradation Block: In TurbNet, the turbulence degradation module learns the physical turbulence degradation operator $\mathcal{T}$ from the input synthetic training data. The primary job of turbulence degradation module is to take clean reconstructed image $\mathbf{J}_{\tilde{\mathbf{I}}}$ corresponding to degraded input image $\tilde{\mathbf{I}}$, apply the learned degradation operator $\mathcal{T}$, to construct back the **re-degraded** input image $\tilde{\mathbf{I}}_{\mathcal{T}}$. This formulation enriches the training set by incorporating additional latent degradation images ($\tilde{\mathbf{I}}_{\mathcal{T}}$), in addition to synthesized degraded images ($\tilde{\mathbf{I}}$), during the training process. Additionally, this module facilitates self-supervised learning without the availability of ground truth. The architecture of this module is the same as Image Reconstruction Block with LoFFN.

Precisely, the work of Degradation Block can be summarized as:

$$\underbrace{\mathbf{J}_{\tilde{\mathbf{I}}}}_{\substack{\text{Reconstructed Clean} \\ \text{Output Image}}} \rightarrow \text{Degradation Operator } \mathcal{T}(\cdot) \rightarrow \underbrace{\tilde{\mathbf{I}}_{\mathcal{T}}}_{\substack{\text{Re-degraded} \\ \text{Output Image}}} \quad (7)$$

Loss Function: TurbNet optimization requires the joint optimization of reconstruction operation and the turbulance degradation operation. Given the synthetic training pair of degraded input $\tilde{\mathbf{I}}$, and corresponding ground truth image $\mathbf{I}$, we formulate following two losses:

$$\underbrace{\mathcal{L}_0}_{\text{Supervised Reconstruction Loss}} = ||\mathbf{J}_{\tilde{\mathbf{I}}} - \mathbf{I}||_1 \quad (8)$$

$$\underbrace{\mathcal{L}_1}_{\text{Self-supervised Reconstruction Loss}} = ||\tilde{\mathbf{I}}_{\mathcal{T}} - \tilde{\mathbf{I}}||_1 \quad (9)$$

where, $\mathcal{L}_0$ is responsible for constructing a clean image $\mathbf{J}_{\tilde{\mathbf{I}}}$ given the degraded input image $\tilde{\mathbf{I}}$, $\mathcal{L}_1$ helps to ensure degradation operator $\mathcal{T}$ can reconstruct the original the original input $\tilde{\mathbf{I}}$ from the reconstructed clean image $\mathbf{J}_{\tilde{\mathbf{I}}}$.

Eventually, the overall loss $\mathcal{L}$ to train TurbNet can be summarized as:

$$\mathcal{L} = \alpha \times \mathcal{L}_0 + (1 - \alpha) \times \mathcal{L}_1 \qquad (10)$$

Overall Pipeline. As shown in Fig. 1(a), TurbNet utilizes a U-shape architecture built upon transformer blocks to extract deep image features. As suggested in [33], an initial convolution-based input projection is used to project the input image to higher dimensional feature space, which can lead to more stable optimization and better results. After obtaining the feature maps, TurbNet jointly learns the turbulence degradation operator $(\mathcal{T})$ along with the reconstructed image $(\mathbf{J}_{\tilde{\mathbf{I}}})$, in contrary to general image restoration methods [2,19,32,37] that directly reconstruct the clean image. This design facilitates spatial adaptivity and long-range dynamics of turbulence effects, plus a self-supervised consistency loss.

Synthetic-to-Real Generalization: With a pre-trained TurbNet model $\mathcal{M}(\cdot)$ using the synthetic data, TurbNet design allows an effective way of generalizing $\mathcal{M}(\cdot)$ on unseen real data (if required) with the help of degradation operator $\mathcal{T}(\cdot)$ in a self-supervised way. Starting from model $\mathcal{M}(\cdot)$, we create a generalization dataset by incorporating unlabelled real data with the synthetic data to fine-tune $\mathcal{M}(\cdot)$. For input images with no ground truth, $\mathcal{M}(\cdot)$ is optimized using Eq. (9), while for input images from labeled synthetic data $\mathcal{M}(\cdot)$ is optimized using Eq. (8 and 9). Note that we incorporate synthetic data into the fine-tuning process to mitigate the issue of catastrophic forgetting during generalization.

4   Large-Scale Training and Testing Datasets

4.1   Training Data: Synthetic Data Generating Scheme

Training a deep neural network requires data, but the real clean-noisy pair of turbulence is nearly impossible to collect. A more feasible approach here is to leverage a powerful turbulence simulator to synthesize the turbulence effects.

Turbulence simulation in the context of deep learning has been reported in [14,23,36]. Their model generates the geometric distortions by repeatedly smoothing a set of random spikes, and the blur is assumed to be spatially invariant Gaussian [13]. We argue that for the face images studied in [14,23,36], the narrow field of view makes their simplified model valid. However, for more complex scenarios, such a simplified model will fail to capture two key phenomena that could cause the training of the network to fail: (1) The instantaneous distortion of the turbulence can vary significantly from one observation to another even if the turbulence parameters are fixed. See Fig. 3(a) for an illustration from a real data. (2) Within the same image, the distortions are spatially varying. See Fig. 3(b).

In order to capture these phenomena, we adopt an advanced simulator [22] to synthesize a large-scale *training* dataset for atmospheric turbulence. The clean

Variation of turbulence strength due to randomness of turbulence   Spatially varying effect of turbulence

Fig. 3. Key turbulence effects requiring attention while designing synthetic dataset.

data used by the simulator is the *Places* dataset [39]. A total of 50,000 images are generated, and the turbulence parameters are configured to cover a wide range of conditions. The details of the simulation can be found in the supplementary material. We remark that this is the first attempt in the literature to systematically generate such a comprehensive and large-scale training dataset.

4.2 Testing Data: Heat Chamber and Text Datasets

Our real benchmarking dataset consists of two parts: the *Heat Chamber Dataset* and the *Turbulent Text Dataset*. Although this paper focuses on single frame restoration, both our benchmarking datasets contain 100 static turbulence degraded frames for each scene. We believe that by doing so, researchers in the field working on multi-frame reconstruction can also benefit from our dataset. Both datasets will be made **publicly available**.

Heat Chamber Dataset. The *Heat Chamber Dataset* is collected by heating the air along the imaging path to artificially create a stronger turbulence effect. The setup for collecting the heat chamber dataset is shown in 4. Turbulence-free ground truth images can be obtained by shutting down the heat source. The images are displayed on a screen placed 20 m away from the camera.

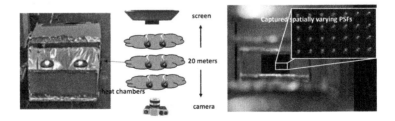

Fig. 4. The setup of heat chamber data collection. We evenly placed three heat chambers along the imaging path. Our dataset captures better spatially varying effect.

We remark that while similar datasets have been collected in [1,10], our data has a clear improvement: we use a long path and more evenly distributed heat so that the turbulence effect is closer to the true long-range effect. The captured images have a better anisoplanatic (spatially varying) effect such that an almost distortion-free frame is less likely to occur compared with the dataset in [1,10]. In addition, our dataset is much large in scale. It contains 2400 different images, which allows for a better evaluation of the learning-based model. Sample images of the *Heat Chamber Dataset* can be found in Fig. 5.

Fig. 5. Sample turbulence degraded images (top) and corresponding ground truth (bottom) from our *Heat Chamber Dataset*. The D/r_0 is estimated to be around 3.

Turbulence Text Dataset. Due to the nature of the problem, it is extremely difficult, if not impossible, to capture ground truth clean images in truly long-range settings. Therefore, we adopt the idea of using the performance of high-level vision task as an evaluation metric for image restoration [16,17]. Specifically, we calculate the detection ratio and longest common subsequence on the output of an OCR algorithm [28,29] as the evaluation metrics. The terms will be defined in Sect. 5.4.

There are several advantages of using text recognition: 1) The degradation induced by atmospheric turbulence, the geometric distortion and the loss of resolution, can be directly reflected by the text patterns. Both types of degradation need to be removed for the OCR algorithms to perform well. 2) The OCR is a mature application. The selected algorithms should be able to recognize the text patterns as long as the turbulence is removed. Other factors such as the domain gap between the training and testing data will not affect the evaluation procedure as much as other high-level vision tasks. 3) An important factor to consider when designing the dataset is whether the difficulty of the task is appropriate. The dataset should neither be too difficult such that the recognition rate cannot be improved by the restoration algorithms nor too easy making all algorithms perform similarly. We can easily adjust the font size and contrast of text patterns to obtain a proper difficulty level.

The *Turbulence Text Dataset* consists of 100 scenes, where each scene contains 5 text sequences. Each scene has 100 static frames. It can be assumed that there is no camera and object motion within the scene, and the observed blur is caused by atmospheric turbulence. The text patterns come in three different scales, which adds variety to the dataset. We also provide labels to crop the individual text patterns from the images. Sample images from the dataset are shown in Fig. 6.

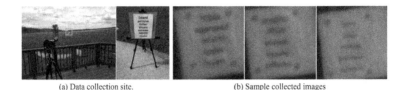

(a) Data collection site.   (b) Sample collected images

Fig. 6. Data collection site of the *Turbulence Text Dataset*. The distance between the camera and the target is 300 m. The D/r_0 is estimated to be in range of 2.5 to 4 (varies due to the temperature change during the collection process). The collected text patterns are in 3 different scales.

Table 1. Performance comparison of state-of-art restoration baselines with respect to TurbNet on synthetic and *Heat Chamber* dataset.

	TDRN [35]	MTRNN [24]	MPRNet [38]	Uformer [32]	Restormer [37]	**TurbNet**
Synthetic dataset						
PSNR	21.35	21.95	21.78	22.03	22.29	**22.76**
SSIM	0.6228	0.6384	0.6410	0.6686	0.6719	**0.6842**
HeatChamber dataset						
PSNR	18.42	18.12	18.68	19.12	19.01	**19.76**
SSIM	0.6424	0.6379	0.6577	0.6840	0.6857	**0.6934**

5   Experiment Results

Implementation Details: TurbNet uses a 4-staged symmetric encoder-decoder architecture, where stage 1, 2, 3, and 4 consist of 4, 6, 6, and 8 MHCA-based transformer layers respectively. Our Reconstruction block and Turbulence Degradation block consist of 4 MHCA-transformer layers enhanced with LoFFN. TurbNet is trained using 50,000 synthetic dataset generated using a physics-based stimulator [22] and MIT Places dataset [39] while synthetic evaluation results are generated on 5,000 synthetic images. Due to resource constraint, our synthetic training uses a batch size of 8 with Adam optimizer. We start our training with learning rate of $1e - 4$, and use the cosine annealing scheduler to gradually decrease the learning rate over the span of 50 epcohs. During training, to modulate between the loss Eq. 8 and 9, we have use α to be 0.9. All the baselines method used in our evaluation has been trained with exactly same settings and same dataset using their official GitHub implementation for fair comparison. Additional implementation details are provided in supplementary materials.

5.1   Synthetic and *Heat Chamber* Dataset Results

We first conduct an experiment on a synthetic testing dataset generated with the same distribution as testing data. In Fig. 7, we show a qualitative comparison between our restored images with ground truth. It can be seen that our results are accurately reconstructed with the assist from estimated turbulence map.

We then compare our results qualitatively with the existing algorithms on both synthetic and *Heat Chamber* dataset. A Visual comparison on the synthetic dataset can be found in Fig. 8. It can be observed that the transformer-based methods generally perform better than the CNN-based methods due to their ability to adapt dynamically to the distortions. The proposed method achieves authentic reconstruction due to its ability to explicitly model the atmospheric turbulence distortion. Table 1 presents the quantitative evaluation of TurbNet wrt. other baselines. TurbNet achieves the best results in both PSNR and SSIM. Note that Uformer [32], and Restomer [37] (designed for classical restoration problems like deblurring, deraining, etc.) uses transformer-based encoder decoder architecture, but their performance is significantly low than TurbNet, which validates the importance of our decoupled (reconstruction and degradation estimation) design.

5.2   *Turbulence Text Dataset* Results

Evaluation Method: In order to evaluate the performance of TurbNet on our real-world turbulence text dataset, we use publicly available OCR detection and recognition algorithms [28,29]. We propose the following two evaluation metrics - Average Word Detection Ratio (**AWDR**), and Average Detected Longest Common Subsequence (**AD − LCS**) defined as follows:

$$\mathbf{AWDR} = \frac{\sum_{Scene=1}^{N} \frac{\text{Word Detected}_{scene}}{\text{Word Count}_{scene}}}{N}, \qquad (11)$$

$$\mathbf{AD - LCS} = \frac{\sum_{Scene=1}^{N} \sum_{Word=1}^{K} \mathcal{LCS}(DetectedString, TrueString)}{N}, \qquad (12)$$

where $\mathcal{LCS}$ represents the Longest Common Subsequence, $TrueString$ represents the ground truth sequence of characters corresponding to a word i in the image, $DetectedString$ represents a sequence of characters recognized by OCR algorithms for word i, and N is the total number of scenes in the test dataset.

Discussion: Figure 9 represents the performance of OCR on the real turbulence impacted images and images restored by TurbNet. It is evident that our restoration model significantly helps in improving the OCR performance by identifying comparatively more words with higher confidence. Table 2 presents the performance gain by TurbNet over the real turbulence degraded text images and their restored version by various state-of-the-art methods. OCR algorithms achieve

Table 2. Performance comparison of state-of-art restoration baselines with respect to TurbNet on our *Turbulence Text Dataset.*

	Raw Input	TDRN [35]	MTRNN [24]	MPRNet [38]	Restormer [37]	**TurbNet**
AWDR	0.623	0.617	0.642	0.633	0.702	**0.758**
AD-LCS	5.076	5.011	5.609	5.374	6.226	**7.314**

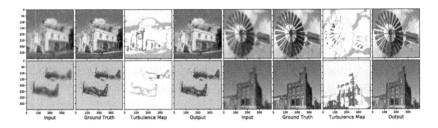

Fig. 7. Qualitative Performance comparison of TurbNet wrt. the ground truth.

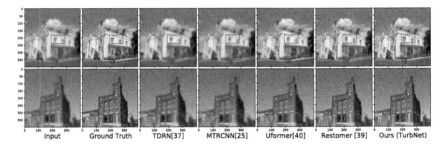

Fig. 8. Qualitative Performance comparison of TurbNet wrt. other SOTA methods.

massive improvements of +0.135 (AWDR) and +2.238 (AD-LCS) when used on images restored by TurbNet compared to being used directly on real images from our proposed test dataset.

5.3 Experimental Validity of the Proposed Model

We conduct two additional experiments to validate the proposed model. The first experiment is an ablation study, where we demonstrate the impact of replacing transformer as feature encoder with U-Net [26] and removing the turbulence map estimation part. The result is reported in 3, where we observe a significant performance drop in both cases. The second experiment is to prove the effectiveness of the extracted turbulence map. We extract a turbulence map from a simulated frame and apply the map back to the ground-truth image. We calculate the PSNR of this re-corrupted image w.r.t. the original turbulence frame. We tested on 10K turbulence frames and the average PSNR is **39.89 dB**, which is a strong evidence that our turbulence map can effectively extract the turbulence information embedded in the distorted frames. A visualization of the experiment can be found in Fig. 10.

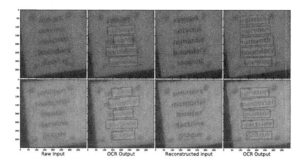

Fig. 9. OCR performance of our reconstruction algorithm for *Turbulance Text Dataset*

Fig. 10. Validation of our turbulence map. Left: groundtruth. Middle: original turbulence frame. Right: groundtruth re-corrupted with the extracted turbulence map.

Table 3. Ablation on Heat Chamber Dataset

Model type	PSNR	SSIM
TurbNet [Ours]	19.76	0.6934
TurbNet - Turbulance Map	19.03 (↓)	0.6852 (↓)
TurbNet - Transformer	18.62 (↓)	0.6481 (↓)

6   Conclusions

In this work, identifying the short-come of existing image restoration algorithms, we propose a novel physics-inspired turbulence restoration model (TurbNet) based on transformer architecture to model spatial adaptivity and long-term dynamics of turbulence effect. We present a synthetic data generation scheme for tuning a sophisticated physics-grounded simulator to generate a large-scale dataset, covering a broad variety of atmospheric turbulence effects. Additionally, we introduce two new large-scale testing datasets that allow for evaluation with classical objective metrics and a new task-driven metric with optical text recognition. Our comprehensive evaluation on realistic and diverse datasets leads to exposing limitations of existing methods and the effectiveness of TurbNet.

Acknowledgement. The research is based upon work supported in part by the Intelligence Advanced Research Projects Activity (IARPA) under Contract No. 2022–21102100004, and in part by the National Science Foundation under the grants CCSS-2030570 and IIS-2133032. The views and conclusions contained herein are those of the authors and should not be interpreted as necessarily representing the official policies, either expressed or implied, of IARPA, or the U.S. Government. The U.S. Government is authorized to reproduce and distribute reprints for governmental purposes notwithstanding any copyright annotation therein.

References

1. Anantrasirichai, N., Achim, A., Kingsbury, N.G., Bull, D.R.: Atmospheric turbulence mitigation using complex wavelet-based fusion. IEEE Trans. Image Process. **22**(6), 2398–2408 (2013). https://doi.org/10.1109/TIP.2013.2249078
2. Chen, H., et al.: Pre-trained image processing transformer. In: 2021 IEEE/CVF Conference on Computer Vision and Pattern Recognition (CVPR), pp. 12294–12305 (2021)
3. Chimitt, N., Chan, S.H.: Simulating anisoplanatic turbulence by sampling intermodal and spatially correlated Zernike coefficients. Opt. Eng. **59**(8), 1–26 (2020). https://doi.org/10.1117/1.OE.59.8.083101
4. Cordonnier, J.B., Loukas, A., Jaggi, M.: On the relationship between self-attention and convolutional layers. arXiv preprint arXiv:1911.03584 (2019)
5. Dosovitskiy, A., et al.: An image is worth 16 × 16 words: transformers for image recognition at scale. arXiv preprint arXiv:2010.11929 (2020)
6. Fried, D.L.: Probability of getting a lucky short-exposure image through turbulence∗. J. Opt. Soc. Am. **68**(12), 1651–1658 (1978). https://doi.org/10.1364/JOSA.68.001651, http://www.osapublishing.org/abstract.cfm?URI=josa-68-12-1651
7. Hardie, R.C., Power, J.D., LeMaster, D.A., Droege, D.R., Gladysz, S., Bose-Pillai, S.: Simulation of anisoplanatic imaging through optical turbulence using numerical wave propagation with new validation analysis. Opt. Eng. **56**(7), 1–16 (2017). https://doi.org/10.1117/1.OE.56.7.071502
8. Hardie, R.C., Rucci, M.A., Dapore, A.J., Karch, B.K.: Block matching and wiener filtering approach to optical turbulence mitigation and its application to simulated and real imagery with quantitative error analysis. Opt. Eng. **56**(7), 071503 (2017)
9. He, R., Wang, Z., Fan, Y., Feng, D.: Atmospheric turbulence mitigation based on turbulence extraction. In: 2016 IEEE International Conference on Acoustics, Speech and Signal Processing (ICASSP), pp. 1442–1446 (2016)
10. Hirsch, M., Sra, S., Schölkopf, B., Harmeling, S.: Efficient filter flow for space-variant multiframe blind deconvolution. In: The IEEE Conference on Computer Vision and Pattern Recognition (CVPR), pp. 607–614 (2010)

11. Kolmogorov, A.N.: The local structure of turbulence in incompressible viscous fluid for very large reynolds' numbers. Akademiia Nauk SSSR Doklady **30**, 301–305 (1941)
12. Lau, C.P., Lai, Y.H., Lui, L.M.: Restoration of atmospheric turbulence-distorted images via RPCA and quasiconformal maps. Inverse Prob. (2019). https://doi.org/10.1088/1361-6420/ab0e4b. Mar
13. Lau, C.P., Lui, L.M.: Subsampled turbulence removal network. Math. Comput. Geom. Data **1**(1), 1–33 (2021). https://doi.org/10.4310/MCGD.2021.v1.n1.a1
14. Lau, C.P., Souri, H., Chellappa, R.: ATFaceGAN: Single face semantic aware image restoration and recognition from atmospheric turbulence. IEEE Trans. Biometrics Behav. Identity Sci. 1 (2021). https://doi.org/10.1109/TBIOM.2021.3058316
15. Leonard, K.R., Howe, J., Oxford, D.E.: Simulation of atmospheric turbulence effects and mitigation algorithms on stand-off automatic facial recognition. In: Proceedings. SPIE 8546, Optics and Photonics for Counterterrorism, Crime Fighting, and Defence VIII, pp. 1–18 (2012)
16. Li, B., Peng, X., Wang, Z., Xu, J.Z., Feng, D.: AOD-Net: all-in-one dehazing network. In: Proceedings of the IEEE International Conference on Computer Vision (2017)
17. Li, B., et al.: Benchmarking single-image dehazing and beyond. IEEE Trans. Image Process. **28**(1), 492–505 (2019). https://doi.org/10.1109/TIP.2018.2867951
18. Li, N., Thapa, S., Whyte, C., Reed, A.W., Jayasuriya, S., Ye, J.: Unsupervised non-rigid image distortion removal via grid deformation. In: Proceedings of the IEEE/CVF International Conference on Computer Vision (ICCV), pp. 2522–2532 (2021)
19. Liu, Z., et al.: Swin transformer: hierarchical vision transformer using shifted windows. arXiv preprint arXiv:2103.14030 (2021)
20. Lou, Y., Ha Kang, S., Soatto, S., Bertozzi, A.: Video stabilization of atmospheric turbulence distortion. Inverse Probl. Imaging **7**(3), 839–861 (2013). https://doi.org/10.3934/ipi.2013.7.839. Aug
21. Mao, Z., Chimitt, N., Chan, S.H.: Image reconstruction of static and dynamic scenes through anisoplanatic turbulence. IEEE Trans. Comput. Imaging **6**, 1415–1428 (2020). https://doi.org/10.1109/TCI.2020.3029401
22. Mao, Z., Chimitt, N., Chan, S.H.: Accelerating atmospheric turbulence simulation via learned phase-to-space transform. In: Proceedings of the IEEE/CVF International Conference on Computer Vision (ICCV), pp. 14759–14768 (2021)
23. Nair, N.G., Patel, V.M.: Confidence guided network for atmospheric turbulence mitigation. In: 2021 IEEE International Conference on Image Processing (ICIP), pp. 1359–1363 (2021). https://doi.org/10.1109/ICIP42928.2021.9506125
24. Park, D., Kang, D.U., Kim, J., Chun, S.Y.: Multi-temporal recurrent neural networks for progressive non-uniform single image deblurring with incremental temporal training. In: Vedaldi, A., Bischof, H., Brox, T., Frahm, J.-M. (eds.) ECCV 2020. LNCS, vol. 12351, pp. 327–343. Springer, Cham (2020). https://doi.org/10.1007/978-3-030-58539-6_20
25. Roggemann, M.C., Welsh, B.M.: Imaging through Atmospheric Turbulence. Laser and Optical Science and Technology. Taylor and Francis (1996)
26. Ronneberger, O., Fischer, P., Brox, T.: U-Net: convolutional networks for biomedical image segmentation. In: Navab, N., Hornegger, J., Wells, W.M., Frangi, A.F. (eds.) MICCAI 2015. LNCS, vol. 9351, pp. 234–241. Springer, Cham (2015). https://doi.org/10.1007/978-3-319-24574-4_28
27. Schmidt, J.D.: Numerical Simulation of Optical Wave Propagation: With Examples in MATLAB. SPIE Press (2010). https://doi.org/10.1117/3.866274

28. Shi, B., Bai, X., Yao, C.: An end-to-end trainable neural network for image-based sequence recognition and its application to scene text recognition. IEEE Trans. Pattern Anal. Mach. Intell. **39**(11), 2298–2304 (2017)

29. Tian, Z., Huang, W., He, T., He, P., Qiao, Yu.: Detecting text in natural image with connectionist text proposal network. In: Leibe, B., Matas, J., Sebe, N., Welling, M. (eds.) ECCV 2016. LNCS, vol. 9912, pp. 56–72. Springer, Cham (2016). https://doi.org/10.1007/978-3-319-46484-8_4

30. Vaswani, A., et al.: Attention is all you need. In: Advances in Neural Information Processing Systems, vol. 30 (2017)

31. Wang, X., Girshick, R.B., Gupta, A.K., He, K.: Non-local neural networks. In: 2018 IEEE/CVF Conference on Computer Vision and Pattern Recognition, pp. 7794–7803 (2018)

32. Wang, Z., Cun, X., Bao, J., Liu, J.: Uformer: a general u-shaped transformer for image restoration. arXiv preprint arXiv:2106.03106 (2021)

33. Xiao, T., Dollar, P., Singh, M., Mintun, E., Darrell, T., Girshick, R.: Early convolutions help transformers see better. In: Advances in Neural Information Processing Systems, vol. 34 (2021)

34. Xie, Y., Zhang, W., Tao, D., Hu, W., Qu, Y., Wang, H.: Removing turbulence effect via hybrid total variation and deformation-guided kernel regression. IEEE Trans. Image Process. **25**(10), 4943–4958 (2016). Oct

35. Yasarla, R., Patel, V.M.: Learning to restore a single face image degraded by atmospheric turbulence using CNNs. arXiv preprint arXiv:2007.08404 (2020)

36. Yasarla, R., Patel, V.M.: Learning to restore images degraded by atmospheric turbulence using uncertainty. In: 2021 IEEE International Conference on Image Processing (ICIP), pp. 1694–1698 (2021). https://doi.org/10.1109/ICIP42928.2021.9506614

37. Zamir, S.W., Arora, A., Khan, S., Hayat, M., Khan, F.S., Yang, M.H.: Restormer: efficient transformer for high-resolution image restoration. arXiv preprint arXiv:2111.09881 (2021)

38. Zamir, S.W., et al.: Multi-stage progressive image restoration. In: Proceedings of the IEEE/CVF Conference on Computer Vision and Pattern Recognition, pp. 14821–14831 (2021)

39. Zhou, B., Lapedriza, A., Khosla, A., Oliva, A., Torralba, A.: Places: a 10 million image database for scene recognition. In: IEEE Trans. Pattern Anal. Mach. Intell. **40**, 1452–1464 (2017)

40. Zhu, X., Milanfar, P.: Removing atmospheric turbulence via space-invariant deconvolution. IEEE Trans. Pattern Anal. Mach. Intell. **35**(1), 157–170 (2013). https://doi.org/10.1109/TPAMI.2012.82

Contextformer: A Transformer with Spatio-Channel Attention for Context Modeling in Learned Image Compression

A. Burakhan Koyuncu[1,2]([⊠]) [ID], Han Gao[4] [ID], Atanas Boev[2] [ID],
Georgii Gaikov[3] [ID], Elena Alshina[2] [ID], and Eckehard Steinbach[1] [ID]

[1] Technical University of Munich, Munich, Germany
`burakhan.koyuncu@tum.de`
[2] Huawei Munich Research Center, Munich, Germany
[3] Huawei Moscow Research Center, Moscow, Russia
[4] Tencent America, Palo Alto, USA

Abstract. Entropy modeling is a key component for high-performance image compression algorithms. Recent developments in autoregressive context modeling helped learning-based methods to surpass their classical counterparts. However, the performance of those models can be further improved due to the underexploited spatio-channel dependencies in latent space, and the suboptimal implementation of context adaptivity. Inspired by the adaptive characteristics of the transformers, we propose a transformer-based context model, named Contextformer, which generalizes the de facto standard attention mechanism to spatio-channel attention. We replace the context model of a modern compression framework with the Contextformer and test it on the widely used Kodak, CLIC2020, and Tecnick image datasets. Our experimental results show that the proposed model provides up to 11% rate savings compared to the standard Versatile Video Coding (VVC) Test Model (VTM) 16.2, and outperforms various learning-based models in terms of PSNR and MS-SSIM.

Keywords: Context model · Learned image compression · Transformers

1 Introduction

Recent works in learned image compression outperform hand-engineered classical algorithms such as JPEG [46] and BPG [8], and even reach the rate-distortion performance of recent versions of video coding standards, such as VVC [1]. The most successful learning-based methods use an autoencoder based on [6,33],

Supplementary Information The online version contains supplementary material available at https://doi.org/10.1007/978-3-031-19800-7_26.

where the entropy of the latent elements is modeled and minimized jointly with an image distortion metric. The entropy modeling relies on two principles – backward and forward adaptation [3]. The former employs a hyperprior estimator utilizing a signaled information source. The latter implements a context model, where previously decoded symbols are used for entropy estimation without a need for signaling. Due to its efficiency, a wide variety of context model architectures were explored in the recent literature [20, 32–34, 38, 39, 52]. We categorize those architectures into the following groups w.r.t. their targets: (1) increased support for spatial dependencies; (2) exploitation of cross-channel dependencies; (3) increased context-adaptivity in the entropy estimation. For instance, we consider the methods such as [13, 14, 26, 52] in the first category since those methods aim to capture long distant relations in the latent space. The 3D context [11, 31, 32] and channel-wise autoregressive context model [34] fall in the second category. In those works, entropy estimation of each latent element can also use information from the spatially co-located elements of previously coded channels. In [34] the authors show that entropy estimation, which mainly relies on cross-channel dependencies, outperforms their previous spatial-only model [33]. Most often, the context models use non-adaptive masked convolutions [29]. Those are location-agnostic [29], i.e., the same kernel is applied to each latent position, which potentially reduces the model performance. Even for a larger kernel size, the performance return is marginal, as only a small set of spatial relations between symbols can be utilized. [20, 39] propose an adaptive context model, where the selection of latent elements to be used is based on pairwise similarities between previously decoded elements. Furthermore, [38] uses a transformer-based context model to achieve context adaptivity for the spatial dimensions. However, those models have limited context adaptivity, as they are partially or not applying adaptive modeling for the cross-channel elements. For instance, in [20], although the primary channel carries on average 60% of the information, the context model does not employ any adaptive mechanism for modeling it.

Attention is a widely used deep learning technique that allows the network to focus on relevant parts of the input and suppress the unrelated ones [36]. In contrast to convolutional networks, attention-based models such as transformers [45] provide a large degree of input adaptivity due to their dynamic receptive field [35]. This makes them a promising candidate for a high-performance context model. Following the success of transformers in various computer vision tasks [10, 16, 17, 22, 38], we propose a transformer-based context model, *Contextformer*. Our contribution is threefold: (1) We propose a variant of the Contextformer, which adaptively exploits long-distance spatial relations in the latent tensor; (2) We extend the Contextformer towards a generalized context model, which can also capture cross-channel relations; (3) We present algorithmic methods to reduce the runtime of our model without requiring additional training.

In terms of PSNR, our model outperforms a variety of learning-based models, as well as VTM 16.2 [43] by a significant margin of 6.9%–10.5% in average bits saving on the Kodak [18], CLIC2020 [44] and Tecnick [2] image datasets. We also show that our model provides better performance than the previous works in a perceptual quality-based metric MS-SSIM [47].

2 Related Work

2.1 Learned Image Compression

Presently, the state-of-the-art in lossy image compression frameworks is fundamentally a combination of variational autoencoders and transform coding [19], where the classical linear transformations are replaced with learned nonlinear transformation blocks, e.g., convolutional neural networks [3]. The encoder applies an analysis transform $g_a(x; \phi)$ mapping the input image x to its latent representation y. This transform serves as dimensionality reduction. The latent representation y is quantized by $Q(\cdot)$ and is encoded into the bitstream. In order to obtain the reconstructed image $\hat{x}$, the decoder reads the quantized latent $\hat{y}$ from the bitstream and applies the synthesis transform $g_s(\hat{y}; \theta)$, which is an approximate inverse of $g_a(\cdot)$.

Aiming to reduce the remaining coding redundancy in latent space, Ballé et al. [5] introduced the factorized density model, which estimates the symbol distribution by using local histograms. During training, a joint optimization is applied to minimize both the symbol entropy and the distortion between the original and the reconstructed image. Knowledge of the probability distribution and coding methods such as arithmetic coding [40] allows for efficient lossless compression of $\hat{y}$. Later, Ballé et al. [6] proposed using a hyperprior, which employs additional analysis and systhesis transforms $h_{a/s}(\cdot)$ and helps with modeling of the distribution $p_{\hat{y}}(\hat{y}|\hat{z})$ conditioned on the side information $\hat{z}$. The side information is modeled with a factorized density model, whereas $p_{\hat{y}}(\hat{y}|\hat{z})$ is modeled as a Gaussian distribution. Their proposed framework can be formulated as

$$\hat{y} = Q(g_a(x; \phi)), \tag{1}$$
$$\hat{x} = g_s(\hat{y}; \theta)), \tag{2}$$
$$\hat{z} = Q(h_a(\hat{y}; \phi_h)), \tag{3}$$
$$p_{\hat{y}}(\hat{y}|\hat{z}) \leftarrow h_s(\hat{z}; \theta_h), \tag{4}$$

and the loss function $\mathcal{L}$ of end-to-end training is

$$\mathcal{L}(\phi, \theta, \phi_h, \theta_h, \psi) = \mathbf{R}(\hat{y}) + \mathbf{R}(\hat{z}) + \lambda \cdot \mathbf{D}(x, \hat{x}) \tag{5}$$
$$= \mathbb{E}[\log_2(p_{\hat{y}}(\hat{y}|\hat{z}))] + \mathbb{E}[\log_2(p_{\hat{z}}(\hat{z}|\psi))] + \lambda \cdot \mathbf{D}(x, \hat{x}), \tag{6}$$

where ϕ, θ, ϕ_h and θ_h are the optimization parameters and ψ denotes the parameters of the factorized density model $p_{\hat{z}}(\hat{z}|\psi)$. λ is the Lagrange multiplier regulating the trade-off between rate $\mathbf{R}(\cdot)$ and distortion $\mathbf{D}(\cdot)$.

2.2   Context Model

Higher compression performance requires more accurate entropy models, which would need an increased amount of side information [33]. To overcome this limitation, Minnen et al. [33] proposed a context model, which estimates the entropy of current latent element $\hat{y}_i$ using the previously coded elements. Their approach extends Eq. (4) to

$$p_{\hat{y}_i}(\hat{y}_i|\hat{z}) \leftarrow g_{ep}(g_{cm}(\hat{y}_{<i}; \boldsymbol{\theta}_{cm}), h_s(\hat{z}; \boldsymbol{\theta}_h); \boldsymbol{\theta}_{ep}), \tag{7}$$

where the context model $g_{cm}(\cdot)$ is implemented as a 2D masked convolution. $g_{ep}(\cdot)$ computes the entropy parameters and $\hat{y}_{<i}$ denotes the previously coded local neighbors of current latent element $\hat{y}_i$. Their proposed 2D context model requires 8.4% fewer bits than BPG [8].

Further improvements of the context model have been proposed (see Figs. 1a to e). In [13,14,52] a multi-scale context model was implemented, which employs multiple masked convolutions with different kernel sizes in order to learn various spatial dependencies simultaneously. [11,31,32] employ 3D masked convolutions in order to exploit cross-channel correlations jointly with the spatial ones.

Minnen and Singh proposed a channel-wise autoregressive context model [34]. It splits the channels of the latent tensor into segments and codes each segment sequentially with the help of a previously coded segment. This reduces the sequential steps and outperforms the 2D context model of [33]. However, this approach uses only cross-channel correlations and omits the spatial ones.

Qian et al. [39] proposed a context model, which combines 2D masked convolutions with template matching to increase the receptive field and provide context adaptivity. They search for a similar patch in the previously coded positions and use the best match as a global reference for the entropy model.

Guo et al. [20] proposed a context model, which can be seen as an extension of [39]. In their approach, the channels of the latent tensor are split into two segments. The first segment is coded with a 2D masked convolution, similar to [34]. Coding of the second segment is done using two different mechanisms: MaskConv+, an "improved" version of the 2D masked convolutions, and a global prediction. Additional to the local neighbors, MaskConv+ uses the spatially co-located elements from the first segment. The global prediction is made by calculating the similarity between all elements from the first segment. The indices of the top k similar elements (from the corresponding position in the first segment) are used to select elements in the second segment and include those in the entropy model. They reported average bits savings of 5.1% over VTM 8.0 [43].

Qian et al. [38] replaced the CNN-based hyperprior and context model with a transformer-based one which increased the adaptivity of the entropy model. They proposed two architectures for their context model – serial and parallel model. The serial model processes the latent tensor sequentially similar to [33]. The parallel one uses the checkboard like grouping prosed in [21] to increase the decoding speed. They achieved competitive performance with some of the CNN-based methods such as [12].

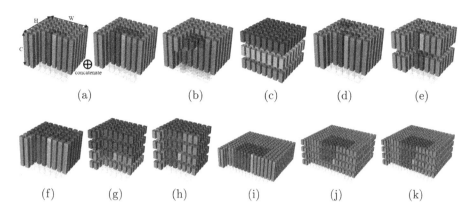

Fig. 1. Illustration of the latent elements used by the context model (■) to estimate the entropy of the current latent (■) in (a– e) for the prior-arts and (f– k) our proposed context model. Previously coded and yet to be coded elements are displayed as (■) and (■), respectively. The displayed prior-art models are (a) multi-scale 2D context [13,14,52], (b) 3D context [11,31,32], (c) channel-wise autoregressive context [34], (d) 2D context with global reference [39], and (e) context with advanced global reference [20]. Note that in (c) each (■) is coded simultaneously by using only a part of the elements presented as (■), and in (e), the primary channel segment is shown at the bottom for better visibility. Our models with different configurations are shown in (f) Contextformer(N_{cs}=1), (g) Contextformer(N_{cs}>1, sfo), (h) Contextformer(N_{cs}>1, cfo). Note that the (serial) transformer-based context model of [38] employs similar mechanism as (f). (i– k) show the versions of our models (f– h) using the sliding window attention. (Color figure online)

2.3   Transformers

Self-attention is an attention mechanism originally proposed for natural language processing [45]. Later, it was adopted in various computer vision tasks, where it outperformed its convolutional counterparts [10,16,17,22].

The general concept of a transformer is as follows. First, an input representation with S sequential elements is mapped into three different representations, query $\boldsymbol{Q} \in \mathbb{R}^{S \times d_q}$, key $\boldsymbol{K} \in \mathbb{R}^{S \times d_k}$ and value $\boldsymbol{V} \in \mathbb{R}^{S \times d_v}$ with separate linear transformations. Then, the attention module dynamically routes the queries with the key-value pairs by applying a scaled dot-product. The attention module is followed by a point-wise multi-layer perceptron (MLP). Additionally, the multi-head attention splits the queries, keys, and values into h sub-representations (so-called heads), and for each head, the attention is calculated separately. The final attention is computed by combining each sub-attention with a learned transformation ($\boldsymbol{W}$). The multi-head attention enables parallelization and each intermediate representation to build multiple relationships.

To preserve coding causality in autoregressive tasks, the attention mechanism has to be limited by a mask for subsequent elements not coded yet. The masked multi-head attention can be formulated as:

$$Attn(\boldsymbol{Q}, \boldsymbol{K}, \boldsymbol{V}) = \text{concat}(head_1, \ldots, head_h)\boldsymbol{W}, \tag{8}$$

$$head_i(\boldsymbol{Q}_i, \boldsymbol{K}_i, \boldsymbol{V}_i) = \text{softmax}\left(\frac{\boldsymbol{Q}_i \boldsymbol{K}_i^T}{d_k} \odot \boldsymbol{M}\right) \boldsymbol{V}_i, \tag{9}$$

where $\boldsymbol{Q}_i \in \mathbb{R}^{S \times \frac{d_q}{h}}$, $\boldsymbol{K}_i \in \mathbb{R}^{S \times \frac{d_k}{h}}$ and $\boldsymbol{V}_i \in \mathbb{R}^{S \times \frac{d_v}{h}}$ are the sub-representations, the mask $\boldsymbol{M} \in \mathbb{R}^{S \times S}$ has ones in its lower triangle and the rest of its values are minus infinity, and $\odot$ stands for the Hadamard product.

3   Our Approach

In this section, we introduce our transformer-based context model, *Contextformer*, which provides context adaptivity and utilizes distant spatial relations in the latent tensor. We present two versions of the model: a simple version, which uses spatial attention; and a more advanced version, which employs attention both in the spatial and channel dimensions for entropy modeling.

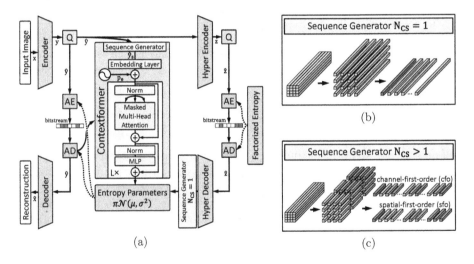

Fig. 2. Illustration of (a) our proposed model with the Contextformer, (b) sequence generator for the Contextformer with spatial attention, Contextformer(N_{cs}=1), and (c) sequence generator for the Contextformer with spatio-channel attention, Contextformer(N_{cs}>1). The prepended start token is shown in dark gray in (b-c). Inspired by [27], we use channel-wise local hyperprior neighbors to increase performance; thus, regardless of the selected N_{cs}, we apply the sequence generator depicted in (b) to the output of the hyperdecoder. (Color figure online)

3.1 Contextformer with Spatial Attention

The proposed Contextformer builds on top of the architecture introduced in [14]. In the encoder, this model employs 3×3 convolution layers with GDN activation function [4] and residual non-local attention modules (RNAB) [50]. The structure of the decoder is very similar to the one of the encoder, with the exception that residual blocks (ResBlock) [11] are used in the first layer to enlarge the receptive field. Additionally, the model adopts a hyperprior network, the multi-scale context model [52] and the universal quantization [53]. This model estimates the distribution $p_{\hat{y}}(\hat{y}|\hat{z})$ with a single Gaussian distribution. In our approach, we use a Gaussian mixture model [12] with 3 mixture components k_m, which is known to increase the accuracy of the entropy model.

In contrast to Cui et al. [14], we use a Contextformer instead of their multi-scale context model, as shown in Fig. 2a. First, the latent $\hat{y} \in \mathbb{R}^{H \times W \times C}$ is rearranged into a sequence of spatial patches $\hat{y}_s \in \mathbb{R}^{\frac{HW}{p_h p_w} \times (p_h p_w C)}$. Here, H, W and C stand for the height, width and number of channels; (p_h, p_w) corresponds to the shape of each patch. Usually, patch-wise processing reduces complexity, especially for large images [16]. However, the latent $\hat{y}$ already has a 16 times lower resolution than the input image, which makes learning an efficient context model harder and leads to a performance drop. To remedy this issue, we set the patch size to 1×1, so each sequential element corresponds to one pixel in the latent tensor (see Fig. 2b).

The Contextformer has L transformer layers with a similar architecture to that of ViT [16]. Each layer requires an intermediate tensor with an embedding size of d_e. Therefore, we apply a learnable linear transformation $\mathbb{R}^{HW \times C} \rightarrow \mathbb{R}^{HW \times d_e}$ (embedding layer). In order to introduce permutation-variance, we add a learned position encoding similar to the one in [16,17], but we apply it to the first layer only. We prepend the latent sequence $\hat{y}_s$ with a zero-valued start token to ensure the causality of coding. We use masking in the attention as described in Eq. (9), and multi-head attention with 12 heads. Multi-head allows our model to independently focus on different channel segments of $\hat{y}$.

3.2 Contextformer with Spatio-Channel Attention

Although multi-head attention is computationally efficient in handling cross-channel dependencies, it can explore relationships in a single channel only partially. For example, consider a Contextformer with a single transformer layer. Given a latent tensor $\hat{y} \in \mathbb{R}^{H \times W \times C}$ and its sequential representation $\hat{y}_s \in \mathbb{R}^{S \times C}$; the n-th sub-representation of the sequence $\hat{y}_s(n, h_i) \in \mathbb{R}^{1 \times \frac{C}{h}}$ can only attend to the previous representations $\hat{y}_s(<n, h_i)$ with the same head index h_i. This means that the attention between different channel segments is not considered. Another limitation arises from the way the model behaves w.r.t. $\hat{y}$. For modeling the entropy of latent element $\hat{y}(i, j, c)$ (with spatial coordinates (i, j) and channel index c), the context model cannot access information from the spatially co-located elements from other channels $\hat{y}(i, j, \neq c)$. This limits exploiting the cross-channel dependencies in $\hat{y}$, and, therefore, the performance of the model.

To remedy this issue, we generate spatio-channel patches in the latent space $\hat{\mathbf{y}}_s \in \mathbb{R}^{\frac{HWC}{p_h p_w p_c} \times (p_h p_w p_c)}$, where p_c corresponds to the size of each channel segment, and total number of channel segments is $N_{cs} = \frac{C}{p_c}$. In a special case of $(p_h, p_w) = (H, W)$, our patch generation method is similar to the slicing method in channel-wise context modeling [34], but our model has a multi-head attention added. In this work, we set p_h and p_w to 1 as already discussed in Sect. 3.1. Splitting the latent tensor into multiple channel segments enables two different coding methods, spatial-first-order (sfo) and channel-first-order (cfo). The first method prioritizes the spatial dimensions and codes all latent elements from a channel segment sequentially before starting with the next segment. The second method prioritizes the channel dimension, and codes all channel segments with the same spatial coordinate sequentially, before coding elements from the next spatial coordinate.

Spatio-channel sequence generation allows the standard transformer to use channel attention, from which a generalized context model can be obtained. To illustrate this, we compare how dependencies in the latent space are handled by Contextformer for various N_{cs}, and how those dependencies are handled by context models in the prior-art.

In case of $N_{cs} = 1$. The attention is limited to a spatial one (see Sect. 3.1). However, such a model provides faster encoding and decoding due to the smaller number of required autoregressive steps and still has better performance than some models in the prior-arts. As illustrated in Fig. 1f, Contextformer ($N_{cs} = 1$) has a larger receptive field than [13,14,52], and also employs learned context adaptivity. Additionally, in [39] the receptive field is limited to a single reference and its neighboring latent elements, whereas Contextformer ($N_{cs} = 1$)'s receptive field is dynamic and theoretically unlimited. Notably, the serial model of [38] (best performing one) uses a similar context model as Contextformer ($N_{cs} = 1$). However, their model has only a sparse-attention mechanism, whereas Contextformer employs the full attention mechanism.

In case of $C \geq N_{cs} > 1$. We achieve a context model that can exploit both spatial and cross-channel dependencies. As shown in Figs. 1g and 1h, both Contextformers ($N_{cs} > 1$) with different coding order handle spatio-channel relationships. Moreover, in [20] only non-primary channel segments could be selected for entropy estimation, while the receptive field of the Contextformer's receptive field can adapt to cover every channel segment. Compared to [38], the Contextformer ($N_{cs} > 1$) provides a more adaptive context model due to the spatio-channel attention. In the extreme case $N_{cs} = C$, the model employs the spatio-channel attention to its full extend by computing the attention between every single latent element. Other implementations can be seen as a simplification of the extreme case for balancing the trade-off between performance and complexity. The Contextformer ($N_{cs} = C$) can be regarded as a 3D context model with a large and adaptive receptive field.

3.3   Handling High-Resolution Images

Although the receptive field size of the Contextformer is theoretically unlimited, computing attention for long input sequences, e.g., high resolution images, is not feasible due to the quadratic increase of memory requirement and computational complexity with increasing the length of the input sequence. Therefore, we have to limit the receptive field of our model and use sliding-window attention as described in [17,37]. Inspired by 3D convolutions, we implemented a 3D sliding-window to traverse the spatio-channel array. Unlike 3D convolutions, the receptive field only slides across spatial dimensions and expands to encompass all elements in the channel dimension. In Figs. 1i to k one can see the sliding-window attention mechanism for various Contextformer variants. For computational efficiency, during training, we used fixed-sized image patches and omitted the sliding-window operations. During inference, we set the size of the receptive field according to the sequence length (HWN_{cs}) used for training.

3.4   Runtime Optimization

Generally, autoregressive processes cannot be efficiently implemented on a GPU due to their serialized nature [21,26,34]. One commonly used approach [15,45] is to pad a set of sequences to have a fixed length, thus enabling the processing of multiple sequences in parallel during training (we refer to this method as Pad&Batch). A straightforward implementation of the sliding-window attention uses dynamic sequence lengths for every position of the window. We call this *dynamic sequence* processing (DS). The padding technique can be combined with the sliding-window by applying masking to the attention mechanism. However, one still needs to calculate attention for each padded element, which creates a bottleneck for the batched processing.

   We propose a more efficient algorithm to parallelize the sliding-window attention. The first step of the algorithm calculates the processing order (or *priority*) for every position of the sliding window and then groups the positions with the same processing order for batch processing. One possible processing order is to follow the number of elements in each window and process them from the smallest to the largest number of elements. We refer to this method as Batched Dynamic Sequence (BDS). Note that transformers are sequence-to-sequence models; they simultaneously compute an output for each element in a sliding window and preserve causality of the sequence due to the masking. Therefore, we can skip computation of intermediate channel segments and calculate the output of the last channel segment for each spatial coordinate of the sliding window, which we refer to as skipping intermediate channel segments (SCS). It is worth mentioning that both the BDS and SCS methods can only be applied in the encoder, where all elements of the latent tensor are simultaneously accessible. For the decoder-side runtime optimization, we adopted the wavefront coding described in [30], which is similar to the partitioning slices used in VVC [42]. We use the same processing priority to the independent sliding windows along the same diagonal, which allows for simultaneous decoding of those windows. More information about the proposed runtime optimization algorithms can be found in the supplementary materials.

4 Implementation Details

We present a few variants of the Contextformer by changing its parameters $\{L, d_e, N_{cs}, co\}$, where L, d_e and N_{cs} correspond to number of layers, embedding size and number of channel segments, and co corresponds to the coding order – either spatial-first (sfo) or channel-first (cfo). For all models, we used the same number of heads h and MLP size of d_{mlp}. We selected the base configuration of the Contextformer as $\{L=8, d_e=384, d_{mlp}=4d_e, h=12, N_{cs}=4, co=cfo\}$. More information about the architectural details can be found in the suplementary materials.

For training of all variants, we used random 256×256 image crops from the Vimeo-90K dataset [49], batch size of 16, and ADAM optimizer [25] with the default settings. We trained our models for 120 epochs ($\sim$1.2M iterations). Following [7], we used the initial learning rate of 10^{-4} and reduced it by half every time the validation loss is nearly constant for 20 epochs. For this purpose, we used the validation set of Vimeo-90K. We selected mean-squared-error (MSE) as the distortion metric $\mathbf{D}(\cdot)$ and trained a set of models with $\lambda \in \{0.002, 0.004, 0.007, 0,014, 0.026, 0.034, 0.070\}$ to cover various bitrates. We also obtained models optimized for MS-SSIM [48] by finetuning the models trained for MSE, in the same fashion for $\sim$500K iterations. By default, we selected both intermediate layer size N of the encoder and decoder, and bottleneck size M as 192. To increase the model capacity at the high target bitrates ($\lambda_{5,6,7}$), we increased M from 192 to 312 by following the common practice [12,33,34].

5 Experimental Results

Unless specified otherwise, we used the base configuration (see Sect. 4) and tested its performance on the Kodak image dataset [18]. We set the spatial receptive field size to 16×16 for the sliding-window attention. We compared the performance with the following models: the 2D context models by Minnen et al. [33] and Cheng et al. [12], the multi-scale 2D context model by Cui et al. [14], the channel-wise autoregressive context model by Minnen and Singh [34], the context model with an advanced global reference by Guo et al. [20], and the transformer-based context model by Qian et al. [38]. When the source was available, we ran the inference algorithms of those methods; in other cases, we took the results from the corresponding publications. For a fair comparison, we used the model from [20] without the GRDN post-filter [24]. Similarly, we used the serial model from [38], since it performs better and is more related to our approach. We also compared with the results achieved by classical compression algorithms such as BPG [8] and VTM 16.2 [43]. In order to test the generalization capability of our model, we also tested its performance on CLIC2020 [44], and Tecnick [2] datasets. Additionally, we present the impact of different configurations of our model on its complexity. More details about the performance comparison, and examples of compression artifacts can be found in the supplementary materials.

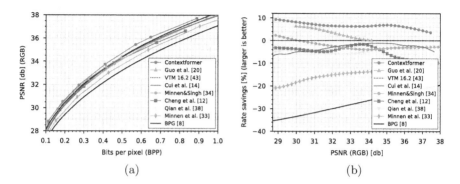

Fig. 3. Illustration of (a) the rate-distortion performance and (b) the rate savings relative to VTM 16.2 as a function of PSNR on the Kodak dataset showing the performance of our model compared to various learning-based and classical codecs.

Performance. In Fig. 3a we show the rate-distortion performance of the Contextformer with a spatio-channel attention mechanism and the comparative performance of prior methods on the Kodak image dateset. Our method qualitatively surpasses the rest in terms of PSNR for all rate points under test. According to the Bjøntegaard Delta rate (BD-Rate) [9], our method achieves average saving of 6.9% over VTM 16.2, while the model in [20] provides 3.7% saving over the same baseline. On average, our model saves 10% more bits compared to the multi-scale 2D context model in [14]. Notably, the only difference between our model and the one in [14] is the context and entropy modeling, and both methods have similar model sizes. The performance of our method and the prior in terms of the generalized BD-Rate metric [34] is shown in Fig. 3b. Our model achieves state-of-the-art performance by reaching 9.3% rate savings for low bitrate and 4% rate savings at the highest quality over VTM 16.2.

We also evaluated our model optimized for MS-SSIM [48]. Figure 4 shows that our model also outperforms previous methods for this perceptual quality metric. On average, our models saves 8.7% more bits than Cheng et al. [12].

Generalization Capability. In order to show the generalization capability, we also evaluated our Contexformer on CLIC2020-Professional and -Mobile [44], and Tecnick [2] datasets. In terms of BD-Rate [9], our model achieves average savings of 9.8%, 5.8%, and 10.5% over VTM 16.2 on those datasets, respectively (see Fig. 6). Evaluating on the generalized BD-Rate metric [34] reveals that our method provides up to 11.9% and 6.6% relative bit savings over VTM 16.2 on CLIC2020-Professional and -Mobile datasets. On Tecnick dataset, the Contextformer saves up to 12.4% more bits over VTM 16.2.

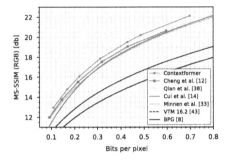

Fig. 4. Illustration of the rate-distortion performance in terms of MS-SSIM on Kodak dataset showing the performance of our model compared to various learning-based and classical codecs. All learned methods were optimized for MS-SSIM.

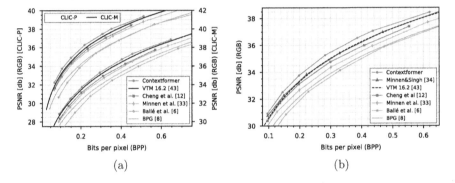

Fig. 5. Comparison of the rate-distortion performance (a) on CLIC2020-Professional (solid line, left vertical axis) and CLIC2020-Mobile (dashed line, right vertical axis) datasets, and (b) on Tecnick dataset.

Contextformer Variants. In Fig. 6a we show the performance of our model for a varying number of channel segments N_{cs} and coding order. From the figure, one can see that increasing the number of channel segments increases the performance of the model since having more channel segments allows the models to explore more of the cross-channel dependencies. However, there is a trade-off between the number of segments and the complexity – the computational cost increases quadratically with raising N_{cs}. According to our observations, training the Contextformer with more than four segments increases training complexity too much to justify the minor performance gains.

On average, the Contextformer (cfo) outperforms the same model in a spatial-first-order (sfo) configuration, which highlights the greater importance of cross-channel dependencies than the spatial ones. For instance, in the Contextformer (sfo), the primary channel segment can only adopt spatial attention due to the coding order. In Fig. 6b we show the distribution of information in each channel segment. The Contextformer (cfo) stores more than 70% of all informa-

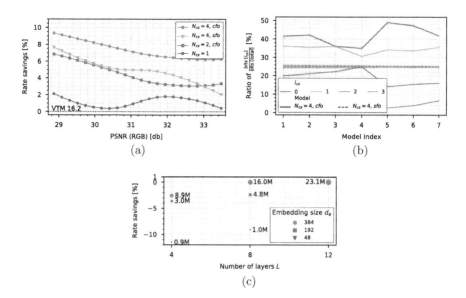

Fig. 6. Various ablation studies conducted with the Contextformer on Kodak dataset. (a) illustrates the rate savings relative to VTM 16.2 for the Contextformer with different number of channel segments N_{cs} and coding order. In (b), the percentile bit occupation per channel segment is shown for models with different coding orders. Each model index depicts a model trained for a specific λ. Notably, increasing the model capacity allocates more bits in the first two segments for cfo variant. (c) is the illustration of the average BD-Rate performance of various model sizes relative to base model. The annotations indicate the total number of entropy and context model parameters.

tion in the first two channel segments, while in Contextformer(sfo) the information is almost equally distributed along with the segments. We observed that the spatial-first coding provides a marginal gain in low target bitrates ($bpp < 0.3$) and images with a uniformly distributed texture such as "kodim02" (in Kodak image dataset). This suggests that spatial dependencies become more pronounced in smoother images.

Model Size. Figure 6c shows the performance of the Contextformers for different model sizes compared to the base configuration. Change in the network depth L and embedding size d_e have similar effects on the performance, whereas best performance can be achieved when both are increased. However, we observed that the return diminishes after a network depth of 8 layers. Since the base model already achieves state-of-the-art performance and further upscaling of models increases the complexity, we did not experiment with larger models. Note that the proposed network of [14], which our model is based on, has approximately the same total number of entropy and context model parameters (17M) as our base model, whereas our model shows additionally 10.1% BD-Rate coding gain on Kodak dataset.

Runtime Complexity. Table 1 shows the encoding and decoding complexity of our model, some of the learning based- prior arts and VTM [43]. We tested the learning-based methods on a single NVIDIA Titan RTX, and ran the VTM [43] on Intel Core i9-10980XE Intel Core i9-10980XE. In our model, we used proposed BDS and SCS optimizations in the encoder and wavefront coding in the decoder. For low resolution images, our methods have close performance to the one of the 3D context. For 4K images, we observed even bigger benefits by the parallelization. The relative encoding time increases only 3x w.r.t. the one on the Kodak dataset, while the increase in number of pixels is 20-fold. Such speed-up shows that encoder methods with online rate-distortion optimization such as [51] have unexplored potential. Moreover, we achieve 9x faster decoding compared to a 3D context model with the proposed wavefront coding.

Table 1. Encoding and decoding time of different compression frameworks.

Method	Enc. Time [s]		Dec. Time [s]	
	Kodak	4K	Kodak	4K
DS	56	1240	62	1440
BDS (ours)	32	600	–	–
BDS&SCS (ours)	8	120	–	–
Wavefront (ours)	40	760	44	820
3D context [11]	4	28	316	7486
2D context [12]	2	54	6	140
VTM 16.2 [43]	420	950	0.8	2.5

6   Conclusion

In this work, we explored learned image compression architectures using a transformer-based context model. We proposed a context model that utilizes a multi-head attention mechanism and uses spatial dependencies in the latent space to model the entropy. Additionally, we also proposed a more generalized attention mechanism, spatio-channel attention, which can constitute a powerful context model. We showed that a compression architecture that employs the spatio-channel attention model achieves state-of-the-art rate-distortion performance.

While using an entropy model with spatio-channel attention brings noticeable gain, it also increases the runtime complexity. We addressed this issue by proposing an algorithm for efficient modeling while keeping the architecture unchanged. Future work will further investigate efficient attention mechanisms (e.g., [23,28,41]) aiming to bridge the gap to a real-time operation.

References

1. Versatile Video Coding. Standard, Rec. ITU-T H.266 and ISO/IEC 23090-3 (2020)
2. Asuni, N., Giachetti, A.: Testimages: a large-scale archive for testing visual devices and basic image processing algorithms. In: STAG, pp. 63–70 (2014)
3. Ballé, J., Chou, P.A., Minnen, D., Singh, S., Johnston, N., Agustsson, E., Hwang, S.J., Toderici, G.: Nonlinear transform coding. IEEE Journal of Selected Topics in Signal Processing 15(2), 339–353 (2020)
4. Ballé, J., Laparra, V., Simoncelli, E.P.: Density modeling of images using a generalized normalization transformation. In: 4th International Conference on Learning Representations, ICLR 2016 (2016)
5. Ballé, J., Laparra, V., Simoncelli, E.P.: End-to-end optimized image compression. In: 5th International Conference on Learning Representations, ICLR 2017 (2017)
6. Ballé, J., Minnen, D., Singh, S., Hwang, S.J., Johnston, N.: Variational image compression with a scale hyperprior. In: International Conference on Learning Representations (2018)
7. Bégaint, J., Racapé, F., Feltman, S., Pushparaja, A.: Compressai: a pyTorch library and evaluation platform for end-to-end compression research. arXiv preprint arXiv:2011.03029 (2020)
8. Bellard, F.: BPG image format (2015). Accessed 01 Jun 2022. https://bellard.org/bpg
9. Bjontegaard, G.: Calculation of average PSNR differences between RD-curves. VCEG-M33 (2001)
10. Carion, Nicolas, Massa, Francisco, Synnaeve, Gabriel, Usunier, Nicolas, Kirillov, Alexander, Zagoruyko, Sergey: End-to-end object detection with transformers. In: Vedaldi, Andrea, Bischof, Horst, Brox, Thomas, Frahm, Jan-Michael. (eds.) ECCV 2020. LNCS, vol. 12346, pp. 213–229. Springer, Cham (2020). https://doi.org/10.1007/978-3-030-58452-8_13
11. Chen, T., Liu, H., Ma, Z., Shen, Q., Cao, X., Wang, Y.: End-to-end learnt image compression via non-local attention optimization and improved context modeling. IEEE Transactions on Image Processing 30, 3179–3191 (2021). DOI: https://doi.org/10.1109/TIP.2021.3058615
12. Cheng, Z., Sun, H., Takeuchi, M., Katto, J.: Learned image compression with discretized gaussian mixture likelihoods and attention modules. In: Proceedings of the IEEE/CVF Conference on Computer Vision and Pattern Recognition, pp. 7939–7948 (2020)
13. Cui, Z., Wang, J., Bai, B., Guo, T., Feng, Y.: G-VAE: A continuously variable rate deep image compression framework. arXiv preprint arXiv:2003.02012 (2020)
14. Cui, Z., Wang, J., Gao, S., Guo, T., Feng, Y., Bai, B.: Asymmetric gained deep image compression with continuous rate adaptation. In: Proceedings of the IEEE/CVF Conference on Computer Vision and Pattern Recognition, pp. 10532–10541 (2021)
15. Devlin, J., Chang, M.W., Lee, K., Toutanova, K.: BERT: Pre-training of deep bidirectional transformers for language understanding. In: Proceedings of the 2019 Conference of the North American Chapter of the Association for Computational Linguistics: Human Language Technologies, vol.1 (Long and Short Papers), pp. 4171–4186. Association for Computational Linguistics, Minneapolis, Minnesota (2019). https://doi.org/10.18653/v1/N19-1423
16. Dosovitskiy, A., et al.: An image is worth 16x16 words: transformers for image recognition at scale. In: International Conference on Learning Representations (2020)

17. Esser, P., Rombach, R., Ommer, B.: Taming transformers for high-resolution image synthesis. In: Proceedings of the IEEE/CVF Conference on Computer Vision and Pattern Recognition, pp. 12873–12883 (2021)
18. Franzen, R.: Kodak lossless true color image suite (1999)
19. Goyal, V.K.: Theoretical foundations of transform coding. IEEE Signal Processing Magazine 18(5), 9–21 (2001)
20. Guo, Z., Zhang, Z., Feng, R., Chen, Z.: Causal contextual prediction for learned image compression. IEEE Transactions on Circuits and Systems for Video Technology (2021)
21. He, D., Zheng, Y., Sun, B., Wang, Y., Qin, H.: Checkerboard context model for efficient learned image compression. In: Proceedings of the IEEE/CVF Conference on Computer Vision and Pattern Recognition, pp. 14771–14780 (2021)
22. Jiang, Y., Chang, S., Wang, Z.: TransGAN: two transformers can make one strong gan. arXiv preprint arXiv:2102.07074 (2021)
23. Katharopoulos, A., Vyas, A., Pappas, N., Fleuret, F.: Transformers are RNNs: fast autoregressive transformers with linear attention. In: III, H.D., Singh, A. (eds.) Proceedings of the 37th International Conference on Machine Learning. Proceedings of Machine Learning Research, 13–18 Jul 2020, vol. 119, pp. 5156–5165. PMLR (2020). https://proceedings.mlr.press/v119/katharopoulos20a.html
24. Kim, D.W., Chung, J.R., Jung, S.W.: GRDN: grouped residual dense network for real image denoising and gan-based real-world noise modeling. In: Proceedings of the IEEE/CVF Conference on Computer Vision and Pattern Recognition Workshops (2019)
25. Kingma, D.P., Ba, J.: Adam: a method for stochastic optimization. arXiv preprint arXiv:1412.6980 (2014)
26. Koyuncu, A.B., Cui, K., Boev, A., Steinbach, E.: Parallelized context modeling for faster image coding. In: 2021 International Conference on Visual Communications and Image Processing (VCIP), pp. 1–5. IEEE (2021)
27. Lee, J., Cho, S., Beack, S.K.: Context-adaptive entropy model for end-to-end optimized image compression. In: 6th International Conference on Learning Representations, ICLR 2018 (2018)
28. Lee-Thorp, J., Ainslie, J., Eckstein, I., Ontanon, S.: FNet: mixing tokens with Fourier transforms. arXiv preprint arXiv:2105.03824 (2021)
29. Li, D., et al.: Involution: inverting the inherence of convolution for visual recognition. In: Proceedings of the IEEE/CVF Conference on Computer Vision and Pattern Recognition, pp. 12321–12330 (2021)
30. Li, M., Ma, K., You, J., Zhang, D., Zuo, W.: Efficient and effective context-based convolutional entropy modeling for image compression. IEEE Transactions on Image Processing 29, 5900–5911 (2020). DOI: 10.1109/TIP.2020.2985225
31. Liu, H., Chen, T., Shen, Q., Ma, Z.: Practical stacked non-local attention modules for image compression. In: CVPR Workshops (2019)
32. Mentzer, F., Agustsson, E., Tschannen, M., Timofte, R., Van Gool, L.: Conditional probability models for deep image compression. In: Proceedings of the IEEE Conference on Computer Vision and Pattern Recognition, pp. 4394–4402 (2018)
33. Minnen, D., Ballé, J., Toderici, G.: Joint autoregressive and hierarchical priors for learned image compression. In: NeurIPS (2018)
34. Minnen, D., Singh, S.: Channel-wise autoregressive entropy models for learned image compression. In: 2020 IEEE International Conference on Image Processing (ICIP), pp. 3339–3343. IEEE (2020)
35. Naseer, M., Ranasinghe, K., Khan, S., Hayat, M., Khan, F.S., Yang, M.H.: Intriguing properties of vision transformers. arXiv preprint arXiv:2105.10497 (2021)

36. Niu, Z., Zhong, G., Yu, H.: A review on the attention mechanism of deep learning. Neurocomputing **452**, 48–62 (2021). https://doi.org/10.1016/j.neucom.2021.03.091. https://www.sciencedirect.com/science/article/pii/S092523122100477X

37. Parmar, N., et al.: Image transformer. In: International Conference on Machine Learning, pp. 4055–4064. PMLR (2018)

38. Qian, Y., Sun, X., Lin, M., Tan, Z., Jin, R.: Entroformer: a transformer-based entropy model for learned image compression. In: International Conference on Learning Representations (2021)

39. Qian, Y., et al.: Learning accurate entropy model with global reference for image compression. In: International Conference on Learning Representations (2020)

40. Rissanen, J., Langdon, G.G.: Arithmetic coding. IBM Journal of research and development 23(2), 149–162 (1979)

41. Roy, A., Saffar, M., Vaswani, A., Grangier, D.: Efficient content-based sparse attention with routing transformers. Transactions of the Association for Computational Linguistics 9, 53–68 (2021)

42. Sullivan, G., Ohm, J., Han, W.J., Wiegand, T.: Overview of the high efficiency video coding standard vol. 22, pp. 1648–1667 (2012)

43. Team, J.V.E.: Versatile video coding (vvc) reference software: Vvc test model (vtm) (2022). Accessed 01 Jun 2022. https://vcgit.hhi.fraunhofer.de/jvet/VVCSoftware/_VTM

44. Toderici, G., et al.: Workshop and challenge on learned image compression (clic2020)

45. Vaswani, A., et al.: Attention is all you need. In: Advances in neural information processing systems, pp. 5998–6008 (2017)

46. Wallace, G.K.: The jpeg still picture compression standard. IEEE Trans. Cons. Electr. **38**(1), xviii-xxxiv (1992)

47. Wang, Z., Simoncelli, E.P., Bovik, A.C.: Multiscale structural similarity for image quality assessment. In: The Thrity-Seventh Asilomar Conference on Signals, Systems & Computers, 2003, vol. 2, pp. 1398–1402. IEEE (2003)

48. Wang, Z., Simoncelli, E.P., Bovik, A.C.: Multiscale structural similarity for image quality assessment. In: The Thrity-Seventh Asilomar Conference on Signals, Systems & Computers, 2003, vol. 2, pp. 1398–1402. IEEE (2003)

49. Xue, T., Chen, B., Wu, J., Wei, D., Freeman, W.T.: Video enhancement with task-oriented flow. International Journal of Computer Vision (IJCV) 127(8), 1106–1125 (2019)

50. Zhang, Y., Li, K., Li, K., Zhong, B., Fu, Y.: Residual non-local attention networks for image restoration. In: International Conference on Learning Representations (2019). https://openreview.net/forum?id=HkeGhoA5FX

51. Zhao, J., Li, B., Li, J., Xiong, R., Lu, Y.: A universal encoder rate distortion optimization framework for learned compression. In: Proceedings of the IEEE/CVF Conference on Computer Vision and Pattern Recognition, pp. 1880–1884 (2021)

52. Zhou, J., Wen, S., Nakagawa, A., Kazui, K., Tan, Z.: Multi-scale and context-adaptive entropy model for image compression. arXiv preprint arXiv:1910.07844 (2019)

53. Ziv, J.: On universal quantization. IEEE Transactions on Information Theory 31(3), 344–347 (1985)

Image Super-Resolution with Deep Dictionary

Shunta Maeda$^{(\boxtimes)}$

Navier Inc., Tokyo, Japan
shunta@navier.co.jp

Abstract. Since the first success of Dong et al., the deep-learning-based approach has become dominant in the field of single-image super-resolution. This replaces all the handcrafted image processing steps of traditional sparse-coding-based methods with a deep neural network. In contrast to sparse-coding-based methods, which explicitly create high/low-resolution dictionaries, the dictionaries in deep-learning-based methods are implicitly acquired as a nonlinear combination of multiple convolutions. One disadvantage of deep-learning-based methods is that their performance is degraded for images created differently from the training dataset (out-of-domain images). We propose an end-to-end super-resolution network with a deep dictionary (SRDD), where a high-resolution dictionary is explicitly learned without sacrificing the advantages of deep learning. Extensive experiments show that explicit learning of high-resolution dictionary makes the network more robust for out-of-domain test images while maintaining the performance of the in-domain test images. Code is available at https://github.com/shuntama/srdd.

Keywords: Super-resolution · Deep dictionary · Sparse representation

1 Introduction

Single-image super-resolution (SISR) is a classical problem in the field of computer vision that predicts a high-resolution (HR) image from its low-resolution (LR) observation. Because this is an ill-posed problem with multiple possible solutions, obtaining a rich prior based on a large number of data points is beneficial for better prediction. Deep learning is quite effective for such problems. The performance of SISR has been significantly improved by using convolutional neural networks (CNN), starting with the pioneering work of Dong et al. in 2014 [9]. Before the dominance of deep-learning-based methods [1,9,10,19,20,23,26,27,41,42,56,57] in this field, example-based methods [4,12,13,16,21,44,45,51,52] were mainly used for learning priors. Among them, sparse coding, which is a representative example-based method, has shown

Supplementary Information The online version contains supplementary material available at https://doi.org/10.1007/978-3-031-19800-7_27.

S. Avidan et al. (Eds.): ECCV 2022, LNCS 13679, pp. 464–480, 2022.
https://doi.org/10.1007/978-3-031-19800-7_27

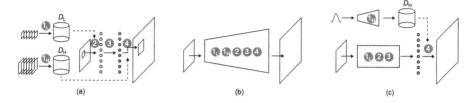

Fig. 1. Schematic illustrations of single image super-resolution with (a) sparse-coding-based approach, (b) conventional deep-learning-based approach, and (c) our approach. The numbers ①-④ indicate each step of the super-resolution process.

state-of-the-art performance [44,45,51]. SISR using sparse coding comprises the following steps, as illustrated in Fig. 1(a): ①$_L$ learn an LR dictionary D_L with patches extracted from LR images, ①$_H$ learn an HR dictionary D_H with patches extracted from HR images, ② represent patches densely cropped from an input image with D_L, ③ map D_L representations to D_H representations, ④ reconstruct HR patches using D_H, then aggregate the overlapped HR patches to produce a final output.

As depicted in Fig. 1(b), Dong et al. [9] replaced all the above handcrafted steps with a multilayered CNN in their proposed method SRCNN to take advantage of the powerful capability of deep learning. Note that, in this method, D_L and D_H are implicitly acquired through network training. Since the SRCNN, various methods have been proposed to improve performance, for example, by deepening the network with residual blocks and skip connections [20,27,41,57], applying attention mechanisms [8,31,34,56], and using a transformer [6,26]. However, most of these studies, including state-of-the-art ones, follow the same formality as SRCNN from a general perspective, where all the processes in the sparse-coding-based methods are replaced by a multilayered network.

One disadvantage of deep-learning-based methods is that their performance is degraded for images created differently from the training dataset [14]. Although there have been several approaches to address this issue, such as training networks for multiple degradations [40,46,49,55,59] and making models agnostic to degradations with iterative optimizations [14,38], it is also important to make the network structure more robust. We hypothesize that D_H implicitly learned inside a multilayered network is fragile to subtle differences in input images from the training time. This hypothesis leads us to the method we propose.

In this study, we propose an end-to-end super-resolution network with a deep dictionary (SRDD), where D_H is explicitly learned through the network training (Fig. 1(c)). The main network predicts the coefficients of D_H and the weighted sum of the elements (or atoms) of D_H produces an HR output. This approach is fundamentally different from the conventional deep-learning-based approach, where the network has upsampling layers inside it. The upsampling process of the proposed method is efficient because the pre-generated D_H can be used as a magnifier for inference. In addition, the main network does not need to maintain the information of the processed image at the pixel level in HR space. Therefore, the network can concentrate only on predicting the coefficients of D_{H}. For in-domain test images, our method shows performance that is not as good as latest ones, but close to the conventional baselines (e.g., CARN). For out-of-domain test images, our method shows superior performance compared to conventional deep-learning-based methods.

2   Related Works

2.1   Sparse-Coding-Based SR

Before the dominance of deep-learning-based methods in the field of SISR, example-based methods showed state-of-the-art performance. The example-based methods exploit internal self-similarity [11,13,16,50] and/or external datasets [4,12,21,44,45,51,52]. The use of external datasets is especially important for obtaining rich prior. In the sparse-coding-based methods [44,45,51,52], which are state-of-the-art example-based methods, high/low-resolution patch pairs are extracted from external datasets to create high/low-resolution dictionaries $D_{\mathrm{H}}/D_{\mathrm{L}}$. The patches cropped from an input image are encoded with D_{L} and then projected onto D_{H} via iterative processing, producing the final output with appropriate patch aggregation.

2.2   Deep-Learning-Based SR

Deep CNN. All the handcrafted steps in the traditional sparse-coding-based approach were replaced with an end-to-end CNN in a fully feed-forward manner. Early methods, including SRCNN [9,19,20], adopted pre-upsampling in which LR input images are first upsampled for the SR process. Because the pre-upsampling is computationally expensive, post-upsampling is generally used in recent models [1,26,27,31,56]. In post-upsampling, a transposed convolution or pixelshuffle [37] is usually used to upsample the features for final output. Although there are many proposals to improve network architectures [25,54], the protocol that directly outputs SR images with post-upsampling has been followed in most of those studies. Few studies have focused on the improvement of the upsampling strategy. Tough some recent works [3,5,60] leveraged the pre-trained latent features as a dictionary to improve output fidelity with rich textures, they used standard upsampling strategies in their proposed networks.

Convolutional Sparse Coding. Although methods following SRCNN have been common in recent years, several fundamentally different approaches have been proposed before and after the proposal of SRCNN. Convolutional sparse coding [15,35,39,47] is one of such methods that work on the entire image differently from traditional patch-based sparse coding. The advantage of convolutional sparse coding is that it avoids the boundary effect in patch-based sparse coding. However, it conceptually follows patch-based sparse coding in that the overall SR process is divided into handcrafted steps. Consequently, its performance lags behind that of end-to-end feed-forward CNN.

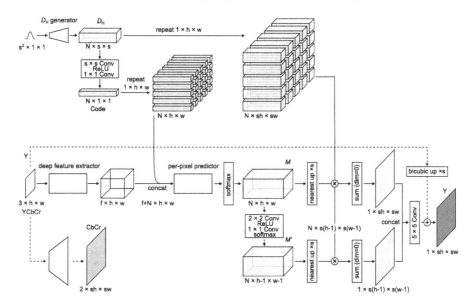

Fig. 2. The overall pipeline of the proposed method. A high-resolution dictionary D_H is generated from random noise. An encoded code of D_H is then concatenated with an extracted feature to be inputted to a per-pixel predictor. The predictor output is used to reconstruct the final output based on D_H.

Robust SR. The performance of deep-learning-based SR is significantly affected by the quality of the input image, especially the difference in conditions from the training dataset [14]. Several approaches have been proposed to make the network more robust against in-domain test images by training with multiple degradations [40,46,49,55,59]. For robustness against out-of-domain test images, some studies aim to make the network agnostic to degradations [14,38]. In these methods, agnostics acquisition is generally limited to specific degradations; therefore, it is important to make the network structure itself more robust.

3   Method

As depicted in Fig. 1(c), the proposed method comprises three components: D_H generation, per-pixel prediction, and reconstruction. The D_H generator generates an HR dictionary D_H from random noise input. The per-pixel predictor predicts the coefficients of D_H for each pixel from an LR YCbCr input. In the reconstruction part, the weighted sum of the elements (or atoms) of D_H produces an HR Y-channel output as a residual to be added to a bicubically upsampled Y channel. The remaining CbCr channels are upscaled with a shallow SR network. We used ESPCN [37] as the shallow SR network in this work. All of these components can be simultaneously optimized in an end-to-end manner; therefore, the same training procedure can be used as in conventional deep-learning-based SR methods. We use L_1 loss function to optimize the network

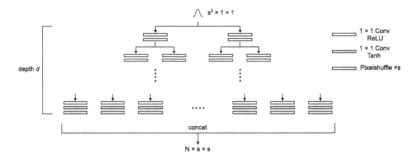

Fig. 3. A generator architecture of a high-resolution dictionary D_{H}. A tree-like network with depth d generates 2^d atoms of size $1 \times s \times s$ from a random noise input, where s is an upscaling factor.

Fig. 4. Learned atoms of $\times 4$ SRDD with $N = 128$. The size of each atom is $1 \times 4 \times 4$. The data range is renormalized to $[0, 1]$ for visualization.

$$L = \frac{1}{M} \sum_{i=1}^{M} ||I_i^{gt} - \Theta(I_i^{lr})||_1, \tag{1}$$

where I_i^{lr} and I_i^{gt} are LR patch and its ground truth. M denotes the number of training image pairs. $\Theta(\cdot)$ represents a function of the SRDD network. Figure 2 illustrates the proposed method in more detail. We describe the design of each component based on Fig. 2 in the following subsections.

3.1 D_{H} Generation

From random noise $\delta^{s^2 \times 1 \times 1}$ ($\in \mathbb{R}^{s^2 \times 1 \times 1}$) with a standard normal distribution, the D_{H} generator generates the HR dictionary $D_{\mathrm{H}}^{N \times s \times s}$, where s is an upscaling factor and N is the number of elements (atoms) in the dictionary. D_{H} is then encoded by $s \times s$ convolution with groups N, followed by ReLU [33] and 1×1 convolution. Each N element of the resultant code $C_{\mathrm{H}}^{N \times 1 \times 1}$ represents each $s \times s$ atom as a scalar value. Although the D_{H} can be trained using a fixed noise input, we found that introducing input randomness improves the stability of the training. A pre-generated fixed dictionary and its code are used in the testing phase. Note that only D_{H} is generated since low-resolution dictionaries (encoding) can be naturally replaced by convolutional operations without excessive increases in computation.

As illustrated in Fig. 3, the D_{H} generator has a tree-like structure, where the nodes consist of two 1×1 convolutional layers with ReLU activation. The final layer has a Tanh activation followed by a pixelshuffling layer; therefore, the data range of the output atoms is $[-1, 1]$. To produce N atoms, depth d of the generator is determined as

Fig. 5. Visualization of sparsity of a prediction map (center) and its complementary prediction map (right). The number of predicted coefficients larger than $1e$–2 is counted for each pixel. More atoms are assigned to the high-frequency parts and the low-frequency parts are relatively sparse.

$$d = \log_2 N. \tag{2}$$

Figure 4 shows generated atoms with $s = 4$ and $N = 128$. We observed that the contrast of the output atoms became stronger as training progressed, and they were almost fixed in the latter half of the training.

3.2   Per-pixel Prediction

We utilize UNet++ [61] as a deep feature extractor in Fig. 2. We slightly modify the original UNet++ architecture: the depth is reduced from four to three, and a long skip connection is added. The deep feature extractor outputs a tensor of size $f \times h \times w$ from the input YCbCr image, where h and w are the height and width of the image, respectively. Then the extracted feature is concatenated with the expanded code of D_{H}

$$C_{\mathrm{H}}^{N \times h \times w} = R_{1 \times h \times w}(C_{\mathrm{H}}^{N \times 1 \times 1}), \tag{3}$$

to be inputted to a per-pixel predictor, where $R_{a \times b \times c}(\cdot)$ denotes the $a \times b \times c$ repeat operations. The per-pixel predictor consists of ten bottleneck residual blocks followed by a softmax function that predicts N coefficients of D_{H} for each input pixel. Both the deep feature extractor and per-pixel predictor contain batch normalization layers [18] before the ReLU activation. The resultant prediction map $M^{N \times h \times w}$ is further convolved with a 2×2 convolution layer to produce a complementary prediction map $M'^{N \times (h-1) \times (w-1)}$. A complementary prediction map is used to compensate for the patch boundaries when reconstructing the final output. The detail of the compensation mechanism is described in the next subsection. Although we tried to replace softmax with ReLU to directly express sparsity, ReLU made the training unstable. We also tried entmax [36], but the performance was similar to that of softmax, so we decided to use softmax for simplicity.

Figure 5 visualizes the sparsity of the prediction map and its complementary prediction map. The number of coefficients larger than $1e-2$ is counted for each pixel to visualize the sparsity. The model with $N = 128$ is used. More atoms are assigned to the high-frequency parts of the image, and the low-frequency parts are relatively sparse. This feature is especially noticeable in the complementary

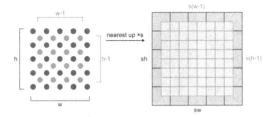

Fig. 6. Schematic illustration of a mechanism to compensate patch boundary with a complementary prediction map, where s is a scaling factor. Left: Prediction map (blue) and its complementary prediction map (orange). Right: Upsampled prediction and complementary prediction maps with centering. (Color figure online)

prediction map. In the high-frequency region, the output image is represented by linear combinations of more than tens of atoms for both maps.

3.3 Reconstruction

The prediction map $M^{N \times h \times w}$ is upscaled to $N \times sh \times sw$ by nearest-neighbor interpolation, and the element-wise multiplication of that upscaled prediction map $U_s(M^{N \times h \times w})$ with the expanded dictionary $R_{1 \times h \times w}(D_{\mathrm{H}}^{N \times s \times s})$ produces $N \times sh \times sw$ tensor T consists of weighted atoms. The $U_s(\cdot)$ denotes $\times s$ nearest-neighbor upsampling. Finally, tensor T is summed over the first dimension, producing output x as

$$x^{1 \times sh \times sw} = \sum_{k=0}^{N-1} T^{N \times sh \times sw}[k, :, :], \qquad (4)$$

$$T^{N \times sh \times sw} = U_s(M^{N \times h \times w}) \otimes R_{1 \times h \times w}(D_{\mathrm{H}}^{N \times s \times s}). \qquad (5)$$

The same sequence of operations is applied to the complementary prediction map to obtain the output x' as follows:

$$x'^{1 \times s(h-1) \times s(w-1)} = \sum_{k=0}^{N-1} T'^{N \times s(h-1) \times s(w-1)}[k, :, :], \qquad (6)$$

$$T'^{N \times s(h-1) \times s(w-1)} = U_s(M'^{N \times (h-1) \times (w-1)}) \otimes R_{1 \times (h-1) \times (w-1)}(D_{\mathrm{H}}^{N \times s \times s}). \quad (7)$$

Note that the same dictionary, D_{H}, is used to obtain x and x'. By centering x and x', as illustrated in Fig. 6, the imperfections at the patch boundaries can complement each other. The final output residual is obtained by concatenating the overlapping parts of the centered x and x' and applying a 5×5 convolution. For non-overlapping parts, x is simply used as the final output.

4 Experiments

4.1 Implementation Details

We adopt a model with 128 atoms (SRDD-128) and a small model with 64 atoms (SRDD-64). The number of filters of the models is adjusted according to the number of atoms. Our network is trained by inputting 48×48 LR patches with a mini-batch size of 32. Following previous studies [1,27,56], random flipping and rotation augmentation is applied to each training sample. We use Adam optimizer [22] with $\beta_1 = 0.9$, $\beta_2 = 0.999$, and $\epsilon = 10^{-8}$. The learning rate of the network except for the D_H generator is initialized as $2e-4$ and halved at [200k, 300k, 350k, 375k]. The total training iterations is 400k. The learning rate of the D_H generator is initialized as $5e-3$ and halved at [50k, 100k, 200k, 300k, 350k]. Parameters of the D_H generator are frozen at 360k iteration. In addition, to stabilize training of the D_H generator, we randomly shuffle the order of output atoms for the first 1k iterations. We use PyTorch to implement our model with an NVIDIA P6000 GPU. Training takes about two/three days for SRDD-64/128, respectively. More training details are provided in the supplementary material.

4.2 Dataset and Evaluation

Training Dataset. Following previous studies, we use 800 HR-LR image pairs of the DIV2K [43] training dataset to train our models. LR images are created from HR images by Matlab bicubic downsampling. For validation, we use initial ten images from the DIV2K validation dataset.

Test Dataset. For testing, we evaluate the models on five standard benchmarks: Set5 [2], Set14 [53], BSD100 [29], Urban100 [16], and Manga109 [30]. In addition to standard test images downsampled with Matlab bicubic function same as in training, we use test images that downsampled by OpenCV bicubic, bilinear, and area functions to evaluate the robustness of the models. In addition, we evaluate the models on real-world ten historical photographs.

Evaluation. We use common image quality metrics peak signal-to-noise ratio (PSNR) and structural similarity index (SSIM) [48] calculated on the Y channel (luminance channel) of YCbCr color space. For evaluation of real-world test images, no-reference image quality metric NIQE [32] is used since there are no ground-truth images. Following previous studies, we ignore s pixels from the border to calculate all the metrics, where s is an SR scale factor.

4.3 Ablation Study

We conduct ablation experiments to examine the impact of individual elements in SRDD. We report the results of SRDD-64 throughout this section. The results of the ablation experiments on Set14 downsampled with Matlab bicubic function are summarized in Table 1.

Batch Normalization. We show the validation curves of SRDD-64 with and without batch normalization layers in Fig. 7. The performance of the proposed model is substantially improved by using batch normalization. This result is in contrast to conventional deep-learning-based SR methods, where batch normalization generally degrades performance [27]. Unlike conventional methods where the network directly outputs the SR image, the prediction network in SRDD

Table 1. Results of ablation experiments on Set14 downsampled with Matlab bicubic function.

	PSNR	SSIM
SRDD-64	28.54	0.7809
SRDD-64 − batch norm	28.49	0.7792
SRDD-64 − bottleneck blocks	28.48	0.7790
SRDD-64 − compensation	28.51	0.7801

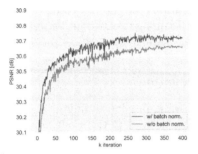

Fig. 7. Validation curves during the training of SRDD-64 with and without batch normalization layers.

predicts the coefficients of D_H for each pixel, which is rather similar to the semantic segmentation task. In this sense, it is natural that batch normalization, which is effective for semantic segmentation [7,24,58], is also effective for the proposed model.

Bottleneck Blocks. We eliminate bottleneck blocks and D_H code injection from the per-pixel predictor. The prediction network becomes close to the plane UNet++ structure with this modification. The performance drops as shown in Table 1, but still demonstrates a certain level of performance.

Compensation Mechanism. As shown in Table 1, removing the compensation mechanism from SRDD-64 degrades the performance. However, the effect is marginal indicates that our model can produce adequate quality outputs without boundary compensation. This result is in contrast to the sparse-coding-based methods, which generally require aggregation with overlapping patch sampling to reduce imperfection at the patch boundary. Because the computational complexity of our compensation mechanism is very small compared to that of the entire model, we adopt it even if the effect is not so large.

4.4 Results on In-Domain Test Images

We conduct experiments on five benchmark datasets, where the LR input images are created by Matlab bicubic downsampling same as in the DIV2K training dataset. Because SRDD is quite shallow and fast compared to current state-of-the-art models, we compare SRDD to relatively shallow and fast models with

Table 2. Quantitative comparison for ×4 SR on benchmark datasets. Best and second best results are highlighted in red and blue, respectively.

Method	Set5 PSNR/SSIM	Set14 PSNR/SSIM	BSD100 PSNR/SSIM	Urban100 PSNR/SSIM	Manga109 PSNR/SSIM
Bicubic	28.42/0.8104	26.00/0.7027	25.96/0.6675	23.14/0.6577	24.89/0.7866
A+ [45]	30.28/0.8603	27.32/0.7491	26.82/0.7087	24.32/0.7183	- / -
SRCNN [9]	30.48/0.8628	27.50/0.7513	26.90/0.7101	24.52/0.7221	27.58/0.8555
FSRCNN [10]	30.72/0.8660	27.61/0.7550	26.98/0.7150	24.62/0.7280	27.90/0.8610
VDSR [19]	31.35/0.8830	28.02/0.7680	27.29/0.0726	25.18/0.7540	28.83/0.8870
DRCN [20]	31.53/0.8854	28.02/0.7670	27.23/0.7233	25.14/0.7510	- / -
LapSRN [23]	31.54/0.8850	28.19/0.7720	27.32/0.7270	25.21/0.7560	29.09/0.8900
DRRN [41]	31.68/0.8888	28.21/0.7720	27.38/0.7284	25.44/0.7638	- / -
MemNet [42]	31.74/0.8893	28.26/0.7723	27.40/0.7281	25.50/0.7630	29.42/0.8942
CARN [1]	32.13/0.8937	28.60/0.7806	27.58/0.7349	26.07/0.7837	30.47/0.9084
IMDN [17]	32.21/0.8948	28.58/0.7811	27.56/0.7353	26.04/0.7838	30.45/ 0.9075
LatticeNet [28]	32.30/0.8962	28.68/0.7830	27.62/0.7367	26.25/0.7873	- / -
SRDD-64	32.05/0.8936	28.54/0.7809	27.54/0.7353	25.89/0.7812	30.16/0.9043
SRDD-128	32.25/0.8958	28.65/0.7838	27.61/0.7378	26.10/0.7877	30.44/0.9084
RCAN [56]	(32.63/0.9002)	(28.87/0.7889)	(27.77/0.7436)	(26.82/0.8087)	(31.22/0.9173)
NLSA [31]	(32.59/0.9000)	(28.87/0.7891)	(27.78/0.7444)	(26.96/0.8109)	(31.27/0.9184)
SwinIR [26]	(32.72/0.9021)	(28.94/0.7914)	(27.83/0.7459)	(27.07/0.8164)	(31.67/0.9226)

Table 3. Execution time of representative models on an Nvidia P4000 GPU for ×4 SR with input size 256 × 256.

	Running time [s]
SRCNN [9]	0.0669
FSRCNN [10]	0.0036
VDSR [19]	0.2636
LapSRN [23]	0.1853
CARN [1]	0.0723
IMDN [17]	0.0351
SRDD-64	0.0842
SRDD-128	0.2196
RCAN [56]	1.5653
NLSA [31]	1.7139
SwinIR [26]	2.1106

roughly 50 layers or less. Note that recent deep SR models usually have hundreds of convolutional layers [56]. We select ten models for comparison: SRCNN [9], FSRCNN [10], VDSR [19], DRCN [20], LapSRN [23], DRRN [41], MemNet [42], CARN [1], IMDN [17], and LatticeNet [28]. We also compare our model with a representative sparse coding-based method A+ [45]. Results for the representative very deep models RCAN [56], NLSA [31], and SwinIR [26] are also shown.

The quantitative results for ×4 SR on benchmark datasets are shown in Table 2. SRDD-64 and SRDD-128 show comparable performances to CARN/IMDN and LatticeNet, respectively. As shown in Table 3, the inference speed of SRDD-64 is also comparable to that of CARN, but slower than IMDN.

474   S. Maeda

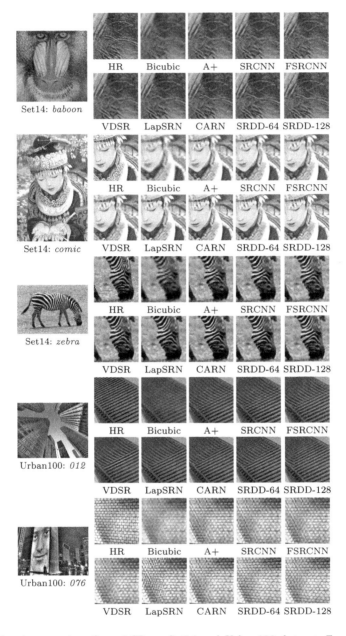

Fig. 8. Visual comparison for ×4 SR on Set14 and Urban100 dataset. Zoom in for a better view.

These results indicate that the overall performance of our method on in-domain test images is close to that of conventional baselines (not as good as state-of-the-art models). The running time of representative deep models are also shown

Table 4. Quantitative results of ×4 SR on Set14 downsampled with three different OpenCV resize functions. Note that the models are trained with Matlab bicubic downsampling.

	Bicubic	Bilinear	Area
	PSNR/SSIM	PSNR/SSIM	PSNR/SSIM
CARN [1]	21.17/0.6310	22.76/0.6805	26.74/0.7604
IMDN [17]	20.99/0.6239	22.54/0.6741	26.60/0.7589
IKC [14]	20.10/0.6031	21.71/0.6558	26.40/0.7554
SRDD-64	21.52/0.6384	23.13/0.6871	27.05/0.7630

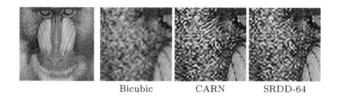

Bicubic   CARN   SRDD-64

Fig. 9. Visual comparison for ×4 SR on Set14 *baboon* downsampled with OpenCV bicubic function.

for comparison. They are about 20 times slower than CARN and SRDD-64. The visual results are provided in Fig. 8.

4.5 Results on Out-of-Domain Test Images

Synthetic Test Images. We conduct experiments on Set14, where the LR input images are created differently from training time. We use bicubic, bilinear, and area downsampling with OpenCV resize functions. The difference between Matlab and OpenCV resize functions mainly comes from the anti-aliasing option. The anti-aliasing is default enabled/unenabled in Matlab/OpenCV, respectively. We mainly evaluate CARN and SRDD-64 because these models have comparable performance on in-domain test images. The state-of-the-art lightweight model IMDN [17] and the representative blind SR model IKC [14] are also evaluated for comparison. The results are shown in Table 4. SRDD-64 outperformed these models by a large margin for the three different resize functions. This result implies that our method is more robust for the out-of-domain images than conventional deep-learning-based methods. The visual comparison on a test image downsampled with OpenCV bicubic function is shown in Fig. 9. CARN overly emphasizes high-frequency components of the image, while SRDD-64 outputs a more natural result.

Real-World Test Images. We conduct experiments on widely used ten historical images to see the robustness of the models on unknown degradations. Because there is no ground-truth image, we adopt a no-reference image quality metric NIQE for evaluation. Table 5 shows average NIQE for representative methods.

Table 5. Results of no-reference image quality metric NIQE on real-world historical images. Note that the models are trained with Matlab bicubic downsampling.

	NIQE (lower is better)
Bicubic	7.342
A+ [45]	6.503
SRCNN [9]	6.267
FSRCNN [10]	6.130
VDSR [19]	6.038
LapSRN [23]	6.234
CARN [1]	5.921
EDSR [27]	5.852
SRDD-64	5.877
SRDD-128	5.896

Fig. 10. Visual comparison for ×4 SR on real-world historical images. Zoom in for a better view.

As seen in the previous subsection, our SRDD-64 shows comparable performance to CARN if compared with in-domain test images. However, on the realistic datasets with the NIQE metric, SRDD-64 clearly outperforms CARN and is close to EDSR. Interestingly, unlike the results on the in-domain test images, the performance of SRDD-64 is better than that of SRDD-128 for realistic degradations. This is probably because representing an HR image with a small number of atoms makes the atoms more versatile. The visual results are provided in Fig. 10.

4.6   Experiments of ×8 SR

To see if our method would work at different scaling factors, we also experiment with the ×8 SR case. We use DIV2K dataset for training and validation. The test

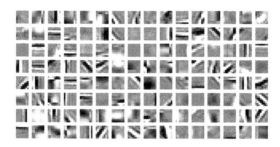

Fig. 11. Learned atoms of ×8 SRDD with $N = 128$. The size of each atom is $1 \times 8 \times 8$. The data range is renormalized to $[0, 1]$ for visualization.

Table 6. Quantitative comparison for ×8 SR on benchmark datasets. Best and second best results are highlighted in red and blue, respectively.

Method	Set5	Set14	BSD100	Urban100	Manga109
	PSNR/SSIM	PSNR/SSIM	PSNR/SSIM	PSNR/SSIM	PSNR/SSIM
Bicubic	24.40/0.6580	23.10/0.5660	23.67/0.5480	20.74/0.5160	21.47/0.6500
SRCNN [9]	25.33/0.6900	23.76/0.5910	24.13/0.5660	21.29/0.5440	22.46/0.6950
FSRCNN [10]	20.13/0.5520	19.75/0.4820	24.21/0.5680	21.32/0.5380	22.39/0.6730
VDSR [19]	25.93/0.7240	24.26/0.6140	24.49/0.5830	21.70/0.5710	23.16/0.7250
LapSRN [23]	26.15/0.7380	24.35/0.6200	24.54/0.5860	21.81/0.5810	23.39/0.7350
MemNet [42]	26.16/0.7414	24.38/0.6199	24.58/0.5842	21.89/0.5825	23.56/0.7387
EDSR [27]	26.96/0.7762	24.91/0.6420	24.81/0.5985	22.51/0.6221	24.69/0.7841
SRDD-64	26.66/0.7652	24.75/0.6345	24.71/0.5926	22.20/0.6034	24.14/0.7621
SRDD-128	26.76/0.7677	24.79/0.6369	24.75/0.5947	22.25/0.6073	24.25/0.7672

images are prepared with the same downsampling function (i.e. Matlab bicubic function) as the training dataset. Figure 11 shows generated atoms of SRDD with $s = 8$ and $N = 128$. The structure of atoms with $s = 8$ is finer than that with $s = 4$, while the coarse structures of both cases are similar. The quantitative results on five benchmark datasets are shown in Table 6. SRDD performs better than the representative shallow models though its performance does not reach representative deep model EDSR.

5   Conclusions

We propose an end-to-end super-resolution network with a deep dictionary (SRDD). An explicitly learned high-resolution dictionary (D_H) is used to upscale the input image as in the sparse-coding-based methods, while the entire network, including the D_H generator, is simultaneously optimized to take full advantage of deep learning. For in-domain test images (images created by the same procedure as the training dataset), the proposed SRDD shows performance that is not as good as latest ones, but close to the conventional baselines (e.g., CARN). For out-of-domain test images, SRDD outperforms conventional deep-learning-based methods, demonstrating the robustness of our model.

The proposed method is not limited to super-resolution tasks but is potentially applicable to other tasks that require high-resolution output, such as high-resolution image generation. Hence, the proposed method is expected to have a broad impact on various tasks. Future works will be focused on the application of the proposed method to other vision tasks. In addition, we believe that our method still has much room for improvement compared to the conventional deep-learning-based approach.

Acknowledgements. I thank Uday Bondi for helpful comments on the manuscript.

References

1. Ahn, N., Kang, B., Sohn, K.-A.: Fast, accurate, and lightweight super-resolution with cascading residual network. In: Ferrari, V., Hebert, M., Sminchisescu, C., Weiss, Y. (eds.) ECCV 2018. LNCS, vol. 11214, pp. 256–272. Springer, Cham (2018). https://doi.org/10.1007/978-3-030-01249-6_16
2. Bevilacqua, M., Roumy, A., Guillemot, C., Alberi-Morel, M.L.: Low-complexity single-image super-resolution based on nonnegative neighbor embedding. In: BMVC (2012)
3. Chan, K.C., Wang, X., Xu, X., Gu, J., Loy, C.C.: Glean: generative latent bank for large-factor image super-resolution. In: CVPR (2021)
4. Chang, H., Yeung, D.Y., Xiong, Y.: Super-resolution through neighbor embedding. In: CVPR (2004)
5. Chen, C., et al.: Real-world blind super-resolution via feature matching with implicit high-resolution priors. arXiv preprint arXiv:2202.13142 (2022)
6. Chen, H., et al.: Pre-trained image processing transformer. In: CVPR (2021)
7. Chen, L.C., Papandreou, G., Schroff, F., Adam, H.: Rethinking atrous convolution for semantic image segmentation. arXiv preprint arXiv:1706.05587 (2017)
8. Dai, T., Cai, J., Zhang, Y., Xia, S.T., Zhang, L.: Second-order attention network for single image super-resolution. In: CVPR (2019)
9. Dong, C., Loy, C.C., He, K., Tang, X.: Learning a deep convolutional network for image super-resolution. In: Fleet, D., Pajdla, T., Schiele, B., Tuytelaars, T. (eds.) ECCV 2014. LNCS, vol. 8692, pp. 184–199. Springer, Cham (2014). https://doi.org/10.1007/978-3-319-10593-2_13
10. Dong, C., Loy, C.C., Tang, X.: Accelerating the super-resolution convolutional neural network. In: Leibe, B., Matas, J., Sebe, N., Welling, M. (eds.) ECCV 2016. LNCS, vol. 9906, pp. 391–407. Springer, Cham (2016). https://doi.org/10.1007/978-3-319-46475-6_25
11. Freedman, G., Fattal, R.: Image and video upscaling from local self-examples. TOG **30**(2), 1–11 (2011)
12. Freeman, W.T., Jones, T.R., Pasztor, E.C.: Example-based super-resolution. CG&A **22**(2), 56–65 (2002)
13. Glasner, D., Bagon, S., Irani, M.: Super-resolution from a single image. In: ICCV (2009)
14. Gu, J., Lu, H., Zuo, W., Dong, C.: Blind super-resolution with iterative kernel correction. In: CVPR (2019)
15. Gu, S., Zuo, W., Xie, Q., Meng, D., Feng, X., Zhang, L.: Convolutional sparse coding for image super-resolution. In: ICCV (2015)

16. Huang, J.B., Singh, A., Ahuja, N.: Single image super-resolution from transformed self-exemplars. In: CVPR (2015)
17. Hui, Z., Gao, X., Yang, Y., Wang, X.: Lightweight image super-resolution with information multi-distillation network. In: ACM Multimedia (2019)
18. Ioffe, S., Szegedy, C.: Batch normalization: accelerating deep network training by reducing internal covariate shift. In: ICML (2015)
19. Kim, J., Lee, J.K., Lee, K.M.: Accurate image super-resolution using very deep convolutional networks. In: CVPR (2016)
20. Kim, J., Lee, J.K., Lee, K.M.: Deeply-recursive convolutional network for image super-resolution. In: CVPR (2016)
21. Kim, K.I., Kwon, Y.: Single-image super-resolution using sparse regression and natural image prior. TPAMI **32**(6), 1127–1133 (2010)
22. Kingma, D.P., Ba, J.: Adam: a method for stochastic optimization. In: ICLR (2014)
23. Lai, W.S., Huang, J.B., Ahuja, N., Yang, M.H.: Deep Laplacian pyramid networks for fast and accurate super-resolution. In: CVPR (2017)
24. Li, H., Xiong, P., An, J., Wang, L.: Pyramid attention network for semantic segmentation. In: BMVC (2018)
25. Li, Y., et al.: NTIRE 2022 challenge on efficient super-resolution: methods and results. In: CVPRW (2022)
26. Liang, J., Cao, J., Sun, G., Zhang, K., Van Gool, L., Timofte, R.: SwinIR: image restoration using Swin transformer. In: ICCV (2021)
27. Lim, B., Son, S., Kim, H., Nah, S., Mu Lee, K.: Enhanced deep residual networks for single image super-resolution. In: CVPRW (2017)
28. Luo, X., Xie, Y., Zhang, Y., Qu, Y., Li, C., Fu, Y.: LatticeNet: towards lightweight image super-resolution with Lattice Block. In: Vedaldi, A., Bischof, H., Brox, T., Frahm, J.-M. (eds.) ECCV 2020. LNCS, vol. 12367, pp. 272–289. Springer, Cham (2020). https://doi.org/10.1007/978-3-030-58542-6_17
29. Martin, D., Fowlkes, C., Tal, D., Malik, J.: A database of human segmented natural images and its application to evaluating segmentation algorithms and measuring ecological statistics. In: ICCV (2001)
30. Matsui, Y., et al.: Sketch-based manga retrieval using manga109 dataset. Multimed. Tools App. **76**(20), 21811–21838 (2017)
31. Mei, Y., Fan, Y., Zhou, Y.: Image super-resolution with non-local sparse attention. In: CVPR (2021)
32. Mittal, A., Soundararajan, R., Bovik, A.C.: Making a "completely blind" image quality analyzer. Signal Process. Lett. **20**(3), 209–212 (2012)
33. Nair, V., Hinton, G.E.: Rectified linear units improve restricted Boltzmann machines. In: ICML (2010)
34. Niu, B., et al.: Single image super-resolution via a holistic attention network. In: Vedaldi, A., Bischof, H., Brox, T., Frahm, J.-M. (eds.) ECCV 2020. LNCS, vol. 12357, pp. 191–207. Springer, Cham (2020). https://doi.org/10.1007/978-3-030-58610-2_12
35. Osendorfer, C., Soyer, H., Smagt, P.: Image super-resolution with fast approximate convolutional sparse coding. In: ICONIP (2014)
36. Peters, B., Niculae, V., Martins, A.F.: Sparse sequence-to-sequence models. In: ACL (2019)
37. Shi, W., et al.: Real-time single image and video super-resolution using an efficient sub-pixel convolutional neural network. In: CVPR (2016)
38. Shocher, A., Cohen, N., Irani, M.: "zero-shot" super-resolution using deep internal learning. In: CVPR (2018)

39. Simon, D., Elad, M.: Rethinking the CSC model for natural images. In: NeurIPS (2019)
40. Soh, J.W., Cho, S., Cho, N.I.: Meta-transfer learning for zero-shot super-resolution. In: CVPR (2020)
41. Tai, Y., Yang, J., Liu, X.: Image super-resolution via deep recursive residual network. In: CVPR (2017)
42. Tai, Y., Yang, J., Liu, X., Xu, C.: MemNet: a persistent memory network for image restoration. In: ICCV (2017)
43. Timofte, R., Agustsson, E., Van Gool, L., Yang, M.H., Zhang, L.: NTIRE 2017 challenge on single image super-resolution: methods and results. In: CVPRW (2017)
44. Timofte, R., De Smet, V., Van Gool, L.: Anchored neighborhood regression for fast example-based super-resolution. In: ICCV (2013)
45. Timofte, R., De Smet, V., Van Gool, L.: A+: adjusted anchored neighborhood regression for fast super-resolution. In: ACCV (2014)
46. Wang, L., et al.: Unsupervised degradation representation learning for blind super-resolution. In: CVPR (2021)
47. Wang, Z., Liu, D., Yang, J., Han, W., Huang, T.: Deep networks for image super-resolution with sparse prior. In: ICCV (2015)
48. Wang, Z., Bovik, A.C., Sheikh, H.R., Simoncelli, E.P.: Image quality assessment: from error visibility to structural similarity. TIP **13**(4), 600–612 (2004)
49. Xu, Y.S., Tseng, S.Y.R., Tseng, Y., Kuo, H.K., Tsai, Y.M.: Unified dynamic convolutional network for super-resolution with variational degradations. In: CVPR (2020)
50. Yang, J., Lin, Z., Cohen, S.: Fast image super-resolution based on in-place example regression. In: CVPR (2013)
51. Yang, J., Wang, Z., Lin, Z., Cohen, S., Huang, T.: Coupled dictionary training for image super-resolution. TIP **21**(8), 3467–3478 (2012)
52. Yang, J., Wright, J., Huang, T.S., Ma, Y.: Image super-resolution via sparse representation. TIP **19**(11), 2861–2873 (2010)
53. Zeyde, R., Elad, M., Protter, M.: On single image scale-up using sparse-representations. In: Curves and Surfaces (2010)
54. Zhang, K., et al.: Aim 2020 challenge on efficient super-resolution: methods and results. In: ECCVW (2020)
55. Zhang, K., Zuo, W., Zhang, L.: Learning a single convolutional super-resolution network for multiple degradations. In: CVPR (2018)
56. Zhang, Y., Li, K., Li, K., Wang, L., Zhong, B., Fu, Y.: Image super-resolution using very deep residual channel attention networks. In: Ferrari, V., Hebert, M., Sminchisescu, C., Weiss, Y. (eds.) ECCV 2018. LNCS, vol. 11211, pp. 294–310. Springer, Cham (2018). https://doi.org/10.1007/978-3-030-01234-2_18
57. Zhang, Y., Tian, Y., Kong, Y., Zhong, B., Fu, Y.: Residual dense network for image super-resolution. In: CVPR (2018)
58. Zhao, H., Shi, J., Qi, X., Wang, X., Jia, J.: Pyramid scene parsing network. In: CVPR (2017)
59. Zhou, R., Susstrunk, S.: Kernel modeling super-resolution on real low-resolution images. In: ICCV (2019)
60. Zhou, S., Chan, K.C., Li, C., Loy, C.C.: Towards robust blind face restoration with codebook lookup transformer. arXiv preprint arXiv:2206.11253 (2022)
61. Zhou, Z., Rahman Siddiquee, M.M., Tajbakhsh, N., Liang, J.: UNet++: a nested u-net architecture for medical image segmentation. In: Stoyanov, D., et al. (eds.) DLMIA/ML-CDS -2018. LNCS, vol. 11045, pp. 3–11. Springer, Cham (2018). https://doi.org/10.1007/978-3-030-00889-5_1

TempFormer: Temporally Consistent Transformer for Video Denoising

Mingyang Song[1,2], Yang Zhang[2(✉)], and Tunç O. Aydın[2]

[1] ETH Zurich, Zurich, Switzerland
[2] DisneyResearch—Studios, Zurich, Switzerland
misong@student.ethz.ch, {yang.zhang,tunc}@disneyresearch.com

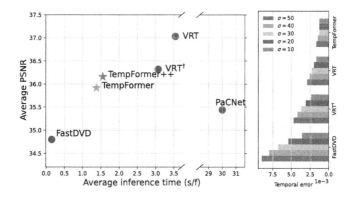

Fig. 1. Left: PSNR (averaged results on noise levels $\sigma = \{10, 20, 30, 40, 50\}$) Vs. Inference time on 480P video sequences. Right: Temporal consistency, the lower the better.

Abstract. Video denoising is a low-level vision task that aims to restore high quality videos from noisy content. Vision Transformer (ViT) is a new machine learning architecture that has shown promising performance on both high-level and low-level image tasks. In this paper, we propose a modified ViT architecture for video processing tasks, introducing a new training strategy and loss function to enhance temporal consistency without compromising spatial quality. Specifically, we propose an efficient hybrid Transformer-based model, *TempFormer*, which composes Spatio-Temporal Transformer Blocks (STTB) and 3D convolutional layers. The proposed STTB learns the temporal information between neighboring frames implicitly by utilizing the proposed *Joint Spatio-Temporal Mixer* module for attention calculation and feature aggregation in each ViT block. Moreover, existing methods suffer from temporal inconsistency artifacts that are problematic in practical cases and distracting to the viewers. We propose a sliding block strategy with recurrent architecture, and use a new loss term, *Overlap* Loss, to alleviate the flickering between adjacent frames. Our method produces state-of-the-art spatio-temporal

Supplementary Information The online version contains supplementary material available at https://doi.org/10.1007/978-3-031-19800-7_28.

denoising quality with significantly improved temporal coherency, and requires less computational resources to achieve comparable denoising quality with competing methods (Fig. 1).

Keywords: Video denoising · Transformer · Temporal consistency

1 Introduction

A major challenge in video processing is efficiently utilizing temporal redundancy. Early methods utilize filtering by explicitly computing spatial and temporal similarity between pixels [17]. Since the emergence of deep learning convolutional neural networks (CNN) have replaced traditional patch-based non-local filtering. One approach for matching pixels temporally is to explicitly align the pixels through optical flow or deformable convolutional networks (DCN) [6,14,29]. There are also works [18,21,24] that avoid flow estimation and only use the capability of CNNs to extract temporal information implicitly.

Transformer networks were initially used in natural language processing [23], and more recently have shown promising performance in vision tasks due to the mechanism of global attention (GA). GA is affordable in some high-level vision tasks, such as object detection and classification [5,10]. However, GA is a severe burden to GPU memory in video denoising tasks, especially when processing high-resolution videos, and the inference speed is unreasonable in practical applications. Swin Transformer [16] computes attention inside non-overlapping spatial windows, and uses shifted windows to extract different patches in each stage to introduce interactions between adjacent windows. Recently, a Transformer-based vision restoration model [14] extrapolates the spatial self attention mechanism within a single image to temporal mutual attention mechanism between adjacent frames. The mutual attention mechanism introduces many additional matrix multiplications, and therefore is inefficient during inference. While ViT needs much fewer parameters compared with CNNs thanks to the content-dependent attention map, it requires larger GPU memory during training.

To introduce interaction between frames inside models, existing methods mainly use temporal sliding windows, that divide a video sequence into blocks with or without overlappings [21,24]. While two neighboring blocks share several common input frames, the denoised frames still contain temporal inconsistency artifacts. Another strategy is the recurrent architecture [18], which has to load a large number of frames in one training step and is inefficient during training.

In this work we propose a model that we call *TempFormer*, which builds upon the Swin Transformer [16]. Our model does not require optical flow and uses the capacity of content-dependent mixer, attention mechanism, with MLP layers to integrate temporal information implicitly. TempFormer only contains explicit spatial attention, and has good efficiency during training and inference. Moreover, we combine the sliding block strategy with recurrent architecture to strengthen the interaction between temporal blocks, and introduce a new loss term to alleviate the incoherency artifacts.

2   Related Work

2.1   Image Denoising

Classical image denoising methods utilize the spatial self-similarity of images. The similarities serve as weights of a filter, and the denoising process is a weighted average of all pixel values within a patch centered at the reference pixel. The Non-Local-Means filter [3] is a famous implementation of such an idea. Recently, the deep-learning based image denoising methods bypass the explicit similarity computation and use the neural network's powerful representation ability to integrate the reference pixel and its spatial neighborhoods [4,15,32–34].

2.2   Video Denoising

In video denoising, sequences are treated as volumes, and the non-linear functions are applied to the noisy pixels and their spatio-temporal neighborhoods. The traditional method VBM4D [17] groups similar volumes together and filters the volumes along four dimensions. Vaksman et al. [22] re-explores the patch-based method, uses K-Nearest Neighbor (KNN) to find all similar patches in the volume for each reference patch, then stacks them together as a kind of data augmentation. In modern deep learning based models, the temporal alignment is performed by optical flow or DCN [29], or their combination [14]. There are also some works that avoid the expensive flow estimation and warping, and use the powerful representation ability of CNNs to perform end-to-end training [21,24].

2.3   Temporal Consistency

The removal of temporal flickering is a common challenge in artistic vision tasks, e.g. colorization, enhancement and style transfer, etc. Some blind methods use an extra model as post-processing on the outputs which were processed frame by frame. Lai et al. [11] proposed a recurrent model that takes frames before and after the processing as inputs and use Temporal Loss to enforce consistency. Lei et al. [12] divide the temporal inconsistency into two types, unimodal and multimodal inconsistency, and proposed a solution to each of them. These existing methods heavily rely on post-processing and lack of efficiency during practical applications. Besides, few attentions were focused on the inconsistency artifacts in the video denoising tasks. The temporal flickering is distracting to the viewers when the noise level is high, especially in the static contents of the video.

2.4   Vision Transformer

Vision Transformer (ViT) has shown promising performance on both high-level vision tasks, such us object detection [8,16,25,28], classification [9,31], and low-level vision tasks, such as image restoration [7,15]. Liu et al. [16] proposed a new backbone for vision tasks, SWin Transformer, that divides image into non-overlapping spatial windows to solve the problem of quadratic computation complexity and uses shifted windows strategy to introduce the connection between neighboring windows. Based on SWin Transformer, Liang et al. [15] applied this new backbone on image restoration tasks. Yang et al. [26] introduced a multi-scale architecture and mix the features with multiple granularities to realize long-range attention. A variation of self-attention (SA) calculation was proposed in [1,30], where a Cross-Covariance attention operation was applied along the feature dimension instead of token dimension in conventional transformers. This modification resulted in linear complexity w.r.t the number of tokens, allowing efficient processing of high-resolution images. Recently, some methods transfer the attention mechanism from the spatial domain to the temporal domain on some video recognition tasks [2,13]. Liang et al. [14] use temporal mutual attention on video restoration tasks as a type of soft warping after motion estimation. The extension from spatial attention to temporal attention is a natural extrapolation, but the boost in the number of attention maps makes training prohibitively expensive when the memory of GPU is limited, and this high computational complexity makes it less practical.

3   Method

Our model is a one-stage model and performs spatial and temporal denoisng simultaneously. For efficiency and temporal coherency reasons our model outputs more than one neighboring frames, namely takes $2 \times m + 1$ frames as inputs and outputs $2 \times n + 1$ frames. This strategy can be described in the following form:

$$\{\hat{I}^t_{-n}, \hat{I}^t_{-n+1}, ..., \hat{I}^t_0, ..., \hat{I}^t_{n-1}, \hat{I}^t_n\} = \Phi(\{\tilde{I}^t_{-m}, \tilde{I}^t_{-m+1}, ..., \tilde{I}^t_0, ..., \tilde{I}^t_{m-1}, \tilde{I}^t_m\}), \quad (1)$$

where $\tilde{I}$ represents the noisy frame of the temporal window $Block^t$, Φ is our video denoising model, and $\hat{I}$ represents the denoised frame of $Block^t$. To introduce communications between neighboring temporal blocks, we set m strictly larger than n so that they share multiple common input frames. We use the setting $m = 2, n = 1$ throughout the rest formulas and visualizations in this paper.

Our training pipeline contains two phases. Firstly, we use TempFormer to perform denoising within each temporal $Block^t$, where the input frames of $Block^t$ can extract information in the Spatio-Temporal Transformer Blocks (STTB). Secondly, to solve the flickering between adjacent temporal blocks, we fine-tune our network to the recurrent architecture, and propose a new loss term to strengthen stability further. See Sect. 3.2 for more detailed information.

3.1   Spatio-Temporal Video Denoising Phase

Overall Architecture. Figure 2 shows the architecture of our model, which is mainly composed of four modules: Wavelet Transform, shallow feature extraction, deep feature extraction, and the image reconstruction module. Firstly, we use Wavelet Transform to decompose the input frames and concatenate all sub-bands along the channel dimension. Secondly, a 3D convolutional layer converts the frequency channels of all sub-bands into shallow features. Next, the deep feature extraction module, which consist of a sequence of Spatial-Temporal Transformer Blocks (STTB), mixes the features of each token spatially and temporally.

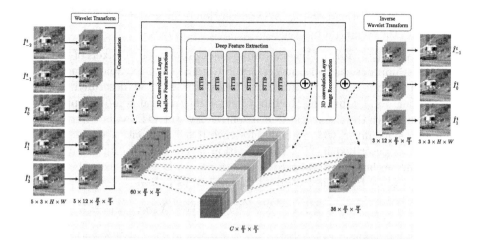

Fig. 2. The architecture of the proposed TempFormer.

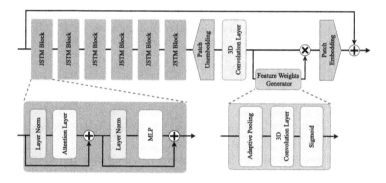

Fig. 3. The architecture of the Spatial-Temporal Transformer Block (STTB).

Following the STTBs, another 3D convolutional layer transforms the features back into the wavelet frequency space. Finally, we use the Inverse Wavelet Transform to convert the frequency sub-bands into high-quality images with the original resolution.

Spatio-Temporal Transformer Block. The architecture of the proposed STTB module is shown in Fig. 3. In Liu et al. [16], the attention layers in SWin Transformer blocks perform spatial mixing followed by feature mixing. In our model, the attention layers perform spatial and temporal mixing jointly, which we call Joint Spatial-Temporal Mixer (JSTM). Inspired by the Residual SWin Transformer Block (RSTB) [15], we use a sequence of JSTMs followed by a convolutional layer at the end to extract deep features. A 3D convolutional layer has been employed to further enhance the temporal feature fusion between neighboring frames. Ghosting artifacts mitigation is challenging for all video processing tasks. We introduce a Feature Weights Generator module within STTB, which consists of an Adaptive pooling, 3D convolutional layer and Sigmoid activation for learning the weight of each feature in channel dimension.

Joint Spatio-Temporal Mixer. Computing GA between all pixels of the video sequence is impractical and unnecessary. Since the channel dimension contains the features from different frames, we follow the method described in SWin Transformer [16], by dividing the input images into several non-overlapping spatial windows with the size $w \times w$. The attention layer of ViT can be interpreted as a spatial tokens mixer, where weights for each token are content-dependent [15]. Moreover, as described in [27], the attention layers can also mix channels. As such, in our method temporal mixing is performed when generating the Queries, Keys and Values from the feature of the tokens, as follows:

$$Q = XP_Q, \quad K = XP_K, \quad V = XP_V, \tag{2}$$

where c is the number of feature channels of a frame, $X \in \mathbb{R}^{w^2 \times 5c}$ is the features of all frames before mixing, $\{P_Q, P_K, P_V\} \in \mathbb{R}^{5c \times 5d}$ are the linear projections that project the features into $\{Q, K, V\} \in \mathbb{R}^{w^2 \times 5d}$. Because we concatenate all input frames along the channel dimension, each $\{\mathbf{q}_{i,j}, \mathbf{k}_{i,j}, \mathbf{v}_{i,j}\} \in \mathbb{R}^{5d}$ integrates the features of all frames at spatial position (i, j), namely $\mathbf{x}_{i,j} \in \mathbb{R}^{5c}$. This process can be described as:

$$\mathbf{q}_{i,j} = \mathbf{x}_{i,j}P_Q, \quad \mathbf{k}_{i,j} = \mathbf{x}_{i,j}P_K, \quad \mathbf{v}_{i,j} = \mathbf{x}_{i,j}P_V, \tag{3}$$

$$\mathbf{q}_{i,j} = cat[\mathbf{q}_{i,j}^{I-2,\dots,2}], \quad \mathbf{k}_{i,j} = cat[\mathbf{k}_{i,j}^{I-2,\dots,2}], \quad \mathbf{v}_{i,j} = cat[\mathbf{v}_{i,j}^{I-2,\dots,2}], \tag{4}$$

where $n \in \{-2, -1, 0, 1, 2\}$, and $\{\mathbf{q}_{i,j}^{I_n}, \mathbf{k}_{i,j}^{I_n}, \mathbf{v}_{i,j}^{I_n}\} \in \mathbb{R}^c$ is the *query*, *key* and *value* of the token in frame n with spatial position (i, j).

Since the motions introduce offsets between pairing pixels in different frames, resulting that the mixing only along the channel dimension is far from enough to integrate the temporal information (as described in Eq. 3). We apply the following spatial mixing which aggregates all the spatial and temporal information to a reference token $\mathbf{y}_{i',j'}^{I_n}$ at spatial location (i', j') of frame I_n $(\langle \cdot , \cdot \rangle : V \times V \to \mathbb{R})$:

$$\mathbf{y}_{i',j'}^{I_n} = \sum_{i=1,j=1}^{i=w,j=w} \frac{\langle \mathbf{q}_{i',j'}^{I_n}, \mathbf{k}_{i,j}^{I_n} \rangle}{norm_{i',j'}^{I_n}} \mathbf{v}_{i,j}^{I_n}, \quad norm_{i',j'}^{I_n} = \sum_{i=1,j=1}^{i=w,j=w} \langle \mathbf{q}_{i',j'}^{I_n}, \mathbf{k}_{i,j}^{I_n} \rangle. \tag{5}$$

The spatio-temporal mixing function (Eqs. 3–4) of attention layer can be visualized in Fig. 4. Above formulas written in matrix form is one of the computations of the attention mechanism in ViT, but we expand the calculation for spatio-temporal feature fusion:

$$Attention(Q, K, V) = SoftMax(\frac{QK^T}{\sqrt{D}} + bias)V, \tag{6}$$

where D is the features length of each token, in our case $D = 5d$, and a trainable relative position *bias*, which can increase the capacity of the model [16]. The following MLP layers in each JSTM act as a temporal mixer. Before feeding the

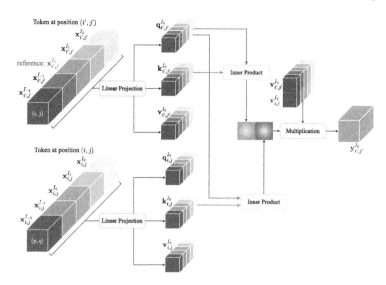

Fig. 4. The visual description of attention layer as implicit temporal mixer. The query $(\mathbf{q}_{i',j'}^{I_0})$, key $(\mathbf{k}_{i',j'}^{I_0})$ and value $(\mathbf{v}_{i',j'}^{I_0})$ of the reference token $\mathbf{x}_{i',j'}^{I_0}$ integrate the features of all frames at position (i',j'). In like manner, the query $(\mathbf{q}_{i,j}^{I_0})$, key $(\mathbf{k}_{i,j}^{I_0})$ and value $(\mathbf{v}_{i,j}^{I_0})$ of the token $\mathbf{x}_{i,j}^{I_0}$ integrate the features of all frames at position (i,j). The attention between $\mathbf{x}_{i',j'}^{I_0}$ and $\mathbf{x}_{i,j}^{I_0}$ fuses the features of all frames at both position (i',j') and (i,j), which performs the spatio-temporal fusion.

tokens to the next STTB, we use a 3D convolutional layer followed by Feature Weights Generator module to extract features further. The end-to-end connection of the STTBs aggregates multiple spatial and temporal mixers together.

Wavelet Decomposition. The size of the attention map, $\text{SoftMax}(QK^T/\sqrt{D}+bias)$ is $w^2 \times w^2$, and is the bottleneck of the inference speed. Inspired by Maggioni et al. [18], we use Wavelet Transform to halve the resolution to make training and inference more efficient. The reduced resolution enables much longer feature embeddings, which is beneficial for the performance of our network. See more comparisons and discussions in the ablation studies in Sect. 4.3.

With the proposed STTB and JSTM module, the spatio-temporal attention can be calculated and learned efficiently. Our proposed model achieved good spatial quality, and the output frames from one $Block^t$ are temporally stable. However, the temporal coherency between adjacent frames that come from neighboring blocks is not as good as those from the same block. As shown in an example Fig. 5, we compute residual images of three consecutive denoised frames from $Block^t$ and $Block^{t+1}$, where larger value means higher difference between consecutive frames. We describe the solution in Sect. 3.2.

3.2   Temporal Coherency Enhancement (TCE) Phase

Recurrent Architecture. To improve the coherency between temporal blocks, we propose a recurrent architecture for fine-tuning the network and add a new

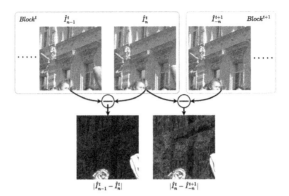

Fig. 5. The visualization of the inconsistency between adjacent frames from one temporal block (left) and from two neighboring temporal blocks (right).

loss term to alleviate flickering further. Despite the $2(m-n)$ common input frames shared in two adjacent blocks, the noise in the remaining $2n+1$ input frames vary in each block, which is the root cause of the incoherency. We modify our model into the recurrent architecture to enforce the connection between two adjacent blocks, namely the first input frame of the $Block^{t+1}$ is the last output frame of the $Block^t$, which can be described as:

$$Block^{t+1} : \{\hat{I}_{-1}^{t+1}, \hat{I}_0^{t+1}, \hat{I}_1^{t+1}\} = \Phi(\{\hat{I}_1^t, \tilde{I}_{-1}^{t+1}, \tilde{I}_0^{t+1}, \tilde{I}_1^{t+1}, \tilde{I}_2^{t+1}\}). \tag{7}$$

The recurrent architecture spreads the information of all frames from the current $Block^t$ to the $Block^{t+1}$ by propagating one denoised frame of $Block^t$ to the first input frame of the $Block^{t+1}$. Such recurrent architecture enhances the connection between neighboring temporal blocks and achieves better temporal consistency, as is shown in Fig. 6.

The substitution of the first noisy input frame with the denoised one provides a solid prior knowledge to each block. However, the reconstruction errors can also propagate to the following blocks. Moreover, the dynamic contents and the static contents with periodical occlusions (e.g., the reliefs which the legs of the dancer sweep over, shown in the blue rectangles of Fig. 6) are still temporally inconsistent. We describe the solution in the next section.

Overlap Loss. To solve the inconsistency of the dynamic contents, we modify the stride when dividing the video sequence so that the neighboring temporal blocks share $2(m-n)+1$ common input frames. Most importantly, an overlapping exists in the output frames of the neighboring blocks. The last output frame of $Block^t$, namely $\hat{I}_n^t$, and the first output frame of $Block^{t+1}$, namely $\hat{I}_{-n}^{t+1}$, should be the same image. Following this idea, we introduce a new loss term as follows:

$$\mathcal{L}_{overlap}^t = |\hat{I}_n^t - \hat{I}_{-n}^{t+1}|, \tag{8}$$

where $\mathcal{L}_{overlap}^t$ is the $l1$ loss between the last output frame of $Block_t$ and the first output frame of $Block_{t+1}$. The total loss $\mathcal{L}_{total}$ is composed of two parts, the

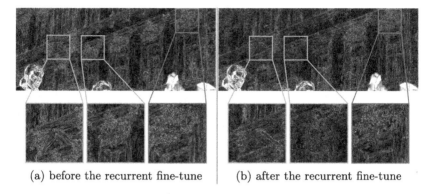

| (a) before the recurrent fine-tune | (b) after the recurrent fine-tune |

Fig. 6. Comparison of the residual figures ($|I^t_{-n} - I^{t+1}_n|$) before and after the recurrent fine-tuning. The contents on the top left corner (blue squares) are static throughout the whole video sequence. For these contents, the temporal consistency is enhanced compared with those without the recurrent fine-tuning. However, the static parts with periodical occlusions (red square) and dynamic regions have limited improvement. (Color figure online)

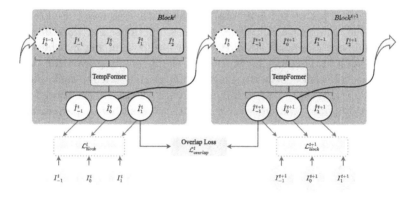

Fig. 7. Illustration of the Recurrent architecture and the Overlap Loss.

first part $\mathcal{L}^t_{block}$ is the loss between the denoised frames $\hat{I}$ and the ground truth I for each temporal block, and the second part is the Overlap Loss $\mathcal{L}^t_{overlap}$. We use a hyper parameter α to balance the spatial loss and the temporal loss, which is shown in the following formula:

$$\mathcal{L}^t_{block} = \frac{1}{2n+1} \sum_{i=-n}^{n} |\hat{I}^t_i - I^t_i|, \tag{9}$$

$$\mathcal{L}_{total} = \frac{1}{T} \sum_{t=0}^{T} \mathcal{L}^t_{block} + \alpha \frac{1}{T-1} \sum_{t=0}^{T-1} \mathcal{L}^t_{overlap}, \tag{10}$$

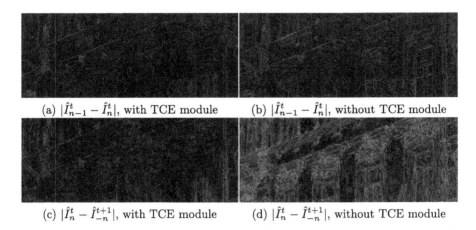

(a) $|\hat{I}^t_{n-1} - \hat{I}^t_n|$, with TCE module   (b) $|\hat{I}^t_{n-1} - \hat{I}^t_n|$, without TCE module

(c) $|\hat{I}^t_n - \hat{I}^{t+1}_{-n}|$, with TCE module   (d) $|\hat{I}^t_n - \hat{I}^{t+1}_{-n}|$, without TCE module

Fig. 8. Comparison of the residual figures with and without the TCE module. Top: residual figures between adjacent frames in one temporal $Block^t$. Bottom: residual figures between adjacent frames from two neighboring $Block^t$ and $Block^{t+1}$.

where T is the index of the temporal blocks in the sequence. Figure 7 shows overview of the recurrent architecture and loss functions. The fine-tuned model achieved promising temporal stability, which is shown in Fig. 8. The temporal consistency between neighboring blocks has significant improvement (Fig. 8(c), (d)), but the coherency between neighboring frames within each block also becomes better (Fig. 8(a), (b)). Compared with the recurrent model without $\mathcal{L}_{overlap}$, the dynamic contents and the static contents with periodical occlusions are also as stable as the ones that are static throughout the sequence.

4   Experiments

4.1   Experimental Setup

Training Strategy. For the temporal sliding windows strategy, we input five neighboring frames and let the model predict three neighboring frames in the middle. During Spatio-Temporal Video Denoising Phase, we process one temporal block in each training step. During Temporal Coherency Enhancement Phase, instead of loading several blocks in one training step, we only load two neighboring blocks($Block^0$ and $Block^1$). For the first temporal block, we substitute the first noisy input frame with the corresponding ground truth to simulate the recurrent architecture. Following our design, we replace the second temporal block's first input frame ($\tilde{I}^1_{-2}$) with the second output frame of the first temporal block ($\hat{I}^0_0$), and add the Overlap Loss to the common output frames ($\hat{I}^0_1$ and $\hat{I}^1_{-1}$).

Datasets. Following the previous works [14,21,22], we use DAVIS 2017 dataset [19] (480P) as training and testing set for qualitative and quantitative evaluations. We train a non-blind model on five noise levels ($\sigma = \{10, 20, 30, 40, 50\}$).

Table 1. Quantitative comparison with existing methods on DAVIS [19] and Set8 [20]. The best and second best methods are written in red and blue colors separately. Comparison of inference time per frame (s/f) on resolution of 480P (*) and 1080P videos (§) respectively. The fastest and second fastest methods are in red and blue respectively. VRT [14] uses temporal block size 12. VRT† [14] uses temporal block size 5.

	σ	FastDVD [21]	PaCNet [22]	VRT [14](†)	TempFormer	TempFormer++
DAVIS	10	39.07	39.97	40.82(40.42)	39.97	40.17
	20	35.95	36.82	38.15(37.49)	37.10	37.36
	30	34.16	34.79	36.52(35.73)	35.40	35.66
	40	32.90	33.34	35.32(34.47)	34.16	34.42
	50	31.92	32.30	34.36(33.47)	33.20	33.44
Set8	10	36.27	37.06	37.88(37.62)	36.97	37.15
	20	33.51	33.94	35.02(34.59)	34.55	34.74
	30	31.88	32.05	33.35(32.82)	33.01	33.20
	40	30.73	30.70	32.15(31.57)	31.86	32.06
	50	29.83	29.66	31.22(30.61)	30.96	31.16
Time* (s/f)		0.15	30	3.54(3.07)	1.38	1.55
Time§ (s/f)		0.68	-	17.67(16.16)	5.88	6.78

4.2 Results

Spatial Accuracy. To compare quantitative results, we use PSNR as the evaluation metric. Inspired by [14], we propose another version of TempFormer with optical flow and warping on RGB space, which we call TempFormer++. Instead of warping both images and features, we only warp RGB images as data augmentation. In this way, there is no change to the architecture of our model. Table 1 reports the average PSNR for each noise level on the Test-Dev 2017 [19] 480P and Set8 [20]. We use the spatial tiling size 128×128 for both VRT [14] and our model, and adjust the other configurations so that both models fully utilize the GPU memory. We use RTX 3090ti as the testing device for evaluating the inference time on 480P and 1080P videos from DAVIS 2017 dataset respectively, and the comparison is shown in last two rows of Table 1.

Since the computation of the attention in ViT is the most expensive module of inference time. With our proposed method, we avoid the time consuming temporal mutual attention calculation and use the proposed STTB and JSTM modules to integrate temporal information implicitly. As a result, our model required approximately 40% inference time compared with VRT [14] with comparable spatial denosing quality on PSNR evaluation, as shown in Table 1. We report temporal consistency evaluation in Sect. 4.2 and Table 2.

Figure 9 shown the qualitative comparison of the results with the existing methods. As shown in the examples, our method produced comparable and even better visual quality to the state-of-the-art (SOTA) method. Note that, on noise level $\sigma = 30$ and $\sigma = 50$ (top and bottom row of Fig. 9), TempFormer restored more detailed pattern and sharper edges than VRT [14] and TempFormer++,

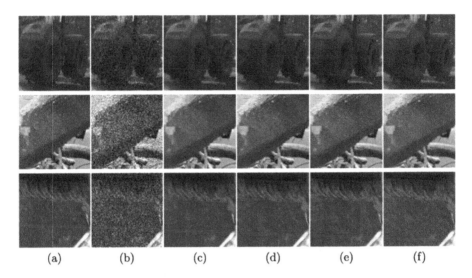

Fig. 9. Visual comparison with other methods. Top row: $\sigma = 30$, middle row: $\sigma = 40$, bottom row: $\sigma = 50$. (a) ground truth. (b) noisy. (c) FastDVD [21]. (d) VRT [14]. (e) TempFormer. (f) TempFormer++.

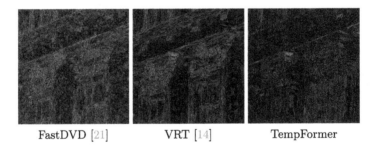

FastDVD [21]   VRT [14]   TempFormer

Fig. 10. Visualization of the residual figure on the static contents from video *berakdance* in DAVIS 2017 [19] 1080P (the reliefs in frame 39 and frame 40). The noise level is $\sigma = 30$. The residual figure of VRT [14] is computed on the junction of two temporal blocks.

which indicated that the failure of optical flow estimation on higher noise level content could produce negative impact on the spatial accuracy.

Temporal Consistency. We qualitatively demonstrate the performance of the temporal consistency by visualizing the residual images of adjacent denoised frames' static region, which is shown in Fig. 10. For a better quantitative comparison (without being influenced by the temporal artifacts in the original dataset), we create a toy video sequence where each frame is identical, and add noise with different random seed for each frame. In this toy sequence, the ground truth of the residual image between adjacent denoised frames is zero everywhere. We estimate the mean absolute error (MAE) between the adjacent output frames

Table 2. Quantitative comparison of temporal consistency. We use one frame from video *skatejump* in DAVIS 2017 [19] 480P to create the toy sequence. VRT [14] uses temporal block size 12. VRT† [14] uses temporal block size 5.

σ	FastDVD [21]	VRT† [14]	VRT [14]	TempFormer
10	3.6×10^{-3}	2.4×10^{-3}	1.7×10^{-3}	1.3×10^{-3}
20	5.4×10^{-3}	3.1×10^{-3}	2.0×10^{-3}	1.3×10^{-3}
30	6.8×10^{-3}	3.7×10^{-3}	2.3×10^{-3}	1.3×10^{-3}
40	8.0×10^{-3}	4.2×10^{-3}	2.6×10^{-3}	1.5×10^{-3}
50	9.0×10^{-3}	4.7×10^{-3}	2.9×10^{-3}	1.7×10^{-3}

denoised by different methods respectively, as shown in Table 2. As long as the whole video sequence is processed block by block, our TCE strategy can alleviate the temporal flickering between frames and neighboring blocks, which resultant significantly better temporal consistency performance than the existing methods. As illustrated in Fig. 10 and Table 2, the temporal consistency of our model outperforms all other state-of-the-art methods, especially under high noise levels. More visual results are provided in the videos contained in the supplementary.

4.3 Ablation Studies

Impact of the channel length and Wavelet Decomposition. In Transformer models, the length of channel is the main factor that effects the performance. We trained our model with two types of configurations where the channel length is 40 (small model) and 120 (large model) per frame respectively. We also trained a TempFormer without Wavelet decomposition to evaluate its impact. Table 3 shows the performance of the models and inference time, which demonstrates the effectiveness of the hyperparameter of the channel length and Wavelet decomposition in our model.

With the Wavelet decomposition, the number of the attention maps is reduced to 1/4 compared with the model without decomposition. As demonstrated in Table 3, in spite of the negative impact on the spatial performance, its boost in inference speed is evident. On the other hand, the halving in spatial resolution allows us to boost in channel length of the model, which achieves good balance between model capacity and efficiency, as shown in the last column of the Table 3. The temporal constraints requires larger capacity of the model, so the model with longer channel has better temporal consistency than the shorter ones, as demonstrated in the comparison at the last row of this table.

Wavelet Transform VS. Pixel Shuffle. Other than the Wavelet Transform, there are some other kinds of decomposition methods that can halve the input resolution. We tested Pixel Shuffle, and Table 4 shows the comparison. Since Wavelet Transform separates low and high frequency sub-bands (horizontal and vertical edges) of the images, and preserves image information better than Pixel Shuffle. The experimental results showed that the model trained with Wavelet

Table 3. Impact of the channel length and Wavelet Decomposition, tested on *breakdance* 1080p in DAVIS 2017 [19] with noise level $\sigma = 30$. S(small model): the length of channel is 40 per frame. L(large model): the length of channel is 120 per frame. Settings: the size of each tile is 128×128, process 8 tiles per batch. (For the PSNR and inference time comparison we use the models before the Temporal Coherency Enhancement Phase.)

	w/o Wavelet	w/ Wavelet	
Model size	S	S	L
PSNR	36.51	36.34	36.59
Inference time(s/f)	4.21	1.43	3.75
Temporal Consistency	✓	✓	✓✓

Table 4. Quantitative comparison between different decomposition methods: Wavelet Transform and Pixel Shuffle. (For this comparison we use the models before the Temporal Coherency Enhancement Phase.)

σ	Wavelet	Pixel Shuffle
10	39.82	39.78
20	36.85	36.81
30	35.10	35.06
40	33.85	33.81
50	32.89	32.84

transform achieved better results. In our methods, we only utilize the Wavelet Transform to reduce the resolution and improve the efficiency. Different from [18], the weights of the kernel in our model are fixed.

5   Conclusions

This paper proposed an effective and efficient SWin Transformer-based video denoising network, TempFormer, which has outperformed most existing methods on additive Gaussian noise, achieved the best temporal coherent denoising results and lower computational complexity than the SOTA video denoiser. Specifically, we introduced the Wavelet Transform as pre-processing to halve the resolution of the video to improve efficiency. For utilizing the temporal information effectively, the spatial and temporal attention has been learned by the proposed Spatial-Temporal Transformer Block and the Joint Spatio-Temporal Mixer modules. Our model achieved both comparable quantitative and qualitative results with approximately 40% inference time requirement of the SOTA method. Moreover, the long-standing temporal inconsistency issue has been solved by the proposed recurrent strategy, together with the Overlap Loss function. The experimental results indicate that the proposed method dramatically enhanced the temporal coherency of the denoised video and almost exterminates the flicker between adjacent frames.

References

1. Ali, A., et al.: XCIT: cross-covariance image transformers. Adv. Neural Inf. Process. Syst. **34**, 1–10 (2021)
2. Bertasius, G., Wang, H., Torresani, L.: Is space-time attention all you need for video understanding. arXiv preprint arXiv:2102.05095 (2021)

3. Buades, A., Coll, B., Morel, J.M.: A non-local algorithm for image denoising. In: 2005 IEEE Computer Society Conference on Computer Vision and Pattern Recognition (CVPR 2005), vol. 2, pp. 60–65. IEEE (2005)
4. Cai, Z., Zhang, Y., Manzi, M., Oztireli, C., Gross, M., Aydin, T.O.: Robust image denoising using kernel predicting networks (2021)
5. Carion, N., Massa, F., Synnaeve, G., Usunier, N., Kirillov, A., Zagoruyko, S.: End-to-end object detection with transformers. In: Vedaldi, A., Bischof, H., Brox, T., Frahm, J.-M. (eds.) ECCV 2020. LNCS, vol. 12346, pp. 213–229. Springer, Cham (2020). https://doi.org/10.1007/978-3-030-58452-8_13
6. Chan, K.C., Zhou, S., Xu, X., Loy, C.C.: BasicVSR++: improving video super-resolution with enhanced propagation and alignment. arXiv preprint arXiv:2104.13371 (2021)
7. Chen, H., et al.: Pre-trained image processing transformer. In: Proceedings of the IEEE/CVF Conference on Computer Vision and Pattern Recognition, pp. 12299–12310 (2021)
8. Dai, X., Chen, Y., Xiao, B., Chen, D., Liu, M., Yuan, L., Zhang, L.: Dynamic head: unifying object detection heads with attentions. In: Proceedings of the IEEE/CVF Conference on Computer Vision and Pattern Recognition, pp. 7373–7382 (2021)
9. Dai, Z., Liu, H., Le, Q., Tan, M.: CoatNet: marrying convolution and attention for all data sizes. Adv. Neural Inf. Process. Syst. **34**, 1–12 (2021)
10. Dosovitskiy, A., et al.: An image is worth 16×16 words: Transformers for image recognition at scale. arXiv preprint arXiv:2010.11929 (2020)
11. Lai, W.-S., Huang, J.-B., Wang, O., Shechtman, E., Yumer, E., Yang, M.-H.: Learning blind video temporal consistency. In: Ferrari, V., Hebert, M., Sminchisescu, C., Weiss, Y. (eds.) ECCV 2018. LNCS, vol. 11219, pp. 179–195. Springer, Cham (2018). https://doi.org/10.1007/978-3-030-01267-0_11
12. Lei, C., Xing, Y., Chen, Q.: Blind video temporal consistency via deep video prior. Adv. Neural Inf. Process. Syst. **33**, 1083–1093 (2020)
13. Li, K., et al.: Uniformer: unified transformer for efficient spatiotemporal representation learning. arXiv preprint arXiv:2201.04676 (2022)
14. Liang, J., et al.: VRT: a video restoration transformer. arXiv preprint arXiv:2201.12288 (2022)
15. Liang, J., Cao, J., Sun, G., Zhang, K., Van Gool, L., Timofte, R.: SwinIR: image restoration using Swin transformer. In: Proceedings of the IEEE/CVF International Conference on Computer Vision, pp. 1833–1844 (2021)
16. Liu, Z., et al.: Swin transformer: hierarchical vision transformer using shifted windows. arXiv preprint arXiv:2103.14030 (2021)
17. Maggioni, M., Boracchi, G., Foi, A., Egiazarian, K.: Video denoising, deblocking, and enhancement through separable 4-d nonlocal spatiotemporal transforms. IEEE Trans. Image Process. **21**(9), 3952–3966 (2012)
18. Maggioni, M., Huang, Y., Li, C., Xiao, S., Fu, Z., Song, F.: Efficient multi-stage video denoising with recurrent spatio-temporal fusion. In: Proceedings of the IEEE/CVF Conference on Computer Vision and Pattern Recognition, pp. 3466–3475 (2021)
19. Perazzi, F., Pont-Tuset, J., McWilliams, B., Van Gool, L., Gross, M., Sorkine-Hornung, A.: A benchmark dataset and evaluation methodology for video object segmentation. In: Proceedings of the IEEE Conference on Computer Vision and Pattern Recognition, pp. 724–732 (2016)
20. Tassano, M., Delon, J., Veit, T.: DVDNet: a fast network for deep video denoising. In: 2019 IEEE International Conference on Image Processing (ICIP), pp. 1805–1809. IEEE (2019)

21. Tassano, M., Delon, J., Veit, T.: FastDVDNet: towards real-time deep video denoising without flow estimation. In: Proceedings of the IEEE/CVF Conference on Computer Vision and Pattern Recognition, pp. 1354–1363 (2020)
22. Vaksman, G., Elad, M., Milanfar, P.: Patch craft: video denoising by deep modeling and patch matching. arXiv preprint arXiv:2103.13767 (2021)
23. Vaswani, A., et al.: Attention is all you need. In: Advances in Neural Information Processing Systems, pp. 5998–6008 (2017)
24. Wang, C., Zhou, S.K., Cheng, Z.: First image then video: A two-stage network for spatiotemporal video denoising. arXiv preprint arXiv:2001.00346 (2020)
25. Xu, M., et al.: End-to-end semi-supervised object detection with soft teacher. In: Proceedings of the IEEE/CVF International Conference on Computer Vision, pp. 3060–3069 (2021)
26. Yang, J., et al.: Focal self-attention for local-global interactions in vision transformers (2021). arXiv preprint arXiv:2107.00641
27. Yu, W., et al.: Metaformer is actually what you need for vision. arXiv preprint arXiv:2111.11418 (2021)
28. Yuan, L., et al.: Florence: a new foundation model for computer vision. arXiv preprint arXiv:2111.11432 (2021)
29. Yue, H., Cao, C., Liao, L., Chu, R., Yang, J.: Supervised raw video denoising with a benchmark dataset on dynamic scenes. In: Proceedings of the IEEE/CVF Conference on Computer Vision and Pattern Recognition, pp. 2301–2310 (2020)
30. Zamir, S.W., Arora, A., Khan, S., Hayat, M., Khan, F.S., Yang, M.H.: Restormer: efficient transformer for high-resolution image restoration. arXiv preprint arXiv:2111.09881 (2021)
31. Zhai, X., Kolesnikov, A., Houlsby, N., Beyer, L.: Scaling vision transformers (2021)
32. Zhang, K., Zuo, W., Chen, Y., Meng, D., Zhang, L.: Beyond a gaussian denoiser: residual learning of deep CNN for image denoising. IEEE Trans. Image Process. **26**(7), 3142–3155 (2017)
33. Zhang, K., Zuo, W., Gu, S., Zhang, L.: Learning deep CNN denoiser prior for image restoration. In: Proceedings of the IEEE Conference on Computer Vision and Pattern Recognition, pp. 3929–3938 (2017)
34. Zhang, K., Zuo, W., Zhang, L.: FFDNet: toward a fast and flexible solution for CNN-based image denoising. IEEE Trans. Image Process. **27**(9), 4608–4622 (2018)

RAWtoBit: A Fully End-to-end Camera ISP Network

Wooseok Jeong and Seung-Won Jung$^{(\boxtimes)}$

Department of Electrical Engineering, Korea University, Seoul, Korea
{561wesd,swjung83}@korea.ac.kr

Abstract. Image compression is an essential and last processing unit in the camera image signal processing (ISP) pipeline. While many studies have been made to replace the conventional ISP pipeline with a single end-to-end optimized deep learning model, image compression is barely considered as a part of the model. In this paper, we investigate the designing of a fully end-to-end optimized camera ISP incorporating image compression. To this end, we propose RAWtoBit network (RBN) that can effectively perform both tasks simultaneously. RBN is further improved with a novel knowledge distillation scheme by introducing two teacher networks specialized in each task. Extensive experiments demonstrate that our proposed method significantly outperforms alternative approaches in terms of rate-distortion trade-off.

Keywords: Camera network · Knowledge distillation · Image compression · Image signal processing pipeline

1 Introduction

The image signal processing (ISP) pipeline is receiving increasing attention from the research community, as mobile devices are equipped with powerful hardware which can be utilized to process more sophisticated operations to boost performance [14]. A typical ISP pipeline includes several local and global operations, such as white balance, demosaicing, color correction, gamma correction, denoising, and tone mapping [22]. Since each of these operations is a research topic on its own, they are often separately optimized for a given ISP pipeline, which can be sub-optimal.

The deep learning-based approach has proven to be effective in various computer vision and image processing tasks, and consequently, many attempts have been made to replace conventional ISPs with convolutional neural networks (CNNs) [14,18,24,30]. While earlier learning-based works only dealt with the ISP components separately, such as demosaicing [32] and denoising[15,35,37], recent studies have paid attention to the design of a unified CNN that performs

Supplementary Information The online version contains supplementary material available at https://doi.org/10.1007/978-3-031-19800-7_29.

all ISP functionalities, which is referred to as an ISP-Net. For example, Schwartz et al. [24] proposed a two-stage ISP-Net for low-level and high-level operations and showed that sharing features between two stages leads to a better result. In [18], correlated ISP components are categorized into two groups and independently trained, followed by joint fine-tuning.

However, most previous ISP-Nets did not consider that sRGB images rendered from RAW are essentially followed by lossy compression, which may substantially alter the image quality. Although some studies [29, 30] have proposed to integrate JPEG simulation as a part of the model to take into account the compression artifacts, they are limited to the simulation, and the standard JPEG is still used to produce a bitstream.

The objective of image compression is to reduce bits required for storing and transmitting an image without largely affecting the perceived quality. Image compression is typically achieved by transforming the image, quantizing the transformed coefficients, and compressing the resultant representation using entropy coding [12]. In particular, the quantization introduces an inevitable error, where coarse quantization leads to bitrate reduction at the expense of distortion increase, giving rise to the rate-distortion trade-off. Under the principle of transform coding [12], many codecs have been developed to improve rate-distortion performance, including JPEG2000 [25] and versatile video coding (VVC) [4]. Most of the components in these existing codecs, however, are designed by human experts much like conventional ISP components, which promote researchers to design a CNN that performs image compression, which is referred to as a Comp-Net [1,2,8,20]. Unlike conventional image compression techniques, Comp-Net is inherently differentiable and performs significantly better than the commonly used JPEG.

The advances in deep learning-based image processing and image compression motivate us to propose a fully end-to-end camera ISP network called RAWtoBit network (RBN). Our RBN takes RAW as an input as other ISP-Nets [18,24,29,30] but outputs a bitstream, which can be decoded to reconstruct a high-quality sRGB image. To this end, we investigate two structures: cascaded and unified. Cascaded structure refers to a simple concatenation of ISP-Net and Comp-Net. However, the performance of Comp-Net can be upper-bounded by ISP-Net, resulting in sub-optimal rate-distortion performance. Unified structure refers to a single network that simultaneously performs the ISP operations and image compression. Although the unified structure can be easily implemented by training a Comp-Net with RAW-sRGB pairs with slight modification in network architecture, such a structure can also lead to sub-optimal rate-distortion performance since Comp-Net is not originally designed to perform complicated ISP operations. Observing that these two naïve approaches suffer from poor rate-distortion performance, we propose RBN to handle both tasks effectively. Furthermore, we present two teacher networks, namely the ISP teacher and the compression teacher, to guide RBN to reach a better rate-distortion trade-off. Experimental results demonstrate that our proposed RBN performs noticeably better than the alternative approaches. Our contribution can be summarized as follows:

- This work is the first attempt to integrate camera ISP and image compression in a single learning framework to the best of our knowledge. Unlike previous studies, our RBN takes RAW data as an input and produces a bitstream as an output.
- We propose a method that distills the knowledge from two teacher models, namely the ISP teacher and the compression teacher, to make RBN effectively performs both ISP and compression tasks.
- Extensive experimental results demonstrate that our RBN with knowledge distillation significantly improves rate-distortion performance over the cascaded or unified structure.

2   Related Work

2.1   Camera ISP Network

An ISP-Net is trained to render sRGB images from RAW sensor data, either by explicitly supervising the subtasks of an ISP or by directly learning a RAW to sRGB mapping function, which in this case learns the necessary subtasks implicitly. Towards the latter approach, Schwartz et al. [24] presented an ISP-Net called DeepISP, where the two-stage network is employed for low-level and high-level operations, and demonstrated that the latter high-level enhancement task could be improved by sharing features from the former low-level task. Chen et al. [6] tackled the challenging problem of low light photography by learning the mapping from a RAW image captured in low light to its corresponding long-exposure sRGB image. Ignatov et al. [14] collected RAW and sRGB image pairs using a smartphone camera and a professional DSLR, respectively. By training a network with a hierarchical structure using such image pairs, their ISP-Net produced sRGB images with better visual quality than those rendered from the smartphone's built-in ISP. Zhang et al. [38] addressed the misalignment problem between RAW and sRGB image pairs [14] and proposed to warp the ground-truth sRGB images to the color corrected RAW images for supervision. However, none of the aforementioned ISP-Nets consider image compression, an essential component of practical camera ISPs.

Meanwhile, Xing et al. [30] proposed an invertible ISP-Net, where the forward pass produces sRGB images and the backward pass reconstructs RAW images. With the differentiable rounding function defined by the Fourier series, JPEG compression is simulated and integrated into the training procedure. Uhm et al. [29] cascaded an ISP-Net and a network that simulates JPEG compression to train the ISP-Net with lossy image compression in consideration. However, these ISP-Nets [29,30] are not trained in a fully end-to-end (i.e., RAW-to-bits) manner and rely on the standard JPEG compression at the inference stage, leading to sub-optimal rate-distortion performance.

2.2   Image Compression Network

Learned image compression has drawn attention from many researchers in recent years, and state-of-the-art methods [10] demonstrate improved rate-distortion performance compared to hand-crafted codecs such as JPEG and JPEG2000. Learning-based methods share the same principle of transform coding as the conventional codecs; however, the nonlinear transformation is performed by a neural network instead of discrete cosine transform or wavelet transform, which are linear transformations, hence capable of learning a more complex representation. The most indispensable component of lossy image compression is undoubtedly the quantization, which is not differentiable, making the design of Comp-Net challenging. Many Comp-Nets thus have applied different strategies to deal with the quantization in the training process, e.g., by adding uniform noise [1] or replacing the derivative of the rounding function with identity function [26].

While early Comp-Nets [27, 28] employed recurrent neural networks, more recent Comp-Nets [1, 26] incorporated an autoencoder structure to minimize distortion and an entropy model estimation network to minimize bitrate. To this end, Ballé et al. [2] proposed to transmit side information to estimate the scale of the zero-mean Gaussian entropy model. Minnen et al. [20] further improved this idea by predicting the mean and scale of the Gaussian entropy model conditioned on hyperprior and decoded latent elements. Cheng et al. [8] achieved comparable performance to the latest VVC standard [4] by embedding attention modules in the network and using Gaussian mixtures as the entropy model. An interested reader can refer to the recent article [13] for a systematic literature review.

2.3   Knowledge Distillation

The main purpose of knowledge distillation (KD) is to transfer knowledge from a large teacher model to a more compact model without significantly compromising the performance. A comprehensive survey on KD [11] categorized existing schemes into three groups: response-based, feature-based, and relation-based KD. We focus on the feature-based KD, where the intermediate features are compared between teacher and student models as a means of knowledge transfer. Since Romero et al. [23] first proved the effectiveness of providing intermediate representation of a teacher model as a hint for training a student model, many approaches have been proposed to find a better form of KD. Zagoruyko et al. [33] proposed to transfer attention maps generated from the intermediate layers. Kim et al. [16] argued that the direct transfer of teacher's knowledge ignores the structural difference between the teacher and student models and introduced "factors", which are the features extracted and paraphrased from the teacher model, as a more effective form of knowledge. Chen et al. [7] developed a framework that can adaptively assign appropriate teacher layers to each student layer by attention allocation.

Although most KD schemes are developed for model compression, some studies have investigated KD from the models which perform related tasks. While not strictly following the general teacher-student principle in KD, Xu et al. [31] proposed to simultaneously perform depth estimation and scene parsing with guidance of intermediate auxiliary tasks such as surface normal estimation and semantic segmentation. Zhang et al. [36] introduced a logit and representation graph for KD from multiple self-supervised auxiliary tasks. Similar to these approaches, we weakly disentangle the main objective into two tasks and perform KD using two teacher networks that better perform each task.

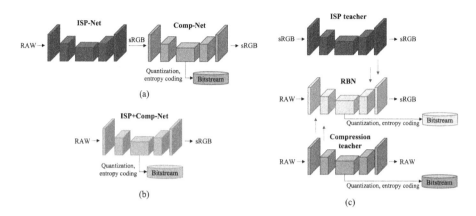

Fig. 1. Different configurations of end-to-end camera ISP networks: (a) Cascaded ISP-Net and Comp-Net, (b) unified ISP+Comp-Net, and (c) our proposed RBN with KD from two teachers. The red arrows represent the KD direction, and the context model for rate estimation is omitted for simplicity. (Color figure online)

3 Proposed Method

The proposed work is the first attempt to integrate ISP-Net and Comp-Net to the best of our knowledge. We thus first present two straightforward configurations of the ISP-Net and Comp-Net integration, namely cascaded structure (Sect. 3.1) and unified structure (Sect. 3.2). We then introduce our RBN, which is also based on the unified structure but specially designed and trained with our KD scheme (Sect. 3.3).

3.1 Cascaded Structure

A naïve approach to combine ISP and lossy compression is to cascade ISP-Net and Comp-Net, as shown in Fig. 1(a). An ISP-Net takes a RAW image $x_r \in \mathbb{R}^{4 \times H/2 \times W/2}$ as an input and produces an sRGB image $\hat{x}_s \in \mathbb{R}^{3 \times H \times W}$, while Comp-Net takes an sRGB image as an input and generates a bitstream which can reconstruct an sRGB image. Both ISP-Net and Comp-Net are separately trained and cascaded. This configuration is not limited to specific ISP-Net and Comp-Net architectures, and in our study, we use LiteISPNet [38] and the context+hyperprior model [20] for ISP-Net and Comp-Net, respectively. In addition, as in [29], one can try fine-tuning ISP-Net in conjunction with Comp-Net to take lossy compression into consideration. We also investigate the effectiveness of this fine-tuning in Sect. 4.

3.2   Unified Structure

Another way to achieve the same objective is to directly train Comp-Net with RAW-sRGB image pairs, as shown in Fig. 1(b). Note that conventional Comp-Nets input and output sRGB images, as shown in Fig. 1(a). However, our target network configuration requires the network to take a RAW image $x_r \in \mathbb{R}^{4 \times H/2 \times W/2}$ as an input and produce a bitstream which can reconstruct an sRGB image $\hat{x}_s \in \mathbb{R}^{3 \times H \times W}$. Consequently, we modify the context+hyperprior model [20] to handle a four-channel input and add an additional inverse generalized divisive normalization (IGDN) and a transposed convolutional layer in the decoder to produce the sRGB image with the target size. The network is trained using the rate-distortion loss [20] while measuring the difference between ground-truth and decoded sRGB images.

Since conventional Comp-Nets, including the context+hyperprior model [20], are not designed to handle complicated ISP functions, it is expected that this unified model cannot perform both ISP and compression functionalities properly. More dedicated architecture design and training methodology are required to realize an effective end-to-end camera ISP, which is the motivation of the proposed RBN.

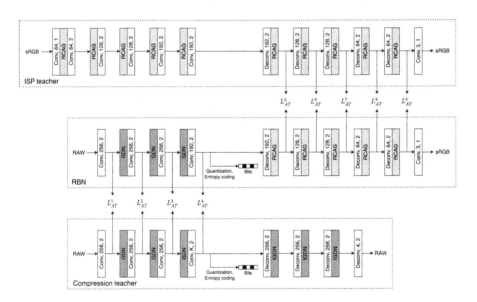

Fig. 2. Network architecture of RBN, consisting of (de)convolutional layers with the specified number of features and stride, RCAG [38], GDN, and IGDN. The applied context model for rate estimation [20] is omitted for simplicity.

3.3   RBN with KD

We now introduce our proposed RBN, which has a more appropriate architecture for the integration of ISP-Net and Comp-Net with a novel KD scheme, as depicted in Fig. 1(c). While the unified structure described in Sect. 3.2 does achieve the main objective of combining ISP-Net and Comp-Net into a single network, the performance is expected to be unsatisfactory in terms of the rate-distortion trade-off. This is because Comp-Net cannot fully handle the transformation of the RAW image into latent representation for compression and necessary ISP operations at the same time. Hence, we design RBN to be capable of performing both tasks with guidance from two teacher networks, namely the ISP teacher and the compression teacher.

Figure 2 illustrates the detailed network architecture of RBN. We design RBN to have a heterogeneous encoder and decoder. The encoder of RBN follows the general structure in image compression with a series of strided convolution and generalized divisive normalization (GDN) [20]. Specifically, we modify the encoder architecture of one of the representative Comp-Nets [20] that sets the number of channels and kernel size as 192 and 5, respectively, to compress a three-channel sRGB image. Since our RBN takes a RAW image that is packed into four channels, the receptive field can grow uncontrollably quickly if a large kernel size is used. Hence, we use the kernel size of 3 while increasing the number of channels to 256. The last convolutional layer produces latent representation with 192 channels. The decoder architecture is modified from LiteISPNet [38], which is one of the state-of-the-art ISP-Nets. In particular, we replace inverse wavelet transform with transposed convolution and use two residual channel attention blocks in the residual channel attention group (RCAG). Note that no skip connection exists between the encoder and decoder since the decoded latent vector alone should be capable of reconstructing an sRGB image. To perform entropy coding and entropy model estimation, we leverage the context+hyperprior model [20], which estimates the mean and scale of the Gaussian entropy model using the spatially adjacent decoded latent elements and hyperprior.

Although RBN can be trained in an end-to-end manner, it may still suffer from sub-optimal rate-distortion performance since joint learning of compression and ISP is challenging. To overcome this issue, on the one hand, we guide the encoder of RBN to focus more on image compression using the compression teacher. As shown in Fig. 2, the compression teacher network takes a RAW image $x_r \in \mathbb{R}^{4 \times H/2 \times W/2}$ and produces a bitstream that can reconstruct a RAW image $\hat{x}_r \in \mathbb{R}^{4 \times H/2 \times W/2}$. Because the encoder of the compression teacher is trained to find compact representation for efficient compression, we consider that the knowledge from the encoder of the compression teacher can be distilled to the encoder of RBN. On the other hand, we guide the decoder of RBN to focus more on reconstructing the sRGB image from the latent representation by using the ISP teacher. As shown in Fig. 2, the ISP teacher is designed as an sRGB autoencoder such that its decoder can best perform the sRGB image reconstruction from low-dimensional latent representation. Consequently, we consider that the knowledge from the decoder of the ISP teacher can be distilled to the decoder of

RBN. Note that except for the last convolutional layer of the compression teacher network, the encoder and decoder pairs between the two teacher networks and RBN have identical structures to facilitate KD.

To perform KD, we adopt the attention transfer [33], where the spatial attention maps evaluated from the intermediate layers of the teacher and student networks are compared. In the original work [33], the attention map is defined as the sum of absolute values along the channel dimension of the output of the intermediate layer. We empirically found it to be ineffective to take absolute values, and thus we define the attention map as the direct sum along the channel dimension:

$$M_j = \sum_{i=1}^{C_j} A_j \left(i, :, : \right), \tag{1}$$

where $A_j \in \mathbb{R}^{C_j \times H_j \times W_j}$ is the output of the j-th intermediate layer, $M_j \in \mathbb{R}^{H_j \times W_j}$ is the attention map of the j-th intermediate layer, C_j, H_j, and W_j are the corresponding channel dimension, height, and width, respectively. This modification is necessary because we apply the attention transfer between the outputs of the convolutional layers and not the ReLU activation, thus taking absolute values can lead to the loss of directional information embedded in the output tensor. The attention loss for KD, L_{AT}, is defined as the mean squared error between the normalized attention maps of the teacher and student networks:

$$
\begin{aligned}
L_{AT} &= \sum_{j=1}^{n_p} \alpha_j L_{AT}^j, \\
L_{AT}^j &= \frac{1}{N_j} \left\| \frac{M_j^S}{\|M_j^S\|_2} - \frac{M_j^T}{\|M_j^T\|_2} \right\|_2^2,
\end{aligned}
\tag{2}
$$

where $\|\cdot\|_2$ measures the L2-norm, $M_j^S (M_j^T)$ is the j-th attention map of the student (teacher) network, n_p is the number of pairs of the attention maps, N_j is the number of elements in the j-th attention map, and α_j is the weight for the j-th loss term. Inspired by [21], we set α_j to make the attention loss relatively higher than the rate-distortion loss during the early training phase, and decay it as the training progresses. In this way, our RBN can initially focus on KD and progressively switch to the main objective of the rate-distortion optimization. To this end, α_j is chosen as:

$$\alpha_j = \alpha_0 \cdot \gamma^{k^2}, \tag{3}$$

where α_0 is the initial value, and γ is the decay factor. α_0 is set to 10^6 for KD between the two encoders and 10^5 for KD between the two decoders, while γ is set to 0.99999 for both cases. In other words, α_j slowly decreases as training epoch k increases. The final loss function is defined as follows:

$$L_{total} = L_R + \lambda L_D + L_{AT}, \tag{4}$$

where L_R and L_D are the rate and distortion loss terms defined in [20], respectively, and the trade-off parameter λ determines the rate-distortion trade-off.

4 Experimental Results

4.1 Implementation Details

Dataset and Settings. To train and test the models, we collected 487 RAW images taken with Nikon D700 from the MIT-Adobe FiveK dataset [5]. As in [29,30,34], the ground-truth sRGB images were rendered using the LibRaw library [19] and split into a ratio of 80:5:15 for training, validation, and testing. The training image patches were randomly extracted from the RAW images with the dimension of $4 \times 128 \times 128$ by four-channel packing (RGGB), and their corresponding patches were extracted from the sRGB images with the dimension of $3 \times 256 \times 256$. Data augmentation, including random flip and rotation, was applied during the training. Our experiments were conducted using PyTorch with Adam optimizer [17] on Intel i9-10980XE and NVIDIA RTX 3090.

Cascaded Structure. We trained a LiteISPNet with the L2 loss. A batch size of 16 was used in this experiment. The model was trained for 24k iterations with the learning rate of 5×10^{-5} and fine-tuned for 2.4k iterations with the learning rate of 5×10^{-6}. For the context+hyperprior model, we leveraged the pre-trained model provided by [3]. We also experimented with the fine-tuning of the LiteISP-Net in conjunction with the context-hyperprior model. In this case, after the pre-training of the LiteISPNet for 24k iterations, fine-tuning was performed in the cascaded configuration while fixing the parameters of the context-hyperprior model.

Unified Structure. The modified context-hyperprior model as described in Sect. 3.2 was trained for 1.6M iterations. We used a batch size of 8 in this experiment. The learning rate was set to 5×10^{-5} and reduced to 5×10^{-6} after 1.5M iterations. The trade-off parameter λ was chosen from the set {0.0035, 0.0067, 0.013, 0.025, 0.0483, 0.0932, 0.18}, resulting seven different models with different rate-distortion performance.

RBN with KD. To train the teacher and student networks, we set the initial learning rate to 5×10^{-5} and then decayed it to 5×10^{-6}. Specifically, the ISP teacher was trained for 580k iterations, where the learning rate was decayed after 480k iterations. The compression teacher network was trained for 2M iterations, where the learning rate was decayed after 1.5M iterations. We trained separate compression teacher models for each rate-distortion trade-off by choosing λ from the set {0.0035, 0.0067, 0.013, 0.0483, 0.0932, 0.18, 0.36} to support seven models with different rate-distortion performance. The channel dimension of the last convolutional layer of the encoder of the compression teacher, i.e., K in Fig. 2, was set to 192 for the three lower bitrate settings ($\lambda = 0.0035, 0.0067, 0.013$) and 320 for the four higher bitrate settings. Our proposed RBN was trained for 1M iterations, where the learning rate was decayed after 900k iterations. We also trained separate RBNs with the same λ values used in the corresponding compression teachers. We used a batch size of 8 in this experiment.

4.2   Performance Comparisons

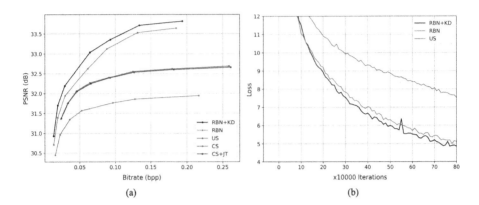

(a)   (b)

Fig. 3. Experimental results: (a) Rate-distortion performance comparisons and (b) training loss for the models trained with $\lambda = 0.18$.

Quantitative Results. The rate-distortion performance of the proposed method is shown in Fig. 3(a), where the average PSNR between the ground-truth and reconstructed sRGB images and average bits per pixel (bpp) were measured from 73 test images. Note that we evaluated bpp in terms of the resolution of the reconstructed sRGB image and not the four-channel packed RAW image. Compared to the baseline approaches such as the cascaded structure (CS) and unified structure (US), RBN outperformed rate-distortion performance, and RBN with KD (RBN+KD) further improved performance. We notice that the performance gap becomes more significant in the high bitrate region, which is important since high-bitrate compression is usually used in practical camera ISPs. Note that the average PSNR between the ground-truth and reconstructed sRGB images obtained by the LiteISPNet used in the cascaded structure is 32.82 dB, which means that the cascaded structure cannot exceed this value regardless of compression rates. Hence the overall rate-distortion performance of the cascaded structure is bounded by the performance of the ISP-Net. As for the joint fine-tuning of the ISP-Net in the cascaded structure (CS+JT), we did not find it effective. We suspect that, unlike the JPEG compression artifacts, which have some form of regularity in that they appear in every 8×8 block boundary, the effect of Comp-Net is more subtle and complex, making it difficult to be effectively captured by the joint fine-tuning of the network. The unified structure performed the worst among the compared methods. This result is expected as the network architecture aims to extract and normalize the features for compression and thus has difficulty performing local and global operations of the ISP. We have also experimented cascading other ISP-Nets with Comp-Net, as well as cascading Comp-Net with ISP-Net, where the result can be found in the supplementary material.

Figure 3(b) shows training loss plots for the unified structure, RBN, and RBN with KD. As suggested in [21], the initial training phase is critical for the network to form a necessary connection to optimize the loss function. By enforcing the network to focus on KD in the initial training stage, the loss of RBN with KD reduced slower than that of RBN in early iterations. However, RBN with KD eventually reached a better optimization point, leading to better rate-distortion performance. It is also clear that the unified structure poorly optimized the rate-distortion loss.

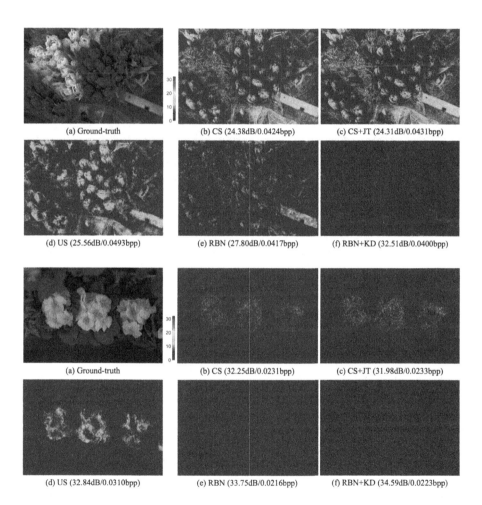

(a) Ground-truth   (b) CS (24.38dB/0.0424bpp)   (c) CS+JT (24.31dB/0.0431bpp)

(d) US (25.56dB/0.0493bpp)   (e) RBN (27.80dB/0.0417bpp)   (f) RBN+KD (32.51dB/0.0400bpp)

(a) Ground-truth   (b) CS (32.25dB/0.0231bpp)   (c) CS+JT (31.98dB/0.0233bpp)

(d) US (32.84dB/0.0310bpp)   (e) RBN (33.75dB/0.0216bpp)   (f) RBN+KD (34.59dB/0.0223bpp)

Fig. 4. Visual comparisons: (a) Ground-truth sRGB image and the error maps between the ground-truth and reconstructed sRGB images for (b) cascaded structure, (c) cascaded structure with joint fine-tuning, (d) unified structure, (e) RBN, and (f) RBN+KD.

Qualitative results The visual comparisons of the proposed methods are shown in Fig. 4. These results were obtained from the models trained with $\lambda = 0.013$ for the unified structure and RBN and $\lambda = 0.0035$ for the cascaded structure. For each method, we visualize the error map between the ground-truth and resultant sRGB images for comparison. It can be seen that the images obtained from the cascaded and unified structures exhibit significant errors. These two structures suffer from not only reproducing image textures such as flower petals but also rendering global color tones, demonstrating that these naïve approaches are insufficient to handle compression and necessary ISP operations at the same time. Meanwhile, the proposed RBN renders sRGB images with less distortion, especially in the texture-rich region. RBN with KD further reduces distortion, yielding the highest image quality at similar compression rates. Additional visual comparison in Fig. 5 clearly shows that RBN with KD renders color more accurately.

(a) Ground-truth   (b) CS   (c) CS+JT   (d) US   (e) RBN   (f) RBN+KD
                    (32.66dB/0.0674bpp) (32.59dB/0.0679bpp) (33.55dB/0.0844bpp) (35.17dB/0.0578bpp) (37.84dB/0.0617bpp)

Fig. 5. Visual comparisons: (a) Ground-truth sRGB image and reconstructed sRGB images obtained by (b) cascaded structure, (c) cascaded structure with joint fine-tuning, (d) unified structure, (e) RBN, and (f) RBN+KD.

4.3   Ablation Studies

We conducted ablation studies on the KD scheme used in the proposed method to verify its effectiveness. Figure 6(a) shows rate-distortion performance for the RBNs trained with guidance from either the ISP teacher or the compression teacher only, as well as the RBNs with full KD and without any KD. The hyperparameters α_0 and γ were kept the same for these four compared models. Unexpectedly, removing either one of the teacher networks resulted in inferior performance even compared with the RBN without KD. We conjecture that the hyperparameter settings of $\alpha_0 = 10^6$ for the encoder, $\alpha_0 = 10^5$ for the decoder, and $\gamma = 0.99999$ were empirically chosen for the KD with two teachers; thus, simply removing one of the teacher networks might not result in a better rate-distortion performance. Next, to verify our claim of the ineffectiveness of deriving the attention map by taking the absolute value of the tensor, we report the result for the model trained with such method in Fig. 6(b). It is clear that the method mentioned above actually hinders the performance of RBN.

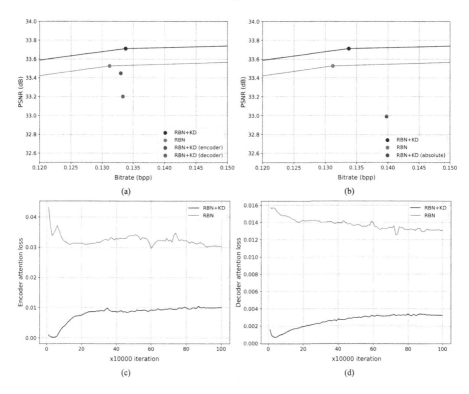

Fig. 6. Ablation studies for models trained with $\lambda = 0.18$: (a) RBNs with different KD strategies and (b) RBNs with different attention maps for KD, and attention loss plots of RBNs with and without KD: (c) encoder and (d) decoder.

Figures 6(c) and (d) show the encoder and decoder attention loss plots for the RBNs trained with and without KD, respectively. Although the RBN without KD was not trained to optimize these attention loss terms, these losses decreased to some extent as the training progressed, which suggests that the attention losses are related to the main objective of the rate-distortion trade-off. In the RBN with KD, the attention losses decreased at the early iterations but then increased since the weight for the attention loss is decreased by (3) as training proceeded. In other words, the optimization with the attention loss in the RBN with KD contributed to finding good initial conditions for the model to reach a better rate-distortion trade-off. Also, note that KD does not incur additional computational cost in the inference stage. Comparison on the computational cost of the experimented models can be found in the supplementary material.

Fig. 7. Samples of the sRGB images rendered from RAW captured with Nikon D7000. The RBN+KD model used for testing was trained with RAW from Nikon D700. Bilinear demosaicing is applied to the RAW for visualization.

4.4 Generalization Test

Since different camera sensors have different characteristics, a dedicated RBN is required for each specific camera model in principle. Here, to test the generalization ability of the RBN with KD trained on the Nikon D700 subset from the MIT-Adobe FiveK dataset [5], we applied the trained model to the test images captured by a different camera sensor. Figure 7 shows some test results on the Nikon D7000 subset from the RAISE dataset [9]. It can be seen that our results still exhibit high contrast and well-adjusted color with rich textures, indicating that sensor-specific training is desired but not mandatory, at least for the sensors from the same manufacturer.

5   Conclusions

In this paper, we presented the first approach to integrate the ISP and image compression into a single framework. To this end, we designed a network called RBN to perform both tasks simultaneously and effectively. Compared to the naïve baselines of the cascaded and unified structures, RBN exhibits significantly better rate-distortion performance. In addition, we further improved RBN by introducing KD from the two teacher networks specialized in each task. Experimental results demonstrated that RBN with KD shows a noticeable performance increase over the alternative approaches. We hope our work inspires further research on the fully end-to-end camera ISP network.

Acknowledgements. This work was supported by the National Research Foundation of Korea (NRF) grant funded by the Korea Government (MSIT) (No. 2022R1A2C2002810).

References

1. Ballé, J., Laparra, V., Simoncelli, E.P.: End-to-end optimized image compression. In: Proceedings of the International Conference on Learning Representations (2017)
2. Ballé, J., Minnen, D., Singh, S., Hwang, S.J., Johnston, N.: Variational image compression with a scale hyperprior. In: Proceedings of the International Conference on Learning Representations (2018)
3. Bégaint, J., Racapé, F., Feltman, S., Pushparaja, A.: CompressAI: a PyTorch library and evaluation platform for end-to-end compression research. arXiv preprint arXiv:2011.03029 (2020)
4. Bross, B., et al.: Overview of the versatile video coding (VVC) standard and its applications. IEEE Trans. Circuits Syst. Video Technol. **31**(10), 3736–3764 (2021)
5. Bychkovsky, V., Paris, S., Chan, E., Durand, F.: Learning photographic global tonal adjustment with a database of input/output image pairs. In: Proceedings of the IEEE/CVF Conference on Computer Vision and Pattern Recognition, pp. 97–104. IEEE (2011)
6. Chen, C., Chen, Q., Xu, J., Koltun, V.: Learning to see in the dark. In: Proceedings of the IEEE/CVF Conference on Computer Vision and Pattern Recognition, pp. 3291–3300 (2018)
7. Chen, D., et al.: Cross-layer distillation with semantic calibration. In: Proceedings of the AAAI Conference on Artificial Intelligence, vol. 35, pp. 7028–7036 (2021)
8. Cheng, Z., Sun, H., Takeuchi, M., Katto, J.: Learned image compression with discretized Gaussian mixture likelihoods and attention modules. In: Proceedings of the IEEE/CVF Conference on Computer Vision and Pattern Recognition, pp. 7939–7948 (2020)
9. Dang-Nguyen, D.T., Pasquini, C., Conotter, V., Boato, G.: Raise: A raw images dataset for digital image forensics. In: Proceedings of the ACM Multimedia Systems Conference, pp. 219–224 (2015)
10. Gao, G., et al.: Neural image compression via attentional multi-scale back projection and frequency decomposition. In: Proceedings of the IEEE/CVF International Conference on Computer Vision, pp. 14677–14686 (2021)
11. Gou, J., Yu, B., Maybank, S.J., Tao, D.: Knowledge distillation: A survey. Int. J. Comput. Vision **129**(6), 1789–1819 (2021)
12. Goyal, V.K.: Theoretical foundations of transform coding. IEEE Signal Process. Mag. **18**(5), 9–21 (2001)
13. Hu, Y., Yang, W., Ma, Z., Liu, J.: Learning end-to-end lossy image compression: A benchmark. IEEE Trans. Pattern Anal. Mach. Intell. (2022)
14. Ignatov, A., Van Gool, L., Timofte, R.: Replacing mobile camera ISP with a single deep learning model. In: Proceedings of the IEEE/CVF Conference on Computer Vision and Pattern Recognition Workshops, pp. 536–537 (2020)
15. Kim, D.W., Ryun Chung, J., Jung, S.W.: GRDN: Grouped residual dense network for real image denoising and GAN-based real-world noise modeling. In: Proceedings of the IEEE/CVF Conference on Computer Vision and Pattern Recognition Workshops, pp. 2086–2094 (2019)
16. Kim, J., Park, S., Kwak, N.: Paraphrasing complex network: Network compression via factor transfer. In: Proceedings of the Advances in Neural Information Processing Systems, vol. 31 (2018)
17. Kingma, D.P., Ba, J.: Adam: A method for stochastic optimization. arXiv preprint arXiv:1412.6980 (2014)

18. Liang, Z., Cai, J., Cao, Z., Zhang, L.: CameraNet: A two-stage framework for effective camera ISP learning. IEEE Trans. Image Process. **30**, 2248–2262 (2021)
19. LibRaw LLC: Libraw (2019). https://www.libraw.org/
20. Minnen, D., Ballé, J., Toderici, G.D.: Joint autoregressive and hierarchical priors for learned image compression. In: Proceedings of the Advances in Neural Information Processing Systems, vol. 31 (2018)
21. Passalis, N., Tzelepi, M., Tefas, A.: Heterogeneous knowledge distillation using information flow modeling. In: Proceedings of the IEEE/CVF Conference on Computer Vision and Pattern Recognition, pp. 2339–2348 (2020)
22. Ramanath, R., Snyder, W.E., Yoo, Y., Drew, M.S.: Color image processing pipeline. IEEE Signal Process. Mag. **22**(1), 34–43 (2005)
23. Romero, A., Ballas, N., Kahou, S.E., Chassang, A., Gatta, C., Bengio, Y.: FitNets: Hints for thin deep nets. In: Proceedings of the International Conference on Learning Representations (2015)
24. Schwartz, E., Giryes, R., Bronstein, A.M.: DeepISP: Toward learning an end-to-end image processing pipeline. IEEE Trans. Image Process. **28**(2), 912–923 (2018)
25. Taubman, D., Marcellin, M.: JPEG2000 image compression fundamentals, standards and practice: Image compression fundamentals, standards and practice, vol. 642. Springer Science & Business Media (2012). https://doi.org/10.1007/978-1-4615-0799-4
26. Theis, L., Shi, W., Cunningham, A., Huszár, F.: Lossy image compression with compressive autoencoders. In: Proceedings of the International Conference on Learning Representations (2017)
27. Toderici, G., et al.: Variable rate image compression with recurrent neural networks. In: Proceedings of the International Conference on Learning Representations (2016)
28. Toderici, G., Vincent, D., Johnston, N., Jin Hwang, S., Minnen, D., Shor, J., Covell, M.: Full resolution image compression with recurrent neural networks. In: Proceedings of the IEEE/CVF Conference on Computer Vision and Pattern Recognition, pp. 5306–5314 (2017)
29. Uhm, K.H., Choi, K., Jung, S.W., Ko, S.J.: Image compression-aware deep camera ISP network. IEEE Access **9**, 137824–137832 (2021)
30. Xing, Y., Qian, Z., Chen, Q.: Invertible image signal processing. In: Proceedings of the IEEE/CVF Conference on Computer Vision and Pattern Recognition, pp. 6287–6296 (2021)
31. Xu, D., Ouyang, W., Wang, X., Sebe, N.: PAD-Net: Multi-tasks guided prediction-and-distillation network for simultaneous depth estimation and scene parsing. In: Proceedings of the IEEE/CVF Conference on Computer Vision and Pattern Recognition, pp. 675–684 (2018)
32. Ye, W., Ma, K.K.: Color image demosaicing using iterative residual interpolation. IEEE Trans. Image Process. **24**(12), 5879–5891 (2015)
33. Zagoruyko, S., Komodakis, N.: Paying more attention to attention: Improving the performance of convolutional neural networks via attention transfer. In: Proceedings of the International Conference on Learning Representations (2017)
34. Zamir, S.W., et al.: CycleISP: Real image restoration via improved data synthesis. In: Proceedings of the IEEE/CVF Conference on Computer Vision and Pattern Recognition, pp. 2696–2705 (2020)
35. Zamir, S.W., et al.: Multi-stage progressive image restoration. In: Proceedings of the IEEE/CVF Conference on Computer Vision and Pattern Recognition, pp. 14821–14831 (2021)

36. Zhang, C., Peng, Y.: Better and faster: Knowledge transfer from multiple self-supervised learning tasks via graph distillation for video classification. In: Proceedings of the International Joint Conference on Artificial Intelligence, pp. 1135–1141 (2018)
37. Zhang, K., Zuo, W., Zhang, L.: FFDNet: Toward a fast and flexible solution for CNN-based image denoising. IEEE Trans. Image Process. **27**(9), 4608–4622 (2018)
38. Zhang, Z., Wang, H., Liu, M., Wang, R., Zhang, J., Zuo, W.: Learning RAW-to-sRGB mappings with inaccurately aligned supervision. In: Proceedings of the IEEE/CVF International Conference on Computer Vision, pp. 4348–4358 (2021)

DRCNet: Dynamic Image Restoration Contrastive Network

Fei Li[1,3,4], Lingfeng Shen[2], Yang Mi[1,4], and Zhenbo Li[1,3,4,5,6(✉)]

[1] College of Information and Electrical Engineering, China Agricultural University, Beijing, China
{leefly072,miy,lizb}@cau.edu.cn
[2] Department of Computer Science, Johns Hopkins University, Maryland, USA
lshen30@jh.edu
[3] National Innovation Center for Digital Fishery, Ministry of Agriculture and Rural Affairs, Beijing, China
[4] Key Laboratory of Agricultural Information Acquisition Technology, Ministry of Agriculture and Rural Affairs, Beijing, China
[5] Key Laboratory of Smart Breeding Technology, Ministry of Agriculture and Rural Affairs, Beijing, China
[6] Precision Agriculture Technology Integrated Scientific Experiment Base, Ministry of Agriculture and Rural Affairs, Beijing, China

Abstract. Image restoration aims to recover images from spatially-varying degradation. Most existing image-restoration models employed static CNN-based models, where the fixed learned filters cannot fit the diverse degradation well. To this end, we propose a novel **D**ynamic Image **R**estoration **C**ontrastive **Net**work (DRCNet) to address this issue. The principal block in DRCNet is the **D**ynamic **F**ilter **R**estoration module (DFR), which mainly consists of the spatial filter branch and the energy-based attention branch. Specifically, the spatial filter branch suppresses spatial noise for varying spatial degradation; the energy-based attention branch guides the feature integration for better spatial detail recovery. To make degraded images and clean images more distinctive in the representation space, we develop a novel **Intra**-class **C**ontrastive **R**egularization (Intra-CR) to serve as a constraint in the solution space for DRCNet. Meanwhile, our theoretical derivation proved Intra-CR owns less sensitivity towards hyper-parameter selection than previous contrastive regularization. DRCNet outperforms previous methods on the ten widely used benchmarks in image restoration. Besides, the ablation studies investigate the impact of the DFR module and Intra-CR, respectively.

Keywords: Image restoration · Dynamic convolution · Contrastive regularization

---

F. Li and L. Shen—Equal contribution.

Supplementary Information The online version contains supplementary material available at https://doi.org/10.1007/978-3-031-19800-7_30.

1   Introduction

Image restoration (IR) is one of the basic tasks in computer vision, which recovers clean images from degraded versions, typically caused by rain [12], noise [25] and blur [23]. It is imperative to restore such degraded images to improve their visual quality. Among the models for IR, most of the achieved progress [24,29] is primarily attributed to static Convolutional Neural Networks (CNN) [16]. However, the image degradation is spatially varying [33], which is incompatible with static CNN that are in a filter sharing manner across spatial domains [6].

Therefore, static CNN-based approaches perform imperfectly when the input image contains noise pixels, as well as severe intensity distortions in different spatial regions [33]. To be specific, static CNN-based [14,17] models have some drawbacks. First, the typical CNN filter is spatial-invariance and content-agnostic, leading to the sub-optimal in IR [33,67]. Second, the fixed learned filters can not automatically fit the diverse input degraded images [17,48]. Considering the limitations mentioned above, we need to design a module to dynamically restore the degraded images since each input image has a variable degree of distortion and specific spatial distribution.

Recently, some efforts [6,48,67] have been made to compensate for the drawbacks of static convolution, enabling the model to flexibly adjust the structure and parameters to be suitable for diverse task demands. Few works [33] have employed dynamic convolution for region-level restoration, which may not effectively reconstruct the fine-grained pixels. To solve this, we propose a new model called **D**ynamic Image **R**estoration **C**ontrastive **Net**work (DRCNet), which consists of two key components: Dynamic Filter Restoration module (DFR) and Intra-Class Contrastive Regularization (Intra-CR). The core component of DRC-Net is DFR, which effectively restores the pixel-level spatial details by using the dynamic mask to suppress spatial noise and applying feature integration. Specifically, there are two principal designs in DFR. One is a spatial filter branch, which masks the noise pixels and applies adaptive feature normalization. The other one is the energy-based attention branch, which is designed to calibrate features dynamically. Moreover, to make degraded images and clean images more distinctive in the representation space, we propose a new contrastive regularization called Intra-CR, serving as a constraint in the solution space. Specifically, Intra-CR constructs negative samples through mixup [62] while existing Contrastive Regularization (CR) construct negative samples by random sampling. Its effectiveness is validated through theoretical derivation and empirical studies.

To summarize, the main contributions of this study are as follows:

- We propose a Dynamic Filter Restoration module **(DFR)** that is adaptive in various image restoration scenes. Such a block enables DRCNet to handle spatial-varying image degradation.
- A novel contrastive regularization is proposed, dubbed **Intra-CR**, to construct intra-class negative samples through mixup. Empirical studies show its superiority over vanilla contrastive regularization, and our theoretical results show that Intra-CR is less sensitive to hyper-parameter selection.

– Extensive experimental results on ten image restoration baselines demonstrate the efficacy of the proposed DRCNet, which achieves state-of-the-art performance.

2   Related Work

2.1   Image Restoration

Early image restoration approaches are based on prior-based models [16,46], sparse models [28], and physical models [4]. Recently, the significant performance improvements in image restoration can be attributed to the architecture of Convolution Neural Networks (CNN) [32,55]. Most CNN-based methods focus on elaborating architecture designs, such as, multi-stage networks [55,60], dense connections [32], and Neural Architecture Search (NAS) [57]. Due to the spatial-varying image degradation, static CNN-based models are less capable than desired to handle this issue [33]. In contrast, we propose the DFR module with dynamic spatial filter and energy-based attention (EA), which is more effective than static CNN.

The most relevant work to our work is SPAIR [33]. However, there are several principal differences between DRCNet and SPAIR. **Operations:** SPAIR is a two-stage framework for IR. In contrast, DFR is a plug-in module that can be easily inserted into any CNN. **Mask construction:** A pre-trained network generates the mask of SPAIR, and it mainly captures the location information of degraded pixels. In contrast, DFR directly generates a mask based on a spatial response map, which also detects degradation intensity automatically. **Spatial adaptability:** The sparse convolution receptive field of SPAIR is limited, and adaptive global context aggregation is performed on degraded pixel locations. In contrast, DFR utilizes adaptive feature normalization and a set of learnable affine parameters to gather relevant features from the whole image. **Attention weight:** SPAIR can not directly build connections between two spatial pixels. It produces weights by conducting a pairwise similar process from four directions. In contrast, DRF obtains weights by utilizing EA (i.e., considering both spatial and channel dimensions) and calibrates features dynamically. **Loss function:** SPAIR utilized $\mathcal{L}_{CE}$ and $\mathcal{L}_1$. In contrast, DRCNet proposes a new Intra-CR loss which utilizes the negative sample and outperforms SPAIR.

2.2   Dynamic Filter

Compared to standard convolution, the dynamic filters can achieve dynamic restoration towards different input features. With the key idea of adaptive inference, dynamic filters are applied to various tasks, such as image segmentation [41], super-resolution [47] and restoration [33]. Dynamic filters can be divided into scale-adaptive [66] and spatially-adaptive filters [32,33]. DFR belongs to the spatially-adaptive category, which can adjust filter values to suit different input features. In particular, dynamic spatially-adaptive filters, such as DRConv

[6], DynamicConv [8] and DDF [67], can automatically assign multiple filters to corresponding spatial regions. However, most dynamic filters are not specifically designed for image restoration, which results in imperfect performance.

2.3   Contrastive Regularization

Contrastive learning (CL) is a self-supervised representation learning paradigm [26] which is based on the assumption that good representation should bring similar images closer while pushing away dissimilar ones. Most existing works often use CL in high-level vision tasks [15]. While some works [44] have demonstrated that contrastive learning can be used as a regularization to remove the haze. Such CR considers all other images in the batch as negative samples, which may lead to sub-optimal performance. Further, only a few works consider that Intra-class CR can improve the generalization. Therefore, in this paper, we construct a new CR method to improve the model generalization for image restoration. The essential distinction between Intra-CR and existing CR is how the negative examples are constructed. Specifically, we construct negative samples by a mixup [62] operation between the clean image and its degraded version.

3   Methods

In this section, we first provide an overview of DRCNet. Then, we detail the proposed DFR module and Intra-CR.

3.1   Dynamic Filter Restoration Network

Due to two- and multi-stage UNet are proven to be effective in encoding broad contextual information [7,18,29,55]. Dynamic Image Restoration Contrastive Net (DRCNet) is designed of two encoder-decoder sub-networks with four down-sampling and up-sampling operations. The overview of DRCNet is shown in Fig. 1. The sub-network first adopts a 3×3 convolution to extract features. Then, the features are processed with four DFR modules for suppressing the degraded pixels and extracting the clean feature in encoders. We employ three ResBlocks [17] in the decoder to reconstruct images with fine spatial details. The restored images are obtained by using a 3×3 convolution to process the decoder output. To link the two sub-networks, we utilize the Cross-Stage Feature Fusion (CSFF) module and Supervised Attention Module (SAM) [55] to fuse the features, which are highlighted by the red dotted lines and green line as illustrated in Fig. 1. Finally, we propose Intra-CR, which serves as a regularization to pull away degraded images and get close to clean images in the representation space.

3.2   Dynamic Filter Restoration Module

The structure of DFR is shown in Fig. 1. The DFR module aims to automatically suppress potential degraded pixels and generate better spatial detail recovery with fewer parameters. Generally, it achieves such goals by constructing three different branches for inputs: (1) spatial filter branch, (2) energy-based attention branch, (3) identity branch. In spatial filter branch, we first utilize a 3×3

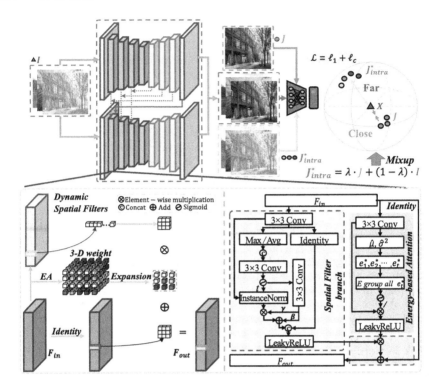

Fig. 1. The architecture of the proposed DRCNet. It consists of two sub-networks and employs the encoder-decoder paradigm to restore images. The core components of Dynamic Filter Restoration module are the spatial filters branch in green color region, and the energy-based attention branch in the pink color region. Moreover, we minimize the L1 reconstruction loss (ℓ_1) with CR (ℓ_c) to better pull the restored image (i.e. anchor, X) to the clear (i.e. positive, J) image and push the restored image away from the degraded (i.e. negative,   ) images. (Color figure online)

convolution to refine the input feature $F \in \mathbb{R}^{C_{in} \times H \times W}$ where C_{in}, H, and W denote the input channel, height, width of the feature maps. Then, we randomly divided the feature map into two parts: one part utilizes our proposed adaptive feature normalization to mask degraded signals, the other to keep context information [7,45]. Finally, we concatenate the two parts to aggregate the features. This operation enables DFR to suppress noise for adaptability to varying spatial degradation, leading to sacrifice of texture details. Therefore, we design an EA branch that focuses on generating the texture details. Besides, the EA branch guides the feature integration between the EA branch and the spatial filter branch [49]. Moreover, the identity branch launches a vanilla transformation with 1×1 convolution to the inputs, which helps maintain the features from the original images. Overall, the whole DFR module can be defined as follows:

$$F'_{(r,i)} = \sum_{j \in \Omega(i)} D_i^{sp}[p_i - p_j]\mathcal{W}_i^{ea}[p_i - p_j]F_{(r,j)} \tag{1}$$

where $F'_{(r,i)}, F_{(r,j)} \in \mathbb{R}$ denotes the output/input feature value at the ith, j^{th} pixel of rth channel. $\Omega(i)$ denotes the k × k convolution window around i^{th} pixel. $D^{sp} \in \mathbb{R}^{h \times w \times k \times k}$ is the spatial dynamic filter with $D_i^{sp} \in \mathbb{R}^{k \times k}$ denoting the filter at i^{th} pixel. $\mathcal{W}^{ea} \in \mathbb{R}^{h \times w \times k \times k}$ is the dynamic attention weights with $\mathcal{W}_i^{ea} \in \mathbb{R}^{k \times k}$ denoting the 3-D attention weights value at i^{th} pixel. To delve into the details of DFR, we detail the two principal modules of DFR: spatial filter branch and energy-based attention branch.

Spatial Filter Branch. Since previous spatially-adaptive IR methods without considering the degraded pixel intensity change, we set out to design an adaptive feature normalization to detect intensity changes and recover them. We first perform convolution on input feature $F_{in} \in \mathbb{R}^{C \times H \times W}$ to extract initial feature and employ max-pooling and average-pooling $F_{max}, F_{avg} \in \mathbb{R}^{1 \times H \times W}$ along the channel to obtain an efficient feature descriptor [56]. The spatial response map $\mathcal{M}_{sr}$ is obtained by a convolution on F_{max}, F_{avg} with sigmoid function, which represents local representation [52] and can be defined as follows:

$$F_{max}, F_{avg} = Conv(F_{in}) \tag{2}$$

$$\mathcal{M}_{sr} = sigmoid\left(Conv\left([F_{max}, F_{avg}]\right)\right) \tag{3}$$

The threshold t in Fig. 1 aims to detect the degraded pixels with a soft distinction. The mask $\mathcal{M}_p \in \mathbb{R}^{1 \times H \times W}$ is 1 when $\mathcal{M}_{sr}$ greater than t, and is 0 otherwise. Specifically, $p \in (h, w)$ represents 2D pixel location. Considering the spatial relationship of $\mathcal{M}_{sr}$, we utilize a convolution layer to obtain a set of learnable parameters expanded along the channel dimension $\gamma_c^i \in \mathbb{R}^{1 \times H \times W}$ and bias $\beta_c^i \in \mathbb{R}^{1 \times H \times W}$, which enhances the feature representation. The computation for γ_c^i, β_c^i is formulated as follows:

$$\gamma_c^i, \beta_c^i = Conv\left(\mathcal{M}_{sr}\right) \tag{4}$$

The μ_c^i and σ_c^i are the channel-wise mean and variance of the features in i-th layer, which relate to global semantic information and local texture [19]:

$$\mu_c^i = \frac{1}{\sum_p \mathcal{M}_i^p} \sum_p F_{in} \odot \mathcal{M}_p \tag{5}$$

$$\sigma_c^i = \sqrt{\frac{1}{\sum_p \mathcal{M}_p} \sum_p \left(F_{in} \odot \mathcal{M}_p - \mu_c^i + \varepsilon\right)} \tag{6}$$

where $\sum_p \mathcal{M}_p$ indicates the number of masked pixels, $\odot$ represents element-wise product, and ε is a small constant to avoid σ_c^i equal to 0. The final feature output of the spatial filter branch is obtained as follows:

$$F_{h,w,c}^i = \gamma_c^i \cdot \frac{F_{in} - \mu_c^i}{\sigma_c^i} + \beta_c^i \tag{7}$$

Energy-Based Attention Branch. The spatial filter branch with adaptive feature normalization suppresses degraded pixels, which may impede the restoration in texture areas. Thus, we introduce the energy-based attention branch to remedy the deficiency of spatial information, which considers the 3-D weights and preserves the details of the textures in the heavily degraded image [49]. Different from the previous works only refined features along either channel or spatial dimensions, we integrate 3D attention in the DFR to directly infer attention weights and calibrate the pixel. Moreover, EA can also leave the clean pixel features and guide the feature integration by calculating the importance score for each pixel.

Specifically, we first obtain the initial feature from a convolution operation. Then, we calculate the mean $\hat{\mu} = \frac{1}{N}\sum_{i=1}^{N} x_i$ and variance $\hat{\sigma}^2 = \frac{1}{N}\sum_{i=1}^{N}(x_i - \hat{\mu})^2$ over all neurons ($N = H \times W$) in that channel. $\hat{\mu}$ and $\hat{\sigma}^2$ are used for calculating the energy function for each pixel, which is the same as re-weighting the input feature map. We minimize the energy of target neuron t and formulate as follows:

$$e_t^* = \frac{4\left(\hat{\sigma}^2 + \delta\right)}{(t - \hat{\mu})^2 + 2\hat{\sigma}^2 + 2\delta} \tag{8}$$

where δ is the coefficient hyper-parameter. The refined features $\tilde{X}$ as follows:

$$\tilde{X} = sigmoid\left(\frac{1}{E}\right) \odot X \tag{9}$$

where E is obtained by grouping all e_t^* across the channel and spatial dimensions. As for the identity branch, it generates identity features by a 1×1 Convolution.

The final feature output of DFR is obtained as follows: (1) we multiply the features of spatial filter branch and EA to obtain the intermediate features (2) we add the intermediate features with identity features to obtain the integrated features, as highlighted by the blue region in Fig. 1. The final features output by the encoder will be fed to the decoder for restored image generation.

3.3   Contrastive Regularization

Previous contrastive regularization [44] simply selected other haze images as negative samples from the same batch, namely **Extra**-class **CR** (Extra-CR), which may result in sub-optimal performance. Thus, we propose a new contrastive regularization method called **Intra**-class **CR** (Intra-CR), which constructs negative samples through mixup [62] between clean images and degraded images.

In a classical IR scenario, a degraded image I is transformed to the restored image X to approximate its clean image J. Specifically, we denote $s = (X, J)$ as the pair of X and J, and $s^* = (X, J^*)$ as the pair of negative sample X and J^*. $\ell_1(s, \theta)$ and $\ell_c(s^*, \theta)$ represent L1 reconstruction loss and contrastive regularizer, where θ represents the model's parameters. Then the empirical risk minimizer for model optimization is given by:

$$\theta_{\alpha,s^*} = \operatorname{argmin}_{\theta \in \Theta} \sum_{s \in S} [\ell_1(s, \theta) + \alpha \cdot \ell_c(s^*, \theta)] \tag{10}$$

where α is the weight to control the balance the reconstruction loss and contrastive regularization. Besides, Intra-CR constructs the negative samples J^* through a mixup operation between degraded images I and clean images J, defined as follows:

$$J^*_{intra} = \lambda \cdot J + (1 - \lambda) \cdot I \qquad (11)$$

where λ is the hyper-parameter in mixup operation, we choose different λ to construct different negative samples. Then we give the theoretical analysis between Intra-CR and Extra-CR. The idea is to compute the parameter change as the weight α changes.

We define the sensitivity of performance towards α as follows:

$$\mathcal{R}_{sen}(s^*) = \left| \lim_{\alpha \to 0} \frac{d\theta_{\alpha,s^*}}{d\alpha} \right| \qquad (12)$$

The sensitivity $\mathcal{R}_{sen}$ is a metric that reflects the how sensitive the model's performance towards α change. Then we give our main theorem:

Theorem 1. *Let s^*_{intra} and s^*_{extra} denote the negative pairs in Intra-CR and Extra-CR, then we obtain $\mathcal{R}_{sen}(s^*_{intra}) < \mathcal{R}_{sen}(s^*_{extra})$.*

The detailed proof is deferred to the supplementary materials. The above theorem indicates that Intra-CR is more stable towards hyper-parameter α than Extra-CR, and such a sensitivity can be reflected through performance changes [61], which will be shown in Sect. 4.6. Then the training objective $\mathcal{L}$ in Intra-CR can be formulated as follows:

$$\mathcal{L} = \ell_1(s, \theta) + \alpha \cdot \frac{\ell_1(G(X), G(J))}{\ell_1(G(X), G(J^*_{intra}))} \qquad (13)$$

where G is a fixed pre-trained VGG19 [39]. $G(\cdot)$ aims to extract hidden features of the images, and we leverage $G(\cdot)$ to compare the common intermediate features between a pair of images. Note that our method is different from the perceptual loss [19], which only adds with positive-pair regularization, but Intra-CR also adopts negative pairs. Besides, our Intra-CR is different from the Extra-CR [44] on negative sample construction. Experiments demonstrate that Intra-CR outperforms Extra-CR in image restoration tasks.

4   Experiments and Analysis

For comprehensive comparisons, the proposed DRCNet is contrasted on three IR tasks in this section: image deraining, denoising, and deblurring.

4.1   Benchmarks and Evaluation

We evaluate our method by Peak Signal-to-Noise Ratio (PSNR) and Structural Similarity Index Measure (SSIM) [42]. As in [55], we report (in parenthesis) the reduce in error for each model relative to the best performing method by RMSE $\left(RMSE \propto \sqrt{10^{-PSNR/10}}\right)$ and DSSIM $(DSSIM = (1 - SSIM)/2)$. Meanwhile, qualitative evaluation is shown through the visualization of different benchmarks. The benchmarks are listed as follows: **Image Deraining.** We employ the same training data as MPRNet [55] which consists of 13,712 clean-rain image pairs, and that of Test100 [59], Rain100H [50], Rain100L [50], Test2800 [13], and Test1200 [58] as testing sets. **Image Denoising**. We train DRCNet on the SIDD medium version [1] dataset with 320 high-resolution images and directly test it on the DND [31] dataset with 50 pairs of real-world noisy images. **Image Deblurring.** We train on the GoPro [29] dataset that contains 2,103 image pairs for training and 1,111 pairs for evaluation and directly apply it to HIDE [38] and RealBlur [36] to demonstrate generalization.

4.2   Implementation Details

Our DRCNet is trained with Adam optimizer [21], and the learning rate is set to 2×10^{-4} by default, and decreased to 1×10^{-7} with cosine annealing strategy [27]. δ in the Eq. (8) is set to 1×10^{-6}, the degraded pixel mask threshold t in Fig. 1 is set to 0.75. Detailed analysis of δ and t will be discussed in our supplementary materials. For Intra-CR, α is set to 0.04, and the number n of negative samples is set to 3. The mixup parameters are selected as $0.90, 0.95, 1.00$. We train our model on 256×256 patches with a batch size of 32 for 4×10^5 iterations. Specifically, we apply random rotation, cropping, and flipping to the images to augment the training data.

4.3   Image Deraining Results

We conduct experiments to illustrate that the proposed DRCNet outperforms prior approaches in visual results and achieves competitive performance in terms of PSNR/SSIM scores on all derain benchmarks, shown in Table 1. For the image deraining task, consistent with prior work [55], Table 1 illustrates that our method significantly advances state-of-the-art by consistently achieving better PSNR/SSIM scores on all derain benchmarks. Compared to the state-of-the-art model HINet [7], we obtain significant performance gains of 0.7dB in PSNR and 0.011 in SSIM, and a 7.76% and 2.7% error reduction averaged across all derain benchmarks. Specifically, the improvement on Rain100L can reach 0.95 dB, which well demonstrates that our model can effectively remove rain streaks. Meanwhile, the qualitative results on image derain samples are illustrated in Fig. 2, which demonstrates that DRCNet produces better visual qualities with fine-detailed structures. In contrast, the output restored images of other comparison methods fail to recover complex textures. Due to the effectiveness of DRF, DRCNet can faithfully recover the texture and structures with fewer parameters.

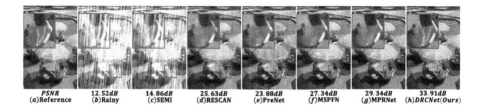

| PSNR
(a)Reference | 12.52dB
(b)Rainy | 14.86dB
(c)SEMI | 25.63dB
(d)RESCAN | 23.88dB
(e)PreNet | 27.34dB
(f)MSPFN | 29.34dB
(g)MPRNet | 33.91dB
(h)DRCNet(Ours) |

Fig. 2. Visual comparisons on the derain test set. Our DRCNet obtains better visual results with more natural details while removing rain.

Table 1. Quantitative results of image deraining.The best and second-best scores are bolden and underlined, respectively. Our DRCNet achieves substantial improvements in PSNR over HINet [7]. 'Params' means the number of parameters (Millions). ↑ denotes higher is better.

Methods	Test100 [59]		Rain100H [50]		Rain100L [50]		Test2800 [13]		Test1200 [58]		Average		Params
	PSNR↑	SSIM↑	PSNR↑	SSIM↑	PSNR↑	SSIM↑	PSNR↑	SSIM↑	PSNR↑	SSIM↑	PSNR↑	SSIM↑	(M)
DerainNet [12]	22.77	0.810	14.92	0.592	27.03	0.884	24.31	0.861	23.38	0.835	22.48	0.796	–
SEMI [43]	22.35	0.788	16.56	0.486	25.03	0.842	24.43	0.782	26.05	0.822	22.88	0.744	–
DIDMDN [58]	22.56	0.818	17.35	0.524	25.23	0.741	28.13	0.867	29.65	0.901	24.58	0.770	0.37
UMRL [51]	24.41	0.829	26.01	0.832	29.18	0.923	29.97	0.905	30.55	0.910	28.02	0.880	0.9
RESCAN [24]	25.00	0.835	26.36	0.786	29.80	0.881	31.29	0.904	30.51	0.882	28.59	0.857	0.15
PreNet [35]	24.81	0.851	26.77	0.858	32.44	0.950	31.75	0.916	31.36	0.911	29.42	0.897	0.16
MSPFN [18]	27.50	0.876	28.66	0.860	32.40	0.933	32.82	0.930	32.39	0.916	30.75	0.903	21
MPRNet [55]	30.27	0.897	30.41	0.890	36.40	0.965	33.64	0.938	32.91	0.916	32.73	0.921	3.64
SPAIR [33]	<u>30.35</u>	<u>0.909</u>	<u>30.95</u>	0.892	36.93	0.969	33.34	0.936	33.04	<u>0.922</u>	32.91	<u>0.926</u>	–
HINet [7]	30.29	0.906	30.65	<u>0.894</u>	<u>37.28</u>	<u>0.970</u>	<u>33.91</u>	<u>0.941</u>	<u>33.05</u>	0.919	<u>33.03</u>	<u>0.926</u>	88.7
DRCNet (Ours)	**32.18**	**0.917**	30.96	0.895	**38.23**	**0.976**	33.89	0.946	**33.40**	**0.94**	**33.73**	**0.933**	18.9

4.4   Image Denoising Results

Table 2 and Fig. 3 show quantitative and qualitative comparisons with other denoising models on the SIDD [1] and DND [31] datasets. DRCNet achieves consistently better PSNR and SSIM. The results show that DRCNet outperforms the state-of-the-art denoising approaches, i.e., 0.37 dB and 0.05 dB over MPRNet on SIDD and DND. In the SSIM metric, DRCNet also has a performance rise compared to MPRNet, boosting from 0.958 to 0.972. It means that the proposed model can successfully restore the detailed regional textures. As the DND dataset does not provide any training images, DRCNet can achieve impressive results, indicating it has good generalization capability. As no training images in DND dataset, DRCNet can achieve impressive results, indicating it has good generalization capability. Generally, our DRCNet provides better image denoise performance on the denoising task, which effectively removes the noise and artifacts while preserving the main structure and contents.

4.5   Image Deblurring Results

Table 3 and Fig. 4 report the image deblurring performance on GoPro [29] and HIDE [38] dataset. Our method achieves 32.82 PSNR and 0.961 in SSIM on

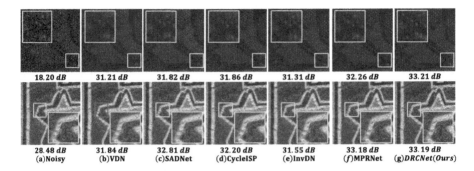

18.20 dB	31.21 dB	31.82 dB	31.86 dB	31.31 dB	32.26 dB	33.21 dB
28.48 dB	31.84 dB	32.81 dB	32.20 dB	31.55 dB	33.18 dB	33.19 dB
(a)Noisy	(b)VDN	(c)SADNet	(d)CycleISP	(e)InvDN	(f)MPRNet	(g)DRCNet(Ours)

Fig. 3. Qualitative comparisons with the existing methods on the denoising datasets. The top row is from SIDD[1] and the down row is from DND[31]. The proposed DRCNet can produce fine-grained texture and high-frequency details.

Table 2. Quantitative results of image denoising on SIDD [1] and DND [31] datasets. We denote the comparison methods using additional training data with *. Following [55], we perform the reduction in error relative to the best-performing algorithm in parenthesis (see Sect. 4.1 for calculation).

| Method | SIDD [1] | | | | DND [31] | | | | Params |
	PSNR↑		SSIM↑		PSNR↑		SSIM↑		(M)
DnCNN [64]	23.66	(84.90%)	0.583	(93.29%)	32.43	(57.44%)	0.790	(79.05%)	0.56
MLP [3]	24.71	(82.96%)	0.641	(92.20%)	34.23	(47.64%)	0.833	(73.65%)	–
BM3D [10]	25.65	(81.01%)	0.685	(91.11%)	34.51	(45.93%)	0.851	(70.47%)	–
CBDNet* [14]	30.78	(65.72%)	0.801	(85.93%)	38.06	(18.62%)	0.942	(24.14%)	4.36
RIDNet* [2]	38.71	(14.59%)	0.951	(42.86%)	39.26	(6.57%)	0.953	(6.38%)	1.49
AINDNet* [20]	38.95	(12.20%)	0.952	(41.67%)	39.37	(5.38%)	0.951	(10.20%)	13.76
VDN [53]	39.28	(8.80%)	0.956	(36.36%)	39.38	(5.27%)	0.952	(8.33%)	7.81
SADNet* [5]	39.46	(6.89%)	0.957	(34.88%)	39.59	(2.95%)	0.952	(8.33%)	0.42
DANet+* [54]	39.47	(6.78%)	0.957	(34.88%)	39.58	(3.06%)	0.955	(2.22%)	9.1
CycleISP* [56]	39.52	(6.25%)	0.957	(34.88%)	39.56	(3.29%)	0.956	(0.00%)	2.8
InvDN [25]	39.28	(8.80%)	0.955	(37.78%)	39.57	(3.17%)	0.952	(8.33%)	2.64
MPRNet [55]	39.71	(4.17%)	0.958	(33.33%)	39.80	(0.58%)	0.954	(4.35%)	15.7
DRCNet (Ours)	**40.08**	(0.00%)	**0.972**	(0.00%)	**39.85**	(0.00%)	**0.956**	(0.00%)	18.9

the GoPro [29] dataset and achieves 31.08 PSNR and 0.94 SSIM on the HIDE dataset. It is worth mentioning that DRCNet is trained only on the GoPro dataset and obtains outstanding performance on the HIDE dataset, validating that the proposed method has good generalization. Moreover, we directly evaluate the GoPro trained model on RealBlur-J, which can further test the generalization of models. Table 3 also shows the experimental results of the DRCNet training and testing on the RealBlur-J dataset. Our DRCNet obtains a performance gain of 0.06 dB on the RealBlur-J subset over the other comparison methods. Overall, the proposed DRCNet outputs restored images with fine-detailed structures and has better visual results than competing methods.

Table 3. Deblurring results. Our method is trained only on the GoPro dataset [29] and directly tested to the HIDE dataset [38] and RealBlur-J [36] datasets. The scores in the PSNR ‡ column were obtained after training and testing on RealBlur-J dataset.

Method	GoPro [29]		HIDE [38]		RealBlur-J [36]			Params
	PSNR	SSIM	PSNR	SSIM	PSNR	SSIM	PSNR‡	(M)
DeblurGAN [22]	28.70	0.858	24.51	0.871	27.97	0.834		–
Nah et al. [29]	29.08	0.914	25.73	0.874	27.87	0.827		11.7
Zhang et al. [63]	29.19	0.913	–	–	27.80	0.847		9.2
DeblurGAN-v2 [23]	29.55	0.934	26.61	0.875	28.70	0.866	29.69	60.9
SRN [34]	30.26	0.934	28.36	0.915	28.56	0.867	31.38	6.8
Shen *et al.* [38]	30.26	0.940	28.89	0.930	–	–		100
DBGAN [65]	31.10	0.942	28.94	0.915	–	–		11.6
MT-RNN [30]	31.15	0.945	29.15	0.918	–	–		2.6
DMPHN [60]	31.20	0.940	29.09	0.924	28.42	0.860		21.7
RADN [32]	31.76	0.952	29.68	0.927	–	–		–
SAPHNet [40]	31.85	0.948	29.98	0.930	–	–		–
SPAIR [33]	32.06	0.953	30.29	0.931	<u>28.81</u>	<u>0.875</u>	<u>31.82</u>	–
MPRNet [55]	32.66	<u>0.959</u>	<u>30.96</u>	<u>0.939</u>	28.70	0.873	31.76	20.1
MIMO-UNet [9]	32.45	0.957	29.99	0.930	27.63	0.873		16.1
HINet [7]	<u>32.71</u>	<u>0.959</u>	30.32	0.932	–	–		88.7
DRCNet(Ours)	**32.82**	**0.961**	**31.08**	**0.940**	**28.87**	**0.881**	**31.85**	18.9

4.6 Ablation Study

To demonstrate the effectiveness of the proposed DRCNet, we conduct ablation studies to analyze the effectiveness of crucial components of DRCNet, including the DFR module and Intra-CR.

Comparison to Other Dynamic Filters. Since there are other proposed dynamic convolution filters, we conduct experiments to compare them in image restoration tasks, as shown in Table 5. We replace the DFR module with three dynamic filters: SACT [11], CondConv [48], UDVD [47], and DDF [67].

Table 5 compares the performance and the parameters of the whole network in various restoration tasks. The experimental results show that models with other dynamic filters obtain significantly worse performance and have more parameters than DFR in the image restoration tasks. Such results validate that DFR is suitable for image restoration tasks.

Effectivenes of DFR. We first construct our base network as baseline, which mainly consists of normal UNet [37] with Resblock [17] in encoding and decoding phrases with SAM and CSFF [55]. Subsequently, we replace DFR module and add the Intra-CR scheme into the base network as follows: (1) **base+SF**: only

Fig. 4. Qualitative comparisons on GoPro [29] test dataset. The deblurred results listed from left to right are from SRN [34], DeblurGANv2 [23], MTRNN [30], SAPHNet [40], MPRNet [55] and ours, respectively.

Table 4. Ablation studies on DRCNet on SIDD benchmark.

Model	CR	PSNR	SSIM	Params (M)	Times (ms)
Base	–	33.25	0.812	12.7	15.2
Base+SF	–	37.76	0.933	15.4	20.1
Base+EA	–	37.12	0.945	13.1	17.7
Base+SF+identity branch	–	38.79	0.925	15.8	21.2
Base+SF+EA	–	38.89	0.965	18.6	22.7
Base+DFR	–	40.01	0.971	18.9	23.9
Base+DFR	Extra-CR	39.95	0.956	–	–
Base+DFR	Intra-CR	**40.08**	**0.972**	–	–

add spatial filter branch (SF) into baseline. (2) **base+EA**: only add energy-based attention branch into baseline. (3) **base+SF+identity branch**: add spatial filter branch and identity branch. (4) **base+SF+EA**: add spatial filter branch and energy-based attention branch. (5) **base+DFR**: add combination of three branches as DFR module. (6) **base+DFR+CR**: add DFR module and Extra-CR. (7) **DRCNet**: the combination of DFR module and Intra-CR for training. The performance of these models is summarized in Table 4.

As shown in Table 4, the spatial filter branch can strengthen DRCNet with more representation power than the base model. Besides, the energy-based attention also improves the model's restoration capacity by dynamically guiding feature integration. Besides, Table 4 shows a significant performance drop in PSNR from 40.01 dB to 33.25 dB by removing the whole DFR, which shows that DFR is a successful and crucial module in DRCNet. Specifically, we show the visualization of intermediate features produced by different branches of DFR. As shown in Fig. 5 (a) denotes that spatial filter can effectively reduce noise, the energy-based attention branch focuses on the textures and sharpness in terms of

SSIM. Besides, the identity branch can further enhance the feature integration. Overall, the combination of the three branches achieves the best results.

Table 5. Comparison of the parameter number and PSNR (dB).

Filter		SACT [11]	CondConv [48]	UDVD [47]	DDF [67]	**DFR**
Params		103.1M	165.7M	95.2M	87.4M	**18.9M**
PSNR	Derain [55]	19.28	23.53	21.72	25.12	**32.39**
	SIDD [1]	27.28	39.43	37.21	39.04	**40.01**
	GoPro [29]	19.97	23.09	27.45	29.01	**32.21**

Effect of Contrastive Regularization. In Table 4, Extra-CR empirically impairs the model performance, indicating that using extra-class images as negative samples in denoising is not beneficial due to easy negative samples. This section illustrates the effectiveness of our Intra-CR. Specifically, we apply Intra-CR and Extra-CR on DRCNet, respectively. Moreover, we vary the value of weight α in Eq. (13) and observe the tendency of Intra-CR and Extra-CR. As shown in Fig. 5 (b), Intra-CR outperforms Extra-CR as α varies from 0 to 0.14. Moreover, Intra-CR achieves more stable results towards α, which matches our theoretical analysis that Intra-CR is less sensitive to α. Overall, the results validate the superiority of our Intra-CR.

Fig. 5. (a) Visualization of intermediate features on images from the GoPro test set [29]. (i-ii) Input blurred image and feature map. (iii-v) Comparisons among the feature map by using spatial filter, energy-based attention and DFR module, respectively. (vi) ground truth feature map; (b) Ablation experiment of comparison between Intra-CR and Extra-CR on SIDD benchmark.

5 Conclusion

In this paper, we propose a dynamic restoration contrastive network (DRCNet) for image restoration with two principal components: Dynamic Filter Restoration module (DFR) and Intra-class contrastive regularization (Intra-CR). The DFR module, built on a spatial filter branch and an energy-based attention branch, benefits from being dynamically adaptive toward spatially varying image degradation. The key insight of Intra-CR is to construct intra-class negative samples, which is accomplished through mixup operations. Through comprehensive evaluation of the performance of DRCNet on various benchmarks, we validate that the DRCNet achieves state-of-the-art results on ten datasets across various restoration tasks. Although DRCNet shows superior performance on three types of degradation, it needs to be trained for each type of degradation with a separate model, which limits the practical utility of the proposed approach. In the future, we will develop an all-in-one model for various restoration tasks.

Acknowledgement. The authors acknowledge the financial support from the Key Research and Development Plan Project of Guangdong Province ($No.\,2020B02020$ 10009) and the National Key R&D Program of China ($No.\,2020YFD0900204$, $2021ZD0113805$). We appreciate the comments from Dr. Linfeng Zhang and the seminar participants at the Center for Deep Learning of Computer vision Research at China Agricultural University, which improves the manuscript significantly.

References

1. Abdelhamed, A., Lin, S., Brown, M.S.: A high-quality denoising dataset for smartphone cameras. In: Proceedings of the IEEE/CVF Conference on Computer Vision and Pattern Recognition (CVPR), pp. 1692–1700 (2018)
2. Anwar, S., Barnes, N.: Real image denoising with feature attention. In: Proceedings of the IEEE/CVF Conference on Computer Vision and Pattern Recognition (CVPR), pp. 3155–3164 (2019)
3. Burger, H.C., Schuler, C.J., Harmeling, S.: Image denoising: Can plain neural networks compete with bm3d? In: Proceedings of the IEEE/CVF Conference on Computer Vision and Pattern Recognition (CVPR), pp. 2392–2399 (2012)
4. Cao, X., Chen, Y., Zhao, Q., Meng, D., Wang, Y., Wang, D., Xu, Z.: Low-rank matrix factorization under general mixture noise distributions. In: Proceedings of the IEEE/CVF International Conference on Computer Vision (ICCV), pp. 1493–1501 (2015)
5. Chang, M., Li, Q., Feng, H., Xu, Z.: Spatial-adaptive network for single image denoising. In: Vedaldi, A., Bischof, H., Brox, T., Frahm, J.-M. (eds.) ECCV 2020. LNCS, vol. 12375, pp. 171–187. Springer, Cham (2020). https://doi.org/10.1007/978-3-030-58577-8_11
6. Chen, J., Wang, X., Guo, Z., Zhang, X., Sun, J.: Dynamic region-aware convolution. In: Proceedings of the IEEE/CVF Conference on Computer Vision and Pattern Recognition (CVPR), pp. 8064–8073 (2021)
7. Chen, L., Lu, X., Zhang, J., Chu, X., Chen, C.: Hinet: Half instance normalization network for image restoration. In: Proceedings of the IEEE/CVF Conference on Computer Vision and Pattern Recognition (CVPR) Workshops, pp. 182–192 (2021)

8. Chen, Y., Dai, X., Liu, M., Chen, D., Yuan, L., Liu, Z.: Dynamic convolution: attention over convolution kernels. In: Proceedings of the IEEE/CVF Conference on Computer Vision and Pattern Recognition (CVPR), pp. 11030–11039 (2020)

9. Cho, S.J., Ji, S.W., Hong, J.P., Jung, S.W., Ko, S.J.: Rethinking coarse-to-fine approach in single image deblurring. In: Proceedings of the IEEE/CVF International Conference on Computer Vision (ICCV), pp. 4641–4650 (2021)

10. Dabov, K., Foi, A., Katkovnik, V., Egiazarian, K.: Image denoising by sparse 3-d transform-domain collaborative filtering. IEEE Trans. Image Process. **16**(8), 2080–2095 (2007)

11. Figurnov, M., et al.: Spatially adaptive computation time for residual networks. In: Proceedings of the IEEE/CVF Conference on Computer Vision and Pattern Recognition (CVPR), pp. 1039–1048 (2017)

12. Fu, X., Huang, J., Ding, X., Liao, Y., Paisley, J.: Clearing the skies: A deep network architecture for single-image rain removal. IEEE Trans. Image Process. **26**(6), 2944–2956 (2017)

13. Fu, X., Huang, J., Zeng, D., Huang, Y., Ding, X., Paisley, J.: Removing rain from single images via a deep detail network. In: Proceedings of the IEEE/CVF Conference on Computer Vision and Pattern Recognition (CVPR), pp. 3855–3863 (2017)

14. Guo, S., Yan, Z., Zhang, K., Zuo, W., Zhang, L.: Toward convolutional blind denoising of real photographs. In: Proceedings of the IEEE/CVF Conference on Computer Vision and Pattern Recognition (CVPR), pp. 1712–1722 (2019)

15. He, K., Fan, H., Wu, Y., Xie, S., Girshick, R.: Momentum contrast for unsupervised visual representation learning. In: Proceedings of the IEEE/CVF Conference on Computer Vision and Pattern Recognition (CVPR), pp. 9729–9738 (2020)

16. He, K., Sun, J., Tang, X.: Single image haze removal using dark channel prior. IEEE Trans. Pattern Anal. Mach. Intell. **33**(12), 2341–2353 (2010)

17. He, K., Zhang, X., Ren, S., Sun, J.: Deep residual learning for image recognition. In: Proceedings of the IEEE/CVF Conference on Computer Vision and Pattern Recognition (CVPR), pp. 770–778 (2016)

18. Jiang, K., et al.: Multi-scale progressive fusion network for single image deraining. In: Proceedings of the IEEE/CVF Conference on Computer Vision and Pattern Recognition (CVPR), pp. 8346–8355 (2020)

19. Johnson, J., Alahi, A., Fei-Fei, L.: Perceptual losses for real-time style transfer and super-resolution. In: Leibe, B., Matas, J., Sebe, N., Welling, M. (eds.) ECCV 2016. LNCS, vol. 9906, pp. 694–711. Springer, Cham (2016). https://doi.org/10.1007/978-3-319-46475-6_43

20. Kim, Y., Soh, J.W., Park, G.Y., Cho, N.I.: Transfer learning from synthetic to real-noise denoising with adaptive instance normalization. In: Proceedings of the IEEE/CVF Conference on Computer Vision and Pattern Recognition (CVPR), pp. 3482–3492 (2020)

21. Kingma, D., Ba, J.: Adam: A method for stochastic optimization (2014)

22. Kupyn, O., Budzan, V., Mykhailych, M., Mishkin, D., Matas, J.: Deblurgan: Blind motion deblurring using conditional adversarial networks. In: Proceedings of the IEEE/CVF Conference on Computer Vision and Pattern Recognition (CVPR), pp. 8183–8192 (2018)

23. Kupyn, O., Martyniuk, T., Wu, J., Wang, Z.: Deblurgan-v2: Deblurring (orders-of-magnitude) faster and better. In: Proceedings of the IEEE/CVF International Conference on Computer Vision (ICCV), pp. 8878–8887 (2019)

24. Li, X., Wu, J., Lin, Z., Liu, H., Zha, H.: Recurrent squeeze-and-excitation context aggregation net for single image deraining. In: Ferrari, V., Hebert, M., Sminchisescu, C., Weiss, Y. (eds.) ECCV 2018. LNCS, vol. 11211, pp. 262–277. Springer, Cham (2018). https://doi.org/10.1007/978-3-030-01234-2_16
25. Liu, Y., et al.: Invertible denoising network: A light solution for real noise removal. In: Proceedings of the IEEE/CVF Conference on Computer Vision and Pattern Recognition (CVPR), pp. 13365–13374 (2021)
26. Lo, Y.C., Chang, C.C., Chiu, H.C., Huang, Y.H., Chang, Y.L., Jou, K.: Clcc: Contrastive learning for color constancy. In: Proceedings of the IEEE/CVF Conference on Computer Vision and Pattern Recognition (CVPR), pp. 8053–8063 (2021)
27. Loshchilov, I., Hutter, F.: Sgdr: Stochastic gradient descent with warm restarts. In: Proceedings of the International Conference on Learning Representations (ICLR) (2016)
28. Mairal, J., Bach, F., Ponce, J., Sapiro, G., Zisserman, A.: Non-local sparse models for image restoration. In: Proceedings of the IEEE/CVF International Conference on Computer Vision (ICCV), pp. 2272–2279 (2009)
29. Nah, S., Hyun Kim, T., Mu Lee, K.: Deep multi-scale convolutional neural network for dynamic scene deblurring. In: Proceedings of the IEEE/CVF Conference on Computer Vision and Pattern Recognition (CVPR), pp. 3883–3891 (2017)
30. Park, D., Kang, D.U., Kim, J., Chun, S.Y.: Multi-temporal recurrent neural networks for progressive non-uniform single image deblurring with incremental temporal training. In: Vedaldi, A., Bischof, H., Brox, T., Frahm, J.-M. (eds.) ECCV 2020. LNCS, vol. 12351, pp. 327–343. Springer, Cham (2020). https://doi.org/10.1007/978-3-030-58539-6_20
31. Plotz, T., Roth, S.: Benchmarking denoising algorithms with real photographs. In: Proceedings of the IEEE/CVF Conference on Computer Vision and Pattern Recognition (CVPR), pp. 1586–1595 (2017)
32. Purohit, K., Rajagopalan, A.: Region-adaptive dense network for efficient motion deblurring. In: Proceedings of the AAAI Conference on Artificial Intelligence, pp. 11882–11889 (2020)
33. Purohit, K., Suin, M., Rajagopalan, A.N., Boddeti, V.N.: Spatially-adaptive image restoration using distortion-guided networks. In: Proceedings of the IEEE/CVF International Conference on Computer Vision (ICCV), pp. 2309–2319 (2021)
34. Ren, D., Shang, W., Zhu, P., Hu, Q., Meng, D., Zuo, W.: Single image deraining using bilateral recurrent network. IEEE Trans. Image Process. **29**, 6852–6863 (2020)
35. Ren, D., Zuo, W., Hu, Q., Zhu, P., Meng, D.: Progressive image deraining networks: A better and simpler baseline. In: Proceedings of the IEEE/CVF Conference on Computer Vision and Pattern Recognition (CVPR), pp. 3937–3946 (2019)
36. Rim, J., Lee, H., Won, J., Cho, S.: Real-world blur dataset for learning and benchmarking deblurring algorithms. In: Vedaldi, A., Bischof, H., Brox, T., Frahm, J.-M. (eds.) ECCV 2020. LNCS, vol. 12370, pp. 184–201. Springer, Cham (2020). https://doi.org/10.1007/978-3-030-58595-2_12
37. Ronneberger, O., Fischer, P., Brox, T.: U-net: Convolutional networks for biomedical image segmentation. In: International Conference on Medical Image Computing and Computer-assisted Intervention, pp. 234–241 (2015)
38. Shen, Z., et al.: Human-aware motion deblurring. In: Proceedings of the IEEE/CVF International Conference on Computer Vision (ICCV), pp. 5572–5581 (2019)
39. Simonyan, K., Zisserman, A.: Very deep convolutional networks for large-scale image recognition. In: Proceedings of the International Conference on Learning Representations (ICLR) (2015)

40. Suin, M., Purohit, K., Rajagopalan, A.: Spatially-attentive patch-hierarchical network for adaptive motion deblurring. In: Proceedings of the IEEE/CVF Conference on Computer Vision and Pattern Recognition (CVPR), pp. 3606–3615 (2020)

41. Thomas, H., Qi, C.R., Deschaud, J.E., Goulette, F., Guibas, L.J.: Kpconv: Flexible and deformable convolution for point clouds. In: Proceedings of the IEEE/CVF International Conference on Computer Vision (ICCV), pp. 6411–6420 (2019)

42. Wang, Z., Bovik, A.C., Sheikh, H.R., Simoncelli, E.P.: Image quality assessment: from error visibility to structural similarity. IEEE Trans. Image Process. **13**(4), 600–612 (2004)

43. Wei, W., Meng, D., Zhao, Q., Xu, Z., Wu, Y.: Semi-supervised transfer learning for image rain removal. In: Proceedings of the IEEE/CVF Conference on Computer Vision and Pattern Recognition (CVPR), pp. 3877–3886 (2019)

44. Wu, H., et al.: Contrastive learning for compact single image dehazing. In: Proceedings of the IEEE/CVF Conference on Computer Vision and Pattern Recognition (CVPR), pp. 10551–10560 (2021)

45. Xie, C., Tan, M., Gong, B., Wang, J., Yuille, A.L., Le, Q.V.: Adversarial examples improve image recognition. In: Proceedings of the IEEE/CVF Conference on Computer Vision and Pattern Recognition (CVPR) (June 2020)

46. Xu, L., Zheng, S., Jia, J.: Unnatural l0 sparse representation for natural image deblurring. In: Proceedings of the IEEE/CVF Conference on Computer Vision and Pattern Recognition (CVPR), pp. 1107–1114 (2013)

47. Xu, Y.S., Tseng, S.Y.R., Tseng, Y., Kuo, H.K., Tsai, Y.M.: Unified dynamic convolutional network for super-resolution with variational degradations. In: Proceedings of the IEEE/CVF Conference on Computer Vision and Pattern Recognition (CVPR), pp. 12496–12505 (2020)

48. Yang, B., Bender, G., Le, Q.V., Ngiam, J.: Condconv: Conditionally parameterized convolutions for efficient inference. In: Advances in Neural Information Processing Systems, pp. 1307–1318 (2019)

49. Yang, L., Zhang, R.Y., Li, L., Xie, X.: Simam: A simple, parameter-free attention module for convolutional neural networks. In: Proceedings of the International Conference on Machine Learning (ICML), pp. 11863–11874 (2021)

50. Yang, W., Tan, R.T., Feng, J., Liu, J., Guo, Z., Yan, S.: Deep joint rain detection and removal from a single image. In: Proceedings of the IEEE/CVF Conference on Computer Vision and Pattern Recognition (CVPR), pp. 1357–1366 (2017)

51. Yasarla, R., Patel, V.M.: Uncertainty guided multi-scale residual learning-using a cycle spinning cnn for single image de-raining. In: Proceedings of the IEEE/CVF Conference on Computer Vision and Pattern Recognition (CVPR), pp. 8405–8414 (2019)

52. Yu, T., et al.: Region normalization for image inpainting. In: Proceedings of the AAAI Conference on Artificial Intelligence, vol. 34, pp. 12733–12740 (2020)

53. Yue, Z., Yong, H., Zhao, Q., Meng, D., Zhang, L.: Variational denoising network: Toward blind noise modeling and removal. In: Advances in Neural Information Processing Systems (2019)

54. Yue, Z., Zhao, Q., Zhang, L., Meng, D.: Dual adversarial network: Toward real-world noise removal and noise generation. In: Vedaldi, A., Bischof, H., Brox, T., Frahm, J.-M. (eds.) ECCV 2020. LNCS, vol. 12355, pp. 41–58. Springer, Cham (2020). https://doi.org/10.1007/978-3-030-58607-2_3

55. Zamir, S.W., et al.: Multi-stage progressive image restoration. In: Proceedings of the IEEE/CVF Conference on Computer Vision and Pattern Recognition (CVPR), pp. 14821–14831 (2021)

56. Zamir, S.W., Arora, A., Khan, S., Hayat, M., Shao, L.: Cycleisp: Real image restoration via improved data synthesis. In: Proceedings of the IEEE/CVF Conference on Computer Vision and Pattern Recognition (CVPR), pp. 2696–2705 (2020)
57. Zhang, H., Li, Y., Chen, H., Shen, C.: Memory-efficient hierarchical neural architecture search for image denoising. In: Proceedings of the IEEE/CVF Conference on Computer Vision and Pattern Recognition (CVPR), pp. 3657–3666 (2020)
58. Zhang, H., Patel, V.M.: Density-aware single image de-raining using a multi-stream dense network. In: Proceedings of the IEEE/CVF Conference on Computer Vision and Pattern Recognition (CVPR), pp. 695–704 (2018)
59. Zhang, H., Sindagi, V., Patel, V.M.: Image de-raining using a conditional generative adversarial network. IEEE Trans. Circuits Syst. Video Technol. **30**(11), 3943–3956 (2019)
60. Zhang, H., Dai, Y., Li, H., Koniusz, P.: Deep stacked hierarchical multi-patch network for image deblurring. In: Proceedings of the IEEE/CVF Conference on Computer Vision and Pattern Recognition (CVPR), pp. 5978–5986 (2019)
61. Zhang, H., Yu, Y., Jiao, J., Xing, E., El Ghaoui, L., Jordan, M.: Theoretically principled trade-off between robustness and accuracy. In: Proceedings of the International Conference on Machine Learning (ICML), pp. 7472–7482 (2019)
62. Zhang, H., Cisse, M., Dauphin, Y.N., Lopez-Paz, D.: Mixup: Beyond empirical risk minimization. In: Proceedings of the International Conference on Learning Representations (ICLR) (2018)
63. Zhang, J., Pan, J., Ren, J., Song, Y., Bao, L., Lau, M.H.: Dynamic scene deblurring using spatially variant recurrent neural networks. In: Proceedings of the IEEE/CVF Conference on Computer Vision and Pattern Recognition (CVPR), pp. 2521–2529 (2018)
64. Zhang, K., Zuo, W., Chen, Y., Meng, D., Zhang, L.: Beyond a gaussian denoiser: Residual learning of deep cnn for image denoising. IEEE Trans. Image Process. **26**(7), 3142–3155 (2017)
65. Zhang, K., et al.: Deblurring by realistic blurring. In: Proceedings of the IEEE/CVF Conference on Computer Vision and Pattern Recognition (CVPR), pp. 2737–2746 (2020)
66. Zhang, R., Tang, S., Zhang, Y., Li, J., Yan, S.: Scale-adaptive convolutions for scene parsing. In: Proceedings of the IEEE/CVF International Conference on Computer Vision (ICCV), pp. 2031–2039 (2017)
67. Zhou, J., Jampani, V., Pi, Z., Liu, Q., Yang, M.H.: Decoupled dynamic filter networks. In: Proceedings of the IEEE/CVF Conference on Computer Vision and Pattern Recognition (CVPR), pp. 6647–6656 (2021)

Zero-Shot Learning for Reflection Removal of Single 360-Degree Image

Byeong-Ju Han[1,2] and Jae-Young Sim[1(✉)]

[1] Ulsan National Institute of Science and Technology, Ulsan, Republic of Korea
{bjhan,jysim}@unist.ac.kr
[2] NAVER Clova, Ulsan, Republic of Korea

Abstract. The existing methods for reflection removal mainly focus on removing blurry and weak reflection artifacts and thus often fail to work with severe and strong reflection artifacts. However, in many cases, real reflection artifacts are sharp and intensive enough such that even humans cannot completely distinguish between the transmitted and reflected scenes. In this paper, we attempt to remove such challenging reflection artifacts using 360-Degree images. We adopt the zero-shot learning scheme to avoid the burden of collecting paired data for supervised learning and the domain gap between different datasets. We first search for the reference image of the reflected scene in a 360-degree image based on the reflection geometry, which is then used to guide the network to restore the faithful colors of the reflection image. We collect 30 test 360-Degree images exhibiting challenging reflection artifacts and demonstrate that the proposed method outperforms the existing state-of-the-art methods on 360-Degree images.

1 Introduction

We often take pictures through the glass, for example, take a picture of the glass showcase in a museum or a gallery. The captured images through the glass exhibit undesired artifacts of the reflected scene. Such reflection artifacts decrease the visibility of the transmitted scene behind the glass and thus degrade the performance of diverse computer vision techniques. For a few decades, attempts have been made to develop efficient reflection removal methods. Whereas many existing methods of reflection removal used multiple glass images taken under constrained environments, the recent learning-based methods achieve outstanding performance by exploiting deep features to separate an input single glass image into transmission and reflection images.

While the existing methods usually assume blurry reflection artifacts associated with the out-of-focus scenes in front of the glass, the actual reflection artifacts exhibit more diverse characteristics than their assumption and often

---

Supplementary Information The online version contains supplementary material available at https://doi.org/10.1007/978-3-031-19800-7_31.

S. Avidan et al. (Eds.): ECCV 2022, LNCS 13679, pp. 533–548, 2022.
https://doi.org/10.1007/978-3-031-19800-7_31

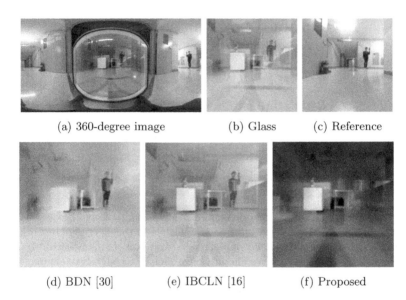

(a) 360-degree image   (b) Glass   (c) Reference

(d) BDN [30]   (e) IBCLN [16]   (f) Proposed

Fig. 1. Reflection removal of a 360-degree image. (a) A 360-degree image, and its pairs of (b) the glass image and (c) the reference image. The reflection removal results obtained by using (d) BDN [30], (e) IBCLN [16], and (f) the proposed method.

become intensive and sharp. Therefore, even the state-of-the-art learning-based methods still suffer from the domain gap between the training and test datasets. In particular, 360-degree cameras, widely used for VR applications, do not focus on a specific object and usually generate the images with sharp reflection artifacts on the glass region as shown in Fig. 1(a). Figures 1(b) and (c) show the cropped images of the glass region and the reference region of the actual reflected scene, respectively, where we see that the reflected scene distinctly emerges in the glass image. As shown in Figs. 1(d) and (e), the existing learning-based methods [16,30] fail to remove such artifacts from the glass image, since the reflection characteristics of 360-degree images are different from that of ordinary images. In such a case, it is more challenging to distinguish which scene is transmitted or reflected in the glass image by even humans. However, we can employ the visual information of the reflected scene within a 360-degree image as a reference to guide the reflection removal effectively.

The only existing reflection removal method [9] for 360-degree images uses a glass image synthesis algorithm for supervised learning, and thus theoretically suffers from the domain gap between the training and test datasets. Moreover, it rarely concerns the cooperation between the two tasks of reflection removal for 360-degree images: image restoration and reference image matching. In this paper, we apply a zero-shot learning framework for reflection removal of 360-degree images that avoids the burden of collecting training datasets and the domain gap between different datasets. Also, the proposed method iteratively estimates the optimal solutions for both the image restoration and the reference matching by alternatively updating the results for a given test image.

We first assume that a 360-degree image is captured by a vertically standing camera in front of the glass plane, and the central region of the 360-degree image is considered as the glass region. Then we investigate the reference information matching to the restored reflection image in a 360-degree image and update the network parameters to recover the transmission and reflection images based on the matched reference information. Consequently, the proposed method provides an outstanding performance to eliminate the reflection artifacts in 360-degree images, as shown in Fig. 1(f).

The main contributions of this work are summarized as follows.

1. To the best of our knowledge, this is the first work to apply a zero-shot learning framework to address the reflection removal problem for a single 360-degree image that avoids the domain gap between different datasets observed in the existing supervised learning methods.
2. The proposed method refines the reference matching by using the reflection geometry on a 360-degree image while adaptively restoring the transmission and reflection images with the guidance of refined references.
3. We collect 30 real test 360-degree images for experiments and demonstrate the proposed method outperforms the state-of-the-art reflection removal techniques.

2   Related Works

In this section, we briefly summarize the existing reflection removal methods. We classify the exiting methods into unsupervised and supervised approaches. The unsupervised approach includes the computational reflection removal methods and the latest zero-shot learning-based image decomposition method that does not need paired datasets for training. In contrast, the supervised approach covers the learning-based single image reflection removal methods.

Unsupervised Approach: The distinct properties of the reflection artifacts appear in the multiple images taken in the particular capturing environments. [5,13,21] removed reflection artifacts in the multiple polarized images according to the unique property of the reflected lights whose intensities are changed by the polarization angles. [20] separated multiple glass images captured as varying focal lengths into two component images to have distinct blurriness. [7,8,17,24,29] analyzed different behaviors of the transmitted and reflected scenes across multiple glass images taken at different camera positions. Furthermore, [19] detected the repeated movement of the transmitted scene in a video. [23] extracted the static image reflected on the front windshield of a car in a black-box video. On the other hand, removing the reflection artifacts from a single glass image is challenging due to the lack of characteristics to distinguish between the transmission and reflection images. [14] selected reflection edges to be removed on a glass image by user assistance. [18] separated the input image into a sharp layer and a blurry layer to obtain the transmission and reflection images under the strong assumption that the reflection images are more blurry than the transmission images.

[15] supposed a glass image causes a large number of the cross-points between two different edges, and separated the glass image into two layers that minimize the total number of the cross-points. In addition, [22] removed spatially repeated visual structures because the lights reflected on the front and back surfaces of the glass window yield the ghosting effects. [6] proposed a general framework that trains a network to decompose the multiple glass images captured in a constrained environment where the transmitted and reflected scenes are dynamic and static, respectively.

While the existing methods require multiple glass images or assume distinct characteristics of the reflection artifacts, the proposed method removes the challenging reflection artifacts exhibiting similar features to the transmission image by detecting reference information in a single 360-degree image.

Supervised Approach: Deep learning-based reflection removal methods have been proposed in recent years. They train the deep networks by using the paired dataset of the glass and transmission images, and provide more reliable results than the computational methods that strongly assume the unique characteristic of reflection artifacts. [4] firstly applied CNN for reflection removal and proposed a framework that two networks are serially connected to restore the gradients and colors of the transmission image, respectively. [25] revised the framework to predict the colors and gradients of the transmission image simultaneously. [30] proposed a novel framework that predicts a transmission image and a reflection image recursively by using the prior result. Similarly, [16] adopted a complete cascade framework that repeats to predict the transmission and reflection images from the glass image by feeding back the prior results of transmission and reflection restoration. [2] tackled locally intensive reflection artifacts by predicting a probability map indicating local regions of dominant reflection artifacts. On the other hand, some methods have tackled the training data issues for supervised learning. [27] defined a novel loss term to train the network parameters regardless of the misalignment between an input glass image and its ground-truth transmission image that is frequently observed in the existing real training datasets. Due to the lack of paired data of real glass and transmission images, [32] modeled a sophisticated image formulation to synthesize glass images, involving the light absorption effect depending on the incident angle of rays on the glass plane. [12] generated synthetic glass images by using a graphical simulator to imitate the reflection physically. [28] utilized the deep networks for reflection removal as well as the glass image synthesis to make more realistic glass images for training. Recently, [9] removed the reflection artifacts using a reference image captured in the opposite direction to the glass window in a panoramic image.

However, all the supervised learning-based methods suffer from the domain gap. [1] demonstrated that the reflection removal performance of the existing methods is determined by the types of reflection artifacts in their training dataset. However, the proposed method adaptively works for a given input image based on a zero-shot learning framework, and also alleviates the burden of collecting training datasets in the supervised learning framework.

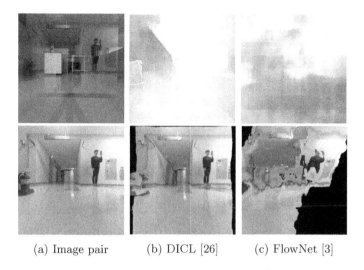

(a) Image pair   (b) DICL [26]   (c) FlowNet [3]

Fig. 2. Image alignment using optical flow estimators. (a) A pair of the rectified glass and reference images on a 360-degree image. The flow maps and the warped reference images are obtained by (b) DICL [26] and (c) FlowNet [3], respectively.

3   Methodology

Since the 360-degree image includes the whole environmental scene around the camera, the glass scene and the associated reflected scene are captured together. The proposed method recovers the transmission and reflection images associated with the glass region in a 360-degree image by bringing relevant information from the reference region including the reflected scene. In this section, we first explain how to search for the reference image based on the reflection geometry in a 360-degree image. Then we introduce the proposed zero-shot learning framework with a brief comparison to the existing method of DDIP [6]. We finally describe the detailed training process of the proposed method in a test time.

3.1   Estimation of Reference Image

We investigate the relationship between the reflection image and the associated reference image. As introduced in [9], the reflection image suffers from the photometric and geometric distortions that make it challenging to distinguish the reflected scene from the transmitted scene on the glass image even using the reference image. The photometric distortion can be generated by external factors like the thickness of glass, the incident angle of light, and the wavelength of light. The image signal processing (ISP) embedded in the camera is also an internal factor of photometric distortion. The geometric distortion between the reflection and reference images is mainly caused by the parallax depending on the distances from the camera to the glass or the objects. The recent techniques [3,26] for optical flow estimation fail to estimate the correct correspondence between the glass

538   B.-J. Han and J.-Y. Sim

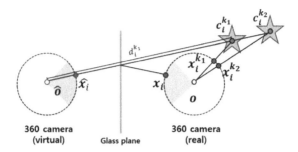

Fig. 3. Configuration for 360-degree image acqusition with reflection. Circles represent the surfaces of unit spheres where the 360-degree images are rendered.

image and the reference image due to the photometric distortion of the reflection image and the mixed transmission image, as shown in Fig. 2.

Reducing the geometric distortion and the photometric distortion can be considered as a chicken-and-egg problem. The reference image well-aligned with the reflection image provides faithful colors for the restoration of reflected scene contents. On the other hand, a well-recovered reflection image yields confident visual features to align the reference image with the reflection image. The proposed method finds reliable reference regions for each pixel in the glass image area based on the reflection geometry. A 360-degree image is captured by the rays projected from the objects in 3D space to the surface of a unit sphere. In particular, the glass region produces additional rays reflected on the glass, and in such cases, we cannot estimate the accurate object locations in 3D space due to the absence of distance information. As shown in Fig. 3, when an object is observed at x_i in the glass region of a 360-degree image, it would be observed at $\hat{x}$ if the glass does not exist. According to the reflection geometry, we calculate the coordinates of the virtual points $\hat{x}_i$ and $\hat{o}$ using the Householder matrix [10] defined by the orientation of the glass plane.

Assuming that the object should be located along the direction of $d_i = \hat{x}_i - \hat{o}$, we consider candidate location of c_i^k for x_i by varying the distance to the object from the virtual origin $\hat{o}$ along d_i. Then we collect the matching candidates x_i^{k}'s by projecting the candidate locations c_i^{k}'s to the unit surface, respectively. In this work, we define the search space including 50 candidate locations of c_i^{k}'s sampled along the direction of d_i to handle the background far from the glass. Then we find the optimal matching point m_i to x_i among x_i^{k}'s of the search space that has the smallest feature difference from x_i. We consider the neighboring pixels to compute a patch-wise feature difference between x_i and x_i^k as

$$\Omega(x_i, x_i^k) = \frac{1}{|\mathcal{N}_i| + 1} \sum_{p_j \in \mathcal{N}_i \cup \{p_i\}} \| F_G(p_j) - F_R(p_j^k) \|_1 \qquad (1)$$

where F_G and F_R represent the arbitrary rectified feature maps of the glass and reference regions in the 360-degree image, respectively, p denotes the pixel

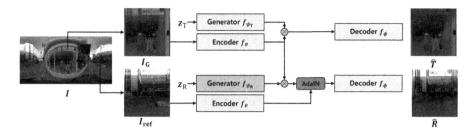

Fig. 4. The overall architecture of the proposed network.

location corresponding to $\boldsymbol{x}$ on the rectified image domain, and $\mathcal{N}_i$ is the neighbor set of $\boldsymbol{p}_i$. In this work, we set the size of $\mathcal{N}_i$ to 24.

Specifically, for a given $\boldsymbol{x}_i$, we search for the two optimal matching points $\boldsymbol{m}_i^c$ and $\boldsymbol{m}_i^g$ in terms of the color and gradient features, respectively. The notation of the training iteration t is omitted for simplification. To search for the color-based matching point $\boldsymbol{m}_i^c$, we set F_G as a reconstructed reflection image $\hat{R}$, and set F_R as the rectified reference image I_{ref}. Note that $\hat{R}$ and $\boldsymbol{m}_i^c$ are iteratively updated for training, and more faithful $\hat{R}$ provides more confident $\boldsymbol{m}_i^c$, and vice versa. The gradient-based matching point $\boldsymbol{m}_i^g$ is obtained by using the gradient of the rectified glass image I_G and I_{ref} for F_G and F_R, respectively. Note that $\boldsymbol{m}_i^c$ and $\boldsymbol{m}_i^g$ provide partially complementary information for reflection recovery. While $\boldsymbol{m}_i^c$ prevents the recovered reflection image from having unfamiliar colors with the reference image, $\boldsymbol{m}_i^g$ makes the recovered reflection image preserve the structure of the glass image.

3.2 Network Architecture

The proposed method is composed of the four sub-networks of encoder, decoder, and two generators, as shown in Fig. 4. We share the network parameters of $\boldsymbol{\theta}$ and $\boldsymbol{\phi}$ for the recovery of the transmission and reflection images, respectively. The encoder gets the rectified images from the 360-degree image and extracts the deep features that are able to reconstruct the input images by the decoder. Since the deep features in the glass image have both of the transmission and reflection features, the generators provide the mask maps to separate the deep features of the glass image into the transmission feature $\boldsymbol{h}_T$ and the reflection feature $\boldsymbol{h}_R$, respectively, given by

$$h_T = f_\theta(I_G) \cdot f_{\psi_T}(\boldsymbol{z}_T), \qquad (2)$$

$$h_R = f_\theta(I_G) \cdot f_{\psi_R}(\boldsymbol{z}_R), \qquad (3)$$

where $\boldsymbol{z}_T$ and $\boldsymbol{z}_R$ represent the different Gaussian random noises and $(\cdot)$ denotes the element-wise multiplication.

However, the photometric distortion of the glass image provides incomplete reflection features to recover the original colors of the reflection image, and the proposed method applies the Adaptive Instance Normalization (AdaIN) [11] on the reflection feature to compensate for the incomplete information. The reflection feature h_R is transformed by the reference feature h_{ref} as

$$\hat{h}_R = \sigma(h_{ref}) \left(\frac{h_R - \mu(h_R)}{\sigma(h_R)} \right) + \mu(h_{ref}), \tag{4}$$

where $h_{ref} = f_\theta(I_{ref})$, and μ and σ denote the operations to compute the average and standard deviation across spatial dimensions. The proposed method finally decodes the reflection image as $\hat{R} = f_\phi(\hat{h}_R)$. Since AdaIN transfers the feature according to the statistics across spatial locations, it relieves the geometric difference between the reflection and reference images. Unlike the reflection recovery, we suppose that the distortion of the transmission is negligible and predict the transmission image via $\hat{T} = f_\phi(h_T)$.

DDIP [6] introduced a general framework that is able to separate the multiple glass images into the transmission and reflection images. It trains the network under a linear formulation for the glass image synthesis. However, recent research [1,9,28] has addressed that such a naive formulation is insufficient to model the actual glass image. On the other hand, the proposed method decomposes the glass image in a deep feature space and synthesizes the glass image by integrating the deep features of the transmission and reflection images instead of simply adding the resulting transmission and reflection color maps. Also note that the proposed method attaches a new branch that brings the reference information from a given 360-degree image to distinguish the reflection image from the transmission image, while DDIP simply demands multiple glass images to involve distinct characteristics between the transmitted and reflected scenes. Please refer to the supplementary material for network architecture details.

3.3   Training Strategy

The proposed method trains the network parameters in a test time for a given instance. Particularly, each network of the proposed framework is trained respectively according to different training losses. For each iteration, the (θ, ϕ), ψ_R, and ψ_T are trained by using three individual Adam optimizers. We update the network parameters during 600 iterations for each test image.

Encoder and Decoder: The parameters of the encoder θ and the decoder ϕ are trained to reconstruct the input image itself according to the reconstruction loss $\mathcal{L}_{recon}$ between a source map X and a target map Y defined as

$$\mathcal{L}_{recon}(X, Y) = \mathcal{L}_{mse}(X, Y) + w_1 \mathcal{L}_{mse}(\nabla X, \nabla Y) \tag{5}$$

where $\mathcal{L}_{mse}$ denotes the mean squared error and w_1 denotes the weight to determine the contribution of the gradient difference for training. We utilize the rectified images I_G and I_{ref} of the glass region and the reference region as training images. The encoder extracts the deep features from I_G and I_{ref} and the decoder outputs the images $\hat{I}_G$ and $\hat{I}_{ref}$ that minimize the auto-encoder loss $\mathcal{L}_A$ defined as

$$\mathcal{L}_A(\theta, \phi) = \mathcal{L}_{recon}(\hat{I}_G, I_G) + \mathcal{L}_{recon}(\hat{I}_{ref}, I_{ref}). \tag{6}$$

In addition, it is helpful to reduce the training time to initialize θ and ϕ by using any photos. For all the following experiments, we used θ and ϕ pre-trained on the natural images in [31] for one epoch.

Mask Generator for Transmission Recovery: Though the network parameters θ, ϕ, and ψ_T are associated with the transmission recovery, ψ_T is only updated by the transmission loss. The gradient prior that the transmission and reflection images rarely have intensive gradients at the same pixel location has been successfully used in reflection removal. We enhance this prior for the two images not to have intensive gradients at *similar* locations. The gradient prior loss $\mathcal{L}_{\mathrm{grad}}$ is defined as

$$\mathcal{L}_{\mathrm{grad}}(\hat{T}, \hat{R}) = \frac{1}{N} \sum_{\boldsymbol{p}_i} |\nabla \hat{T}(\boldsymbol{p}_i)||\nabla \hat{R}^*(\boldsymbol{p}_i)|, \qquad (7)$$

where N represents the total number of pixels and $\nabla \hat{R}^*(\boldsymbol{p}_i)$ denotes the gradient having the maximum magnitude around $\boldsymbol{p}_i$, i.e. $\nabla \hat{R}^*(\boldsymbol{p}_i) = \max_{\boldsymbol{p}_j \in \mathcal{W}_i} |\nabla \hat{R}(\boldsymbol{p}_j)|$ where $\mathcal{W}_i$ denotes the set of pixels within a local window centered at $\boldsymbol{p}_i$. We empirically set the window size to 5. We also evaluate the additional reconstruction loss for the glass image by synthesizing a glass image using the recovered transmission and reflection images. For glass image synthesis, the existing methods [16,30,31] manually modify the reflection image to imitate the photometric distortion of reflection and combine them according to the hand-crafted image formation models. However, we obtain the distorted reflection image $\bar{R}$ by deactivating AdaIN of the proposed framework as $\bar{R} = f_\phi(f_\theta(I_G) \cdot f_{\psi_R}(\boldsymbol{z}_R))$ and synthesize the glass image by using the encoder and decoder as $\tilde{I}_G = f_\phi(f_\theta(\hat{T}) + f_\theta(\bar{R}))$. The transmission loss $\mathcal{L}_T$ is defined as

$$\mathcal{L}_T(\psi_T) = \mathcal{L}_{\mathrm{recon}}(\tilde{I}_G, I_G) + w_2 \mathcal{L}_{\mathrm{grad}}(\hat{T}, \hat{R}). \qquad (8)$$

Mask Generator for Reflection Recovery: While the transmission image is hypothetically estimated by applying the gradient prior, the reflection image has a reference color map R and a reference gradient map $\mathcal{M}$ obtained by the reference matching process, such that $R(\boldsymbol{p}_i) = I(\boldsymbol{m}_i^c)$ and $\mathcal{M}(\boldsymbol{p}_i) = \nabla I(\boldsymbol{m}_i^g)$ where $\boldsymbol{p}_i$ denotes the pixel location corresponding to $\boldsymbol{x}_i$ in the rectified image. The total reflection loss $\mathcal{L}_R$ is given by

$$\mathcal{L}_R(\psi_R) = \mathcal{L}_{\mathrm{recon}}(\tilde{I}_G, I_G) + w_3 \mathcal{L}_{\mathrm{mse}}(\hat{R}, R) + w_4 \mathcal{L}_{\mathrm{mse}}(\nabla \hat{R}, \mathcal{M}). \qquad (9)$$

4   Experimental Results

This section provides the experimental results on ten 360-degree images to discuss the effectiveness of each part of the proposed method and compare the proposed method with the state-of-the-art methods qualitatively and quantitatively. In this work, we set the weight of w_1 for $\mathcal{L}_A$ to 1 and the weights of w_1, w_2, w_3, and w_4 for $\mathcal{L}_T$ and $\mathcal{L}_R$ to 10, 3, 5, and 50, respectively. Please see the supplementary results for more experimental results.

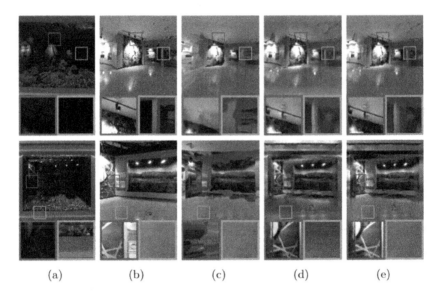

     (a)   (b)   (c)   (d)   (e)

Fig. 5. Effect of feature matching for reference searching. (a) Glass images and (b) reference images rectified from 360-degree images. The reflection recovery results are obtained by the proposed methods using the (c) color-based matching, (d) gradient-based matching, and (e) both of them.

4.1   Ablation Study

Feature Matching for Reference Searching: The proposed method utilizes the color of the recovered reflection image and the gradient of the glass images to determine the matching points to bring the information to recover the reflection image. We tested the comparative methods that utilize either of the color-based matching points or the gradient-based matching points to search for the reference images. Figure 5 shows the glass and reference images in the 360-degree images captured in front of the fish tanks of an aquarium. As shown in Figs. 5c and 5d, the method using only the color-based matching destroys the reflected scene structures, and the method using only the gradient-based matching fails to recover the original color of the reflection image faithfully. However, when using both of the matching together, the proposed method recovers realistic colors while preserving the reflected scene structures. Note that the rectified reference image and the recovered reflection image are misaligned due to the geometric distortion.

Glass Synthesis Loss: Although the gradient prior provides a good insight for image decomposition, it may result in a homogeneous image where all pixels have small gradients. We can alleviate this problem by using the glass synthesis loss $\mathcal{L}_{\mathrm{recon}}(\tilde{I}_{\mathrm{G}}, I_{\mathrm{G}})$. Figure 6 shows the effect of the glass synthesis loss. The proposed method without $\mathcal{L}_{\mathrm{recon}}(\tilde{I}_{\mathrm{G}}, I_{\mathrm{G}})$ provides the significantly blurred transmission images as shown in Fig. 6b where the mannequins behind the glass are

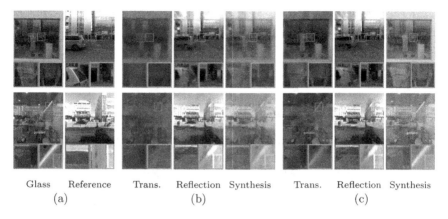

Glass   Reference   Trans.   Reflection   Synthesis   Trans.   Reflection   Synthesis
(a)   (b)   (c)

Fig. 6. Effect of the glass synthesis loss $\mathcal{L}_{\mathrm{recon}}(\tilde{I}_{\mathrm{G}}, I_{\mathrm{G}})$. (a) Glass and reference images rectified from 360-degree images. The triplets of the recovered transmission, reflection, and synthesized glass images obtained by the proposed method (b) without $\mathcal{L}_{\mathrm{recon}}(\tilde{I}_{\mathrm{G}}, I_{\mathrm{G}})$ and (c) with $\mathcal{L}_{\mathrm{recon}}(\tilde{I}_{\mathrm{G}}, I_{\mathrm{G}})$.

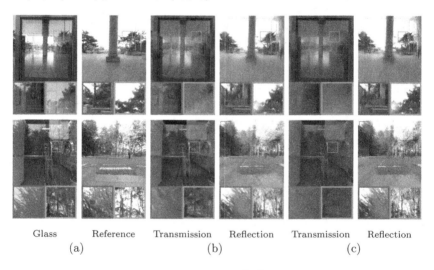

Glass   Reference   Transmission   Reflection   Transmission   Reflection
(a)   (b)   (c)

Fig. 7. Effect of the gradient prior loss $\mathcal{L}_{\mathrm{grad}}(\hat{T}, \hat{R})$. (a) Glass and reference images rectified from 360-degree images. The pairs of the recovered transmission and reflection images obtained by the proposed method (b) without $\mathcal{L}_{\mathrm{grad}}(\hat{T}, \hat{R})$ and (c) with $\mathcal{L}_{\mathrm{grad}}(\hat{T}, \hat{R})$.

disappeared from the recovered transmission image and the synthesized glass image. In contrary, the proposed method using $\mathcal{L}_{\mathrm{recon}}(\tilde{I}_{\mathrm{G}}, I_{\mathrm{G}})$ enforces the synthesized glass images to have the image context not detected in the reflection image, which preserves the context of the transmitted scene.

Gradient Prior Loss: The ablation study for the gradient prior loss $\mathcal{L}_{\mathrm{grad}}$ shows how it affects the resulting transmission images. As shown in Fig. 7,

Fig. 8. Qualitative comparison of the reflection removal performance. (a) Pairs of the glass and reference images in 360-degree images. The results of the recovered transmission and reflection images obtained by (b) RS [18], (c) PRR [31], (d) BDN [30], (e) IBCLN [16], (f) PBTI [12], and (g) the proposed method.

whereas the method without the gradient prior loss often remains the sharp edges of the intensive reflection artifacts in the transmission images, the proposed method trained with $\mathcal{L}_{\mathrm{grad}}$ successfully suppresses such reflection edges.

4.2 Qualitative Comparison

Since there are no existing methods of unsupervised reflection removal for a single 360-degree image, we compared the proposed method with the representative unsupervised method [18] and the state-of-the-art supervised methods [12,16, 30,31] that remove the reflection artifacts from a single glass image. The rectified images of the glass regions in 360-degree images are given as input images for the existing methods. Most of the reflection removal methods restore not only the transmission image but also the reflection image, and thus we evaluate the quality of the recovered transmission and reflection images together.

Figure 8 shows the reflection removal results for three challenging glass images that make it hard for even humans to distinguish between the transmission and reflection images. Due to the absence of the ground truth images, the rectified images of the misaligned reference regions in the 360-degree images are inferred to display the reflected scenes. The unsupervised method RS [18] targets to remove blurred reflection artifacts and therefore rarely removed the reflection artifacts on the test glass images. Also, the existing learning-based methods failed to detect the reflection artifacts because they are mainly trained by the synthesized glass images where the reflection images are manually blurred and attenuated except PBTI [12]. PBTI generates realistic glass images by using a graphic simulator, and suppressed the grey and homogeneous reflection artifacts from the sky as shown in the first image in Fig. 8, however, it failed to remove the colorful and structural reflection artifacts in the other glass images. On the other hand, the proposed method successfully estimated the reflection images and suppressed the challenging reflection artifacts with the guidance of the reference regions estimated in the 360-degree images.

4.3 Quantitative Comparison

We simply synthesize the glass images in 360-degree images without reflection artifacts. In practice, we set the center area of a 360-degree image as the glass region and suppose an arbitrary depth of the region opposite to the glass region as a reflected scene. Then we compose the transmission image in the glass region according to the conventional linear glass image formulation. Table 1 quantitatively compare the performance of the reflection removal methods using 12 synthetic 360-degree images, where '-T' and '-R' denote the comparison for the transmission and reflection images, respectively. We see that the proposed method ranks the first among the compared methods in terms of all the metrics except SSIM-T. However, note that the input glass image itself, without any processing, yields the SSIM-T score of 0.666, even higher than that of the most methods. It means that the quantitative measures are not sufficient to reflect the actual performance of the reflection removal, and the qualitative comparison on real test datasets is much more informative.

Table 1. Comparison of the quantitative performance of reflection removal.

Method	Input	RS [18]	PRR [31]	BDN [30]	IBCLN [16]	PBTI [12]	Prop
PSNR-T	12.19	15.10	14.30	12.12	12.80	12.70	19.08
PSNR-R	–	10.36	10.85	9.08	12.28	12.46	28.31
SSIM-T	0.666	0.655	0.675	0.620	0.580	0.626	0.647
SSIM-R	–	0.448	0.296	0.428	0.507	0.531	0.852

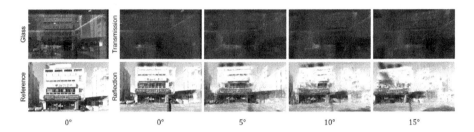

Fig. 9. Layer separation results accroding to different angles of the glass plane orientation.

4.4   Limitations

The angular deviation of the glass plane orientation may cause large displacement of the matching candidates in 3D space, and thus degrade the performance of the proposed method. Figure 9 shows this limitation where the recovered transmission images remain lots of the reflection artifacts in the glass regions as the angular deviation of the glass plane orientation increases. Moreover, since the proposed method highly depends on the quality of the reference image captured by the camera, it fails to remove the reflected camera contents itself and it often fails to recover the transmission and/or reflection images when the reference image is overexposed due to intense ambient light.

5   Conclusion

This paper proposes a novel reflection removal method for 360-degree images by applying the zero-shot learning scheme. Based on reflection geometry, the proposed method searches for reliable references from outside the glass region in the 360-degree image. And then, it adaptively restores the truthful colors for the transmission and reflection images according to the searched references. Experimental results demonstrate that the proposed method provides outstanding reflection removal results compared to the existing state-of-the-art methods for 360-degree images.

Acknowledgments. This work was supported by the National Research Foundation of Korea within the Ministry of Science and ICT (MSIT) under Grant 2020R1A2B5B01002725, and by Institute of Information & communications Technology Planning & Evaluation (IITP) grant funded by the Korea government(MSIT) (No.2021-0-02068, Artificial Intelligence Innovation Hub) and (No.2020-0-01336, Artificial Intelligence Graduate School Program(UNIST)).

References

1. Chenyang, L., et al.: A categorized reflection removal dataset with diverse real-world scenes. In: CVPRW (2022)
2. Dong, Z., Xu, K., Yang, Y., Bao, H., Xu, W., Lau, R.W.: Location-aware single image reflection removal. In: ICCV (2021)
3. Dosovitskiy, A., et al.: FlowNet: learning optical flow with convolutional networks. In: ICCV (2015)
4. Fan, Q., Yang, J., Hua, G., Chen, B., Wipf, D.: A generic deep architecture for single image reflection removal and image smoothing. In: ICCV (2017)
5. Farid, H., Adelson, E.H.: Separating reflections and lighting using independent components analysis. In: CVPR (1999)
6. Gandelsman, Y., Shocher, A., Irani, M.: "Double-dip": unsupervised image decomposition via coupled deep-image-priors. In: CVPR (2019)
7. Guo, X., Cao, X., Ma, Y.: Robust separation of reflection from multiple images. In: CVPR (2014)
8. Han, B.J., Sim, J.Y.: Glass reflection removal using co-saliency-based image alignment and low-rank matrix completion in gradient domain. IEEE TIP $27(10)$, 4873–4888 (2018)
9. Hong, Y., Zheng, Q., Zhao, L., Jiang, X., Kot, A.C., Shi, B.: Panoramic image reflection removal. In: CVPR (2021)
10. Householder, A.S.: Unitary triangularization of a nonsymmetric matrix. J. ACM **5**, 339–342 (1958)
11. Huang, X., Belongie, S.: Arbitrary style transfer in real-time with adaptive instance normalization. In: ICCV (2017)
12. Kim, S., Huo, Y., Yoon, S.E.: Single image reflection removal with physically-based training images. In: CVPR (2020)
13. Kong, N., Tai, Y.W., Shin, J.S.: A physically-based approach to reflection separation: from physical modeling to constrained optimization. IEEE TPAMI **36**(2), 209–221 (2014)
14. Levin, A., Weiss, Y.: User assisted separation of reflections from a single image using a sparsity prior. IEEE TPAMI **29**(9), 1647–1654 (2007)
15. Levin, A., Zomet, A., Weiss, Y.: Separating reflections from a single image using local features. In: CVPR (2004)
16. Li, C., Yang, Y., He, K., Lin, S., Hopcroft, J.E.: Single image reflection removal through cascaded refinement. In: CVPR (2020)
17. Li, Y., Brown, M.S.: Exploiting reflection change for automatic reflection removal. In: ICCV (2013)
18. Li, Y., Brown, M.S.: Single image layer separation using relative smoothness. In: CVPR (2014)
19. Sarel, B., Irani, M.: Separating transparent layers of repetitive dynamic behaviors. In: ICCV (2005)

20. Schechner, Y.Y., Kiryati, N., Shamir, J.: Blind recovery of transparent and semire-flected scenes. In: CVPR (2000)
21. Schechner, Y.Y., Shamir, J., Kiryati, N.: Polarization and statistical analysis of scenes containing a semireflector. J. Opt. Soc. Amer. **17**(2), 276–284 (2000)
22. Shih, Y., Krishnan, D., Durand, F., Freeman, W.T.: Reflection removal using ghost-ing cues. In: CVPR (2015)
23. Simon, C., Park, I.K.: Reflection removal for in-vehicle black box videos. In: CVPR (2015)
24. Sinha, S.N., Kopf, J., Goesele, M., Scharstein, D., Szeliski, R.: Image-based ren-dering for scenes with reflections. ACM TOG **31**(4), 100:1–100:10 (2012)
25. Wan, R., Shi, B., Duan, L.Y., Tan, A.H., Kot, A.C.: CRRN: multi-scale guided concurrent reflection removal network. In: CVPR (2018)
26. Wang, J., Zhong, Y., Dai, Y., Zhang, K., Ji, P., Li, H.: Displacement-invariant matching cost learning for accurate optical flow estimation. In: NeurIPS (2020)
27. Wei, K., Yang, J., Fu, Y., David, W., Huang, H.: Single image reflection removal exploiting misaligned training data and network enhancements. In: CVPR (2019)
28. Wen, Q., Tan, Y., Qin, J., Liu, W., Han, G., He, S.: Single image reflection removal beyond linearity. In: CVPR (2019)
29. Xue, T., Rubinstein, M., Liu, C., Freeman, W.T.: A computational approach for obstruction-free photography. ACM TOG **34**(4), 79:1–79:11 (2015)
30. Yang, J., Gong, D., Liu, L., Shi, Q.: Seeing deeply and bidirectionally: a deep learning approach for single image reflection removal. In: ECCV (2018)
31. Zhang, X., Ng, R., Chen, Q.: Single image reflection separation with perceptual losses. In: CVPR (2018)
32. Zheng, Q., Shi, B., Chen, J., Jiang, X., Duan, L.Y., Kot, A.C.: Single image reflec-tion removal with absorption effect. In: CVPR (2021)

Transformer with Implicit Edges for Particle-Based Physics Simulation

Yidi Shao[1(✉)] , Chen Change Loy[1] , and Bo Dai[2]

[1] S-Lab for Advanced Intelligence, Nanyang Technological University,
Singapore, Singapore
yidi001@e.ntu.edu.sg, ccloy@ntu.edu.sg
[2] Shanghai AI Laboratory, Shanghai, China
daibo@pjlab.org.cn

Abstract. Particle-based systems provide a flexible and unified way to simulate physics systems with complex dynamics. Most existing data-driven simulators for particle-based systems adopt graph neural networks (GNNs) as their network backbones, as particles and their interactions can be naturally represented by graph nodes and graph edges. However, while particle-based systems usually contain hundreds even thousands of particles, the explicit modeling of particle interactions as graph edges inevitably leads to a significant computational overhead, due to the increased number of particle interactions. Consequently, in this paper we propose a novel Transformer-based method, dubbed as Transformer with Implicit Edges (TIE), to capture the rich semantics of particle interactions in an edge-free manner. The core idea of TIE is to decentralize the computation involving pair-wise particle interactions into per-particle updates. This is achieved by adjusting the self-attention module to resemble the update formula of graph edges in GNN. To improve the generalization ability of TIE, we further amend TIE with learnable material-specific abstract particles to disentangle global material-wise semantics from local particle-wise semantics. We evaluate our model on diverse domains of varying complexity and materials. Compared with existing GNN-based methods, without bells and whistles, TIE achieves superior performance and generalization across all these domains. Codes and models are available at https://github.com/ftbabi/TIE_ECCV2022.git. (Bo Dai completed this work when he was with S-Lab, NTU.)

1 Introduction

Particle-based physics simulation not only facilitates the exploration of underlying principles in physics, chemistry and biology, it also plays an important role in computer graphics, *e.g.*, enabling the creation of vivid visual effects such as explosion and fluid dynamic in films and games. By viewing a system as a composition of particles, particle-based physics simulation imitates system dynamics according

---

Supplementary Information The online version contains supplementary material available at https://doi.org/10.1007/978-3-031-19800-7_32.

S. Avidan et al. (Eds.): ECCV 2022, LNCS 13679, pp. 549–564, 2022.
https://doi.org/10.1007/978-3-031-19800-7_32

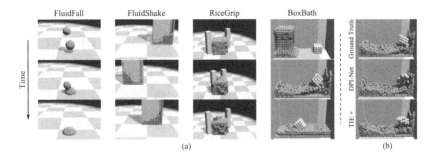

Fig. 1. (a). Samples from base domains. *FluidFall* contains two drops of water. *Fluid-Shake* simulates a block of water in a moving box. *RiceGrip* has a deformable object squeezed by two grippers. *BoxBath* contains a rigid cubic washed by water. (b). Samples from *BunnyBath*, where we change the rigid cube into bunny for generalization test. We compare our TIE with DPI-Net, which achieves the best performances on *BunnyBath* among previous methods. While the bunny is flooded upside down in ground truth, TIE rollouts more faithful results especially in terms of the bunny's posture and fluid dynamics. More comparisons can be found in Sect. 4.2.

to the states of particles as well as their mutual interactions. In this way, although different systems may contain different materials and follow different physical laws, they can be simulated in a unified manner with promising quality.

Recent approaches for particle-based physics simulation [2,12,17,22,23,25] often adopt a graph neural network (GNN) [10] as the backbone network structure, where particles are treated as graph nodes, and interactions between neighboring particles are explicitly modeled as edges. By explicitly modeling particle interactions, existing methods effectively capture the semantics emerging from those interactions (*e.g.*, the influences of action-reaction forces), which are crucial for accurate simulation of complex system. However, such an explicit formulation requires the computation of edge features for all valid interactions. Since a particle-based system usually contains hundreds even thousands of densely distributed particles, the explicit formulation inevitably leads to significant computational overhead, limiting the efficiency and scalability of these GNN-based approaches.

In this paper, instead of relying on GNN, we propose to adopt Transformer as the backbone network structure for particle-based physics simulation. While particle interactions are represented as graph edges in GNN, in Transformer they are captured by a series of self-attention operations, in the form of dot-products between tokens of interacting particles. Consequently, in Transformer only particle tokens are required to simulate a system, leading to significantly reduced computational complexity when compared to GNN-based approaches.

The vanilla Transformer, however, is not directly applicable for effective simulation, since the rich semantics of particle interactions cannot be fully conveyed by the dot-products in self-attention operations. In this work, we address the problem via a novel modification to the self-attention operation that resembles the effect of edges in GNN but exempts from the need of explicitly modeling them. Specifically, each particle token is decomposed into three tokens, namely a state token, a receiver token, and a sender token. In particular, the state token keeps track of the particle state, the receiver token describes how the particle's state would change, and the sender token indicates how the particle will affect its interacting neighbors. By taking receiver tokens and sender tokens as both keys and values, while state tokens are queries, the stucture of edges in GNN can be equally represented by attention module in Transformer. To further trace the edge semantics in GNN, motivated by the process of normalizations for edges, both receiver and sender tokens are first decentralized in our attention module. Then we recover the standard deviations of edges from receiver and sender tokens, and apply the recovered scalar values as part of attention scores. Thus, the edge features can be effectively revived in Transformer. Moreover, to improve the generalization ability of the proposed method, we further propose to assign a learnable abstract particle for each type of material, and force particles of the same material to interact with their corresponding abstract particle, so that global semantics shared by all particles of the same material can be disentangled from local particle-level semantics.

Our method, dubbed as **T**ransformer with **I**mplicit **E**dges for Particle-based Physics Simulation (TIE), possesses several advantages over previous methods. First, thanks to the proposed edge-free design, TIE maintains the same level of computational complexity as in the vanilla Transformer, while combines the advantages of both Transformer and GNN. TIE not only inherits the self-attention operation from Transformer that can naturally attend to essential particles in the dynamically changing system, TIE is also capable of extracting rich semantics from particle interactions as GNN, without suffering from its significant computational overhead. Besides, the introduction of learnable abstract particles further boosts the performance of TIE in terms of generality and accuracy, by disentangling global semantics such as the intrinsic characteristics of different materials. For instance, after learning the dynamics of water, TIE can be directly applied to systems with varying numbers and configurations of particles, mimicking various effects including waterfall and flood.

To demonstrate the effectiveness of TIE, a comprehensive evaluation is conducted on four standard environments commonly used in the literature [12, 22], covering domains of different complexity and materials, where TIE achieves superior performance across all these environments compared to existing methods. Attractive properties of TIE, such as its strong generalization ability, are also studied, where we adjust the number and configuration of particles in each environments to create unseen systems for TIE to simulate without re-training. Compared to previous methods, TIE is able to obtain more realistic simulation results across most unseen systems. For example, after changing the shape from cube to bunny in *BoxBath*, the MSEs achieved by TIE is at least 30% lower than previous methods.

2   Related Work

Physics Simulation by Neural Networks. There are many different kind of representations for physics simulations. Grid-based methods [11, 24, 28] adopt convolutional architectures for learning high-dimensional physical system, while mesh-based simulations [3,9,14,18–20,30] typically simulate objects with continuous surfaces, such as clothes, rigid objects, surfaces of water and so on.

Many studies [2,12,17,22,23,25] simulate physics on particle-based systems, where all objects are represented by groups of particles. Specifically, Interaction Network (IN) [2] simulated interactions in object-level. Smooth Particle Networks (SPNets) [23] implemented fluid dynamics using position-based fluids [15]. Hierarchical Relation Network (HRN) [17] predicted physical dynamics based on hierarchical graph convolution. Dynamic Particle Interaction Networks (DPI-Net) [12] combined dynamic graphs, multi-step spatial propagation, and hierarchical structure to simulate particles. CConv [25] used spatial convolutions to simulate fluid particles. Graph Network-based Simulators (GNS) [22] computed dynamics via learned message-passing.

Previous work mostly adopted graph networks for simulations. They extracted potential semantics by explicitly modeling edges and storing their embeddings, and required each particle to interact with all its nearby particles without selective mechanism. In contrast, our TIE is able to capture semantics in edges in an edge-free manner, and selectively focus on necessary particle interactions through attention mechanism. Experiments show that TIE is more efficient, and surpasses existing GNN-based methods.

Transformer. Transformer [26] was designed for machine translation and achieved state-of-the-art performance in many natural language processing tasks [4,6,21]. Recently, Transformer starts to show great expandability and applicability in many other fields, such as computer vision [5,7,13,27,29], and graph representations [8,31,32]. To our knowledge, no attempt has been made to apply Transformer on physics simulation.

Our TIE inherits the multi-head attention mechanism, contributing to dynamically model the potential pattern in particle interactions. Though Graph Transformer [8], which we refer as GraphTrans for short, is also Transformer-based model on graphs, it still turns to explicitly modeling each valid edge to enhance the semantics of particle tokens, failing to make full use of attention mechanism to describe the relations among tokens in a more efficient manner. We adopt GraphTrans [8] in particle-based simulation and compare it with TIE in experiments. Quantitative and qualitative results show that TIE achieves more faithful rollouts in a more efficient way.

3   Methodology

3.1   Problem Formulation

For a particle-based system composed of N particles, we use $\mathcal{X}^t = \{x_i^t\}_{i=1}^{N}$ to denote the system state at time step t, where x_i^t denotes the state of i-th particle. Specifically, $x_i^t = [p_i^t, q_i^t, a_i]$, where $p_i^t, q_i^t \in \mathbb{R}^3$ refer to position and velocity, and $a_i \in \mathbb{R}^{d_a}$ represents fixed particle attributes such as its material type. The goal of a simulator is to learn a model $\phi(\cdot)$ from previous rollouts of a system to causally predict a rollout trajectory in a specific time period conditioned on the initial system state $\mathcal{X}^0$. The prediction runs in a recursive manner, where the simulator will predict the state $\hat{\mathcal{X}}^{t+1} = \phi(\mathcal{X}^t)$ at time step $t+1$ based on the state $\mathcal{X}^t = \{x_i^t\}$ at time step t. In practice, we will predict the velocities of particles $\hat{Q}^{t+1} = \{\hat{q}_i^{t+1}\}$, and obtain their positions via $\hat{p}_i^{t+1} = p_i^t + \Delta t \cdot \hat{q}_i^{t+1}$, where Δt is a domain-specific constant. In the following discussion, the time-step t is omitted to avoid verbose notations.

3.2   GNN-Based Approach

As particle-based physics systems can be naturally viewed as directed graphs, a straightforward solution for particle-based physics simulation is applying graph neural network (GNN) [2,12,17,22,23]. Specifically, we can regard particles in the system as graph nodes, and interactions between pairs of particles as directed edges. Given the states of particles $\mathcal{X} = \{x_i\}_{i=1}^N$ at some time-step, to predict the velocities of particles in the next time-step, GNN will at first obtain the initial node features and edge features following:

$$v_i^{(0)} = f_V^{\text{enc}}(x_i), \tag{1}$$

$$e_{ij}^{(0)} = f_E^{\text{enc}}(x_i, x_j), \tag{2}$$

where $v_i, e_{ij} \in \mathbb{R}^{d_h}$ are d_h dimensional vectors, and $f_V^{\text{enc}}(\cdot), f_E^{\text{enc}}(\cdot)$ are respectively the node and edge encoders. Subsequently, GNN will conduct L rounds of message-passing, and obtain the velocities of particles as:

$$e_{ij}^{(l+1)} = f_E^{\text{prop}}(v_i^{(l)}, v_j^{(l)}, e_{ij}^{(l)}), \tag{3}$$

$$v_i^{(l+1)} = f_V^{\text{prop}}(v_i^{(l)}, \sum_{j \in \mathcal{N}_i} e_{ij}^{(l+1)}), \tag{4}$$

$$\hat{q}_i = f_V^{\text{dec}}(v_i^{(L)}), \tag{5}$$

where $\mathcal{N}_i$ indicates the set of neighbors of i-th particle, and $f_E^{\text{prop}}(\cdot), f_V^{\text{prop}}(\cdot)$ and $f_V^{\text{dec}}(\cdot)$ are respectively the node propagation module, the edge propagation module as well as the node decoder. In practice, $f_V^{\text{enc}}(\cdot), f_E^{\text{enc}}(\cdot), f_E^{\text{prop}}(\cdot), f_V^{\text{prop}}(\cdot)$ and $f_V^{\text{dec}}(\cdot)$ are often implemented as multi-layer perceptrons (MLPs). Moreover, a window function g is commonly used to filter out interactions between distant particles and reduce computational complexity:

$$g(i, j) = \mathbf{1}\left(\|p_i - p_j\|_2 < R\right), \tag{6}$$

where $\mathbf{1}(\cdot)$ is the indicator function and R is a pre-defined threshould.

3.3   From GNN to Transformer

To accurately simulate the changes of a system over time, it is crucial to exploit the rich semantics conveyed by the interactions among particles, such as the energy transition of a system when constrained by material characteristics and

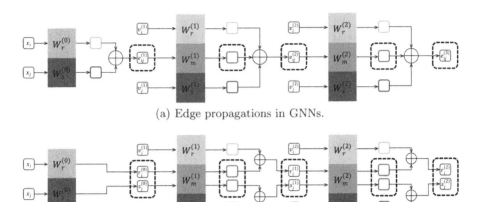

(a) Edge propagations in GNNs.

(b) Implicit edge propagations in TIE.

Fig. 2. We demonstrate the propagations for edges in GNNs and TIE, where explicit or implicit edges are shown in red boxes. The process of MLP in each layer is splitted into blocks of square followed by summations. Different blocks of MLP are shown by square areas with different colors. The key idea of TIE is that TIE replaces the explicit edges $e_{ij}^{(l+1)}$ by receiver tokens $r_i^{(l)}$ and sender tokens $s_j^{(l)}$. When only considering the trainable weights of each MLP, the summation of receiver and sender tokens within a red box equals to the edge within the same depth of red box, as shown in Eq. 12. From the indexes we can know, the behaviors of node i and j are independent in Figure (b), thus TIE does not include explicit edges. (Color figure online)

physical laws. While GNN achieves this by explicitly modeling particle interactions as graph edges, such a treatment also leads to substantial computational overhead. Since a particle-based system contains hundreds even thousands of particles, and particles of a system are densely clustered together, this issue significantly limits the efficiency of GNN-based approaches.

Inspired by recent successes of Transformer [26] that applies computational efficient self-attention operations to model the communication among different tokens, in this paper we propose a Transformer-based method, which we refer to as Transformer with Implicit Edges, TIE, for particle-based physics simulation. We first describe how to apply a vanilla Transformer in this task. Specifically, we assign a token to each particle of the system, and therefore particle interactions are naturally achieved by L blocks of multi-head self-attention modules. While the token features are initialized according to Eq. 1, they will be updated in the l-th block as:

$$\omega_{ij} = (W_Q^{(l)} \boldsymbol{v}_i^{(l)})^\top \cdot (W_K^{(l)} \boldsymbol{v}_j^{(l)}), \tag{7}$$

$$\boldsymbol{v}_i^{(l+1)} = \sum_j \frac{\exp(\omega_{ij}/\sqrt{d})}{\sum_k \exp(\omega_{ik}/\sqrt{d})} \cdot (W_V^{(l)} \boldsymbol{v}_j^{(l)}), \tag{8}$$

where d is the dimension of features, and $W_Q^{(l)}, W_K^{(l)}, W_V^{(l)}$ are weight matrices for queries, keys, and values. Following the standard practice, a mask is generated according to Eq. 6 to mask out distant particles when computing the attention. And finally, the prediction of velocities follows Eq. 5.

Although the vanilla Transformer provides a flexible approach for particle-based simulation, directly applying it leads to inferior simulation results as shown in our experiments. In particular, the vanilla Transformer uses attention weights that are scalars obtained via dot-product, to represent particle interactions, which are insufficient to reflect the rich semantics of particle interactions. To combine the merits of GNN and Transformer, TIE modify the self-attention operation in the vanilla Transformer to *implicitly* include edge features as in GNN in an edge-free manner. In Fig. 2 we include the comparison between our proposed implicit edges and the explicit edges in GNN. Specifically, since f_E^{prop} in Eq. 3 and f_E^{enc} in Eq. 2 are both implemented as an MLP in practice, by expanding Eq. 3 recursively and grouping terms respectively for i-th and j-th particle we can obtain:

$$r_i^{(0)} = W_r^{(0)} x_i, \qquad s_j^{(0)} = W_s^{(0)} x_j, \tag{9}$$

$$r_i^{(l)} = W_r^{(l)} v_i^{(l)} + W_m^{(l)} r_i^{(l-1)}, \tag{10}$$

$$s_j^{(l)} = W_s^{(l)} v_j^{(l)} + W_m^{(l)} s_j^{(l-1)}, \tag{11}$$

$$e_{ij}^{(l+1)} = r_i^{(l)} + s_j^{(l)}, \tag{12}$$

where the effect of an explicit edge can be effectively achieved by two additional tokens, which we refer to as the receiver token r_i and the sender token s_j. The detained expansion of Eq. 3 can be found in the supplemental material. Following the above expansion, TIE thus assigns three tokens to each particle of the system, namely a receiver token r_i, a sender token s_i, and a state token v_i. The state token is similar to the particle token in the vanilla Transformer, and its update formula combines the node update formula in GNN and the self-attention formula in Transformer:

$$\omega'_{ij} = (W_Q^{(l)} v_i^{(l)})^\top r_i^{(l)} + (W_Q^{(l)} v_i^{(l)})^\top s_j^{(l)}, \tag{13}$$

$$v_i^{(l+1)} = r_i^{(l)} + \sum_j \frac{\exp(\omega'_{ij}/\sqrt{d})}{\sum_k \exp(\omega'_{ik}/\sqrt{d})} \cdot s_j^{(l)}. \tag{14}$$

We refer to Eq. 14 as an implicit way to incorporate the rich semantics of particle interactions, since TIE approximates graph edges in GNN with two additional tokens per particle, and more importantly these two tokens can be updated, along with the original token, separately for each particle, avoiding the significant computational overhead. To interpret the modified self-attention in TIE, from the perspective of graph edges, we decompose them into the receiver tokens and the sender tokens, maintaining two extra paths in the Transformer's self-attention module. As for the perspective of self-attention, the receiver tokens and the sender tokens respectively replace the original keys and values.

In practice, since GNN-based methods usually incorporate LayerNorm [1] in their network architectures that computes the mean and std of edge features to improve their performance and training speed, we can further modify the self-attention in Eq. 13 and Eq. 14 to include the effect of normalization as well:

$$\left(\sigma_{ij}^{(l)}\right)^2 = \frac{1}{d}(\boldsymbol{r}_i^{(l)})^\top \boldsymbol{r}_i^{(l)} + \frac{1}{d}(\boldsymbol{s}_j^{(l)})^\top \boldsymbol{s}_j^{(l)} + \frac{2}{d}(\boldsymbol{r}_i^{(l)})^\top \boldsymbol{s}_j^{(l)} - (\mu_{r_i}^{(l)} + \mu_{s_j}^{(l)})^2, \quad (15)$$

$$\omega_{ij}'' = \frac{(W_Q^{(l)}\boldsymbol{v}_i^{(l)})^\top (\boldsymbol{r}_i^{(l)} - \mu_{r_i}^{(l)}) + (W_Q^{(l)}\boldsymbol{v}_i^{(l)})^\top (\boldsymbol{s}_j^{(l)} - \mu_{s_j}^{(l)})}{\sigma_{ij}^{(l)}}, \quad (16)$$

$$\boldsymbol{v}_i^{(l+1)} = \sum_j \frac{\exp(\omega_{ij}''/\sqrt{d})}{\sum_k \exp(\omega_{ik}''/\sqrt{d})} \cdot \frac{(\boldsymbol{r}_i^{(l)} - \mu_{r_i}^{(l)}) + (\boldsymbol{s}_j^{(l)} - \mu_{s_j}^{(l)})}{\sigma_{ij}^{(l)}}, \quad (17)$$

where $\mu_{r_i}^{(l)}$ and $\mu_{s_j}^{(l)}$ are respectively the mean of receiver tokens and sender tokens after l-th block. Detailed deduction can be found in the supplemental material.

3.4   Abstract Particles

To further improve the generalization ability of TIE and disentangle global material-specific semantics from local particle-wise semantics, we further equip TIE with material-specific abstract particles.

For N_a types of materials, TIE respectively adopts N_a abstract particles $A = \{\boldsymbol{a}_k\}_{k=1}^{N_a}$, each of which is a virtual particle with a learnable state token. Ideally, the abstract particle $\boldsymbol{a}_k$ should capture the material-specific semantics of k-th material. They act as additional particles in the system, and their update formulas are the same as normal particles. Unlike normal particles that only interact with neighboring particles, each abstract particle is forced to interact with all particles belonging to its corresponding material. Therefore with N_a abstract particles TIE will have $N + N_a$ particles in total: $\{\boldsymbol{a}_1, \cdots, \boldsymbol{a}_{N_a}, \boldsymbol{x}_1, \cdots, \boldsymbol{x}_N\}$. Once TIE is trained, abstract particles can be reused when generalizing TIE to unseen domains that have same materials but vary in particle amuont and configuration.

3.5   Traning Objective and Evaluation Metric

To train TIE with existing rollouts of a domain, the standard mean square error (MSE) loss is applied to the output of TIE:

$$\text{MSE}(\hat{Q}, Q) = \frac{1}{N} \sum_i \|\hat{\boldsymbol{q}}_i - \boldsymbol{q}_i\|_2^2, \quad (18)$$

where $\hat{Q} = \{\hat{\boldsymbol{q}}_i\}_{i=1}^N$ and $Q = \{\boldsymbol{q}_i\}_{i=1}^N$ are respectively the estimation and the ground truth, and $\|\cdot\|_2$ is the L2 norm.

Table 1. We report M^3SEs (1e−2) results on four base domains, while keep the models' number of parameters similar to each other. TIE achieves superior performance on all domains without suffering from its significant computational overhead. When adding trainable abstract particles, TIE, marked by +, further improves performance on *RiceGrip* and *BoxBath*, which involve complex deformations and multi-material interactions respectively.

Methods	FluidFall		FluidShake		RiceGrip		BoxBath	
	M^3 SE	# Para	M^3 SE	# Para	M^3 SE	# Para	M^3 SE	# Para
DPI-Net [12]	0.08 ± 0.05	0.61M	1.38 ± 0.45	0.62M	0.13 ± 0.09	1.98M	1.33 ± 0.29	1.98M
CConv [25]	0.08 ± 0.02	0.84M	1.41 ± 0.46	0.84M	N/A	N/A	N/A	N/A
GNS [22]	0.09 ± 0.02	0.70M	1.66 ± 0.37	0.70M	0.40 ± 0.16	0.71M	1.56 ± 0.23	0.70M
GraphTrans [8]	0.04 ± 0.01	0.77M	1.36 ± 0.37	0.77M	0.12 ± 0.11	0.78M	1.27 ± 0.25	0.77M
TIE (Ours)	0.04 ± 0.01	0.77M	$\mathbf{1.22 \pm 0.37}$	0.77M	0.13 ± 0.12	0.78M	1.35 ± 0.35	0.77M
TIE+ (Ours)	$\mathbf{0.04 \pm 0.00}$	0.77M	1.30 ± 0.41	0.77M	$\mathbf{0.08 \pm 0.08}$	0.78M	$\mathbf{0.92 \pm 0.16}$	0.77M

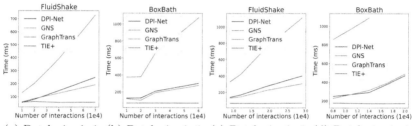

(a) Batch size is 1. (b) Batch size is 1. (c) Batch size is 4. (d) Batch size is 4.

Fig. 3. We report averaged models' training time for each iteration. The batch size in (a) and (b) is set to 1, while the batch size in (c) and (d) is set to 4. As the number of interactions increases, the time cost for TIE+ remains stable, while other models spend more time to train due to the computational overhead introduced by extra interactions.

In terms of evaluation metric, since a system usually contains multiple types of materials with imbalanced numbers of particles, to better reflect the estimation accuracy, we apply the Mean of Material-wise MSE (M^3SE) for evaluation:

$$M^3SE(\hat{Q}, Q) = \frac{1}{K} \sum_k \frac{1}{N_k} \sum_i \|\hat{q}_{i,k} - q_{i,k}\|_2^2, \qquad (19)$$

where K is the number of material types, N_k is the number of particles belonging to the k-th material. M^3SE is equivalent to the standard MSE when $K = 1$.

4 Experiments

We adopt four domains commonly used in the literature [12,22,25] for evaluation. *FluidFall* is a basic simulation for two droplets of water with 189 particle in total; *FluidShake* is more complex and simulate the water in a randomly moving box, containing 450 to 627 fluid particles; *BoxBath* simulates the water washing a rigid cube in fixed box with 960 fluid particles and 64 rigid particles; *Rice-Grip* simulates the interactions between deformable rice and two rigid grippers, including 570 to 980 particles. Samples are displayed in Fig. 1. To explore the effectiveness of our model, we compare TIE with four representative approaches: DPI-Net [12], CConv [25], GNS [22], and GraphTrans [8].

Implementation Details. TIE contains $L = 4$ blocks. For multi-head self-attention version, The receiver tokens and sender tokens are regarded as the projected keys and values for each head. After projecting the concatenated state tokens from all heads, a two-layer MLPs is followed with dimensions 256 and 128. The concatenated receiver tokens and sender tokens are directly projected by one layer MLP with dimensions 128. The rest hidden dimensions are 128 for default. We train four models independently on four domains, with 5 epochs on *FluidShake* and *BoxBath*, 13 epochs on *FluidFall*, and 20 epochs on *RiceGrip*. On *BoxBath*, all models adopt the same strategy to keep the shape of the rigid object following [12]. We adopt MSE on velocities as training loss for all models. The neighborhood radius R in Eq. 6 is set to 0.08. We adopt Adam optimizer with an initial learning rate of 0.0008, which has a decreasing factor of 0.8 when the validation loss stops to decrease after 3 epochs. The batch size is set to 16 on all domains. All models are trained and tested on V100 for all experiments, with no augmentation involved.

4.1 Basic Domains

Quantitative results are provided in Table 1, while qualitative results are shown in Fig. 4. TIE achieves superior performances on all domains. The effectiveness of abstract particles are more obvious for *RiceGrip* and *BoxBath*, which involve complex materials or multi-material interactions.

Performance Comparison. We compare TIE with four representative approaches: DPI-Net [12], CConv [25], GNS [22], and GraphTrans [8]. Since DPI-Net and GNS adopt message-passing graph networks for particle-based simulations, we set the number of propagation steps as four for both models, except that DPI-Net adopts a total number of six propagation steps on *BoxBath* and *RiceGrip*, where hierarchical structures are adopted. For CConv, which designs convolutional layers carefully tailored to modeling fluid dynamics, such as an SPH-like local kernel [16], we only report the results on fluid-based domains. As shown in Table 1, TIE achieves superior performances on most domains, while TIE+, which has abstract particles, further improves the performances especially on *RiceGrip* and *BoxBath*, suggesting the effectiveness of abstract particles in modeling complex deformations and multi-materials interactions. For qualitative results in Fig. 4, our model can predict more faithful rollouts on all domains.

Efficiency Comparison. The training time for models with varying batch size is shown in Fig. 3. For simplicity, the number of particles is fixed and only number of interactions varies in Fig. 3. Since TIE uses implicit edges to model particle interactions and significantly reduces computational overhead, TIE has the

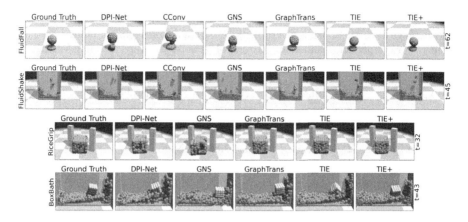

Fig. 4. Qualitative results on base domains. TIE is able to achieve more faithful results on all domains. On *FluidFall*, TIE is able to better maintain the shape before the droplets merge and handle redundant neighbors, which are introduced from two different droplets when they move closer to each other. The relative positions of the droplets are also closer the the ground truth. On *FluidShake*, TIE can predict two faithful blocks of water on the top right. On *RiceGrip*, when focusing on the areas compressed by the grippers, the rice restores its position more faithfully in TIE. On *BoxBath*, the rigid cube predicted by TIE is pushed far away enough from the right wall, and the positions for the cube by TIE+ is much closer to the ground truth. The fluid particles predicted by our models are also more faithful.

fastest training speed against general GNN-based simulators (CConv [25] is a specialized simulator for systems containing only fluid) as shown in Fig. 3 (a) and (b). When it comes to batch size larger than 1, GNN-based methods need pad edges for each batch, leading to extra computational cost. On the other hand, TIE only need the corresponding attention masks to denote the connectivities without further paddings, which is faster to train on large batch size. We does not report the speed of GraphTrans with more than 1.4×10^4 interactions due to the limit of memory. In terms of testing speed, it is hard to compare different methods directly since different simulation results will lead to different amount of valid particle interactions.

4.2 Generalizations

As shown in Table 2, we generate more complex domains to challenge the robustness of our full model TIE+. Specifically, we add more particles for *FluidShake* and *RiceGrip*, which we refer to as *L-FluidShake* and *L-RiceGrip* respectively. The *L-FluidShake* includes 720 to 1368 particles, while *L-RiceGrip* contains 1062 to 1642 particles. On *BoxBath*, we change the size and shape of rigid object. Specifically, we add more fluid particles in *Lfluid-BoxBath* to 1280 fluid particles, while we enlarge the rigid cube in *L-BoxBath* to 125 particles. We also change the shape of the rigid object into ball and bunny, which we refer to *Ball-Box* and *BunnyBath* respectively. Details of generalized environments settings and results can be found in supplementary materials.

Table 2. M^{3}SEs on generalizations. The lists of numbers in *FluidShake* and *RiceGrip* are the range of particles, while the tuples in *BoxBath* denotes number of fluid particles, number of rigid particles, and shape of rigid objects respectively. Training settings are marked by *. TIE + achieves the best results on most cases.

Methods	FluidShake [450,627]*		RiceGrip [570,980]*	
	[720,1013]	[1025,1368]	[1062,1347]	[1349,1642]
DPI-Net [12]	2.13 ± 0.55	2.78 ± 0.84	0.23 ± 0.13	0.38 ± 0.67
CConv [25]	2.01 ± 0.55	**2.43 ± 0.81**	N/A	N/A
GNS [22]	2.61 ± 0.44	3.41 ± 0.59	0.47 ± 0.20	0.51 ± 0.28
GraphTrans [8]	2.68 ± 0.52	3.97 ± 0.70	0.20 ± 0.13	0.22 ± 0.18
TIE+ (Ours)	**1.92 ± 0.47**	2.46 ± 0.65	**0.17 ± 0.11**	**0.19 ± 0.15**
Methods	**BoxBath** (960,64,cube)*			
	(1280,64,cube)	(960,125,cube)	(960,136,ball)	(960,41,bunny)
DPI-Net [12]	1.70 ± 0.22	3.22 ± 0.88	2.86 ± 0.99	2.04 ± 0.79
GNS [22]	2.97 ± 0.48	2.97 ± 0.71	3.50 ± 0.67	2.17 ± 0.37
GraphTrans [8]	1.88 ± 0.25	1.50 ± 0.30	1.71 ± 0.34	2.22 ± 0.61
TIE+ (Ours)	**1.57 ± 0.18**	**1.49 ± 0.19**	**1.45 ± 0.27**	**1.39 ± 0.48**

Quantitative results are summarized in Table 2, while qualitative results are depicted in Fig. 5. As shown in Table 2, TIE+ achieves lower M^{3}SEs on most domains, while having more faithful rollouts in Fig. 5. On *L-FluidShake*, TIE+ maintains the block of fluid in the air and predicts faithful wave on the surface. On *L-RiceGrip*, while DPI-Net and GNS have difficulties in maintaining the shape, the rice predicted by GraphTrans is compressed more densely only in the center areas where the grips have reached, the left side and right side of the rice does not deform properly compared with the ground truth. In contrast, TIE+ is able to maintains the shape of the large rice and faithfully deform the whole rice after compressed. On generalized *BoxBath*, TIE+ is able to predict faithful rollout when the fluid particles flood the rigid objects into the air or when the wave of the fluid particles starts to push the rigid object after the collision. Even when the rigid object changes to bunny with more complex surfaces, TIE+ generates more accurate predictions for both fluid particles and rigid particles.

4.3   Ablation Studies

We comprehensively analyze our TIE and explore the effectiveness of our model in the following aspects: (a) with and without implicit edges; (b) with and without normalization effects in attention; (c) with and without abstract particles; and (d) the sensitiveness to R. The experiments for (a), (b), and (d) are conducted on *FluidShake* and *L-FluidShake*, while experiment (c) is conducted on *BoxBath*. The quantitative results are in Table 3 and Table 4.

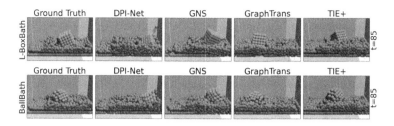

Fig. 5. Qualitative results on generalized domains. Here we only show part of results on generalized *BoxBath*, where we mainly change the shape and size of the rigid object. TIE+ can predict more faithful movements of the rigid object, while the fluid particles are also vivid. More details can be found in supplementary materials.

Table 3. Ablation studies. We comprehensively explore the effectiveness of TIE, including the effectiveness of implicitly modeling of edges, normalization effects in attention, and abstract particles. We report $M^3SEs(1e-2)$ on *FluidShake* and *L-FluidShake*, which are complex domains involving outer forces.

Configurations	A(Transformer)	B	C(TIE)	D(TIE+)
Implicit edges		✓	✓	✓
Normalization			✓	✓
Abstract particles				✓
FluidShake	2.75 ± 0.86	1.52 ± 0.39	1.22 ± 0.37	1.30 ± 0.41
L-FluidShake	8.18 ± 3.15	3.17 ± 0.94	2.40 ± 0.74	2.16 ± 0.62

Effectiveness of Implicit Edges. We apply vanilla Transformer encoders by configuration A, while TIE in configuration B does not adopt the interaction attention, making sure the only difference is the edge-free structure. The hidden dimension and number of blocks are the same, while TIE is a little larger because of the extra projections for receiver and sender tokens. As shown in Table 3, the original Transformer achieves worse performances, suggesting the scalar attention scores alone are insufficient to capture rich semantics of interactions among particles. In contrast, implicit way of modeling edges enables TIE to take advantages of GNN methods and recover more semantics of particle interactions.

Effectiveness of Normalization Effects in Attention. We follow configuration C to build TIE, which includes Eq. 17. Comparing configuration B and C in Table 3, we find that the normalization effects brings benefits to TIE on both base and generalized domains. Such structure further enables TIE to trace the rice semantics from edges, leading to more stable and robust performances.

Effectiveness of Abstract Particles. As shown in Table 4, we replace the abstract particles with dummy particles, which are zero initialized vectors with fixed values but have the same connectivities as abstract particles. Thus, the dummy particles could not capture the semantics of materials during training. TIE with dummy particles slightly improve the performances on base domains,

Table 4. Ablation studies on abstract particles and sensitiveness to radius R. To explore the material-aware semantics extracted by abstract particles, we conduct experiments on *BoxBath* and the generalized domains *BunnyBath*, where the rigid cube is replaced by bunny. We replace abstract particles with dummy particles, which are zero constant vectors and have same connectivities as abstract particles. TIE marked by "dummy" adopts dummy particles. The sensitiveness is on the right part. We report $M^3SEs(1e-2)$ on *FluidShake*. Our default setting on all domains is marked by $*$.

Methods	BoxBath		Methods	FluidShake		
	(960,64,cube)*	(960,41,bunny)		$R = 0.07$	$R^* = 0.08$	$R = 0.09$
TIE	1.35 ± 0.35	1.50 ± 0.45	DPI-Net	2.60 ± 0.56	1.38 ± 0.45	1.66 ± 0.48
TIE dummy	1.21 ± 0.28	1.96 ± 0.71	GraphTrans	1.97 ± 0.48	1.36 ± 0.37	1.36 ± 0.38
TIE+	0.92 ± 0.16	1.39 ± 0.48	TIE	1.60 ± 0.37	1.22 ± 0.37	1.31 ± 0.40

suggesting that the extra connectivities introduced by abstract particles benefit little on TIE. TIE+ achieves more stable and robust performances, suggesting that the abstract particles are able to effectively disentangle the domain-specific semantics, i.e., the outer forces introduced by walls, and materials-specific semantics, i.e., the pattern of fluid particle dynamics.

Sensitiveness to R. Quantitative results are reported on *FluidShake*. As shown in Table 4, when R is smaller, models tend to have a drop in accuracies due to the insufficient particle interactions. When R is greater, the drop of accuracies for DPI-Net is caused by redundant interactions due to the high flexibility of fluid moving patterns. In all cases, TIE achieves superior performances more efficiently, suggesting the effectiveness and robustness of our model.

5   Conclusion

In this paper, we propose Transformer with Implicit Edges (TIE), which aims to trace edge semantics in an edge-free manner and introduces abstract particles to simulate domains of different complexity and materials, Our experimental results show the effectiveness and efficiency of our edge-free structure. The abstract particles enable TIE to capture material-specific semantics, achieving robust performances on complex generalization domains. Finally, TIE makes a successful attempt to hybrid GNN and Transformer into physics simulation and achieve superior performances over existing methods, showing the potential abilities of implicitly modeling edges in physics simulations.

Acknowledgement. This study is supported under the RIE2020 Industry Alignment Fund Industry Collaboration Projects (IAF-ICP) Funding Initiative, as well as cash and in-kind contribution from the industry partner(s). It is also supported by Singapore MOE AcRF Tier 2 (MOE-T2EP20221-0011) and Shanghai AI Laboratory.

References

1. Ba, L.J., Kiros, J.R., Hinton, G.E.: Layer normalization. CoRR (2016)
2. Battaglia, P.W., Pascanu, R., Lai, M., Rezende, D.J., Kavukcuoglu, K.: Interaction networks for learning about objects, relations and physics. In: Advances in Neural Information Processing Systems 29: Annual Conference on Neural Information Processing Systems 2016, 5–10 December 2016, Barcelona, Spain (2016)
3. Bronstein, M.M., Bruna, J., LeCun, Y., Szlam, A., Vandergheynst, P.: Geometric deep learning: going beyond Euclidean data. IEEE Sign. Process. Mag. **34**, 18–42 (2017)
4. Brown, T.B., et al.: Language models are few-shot learners. In: Advances in Neural Information Processing Systems 33: Annual Conference on Neural Information Processing Systems 2020, NeurIPS 2020, 6–12 December 2020, virtual (2020)
5. Carion, N., Massa, F., Synnaeve, G., Usunier, N., Kirillov, A., Zagoruyko, S.: End-to-end object detection with transformers. In: Vedaldi, A., Bischof, H., Brox, T., Frahm, J.-M. (eds.) ECCV 2020. LNCS, vol. 12346, pp. 213–229. Springer, Cham (2020). https://doi.org/10.1007/978-3-030-58452-8_13
6. Devlin, J., Chang, M., Lee, K., Toutanova, K.: BERT: pre-training of deep bidirectional transformers for language understanding. In: Proceedings of the 2019 Conference of the North American Chapter of the Association for Computational Linguistics: Human Language Technologies, NAACL-HLT 2019, Minneapolis, MN, USA, 2–7 June 2019, Volume 1 (Long and Short Papers) (2019)
7. Dosovitskiy, A., et al.: An image is worth 16×16 words: transformers for image recognition at scale. In: 9th International Conference on Learning Representations, ICLR 2021, Virtual Event, Austria, 3–7 May 2021 (2021)
8. Dwivedi, V.P., Bresson, X.: A generalization of transformer networks to graphs. CoRR (2020)
9. Hanocka, R., Hertz, A., Fish, N., Giryes, R., Fleishman, S., Cohen-Or, D.: MeshCNN: a network with an edge. ACM Trans. Graph. **38**, 1–12 (2019)
10. Kipf, T.N., Welling, M.: Semi-supervised classification with graph convolutional networks. CoRR (2016)
11. Lee, S., You, D.: Data-driven prediction of unsteady flow over a circular cylinder using deep learning. J. Fluid Mech. **879**, 217–254 (2019)
12. Li, Y., Wu, J., Tedrake, R., Tenenbaum, J.B., Torralba, A.: Learning particle dynamics for manipulating rigid bodies, deformable objects, and fluids. In: 7th International Conference on Learning Representations, ICLR 2019, New Orleans, LA, USA, 6–9 May 2019 (2019)
13. Liu, Z., et al.: Swin Transformer: Hierarchical vision transformer using shifted windows. CoRR (2021)
14. Luo, R., et al.: NNWarp: neural network-based nonlinear deformation. IEEE Trans. Vis. Comput. Graph. **26**, 1745–1759 (2020)
15. Macklin, M., Müller, M.: Position based fluids. ACM Trans. Graph. **34**, 1–12 (2013)
16. Monaghan, J.J.: Smoothed particle hydrodynamics. Annu. Rev. Astronom. Astrophys. **30**, 543–574 (1992)
17. Mrowca, D., et al.: Flexible neural representation for physics prediction. In: Advances in Neural Information Processing Systems 31: Annual Conference on Neural Information Processing Systems 2018, NeurIPS 2018, 3–8 December 2018, Montréal, Canada (2018)
18. Nash, C., Ganin, Y., Eslami, S.M.A., Battaglia, P.W.: PolyGen: an autoregressive generative model of 3D meshes. In: Proceedings of the 37th International Conference on Machine Learning, ICML 2020, 13–18 July 2020, Virtual Event (2020)

19. Pfaff, T., Fortunato, M., Sanchez-Gonzalez, A., Battaglia, P.W.: Learning mesh-based simulation with graph networks. In: 9th International Conference on Learning Representations, ICLR 2021, Virtual Event, Austria, 3–7 May 2021 (2021)
20. Qiao, Y., Liang, J., Koltun, V., Lin, M.C.: Scalable differentiable physics for learning and control. In: Proceedings of the 37th International Conference on Machine Learning, ICML 2020, 13–18 July 2020, Virtual Event (2020)
21. Radford, A., Wu, J., Child, R., Luan, D., Amodei, D., Sutskever, I., et al.: Language models are unsupervised multitask learners. OpenAI blog (2019)
22. Sanchez-Gonzalez, A., Godwin, J., Pfaff, T., Ying, R., Leskovec, J., Battaglia, P.W.: Learning to simulate complex physics with graph networks. In: Proceedings of the 37th International Conference on Machine Learning, ICML 2020, 13–18 July 2020, Virtual Event (2020)
23. Schenck, C., Fox, D.: SPNets: differentiable fluid dynamics for deep neural networks. In: 2nd Annual Conference on Robot Learning, CoRL 2018, Zürich, Switzerland, 29–31 October 2018, Proceedings (2018)
24. Thuerey, N., Weißenow, K., Prantl, L., Hu, X.: Deep learning methods for Reynolds-averaged Navier-stokes simulations of airfoil flows. AIAA J. **58**, 25–36 (2020)
25. Ummenhofer, B., Prantl, L., Thuerey, N., Koltun, V.: Lagrangian fluid simulation with continuous convolutions. In: 8th International Conference on Learning Representations, ICLR 2020, Addis Ababa, Ethiopia, 26–30 April 2020 (2020)
26. Vaswani, A., et al.: Attention is all you need. In: Advances in Neural Information Processing Systems 30: Annual Conference on Neural Information Processing Systems 2017, 4–9 December 2017, Long Beach, CA, USA (2017)
27. Wang, H., Zhu, Y., Adam, H., Yuille, A.L., Chen, L.: MaX-DeepLab: end-to-end panoptic segmentation with mask transformers. In: IEEE Conference on Computer Vision and Pattern Recognition, CVPR 2021, virtual, 19–25 June 2021 (2021)
28. Wang, R., Kashinath, K., Mustafa, M., Albert, A., Yu, R.: Towards physics-informed deep learning for turbulent flow prediction. In: KDD 2020: The 26th ACM SIGKDD Conference on Knowledge Discovery and Data Mining, Virtual Event, CA, USA, 23–27 August 2020 (2020)
29. Wang, X., Girshick, R.B., Gupta, A., He, K.: Non-local neural networks. In: 2018 IEEE Conference on Computer Vision and Pattern Recognition, CVPR 2018, Salt Lake City, UT, USA, 18–22 June 2018 (2018)
30. Weng, Z., Paus, F., Varava, A., Yin, H., Asfour, T., Kragic, D.: Graph-based task-specific prediction models for interactions between deformable and rigid objects. CoRR (2021)
31. Zhang, J., Zhang, H., Xia, C., Sun, L.: Graph-Bert: only attention is needed for learning graph representations. CoRR (2020)
32. Zhou, D., Zheng, L., Han, J., He, J.: A data-driven graph generative model for temporal interaction networks. In: KDD 2020: The 26th ACM SIGKDD Conference on Knowledge Discovery and Data Mining, Virtual Event, CA, USA, 23–27 August 2020 (2020)

Rethinking Video Rain Streak Removal: A New Synthesis Model and a Deraining Network with Video Rain Prior

Shuai Wang[1], Lei Zhu[2,3]([✉]), Huazhu Fu[4], Jing Qin[5], Carola-Bibiane Schönlieb[6], Wei Feng[7], and Song Wang[8]

[1] Tianjin University, Tianjin, China
[2] The Hong Kong University of Science and Technology (Guangzhou), Guangzhou, China
leizhu@ust.hk
[3] The Hong Kong University of Science and Technology, Clear Water Bay, Hong Kong
[4] IHPC, ASTAR, Singapore, Singapore
[5] The Hong Kong Polytechnic University, Hung Hom, Hong Kong
[6] University of Cambridge, Cambridge, UK
[7] School of Computer Science and Technology, Tianjin University, Tianjin, China
[8] University of South Carolina, Columbia, USA

Abstract. Existing video synthetic models and deraining methods are mostly built on a simplified video rain model assuming that rain streak layers of different video frames are uncorrelated, thereby producing degraded performance on real-world rainy videos. To address this problem, we devise a new video rain sy nthesis model with the concept of rain streak motions to enforce a consistency of rain layers between video frames, thereby generating more realistic rainy video data for network training, and then develop a recurrent disentangled deraining network (RDD-Net) based on our video rain model for boosting video deraining. More specifically, taking adjacent frames of a key frame as the input, our RDD-Net recurrently aggregates each adjacent frame and the key frame by a fusion module, and then devise a disentangle model to decouple the fused features by predicting not only a clean background layer and a rain layer, but also a rain streak motion layer. After that, we develop three attentive recovery modules to combine the decoupled features from different adjacent frames for predicting the final derained result of the key frame. Experiments on three widely-used benchmark datasets and a collected dataset, as well as real-world rainy videos show that our RDD-Net quantitatively and qualitatively outperforms state-of-the-art deraining methods. Our code, our dataset, and our results on four datasets are released at https://github.com/wangshauitj/RDD-Net.

Keywords: Video deraining · New video deraining model · Video rain direction prior · Disentangled feature learning

© The Author(s), under exclusive license to Springer Nature Switzerland AG 2022
S. Avidan et al. (Eds.): ECCV 2022, LNCS 13679, pp. 565–582, 2022.
https://doi.org/10.1007/978-3-031-19800-7_33

1   Introduction

As the most common type of rain degradation, rain streaks often cause the visibility degradation in captured rainy images or videos, and thus lead to failure of outdoor computer vision systems, which generally take clean video frames as input by default. Rain streaks also lower the subsequent video analysis since they partially occlude a background scene, change image appearance, make the scene blurred, etc. A number of methods have been developed to remove rain streaks in past decades. They are typically classified by their input type. Single-image methods [7,20,21,26,37,41,44] remove rain streaks given only a single image by examining image priors of the underlying background scene and rain streaks, while video-based methods [22,27,36,38] leverage rich temporal information across video frames to locate and remove rain streaks.

Traditionally, most video deraining methods attempt to generalize the single-image rain models to videos [22,23,38], and, in principle, the formulation is:

$$I_t = B_t + S_t, \text{ where } t \in [1, T], \tag{1}$$

where I_t is the t-th frame of the video with rain streaks, B_t is the corresponding rain-free background layer, while S_t is the rain streak layer. T is the total number of frames. As shown in Fig. 1(a), these methods often assume that rain streaks

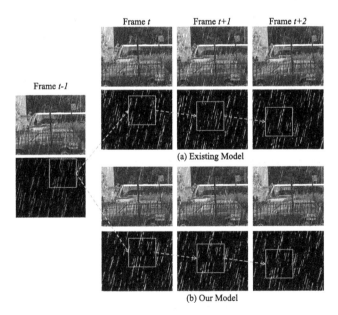

Fig. 1. Synthesized rain streak images and rainy video frames using (a) the existing video rain synthesis model [36] and (b) our proposed video rain synthesis model with rain streak motion. Apparently, the rain streaks at the yellow rectangle move along the dominated rain direction of the video in our method, while these synthesized rain streaks in existing models are not correlated.

at adjacent video frames are independent and identically distributed random samples. Recently, several researchers further modified this model by considering other rain degradation factors (*e.g.*, fog) [36], or rain occlusions [22,23]. However, *without considering the temporal coherence among frames, in these models, the rain streak layers of neighboring frames are discontinuous and messy.* To the end, the rainy videos synthesized based on these models are not realistic as real rainy videos, such that the video deraining models trained on these synthesized videos cannot achieve satisfactory results on real rainy videos.

In this paper, we rethink the video rain streak removal problem, based on a video rain observation (prior) that rain streaks usually fall within a limited region along the directions in dynamic video scenes, which indicates that rain streaks often moves along several directions. Thus, we introduce a concept of "**rain streak motion**" to model such a video rain prior. Specifically, we devise a new video rain synthesis model embedding the motions of rain streaks, as shown in Fig. 1(b). Simultaneously, we also develop a novel recurrent disentangled deraining network (RDD-Net) to recurrently estimate additional rain motion from adjacent video frames for boosting video deraining. In our RDD-Net, we first develop a disentangling temporal (DT) module to decouple temporal features of adjacent video frames to sequentially predict a rain streak layer, a rain motion layer, and a rain-free background layer according to our video rain synthesis model. Then, we develop attentive recovery (AR) modules to integrate multiple output layers for generating our final result of video deraining. Overall, the major contributions of this work are:

- First, in this paper, we introduce a new prior of "**rain streak motion**", which models the rain streak motion in video. Based on this term, we devise a new video rain synthesis model to generate a more realistic rainy video dataset for network training.
- Second, we devise a novel recurrent disentangled deraining network (RDD-Net) by attentively aggregating predictions from temporal features of adjacent video frames.
- Third, a disentangled temporal (DT) module is introduced to disentangle temporal features from each pair of adjacent video frames into several features for predicting rain streak layers, rain motion layers, and clean background layers in sequence based on our video rain synthesis model. Simultaneously, an attentive recovery (AR) module is utilized to integrate three predictions of multiple DT modules for fully exploiting complementary information among these predictions, and generate the final video deraining result.
- Final, we evaluate the proposed method on real-world rainy videos and four synthesized video datasets (three widely-used benchmarks and a new synthesized video dataset) by comparing it with state-of-the-art deraining methods. The experimental results show that the proposed method outperforms all competitors on all benchmarks and real hazy images. Overall, Our method sets a new state-of-the-art baseline on video deraining.

2   Related Work

2.1   Single-Image Rain Streak Removal

Early single-image deraining methods examined diverse image priors based on the statistics of the rainy and clean images for removing rain streaks of the single input rainy image. [6,12,16,21,25,29,44]. Inspired by the observation that rain streaks usually fall within a narrow band of directions, Zhu et al. [44] developed rain direction prior, sparse prior, and rain patch prior to form a joint optimization for image deraining. These methods suffers from failures in handling complex rainy cases [20,41], since their hand-crafted image priors are not always correct [44].

Recent methods [43] mainly focused on designing different convolutional neural networks (CNNs) to address image deraining from collected data. Fu et al. [7] learned a mapping between rainy and clean detail layers, and then add a predicted detail layer into a low-pass filtered base layer for outputting a derained image. Then, Yang et al. [37] presented a multi-task deep learning architecture to jointly detect and remove rain streaks from CNN features of a contextualized dilated network. Later CNNs utilized a residual learning to learn a rain streak image for image deraining [18]. More recently, Zhang et al. [41] classified the rain density of the input rainy image and incorporated the density information to multiple densely-connected blocks for predicting a rain streak image. Ren et al. [26] combined ResNet, recurrent layers, and a multi-stage recursion for building a deraining network. Jiang et al. [13] formulated a multi-scale progressive fusion network (MSPFN) to unify the input image scales and hierarchical deep features for image deraining. Although we can generalize image deraining methods to remove rain streaks of a video in a frame by frame manner, the temporal information among video frames enables video deraining methods to work better than image deraining ones [19,22,36,38].

2.2   Video Rain Streak Removal

Garg and Nayar first modeled the video rain and addressed video rain streak removal [9,10]. Many subsequent methods [1–4,6,17,24,27,28,30,31,42] examined more hand-crafted intrinsic priors of rain streaks and clean background details for video deraining. Wei et al. [34] encoded the rain streaks as a patch-based mixture of Gaussians to make the developed method to better adapt a wider range of rain variations. Please see [23] for reviewing video deraining methods with diverse hand-crafted priors.

Recently, deep neural networks [5,23,38] have also been employed to handle video deraining. Li et al. [19] formulated a multiscale convolutional sparse coding to decompose the rain layer into different levels of rain streaks with physical meanings for video deraining. Yang et al. [36] constructed a two-stage recurrent network with dual-level flow regularizations for video deraining. Recently, Yan et al. [35] developed a self-alignment network with transmission-depth consistency to solve the problem of rain accumulation. To address the gap between synthetic and real dataset, Yue et al. [39] presented a semi-supervised video deraining method with a dynamical rain generator. Although improving overall visibility of input rainy videos, existing CNN-based video deraining methods often randomly synthesized rain streak layers of neighboring video frames without considering motions of rain streaks. *Hence, these synthesized videos do not have realistic rain streaks, thereby degrading deraining performance when training video deraining network on these synthesized data.* To alleviate this issue, we devise a new video rain model with rain streak motions to more accurately model rain streak layers of videos and develop a video deraining network based on the new rain model for enhancing video deraining performance.

3   Video Rain Synthesis Model

Observing a video rain prior that rain streaks often fall within a limited range along the directions in real rainy, even for heavy rain, we introduce a new concept of "**rain streak motion**" to model this phenomenon. With the concept of rain streak motion, we can figure out two kinds of rain streaks contributing to the rain streak layer in the rain video. *First*, the new rain streaks will appear when the video camera moves to capture a dynamic scene. *Second* and more importantly, some rain streaks in the $(t-1)$-th frame moves along the dominated rain direction into the t-th video frame to form its rain streaks. Thus, we propose a new video rain synthesis model by embedding these two kinds of rain streaks:

$$I_t = \begin{cases} B_1 + S_1, & t = 1, \\ B_t + (S_{t-1} \bigoplus M_{(t-1)\to t}) + R_t, & t \in [2, T], \end{cases} \tag{2}$$

where S_{t-1} and S_t denote the rain streak layers in $(t-1)$-th and t-th video frames, respectively. $M_{(t-1)\to t}$ is the rain streak motion from the $(t-1)$-th frame to the t-th frame, which represents the dominated rain streak directions of a rainy video. It is computed by multiplying a random integer with the rain streak angle of the first rain streak map S_1. R_t denotes the new rain streaks, which appear due to the camera movement when taking the video, $\bigoplus$ represents the point-wise addition between S_{t-1} and $M_{(t-1)\to t}$.

Figure 1 shows the synthesized rain streak images and the corresponding rainy video frames by using the traditional method (Fig. 1(a)) and our model (Fig. 1(b)), respectively. It is clearly observed that the rain streaks in adjacent frames generated from the traditional model are uncorrelated and, somehow, messy, while our rain model generates more consistent rain streaks along a dominated rain direction, as shown in the yellow rectangles of Fig. 1(b), which more faithfully reflects real rainy scenes. In this regard, the networks trained on our synthesized rain videos have potential to achieve better deraining performance on real rain videos than those trained on previous synthesized training datasets.

Difference of "Rain Motion" in Gary's Model. Gary et al. [10] presented a raindrop oscillation model to render a complex falling raindrop (i.e., rain motion among pixels of an image) produce for generating a realistic rain streak image, or generating rain streak maps for all video frames independently, which totally ignores the rain streak movement between video frames. Unlike this, our rain video model at Eq. (2) takes the rain streak map S (S can be generated by Gary's method) of the first video frame as the input, and then follows the rain streak direction (i.e., rain motion) of the input rain streak map to generate the rain streak maps of all other video frames. Hence, the usage of the rain motion in our video rain model and Gary's model [10] are different. More importantly, our video rain model equation enables us to formulate a CNN to decompose the rain motion, rain streak, and non-rain background and our network outperforms state-of-the-art methods in four synthesized datasets and real data.

4   Proposed Deraining Network

Figure 2 shows the illustration of the proposed recurrent disentangled video deraining network (RDD-Net). The intuition behind our RDD-Net is to recurrently disentangle temporal features from adjacent frames for predicting a background layer, a rain streak layer, and a rain motion layer, and then attentively integrate these predictions from multiple adjacent frames to produce the derained results.

RDD-Net takes $2n+1$ video frames $\{I_{t-n}, \ldots, I_{t-1}, I_t, I_{t+1}, \ldots, I_{t+n}\}$ as the inputs and predicts a derained result of the target frame I_t. To leverage video temporal information, our RDD-Net starts by grouping the input $2n+1$ video frames into $2n$ image pairs, i.e., $\{(I_t, I_{t-n}), \ldots, (I_t, I_{t-1}), (I_t, I_{t+1}), \ldots, (I_t, I_{t+n})\}$. Then, for the first image pair (I_t, I_{t-n}), we apply a 3×3 convolution on $[I_t, I_{t-n}]$ (i.e., concatenation of I_t and I_{t-n}) to generate a feature map (denoted as "Y_1"), while apply a 3×3 convolution on the target video frame I_t to obtain features X_1. To further extract the rain motion of (I_t, I_{t-n}), we devise a disentangled temporal (DT) module and pass X_1 and Y_1 into the DT module to

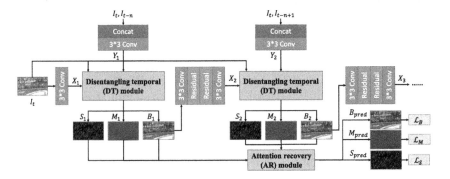

Fig. 2. Schematic illustration of the proposed recurrent disentangled video deraining network (RDD-Net). S_{pred}, M_{pred}, and B_{pred} denote predictions of the rain layer, the rain motion layer, and the clean background layer for the input target video frame I_t. $\{I_{t-n}, \ldots, I_{t-1}, I_{t+1}, \ldots, I_{t+n}\}$ are $2n$ adjacent video frames of I_t.

predict a background image B_1, a rain streak image S_1, and a rain motion image M_1, according to our video rain model defined in Eq. 2.

After that, we utilize a 3×3 convolution, two residual blocks, and a 3×3 convolution on B_1 to produce features X_2, and a 3×3 convolution is applied on the subsequent image pair (I_t, I_{t-n-1}) to obtain features Y_2. Meanwhile, the second DT module is utilized to compute another three image B_2, S_2, and M_2 from X_2 and Y_2. By repeating this process, we can use DT modules to sequentially predict the background image, the rain streak image, and the rain motion image for all $2n$ image pairs. Finally, we develop an attention recovery (AR) module to predict a final background image (see P_B of Fig. 2) from $\{B_1, ..., B_{2n}\}$, an AR module to predict a final rain-free image P_S from $\{S_1, ..., S_{2n}\}$, and an AR module to predict a rain motion image P_M from $\{M_1, ..., M_{2n}\}$ for the target video frame I_t,

Loss Function. Unlike existing video deraining methods only predicting the rain and background layers, our RDD-Net predicts an additional rain motion map for each target frame. Hence, the total loss $\mathcal{L}_{total}$ of our RDD-Net is:

$$\mathcal{L}_{total} = \mathcal{L}_S + \mathcal{L}_M + \mathcal{L}_B,$$

$$where \ \mathcal{L}_S = \|S_{pred} - S_{gt}\|_1, \mathcal{L}_M = \|M_{pred} - M_{gt}\|_1, \mathcal{L}_B = \|B_{pred} - B_{gt}\|_1. \tag{3}$$

Here, S_{pred} and S_{gt} denote the predicted rain layer and the corresponding ground truth. M_{pred} and M_{gt} are the predicted rain motion layer and the corresponding ground truth. B_{pred} and B_{gt} denote the predicted background layer and the corresponding ground truth. $\mathcal{L}_S$ is the prediction loss of S_{pred} and S_{gt}, and we use L_1 loss to compute $\mathcal{L}_S$. $\mathcal{L}_M$ is the L_1 loss of M_{pred} and M_{gt}, while $\mathcal{L}_B$ is the L_1 loss of B_{pred} and B_{gt}.

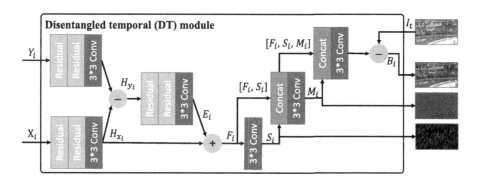

Fig. 3. Schematic illustration of the DT module of our RDD-Net.

4.1   Disentangling Temporal (DT) Module

Existing video deraining networks [36,38] predict a rain layer and a background layer by capturing the temporal correlations of adjacent video frames. As presented in our video rain model (see Eq. 2), rain motions enable us to more accurately approximate the underlying rain streak distributions over rainy videos. In this regard, we develop a disentangled temporal (DT) module to learn temporal features from adjacent video frames and decouple these temporal features to sequentially compute a rain layer, a clean background layer, and a rain motion layer since they are intrinsically correlated.

Figure 3 shows the schematic illustration of the disentangled temporal (DT) module, which takes features X_i of the target video frame, another features (Y_i) from two adjacent video frames, and the target video frame I_t as the inputs. To learn the temporal features, our DT module starts by fusing features of adjacent video frames. We first apply two residual blocks and a 3×3 convolution on X_i to obtain H_{x_i}, and two residual blocks and a 3×3 convolution are utilized on Y_i to obtain H_{y_i}. After that, we subtract H_{y_i} from H_{x_i} and apply two residual blocks and a 3×3 convolution on the subtraction result to obtain features E_i. We then add E_i and H_{x_i} to obtain the temporal feature map (denoted as F_s) of adjacent video frames. Mathematically, the temporal feature map F_s is computed by

$$F_s = H_{x_i} + \mathcal{D}_1(H_{x_i} - H_{y_i}), \text{ where } H_{x_i} = \mathcal{D}_2(X_i), \text{ and } H_{y_i} = \mathcal{D}_3(Y_i). \quad (4)$$

Here, $\mathcal{D}_1$, $\mathcal{D}_2$, and $\mathcal{D}_3$ denote three blocks, which has two residual blocks and a 3×3 convolution. And $\mathcal{D}_1$, $\mathcal{D}_2$, and $\mathcal{D}_3$ do not share the same convolutional parameters.

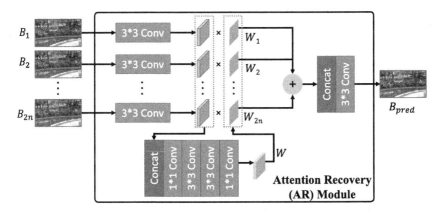

Fig. 4. Schematic illustration of the attentive recovery (AR) module of our RDD-Net.

Once obtaining the temporal feature map F_s (see Eq. 4), our DT module predicts the clean background layer, the rain layer, and the rain motion layer one by one. Specifically, F_i is passed to a 3×3 convolutional layer to predict a rain layer S_i. Then, we concatenate the obtained rain layer S_i with the temporal feature map F_i and utilize a 3×3 convolutional layer on the concatenation result (see $[F_i, S_i]$ of Fig. 3) to compute a rain motion layer M_i. Finally, we subtract a result of a 3×3 convolutional layer on the concatenation (see $[F_i, S_i, M_i]$ of Fig. 3) of F_i, S_i, and M_i from the target video frame I_t to get a clean background layer B_i. In summary, the rain layer S_i, the rain motion layer M_i, and the clean background layer B_i are computed as:

$$S_i = conv(F_i), M_i = conv([F_i, S_i]), B_i = I_t - conv([F_i, S_i, M_i]), \quad (5)$$

where $conv$ denotes a 3×3 convolutional layer, and three $conv$ operations for computing S_i, M_i, and B_i do not share convolutional parameters.

4.2 Attention Recovery (AR) Module

Rather than stacking or warping adjacent video frames together in most video restoration networks, our method follows a back-projection framework [11] to treat each adjacent frame as a separate source of temporal information, and then recurrently combine multiple sources from several adjacent video frames, as shown in Fig. 2. Unlike simply concatenating predictions at each recurrent step in original back-projection framework, we find that there are complemental information among these prediction results at different recurrent steps. Hence, we develop an attention recovery (AR) module to attentively aggregate these different predictions for further improving the network prediction accuracy. Note that our DT module at each recurrent step has three predictions, including a rain layer prediction, a rain motion layer prediction, and a clean background layer prediction; see Fig. 3. In this regard, we develop an AR module to aggregate $2n$ background predictions (i.e., $\{B_1, B_2, \ldots, B_{2n}\}$) to produce a final result of estimating the background layer of the target video frame I_t. Meanwhile, we develop an AR module to aggregate $2n$ rain layer predictions (i.e., $\{S_1, S_2, \ldots, S_{2n}\}$) to produce a final result of estimating the rain layer of I_t, while another AR module is devised to aggregate $2n$ rain motion layer predictions (i.e., $\{M_1, M_2, \ldots, M_{2n}\}$) to produce a final result of estimating the rain motion layer of I_t.

Here, we only show the schematic illustration of the developed AR module of computing a final background layer; see Fig. 4. Specifically, taking $2n$ predictions

Table 1. Quantitative comparisons of our network and compared methods on three widely-used video rain streak removal benchmark datasets. Best results are denoted in red and the second best results are denoted in blue.

		CVPR'17	TIP'15	CVPR'17	CVPR'18	ICCV'15	ICCV'17	TIP'18	CVPR'18	CVPR'18	CVPR'19	CVPR'20	CVPR'21
Dataset	Metric	DetailNet [8]	TCLRM [17]	JORDER [37]	MS-CSC [19]	DSC [25]	SE [34]	FastDerain [15]	J4RNet [23]	SpacCNN [5]	FCDN [36]	SLDNet [38]	S2VD [39]	RDD-Net
RainSynLight25	PSNR↑	25.72	28.77	30.37	25.58	25.63	26.56	29.42	32.96	32.78	35.80	34.28	34.66	35.61
	SSIM↑	0.8572	0.8693	0.9235	0.8089	0.9328	0.8683	0.9434	0.9239	0.9622	0.9586	0.9403	0.9766
RainSynHeavy25	PSNR↑	16.50	17.31	20.20	16.96	17.33	16.76	19.25	24.13	21.21	27.72	26.51	27.03	32.39
	SSIM↑	0.5441	0.4956	0.6335	0.5049	0.5036	0.5293	0.5385	0.7163	0.5854	0.8239	0.7966	0.8255	0.9518
NTURain	PSNR↑	30.13	29.98	32.61	27.31	29.20	25.73	30.32	32.14	33.11	36.05	34.89	37.37	37.71
	SSIM↑	0.9220	0.9199	0.9482	0.7870	0.9137	0.7614	0.9262	0.9480	0.9474	0.9676	0.9540	0.9683	0.9720

Table 2. Quantitative comparisons of our network and compared methods on our synthesized rainy video dataset. Best results are denoted in red and the second best results are denoted in blue.

	CVPR'16	CVPR'17	CVPR'17	CVPR'19	CVPR'20	ACM MM'20	CVPR'21	CVPR'17	TIP'18	CVPR'18	CVPR'19	CVPR'20	CVPR'21
Metric	LP [21]	JORDER [37]	DetailNet [8]	PReNet [26]	MSPFN [13]	DCSFN [32]	MPRNet [40]	DIP [14]	FastDerain [15]	MS-CSC [19]	FCDN [36]	SLDNet [38]	S2VD [39]	RDD-Net
PSNR↑	19.42	15.94	21.42	27.06	22.99	26.77	28.42	19.35	23.66	17.36	24.81	20.31	24.09	31.82
SSIM↑	0.6841	0.5334	0.7826	0.9077	0.8325	0.9052	0.9203	0.6518	0.7893	0.5968	0.8658	0.6272	0.7944	0.9424

of the clean background layer as the inputs, our AR module first utilize a 3×3 convolutional layer on each background layer prediction to obtain $2n$ feature maps, which are denoted as $\{Q_1, Q_2, \ldots, Q_{2n}\}$. Then, we concatenate these $2n$ feature maps and utilize four convolutional layers and a softmax layer on the concatenated feature map to produce an attention map W with $2n$ channels. The four convolutional layers includes a 1×1 convolution, two 3×3 convolutions, and a 1×1 convolution. After that, we multiply all $2n$ channels of W with $2n$ feature maps to produce weighted feature maps, which are then added together to produce the final background layer prediction (see B_{pred} of Fig. 4) by using a 3×3 convolutional layer. Hence, B_{pred} is computed by:

$$B_{pred} = conv(cat(W_1 Q_1, W_2 Q_2, \ldots, W_{2n} Q_{2n})), \qquad (6)$$

where $conv$ denotes a 3×3 convolution. $cat(\cdot)$ is a feature concatenation operation.

5 Experiments

Benchmark Datasets. We evaluate the effectiveness of our network on three widely-used benchmark datasets and a new dataset (denoted as "RainMotion") synthesized in our work. Table 3 summarizes the details of four video deraining datasets. Three benchmark datasets are RainSynLight25 [23] with 215 light rain videos, RainSynComplex25 [23] with 215 heavy rain videos, and NTURain [5] with 24 rain videos. Regarding our dataset, we use the same 16 clean background videos (8 videos for training and 8 videos for testing) of NTURain [5] to generate 80 rain videos based on our video rain model (see Eq. 2). Specifically, for each clean background videos with k frames, we first generate five large rain streak masks (with 10 times spatial resolutions of the clean video frame), including three masks obtained by using Photoshop, a mask randomly selected from RainSynComplex25 [23], and a mask from [10], and the spatial resolution of each rain streak mask is than that of the clean video frame. Then, k images are cropped from each rain streak mask along the rain direction of the mask to simulate the

Table 3. Comparison between different datasets.

Dataset	Split	Video Num	Video Length	Video Frame Num
RainSynLight25	train	190	9	1710
	test	25	31	775
RainSynHeavy25	train	190	9	1720
	test	25	31	755
NTURain	train	24	80–138	-
	test	8	116–298	-
Our RainMotion	train	40	50	2000
	test	40	20	800

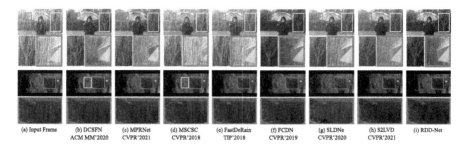

| (a) Input Frame | (b) DCSFN ACM MM'2020 | (c) MPRNet CVPR'2021 | (d) MSCSC CVPR'2018 | (e) FastDeRain TIP'2018 | (f) FCDN CVPR'2019 | (g) SLDNe CVPR'2020 | (h) S2LVD CVPR'2021 | (i) RDD-Net |

Fig. 5. Visual comparison of different deraining methods on a real rain video sequence. The blue box indicates the comparison of rain streak removal. The red box indicates the comparison of detail retention. (Color figure online)

rain with video rain motion, and then we add these k images with the clean background layer to generate a rainy video. By doing so, we can obtain five rainy videos for each background video, thereby resulting in 40 rainy videos in our training set, and 40 rainy videos in our testing set.

Implementation Details. We implement our RDD-Net with PyTorch, and use the Adam optimizer to train the network on a NVIDIA GTX 2080Ti. We empirically set $n=3$, which means that our network receives seven frames as the inputs for video deraining; see our network in Fig. 2. We crop the target video frame to 128×128. The initial learning rate, weight decay, and batch size are empirically set as 0.0001, 0.00005 and 8, respectively. The total epoch number is empirically set as 1500 for RainSynLight25, 1500 for RainSynComplex25, 150 for NTURain, and 500 for RainMotion. Our RDD-Net contains 30.64 MB parameters, and the average running time of our network is about 0.8633s for one video frame with a resolution of 832×512. We employed peak signal to noise ratio (PSNR) and structural similarity index (SSIM) [33] to quantitatively compare different methods.

Comparative Methods. We compare our network against 18 state-of-the-art methods, including eight single-image deraining methods, and ten video deraining methods. Eight single-image deraining methods are DSC [25], LP [21], DetailNet [8], JORDER [37], PReNet [26], MSPFN [13], DCSFN [32], and MPR-

| PSNR/SSIM= | 19.26/0.6830 | 20.24/0.6930 | 22.34/0.7703 | 23.70/0.7868 | 24.29/0.8401 | 21.83/0.7105 | 24.80/0.8244 | 27.87/0.9035 | ∞/1 |

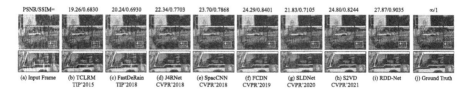

| (a) Input Frame | (b) TCLRM TIP'2015 | (c) FastDeRain TIP'2018 | (d) J4RNet CVPR'2018 | (e) SpacCNN CVPR'2018 | (f) FCDN CVPR'2019 | (g) SLDNet CVPR'2020 | (h) S2VD CVPR'2021 | (i) RDD-Net | (j) Ground Truth |

Fig. 6. Visual comparison of different deraining methods on RainSynHeavy25 dataset. The blue box indicates the comparison of rain streak removal. The red box indicates the comparison of detail retention. (Color figure online)

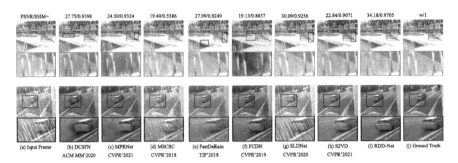

Fig. 7. Visual comparison of different deraining methods on RainMotion dataset. The blue box indicates the comparison of rain streak removal. The red box indicates the comparison of detail retention. (Color figure online)

Net [40], while ten video deraining techniques are TCLRM [17], DIP [14], MS-CSC [19], SE [34], FastDerain [15], J4RNet [23], SpacCNN [5], FCDN [36], SLD-Net [39] and S2VD [39]. To provide fair comparisons, we obtain FCDN's results from the authors. For other comparing methods, we use their public implementations, and re-train these networks on same benchmark datasets to obtain their best performance for a fair comparison.

5.1   Results on Real-World Rainy Videos

To evaluate the effectiveness of our video raining network, we collect 11 real-world rainy videos from Youtube website by comparing our network against state-of-the-art methods. Figure 5 shows the derained results produced by our network and compared methods on real-world video frames. Apparently, DCSFN, MPRNet, MSCSC, FastDeRain, SLDNet and S2VD cannot fully remove rain streaks. Although eliminating rain streaks, FCDN tends to over-smooth clean background details. On the contrary, our method effectively removes rain streaks and better maintains background details than FCDN; see these magnified tree regions of Figs. 5(f) and (i).

Table 4. Quantitative comparisons of ablation study on the RainMotion dataset.

Network	DT	AR	PSNR↑	SSIM ↑
basic	×	×	30.89	0.9351
basic+DT	✓	×	31.22	0.9367
our method	✓	✓	**31.82**	**0.9423**

5.2 Results on Synthetic Videos

Quantitative Comparison. Table 1 reports PSNR and SSIM scores of our network and compared methods on the three existing benchmark datasets, while Table 2 compares the metrics results on our RainMotion dataset. As presented in Table 1, FCDN and S2VD has largest PSNR and SSIM scores among all compared methods. Compared with these two methods, our method has achieved a PSNR improvement of 7.85% and a SSIM improvement of 1.50% on RainSyn-Light25, a PSNR improvement of 16.85% and a SSIM improvement of 12.88% on RainSynHeavy25, and a PSNR improvement of 0.91% and a SSIM improvement of 0.38% on NTURain. Moreover, our method has larger PSNR and SSIM scores than all the competitors on our dataset, demonstrating that our network can more accurately recover clean video backgrounds; see Table 2.

Visual Comparison. Figure 6 shows the visual comparison between our network and state-of-the-art methods on an input rainy frame of RainSynHeavy25, which is the most challenging among existing benchmark datasets. Apparently, after removing rain streaks, our method can better preserve clean background image than state-of-the-art methods. It shows that our method has a more accurate video deraining result, which is further verified by the superior PSNR/SSIM values of our method. Moreover, Fig. 7 presents visual comparisons between our network and state-of-the-art methods on our dataset. From these visual results, we can find that DCSFN, MPRNet and S2VD tend to produce artifacts with dark pixels, while MSCSC, FastDeRain and SLDNet maintain many rain steaks in their derained results. FCDN also cannot fully remove rain streaks, such as the grass region at the second row of Fig. 7. By progressively predicting additional rain motions, our RDD-Net can effectively eliminate rain streaks and better maintain non-rain background details; see our larger PSNR/SSIM scores.

5.3 Ablation Study

Baseline Design. We also conduct ablation study experiments on the RainMotion dataset to evaluate two major modules (i.e., DT module and AR module) of our network. To do so, we construct two baseline networks. The first baseline (denoted as "basic") is to remove all AR modules from our network and modifying DT modules to predict only clean background layers for video deraining. It means that all DT modules in "basic" do not predict rain motion layers and rain streak layers. The second baseline (denoted as "basic+DT") is to add DT modules into "basic".

Quantitative Comparison. Table 4 reports PSNR and SSIM scores of our method and two constructed baseline networks. First, "basic+DT" has a larger PSNR and SSIM scores than "basic", demonstrating that utilizing our DT modules to decouple temporal features for predicting additional rain streak layers and rain motions layers helps our network to better recover the underlying clean background layer. Moreover, our network outperforms "basic+DT" in terms of

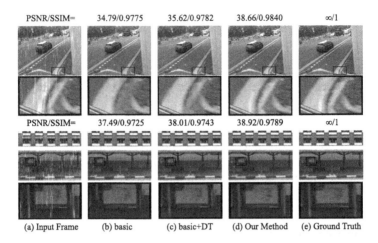

| PSNR/SSIM= | 34.79/0.9775 | 35.62/0.9782 | 38.66/0.9840 | ∞/1 |

| PSNR/SSIM= | 37.49/0.9725 | 38.01/0.9743 | 38.92/0.9789 | ∞/1 |

(a) Input Frame   (b) basic   (c) basic+DT   (d) Our Method   (e) Ground Truth

Fig. 8. Visual comparison of ablation study. (a) Input video rain frame. The results of (b) basic, (c) basic+DT, (d) our method, and (e) ground truths.

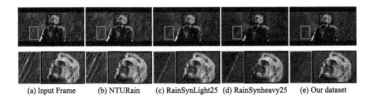

(a) Input Frame   (b) NTURain   (c) RainSynLight25 (d) RainSynheavy25   (e) Our dataset

Fig. 9. Results of our network trained on different datasets.

PSNR and SSIM metrics. It indicates that leveraging our AR modules to attentively aggregate predictions of different recurrent steps enables our network to achieve superior video deraining performance.

Visual Comparison. Figure 8 shows derained results produced by our network and two baseline networks for different rain video frames. Apparently, "basic" and "basic+DT" tend to over-smooth background details when removing rain streaks of the video frames. On the contrary, our method is capable to better preserve these background details; as shown in Fig. 8. Moreover, our method has the larger PSNR and SSIM values than baseline networks, showing the superior video deraining performance of our method.

5.4 Discussions

Advantage of Our Dataset. One of main advantages of our dataset is that we introduce the **rain streak motion** to generate a more realistic rainy video data for network training. To prove the this advantage over other datasets, we re-train our network on our dataset and other three datasets (i.e., NTURain, RainSynLight25, and RainSynheavy25), separately, and test them on the same

Table 5. The results of our network with and without $\mathcal{L}_S$ and $\mathcal{L}_M$ on RainMotion.

	w/o $\mathcal{L}_S, \mathcal{L}_M$	w/o $\mathcal{L}_S$	w/o $\mathcal{L}_M$	RDD-Net
PSNR↑	30.68	31.09	30.92	**31.82**
SSIM↑	0.9353	0.9372	0.9364	**0.9423**

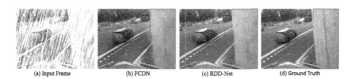

(a) Input Frame   (b) FCDN   (c) RDD-Net   (d) Ground Truth

Fig. 10. A failure case of our RDD-Net.

real-world rainy videos. Figure 9 shows the results, where our network trained on our dataset (e) gets better result than those trained on other datasets.

The Effect of the Video Rain Prior. Compared to existing methods, our network utilizes additional supervisions (i.e., $\mathcal{L}_S$ and $\mathcal{L}_M$) on predicting the rain motion image (i.e., video rain prior) and the non-rain clean image for training due to the disentangled feature learning. Table 5 reports PSNR and SSIM scores of our method with and without $\mathcal{L}_S$ and $\mathcal{L}_M$. It shows that the performance of our network is reduced when removing $\mathcal{L}_S$ or $\mathcal{L}_M$, showing that the additional $\mathcal{L}_S$ and $\mathcal{L}_M$ help our network to achieve a better video deraining accuracy. Moreover, our method without $\mathcal{L}_S$ or $\mathcal{L}_M$ (see $w/o\mathcal{L}_S, \mathcal{L}_M$ of Table 5) still outperforms all existing video deraining methods, since the largest PSNR and SSIM scores of existing methods are 28.42 and 0.9203 (*i.e.*, MPRNet in Table 2).

Failure Cases. Like other video deraining methods, our method cannot work well for a very heavy rain case, where the background details are almost completely covered by rain streaks; see Fig. 10 for an example input and results of FCDN and our method. We argue that such heavy rain case is rare in our daily life, and we can alleviate this issue by generating or collecting similar video data samples.

6   Conclusion

This paper presents a novel network for video rain streak removal. One of our key contributions is to devise a new video rain model by first embedding rain streak motions and collect a new dataset based on the rain model. The second contribution is the development of a novel network for video rain streak removal by decoupling the aggregated features from each pair of adjacent video frames into features for predicting a background layer, a rain motion, a background layer, and a rain layer, and then attentively integrate decoupled features from several pairs of adjacent frames. Experimental results on benchmark datasets and real-world rainy videos show that our network consistently outperforms state-of-the-art methods by a large margin. In future, we will also incorporate other rain degrading factors (e.g., fog/haze/raindrops) into our video rain model to further improve the robustness of our video rain streak removal network.

Acknowledgement. The work is supported by the National Natural Science Foundation of China (Grant No. 61902275, NSFC-U1803264), and a grant of Hong Kong Research Grants Council under General Research Fund (no. 15205919).

References

1. Barnum, P.C., Narasimhan, S., Kanade, T.: Analysis of rain and snow in frequency space. IJCV **86**(2–3), 256–274 (2010)
2. Bossu, J., Hautière, N., Tarel, J.P.: Rain or snow detection in image sequences through use of a histogram of orientation of streaks. IJCV **93**(3), 348–367 (2011)
3. Brewer, N., Liu, N.: Using the shape characteristics of rain to identify and remove rain from video. In: da Vitoria Lobo, N., et al. (eds.) SSPR /SPR 2008. LNCS, vol. 5342, pp. 451–458. Springer, Heidelberg (2008). https://doi.org/10.1007/978-3-540-89689-0_49
4. Chen, J., Chau, L.P.: A rain pixel recovery algorithm for videos with highly dynamic scenes. IEEE TIP **23**(3), 1097–1104 (2013)
5. Chen, J., Tan, C.H., Hou, J., Chau, L.P., Li, H.: Robust video content alignment and compensation for rain removal in a CNN framework. In: CVPR, pp. 6286–6295 (2018)
6. Chen, Y.L., Hsu, C.T.: A generalized low-rank appearance model for spatio-temporally correlated rain streaks. In: ICCV, pp. 1968–1975 (2013)
7. Fu, X., Huang, J., Ding, X., Liao, Y., Paisley, J.: Clearing the skies: a deep network architecture for single-image rain removal. IEEE TIP **26**(6), 2944–2956 (2017)
8. Fu, X., Huang, J., Zeng, D., Huang, Y., Ding, X., Paisley, J.: Removing rain from single images via a deep detail network. In: CVPR, pp. 3855–3863 (2017)
9. Garg, K., Nayar, S.K.: Detection and removal of rain from videos. In: CVPR, pp. 528–535 (2004)
10. Garg, K., Nayar, S.K.: Photorealistic rendering of rain streaks. ACM Trans. Graph. (TOG) **25**(3), 996–1002 (2006)
11. Haris, M., Shakhnarovich, G., Ukita, N.: Recurrent back-projection network for video super-resolution. In: CVPR (2019)
12. Huang, D.A., Kang, L.W., Wang, Y.C.F., Lin, C.W.: Self-learning based image decomposition with applications to single image denoising. IEEE Trans. Multimed. **16**(1), 83–93 (2014)
13. Jiang, K., et al.: Multi-scale progressive fusion network for single image deraining. In: CVPR, pp. 8346–8355 (2020)
14. Jiang, T.X., Huang, T.Z., Zhao, X.L., Deng, L.J., Wang, Y.: A novel tensor-based video rain streaks removal approach via utilizing discriminatively intrinsic priors. In: CVPR, pp. 4057–4066 (2017)
15. Jiang, T.X., Huang, T.Z., Zhao, X.L., Deng, L.J., Wang, Y.: FastDeRain: a novel video rain streak removal method using directional gradient priors. IEEE TIP **28**(4), 2089–2102 (2018)
16. Kang, L.W., Lin, C.W., Fu, Y.H.: Automatic single-image-based rain streaks removal via image decomposition. IEEE TIP **21**(4), 1742–1755 (2012)

17. Kim, J.H., Sim, J.Y., Kim, C.S.: Video deraining and desnowing using temporal correlation and low-rank matrix completion. IEEE TIP **24**(9), 2658–2670 (2015)
18. Li, G., He, X., Zhang, W., Chang, H., Dong, L., Lin, L.: Non-locally enhanced encoder-decoder network for single image de-raining. In: ACM Multimedia, pp. 1056–1064 (2018)
19. Li, M., et al.: Video rain streak removal by multiscale convolutional sparse coding. In: CVPR, pp. 6644–6653 (2018)
20. Li, X., Wu, J., Lin, Z., Liu, H., Zha, H.: Recurrent squeeze-and-excitation context aggregation net for single image deraining. In: ECCV, pp. 254–269 (2018)
21. Li, Y., Tan, R.T., Guo, X., Lu, J., Brown, M.S.: Rain streak removal using layer priors. In: CVPR, pp. 2736–2744 (2016)
22. Liu, J., Yang, W., Yang, S., Guo, Z.: D3R-Net: dynamic routing residue recurrent network for video rain removal. IEEE TIP **28**(2), 699–712 (2018)
23. Liu, J., Yang, W., Yang, S., Guo, Z.: Erase or fill? Deep joint recurrent rain removal and reconstruction in videos. In: CVPR, pp. 3233–3242 (2018)
24. Liu, P., Xu, J., Liu, J., Tang, X.: Pixel based temporal analysis using chromatic property for removing rain from videos. Comput. Inf. Sci. **2**(1), 53–60 (2009)
25. Luo, Y., Xu, Y., Ji, H.: Removing rain from a single image via discriminative sparse coding. In: ICCV, pp. 3397–3405 (2015)
26. Ren, D., Zuo, W., Hu, Q., Zhu, P., Meng, D.: Progressive image deraining networks: a better and simpler baseline. In: CVPR, pp. 3937–3946 (2019)
27. Ren, W., Tian, J., Han, Z., Chan, A., Tang, Y.: Video desnowing and deraining based on matrix decomposition. In: CVPR, pp. 4210–4219 (2017)
28. Santhaseelan, V., Asari, V.K.: Utilizing local phase information to remove rain from video. IJCV **112**(1), 71–89 (2015)
29. Sun, S.H., Fan, S.P., Wang, Y.C.F.: Exploiting image structural similarity for single image rain removal. In: IEEE ICIP, pp. 4482–4486 (2014)
30. Tripathi, A.K., Mukhopadhyay, S.: A probabilistic approach for detection and removal of rain from videos. IETE J. Res. **57**(1), 82–91 (2011)
31. Tripathi, A., Mukhopadhyay, S.: Video post processing: low-latency spatiotemporal approach for detection and removal of rain. IET Image Proc. **6**(2), 181–196 (2012)
32. Wang, C., Xing, X., Wu, Y., Su, Z., Chen, J.: DCSFN: deep cross-scale fusion network for single image rain removal. In: Proceedings of the 28th ACM International Conference on Multimedia, pp. 1643–1651 (2020)
33. Wang, Z., Bovik, A.C., Sheikh, H.R., Simoncelli, E.P.: Image quality assessment: from error visibility to structural similarity. IEEE TIP **13**(4), 600–612 (2004)
34. Wei, W., Yi, L., Xie, Q., Zhao, Q., Meng, D., Xu, Z.: Should we encode rain streaks in video as deterministic or stochastic? In: ICCV, pp. 2516–2525 (2017)
35. Yan, W., Tan, R.T., Yang, W., Dai, D.: Self-aligned video deraining with transmission-depth consistency. In: CVPR, pp. 11966–11976 (2021)
36. Yang, W., Liu, J., Feng, J.: Frame-consistent recurrent video deraining with dual-level flow. In: CVPR, pp. 1661–1670 (2019)
37. Yang, W., Tan, R.T., Feng, J., Liu, J., Guo, Z., Yan, S.: Joint rain detection and removal from a single image. In: CVPR, pp. 1685–1694 (2017)
38. Yang, W., Tan, R.T., Wang, S., Liu, J.: Self-learning video rain streak removal: when cyclic consistency meets temporal correspondence. In: CVPR, pp. 1720–1729 (2020)
39. Yue, Z., Xie, J., Zhao, Q., Meng, D.: Semi-supervised video deraining with dynamical rain generator. In: CVPR, pp. 642–652 (2021)
40. Zamir, S.W., et al.: Multi-stage progressive image restoration. In: CVPR (2021)

41. Zhang, H., Patel, V.M.: Density-aware single image de-raining using a multi-stream dense network. In: CVPR, pp. 695–704 (2018)
42. Zhang, X., Li, H., Qi, Y., Leow, W.K., Ng, T.K.: Rain removal in video by combining temporal and chromatic properties. In: IEEE International Conference on Multimedia and Expo, pp. 461–464 (2006)
43. Zhu, L., et al.: Learning gated non-local residual for single-image rain streak removal. IEEE Trans. Circuits Syst. Video Technol. **31**(6), 2147–2159 (2020)
44. Zhu, L., Fu, C.W., Lischinski, D., Heng, P.A.: Joint bi-layer optimization for single-image rain streak removal. In: ICCV, pp. 2526–2534 (2017)

Super-Resolution by Predicting Offsets: An Ultra-Efficient Super-Resolution Network for Rasterized Images

Jinjin Gu[1]([⊠]), Haoming Cai[2], Chenyu Dong[3], Ruofan Zhang[3], Yulun Zhang[4], Wenming Yang[3], and Chun Yuan[3,5]([⊠])

[1] The University of Sydney, Camperdown, Australia
`jinjin.gu@sydney.edu.au`
[2] University of Maryland, College Park, USA
`hmcai@umd.edu`
[3] Tsinghua Shenzhen International Graduate School,
Tsinghua University, Shenzhen, China
{`dcy20,zrf20`}`@mails.tsinghua.edu.cn`,
{`yang.wenming,yuanc`}`@sz.tsinghua.edu.cn`
[4] ETH Zürich, Zürich, Switzerland
[5] Peng Cheng National Laboratory, Shenzhen, China

Abstract. Rendering high-resolution (HR) graphics brings substantial computational costs. Efficient graphics super-resolution (SR) methods may achieve HR rendering with small computing resources and have attracted extensive research interests in industry and research communities. We present a new method for real-time SR for computer graphics, namely Super-Resolution by Predicting Offsets (SRPO). Our algorithm divides the image into two parts for processing, i.e., sharp edges and flatter areas. For edges, different from the previous SR methods that take the anti-aliased images as inputs, our proposed SRPO takes advantage of the characteristics of rasterized images to conduct SR on the rasterized images. To complement the residual between HR and low-resolution (LR) rasterized images, we train an ultra-efficient network to predict the offset maps to move the appropriate surrounding pixels to the new positions. For flat areas, we found simple interpolation methods can already generate reasonable output. We finally use a guided fusion operation to integrate the sharp edges generated by the network and flat areas by the interpolation method to get the final SR image. The proposed network only contains 8,434 parameters and can be accelerated by network quantization. Extensive experiments show that the proposed SRPO can achieve superior visual effects at a smaller computational cost than the existing state-of-the-art methods.

1 Introduction

With the popularity of 4K or even 8K display devices, rendering graphics at ultra-high resolution and high frame rates has attracted extensive research interests in industry and research communities. However, achieving such a goal is very

S. Avidan et al. (Eds.): ECCV 2022, LNCS 13679, pp. 583–598, 2022.
https://doi.org/10.1007/978-3-031-19800-7_34

challenging, as rendering graphics at high resolutions will bring huge computational costs, which poses severe challenges to graphics algorithms and graphic computing devices. Especially for mobile devices, the huge computational cost also means high power consumption. Finding ways to enjoy high resolutions and high frame rates without compromising graphics quality as much as possible has become an imperative issue.

In addition to compromising graphics effects and texture quality, there is a new paradigm in recent years to render low-resolution (LR) images first and then super-resolve them to obtain high-resolution (HR) images. NVIDIA Deep Learning Super Sampling (DLSS) technology and AMD FidelityFX Super Resolution (FSR) are two representative solutions that follow this new paradigm. However, the poor visual effect and computationally unfriendly features of these super-resolution (SR) methods restrict the application of such techniques. For example, FSR uses traditional filtering methods to upsample and sharpen LR images. This method is relatively easy to deploy on various graphics computing devices, but its visual effect is far from ideal. DLSS uses state-of-the-art deep learning-based SR methods to obtain better perceptual effects, but deep networks' high computational cost makes such a solution only available on dedicated acceleration devices called NVIDIA Tensor Core. There is no solution available for other devices that do not have such powerful neural computing power.

Deep learning-based SR methods (SR networks) directly map LR rendered images to HR rendered images with many stacked convolutional layers/filters. One of the reasons for its success is to use a large number of learnable parameters in exchange for sufficient model capacity. Some successful SR networks even contain tens of millions of parameters, e.g., EDSR [19], and RRDBNet [27]. The state-of-the-art efficiency-oriented SR network also contains more than 200k parameters, far short of real-time SR requirements. An efficient deep model can be very "shallow" for widely deployed graphic devices, i.e., only three or fewer convolutional layers. However, within this constraint, deep learning has no precedent for success.

In this paper, we propose an ultra-efficient SR method for computer graphics, especially for mobile platforms and their graphics applications. Some observations inspire our approach. Firstly, we argue that generating rich, detailed textures for small SR networks is difficult. In this case, keeping the edges of the SR image sharp is the most effective way to improve the perceptual effect. Our method is mainly used to generate such sharp edges. Secondly, SR is generally performed on anti-aliased images (i.e., FSR) because anti-aliased images typically have gradient distributions and visual effects similar to natural images. It is very straightforward to borrow an algorithm that works on natural images for anti-aliased images. However, the edges of the anti-aliased images have more complex gradient distributions, and it is difficult for small SR networks to handle such complex gradient changes. Rasterized images have simpler color changes, obvious truncation of edges, and similar distributions under various rendering engines than anti-aliased images. These properties allow us to perform SR on rasterized images using simple operations without wasting the model's capacity to generate sharp edges.

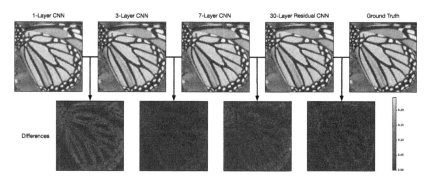

Fig. 1. For SR networks, the processing of edges is very important. It can be seen that the 3-layer network mainly improves the edge compared to the network with only one layer. Continuing to increase the network to seven layers did not bring significant changes. Until we deepen the network to 30 layers, the network cannot generate sharper edges. Nevertheless, for the real-time SR problem explored in this paper, how to use a 3-layer network to generate as sharp, visually pleasing edges as possible is the key issue.

In the light of the above discussion, we propose to perform SR directly on rasterized images. The difference between HR and LR rasterized images usually occurs in the change of edge pixels. This change is spatially abrupt (the "jagged" edges), and it is difficult to make up for this difference with a simple convolutional network. Our method predicts offsets that shift surrounding similarly colored pixels to their desired positions to compensate for this sharp difference. The new SR rasterized image obtained by this method retains the characteristics of the rasterized image well and can produce sharp edges. We fuse these edges with other areas obtained by the interpolation method to get the final output image. With subsequent anti-aliasing (AA) algorithm, we can obtain super-resolved rendered graphics at a small cost. Our final method uses only a three-layer convolutional neural network, which can also be quantized and accelerated and run on various devices with 8-bit integer without loss of final effects. We present extensive experiments, and the final results show sharp edges and good visual performance.

2   Related Work

Anti-aliasing is a longstanding problem in computer graphics. Aliasing occurs when sampling is insufficient during rendering because each pixel can only belong to a specific object and receive a unique pixel value, so jagged and saw-toothed effects can appear at the edges of such an object. Using higher sampling rates is the most straightforward solution to ameliorate aliasing effects, i.e., super-sample anti-aliasing (SSAA) and multisample anti-aliasing (MSAA). These approaches are computationally expensive and difficult to be compatible with modern rendering methods such as deferred lighting/shading, and thus not

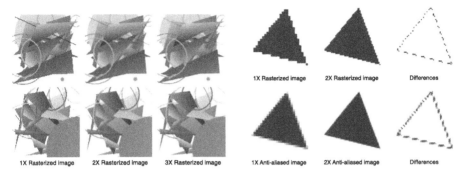

Fig. 2. Samples of the generated training images. We rendered 300 images of random geometric objects with random gradient colors, including triangles, circles, rings, lines and bezier curves.

Fig. 3. The differences between the rasterized images and the anti-aliased images. The residual images are between the nearest neighbor upsampled LR image and the HR image.

suitable for real-time applications for mobile devices. Another alternative anti-aliasing paradigm is optimising the visual effects of rasterized images through image post-processing methods. The most used alternative to MSAA was edge detection and blurring, which is simple, but the results are significantly lower quality than MSAA. In 2009, Reshetov proposed morphological anti-aliasing (MLAA) [23] that performs anti-aliasing with rule-based pixel blending according to certain patterns in the neighborhood. MLAA has gained extensive attention and applications and inspired many post-processing AA algorithms, e.g., FXAA, SMAA [12], Filmic SMAA and DLAA. Most of these algorithms have already been applied and created good visual effects. However, AA algorithms do not increase the resolution of the rendered image, and they can only reduce jagged artifacts at the native resolution.

Super-Resolution (SR) aims at creating HR images according to the LR observations. The simplest way to perform SR is through interpolation-based methods that generate HR pixels by averaging neighboring LR pixels, e.g., bicubic, bilinear and Lanczos. These methods are computationally efficient, but the results are over-smoothed as the interpolated pixels are locally similar to neighbouring pixels and thus have insufficient visual effects. AMD FSR algorithm first employs a Lanzocs-like upsampling method and uses a sharpening filter to optimize overly smooth edges. A new fundamental paradigm shift in image processing has resulted from the development of data-driven or learning-based methods in recent years. Since Dong et al. [5] introduce the first SR network, plenty of deep learning based SR methods have been proposed, including deeper networks [6,14,24], recurrent architectures [15,25], residual architectures [17–19,27], and attention networks [3,4,31]. Network-based methods are also used in computer graphics [13,26]. More related to this work, Xiao et al. [29] propose a dense video SR network for graphics rendering. These SR networks can achieve impressive SR results, but the massive parameters and the expensive computational cost limit

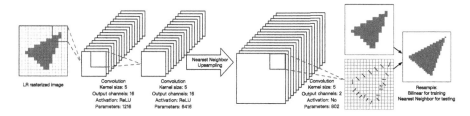

Fig. 4. The proposed SRPO network architecture. The whole network contains only three convolution layers, and no other computationally expensive operation is used. The output of this network is a two-channel offset map instead of a three-channel image.

their practice in real applications. The development of lightweight SR networks is also a popular research topic. [24] propose sub-pixel upsampling operation for SR networks and propose ESPCN as an early attempt in this field. [1] propose CARN that uses group convolution and implements a cascading mechanism upon a residual network for efficient SR. IMDN [11] extracts hierarchical features step-by-step by split operations and then aggregates them by simply using a 1×1 convolution Zhao et al. [33] construct an effective network with pixel attention, and the entire network contains only 200K parameters. Despite several years of attempts in this direction, even today's state-of-the-art network is far from being applied to real-time image rendering. More related to this work, [20] proposes edge-SR (eSR), a set of shallow convolutional layer SR networks that upscale images for edge devices. This level of computational overhead is likely to be used in real-time rendering. Thus we will also focus on the comparison with edge-SR in this paper.

3   Method

The methods studied in this paper all have strict computational constraints. It is difficult for the network to generate so-called "rich textures" with a small capacity. The resulting images are hardly any real improvement over more straightforward interpolation methods [20]. To generate realistic rich textures, we need to exponentially enlarge the networks we used, or even use generative adversarial models [10,27] (see Fig. 1). Many works reveal that a human's perception of an image's structure greatly affects the whole image's subjective perception [8–10,28]. Sharp edges are among the most critical parts affecting this structure's perception. With limited resources, we argue that enhancing the edges is more appropriate than generating textures in complex and challenging areas, as the interpolation method can already be an economical choice for these areas. Our method first upsamples the image using interpolation to ensure comparable results in areas other than edges. It then generates images with fine and sharp edges through the proposed network. At last, we combine the advantages of both through a fusion operation. We first introduce the proposed SRPO network in Sect. 3.1 and then describe the fusion method in Sect. 3.2.

3.1 SRPO Network

Motivation. We first describe the motivation for our proposed SRPO network. The graphics rendering pipeline can be summarized as four stages [2]: application stage, geometry processing stage, rasterization stage and pixel processing stage. The geometric primitive is sampled and discretized into rasterized images in the rasterization stage. The pixel processing stage involves pixel shading and blending operations. The post-processing anti-aliasing step is also implemented at the end of this stage. The current real-time graphics SR methods (e.g., AMD FSR) usually take the anti-aliased images as inputs, as these images have similar edges to natural ones. Under severe computation constraints, we can only use a minimal number of convolution or filtering operations to process the LR anti-aliased images. The method at this time does not have a significantly larger model capacity than the linear models, making it very difficult to generate sharp edges.

Our network design begins with the observations of the rasterized and anti-aliased images. As shown in Fig. 3, the rasterized image shows a jagged-like appearance, while the anti-aliased image has complex grayscale pixels along the edges. These edges make the image look more natural because they simulate the gradient distribution in natural images. At higher resolutions, rasterized images still exhibit the same jagged edges, and its anti-aliased images use finer-grained gradients to retouch the edges of the image. The residuals are equally complex due to the complex edges of both HR and LR anti-aliased images. This requires SR methods to generate complex residual images to compensate for it. On the contrary, the residuals of rasterized images are very regular. We only need to make up for this part of the pixel difference to get an HR rasterised image. This inspires us to develop an SR method on rasterized images at a small cost.

We further dive into the difference between high and low resolution rasterized images. When converting an LR rasterized image to an HR rasterized image, we only need to change the image at the edges from background pixel values to foreground pixel values, or vice versa. The pixel values that need to be changed can usually be found directly from the surrounding – *we can move the appropriate surrounding pixels to the new positions to complete the upsampling of the rasterized image.* In this paper, we use a pixel-level offset map to represent the movement of pixels. Our experiments show that such an offset can be obtained simply by training an ultra-lightweight network. This leads us to our approach: SR by predicting offsets (SRPO).

Network Architecture. We train a simple convolutional neural network F to predict the pixel-level offset map. This network takes the three-channel LR rasterized image $I^{LR} \in \mathbb{R}^{3 \times H \times W}$ as input and outputs a two-channel (x-axis and y-axis) offset map $\Omega = F(I^{LR}), \Omega \in \mathbb{R}^{2 \times sH \times sW}$, where s is the SR factor. The values in Ω indicate which pixel in I^{LR} the current pixel is composed of. For example, $(0,0)$ means no offset, that is, the corresponding pixels in I^{LR} are directly used for filling HR results. $(-1,-1)$ means to use the pixel relative to the lower-left corner of the current pixel. According to Fig. 3, most of the offsets should be 0. The super-resolved rasterized image $I_\Omega^{SR} \in \mathbb{R}^{3 \times sh \times sw}$ can be obtained by projecting the pixels of I^{LR} according to the offset map $I_\Omega^{SR} = P_{\text{nearest}}(I^{LR}, \Omega)$. The subscript nearest indicates that the projection process uses the nearest neighbor resampling method (the offsets are rounded) to produce similar sharp jagged edges.

The architecture of the proposed network is illustrated in Fig. 4. The whole network consists of two convolution layers. The first convolution layer extracts features from I^{LR} and generates 16 feature maps. The second convolution layer performs a non-linear mapping to these feature maps and generates the other 16 feature maps. For these two layers, the kernel size is set to 5×5, and the activation function is ReLU [7]. Note that the computation time of such a layer is only about two milliseconds for a 720P input image when using 8-bit integers for low-precision computations on some specially optimized computing devices. A nearest neighbor upsampling operation is performed on the feature maps produced by the second convolutional layer. At last, we use another convolution layer to aggregate the upsampled 16 feature maps to the offset map Ω. The entire network contains 8434 learnable parameters.

Network Training. The proposed network is trained self-super-vised as the ground truth offset maps are unavailable. The self-supervised learning process is modelled based on the fact that the projected I_Ω^{SR} should be close to the ground truth HR rasterized image I^{HR}. Recall that we want the result of the network could preserve image edges/structure information; the objective function can be formulated using SSIM loss [28,32]. The SSIM loss for pixel $[i, j]$ is defined as:

$$\mathcal{L}(i,j) = \frac{2\mu(I_\Omega^{SR})_{[i,j]}\mu(I^{HR})_{[i,j]} + C_1}{\mu(I_\Omega^{SR})_{[i,j]}^2 + \mu(I^{HR})_{[i,j]}^2 + C1} \times \frac{2\sigma(I_\Omega^{SR}, I^{HR})_{[i,j]} + C_2}{\sigma(I_\Omega^{SR})_{[i,j]}^2 + \sigma(I^{HR})_{[i,j]}^2 + C_2}, \quad (1)$$

where the subscript $[i,j]$ indicates pixel index, C_1 and C_2 are constant, $\mu(\cdot)$, $\sigma(\cdot)$, $\sigma(\cdot, \cdot)$ represent means, standard deviations and cross-covariance, and we omitted the dependence of means and standard deviations. The SSIM loss for the whole image is $\mathcal{L} = \frac{1}{s^2 WH} \sum_i^W \sum_j^H 1 - \mathcal{L}(i,j)$. Means and standard deviations are computed with a Gaussian filter. The resampling method used in the projection process can not be the nearest neighbor method during training as it produces only discrete results and is non-differentiable. We use differentiable resampling methods such as bilinear during training to ensure the back-propagation of the network. Training using Eq. (1) can automatically generate reasonable offset maps, although we do not know which offset map is optimal.

For the training data, obtaining real aligned data for training is challenging under most circumstances. For example, one may need to prepare a lot of aligned HR-LR image pairs for training to enable NVIDIA DLSS in one game. In this paper, we show that we can use general and simple rendered images for training, and the effect of the model can be well generalized to various game scenarios. Recall that the network generates sharp edges while upsampling of other areas is done by interpolation methods. Thus our training data only needs to contain

(a) Offset-SR   (b) Interpolation Result   (c) Offset Map   (d) Final Result

Fig. 5. We combine the edges in the offset-SR I_Ω^{SR} (a) and other areas in the interpolation upsampling result $I_\uparrow^{SR}$ (b) through the offset map (c). The final result is shown in (d). As can be seen, there are some non-smooth color transitions in (a) (see the red arrow) because the offset is zero in those places. Its actual effect is the effect of nearest neighbor upsampling. The final effect avoids this while preserving the edges (see the blue arrow). (Color figure online)

a wide variety of edges. We rendered 300 images of random geometric objects with random gradient colors, including triangles, circles, rings, lines and bezier curves. Figure 2 shows some image examples used for training. The LR training images are of size 128×128 and the $\times 2$ and the $\times 3$ HR images are of size 256×256 and 384×384, respectively.

For optimization, we use Adam optimizer [16] with $\beta_1 = 0.9$, $\beta_2 = 0.99$. The initial learning rate is 3×10^{-4} and halved every 7k iterations. In the training phase, we set total 40k iterations for our model. The mini-batch size is set to 16.

3.2 Offset-Guided Image Fusion

Although the obtained the SRPO result I_Ω^{SR} can bring images with sharp edges, the rest areas of the image are similar to the effect of nearest neighbour upsampling (the offsets of these areas are close to zero) and cannot be directly used as the final output. An example is show in Fig. 5(a). For convenience, we use the term I_Ω^{SR} as offset-SR. Simple interpolation methods can obtain reasonable upsampling results for these relatively flat areas. In this work, we use the Lanczos interpolation method, and we use $I_\uparrow^{SR}$ to represent the result. Next, we compute the linear combination of the corresponding pixels of the two images to fuse the sharp edges of the offset-SR I_Ω^{SR} with other areas of interpolated image $I_\uparrow^{SR}$. The final result can be formulated as $I^{SR} = \alpha \odot I_\Omega^{SR} + (1-\alpha) \odot I_\uparrow^{SR}$, where the $\alpha \in [0,1]$ is the blending mask, $\odot$ is the element-wise product. The offset map Ω contains the movement information for every pixel. If one pixel is replaced with another value during projection, this pixel belongs to an edge. We can use the offset map as the blending mask only with some processing: $\alpha_{[i,j]} = \omega_k \otimes \mathbb{I}\{\lfloor \Omega_{[i,j]} \rceil \neq 0\}$, where $\mathbb{I}\{\cdot\}$ is the indicator function and ω represent a 3×3 Gaussian blur filter with sigma 1.5.

Table 1. The quantitative results, the amount of floating-point operations and parameters of the different networks involved in our experiments. ↑ means the higher the better while ↓ means the lower the better.

Method	Parameters	FLOPs (G)	Metrics		
			PSNR ↑	SSIM ↑	LPIPS ↓
FSRCNN	12.64K	20.54	27.26	0.8343	0.1687
ESPCN	8.10K	6.30	27.16	0.8195	0.1775
eSR-CNN	1.97K	1.53	27.28	0.8495	0.1547
eSR-TM	1.57K	1.22	27.20	0.8506	0.1676
eSR-TR	0.6K	0.47	27.22	0.8490	0.1714
eSR-Max	0.036K	0.03	27.03	0.8504	0.1513
AMD FSR	-	-	27.56	0.8639	0.1650
SRPO (ours)	8.43K	8.50	26.97	0.8532	0.1501

4   Experiments

4.1   Comparison

We prepared our testing data using Unreal Engine 4 with online downloaded scenes and assets. We render the testing image with one sample per pixel under different resolutions and keep the rasterized and anti-aliased images. We also applied MLAA anti-aliasing for the HR rasterized images for the final comparison. All the tests are conducted using tone-mapped images. There are nine different scenes and hundreds of images, including a wide range of possible scenes in video games, e.g., city streets, gardens, palaces, people, indoor rooms, and spaceship interiors.

We first present a qualitative comparison of the proposed and existing methods. For the comparison, we include two classic light-weight SR networks FSR-CNN[1] [6] and ESPCN[2] [24], a series of SR networks designed for edge computing called eSR[3] [20] and AMD FSR. Note that FSRCNN includes seven layers and is not designed for real-time processing. We include them only for comparison. All the trainable methods are re-trained using our paired data for the best performance. For the AMD FSR method, we use the open-source implementation. Except for FSR, all the networks are trained and tested using Pytorch framework [22].

Figure 6 show some representative regions in our test set. It can be observed that the proposed method produces sharp edges very close to HR images. This

---

[1] For FSRCNN, we use the hyper-parameter of $D = 56$, $S = 12$ and $M = 4$.

[2] For ESPCN, we use the hyper-parameter of $D = 22$ and $S = 32$.

[3] For eSR family, we select four versions of eSR: eSR-MAX with $K = 3$ and $C = 1$; eSR-TR with $K = 5$ and $C = 2$; eSR-TM with $K = 7$ and $C = 4$; eSR-CNN with $C = 4$, $D = 3$ and $S = 6$.

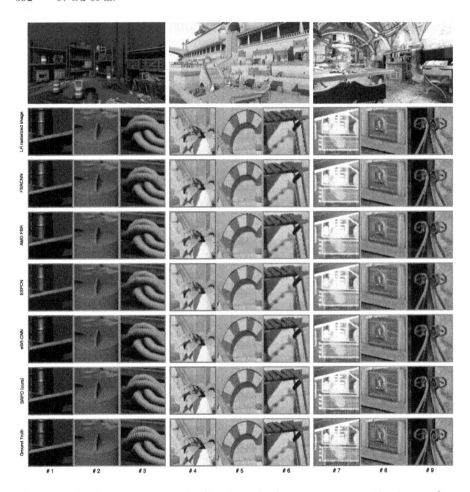

Fig. 6. Qualitative comparison of different methods using representative images from our test datasets. The SR factor is 2.

greatly improves the overall perceptual quality of SR images. While other methods use neural networks to directly predict output pixels, producing such sharp edges is difficult. The overall visual effect tends to be blurred. At some significant jagged edges (see the example #1, #2 and #6 in Fig. 6), the images generated by the other methods still show the jaggedness of the LR image but are only blurred. The proposed method performs well in these domains to remove aliasing amplification caused by upsampling. We can also observe that the proposed method still outperforms other methods even on some less apparent edges (without strong color contrast, see #8 in Fig. 6). The proposed SRPO does not regard these areas as edges that need to recover by moving pixels. The blending process provides suitable fallbacks for additional robustness. If the result of SRPO leaves any edge unprocessed (the corresponding offsets are all zeros), The whole method will go back to interpolation upsampling.

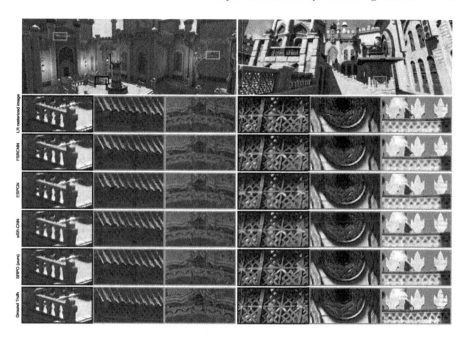

Fig. 7. Qualitative comparison of different methods using representative images from our test datasets. The SR factor is 3. Compared with ×2 SR, a larger SR factor brings challenges to all the methods. However, the proposed method can still produce sharp edges. This is mainly attributed to its paradigm of predicting offsets.

Generally, upsampling with a larger SR factor in real-time rendering will significantly drop image quality. Here we show the comparison results under a higher SR factor of 3 in Fig. 7. For this experiment, we compare with FSRCNN ($D = 56$, $S = 12$ and $M = 4$), ESPCN ($D = 16$ and $S = 6$) and eSR-CNN ($C = 8$, $D = 3$, $S = 15$). The proposed network remains the same architecture as the SR factor 2, only changing the upsampling to ×3. The FSR does not have ×2 version. As one can see, the proposed method maintains a good performance on the edges and surpasses the existing methods.

We next present the quantitative comparison of different methods. The comparison results are shown in Table 1. We also show the parameter numbers and floating-point operations [21] (FLOPs) of these methods. Since the optimization of some operations under different hardware environments is different, we use FLOPs to indicate the computational costs for each method without loss of generality. The FLOPs is calculated through a $3 \times 1280 \times 720$ (720p) image. It can be seen that since we do not optimize using pixel-wise losses such as l_1 and l_2-norm, the PSNR value of the proposed method is relatively low. But for the other two indicators, SSIM [28], and LPIPS [30], which are considered to be more relevant to human subjective evaluation [8], the proposed method achieves the level of superior or sub-optimal. This illustrates the pleasing visual effect of the proposed method.

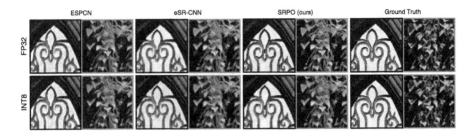

Fig. 8. The comparison of quantization effects. For ESPCN and eSR-CNN, the quantization process introduces artifacts that significantly affect image quality. The proposed method is robust to small perturbations because the offset used in the end should be changed to a rounded version.

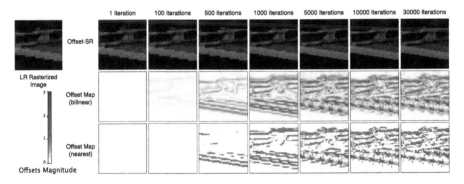

Fig. 9. The visualization of the intermediate training results. The offset maps (bilinear) indicate the float-point offsets used during training (bilinear resampling). The offset maps (nearest) indicate the rounded offsets. The color shows the magnitudes of the offset vectors. (Color figure online)

4.2 Quantization

The computation of deep learning methods involves intensive operations. Typically, deep learning training is conducted using 32-bit floating-point numbers. While efforts are being made to develop efficient SR networks, reducing inference computations to lower bit-depth representations can improve efficiency and reduce power consumption. For example, half-precision (16-bit) computations tend to be more efficient, and some advanced processing units can support 8-bit integer computations with greater efficiency. The throughput of 8-bit integer computations is almost twice that of half-precision and 4 times of single-precision. The good news is that more and more integrated circuits, especially mobile SoCs (system on a chip) have already integrated such advanced processing units, enabling similar technology to be applied on a larger scale. After training using single-precision (FP32), we apply static quantization [26] to all the layers of our network.

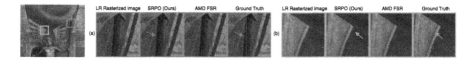

Fig. 10. Some failure cases of the proposed method. In case (a), the network cannot identify edges with such slopes due to the limited receptive field. In case (b), the network did not recognize this edge due to the low edge contrast.

As shown in Fig. 8, for other methods, quantization brings severe performance degradation and artifacts due to insufficient precision. There are two reasons for this phenomenon. First, since the existing network outputs pixel intensity values, the number of intensity values that the network can generate under an 8-bit integer is small. Artifacts due to loss of accuracy are unavoidable. Second, since the network involved in this paper is itself a small model, further quantification has a more noticeable impact on the final effect.

The method proposed in this paper is additionally robust to the loss of computing precision because the offset output by our method itself needs to be rounded. Although the raw output of the SRPO network will also be affected, a certain loss of precision will not significantly change the rounded offset (unless the value itself is around 0.5). Shifted pixels can retain their original precision (even for 16-bit high-dynamic images). Therefore, the proposed method is more suitable for quantification.

4.3 Interpretation of the Learning Process

We take a deep dive into the learning process of the proposed self-supervised scheme. Recall that we do not have any prior knowledge about what kind of offset map it should be. However, the self-supervised training automatically generates the desired offset. In Fig. 9, we visualize the training of the SRPO network. We have the following findings. Firstly, the training of offset is not achieved overnight. In the initial stage of training, although the output offset-sr does not change, the floating-point part of the offset has been evolving (see 1 and 100 iterations). The offset that significantly impacts the result during the training process will have a larger loss value, which the network will quickly learn. For example, the lower boundary of the orange horizontal bar in Fig. 9 learns faster than the upper boundary because the gradient of the lower boundary is larger than the upper boundary. As training progresses, complex structures appear in the optimized offset map. If the automatic learning of the network does not reveal it, such a complex structure is challenging to be summed up by the rules of manual design. The self-supervised learning paradigm plays an important role in this work.

4.4 Limitations

The first limitation is the scope of application of the proposed method. Many advanced graphic technologies in the industry like temporal supersampling, checkerboard rendering, variable-rate shading, or dynamic resolution scaling may affect the ideal condition of the rasterized images assumed in this work. However, we found that there can be little overlap between these techniques and the goals of this paper. The techniques described herein are more applicable to mobile devices and their graphics applications. On these devices, most advanced graphics techniques are difficult to apply. The proposed method is more suitable for these simpler graphics applications, which are equally important.

Secondly, the limited capacity of the proposed network also brings limitations. The first problem is that although the network is already very small and can be quantized, it may still not be enough for very high frame rate processing. We need more advanced network architecture designs, quantization methods, and computing devices to overcome this problem. Also, due to the limited network depth and receptive field, the results of SRPO still have some aliasing for some difficult edges, see Fig. 10(a). This is because detecting a line with such a slope requires a larger receptive field, which is difficult for a network with only three layers to achieve. Another limitation is the edges with low contrast, as shown in Fig. 10(b). In these areas, the network is hard to identify whether the pixel changes are caused by an edge or noise and color gradient.

There are many more challenging sources of aliasing in computer graphics, such as sub-pixel aliasing, thin ropes, thin objects that disappear and appear partially or entirely and shading aliasing. The proposed method can be expected to suffer from challenges, but these scenarios are also challenging to existing solutions. This paper is still a solid step in this direction.

5 Conclusion

In this paper, we propose a new method for real-time rendering. The proposed method uses an SRPO network to obtain images with sharp edges and then combines these edges with interpolation results. The SRPO network does not directly generate pixels. Instead, it moves appropriate surrounding pixels in LR rasterized image to the new positions to form the upsampled rasterized image. We also investigate the quantization effect of the proposed method. The proposed method can generate SR results with sharp edges and show good visual quality with less than 10K parameters.

Acknowledgement. This work was partly supported by SZSTC Grant No. JCYJ20190809172201639 and WDZC20200820200655001, Shenzhen Key Laboratory ZDSYS20210623092001004. We sincerely thank Yongfei Pu, Yuanlong Li, Jieming Li and Yuanlin Chen for contributing to this study.

References

1. Ahn, N., Kang, B., Sohn, K.A.: Fast, accurate, and lightweight super-resolution with cascading residual network. In: ECCV, pp. 252–268 (2018)
2. Akenine-Moller, T., Haines, E., Hoffman, N.: Real-Time Rendering. AK Peters/CRC Press (2019)
3. Chen, H., Gu, J., Zhang, Z.: Attention in attention network for image super-resolution. arXiv preprint arXiv:2104.09497 (2021)
4. Dai, T., Cai, J., Zhang, Y., Xia, S.T., Zhang, L.: Second-order attention network for single image super-resolution. In: CVPR, pp. 11065–11074 (2019)
5. Dong, C., Loy, C.C., He, K., Tang, X.: Image super-resolution using deep convolutional networks. TPAMI **38**(2), 295–307 (2015)
6. Dong, C., Loy, C.C., Tang, X.: Accelerating the super-resolution convolutional neural network. In: Leibe, B., Matas, J., Sebe, N., Welling, M. (eds.) ECCV 2016. LNCS, vol. 9906, pp. 391–407. Springer, Cham (2016). https://doi.org/10.1007/978-3-319-46475-6_25
7. Glorot, X., Bordes, A., Bengio, Y.: Deep sparse rectifier neural networks. In: Proceedings of the Fourteenth International Conference on Artificial Intelligence and Statistics, pp. 315–323. JMLR Workshop and Conference Proceedings (2011)
8. Jinjin, G., Haoming, C., Haoyu, C., Xiaoxing, Y., Ren, J.S., Chao, D.: PIPAL: a large-scale image quality assessment dataset for perceptual image restoration. In: Vedaldi, A., Bischof, H., Brox, T., Frahm, J.-M. (eds.) ECCV 2020. LNCS, vol. 12356, pp. 633–651. Springer, Cham (2020). https://doi.org/10.1007/978-3-030-58621-8_37
9. Gu, J., et al.: NTIRE 2022 challenge on perceptual image quality assessment. In: CVPR Workshops, pp. 951–967 (2022)
10. Gu, J., Shen, Y., Zhou, B.: Image processing using multi-code GAN prior. In: CVPR, pp. 3012–3021 (2020)
11. Hui, Z., Gao, X., Yang, Y., Wang, X.: Lightweight image super-resolution with information multi-distillation network. In: ACM MM, pp. 2024–2032 (2019)
12. Jimenez, J., Echevarria, J.I., Sousa, T., Gutierrez, D.: SMAA: enhanced subpixel morphological antialiasing. In: Computer Graphics Forum, vol. 31, pp. 355–364. Wiley Online Library (2012)
13. Kaplanyan, A.S., Sochenov, A., Leimkühler, T., Okunev, M., Goodall, T., Rufo, G.: DeepFovea: neural reconstruction for foveated rendering and video compression using learned statistics of natural videos. TOG **38**(6), 1–13 (2019)
14. Kim, J., Kwon Lee, J., Mu Lee, K.: Accurate image super-resolution using very deep convolutional networks. In: CVPR, pp. 1646–1654 (2016)
15. Kim, J., Kwon Lee, J., Mu Lee, K.: Deeply-recursive convolutional network for image super-resolution. In: CVPR, pp. 1637–1645 (2016)
16. Kingma, D.P., Ba, J.: Adam: a method for stochastic optimization. arXiv preprint arXiv:1412.6980 (2014)
17. Ledig, C., et al.: Photo-realistic single image super-resolution using a generative adversarial network. In: CVPR, pp. 4681–4690 (2017)
18. Li, Z., et al.: Blueprint separable residual network for efficient image super-resolution. In: CVPR, pp. 833–843 (2022)
19. Lim, B., Son, S., Kim, H., Nah, S., Mu Lee, K.: Enhanced deep residual networks for single image super-resolution. In: CVPR Workshops, pp. 136–144 (2017)
20. Michelini, P.N., Lu, Y., Jiang, X.: edge-SR: super-resolution for the masses. In: WACV, pp. 1078–1087 (2022)

21. Molchanov, P., Tyree, S., Karras, T., Aila, T., Kautz, J.: Pruning convolutional neural networks for resource efficient inference. arXiv preprint arXiv:1611.06440 (2016)
22. Paszke, A., et al.: PyTorch: an imperative style, high-performance deep learning library. In: NeurIPS, vol. 32, pp. 8026–8037 (2019)
23. Reshetov, A.: Morphological antialiasing. In: Proceedings of the Conference on High Performance Graphics, pp. 109–116 (2009)
24. Shi, W., et al.: Real-time single image and video super-resolution using an efficient sub-pixel convolutional neural network. In: CVPR, pp. 1874–1883 (2016)
25. Tai, Y., Yang, J., Liu, X.: Image super-resolution via deep recursive residual network. In: CVPR, pp. 3147–3155 (2017)
26. Thomas, M.M., Vaidyanathan, K., Liktor, G., Forbes, A.G.: A reduced-precision network for image reconstruction. TOG **39**(6), 1–12 (2020)
27. Wang, X., et al.: ESRGAN: enhanced super-resolution generative adversarial networks. In: Leal-Taixé, L., Roth, S. (eds.) ECCV 2018. LNCS, vol. 11133, pp. 63–79. Springer, Cham (2019). https://doi.org/10.1007/978-3-030-11021-5_5
28. Wang, Z., Bovik, A.C., Sheikh, H.R., Simoncelli, E.P.: Image quality assessment: from error visibility to structural similarity. TIP **13**(4), 600–612 (2004)
29. Xiao, L., Nouri, S., Chapman, M., Fix, A., Lanman, D., Kaplanyan, A.: Neural supersampling for real-time rendering. TOG **39**(4), 142-1 (2020)
30. Zhang, R., Isola, P., Efros, A.A., Shechtman, E., Wang, O.: The unreasonable effectiveness of deep features as a perceptual metric. In: CVPR, pp. 586–595 (2018)
31. Zhang, Y., Li, K., Li, K., Wang, L., Zhong, B., Fu, Y.: Image super-resolution using very deep residual channel attention networks. In: ECCV, pp. 286–301 (2018)
32. Zhao, H., Gallo, O., Frosio, I., Kautz, J.: Loss functions for image restoration with neural networks. IEEE Trans. Comput. Imaging **3**(1), 47–57 (2016)
33. Zhao, H., Kong, X., He, J., Qiao, Yu., Dong, C.: Efficient image super-resolution using pixel attention. In: Bartoli, A., Fusiello, A. (eds.) ECCV 2020. LNCS, vol. 12537, pp. 56–72. Springer, Cham (2020). https://doi.org/10.1007/978-3-030-67070-2_3

Animation from Blur: Multi-modal Blur Decomposition with Motion Guidance

Zhihang Zhong[1,3], Xiao Sun[2], Zhirong Wu[2], Yinqiang Zheng[1(✉)], Stephen Lin[2], and Imari Sato[1,3]

[1] The University of Tokyo, Tokyo, Japan
`zhong@is.s.u-tokyo.ac.jp, yqzheng@ai.u-tokyo.ac.jp`
[2] Microsoft Research Asia, Beijing, China
[3] National Institute of Informatics, Tokyo, Japan

Abstract. We study the challenging problem of recovering detailed motion from a single motion-blurred image. Existing solutions to this problem estimate a single image sequence without considering the motion ambiguity for each region. Therefore, the results tend to converge to the mean of the multi-modal possibilities. In this paper, we explicitly account for such motion ambiguity, allowing us to generate multiple plausible solutions all in sharp detail. The key idea is to introduce a motion guidance representation, which is a compact quantization of 2D optical flow with only four discrete motion directions. Conditioned on the motion guidance, the blur decomposition is led to a specific, unambiguous solution by using a novel two-stage decomposition network. We propose a unified framework for blur decomposition, which supports various interfaces for generating our motion guidance, including human input, motion information from adjacent video frames, and learning from a video dataset. Extensive experiments on synthesized datasets and real-world data show that the proposed framework is qualitatively and quantitatively superior to previous methods, and also offers the merit of producing physically plausible and diverse solutions. Code is available at https://github.com/ zzh-tech/Animation-from-Blur.

Keywords: Deblurring · Multi-modal image-to-video · Deep learning

1 Introduction

Motion blur appears in an image when the recorded scene undergoes change during the exposure period of the camera. Although such blur may impart a dynamic quality to a photograph, it is often desirable to invert this blur to produce a sharper image with clearer visual detail. Conventionally, this deblurring task is treated as a one-to-one mapping problem, taking a motion blurred image

Supplementary Information The online version contains supplementary material available at https://doi.org/10.1007/978-3-031-19800-7_35.

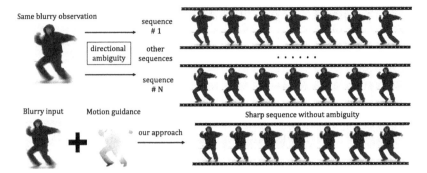

Fig. 1. This paper studies the challenging problem of recovering the sharp image sequence from blurry input caused by relative motion. We first identify the fundamental directional motion ambiguity in this problem, which prevents the network to learn effectively. In order to solve this ambiguity, we propose to use motion as a guidance for conditional blur decomposition. Our approach demonstrates strong performance for recovering sharp visual details in motions

as input and producing a single output image corresponding to a single time instant during the exposure. Recently, attention has been drawn to a more challenging problem of extracting an image sequence [11] instead, where the images correspond to multiple time instances that span the exposure period, thus forming a short video clip from the blurred motion.

Blur decomposition from a single blurry image faces the fundamental problem of motion ambiguity [27]. Each independent and uniform motion blurred region in an image can correspond to either a forward or a backward motion sequence, both of which are plausible without additional knowledge. With multiple motion blurred regions in an image, the number of potential solutions increases exponentially, with many that are physically infeasible. For example, in Fig. 1, there exists multiple human dance movements that can correspond to the same observed blurry image, since the movement of each limb of the dancer can be independent. However, existing methods for blur decomposition are designed to predict a single solution among them. Moreover, this directional ambiguity brings instability to the training process, especially when the motion pattern is complex. As a result, this ambiguity, when left unaddressed as in current methods, would lead to poorly diversified and low-quality results.

In this work, we introduce a motion guidance representation to tackle the inherent directional motion ambiguity. The motion guidance is an optical flow representation quantized into four major quadrant directions, describing the motion field only roughly. Given the input blurry image, conditioned on the compact motion guidance, the blur decomposition now becomes a nearly deterministic one-to-one mapping problem without directional ambiguity. Empirically, we find that the decomposition network shows significantly better training convergence with this conditioning on an additional guidance input.

Given the blurry image and additional motion guidance as inputs, we propose a two-stage blur decomposition network to predict the image sequence. The first stage expands the blurry image into an image sequence based on the motion guidance, and the second stage refines the visual details in a residual fashion to generate high-quality images. Our unified framework supports various interfaces for motion guidance acquisition: 1) Through a guidance predictor network learned from a dataset. The guidance predictor network is a VAE-GAN [18,44] which learns a multi-modal distribution over plausible guidances. During inference, given an input blurry image together with sampled noises, the predictor can produce multiple guidance maps. 2) By additional information of dense optical flow computed from temporal frames. When the blurry image input is captured and sampled from a video sequence. The optical flow field between the blurry input and its adjacent frame can be used to compute the motion guidance. This motion guidance reflects the actual motion direction. 3) Through user input. Since the guidance is simple and compact, it can be annotated by outlining the region contours and their motion directions interactively.

To train our model, we synthesize blurry images from high speed videos following the pipeline of REDS [22]. Specifically, we validate the performance of our model on human dance videos from Aist++ [20] which only contain motion blur caused by human movement from a static camera, and general scene videos (GOPRO [23], DVD [31]), which are dominated by camera motion. Our approach provides a significant qualitative and quantitative improvement over previous methods by introducing a novel motion guidance representation to address the fundamental directional ambiguity in blur decomposition. Furthermore, due to the compactness of motion guidance representation, our unified framework may only need to be trained once, while supporting various decomposition scenarios under different modalities. The motion guidance obtained through different interfaces and their corresponding decomposition results reflect physically plausible and diverse solutions from our multi-modal framework.

2   Related Works

In this section, we review the related literature on image and video deblurring, blur decomposition, as well as multi-modal image translation.

2.1   Deblurring

Deblurring refers to the task of estimating a sharp image from a blurry input, where the blur is often caused by scene or camera motion. Traditional deblurring methods model the blur as a blur kernel operating on a sharp image via a convolution operation. A number of useful priors have been proposed to infer the latent sharp image and the corresponding blur kernel, such as total variation [3], hyper-Laplacian [15], image sparsity [19], and l_0-norm gradient [36]. Recently, image and video deblurring has benefited from the advancement of deep convolution neural networks (CNNs). A coarse-to-fine pyramid CNN structure is widely used for the single-image deblurring task and achieves impressive performance [23,32,38]. Also, generative adversarial networks (GANs) have been adopted to improve the perceptual quality of deblurring results [16,17]. Temporal dependency across adjacent frames is another source of information which could be utilized to recover the sharp image [31,34]. Recurrent architectures are shown be effective at exploiting such temporal information [13,24,41,42]. Extensive studies in these works demonstrate that deep neural networks are able to approximate blur kernels well in an implicit way.

2.2   Blur Decomposition

Blur decomposition attempts to recover the full image sequence from a blurry input caused by object and camera motion during the exposure time. [11] are the first to tackle this problem and propose a pairwise order-invariant loss to improve convergence in training. [27] present a method that extracts a motion representation from the blurry image through self-supervised learning, and then feeds it into a recurrent video decoder to generate a sharp image sequence. [2] utilize an encoder-decoder structure with a spatial transformer network to estimate the middle frame and other frames simultaneously with a transformation consistency loss. Assuming that the background is known, DeFMO [28] embeds a blurred object into a latent space, from which it is rendered into an image sequence that is constrained to be sharp, time-consistent, and independent of the background.

When the input is a blurry video, [10] design a cascade scheme, *i.e.*, deblurring followed by interpolation, to tackle the problem. To avoid errors introduced in the first stage, Shen *et al.* propose BIN [29] with a pyramid module and an inter-pyramid recurrent module to jointly estimate the latent sharp sequence. [1] achieve blurry video decomposition by first estimating the optical flow and then predicting the latent sequence by warping the decoded features. In addition, methods for blur decomposition also consider exploiting high-frequency temporal information from event cameras [21,25].

None of the existing methods address the fundamental ambiguity that exists with motion directions. We are the first to address this by conditioning the decomposition process via a novel motion guidance approach. We also design a flexible blur decomposition network, which can produce diverse decomposition results using guidance from the proposed interfaces for different modalities.

2.3   Image-to-Image/Video Translation

Our work is related to image-to-image translation networks [9] with applications for image synthesis [26] and style transfer [43]. GANs [6,12] and VAEs [14] are two popular approaches for training generative models. Both models can easily be conditioned by feeding additional inputs, such as in conditional VAE [30] and infoGAN [4]. Blur decomposition can be formulated as a similar image-to-image translation problem. However, the inherent motion ambiguity in the blurry image prevents the model from converging to a single optimal solution.

We thus introduce a new motion guidance representation to disambiguate the motion directions.

Multi-modal image translation is a promising direction to generate a distribution of results given a single input. Approaches along this direction combine VAE and GAN, so that stochastic variables in VAE could sample from a distribution, while GAN is used to encourage realistic generations. Notable works include VAE-GAN [18] and BicycleGAN [44]. Our guidance predictor follows VAE-GAN [18] to generate multi-modal motion guidance. We note that this technical element is not among the contributions of our paper.

Learning to animate a static image is a fascinating application. Learning-based methods either predict the motion field [5,7] which is later used to generate videos, or directly predict the next frames [37,39]. Our work focuses on animating a specific kind of input image with motion blur, which is physically informative to recover the image sequence.

3   Methodology

The Blur Decomposition Problem. A blurred image can be considered as an average of successive relatively sharp images over the exposure time

$$I_b = \frac{1}{T} \int_0^T I^t dt, \tag{1}$$

which can be approximately expressed in the following discrete form when T is large enough, $i.e.$, $I^1 \cdots I^T$ is a high-frame-rate sequence

$$\frac{1}{T}(I^1 + ... + I^T) = I_b. \tag{2}$$

Note that this image averaging process is simulated in an approximately linear space through applying inverse gamma calibration to RGB images [22,23]. Our goal is to invert this blurring process to estimate a finite sequence of sharp images which are uniformly distributed over the exposure time

$$I_b \xrightarrow{\mathbf{D}} \mathbf{I} = \{I^t, t \in 1, \cdots T\}. \tag{3}$$

This is a highly ill-posed problem because given the blurry image I_b, there are infinitely many solutions per pixel (u, v) among the sharp images if these sharp images are treated as independent

$$\frac{1}{T}(I^1(u,v) + ... + I^T(u,v)) = I_b(u,v). \tag{4}$$

However, assuming the images exist in succession over a short period of time and that the pixels are rarely affected by saturation and occlusions/disocclusions, then the following holds true: the pixels in these images are highly correlated

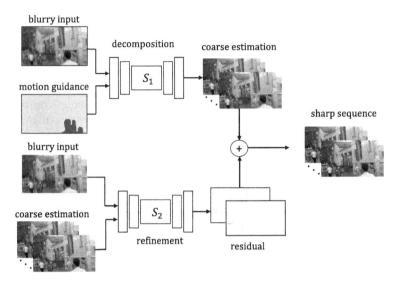

Fig. 2. Architecture of our motion guided blur decomposition network. It consists of two successive stages. The first stage S_1 concatenates the blurry image I_b and motion guidance G as input and outputs a rough image sequence. The second stage S_2 then refines the visual details in a residual fashion

and their dependencies can be described by the optical flow F^t of a sharp image I^t to its next frame I^{t+1},

$$I^t(u, v) = I^{t+1}(F^t(u, v)). \tag{5}$$

Supposing that we are given the optical flow fields for all frames in the target sequence $\mathbf{F} = \{F^t, t \in 1, \cdots T - 1\}$, Eqs. 4 and 5 form a linear system which can be solved with a unique solution. In other words, the ground truth motions between sharp images resolve the ambiguity problem in Eq. 3.

Motion-Guided Decomposition. We propose to solve the decomposition problem in Eq. 3 in two steps. The first step estimates the motions $\mathbf{F}$ during the exposure time, *e.g.*, by learning a motion predictor $\mathcal{P}$ for the blurry image,

$$I_b \overset{\mathcal{P}}{\longmapsto} \hat{\mathbf{F}}. \tag{6}$$

The second step learns a motion guided decomposition network $\mathcal{S}$ that takes both the blurry image and an estimated motion guidance as input to predict the sharp image sequence,

$$(I_b, \hat{\mathbf{F}}) \overset{\mathcal{S}}{\longmapsto} \mathbf{I} = \{\hat{I}^t, t \in 1, \cdots T\}. \tag{7}$$

As a result, the ambiguity is explicitly decoupled from the decomposition network $\mathcal{S}$, and only exists in the motion predictor $\mathcal{P}$.

Predicting the motion guidance with frame-wise optical flow would still be a difficult task. In practice, motion ambiguity will be complex, because the ambiguities of the independent moving regions in the image can be arbitrarily combined. However, we notice that the ambiguity mainly lies in the forward and backward directions of the motions, and hence the motion guidance does not need to be precise to frame-wise and continuous values to resolve the ambiguity. We therefore propose a compact motion guidance representation to replace the accurate optical flow, which enables the decomposition network to adapt to different input modalities. In the following, we describe the compact motion guidance representation in Sect. 3.1, the blur decomposition network conditioned on the motion guidance in Sect. 3.2, and three distinct interfaces for acquiring the motion guidance in Sect. 3.3.

3.1   Motion Guidance Representation

Given accurate dense optical flow sequence $\mathbf{F} = \{F^t, t \in 1, \cdots T - 1\}$, the blur decomposition problem can be solved without ambiguity. However, dense optical flow sequence is difficult to obtain and to predict accurately, and hence it may not be an ideal representation as a guidance.

We notice that the ambiguity for blur decomposition is in the motion directions. For example, if $\mathbf{F} = \{F^1, ..., F^{T-1}\}$ is one possible motion of the blurry image I_b and the corresponding sharp image sequence is $\mathbf{I} = \{I^1, ..., I^T\}$, then there also exists another reverse motion $\mathbf{F}_{\mathrm{bac}} = \{F_{\mathrm{bac}}^{T-1}, ..., F_{\mathrm{bac}}^1\}$ with the corresponding sharp image sequence $\mathbf{I}_{\mathrm{inv}} = \{I^T, ..., I^1\}$ which leads to the same blurry image I_b, where F_{bac}^t is the backward optical flow between I^t and I^{t+1}. Providing a crude motion direction may be sufficient to resolve the ambiguity.

Motivated by this observation, we design a compact guidance representation by motion quantization. We first assume that the motion directions within the exposure time do not change abruptly. This is generally true when the shutter speed is not extremely slow compared with object motion. We thus use the aggregated flow to represent the motion pattern for the full sequence $\bar{F} = \sum_1^T F^t$. We further quantize the aggregated flow into four quadrant directions and an additional motionless class which takes flows below a certain magnitude. Empirically, we find four quadrant directions to be adequate for disambiguating motion directions. We denote the motion guidance as G.

3.2   Motion Guided Blur Decomposition Network

Given the blurry image and the motion guidance, the sharp image sequence is predicted via a blur decomposition network $\mathcal{S}$. Once the model is trained, it can be used to decompose a blurry image into different sharp image sequences simply by providing it with the corresponding motion guidance. In this section, we illustrate the model architecture and training loss in detail.

Training the network requires a dataset of triplet samples $(I_b, G, \mathbf{I})$, consisting of the blurry image I_b, the ground truth sharp image sequence $\mathbf{I}$, and motion guidance G derived from $\mathbf{I}$. We follow the common practice [22,23] of synthesizing

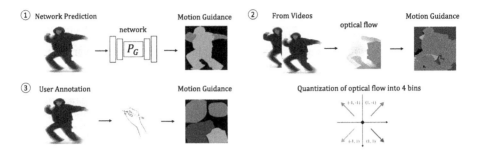

Fig. 3. Motion guidance acquisition. We represent motion guidance as a quantized motion vector into 4 quadrant directions. Due to its compactness, the guidance could be obtained from a network, videos or user annotations

a blurry image by accumulating sharp images over time according to Eq. 2, which is implemented in linear space through inverse gamma calibration. We use a off-the-shelf optical flow estimator [33] for deriving $\mathbf{F}$ and the guidance G.

Figure 2 illustrates our two-stage workflow of $\mathcal{S}$. The first stage estimates a rough dynamic image sequence, and the second stage refines the visual details in a residual fashion. Both networks adopt a similar encoder-decoder architecture. The architecture details can be found in the supplementary materials. The two-stage blur decomposition network outputs the sharp image sequence prediction $\hat{\mathbf{I}}$. We adopt commonly used $\mathcal{L}_2$ loss function for supervising the decomposition,

$$\mathcal{L}_2 = \|\mathbf{I} - \hat{\mathbf{I}}\|_2^2. \tag{8}$$

3.3 Motion Guidance Acquisition

We provide three interfaces to acquire the motion guidance: learning to predict the motion guidance, motion from video, and user input, as illustrated in Fig. 3.

Multi-modal Motion Prediction Network. The directional ambiguity now exists in the motion guidance representation. To account for the ambiguity, we train a multi-modal network to generate multiple physically plausible guidances given a blurry image. We follow the framework of cVAE-GAN [18,30] for multi-modal image translation as shown in Fig. 4.

The guidance prediction network comprises an encoder $\mathcal{P}_E$ and a generator $\mathcal{P}_G$. The encoder $\mathcal{P}_E$ converts the ground truth guidance into a latent stochastic variable by $\mathbf{z} = \mathcal{P}_E(G)$, and the generator predicts the guidance given the latent code and the blurry input $\hat{G} = \mathcal{P}_G(\mathbf{z}, I_b)$. The latent variable $\mathbf{z}$ is considered to follow a Gaussian distribution $\mathcal{N}(0, 1)$, and this stochastic variable is used to model the directional distribution that exists in the motion space. At the testing phase, multi-modal motion predictions can be generated by randomly sampling the latent vector $\mathbf{z}$ from a Gaussian distribution.

The overall network is trained with a combination of a GAN loss $\mathcal{L}_{\mathrm{GAN}}$ on the guidance predictions, a VAE loss $\mathcal{L}_{\mathrm{VAE}}$, and a Kullback-Leibler (KL) divergence

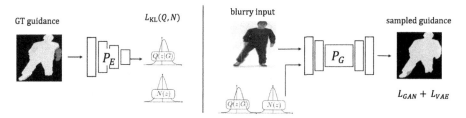

Fig. 4. Framework of the multi-modal motion guidance prediction network.
We mainly follow the cVAE-GAN [18,30], and adapt it to our problem to generate
multiple physically plausible guidances from a blurry image

loss $\mathcal{L}_{\mathrm{KL}}$ for the stochastic variable $\mathbf{z}$ as in [44],

$$
\begin{aligned}
\mathcal{L}_{\text{guidance}} =&\lambda_1 \mathcal{L}_{\mathrm{GAN}}(\mathcal{P}_E, \mathcal{P}_G) \\
&+ \lambda_2 \mathcal{L}_{\mathrm{VAE}}(\mathcal{P}_E, \mathcal{P}_G) + \lambda_3 \mathcal{L}_{\mathrm{KL}}(\mathbf{z}||\mathcal{N}(0,1)),
\end{aligned}
\tag{9}
$$

where $\lambda_1, \lambda_2, \lambda_3$ are mixing coefficients for the losses. The architecture details
can be found in the supplementary materials.

Motion from Video. We assume that the motion direction does not change
abruptly in a short time. Thus, the motion direction in the blurry image can be
approximated by the motion to the adjacent frames, if a video is provided. Hence,
our method can be directly applied to video deblurring without any modification.
In the experiment, our method is also compared with the state-of-the-art video
deblurring methods and shows better performance.

Human Annotation. The compact quantized motion guidance provides a
friendly interface to our blur decomposition network. Given a blurry image,
the user can generate multiple plausible sharp video clips simply by drawing the
outlines of the blurry regions and arbitrarily specifying their motion directions.

4 Experiments

We show the details of the used datasets in Sect. 4.1, single image and video
decomposition results in Sect. 4.2 and Sect. 4.3, real-world evaluation in Sect. 4.4,
guidance robustness analysis in Sect. 4.5, as well as ablation study in Sect. 4.6.

4.1 Datasets

Existing dataset for blur decomposition [29] introduces 1/3 temporal overlaps
between adjacent blurred frames. This violates the actual blur occurred in real
world. We thus create datasets by our own where blurry frames have almost no
temporal overlaps. One of our datasets for general scenes (GenBlur) consists of
high-fps videos used by related works [11,27], but with a better pipeline [22] to
simulate the formation of blur.

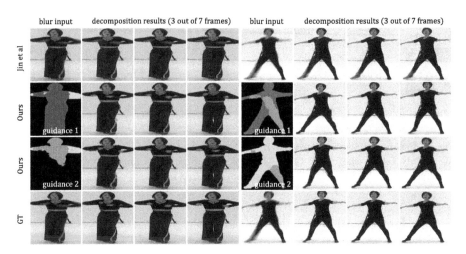

Fig. 5. Qualitative comparison with single image decomposition baseline method [11]. Given a blurry image, our method can generate multiple physically plausible motion guidance and recover distinct sharp image sequences based on each motion guidance. The baseline Jin *et al.* fails, resulting in a sequence with little motion. Please pay attention to the motion on the hands of the left dancer and the legs of the right dancer

GenBlur. We synthesize the GenBlur dataset using high-frame-rate (240fps) videos from GOPRO [23], DVD [31], and videos collected by ourselves. To suppress noise and video compression artifact [24], the image resolution is uniformly down-sampled to 960×540. We follow a widely used blur synthesis technique proposed in [22], that first employs an off-the-shelf CNN [8] to interpolate frames into a much higher fps (240fps → 7680fps) to avoid unnatural spikes or steps in the blurred trajectory [35]. In the interpolated videos, sets of 128 frames (non-overlapping) are averaged in linear space through inverse gamma calibration to synthesize blurred images. Instead of using all the 128 frames as ground truth clear images, we evenly sample 7 images among them to keep consistent with the previous work [11]. There are 161 and 31 videos for the train and test set, respectively. This dataset consists mainly of urban scenes, and the motion is dominated by camera ego-motion.

B-Aist++. The problem arising from directional ambiguity is particularly severe when there are multiple independent motions in the image. We thus synthesize another dataset specifically to highlight this issue by using videos from a dance dataset Aist++ [20] which contains complex human body movements by professional dancers. We use the same pipeline as for GenBlur to synthesize blurry images and corresponding sharp image sequences. The synthesized blurry dataset is denoted as B-Aist++. There are 73 and 32 videos for the train and test set. The images are in resolution of 960×720. This dataset contains complex human motion and the camera is stationary.

4.2   Blurry Image Decomposition

Qualitative Evaluation. We qualitatively compare our result with the state-of-the-art single image based blurry decomposition method [11] in Fig. 5. B-Aist++ is used for comparison because of its complex directional ambiguities. In the second and third rows, we demonstrate diversity in our blur decomposition results through the use of different motion guidance sampled from our motion predictor $\mathcal{P}$. Ground-truth is presented in the last row.

Existing methods such as [11] are unable to resolve the directional ambiguity in motion blur. For example, for the blur in the second dancer's legs, they cannot determine whether the legs are being spread out or drawn in. Consequently, in the case of data with high directional ambiguity such as B-Aist++, the moving range of the generated sharp frames is limited. In contrast, our multi-modal method incorporates directional guidance to remove ambiguity, leading to multiple coherent natural motions that look physically plausible. To better perceive the temporal variation in the decomposition results, we strongly recommend the reader to check out the videos in our supplementary materials.

Table 1. Quantitative evaluation of single blurry image decomposition. For our method, we predict multiple motion guidance from our guidance predictor network. $P_\#$ denotes we evaluate $\#$ number of plausible decomposition results for each input, and choose the best case. The results of Jin *et al.* [11] represent the best performance calculated as using either the forward or reverse outputs, following the original paper. Our approach outperforms Jin *et al.* [11] by a large margin even with a single sampling

Dataset Method	B-Aist++			GenBlur		
	PSNR ↑	SSIM ↑	LPIPS ↓	PSNR ↑	SSIM ↑	LPIPS ↓
Jin *et al.* [11]	17.01	0.540	0.192	20.88	0.621	0.283
Ours ($\mathcal{P}_1$)	19.97	0.860	0.089	23.41	0.737	0.267
Ours ($\mathcal{P}_3$)	22.44	0.898	0.068	23.56	0.740	0.263
Ours ($\mathcal{P}_5$)	**23.49**	**0.911**	**0.060**	**23.61**	**0.741**	**0.260**

Quantitative Evaluation. We report quantitative comparison results on B-Aist++ and GenBlur in Table 1. Following common practice, PSNR, SSIM and LPIPS [40] are used as evaluation metrics. Our method can generate multiple decomposition results by sampling multiple motion guidances from the motion predictor $\mathcal{P}$. In the table, $\mathcal{P}_\#$ denotes that $\#$ motion guidances are sampled from the predictor and the best result among the samples is reported. It can be seen that our method outperforms Jin *et al.* [11] by a large margin and more samples leads to better best results.

4.3   Blurry Video Decomposition

Qualitative Evaluation. As explained in Sect. 3.3, our method can be directly applied to video based decomposition without modification. The motion

Blur video input   BIN   Ours   BIN   Ours   GT

Fig. 6. Qualitative comparison with blurry video decomposition baseline method BIN [29]. Our approach uses the guidance calculated from the input video itself. For close up investigation, our method recovers much sharper visual details than the baseline method, *e.g.*, the text in the blurry input

Table 2. Quantitative evaluation of blurry video decomposition. The motion guidance for our method is obtained from the optical flow in the input blurry video. Our method outperforms the baseline BIN [29] by a large margin of 1.16 dB and 2.22 dB absolute PSNR on B-AIST++ and GenBlur respectively

Dataset Method	B-Aist++			GenBlur		
	PSNR ↑	SSIM ↑	LPIPS ↓	PSNR ↑	SSIM ↑	LPIPS ↓
BIN [29]	22.84	0.903	0.068	24.82	0.805	0.157
Ours (guidance from video)	**24.03**	**0.911**	**0.067**	**27.04**	**0.858**	**0.122**

guidance used for our decomposition network is quantized from the optical flow between adjacent frames.

Figure 6 presents a visual comparison between our result and the state-of-the-art video-based method BIN [29] on general scenes (GenBlur). Our decomposition results surpass those of the video-based model, with much clearer details. It is worth noting that since the adjacent frames themselves are blurred, the estimated optical flows are not accurate. However, due to the effective direction augmentation and the need for only coarse directional guidance, the learned decomposition network is robust and effective. Also, please see the videos in our supplementary for better perception.

Quantitative Evaluation. When comparing with the video-based method BIN [29], we use motion guidance estimated from adjacent frames using the off-the-shelf flow estimator [33], denoted as *vid.* in Table 2. Our method is clearly superior to [29] in terms of all metrics.

4.4   Real-World Evaluation

We further captured real-world blurry image for validating the generalization ability of the proposed method. Because the blurry image is captured in real world, no ground truth sharp image sequences can be used for quantitative evaluation. We display the visual results on real-world data when a user provides directional guidance in Fig. 7. The results demonstrate that our method can generalize well on real data. We also show real-world evaluations with the guidance prediction network in the appendix.

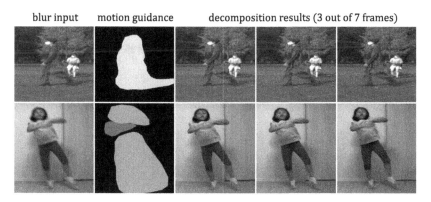

Fig. 7. Results on real-world captured blurry image. We manually provide the motion guidance and recover the image sequence using our decomposition network. Although trained on synthetic data, our model successfully generalizes on real-world data. Please notice the relative position between the door frame and the legs of the girl in the bottom

4.5   Robustness of Motion Guidance

The errors of motion guidance may come from two sources: one by incorrect prediction or human annotation, one by optical flow quantization. For the first case, the model may tolerate guidance errors in the sharp regions. We demonstrate this by showing results using fit, dilated, and eroded guidance in Fig. 8. The decomposition model may identify the pixels are non-blurry and preserve the original details, no matter what guidance prediction is given (dilate result). The model cannot recover a blurry region and may introduce artifacts if it is not provided with a meaningful guidance (erode result). For the second case, please refer to the ablation experiment in the supplementary material, which shows that quantization into 4 bins is sufficient to achieve good performance.

| fit | fit result | dilate | dilate result | erode | erode result |

Fig. 8. The influence of incorrect prediction or human annotation. Our approach may tolerate guidance errors in the sharp regions

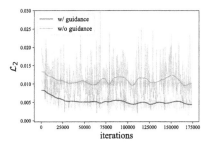

Fig. 9. Training curves for the decomposition network with and without motion guidance. With extra guidance input to disambiguate the motion direction, the network is able to fit to the data a lot easier

Table 3. Ablation studies on decomposition network architecture. We ablate the effectiveness of refinement work by studying 1-stage estimation and 2-stage estimation. The refinement network significantly improves the performance. 1-stage and 2-stage models are set to similar sizes by adjusting channel numbers, for fair comparison

Method	PSNR ↑	SSIM ↑	LPIPS ↓
1-stage	24.47	0.912	0.074
2-stage	**25.45**	**0.933**	**0.054**

4.6 Ablation Studies

We present ablation studies on motion guidance and the multi-stage architecture. The experiments are conducted on B-Aist++ and the metrics are calculated using ground-truth motion guidance. Based on Fig. 9, introducing motion guidance in the training stage greatly improves convergence by eliminating directional ambiguity. Table 3 shows that introducing a two-stage coarse-and-refinement pipeline while maintaining the model size may bring about 1dB gain.

5 Conclusions

In this work, we address the problem of recovering a sharp motion sequence from a motion-blurred image. We bring to light the issue of directional ambiguity and propose the first solution to this challenging problem by introducing motion guidance to train networks. The proposed method can adapt to blurry input of different modalities by using the corresponding interfaces including a multi-modal prediction network, motion from video, and user annotation. The motion sequences generated by our method are superior to existing methods in terms of quality and diversity.

Acknowledgement. This work was supported by D-CORE Grant from Microsoft Research Asia, JSPS KAKENHI Grant Numbers 22H00529, and 20H05951, and JST, the establishment of university fellowships towards the creation of science technology innovation, Grant Number JPMJFS2108.

References

1. Argaw, D.M., Kim, J., Rameau, F., Kweon, I.S.: Motion-blurred video interpolation and extrapolation. In: AAAI Conference on Artificial Intelligence (2021)
2. Argaw, D.M., Kim, J., Rameau, F., Zhang, C., Kweon, I.S.: Restoration of video frames from a single blurred image with motion understanding. In: Proceedings of the IEEE/CVF Conference on Computer Vision and Pattern Recognition Workshops, pp. 701–710 (2021)
3. Chan, T.F., Wong, C.K.: Total variation blind deconvolution. IEEE Trans. Image Process. **7**(3), 370–375 (1998)
4. Chen, X., Duan, Y., Houthooft, R., Schulman, J., Sutskever, I., Abbeel, P.: Infogan: Interpretable representation learning by information maximizing generative adversarial nets. In: Proceedings of the 30th International Conference on Neural Information Processing Systems. pp. 2180–2188 (2016)
5. Endo, Y., Kanamori, Y., Kuriyama, S.: Animating landscape: self-supervised learning of decoupled motion and appearance for single-image video synthesis. arXiv preprint arXiv:1910.07192 (2019)
6. Goodfellow, I., et al.: Generative adversarial nets. In: Advances in Neural Information Processing Systems, vol. 27 (2014)
7. Holynski, A., Curless, B.L., Seitz, S.M., Szeliski, R.: Animating pictures with Eulerian motion fields. In: Proceedings of the IEEE/CVF Conference on Computer Vision and Pattern Recognition, pp. 5810–5819 (2021)
8. Huang, Z., Zhang, T., Heng, W., Shi, B., Zhou, S.: Rife: real-time intermediate flow estimation for video frame interpolation. arXiv preprint arXiv:2011.06294 (2020)
9. Isola, P., Zhu, J.Y., Zhou, T., Efros, A.A.: Image-to-image translation with conditional adversarial networks. In: Proceedings of the IEEE Conference on Computer Vision and Pattern Recognition, pp. 1125–1134 (2017)
10. Jin, M., Hu, Z., Favaro, P.: Learning to extract flawless slow motion from blurry videos. In: Proceedings of the IEEE/CVF Conference on Computer Vision and Pattern Recognition, pp. 8112–8121 (2019)
11. Jin, M., Meishvili, G., Favaro, P.: Learning to extract a video sequence from a single motion-blurred image. In: Proceedings of the IEEE Conference on Computer Vision and Pattern Recognition, pp. 6334–6342 (2018)
12. Karras, T., Laine, S., Aila, T.: A style-based generator architecture for generative adversarial networks. In: Proceedings of the IEEE/CVF Conference on Computer Vision and Pattern Recognition, pp. 4401–4410 (2019)
13. Kim, T.H., Lee, K.M., Scholkopf, B., Hirsch, M.: Online video deblurring via dynamic temporal blending network. In: Proceedings of the IEEE International Conference on Computer Vision, pp. 4038–4047 (2017)
14. Kingma, D.P., Welling, M.: Auto-encoding variational bayes. arXiv preprint arXiv:1312.6114 (2013)
15. Krishnan, D., Fergus, R.: Fast image deconvolution using hyper-Laplacian priors. Adv. Neural. Inf. Process. Syst. **22**, 1033–1041 (2009)

16. Kupyn, O., Budzan, V., Mykhailych, M., Mishkin, D., Matas, J.: Deblurgan: Blind motion deblurring using conditional adversarial networks. In: Proceedings of the IEEE Conference on Computer Vision and Pattern Recognition, pp. 8183–8192 (2018)
17. Kupyn, O., Martyniuk, T., Wu, J., Wang, Z.: Deblurgan-v2: deblurring (orders-of-magnitude) faster and better. In: Proceedings of the IEEE/CVF International Conference on Computer Vision, pp. 8878–8887 (2019)
18. Larsen, A.B.L., Sønderby, S.K., Larochelle, H., Winther, O.: Autoencoding beyond pixels using a learned similarity metric. In: International Conference on Machine Learning, pp. 1558–1566. PMLR (2016)
19. Levin, A., Weiss, Y., Durand, F., Freeman, W.T.: Understanding and evaluating blind deconvolution algorithms. In: 2009 IEEE Conference on Computer Vision and Pattern Recognition, pp. 1964–1971. IEEE (2009)
20. Li, R., Yang, S., Ross, D.A., Kanazawa, A.: AI choreographer: music conditioned 3D dance generation with AIST++. In: Proceedings of the IEEE/CVF International Conference on Computer Vision, pp. 13401–13412 (2021)
21. Lin, S., et al.: Learning event-driven video deblurring and interpolation. In: Vedaldi, A., Bischof, H., Brox, T., Frahm, J.-M. (eds.) ECCV 2020. LNCS, vol. 12353, pp. 695–710. Springer, Cham (2020). https://doi.org/10.1007/978-3-030-58598-3_41
22. Nah, S., et al.: Ntire 2019 challenge on video deblurring and super-resolution: dataset and study. In: Proceedings of the IEEE/CVF Conference on Computer Vision and Pattern Recognition Workshops (2019)
23. Nah, S., Kim, T.H., Lee, K.M.: Deep multi-scale convolutional neural network for dynamic scene deblurring. In: Proceedings of the IEEE Conference on Computer Vision and Pattern Recognition, pp. 3883–3891 (2017)
24. Nah, S., Son, S., Lee, K.M.: Recurrent neural networks with intra-frame iterations for video deblurring. In: Proceedings of the IEEE/CVF Conference on Computer Vision and Pattern Recognition, pp. 8102–8111 (2019)
25. Pan, L., Scheerlinck, C., Yu, X., Hartley, R., Liu, M., Dai, Y.: Bringing a blurry frame alive at high frame-rate with an event camera. In: Proceedings of the IEEE/CVF Conference on Computer Vision and Pattern Recognition, pp. 6820–6829 (2019)
26. Park, T., Liu, M.Y., Wang, T.C., Zhu, J.Y.: Semantic image synthesis with spatially-adaptive normalization. In: Proceedings of the IEEE/CVF Conference on Computer Vision and Pattern Recognition, pp. 2337–2346 (2019)
27. Purohit, K., Shah, A., Rajagopalan, A.: Bringing alive blurred moments. In: Proceedings of the IEEE/CVF Conference on Computer Vision and Pattern Recognition, pp. 6830–6839 (2019)
28. Rozumnyi, D., Oswald, M.R., Ferrari, V., Matas, J., Pollefeys, M.: DeFMO: deblurring and shape recovery of fast moving objects. In: Proceedings of the IEEE/CVF Conference on Computer Vision and Pattern Recognition, pp. 3456–3465 (2021)
29. Shen, W., Bao, W., Zhai, G., Chen, L., Min, X., Gao, Z.: Blurry video frame interpolation. In: Proceedings of the IEEE/CVF Conference on Computer Vision and Pattern Recognition, pp. 5114–5123 (2020)
30. Sohn, K., Lee, H., Yan, X.: Learning structured output representation using deep conditional generative models. Adv. Neural. Inf. Process. Syst. **28**, 3483–3491 (2015)
31. Su, S., Delbracio, M., Wang, J., Sapiro, G., Heidrich, W., Wang, O.: Deep video deblurring for hand-held cameras. In: Proceedings of the IEEE Conference on Computer Vision and Pattern Recognition, pp. 1279–1288 (2017)

32. Tao, X., Gao, H., Shen, X., Wang, J., Jia, J.: Scale-recurrent network for deep image deblurring. In: Proceedings of the IEEE Conference on Computer Vision and Pattern Recognition, pp. 8174–8182 (2018)

33. Teed, Z., Deng, J.: RAFT: recurrent all-pairs field transforms for optical flow. In: Vedaldi, A., Bischof, H., Brox, T., Frahm, J.-M. (eds.) ECCV 2020. LNCS, vol. 12347, pp. 402–419. Springer, Cham (2020). https://doi.org/10.1007/978-3-030-58536-5_24

34. Wang, X., Chan, K.C., Yu, K., Dong, C., Change Loy, C.: EDVR: video restoration with enhanced deformable convolutional networks. In: Proceedings of the IEEE/CVF Conference on Computer Vision and Pattern Recognition Workshops (2019)

35. Wieschollek, P., Hirsch, M., Scholkopf, B., Lensch, H.: Learning blind motion deblurring. In: Proceedings of the IEEE International Conference on Computer Vision, pp. 231–240 (2017)

36. Xu, L., Zheng, S., Jia, J.: Unnatural l0 sparse representation for natural image deblurring. In: Proceedings of the IEEE Conference on Computer Vision and Pattern Recognition, pp. 1107–1114 (2013)

37. Xue, T., Wu, J., Bouman, K.L., Freeman, W.T.: Visual dynamics: probabilistic future frame synthesis via cross convolutional networks. arXiv preprint arXiv:1607.02586 (2016)

38. Zhang, H., Dai, Y., Li, H., Koniusz, P.: Deep stacked hierarchical multi-patch network for image deblurring. In: Proceedings of the IEEE/CVF Conference on Computer Vision and Pattern Recognition, pp. 5978–5986 (2019)

39. Zhang, J., et al.: DTVNet: dynamic time-lapse video generation via single still image. In: Vedaldi, A., Bischof, H., Brox, T., Frahm, J.-M. (eds.) ECCV 2020. LNCS, vol. 12350, pp. 300–315. Springer, Cham (2020). https://doi.org/10.1007/978-3-030-58558-7_18

40. Zhang, R., Isola, P., Efros, A.A., Shechtman, E., Wang, O.: The unreasonable effectiveness of deep features as a perceptual metric. In: Proceedings of the IEEE Conference on Computer Vision and Pattern Recognition, pp. 586–595 (2018)

41. Zhong, Z., Gao, Y., Zheng, Y., Zheng, B.: Efficient spatio-temporal recurrent neural network for video deblurring. In: Vedaldi, A., Bischof, H., Brox, T., Frahm, J.-M. (eds.) ECCV 2020. LNCS, vol. 12351, pp. 191–207. Springer, Cham (2020). https://doi.org/10.1007/978-3-030-58539-6_12

42. Zhou, S., Zhang, J., Pan, J., Xie, H., Zuo, W., Ren, J.: Spatio-temporal filter adaptive network for video deblurring. In: Proceedings of the IEEE/CVF International Conference on Computer Vision, pp. 2482–2491 (2019)

43. Zhu, J.Y., Park, T., Isola, P., Efros, A.A.: Unpaired image-to-image translation using cycle-consistent adversarial networks. In: Proceedings of the IEEE International Conference on Computer Vision, pp. 2223–2232 (2017)

44. Zhu, J.Y., et al.: Multimodal image-to-image translation by enforcing bi-cycle consistency. In: Advances in Neural Information Processing Systems, pp. 465–476 (2017)

AlphaVC: High-Performance and Efficient Learned Video Compression

Yibo Shi, Yunying Ge, Jing Wang$^{(\boxtimes)}$, and Jue Mao

Huawei Technologies, Beijing, China
wangjing215@huawei.com

Abstract. Recently, learned video compression has drawn lots of attention and show a rapid development trend with promising results. However, the previous works still suffer from some critical issues and have a performance gap with traditional compression standards in terms of widely used PSNR metric. In this paper, we propose several techniques to effectively improve the performance. First, to address the problem of accumulative error, we introduce a conditional-I-frame as the first frame in the GoP, which stabilizes the reconstructed quality and saves the bit-rate. Second, to efficiently improve the accuracy of inter prediction without increasing the complexity of decoder, we propose a pixel-to-feature motion prediction method at encoder side that helps us to obtain high-quality motion information. Third, we propose a probability-based entropy skipping method, which not only brings performance gain, but also greatly reduces the runtime of entropy coding. With these powerful techniques, this paper proposes AlphaVC, a high-performance and efficient learned video compression scheme. To the best of our knowledge, AlphaVC is the first E2E AI codec that exceeds the latest compression standard VVC on all common test datasets for both PSNR (-28.2% BD-rate saving) and MSSSIM (-52.2% BD-rate saving), and has very fast encoding (0.001x VVC) and decoding (1.69x VVC) speeds.

1 Introduction

Video data is reported to occupy more than 82% of all consumer Internet traffic [10], and is expected to see the rapid rate of growth in the next few years, especially the high-definition videos and ultra high-definition videos. Therefore, video compression is a key requirement for the bandwidth-limited Internet. During the past decades, several video coding standards were developed, such as H.264 [35], H.265 [29], and H.266 [7]. These methods are based on hand-designed modules such as block partition, inter prediction and transform [2], etc. While these traditional video compression methods have made a promising performance, their performance are limited since the modules are artificially designed and optimized separately.

SupplementaryInformation The online version contains supplementary material available at https://doi.org/10.1007/978-3-031-19800-7_36.

Recently, learned image compression [8,11,15,26] based on variational auto-encoder [20] has shown great potential, achieving better performance than traditional image codecs [5,7,32]. Inspired by the learned image compression, and combined with the idea of traditional video codecs, many learning-based video compression approaches [1,14,16,17,19,21,24,27] were proposed.

Given the reference frame, variant kinds of motion compensation (alignment) methods were proposed like scale-space alignment [1], feature-based alignment [19], multi-scale feature-based alignment [28]. These methods aim to improve the diversity of motion compensation and result in more compression-friendly predictions. However, such methods increase the complexity on both encoder and decoder side. Inspired by AMVP (Advanced Motion Vector Prediction) on traditional video compression methods [29], we expect the encoder side to predict a more accurate motion information. Further, at the encoder side of AlphaVC, we propose a pixel-to-feature motion prediction method that can obtain high-quality motion information without increasing the complexity of the decoder.

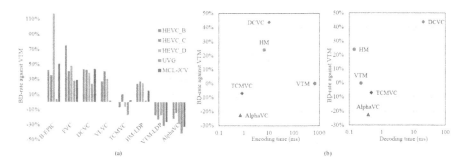

Fig. 1. (a): BD-rate against VTM in terms of PSNR (Lower is better). (b): BD-rate against VTM as a function of encoding/decoding time on 1080p videos.

Existing learned video compression can be divided into two categories: Low-Delay P mode and Low-Delay B/Random-Access mode. For the Low-Delay P mode, the methods [1,16,19,28] only include the P(predictive)-frames and I(image)-frames. For the Low-Delay B or Random-Access mode, the methods [14,27] insert the B(bidirectional predictive) frames into the GoP to improve compression performance. AlphaVC focuses on the Low-Delay P mode. In this mode, due to the accumulation error in P-frame [23], most existing methods have to use the inefficient I-frame as the first frame in limited length GoP. Unlike the existing methods, we overcome this issue by introducing a conditional I-frame (cI-frame) as the first frame in the GoP, which stabilizes the reconstructed quality and achieves better performance.

In addition, we all know that the entropy coding [13,18] can only run serially will increase the runtime. Moreover, the auto-regressive entropy module [26], which significantly increase the decoding time, is always used on learned image codecs for a higher compression ratio. We found that most elements of the latents usually have very low information entropy, which means the probability distributions of these elements estimated by entropy module always is highly concentrated. Inspired by this, we propose an efficient probability-based entropy skipping method (Skip) which can significantly save runtime in entropy coding, and achieve higher performance without auto-regressive.

With the help of the above technologies, AlphaVC achieves the highest E2E compression performance while being very efficient. As shown in Fig. 1, the proposed AlphaVC outperforms VTM-IPP/VTM-LDP by 28.2%/6.59%, where the VTM is the official software of H.266/VVC, the IPP denotes the configuration using one reference frame and flat QP, and the LDP denotes the better configuration using multiple references and dynamic QP. Note the configuration of AlphaVC is the same as IPP. To the best of our knowledge, AlphaVC is the only learning-based video codec that can consistently achieve comparable or better performance with VTM-LDP in terms of PSNR on all common test datasets. Comparing with the state-of-the-art learning-based video codecs [28], AlphaVC reduces the BD-rate by about 25% while faster encoding and decoding.

Our contributions are summarized as follows:

1. We introduce a new type of frame named conditional-I frame (cI-frame) and propose a new coding mode for learned video compression. It can effectively save the bit rate of I-frame and alleviate the problem of accumulated error.
2. The proposed motion prediction method, utilizing the idea of pixel-to-feature and global-to-local, can significantly improve the accuracy of inter-frame prediction without increasing decoding complexity.
3. An efficient method in entropy estimation module and entropy coding have higher performance and faster encoding and decoding time.

2   Related Work

2.1   Image Compression

In the past decades, the traditional image compression methods like JPEG [32], JPEG2000 [9] and BPG [5] can efficiently reduce the image size. Those methods have achieved a high performance by exploiting the hand-crafted techniques, such as DCT [2]. Recently, thanks to variational autoencoder (VAE) [20] and scalar quantization assumption [3], the learning-based image compression methods have achieved great progress. With the optimization of entropy estimation modules [4, 26] and network structure [8, 11], the learning-based image compression methods have achieved better performance than the traditional image compression codecs on common metrics, such as PSNR and MS-SSIM [34].

2.2   Video Compression

Video compression is a more challenging problem compared to image compression. There is a long history of progress for hand-designed video compression methods, and several video coding standards have been proposed, such as H.264(JM) [35], H.265(HM) [29] and more recently H.266(VTM) [7]. With the development of video coding standards, the traditional video compression methods made significant improvements and provided a strong baseline. Even they have shown a good performance, these algorithms are limited by the hand-designed strategy and the difficult to optimize jointly.

Recently, learning-based video compression has become a new direction. Following the traditional video compression framework, Lu et al. proposed the end-to-end optimized video compression framework DVC [24], in which the neural networks are used to replace all the critical components in traditional video compression codec. Then, the exploration direction of existing approaches can be classified into three categories. One category of approaches focuses on the motion compensation (alignment) method to improve the accuracy of inter prediction. For example, SSF [1] designed a scale-space flow to replace the bilinear warping operation. Hu et al. [19] propose the FVC framework, which apply transformation in feature space with deformable convolution [12]. Later Sheng et al. introduce multi-scale in feature space transformation [28]. Another popular direction is the design of auto-encoder module. Such as Habibian et al. [17] use a 3D spatio-temporal autoencoder network to directly compress multiple frames. Li et al. [21] use the predicted frame as the input of encoder, decoder, instead of explicitly computing the residual. The third category extends the learned video compression to more codec functions, like B-frame [14,27], utilizing multiple reference frames [19].

3   Method

3.1   Overview

Let $\mathcal{X} = \{\mathbf{X}_1, \mathbf{X}_2, \dots\}$ denote a video sequence, video codecs usually break the full sequence into groups of pictures (GoP). Due to the accumulative error of P-frames, in low delay P mode, which is AlphaVC adopted, each group needs to start with an I-frame and then follow P-frames. In AlphaVC, we propose a new codecing mode in GoP, including three types of frames. As shown in Fig. 2(a), the I-frame is only used for the first frame. For other groups, we propose to start with conditional-I-frame instead of I-frame. The Conditional-I-frame (named cI-frame), which uses the reference frame as condition of entropy to reduce the bit-rate, stabilises the reconstructed quality like I-frame, and meanwhile has a high compression rate. The details of each type of our P-frame and cI-frame are summarized as follows:

P-Frame. First of all, we define the P-Frame in learned video compression as a class of methods that has the following form on decoder side:

$$\hat{\mathbf{X}}_t = D_p(H_{\text{align}}(\hat{\mathbf{X}}_{t-1}, \hat{\mathbf{m}}_t), \hat{\mathbf{r}}_t) \tag{1}$$

where $D_p(\cdot), H_{\text{align}}(\cdot)$ denote the method of reconstruction and alignment, $\hat{\mathbf{m}}_t, \hat{\mathbf{r}}_t$ are the quantized latent representation of motion, residual. Note that the quantized latent representation is the features to be encoded after the encoder and

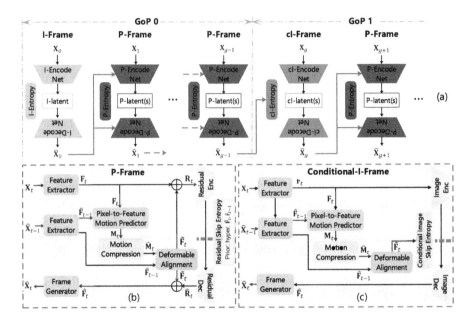

Fig. 2. Overview of our proposed video compression scheme. (a): Two kinds of GoP. (b): The framework of P-frame. (c): The framework of cI-frame.

quantization. That is, the reference frame $\hat{\mathbf{X}}_{t-1}$ will participate in and affect the reconstruction of current frame, which means that the consecutive P-frame will generate cumulative errors.

In this paper, we use the feature-align based P-frame framework, Fig. 2(b) sketches our P-frame compression framework. We first transform $\hat{\mathbf{X}}_{t-1}, \mathbf{X}_t$ into feature space $\hat{\mathbf{F}}_{t-1}, \mathbf{F}_t$. Then motion predictor will generate the predicted motion $\mathbf{M}_t$ and the predicted motion will be compressed by motion compression model. The predicted feature $\tilde{\mathbf{F}}_t$ is generated by deformable alignment [12] with the reconstructed motion $\hat{\mathbf{M}}_t$ and reference feature $\hat{\mathbf{F}}_{t-1}$. Finally, the residual in feature-based $\mathbf{R}_t = \mathbf{F}_t - \tilde{\mathbf{F}}_t$ will be compressed by residual compression model. The reconstructed feature $\hat{\mathbf{F}}_t = \hat{\mathbf{R}}_t + \tilde{\mathbf{F}}_t$ is transformed into the current reconstruct frame $\hat{\mathbf{X}}_t$ with frame generator.

Both the motion compression model and residual compression model are implemented by auto-encoder structure [4], including an encoder module, decoder module and the proposed entropy estiamtion module. The network structure of auto-encoder part is the same as FVC [19]. To further reduce redundant information, we introduce the temporal and structure prior for the entropy estimation module in both motion and residual compression models:

$$
\begin{aligned}
&\mathbb{E}_{\hat{\mathbf{m}}_t \sim p_t}[-\log_2 q_t(\hat{\mathbf{m}}_t | \hat{\mathbf{F}}_{t-1}, \hat{\mathbf{m}}_{t-1})] \\
&\mathbb{E}_{\hat{\mathbf{r}}_t \sim p_t}[-\log_2 q_t(\hat{\mathbf{r}}_t | \tilde{\mathbf{F}}_t, \hat{\mathbf{r}}_{t-1})]
\end{aligned}
\tag{2}
$$

the reference feature $\hat{\mathbf{F}}_{t-1}$ and previous quantized motion latent representation $\hat{\mathbf{m}}_{t-1}$ are structure and temporal priors of $\hat{\mathbf{m}}_t$ respectively, and the predicted feature $\tilde{\mathbf{F}}_t$ and previous quantized residual latent representation $\hat{\mathbf{r}}_{t-1}$ are structure and temporal priors of $\hat{\mathbf{r}}_t$ respectively.

Conditional-I-Frame (cI-Frame). We introduce a new type of frame called the cI-frame like [22], which can be formulated as:

$$
\begin{aligned}
&\text{Auto-Encoder}: \hat{\mathbf{y}}_t = Q(E_{cI}(\mathbf{X}_t)), \hat{\mathbf{X}}_t = D_{cI}(\hat{\mathbf{y}}_t), \\
&\text{Entropy}: R(\hat{\mathbf{y}}_t|\hat{\mathbf{X}}_{t-1}) = \mathbb{E}_{\hat{\mathbf{y}}_t \sim p_t}[-\log_2 q_t(\hat{\mathbf{y}}_t|H_{\text{align}}(\hat{\mathbf{X}}_{t-1}, \hat{\mathbf{m}}_t))],
\end{aligned}
\tag{3}
$$

where $\hat{\mathbf{y}}_t$ is the quantized latent representation of $\mathbf{X}_t$, $E_{cI}(\cdot), Q(\cdot), D_{cI}(\cdot)$ denote the function of cI encoder module, quantization and reconstruction. That is, cI-frame reduces the inter redundant information through the entropy conditioned on $\hat{\mathbf{X}}_{t-1}$. For cI-frame, the input of the autoencoder does not use the reference frames, thus make the reconstructed quality stable. Further, we use cI-frame as the first frame in the GoP excluding the first GoP, which not only stabilizes the sequence quality like I-frame, but also improves the compression ratio, thereby alleviating the problem of accumulated errors.

The framework for cI-frame is shown in Fig. 2(c). The feature extractor, motion prediction and motion compression part share the same structure with P-frame framework. $\tilde{\mathbf{F}}_t$ is only used as the prior, the current feature $\mathbf{F}_t$ will be the only input of the encoder.

Furthermore, we propose two novel strategies in both P-frame and cI-frame, named pixel-to-feature motion prediction (P2F MP) and probability-based entropy skipping method (Skip), to improve the accuracy of inter prediction and coding efficiency.

3.2   Pixel-to-Feature Motion Prediction

Inter-frame prediction is a critical module to improve the efficiency of inter-frame coding, since it determines the accuracy of the predicted frame. We propose pixel-to-feature motion prediction to fully exploit the diversity of feature-based alignment and the state-of-the-art optical flow network. The illustration is shown in Fig. 3.

Given the previous reconstructed frame $\hat{\mathbf{X}}_{t-1}$ and the current frame $\mathbf{X}_t$, the optical flow in pixel space $\mathbf{M}_t^{\text{pixel}}$ will be generated by a state-of-the-art optical flow network [30,31]. The pixel space motion $\mathbf{M}_t^{\text{pixel}}$ is then used to initialize a motion in feature space $\mathbf{M}_t^{\text{init}}$. Then, we apply the deformable alignment $D(\cdot, \cdot)$ to the reference feature $\hat{\mathbf{F}}_{t-1}$ by $\mathbf{M}_t^{\text{init}}$:

$$
\bar{\mathbf{F}}_t = D(\hat{\mathbf{F}}_{t-1}, \mathbf{M}_t^{\text{init}})
\tag{4}
$$

After initial alignment, the motion local refinement network will refine the initial motion locally according to the initially aligned feature $\bar{\mathbf{F}}_t$ and the target feature $\mathbf{F}_t$, and then generate the final predicted motion $\mathbf{M}_t$.

$$
\mathbf{M}_t = \text{Refine}(\bar{\mathbf{F}}_t, \mathbf{F}_t) + \mathbf{M}_t^{\text{init}}
\tag{5}
$$

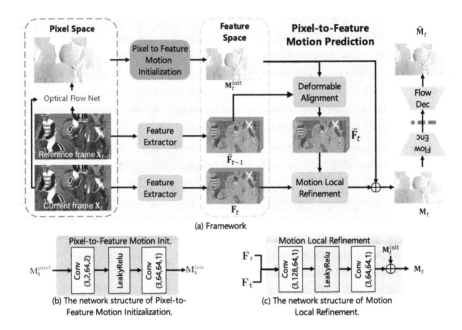

Fig. 3. Illustration of our proposed pixel-to-feature motion prediction module.

Finally, the predicted motion will be compressed to reconstruct motion $\hat{\mathbf{M}}_t$ through motion compression model.

Unlike existing methods, AlphaVC neither learn motion directly from features [19] that are difficult to fit through convolutions nor compress the generated optical flow directly [24]. We follow pixel-to-feature and global-to-local principles, first generate the feature space motion before coding with optical flow, then performing further fine-tuning through alignment feedback. Experiments show that this method greatly improves the accuracy of inter-frame prediction without affecting the decoding complexity and running time.

3.3   Probability-Base Entropy Skipping Method

For a latent representation variable $\mathbf{v}$ in learned image or video compression, we first quantize it with round-based quantization $\hat{\mathbf{v}} = [\mathbf{v}]$, and estimate the probability distribution of $\mathbf{v}$ by an entropy estimation module with some priors, such as hyper [4], context [26], etc. Then $\hat{\mathbf{v}}$ is compressed into the bitstream by entropy coding like arithmetic coding [18], asymmetric numeral system [13]. In video compression, due to the introduction of the reference frame, the entropy of quantized latent representation variables like $\hat{\mathbf{m}}_t, \hat{\mathbf{r}}_t$ in P-frame is very small, especially in low bit-rate. That means the probability distributions of most elements in the latent variable are concentrated. If it is slightly off-center for such an element, we will encode it to bitstream with a high cost. In other words, if we skip these elements without encoding/decoding and replace them with the peak of probability distribution, we can save both bit-rate and runtime of entropy coding with little error expectations. Inspired by this idea, we propose an efficient probability-based entropy skipping method (Skip).

For a latent representation variable $\mathbf{v}$, we define $\mathcal{Q}$ as the probability density set of $\mathbf{v}$ estimated by its entropy module. The value which has the maximum probability density of the i-th element is calculated as:

$$\theta_i = \arg\max_{\theta_i} q_i(\theta_i) \tag{6}$$

The probability that the element v_i is close to θ_i can be computed by:

$$q_i^{\mathrm{max}} = \int_{\theta_i-0.5}^{\theta_i+0.5} q_i(x)\, dx \tag{7}$$

If the probability q_i^{max} is high enough, we will not encode/decode the element to/from the bitstream, and replace the value with θ_i. After this operation, the quantized latent representation will become $\hat{\mathbf{v}}^{\mathrm{s}}$:

$$\hat{v}_i^{\mathrm{s}} = \begin{cases} \theta_i, & q_i^{\mathrm{max}} >= \tau \\ [v_i], & q_i^{\mathrm{max}} < \tau \end{cases} \tag{8}$$

where τ is a threshold to determine whether to skip.

In our paper, we use gaussian distribution as the estimated probability density of all the quantized latent representations. Hence the Eq. 6 and Eq. 7 can be easily solved as:

$$\theta_i = \mu_i, q_i^{\mathrm{max}} = \mathrm{erf}(\frac{1}{2\sqrt{2}\sigma_i}). \tag{9}$$

It can be seen that q_i^{max} is the monotone function of σ_i, we use σ_i as the condition of Eq. 8 to further reduce the computational complexity:

$$\hat{v}_i^{\mathrm{s}} = \begin{cases} \mu_i, & \sigma_i < \tau_\sigma \\ [v_i], & \sigma_i >= \tau_\sigma \end{cases} \tag{10}$$

There are two benefits of Skip. First, it can dynamically reduce the number of elements that need to be entropy encoded, significantly reducing the serial CPU runtime. Second, we can better trade-off errors and bit rates for elements with high determinism, thereby achieving high compression performance.

3.4 Loss Function

Our proposed AlphaVC targets to jointly optimize the rate-distortion (R-D) cost.

$$L = R + \lambda \cdot D = (R_0^{\mathrm{I}} + \lambda \cdot D_0^{\mathrm{I}}) + \sum_{t=1}^{T-1}(R_t^{\mathrm{p}} + \lambda \cdot D_t^{\mathrm{p}}) + (R_{\mathrm{T}}^{\mathrm{cI}} + \lambda \cdot D_{\mathrm{T}}^{\mathrm{cI}}) \tag{11}$$

where the training GoP size is T, λ controls the trade-off, $R_0^{\mathrm{I}} - D_0^{\mathrm{I}}$, $R_t^{\mathrm{p}} - D_t^{\mathrm{p}}$ and $R_{\mathrm{T}}^{\mathrm{cI}} - D_{\mathrm{T}}^{\mathrm{cI}}$ represent the rate-distortion of the 0-th I-frame, the t-th P-frame and the T-th cI-frame, respectively.

4   Experiments

4.1   Setup

Training. We train our model on the Vimeo-90k dataset. This dataset consists of 4278 videos with 89800 independent shots that are different from each other in content. We randomly crop the frames to patches of size 256×256, and start training from scratch. We train the models with Adam optimizer for 60 epochs, where the batchsize was set to 8 and learning rate was initially set to $1e-4$ and reduced to half for 30 epochs. The skip operation will been enabled during training. The loss function is the joint rate-distortion loss as shown in Eq. 11, where the multiplier λ is chosen from (0.07, 0.05, 0.01, 0.005, 0.001, 0.0007) for the MSE optimization. The MS-SSIM optimized models are finetuned from MSE-optimized model with $\lambda = 0.03, 0.01, 0.007, 0.005, 0.001$.

Testing. We evaluate our proposed algorithm on the HEVC datasets [6] (Class B, C, D, E), the UVG datasets [25], and the MCL-JCV datasets [33]. The HEVC datasets contain 16 videos with different resolution 416×240, 832×480 and 1920×1080. The UVG and MCL-JVC datasets contain 7 and 30 1080p videos, respectively. The GoP size in AlphaVC is set to 20 for all testing datasets.

Camparision. Both IPP and LDP configuration of VTM-10.0 and HM-16.20 are used for comparision. The IPP only references the previous frame, and each P-frame has the flat QP, which is the same configuration with AlphaVC. The LDP is the default low-delay P configuration that references multiple previous frames and has dynamic QP for each P-frame. In addition, state-of-the-art learning-based video compression methods, i.e., FVC (CVPR'21) [19], DCVC (NIPS'21) [21], B-EPIC (ICCV'21) [27], VLVC (2021) [14], TCMVC (2021) [28]. Note that, B-EPIC and VLVC don't belong to IPPP mode, due to the introduction of B-frame.

4.2   Experiment Results

Performance. Figure 4, 5 shows the experimental results on all testing datasets. It is obvious that AlphaVC achieves the bset performance of all methods. In terms of MS-SSIM, AlphaVC significantly outperforms all the other methods over the entire bitrate range and on all the datasets. In terms of PSNR, AlphaVC significantly outperforms all the learning-based codecs and VTM-IPP, and even outperforms VTM-LDP in most situations. As mentioned before, VTM-LDP references multiple previous frames and has dynamic QP for each P-frame. which is not adopted by AlphaVC.

Table 1 and Table 2 show the BD-rate savings in PSNR and MS-SSIM that anchored by VTM-IPP. In terms of PSNR, AlphaVC achieves an average 28.2% bitrate saving compared to VTM-IPP, outperforming all the reported methods, including the stronger VTM-LDP (23.5% bitrate saving). In the worst case,

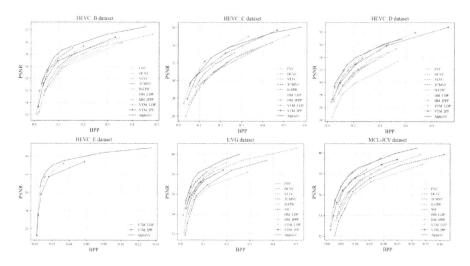

Fig. 4. PSNR based R-D Curves of traditional codecs and state-of-the-art learning-based codecs on each datasets. The red solid line is AlphaVC. Traditional codecs are all represented by solid lines, and other learning-based codecs are represented by dotted lines. (Color figure online)

Table 1. BD-rate calculated by PSNR with the anchor of VTM-IPP. Red means more bits ($> 3\%$) required. Green means fewer bits ($< -3\%$) required.

	VTM-IPP	VTM-LDP	HM-IPP	HM-LDP	SSF	FVC	DCVC	VLVC	TCMVC	B-EPIC	AlphaVC
HEVC_B	0	−17.9%	55.2%	24.0%	-	75.4%	43.7%	27.1%	−6.92%	42.5%	−22.5%
HEVC_C	0	−23.1%	38.6%	27.1%	-	40.9%	42.8%	40.8%	10.2%	35.6%	−14.9%
HEVC_D	0	−17.9%	35.7%	24.9%	-	47.9%	38.6%	30.5%	−6.61%	117.%	−29.0%
UVG	0	−31.9%	18.5%	1.99%	57.7%	28.4%	24.0%	2.15%	−17.3%	3.78%	−41.7%
MCL-JCV	0	−26.6%	26.3%	15.2%	50.6%	29.3%	43.8%	-	2.32%	50.6%	−32.9%
Avg	0	−23.5%	35.6%	19.7%	54.2%	44.4%	38.6%	25.1%	−3.66%	49.9%	−28.2%

AlphaVC also achieves a BD-rate saving of 14.9% showing a good stability. In terms of MS-SSIM, learning-based codecs generally have better performances than traditional codecs, among with AlphaVC performing the best, by saving an additional 8% bitrate over the best SOTA TCMVC.

Complexity. The MAC(Multiply Accumulate) of the P-frame at the decoding side is about 1.13M/pixel, and the cI-frame is about 0.98M/pixel. We use arithmetic coding for the complete entropy encoding and decoding process, and 1080p videos to evaluate the runtime. The runtime of the encoding side includes model inference, data transmission from GPU to CPU and entropy encoding, and the runtime of the decoding side includes entropy decoding, data transmission and model inference. The comparison results are shown in Table 3, in which running platform of AlphaVC is Intel(R) Xeon(R) Gold 6278C CPU and NVIDIA V100

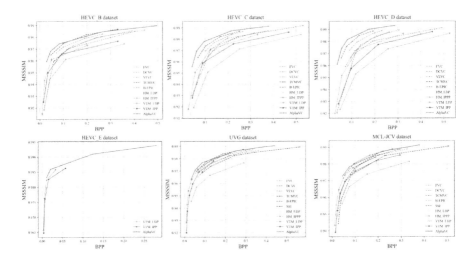

Fig. 5. MS-SSIM based R-D Curves.

Table 2. BD-rate calculated by MS-SSIM with the anchor of VTM-PVC-IPP. Red means more bits ($> 3\%$) required. Green means fewer bits ($< -3\%$) required.

	VTM-IPP	VTM-LDP	HM-IPP	HM-LDP	SSF	FVC	DCVC	VLVC	TCMVC	B-EPIC	AlphaVC
HEVC_B	0	−20.5%	54.6%	17.4%	-	−21.3%	−16.0%	−42.5%	−53.5%	−7.1%	−61.6%
HEVC_C	0	−20.7%	53.6%	12.8%	-	−22.2%	−12.8%	−41.6%	−47.6%	−15.4%	−58.9%
HEVC_D	0	−27.2%	39.3%	-1.5%	-	−34.7%	−33.0%	−49.6%	−60.7%	−21.5%	−67.2%
UVG	0	−26.7%	56.3%	20.2%	33.9%	11.5%	10.9%	−12.9%	−22.0%	−1.63%	−32.9%
MCL-JCV	0	−26.0%	49.6%	14.5%	−4.5%	−18.8%	−17.9%	-	−38.8%	−19.9%	−40.5%
Avg	0	−24.2%	49.9%	11.5%	14.7%	−17.1%	−13.7%	−36.6%	−44.5%	−13.1%	−52.2%

GPU. The encoding and decoding times of AlphaVC on a 1080p frame average about 715 ms and 379 ms. The encoding time is about 1000x faster than VTM, and the decoding time is similar to VTM (1.69x). Even though AlphaVC uses more parameters than TCMVC, it is still faster. The main reason is the proposed probability-based skip entropy technique, which significantly reduces the running time on CPU. In addition, we can find that the cI-frame is slower than P-frame although the cI-frame has less complexity. This is also because the bit-rate in the cI-frame is higher, and the number of skipping elements in the cI-frame is fewer.

4.3 Ablation Study and Analysis

Frame Analysis. We use three types of frame in AlphaVC: I-frame, cI-frame and P-frame. To justify this approach and evaluate each type of frame, we train two additional models AlphaVC-P and AlphaVC-cI. AlphaVC-P only includes I-frame and P-frame, and the GoP size is the same with AlphaVC in the test

Table 3. Complexity on 1080p video. We compare our AlphaVC including cI-Frame and p-Frame with traditional codecs and TCMVC. The time ratio is calculated with the anchor of VTM.

Method	Params.	Enc-T (s)	Dec-T (s)	Enc-T ratio	Dec-T ratio
VTM-10.0-IPP	–	661.9	0.224	1.0000	1.0000
HM-16.40-IPP	–	26.47	0.140	0.0400	0.6250
TCMVC	10.7M	0.827	0.472	0.0012	2.1071
AlphaVC	63.7M	0.715	0.379	0.0011	1.6920
AlphaVC-cI	29.9M	0.733	0.580	0.0011	2.5893
AlphaVC-P	33.8M	0.685	0.365	0.0010	1.6295

phase. AlphaVC-cI only includes I-frame and cI-frame, and there is no group in AlphaVC-cI, I-frame is only used in the first frame and all subsequent frames are cI-frames. The R-D performance is shown in Fig. 6(a), AlphaVC-P achieves comparable performance with VTM_IPP, and AlphaVC-cI only achieves comparable performance with HM_IPP. The reason may be that cI-frame utilizes reference frames in a more implicityly way: as the condition of entropy. The reason is that, although the cI-frame is not good enough, it is stable and has no accumulated error as shown in Fig. 6(b). By combining these two types of frame, AlphaVC achieves better R-D performance for the following two reasons:

1. The accumulated error of P-frame in AlphaVC is smaller than the P-frame in AlphaVC-P. (see in Fig. 6(b)).
2. The performance of cI-frame is much better than I-frame (see in Fig. 6, similar distortion with smaller rate).

Effectiveness of Different Components. We demonstrate the effectiveness of our proposed components with AlphaVC-P as the anchor. We gradually remove the P2F MP, Skip in $\hat{m}$ and Skip in $\hat{r}$ from AlphaVC-P. Note that, without P2F MP, the current feature and reference feature will be fed to the motion compression module directly. The BD-Rate savings against AlphaVC-P are presented in Table 4(b). Moreover, a more intuitive analysis for the proposed methods is shown in Fig. 7.

As shown in Table 4(b), P2F MP brings 10.4% BD-rate saving. From Fig. 7(b), we can see that the compressed motion with P2F MP is more accurate and with smaller entropy.

To analyze Skip, we first explore the relationship between the replacement error, and the variance of Gaussian distribution as shown in Fig. 7(c). Notice that the replacement error is highly correlated with variance, and elements with smaller variance have small errors. Therefore, skipping the entropy coding of these elements will not cause any loss, and may even improve performance. Due to the smoothness of motion information, the Skip ratio of motion latents is as high as 90% at each quality level as shown in Fig. 7(d), The Skip ratio

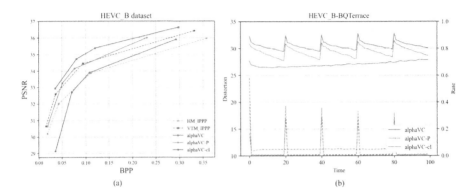

(a)   (b)

Fig. 6. Comparison with each type of frame in AlphaVC. AlphaVC-P only include P-frame and I-frame, the GoP size is 20 samed as AlphaVC. AlphaVC-cI only include cI-frame and I-frame, only the first frame uses the I-frame. (a): R-D performance of AlphaVC, AlphaVC-P and AlphaVC-cI under PSNR on HEVC class B dataset. (b): Example of performance comparison for each type of frame, the tested sequence is BQTerrace in class B. The solid line indicates the curve of distortion, the dashed line indicates the curve of rate.

Table 4. Effectiveness of our different components. The BD-rate values are computed under PSNR on HEVC class B dataset.

(a)				(b)				
I-frame	✓	✓	✓	P2F MP	✓			
P-frame	✓	✓		Skip in M.	✓	✓		
cI-frame	✓		✓	Skip in R.	✓	✓	✓	
BD-Rate	0%	21.4%	92.7%	BD-Rate	0%	10.4%	18.6%	37.5%

of residual latents gradually increases (60%–90%) with the decrease of quality. With the number of skipped elements increases, we can clearly see in Fig. 7(d) that the runtime of entropy coding on CPU is greatly reduced. In addition, as shown in Table 4(b), the probability-based skip entropy method can also improve performance obviously.

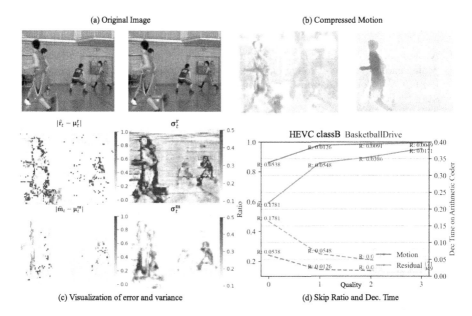

Fig. 7. Analysis of methods. (a): Two adjacent original frames of HEVC classB BasketballDrive. (b): Left/Right: The compressed motion wo/w our motion prediction module. (c): Visualization of variance of gaussian distortion σ and error after replacement. (d): Example result of the average skip ratio and arithmetic decoding time at 4 different bit rates, the ratio is calculated by skipped elements/total elements. The motion and residual latents are shown in the red and yellow curve, respectively. The solid and dotted curves represent ratio and time, respectively. The number on curves indicates bit-rate(BPP). (Color figure online)

5   Conclusion

This paper proposed a high-performance and efficient learned video compression approach named AlphaVC. Specifically, we designed a new coding mode including three types of frame: I-frame, P-frame, and cI-frame, to reduce the bit rate of I-frame and mitigate the accumulative error. We then proposed two efficient techniques: P2F MP for improving the accuracy of inter-frame prediction at the encoder side, and Skip for reducing entropy and speeding up runtime. Experimental results show that AlphaVC outperforms H.266/VVC in terms of PSNR by 28% under the same configuration, meanwhile AlphaVC has the comparable decoding time compared with VTM. To the best of our knowledge, AlphaVC is the first learned video compression scheme achieving such a milestone result that outperforms VTM-IPP over the entire bitrate range and on all common test datasets.

We believe that our proposed AlphaVC provides some novel and useful techniques that can help researcheres to further develop the next generation video codecs with more powerful compression.

References

1. Agustsson, E., Minnen, D., Johnston, N., Balle, J., Hwang, S.J., Toderici, G.: Scale-space flow for end-to-end optimized video compression. In: Proceedings of the IEEE/CVF Conference on Computer Vision and Pattern Recognition, pp. 8503–8512 (2020)
2. Ahmed, N., Natarajan, T., Rao, K.R.: Discrete cosine transform. IEEE Trans. Comput. **100**(1), 90–93 (1974)
3. Ballé, J., Laparra, V., Simoncelli, E.P.: End-to-end optimization of nonlinear transform codes for perceptual quality. In: 2016 Picture Coding Symposium (PCS), pp. 1–5. IEEE (2016)
4. Ballé, J., Minnen, D., Singh, S., Hwang, S.J., Johnston, N.: Variational image compression with a scale hyperprior. arXiv preprint arXiv:1802.01436 (2018)
5. Bellard, F.: BPG image format (2014). www.bellard.org/bpg/. Accessed 05 Aug 2016
6. Bossen, F.: Common test conditions and software reference configurations, document jctvc-l1100. JCT-VC, San Jose, CA (2012)
7. Bross, B., Chen, J., Ohm, J.R., Sullivan, G.J., Wang, Y.K.: Developments in international video coding standardization after AVC, with an overview of versatile video coding (VVC). Proc. IEEE **109**(9), 1463–1493 (2021)
8. Cheng, Z., Sun, H., Takeuchi, M., Katto, J.: Learned image compression with discretized gaussian mixture likelihoods and attention modules. In: Proceedings of the IEEE/CVF Conference on Computer Vision and Pattern Recognition, pp. 7939–7948 (2020)
9. Christopoulos, C., Skodras, A., Ebrahimi, T.: The JPEG2000 still image coding system: an overview. IEEE Trans. Consum. Electron. **46**(4), 1103–1127 (2000)
10. Cisco: Cisco annual internet report (2018–2023) white paper. www.cisco.com/c/en/us/solutions/collateral/executive-perspectives/annual-internet-report/white-paper-c11-741490.html (2020)
11. Cui, Z., Wang, J., Gao, S., Guo, T., Feng, Y., Bai, B.: Asymmetric gained deep image compression with continuous rate adaptation. In: Proceedings of the IEEE/CVF Conference on Computer Vision and Pattern Recognition, pp. 10532–10541 (2021)
12. Dai, J., et al.: Deformable convolutional networks. In: Proceedings of the IEEE International Conference on Computer Vision, pp. 764–773 (2017)
13. Duda, J.: Asymmetric numeral systems. arXiv preprint arXiv:0902.0271 (2009)
14. Feng, R., Guo, Z., Zhang, Z., Chen, Z.: Versatile learned video compression. arXiv preprint arXiv:2111.03386 (2021)
15. Guo, T., Wang, J., Cui, Z., Feng, Y., Ge, Y., Bai, B.: Variable rate image compression with content adaptive optimization. In: Proceedings of the IEEE/CVF Conference on Computer Vision and Pattern Recognition Workshops, pp. 122–123 (2020)
16. Guo, Z., Feng, R., Zhang, Z., Jin, X., Chen, Z.: Learning cross-scale prediction for efficient neural video compression. arXiv preprint arXiv:2112.13309 (2021)
17. Habibian, A., Rozendaal, T.v., Tomczak, J.M., Cohen, T.S.: Video compression with rate-distortion autoencoders. In: Proceedings of the IEEE/CVF International Conference on Computer Vision, pp. 7033–7042 (2019)
18. Howard, P.G., Vitter, J.S.: Arithmetic coding for data compression. Proc. IEEE **82**(6), 857–865 (1994)

19. Hu, Z., Lu, G., Xu, D.: FVC: a new framework towards deep video compression in feature space. In: Proceedings of the IEEE/CVF Conference on Computer Vision and Pattern Recognition, pp. 1502–1511 (2021)

20. Kingma, D.P., Welling, M.: Auto-encoding variational Bayes. arXiv preprint arXiv:1312.6114 (2013)

21. Li, J., Li, B., Lu, Y.: Deep contextual video compression. In: Advances in Neural Information Processing Systems, vol. 34 (2021)

22. Liu, J., et al.: Conditional entropy coding for efficient video compression. In: Vedaldi, A., Bischof, H., Brox, T., Frahm, J.-M. (eds.) ECCV 2020. LNCS, vol. 12362, pp. 453–468. Springer, Cham (2020). https://doi.org/10.1007/978-3-030-58520-4_27

23. Lu, G., et al.: Content adaptive and error propagation aware deep video compression. In: Vedaldi, A., Bischof, H., Brox, T., Frahm, J.-M. (eds.) ECCV 2020. LNCS, vol. 12347, pp. 456–472. Springer, Cham (2020). https://doi.org/10.1007/978-3-030-58536-5_27

24. Lu, G., Zhang, X., Ouyang, W., Chen, L., Gao, Z., Xu, D.: An end-to-end learning framework for video compression. IEEE Trans. Pattern Anal. Mach. Intell. **43**(10), 3292–3308 (2020)

25. Mercat, A., Viitanen, M., Vanne, J.: UVG dataset: 50/120fps 4k sequences for video codec analysis and development. In: Proceedings of the 11th ACM Multimedia Systems Conference, pp. 297–302 (2020)

26. Minnen, D., Ballé, J., Toderici, G.D.: Joint autoregressive and hierarchical priors for learned image compression. In: Advances in Neural Information Processing Systems, vol. 31 (2018)

27. Pourreza, R., Cohen, T.: Extending neural p-frame codecs for b-frame coding. In: Proceedings of the IEEE/CVF International Conference on Computer Vision, pp. 6680–6689 (2021)

28. Sheng, X., Li, J., Li, B., Li, L., Liu, D., Lu, Y.: Temporal context mining for learned video compression. arXiv preprint arXiv:2111.13850 (2021)

29. Sullivan, G.J., Ohm, J.R., Han, W.J., Wiegand, T.: Overview of the high efficiency video coding (HEVC) standard. IEEE Trans. Circuits Syst. Video Technol. **22**(12), 1649–1668 (2012)

30. Sun, D., Yang, X., Liu, M.Y., Kautz, J.: PWC-Net: CNNs for optical flow using pyramid, warping, and cost volume. In: Proceedings of the IEEE Conference on Computer Vision and Pattern Recognition, pp. 8934–8943 (2018)

31. Teed, Z., Deng, J.: RAFT: recurrent all-pairs field transforms for optical flow. In: Vedaldi, A., Bischof, H., Brox, T., Frahm, J.-M. (eds.) ECCV 2020. LNCS, vol. 12347, pp. 402–419. Springer, Cham (2020). https://doi.org/10.1007/978-3-030-58536-5_24

32. Wallace, G.K.: The JPEG still picture compression standard. IEEE Trans. Consum. Electron. **38**(1), xviii-xxxiv (1992)

33. Wang, H., et al.: MCL-JCV: a JND-based H. 264/AVC video quality assessment dataset. In: 2016 IEEE International Conference on Image Processing (ICIP), pp. 1509–1513. IEEE (2016)

34. Wang, Z., Simoncelli, E.P., Bovik, A.C.: Multiscale structural similarity for image quality assessment. In: The Thrity-Seventh Asilomar Conference on Signals, Systems & Computers, 2003, vol. 2, pp. 1398–1402. IEEE (2003)

35. Wiegand, T., Sullivan, G.J., Bjontegaard, G., Luthra, A.: Overview of the H. 264/AVC video coding standard. IEEE Trans. Circuits Syst. Video Technol. **13**(7), 560–576 (2003)

Content-Oriented Learned Image Compression

Meng Li, Shangyin Gao, Yihui Feng, Yibo Shi, and Jing Wang[✉]

Huawei Technologies, Beijing, China
wangjing215@huawei.com

Abstract. In recent years, with the development of deep neural networks, end-to-end optimized image compression has made significant progress and exceeded the classic methods in terms of rate-distortion performance. However, most learning-based image compression methods are unlabeled and do not consider image semantics or content when optimizing the model. In fact, human eyes have different sensitivities to different content, so the image content also needs to be considered. In this paper, we propose a content-oriented image compression method, which handles different kinds of image contents with different strategies. Extensive experiments show that the proposed method achieves competitive subjective results compared with state-of-the-art end-to-end learned image compression methods or classic methods.

Keywords: Image compression · Content-oriented · Loss metric

1 Introduction

An uncompressed image usually contains tremendous data that is expensive to store or transmit. Therefore, image compression, or image codec, which aims to reduce redundant information in image data for efficient storage and transmission, is an essential part of real-world applications. The frameworks of traditional image compression methods such as JPEG [25], JPEG2000 [24] and BPG [6] are sophistically designed, which usually include modules of prediction, transformation, quantization, and entropy coding. However, each module in the frameworks is optimized separately, making it hard to achieve global optimality.

In recent years, with the development of deep learning, end-to-end (E2E) learned image compression methods are proposed. Compared with traditional codecs, the biggest advantage of E2E methods is that the whole framework can be jointly optimized, making it has a greater protential in compression efficiency. Impressively, it takes only five years for E2E image compression to outpace the traditional methods that have developed for 30 years in terms of rate-distortion performance. Mainstream E2E image compression methods rely on the variational autoencoder (VAE) [3,4,15,21] or generative adversarial network (GAN) [1,2,20,22] to compress images, and various loss metrics such as Mean Squared Error (MSE), Multi-Scale Structural Similarity Index (MS-SSIM) [27], Learned

S. Avidan et al. (Eds.): ECCV 2022, LNCS 13679, pp. 632–647, 2022.
https://doi.org/10.1007/978-3-031-19800-7_37

Fig. 1. Reconstructed image with different methods at a similar bitrate.

Perceptual Image Patch Similarity (LPIPS) [28], etc. are used to optimize the model. Most existing methods optimized all regions of the image in the same way, and have different distortions at low bit rates. For example, Minnen [21] used MSE metric to train a VAE image compression network. In this optimization, structural information such as text and lines are correctly perserved, but the reconstructed image will become too blurry. Mentzer [20] tried to improve the image quality by introducing GAN and LPIPS. In this optimization, the informative details are well preserved, but the structural information is distorted, such as distorted text, warped face (demonstrate in the left part of Fig. 1).

Image content plays an important role in human perception, and human eyes have different sensitivities to different content. However, the influence of image content has been largely ignored in learning-based image compression. Different regions of the images have different properties, so the training strategy should also be different. For example, pixels in flat or texture regions are strongly correlated, and it is better to use loss metrics with a large receptive field. In contrast, pixels in edge or structure reagions have little correlation with their neighborhoods, and it is better to use loss metrics with a small receptive field. The usage of paintbrushes is a good analogy to describe it, large paintbrushes are usually used to make large textures and to lay large color blocks, while small paintbrushes are usually used to draw fine lines and color dots. Besides, for some special regions, like small face, it is needed to use more strict constraints to avoid deformation. As a result, to address the problems above, we propose a content-oriented image compression scheme, which is suitable for most of the existing frameworks. Specifically, in the training stage, we divide the image into different regions, and use different loss metrics according to their characteristics.

To the best of our knowledge, this is the first content-oriented image compression method that improves the visual perceptual quality without changing the architecture. An instance is shown in Fig. 1, which demonstrates the superiority of our method. The contributions of this paper are summarized as follows:

1. We propose a content-oriented E2E image compression scheme, in which we use different loss metrics in different regions. The region masks are used only in the training stage, and no extra information is needed in the encoding and decoding stage.
2. To evaluate the scheme, we design a GAN-based architecture as an instance to show the effectiveness. Several classic and E2E methods are used for comparison, and our method shows the best performance.

2 Related Work

2.1 Loss Metrics

MAE/MSE Loss. MSE and the mean absolute error (MAE) are two of the most commonly used loss metrics in image compression. MAE and MSE metrics assume pixel-wise independence, and constrints the accuracy of the corresponding pixels. However, the main drawback of MSE loss metric mostly yields an oversmoothed reconstruction, which results in a lack of high-frequency details in the edges and textures. Given an image x and its reconstructed version $\tilde{x}$, the MAE and MSE loss are computed by:

$$\mathcal{L}_{mae} = \mathbb{E}\|x - \tilde{x}\|_1$$
$$\mathcal{L}_{mse} = \mathbb{E}\|x - \tilde{x}\|_2^2 \tag{1}$$

Laplacian Loss. Laplacian is a differential operator given by the divergence of the gradient, which is always used to detect the high-frenquency component of images. The Laplacian loss is defined as the mean-squared distance between their Laplacians:

$$\mathcal{L}_{lap} = \mathbb{E}\|L(x) - L(\tilde{x})\|_2^2 \tag{2}$$

where $\mathcal{L}_{lap}$ is the Laplacian loss value. As shown in Eq. 2, it is also a point-to-point loss metric, which constraints the Laplacians of the corresponding location. By doing this, the high-frenquency component of the area is preserved.

LPIPS Loss. LPIPS is a state-of-the-art perceptual metric proposed by Zhang [28]. He uses architectures trained for classification as feature extractors, and leverages the power of the features to judge the similarity between the reconstructed image and the original one, which is computed by:

$$\mathcal{L}_{lpips} = \sum_k \tau^k \left(f^k(x) - f^k(\tilde{x})\right) \tag{3}$$

where f denotes the feature extractor, and τ^k computes the score of features from the k-th layer of the architecture. The LPIPS value is the averaged score of all layers. It is a loss metric with a large receptive field, which constraints the distribution of corresponding location. The LPIPS metrics makes images more semantically similar, which is more consistent with human perception. However, the absence of point to point constraints may result in geometric distortion.

GAN Loss. GAN is widely used for perceptual image compression. By taking advantage of adversarial training, GAN-based architectures can produce more photo-realistic images. It contains two rivaling networks: the generator G is used to generate an image $\tilde{x} = G(\hat{y})$ that is consistent with the input image distribution p_x, and the discriminator D is used to predict if the input image is an image generated by G. The goal of GAN for G is to produce images that are real enough to fool D. In the procedure of training, the image produced by G becomes more and more authentic, and D becomes more and more discriminating, finally reaching a balance.

2.2   Learned Image Compression Methods

Many E2E image compression methods take advantage of VAE as its backbone, which usually consists of four components: the encoder, the quantizer, the entropy module and the decoder. The encoder is used to encode the input image x into a latent representation y, which is then quantized to $\hat{y}$ by the quantizer. The entropy module, which is used to estimate the distribution of $\hat{y}$, plays an important role in minimizing the rate-distortion cost. Finally, the quantified feature $\hat{y}$ is transformed to reconstruct the image $\tilde{x}$. The framework is directly optimized for the rate-distortion trade-off, that is: $\mathcal{L}_{RD} = R + \lambda d$. Where R represents the bitrate which is lower-bounded by the entropy of the discrete probability distribution of $\hat{y}$, d is the reconstruction distortion, λ controls the trade-off. The framework is first proposed by Ballé in reference [3], where they introduced the widely used generalized divisive normalization (GDN) transform. In their following works, they proposed the hyper prior [4] to better exploit the probability distribution of the latent feature. And in [15,21], spacial context structure is proposed to improve the performance of the entropy module.

On the basis of above works, some researchers proposed to use GAN and some perceptual metrics (e.g. LPIPS) to improve the visual perceptual quality. Rippel [22] first introduced the effectiveness of GAN in generating perceptual friendly images at an extremely low bitrate. In the following works, Agustsson [1], Akutsu [2], Dash [10] also make use of GAN loss to improve the perceptual quality of reconstruction images. According to rate-distortion-perception theory presented in [5], Mentzer combines MSE (Mean squared error), LPIPS and GAN loss to generate images of competitive perceptual quality [20]. In this paper, we also use a GAN-based architecture, and what distinguishes us from previous works is that we take the image contents into consideration, and adopt different strategies on different target regions.

Another related topic of the work is content-related image compression. Li introduced a content-weighted importance map to guide the allocation of local bit rate [17]. Similarly, Cai proposed a CNN based ROI image compression method to allocate more bits to the ROI areas [7]. Besides, Zhang proposed an attention-guided dual-layer image compression, which employs a CNN module to predict those pixels on and near a saliency sketch within ROI that are critical to perceptual quality [29]. However, most of the existing content-related works need to change the architecture and allocate more bits in important fields, thus increasing the network complexity and reducing the compression efficiency. Different from above, we proposed a content-oriented image compression method by adopting different loss strategies on different areas. The advantage is that our scheme can be applied in most of the previous works without changing the architecture. Besides, the image content masks are learned by the network during the training, so no extra information is needed when encoding or decoding an image.

3   Method

3.1   Framework of Our Method

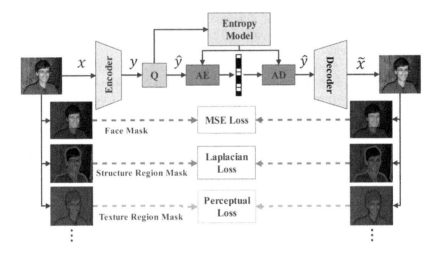

Fig. 2. Framework of our method.

From Sect. 2.1, it is easy to deduce that different loss functions are suitable for different image contents. However, existing learned image compression always optimizes the whole image with the same loss function. In existing content-related image compression methods, important maps [17], ROI masks [7], or other extra information need to be encoded as part of the codestream. One the one hand, such methods require changing the encoder-decoder structure to make the architecture more complex by adding a special module to extract the important maps or ROI masks, on the other hand, they also increase the extra bits that inevitably degrade the coding efficiency. This problem can be overcome if the architecture is 'clever' enough to distinguish different image contents and employ different compression strategies. The whole framework of our method is shown in Fig. 2. The mask information is only used to select different loss functions during the training phase and not needed in the inference phase.

As shown in Fig. 2, E2E image compression is transformed from unlabeled to labeled learning. The choice of the loss functions depends on the classification of image regions. According to the previous analysis, we divide the image into three image regions, namely texture region, structure region, and small face region.

Structure Region. Structure regions usually have strong gradients and have little statistical correlation with very close neighborhoods due to the abrupt changes in pixels. And loss function with large receptive field will introduce additional noise, which is not acceptable for a precise edge reconstruction. The human eye is sensitive to the sharpness and the pixel-wise correctness of the structure, so a point-wise loss function is more suitable. However, MSE will lead to a blurred reconstruction, affecting the subjective visual perception. As shown in Fig. 3 [19], considering a simple 1-dimensional case. If the model is only optimized in image space by the L1 or MSE loss, we usually get a reconstructed sequence as Fig. 3(b) given an input testing sequence whose ground-truth is a sharp edge as Fig. 3(a). The model fails to recover sharp edges for the reason that the model tends to give a statistical average. If a second-order gradient constraint is added to the optimization objective as Fig. 3(f), the probability of recovering Fig. 3(c) is increased significantly. As a results, we choose the Laplacian loss in structure region. The structure loss function is as follows:

$$\mathcal{L}_{stru} = M_{stru} \circ \mathcal{L}_{lap} \qquad (4)$$

where M_{stru} denotes the mask of the structure region, $\mathcal{L}_{lap}$ is computed with Eq. 2. We use Laplacian edge detector to generate the M_{stru}, which will be introduced in Sect. 4.1.

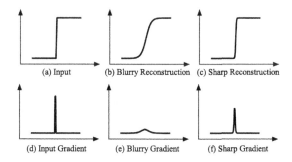

| (a) Input | (b) Blurry Reconstruction | (c) Sharp Reconstruction |
| (d) Input Gradient | (e) Blurry Gradient | (f) Sharp Gradient |

Fig. 3. An illumination of a simple 1-D case. The first row shows the pixel sequences and the second row shows their corresponding gradients.

Texture Region. Unlike structure regions, texture regions always have more details and domain pixels are highly correlated. It is difficult for the human eyes to perceive pixel-by-pixel correctness, and people are more concerned about the distribution of the texture. Existing perceptual optimization based methods [20] have achieved very compelling texture reconstruction results. Therefore, we use the perceptual loss in this region. In our work, the perceptual loss are constituted of three part: MAE loss, LPIPS loss, and GAN loss. The formulation can be denoted by:

$$\mathcal{L}_{per} = M_{tex} \circ (\alpha \cdot \mathcal{L}_{mae} + \beta \cdot \mathcal{L}_{LPIPS} + \delta \cdot \mathcal{L}_{GAN}) \tag{5}$$

where M_{tex} denotes the mask of the texture region, $\mathcal{L}_{mae}$, $\mathcal{L}_{LPIPS}$ are computed with Eqs. 1, 3, $\mathcal{L}_{GAN}$ will be introduced in Sect. 3.2. In our work, the VGG [23] network is chosen as the backbone to compute the LPIPS loss.

Small Face Region. In our framework, the facial regions will be classified as texture regions and optimised with perceptual loss if not intervened. In this case, larger faces can be well reconstructed, but small faces may be warped, as shown on the left side of Fig. 1. Therefore, we adopt a different loss function for regions of the small faces. Generally, people are very sensitive to the correctness of the face structure, for which an accurate reconstruction is necessary. Therefore, we use a stricter constraint loss, the MSE loss, for the facial image reconstruction.

$$\mathcal{L}_{sface} = M_{sface} \circ \mathcal{L}_{mse} \tag{6}$$

where the M_{sface} denotes the mask of the small face regions, and $\mathcal{L}_{mse}$ is computed with Eq. 1. We use the well-known YOLO-face to detect the faces in the image, and $\mathcal{L}_{sface}$ is only adopted to small faces. The bitrate of the quantized latent representation $\hat{y}$ is estimated by the entropy module denoted by P, $R(\hat{y}) = -\log(P(\hat{y}))$. Finally, the loss function of the whole image is summaried as:

$$\mathcal{L}_{total} = \eta R(\hat{y}) + \epsilon \mathcal{L}_{stru} + \mathcal{L}_{per} + \gamma \mathcal{L}_{sface} \tag{7}$$

where η, ϵ and γ are weights of corresponding loss metrics. Because people usually pay more attention to faces of the images, we intentionally allocate more bits on small faces by using a larger γ. Note that the masks are binary-valued and mutually exclusive. And the priority of the masks is different, specifically, from high to low: the facial mask, the structure mask and the texture mask. In other words, the structure mask doesn't cover the facial areas, and the texture mask doesn't cover the facial and structure areas.

3.2   Architecture

To prove the effectiveness of our method, we design an E2E image compression architecture, as shown in Fig. 4. It consists of four parts: the encoder E, the decoder/generator G, the entropy module P, and the discriminator D.

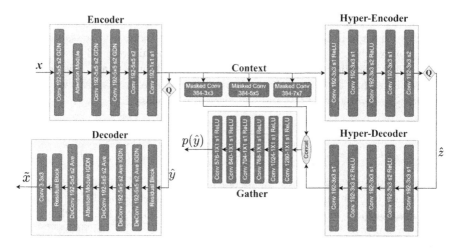

Fig. 4. The architecture of our method. $Conv192 - 5 \times 5$ is a convolution with 192 output channels, with 5×5 filters. $DeConv$ is a deconvolution operation. $s2$ means the stride of this convolution or deconvolution is 2. Ave means average pooling. GDN or $ReLU$ is used to increase the non-linearity.

Autoencoder. For the encoder and generator/decoder, GDN [3] is used to normalize the intermediate feature and also play a role of non-linearity element. Besides, to capture the global dependencies between features, we introduced the attention module (the residual non-local attention block, RNAB) [30] integrated into the architecture. It is well-known that deconvolution operation, or transposed convolution always generates checkerboard artifacts on the reconstructed image. The main reason is, the up-sampled feature map generated by deconvolution can be considered as the result of periodical shuffling of multiple intermediate feature maps computed from the input feature map by independent convolutions [12]. As a result, adjacent pixels on the output feature map are not directly related, resulting in checkerboard artifacts. To alleviate this issue, we add an extra average pooling layer after every deconvolution layer to strengthen the association between adjacent pixels.

Entropy Model. We adopt the context-based model [21] to extract side information z, which is used to model the distribution of latent representation $\hat{y}$. And uniform noise U(-1/2,1/2) is used to simulate quantization in the hyperencoder and when estimating $p(\hat{y}|z)$. The distribution of $\hat{y}$ is modeled with an asymmetric Gaussian entropy model [9], which can be denoted by:

$$p_{\hat{y}|\hat{z}}(\hat{y} \mid \hat{z}) \sim N\left(\mu, \sigma_l^2, \sigma_r^2\right) \tag{8}$$

where μ represent the mean of the latent representation, σ_l^2 and σ_r^2 represent the estimated left-scale and right-scale parameter, respectively. The asymmetric Gaussian model has stronger representation ability when the entropy estimation do not obey the Gaussian distribution.

Discriminator. In our framework, adversarial training is adopted to improve the perceptual quality of the reconstructed images. Instead of a standard discriminator, we borrow the relativistic average discriminator [13] used in [26], which tries to predict the probability that a groundtruth image x is relatively more realistic than a generated one $\tilde{x}$, on average. The loss is divided into two parts, the generator loss $\mathcal{L}_D^{Ra}$, and the discriminator loss $\mathcal{L}_G^{Ra}$:

$$
\begin{aligned}
\mathcal{L}_D^{Ra} &= -\mathbb{E}_x \left[\log \left(D_{Ra} \left(x, \tilde{x} \right) \right) \right] - \mathbb{E}_{\tilde{x}} \left[\log \left(1 - D_{Ra} \left(\tilde{x}, x \right) \right) \right] \\
\mathcal{L}_G^{Ra} &= -\mathbb{E}_x \left[\log \left(1 - D_{Ra} \left(x, \tilde{x} \right) \right) \right] - \mathbb{E}_{\tilde{x}} \left[\log \left(D_{Ra} \left(\tilde{x}, x \right) \right) \right]
\end{aligned}
\tag{9}
$$

where $D_{Ra} \left(x, \tilde{x} \right) = \sigma \left(C \left(x \right) - \mathbb{E}_{\tilde{x}} \left[C \left(\tilde{x} \right) \right] \right)$. $C \left(x \right)$ and $C \left(\tilde{x} \right)$ are the the non-transformed discriminator ouput. σ is the sigmoid function, and $\mathbb{E}_x [\cdot]$ computes the average output. Moreover, the PatchGAN discriminator [16], which has been proven to improve the quality of the generated images, is also utilized in our architecture. The PatchGAN has fewer parameters. And it not only preserves more texture but can also be applied to images of arbitrary sizes. The detailed architecture of our discriminator is shown in Fig. 5.

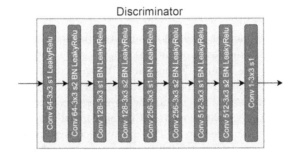

Fig. 5. The architecture of discriminator. Same notation is used as in Fig. 4.

3.3   Implementation of Masked Perceptual Loss

Usuallym, Adding a pixel-level mask to MSE or MAE is easy with simple point-wise multiplication. But it is a little harder to used on LPIPS or GAN losses, because these two loss functions compute the feature losses and cannot correspond to mask pixel-to-pixel. In this section, we propose a method called 'real value replacement' to solve the problem.

Consider the mask M_{tex}, the original image x, and the reconstructed image $\tilde{x}$, we replace the value of the mask part of $\tilde{x}$ with the corresponding value of x to get the replaced reconstructed image $\tilde{x}'$:

$$
\tilde{x}' = (1 - M_{tex}) \circ x + M_{tex} \circ \tilde{x}
\tag{10}
$$

Then calculate the loss function directly with x and $\tilde{x}'$ to estimate the masked loss:

$$M_{tex} \circ \mathcal{L}_{LPIPS}(x, \tilde{x}) \approx \mathcal{L}_{LPIPS}(x, \tilde{x}')$$
$$M_{tex} \circ \mathcal{L}_{GAN}(x, \tilde{x}) \approx \mathcal{L}_{GAN}(x, \tilde{x}') \tag{11}$$

4 Experiment

4.1 Training Details

Due to the adoption of face loss, a large number of face images are required for training. For this purpose, we use the well-known MSCOCO dataset [18] as our training set, and Kodak dataset [14] as our testing set. It is notoriously hard to train GANs for image generation, so the training procedure is divided into two stages. In the first stage, we only use the MSE as the distortion loss to guide the optimization at the pixel level reconstruction. The optimization target in the first stage is to minimize $\mathcal{L}_{RD} = \eta R + \mathcal{L}_{mse}$. Using the first stage result as the pre-trained model, we can train the perceptual optimized model with the loss function Eq. 7 mentioned in Sect. 3.2 in the second stage. During the training phase, we randomly crop the images into patches of size 256×256 and set the batch size to 8. The initial learning rate is set to 0.0001 and halved at 160k and 500k iteration. We use kaiming initialization [11] to initialize all our models. The weights of the loss are set: $\alpha = 0.01$, $\beta = 1$, $\gamma = 0.2$, $\delta = 0.0005$, and $\epsilon = 0.3$. We only modify η for different target bit-rates.

In order to use different loss metrics on different regions of the images, the masks of different content regions are required. In our experiment, the faces in the images are detected using the well-known YOLO-face [8]. Then the coordinate information of the faces is stored in an XML file, which is used to generate the face masks in the training phase. By doing this, we can save the face detection time during training the model. For structure region masks, due to the low complexity of edge detection, we do not generate masks in advance, but directly use Laplacian edge detectors to detect structure regions during training.

4.2 Ablation Study

Ablation on the Loss Metric. In order to show the effectiveness of the proposed, we conduct several comparative experiments as follows.

- Case 1, the model is optimized only with MSE loss. (MSE)
- Case 2, the model is optimized with MAE, LPIPS and GAN loss. (Perceptual)
- Case 3, the model is optimized with MAE, LPIPS, GAN and Laplacian loss. (Perceptual + Lap)
- Case 4, the model is optimized with MAE, LPIPS, GAN, Laplacian and face loss. (Perceptual + Lap & face)

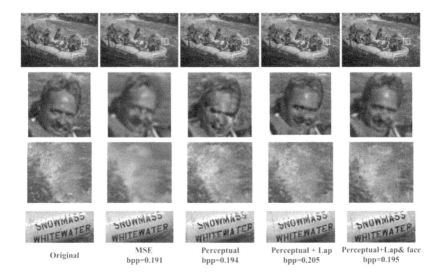

| Original | MSE
bpp=0.191 | Perceptual
bpp=0.194 | Perceptual + Lap
bpp=0.205 | Perceptual+Lap& face
bpp=0.195 |

Fig. 6. Comparison of different loss strategies.

(a) with HIFIC discriminator (b) with our discriminator

Fig. 7. Comparison of the discriminators

(a) without average pooling   (b) with average pooling

Fig. 8. Ablation on the average pooling

Take the image kodim14 an example, the visual comparison of different cases is shown in Fig. 6. All of these cases are compressed at a similar bitrate, around 0.2 bpp. Overall, it can be clearly observed that the reconstructed image in case 5 has high-fidelity facial features, clear and correct text, informatively detailed backgrounds and an overall harmonious visual quality. Specifically, in case 1, the faces and water waves are too blurred, which attributes to the property of the MSE loss function. In case 2, with the help of additional loss functions GAN and LPIPS, the informative details of water waves are restored, but the facial features and text are severely warped. In case 3, with the help of additional edge loss, not only the informative details of water waves are restored, but the text distortion phenomenon also disappears. However, the facial distortion remains. Until all the losses are added, in case 5, the best visual effect is achieve in all the areas. Through the ablation study, we can draw two conclusions: (1) the architecture proposed in 3.3 is able to distinguish different image contents; (2) adopting appropriate loss function for different image content helps improve the visual quality of reconstructed images.

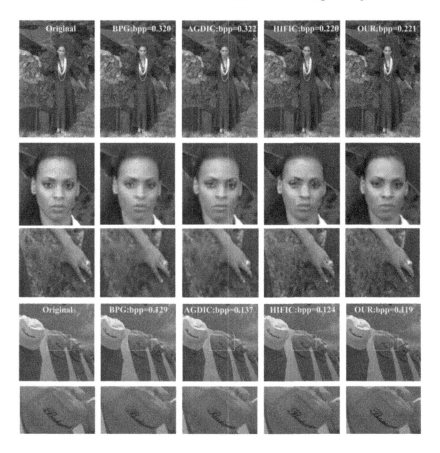

Fig. 9. Compressed results of kodim18 using different methods.

Ablation on the Architecture. In order to get better result, we choose the better components in our architecture, such as the asymmetric Gaussian entropy model, the relatively average discriminator,and the average pooling. We have done relevant experiments to demonstrate the effectiveness of our architecture. The results show that with the help of the asymmetric Gaussian model, we achieve about 0.68% BD-rate reduction compared with the general Gaussian entropy model. We also tested the effectiveness of our disriminator, and the result shown in Fig. 7 proves that our discriminator can preserve more details than that of HIFIC. Besides, Fig. 8 shows that the average polling can alleviate the checkerboard artifacts.

4.3   Visual Results

To show the advantage of our method, we compare our method (named COLIC) with BPG, Asymmetric Gained Deep Image Compression (AGDIC) optimized with MSE [9] and High-Fidelity Generative Image Compression (HIFIC, SOTA

644   M. Li et al.

perceptual optimized method) [20].Since BPG and AGDIC are not perceptual-optimized, we select relatively higher bitrates for them. The visual results are shown in Fig. 9, in which the cropped blocks highlight the reconstruction of certain regions, such as textures, texts, and small faces. As can be seen from Fig. 9, although BPG and AGDIC can maintain the correct facial structure and achieve relatively better results in text area, the texture results are over-smoothed. As shown in the third row, the background generated by BPG and AGDIP is too blurry. On the contrary, although HIFIC can reconstruct the informative details, it will lead to the distortion of face and text. As shown in the second and fifth rows, the face and text generated by HIFIC are overwarpped. Compared to these results, it is clear that our proposed COLIC achieves the best visual effects. It handles all these situations better, recovering more texture detail, correct small face and text structure.

More examples of comparison with HIFIC are shown in Fig. 10. Compared with HIFIC, COLIC can not only recover similar informative texture regions, such as the spray, but also better structured regions such as lines, textures and small faces. In a word, COLIC can achieve better visual effects.

Fig. 10. Compressed results of kodim18 using different methods.

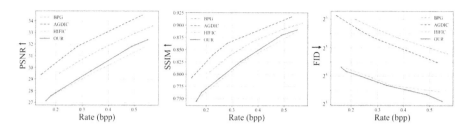

Fig. 11. Rate-distortion and -perception curves on Kodak. Arrows indicate whether lower is better (↓), or higher is better (↑).

4.4 Statistics Result

In this section, we use metrics such as PSNR, SSIM, and FID to quantify our results. PSNR and SSIM are widely used in various digital image evaluations, which compute the average pixel-wise distance and structural similarity between the two images. Unlike PSNR, SSIM, which measure the similarity between individual images pairs, FID assesses the similarity between the distribution of the reference images and the generated/distorted images. FID is a good metric for evaluating the subjective results and is widely used for super-resolution or generative tasks.

The R-D curves of COLIC, BPG, AGDIC and HIFIC are shown in Fig. 11. Compared with BPG and AGDIC, as expected, COLIC and HIFIC dominate in perceptual metric FID, but relatively poor on objective metrics PSNR and SSIM, which can be explained by the rate-distortion-perception theory [5] that they sacrifice some objective performance to improve the perceptual quality. In order to improve the visual quality, we sacrifice some of the objective metrics. Compared with HIFIC, COLIC achieves better results on both objective and perceptual metrics. It attributes to the better optimization loss that imposes the correct constraints on the structure region, the better network structure that with better reconstruction ability, and better training strategy.

5 Conclusion

In this work, we propose a content-oriented image compression scheme, which can be used in most existing methods. We suggest that different loss metrics should be used on different image contents according to their characteristics. And a GAN-based architecture is designed to prove the effectiveness of our scheme. Experiments clearly show the superiority of our method on visual quality as well as different metrics. In fact, the effectiveness of this method demostrates that existing encoders and decoders are 'smart' enough to distinguish different image regions and employ different reconstruction strategies with the guidance of different training loss. Therefore, human perceptual priors can be better utilized through supervised training methods to obtain better subjective results.

References

1. Agustsson, E., Tschannen, M., Mentzer, F., Timofte, R., Van Gool, L.: Generative adversarial networks for extreme learned image compression. In: 2019 IEEE/CVF International Conference on Computer Vision (ICCV), pp. 221–231 (2019). https://doi.org/10.1109/ICCV.2019.00031

2. Akutsu, H., Suzuki, A., Zhong, Z., Aizawa, K.: Ultra low bitrate learned image compression by selective detail decoding. In: 2020 IEEE/CVF Conference on Computer Vision and Pattern Recognition Workshops (CVPRW), pp. 524–528 (2020). https://doi.org/10.1109/CVPRW50498.2020.00067

3. Ballé, J., Laparra, V., Simoncelli, E.: End-to-end optimized image compression. In: Proceedings of the International Conference on Learning Representations (ICLR) (2017)

4. Ballé, J., Minnen, D., Singh, S., Hwang, S., Johnston, N.: Variational image compression with a scale hyperprior. In: Proceedings of the International Conference on Learning Representations (ICLR) (2018)

5. Blau, Y., Michaeli, T.: Rethinking lossy compression: the rate-distortion-perception tradeoff. In: Chaudhuri, K., Salakhutdinov, R. (eds.) Proceedings of the 36th International Conference on Machine Learning, vol. 97, pp. 675–685 (2019)

6. BPG: Bpg image format (2014). https://bellard.org/bpg/. Accessed 7 Mar 2022

7. Cai, C., Chen, L., Zhang, X., Gao, Z.: End-to-end optimized ROI image compression. IEEE Trans. Image Process. **29**, 3442–3457 (2020). https://doi.org/10.1109/TIP.2019.2960869

8. Chen, W., Huang, H., Peng, S., Zhou, C., Zhang, C.: YOLO-face: a real-time face detector. Vis. Comput. **37**(4), 805–813 (2020). https://doi.org/10.1007/s00371-020-01831-7

9. Cui, Z., Wang, J., Gao, S., Guo, T., Feng, Y., Bai, B.: Asymmetric gained deep image compression with continuous rate adaptation. In: Proceedings of the IEEE/CVF Conference on Computer Vision and Pattern Recognition (CVPR), pp. 10532–10541 (2021)

10. Dash, S., Kumaravelu, G., Naganoor, V., Raman, S.K., Ramesh, A., Lee, H.: Compressnet: Generative compression at extremely low bitrates. In: 2020 IEEE Winter Conference on Applications of Computer Vision (WACV), pp. 2314–2322 (2020). https://doi.org/10.1109/WACV45572.2020.9093415

11. He, K., Zhang, X., Ren, S., Sun, J.: Delving deep into rectifiers: surpassing human-level performance on imagenet classification. In: 2015 IEEE International Conference on Computer Vision (ICCV), pp. 1026–1034 (2015). https://doi.org/10.1109/ICCV.2015.123

12. Hongyang, G., Hao, Y., Zhengyang, W., Shuiwang, J.: Pixel deconvolutional networks. In: Proceedings of the International Conference on Learning Representations (ICLR) (2018)

13. Jolicoeur-Martineau, A.: The relativistic discriminator: a key element missing from standard gan. In: Proceedings of the International Conference on Learning Representations (ICLR) (2019)

14. Kodak, E.: Kodak lossless true color image suite: photocd pcd0992 (1993). http://r0k.us/graphics/kodak/. Accessed 7 Mar 2022

15. Lee, J., Cho, S., Beack, S.K.: Context-adaptive entropy model for end-to-end optimized image compression. In: Proceedings of the International Conference on Learning Representations (ICLR) (2018)

16. Li, C., Wand, M.: Precomputed real-time texture synthesis with markovian generative adversarial networks. In: Leibe, B., Matas, J., Sebe, N., Welling, M. (eds.) ECCV 2016. LNCS, vol. 9907, pp. 702–716. Springer, Cham (2016). https://doi.org/10.1007/978-3-319-46487-9_43

17. Li, M., Zuo, W., Gu, S., Zhao, D., Zhang, D.: Learning convolutional networks for content-weighted image compression. In: 2018 IEEE/CVF Conference on Computer Vision and Pattern Recognition, pp. 3214–3223 (2018). https://doi.org/10.1109/CVPR.2018.00339

18. Lin, T.-Y., et al.: Microsoft COCO: common objects in context. In: Fleet, D., Pajdla, T., Schiele, B., Tuytelaars, T. (eds.) ECCV 2014. LNCS, vol. 8693, pp. 740–755. Springer, Cham (2014). https://doi.org/10.1007/978-3-319-10602-1_48

19. Ma, C., Rao, Y., Cheng, Y., Chen, C., Lu, J., Zhou, J.: Structure-preserving super resolution with gradient guidance, pp. 7766–7775 (2020). https://doi.org/10.1109/CVPR42600.2020.00779

20. Mentzer, F., Toderici, G., Tschannen, M., Agustsson, E.: High-fidelity generative image compression. In: Advances in Neural Information Processing Systems (NeurIPS) (2020)

21. Minnen, D., Ballé, J., Toderici, G.: Joint autoregressive and hierarchical priors for learned image compression. In: Proceedings of the 32nd International Conference on Neural Information Processing Systems, pp. 10794–10803 (2018)

22. Rippel, O., Bourdev, L.: Real-time adaptive image compression. In: Proceedings of the 34th International Conference on Machine Learning, vol. 70, pp. 2922–2930. PMLR (2017)

23. Simonyan, K., Zisserman, A.: Very deep convolutional networks for large-scale image recognition. In: International Conference on Learning Representations (2015)

24. David, S.T.: Jpeg 2000: image compression fundamentals, standards and practice. J. Electron. Imaging **11**(2), 286 (2002)

25. Wallace, G.: The jpeg still picture compression standard. IEEE Trans. Consum. Electron. **38**(1), 18–34 (1992). https://doi.org/10.1109/30.125072

26. Wang, X., et al.: Esrgan: enhanced super-resolution generative adversarial networks. In: Proceedings of the European Conference on Computer Vision (ECCV) Workshops (2018)

27. Wang, Z., Simoncelli, E., Bovik, A.: Multiscale structural similarity for image quality assessment. In: The Thrity-Seventh Asilomar Conference on Signals, Systems Computers, 2003, vol. 2, pp. 1398–1402 (2003). https://doi.org/10.1109/ACSSC.2003.1292216

28. Zhang, R., Isola, P., Efros, A.A., Shechtman, E., Wang, O.: The unreasonable effectiveness of deep features as a perceptual metric. In: Proceedings of the IEEE Conference on Computer Vision and Pattern Recognition (CVPR) (2018)

29. Zhang, X., Wu, X.: Attention-guided image compression by deep reconstruction of compressive sensed saliency skeleton. In: Proceedings of the IEEE/CVF Conference on Computer Vision and Pattern Recognition (CVPR), pp. 13354–13364 (2021)

30. Zhang, Y., Li, K., Li, K., Zhong, B., Fu, Y.R.: Residual non-local attention networks for image restoration. ArXiv abs/1903.10082 (2019)

RRSR:Reciprocal Reference-Based Image Super-Resolution with Progressive Feature Alignment and Selection

Lin Zhang[1,3,5,6], Xin Li[2], Dongliang He[2(✉)], Fu Li[2], Yili Wang[4],
and Zhaoxiang Zhang[1,3,5,7(✉)]

[1] Institute of Automation, Chinese Academy of Sciences, Beijing, China
{zhanglin2019,zhaoxiang.zhang}@ia.ac.cn
[2] Department of Computer Vision Technology (VIS), Baidu Inc., Beijing, China
{lixin41,hedongliang01,lifu}@baidu.com
[3] University of Chinese Academy of Sciences, Beijing, China
[4] Tsinghua University, Beijing, China
wangyili20@mails.tsinghua.edu.cn
[5] National Laboratory of Pattern Recognition, CASIA, Beijing, China
[6] School of Future Technology, UCAS, Beijing, China
[7] Center for Artificial Intelligence and Robotics, HKISI_CAS, Beijing, China

Abstract. Reference-based image super-resolution (RefSR) is a promising SR branch and has shown great potential in overcoming the limitations of single image super-resolution. While previous state-of-the-art RefSR methods mainly focus on improving the efficacy and robustness of reference feature transfer, it is generally overlooked that a well reconstructed SR image should enable better SR reconstruction for its similar LR images when it is referred to as. Therefore, in this work, we propose a reciprocal learning framework that can appropriately leverage such a fact to reinforce the learning of a RefSR network. Besides, we deliberately design a progressive feature alignment and selection module for further improving the RefSR task. The newly proposed module aligns reference-input images at multi-scale feature spaces and performs reference-aware feature selection in a progressive manner, thus more precise reference features can be transferred into the input features and the network capability is enhanced. Our reciprocal learning paradigm is model-agnostic and it can be applied to arbitrary RefSR models. We empirically show that multiple recent state-of-the-art RefSR models can be consistently improved with our reciprocal learning paradigm. Furthermore, our proposed model together with the reciprocal learning strategy sets new state-of-the-art performances on multiple benchmarks.

Keywords: Reference-based image super-resolution · Reciprocal learning · Reference-input feature alignment

L. Zhang and X. Li—Joint First Authors.
Work done during an internship at Baidu Inc.

Supplementary Information The online version contains supplementary material available at https://doi.org/10.1007/978-3-031-19800-7_38.

1   Introduction

Image super-resolution (SR), which aims to reconstruct the corresponding high-resolution (HR) image with natural and sharp details from a low-resolution (LR) image, is an important image processing technique in computer vision. It has broad applications in surveillance [44], medical imaging [4], and astronomy [8], etc. With the prosperity of convolutional neural networks (CNN) [7,9,29], numerous CNN-based SR methods [2,17,18,46] are proposed, and considerable improvements have been achieved. However, due to the inevitable information loss of the LR images, the SR results often suffer from blurry textures or unrealistic artifacts. As an relaxation to this ill-posed problem, reference-based image super-resolution (RefSR) aims to super-resolve the input LR image with an external HR reference image, which can be acquired from web-searching, photo albums, private repositories, etc. In this manner, similar textures are transferred from the reference image to provide accurate details for the reconstruction of target HR image.

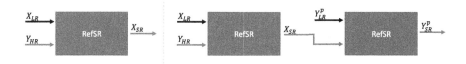

Fig. 1. Left: Traditional RefSR. Right: Our proposed reciprocal training RefSR.

In recent years, there has been extensive research on RefSR. A general pipeline for RefSR is as follows: (1) *Search the correlated content in the reference image.* (2) *Align the matched patterns with the input LR features.* (3) *Fuse the aligned features from reference image into input LR features and then reconstruct target HR image.* To obtain correspondences between the input image and the reference image, some methods [49] directly make use of optical flow, some [28] leverage deformable convolutional networks, and the others [48] perform dense patch matching. C^2-Matching [15] combined dense patch matching with modulated deformable convolution and achieved state-of-the-art performance. MASA [20] proposed a spatial adaptation module to boost the network robustness when there exists a large disparity in distribution. Prior research works focused on leveraging the reference image to the largest extent to improve reconstruction of the target HR image, while little attention is paid to whether the reconstructed SR result can be leveraged to improve the RefSR itself.

In this paper, we introduce a novel **R**eciprocal training strategy for **R**eference-based **S**uper-**R**esolution (RRSR) paradigm, as shown in Fig. 1. Intuitively, if an SR output X_{SR} can be used as reference in turn to boost the performance of super-resolving its similar LR images, X_{SR} should be with clear and sharp context. Therefore, unlike the previous RefSR methods, we treat the

SR output of a RefSR model as reference image and require it to assist in super-resolving a LR variant of the original reference. With such a learning paradigm, the RefSR model can be reinforced to be more robust. Besides the reciprocal learning framework, we also propose a **F**eature **A**lignment and **S**election (FAS) module for more accurate reference feature transfer to enhance the capability of the RefSR model. We progressively refine the reference feature alignment at different feature scales by stacking FAS multiple times. Moreover, a set of reference-aware learnable filters is used in FAS for learning to select the most relevant reference features. Our model achieves state-of-the-art performance for the RefSR task. In summary, our contributions are as follows.

- To the best of our knowledge, we are the first to introduce reciprocal learning training strategy to RefSR task. We try this reciprocal learning training strategy on multiple RefSR frameworks and achieve consistent performance improvements.
- We propose a novel Feature Alignment and Selection (FAS) module for better reference feature utilization. More specifically, we use multiple progressive feature alignment and feature selection with reference-aware learnable filters.
- Without any bells and whistles, experiments and user studies show that our method obtains favorable performance on several benchmarks. Specially, on the most widely used CUFED5 [37] dataset, 0.59 dB PSNR gain is achieved compared to prior state-of-the-art.

2   Related Work

In this section, we first briefly introduce the current mainstream research methods for single image super-resolution and reference-based image super-resolution. Then, we discuss weight generating networks and reciprocal learning which are related to our work.

Single Image Super-Resolution. In recent years, learning-based approaches with deep convolutional networks achieve promising results in SISR. Dong *et al.* [2] first introduced a 3-layer convolutional network to represent the image mapping function between LR images and HR images. Ledig *et al.* [17] used residual blocks which are originally designed for high-level tasks and brought a significant reduction in reconstruction error. With elaborate analysis, lim *et al.* [18] removed the batch normalization layers [12] and developed a new training procedure to achieve better SR performance. Zhang *et al.* [46] and Dai *et al.* [1] introduced channel attention [9] to explore inter-channel correlations. Recently, a lot of works [1,19,23,24,47] adopted non-local attention to model long-range feature relationships, further improving SR performance. Moreover, the PSNR-oriented methods lead to overly-smooth textures, another branch of works aiming at improving the perceptual quality have been proposed. Johnson *et al.* [16] combined MSE with the perception loss based on high-level convolutional features [29]. Generative adversarial network (GAN) [3] prior was also introduced into SR tasks by [17] and further refined by [27,36,45].

Reference-Based Image Super-Resolution. Different from SISR, whose only input is an LR image, RefSR [42,49] use an additional reference image, which greatly improves the SR reconstruction. The RefSR methods transfer the fine details of the external reference images to the regions with similar textures in the input LR image, so that the SR reconstruction obtains more abundant high-frequency components. Zhang *et al.* [48] performed a multi-scale feature transfer by conducting local patch matching in the feature space and fusing multiple swapped features to the input LR features. This enables the network with strong robustness even when irrelevant reference images are given. Subsequently, TTSR [40] unfroze the parameters of VGG extractor [29] and proposed a cross-scale feature integration module to merge multi-scale features, which enhances the feature representation. MASA [20] designed a coarse-to-fine patch matching scheme to reduce the computational complexity and a spatial adaption module to boost the robustness of the network when the input and the reference differ in color distributions.

C^2-Matching [15] proposed a contrastive correspondence network to perform scale and rotation robust matching between input images and reference images. Although C^2-Matching greatly improves the matching accuracy, there is still room for improvement in terms of alignment. Besides, C^2-Matching did not filter and select the reference features and ignored the potential large disparity in distributions between the LR and Ref images. We conduct a multiple times progressive tuning at each feature scale to further improve reference feature alignment. Besides, we design some reference-aware learnable filters to select reference features.

Weight Generating Networks. Unlike classical neural networks, where the weight parameters are frozen after training, weight generating networks [5,13, 21,39] dynamically produce the weight parameters conditioned on the latent vectors or the input. Ha *et al.* [5] proposed the HyperNetworks that uses an extra network to generate the weight parameters for the main network. Instead of learning input-agnostic weights, Jia *et al.* [13] and Yang *et al.* [39] suggested learning different weights for different samples. Thanks to its powerful representational capability and customizability, weight generating networks have been modified successfully for image denoising [25,38], instance segmentation [33], neural rendering [30] and scale-arbitrary SR [10,34]. In this work, we extend the idea to generate a set of reference-aware filters for reference feature selection.

Reciprocal Learning. Unlike these RefSR methods which focused on reference feature transfer, we propose a reciprocal training strategy by using a RefSR result image as a new reference and conducting a RefSR for the second time. Throughout the literature of reciprocal learning [6,14,26,31,43], it generally involves a pair of parallel learning processes, excavates the relation between them and constructs a learning-feedback loop, thus promoting the primal learning process. In neural machine translation, He *et al.* [6] created a closed-loop, learning English-to-French translation (source → target) versus learning French-to-English translation (target → source), and both learning processes are improved by generated feedback signals. Similar strategies have been applied successfully to unpaired image-to-image translation such as DualGAN [41]. More recently, Sun *et al.* [31] designed two coupling networks, one predicting future human trajectories and the other for past human trajectories, and achieved great improvement on human trajectory prediction task by jointly optimizing two models under the reciprocal constraint. In this paper, we make a conjecture that an ideal SR result can also served as a new reference image and provide high-frequency information to other similar LR images. Hence, we propose a reciprocal training strategy for RefSR.

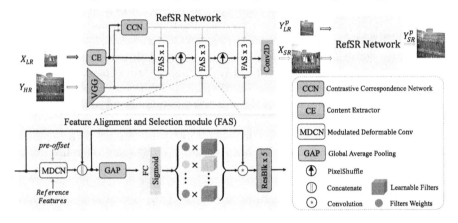

Fig. 2. An overview of RRSR with **Reciprocal Target-Reference Reconstruction** (top) and **Progressive Feature Alignment and Selection** (bottom-left). By creating an extra branch that super-resolves reference LR, Reciprocal Target-Reference Reconstruction constructs a dual task, i.e., reference → target and target → reference, thus improving both target reconstruction and reference reconstruction. We progressively refine the reference feature alignment at $2\times$ and $4\times$ feature scales by stacking FAS multiple times. Moreover, a set of reference-aware learnable filters is used in FAS for learning to select the most relevant reference features.

3   Approach

The overall architecture of the proposed method is shown in Fig. 2. Reciprocal learning paradigm is designed to boost the training of the reference-based image super-resolution network (RefSR Network). Intuitively, if a super-resolved output is well reconstructed, it can be qualified to serve as reference image for super-resolving the low-resolution version of the original reference image. Therefore, in our framework, the original high-resolution reference image Y_{HR} is leveraged to help the reconstruction of high-resolution version X_{SR} for a given low-resolution input X_{LR}. In turn, we treat X_{SR} as reference and require the network to well reconstruct Y_{SR}^{p} by super-resolving its low-resolution counterpart Y_{LR}^{p}. Note that, we did not directly super-resolve Y_{LR}, but a warped version Y_{LR}^{p} is fed into the RefSR network. Such a learning paradigm is termed as **R**eciprocal **T**arget-**R**eference **R**econstruction (RTRR) in this paper.

Our RefSR network is largely inspired by the C^2-Matching [15], meanwhile, a novel feature alignment and selection module (FAS) is proposed and progressively stacked for more accurate reference feature transformation. Specifically, a

VGG network and a context encoder (CE) are used to encode the high-resolution reference image and the input low-resolution image, respectively. Then, a contrastive correspondence network (CCN) is applied for predicting the pre-offset of input and reference at feature space. Subsequently, our proposed FAS module takes as input the pre-offset, input image feature, and the reference feature at different scales to progressively transfer reference features to the input feature space for high-resolution output reconstruction. We will present details of our reciprocal learning paradigm and the feature alignment and selection module in Sect. 3.1 and Sect. 3.2, respectively.

3.1 Reciprocal Target-Reference Reconstruction

Given the success of reciprocal learning in many research fields, we postulate that RefSR would also benefit from a carefully designed reciprocal learning strategy since the roles of input and reference could switch mutually. Intuitively, if a super-resolved image is well reconstructed with clear and sharp context, it should be suitable to serve as reference image to guide the super-resolution reconstruction of other similar LR images. Specifically, for reference-based image super-resolution scenario, a straightforward way to compose a reciprocal learning framework is to use the output image X_{SR}, which is reconstructed by referring to the original reference image Y_{HR} via a RefSR network, as reference for super-resolving the down-sampled reference image Y_{LR} by using the RefSR a second time to generate Y_{SR}. We adopt ℓ_1 loss as the reconstruction objective, then the two pass RefSR reconstruction and reciprocal loss to be optimized can be represented as:

$$\mathcal{L}_{rec} = \|X_{HR} - X_{SR}\|_1, \quad X_{SR} = RefSR(X_{LR}, Y_{HR}), \tag{1}$$

$$\mathcal{L}_{RTRR} = \|Y_{HR} - Y_{SR}\|_1, \quad Y_{SR} = RefSR(Y_{LR}, X_{SR}), \tag{2}$$

Note that, during the two phases, the parameters of RefSR networks are shared.

However, with such straightforward configuration, the reciprocal learning framework will collapse. That is because Y_{HR} is the input of the first RefSR stage as reference, then the whole process combining Eq. 1 and Eq. 2 becomes an auto-encoder for Y_{HR}. The auto-encoder will push the first RefSR stage to keep X_{SR} having as much Y_{HR} information as possible for better reconstructing Y_{SR}, and the $\mathcal{L}_{RTRR}$ drops quickly such that the capability of RefSR network is not enhanced.

To prevent RefSR from collapsing, we introduce a simple yet effective mechanism for processing Y_{HR}. In the second RefSR phase, under the condition that X_{SR} is the reference image, we apply a random perspective transformation on the original Y_{LR} and Y_{HR} to obtain the training image pair $(Y_{LR}^{\mathcal{P}}, Y_{HR}^{\mathcal{P}})$. A process of perspective transformation is shown in Fig. 3. Because $Y_{SR}^{\mathcal{P}}$ and Y_{HR} are quite different, the reconstruction of $Y_{SR}^{\mathcal{P}}$ will not force X_{SR} to be same as Y_{HR}. The revised RTRR loss then becomes as follows:

$$\mathcal{L}_{RTRR} = \|Y_{HR}^{\mathcal{P}} - Y_{SR}^{\mathcal{P}}\|_1, \quad Y_{SR}^{\mathcal{P}} = RefSR(Y_{LR}^{\mathcal{P}}, X_{SR}). \tag{3}$$

$$I_{crop} \qquad\qquad\qquad I_{crop}^{p}$$

Fig. 3. Illustration for perspective transformation. Given an image I and a rectangular bounding box, we can get four new vertices by randomly perturbing the four vertices of the box in a fixed area. Then we can use these two sets of vertices to compute an perspective transformation matrix which is used to transfer I to I^{p}. Finally we crop I^{p} with the original box to get a perspective transformation variant I_{crop}^{p} of I_{crop}. (Color figure online)

To minimize $\mathcal{L}_{RTRR}$, $Y_{SR}^{\mathcal{P}}$ should be well reconstructed, which in turn depends on the quality of its reference image X_{SR}. Thus optimizing the RefSR result $Y_{SR}^{\mathcal{P}}$ at the second phase can also help optimize the first SR result X_{SR}. The proposed reciprocal target-reference reconstruction (RTRR) training strategy is model-agnostic and can be leveraged to improve arbitrary reference-based SR networks. We empirically show improvements of C^2-Matching [15], MASA-SR [20] and TTSR [40] by using our RTRR configuration in Sect. 4.4.

3.2 Progressive Feature Alignment and Selection

Our RefSR network is based on C^2-Matching [15] considering its state-of-the-art performance. We also propose progressive feature alignment and selection to further improve its capability. As shown in Fig. 2, a *Content Extractor* is used to extract features $F_{X_{LR}}$ from X_{LR}. Multi-scale ($1\times$, $2\times$ and $4\times$) reference image features $F_{Y_{HR}}^{s}$ are extracted by a *VGG* extractor, where $s = 1, 2, 4$. A pretrained *Contrastive Correspondence Network* is used to obtain the relative target offsets of the LR input and reference images. These offsets are used as *pre-offsets* for reference feature alignment. We use the *Modulated Deformable Convolution* (MDCN) in C^2-Matching [15] to align the reference features. But unlike C^2-Matching [15], we propose a progressive feature alignment and selection module (PFAS) for better aggregating information from the reference image.

First, an MDCN is used to initially align reference features $F_{Y_{HR}}^{s}$ to LR image features by the *pre-offsets*. Then the aligned reference features and the LR features are concatenated together to get a merged feature F_{merge}^{s}. In real scenarios, there may be many differences between input and reference images in terms of color, style, intensity, etc. Therefore, the features of the reference images should be elaborately selected. We design a reference-aware feature selection mechanism to selectively exploit reference features. Reference-aware information is obtained by applying a global average pooling GAP to F_{merge}^{s}. Then it is used to generate routing weights:

$$(\alpha_1, \alpha_2, \ldots, \alpha_K) = \sigma(f(GAP(F_{merge}^{s}))), \tag{4}$$

where $f(\cdot)$ and $\sigma(\cdot)$ denote fully-connected layer and sigmoid activation. These routing weights are expected to combine K learnable template filters $E_k, k \in \{1, 2, ..., K\}$ which are applied onto F_{merge} to choose the features:

$$
\begin{aligned}
F_{selected}^s &= \alpha_1(E_1 * F_{merge}^s) + \alpha_2(E_2 * F_{merge}^s) + \ldots + \alpha_K(E_K * F_{merge}^s) \\
&= (\alpha_1 E_1 + \alpha_2 E_2 + \ldots + \alpha_K E_K) * F_{merge}^s,
\end{aligned}
\tag{5}
$$

where $*$ denotes convolution operation. It can be seen that it is equivalent to predict a reference-aware filter, which is eventually used to process the F_{merge}^s for feature selection. Unlike static convolution, the reference-aware filter is adaptively conditioned on input and reference. It is demonstrated in Sect. 4.4 that our network benefits from the reference-aware feature selection to produce better results for reference-based SR. At the last of the module, there are several residual blocks to fuse the selected and aligned reference features with LR features. Furthermore, we use the module three times at the 2× and 4× scale to progressively refine the feature alignment and selection. In this way, the details in the LR and reference features are enhanced and aggregated.

3.3   Loss Functions

Our overall objective is formulated as

$$
\mathcal{L} = \lambda_{rec}\mathcal{L}_{rec} + \lambda_{RTRR}\mathcal{L}_{RTRR} + \lambda_{per}\mathcal{L}_{per} + \lambda_{adv}\mathcal{L}_{adv}.
\tag{6}
$$

The reconstruction loss $\mathcal{L}_{rec}$ and the reciprocal loss $\mathcal{L}_{RTRR}$ have been introduced in Sect. 3.1. To generate sharp and visually pleasing images, we employ perceptual loss $\mathcal{L}_{per}$ and adversarial loss $\mathcal{L}_{adv}$ introduced in [48] to help the training of the network.

4   Experiments

4.1   Datasets and Metrics

Following [15,28,40,48], we use the training set of CUFED5 [37,48] as our training dataset, which contains 11,781 training pairs. Each pair consists of a target HR image and a corresponding reference HR image, both at about 160×160 resolution. We evaluate SR results on the testing set of CUFED5, Sun80 [32], Urban100 [11], Manga109 [22] and the newly proposed WR-SR [15]. The testing set of CUFED5 contains 126 pairs, and each consists of an HR image and five reference images with different similarity levels based on SIFT feature matching. In order to be consistent with the previous methods, we pad each reference image to the left-top corner in each 500×500 zero image and stitch them to obtain a 2500×500 image as the reference image. The Sun80 dataset contains 80 natural images, and each with 20 web-searching references. The reference image is randomly selected from them. The Urban100 dataset contains 100 building images, lacking references. Because of self-similarity in the building image,

Table 1. We report PSNR/SSIM (higher is better) of different SR methods on the testing set of CUFED5 [37,48], Sun80 [32], Urban100 [11], Manga109 [22], and WR-SR [15]. Methods are grouped by SISR methods (top) and reference-based methods (bottom). Urban100 indicated with † lacks an external reference image and all the methods essentially degrade to be SISR methods. The best and the second best results are shown in red and blue, respectively

Method	CUFED5 [37,48] PSNR↑/SSIM↑	Sun80 [32] PSNR↑/SSIM↑	Urban100† [11] PSNR↑/SSIM↑	Manga109 [22] PSNR↑/SSIM↑	WR-SR [15] PSNR↑/SSIM↑
SRCNN [2]	25.33/0.745	28.26/0.781	24.41/0.738	27.12/0.850	27.27/0.767
EDSR [18]	25.93/0.777	28.52/0.792	25.51/0.783	28.93/0.891	28.07/0.793
RCAN [46]	26.06/0.769	29.86/0.810	25.42/0.768	29.38/0.895	28.25/0.799
NLSN [23]	26.53/0.784	30.16/0.816	26.28/0.793	30.47/0.911	28.07/0.794
SRGAN [17]	24.40/0.702	26.76/0.725	24.07/0.729	25.12/0.802	26.21/0.728
ENet [27]	24.24/0.695	26.24/0.702	23.63/0.711	25.25/0.802	25.47/0.699
ESRGAN [36]	21.90/0.633	24.18/0.651	20.91/0.620	23.53/0.797	26.07/0.726
RankSRGAN [45]	22.31/0.635	25.60/0.667	21.47/0.624	25.04/0.803	26.15/0.719
CrossNet [49]	25.48/0.764	28.52/0.793	25.11/0.764	23.36/0.741	–
SRNTT [48]	25.61/0.764	27.59/0.756	25.09/0.774	27.54/0.862	26.53/0.745
SRNTT-*rec* [48]	26.24/0.784	28.54/0.793	25.50/0.783	28.95/0.885	27.59/0.780
TTSR [40]	25.53/0.765	28.59/0.774	24.62/0.747	28.70/0.886	26.83/0.762
TTSR-*rec* [40]	27.09/0.804	30.02/0.814	25.87/0.784	30.09/0.907	27.97/0.792
C^2-Matching [15]	27.16/0.805	29.75/0.799	25.52/0.764	29.73/0.893	27.80/0.780
C^2-Matching-*rec* [15]	28.24/0.841	30.18/0.817	26.03/0.785	30.47/0.911	28.32/0.801
MASA [20]	24.92/0.729	27.12/0.708	23.78/0.712	27.44/0.849	25.76/0.717
MASA-*rec* [20]	27.54/0.814	30.15/0.815	26.09/0.786	30.28/0.909	28.19/0.796
SSEN [28]	25.35/0.742	–	–	–	–
SSEN-*rec* [28]	26.78/0.791	–	–	–	–
DCSR [35]	25.39/0.733	–	–	–	–
DCSR-*rec* [35]	27.30/0.807	–	–	–	–
Ours	28.09/0.835	29.57/0.793	25.68/0.767	29.82/0.893	27.89/0.784
Ours-*rec*	28.83/0.856	30.13/0.816	26.21/0.790	30.91/0.913	28.41/0.804

the corresponding LR image is treated as the reference image. The Manga109 dataset contains 109 manga images without references. Since all the images in Manga109 are the same category (manga cover) and some similar patterns occur across the images, we randomly sample an HR image from the dataset as the reference image. The WR-SR dataset, which is proposed by [15] to cover more diverse categories, contains 80 image pairs, each target image accompanied by a web-searching reference image. All the LR images are obtained by bicubically downsampling the HR images with the scale factor 4×. All the results are evaluated in PSNR and SSIM on Y channel in the transformed YCbCr color space.

4.2   Training Details

We train our RefSR network for 255K iterations with a mini-batch size of 9, using Adam optimizer with parameters $\beta_1 = 0.9$ and $\beta_2 = 0.999$. The initial learning rate is set to 1e−4. The weight coefficients for λ_{rec}, λ_{RTRR}, λ_{per} and λ_{adv} are set to 1, 0.4, 1e−4 and 1e−6, respectively. The perspective transformation perturbation range in RTRR of the vertex is $[-20, -5]$ and $[5, 20]$ both horizontally and vertically. The reason why $[-5, 5]$ is not used because the perturbation must be guaranteed to exceed a certain magnitude, otherwise the perturbed image Y_{LR}^P is too similar to Y_{LR}, which hinders the performance. The number of learnable filters in each FAS module is 16. In order to keep the network complexity close to C^2-Matching, the number of res-blocks in a FAS is 5, and other network parameters are the same as C^2-Matching. Please refer to supplementary material for the network implementation details. The input LR patch size is 40×40, corresponding to a 160×160 ground-truth HR patch. During training, we augment the training data with randomly horizontal flipping, randomly vertical flipping, and random $90°$ rotation.

4.3   Comparison with State-of-the-Art Methods

Quantitative Comparison. We quantitatively compare our method with previous state-of-the-art SISR methods and reference-based SR methods. SISR methods include SRCNN [2], EDSR [18], RCAN [46], NLSN [23], SRGAN [17], ENet [27], ESRGAN [36], and RankSRGAN [45]. As for reference-based SR methods, CrossNet [49], SRNTT [48], TTSR [40], SSEN [28], DCSR [35], C^2-Matching [15], and MASA [20] are included. All the reference-based methods except CrossNet have a PSNR-oriented variant (training without GAN loss and perceptual loss), marked with the suffix '-*rec*'.

As shown in Table 1, our proposed method can outperform almost all comparative methods. On the standard CUFED5 benchmark, our method shows a significant improvement of 0.59 dB over the previous state-of-the-art C^2-Matching. On the Sun80 and Urban100 datasets, our method performs comparably to the state-of-the-art methods. Because on the Urban100 dataset, the reference image is the input image itself, reference-based methods have no advantage over SISR methods. As for the Manga109 dataset, the performance of our method surpasses the second-place candidate by a large margin of 0.44 dB. Moreover, our method still achieves the best performance on the WR-SR dataset.

Qualitative Comparison. Figure 4 shows some visual results for qualitative comparisons. We compare our method with current top-performing methods, ESRGAN [36], RankSRGAN [45], TTSR [40], MASA [20], and C^2-Matching [15]. As demonstrated by the examples, our method can extract the correlated information from reference HR image and correctly transfer it to finer HR reconstruction in both sharpness and details. As shown in the second example, our approach recovers a clear plausible face while other methods fail. Even though C^2-Matching achieves a comparable result, artifacts appeared in the left eye. Besides, as shown in the bottom example, only the proposed method recovers the exact two Chinese characters. More visual comparisons are provided in supplementary material.

Following the convention, we also conduct a user study to compare our method with the above methods. Exactly, in each test, we present every participant with two super-resolution results, one predicted by our method and

Input LR	ESRGAN [36]	RankSRGAN [45]	TTSR [40]
Reference HR	MASA [20]	C^2-Matching [15]	Ours

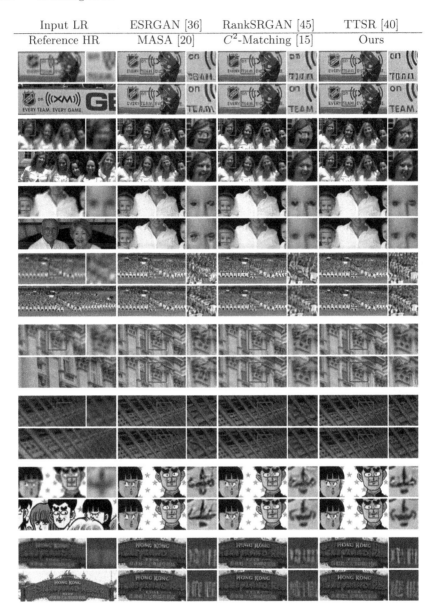

Fig. 4. Comparisons on the testing set of CUFED5 [37,48] (the first four examples), Sun80 [32] (the fifth example), Urban100 [11] (the sixth example), Manga109 [22] (the seventh example) and WR-SR [15] (the eighth example). Our method is able to discover highly related content in reference HR and properly transfer it to restore sharper and more natural textures than the prior works.

another predicted by one of the other methods. A total number of 50 users are

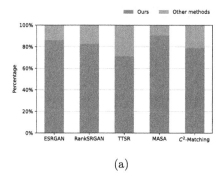
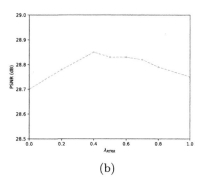

(a)   (b)

Fig. 5. (a) User study results. Values on Y-axis indicate the voting percentage for preferring our method. (b) Influence of λ_{RTRR}.

asked to compare the visual quality. As shown in Fig. 5(a), the participants favor our results against other state-of-the-arts methods.

4.4   Ablation Study

In this section, we verify the effectiveness of different modules in our approach. The testing set of CUFED5 is used for evaluating model. As shown in left of the Table 2, starting with a C^2-Matching baseline model, we separately evaluate the impact of the progressive feature alignment (PFA) and the reference-aware feature selection (RAS) in the proposed Progressive Feature Alignment and Selection (PFAS). Then we demonstrate the effectiveness of the RTRR training strategies.

Reciprocal Target-Reference Reconstruction. We introduce the RTRR training strategies on C^2-Matching [15], MASA [20] and TTSR [40], since these methods are open-sourced. The right part of the Table 2 shows the influence of the RTRR. It can be seen that all methods have consistent improvement, especially a 0.24 dB in C^2-Matching. We notice that the improvement of MASA and TTSR with RTRR is slightly smaller, because the SR results of these two methods are a little worse and RTRR relies on the SR results to do the second time RefSR.

Table 2. Left: Ablation study to analyze the effectiveness of each component of our RRSR. Right: Ablation study on our reciprocal target-reference reconstruction. Asterisks represent our achieved results, not official results

Model	PFA	RAS	RTRR	PSNR ↑ / SSIM↑
Baseline(C^2-Matching*)				28.40 / 0.846
Baseline+PFA	✓			28.63 / 0.851
Baseline+PFA+RAS	✓	✓		28.70 / 0.853
Baseline+PFA+RAS+RTRR	✓	✓	✓	28.83 / 0.856

Model	RTRR	PSNR ↑ / SSIM↑
C^2-Matching*		28.40 / 0.846
C^2-Matching*+RTRR	✓	28.64 / 0.853
MASA*		27.47 / 0.815
MASA*+RTRR	✓	27.58 / 0.818
TTSR*		27.03 / 0.800
TTSR*+RTRR	✓	27.17 / 0.804

Fig. 6. Qualitative comparisons of ablation study on RTRR. The first column shows the input image and the reference image. On the right side of them, we zoom in a small region for better analysis. To take a close look, we find that a ghost of from reference image occurs in the SR result of a model with reciprocal learning but no perspective transformation (RTRR w/o PT). (Color figure online)

We study the effect of the coefficient λ_{RTRR} of the $\mathcal{L}_{RTRR}$ loss. As shown in Fig. 5(b), The PSNR of the model with the RTRR is significantly higher than that without. But as the λ_{RTRR} increases beyond 0.4, the results start to drop. It's easy to understand because in the inference phase, we use the first time RRSR instead of the second which with the SR image X_{SR} as a reference image. There is a data distribution gap between the SR result and a real HR image when used as a reference, so λ_{RTRR} should not be too large.

Figure 6 intuitively illustrates the important role of the perspective transformation used to generate the input image Y_{LR}^{P} for second time RRSR. The SR result image of a model with reciprocal learning but no perspective transformation have reference image textures and the reason has been explained in Sect. 3.1, these textures are used for generating SR result of the second time RRSR. From Fig. 6 we can also see with the RRTR, the output SR images have more clear and realistic textures. More experiments and discussions of perspective transformation are in supplementary material.

Progressive Feature Alignment and Selection. As indicated in the left of the Table 2, We verify the effects of the PFA which has an PSNR improvement of 0.23 dB. Figure 7 shows the visualized feature maps after different alignments module on 4× feature scale. It can be seen that the textures of feature maps gradually become clear after passing through multiple alignments.

Fig. 7. Feature visualization at different PFA states on 4× feature scale. The quality of features is improved progressively.

(a)   (b)

Fig. 8. Qualitative comparisons of ablation study on reference-aware feature selection. There are color and style differences between input and reference images in (a) and (b). Models equipped with RAS can reproduce sharper textures.

Furthermore, we assess the impact of RAS and get a PSNR gain of 0.07dB. Figure 8 shows the the influence of the RAS module. When the reference images are very different in color, lighting, style, etc., with the RAS module, our method can better select reference features to generate more clear textures. Finally, we analyz the influence of the number of learnable filters in RAS. We try the learnable filters' number of 8, 16 and 32, and find that compared to 16, the PSNRs of the others decrease slightly by around 0.02 dB. We also compare RAS with feature alignment methods based on statistics in supplementary material.

5   Conclusion

In this paper, we propose a novel reciprocal learning strategy for reference-based image super-resolution (RefSR). In addition, in order to transfer more accurate reference features, we design a progressive feature alignment and selection module. Extensive experimental results have demonstrated the superiority of our proposed RefSR model against recent state-of-the-art framework named C^2-Matching. We also validate that the reciprocal learning strategy is model-agnostic and it can be applied to improve arbitrary RefSR models. Specifically, our reciprocal learning method consistently improves three recent state-of-the-art RefSR frameworks. Combining the reciprocal learning and progressive feature alignment and selection strategies, we set new state-of-the-art RefSR performances on multiple benchmarks.

Acknowledgments. We thank Qing Chang, He Zheng, and anonymous reviewers for helpful discussions. This work was supported in part by the Major Project for New Generation of AI (No. 2018AAA0100400), the National Natural Science Foundation of China (No. 61836014, No. U21B2042, No. 62072457, No. 62006231) and in part by the Baidu Collaborative Research Project.

References

1. Dai, T., Cai, J., Zhang, Y., Xia, S.T., Zhang, L.: Second-order attention network for single image super-resolution. In: Proceedings of the IEEE Conference on Computer Vision and Pattern Recognition (CVPR) (2019)
2. Dong, C., Loy, C.C., He, K., Tang, X.: Learning a deep convolutional network for image super-resolution. In: Fleet, D., Pajdla, T., Schiele, B., Tuytelaars, T. (eds.) ECCV 2014. LNCS, vol. 8692, pp. 184–199. Springer, Cham (2014). https://doi.org/10.1007/978-3-319-10593-2_13
3. Goodfellow, I., et al.: Generative adversarial nets. In: Advances in Neural Information Processing Systems (NeurIPS) (2014)
4. Greenspan, H.: Super-resolution in medical imaging. Comput. J. **52**(1), 43–63 (2009)
5. Ha, D., Dai, A., Le, Q.V.: Hypernetworks. In: International Conference on Learning Representations (ICLR) (2017)
6. He, D., et al.: Dual learning for machine translation. In: Advances in Neural Information Processing Systems (NeurIPS) (2016)
7. He, K., Zhang, X., Ren, S., Sun, J.: Deep residual learning for image recognition. In: Proceedings of the IEEE Conference on Computer Vision and Pattern Recognition (CVPR) (2016)
8. Holden, S.J., Uphoff, S., Kapanidis, A.N.: Daostorm: an algorithm for high-density super-resolution microscopy. Nat. Meth. **8**(4), 279–280 (2011)
9. Hu, J., Shen, L., Sun, G.: Squeeze-and-excitation networks. In: Proceedings of the IEEE Conference on Computer Vision and Pattern Recognition (CVPR) (2018)
10. Hu, X., Mu, H., Zhang, X., Wang, Z., Tan, T., Sun, J.: Meta-sr: a magnification-arbitrary network for super-resolution. In: Proceedings of the IEEE Conference on Computer Vision and Pattern Recognition (CVPR) (2019)
11. Huang, J.B., Singh, A., Ahuja, N.: Single image super-resolution from transformed self-exemplars. In: Proceedings of the IEEE Conference on Computer Vision and Pattern Recognition (CVPR) (2015)
12. Ioffe, S., Szegedy, C.: Batch normalization: accelerating deep network training by reducing internal covariate shift. In: Proceedings of the International Conference on Machine Learning (ICML) (2015)
13. Jia, X., De Brabandere, B., Tuytelaars, T., Gool, L.V.: Dynamic filter networks. In: Advances in Neural Information Processing Systems (NeurIPS) (2016)
14. Jiang, H., et al.: Reciprocal feature learning via explicit and implicit tasks in scene text recognition. In: Lladós, J., Lopresti, D., Uchida, S. (eds.) ICDAR 2021. LNCS, vol. 12821, pp. 287–303. Springer, Cham (2021). https://doi.org/10.1007/978-3-030-86549-8_19
15. Jiang, Y., Chan, K.C., Wang, X., Loy, C.C., Liu, Z.: Robust reference-based super-resolution via c2-matching. In: Proceedings of the IEEE Conference on Computer Vision and Pattern Recognition (CVPR) (2021)

16. Johnson, J., Alahi, A., Fei-Fei, L.: Perceptual losses for real-time style transfer and super-resolution. In: Leibe, B., Matas, J., Sebe, N., Welling, M. (eds.) ECCV 2016. LNCS, vol. 9906, pp. 694–711. Springer, Cham (2016). https://doi.org/10.1007/978-3-319-46475-6_43

17. Ledig, C., et al.: Photo-realistic single image super-resolution using a generative adversarial network. In: Proceedings of the IEEE Conference on Computer Vision and Pattern Recognition (CVPR) (2017)

18. Lim, B., Son, S., Kim, H., Nah, S., Lee, K.M.: Enhanced deep residual networks for single image super-resolution. In: Proceedings of the IEEE Conference on Computer Vision and Pattern Recognition (CVPR) Workshops (2017)

19. Liu, D., Wen, B., Fan, Y., Loy, C.C., Huang, T.S.: Non-local recurrent network for image restoration. In: Advances in Neural Information Processing Systems (NeurIPS) (2018)

20. Lu, L., Li, W., Tao, X., Lu, J., Jia, J.: Masa-sr: matching acceleration and spatial adaptation for reference-based image super-resolution. In: Proceedings of the IEEE Conference on Computer Vision and Pattern Recognition (CVPR) (2021)

21. Ma, N., Zhang, X., Huang, J., Sun, J.: WeightNet: revisiting the design space of weight networks. In: Vedaldi, A., Bischof, H., Brox, T., Frahm, J.-M. (eds.) ECCV 2020. LNCS, vol. 12360, pp. 776–792. Springer, Cham (2020). https://doi.org/10.1007/978-3-030-58555-6_46

22. Matsui, Y., et al.: Sketch-based manga retrieval using manga109 dataset. Multimedia Tools Appl. **76**(20), 21811–21838 (2016). https://doi.org/10.1007/s11042-016-4020-z

23. Mei, Y., Fan, Y., Zhou, Y.: Image super-resolution with non-local sparse attention. In: Proceedings of the IEEE Conference on Computer Vision and Pattern Recognition (CVPR) (2021)

24. Mei, Y., Fan, Y., Zhou, Y., Huang, L., Huang, T.S., Shi, H.: Image super-resolution with cross-scale non-local attention and exhaustive self-exemplars mining. In: Proceedings of the IEEE Conference on Computer Vision and Pattern Recognition (CVPR) (2020)

25. Mildenhall, B., Barron, J.T., Chen, J., Sharlet, D., Ng, R., Carroll, R.: Burst denoising with kernel prediction networks. In: Proceedings of the IEEE Conference on Computer Vision and Pattern Recognition (CVPR) (2018)

26. Pham, H., Dai, Z., Xie, Q., Le, Q.V.: Meta pseudo labels. In: Proceedings of the IEEE Conference on Computer Vision and Pattern Recognition (CVPR) (2021)

27. Sajjadi, M.S., Scholkopf, B., Hirsch, M.: Enhancenet: single image super-resolution through automated texture synthesis. In: Proceedings of the IEEE Conference on Computer Vision and Pattern Recognition (CVPR) (2017)

28. Shim, G., Park, J., Kweon, I.S.: Robust reference-based super-resolution with similarity-aware deformable convolution. In: Proceedings of the IEEE Conference on Computer Vision and Pattern Recognition (CVPR) (2020)

29. Simonyan, K., Zisserman, A.: Very deep convolutional networks for large-scale image recognition. In: International Conference on Learning Representations (ICLR) (2015)

30. Sitzmann, V., Zollhöfer, M., Wetzstein, G.: Scene representation networks: continuous 3d-structure-aware neural scene representations. In: Advances in Neural Information Processing Systems (NeurIPS) (2019)

31. Sun, H., Zhao, Z., He, Z.: Reciprocal learning networks for human trajectory prediction. In: Proceedings of the IEEE Conference on Computer Vision and Pattern Recognition (CVPR) (2020)

32. Sun, L., Hays, J.: Super-resolution from internet-scale scene matching. In: IEEE International Conference on Computational Photography (ICCP) (2012)
33. Tian, Z., Shen, C., Chen, H.: Conditional convolutions for instance segmentation. In: Vedaldi, A., Bischof, H., Brox, T., Frahm, J.-M. (eds.) ECCV 2020. LNCS, vol. 12346, pp. 282–298. Springer, Cham (2020). https://doi.org/10.1007/978-3-030-58452-8_17
34. Wang, L., Wang, Y., Lin, Z., Yang, J., An, W., Guo, Y.: Learning a single network for scale-arbitrary super-resolution. In: Proceedings of the IEEE International Conference on Computer Vision (ICCV) (2021)
35. Wang, T., Xie, J., Sun, W., Yan, Q., Chen, Q.: Dual-camera super-resolution with aligned attention modules. In: Proceedings of the IEEE International Conference on Computer Vision (ICCV) (2021)
36. Wang, X., et al.: Esrgan: enhanced super-resolution generative adversarial networks. In: Proceedings of the European Conference on Computer Vision (ECCV) Workshops (2018)
37. Wang, Y., Lin, Z., Shen, X., Mech, R., Miller, G., Cottrell, G.W.: Event-specific image importance. In: Proceedings of the IEEE Conference on Computer Vision and Pattern Recognition (CVPR) (2016)
38. Xia, Z., Perazzi, F., Gharbi, M., Sunkavalli, K., Chakrabarti, A.: Basis prediction networks for effective burst denoising with large kernels. In: Proceedings of the IEEE Conference on Computer Vision and Pattern Recognition (CVPR) (2020)
39. Yang, B., Bender, G., Le, Q.V., Ngiam, J.: Condconv: conditionally parameterized convolutions for efficient inference. In: Advances in Neural Information Processing Systems (NeurIPS) (2019)
40. Yang, F., Yang, H., Fu, J., Lu, H., Guo, B.: Learning texture transformer network for image super-resolution. In: Proceedings of the IEEE Conference on Computer Vision and Pattern Recognition (CVPR) (2020)
41. Yi, Z., Zhang, H., Tan, P., Gong, M.: Dualgan: unsupervised dual learning for image-to-image translation. In: Proceedings of the IEEE International Conference on Computer Vision (ICCV) (2017)
42. Yue, H., Sun, X., Yang, J., Wu, F.: Landmark image super-resolution by retrieving web images. IEEE Trans. Image Proc. (TIP) **22**(12), 4865–4878 (2013)
43. Zagalsky, A., et al.: The design of reciprocal learning between human and artificial intelligence. In: Proceedings of the ACM on Human-Computer Interaction (2021)
44. Zhang, L., Zhang, H., Shen, H., Li, P.: A super-resolution reconstruction algorithm for surveillance images. Sig. Proc. **90**(3), 848–859 (2010)
45. Zhang, W., Liu, Y., Dong, C., Qiao, Y.: Ranksrgan: generative adversarial networks with ranker for image super-resolution. In: Proceedings of the IEEE International Conference on Computer Vision (ICCV) (2019)
46. Zhang, Y., Li, K., Li, K., Wang, L., Zhong, B., Fu, Y.: Image super-resolution using very deep residual channel attention networks. In: Proceedings of the European Conference on Computer Vision (ECCV) (2018)
47. Zhang, Y., Li, K., Li, K., Zhong, B., Fu, Y.: Residual non-local attention networks for image restoration. In: International Conference on Learning Representations (ICLR) (2019)
48. Zhang, Z., Wang, Z., Lin, Z., Qi, H.: Image super-resolution by neural texture transfer. In: Proceedings of the IEEE Conference on Computer Vision and Pattern Recognition (CVPR) (2019)
49. Zheng, H., Ji, M., Wang, H., Liu, Y., Fang, L.: Crossnet: an end-to-end reference-based super resolution network using cross-scale warping. In: Proceedings of the European Conference on Computer Vision (ECCV) (2018)

Contrastive Prototypical Network with Wasserstein Confidence Penalty

Haoqing Wang and Zhi-Hong Deng$^{(\boxtimes)}$

School of Artificial Intelligence, Peking University, Beijing, China
{wanghaoqing,zhdeng}@pku.edu.cn

Abstract. Unsupervised few-shot learning aims to learn the inductive bias from unlabeled dataset for solving the novel few-shot tasks. The existing unsupervised few-shot learning models and the contrastive learning models follow a unified paradigm. Therefore, we conduct empirical study under this paradigm and find that pairwise contrast, meta losses and large batch size are the important design factors. This results in our CPN (Contrastive Prototypical Network) model, which combines the prototypical loss with pairwise contrast and outperforms the existing models from this paradigm with modestly large batch size. Furthermore, the one-hot prediction target in CPN could lead to learning the sample-specific information. To this end, we propose Wasserstein Confidence Penalty which can impose appropriate penalty on overconfident predictions based on the semantic relationships among pseudo classes. Our full model, CPNWCP (Contrastive Prototypical Network with Wasserstein Confidence Penalty), achieves state-of-the-art performance on miniImageNet and tieredImageNet under unsupervised setting. Our code is available at https://github.com/Haoqing-Wang/CPNWCP.

Keywords: Unsupervised few-shot learning · Contrastive learning · Confidence penalty · Wasserstein distance

1 Introduction

Humans have the ability to learn from limited labeled data, yet it is still a challenge for modern machine learning systems. Few-shot learning [15,27,40,44,53] is proposed to imitate this ability and has attracted significant attention from the machine learning community recently. Before solving novel few-shot tasks, most models typically learn task-shared inductive bias from sufficient labeled data (base dataset). However, obtaining sufficient labeled data for certain domains may be difficult or even impossible in practice, such as satellite imagery and skin diseases. When only the unlabeled data from the same domain as the novel tasks is available, we can learn the inductive bias in the unsupervised manner, which is formalized as the unsupervised few-shot learning.

Existing unsupervised few-shot learning models focus on constructing pseudo training tasks from unlabeled dataset with clustering based methods [21,23] or

© The Author(s), under exclusive license to Springer Nature Switzerland AG 2022
S. Avidan et al. (Eds.): ECCV 2022, LNCS 13679, pp. 665–682, 2022.
https://doi.org/10.1007/978-3-031-19800-7_39

data augmentation based methods [25, 26, 54]. The latter ones usually achieve better performance, which randomly select a batch of samples from the unlabeled dataset and generate in-class samples for each one to form the support and query set via hand-craft or learnable data augmentations [25, 26, 54]. The synthetic pseudo tasks are used to train the meta-learning models [27, 40, 43].

Concurrently, contrastive learning [9, 11, 16, 51] achieves outstanding success in the field of self-supervised representation learning and can be directly used in unsupervised few-shot learning. These models also randomly select a batch of samples from the unlabeled dataset and generate different views for each one via well-designed data augmentations. The key motivation is to push the views of the same sample (positive pair) close to each other and the views of different samples (negative pair) away from each other in embedding space. To this end, they propose different contrastive losses, such as a lower bound on the mutual information [9, 18], the asymmetric similarity loss [16] or the difference between the cross-correlation matrix and the identity matrix [51].

If we consider the contrastive loss as a meta-learning objective where the augmented views form a training sub-task, the contrastive learning models are essentially the same as the data augmentation based unsupervised few-shot learning models. Therefore, we take a closer look at this paradigm and conduct empirical study to find the key design factors, as shown in Sect. 4.3. Concretely, the contrastive learning models typically can achieve better performance than unsupervised few-shot learning models, while we find their superiority actually comes from the larger batch size and pairwise contrast. Although the key motivation is appropriate, the specific contrastive losses (e.g., a lower bound on the mutual information) are not as suitable for few-shot learning as some meta losses, which limits its performance. Therefore, we combine the prototypical loss [40] with pairwise contrast and get CPN (Contrastive Prototypical Network). With the modestly large batch size, CPN outperforms both the unsupervised few-shot learning models and the contrastive learning models.

Furthermore, some negative pairs could be semantically similar or even belong to the same semantic class in CPN. This problem is also referred to as "class collision" [3] or "sampling bias" [12, 48] in contrastive learning, as shown in Fig. 1(a). Using one-hot prediction target could overly push view b_2 close to view b_1 while away from view a_1 and make the representations ignoring the semantic information about birds and learning the sample-specific information, like background and color distribution. Therefore, we make the prediction distribution in CPN approximating a latent distribution (e.g., the uniform distribution) to prevent overconfident one-hot prediction during training. The most related methods, Label Smoothing [33, 41] and Confidence Penalty [34], use f-divergence to measure the difference between the prediction distribution and the latent distribution. However, f-divergence does not consider the semantic relationships among classes, since the difference in the prediction probability of each class is computed independently. Instead, we use the Wasserstein distance [7] which can impose appropriate penalty based on the semantic relationships among classes. We solve the optimal transport problem using Sinkhorn iteration [1, 13] which works well with the automatic differentiation libraries for deep

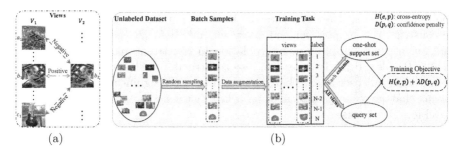

(a)   (b)

Fig. 1. (a) Some negative pairs (e.g., (a_1, b_2)) may be semantically similar or even belong to the same semantic class. (b) Overview of our CPNWCP model. We select a batch of samples and generate in-class samples for each one via data augmentations. We combine the prototypical loss with pairwise contrast. To alleviate the problem of learning sample-specific information, we propose Wasserstein Confidence Penalty which make the prediction distribution approximating the uniform distribution.

learning, without computing the second-order gradients. This method is denoted as Wasserstein Confidence Penalty, which effectively alleviates the problem of learning sample-specific information.

The framework of our full model, CPNWCP (Contrastive Prototypical Network with Wasserstein Confidence Penalty), is shown in Fig. 1(b). The main contributions of this work are as follows:

- Under a unified paradigm of contrastive learning and unsupervised few-shot learning, we conduct empirical study and find that pairwise contrast, meta losses and large batch size are the key factors to the satisfactory performance on novel few-shot tasks, which results in our CPN model.
- To prevent CPN from learning sample-specific information, we propose Wasserstein Confidence Penalty which significantly improves the performance of CPN and outperforms the f-divergence based confidence penalty methods.
- Our CPNWCP model achieves state-of-the-art performance on standard unsupervised few-shot learning datasets, miniImageNet and tieredImageNet.

2   Related Work

Unsupervised Few-Shot Learning. Although various few-shot learning models [5,15,27,40,53] have achieved impressive performance, they rely on sufficient labeled data during training, which is difficult to acquire in some domains. Unsupervised few-shot learning [2,21,23,25,26,50,54] aims to learn the task-shared inductive bias from the unlabeled dataset. These models generate pseudo few-shot tasks to train the meta-learning models through various techniques. [21,23] construct the partitions of unlabeled dataset through clustering in the embedding space and thus obtain the pseudo labels. [2,25,50,54] randomly select a batch of samples with small batch size (e.g., 5) and each sample is assumed from the different class. They generate the in-class samples via data augmentations to construct the support set and query set. LASIUM [26] generate the in-class and out-of-class samples via interpolation in the latent space of a generative model. Besides, ProtoTransfer [30] also constructs few-shot tasks via data augmentations, but uses a large batch size and achieves significant improvement. It means that large batch size may be a key factor to the good performance on novel few-shot tasks.

Contrastive Learning. Contrastive learning [4,9,18,45,51] is a successful self-supervised representation learning [24,46] framework that learns well-generalizing representations from large scale unlabeled dataset. In the training phase, they typically select a batch of samples from the unlabeled dataset and generate different views for each sample via data augmentations. Generally, they push the views from the same sample (positive pair) close to each other and the views from different samples (negative pair) away from each other in the embedding space. The training objectives are typically to maximize the lower bound on the mutual information [4,9,18,20,47] or make the cross-correlation matrix between positive pair as close to the identity matrix as possible [51], which indirectly learn semantic relevance among samples (linear separability or proximity in the embedding space) and not as suitable for few-shot learning as some meta-losses. Contrastive learning avoids representation collapse via large batch size and it also adapts pairwise contrast, i.e., each view is compared with all other views from the same sample, which is helpful for learning useful representations. Chuang et al. [12] and Wei et al. [48] point out the "sampling bias" problem, and propose a debiased objective and consistency regularization respectively.

Confidence Penalty. For a network, over-confident prediction is a symptom of overfitting. For this end, Label Smoothing [33,41,52] relaxes the one-hot label to a soft version which is equivalent to adding uniform label noise. Confidence Penalty [34] penalizes low entropy prediction following the maximum entropy principle [22]. They essentially make the prediction distribution approximating a latent distribution, such as the uniform distribution or a learnable distribution [52]. Both Label Smoothing and Confidence Penalty use f-divergence to measure the difference between distributions, which ignores the semantic relationships among classes. We explore the Wasserstein distance and introduce the semantic relationships with cost matrix. With semantic relationships as prior information, our Wasserstein Confidence Penalty can impose appropriate penalty and outperforms both Label Smoothing and Confidence Penalty in CPN.

3   Methodology

3.1   Preliminaries

Few-shot learning aims to obtain the model which can efficiently and effectively solve novel few-shot tasks. Each few-shot task contains a support set $\mathcal{S}$ and a query set $\mathcal{Q}$. When the support set $\mathcal{S}$ contains N classes with K samples in each class, the few-shot task is called a N-way K-shot task, and $N = 5$ and

$K = 1$ or 5 is the standard setting. The query set $\mathcal{Q}$ contains the samples from the same classes with the support set $\mathcal{S}$. We need to classify the samples in the query set correctly based on the few labeled data from the support set. Since K is typically very small, this is challenging for modern deep learning models. To this end, one can learn the inductive bias from a large base training set $\mathcal{D}$, which has completely disjoint classes with the novel tasks. Meta-learning models [15,27,40] adapt *episode* training [42], where few-shot training tasks are constructed from the base training set $\mathcal{D}$. Some non-episodical transfer learning models [10,14,55] also achieve comparable performance.

In most cases, the large base training set $\mathcal{D}$ is labeled, so we can easily construct few-shot training tasks based on labels. However, obtaining sufficient labeled dataset is difficult or even impossible for some domains, e.g., satellite imagery and skin diseases, so we assume the training set is unlabeled in this work and learn the inductive bias in the unsupervised manner.

3.2 Contrastive Prototypical Network

We first describe a unified paradigm, and then take the data augmentation based unsupervised few-shot learning models, contrastive learning models and our CPN model as its special cases.

Given an unlabeled dataset $\mathcal{D}$, samples $\{x_i\}_{i=1}^N$ are randomly selected and each x_i represents a pseudo class. For each x_i, in-class samples $\{v_i^j\}_{j=1}^M$ are generated via manually or learnable data augmentations. For a specific problem, the loss function $\mathcal{L}$ is designed and calculated on the sub-dataset $\{v_i^j\}_{i=1,j=1}^{N,M}$ and the sub-task training objective is

$$\min_\theta \mathbb{E}_{p(\{v_i^j\}_{i=1,j=1}^{N,M})}[\mathcal{L}(\{v_i^j\}_{i=1,j=1}^{N,M}, \theta)] \tag{1}$$

where θ represents the model parameters. We denote this paradigm as the *Sampling-Augmentation* paradigm.

Data augmentation based unsupervised few-shot learning models [25,26,54] follow this paradigm and achieve outstanding performance. Let $M = S + Q$, the augmented samples $\{v_i^j\}_{i=1,j=1}^{N,M}$ constitute a pseudo S-shot training task with $N \cdot S$ samples as the support set $\mathcal{S}$ and the $N \cdot Q$ samples as the query set $\mathcal{Q}$. These pseudo few-shot tasks can be directly used to train the meta-learning models, which means $\mathcal{L}$ can be various meta losses and the training objective is

$$\min_\theta \mathbb{E}_{p(\{v_i^j\}_{i=1,j=1}^{N,M})}[\mathcal{L}^{meta}(\{v_i^j\}_{i=1,j=S+1}^{N,M}, \psi)], \quad \psi = \mathcal{A}(\{v_i^j\}_{i=1,j=1}^{N,S}, \theta) \tag{2}$$

where $\mathcal{A}$ is a base learner and ψ is the task solution. Following the *episode* training, N is typically set small while M is set large, such as $N = 5$ and $M = 5 + 15$. This setting is popular in the few-shot learning, since it makes the training setting aligning with the test scenario. However, we find that the small batch size is not suitable for unsupervised few-shot learning, as shown in Fig. 2.

Most contrastive learning models [4,9,18,20] also follow this paradigm and achieve outstanding success in the field of self-supervised representation learning.

It is usually assumed that different views $\{v_i^j\}_{j=1}^M$ share the semantic information from the input x_i, so the view-invariant representations are expected. For example, many contrastive learning models [9,18,20,49] maximize the mutual information between the representations of positive pair, and the training loss is the InfoNCE lower bound estimate [35]. M is typically set 2 for simplicity and the training objective is

$$\min_\theta \mathbb{E}_{p(\{v_i^j\}_{i=1,j=1}^{N,2})} \left[-\frac{1}{2N} \sum_{i=1}^{N} \sum_{j,l=1;j\neq l}^{2} \ln \frac{\exp(h_\theta(g_\theta(v_i^j), g_\theta(v_i^l)))}{\sum_{s=1}^{N} \sum_{t=1,(s,t)\neq(i,j)}^{2} \exp(h_\theta(g_\theta(v_i^j), g_\theta(v_s^t)))} \right] \quad (3)$$

where g_θ is an encoder network and h_θ contains a multilayer perceptron used to calculate the InfoNCE lower bound. Each view v_i^j is compared with all other views $\{v_i^l\}_{l=1}^M, l \neq j$ from the same sample x_i, i.e., pairwise contrast, which is useful in unsupervised few-shot learning, as shown in Table 3. The batch size N is typically set large to avoid representation collapse, such as $N = 4096$ in SimCLR [9]. Although the contrastive learning models can be applied in unsupervised few-shot learning, their training losses indirectly learn the semantic relevance among samples, e.g., using mutual information or cross-correlation matrix [51], which are not as suitable as directly comparing the representations of different views, like prototypical loss, as shown in Fig. 2.

Our CPN model combines the advantages of both the contrastive learning models and the data augmentation based unsupervised few-shot learning models. We adopt a big batch size and introduce pairwise contrast to a widely used meta loss, prototypical loss [40]. The training objective is

$$\min_\theta \mathbb{E}_{p(\{v_i^j\}_{i=1,j=1}^{N,M})} \left[-\frac{1}{NM^2} \sum_{l=1}^{M} \sum_{i=1}^{N} \sum_{j=1}^{M} \ln \frac{\exp(-\|g_\theta(v_i^j) - g_\theta(v_i^l)\|^2)}{\sum_{k=1}^{N} \exp(-\|g_\theta(v_i^j) - g_\theta(v_k^l)\|^2)} \right] \quad (4)$$

The l-th view $\{v_i^l\}_{i=1}^N$ is used as the one-shot support set to classify all the views. We directly compare the representations of different views without using the multilayer perceptron to calculate mutual information estimation. With modestly large batch size, our CPN outperforms both the unsupervised few-shot learning models and some classical contrastive learning models.

In addition to the empirical study, we also provide some theoretical or intuitive justification for the above key factors.

1) *Pairwise contrast.* Each positive pair provides supervised information to each other under the unsupervised setting [45], and the model learns semantic knowledge from the shared information between views. Obviously, pairwise contrast brings more shared information between views which contains more useful knowledge. Concretely, assuming there are M views, we have $I_{pc} = \sum_{l=1}^{M} \sum_{k\neq l} I(v_l, v_k) \geq I_{w/o\ pc} = \sum_{k\neq 1} I(v_1, v_k)$, where 'pc' represents 'pairwise contrast' and we set view v_1 as the anchor view when without pairwise contrast.

2) *Meta losses.* Compared with the contrastive losses which indirectly learn the semantic relevance among samples via mutual information or cross-correlation matrix, the meta losses typically directly compare the representations of different

views (especially the metric-based meta losses), and are more suitable for few-shot scenarios, i.e., semantic matching between support and query samples.

3) *Large batch size.* In the instance discrimination task, the number of classes is directly related to the batch size. Our CPN and some contrastive learning models adopt the cross-entropy loss and may encounter log-K curse [8]. Concretely, the cross-entropy loss is $\mathbf{H} = -\log \frac{\exp(s_y)}{\sum_{i=1}^{N} \exp(s_i)} = \log(1 + \sum_{i \neq y} \exp(s_i - s_y))$, where $(s_1, \cdots, s_N)$ is the prediction logits. After several training epochs, s_y is significantly larger than $s_i, i \neq y$ and $\exp(s_i - s_y), i \neq y$ are small, so $\mathbf{H} \approx \log(1 + (N-1)\epsilon)$ with ϵ is a small constant. When we use a small batch size, $\mathbf{H} \approx (N-1)\epsilon \approx 0$ and floating-point precision can lead to large gradient variance, hurting performance.

3.3 Wasserstein Confidence Penalty

As shown in Fig. 1(a), some negative pairs in CPN could be semantically similar or even belong to the same semantic class. Using the one-hot prediction target as in Eq. (4) could overly push the semantically similar negative pairs away from each other, which has the risk of learning sample-specific information rather than generalizing semantic information in the representations.

Further, when we use a large batch size, this problem becomes serious since the probability that the samples from the same semantic class appear in the selected batch significantly increases. For this end, we make the prediction distribution approximating a latent distribution during training to prevent over-confident prediction, which we denote as confidence penalty. For CPN, when we use $\{v_i^l\}_{i=1}^{N}$ as one-shot support set, the prediction distribution of a view v is $p_\theta^l(i|v) = \frac{\exp(-\|g_\theta(v) - g_\theta(v_i^l)\|^2)}{\sum_{k=1}^{N} \exp(-\|g_\theta(v) - g_\theta(v_k^l)\|^2)}$. We introduce a plug-and-play confidence penalty term $D(p_\theta^l(i|v), q)$, where $D(\cdot, \cdot)$ is a distance metric between distributions and q represents a latent distribution. Therefore, the Eq. (4) becomes

$$\min_\theta \mathbb{E}_{p(\{v_i^j\}_{i=1,j=1}^{N,M})} \left[\frac{1}{NM^2} \sum_{l=1}^{M} \sum_{i=1}^{N} \sum_{j=1}^{M} \left(-\ln p_\theta^l(i|v_i^j) + \lambda D(p_\theta^l(i|v_i^j), q) \right) \right] \quad (5)$$

where λ is a weight coefficient. The ideal choice for distribution q is the ground-truth class distribution in the instance classification task, which has non-ignorable probability in the semantically similar pseudo classes and we can not obtain it without labels. Therefore, we simply set q as the uniform distribution, i.e., $q_k = 1/N, k = 1, \cdots, N$. For distance metric D, we consider different choices.

For simplicity, let e be a one-hot distribution and p be the prediction distribution, a widely-used choice for distance metric $D(p, q)$ is the f-divergence $D(p, q) = \sum_{k=1}^{N} f(p_k/q_k) \cdot q_k$, where f is a convex function with $f(1) = 0$. When $f(z) = z \ln z$, the f-divergence becomes the Kullback-Leibler divergence $D(p, q) = KL(p\|q) = \sum_{k=1}^{N} p_k \ln p_k + \ln N$. This is the regularization term from [34], named Confidence Penalty. It penalizes low entropy prediction distributions following the maximum entropy principle [22] and is also used in reinforcement learning [29,32]. When $f(z) = -\ln z$, the f-divergence becomes the reverse Kullback-Leibler divergence $KL(q\|p)$ and this regularization term is equivalent to Label Smoothing [33,41]. Concretely, $H(e,p) + \lambda KL(q\|p) = H(e + \lambda q, p) - \lambda \ln N$, where $H(e,p) = -\sum_{k=1}^{N} e_k \ln p_k$ is cross-entropy. $e + \lambda q$ is equivalent to $(1-\alpha)e + \alpha q$, which is just the target distribution in Label Smoothing and α is typically set 0.1. When $f(z) = [(z+1)\ln(2/(z+1)) + z\ln z]/2$, we get a symmetric f-divergence, Jensen-Shannon divergence.

The difference in the probability of each class is computed independently in f-divergence and the structural information, i.e., the semantic relationships among different classes, is ignored. For this end, we use the Wasserstein distance [7] $W(p,q)$ to introduces the semantic relationships as the prior knowledge. To calculate $W(p,q)$, we need to solve the optimal transport problem

$$\min_{T} \quad \sum_{i=1}^{N}\sum_{j=1}^{N} T_{ij} \cdot C_{ij} \tag{6}$$

$$s.t. \quad T_{ij} \geq 0, i = 1, \cdots, N, j = 1, \cdots, N$$

$$\sum_{j=1}^{N} T_{ij} = p_i, i = 1, \cdots, N; \quad \sum_{i=1}^{N} T_{ij} = q_j, j = 1, \cdots, N$$

where $T \in \mathbb{R}^{N \times N}$ is a transportation matrix and $C \in \mathbb{R}^{N \times N}$ is the cost matrix. C_{ij} represents the cost of transporting per unit probability from class i to class j. T_{ij} represents the amount of the probability transported from class i to class j. Let the solution of the problem (6) be T^*, which is the matching flows with the minimum cost between p and q, we have $W(p,q) = \sum_{i=1}^{N}\sum_{j=1}^{N} T_{ij}^* \cdot C_{ij}$. The cost matrix C is the key to introduce the structural information. C_{ij} can be understood as the cost of misclassifying a sample from class i to class j. Intuitively, the higher the semantic similarity between class i and class j, the smaller the transportation cost C_{ij} should be. Therefore, we define the transportation cost as a decreasing function of class similarity

$$C_{ij} = \gamma \cdot (1 - S_{ij}) + \mathbb{I}_{i=j} \tag{7}$$

where γ is a scaling factor, $\mathbb{I}_{i=j}$ is an indicator function in the condition $i = j$ and is used to avoid zero cost, and S_{ij} represents the semantic similarity between class i and class j. Although this definition can not satisfy $W(p,p) = 0$, we find avoiding zero cost can achieve better performance in practice. In the batch of samples $\{x_i\}_{i=1}^{N}$, we label each x_i as a pseudo class i. Considering that mean can weaken sample differences and highlight intra-class commonality, we use the mean of the representations of views $\{v_i^j\}_{j=1}^{M}$ to represent each pseudo class i and use their cosine similarity as the class similarity, i.e., $S_{ij} = \frac{r_i^T r_j}{\|r_i\|\|r_j\|}$ with $r_i = \frac{1}{M}\sum_{j=1}^{M} g_\theta(v_i^j)$. We thus can measure the difference between distributions in a way that is sensitive to semantic relationships among classes.

To solve the problem (6), we use the Sinkhorn iteration [1,13] which enforces a simple structure on the optimal transportation matrix and can quickly solve

Table 1. Few-shot classification accuracy(%) with 95% confidence interval on 10,000 5-way K-shot tasks randomly sampled from miniImageNet.

Model	1-shot	5-shot	20-shot	50-shot
Train from scratch [21]	27.59 ± 0.59	38.48 ± 0.66	51.53 ± 0.72	59.63 ± 0.74
CACTUs-ProtoNet [21]	39.18 ± 0.71	53.36 ± 0.70	61.54 ± 0.68	63.55 ± 0.64
CACTUs-MAML [21]	39.90 ± 0.74	53.97 ± 0.70	63.84 ± 0.70	69.64 ± 0.63
UMTRA [25]	39.93	50.73	61.11	67.15
ULDA-ProtoNet [36]	40.63 ± 0.61	56.18 ± 0.59	64.31 ± 0.51	66.43 ± 0.47
ULDA-MetaOptNet [36]	40.71 ± 0.62	54.49 ± 0.58	63.58 ± 0.51	67.65 ± 0.48
LASIUM-ProtoNet [26]	40.05 ± 0.60	52.53 ± 0.51	59.45 ± 0.48	61.43 ± 0.45
LASIUM-MAML [26]	40.19 ± 0.58	54.56 ± 0.55	65.17 ± 0.49	69.13 ± 0.49
ArL-RelationNet [54]	36.37 ± 0.92	46.97 ± 0.86	–	–
ArL-ProtoNet [54]	38.76 ± 0.84	51.08 ± 0.84	–	–
ArL-SoSN [54]	41.13 ± 0.84	55.39 ± 0.79	–	–
SimCLR [9]	40.91 ± 0.19	57.22 ± 0.17	65.74 ± 0.15	67.83 ± 0.15
BYOL [16]	39.81 ± 0.18	56.65 ± 0.17	64.58 ± 0.15	66.69 ± 0.15
BarTwins [51]	39.02 ± 0.18	57.20 ± 0.17	65.26 ± 0.15	67.42 ± 0.14
ProtoCLR [30]	44.89 ± 0.58	63.35 ± 0.54	72.27 ± 0.45	74.31 ± 0.45
CPNWCP (ours)	**47.93 ± 0.19**	**66.44 ± 0.17**	**75.69 ± 0.14**	**78.20 ± 0.13**
ProtoNet-Sup [40]	49.42 ± 0.78	68.20 ± 0.66	–	–

the optimal transport problem. The gradients can be back-propagated along the iteration process, so it works well with the automatic differentiation libraries for deep learning. Besides, there is no gradient calculation in the forward iterations, so the optimization process does not need to calculate the second-order gradients. This regularization method is denoted as Wasserstein Confidence Penalty.

We apply Wasserstein Confidence Penalty to CPN and get CPNWCP (Contrastive Prototypical Network with Wasserstein Confidence Penalty) model which has the training objective of Eq. (5).

4 Experiments

4.1 Experimental Settings

Datasets. We evaluate the models on two standard few-shot learning benchmarks, miniImageNet [42] and tieredImageNet [38]. The miniImageNet dataset is a subset of ImageNet [39] and consists of 100 classes with 600 images per class. Following the commonly-used protocol from [37], we use 64 classes as the base training set, 16 and 20 classes as validation set and test set respectively. The tieredImageNet dataset is a larger subset of ImageNet, composed of 608 classes grouped into 34 high-level categories. These categories are divided into 20 categories for training, 6 categories for validation and 8 categories for test,

Table 2. Few-shot classification accuracy(%) with 95% confidence interval on 10,000 5-way K-shot tasks randomly sampled from tieredImageNet.

Model	1-shot	5-shot	20-shot	50-shot
Train from scratch [36]	26.27 ± 1.02	34.91 ± 0.63	38.14 ± 0.58	38.67 ± 0.44
ULDA-ProtoNet [36]	41.60 ± 0.64	56.28 ± 0.62	64.07 ± 0.55	66.00 ± 0.54
ULDA-MetaOptNet [36]	41.77 ± 0.65	56.78 ± 0.63	67.21 ± 0.56	71.39 ± 0.53
SimCLR [9]	35.60 ± 0.17	52.88 ± 0.19	61.09 ± 0.17	63.47 ± 0.17
BYOL [16]	37.11 ± 0.18	52.71 ± 0.19	60.56 ± 0.17	62.68 ± 0.16
BarTwins [51]	35.39 ± 0.17	52.01 ± 0.18	60.19 ± 0.17	62.57 ± 0.16
CPNWCP (ours)	**45.00 ± 0.19**	**62.96 ± 0.19**	**72.84 ± 0.17**	**76.03 ± 0.15**
ProtoNet-Sup [40]	53.31 ± 0.89	72.69 ± 0.74	–	–

which corresponds to 351, 97 and 160 classes respectively. In order to simulate the unsupervised setting, we do not use the labels in the training set during training, nor do we use the labeled validation set to select the best checkpoint.

Implementation Details. For fair comparison with previous models [21,25,26,30, 36,54], we use Conv4 as the backbone which consists of four convolutional blocks with 64 filters for each convolutional layer. We also perform a series of experiments on ResNet12 [19] for comprehensive study. For all experiments, we use random cropping, flip and random color distortion as the data augmentations, like in [25,30]. The models are trained for 600 epochs using Adam optimizer with the learning rate of 1e-3. We set the batch size $N = 64$ for miniImageNet and $N = 192$ for tieredImageNet. The number of augmented views for each sample is set $M = 4$ for Conv4 and $M = 8$ for ResNet12. For different datasets and backbones, we set the regularization coefficient $\lambda = 1$ and choose scaling factor γ from $\{6, 8, 10, 12\}$. We set the number of Sinkhorn iteration as 5. For Label Smoothing, we choose the label relaxation factor α from $\{0.1, 0.01, 0.001\}$.

Evaluation Protocol. We evaluate the models in the standard 5-way 1-shot/5-shot tasks and the tasks with more support samples, i.e., 5-way 20-shot/50-shot tasks. We use 10,000 randomly sampled few-shot tasks with 15 query samples per class, and report the average accuracy (%) as well as 95% confidence interval. Unless otherwise specified, all non-meta-learning models, including our models and contrastive learning models, use a prototype-based nearest neighbor classifier [40] to solve the novel few-shot tasks based on the pre-trained backbone.

4.2   Comparison with State-Of-The-Arts

We compare our full model, CPNWCP, with existing unsupervised few-shot learning models [21,25,26,30,36,54] and classical contrastive learning models [9,16,51]. Among them, Medina et al. [30] uses a large batch size prototypical loss but not pairwise contrast and Wasserstein Confidence Penalty. We report its

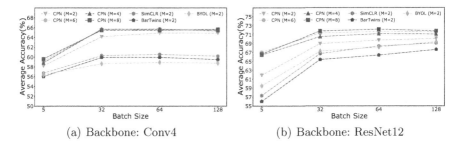

(a) Backbone: Conv4   (b) Backbone: ResNet12

Fig. 2. Average few-shot classification accuracy across four different settings (5-way 1-shot/5-shot/20-shot/50-shot) on miniImageNet with varying batch size.

Table 3. Few-shot classification accuracy(%) with 95% confidence interval on 10,000 5-way K-shot tasks sampled from miniImageNet. 'PC' represents 'pairwise contrast'.

Model	Backbone	1-shot	5-shot	20-shot	50-shot
CPN w/o PC	Conv4	46.08 ± 0.19	63.89 ± 0.17	72.59 ± 0.14	74.81 ± 0.14
CPN		46.96 ± 0.19	64.75 ± 0.17	73.31 ± 0.14	75.63 ± 0.14
CPN w/o PC	ResNet12	48.80 ± 0.19	69.09 ± 0.16	78.54 ± 0.13	80.83 ± 0.12
CPN		50.01 ± 0.18	70.73 ± 0.16	80.33 ± 0.13	82.74 ± 0.11

results without further fine-tuning for fairness, i.e., the results of ProtoCLR. The results of training a classifier on the support set from scratch is used as the lower bound for performance. The results of supervised ProtoNet [40] are also provided as the supervised baseline. Table 1 and Table 2 provide the results on miniImageNet and tieredImageNet respectively, and the best unsupervised result in each setting is in bold. All models use Conv4 as the backbone for fair comparison. As we can see, our CPNWCP outperforms all previous unsupervised few-shot learning models and classical contrastive learning models with a large margin, and achieves the performance much closer to the supervised baseline. Besides, many unsupervised methods (e.g., ULDA, SimCLR and our CPNWCP) have a larger gap to the supervised baseline on tieredImageNet than that on miniImageNet. The reason may be that, the classes in tieredImageNet are structural and there are many similar classes under the same category. These classes rely on label information to be well discriminated for learning relevant semantic knowledge, which is not friendly to unsupervised learning. Despite tieredImageNet is a more difficult dataset, our CPNWCP still significantly outperforms existing baselines.

4.3   Empirical Study on Sampling-Augmentation Paradigm

As shown in Table 1, contrastive learning models [9, 16, 51] outperform the models [21, 25, 26, 36, 54] which construct pseudo few-shot tasks with small batch size, but are inferior to the model [30] using large batch size and prototypical loss. This inspires us that when some meta losses are combined with large batch size,

Table 4. Few-shot classification accuracy(%) with 95% confidence interval on 10,000 5-way K-shot tasks sampled from miniImageNet. We provide the results of Consistency Regularization ('+CR') [48], Label Smoothing ('+LS') [41], Confidence Penalty ('+CP') [34], Jensen-Shannon Confidence Penalty ('+JSCP') and our Wasserstein Confidence Penalty ('+WCP').

Model	Backbone	1-shot	5-shot	20-shot	50-shot
CPN	Conv4	46.96 ± 0.19	64.75 ± 0.17	73.31 ± 0.14	75.63 ± 0.14
+ CR [48]		47.33 ± 0.19	65.15 ± 0.17	73.28 ± 0.14	75.50 ± 0.14
+ LS [41]		47.19 ± 0.19	65.22 ± 0.17	74.21 ± 0.14	76.71 ± 0.13
+ CP [34]		47.22 ± 0.19	65.46 ± 0.17	74.52 ± 0.14	77.05 ± 0.13
+ JSCP		46.82 ± 0.19	64.89 ± 0.17	73.92 ± 0.14	76.37 ± 0.13
+ WCP (ours)		**47.93 ± 0.19**	**66.44 ± 0.17**	**75.69 ± 0.14**	**78.20 ± 0.13**
CPN	ResNet12	50.01 ± 0.18	70.73 ± 0.16	80.33 ± 0.13	82.74 ± 0.11
+ CR [48]		51.85 ± 0.19	72.23 ± 0.16	81.35 ± 0.12	83.28 ± 0.11
+ LS [41]		50.41 ± 0.19	71.10 ± 0.16	80.97 ± 0.12	83.61 ± 0.11
+ CP [34]		50.71 ± 0.18	71.29 ± 0.16	81.11 ± 0.12	83.91 ± 0.11
+ JSCP		49.87 ± 0.18	70.53 ± 0.16	81.01 ± 0.13	83.19 ± 0.11
+ WCP (ours)		**53.56 ± 0.19**	**73.21 ± 0.16**	**82.18 ± 0.12**	**84.35 ± 0.11**

the contrastive losses have no advantage any more. Therefore, we empirically study three important factors in the Sampling-Augmentation paradigm: the loss function $\mathcal{L}$, the batch size N and the view number M. We consider three classical contrastive losses [9,16,51] and a meta loss [40]. N is chosen from $\{5, 32, 64, 128\}$ and M is chosen from $\{2, 4, 6, 8\}$. For fair comparison, we introduce pairwise contrast from contrastive learning to the prototypical loss, i.e., each view is used as the one-shot support set to classify other views.

Considering that using the prototype-based nearest-neighbor classifier seems unfair for the comparison between the prototypical loss and contrastive losses, we provide the results with ridge regression classifier [6] in Fig. 2 which examines linear separability. 'CPN' represents prototypical loss with pairwise contrast, 'SimCLR', 'BYOL' and 'BarTwins' represent contrastive losses with pairwise contrast. Similar to Table 1, contrastive learning models with large batch size $N = 64$ outperform the prototypical loss with small batch size $N = 5$. But when the batch size is the same, contrastive learning models consistently perform worse than the prototypical loss. Besides, more augmented views lead to better performance due to increased view diversity, especially for large backbone.

To explore the effect of pairwise contrast, we evaluate the performance of CPN without pairwise contrast, i.e., only using one randomly selected view $\{v_i^l\}_{i=1}^N$ as the one-shot support set to classify all views. The comparison results are shown in Table 3, where we still use a prototype-based nearest neighbor classifier [40]. We set ($N = 64$, $M = 4$) for Conv4 and ($N = 64$, $M = 8$) for ResNet12. As we can see, pairwise contrast achieves consistent performance improvement under different task settings and backbones, especially for large backbone. This shows its potential for larger backbones.

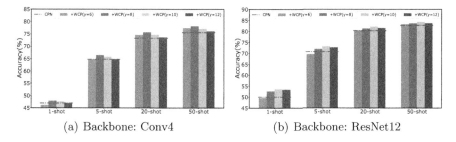

(a) Backbone: Conv4   (b) Backbone: ResNet12

Fig. 3. Few-shot classification accuracy (%) on 10,000 5-way 1-shot/5-shot/20-shot/50-shot tasks sampled from miniImageNet. We provide the results of Wasserstein Confidence Penalty with different scaling factor $\gamma = \{6, 8, 10, 12\}$. The results of CPN are also provided for clear comparison.

4.4 Ablation Study on Confidence Penalty

As we analyze in Sect. 3.3, since some negative pairs could be semantically similar or even from the same semantic class, using one-hot prediction target has the risk of learning sample-specific information instead of generalizing semantic information. This problem is also referred as 'sampling bias' [12] in contrastive learning, and Wei et al. [48] proposes Consistency Regularization to alleviate this problem, which can be directly used in CPN. In this work, we propose to make the prediction distribution approximating a latent distribution to prevent overconfident one-hot prediction. We consider different distance metrics between distributions and compare their effect in CPN, including classical f-divergences and Wasserstein distance. We conduct experiments on miniImageNet and use both Conv4 and ResNet12 as backbone for comprehensive study.

The few-shot classification results are shown in Table 4 and the best result in each setting is in bold. Most regularization methods consistently improve the performance of CPN. Using Jensen-Shannon divergence ('+JSCP') is inferior to using Kullback-Leibler divergence ('+CP' and '+LS'), which means symmetry is not required for the distance metric between the prediction distribution and the latent distribution. Using the Wasserstein distance ('+WCP') outperforms all f-divergence based confidence penalty methods ('+LS', '+CP' and '+JSCP'), which means imposing appropriate penalty based on the semantic relationships among classes helps to learn more general semantic information. Our Wasserstein Confidence Penalty also significantly outperforms the Consistency Regularization ('+CP') [48] in unsupervised few-shot learning.

We also explore the performance of Wasserstein Confidence Penalty with different scaling factor γ, which controls the probability transportation cost between classes. We conduct experiments under the same settings as above and the results are shown in Fig. 3. We provide the results of CPN for clear comparison. As we can see, Wasserstein Confidence Penalty is robust to different γ and can achieve consistent improvement with most candidate scaling factors.

Furthermore, Guo et al. [17] points that although many modern neural networks have better performance, they are poorly calibrated and over-confident.

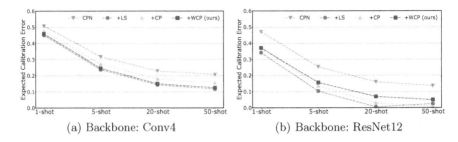

(a) Backbone: Conv4   (b) Backbone: ResNet12

Fig. 4. Expected Calibration Error on different backbones (Conv4 and ResNet12) and settings (5-way 1-shot/5-shot/20-shot/50-shot). We provide the results of CPN model and various confidence penalty methods: Label Smoothing ('+LS') [41], Confidence Penalty ('+CP') [34] and our Wasserstein Confidence Penalty ('+WCP').

In other words, the confidence of their predictions cannot accurately represent their accuracy, which is potentially harmful in many real-world decision making systems. To measure calibration, the authors propose the estimated Expected Calibration Error (ECE), and it is widely used nowadays. Some works [28,33,52] shows that Label Smoothing and Confidence Penalty can improve the calibration of the models in supervised learning. Here we explore whether various confidence penalty methods can improve the calibration of CPN under unsupervised setting. For fair comparison, we calculate the estimated Expected Calibration Error without temperature scaling which not only improves calibration, but also hides the trends in calibration among models [31]. The results calculated on 10,000 sampled tasks are shown in Fig. 4 and the corresponding accuracy is provided in Table 4. As we can see, the models have better calibration property as the support shot increases, which means we can use more support data to simultaneously increase accuracy and improve calibration. Various confidence penalty methods not only improve the few-shot classification accuracy, but also improve the calibration of CPN. Although Label Smoothing has the best calibration property, our Wasserstein Confidence Penalty achieves comparable calibration results and better accuracy on novel few-shot tasks.

5   Conclusions

In this work, we investigate existing unsupervised few-shot learning models and contrastive learning models and find a unified paradigm above them. To find the key design factors for unsupervised few-shot learning, we conduct empirical study and propose CPN model which combines the prototypical loss with pairwise contrast from contrastive learning. Besides, we also provide theoretical or intuitive justification for these key factors. Furthermore, when using a large batch size, CPN has the risk of learning sample-specific information. To this end, we propose Wasserstein Confidence Penalty to prevent overconfident one-hot prediction. Our full model, CPNWCP (Contrastive Prototypical Network with Wasserstein Confidence Penalty), achieves state-of-the-art performance in unsupervised few-shot learning. Besides, Wasserstein Confidence Penalty can also be used in contrastive learning to alleviate the 'sampling bias' problem and we will explore its effect in the future work.

References

1. Altschuler, J., Weed, J., Rigollet, P.: Near-linear time approximation algorithms for optimal transport via Sinkhorn iteration. Adv. Neural. Inf. Process. Syst. **2017**, 1965–1975 (2017)
2. Antoniou, A., Storkey, A.J.: Assume, augment and learn: unsupervised few-shot meta-learning via random labels and data augmentation. CoRR (2019)
3. Arora, S., Khandeparkar, H., Khodak, M., Plevrakis, O., Saunshi, N.: A theoretical analysis of contrastive unsupervised representation learning. In: 36th International Conference on Machine Learning, ICML 2019, pp. 9904–9923. International Machine Learning Society (IMLS) (2019)
4. Bachman, P., Hjelm, R.D., Buchwalter, W.: Learning representations by maximizing mutual information across views. Adv. Neural. Inf. Process. Syst. **32**, 15535–15545 (2019)
5. Baik, S., Choi, J., Kim, H., Cho, D., Min, J., Lee, K.M.: Meta-learning with task-adaptive loss function for few-shot learning. In: Proceedings of the IEEE/CVF International Conference on Computer Vision, pp. 9465–9474 (2021)
6. Bertinetto, L., Henriques, J.F., Torr, P.H.S., Vedaldi, A.: Meta-learning with differentiable closed-form solvers. In: 7th International Conference on Learning Representations (2019)
7. Bogachev, V.I., Kolesnikov, A.V.: The Monge-Kantorovich problem: achievements, connections, and perspectives. Russ. Math. Surv. **67**(5), 785–890 (2012)
8. Chen, J., et al.: Simpler, faster, stronger: breaking the log-k curse on contrastive learners with flatnce. CoRR abs/2107.01152 (2021)
9. Chen, T., Kornblith, S., Norouzi, M., Hinton, G.: A simple framework for contrastive learning of visual representations. In: International Conference on Machine Learning, pp. 1597–1607. PMLR (2020)
10. Chen, W., Liu, Y., Kira, Z., Wang, Y.F., Huang, J.: A closer look at few-shot classification. In: 7th International Conference on Learning Representations, ICLR 2019, New Orleans, LA, USA, 6–9 May 2019. OpenReview.net (2019). www.openreview.net/forum?id=HkxLXnAcFQ
11. Chen, X., He, K.: Exploring simple siamese representation learning. In: IEEE Conference on Computer Vision and Pattern Recognition, 2021. Computer Vision Foundation/IEEE (2021)
12. Chuang, C.Y., Robinson, J., Lin, Y.C., Torralba, A., Jegelka, S.: Debiased contrastive learning. Adv. Neural. Inf. Process. Syst. **33**, 8765–8775 (2020)
13. Cuturi, M.: Sinkhorn distances: lightspeed computation of optimal transport. Adv. Neural Inf. Process. Syst. **26**, 2292–2300 (2013)
14. Dhillon, G.S., Chaudhari, P., Ravichandran, A., Soatto, S.: A baseline for few-shot image classification. In: 8th International Conference on Learning Representations, 2020 (2020)
15. Finn, C., Abbeel, P., Levine, S.: Model-agnostic meta-learning for fast adaptation of deep networks. In: Proceedings of the 34th International Conference on Machine Learning-Volume 70, pp. 1126–1135. JMLR. org (2017)

16. Grill, J.B., et al.: Bootstrap your own latent: a new approach to self-supervised learning. In: Neural Information Processing Systems (2020)
17. Guo, C., Pleiss, G., Sun, Y., Weinberger, K.Q.: On calibration of modern neural networks. In: International Conference on Machine Learning, pp. 1321–1330. PMLR (2017)
18. He, K., Fan, H., Wu, Y., Xie, S., Girshick, R.: Momentum contrast for unsupervised visual representation learning. In: Proceedings of the IEEE/CVF Conference on Computer Vision and Pattern Recognition, pp. 9729–9738 (2020)
19. He, K., Zhang, X., Ren, S., Sun, J.: Deep residual learning for image recognition. In: Proceedings of the IEEE Conference on Computer Vision and Pattern Recognition, pp. 770–778 (2016)
20. Hjelm, R.D., et al.: Learning deep representations by mutual information estimation and maximization. In: International Conference on Learning Representations (2018)
21. Hsu, K., Levine, S., Finn, C.: Unsupervised learning via meta-learning. In: 7th International Conference on Learning Representations (2019)
22. Jaynes, E.T.: Information theory and statistical mechanics. Phys. Rev. **106**(4), 620 (1957)
23. Ji, Z., Zou, X., Huang, T., Wu, S.: Unsupervised few-shot feature learning via self-supervised training. Front. Comput. Neurosci. **14**, 83 (2020)
24. Jing, L., Tian, Y.: Self-supervised visual feature learning with deep neural networks: a survey. IEEE Trans. Pattern Anal. Mach. Intell. **43**(11), 4037–4058 (2020)
25. Khodadadeh, S., Bölöni, L., Shah, M.: Unsupervised meta-learning for few-shot image classification. In: Wallach, H.M., Larochelle, H., Beygelzimer, A., d'Alché-Buc, F., Fox, E.B., Garnett, R. (eds.) Advances in Neural Information Processing Systems 32: Annual Conference on Neural Information Processing Systems, pp. 10132–10142 (2019)
26. Khodadadeh, S., Zehtabian, S., Vahidian, S., Wang, W., Lin, B., Bölöni, L.: Unsupervised meta-learning through latent-space interpolation in generative models. In: 9th International Conference on Learning Representations (2021)
27. Lee, K., Maji, S., Ravichandran, A., Soatto, S.: Meta-learning with differentiable convex optimization. In: Proceedings of the IEEE Conference on Computer Vision and Pattern Recognition, pp. 10657–10665 (2019)
28. Lienen, J., Hüllermeier, E.: From label smoothing to label relaxation. In: Proceedings of the 35th AAAI Conference on Artificial Intelligence, AAAI (2021)
29. Luo, Y., Chiu, C.C., Jaitly, N., Sutskever, I.: Learning online alignments with continuous rewards policy gradient. In: 2017 IEEE International Conference on Acoustics, Speech and Signal Processing (ICASSP), pp. 2801–2805. IEEE (2017)
30. Medina, C., Devos, A., Grossglauser, M.: Self-supervised prototypical transfer learning for few-shot classification. arXiv preprint arXiv:2006.11325 (2020)
31. Minderer, M., et al.: Revisiting the calibration of modern neural networks. Adv. Neural Inf. Process. Syst. **34** (2021)
32. Mnih, V., et al.: Asynchronous methods for deep reinforcement learning. In: International Conference on Machine Learning, pp. 1928–1937. PMLR (2016)
33. Müller, R., Kornblith, S., Hinton, G.E.: When does label smoothing help? Adv. Neural. Inf. Process. Syst. **32**, 4694–4703 (2019)
34. Pereyra, G., Tucker, G., Chorowski, J., Kaiser, L., Hinton, G.E.: Regularizing neural networks by penalizing confident output distributions. In: 5th International Conference on Learning Representations, ICLR 2017, Toulon, France, 24–26 April 2017, Workshop Track Proceedings (2017)

35. Poole, B., Ozair, S., van den Oord, A., Alemi, A., Tucker, G.: On variational bounds of mutual information. In: International Conference on Machine Learning, pp. 5171–5180. PMLR (2019)
36. Qin, T., Li, W., Shi, Y., Gao, Y.: Unsupervised few-shot learning via distribution shift-based augmentation. arXiv preprint arXiv:2004.05805 2 (2020)
37. Ravi, S., Larochelle, H.: Optimization as a model for few-shot learning. In: 5th International Conference on Learning Representations (2017)
38. Ren, M., et al.: Meta-learning for semi-supervised few-shot classification. In: 6th International Conference on Learning Representations (2018)
39. Russakovsky, O., et al.: ImageNet large scale visual recognition challenge. Int. J. Comput. Vision **115**(3), 211–252 (2015)
40. Snell, J., Swersky, K., Zemel, R.: Prototypical networks for few-shot learning. In: Advances in Neural Information Processing Systems, pp. 4077–4087 (2017)
41. Szegedy, C., Vanhoucke, V., Ioffe, S., Shlens, J., Wojna, Z.: Rethinking the inception architecture for computer vision, In: Proceedings of the IEEE Conference on Computer Vision and Pattern Recognition, pp. 2818–2826 (2016)
42. Vinyals, O., Blundell, C., Lillicrap, T., Wierstra, D., et al.: Matching networks for one shot learning. Adv. Neural Inf. Process. Syst. **29**, 3630–3638 (2016)
43. Wang, H., Deng, Z.H.: Few-shot learning with LSSVM base learner and transductive modules. arXiv preprint arXiv:2009.05786 (2020)
44. Wang, H., Deng, Z.H.: Cross-domain few-shot classification via adversarial task augmentation. In: Proceedings of the Thirtieth International Joint Conference on Artificial Intelligence (2021)
45. Wang, H., Guo, X., Deng, Z.H., Lu, Y.: Rethinking minimal sufficient representation in contrastive learning. In: Proceedings of the IEEE/CVF Conference on Computer Vision and Pattern Recognition, pp. 16041–16050 (2022)
46. Wang, H., Mai, H., Deng, Z.H., Yang, C., Zhang, L., Wang, H.Y.: Distributed representations of diseases based on co-occurrence relationship. Expert Syst. Appl. **183**, 115418 (2021)
47. Wang, X., Zhang, R., Shen, C., Kong, T., Li, L.: Dense contrastive learning for self-supervised visual pre-training. In: Proceedings of the IEEE/CVF Conference on Computer Vision and Pattern Recognition, pp. 3024–3033 (2021)
48. Wei, C., Wang, H., Shen, W., Yuille, A.L.: CO2: consistent contrast for unsupervised visual representation learning. In: 9th International Conference on Learning Representations (2021)
49. Wu, Z., Xiong, Y., Yu, S.X., Lin, D.: Unsupervised feature learning via nonparametric instance discrimination. In: Proceedings of the IEEE Conference on Computer Vision and Pattern Recognition, pp. 3733–3742 (2018)
50. Ye, H., Han, L., Zhan, D.: Revisiting unsupervised meta-learning: amplifying or compensating for the characteristics of few-shot tasks. CoRR (2020)
51. Zbontar, J., Jing, L., Misra, I., LeCun, Y., Deny, S.: Barlow twins: self-supervised learning via redundancy reduction. In: Proceedings of the 38th International Conference on Machine Learning, ICML 2021, 18–24 July 2021, Virtual Event. PMLR (2021)
52. Zhang, C.B., et al.: Delving deep into label smoothing. IEEE Trans. Image Process. **30**, 5984–5996 (2021)
53. Zhang, C., Cai, Y., Lin, G., Shen, C.: Deepemd: few-shot image classification with differentiable earth mover's distance and structured classifiers. In: Proceedings of the IEEE/CVF Conference on Computer Vision and Pattern Recognition, pp. 12203–12213 (2020)

54. Zhang, H., Koniusz, P., Jian, S., Li, H., Torr, P.H.S.: Rethinking class relations: absolute-relative supervised and unsupervised few-shot learning. In: IEEE Conference on Computer Vision and Pattern Recognition, CVPR 2021, virtual, 19–25 June 2021 (2021)
55. Ziko, I.M., Dolz, J., Granger, E., Ayed, I.B.: Laplacian regularized few-shot learning. In: Proceedings of the 37th International Conference on Machine Learning, 2020 (2020)

Learn-to-Decompose: Cascaded Decomposition Network for Cross-Domain Few-Shot Facial Expression Recognition

Xinyi Zou[1], Yan Yan[1(✉)], Jing-Hao Xue[2], Si Chen[3], and Hanzi Wang[1]

[1] Xiamen University, Xiamen, China
{yanyan,hanzi.wang}@xmu.edu.cn
[2] University College London, London, UK
jinghao.xue@ucl.ac.uk
[3] Xiamen University of Technology, Xiamen, China
chensi@xmut.edu.cn

Abstract. Most existing compound facial expression recognition (FER) methods rely on large-scale labeled compound expression data for training. However, collecting such data is labor-intensive and time-consuming. In this paper, we address the compound FER task in the *cross-domain few-shot learning* (FSL) setting, which requires only a few samples of compound expressions in the target domain. Specifically, we propose a novel cascaded decomposition network (CDNet), which cascades several learn-to-decompose modules with shared parameters based on a sequential decomposition mechanism, to obtain a transferable feature space. To alleviate the overfitting problem caused by limited base classes in our task, a partial regularization strategy is designed to effectively exploit the best of both episodic training and batch training. By training across similar tasks on multiple basic expression datasets, CDNet learns the ability of *learn-to-decompose* that can be easily adapted to identify unseen compound expressions. Extensive experiments on both in-the-lab and in-the-wild compound expression datasets demonstrate the superiority of our proposed CDNet against several state-of-the-art FSL methods. Code is available at: https://github.com/zouxinyi0625/CDNet.

Keywords: Compound facial expression recognition · Cross-domain few-shot learning · Feature decomposition · Regularization

1 Introduction

Automatic facial expression recognition (FER) is an important computer vision task with a variety of applications, such as mental assessment, driver fatigue surveillance, and interaction entertainment [16].

Supplementary Information The online version contains supplementary material available at https://doi.org/10.1007/978-3-031-19800-7_40.

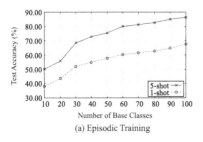
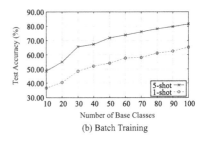

(a) Episodic Training   (b) Batch Training

Fig. 1. Test accuracy obtained by (a) an episodic training-based FSL method (ProtoNet [28]) and (b) a batch training-based FSL method (BASELINE [3]) with the different numbers of base classes on a widely used FSL benchmark (CUB [32])

The conventional FER task [25,34,36] aims to classify the input facial images into several basic expression categories (including anger, disgust, fear, happiness, sadness, surprise, contempt, and neutral). Unfortunately, the above basic expression categories cannot comprehensively describe the diversity and complexity of human emotions in practical scenarios. Later, Du *et al.* [7] further define compound expression categories. Typically, compound expressions are much more fine-grained and difficult to be identified than basic expressions. Most existing work on compound FER [13,27] depends heavily on large-scale labeled compound expression data. However, annotating such data is time-consuming since the differences between compound expressions are subtle.

To avoid expensive annotations, few-shot learning (FSL) has emerged as a promising learning scheme. Very recently, Zou *et al.* [42] first study cross-domain FSL for compound FER. Our paper is under the same problem setting as [42], where easily-accessible basic expression datasets and the compound expression dataset are used for training and testing, respectively. However, unlike [42], we address this problem from the perspective of feature decomposition and develop a novel regularization strategy for better performance.

A key issue of FSL is how to obtain a transferable feature space. Two popular paradigms to learn such a space are episodic training and batch training. Episodic training-based methods [19,28,31] construct few-shot tasks to learn knowledge transfer across similar tasks. Batch training-based methods [1,3,30] learn a classification model to capture the information of all base classes. Note that, different from popular FSL tasks (such as image classification), which leverage a large number of base classes for training, our FER task involves only limited base classes (i.e., the number of classes in basic expression datasets is small). Hence, for episodic training-based methods, the sampled few-shot tasks are highly overlapped, leading to overfitting to the seen tasks. On the other hand, for batch training-based methods, the global view knowledge learned from limited base classes fails to be transferred to a novel task due to their inferior meta-learning ability. As shown in Fig. 1, the performance of exiting FSL methods drops substantially with the decreasing number of base classes.

To alleviate the overfitting problem caused by limited base classes, one reasonable way is to impose the batch training-based regularization to episode training. Although some methods [2,40] employ the batch training as an auxiliary task, they do not work on the case of limited base classes. EGS-Net [42] applies full regularization of batch training to facilitate the training. However, the inferior meta-learning ability of batch training will unavoidably affect episodic training when full regularization is used. Therefore, it is significant to investigate how to exploit the best of both episodic training and batch training under limited base classes.

In this paper, we propose a novel cascaded decomposition network (CDNet), which cascades several learn-to-decompose (LD) modules with shared parameters in a sequential way, for compound FER. Our method is inspired by the RGB decomposition, where colors are represented by combinations of R, G, and B values. Once a model learns the ability of RGB decomposition from existing colors, it can be easily adapted to infer new colors. In the same spirit, we aim to represent facial expressions as weighted combinations of expression prototypes. The expression prototypes encode the underlying generic knowledge across expressions while their weights characterize adaptive embeddings of one expression. Building on our cascaded decomposition, a partial regularization strategy is designed to effectively integrate episodic training and batch training.

Specifically, an LD module, consisting of a decomposition block and a weighting block, learns an expression prototype and its corresponding weight, respectively. Based on the sequential decomposition mechanism, CDNet cascades LD modules with shared parameters to obtain weighted expression prototypes and reconstruct the expression feature. During the episodic training of CDNet, we further leverage the batch training-based pre-trained model to regularize only the decomposition block (instead of full regularization on the whole LD module). In this way, a generic LD module can be effectively learned under the supervision of the pre-trained model holding the global view of all base classes. By training across similar tasks with our designed partial regularization, CDNet is enabled to have the ability of learn-to-decompose that can be adapted to a novel task.

In summary, our main contributions are given as follows:

- We propose a novel CDNet for compound FER in the cross-domain FSL setting. An LD module is repeatedly exploited to extract the domain-agnostic expression feature from multi-source domains via a sequential decomposition mechanism. Based on the trained model, we can easily construct a transferable feature space for the compound FER task in the target domain.
- We develop a partial regularization strategy to combine the benefits of episodic training and batch training. Such a way can greatly alleviate the overfitting problem caused by limited base classes in our task and simultaneously maintain the meta-learning ability of the whole model.
- We perform extensive ablation studies to validate the importance of each component of CDNet. Experimental results show that CDNet performs favorably against state-of-the-art FSL methods for compound FER.

2   Related Work

2.1   Facial Expression Recognition

Basic FER. Based on the Ekman and Friesen's study [8], the conventional FER task classifies an input facial image into one of the basic expression categories. In this paper, we refer to the conventional FER task as the basic FER. A large number of basic FER methods [24,25,33] have been proposed to extract discriminative expression features. Recently, Ruan *et al.* [25] introduce a decomposition module to model action-aware latent features for basic FER. Different from the parallel design in [25], we aim to learn a generic LD module by developing a sequential decomposition mechanism and a partial regularization strategy, enabling our model to obtain transferable features in the FSL setting.

Compound FER. Li *et al.* [18] design a novel separate loss to maximize the intra-class similarity and minimize the inter-class similarity for compound FER. Zhang *et al.* [37] propose a coarse-to-fine two-stage strategy to enhance the robustness of the learned feature. Note that the above methods often require large-scale labeled compound expression data for training. Unfortunately, annotating these data is expensive and requires the professional guidance of psychology.

Few-Shot FER. Ciubotaru *et al.* [5] revisit popular FSL methods on basic FER. Recently, Zhu *et al.* [41] construct a convolutional relation network (CRN) to identify novel basic expression categories. The work most relevant to ours is EGS-Net [42], which first investigates compound FER in the cross-domain FSL setting. Different from [42], we propose CDNet to obtain multiple weighted expression prototypes and reconstruct a transferable expression feature space.

2.2   Few-Shot Learning

Episodic Training-Based FSL. Based on what a model is expected to meta-learn [20], various episodic training-based methods (such as learn-to-measure [28,29], learn-to-fine-tune [10,15], and learn-to-parameterize [12,38]) have been developed. In this paper, inspired by the fact that different colors can be reconstructed by a linear combination of R, G, and B values, we represent expression categories by combinations of expression prototypes. Technically, we cascade several LD modules with shared parameters in a sequential decomposition way to enforce the model to have the ability of learn-to-decompose by episodic training.

Batch Training-Based FSL. Recently, Chen *et al.* [3] reveal that a simple baseline with a cosine classifier can achieve surprisingly competing results. Tian *et al.* [30] boost the performance with self-distillation. Afrasiyabi *et al.* [1] develop a strong baseline with a novel angular margin loss and an early-stopping strategy. However, the meta-learning ability of batch training-based methods is inferior, especially when the number of base classes is limited as in our task.

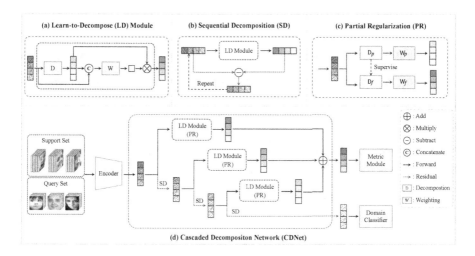

Fig. 2. Overview of the proposed CDNet. It contains three main parts: (a) an LD module to extract an expression prototype and its corresponding weight, (b) a sequential decomposition mechanism to integrate shared LD modules, and (c) a partial regularization strategy to regularize the training. (d) CDNet is trained to obtain a transferable expression feature space that can be easily adapted to a novel compound FER task

Hybrid FSL. A simple way to combine episodic training and batch training is Meta-Baseline [4], which pre-trains the model by batch training and fine-tunes it by episodic training. Chen *et al.* [2] take the classification task as an auxiliary task to stabilize the training. Zhou *et al.* [40] introduce binocular mutual learning (BML) to use the complementary information of the two paradigms. The above methods focus on popular FSL tasks with a large number of base classes for training. However, our FER task involves only limited base classes. As a result, these methods do not work well in our case. In this paper, a partial regularization strategy is proposed to address the limited base classes problem by properly exploiting the advantages of the two training paradigms.

3 The Proposed Method

3.1 Problem Definition

In this paper, as done in EGS-Net [42], we consider the compound FER task in the cross-domain FSL setting, where only a few novel class samples are required to identify a compound expression category in the target domain.

Given a labeled training set $\mathcal{D}_{train}$ (consisting of C_{base} base classes), we aim to learn a model that can be well generalized to the test set $\mathcal{D}_{test}$ (consisting of C_{novel} novel classes). In our setting, the base classes are the basic expression categories, while the novel classes are the compound expression categories. To enrich the diversity of the training set and handle the discrepancy between source and target domains, multiple easily-accessible basic expression datasets (i.e., the multi-source domains) are used. Note that the base classes and novel classes are disjoint, and the number of base classes is limited in our task.

After training the model on $\mathcal{D}_{train}$, few-shot tasks are constructed on $\mathcal{D}_{test}$ to evaluate the performance of the learned model in the target domain. The goal of a few-shot task is to classify the query images with the reference of the support images. Each few-shot task (an N-way K-shot task) samples N classes from the C_{novel} classes, and each class contains K labeled support samples and Q unlabeled query samples. In this paper, following the representative FSL method [28], a query image is simply assigned to its nearest class in the learned expression feature space. Hence, the key question of our task is how to construct a transferable expression feature space given limited base classes in $\mathcal{D}_{train}$.

3.2   Overview

An overview of the proposed CDNet is shown in Fig. 2. CDNet is composed of several learn-to-decompose (LD) modules with shared parameters. Each LD module (Fig. 2(a)) consists of a decomposition block to extract an expression prototype and a weighting block to output the corresponding weight. Specifically, given an input feature from the encoder, an LD module first generates a weighted prototype, while the residual feature (obtained by subtracting the weighted prototype from the input feature) is then fed into the subsequent LD module. Based on a sequential decomposition mechanism (Fig. 2(b)), the LD module is repeatedly used to extract weighted prototypes progressively. Finally, the expression feature, which is obtained by combining all the weighted prototypes, models the domain-agnostic expression information. Meanwhile, the final residual feature captures the domain-specific information by identifying the input domain. As a consequence, CDNet can be well generalized to the unseen target domain.

The training of CDNet involves two stages. In the first stage, CDNet is pre-trained in a batch training manner to capture the global view information of all base classes on the whole $\mathcal{D}_{train}$. In the second stage, CDNet is fine-tuned in an episode training manner under the regularization of the pre-trained model. To alleviate the overfitting problem caused by limited base classes, a novel partial regularization strategy (Fig. 2(c)) is developed to regularize the training in this stage. By training across similar tasks with proper regularization, CDNet learns the ability of learn-to-decompose that can be easily adapted to a novel task.

3.3   Cascaded Decomposition Network (CDNet)

CDNet consists of shared LD modules to reconstruct the transferable expression feature based on a novel sequential decomposition mechanism. In the following, we will elaborate the LD module and the sequential decomposition mechanism.

LD Module. The LD module consists of a decomposition block and a weighting block. Specifically, given an input feature $x \in \mathbb{R}^d$, where d denotes the dimension of the given feature, x is first fed into a decomposition block $D(\cdot)$ to extract

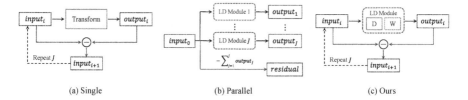

(a) Single   (b) Parallel   (c) Ours

Fig. 3. Variants of the proposed CDNet. (a) A single transformation module which directly obtains a weighted prototype. (b) The parallel mechanism which simultaneously integrates multiple LD modules. (c) Our method which cascades the two-block LD modules with shared parameters based on a sequential decomposition mechanism

an expression prototype. The decomposition block includes a transform matrix $P \in \mathbb{R}^{d \times d}$ and a PReLU activation layer $\sigma(\cdot)$. Mathematically, the expression prototype $\boldsymbol{p}$ is computed as

$$
\begin{aligned}
\boldsymbol{p} &= D(\boldsymbol{x}) \\
&= \sigma(P(\boldsymbol{x})).
\end{aligned}
\tag{1}
$$

Then, the extracted prototype $\boldsymbol{p}$ and the input feature $\boldsymbol{x}$ are concatenated, and they are fed into a weighting block $W(\cdot)$ to compute the corresponding weight $\alpha = W([\boldsymbol{x}, \boldsymbol{p}])$, where $[\cdot, \cdot]$ represents the concatenation operation. The weighting block contains a three-layer perceptron. Finally, the output of the LD module is the weighted prototype $\boldsymbol{f}$, which can be written as

$$
\begin{aligned}
\boldsymbol{f} &= \alpha \cdot \boldsymbol{p} \\
&= W([\boldsymbol{x}, D(\boldsymbol{x})]) \cdot D(\boldsymbol{x}).
\end{aligned}
\tag{2}
$$

Note that, instead of using a single transformation module (Fig. 3(a)), we use two sequential blocks to obtain a weighted prototype (Fig. 3(c)). Such a way can better learn the expression prototype and enable us to impose the regularization only on the decomposition block. This is helpful to transfer the global view knowledge of all base classes by batch training and simultaneously preserve the meta-learning ability of the whole model by episodic training.

Sequential Decomposition Mechanism. A single weighted prototype cannot comprehensively provide the representation of the expression feature. The residual feature also contains the discriminative information for expression classification. Therefore, multiple weighted prototypes are desirable.

As shown in Fig. 3(b), a straightforward way to learn multiple weighted prototypes is to use multiple different LD modules in a parallel way, where a separate LD module is required to compute a weighted prototype. However, multiple LD modules with different parameters are not suitable to be adapted to a novel task, since the inference ability of over-parameterized LD modules is weak for each meta-task involving only few training samples. Here, we propose a sequential decomposition mechanism (Fig. 3(c)), which cascades the LD modules with shared parameters to obtain multiple weighted prototypes progressively. In this way, a generic LD module can be learned by repeatedly using it for training.

Specifically, the original feature $\boldsymbol{x}_0$ from the feature encoder is fed into the LD module to obtain the first weighted prototype $\boldsymbol{f}_1$ by Eq. (2), that is, $\boldsymbol{f}_1 = \alpha_1 \cdot \boldsymbol{p}_1$, where $\boldsymbol{p}_1$ and α_1 denote the first expression prototype and its corresponding weight, respectively. Then, the residual feature is computed by subtracting the weighted prototype $\boldsymbol{f}_1$ from the original feature $\boldsymbol{x}_0$, and is further fed into the same LD module to obtain the second weighted prototype $\boldsymbol{f}_2$. The process is repeated several times to get the weighted prototypes progressively. For the i-th LD module, its input $\boldsymbol{input}_i$ and output $\boldsymbol{output}_i$ are defined as

$$\boldsymbol{input}_i = \begin{cases} \boldsymbol{x}_0 & , i = 1 \\ \boldsymbol{x}_0 - \sum_{k=1}^{i-1} \alpha_k \boldsymbol{p}_k & , i > 1, \end{cases} \tag{3}$$

$$\boldsymbol{output}_i = \alpha_i \boldsymbol{p}_i, \tag{4}$$

where $\boldsymbol{x}_0$ is the original feature. $\boldsymbol{p}_i = \mathrm{D}(\boldsymbol{input}_i)$ and $\alpha_i = \mathrm{W}([\boldsymbol{input}_i, \boldsymbol{p}_i])$ respectively denote the i-th expression prototype and its corresponding weight.

Finally, the expression feature is reconstructed by combining all the weighted prototypes to recognize the expression. At the same time, the residual feature is used to identify the input domain, encoding the domain-specific information. Mathematically, the output of CDNet that cascades J LD modules is

$$\mathrm{CDNet}(\boldsymbol{x}_0) = \begin{cases} \boldsymbol{r}_e = \sum_{k=1}^{J} \alpha_k \boldsymbol{p}_k \\ \boldsymbol{r}_d = \boldsymbol{x}_0 - \boldsymbol{r}_e, \end{cases} \tag{5}$$

where $\boldsymbol{r}_e$ and $\boldsymbol{r}_d$ represent the domain-agnostic expression feature and the domain-specific residual feature, respectively.

By disentangling the domain information from the given feature, we are able to extract a domain-agnostic expression feature. Therefore, we overcome the discrepancy between source and target domains, thus facilitating the recognition of compound expressions in the target domain.

3.4   Training Process

CDNet is first pre-trained by batch training, and then fine-tuned by episodic training. In particular, a partial regularization strategy is designed to take full advantage of the two training paradigms under the limited base class setting.

Pre-training Stage. In this stage, CDNet is pre-trained in the batch training manner to obtain initial parameters. Moreover, the pre-trained decomposition block is used to regularize the fine-tuning stage. For each iteration, we sample a batch of data from a randomly selected source domain. A sample is denoted as $(\boldsymbol{I}, y_e, y_d)$, where $\boldsymbol{I}$, y_e, and y_d are the image, the expression label, and the domain label of the sample, respectively. $\boldsymbol{I}$ is fed into the feature encoder to obtain the original feature $\boldsymbol{x}_0$, which is further passed through CDNet to extract the expression feature $\boldsymbol{r}_e$ and the residual feature $\boldsymbol{r}_d$, according to Eq. (5).

On one hand, r_e is used to make prediction of the expression category, and the classification loss $\mathcal{L}_{cls}^p$ is defined by the popular cross-entropy loss:

$$\mathcal{L}_{cls}^p = -\sum_{c=1}^{C_e} \mathbb{1}_{[c=y_e]}\log(\mathrm{F}_e(r_e)), \tag{6}$$

where $\mathrm{F}_e(\cdot)$ is a linear expression classifier (i.e., a fully-connected layer), C_e is the number of basic expression categories, and $\mathbb{1}_{[c=y_e]}$ equals to 1 when $c = y_e$, and 0 otherwise.

On the other hand, r_d is used to identify the input domain, so that the learned expression feature is domain-agnostic and can be better adapted to the unseen target domain. The domain classification loss $\mathcal{L}_d^p$ is also the cross-entropy loss between the predicted results $\hat{y}_d$ and the ground-truth y_d:

$$\mathcal{L}_d^p = -\sum_{c=1}^{C_d} \mathbb{1}_{[c=y_d]}\log(\mathrm{F}_d(r_d)), \tag{7}$$

where $\mathrm{F}_d(\cdot)$ is a domain classifier (i.e., a two-layer perceptron) and C_d is the number of source domain categories.

Therefore, the total loss in this stage is the joint loss of $\mathcal{L}_{cls}^p$ and $\mathcal{L}_d^p$:

$$\mathcal{L}_p = \mathcal{L}_{cls}^p + \lambda_d^p \mathcal{L}_d^p, \tag{8}$$

where λ_d^p is the balance weight in the pre-training stage.

Fine-Tuning Stage. In this stage, CDNet is fine-tuned to learn transferable knowledge across similar tasks by episodic training. For each episode, an FSL task of N classes is sampled on a randomly selected source domain. The support set $\mathbb{S} = \{\mathbb{I}_s, \mathbb{Y}_s\}$ and the query set $\mathbb{Q} = \{\mathbb{I}_q, \mathbb{Y}_q\}$ are constructed with K support samples and Q query samples of each class, where $\mathbb{I}_*$ and $\mathbb{Y}_*$ denote the image set and the corresponding label set. All the images are subsequently fed into the feature encoder and CDNet to obtain the expression feature and the domain-specific residual feature. The expression feature and the domain-specific residual feature of an image in $\mathbb{S}$ ($\mathbb{Q}$) are denoted as r_e^s (r_e^q) and r_d^s (r_d^q), respectively.

The expression feature obtained by CDNet is used for expression classification. Following the representative ProtoNet [28], each query image is assigned to its nearest support class center in the learned feature space. The expression classification loss of a query image is

$$\mathcal{L}_{cls}^f = -\sum_{n=1}^{N} \mathbb{1}_{[n=y_q]}\log(\mathrm{softmax}(-\mathcal{M}(r_e^q, R_n))), \tag{9}$$

where r_e^q and y_q are the expression feature and the expression label of the query image, respectively. $R_n = \frac{1}{K}\sum_{k=1}^{K}(r_e^s)_k^n$ represents the center of class n, where $(r_e^s)_k^n$ is the expression feature of the k-th image in class n in the support set. $\mathcal{M}(\cdot)$ denotes the metric module (the Euclidean distance is used). N is the number of sampled classes. $\mathrm{softmax}(\cdot)$ denotes the softmax function.

The domain classification loss $\mathcal{L}_d^f$ is similar to Eq. (7), where all the support samples and query samples are used to compute the domain classification loss.

Finally, instead of applying full regularization to the whole LD module, we leverage partial regularization, which imposes regularization only on the decomposition block. In this way, the decomposition block learns the generic expression prototype while the weighting block learns adaptive weights without being affected by batch training. Mathematically, a regularization loss is designed to enforce the output of the decomposition block in the fine-tuning stage to be close to that of the pre-trained decomposition block. That is,

$$\mathcal{L}_r^f = \sum_{i=1}^{J} ||\mathrm{D}_p(\boldsymbol{input}_i) - \mathrm{D}_f(\boldsymbol{input}_i)||_2^2, \tag{10}$$

where $\mathrm{D}_p(\cdot)$ and $\mathrm{D}_f(\cdot)$ are the decomposition blocks in the pre-training stage and the fine-tuning stage, respectively. J is the number of cascaded LD modules.

Overall, the total loss of the fine-tuning stage is formulated as

$$\mathcal{L}_f = \mathcal{L}_{cls}^f + \lambda_d^f \mathcal{L}_d^f + \lambda_r^f \mathcal{L}_r^f, \tag{11}$$

where λ_d^f and λ_r^f are the balance weights in the fine-tuning stage.

4   Experiments

4.1   Datasets

Our CDNet is trained on multiple basic expression datasets and tested on the compound expression dataset.

Basic Expression Datasets. We use five basic expression datasets, including three in-the-lab datasets (CK+ [21], MMI [22], and Oulu-CASIA [39])), and two in-the-wild datasets (the basic expression subset of RAF-DB [17] and SFEW [6]), to form the training set. **Compound Expression Datasets** Three compound expression datasets (CFEE [7], EmotioNet [9], and RAF-DB) are used to evaluate the performance of the learned model. To ensure the disjointness between base classes and novel classes, only the compound expression subsets of these datasets, denoted as CFEE_C, EmotioNet_C, and RAF_C, are used for testing. The details of these datasets are given in supplementary materials.

4.2   Implementation Details

Our method is implemented with PyTorch. All the facial images are first aligned and resized to 256×256. Then, they are randomly cropped to 224×224, following by a random horizontal flip and color jitter as data augmentation for training. To address the different numbers of classes and the different label sequences of multi-source domains, we use a mapping function to unify the labels. The encoder of our CDNet is ResNet-18, which is pre-trained on the MS-Celeb-1M dataset

Table 1. The details of the baseline method and 6 variants of CDNet

Methods	Decomposition module	Decomposition mechanism	Regularization
Baseline	×	×	×
Single	Single transformation	Sequential	Full
Parallel	LD	Parallel	Partial
Decompose	LD	Sequential	×
CDNet_Full	LD	Sequential	Full
CDNet_Fix	LD	Sequential	Partial (Fix)
CDNet (ours)	LD	Sequential	Partial

[14]. The number of the cascaded LD modules (whose detailed architecture is given in supplementary materials) J is set to 3 by default.

Our model is trained using the Adam algorithm with the learning rate of 0.0001, $\beta_1 = 0.500$, and $\beta_2 = 0.999$. For the pre-training stage, the model is optimized by 10,000 iterations and each iteration samples a mini-batch (with the batch size of 16) from a randomly selected source domain. The balance weight λ_d^t in Eq. (8) is empirically set to 1.0. For the fine-tuning stage, the model is fine-tuned by 100 episodes and each episode contains 100 few-shot tasks. For a few-shot task, we set the number of classes $N = 5$, the number of support samples $K = 1$ or 5, and the number of query samples $Q = 16$ for each class. The balance weights λ_d^f and λ_r^f in Eq. (11) are set to 0.01 and 1.0, respectively. The influence of different balance weights is shown in supplementary materials. The accuracy of 1,000 few-shot tasks sampled on the test set is used for evaluation.

4.3   Ablation Studies

The details of the compared variants of CDNet are shown in Table 1. ProtoNet [28], which adopts ResNet-18 as the encoder, is taken as the baseline method.

Influence of the LD Module. To validate the effectiveness of our proposed LD module, we replace the LD module with a single transformation module (as shown in Fig. 3(a)) to obtain the weighted prototype. We denote our method based on the single module as "Single". We also evaluate a variant of CDNet (denoted as "CDNet_Full"), which applies the pre-trained LD module to supervise the output of the whole LD module during the fine-tuning stage. The comparison results are shown in Table 2.

Compared with CDNet, the "Single" method performs worse since it can only impose full regularization on the whole transformation module. Moreover, the "CDNet_Full" method obtains better accuracy than the "Single" method. This indicates the superiority of obtaining the weighted prototype in our two-block LD module. By learning the expression prototype and its weight individually, we can fully exploit the generic information across basic expressions, which can facilitate the extraction of a transferable expression feature.

Table 2. Influence of the key modules. Test accuracy (%) of 5-way few shot classification tasks with 95% confidence intervals on three different datasets. "Pre" indicates that the pre-trained model is used as an initialization in the second stage

Pre	Method	CFEE_C		EmotioNet_C		RAF_C	
		1-shot	5-shot	1-shot	5-shot	1-shot	5-shot
✗	Baseline	53.29 ± 0.73	66.60 ± 0.60	50.15 ± 0.66	60.04 ± 0.56	39.12 ± 0.56	58.41 ± 0.46
✗	Single	53.67 ± 0.72	67.25 ± 0.61	50.72 ± 0.65	60.62 ± 0.56	40.59 ± 0.57	59.40 ± 0.46
✗	Parallel	53.83 ± 0.73	67.53 ± 0.60	51.84 ± 0.67	61.21 ± 0.58	41.11 ± 0.57	60.48 ± 0.45
✗	Decompose	53.78 ± 0.72	67.60 ± 0.61	51.16 ± 0.67	60.75 ± 0.58	40.75 ± 0.57	59.69 ± 0.44
✗	CDNet_Full	54.23 ± 0.70	67.82 ± 0.59	51.72 ± 0.68	61.47 ± 0.60	41.51 ± 0.59	60.25 ± 0.45
✗	CDNet	54.55 ± 0.71	68.09 ± 0.62	52.76 ± 0.67	61.76 ± 0.57	42.02 ± 0.58	61.75 ± 0.44
✓	Baseline	53.43 ± 0.71	66.75 ± 0.60	51.31 ± 0.67	60.68 ± 0.59	42.30 ± 0.58	60.19 ± 0.43
✓	Single	54.37 ± 0.71	67.44 ± 0.59	53.13 ± 0.65	61.47 ± 0.58	43.22 ± 0.58	60.94 ± 0.45
✓	Parallel	54.72 ± 0.72	67.66 ± 0.59	54.27 ± 0.68	61.74 ± 0.59	44.78 ± 0.60	61.29 ± 0.43
✓	Decompose	55.17 ± 0.71	67.85 ± 0.59	53.01 ± 0.68	61.60 ± 0.60	43.78 ± 0.59	61.00 ± 0.43
✓	CDNet_Full	55.91 ± 0.73	68.37 ± 0.60	54.11 ± 0.68	61.99 ± 0.61	45.69 ± 0.59	61.59 ± 0.42
✓	CDNet_Fix	56.45 ± 0.72	68.54 ± 0.61	54.60 ± 0.68	62.50 ± 0.60	45.90 ± 0.60	62.12 ± 0.43
✓	CDNet	$\mathbf{56.99} \pm \mathbf{0.73}$	$\mathbf{68.98} \pm \mathbf{0.60}$	$\mathbf{55.16} \pm \mathbf{0.67}$	$\mathbf{63.03} \pm \mathbf{0.59}$	$\mathbf{46.07} \pm \mathbf{0.59}$	$\mathbf{63.03} \pm \mathbf{0.45}$

Influence of the Sequential Decomposition Mechanism. In Table 2, we compare our sequential decomposition mechanism with the parallel mechanism (Fig. 3(b)) that obtains multiple weighted prototypes using different LD modules. Our method based on the parallel mechanism is denoted as "Parallel".

CDNet with our sequential decomposition mechanism outperforms that with the parallel mechanism. The inference ability of the "Parallel" method is weak due to over-parameterized LD modules when only a small number of training samples are available. These results show the effectiveness of using a generic LD module to obtain the weighted prototypes progressively in the FSL setting.

Influence of the Cascaded Decomposition Design. We evaluate the performance of our cascaded decomposition design (denoted as "Decompose") in Table 2. We can see that the "Decompose" method performs better than the baseline method, and the improvements are more evident when using a batch training-based pre-trained model. With the ability of learn-to-decompose, our method can extract transferable features for the novel compound FER, especially on the more difficult 1-shot classification task.

Figure 4 further illustrates t-SNE visualization results of the learned feature space by the baseline method and our CDNet. Clearly, the domain gap between the source and target domains is greatly reduced by our CDNet. By disentangling the domain-specific information from the original feature, the learned expression feature is domain-agnostic, alleviating the domain discrepancy between the source and target domains. The superiority of using a decomposition-based design is further illustrated in supplementary materials.

Influence of Regularization. We also compare the CDNet methods with and without our regularization strategy (denoted as "CDNet" and "Decompose",

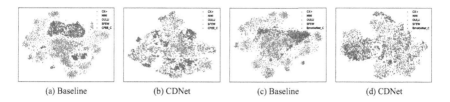

| (a) Baseline | (b) CDNet | (c) Baseline | (d) CDNet |

Fig. 4. t-SNE visualization of the extracted feature obtained by (a) the Baseline method and (b) CDNet on multi-source domains and a target domain (CFEE_C). The target domain is marked in red. The domain discrepancy between multi-source domains and the target domain is reduced by our CDNet, facilitating our cross-domain FER task. (c-d) A similar pattern can be found for another target domain (EmotioNet_C). (Color figure online)

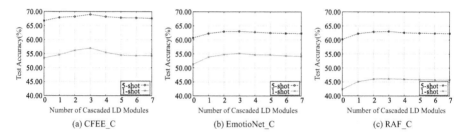

Fig. 5. Influence of the number of cascaded LD modules on three different datasets. The average accuracy of 5-way few-shot classification tasks is reported

respectively) in Table 2. We can see that the recognition accuracy is greatly improved when our regularization strategy is used. This validates the importance of imposing the partial regularization from a pre-trained block (which holds the global view) during episodic training.

Moreover, we compare the proposed partial regularization strategy with two variants ("CDNet_Full" and "CDNet_Fix"). From Table 2, the "CDNet_Full" method achieves worse results than the other two regularization variants. This can be ascribed to the poor "meta-learning" ability of the pre-trained model, deteriorating the transfer ability of the fine-tuning stage. "CDNet_Fix" fixes the pre-trained decomposition block and only fine-tunes the weighting block to obtain adaptive weights. It alleviates the overfitting problem with the fixed decomposition block, but the inference ability of the fixed decomposition block is still poor. Our method with the proposed partial regularization strategy obtains the highest recognition accuracy among the three regularization variants.

Influence of the Pre-training Stage. In Table 2, all the variants with the pre-trained initialization achieve higher accuracy. The improvements on CDNet are more evident than those on the baseline method. This shows the importance of preserving a global view for feature decomposition in our FER task.

Influence of the Number of Cascaded LD Modules. We also evaluate the performance with the different numbers of cascaded LD modules, as shown in Fig. 5. The 0-layer CDNet indicates the baseline method. Compared with the baseline method, CDNet with a single LD module can improve the accuracy by disentangling the expression feature and the domain-specific residual feature. The performance of CDNet is further boosted when two or three shared LD modules are cascaded to obtain weighted prototypes. This indicates that the residual feature from the first decomposition contains the expression information. However, when more cascaded LD modules are used, the accuracy decreases especially on the CFEE_C dataset. In such a case, the residual feature is less informative, thus reducing the discrimination of the learned feature. Our method achieves the best performance when the number of cascaded LD modules is 3.

4.4   Comparison with State-of-the-Art Methods

Table 3 shows the performance comparisons between our developed CDNet and several state-of-the-art FSL methods. For a fair comparison, we report the results of the competing methods using the source codes provided by respective authors under the same settings as ours.

Table 3. Comparisons with state-of-the-art FSL methods. Test accuracy (%) of 5-way few-shot classification tasks with 95% confidence intervals on three different datasets

Method	CFEE_C		EmotioNet_C		RAF_C	
	1-shot	5-shot	1-shot	5-shot	1-shot	5-shot
(a) Episodic training-based FSL methods						
ProtoNet [28]	53.29 ± 0.73	66.60 ± 0.60	50.15 ± 0.66	60.04 ± 0.56	39.12 ± 0.56	58.41 ± 0.46
MatchingNet [31]	52.31 ± 0.69	62.24 ± 0.61	48.64 ± 0.63	54.19 ± 0.58	34.84 ± 0.54	52.45 ± 0.44
RelationNet [29]	50.58 ± 0.68	63.17 ± 0.60	48.33 ± 0.68	56.27 ± 0.58	36.18 ± 0.54	53.45 ± 0.46
GNN [11]	54.01 ± 0.74	64.26 ± 0.63	49.49 ± 0.68	58.67 ± 0.59	38.74 ± 0.56	57.15 ± 0.47
DSN [26]	49.61 ± 0.73	60.03 ± 0.62	48.25 ± 0.68	54.89 ± 0.58	40.09 ± 0.55	52.49 ± 0.47
InfoPatch [19]	54.19 ± 0.67	67.29 ± 0.56	48.14 ± 0.61	59.84 ± 0.55	41.02 ± 0.52	57.98 ± 0.45
(b) Batch training-based FSL methods						
softmax [3]	54.32 ± 0.73	66.35 ± 0.62	51.60 ± 0.68	61.83 ± 0.59	42.16 ± 0.59	58.57 ± 0.45
cosmax [3]	54.97 ± 0.71	67.89 ± 0.61	50.87 ± 0.65	61.10 ± 0.56	40.87 ± 0.56	57.67 ± 0.46
arcmax [1]	55.29 ± 0.71	67.72 ± 0.60	50.73 ± 0.65	61.70 ± 0.56	41.28 ± 0.57	57.94 ± 0.46
rfs [30]	54.96 ± 0.73	65.71 ± 0.61	51.91 ± 0.67	61.94 ± 0.57	43.05 ± 0.59	60.08 ± 0.46
LR+DC [35]	53.20 ± 0.73	64.18 ± 0.66	52.09 ± 0.70	60.12 ± 0.58	42.90 ± 0.60	56.74 ± 0.46
STARTUP [23]	54.89 ± 0.72	67.79 ± 0.61	52.61 ± 0.69	61.95 ± 0.57	43.97 ± 0.60	59.14 ± 0.47
(c) Hybrid FSL methods						
Meta-Baseline [4]	55.17 ± 0.74	67.15 ± 0.61	52.36 ± 0.67	62.01 ± 0.59	43.54 ± 0.61	61.59 ± 0.44
OAT [2]	54.28 ± 0.75	67.88 ± 0.62	52.92 ± 0.66	61.85 ± 0.59	42.75 ± 0.60	60.41 ± 0.43
BML [40]	52.42 ± 0.71	66.72 ± 0.61	51.31 ± 0.66	58.77 ± 0.57	41.91 ± 0.55	59.72 ± 0.45
EGS-Net [42]	56.65 ± 0.73	68.38 ± 0.60	51.62 ± 0.66	60.52 ± 0.56	44.07 ± 0.60	61.90 ± 0.46
CDNet (ours)	$\mathbf{56.99} \pm 0.73$	$\mathbf{68.98} \pm 0.60$	$\mathbf{55.16} \pm 0.67$	$\mathbf{63.03} \pm 0.59$	$\mathbf{46.07} \pm 0.59$	$\mathbf{63.03} \pm 0.45$

From Table 3, the episodic training-based methods suffer from the overfitting problem caused by highly overlapped sampled tasks under the limited base class setting in our task. The batch training-based methods perform better than the episodic training-based methods since the extracted global view information is not easily affected by overlapped sampled tasks.

Existing hybrid FSL methods combine the two training paradigms to facilitate the training. For example, Meta-Baseline [4] pre-trains the model by batch training and fine-tunes it by episodic training. OAT [2] proposes an organized auxiliary task co-training method, which organizes the batch training and episodic training in an orderly way to stabilize the training process. BML [40] aggregates the complementary information of the batch training branch and the episodic training branch for the meta-test tasks. However, they do not focus on the limited base class setting. Very recently, EGS-Net [42] uses a joint and alternate learning framework to alleviate the problem of limited base classes. Different from EGS-Net, we incorporate a novel partial regularization strategy into CDNet to take full advantage of the two training paradigms. Results show that our method outperforms the above methods for both the 1-shot and 5-shot few-shot classification tasks on all the compound expression datasets.

5   Conclusions

In this paper, we address compound FER in the cross-domain FSL setting, which alleviates the burden of collecting large-scale labeled compound FER data. Based on a proposed sequential decomposition mechanism, we develop a novel CDNet consisting of cascaded LD modules with shared parameters to learn a transferable feature space. In particular, a partial regularization strategy is designed to take full advantage of episodic training and batch training. In this way, we prevent the model from overfitting to highly-overlapped seen tasks due to limited base classes and enable the trained model to have the ability of learn-to-decompose. Experimental results show the effectiveness of our proposed method against several state-of-the-art FSL methods on various compound FER datasets.

Acknowledgement. This work was partly supported by the National Natural Science Foundation of China under Grants 62071404, U21A20514, and 61872307, by the Open Research Projects of Zhejiang Lab under Grant 2021KG0AB02, by the Natural Science Foundation of Fujian Province under Grant 2020J01001, and by the Youth Innovation Foundation of Xiamen City under Grant 3502Z20206046.

References

1. Afrasiyabi, A., Lalonde, J.-F., Gagné, C.: Associative alignment for few-shot image classification. In: Vedaldi, A., Bischof, H., Brox, T., Frahm, J.-M. (eds.) ECCV 2020. LNCS, vol. 12350, pp. 18–35. Springer, Cham (2020). https://doi.org/10.1007/978-3-030-58558-7_2
2. Chen, M., et al.: Diversity transfer network for few-shot learning. In: AAAI Conference on Artificial Intelligence, vol. 34, pp. 10559–10566 (2020)

3. Chen, W.Y., Liu, Y.C., Kira, Z., Wang, Y.C., Huang, J.B.: A closer look at few-shot classification. In: International Conference on Learning Representations (2019)
4. Chen, Y., Liu, Z., Xu, H., Darrell, T., Wang, X.: Meta-Baseline: exploring simple meta-learning for few-shot learning. In: IEEE/CVF International Conference on Computer Vision, pp. 9062–9071 (2021)
5. Ciubotaru, A.N., Devos, A., Bozorgtabar, B., Thiran, J.P., Gabrani, M.: Revisiting few-shot learning for facial expression recognition. arXiv preprint arXiv:1912.02751 (2019)
6. Dhall, A., Goecke, R., Lucey, S., Gedeon, T.: Static facial expression analysis in tough conditions: data, evaluation protocol and benchmark. In: IEEE International Conference on Computer Vision Workshops, pp. 2106–2112 (2011)
7. Du, S., Tao, Y., Martinez, A.M.: Compound facial expressions of emotion. Proc. Natl. Acad. Sci. **111**(15), E1454–E1462 (2014)
8. Ekman, P., Friesen, W.V.: Constants across cultures in the face and emotion. J. Pers. Soc. Psychol. **17**(2), 124–129 (1971)
9. Fabian Benitez-Quiroz, C., Srinivasan, R., Martinez, A.M.: EmotioNet: an accurate, real-time algorithm for the automatic annotation of a million facial expressions in the wild. In: IEEE/CVF Conference on Computer Vision and Pattern Recognition, pp. 5562–5570 (2016)
10. Finn, C., Abbeel, P., Levine, S.: Model-agnostic meta-learning for fast adaptation of deep networks. In: International Conference on Machine Learning, pp. 1126–1135 (2017)
11. Garcia, V., Bruna, J.: Few-shot learning with graph neural networks. In: International Conference on Learning Representations (2018)
12. Gidaris, S., Komodakis, N.: Dynamic few-shot visual learning without forgetting. In: IEEE/CVF Conference on Computer Vision and Pattern Recognition, pp. 4367–4375 (2018)
13. Guo, J., et al.: Multi-modality network with visual and geometrical information for micro emotion recognition. In: IEEE International Conference on Automatic Face and Gesture Recognition, pp. 814–819 (2017)
14. Guo, Y., Zhang, L., Hu, Y., He, X., Gao, J.: MS-Celeb-1M: a dataset and benchmark for large-scale face recognition. In: Leibe, B., Matas, J., Sebe, N., Welling, M. (eds.) ECCV 2016. LNCS, vol. 9907, pp. 87–102. Springer, Cham (2016). https://doi.org/10.1007/978-3-319-46487-9_6
15. Lee, Y., Choi, S.: Gradient-based meta-learning with learned layerwise metric and subspace. In: International Conference on Machine Learning, pp. 2927–2936 (2018)
16. Li, S., Deng, W.: Deep facial expression recognition: a survey. IEEE Trans. Affect. Comput. (2020)
17. Li, S., Deng, W., Du, J.: Reliable crowdsourcing and deep locality-preserving learning for expression recognition in the wild. In: IEEE/CVF Conference on Computer Vision and Pattern Recognition, pp. 2852–2861 (2017)
18. Li, Y., Lu, Y., Li, J., Lu, G.: Separate loss for basic and compound facial expression recognition in the wild. In: Asian Conference on Machine Learning, pp. 897–911 (2019)
19. Liu, C., et al.: Learning a few-shot embedding model with contrastive learning. In: AAAI Conference on Artificial Intelligence, vol. 35, pp. 8635–8643 (2021)
20. Lu, J., Gong, P., Ye, J., Zhang, C.: Learning from very few samples: a survey. arXiv preprint arXiv:2009.02653 (2020)

21. Lucey, P., Cohn, J.F., Kanade, T., Saragih, J., Ambadar, Z., Matthews, I.: The extended Cohn-Kanade dataset (CK+): a complete dataset for action unit and emotion-specified expression. In: IEEE Computer Society Conference on Computer Vision and Pattern Recognition Workshops, pp. 94–101 (2010)

22. Pantic, M., Valstar, M., Rademaker, R., Maat, L.: Web-based database for facial expression analysis. In: IEEE International Conference on Multimedia and Expo, pp. 317–321 (2005)

23. Phoo, C.P., Hariharan, B.: Self-training for few-shot transfer across extreme task differences. In: International Conference on Learning Representations (2021)

24. Ruan, D., Yan, Y., Chen, S., Xue, J.H., Wang, H.: Deep disturbance-disentangled learning for facial expression recognition. In: ACM International Conference on Multimedia, pp. 2833–2841 (2020)

25. Ruan, D., Yan, Y., Lai, S., Chai, Z., Shen, C., Wang, H.: Feature decomposition and reconstruction learning for effective facial expression recognition. In: IEEE/CVF Conference on Computer Vision and Pattern Recognition, pp. 7660–7669 (2021)

26. Simon, C., Koniusz, P., Nock, R., Harandi, M.: Adaptive subspaces for few-shot learning. In: IEEE/CVF Conference on Computer Vision and Pattern Recognition, pp. 4136–4145 (2020)

27. Slimani, K., Lekdioui, K., Messoussi, R., Touahni, R.: Compound facial expression recognition based on highway CNN. In: New Challenges in Data Sciences: Acts of the Second Conference of the Moroccan Classification Society, pp. 1–7 (2019)

28. Snell, J., Swersky, K., Zemel, R.S.: Prototypical networks for few-shot learning. In: Advances in Neural Information Processing Systems, pp. 4077–4087 (2017)

29. Sung, F., Yang, Y., Zhang, L., Xiang, T., Torr, P.H., Hospedales, T.M.: Learning to compare: relation network for few-shot learning. In: IEEE/CVF Conference on Computer Vision and Pattern Recognition, pp. 1199–1208 (2018)

30. Tian, Y., Wang, Y., Krishnan, D., Tenenbaum, J.B., Isola, P.: Rethinking few-shot image classification: a good embedding is all you need? In: Vedaldi, A., Bischof, H., Brox, T., Frahm, J.-M. (eds.) ECCV 2020. LNCS, vol. 12359, pp. 266–282. Springer, Cham (2020). https://doi.org/10.1007/978-3-030-58568-6_16

31. Vinyals, O., Blundell, C., Lillicrap, T., Kavukcuoglu, K., Wierstra, D.: Matching networks for one shot learning. In: Advances in Neural Information Processing Systems, pp. 3630–3638 (2016)

32. Wah, C., Branson, S., Welinder, P., Perona, P., Belongie, S.: The Caltech-UCSD Birds-200-2011 dataset (2011)

33. Wang, C., Wang, S., Liang, G.: Identity- and pose-robust facial expression recognition through adversarial feature learning. In: ACM International Conference on Multimedia, pp. 238–246 (2019)

34. Wang, K., Peng, X., Yang, J., Lu, S., Qiao, Y.: Suppressing uncertainties for large-scale facial expression recognition. In: IEEE/CVF Conference on Computer Vision and Pattern Recognition, pp. 6897–6906 (2020)

35. Yang, S., Liu, L., Xu, M.: Free lunch for few-shot learning: distribution calibration. In: International Conference on Learning Representations (2021)

36. Zeng, J., Shan, S., Chen, X.: Facial expression recognition with inconsistently annotated datasets. In: European Conference on Computer Vision, pp. 222–237 (2018)

37. Zhang, Z., Yi, M., Xu, J., Zhang, R., Shen, J.: Two-stage recognition and beyond for compound facial emotion recognition. In: IEEE International Conference on Automatic Face and Gesture Recognition, pp. 900–904 (2020)

38. Zhao, F., Zhao, J., Yan, S., Feng, J.: Dynamic conditional networks for few-shot learning. In: European Conference on Computer Vision, pp. 19–35 (2018)

39. Zhao, G., Huang, X., Taini, M., Li, S.Z., Pietikälnen, M.: Facial expression recognition from near-infrared videos. Image Vis. Comput. **29**(9), 607–619 (2011)
40. Zhou, Z., Qiu, X., Xie, J., Wu, J., Zhang, C.: Binocular mutual learning for improving few-shot classification. In: IEEE/CVF International Conference on Computer Vision, pp. 8402–8411 (2021)
41. Zhu, Q., Mao, Q., Jia, H., Noi, O.E.N., Tu, J.: Convolutional relation network for facial expression recognition in the wild with few-shot learning. Expert Syst. Appl. **189**, 116046 (2022)
42. Zou, X., Yan, Y., Xue, J.H., Chen, S., Wang, H.: When facial expression recognition meets few-shot learning: a joint and alternate learning framework. In: AAAI Conference on Artificial Intelligence (2022)

Self-support Few-Shot Semantic Segmentation

Qi Fan[1], Wenjie Pei[2(✉)], Yu-Wing Tai[1,3], and Chi-Keung Tang[1]

[1] HKUST, Clear Water Bay, Hong Kong
`cktang@cs.ust.hk`
[2] Harbin Institute of Technology, Shenzhen, China
`wenjiecoder@outlook.com`
[3] Kuaishou Technology, Beijing, China

Abstract. Existing few-shot segmentation methods have achieved great progress based on the support-query matching framework. But they still heavily suffer from the limited coverage of intra-class variations from the few-shot supports provided. Motivated by the simple Gestalt principle that pixels belonging to the same object are more similar than those to different objects of same class, we propose a novel self-support matching strategy to alleviate this problem, which uses query prototypes to match query features, where the query prototypes are collected from high-confidence query predictions. This strategy can effectively capture the consistent underlying characteristics of the query objects, and thus fittingly match query features. We also propose an adaptive self-support background prototype generation module and self-support loss to further facilitate the self-support matching procedure. Our self-support network substantially improves the prototype quality, benefits more improvement from stronger backbones and more supports, and achieves SOTA on multiple datasets. Codes are at https://github.com/fanq15/SSP.

Keywords: Few-shot semantic segmentation · Self-support prototype (SSP) · Self-support matching · Adaptive background prototype generation

1 Introduction

Semantic segmentation has achieved remarkable advances tapping into deep learning networks [28,33,41] and large-scale datasets such as [4,14,90]. However, current high-performing semantic segmentation methods rely heavily on laborious pixel-level annotations, which has expedited the recent development of few-shot semantic segmentation (FSS).

This research was supported by Kuaishou Technology, the Research Grant Council of the HKSAR (16201420), and NSFC fund (U2013210, 62006060).

Supplementary Information The online version contains supplementary material available at https://doi.org/10.1007/978-3-031-19800-7_41.

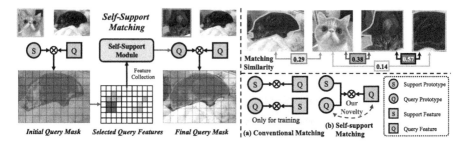

Fig. 1. The *left* image illustrates the core idea of our self-support matching. We use the initial query mask prediction to collect query features in high-confidence regions and then use the generated **query prototype** to perform **self-matching** with **query features**. The *right top* image illustrates the motivation of our self-support matching: pixels/regions of the same objects are more similar than those from different objects. The numbers in boxes represent the cosine similarities between two objects. The *right bottom* image illustrates that our self-support matching is fundamentally distinct from conventional matching methods

Few-shot semantic segmentation aims to segment arbitrary novel classes using only a few support samples. The dilemma is that the support images are limited and fixed (usually $\{1, 3, 5, 10\}$ supports per class), while the query images can be massive and arbitrary. Limited few-shot supports can easily fail to cover underlying appearance variations of the target class in query images, regardless of the support quality. This is clearly caused by the inherent data scarcity and diversity, two long standing issues in few-shot learning.

Existing methods try to solve the problem by making full use of the limited supports, such as proposing better matching mechanism [31,53,67,71,80, 84,93] or generating representative prototypes [26,37,44,55,60,62,68,78,79,85]. Despite their success, they still cannot fundamentally solve the appearance discrepancy problem, bounded by the scarce few-shot supports.

We propose a novel self-support matching strategy to narrow the matching appearance discrepancy. This strategy uses query prototypes to match query features, or in other words, use the query feature to self-support itself. We thus call the query prototype as *self-support prototype* because of its self-matching property. This new idea is motivated by the classical Gestalt law [40] that pixels belonging to the same object are more similar than those to different objects.

Refer to Fig. 1 for a high-level understanding of our novel self-support matching. First we generate the initial mask predictions by directly matching the support prototype and query features. Based on the initial query mask, we collect confident query features to generate the self-support prototype, which is used to perform matching with query features. Our *self-support module (SSM)* collects confident features of the cat head which are used to segment the entire black cat. Our model is optimized on base classes to retrieve other object parts supported by object fragments, *i.e.*, self-support prototype.

We apply our self-support module on both foreground and background prototypes for self-support matching. While SSM directly benefits foreground prototypes, note that the background is usually cluttered, which does not have the global semantic commonality shared among all background pixels. Thus, rather than generating a global background prototype by aggregating all the background pixels, we propose to adaptively generate self-support background prototypes for each query pixel, by dynamically aggregating similar background pixels in the query image. The *adaptive self-support background prototype (ASBP)* is motivated by the fact that separate background regions have local semantic similarity. Finally, we propose a *self-support loss (SSL)* to further facilitate the self-support procedure.

Our self-support matching strategy is thus fundamentally different than conventional support-query matching. We use the flexible self-support prototypes to match query features, which can effectively capture the consistent underlying characteristics of the query objects, and thus fittingly match query features. As shown in Fig. 1, the cats in the query and support images are very different in color, parts and scales, The garfield cat support has large appearance discrepancy to the black cat query, and undoubtedly conventional support-query matching produces inferior segmentation. In our self-support matching, our self-support prototype (the black cat head) is more consistent to the query (the entire black cat), and thus our method produces satisfactory results.

We are the first to perform self-support matching between query prototype and query features. As shown in Fig. 1, our self-support matching fundamentally differs from conventional matching. Other methods learn better support prototypes for support-query matching from extra unlabeled images (PPNet [55] and MLC [79]) or builds various support prototype generation modules [44,68,78] or feature priors (PFENet [70]) based on support images. Although PANet [72] and CRNet [54] also explore query prototypes, they use *query prototypes* to match *support features* as a query-support matching only for auxiliary training, and cannot solve the appearance discrepancy.

Our self-support method significantly improves the prototype quality by alleviating the intra-class appearance discrepancy problem, evidenced by the performance boost on multiple datasets in our experimental validation. Despite the simple idea, our self-support method is very effective and has various advantages, such as benefiting more from stronger backbone and more supports, producing high-confidence predictions, more robustness to weak support labels, higher generalization to other methods and higher running efficiency. We will substantiate these advantages with thorough experiments. In summary, our contributions are:

- We propose novel self-support matching and build a novel self-support network to solve the appearance discrepancy problem in FSS.
- We propose self-support prototype, adaptive self-support background prototype and self-support loss to facilitate our self-support method.
- Our self-support method benefits more improvement from stronger backbones and more supports, and outperforms previous SOTAs on multiple datasets with many desirable advantages.

2   Related Works

Semantic Segmentation. Semantic segmentation is a fundamental computer vision task to produce pixel-wise dense semantic predictions. The state-of-the-art has recently been greatly advanced by the end-to-end fully convolutional network (FCN) [56]. Subsequent works have since followed this FCN paradigm and contributed many effective modules to further promote the performance, such as encoder-decoder architectures [3,10,12,64], image and feature pyramid modules [9,38,48,49,88], context aggregation modules [24,25,32,35,82,86,89,92] and advance convolution layers [8,13,61,81]. Nevertheless, the above segmentation methods rely heavily on abundant pixel-level annotations. This paper aims to tackle the semantic segmentation problem in the few-shot scenario.

Few-Shot Learning. Few-shot learning targets at recognizing new concepts from very few samples. This low cost property has attracted a lot of research interests over the last years. There are three main approaches. The first is the transfer-learning approach [11,15,27,63] by adapting the prior knowledge learned from base classes to novel classes in a two-stage finetuning procedure. The second is the optimized-based approach [2,5,23,29,30,42,43,65], which rapidly updates models through meta-learning the optimization procedures from a few samples. The last is the metric-based approach [1,16,34,39,45,46], which applies a siamese network [39] on support-query pairs to learn a general metric for evaluating their relevance. Our work, including many few-shot works [21,22,36,77,87] on various high-level computer vision tasks, are inspired by the metric-based approach.

Few-Shot Semantic Segmentation. Few-shot semantic segmentation is pioneered by Shaban *et al.* [66]. Later works have mainly adopted the metric-based mainstream paradigm [17] with various improvements, *e.g.*, improving the matching procedure between support-query images with various attention mechanisms [53,67,80], better optimizations [52,91], memory modules [74,76], graph neural networks [71,75,84], learning-based classifiers [57,69], progressive matching [31,93], or other advanced techniques [47,51,59,83].

We are the first to perform self-support matching between query prototype and query features. Our self-support matching method is also related to the prototype generation methods. Some methods leverage extra unlabeled data [55,79] or feature priors [70] for further feature enhancement. Other methods generate representative support prototypes with various techniques, *e.g.*, attention mechanism [26,85], adaptive prototype learning [44,62,68], or various prototype generation approaches [60,78]. Although the query prototype has been explored in some methods [54,72], they only use query prototypes to match support features for prototype regularization. Finally, existing methods heavily suffer from the intra-class discrepancy problem in the support-query matching. On the other hand, we propose a novel self-support matching strategy to effectively address this matching problem.

3   Self-support Few-Shot Semantic Segmentation

Given only a few support images, few-shot semantic segmentation aims to segment objects of novel classes using the model generalized from base classes. Existing mainstream few-shot semantic segmentation solution can be formulated as follows: The input support and query images $\{I_s, I_q\}$ are processed by a

Table 1. Cosine similarity for cross/intra object pixels

FG pixels similarity		BG pixels similarity	
Cross-object	Intra-object	Cross-image	Intra-image
0.308	$0.416_{\uparrow 0.108}$	0.298	$0.365_{\uparrow 0.067}$

weight-shared backbone to extract image features $\{\mathcal{F}_s, \mathcal{F}_q\} \in \mathbb{R}^{C \times H \times W}$, where C is the channel size and $H \times W$ is the feature spatial size. Then the support feature $\mathcal{F}_s$ and its groundtruth mask $\mathcal{M}_s$ are fed into the masked average pooling layer to generate the support prototype vectors $\mathcal{P}_s = \{\mathcal{P}_{s,f}, \mathcal{P}_{s,b}\} \in \mathbb{R}^{C \times 1 \times 1}$ for foreground and background regions respectively. Finally, two distance maps $\mathcal{D} = \{\mathcal{D}_f, \mathcal{D}_b\}$ are generated by evaluating the cosine similarity between $\mathcal{P}_s$ and $\mathcal{F}_q$, which is then processed by a softmax operation as the final prediction $\mathcal{M}_1 = \text{softmax}(\mathcal{D})$.

3.1 Motivation

Current FSS methods rely heavily on the support prototype to segment query objects, by densely matching each query pixel with the support prototype. However, such cross-object matching severely suffers from intra-class appearance discrepancy, where objects in support and query can look very different even belonging to the same class. Such high intra-class variation cannot be reconciled by only a few supports, thus leading to poor matching results due to the large appearance gap between the query and supports.

To validate the relevance of Gestalt law [40] in narrowing such appearance discrepancy, we statistically analyze the feature cosine similarity of cross-object and intra-object pixels of Pascal VOC [18], where the pixel features are extracted from the ImageNet [14]-pretrianed ResNet-50 [33]. Table 1 shows that pixels belonging to the same object are much more similar than the cross-object pixels. Notably, background pixels share similar characteristics on their own, where intra-image background pixels are much more similar than cross-image pixels.

Thus, we propose to leverage the query feature to generate self-support prototypes to match the query feature itself. Notably, such prototype aligns the query along the homologous query features and thus can significantly narrow the feature gap between the support and query. In hindsight, the crucial reason the self-support matching works better than traditional support-query matching is that for a given visual object class, the intra-object similarities are much higher than the cross-object similarities.

3.2 Self-support Prototype

Our core idea (Fig. 2) is to aggregate query features to generate the query prototype and use it to self-support the query feature itself.

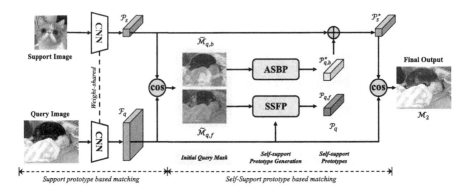

Fig. 2. Overall self-support network architecture. We first generate the initial mask predictions using the traditional support prototype based matching network. Then we leverage the initial query mask to aggregate query features to generate self-support prototypes, *i.e.*, the self-support foreground prototype (SSFP) and adaptive self-support background prototype (ASBP). Finally, we combine the support prototype and self-support prototypes to perform matching with query features

To recap, the regular support prototype generation procedure is:

$$\mathcal{P}_s = MAP(\mathcal{M}_s, \mathcal{F}_s), \tag{1}$$

where MAP is the masked average pooling operation, which is used to generate the matching prediction with query feature $\mathcal{F}_q$:

$$\mathcal{M}_1 = \mathrm{softmax}(\mathrm{cosine}(\mathcal{P}_s, \mathcal{F}_q)), \tag{2}$$

where cosine is the cosine similarity metric.

Now, we can generate the query prototype $\mathcal{P}_q$ in the same manner, except the groundtruth masks of query images $\mathcal{M}_q$ are unavailable during inference. Thus, we need to use a predicted query mask $\widetilde{\mathcal{M}}_q$ to aggregate query features. The query prototype generation procedure can be formulated as:

$$\mathcal{P}_q = MAP(\widetilde{\mathcal{M}}_q, \mathcal{F}_q), \tag{3}$$

where $\widetilde{\mathcal{M}}_q = \mathbb{1}(\mathcal{M}_1 > \tau)$, and $\mathcal{M}_1$ is the estimated query mask generated by Eq. 2, $\mathbb{1}$ is the indicator function. The mask threshold τ is used to control the query feature sampling scope which is set as $\{\tau_{fg} = 0.7, \tau_{bg} = 0.6\}$ for foreground and background query masks respectively. The estimated self-support prototype $\mathcal{P}_q = \{\mathcal{P}_{q,f}, \mathcal{P}_{q,b}\}$ will be utilized to match query features.

We understand the reader's natural concern about the quality of self-support prototype, which is generated based on the estimated query mask, *i.e.*, whether the estimated mask is capable of effective self-support prototype generation. We found that even the estimated query mask is not perfect, as long as it covers some representative object fragments, it is sufficient to retrieve other regions of

Table 2. The 1-shot matching results (mIoU) of support/self-support prototypes aggregated from full/partial objects

Object ratio	Full	10%	1%	1%+noise
Support prototype	58.2	57.1	52.4	48.7
Self-support prototype	83.0	82.5	79.2	74.6

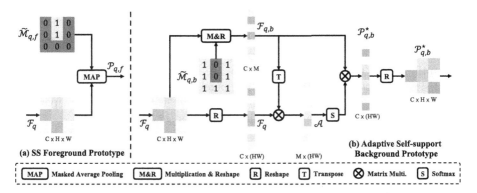

Fig. 3. Prototype generations of (a) self-support (SS) foreground prototype and (b) adaptive self-support background prototype

the same object. To validate partial object or object fragment is capable of supporting the entire object, we train and evaluate models with partial prototypes, which are aggregated from randomly selecting features based on the groundtruth mask labels. We conduct the 1-shot segmentation experiments on Pascal VOC dataset with the ResNet-50 backbone. As shown in Table 2, while reducing the aggregated object regions for prototype generation, our self-support prototype consistently achieves high segmentation performance. By contrast, the traditional support prototype consistently obtains much inferior performance, even using perfect support features from the entire object.

We further introduce noisy features (with 20% noise ratio) into partial prototypes to mimic realistic self-support generation during inference, by randomly selecting image features from non-target regions and aggregating these features into the above partial prototypes. To our pleasant surprise, our self-support prototype still works much better than the traditional support prototype in such noisy situation. Note that each image may contain multiple objects, thus the good performance indicates that our self-support prototype can also handle well the multiple objects scenarios. These results confirm the practicability and advantages of our self-support prototypes in the realistic applications.

3.3 Adaptive Self-support Background Prototype

Foreground pixels share semantic commonalities [19,20], which constitutes the rationale behind our self-support prototype generation and matching procedure

708   Q. Fan et al.

between query feature and support prototypes for foreground objects. Therefore, we can utilize a masked average pooling to generate the self-support foreground prototype (Fig. 3(a)):

$$\mathcal{P}_{q,f} = MAP(\widetilde{\mathcal{M}}_{q,f}, \mathcal{F}_q), \tag{4}$$

where $\widetilde{\mathcal{M}}_{q,f}$ is the aforementioned estimated query mask.

On the other hand, background can be cluttered, where commonalities can be reduced to local semantic similarities in disjoint regions, without a global semantic commonality shared among all background pixels. For example, for a query image with dog as the target class, other objects such as person and car are both treated as background, but they are different in both appearance and semantic levels. This observation is also validated by the smaller background pixel similarity compared to foreground pixels as shown in Table 1, especially in the intra-object/image situation. This motivates us to generate multiple self-support background prototypes for different query semantic regions.

A straightforward solution is to directly group multiple background prototypes using a clustering algorithm, and then choose the most similar prototype at each query pixel for background matching. This explicit background grouping heavily relies on the clustering algorithm, which is unstable and time-consuming. Therefore, we propose a more flexible and efficient method to adaptively generate self-support background prototypes for each query pixel (Fig. 3(b)).

The idea is to dynamically aggregate similar background pixels for each query pixel to generate adaptive self-support background prototypes. Specifically, we first gather the background query features $\mathcal{F}_{q,b} \in \mathbb{R}^{C \times M}$ through the masked multiplication on the query feature $\mathcal{F}_q$ with the background mask $\widetilde{\mathcal{M}}_{q,b}$, where M is the pixel number of the background region. Then we can generate the affinity matrix $\mathcal{A}$ between pixels of the reshaped background query feature $\mathcal{F}_{q,b}$ and full query feature $\mathcal{F}_q$ through a matrix multiplication operation $MatMul$:

$$\mathcal{A} = MatMul(\mathcal{F}_{q,b}^T, \mathcal{F}_q), \tag{5}$$

where $\mathcal{A}$ is in size of $\mathbb{R}^{M \times (H \times W)}$. The affinity matrix is normalized through a softmax operation along the first dimension, which is used to weighted aggregate background query features for each query pixel to generate the adaptive self-support background prototypes $\mathcal{P}_{q,b}^{\star} \in \mathbb{R}^{C \times H \times W}$:

$$\mathcal{P}_{q,b}^{\star} = MatMul(\mathcal{F}_{q,b}, \mathrm{softmax}(\mathcal{A})). \tag{6}$$

The self-support prototype is updated with the adaptive self-support background prototype: $\mathcal{P}_q = \{\mathcal{P}_{q,f}, \mathcal{P}_{q,b}^{\star}\}$.

3.4 Self-support Matching

We weighted combine the support prototype $\mathcal{P}_s$ and self-support prototype $\mathcal{P}_q$:

$$\mathcal{P}_s^{\star} = \alpha_1 \mathcal{P}_s + \alpha_2 \mathcal{P}_q, \tag{7}$$

where α_1 and α_2 are the tuning weights and we set $\alpha_1 = \alpha_2 = 0.5$ in our experiments. Then we compute the cosine distance between the augmented support prototype $\mathcal{P}_s^{\star}$ and query feature $\mathcal{F}_q$ to generate the final matching prediction:

$$\mathcal{M}_2 = \text{softmax}(\text{cosine}(\mathcal{P}_s^{\star}, \mathcal{F}_q)). \tag{8}$$

Then we apply the training supervision on the generated distance maps:

$$\mathcal{L}_m = BCE(\text{cosine}(\mathcal{P}_s^{\star}, \mathcal{F}_q), \mathcal{G}_q), \tag{9}$$

where BCE is the binary cross entropy loss and $\mathcal{G}_q$ is the groundtruth mask of the query image.

To further facilitate the self-support matching procedure, we propose a novel query self-support loss. For the query feature $\mathcal{F}_q$ and its prototype $\mathcal{P}_q$, we apply the following training supervision:

$$\mathcal{L}_q = BCE(\text{cosine}(\mathcal{P}_q, \mathcal{F}_q), \mathcal{G}_q). \tag{10}$$

We can apply the same procedure on the support feature to introduce the support self-matching loss $\mathcal{L}_s$.

Finally, we train the model in an end-to-end manner by jointly optimizing all the aforementioned losses:

$$\mathcal{L} = \lambda_1 \mathcal{L}_m + \lambda_2 \mathcal{L}_q + \lambda_3 \mathcal{L}_s, \tag{11}$$

where $\lambda_1 = 1.0, \lambda_2 = 1.0, \lambda_3 = 0.2$ are the loss weights.

4   Experiments

Datasets. We conduct experiments on two FSS benchmark datasets: PASCAL-5^i [18] and COCO-20^i [50]. We follow previous works [70,79] to split the data into four folds for cross validation, where three folds are used for training and the remaining one for evaluation. During inference, we randomly sample 1,000/4,000 support-query pairs to perform evaluation for PASCAL-5^i and COCO-20^i, respectively. We use the popular mean Intersection-over-Union (mIoU, $\uparrow^1$) as the default metric to evaluate our model under 1-shot and 5-shot settings. We also apply the Mean Absolute Error (MAE, $\downarrow$) to evaluate our prediction quality. By default, all analyses are conducted on PASCAL-5^i dataset with ResNet-50 backbone in the 5-shot setting.

Implementation Details. We adopt the popular ResNet-50/101 [33] pretrained on ImageNet [14] as the backbone. Following previous work MLC [79], we discard the last backbone stage and the last ReLU for better generalization. We use SGD to optimize our model with the 0.9 momentum and 1e-3 initial learning rate, which decays by 10 times every 2,000 iterations. The model is trained for 6,000 iterations where each training batch contains 4 support-query pairs. Both images and masks are resized and cropped into (473, 473) and augmented with random horizontal flipping. The evaluation is performed on the original image.

---

[1] The "$\uparrow$" ("$\downarrow$") means that the higher (lower) is better.

Table 3. Quantitative comparison results on PASCAL-5^i dataset. The **best** and second best results are highlighted with **bold** and underline, respectively

Method	Backbone	1-shot					5-shot					Params
		fold0	fold1	fold2	fold3	Mean	fold0	fold1	fold2	fold3	Mean	
PANet [72]	Res-50	44.0	57.5	50.8	44.0	49.1	55.3	67.2	61.3	53.2	59.3	23.5 M
PPNet [55]		48.6	60.6	55.7	46.5	52.8	58.9	68.3	66.8	58.0	63.0	31.5 M
PFENet [70]		61.7	69.5	55.4	56.3	60.8	63.1	70.7	55.8	57.9	61.9	34.3 M
CWT [57]		56.3	62.0	59.9	47.2	56.4	61.3	68.5	68.5	56.6	63.7	-
HSNet [59]		**64.3**	70.7	60.3	**60.5**	**64.0**	**70.3**	**73.2**	67.4	**67.1**	**69.5**	26.1 M
MLC [79]		59.2	**71.2**	65.6	52.5	62.1	63.5	71.6	71.2	58.1	66.1	**8.7 M**
SSP (Ours)		61.4	67.2	65.4	49.7	60.9	68.0	72.0	74.8	60.2	68.8	**8.7 M**
SSP$_{refine}$		60.5	67.8	**66.4**	51.0	61.4	67.5	72.3	**75.2**	62.1	69.3	**8.7 M**
FWB [60]	Res-101	51.3	64.5	56.7	52.2	56.2	54.8	67.4	62.2	55.3	59.9	43.0 M
PPNet [55]		52.7	62.8	57.4	47.7	55.2	60.3	70.0	69.4	60.7	65.1	50.5 M
PFENet [70]		60.5	69.4	54.4	55.9	60.1	62.8	70.4	54.9	57.6	61.4	53.4 M
CWT [57]		56.9	65.2	61.2	48.8	58.0	62.6	70.2	68.8	57.2	64.7	-
HSNet [59]		**67.3**	**72.3**	62.0	**63.1**	**66.2**	**71.8**	74.4	67.0	**68.3**	70.4	45.2 M
MLC [79]		60.8	71.3	61.5	56.9	62.6	65.8	74.9	71.4	63.1	68.8	**27.7 M**
SSP (Ours)		63.7	70.1	66.7	55.4	64.0	70.3	76.3	77.8	65.5	72.5	**27.7 M**
SSP$_{refine}$		63.2	70.4	**68.5**	56.3	64.6	70.5	**76.4**	**79.0**	66.4	**73.1**	**27.7 M**

4.1   Comparison with State-of-the-Arts

To validate the effectiveness of our method, we conduct extensive comparisons with SOTA methods under different backbone networks and few-shot settings.

PASCAL-5^i. We present the results of our self-support method and the improved version with one extra self-support refinement. As shown in Table 3, our method substantially outperforms MLC [79] by a large margin in the 5-shot setting, with the improvement jumping from 2.7% to 3.7% with the ResNet-50 backbone replaced by the stronger ResNet-101 network. In the 1-shot setting, our slightly inferior performance is remedied by using the stronger ResNet-101 backbone, where we surpass MLC [79] by 1.4% improvement. We can further promote the overall performance on PASCAL-5^i up to 73.1% with the self-support refinement, which is a simple and straightforward extension by repeating the self-support procedure. It surpasses the previous SOTA [59] by 2.7%. Note that our method is non-parametric and thus our model uses fewest parameters while achieving the best performance.

COCO-20^i. This is a very challenging dataset whose images usually contain multiple objects against a complex background. As shown in Table 4, our method obtains comparable or best results with the ResNet-50 backbone. When equipped with the stronger ResNet-101 backbone, our method significantly outperforms MLC [79] with 1.3/1.8% improvements in 1/5-shot settings. To fairly compare to HSNet [59], we adopt their evaluation protocol to evaluate our method. Our method achieves SOTA when using the ResNet-101 backbone. Our method also performs best on FSS-1000 [47], shown in the supplementary material.

Table 4. Quantitative comparison results on COCO-20^i dataset. * denotes the results are evaluated on the HSNet's evaluation protocol

Method	Backbone	1-shot					5-shot					Params
		fold0	fold1	fold2	fold3	Mean	fold0	fold1	fold2	fold3	Mean	
PANet [72]	Res-50	31.5	22.6	21.5	16.2	23.0	45.9	29.2	30.6	29.6	33.8	23.5 M
PPNet [55]		36.5	26.5	26.0	19.7	27.2	48.9	31.4	36.0	30.6	36.7	31.5 M
CWT [57]		32.2	36.0	31.6	31.6	32.9	40.1	43.8	39.0	42.4	41.3	-
MLC [79]		**46.8**	35.3	26.2	27.1	33.9	**54.1**	41.2	34.1	33.1	40.6	**8.7 M**
SSP (Ours)		46.4	35.2	27.3	25.4	33.6	53.8	41.5	36.0	33.7	41.3	**8.7 M**
HSNet* [59]		36.3	**43.1**	**38.7**	**38.7**	**39.2**	43.3	**51.3**	**48.2**	**45.0**	**46.9**	26.1 M
SSP* (Ours)		35.5	39.6	37.9	36.7	37.4	40.6	47.0	45.1	43.9	44.1	**8.7 M**
PMMs [78]	Res-101	29.5	36.8	28.9	27.0	30.6	33.8	42.0	33.0	33.3	35.5	38.6 M
CWT [57]		30.3	36.6	30.5	32.2	32.4	38.5	46.7	39.4	43.2	42.0	-
MLC [79]		50.2	37.8	27.1	30.4	36.4	57.0	46.2	37.3	37.2	44.4	**27.7 M**
SSP (Ours)		**50.4**	39.9	30.6	30.0	37.7	**57.8**	47.0	40.2	39.9	46.2	**27.7 M**
HSNet* [59]		37.2	44.1	42.4	**41.3**	41.2	45.9	53.0	**51.8**	47.1	49.5	45.2 M
SSP* (Ours)		39.1	**45.1**	**42.7**	41.2	**42.0**	47.4	**54.5**	50.4	**49.6**	**50.2**	**27.7 M**

Table 5. Self-support model ablation results. "SSM" denotes the self-support module (containing the self-support foreground/background prototypes), "SSL" denotes the self-support loss and "ASBP" denotes the adaptive self-support background prototype

SSM	SSL	ASBP	fold0	fold1	fold2	fold3	Mean
			62.2	70.5	70.7	55.7	64.8
✓			65.3	71.1	73.6	59.2	67.3$_{\uparrow 2.5}$
	✓		63.6	71.0	71.7	56.3	65.7$_{\uparrow 0.9}$
✓	✓		67.0	**72.4**	72.9	59.9	68.1$_{\uparrow 3.3}$
✓		✓	67.0	71.4	74.7	59.8	68.2$_{\uparrow 3.4}$
✓	✓	✓	**68.0**	72.0	**74.8**	**60.2**	**68.8**$_{\uparrow 4.0}$

Note that our method benefits more improvement from stronger backbones and more supports because they provide better self-support prototypes, which will be validated later in Table 8.

4.2 Ablation Studies

As shown in Table 5, our self-support module significantly improves the performance by 2.5%. The self-support loss further facilitates the self-support procedure and promotes the performance to 68.1%. The baseline model also benefits from the extra supervision of self-support loss. After equipped with the adaptive self-support background prototype, the self-support module can obtain extra 0.9% gain. Integrating all modules, our self-support method significantly improves the performance from 64.8% to 68.8% based on the strong baseline.

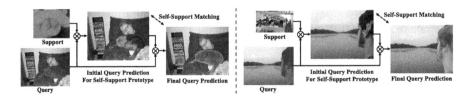

Fig. 4. Visualization for the working mechanism of our self-support matching. We omit the original support in self-support matching and the first row caption for clarity

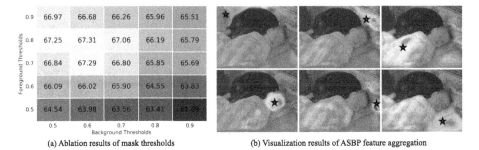

(a) Ablation results of mask thresholds   (b) Visualization results of ASBP feature aggregation

Fig. 5. (a) Results of mask threshold variations for self-support prototypes. (b) Visualization of the feature aggregation for adaptive self-support background prototypes (ASBP) at each star-marked position. They are aggregated from the activated background regions

4.3   Self-support Analysis

We conduct extensive experiments and analysis to understand our method.

Self-support Working Mechanism. As shown in Fig. 4, we first generate the *Initial* query predictions using the support prototype (as in Eq. 2), and leverage the confident predictions to extract query features to generate self-support prototype (as in Eq. 3). Then we use the self-support prototype to match with query features (as in Eq. 8) and produce the final output. Note that because of the large inter-object/inter-background variation, the *Init* predictions usually only capture some small representative regions, *e.g.*, the cat/dog heads. Notwithstanding, our self-support method can handle well these hard cases by bridging the gap between query and support prototypes.

Mask Threshold. The threshold τ controls the query feature selection for self-support prototype generation (as in Eq. 3). While we need to select high-confidence features for the foreground prototype, the background prototype requires more query features with a relative low threshold. This is because foreground pixels exhibit strong similarities with relatively low noise tolerance, while background is cluttered and the aggregated diverse features should tolerate more noises. Figure 5(a) summarizes the model performance on Pascal dataset with different thresholds, where a good balance between foreground and background thresholds are respectively $\tau_{fg} \in [0.7, 0.9]$ and $\tau_{bg} \in [0.5, 0.7]$.

Table 6. Ablation results of self-support module (SSM) by respectively removing foreground support prototype (FP), background support prototype (BP), self-support foreground prototype (SFP) and self-support background prototype (SBP)

SSM	w/o FP	w/o BP	w/o SFP	w/o SBP
67.3	$66.0_{\downarrow 1.3}$	$67.2_{\downarrow 0.1}$	$66.5_{\downarrow 0.8}$	$65.6_{\downarrow 1.7}$

Table 7. Comparison with self-attention modules. "$\dagger$" means the improved version by removing the transformation layer

Baseline	NL [73]	NL† [73]	GCNet [7]	Our SSM
64.8	$62.1_{\downarrow 2.7}$	$64.3_{\downarrow 0.5}$	$63.9_{\downarrow 0.9}$	$\mathbf{67.3_{\uparrow 2.5}}$

Prototype Ablation. We investigate the effect of each of the prototypes by respectively removing them from the overall prototype. Table 6 summarizes the results. Both our self-support foreground and background prototypes play a critical role to account for good matching performance. The support foreground prototype is also essential for the prototype quality thanks to its foreground semantic information aggregated from multiple support images. The support background prototype can be discarded with slight impact because of the large background variation between query and support.

Distinction from Self-attention. Readers may compare our self-support method with self-attention mechanisms. Our self-support method shares some concepts but is different from self-attention. Self-attention augments the image feature at each position by weighted aggregation of the features from all positions according to the affinity matrix. In contrast, our self-support method leverages representative query features to generate prototypes according to the query-support matching results. In Table 7 we experiment with multiple self-attention modules on the baseline. Unfortunately, all of them impose various degrees of harm on the matching performance, which are resulted by their self-attention augmentation which can destroy feature similarity between query and supports.

Adaptive self-support Background Prototype. This is designed to address the background clutter problem by adaptively aggregating background prototypes for each position. As shown in Fig. 5(b), the target cat is lying on a cluttered background consisting of the wardrobe, bed, quilt, baby, pillow and sheet. For each star-marked query position, the self-support background prototypes are aggregated from the corresponding semantic regions. Note that this adaptive background prototype generation is specifically designed for self-support prototypes, which cannot be directly applied to support prototype generation because it will collapse to trivial solutions by greedily aggregating similar pixels without semantic consideration.

Table 8. Comparison with other methods on performance improvement across different backbones and support shots

	PFENet [70]	ReRPI [6]	CWT [57]	MLC [79]	Ours
R50 → R101	−0.5	−1.2	+1.0	+2.7	**+3.7**
1shot → 5shot	+1.3	+6.2	+6.7	+6.2	**+8.5**

4.4   Self-support Advantages

Our self-support method has many desirable properties.

Benefits from Backbones and Supports. As shown before, our self-support method benefits more improvement from stronger backbones and more supports. Table 8 summarizes the improvement of different methods. When switching the backbone from ResNet-50 to ResNet-101, our method obtains 3.7% performance improvement, while other methods obtain at most 2.7% improvement or even performance degradation. Our method also obtains the largest improvement of 8.5% by increasing support images from 1-shot to 5-shot. The behind reason is that our self-support method benefits from the Matthew effect [58] of accumulated advantages, where better predictions induce better self-support prototypes and produce better predictions.

High-Confident Predictions. Our self-support method not only improves hard segmentation results with 0–1 labels, but also improves the soft confidence scores to produce high-confident predictions. As shown in Table 9, our self-support method significantly reduces the Mean Absolute Error (MAE) by 4.9% compared to the baseline. We further evaluate the MAE in the truth positive (TP) regions for a fair comparison, where the MAE can still be largely reduced by 5.0%. These results demonstrate that our self-support method can significantly improve the output quality by producing high-confident predictions, a desirable property for many real-world applications.

Robust to Weak Support Labels. As shown in Table 10, when replacing the support mask with bounding box or scribble annotations for prototype generation, our self-support method still works very well with high robustness against support noises. This is because our method mainly relies on self-support prototypes and thus is less affected by from noisy support prototypes.

Generalized to Other Methods. Our self-support method is general and can be applied to other methods. As shown in Table 11, equipped with our self-support module, both the strong PANet [72] and PPNet [55] report further boost in their performance by a large improvement.

High Efficiency. Our self-support method is very efficient, which is a non-parametric method with few extra computation and ∼28 FPS running speed on a Tesla V100 GPU (with the ResNet-50 backbone in the 1-shot setting).

Table 9. Results of prediction quality in MAE ($\downarrow$) metric. "All/TP" means evaluating models on all/truth positive regions of the image

	Baseline	SSM	SSM+SSL	SSM+ASBP	Full
All	17.6	$14.6_{\downarrow 3.0}$	$14.8_{\downarrow 2.8}$	$12.9_{\downarrow 4.7}$	$\mathbf{12.7}_{\downarrow \mathbf{4.9}}$
TP	13.2	$9.6_{\downarrow 3.6}$	$10.1_{\downarrow 3.1}$	$\mathbf{7.8}_{\downarrow \mathbf{5.4}}$	$8.2_{\downarrow 5.0}$

Table 10. Results of using weak support annotations

	Mask	Scribble	Bounding box
Baseline	64.8	$63.3_{\downarrow 1.5}$	$61.7_{\downarrow 3.1}$
Ours	68.8	$68.0_{\downarrow 0.8}$	$66.9_{\downarrow 2.1}$

Table 11. Results of applying our method to other models

PANet [72]	PANet + Ours	PPNet [55]	PPNet + Ours
55.7	$58.3_{\uparrow 2.6}$	62.0	$64.2_{\uparrow 2.2}$

5 Conclusion

In this paper, we address the critical intra-class appearance discrepancy problem inherent in few-shot segmentation, by leveraging the query feature to generate self-support prototypes and perform self-support matching with query features. This strategy effectively narrows down the gap between support prototypes and query features. Further, we propose an adaptive self-support background prototype and a self-support loss to facilitate the self-support procedure. Our self-support network has various desirable properties, and achieves SOTA on multiple benchmarks. We have thoroughly investigated the self-support procedure with extensive experiments and analysis to substantiate its effectiveness and deepen our understanding on its working mechanism.

References

1. Allen, K., Shelhamer, E., Shin, H., Tenenbaum, J.: Infinite mixture prototypes for few-shot learning. In: ICML (2019)
2. Antoniou, A., Edwards, H., Storkey, A.: How to train your MAML. In: ICLR (2019)
3. Badrinarayanan, V., Kendall, A., Cipolla, R.: SegNet: a deep convolutional encoder-decoder architecture for image segmentation. IEEE TPAMI **39**, 2481–2495 (2017)
4. Benenson, R., Popov, S., Ferrari, V.: Large-scale interactive object segmentation with human annotators. In: CVPR (2019)
5. Bertinetto, L., Henriques, J.F., Torr, P.H., Vedaldi, A.: Meta-learning with differentiable closed-form solvers. In: ICLR (2019)

6. Boudiaf, M., Kervadec, H., Masud, Z.I., Piantanida, P., Ben Ayed, I., Dolz, J.: Few-shot segmentation without meta-learning: a good transductive inference is all you need? In: CVPR (2021)

7. Cao, Y., Xu, J., Lin, S., Wei, F., Hu, H.: GCNet: non-local networks meet squeeze-excitation networks and beyond. In: CVPRW (2019)

8. Chen, L.C., Papandreou, G., Kokkinos, I., Murphy, K., Yuille, A.L.: DeepLab: semantic image segmentation with deep convolutional nets, Atrous convolution, and fully connected CRFs. IEEE TPAMI **40**, 834–848 (2017)

9. Chen, L.C., Yang, Y., Wang, J., Xu, W., Yuille, A.L.: Attention to scale: scale-aware semantic image segmentation. In: CVPR (2016)

10. Chen, L.-C., Zhu, Y., Papandreou, G., Schroff, F., Adam, H.: Encoder-decoder with Atrous separable convolution for semantic image segmentation. In: Ferrari, V., Hebert, M., Sminchisescu, C., Weiss, Y. (eds.) ECCV 2018. LNCS, vol. 11211, pp. 833–851. Springer, Cham (2018). https://doi.org/10.1007/978-3-030-01234-2_49

11. Chen, W.Y., Liu, Y.C., Kira, Z., Wang, Y.C.F., Huang, J.B.: A closer look at few-shot classification. In: ICLR (2019)

12. Cheng, B., et al.: SPGNet: semantic prediction guidance for scene parsing. In: ICCV (2019)

13. Dai, J., et al.: Deformable convolutional networks. In: ICCV (2017)

14. Deng, J., Dong, W., Socher, R., Li, L.J., Li, K., Fei-Fei, L.: ImageNet: a large-scale hierarchical image database. In: CVPR (2009)

15. Dhillon, G.S., Chaudhari, P., Ravichandran, A., Soatto, S.: A baseline for few-shot image classification. In: ICLR (2019)

16. Doersch, C., Gupta, A., Zisserman, A.: CrossTransformers: spatially-aware few-shot transfer. In: NeurIPS (2020)

17. Dong, N., Xing, E.P.: Few-shot semantic segmentation with prototype learning. In: BMVC (2018)

18. Everingham, M., Van Gool, L., Williams, C.K., Winn, J., Zisserman, A.: The Pascal visual object classes (VOC) challenge. IJCV **83**, 303–338 (2010). https://doi.org/10.1007/s11263-009-0275-4

19. Fan, Q., et al.: Group collaborative learning for co-salient object detection. In: CVPR (2021)

20. Fan, Q., Ke, L., Pei, W., Tang, C.-K., Tai, Y.-W.: Commonality-parsing network across shape and appearance for partially supervised instance segmentation. In: Vedaldi, A., Bischof, H., Brox, T., Frahm, J.-M. (eds.) ECCV 2020. LNCS, vol. 12353, pp. 379–396. Springer, Cham (2020). https://doi.org/10.1007/978-3-030-58598-3_23

21. Fan, Q., Tang, C.K., Tai, Y.W.: Few-shot video object detection. arXiv preprint arXiv:2104.14805 (2021)

22. Fan, Q., Zhuo, W., Tang, C.K., Tai, Y.W.: Few-shot object detection with attention-RPN and multi-relation detector. In: CVPR (2020)

23. Finn, C., Abbeel, P., Levine, S.: Model-agnostic meta-learning for fast adaptation of deep networks. In: ICML (2017)

24. Fu, J., et al.: Dual attention network for scene segmentation. In: CVPR (2019)

25. Fu, J., et al.: Adaptive context network for scene parsing. In: ICCV (2019)

26. Gairola, S., Hemani, M., Chopra, A., Krishnamurthy, B.: SimPropNet: improved similarity propagation for few-shot image segmentation. In: IJCAI (2020)

27. Gidaris, S., Komodakis, N.: Dynamic few-shot visual learning without forgetting. In: CVPR (2018)

28. Goodfellow, I., Bengio, Y., Courville, A.: Deep Learning. MIT Press, Cambridge (2016)

29. Gordon, J., Bronskill, J., Bauer, M., Nowozin, S., Turner, R.: Meta-learning probabilistic inference for prediction. In: ICLR (2019)
30. Grant, E., Finn, C., Levine, S., Darrell, T., Griffiths, T.: Recasting gradient-based meta-learning as hierarchical Bayes. In: ICLR (2018)
31. He, H., Zhang, J., Thuraisingham, B., Tao, D.: Progressive one-shot human parsing. In: AAAI (2021)
32. He, J., Deng, Z., Zhou, L., Wang, Y., Qiao, Y.: Adaptive pyramid context network for semantic segmentation. In: CVPR (2019)
33. He, K., Zhang, X., Ren, S., Sun, J.: Deep residual learning for image recognition. In: CVPR (2016)
34. Hou, R., Chang, H., Ma, B., Shan, S., Chen, X.: Cross attention network for few-shot classification. In: NeurIPS (2019)
35. Huang, Z., Wang, X., Huang, L., Huang, C., Wei, Y., Liu, W.: CCNET: criss-cross attention for semantic segmentation. In: ICCV (2019)
36. Kang, B., Liu, Z., Wang, X., Yu, F., Feng, J., Darrell, T.: Few-shot object detection via feature reweighting. In: ICCV (2019)
37. Kim, S., Chikontwe, P., Park, S.H.: Uncertainty-aware semi-supervised few shot segmentation. In: IJCAI (2021)
38. Kirillov, A., Girshick, R., He, K., Dollár, P.: Panoptic feature pyramid networks. In: CVPR (2019)
39. Koch, G., Zemel, R., Salakhutdinov, R.: Siamese neural networks for one-shot image recognition. In: ICMLW (2015)
40. Koffka, K.: Principles of Gestalt Psychology. Routledge, Milton Park (1935)
41. Krizhevsky, A., Sutskever, I., Hinton, G.E.: ImageNet classification with deep convolutional neural networks. In: NeurIPS (2012)
42. Lee, K., Maji, S., Ravichandran, A., Soatto, S.: Meta-learning with differentiable convex optimization. In: CVPR (2019)
43. Lee, Y., Choi, S.: Gradient-based meta-learning with learned layerwise metric and subspace. In: ICML (2018)
44. Li, G., Jampani, V., Sevilla-Lara, L., Sun, D., Kim, J..: Adaptive prototype learning and allocation for few-shot segmentation. In: CVPR (2021)
45. Li, H., Eigen, D., Dodge, S., Zeiler, M., Wang, X.: Finding task-relevant features for few-shot learning by category traversal. In: CVPR (2019)
46. Li, W., Wang, L., Xu, J., Huo, J., Gao, Y., Luo, J.: Revisiting local descriptor based image-to-class measure for few-shot learning. In: CVPR (2019)
47. Li, X., Wei, T., Chen, Y.P., Tai, Y.W., Tang, C.K.: FSS-1000: a 1000-class dataset for few-shot segmentation. In: CVPR (2020)
48. Lin, G., Milan, A., Shen, C., Reid, I.: RefineNet: multi-path refinement networks for high-resolution semantic segmentation. In: CVPR (2017)
49. Lin, G., Shen, C., Van Den Hengel, A., Reid, I.: Efficient piecewise training of deep structured models for semantic segmentation. In: CVPR (2016)
50. Lin, T.Y., et al.: Microsoft COCO: common objects in context. In: Fleet, D., Pajdla, T., Schiele, B., Tuytelaars, T. (eds.) ECCV 2014. LNCS, vol. 8693, pp. 740–755. Springer, Cham (2014). https://doi.org/10.1007/978-3-319-10602-1_48
51. Liu, B., Ding, Y., Jiao, J., Ji, X., Ye, Q.: Anti-aliasing semantic reconstruction for few-shot semantic segmentation. In: CVPR (2021)
52. Liu, C., et al.: Learning a few-shot embedding model with contrastive learning. In: AAAI (2021)
53. Liu, L., Cao, J., Liu, M., Guo, Y., Chen, Q., Tan, M.: Dynamic extension nets for few-shot semantic segmentation. In: ACM MM (2020)

54. Liu, W., Zhang, C., Lin, G., Liu, F.: CRNet: cross-reference networks for few-shot segmentation. In: CVPR (2020)
55. Liu, Y., Zhang, X., Zhang, S., He, X.: Part-aware prototype network for few-shot semantic segmentation. In: Vedaldi, A., Bischof, H., Brox, T., Frahm, J.-M. (eds.) ECCV 2020. LNCS, vol. 12354, pp. 142–158. Springer, Cham (2020). https://doi.org/10.1007/978-3-030-58545-7_9
56. Long, J., Shelhamer, E., Darrell, T.: Fully convolutional networks for semantic segmentation. In: CVPR (2015)
57. Lu, Z., He, S., Zhu, X., Zhang, L., Song, Y.Z., Xiang, T.: Simpler is better: few-shot semantic segmentation with classifier weight transformer. In: ICCV (2021)
58. Merton, R.K.: The Matthew effect in science: the reward and communication systems of science are considered. Science **159**, 56–63 (1968)
59. Min, J., Kang, D., Cho, M.: Hypercorrelation squeeze for few-shot segmentation. In: ICCV (2021)
60. Nguyen, K., Todorovic, S.: Feature weighting and boosting for few-shot segmentation. In: ICCV (2019)
61. Noh, H., Hong, S., Han, B.: Learning deconvolution network for semantic segmentation. In: ICCV (2015)
62. Ouyang, C., Biffi, C., Chen, C., Kart, T., Qiu, H., Rueckert, D.: Self-supervision with Superpixels: training few-shot medical image segmentation without annotation. In: Vedaldi, A., Bischof, H., Brox, T., Frahm, J.-M. (eds.) ECCV 2020. LNCS, vol. 12374, pp. 762–780. Springer, Cham (2020). https://doi.org/10.1007/978-3-030-58526-6_45
63. Qi, H., Brown, M., Lowe, D.G.: Low-shot learning with imprinted weights. In: CVPR (2018)
64. Ronneberger, O., Fischer, P., Brox, T.: U-Net: convolutional networks for biomedical image segmentation. In: Navab, N., Hornegger, J., Wells, W.M., Frangi, A.F. (eds.) MICCAI 2015. LNCS, vol. 9351, pp. 234–241. Springer, Cham (2015). https://doi.org/10.1007/978-3-319-24574-4_28
65. Rusu, A.A., et al.: Meta-learning with latent embedding optimization. In: ICLR (2019)
66. Shaban, A., Bansal, S., Liu, Z., Essa, I., Boots, B.: One-shot learning for semantic segmentation. In: BMVC (2017)
67. Siam, M., Doraiswamy, N., Oreshkin, B.N., Yao, H., Jagersand, M.: Weakly supervised few-shot object segmentation using co-attention with visual and semantic embeddings. In: IJCAI (2020)
68. Siam, M., Oreshkin, B.N., Jagersand, M.: AMP: adaptive masked proxies for few-shot segmentation. In: ICCV (2019)
69. Tian, P., Wu, Z., Qi, L., Wang, L., Shi, Y., Gao, Y.: Differentiable meta-learning model for few-shot semantic segmentation. In: AAAI (2020)
70. Tian, Z., Zhao, H., Shu, M., Yang, Z., Li, R., Jia, J.: Prior guided feature enrichment network for few-shot segmentation. IEEE TPAMI **44**, 1050–1065 (2020)
71. Wang, H., Zhang, X., Hu, Y., Yang, Y., Cao, X., Zhen, X.: Few-shot semantic segmentation with democratic attention networks. In: Vedaldi, A., Bischof, H., Brox, T., Frahm, J.-M. (eds.) ECCV 2020. LNCS, vol. 12358, pp. 730–746. Springer, Cham (2020). https://doi.org/10.1007/978-3-030-58601-0_43
72. Wang, K., Liew, J.H., Zou, Y., Zhou, D., Feng, J.: PANet: few-shot image semantic segmentation with prototype alignment. In: ICCV (2019)
73. Wang, X., Girshick, R., Gupta, A., He, K.: Non-local neural networks. In: CVPR (2018)

74. Wu, Z., Shi, X., Lin, G., Cai, J.: Learning meta-class memory for few-shot semantic segmentation. In: ICCV (2021)

75. Xie, G.S., Liu, J., Xiong, H., Shao, L.: Scale-aware graph neural network for few-shot semantic segmentation. In: CVPR (2021)

76. Xie, G.S., Xiong, H., Liu, J., Yao, Y., Shao, L.: Few-shot semantic segmentation with cyclic memory network. In: ICCV (2021)

77. Yan, X., Chen, Z., Xu, A., Wang, X., Liang, X., Lin, L.: Meta R-CNN: towards general solver for instance-level low-shot learning. In: ICCV (2019)

78. Yang, B., Liu, C., Li, B., Jiao, J., Ye, Q.: Prototype mixture models for few-shot semantic segmentation. In: Vedaldi, A., Bischof, H., Brox, T., Frahm, J.-M. (eds.) ECCV 2020. LNCS, vol. 12353, pp. 763–778. Springer, Cham (2020). https://doi.org/10.1007/978-3-030-58598-3_45

79. Yang, L., Zhuo, W., Qi, L., Shi, Y., Gao, Y.: Mining latent classes for few-shot segmentation. In: ICCV (2021)

80. Yang, X., et al.: BriNet: towards bridging the intra-class and inter-class gaps in one-shot segmentation. In: BMVC (2020)

81. Yu, F., Koltun, V., Funkhouser, T.: Dilated residual networks. In: CVPR (2017)

82. Yuan, Y., Chen, X., Wang, J.: Object-contextual representations for semantic segmentation. In: Vedaldi, A., Bischof, H., Brox, T., Frahm, J.-M. (eds.) ECCV 2020. LNCS, vol. 12351, pp. 173–190. Springer, Cham (2020). https://doi.org/10.1007/978-3-030-58539-6_11

83. Zhang, B., Xiao, J., Qin, T.: Self-guided and cross-guided learning for few-shot segmentation. In: CVPR (2021)

84. Zhang, C., Lin, G., Liu, F., Guo, J., Wu, Q., Yao, R.: Pyramid graph networks with connection attentions for region-based one-shot semantic segmentation. In: ICCV (2019)

85. Zhang, C., Lin, G., Liu, F., Yao, R., Shen, C.: CANet: class-agnostic segmentation networks with iterative refinement and attentive few-shot learning. In: CVPR (2019)

86. Zhang, F., et al.: ACFNet: attentional class feature network for semantic segmentation. In: ICCV (2019)

87. Zhang, H., Zhang, L., Qi, X., Li, H., Torr, P.H.S., Koniusz, P.: Few-shot action recognition with permutation-invariant attention. In: Vedaldi, A., Bischof, H., Brox, T., Frahm, J.-M. (eds.) ECCV 2020. LNCS, vol. 12350, pp. 525–542. Springer, Cham (2020). https://doi.org/10.1007/978-3-030-58558-7_31

88. Zhao, H., Shi, J., Qi, X., Wang, X., Jia, J.: Pyramid scene parsing network. In: CVPR (2017)

89. Zhao, H., et al.: PSANet: point-wise spatial attention network for scene parsing. In: Ferrari, V., Hebert, M., Sminchisescu, C., Weiss, Y. (eds.) ECCV 2018. LNCS, vol. 11213, pp. 270–286. Springer, Cham (2018). https://doi.org/10.1007/978-3-030-01240-3_17

90. Zhou, B., Zhao, H., Puig, X., Fidler, S., Barriuso, A., Torralba, A.: Scene parsing through ADE20K dataset. In: CVPR (2017)

91. Zhu, K., Zhai, W., Zha, Z.J., Cao, Y.: Self-supervised tuning for few-shot segmentation. In: IJCAI (2020)

92. Zhu, Z., Xu, M., Bai, S., Huang, T., Bai, X.: Asymmetric non-local neural networks for semantic segmentation. In: ICCV (2019)

93. Zhuge, Y., Shen, C.: Deep reasoning network for few-shot semantic segmentation. In: ACM MM (2021)

Few-Shot Object Detection with Model Calibration

Qi Fan[1], Chi-Keung Tang[1(✉)], and Yu-Wing Tai[1,2]

[1] The Hong Kong University of Science and Technology,
Clear Water Bay, Hong Kong
cktang@cs.ust.hk
[2] Kuaishou Technology, Beijing, China

Abstract. Few-shot object detection (FSOD) targets at transferring knowledge from known to unknown classes to detect objects of novel classes. However, previous works ignore the model bias problem inherent in the transfer learning paradigm. Such model bias causes overfitting toward the training classes and destructs the well-learned transferable knowledge. In this paper, we pinpoint and comprehensively investigate the model bias problem in FSOD models and propose a simple yet effective method to address the model bias problem with the facilitation of model calibrations in three levels: 1) Backbone calibration to preserve the well-learned prior knowledge and relieve the model bias toward base classes, 2) RPN calibration to rescue unlabeled objects of novel classes and, 3) Detector calibration to prevent the model bias toward a few training samples for novel classes. Specifically, we leverage the overlooked classification dataset to facilitate our model calibration procedure, which has only been used for pre-training in other related works. We validate the effectiveness of our model calibration method on the popular Pascal VOC and MS COCO datasets, where our method achieves very promising performance. Codes are released at https://github.com/fanq15/FewX.

Keywords: Few-shot object detection · Model bias · Model calibration · Uncertainty-aware RPN · Detector calibration

1 Introduction

Object detection [25,57,76] is a fundamental and well-studied research problem in computer vision, which is instrumental in many down-stream vision tasks and applications. Current deep learning based methods have achieved significant performance on object detection task by leveraging abundant well-annotated training samples. However, box-level annotation for object detection is very time and labor consuming, and it is impossible to annotate every class in the real world. Typical object detection models [58,62,74,75] degrade when labeled training

This research was supported in part by Kuaishou Technology, and the Research Grant Council of the Hong Kong SAR under grant No. 16201420.

Table 1. The bias source of each detection module and the performance improvement from our calibrated model on COCO [59]

Module	Biased model		Calibrated model
	Bias source	mAP	mAP
RPN	Base class	11.3	11.8 (*+0.5*)
Backbone	Base class		14.7 (*+3.4*)
Detector	Novel samples		11.9 (*+0.6*)
Overall	All above		15.1 (*+3.8*)

data are scarce, and fail to detect novel classes unseen in the training set. Few-shot object detection (FSOD) [8,21,40] targets at solving this problem. Given only a few support samples of novel classes, FSOD model can detect objects of the target novel classes in query images.

Few-shot object detection is an emerging task and has received considerable attention very recently. Some works [39,93,94] detect query objects by exploring the relationship between support and query images through a siamese network equipped with meta learning. Other works [90,92,107] adopt a fine-tuning strategy to transfer knowledge priors from base classes to novel classes which have very few annotated samples.

Despite their success, a critical intrinsic issue of few-shot object detection has long been neglected by these previous works: the model bias problem. The problem is caused by the extremely unbalanced training datasets between the base and novel classes. Specifically, to learn general and transferable knowledge, the model is first trained on base classes with numerous annotated samples, where the potential novel classes are labeled as background. Therefore, the model will bias toward only recognizing base classes and reject novel classes in RPN [76]. Second, the backbone feature will bias toward the base classes under the biased training supervision, where the feature distribution learned from the abundant classes from the pretraining dataset [12] will be destroyed with the backbone overfitting to the limited base classes. Third, when the detector is finetuned on novel classes, the very few training samples cannot represent the real class statistics. Therefore, the model will bias toward the limited training samples of novel classes, and thus cannot generalize well to the real data distribution, which can not solved by the class-imbalance learning methods [10,13,41,42,88].

The model bias problem has not been given adequate research attention in previous works. There are only few common practices to prevent model bias. A naive and common practice is to leverage a large-scale classification dataset with numerous classes, *e.g.*, ImageNet [12], to pretrain the model for better and general prior knowledge to alleviate the model bias toward base classes. Granted that the ImageNet pretraining provides better prior knowledge with the fully-supervised [32] or self-supervised learning [30,34,55], the pertinent model still biases to base classes because of the lack of explicit bias constraints. Fan *et al.* [21] proposes another solution to further alleviate this problem, by leveraging an object detection dataset with numerous training classes to prevent overfitting toward base classes. While this work has significantly improved the generalization performance on novel classes, and such improvement has validated the model bias problem in existing FSOD methods, this approach requires to establish a large-scale dataset for few-shot object detection, which is expensive and hard to generalize to other high-level few-shot tasks.

Previous works [21,90,92] either have limited performance or require extra annotated dataset. In this paper, we pinpoint and thoroughly investigate the model bias problems in each detection module and present a simple but effective method to calibrate the model from three levels to address the model bias problem: RPN calibration, detector calibration and backbone calibration. Table 1 presents the model bias problem and the bias source for different detection modules, and the performance improvement from our model calibration.

Specifically, *RPN calibration* is designed to calibrate the biased RPN by identifying potential objects of the novel classes and rectify their training labels. We propose Uncertainty-Aware RPN (UA-RPN) to evaluate the uncertainty of each proposal, and exploit such uncertainty to mine novel classes. The *detector calibration* is designed to leverage the feature statistics of both base and novel classes to generate proposal features for unbiased detector training. For the *backbone calibration*, we propose to leverage the overlooked classification dataset, *i.e.*, ImageNet dataset to address the model bias problem, which is freely available but is only used for pretraining in other FSOD works. The backbone is jointly trained on both detection and classification datasets with pseudo box annotations to bridge the domain gap. In summary, our paper has three contributions:

- We identify and thoroughly inspect the model bias problem of each detection module in existing few-shot object detection methods.
- We propose to address the model bias problem from three levels via backbone calibration, RPN calibration and detector calibration. We leverage the overlooked classification dataset to further facilitate our model calibration procedure.
- We verify the effectiveness of our method on two datasets and show that our method achieves very promising performance.

2 Related Works

Object Detection. One-stage detectors [58,61,62,74,75,101] directly predict classes and locations of anchors densely on the extracted backbone features in a single-shot manner. These methods [45,69,79,84,89,102,104,108] usually have fast inference at the expense of detection performance. But the recently proposed anchor-free algorithms [17,44,46,63,65,86,98,106] have significantly boosted the performance with competitive running speed at the same time. Two-stage detectors, which are pioneered and represented by R-CNN methods [25,57,76], first generate candidate proposals likely to contain objects, using traditional techniques [87] or a jointly optimized region proposal network (RPN) [76]. Then these proposals are refined for accurate locations and classified into different classes. These methods [3,5,6,11,31,33,54,68,73,80–82] usually have higher detection performance but are slower with its two-stage pipeline. Overall, even these methods perform excellently on multiple object detection datasets, they can only detect objects of training classes and cannot generalize to detecting novel classes.

Few-Shot Learning. Recent few-shot classification methods can be roughly classified into two approaches depending on the prior knowledge learning and adaptation methods. The first approaches few-shot classification as a meta-learning problem by metric-based or optimization-based methods. The metric-based approaches [1,15,35,43,51,52] leverage a siamese network [43] to learn feature embedding of both support and query images and evaluate their relevance using a general distance metric regardless of their categories. The optimized-based approaches [2,4,23,26,27,47,48,78] meta-learn the learning procedures to rapidly update models online with few examples. The second is the recently proposed transfer-learning approach [9,14,24,70] which consists of two separate training stages. These methods first pretrain model on base classes to obtain transferable backbone features at the first stage, and then finetune high-level layers to adapt to novel classes at the second stage. This simple transfer-learning procedure obtains strong performance as validated by multiple recent works [60,85,109]. Our work is inspired by the transfer learning approach, with the idea applied in the few-shot object detection task.

Few-Shot Object Detection. Until now, few-shot learning has achieved impressive progress on multiple important computer vision tasks [19,20,53,64], *e.g.*, semantic segmentation [16,37,67], human motion prediction [28] and object detection [8]. The FSOD methods can be classified into two approaches: meta-learning and transfer-learning methods. The meta-learning methods adopt a siamese network to detect novel classes in query images based on the similarity with given support images. Fan *et al.* [21] proposes attention-rpn and multi-relation detector for better similarity measurement. FR [39] proposes a meta feature learner and a reweighting module to quickly adapt to novel classes. Other methods improve the meta-learning based FSOD methods with different modules, *e.g.*, joint feature embedding [93], support-query mutual guidance [100], dense relation distillation [36] and others [50,93,94]. Transfer-learning methods first train a model on base classes followed by finetuning the model on novel classes to gain good generalization ability. TFA [90] introduces a cosine similarity classifier to detect novel classes. MSPR [92] proposes a multi-scale positive sample refinement module to enrich FSOD object scales. Techniques have been proposed to improve the transfer-learning FSOD methods, *e.g.*, semantic relation reasoning [107], hallucinator network [103], contrastive proposal encoding [83], and others [7,8,22,29,40,49,56,71,91,97]. Our work belongs to the transfer-learning approach. Notably, we identify the model bias problem in existing FSOD models, and propose corresponding model calibration modules to address the bias problems so as to make the trained model generalize better on novel classes. It is also promising to apply our method to the zero-shot task [99].

3   FSOD with Model Calibration

The few-shot object detection (FSOD) task is formally defined as following: given two disjoint classes, base class and novel class, where the base class dataset D_b contains massive training samples for each class, whereas the novel class dataset D_n has very few (usually no more than 10) annotated instances per class. The base class dataset D_b has been available for model training. The novel class dataset D_n has however been unavailable until now. FSOD targets at detecting all objects of the novel classes for any given input images by transferring knowledge learned from the base class dataset. The performance is measured by average precision (AP) [59] of the novel classes.

Table 2. Model bias problem

	Stage 1	Stage 2
Training data	Base classes	Novel classes
Data volume	Massive	Few
Biased module	Backbone & RPN	Detector
Bias toward	Base classes	Novel samples

Current methods usually take a two-stage training scheme: the base training stage (stage-1) is conducted on the base dataset D_b to extract transferable knowledge. The novel finetuning stage (stage-2) is conducted on the novel dataset D_n for generalization on novel classes. Because D_n contains very few training samples, the backbone weights are frozen, and only the detector and RPN are trained in the novel finetuning stage. This two-stage training scheme results in a model bias problem, as shown in Table 2. In this paper, we propose to calibrate the FSOD model to solve the model bias problem from three levels: backbone calibration, RPN calibration, and detector calibration, as shown in Fig. 1.

3.1   Backbone Calibration

For few-shot object detection task, a common practice is to pretrain the backbone on a large-scale *classification* dataset, *e.g.*, ImageNet [12], to obtain good feature initialization for faster training convergence, while simultaneously providing general prior data distribution for good generalization on novel classes. However, the separate, two-stage training of FSOD impedes the generalization gain for novel classes, which is only finetuned in the second training stage. The key reason is that the base classes with massive training samples significantly change the backbone feature distribution in the first training stage. The model is trained to fit the data distribution of the limited base classes (less than 100 classes) at the expense of losing the general distribution learned from massive classes (at least 1000 classes) in the pretraining stage. The backbone biases toward base classes, thus impeding the generalization on novel classes.

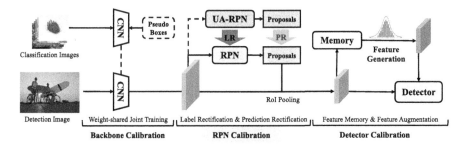

Fig. 1. Overall network architecture. The detection image is fed into the convolutional backbone which is jointly trained with classification images alongside with pseudo boxes. The feature of detection images is then processed by RPN and UA-RPN (uncertainty-aware RPN) to generate proposals. The UA-RPN provides the regular RPN with label rectification (LR) and prediction rectification (PR). The proposal features generated by RoI pooling are fed to the feature memory module to generate features for novel classes. The detector processes both the original and generated proposal features and outputs object detection predictions

Although the base class training stage can destroy the well-learned class distribution from pretraining, it does provide model location supervision by enabling novel *object detection*. In practice, the detection performance on novel classes will significantly degrade if we discard the base class training stage. This paradox motivates us to find a good solution to simultaneously preserve the well-learned class distribution while enabling location supervision. In this paper, we propose to achieve this by providing the backbone with an implicit feature constraint in the base training stage, so as to keep the well-learned data distribution covering massive classes, while enabling the object detection training under the location supervision from base classes.

A naive solution is to jointly train the backbone on both the large-scale classification dataset and object detection dataset to keep both of their data properties. But we find that the classification and detection tasks are not well compatible, where the classification task always dominates the training procedure while significantly degrading the object detection performance. Therefore, we propose to equip the classification images with *pseudo box* annotations to transform the classification dataset into object detection dataset.

The classification images have a desirable property: most images are dominated by the salient objects of the labeled target class. We make use this attribute to generate pseudo boxes for target objects. We utilize a pretrained salient object detection (SOD) model [72] to detect salient objects in classification images. Then we remove SOD mask outliers and only keep the largest contiguous region as the salient region, and generate corresponding pseudo box.

We jointly train the model with a weight-shared backbone on both the detection dataset and classification dataset equipped with pseudo boxes. Specifically, for the detection branch, we keep the training setting as other FSOD methods. For the backbone trained on the classification dataset, we use a smaller input

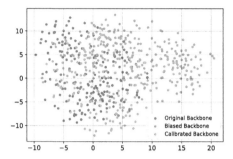

Fig. 2. The t-SNE visualization for feature distributions of original, biased and calibrated backbones

size to fit its original image size. In this way, the model can be trained to perform object detection task while simultaneously keeping the data distribution learned from massive classes of the classification dataset. Note that our backbone calibration is scalable to the number of classes in the classification dataset, where more classes will produce better data distribution and thus better detection performance.

Our backbone calibration method significantly alleviates the backbone bias toward limited detection classes. This is achieved through the distribution calibration from abundantly available classes of the jointly trained classification task. To show the backbone bias problem and the effect of our backbone calibration, we use t-SNE [66] to plot the respective feature distribution of the original, biased and calibrated backbone feature. As shown in Fig. 2, for the same input images, the feature distribution of the biased backbone suffer obvious drift from the well-learned distribution of the original backbone. After our model calibration, the backbone feature distribution is well aligned to the original distribution which is closer to the real data distribution.

3.2   RPN Calibration

The region proposal network (RPN) is designed to generate proposals for potential objects, which is trained in a class-agnostic manner. Thus RPN is widely regarded as a general object detection module capable of detecting arbitrary known or unknown classes [38]. However, we find that RPN is general only for the known training classes, with its performance significantly degrading on unknown novel classes for the following two intrinsic reasons.

First, there are no training samples available for novel classes and thus the RPN cannot be trained with the supervision signals of novel classes. Notwithstanding, the RPN generalization ability on novel classes (RPN still can detect some objects of novel classes) is derived from supervision signals of the similar training classes, *e.g.*, RPN trained on horse and sheep can detect zebra, but the performance is not as satisfactory as the training classes. Second, negative supervision signals on novel classes may in fact be present. Note that the training images from RPN probably contain objects of novel classes, but they are not

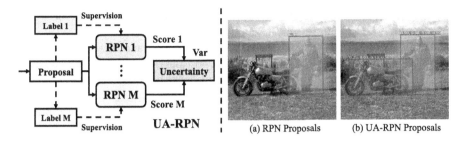

Fig. 3. Uncertainty-aware RPN (UA-RPN) and visualization for proposals of the biased RPN and our UA-RPN. The proposals are visualized with semi-transparent insets, with the most confident proposals highlighted with solid rectangular outlines. The base and novel classes are represented by   and red proposals respectively (Color figure online)

labeled and therefore are regarded as background during training. This inadvertent ignorance can further reduce the RPN generalization ability on novel classes. To make things worse, FSOD models further suffer from the biased RPN problem because of its two-stage training scheme, where the novel classes are totally unlabeled in first base training stage.

We propose to calibrate the biased RPN by rectifying the labels and predictions of potential objects of novel classes. The challenge lies on the object discovery of novel classes. We find an interesting attribute for the RPN proposals of novel classes: their object scores drastically fluctuate across different images even for objects of the same novel class, while the base classes almost *always* have stable high object scores. This means proposals of novel classes has higher prediction uncertainty compared to pure background and base classes. On the one hand, the RPN is trained to identify class-agnostic objects irrespective of classes. On the other hand, some objects of novel classes are regarded as background during training. This observation motivates us to leverage the prediction *uncertainty* to identify objects of novel classes.

We propose uncertainty-aware RPN (**UA-RPN**) to rectify the RPN training labels and predictions for RPN calibration. Our method is inspired by a widely used uncertainty estimation method M-head [77], which models deterministic features with a shared backbone, as well as *stochastic* features with multiple different predictors, where the multiple predicted hypotheses are utilized to represent the uncertainty. Our UA-RPN extends the M-head idea to estimate the uncertainty of proposals, as shown in Fig. 3. Specifically, we first build M separate RPN heads f_m with the same architecture. Each RPN shares the same input backbone feature x and generates one object score prediction for each proposal. Therefore, we can obtain M object scores for each proposal.

$$f(x) = (f_1(x), f_2(x), ..., f_M(x)) \tag{1}$$

Then we compute the variance *Var*

$$Var(f(x)) = \frac{\sum_{m=1}^{M}(f_m(x) - \mu)^2}{M - 1} \tag{2}$$

of these multiple predictions for each proposal to represent the prediction uncertainty, where μ is the mean of $f(x)$.

With the aforementioned M prediction heads, we want their predictions to be different for the samples of novel classes, so that the prediction variance can be used to evaluate uncertainty. Thus, we propose the following two designs to make UA-RPN more uncertainty-aware.

The first is training UA-RPN with diverse label assignments, where different RPN heads have different supervision labels for the same proposal. Because we target at discovering novel classes from cluttered background, we only change the labels of background proposals, where some background proposals are selectively ignored under different label assignments. For the regular RPN, the proposals are labeled as background when the overlap OV with the groundtruth bounding boxes satisfies $OV \in [0.0, 0.3]$ and those proposals with $OV \in (0.3, 0.7)$ are ignored during training. For our UA-RPN, we set different OVs for the background label assignment of different RPN heads to improve the supervision ambiguity and diversity. Those original background proposals which are not in accordance to the label assignment are ignored during training.

The second design is to detach UA-RPN from the backbone gradients so that the backbone and UA-RPN are separately optimized. This separate optimization not only avoids the backbone feature from the ambiguity supervision of UA-RPN, but also ensures the independent training for different heads of UA-RPN.

During training, those background proposals with large uncertainty $Var > \alpha$ are regarded as potential objects of novel classes, for which we rectify their labels to foreground. During testing, the predicted object scores of UA-RPN are used to rectify the RPN predictions through an average operation. The above rectifications are performed in a module ensemble manner with only a few extra computation, thanks to the light-weight design of UA-RPN.

We analyze proposal scores of both base and novel classes to illustrate the RPN bias problem and our RPN calibration. As shown in Fig. 3, the regular RPN fails to detect the novel class caused by its training bias, while our UA-RPN successfully detects the object of this novel "motorbike". Note that the proposal of novel classes has diverse object scores from multiple heads of UA-RPN and therefore their uncertainty (variance) is very high, while the base class proposal has consistently high object scores with low uncertainty.

3.3 Detector Calibration

The biased detector is mainly caused by the limited training samples in the novel finetuning stage. With numerous labeled samples in the base training stage to represent the real data distribution of base classes, the detector can be optimized to the unbiased base classes and generalize well in inference. However, in the novel finetuning stage, there are only a few training samples for each novel class, which is insufficient to represent the real data distribution of novel classes. Thus the model can easily overfit to the biased distribution underrepresented by these few samples.

We propose to calibrate the biased detector by providing rectified proposal features with the help of base classes. This idea is motivated by the fact that different classes share some commonalities, *e.g.*, horse and cow share similar legs and bodies. We can accurately estimate the data distribution of base classes under the supervision of numerous training samples. Then we can retrieve the similar base classes for novel classes, and leverage the accurate distribution estimation to rectify the data distribution. With the rectified distribution estimation, we can generate unbiased proposal features to train the detector for detector calibration. This idea has been validated in other few-shot learning tasks [95,96].

We assume the class feature distribution is Gaussian. Then we leverage a feature memory module to accumulate the feature prototype statistics of both base and novel classes. The global prototype of class c is denoted as P_c. For each image i during training, we select all proposal features F_c of the target class and accumulate them into the global prototype: $P_c \leftarrow mP_c + (1-m)F_c^i$, where m is the update momentum and set as 0.999 in our experiments. In this way, the class prototype is iteratively updated during training in an exponential moving average manner. The feature memory encodes various objects in the dataset for each class, and thus the representative prototype can capture transferable commonalities shared among base and novel classes with higher chance.

The class prototypes effectively represent the feature statistics of each class under the Gaussian distribution assumption. For a novel class n, we compute the cosine similarity S between its prototype P_n and all base class prototypes P_b. Then we select the prototype of the most similar base class P_{bs}, where $bs = \mathrm{argmax}(S)$. Then we calibrate the novel class prototype as $\hat{P}_n = \gamma P_n + (1-\gamma)P_{bs}$, where γ is the adjustable weight and we adopt $\gamma = 0.5$ in our experiments. Then we utilize a Gaussian distribution $F_G \sim N(\hat{P}_n, 1)$ to generate features F_G for this novel class.

We perform detector calibration in the novel finetuning stage, where we fix the backbone and only finetune the detector and RPN. We use the generated feature F_G with the original proposal feature F_O to jointly train the detector. There are at most 32 generated features for each foreground class.

4 Experiments

In this section, we conduct extensive experiments to validate the model bias problem in current FSOD models, and demonstrates the effectiveness of our proposed model calibration modules.

4.1 Experimental Settings

Datasets. Our experiments are conducted on MS COCO [59] and Pascal VOC [18] datasets. MS COCO dataset contains 80 classes and we follow previous works [21,39,90] to split them into two separate sets, where the 20 classes overlapping with Pascal VOC dataset are treated as novel classes, with the remaining 60 classes regarded as base classes. We utilize the 5K images of the val2017 set

Table 3. Ablation studies on different calibration (Cal.) cooperations

RPN	Detector	Backbone	AP	AP_{50}	AP_{75}
			11.3	20.9	11.0
Cal			11.8	21.5	11.8
	Cal		12.0	22.1	11.9
		Cal	14.7	25.8	14.6
Cal	Cal		12.2	23.0	11.6
Cal	Cal	Cal	15.1	27.2	14.6

for evaluation, and train2017 set with around 80K images for training. We use the support samples of novel classes in FSOD [21] to finetune our model on MS COCO dataset. As for Pascal VOC dataset which contains 20 classes, random split is done to produce 5 novel classes and 15 base classes. Specifically, there are three random class split groups, and we follow the split setting of previous works [83,90] for a fair comparison. The VOC 2007 and VOC 2012 trainval sets are utilized for training, and VOC 2007 test set are used for evaluation.

Training and Evaluation. The model is first trained on base classes and then finetuned on novel classes. Specifically, the instance number K of novel classes for finetuning is $K = 5, 10$ for MS COCO dataset, and $K = 1, 2, 3, 5, 10$ for Pascal VOC dataset. The model is evaluated multiple times on novel classes with average precision (AP) as the evaluation metric. We report the COCO-style mAP on COCO dataset and AP_{50} on Pascal VOC dataset, which are the common practice to fit the dataset characteristics.

Model Details. We adopt the pretrained U^2-Net [72] salient object detection network to generate pseudo boxes. We reuse ImageNet [12] dataset for backbone calibration, which is only used for model pretraining in other works. UA-RPN has $M = 4$ RPNs with different $OV \in [0.01, 0.3], [0.1, 0.3], [0.15, 0.3], [0.2, 0.3]^1$. We dynamically set α by selecting top-1,000 uncertain proposals.

Implementation Details. We adopt Faster R-CNN [76] with Feature Pyramid Network [57] (FPN) as our basic detection framework, with the ResNet-50 [32] backbone pretrained on ImageNet [12] dataset. We use SGD to optimize our model with weight decay of $5e^{-5}$ and momentum of 0.9. The model is trained 50,000 iterations at the base training stage. The learning rate is set as 0.02 in the first 30,000 iterations, which decays by 10× for every 10,000 iterations. For the novel class finetuning stage, the model is trained 3,000 iterations with 0.01 initial learning rate, which decays by 10× upon reaching the 2,000-th iteration. The object detection images are resized with the fixed height/width ratio, where the shorter image side is resized to 600 while the longer side is capped at 1,000.

---

[1] Proposals with $OV \in \{[0, 0.01), [0, 0.1), [0, 0.15), [0, 0.2)\}$ are respectively ignored during training for each UA-RPN head.

4.2   Ablation Studies

Table 3 shows that each model calibration module improves the detection performance, and their combination promotes the overall performance from 11.3 to 15.1 AP. We further conduct extensive experiments on MS COCO dataset to investigate the efficacy of our model calibration on handling model bias in different modules.

Backbone Calibration. The backbone bias is introduced at the base training stage, where the generalized feature distribution learned from massive classes can be scrapped. This problem is effectively relieved by our backbone calibration module, where the generalization performance on novel classes is significantly improved by 3.4 AP. (Table 4)

Table 4. Ablation studies on backbone calibrations. "CAM" denotes class activation map, PB denotes pseudo boxes, and † means with careful hyperparameter tuning

Backbone	AP	AP_{50}	AP_{75}
Baseline	11.3	20.9	11.0
Cal. Backbone	14.7	25.8	14.6
Cal. w/725 Cls	14.2	25.4	13.9
Cal. w/Rand. 500 Cls	13.9	24.7	13.8
Cal. w/Rand. 300 Cls	13.3	25.3	12.7
Cal. w/Rand. 100 Cls	12.3	22.2	12.1
Cal. w/CAM	14.4	27.5	13.3
Cal. w/o PB	7.5	16.2	5.8
Cal. w/o PB†	14.2	27.1	13.2

Discussions. Concerns about backbone calibration include:

Does the performance gain come from the overlapped classes in the ImageNet dataset? The performance gain mainly comes from the well-learned feature distribution covering the massive classes. To remove any effect of the overlapped classes, we use a purified ImageNet [12] dataset to calibrate the backbone, which contains 725 classes by removing all classes similar to the novel classes in MS COCO. Compared to the backbone calibrated on the full ImageNet dataset, the performance slightly degrades by 0.5 AP. With 500 randomly selected classes, the performance with model calibration only degrades by 0.8 AP. These results validate that the improvement of backbone calibration is mainly derived from the massive classes, rather than from the overlapped classes. We also present the performance with 100 and 300 randomly selected classes to further show the impact of the class diversity on backbone calibration.

Does the performance gain come from the pretrained SOD model? To address this concern, we utilize class activated map [105] (CAM) to generate pseudo boxes, which is an unsupervised method and the pseudo mask can be directly generated from the pretrained classification model. The performance only

Table 5. Ablation studies for UA-RPN. "DT" denotes detaching UA-RPN gradient from backbone, "LA" denotes label assignment for background proposals, "LR" denotes label rectification and "PR" denotes prediction rectification

Method	Stage1 AR		Stage2 AR		AP
	@100	@1000	@100	@1000	
RPN	17.1	35.3	26.1	38.6	11.3
Cal. RPN	20.1	37.4	28.5	39.6	11.8
Cal. w/o DT	19.2	37.0	26.9	39.2	10.2
Cal. w/o LA	17.5	35.5	26.5	38.7	11.5
Cal. w/o LR	19.1	37.1	27.9	39.0	11.6
Cal. w/o PR	18.5	36.7	27.0	39.4	11.4

Table 6. Experimental results on Pascal VOC dataset. The **best** and <u>second best</u> results are highlighted with **bold** and <u>underline</u>, respectively

Method	Novel set 1					Novel set 2					Novel set 3				
	1	2	3	5	10	1	2	3	5	10	1	2	3	5	10
LSTD [8]	8.2	1.0	12.4	29.1	38.5	11.4	3.8	5.0	15.7	31.0	12.6	8.5	15.0	27.3	36.3
FSRW [39]	14.8	15.5	26.7	33.9	47.2	15.7	15.3	22.7	30.1	40.5	21.3	25.6	28.4	42.8	45.9
MetaRCNN [94]	19.9	25.5	35.0	45.7	51.5	10.4	19.4	29.6	34.8	45.4	14.3	18.2	27.5	41.2	48.1
FsDetView [93]	24.2	35.3	42.2	49.1	57.4	21.6	24.6	31.9	37.0	45.7	21.2	30.0	37.2	43.8	49.6
MSPR [92]	41.7	–	**51.4**	55.2	61.8	24.4	–	39.2	39.9	47.8	35.6	–	42.3	48.0	49.7
TFA [90]	39.8	36.1	44.7	55.7	56.0	23.5	26.9	34.1	35.1	39.1	30.8	34.8	42.8	49.5	49.8
FSCE [83]	<u>44.2</u>	43.8	**51.4**	<u>61.9</u>	**63.4**	27.3	29.5	**43.5**	<u>44.2</u>	**50.2**	<u>37.2</u>	<u>41.9</u>	**47.5**	**54.6**	**58.5**
DCNet [36]	33.9	37.4	43.7	51.1	59.6	23.2	24.8	30.6	36.7	46.6	32.3	34.9	39.7	42.6	50.7
SRR-FSD [107]	**47.8**	**50.5**	<u>51.3</u>	55.2	56.8	<u>32.5</u>	**35.3**	39.1	40.8	43.8	**40.1**	41.5	<u>44.3</u>	46.9	46.4
Ours	40.1	<u>44.2</u>	51.2	**62.0**	<u>63.0</u>	**33.3**	<u>33.1</u>	<u>42.3</u>	**46.3**	**52.3**	36.1	**43.1**	43.5	<u>52.0</u>	<u>56.0</u>

degrades by 0.3 AP with the inaccurate CAM generated pseudo boxes. We also directly and jointly train the model on both detection and classification datasets without pseudo boxes. The performance dramatically degrades to 7.5 AP because of the dominating classification branch. But with careful hyperparameter tuning by reducing the loss weights from the classification branch, the performance can reach 14.2 AP. These results validates that the backbone calibration can be *only* slightly affected by the pseudo box quality.

Does the backbone calibration introduce extra data? Our method does not introduce any extra data. We only reuse ImageNet dataset, which is a free resource, to perform backbone calibration. Other FSOD methods however only use ImageNet for model pretraining.

RPN Calibration. Table 5 validates the effectiveness of our proposed UA-RPN, where the baseline RPN only has 17.1/35.3 AR@100/1000 on novel classes in the base training stage (stage 1), while the performance on base classes can reach 42.1/49.8 AR@100/1000. The performance of the former on novel classes is only improved to 26.1/38.6 AR@100/1000 after the novel finetuning stage. These

Table 7. Experimental 5-shot results on MS COCO dataset

Backbone	Publication	AP	AP_{50}	AP_{75}
FSRW [39]	ICCV'19	5.6	12.3	4.6
MetaRCNN [94]	ICCV'19	8.7	19.1	6.6
FSOD [21]	CVPR'20	11.1	20.4	10.6
MSPR [92]	ECCV'20	9.8	17.9	9.7
FsDetView [93]	ECCV'20	12.5	27.3	9.8
TFA [90]	ICML'20	10.0	–	9.3
SRR-FSD [107]	CVPR'21	11.3	23.0	9.8
FSCE [83]	CVPR'21	11.9	–	10.5
DCNet [36]	CVPR'21	12.8	23.4	11.2
Ours	–	**15.1**	**27.2**	**14.6**

results indicate the serious RPN bias toward the base classes, which adversely affects the generalization ability on the novel classes. With our RPN calibration, the recall of the novel classes on both stage 1 and stage 2 is significantly improved, and the overall detection AP performance is also improved by 0.5 AP. We further validate the effectiveness of separate modules in UA-RPN. The gradient detaching is essential for keeping the detection performance by separating UA-RPN gradients from backbone. The diverse label assignment affects the uncertainty of UA-RPN and therefore is essential for the recall of novel classes. Both the label and prediction rectifications are beneficial to the proposal recall and detection performance of novel classes.

Detector Calibration. We evaluate the models on the training samples of novel classes to demonstrate the detector bias. The detection performance on the training samples reaches 61.7 AP, while the generalization performance on testing samples is only 11.3 AP. The large performance gap between training and testing samples indicates the serious detector bias toward the training samples. Equipped with our detector calibration, the performance on testing samples can be improved from 11.3 to 11.9 AP, with the performance gap also reduced by relieving the overfitting on training samples.

4.3   Comparison with SOTAs

We conduct comparison experiments with state-of-the-art methods on Pascal VOC and MS COCO datasets. Pascal VOC contains more median-sized and large objects and thus the detection performance is much higher than that on MS COCO dataset. As shown in Table 6, out method performs better or comparable to other methods in all class splits. MS COCO is a challenging dataset even for fully-supervised methods. As shown in Table 7, with the proposed model calibration, our model significantly outperforms other methods by a large margin of 2.5 AP, with the detection performance reaching 15.1 AP.

5 Conclusion

Few-shot object detection (FSOD) has recently achieved remarkable progress. However, previous FSOD works have ignored the intrinsic model bias problem in transfer learning. The model bias problem causes overfitting toward training classes while destructing the well-learned transferable knowledge. In this paper, we identify and perform a comprehensive study on the model bias problem in FSOD, and propose a simple yet effective method to address the problem, making use of the ImageNet dataset not limited to pre-training as done in other works. Specifically, we perform model calibrations in three levels: 1) *backbone calibration* to preserve the well-learned prior knowledge which relieves the model from bias towards base classes; 2) *RPN calibration* to rescue unlabeled objects of novel classes; and 3) *detector calibration* to prevent model bias towards a small number of training samples of the novel classes. Extensive experiments and analysis substantiate the effectiveness of our model calibration method.

References

1. Allen, K., Shelhamer, E., Shin, H., Tenenbaum, J.: Infinite mixture prototypes for few-shot learning. In: ICML (2019)
2. Antoniou, A., Edwards, H., Storkey, A.: How to train your MAML. In: ICLR (2019)
3. Bell, S., Zitnick, C.L., Bala, K., Girshick, R.: Inside-outside net: detecting objects in context with skip pooling and recurrent neural networks. In: CVPR (2016)
4. Bertinetto, L., Henriques, J.F., Torr, P.H., Vedaldi, A.: Meta-learning with differentiable closed-form solvers. In: ICLR (2019)
5. Cai, Z., Fan, Q., Feris, R.S., Vasconcelos, N.: A unified multi-scale deep convolutional neural network for fast object detection. In: Leibe, B., Matas, J., Sebe, N., Welling, M. (eds.) ECCV 2016. LNCS, vol. 9908, pp. 354–370. Springer, Cham (2016). https://doi.org/10.1007/978-3-319-46493-0_22
6. Cai, Z., Vasconcelos, N.: Cascade R-CNN: delving into high quality object detection. In: CVPR (2018)
7. Cao, Y., et al.: Few-shot object detection via association and discrimination. In: NeurIPS (2021)
8. Chen, H., Wang, Y., Wang, G., Qiao, Y.: LSTD: a low-shot transfer detector for object detection. In: AAAI (2018)
9. Chen, W.Y., Liu, Y.C., Kira, Z., Wang, Y.C.F., Huang, J.B.: A closer look at few-shot classification. In: ICLR (2019)
10. Cui, Y., Jia, M., Lin, T.Y., Song, Y., Belongie, S.: Class-balanced loss based on effective number of samples. In: CVPR (2019)
11. Dai, J., Li, Y., He, K., Sun, J.: R-FCN: object detection via region-based fully convolutional networks. In: NeurIPS (2016)
12. Deng, J., Dong, W., Socher, R., Li, L.J., Li, K., Fei-Fei, L.: ImageNet: a large-scale hierarchical image database. In: CVPR (2009)
13. Deng, J., Guo, J., Xue, N., Zafeiriou, S.: ArcFace: additive angular margin loss for deep face recognition. In: CVPR (2019)
14. Dhillon, G.S., Chaudhari, P., Ravichandran, A., Soatto, S.: A baseline for few-shot image classification. In: ICLR (2019)

15. Doersch, C., Gupta, A., Zisserman, A.: CrossTransformers: spatially-aware few-shot transfer. In: NeurIPS (2020)
16. Dong, N., Xing, E.P.: Few-shot semantic segmentation with prototype learning. In: BMVC (2018)
17. Duan, K., Bai, S., Xie, L., Qi, H., Huang, Q., Tian, Q.: CenterNet: keypoint triplets for object detection. In: ICCV (2019)
18. Everingham, M., Van Gool, L., Williams, C.K., Winn, J., Zisserman, A.: The Pascal visual object classes (VOC) challenge. IJCV **88**, 303–338 (2010). https://doi.org/10.1007/s11263-009-0275-4
19. Fan, Q., Ke, L., Pei, W., Tang, C.-K., Tai, Y.-W.: Commonality-parsing network across shape and appearance for partially supervised instance segmentation. In: Vedaldi, A., Bischof, H., Brox, T., Frahm, J.-M. (eds.) ECCV 2020. LNCS, vol. 12353, pp. 379–396. Springer, Cham (2020). https://doi.org/10.1007/978-3-030-58598-3_23
20. Fan, Q., Tang, C.K., Tai, Y.W.: Few-shot video object detection. arXiv preprint arXiv:2104.14805 (2021)
21. Fan, Q., Zhuo, W., Tang, C.K., Tai, Y.W.: Few-shot object detection with attention-RPN and multi-relation detector. In: CVPR (2020)
22. Fan, Z., Ma, Y., Li, Z., Sun, J.: Generalized few-shot object detection without forgetting. In: CVPR (2021)
23. Finn, C., Abbeel, P., Levine, S.: Model-agnostic meta-learning for fast adaptation of deep networks. In: ICML (2017)
24. Gidaris, S., Komodakis, N.: Dynamic few-shot visual learning without forgetting. In: CVPR (2018)
25. Girshick, R.: Fast R-CNN. In: ICCV (2015)
26. Gordon, J., Bronskill, J., Bauer, M., Nowozin, S., Turner, R.: Meta-learning probabilistic inference for prediction. In: ICLR (2019)
27. Grant, E., Finn, C., Levine, S., Darrell, T., Griffiths, T.: Recasting gradient-based meta-learning as hierarchical bayes. In: ICLR (2018)
28. Gui, L.-Y., Wang, Y.-X., Ramanan, D., Moura, J.M.F.: Few-shot human motion prediction via meta-learning. In: Ferrari, V., Hebert, M., Sminchisescu, C., Weiss, Y. (eds.) ECCV 2018. LNCS, vol. 11212, pp. 441–459. Springer, Cham (2018). https://doi.org/10.1007/978-3-030-01237-3_27
29. Han, G., He, Y., Huang, S., Ma, J., Chang, S.F.: Query adaptive few-shot object detection with heterogeneous graph convolutional networks. In: ICCV (2021)
30. He, K., Fan, H., Wu, Y., Xie, S., Girshick, R.: Momentum contrast for unsupervised visual representation learning. In: CVPR (2020)
31. He, K., Gkioxari, G., Dollár, P., Girshick, R.: Mask R-CNN. In: ICCV (2017)
32. He, K., Zhang, X., Ren, S., Sun, J.: Deep residual learning for image recognition. In: CVPR (2016)
33. He, Y., Zhu, C., Wang, J., Savvides, M., Zhang, X.: Bounding box regression with uncertainty for accurate object detection. In: CVPR (2019)
34. Hénaff, O.J., Koppula, S., Alayrac, J.B., Van den Oord, A., Vinyals, O., Carreira, J.: Efficient visual pretraining with contrastive detection. In: ICCV (2021)
35. Hou, R., Chang, H., Ma, B., Shan, S., Chen, X.: Cross attention network for few-shot classification. In: NeurIPS (2019)
36. Hu, H., Bai, S., Li, A., Cui, J., Wang, L.: Dense relation distillation with context-aware aggregation for few-shot object detection. In: CVPR (2021)
37. Hu, T., Yang, P., Zhang, C., Yu, G., Mu, Y., Snoek, C.G.M.: Attention-based multi-context guiding for few-shot semantic segmentation. In: AAAI (2019)

38. Joseph, K., Khan, S., Khan, F.S., Balasubramanian, V.N.: Towards open world object detection. In: CVPR (2021)
39. Kang, B., Liu, Z., Wang, X., Yu, F., Feng, J., Darrell, T.: Few-shot object detection via feature reweighting. In: ICCV (2019)
40. Karlinsky, L., et al.: RepMet: representative-based metric learning for classification and few-shot object detection. In: CVPR (2019)
41. Khan, S., Hayat, M., Zamir, S.W., Shen, J., Shao, L.: Striking the right balance with uncertainty. In: CVPR (2019)
42. Khan, S.H., Hayat, M., Bennamoun, M., Sohel, F.A., Togneri, R.: Cost-sensitive learning of deep feature representations from imbalanced data. IEEE TNNLS **29**(8), 3573–3587 (2017)
43. Koch, G., Zemel, R., Salakhutdinov, R.: Siamese neural networks for one-shot image recognition. In: ICML Workshop (2015)
44. Kong, T., Sun, F., Liu, H., Jiang, Y., Li, L., Shi, J.: FoveaBox: beyound anchor-based object detection. IEEE TIP **29**, 7389–7398 (2020)
45. Kong, T., Sun, F., Yao, A., Liu, H., Lu, M., Chen, Y.: RON: reverse connection with objectness prior networks for object detection. In: CVPR (2017)
46. Law, H., Deng, J.: CornerNet: detecting objects as paired keypoints. In: Ferrari, V., Hebert, M., Sminchisescu, C., Weiss, Y. (eds.) Computer Vision – ECCV 2018. LNCS, vol. 11218, pp. 765–781. Springer, Cham (2018). https://doi.org/10.1007/978-3-030-01264-9_45
47. Lee, K., Maji, S., Ravichandran, A., Soatto, S.: Meta-learning with differentiable convex optimization. In: CVPR (2019)
48. Lee, Y., Choi, S.: Gradient-based meta-learning with learned layerwise metric and subspace. In: ICML (2018)
49. Li, A., Li, Z.: Transformation invariant few-shot object detection. In: CVPR (2021)
50. Li, B., Yang, B., Liu, C., Liu, F., Ji, R., Ye, Q.: Beyond max-margin: class margin equilibrium for few-shot object detection. In: CVPR (2021)
51. Li, H., Eigen, D., Dodge, S., Zeiler, M., Wang, X.: Finding task-relevant features for few-shot learning by category traversal. In: CVPR (2019)
52. Li, W., Wang, L., Xu, J., Huo, J., Gao, Y., Luo, J.: Revisiting local descriptor based image-to-class measure for few-shot learning. In: CVPR (2019)
53. Li, X., Wei, T., Chen, Y.P., Tai, Y.W., Tang, C.K.: FSS-1000: a 1000-class dataset for few-shot segmentation. In: CVPR (2020)
54. Li, Y., Chen, Y., Wang, N., Zhang, Z.: Scale-aware trident networks for object detection. In: ICCV (2019)
55. Li, Y., Xie, S., Chen, X., Dollar, P., He, K., Girshick, R.: Benchmarking detection transfer learning with vision transformers. arXiv preprint arXiv:2111.11429 (2021)
56. Li, Y., et al.: Few-shot object detection via classification refinement and distractor retreatment. In: CVPR (2021)
57. Lin, T.Y., Dollár, P., Girshick, R., He, K., Hariharan, B., Belongie, S.: Feature pyramid networks for object detection. In: CVPR (2017)
58. Lin, T.Y., Goyal, P., Girshick, R., He, K., Dollár, P.: Focal loss for dense object detection. In: ICCV (2017)
59. Lin, T.-Y., et al.: Microsoft COCO: common objects in context. In: Fleet, D., Pajdla, T., Schiele, B., Tuytelaars, T. (eds.) ECCV 2014. LNCS, vol. 8693, pp. 740–755. Springer, Cham (2014). https://doi.org/10.1007/978-3-319-10602-1_48
60. Liu, B., et al.: Negative margin matters: understanding margin in few-shot classification. In: Vedaldi, A., Bischof, H., Brox, T., Frahm, J.-M. (eds.) ECCV 2020.

LNCS, vol. 12349, pp. 438–455. Springer, Cham (2020). https://doi.org/10.1007/978-3-030-58548-8_26

61. Liu, S., Huang, D., Wang, Y.: Receptive field block net for accurate and fast object detection. In: Ferrari, V., Hebert, M., Sminchisescu, C., Weiss, Y. (eds.) ECCV 2018. LNCS, vol. 11215, pp. 404–419. Springer, Cham (2018). https://doi.org/10.1007/978-3-030-01252-6_24

62. Liu, W., et al.: SSD: single shot multibox detector. In: Leibe, B., Matas, J., Sebe, N., Welling, M. (eds.) ECCV 2016. LNCS, vol. 9905, pp. 21–37. Springer, Cham (2016). https://doi.org/10.1007/978-3-319-46448-0_2

63. Liu, W., Liao, S., Ren, W., Hu, W., Yu, Y.: High-level semantic feature detection: a new perspective for pedestrian detection. In: CVPR (2019)

64. Liu, Y., Zhang, X., Zhang, S., He, X.: Part-aware prototype network for few-shot semantic segmentation. In: Vedaldi, A., Bischof, H., Brox, T., Frahm, J.-M. (eds.) ECCV 2020. LNCS, vol. 12354, pp. 142–158. Springer, Cham (2020). https://doi.org/10.1007/978-3-030-58545-7_9

65. Lu, X., Li, B., Yue, Y., Li, Q., Yan, J.: Grid R-CNN. In: CVPR (2019)

66. Van der Maaten, L., Hinton, G.: Visualizing data using t-SNE. J. Mach. Learn. Res. **9**, 2579–2605 (2008)

67. Michaelis, C., Bethge, M., Ecker, A.S.: One-shot segmentation in clutter. In: ICML (2018)

68. Najibi, M., Rastegari, M., Davis, L.S.: G-CNN: an iterative grid based object detector. In: CVPR (2016)

69. Nie, J., Anwer, R.M., Cholakkal, H., Khan, F.S., Pang, Y., Shao, L.: Enriched feature guided refinement network for object detection. In: ICCV (2019)

70. Qi, H., Brown, M., Lowe, D.G.: Low-shot learning with imprinted weights. In: CVPR (2018)

71. Qiao, L., Zhao, Y., Li, Z., Qiu, X., Wu, J., Zhang, C.: DeFRCN: decoupled Faster R-CNN for few-shot object detection. In: ICCV (2021)

72. Qin, X., Zhang, Z., Huang, C., Dehghan, M., Zaiane, O.R., Jagersand, M.: U2-Net: going deeper with nested U-structure for salient object detection. PR **106**, 107404 (2020)

73. Qin, Z., et al.: ThunderNet: towards real-time generic object detection on mobile devices. In: ICCV (2019)

74. Redmon, J., Divvala, S., Girshick, R., Farhadi, A.: You only look once: unified, real-time object detection. In: CVPR (2016)

75. Redmon, J., Farhadi, A.: YOLO9000: better, faster, stronger. In: CVPR (2017)

76. Ren, S., He, K., Girshick, R., Sun, J.: Faster R-CNN: towards real-time object detection with region proposal networks. In: NeurIPS (2015)

77. Rupprecht, C., et al.: Learning in an uncertain world: representing ambiguity through multiple hypotheses. In: ICCV (2017)

78. Rusu, A.A., et al.: Meta-learning with latent embedding optimization. In: ICLR (2019)

79. Shen, Z., Liu, Z., Li, J., Jiang, Y.G., Chen, Y., Xue, X.: DSOD: learning deeply supervised object detectors from scratch. In: ICCV (2017)

80. Shrivastava, A., Gupta, A.: Contextual priming and feedback for Faster R-CNN. In: Leibe, B., Matas, J., Sebe, N., Welling, M. (eds.) ECCV 2016. LNCS, vol. 9905, pp. 330–348. Springer, Cham (2016). https://doi.org/10.1007/978-3-319-46448-0_20

81. Shrivastava, A., Gupta, A., Girshick, R.: Training region-based object detectors with online hard example mining. In: CVPR (2016)

82. Singh, B., Najibi, M., Davis, L.S.: SNIPER: efficient multi-scale training. In: NeurIPS (2018)
83. Sun, B., Li, B., Cai, S., Yuan, Y., Zhang, C.: FSCE: few-shot object detection via contrastive proposal encoding. In: CVPR (2021)
84. Tan, M., Pang, R., Le, Q.V.: EfficientDet: scalable and efficient object detection. In: CVPR (2020)
85. Tian, Y., Wang, Y., Krishnan, D., Tenenbaum, J.B., Isola, P.: Rethinking few-shot image classification: a good embedding is all you need? In: Vedaldi, A., Bischof, H., Brox, T., Frahm, J.-M. (eds.) ECCV 2020. LNCS, vol. 12359, pp. 266–282. Springer, Cham (2020). https://doi.org/10.1007/978-3-030-58568-6_16
86. Tian, Z., Shen, C., Chen, H., He, T.: FCOS: fully convolutional one-stage object detection. In: ICCV (2019)
87. Uijlings, J.R., Van De Sande, K.E., Gevers, T., Smeulders, A.W.: Selective search for object recognition. IJCV **104**, 154–171 (2013). https://doi.org/10.1007/s11263-013-0620-5
88. Wang, H., et al.: CosFace: large margin cosine loss for deep face recognition. In: CVPR (2018)
89. Wang, T., Anwer, R.M., Cholakkal, H., Khan, F.S., Pang, Y., Shao, L.: Learning rich features at high-speed for single-shot object detection. In: ICCV (2019)
90. Wang, X., Huang, T.E., Darrell, T., Gonzalez, J.E., Yu, F.: Frustratingly simple few-shot object detection. In: ICML (2020)
91. Wu, A., Han, Y., Zhu, L., Yang, Y.: Universal-prototype enhancing for few-shot object detection. In: ICCV (2021)
92. Wu, J., Liu, S., Huang, D., Wang, Y.: Multi-scale positive sample refinement for few-shot object detection. In: Vedaldi, A., Bischof, H., Brox, T., Frahm, J.-M. (eds.) ECCV 2020. LNCS, vol. 12361, pp. 456–472. Springer, Cham (2020). https://doi.org/10.1007/978-3-030-58517-4_27
93. Xiao, Y., Marlet, R.: Few-shot object detection and viewpoint estimation for objects in the wild. In: Vedaldi, A., Bischof, H., Brox, T., Frahm, J.-M. (eds.) ECCV 2020. LNCS, vol. 12362, pp. 192–210. Springer, Cham (2020). https://doi.org/10.1007/978-3-030-58520-4_12
94. Yan, X., Chen, Z., Xu, A., Wang, X., Liang, X., Lin, L.: Meta R-CNN: towards general solver for instance-level low-shot learning. In: ICCV (2019)
95. Yang, L., Zhuo, W., Qi, L., Shi, Y., Gao, Y.: Mining latent classes for few-shot segmentation. In: ICCV (2021)
96. Yang, S., Liu, L., Xu, M.: Free lunch for few-shot learning: distribution calibration. In: ICLR (2021)
97. Yang, Y., Wei, F., Shi, M., Li, G.: Restoring negative information in few-shot object detection. In: NeurIPS (2020)
98. Yang, Z., Liu, S., Hu, H., Wang, L., Lin, S.: RepPoints: point set representation for object detection. In: ICCV (2019)
99. Zareian, A., Rosa, K.D., Hu, D.H., Chang, S.F.: Open-vocabulary object detection using captions. In: CVPR (2021)
100. Zhang, L., Zhou, S., Guan, J., Zhang, J.: Accurate few-shot object detection with support-query mutual guidance and hybrid loss. In: CVPR (2021)
101. Zhang, S., Chi, C., Yao, Y., Lei, Z., Li, S.Z.: Bridging the gap between anchor-based and anchor-free detection via adaptive training sample selection. In: CVPR (2020)
102. Zhang, S., Wen, L., Bian, X., Lei, Z., Li, S.Z.: Single-shot refinement neural network for object detection. In: CVPR (2018)

103. Zhang, W., Wang, Y.X.: Hallucination improves few-shot object detection. In: CVPR (2021)
104. Zhang, Z., Qiao, S., Xie, C., Shen, W., Wang, B., Yuille, A.L.: Single-shot object detection with enriched semantics. In: CVPR (2018)
105. Zhou, B., Khosla, A., Lapedriza, A., Oliva, A., Torralba, A.: Learning deep features for discriminative localization. In: CVPR (2016)
106. Zhou, X., Zhuo, J., Krahenbuhl, P.: Bottom-up object detection by grouping extreme and center points. In: CVPR (2019)
107. Zhu, C., Chen, F., Ahmed, U., Savvides, M.: Semantic relation reasoning for shot-stable few-shot object detection. In: CVPR (2021)
108. Zhu, R., et al.: ScratchDet: training single-shot object detectors from scratch. In: CVPR (2019)
109. Ziko, I., Dolz, J., Granger, E., Ayed, I.B.: Laplacian regularized few-shot learning. In: ICML (2020)

Self-Supervision Can Be a Good Few-Shot Learner

Yuning Lu[1]([✉]), Liangjian Wen[2], Jianzhuang Liu[2], Yajing Liu[1],
and Xinmei Tian[1,3]

[1] University of Science and Technology of China, Hefei, China
{lyn0,lyj123}@mail.ustc.edu.cn
[2] Huawei Noah's Ark Lab, Shenzhen, China
{wenliangjian1,liu.jianzhuang}@huawei.com
[3] Institute of Artificial Intelligence, Hefei Comprehensive National Science Center,
Hefei, China
xinmei@ustc.edu.cn

Abstract. Existing few-shot learning (FSL) methods rely on training with a large labeled dataset, which prevents them from leveraging abundant unlabeled data. From an information-theoretic perspective, we propose an effective unsupervised FSL method, learning representations with self-supervision. Following the InfoMax principle, our method learns comprehensive representations by capturing the intrinsic structure of the data. Specifically, we maximize the mutual information (MI) of instances and their representations with a low-bias MI estimator to perform self-supervised pre-training. Rather than supervised pre-training focusing on the discriminable features of the seen classes, our self-supervised model has less bias toward the seen classes, resulting in better generalization for unseen classes. We explain that supervised pre-training and self-supervised pre-training are actually maximizing different MI objectives. Extensive experiments are further conducted to analyze their FSL performance with various training settings. Surprisingly, the results show that self-supervised pre-training can outperform supervised pre-training under the appropriate conditions. Compared with state-of-the-art FSL methods, our approach achieves comparable performance on widely used FSL benchmarks without any labels of the base classes.

Keywords: Few-shot image classification · Self-supervised learning

1 Introduction

Training a reliable model with limited data, also known as few-shot learning (FSL) [22,43,48,53,59,65,71], remains challenging in computer vision. The core idea of FSL is to learn a prior which can solve unknown downstream tasks.

This work was done during an internship in Huawei Noah's Ark Lab.

Supplementary Information The online version contains supplementary material available at https://doi.org/10.1007/978-3-031-19800-7_43.

Despite various motivations, most existing methods are *supervised*, requiring a large labeled (base) dataset [61,75] to learn the prior. However, collecting a large-scale base dataset is expensive in practice. Depending on supervision also does not allow the full use of abundant unlabeled data.

Several unsupervised FSL works [3,35,37,38,57] attempt to solve the problem of *label dependency*. Most of them share a similar motivation of applying existing meta-learning methods (i.e., the popular supervised FSL solutions) to unsupervised data. Instead of leveraging category labels, these approaches generate (meta-)training tasks (or *episodes*) via different unsupervised ways, such as data augmentation [37] or pseudo labels [35]. Despite their worthy attempts, they still have a large performance gap compared with the top supervised FSL methods. Recent work [39] indicates that the episodic training of meta-learning is data-inefficient in that it does not sufficiently exploit the training batch. Several studies [10,19,28,71] of (supervised) FSL also show that a simple pre-training-&-fine-tuning approach outperforms many sophisticated meta-learning methods.

From an information-theoretic perspective, we propose an effective unsupervised FSL method, i.e., learning the representations with self-supervised pre-training. Following the principle of InfoMax [46], the goal of our method is to preserve more information about high-dimensional raw data in the low-dimensional learned representations. In contrast to supervised pre-training [71], self-supervised pre-training focuses on capturing the intrinsic structure of the data. It learns comprehensive representations instead of the most discriminative representations about the base categories. Specifically, our self-supervised pre-training maximizes the mutual information (MI) between the representations of augmented views of the same instance. It is a lower bound of MI between the instance and its representations. Many contrastive learning methods [8,31,52] maximize MI by optimizing a loss based on Noise-Contrastive Estimation [29] (also called InfoNCE [52]). However, recent progress [56,66,77] shows that the MI estimation based on InfoNCE has *high bias*. We alternatively employ a low-bias MI estimator following the MI neural estimation [4] to address the issue. The experiments in FSL demonstrate the effectiveness of our approach.

To better understand self-supervision and supervision in FSL, we explain that they are maximizing different MI targets. We further construct comprehensive experiments to analyze their different behaviors in FSL across various settings (i.e., backbones, data augmentations, and input sizes). The experiment results surprisingly show that, with appropriate settings, self-supervision *without* any labels of the base dataset can outperform supervision while exhibiting better scalability for network depth. We argue that self-supervision learns less bias toward the base classes than supervision, resulting in better generalization ability for unknown classes. In this manner, extending the network depth can learn more powerful representations without over-fitting to the seen classes.

The scalability of network depth provides an opportunity to use a deep model to guide the learning of a shallow model in FSL. We formulate this problem of unsupervised knowledge distillation as maximizing MI between the representations of different models. Consequently, we propose a simple yet effective loss to perform the knowledge distillation *without* labels. To the best of our knowledge, existing supervised FSL methods [20,71] only perform the knowledge distillation between shallow models. In summary, our contributions are:

- From an information-theoretic perspective, we propose an effective unsupervised FSL approach that learns representations with self-supervision. Our method maximizes the MI between the instances and their representations with a low-bias MI estimator.
- We indicate that the self-supervised pre-training and supervised pre-training maximize different targets of MI. We construct comprehensive experiments to analyze the difference between them for the FSL problem.
- We present a simple yet effective self-supervised knowledge distillation for unsupervised FSL to improve the performance of a small model.
- Extensive experiments are conducted to demonstrate the advantages of our method. Our *unsupervised* model achieves comparable results with the state-of-the-art *supervised* FSL ones on widely used benchmarks, i.e., *mini*-ImageNet [75] and *tiered*-ImageNet [61], without any labels of the base classes.

2   Related Work

Few-Shot Learning (FSL). The pioneering works of FSL date back to the Bayesian approach [40,44]. In recent years, several papers [23,43,53,63,65,75] address the problem with a meta-learning paradigm, where the model learns from a series of simulated learning tasks that mimic the real few-shot circumstances. Due to its elegant form and excellent results, it has attracted great interest. However, recent studies [10,28,71] show that pre-training an embedding model with the classification loss (cross-entropy) is a simple but tough-to-beat baseline in FSL. Subsequently, many studies [13,47,49,55,67] focus on how to learn a good embedding instead of designing complex meta-learning strategies. Although considerable progress has been made, the aforementioned approaches rely on the annotation of the base classes, limiting their applications. In addition, most existing supervised methods [10,22,43,51,53,65,71,75] achieve their best results with a relatively shallow backbone, e.g., ResNet-10/12. Our paper demonstrates that it is possible to build an effective and scalable few-shot learner without any labels of the base classes. It suggests that we should rethink the significance of label information of the base dataset in FSL.

InfoMax Principle in FSL. Some recent studies [5,19] address the problem of transductive FSL, where unlabeled query samples are utilized in the downstream fine-tuning, from the information-theoretic perspective. The most related work [5] introduces the InfoMax principle [46] to perform transductive fine-tuning. It maximizes the MI between the representations of query samples and their predicted labels during fine-tuning, while ours maximizes the MI between base samples and their representations during pre-training.

Self-supervised Learning (SSL). A self-supervised model learns representations in an unsupervised manner via various pretext tasks, such as colorization [41,82], inpainting [54], and rotation prediction [26]. One of the most competitive methods is contrastive learning [8,30,31,34,52,69], which aligns the representation of samples from the same instance (the positive pair, e.g., two augmented views of the same image). A major problem of contrastive learning is the *representation collapse*, i.e., all outputs are a constant. One solution is the uniformity regularization, which encourages different images (the negative pair) to have dissimilar representations. Recent works [8,31] typically optimize the InfoNCE loss [29,52] to perform both alignment and uniformity, which is considered to maximize the MI between different views. Since InfoNCE can be decomposed into alignment and uniformity terms [9,76], many works introduce new forms of uniformity (and/or alignment) to design new objectives. Barlow Twins [81] encourages the representations to be dissimilar for different channels, not for different samples. Chen and Li [9] propose to explicitly match the distribution of representations to a prior distribution of high entropy as a new uniformity term. Some recent works [12,27,72] introduce asymmetry in the alignment of the positive pair to learn meaningful representations without explicit uniformity.

FSL with SSL. In natural language processing, self-supervised pre-training shows superior performance on few-shot learning [7]. However, the application of SSL in the few-shot image classification is still an open problem. Most works [25,49,67] leverage the pretext task of SSL as an auxiliary loss to enhance the representation learning of supervised pre-training. The performance of these methods degrades drastically without supervision. Another way is unsupervised FSL [3,35,37,38,42,50,57], whose setting is the same as ours. Most of these works [3,35,37,38,50,57] simply adapt existing supervised meta-learning methods to the unsupervised versions. For example, CACTUs [35] uses a clustering method to obtain pseudo-labels of samples and then applies a meta-learning algorithm. Their performance is still limited by the downstream meta-learning methods, having a large gap with the top supervised FSL methods. In addition, the recent work [21] evaluates existing self-supervised methods on a benchmark [28] of cross-domain few-shot image classification, where there is a large domain shift between the data of base and novel classes. Our approach also obtains the state-of-the-art results on this benchmark [28] compared with other self-supervised and supervised methods (see our supplementary materials). Besides, similar works in continuous [24] and open-world learning [18] also employ SSL to enhance their performances, which can relate to FSL since these fields all aim to generalize the learned representations to the novel distribution. Chen *et al.* [16] suggest that, in the *transductive* setting, the existing SSL method (MoCo v2 [11]) can achieve competitive results with supervised FSL methods. However, their transductive FSL method requires the data of test classes for unsupervised pre-training, which is somewhat contrary to the motivation of FSL.

3 Method

3.1 Preliminaries

FSL Setup. In few-shot image classification, given a base dataset $\mathcal{D}_{base} = \{(x_i, y_i)\}$, the goal is to learn a pre-trained (or meta-) model that is capable of

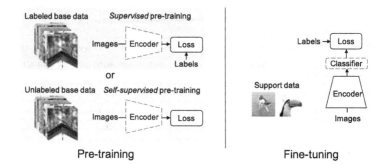

Fig. 1. The overview of pre-training-&-fine-tuning approach in FSL. (Left) In the pre-training stage, an encoder network is trained on a labeled (or unlabeled) base dataset with a supervised (or self-supervised) loss. **(Right)** In the fine-tuning stage, a linear classifier (e.g., logistic regression) is trained on the embeddings of a few support samples with the frozen pre-trained encoder.

effectively solving the downstream few-shot task T, which consists of a support set $\mathcal{S} = \{(x_s, y_s)\}_{s=1}^{N*K}$ for adaptation and a query set $\mathcal{Q} = \{x_q\}_{q=1}^{Q}$ for prediction, where y_s is the class label of image x_s. As an N-way K-shot classification task T, K is relatively small (e.g., 1 or 5 usually) and the N novel categories are not in $\mathcal{D}_{base}$.

FSL with Supervised Pre-training. Recent works [10,71] show that a simple pre-training-&-fine-tuning approach is a strong baseline for FSL. These methods pre-train an encoder (e.g., a convolution neural network) on $\mathcal{D}_{base}$ with the standard classification objective. In downstream FSL tasks, a simple linear classifier (e.g., logistic regression in our case) is trained on the output features of the fixed encoder network with the support samples. Finally, the pre-trained encoder with the adapted classifier is used to infer the query samples (as shown in Fig. 1).

Unsupervised FSL Setup. In contrast to supervised FSL where $\mathcal{D}_{base} = \{(x_i, y_i)\}$, only the unlabeled dataset $\mathcal{D}_{base} = \{x_i\}$ is available in the pre-training (or meta-training) stage for unsupervised FSL. Our self-supervised pre-training approach follows the standard pre-training-&-fine-tuning strategy discussed above, except that the base dataset is *unlabeled* (as shown in Fig. 1). Note that, for a fair comparison, our model is *not* trained on any additional (unlabeled) data.

3.2   Self-supervised Pre-training for FSL

Self-supervised Pre-training and Supervised Pre-training Maximize Different MI Targets. Supervised pre-training aims to reduce the classification loss on the base dataset toward zero. A recent study [74] shows that there is a pervasive phenomenon of *neural collapse* in the supervised training process, where the representations of within-class samples collapse to the class mean. It means the conditional entropy $H(Z|Y)$ of hidden representations Z given the class label Y is small. In fact, Boudiaf et al. [6] indicate that minimizing the cross-entropy loss is equivalent to maximizing the mutual information $I(Z;Y)$ between *representations* Z and *labels* Y. Qin et al. [58] also prove a similar result.

Maximizing $I(Z;Y)$ is beneficial for recognition on the base classes. However, since FSL requires the representations generalizing on the novel classes, overfitting to the base classes affects the performance of FSL. In this paper, following the InfoMax principle [46], our method aims to preserve the raw data information as much as possible in the learned representations. Theoretically, we maximize another MI target, i.e., the mutual information $I(Z;X)$ between *representations* Z and *data* X, to learn meaningful representations for FSL. Comparing the two MI objectives $I(Z;Y)$ and $I(Z;X)$, the supervised representations are only required to contain information about the associated labels of the images. In contrast, the representations with self-supervision are encouraged to contain comprehensive information about the data with less bias toward the base labels.

In practice, the calculation of $I(Z;X)$ is intractable. We maximize an alternative MI objective $I(Z^1;Z^2) = I(f(X^1);f(X^2))$, which is a lower bound of $I(Z;X)$ [73], where X^1 and X^2 are two augmented views of X obtained by some data augmentations, and f is the encoder network. In addition, our encoder $f(\cdot) = h_{proj} \circ g(\cdot)$ consists of a backbone $g(\cdot)$ (e.g., ResNet) and an extra *projection* head $h_{proj}(\cdot)$ (e.g., MLP) following contrastive learning methods [8,11], as shown in Fig. 3a. The projection head is only used in the pre-training stage. In the fine-tuning stage, the linear classifier is trained on the representations before the projection head. Next, we introduce two MI estimators for $I(Z^1,Z^2)$ and describe how to perform self-supervised pre-training with them.

Maximizing $I(Z^1;Z^2)$ with I_{NCE} and I_{MINE}. Many contrastive learning methods [8,52] maximize $I(Z^1;Z^2)$ with the *InfoNCE* estimator proposed in [52]:

$$I(Z^1;Z^2) = I(f(X^1);f(X^2)) \tag{1}$$

$$\geq \underset{p(x^1,x^2)}{\mathbb{E}}[C(x^1,x^2)] - \underset{p(x^1)}{\mathbb{E}}[\log(\underset{p(x^2)}{\mathbb{E}}[e^{C(x^1,x^2)}])] \triangleq I_{NCE}(Z^1;Z^2), \tag{2}$$

where $p(x^1,x^2)$ is the joint distribution (i.e., $(x^1,x^2) \sim p(x^1,x^2)$, and (x^1,x^2) is a positive pair) and the critic $C(x^1,x^2)$ is parameterized by the encoder f, e.g., $C(x^1,x^2) = f^T(x^1)f(x^2)/\tau$ with τ being temperature. Given a training batch $\{x_i\}_{i=1}^{2B}$ where x_i and x_{i+B} are positive pair $(i \leq B)$, the well-known method SimCLR [8] minimizes the contrastive loss[1] based on I_{NCE}:

$$\mathcal{L}_{NCE} = -\underbrace{\frac{1}{B}\sum_{i=1}^{B} z_i^T z_{i+B}/\tau}_{Alignment} + \underbrace{\frac{1}{2B}\sum_{i=1}^{2B}\log(\sum_{j \neq i} e^{z_i^T z_j/\tau})}_{Uniformity}, \tag{3}$$

where $z_i = f(x_i)$. Despite the great success of I_{NCE} in contrastive learning, the problem is that I_{NCE} has high bias, especially when the batch size is small and MI is large. For detailed discussions we refer the reader to [56,66].

---

[1] Alignment: the difference between representation of two views of the same sample should be minimized. Uniformity: the difference between representation of two different samples should be maximized.

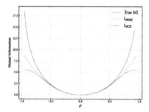

Fig. 2. We estimate MI between two multivariate Gaussians with the component-wise correlation ρ (see the supplementary materials for details). When the true MI is large, I_{NCE} has a high bias compared with I_{MINE}.

Our work employs another MI estimator I_{MINE} following recent progress in the MI neural estimation [4], which has lower bias than I_{NCE} [56,66]:

$$I_{MINE}(Z^1; Z^2) \triangleq \underset{p(x^1,x^2)}{\mathbb{E}}[C(x^1,x^2)] - \log(\underset{p(x^1)\otimes p(x^2)}{\mathbb{E}}[e^{C(x^1,x^2)}]), \qquad (4)$$

where $p(x^1) \otimes p(x^2)$ is the product of the marginal distributions. We construct a simple experiment on the synthetic data to compare the estimation bias of I_{NCE} and I_{MINE}, as shown in Fig. 2. Based on $I_{MINE}(Z^1; Z^2)$, we can further propose a novel contrastive loss for self-supervised pre-training:

$$\mathcal{L}_{MINE} = \underbrace{-\frac{1}{B}\sum_{i=1}^{B} z_i^T z_{i+B}/\tau}_{Alignment} + \underbrace{\log(\sum_{i=1}^{2B}\sum_{z_j \in Neg(z_i)} e^{z_i^T z_j/\tau})}_{Uniformity}, \qquad (5)$$

where $Neg(z_i)$ denotes the collection of negative samples of z_i.

Improving $\mathcal{L}_{MINE}$ with Asymmetric Alignment. We can decompose both $\mathcal{L}_{MINE}$ (Eq. 5) and $\mathcal{L}_{NCE}$ (Eq. 3) into two terms: the *alignment* term encourages the positive pair to be close, and the *uniformity* term pushes the negative pair away. In fact, the uniformity term is a regularization used to avoid the *representation collapse*, i.e., the output representations are the same for all samples [76]. Alternatively, without the uniformity term, recent work SimSiam [12] suggests that the Siamese model can learn meaningful representations by introducing asymmetry in the alignment term and obtains better results.

In our experiments (Table 1), when using the common data augmentation strategy [11,12], SimSiam is slightly better than models with contrastive loss ($\mathcal{L}_{NCE}$ or $\mathcal{L}_{MINE}$). However, we empirically find that the SimSiam model fails to learn stably in FSL when using *stronger* data augmentation. When the variations in the positive pairs are large, the phenomenon of *dimensional collapse* [36] occurs in SimSiam, i.e., a part of dimensionality of the embedding space vanishes (as shown in Fig. 6). In contrast, models with uniformity regularization do not suffer from significant dimensional collapse. This paper further improve $\mathcal{L}_{MINE}$ with the asymmetric alignment:

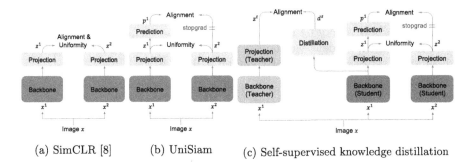

(a) SimCLR [8]   (b) UniSiam   (c) Self-supervised knowledge distillation

Fig. 3. (a) SimCLR [8] for comparison. (b) Our UniSiam for self-supervised pre-training. (c) The architecture of our self-supervised knowledge distillation.

$$\mathcal{L}_{AMINE} = -\underbrace{\frac{1}{2B}\sum_{i=1}^{B}(p_i^T SG(z_{i+B}) + p_{i+B}^T SG(z_i))}_{Asymmetric\ Alignment} + \underbrace{\lambda \log(\sum_{i=1}^{2B}\sum_{z_j \in Neg(z_i)} e^{z_i^T z_j/\tau})}_{Uniformity}, \quad (6)$$

where λ is a weighting hyper-parameter, $p_i = h_{pred}(z_i)$ is the output of the additional *prediction* head $h_{pred}(\cdot)$ [12], and the SG (stop gradient) operation indicates that the back-propagation of the gradient stops here. Similar to the projection head, the prediction head is only used in the pre-training stage. Compared with SimSiam, our method can learn with stronger data augmentation to improve the invariance of the representations, resulting in better out-of-distribution generalization for FSL. Since our model can be considered as Sim**Siam** with the **Uni**formity regularization, we term it UniSiam (as shown in Fig. 3b).

Thus, we obtain the final self-supervised pre-training loss $\mathcal{L}_{AMINE}$ (Eq. 6). We can train our UniSiam model by minimizing this objective. After self-supervised pre-training, the pre-trained backbone can be used in FSL tasks by training a classifier on the output embeddings (discussed in Sect. 3.1). Note that the projection head and prediction head are removed in the fine-tuning stage. Next, we introduce how to perform self-supervised knowledge distillation with a pre-trained UniSiam model.

3.3   Self-supervised Knowledge Distillation for Unsupervised FSL

A large model (teacher) trained with the self-supervised loss (Eq. 6) can be used to guide the learning of a small self-supervised model (student)[2]. In [70], the knowledge transfer from a teacher model to a student model is defined as maximizing the mutual information $I(X^s; X^t)$ between the representations of them. Maximizing the objective is equivalent to minimizing the conditional entropy $H(X^t|X^s)$, since $I(X^s; X^t) = H(X^t) - H(X^t|X^s)$ and the teacher model is fixed. It means the difference between their outputs should be as small as possible. So, simply aligning the outputs of them can achieve the purpose.

---

[2] While larger models have better performance, training a smaller model is also meaningful since it can be more easily deployed in practical scenarios such as edge devices.

Specifically, as shown in Fig. 3c, the pre-trained teacher encoder $f^t(\cdot)$ (consisting of the backbone $g^t(\cdot)$ and the projection head $h^t_{proj}(\cdot)$) is used to guide the training of the student backbone $g^s(\cdot)$ with a distillation head $h_{dist}(\cdot)$. The self-supervised distillation objective can be written as:

$$\mathcal{L}_{dist} = -\frac{1}{2B}\sum_{i=1}^{2B}(d_i^s)^T z_i^t, \qquad (7)$$

where $d^s = h_{dist} \circ g^s(x)$ is the output of the distillation head on the student backbone, and $z^t = h^t_{proj} \circ g^t(x)$ is the output of the teacher model. Finally, the total objective that combines both distillation and pre-training is:

$$\mathcal{L} = \alpha\mathcal{L}_{AMINE} + (1-\alpha)\mathcal{L}_{dist}, \qquad (8)$$

where α is a hyper-parameter. We set $\alpha = 0.5$ for all our experiments. Given a large UniSiam model pre-trained by Eq. 6, we can employ it as a teacher network to guide the training of a small model (from scratch) by minimizing Eq. 8.

4   Experiments

4.1   Datasets and Settings

Datasets. We perform experiments on two widely used few-shot image classification datasets, *mini*-ImageNet [75] and *tiered*-ImageNet [61]. *mini*-ImageNet [75] is a subset of ImageNet [62], which contains 100 classes with 600 images per class. We follow the split setting used in previous works [60], which randomly select 64, 16, and 20 classes for training, validation, and testing, respectively. *tiered*-ImageNet [61] is a larger subset of ImageNet with 608 classes and about 1300 images per class. These classes are grouped into 34 high-level categories and then divided into 20 categories (351 classes) for training, 6 categories (97 classes) for validation, and 8 categories (160 classes) for testing.

Implementation Details. We use the networks of ResNet family [32] as our backbones. The projection and prediction heads of UniSiam are MLPs with the same setting as SimSiam [12], except that the ResNets without bottleneck blocks (e.g., ResNet-18) on *mini*-ImageNet use 512 output dimensions to avoid over-fitting. The distillation head is a 5-layer MLP with batch normalization applied to each hidden layer. All the hidden fully-connected layers are 2048-D, except that the penultimate layer is 512-D. We find that this distillation head structure, which is similar to the combination of the projection and the prediction (as shown in Fig. 3c), is suited for the knowledge distillation. The output vectors of the projection, prediction, and distillation heads are normalized by their L2-norm [79]. More implementation details can be found in the supplementary materials.

4.2   Self-supervised Vs. Supervised Pre-training in FSL

In this subsection, we explore how several factors (network depth, image size, and data augmentation) affect the FSL performance of self-supervised and supervised

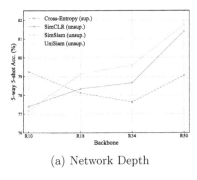

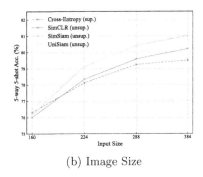

(a) Network Depth   (b) Image Size

Fig. 4. Effect of network depth and image size. (a) Self-supervised methods have better scalability for network depth compared to supervised pre-training in FSL. (b) A larger image size improves the FSL performance of self-supervised methods. Note that unsupervised (unsup.) approaches perform pre-training on the base dataset *without* any labels.

pre-training. On *mini*-ImageNet, we compare supervised pre-training (training with the cross-entropy loss [71]) with our self-supervised UniSiam and two recent SSL models SimCLR [8] and SimSiam [12]. SimCLR is an well-known contrastive learning method that optimizes L_{NCE} (Eq. 3), and SimSiam is a relevant baseline to our UniSiam (i.e., $\lambda = 0$ in Eq. 6). More detailed comparison among the self-supervised methods is in Sect 4.3.

For a fair comparison, all methods use the same SGD optimization with cosine learning decay for 400 epochs, with batch size 256. Other hyper-parameters in each algorithm are chosen optimally using the grid search. To evaluate their performances in FSL, after pre-training on the base dataset of *mini*-ImageNet (i.e., the data of the training classes), we train a logistic regression classifier (with their fixed representations) for each few-shot classification task, which is sampled from the testing classes of *mini*-ImageNet. The reported results are the average of the accuracies on 3000 tasks for each method. More details about the baselines and evaluation can be found in the supplementary materials. Note that our self-supervised knowledge distillation is *not* used in this experiment.

Network Depth. Figure 4a compares the performances of different methods with various depths of ResNet (i.e., ResNet-10/18/34/50). The input image size is 224×224. We use the data augmentation (DA) strategy, widely used in self-supervised learning [11,12], termed *default DA*. The details of the default DA are described in the supplementary materials.

We can find that when the backbone is shallow (i.e., ResNet-10), supervised pre-training has an advantage compared to self-supervised methods. However, as the network deepens, the self-supervised methods gradually outperform the supervised one. When the backbone changes from ResNet10 to ResNet50, the performance improvement of the self-supervised approach is larger than 4%. In contrast, the performance of supervised pre-training is decreased by 0.2%.

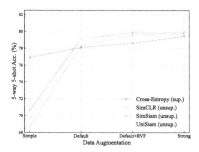

Fig. 5. Effect of data augmentation. Stronger data augmentation can substantially improve the performances of the self-supervised pre-training compared to supervised pre-training.

Image Size. Figure 4b shows the performances of different approaches with various input sizes (160×160, 224×224, 288×288, and 384×384). All methods use ResNet-18 as the backbone with the default DA strategy. We find that a larger image size is more important for self-supervised methods. When the image size is small (i.e., 160×160), the performances of different methods are close. However, when the image size increases, self-supervised methods have larger performance gains compared with supervised pre-training. Although a larger image size can bring significant performance improvement, we still use the image size of 224×224 in other experiments following the typical setting in the community.

Data Augmentation. Figure 5 shows the performances of various pre-training methods with different levels of data augmentation. All mehtods use the ResNet-18 backbone with input size 224 × 224. Here we introduces two effective DA for FSL: *RandomVerticalFlip* (RVF) and *RandAugment* (RA) [17]. We set 4 levels of DA (from slight to heavy) as follows: (1) "Simple" denotes the strategy used for traditional supervised pre-training (including *RandomResizedCrop*, *ColorJitter*, and *RandomHorizontalFlip*), (2) "Default" is the same as the default DA mentioned above, (3) "Default+RVT" denotes the default DA plus the RVF, and (4) "Strong" represents the default DA plus RVF and RA.

Supervised pre-training can bring more information than self-supervised methods in the case of simple DA. However, default DA substantially improves the performances of the self-supervised methods, but it has a limited gain for supervised pre-training. In addition, RVF can further improve the performances of all methods. RA improves the performances of most methods, except for SimSiam. We consider that the strong data augmentation leads to the dimensional collapse of SimSiam, as shown in the next subsection.

4.3   Self-supervised Pre-training with Strong Augmentation

We compare SimCLR, SimSiam, and the variants of our UniSiam under default and strong DA (in Table 1). We observe that self-supervised pre-training with the uniformity term obtains a larger improvement from strong DA compared with

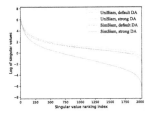

Fig. 6. Singular value spectrum of embedding space. The uniformity regularization alleviates the dimensional collapse under strong DA.

Table 1. Comparison of self-supervised methods under default and strong data augmentations. We report their 5-way 5-shot accuracy (%) on *mini*-ImageNet. "symm." and "asymm." denote using the symmetric alignment (Eq. 3 or Eq. 5) and the asymmetric alignment (Eq. 6) respectively.

Method	Align	Uniform	R18		R50	
			DefaultDA	StrongDA	DefaultDA	StrongDA
SimCLR	symm	NCE (Eq. 3)	78.34 ± 0.27	79.66 ± 0.27	81.42 ± 0.25	81.51 ± 0.26
SimSiam	asymm.	–	$\mathbf{79.13 \pm 0.26}$	79.85 ± 0.27	81.75 ± 0.24	79.66 ± 0.27
UniSiam	symm	MINE (Eq. 5)	78.04 ± 0.27	80.72 ± 0.26	81.45 ± 0.24	82.84 ± 0.24
	asymm	NCE (Eq. 3)	78.95 ± 0.26	80.66 ± 0.26	81.51 ± 0.24	82.54 ± 0.24
	asymm	MINE (Eq. 5)	79.11 ± 0.25	$\mathbf{81.13 \pm 0.26}$	$\mathbf{81.93 \pm 0.24}$	$\mathbf{83.18 \pm 0.24}$

SimSiam. In addition, the uniformity term of $\mathcal{L}_{MINE}$ has a more significant improvement than the uniformity term of $\mathcal{L}_{NCE}$. Asymmetric alignment can also improve the FSL performance than the symmetric alignment.

To further demonstrate the importance of uniformity, we visualize the singular value spectrum of the embedding space of SimSiam and our UniSiam under different DAs in Fig. 6. The backbone is ResNet-50. Both SimSiam and UniSiam have a flat singular value spectrum when using the default DA. However, when DA is strong, some singular values of SimSiam are reduced. It means the features of SimSiam fall into a lower-dimensional subspace. This phenomenon is termed dimensional collapse by [36]. In contrast, the singular value spectrum of UniSiam is flat even with strong DA, which indicates the significance of the uniformity.

4.4 Our Self-supervisied Knowledge Distillation

The previous work RFS [71] employs the standard knowledge distillation [33] to improve the supervised pre-training model in FSL. However, it is based on the logits that cannot be applied in unsupervised FSL. We use the standard knowledge distillation to transfer knowledge from a large supervised pre-training model to small ones, being a compared baseline to our self-supervised knowledge distillation (as shown in Table 2). Note that our method does not use any labels in the pre-training and the distillation stage. All methods use the default DA and the image size of 224×224. We can see that our knowledge distillation approach

Table 2. Effect of our self-supervised knowledge distillation. We report the 5-way 5-shot classification accuracy (%) on the *mini*-ImageNet dataset.

	Teacher		Student		
	ResNet-50	distillation	ResNet-10	ResNet-18	ResNet-34
RFS [71] (sup.)	79.05 ± 0.26	N	79.25 ± 0.26	78.12 ± 0.26	77.63 ± 0.27
		Y	79.44 ± 0.25	80.15 ± 0.25	80.55 ± 0.26
UniSiam (unsup.)	81.93 ± 0.24	N	76.94 ± 0.27	79.11 ± 0.25	79.69 ± 0.26
		Y	78.58 ± 0.26	80.35 ± 0.26	81.39 ± 0.25

Table 3. Comparison to previous works on *mini*-ImageNet, using the averaged 5-way classification accuracy (%) with the 95% confidence interval on the testing split. Note that UniSiam+dist is trained by our self-supervised knowledge distillation (Fig. 3c) with ResNet-50 being the teacher's backbone. †: the results obtained from [10]. ‡: the results are from our implementations. Models that use knowledge distillation are tagged with the suffix "+*dist*."

Backbone	Method	Size		1-shot	5-shot
	Δ-Encoder [64]	224	sup	59.9	69.7
	SNCA [78]	224	sup	57.8 ± 0.8	72.8 ± 0.7
	iDeMe-Net [15]	224	sup	59.14 ± 0.86	74.63 ± 0.74
	Robust+dist [20]	224	sup	63.73 ± 0.62	81.19 ± 0.43
	AFHN [45]	224	sup	62.38 ± 0.72	78.16 ± 0.56
	ProtoNet+SSL [67]	224	sup.+ssl	–	76.6
	Neg-Cosine [47]	224	sup	62.33 ± 0.82	80.94 ± 0.59
ResNet-18	Centroid Alignment [2]	224	sup	59.88 ± 0.67	80.35 ± 0.73
	PSST [14]	224	sup.+ssl	59.52 ± 0.46	77.43 ± 0.46
	UMTRA‡ [37]	224	unsup	43.09 ± 0.35	53.42 ± 0.31
	ProtoCLR‡ [50]	224	unsup	50.90 ± 0.36	71.59 ± 0.29
	SimCLR‡ [8]	224	unsup	62.58 ± 0.37	79.66 ± 0.27
	SimSiam‡ [12]	224	unsup.	62.80 ± 0.37	79.85 ± 0.27
	UniSiam (Ours)	224	unsup	63.26 ± 0.36	81.13 ± 0.26
	UniSiam+dist (Ours)	224	unsup.	$\mathbf{64.10 \pm 0.36}$	$\mathbf{82.26 \pm 0.25}$
ResNet-34	MatchingNet‡ [75]	224	sup	53.20 ± 0.78	68.32 ± 0.66
	ProtoNet‡ [65]	224	sup	53.90 ± 0.83	74.65 ± 0.64
	MAML‡ [22]	224	sup	51.46 ± 0.90	65.90 ± 0.79
	RelationNet‡ [68]	224	sup	51.74 ± 0.83	69.61 ± 0.67
	Baseline [10]	224	sup	49.82 ± 0.73	73.45 ± 0.65
	Baseline++ [10]	224	sup.	52.65 ± 0.83	76.16 ± 0.63
	SimCLR‡ [8]	224	unsup	63.98 ± 0.37	79.80 ± 0.28
	SimSiam‡ [12]	224	unsup.	63.77 ± 0.38	80.44 ± 0.28
	UniSiam (Ours)	224	unsup	64.77 ± 0.37	81.75 ± 0.26
	UniSiam+dist (Ours)	224	unsup	$\mathbf{65.55 \pm 0.36}$	$\mathbf{83.40 \pm 0.24}$

improves the performances of the smaller networks. Although the distillation loss allows supervised pre-training models to capture the relationships between classes to learn information beyond labels, our model after distillation still outperforms them when the backbones are larger (ResNet-18 and ResNet-34).

Table 4. Comparison to previous FSL works on *tiered*-ImageNet, using the averaged 5-way classification accuracy (%) on the testing split. ‡: the results are from our implementations. ResNet-50 is the teacher's backbone.

Method	Backbone (#Params)	Size	MACs		1-shot	5-shot
MetaOptNet [43]	ResNet-12 (8.0M)	84	3.5G	sup	65.99±0.72	81.56±0.53
RFS+dist [71]	ResNet-12 (8.0M)	84	3.5G	sup	**71.52±0.72**	**86.03±0.49**
BML [83]	ResNet-12 (8.0M)	84	3.5G	sup	68.99±0.50	85.49±0.34
Roubst+dist [20]	ResNet-18 (11.2M)	224	1.8G	sup	70.44±0.32	85.43±0.21
Centroid Alignment [2]	ResNet-18 (11.2M)	224	1.8G	sup	69.29±0.56	85.97±0.49
SimCLR‡ [8]	ResNet-18 (11.2M)	224	1.8G	unsup	63.38±0.42	79.17±0.34
SimSiam‡ [12]	ResNet-18 (11.2M)	224	1.8G	unsup.	64.05±0.40	81.40±0.30
UniSiam (Ours)	ResNet-18 (11.2M)	224	1.8G	unsup	65.18±0.39	82.28±0.29
UniSiam+dist (Ours)	ResNet-18 (11.2M)	224	1.8G	unsup.	67.01±0.39	84.47±0.28
LEO [63]	WRN-28-10 (36.5M)	84	41G	sup	66.33±0.05	81.44±0.09
CC+Rot [25]	WRN-28-10 (36.5M)	84	41G	sup.+ssl	**70.53±0.51**	84.98±0.36
FEAT [80]	WRN-28-10 (36.5M)	84	41G	sup.	70.41±0.23	84.38±0.16
UniSiam (Ours)	ResNet-34 (21.3M)	224	3.6G	unsup	67.57±0.39	84.12±0.28
UniSiam+dist (Ours)	ResNet-34 (21.3M)	224	3.6G	unsup	68.65±0.39	85.70±0.27
UniSiam (Ours)	ResNet-50 (23.5M)	224	4.1G	unsup	69.11±0.38	85.82±0.27
UniSiam+dist (Ours)	ResNet-50 (23.5M)	224	4.1G	unsup	69.60±0.38	**86.51±0.26**

4.5 Comparison with the State-of-the-Art

We compare with state-of-the-art FSL approaches in Table 3 and Table 4. Our method uses the strong DA and the image size of 224×224. In addition, we reimplement two unsupervised FSL methods (ProtoCLR [50] and UMTRA [37]) with the same DA strategy (strong DA) on *mini*-ImageNet. More baseline details are in the supplementary materials. On *mini*-ImageNet, our unsupervised UniSiam achieves the state-of-the-art results compared to other supervised methods with the ResNet-18 and ResNet-34 backbones. UniSiam also has a significant improvement than some methods that incorporate self-supervised objective and supervised pre-training ("sup.+ssl"). In addition, our method outperforms previous unsupervised FSL methods [37,50] by a larger margin.

On *tiered*-ImageNet, since only a few studies use standard ResNet [32] as their backbones, we also compare with some methods that use other backbones. For a fair comparison, we count the number of parameters and MACs of different backbones. Note that ResNet-12 modifies the original architecture of ResNet (e.g., larger channel dimensions). It has a larger computation overhead than standard ResNet-18, even with a smaller input size. Our method with a shallow backbone ResNet-18 is slightly worse than top supervised FSL methods on *tiered*-ImageNet. The main reasons are twofold. One is that increasing the number of classes alleviates the overfitting problem of supervised methods on the *tiered*-ImageNet dataset. The more important reason is that existing FSL methods utilize a variety of techniques to implicitly alleviate the problem of over-fitting to the base classes. For example, *Robust+dist* [20] trains 20 different networks to learn diverse information for avoiding overfitting. *RFS+dist* [71] repeats self-distillation many times, which can capture the relation between the classes to learn more information beyond the labels. However, these methods require complicated processes and troublesome human designs, which limit their application and scalability. In contrast, our self-supervised UniSiam is a concise and effective approach that fundamentally avoids bias. When the backbone (i.e., ResNet-34) has similar computational overhead, UniSiam also achieves comparable results with the state-of-the-art supervised FSL methods on *tiered*-ImageNet.

5   Conclusion

This paper proposes an effective few-shot learner without using any labels of the base dataset. From a unified information-theoretic perspective, our self-supervised pre-training learns good embeddings with less bias toward the base classes for FSL by maximizing the MI of the instances and their representations. Compared with state-of-the-art supervised FSL methods, our UniSiam achieves comparable results on two popular FSL benchmarks. Considering the simplicity and effectiveness of the proposed approach, we believe it would motivate other researchers to rethink the role of label information of the base dataset in FSL.

Acknowledgement. The research was supported by NSFC No. 61872329, and by MindSpore [1] which is a new deep learning computing framework.

References

1. MindSpore. www.mindspore.cn/
2. Afrasiyabi, A., Lalonde, J.-F., Gagné, C.: Associative alignment for few-shot image classification. In: Vedaldi, A., Bischof, H., Brox, T., Frahm, J.-M. (eds.) ECCV 2020. LNCS, vol. 12350, pp. 18–35. Springer, Cham (2020). https://doi.org/10.1007/978-3-030-58558-7_2
3. Antoniou, A., Storkey, A.: Assume, augment and learn: Unsupervised few-shot meta-learning via random labels and data augmentation. arxiv:1902.09884 (2019)
4. Belghazi, M.I., et al.: Mutual information neural estimation. In: ICML (2018)
5. Boudiaf, M., et al.: Transductive information maximization for few-shot learning. In: NeurIPS (2020)
6. Boudiaf, M., Rony, J., Masud, Z.I., Granger, E., Pedersoli, M., Piantanida, P., Ayed, I.B.: A unifying mutual information view of metric learning: Cross-entropy vs. pairwise losses. In: ECCV (2020)
7. Brown, T.B., Mann, B., et al.: Language models are few-shot learners. In: NeurIPS (2020)
8. Chen, T., Kornblith, S., Norouzi, M., Hinton, G.: A simple framework for contrastive learning of visual representations. In: ICML (2020)
9. Chen, T., Li, L.: Intriguing properties of contrastive losses. arXiv:2011.02803 (2020)
10. Chen, W.Y., Liu, Y.C., Kira, Z., Wang, Y.C.F., Huang, J.B.: A closer look at few-shot classification. In: ICLR (2019)

11. Chen, X., Fan, H., Girshick, R., He, K.: Improved baselines with momentum contrastive learning. arXiv:2003.04297 (2020)
12. Chen, X., He, K.: Exploring simple Siamese representation learning. In: CVPR (2021)
13. Chen, Y., Wang, X., Liu, Z., Xu, H., Darrell, T.: A new meta-baseline for few-shot learning. arXiv:2003.04390 (2020)
14. Chen, Z., Ge, J., Zhan, H., Huang, S., Wang, D.: Pareto self-supervised training for few-shot learning. In: CVPR (2021)
15. Chen, Z., Fu, Y., Wang, Y.X., Ma, L., Liu, W., Hebert, M.: Image deformation meta-networks for one-shot learning. In: CVPR (2019)
16. Chen, Z., Maji, S., Learned-Miller, E.: Shot in the dark: few-shot learning with no base-class labels. In: CVPRW (2021)
17. Cubuk, E.D., Zoph, B., Shlens, J., Le, Q.: RandAugment: practical automated data augmentation with a reduced search space. In: NeurIPS (2020)
18. Dhamija, A.R., Ahmad, T., Schwan, J., Jafarzadeh, M., Li, C., Boult, T.E.: Self-supervised features improve open-world learning. arXiv:2102.07848 (2021)
19. Dhillon, G.S., Chaudhari, P., Ravichandran, A., Soatto, S.: A baseline for few-shot image classification. In: ICLR (2020)
20. Dvornik, N., Mairal, J., Schmid, C.: Diversity with cooperation: ensemble methods for few-shot classification. In: ICCV (2019)
21. Ericsson, L., Gouk, H., Hospedales, T.M.: How well do self-supervised models transfer? arXiv:2011.13377 (2020)
22. Finn, C., Abbeel, P., Levine, S.: Model-agnostic meta-learning for fast adaptation of deep networks. In: ICML (2017)
23. Flennerhag, S., Rusu, A.A., Pascanu, R., Visin, F., Yin, H., Hadsell, R.: Meta-learning with warped gradient descent. In: ICLR (2020)
24. Gallardo, J., Hayes, T.L., Kanan, C.: Self-supervised training enhances online continual learning. In: BMVC (2021)
25. Gidaris, S., Bursuc, A., Komodakis, N., Perez, P.P., Cord, M.: Boosting few-shot visual learning with self-supervision. In: ICCV (2019)
26. Gidaris, S., Singh, P., Komodakis, N.: Unsupervised representation learning by predicting image rotations. In: ICLR (2018)
27. Grill, J.B., et al.: Bootstrap your own latent: a new approach to self-supervised learning. In: NeurIPS (2020)
28. Guo, Y., Codella, N.C., Karlinsky, L., Codella, J.V., Smith, J.R., Saenko, K., Rosing, T., Feris, R.: A Broader study of cross-domain few-shot learning. In: Vedaldi, A., Bischof, H., Brox, T., Frahm, J.-M. (eds.) ECCV 2020. LNCS, vol. 12372, pp. 124–141. Springer, Cham (2020). https://doi.org/10.1007/978-3-030-58583-9_8
29. Gutmann, M., Hyvärinen, A.: Noise-contrastive estimation: A new estimation principle for unnormalized statistical models. In: AISTATS (2010)
30. Hadsell, R., Chopra, S., LeCun, Y.: Dimensionality reduction by learning an invariant mapping. In: CVPR (2006)
31. He, K., Fan, H., Wu, Y., Xie, S., Girshick, R.: Momentum contrast for unsupervised visual representation learning. In: CVPR (2020)
32. He, K., Zhang, X., Ren, S., Sun, J.: Deep residual learning for image recognition. In: CVPR (2016)
33. Hinton, G., Vinyals, O., Dean, J.: Distilling the knowledge in a neural network. arXiv:1503.02531 (2015)
34. Hjelm, R.D., et al.: Learning deep representations by mutual information estimation and maximization. In: ICLR (2018)

35. Hsu, K., Levine, S., Finn, C.: Unsupervised learning via meta-learning. In: ICLR (2018)
36. Jing, L., Vincent, P., LeCun, Y., Tian, Y.: Understanding dimensional collapse in contrastive self-supervised learning. In: ICLR (2021)
37. Khodadadeh, S., Boloni, L., Shah, M.: Unsupervised meta-learning for few-shot image classification. In: NeurIPS (2019)
38. Khodadadeh, S., Zehtabian, S., Vahidian, S., Wang, W., Lin, B., Boloni, L.: Unsupervised meta-learning through latent-space interpolation in generative models. In: ICLR (2021)
39. Laenen, S., Bertinetto, L.: On episodes, prototypical networks, and few-shot learning. In: NeurIPS (2021)
40. Lake, B.M., Salakhutdinov, R., Tenenbaum, J.B.: Human-level concept learning through probabilistic program induction. Science (2015)
41. Larsson, G., Maire, M., Shakhnarovich, G.: Learning representations for automatic colorization. In: Leibe, B., Matas, J., Sebe, N., Welling, M. (eds.) ECCV 2016. LNCS, vol. 9908, pp. 577–593. Springer, Cham (2016). https://doi.org/10.1007/978-3-319-46493-0_35
42. Lee, D.B., Min, D., Lee, S., Hwang, S.J.: Meta-GMVAE: mixture of Gaussian VAE for unsupervised meta-learning. In: ICLR (2021)
43. Lee, K., Maji, S., Ravichandran, A., Soatto, S.: Meta-learning with differentiable convex optimization. In: CVPR (2019)
44. Li, F.F., Rob, F., Pietro, P.: One-shot learning of object categories. In: Trans. Pattern Anal. Mach. Intell. 28, 594–611 (2006)
45. Li, K., Zhang, Y., Li, K., Fu, Y.: Adversarial feature hallucination networks for few-shot learning. In: CVPR (2020)
46. Linsker, R.: Self-organization in a perceptual network. Computer 21, 105–117 (1988)
47. Liu, B., et al.: Negative margin matters: understanding margin in few-shot classification. In: Vedaldi, A., Bischof, H., Brox, T., Frahm, J.-M. (eds.) ECCV 2020. LNCS, vol. 12349, pp. 438–455. Springer, Cham (2020). https://doi.org/10.1007/978-3-030-58548-8_26
48. Lu, Y., Liu, J., Zhang, Y., Liu, Y., Tian, X.: Prompt distribution learning. In: CVPR (2022)
49. Mangla, P., Kumari, N., Sinha, A., Singh, M., Krishnamurthy, B., Balasubramanian, V.N.: Charting the right manifold: Manifold mixup for few-shot learning. In: WACV (2020)
50. Medina, C., Devos, A., Grossglauser, M.: Self-supervised prototypical transfer learning for few-shot classification. In: ICMLW (2020)
51. Mishra, N., Rohaninejad, M., Chen, X., Abbeel, P.: A simple neural attentive meta-learner. In: ICLR (2018)
52. van den Oord, A., Li, Y., Vinyals, O.: Representation learning with contrastive predictive coding. arXiv:1807.03748 (2018)
53. Oreshkin, B.N., López, P.R., Lacoste, A.: TADAM: task dependent adaptive metric for improved few-shot learning. In: NeurIPS (2018)
54. Pathak, D., Krahenbuhl, P., Donahue, J., Darrell, T., Efros, A.A.: Context encoders: feature learning by inpainting. In: CVPR (2016)
55. Phoo, C.P., Hariharan, B.: Self-training for few-shot transfer across extreme task differences. arXiv:2010.07734 (2020)
56. Poole, B., Ozair, S., van den Oord, A., Alemi, A.A., Tucker, G.: On variational bounds of mutual information. In: ICML (2019)

57. Qin, T., Li, W., Shi, Y., Yang, G.: Unsupervised few-shot learning via distribution shift-based augmentation. arxiv:2004.05805 (2020)
58. Qin, Z., Kim, D., Gedeon, T.: Neural network classifiers as mutual information evaluators. In: ICMLW (2021)
59. Radford, A., et al.: Learning transferable visual models from natural language supervision. In: ICML (2021)
60. Ravi, S., Larochelle, H.: Optimization as a model for few-shot learning. In: ICLR (2017)
61. Ren, M., et al.: Meta-learning for semi-supervised few-shot classification. arXiv:1803.00676 (2018)
62. Russakovsky, O., et al.: ImageNet large scale visual recognition challenge. Int. J. Ccomput. Vis. **115**, 211–252 (2015)
63. Rusu, A., et al.: Meta-learning with latent embedding optimization. In: ICLR (2018)
64. Schwartz, E., et al.: Delta-encoder: an effective sample synthesis method for few-shot object recognition. In: NeurIPS (2018)
65. Snell, J., Swersky, K., Zemel, R.S.: Prototypical networks for few-shot learning. In: NeurIPS (2017)
66. Song, J., Ermon, S.: Understanding the limitations of variational mutual information estimators. In: ICLR (2020)
67. Su, J.-C., Maji, S., Hariharan, B.: When does self-supervision improve few-shot learning? In: Vedaldi, A., Bischof, H., Brox, T., Frahm, J.-M. (eds.) ECCV 2020. LNCS, vol. 12352, pp. 645–666. Springer, Cham (2020). https://doi.org/10.1007/978-3-030-58571-6_38
68. Sung, F., Yang, Y., Zhang, L., Xiang, T., Torr, P.H., Hospedales, T.M.: Learning to compare: Relation network for few-shot learning. In: CVPR (2018)
69. Tian, Y., Krishnan, D., Isola, P.: Contrastive multiview coding. In: Vedaldi, A., Bischof, H., Brox, T., Frahm, J.-M. (eds.) ECCV 2020. LNCS, vol. 12356, pp. 776–794. Springer, Cham (2020). https://doi.org/10.1007/978-3-030-58621-8_45
70. Tian, Y., Krishnan, D., Isola, P.: Contrastive representation distillation. In: ICLR (2020)
71. Tian, Y., Wang, Y., Krishnan, D., Tenenbaum, J.B., Isola, P.: Rethinking Few-shot image classification: a good embedding is all you need? In: Vedaldi, A., Bischof, H., Brox, T., Frahm, J.-M. (eds.) ECCV 2020. LNCS, vol. 12359, pp. 266–282. Springer, Cham (2020). https://doi.org/10.1007/978-3-030-58568-6_16
72. Tian, Y., Chen, X., Ganguli, S.: Understanding self-supervised learning dynamics without contrastive pairs. arXiv:2102.06810 (2021)
73. Tschannen, M., Djolonga, J., Rubenstein, P.K., Gelly, S., Lucic, M.: On mutual information maximization for representation learning. In: ICLR (2020)
74. Vardan, P., Han, X.Y., Donoho, D.L.: Prevalence of neural collapse during the terminal phase of deep learning training. PNAS (2020)
75. Vinyals, O., Blundell, C., Lillicrap, T., Wierstra, D., et al.: Matching networks for one shot learning. In: NeurIPS (2016)
76. Wang, T., Isola, P.: Understanding contrastive representation learning through alignment and uniformity on the hypersphere. In: ICML (2020)
77. Wen, L., Zhou, Y., He, L., Zhou, M., Xu, Z.: Mutual information gradient estimation for representation learning. In: ICLR (2020)
78. Wu, Z., Efros, A.A., Yu, S.X.: Improving generalization via scalable neighborhood component analysis. In: Ferrari, V., Hebert, M., Sminchisescu, C., Weiss, Y. (eds.) ECCV 2018. LNCS, vol. 11211, pp. 712–728. Springer, Cham (2018). https://doi.org/10.1007/978-3-030-01234-2_42

79. Wu, Z., Xiong, Y., Yu, S.X., Lin, D.: Unsupervised feature learning via non-parametric instance discrimination. In: CVPR (2018)
80. Ye, H.J., Hu, H., Zhan, D.C., Sha, F.: Few-shot learning via embedding adaptation with set-to-set functions. In: CVPR (2020)
81. Zbontar, J., Jing, L., Misra, I., LeCun, Y., Deny, S.: Barlow twins: Self-supervised learning via redundancy reduction. arXiv:2103.03230 (2021)
82. Zhang, R., Isola, P., Efros, A.A.: Colorful Image colorization. In: Leibe, B., Matas, J., Sebe, N., Welling, M. (eds.) ECCV 2016. LNCS, vol. 9907, pp. 649–666. Springer, Cham (2016). https://doi.org/10.1007/978-3-319-46487-9_40
83. Zhou, Z., Qiu, X., Xie, J., Wu, J., Zhang, C.: Binocular mutual learning for improving few-shot classification. In: ICCV (2021)

Author Index

Printed in the United States
by Baker & Taylor Publisher Services